SmartSuite® Millennium Edition Bible

SmartSuite®
Millennium Edition
Bible

Lisa A. Bucki

with Elaine Marmel and David Plotkin

IDG Books Worldwide, Inc.
An International Data Group Company

Foster City, CA ✦ Chicago, IL ✦ Indianapolis, IN ✦ New York, NY

SmartSuite® Millennium Edition Bible

Published by
IDG Books Worldwide, Inc.
An International Data Group Company
919 E. Hillsdale Blvd., Suite 400
Foster City, CA 94404
www.idgbooks.com (IDG Books Worldwide Web site)

Library of Congress Catalog Card Number: 98-70264

ISBN: 0-7645-3147-6

Printed in the United States of America

10 9 8 7 6 5 4 3 2 1

1B/QR/QX/ZY/FC

Distributed in the United States by IDG Books Worldwide, Inc.

Distributed by Macmillan Canada for Canada; by Transworld Publishers Limited in the United Kingdom; by IDG Norge Books for Norway; by IDG Sweden Books for Sweden; by Woodslane Pty. Ltd. for Australia; by Woodslane (NZ) Ltd. for New Zealand; by Addison Wesley Longman Singapore Pte Ltd. for Singapore, Malaysia, Thailand, Indonesia, and Korea; by Norma Comunicaciones S.A. for Colombia; by Intersoft for South Africa; by International Thomson Publishing for Germany, Austria, and Switzerland; by Toppan Company Ltd. for Japan; by Distribuidora Cuspide for Argentina; by Livraria Cultura for Brazil; by Ediciencia S.A. for Ecuador; by Ediciones ZETA S.C.R. Ltda. for Peru; by WS Computer Publishing Corporation, Inc., for the Philippines; by Unalis Corporation for Taiwan; by Contemporanea de Ediciones for Venezuela; by Computer Book & Magazine Store for Puerto Rico; by Express Computer Distributors for the Caribbean and West Indies. Authorized Sales Agent: Anthony Rudkin Associates for the Middle East and North Africa.

For general information on IDG Books Worldwide's books in the U.S., please call our Consumer Customer Service department at 800-762-2974. For reseller information, including discounts and premium sales, please call our Reseller Customer Service department at 800-434-3422.

For information on where to purchase IDG Books Worldwide's books outside the U.S., please contact our International Sales department at 650-655-3200.

For information on foreign language translations, please contact our Foreign & Subsidiary Rights department at 650-655-3021 or fax 650-655-3281 or fax 650-3281.

For sales inquiries and special prices for bulk quantities, please contact our Sales department at 650-655-3200 or write to the address above.

For information on using IDG Books Worldwide's books in the classroom or for ordering examination copies, please contact our Educational Sales department at 800-434-2086 or fax 317-596-5499.

For press review copies, author interviews, or other publicity information, please contact our Public Relations department at 650-655-3000 or fax 650-655-3299.

For authorization to photocopy items for corporate, personal, or educational use, please contact Copyright Clearance Center, 222 Rosewood Drive, Danvers, MA 01923, or fax 978-750-4470.

is a trademark under exclusive license to IDG Books Worldwide, Inc., from International Data Group, Inc.

ABOUT IDG BOOKS WORLDWIDE

Welcome to the world of IDG Books Worldwide.

IDG Books Worldwide, Inc., is a subsidiary of International Data Group, the world's largest publisher of computer-related information and the leading global provider of information services on information technology. IDG was founded more than 25 years ago and now employs more than 8,500 people worldwide. IDG publishes more than 275 computer publications in over 75 countries (see listing below). More than 90 million people read one or more IDG publications each month.

Launched in 1990, IDG Books Worldwide is today the #1 publisher of best-selling computer books in the United States. We are proud to have received eight awards from the Computer Press Association in recognition of editorial excellence and three from *Computer Currents'* First Annual Readers' Choice Awards. Our best-selling *...For Dummies*® series has more than 50 million copies in print with translations in 38 languages. IDG Books Worldwide, through a joint venture with IDG's Hi-Tech Beijing, became the first U.S. publisher to publish a computer book in the People's Republic of China. In record time, IDG Books Worldwide has become the first choice for millions of readers around the world who want to learn how to better manage their businesses.

Our mission is simple: Every one of our books is designed to bring extra value and skill-building instructions to the reader. Our books are written by experts who understand and care about our readers. The knowledge base of our editorial staff comes from years of experience in publishing, education, and journalism — experience we use to produce books for the '90s. In short, we care about books, so we attract the best people. We devote special attention to details such as audience, interior design, use of icons, and illustrations. And because we use an efficient process of authoring, editing, and desktop publishing our books electronically, we can spend more time ensuring superior content and spend less time on the technicalities of making books.

You can count on our commitment to deliver high-quality books at competitive prices on topics you want to read about. At IDG Books Worldwide, we continue in the IDG tradition of delivering quality for more than 25 years. You'll find no better book on a subject than one from IDG Books Worldwide.

John Kilcullen
CEO
IDG Books Worldwide, Inc.

Steven Berkowitz
President and Publisher
IDG Books Worldwide, Inc.

Eighth Annual Computer Press Awards ≥ 1992

Ninth Annual Computer Press Awards ≥ 1993

Tenth Annual Computer Press Awards ≥ 1994

Eleventh Annual Computer Press Awards ≥ 1995

IDG Books Worldwide, Inc., is a subsidiary of International Data Group, the world's largest publisher of computer-related information and the leading global provider of information services on information technology. International Data Group publishes over 275 computer publications in over 75 countries. More than 90 million people read one or more International Data Group's publications each month. International Data Group's publications include: **ARGENTINA:** Buyer's Guide, Computerworld Argentina, PC World Argentina; **AUSTRALIA:** Australian Macworld, Australian PC World, Australian Reseller News, Computerworld, IT Casebook, Network World, Publish, Webmaster; **AUSTRIA:** Computerwelt Osterreich, Networks Austria, PC Tip Austria; **BANGLADESH:** PC World Bangladesh; **BELARUS:** PC World Belarus; **BELGIUM:** Data News; **BRAZIL:** Annuário de Informática, Computerworld, Connections, Macworld, PC Player, PC World, Publish, Reseller News, Supergamepower; **BULGARIA:** Computerworld Bulgaria, Network World Bulgaria, PC & MacWorld Bulgaria; **CANADA:** CIO Canada, Client/Server World, ComputerWorld Canada, InfoWorld Canada, NetworkWorld Canada, WebWorld; **CHILE:** Computerworld Chile, PC World Chile; **COLOMBIA:** Computerworld Colombia, PC World Colombia; **COSTA RICA:** PC World Centro America; **THE CZECH AND SLOVAK REPUBLICS:** Computerworld Czechoslovakia, Macworld Czech Republic, PC World Czechoslovakia; **DENMARK:** Communications World Danmark, Computerworld Danmark, Macworld Danmark, PC World Danmark, Techworld Denmark; **DOMINICAN REPUBLIC:** PC World Republica Dominicana; **ECUADOR:** PC World Ecuador; **EGYPT:** Computerworld Middle East, PC World Middle East; **EL SALVADOR:** PC World Centro America; **FINLAND:** MikroPC, Tietoverkko, Tietoviikko; **FRANCE:** Distributique, Hebdo, Info PC, Le Monde Informatique, Macworld, Reseaux & Telecoms, WebMaster France; **GERMANY:** Computer Partner, Computerwoche, Computerwoche Extra, Computerwoche FOCUS, Global Online, Macwelt, PC Welt; **GREECE:** Amiga Computing, GamePro Greece, Multimedia World; **GUATEMALA:** PC World Centro America; **HONDURAS:** PC World Centro America; **HONG KONG:** Computerworld Hong Kong, PC World Hong Kong, Publish in Asia; **HUNGARY:** ABCD CD-ROM, Computerworld Szamitastechnika, Internetto online Magazine, PC World Hungary, PC-X Magazin Hungary; **ICELAND:** Tolvuheimur PC World Island; **INDIA:** Information Communications World, Information Systems Computerworld, PC World India, Publish in Asia; **INDONESIA:** InfoKomputer PC World, Komputek Computerworld, Publish in Asia; **IRELAND:** ComputerScope, PC Live!; **ISRAEL:** Macworld Israel, People & Computers/Computerworld; **ITALY:** Computerworld Italia, Macworld Italia, Networking Italia, PC World Italia; **JAPAN:** DTP World, Macworld Japan, Nikkei Personal Computing, OS/2 World Japan, SunWorld Japan, Windows NT World, Windows World Japan; **KENYA:** PC World East African; **KOREA:** Hi-Tech Information, Macworld Korea, PC World Korea; **MACEDONIA:** PC World Macedonia; **MALAYSIA:** Computerworld Malaysia, PC World Malaysia, Publish in Asia; **MALTA:** PC World Malta; **MEXICO:** Computerworld Mexico, PC World Mexico; **MYANMAR:** PC World Myanmar; **NETHERLANDS:** Computer! Totaal, LAN Internetworking Magazine, LAN World Buyers Guide, Macworld Netherlands, Net, WebWereld; **NEW ZEALAND:** Absolute Beginners Guide and Plain & Simple Series, Computer Buyer, Computer Industry Directory, Computerworld New Zealand, MTB, Network World, PC World New Zealand; **NICARAGUA:** PC World Centro America; **NORWAY:** Computerworld Norge, CW Rapport, Datamagasinet, Financial Rapport, Kursguide Norge, Macworld Norge, Multimediaworld Norge, PC World Ekspress Norge, PC World Nettverk, PC World Norge, PC World ProduktGuide Norge; **PAKISTAN:** Computerworld Pakistan; **PANAMA:** PC World Panama; **PEOPLE'S REPUBLIC OF CHINA:** China Computer Users, China Computerworld, China InfoWorld, China Telecom World Weekly, Computer & Communication, Electronic Design China, Electronics Today, Electronics Weekly, Game Software, PC World China, Popular Computer Week, Software World, Telecom World; **PERU:** Computerworld Peru, PC World Profesional Peru, PC World SoHo Peru; **PHILIPPINES:** Click!, Computerworld Philippines, PC World Philippines, Publish in Asia; **POLAND:** Computerworld Poland, Computerworld Special Report Poland, Cyber, Macworld Poland, Networld Poland, PC World Komputer; **PORTUGAL:** Cerebro/PC World, Computerworld/Correio Informático, Dealer World Portugal, Mac*In/PC*In Portugal, Multimedia World; **PUERTO RICO:** PC World Puerto Rico; **ROMANIA:** Computerworld Romania, PC World Romania, Telecom Romania; **RUSSIA:** Computerworld Russia, Mir PK, Publish, Seti; **SINGAPORE:** Computerworld Singapore, PC World Singapore, Publish in Asia; **SLOVENIA:** Monitor; **SOUTH AFRICA:** Computing SA, Network World SA, Software World SA; **SPAIN:** Communicaciones World España, Computerworld España, Dealer World España, Macworld España, PC World España; **SRI LANKA:** Infolink PC World; **SWEDEN:** CAP&Design, Computer Sweden, Corporate Computing Sweden, Internetworld Sweden, it.branschen, Macworld Sweden, MaxiData Sweden, MikroDatorn, Nätverk & Kommunikation, PC World Sweden, PCaktiv, Windows World Sweden; **SWITZERLAND:** Computerworld Schweiz, Macworld Schweiz, PCtip; **TAIWAN:** Computerworld Taiwan, Macworld Taiwan, NEW ViSiON/Publish, PC World Taiwan, Windows World Taiwan; **THAILAND:** Publish in Asia, Thai Computerworld; **TURKEY:** Computerworld Turkiye, Macworld Turkiye, Network World Turkiye, PC World Turkiye; **UKRAINE:** Computerworld Kiev, Multimedia World Ukraine, PC World Ukraine; **UNITED KINGDOM:** Acorn User UK, Amiga Action UK, Amiga Computing UK, Apple Talk UK, Computing, Macworld, Parents and Computers UK, PC Advisor, PC Home, PSX Pro, The WEB; **UNITED STATES:** Cable in the Classroom, CIO Magazine, Computerworld, DOS World, Federal Computer Week, GamePro Magazine, InfoWorld, I-Way, Macworld, Network World, PC Games, PC World, Publish, Video Event, THE WEB Magazine, and WebMaster; online webzines: JavaWorld, NetscapeWorld, and SunWorld Online; **URUGUAY:** InfoWorld Uruguay; **VENEZUELA:** Computerworld Venezuela, PC World Venezuela; and **VIETNAM:** PC World Vietnam.   5/7/98

Credits

Acquisitions Editor
Andy Cummings

Development Editors
Valerie Perry
Susannah Pfalzer

Technical Editors
David Wall
Maryann Brown

Copy Editors
Luann Rouff
Michael D. Welch

Project Coordinator
Susan Parini

Cover Design
Murder By Design

Graphics and Production Specialists
Mario Amador
Jude Levinson
Linda Marousek
Hector Mendoza
Christopher Pimentel
Elsie Yim

Quality Control Specialists
Mick Arellano
Mark Schumann

Proofreaders
Mary C. Barnack
Annie Sheldon

Indexer
Sharon Duffy

About the Authors

Author and publishing consultant **Lisa A. Bucki** has written or coauthored more than 15 titles during more than eight years in the computer book industry. She has also contributed chapters covering numerous computer subjects such as online communications, presentation graphics, multimedia, and more for other books in addition to training users and managing more than 100 book projects for a number of publishers.

Elaine Marmel is President of Marmel Enterprises, Inc., an organization that specializes in technical writing and software training. Elaine spends most of her time writing and has authored and coauthored more than 25 books about software products. In addition, Elaine is a contributing editor to *Inside Peachtree for Windows* and *Inside QuickBooks for Windows*, monthly magazines.

David Plotkin is a Senior Data Administrator for Longs Drug Stores in Walnut Creek, California. He designs computer systems, specializing in databases and database systems. He has written several books on computers and computer software, and has contributed numerous chapters to other books.

To Steve and Bo, who prop me up at the computer in the morning to set me on my way and provide a seemingly endless supply of support and love.

—Lisa A. Bucki

Foreword

In an age when the Internet and other advanced technologies are drastically changing the way people use software, the desktop application suite has become an indispensable computing tool. From the start, Lotus has strived to address current computing challenges with vision, innovation, and responsiveness to our customers' needs. Lotus doesn't follow the industry trends—we set them. Today, SmartSuite Millennium Edition delivers a powerhouse of tightly integrated applications that equip you with tools and technologies for computing into the future.

Our vision has resulted in unmatched integration with the World Wide Web, enabling you to harness the power of the Internet to communicate with partners, colleagues, and customers around the world. In the Millennium Edition, we introduce a brand new application that is truly the most natural extension of the desktop application suite. Lotus FastSite makes Internet and intranet publishing so easy that anyone can do it. With exciting ideas such as FastSite, our vision continues to enable millions of desktop users around the world to compete and succeed in business every day.

At Lotus, we build innovation into everything we do, fully exploiting the power of emerging technologies. For example, speech recognition is now seamlessly integrated into SmartSuite. We introduced Java-based Lotus eSuite to the world and ensured that data can be easily and intelligently shared between SmartSuite and eSuite. Together with IBM, we're leading the way in designing applications that are ready for the Year 2000. And as Lotus 1-2-3 celebrates its 15th anniversary, its all-new, state-of-the-art features position it to revolutionize the world—again!

But perhaps we're best at turning your feedback into products that truly meet your needs. You asked for compatibility. SmartSuite users can now share data with almost any popular desktop application. You asked for integration with critical enterprise applications. We have provided unparalleled integration with Lotus Notes and Lotus Domino, as well as with SAP, PeopleSoft, Oracle, and many others. You asked for ease of use. We've simplified access to features, built in natural-language help, and now let you choose the menu you'd like to use. Years of technical expertise and direct customer relationships have honed our knack for delivering software features that are both cutting-edge and simple to use.

The power of the SmartSuite Millennium Edition combined with the road map in the *SmartSuite Millennium Edition Bible* from IDG Books Worldwide offers you a recipe for instant productivity. This book provides you with time-saving tips, instructions, and advice that you can use today to create, discover, publish, share, and analyze information.

On behalf of the entire Lotus team, I'd like to thank you for your support and wish you a successful computing journey into the new millennium.

Penny D. Scharfman
Group Marketing Manager
Lotus SmartSuite

Preface

Working with new software or experimenting with new features doesn't have to be a pain in the neck. We've developed the *SmartSuite Millennium Edition Bible* to ease you through the process of working with the eight applications in the Millennium Edition of Lotus SmartSuite:

- ✦ Word Pro
- ✦ 1-2-3
- ✦ Freelance Graphics
- ✦ Approach
- ✦ Organizer
- ✦ FastSite
- ✦ ScreenCam
- ✦ ViaVoice

If you're working with SmartSuite for the first time, or are an experienced user who needs a solid reference and an introduction to the features in the new version, think of this book as your personal guide. It offers everything you need to learn any or all of the SmartSuite applications.

Yes, this book is a comprehensive reference that presents the steps for tasks you can complete in SmartSuite. But this book also puts those steps in context for you, providing detailed examples; targeted tips and warnings; and ideas for using features to tackle challenges in the real world—your world.

Is This Book for You?

This book can be a lifesaver, no matter what your situation is with SmartSuite. If you've just joined a new company that uses SmartSuite, or your company has just adopted SmartSuite, read the first two chapters to get an overview of common SmartSuite techniques and read the first chapter covering each application. These chapters teach you an ample number of skills so you can make your way around.

If you have some experience using SmartSuite, you can delve into the subsequent chapters covering each application to discover features that move you beyond "muddling through" to "kicking butt." Likewise, if you never know what kind of critical project your boss will throw at you on any given day, this book can help you discover time-saving (and career-enhancing) features.

This book also contains coverage to appeal to more advanced users, or those who need a thorough understanding of a particular application or subject area. For example, the book provides expansive coverage of SmartSuite's Internet and communication features.

How This Book Is Organized

As in other reference books, each chapter in this book offers self-contained coverage of its topics. If you need only occasional help, you can dip into selected chapters as needed. If you're just getting started, however, you'll find that later chapters build on the techniques presented earlier in the book, so you can start at the beginning of the coverage for each application and work through it to build your skills. If you just need help when you can't get a particular feature to work, rely on the information herein.

We've divided the book into the following eight parts:

Part I: Your First Look at SmartSuite. This part introduces SmartSuite and the basics of using its applications, including an overview of the SmartSuite applications and how to use SmartCenter.

Part II: Word Pro. To learn how to use Word Pro to create impressive letters, memos, and other documents, rely on the chapters found in this part. You'll learn how to create, format, print, and organize your documents. You'll also learn how to use styles and scripts, and how to import and export information.

Part III: 1-2-3. A couple of generations of bean counters have relied on the 1-2-3 spreadsheet program to organize and calculate numerical information. This part enumerates all the 1-2-3 features that you can put to work.

Part IV: Freelance Graphics. This part of the book presents everything you need to create great slide shows with Freelance Graphics. You'll find out how to create presentations, develop presentation content, add charts, and run a slide show.

Part V: Approach. Database management can intimidate even hardy computer users. The chapters in this part reveal how straightforward and indispensable the Approach database program really is.

Part VI: Organizing Your Life. With downsizing and an employment crunch, we all need to be as efficient as possible to keep our jobs and to position ourselves for even better employment. This part explains how to use Organizer to organize yourself, and how to use the SmartCenter and SmartIcon bars to organize SmartSuite.

Part VII: SmartSuite Online. We all enjoy more ways to connect with each other online than ever before. Accordingly, SmartSuite offers more online features for connecting with other users than ever before, and this part details those features. You'll learn how to use FastSite to create a Web site, how to use SmartSuite's Internet features, and how to create Web pages using other SmartSuite applications.

Part VIII: Exploiting Other Features. This book's concluding chapters cover special-purpose SmartSuite features. We'll show you how to use ScreenCam, how to share information between documents, and how to use ViaVoice to select commands and enter content using your own voice.

Conventions This Book Uses

In a book this large, you need signposts to help you find your way. Numbered and bulleted lists break up the text and help you digest information more easily. The illustrations include as much information as possible so the book shows you — as well as tells you — what to do.

The book also includes special types of information highlighted with eye-catching icons in the margin. These icons point out power hints, trouble spots, other points to find more information, and interesting and useful tangents.

This icon highlights an interesting, perhaps more advanced, aspect of the current topic.

This icon points out shortcuts and killer techniques. More proficient users, in particular, should skim the text for these icons to beef up skills without reading about already-mastered techniques.

In every software program, some of the things you do may lead to an unwanted, frustrating outcome. Be on the lookout for these icons, which point out pitfalls to steer clear of.

This icon sends you to other places in the book for more information about something we mention.

SmartSuite programs share common features, and sometimes common information. This icon identifies instances where you can use the SmartSuite applications together for greater impact.

Sidebars

Sidebars (that look like this) give more detailed side coverage of topics or present examples that require more than a couple of steps. If you need to learn a feature in a hurry, you can bypass the sidebars. If you're looking to learn as much as possible, however, zero in on these features also.

Where Should I Start?

Chapter 3 provides the first coverage of Word Pro, SmartSuite's word processor. Start with this chapter if you need to crank out your first letter or memo.

Need to crunch numbers? Go directly to Chapter 8, which leads off the coverage for Lotus 1-2-3, the longtime workhorse of the spreadsheet world.

When you need to put together your first sales presentation, but only have a couple of hours to develop the content and the layout, turn to Chapter 14. This chapter introduces the Freelance Graphics presentation graphics program offered in SmartSuite.

If you think a database is some kind of stand that holds up your computer, go quickly to Chapter 20, which starts by explaining how to use the Approach database management program to capture, sort, and report lists of information.

Learn how to use Lotus Organizer to manage your appointments, to-do tasks, and contacts in Chapters 25 and 26.

To begin working with FastSite to pull together your files into an attractive Web site, turn to Chapter 29.

Help Online from the L-Team

You can rarely have enough varied resources to assist you with your ongoing and momentary computing needs. A library filled with well-written books from IDG Books Worldwide — coupled with a team of friendly, helpful, knowledgeable, and willing voices available to speak to your express and immediate concerns — forms a satisfying combination. To help members of its user community like you, Lotus supplies a team of dedicated, hand-picked, expert volunteer voices — the Lotus L-Team — to supplement its Web site and technical support team. You can find the L-Team via the Lotus CompuServe Forums. From locations across the United States and other nations, the multitalented L-Team could best be classed as a living, up-to-date, encyclopedic resource. The team consists of authors (computing and otherwise, one of our very own included), university professors, technicians, software developers, business owners, radio hosts, and other expert users. The L-Team members are real people who share their personal time to give you quality professional assistance with Lotus software. CompuServe members may take advantage of this valuable resource by typing in the "Go" words **LotusA**, **LotusB**, **LotusC**, **LotusM**, **LotusN**, or **WordPro**.

Acknowledgments

IDG brought together the talents of many people to produce this book, the best SmartSuite guide available (in my humble opinion). In addition to those of us who slaved over the writing, dozens of others contributed expertise, efforts, and information to enhance the book's content and shepherd it from raw text to finished volume.

Thanks to Andy Cummings and Nancy Stevenson at IDG Books Worldwide, who encouraged me to take on this project, and provided ample support to me and my coauthors, even when stamina and time were in short supply. Andy deserves special kudos for developing a strong relationship with Lotus, so we could verify technical information or untangle new features for readers.

The book's contributing authors, Elaine Marmel, Dave Plotkin, Micheline Long, Brian Underdahl, and Charles Brannon, deserve substantial thanks and praise for sacrificing vital free time to write crisp, thorough, informative, and inviting chapters. And Brian Underdahl batted cleanup near the end of the project, pushing this title toward timely publication. Thanks, everyone.

IDG's editorial team provided expert guidance in refining the text and ensuring the accuracy of the final product you now hold. Thank you to Susannah Pfalzer and Valerie Perry who supervised this monster, guiding us to make improvements and tracking all the pieces. Thanks to technical editors David Wall and Maryann Brown, who tested, checked, and rechecked every step. Thank you to copy editors Luann Rouff and Michael Welch for fine-tuning the writing and ensuring clarity. And thanks to the production department team, coordinated by Susan Parini, that beautifully formatted the pages bound herein.

Several folks at Lotus Development Corporation also provided invaluable help that enabled us to present a thorough — and timely — product to you. In particular, Craig Colwell (SmartSuite Product Manager) met with Andy Cummings and provided continuous support regarding technical issues and areas to emphasize in the book to best serve you, our readers. Thanks, Craig. Thanks also go to SmartSuite Product Manager Adam Frary, and to Craig Colwell's other Lotus colleagues: Barbara Fox, Gail Hughes, Paul Nott, Heidi Votaw, and Will Williams. And finally, thanks to Penny D. Scharfman for providing this book's foreword.

—*Lisa A. Bucki, Lead Author*

Contents at a Glance

Contents

Chapter 12: Previewing and Printing a Worksheet 383

Chapter 13: Using Data Management and Analysis Tools 391

Chapter 14: Saving Time with Power 1-2-3 Features............................409

Part IV: Freelance Graphics — 437

Chapter 15: Starting, Saving, and Opening Presentations — 439

Chapter 16: Developing the Presentation Content — 465

Part V: Approach   587

Chapter 28: Working with SmartIcon Bars 823

Part VII: SmartSuite Online   837

Chapter 29: Using FastSite to Create a Web Site 839

Your First Look at SmartSuite

This part introduces SmartSuite and the basics of using its applications. You'll learn how to start and quit applications, use application window features, give commands, enter information in dialog boxes, choose options in InfoBoxes, create and manage files, print, and get help. This part also discusses the SmartCenter, which organizes application startup shortcuts and other special features in drawers and folders.

Getting Started with SmartSuite Applications

With SmartSuite Millennium Edition installed on your system, you have access to applications and tools that enable you to handle nearly every business computing need. This chapter previews the parts of SmartSuite and explains how to start a SmartSuite application. The chapter covers operations you need to know in all the applications, including working with windows, choosing commands, creating and working with files, printing, and getting help.

Introducing SmartSuite Applications and Tools

Lotus SmartSuite Millennium Edition provides a group of applications and capabilities that enable you to use your computer to complete any key business task. Lotus built the SmartSuite applications to work smoothly with one another, with Windows, and with other applications set up on your system, such as your Internet browser program. The applications can share information and they feature a consistent look and consistent tools — the command for opening a file in one application is the same in another application. This approach ensures you'll be as confident and productive as possible when using any of the SmartSuite applications.

About SmartSuite's Applications

The six primary SmartSuite applications handle many mission-critical business tasks, from creating a simple letter to managing all of the customer and financial information for your company. The key SmartSuite applications include the following:

✦ **Word Pro.** Word processors are the most-used software application in business. Word Pro, SmartSuite's word processor, provides features for creating all types of documents, from simple memos to multicolumn, highly graphical newsletters. Whether you want to type a quick note or prepare a career-making report, Word Pro can help you make documents accurate, well-organized, and attractive.

✦ **1-2-3.** When you need to crunch numbers, you can launch the 1-2-3 spreadsheet program that's part of SmartSuite. 1-2-3 helps you organize numbers in a grid of rows and columns called a *worksheet*. Once you've captured the data, 1-2-3 can sort it, chart it, calculate it, and more. Preprogrammed formulas called @*functions* provide the mathematical and statistical expertise that you need to generate timely, precise information for business decision-making. Finally, 1-2-3 provides a number of features for formatting data, so you can highlight key stats or simply make the whole worksheet more appealing.

Note

Word Pro's ancestor, Ami Pro, was the first leading word processor to introduce easy-to-use document design features such as borders and columns. And 1-2-3 evolved from the first-ever spreadsheet program. These two products have a long history of new feature innovation.

✦ **Freelance Graphics.** As hardware has become more powerful and less expensive, users have gained the computing power that makes interactive onscreen presentations less clunky and more striking, incorporating better graphics, sounds, and animation. With Freelance Graphics, SmartSuite's presentation graphics program, you can build a presentation that you can print, display as slides or overheads, or even run sequentially onscreen. Whether you're creating simple bulleted-list handouts for a meeting or need to use your notebook computer to display a proposal presentation for a customer, Freelance Graphics provides the tools you need.

✦ **Approach.** Database programs help you organize and manage sets of information, like the key statistics about each product your company offers, or information about each employee. The Approach database application in SmartSuite can create very simple databases holding contact information, or complicated ones that hold dozens of types of information. Approach can sort information, summarize it, relate or compare information in more than one database, and generate attractive reports, so you can focus on the important facts and clues that data holds.

✦ **Organizer.** Before Lotus integrated it into SmartSuite, Lotus Organizer was the leading *personal information manager (PIM)* application. Using Organizer, you can track your appointments on a calendar, take notes, create a to-do list, create a contact list, and make calls.

✦ **FastSite.** SmartSuite offers the new FastSite program, which you can use to pull together information into a Web site that you can publish on the Internet. FastSite provides tools to help you better organize the pages in your site, control the links between pages in the site, and apply a uniform look to the pages.

SmartSuite offers one other application, ScreenCam. ScreenCam enables you to record actions you perform onscreen in another application. On systems equipped with a microphone, you also can capture your voice as you describe what you're doing onscreen. ScreenCam saves the onscreen action and voice annotation together in a movie file. When you need to communicate key details about a document or teach others how to use a particular program or tool, you can record that information in a ScreenCam movie, and send it to your colleagues.

About Other SmartSuite Features

Other beneficial features in SmartSuite provide functions that set SmartSuite apart from other software suites and provide you even more capabilities and flexibility for accomplishing your work. This book covers all these key features in SmartSuite applications:

✦ The SuiteStart buttons, described in the next section, provide the fastest way to start a SmartSuite application.

✦ SmartCenter appears as a bar along the top of your Windows desktop, and uses "drawers" and "folders" to organize files, application startup icons, help files, and special features such as a thesaurus. The SmartCenter provides a fast way for you to open files and applications, as well as tools you can use without launching another SmartSuite application.

Chapter 2, "Saving Time with SmartCenter," gives you more details about working with SuiteStart buttons and the SmartCenter.

✦ Team Computing features enable you to route files for comments, send messages to team members, and more. These features provide an automated way to get and integrate feedback for a project.

✦ Built-in Internet features enable you to save files to an Internet location, find information on the World Wide Web from within a SmartSuite application, and even save information as a Web page.

✦ New ViaVoice technology enables you to speak into a microphone to enter information in Word Pro as an alternative to using your keyboard to perform this task.

Starting a SmartSuite Application

Starting an application opens it onscreen in its own window so that you can begin using it to create a particular type of document. For your convenience, Lotus built a few different application startup methods into SmartSuite so that you can use the most convenient method given the operation at hand and any other applications you have open.

As with other Windows applications, you can use the Start menu on the Windows taskbar to launch a SmartSuite application. Click the Start button at the left end of the taskbar to open the Start menu. Move the mouse pointer up to highlight the Programs option. The Programs menu appears; it holds commands for starting Windows accessories, as well as several folders holding application startup commands. Move the mouse pointer to the right and down to highlight the Lotus SmartSuite folder option, which displays a menu of SmartSuite application startup commands, as shown in Figure 1-1. Move the mouse pointer to the right, then up as needed to highlight the startup command for the application you'd like to work with, and then click the command.

Click one of these startup commands.

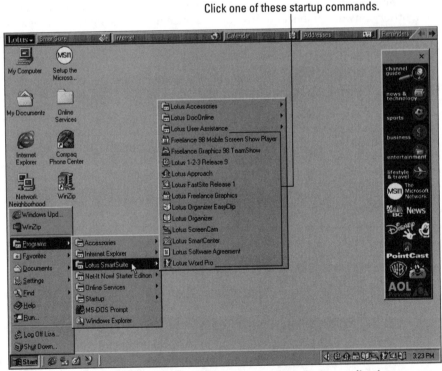

Figure 1-1: Use the Windows Start menu to open a SmartSuite application so you can begin working.

Starting a SmartSuite application, choosing a command, and virtually every other action in a SmartSuite application is the same, whether you're using Windows 95, Windows 98, or Windows NT 4 or later.

SmartCenter provides a second method for opening a SmartSuite application. Because the SmartCenter appears at the top of the screen by default, like menus in Windows programs, you may feel more comfortable using it to start a SmartSuite application.

The SmartCenter bar displays a number of *drawers*, each of which looks like a rectangle or elongated button on the SmartCenter. The first drawer, labeled SmartSuite, holds *shortcuts* (small pictures or icons that you select to perform an action such as launching SmartSuite applications), along with *folders* in which you can store files you create with SmartSuite. To use the SmartCenter to launch a SmartSuite application, follow these steps:

1. Click the SmartSuite drawer, which is the first one to the right of the Lotus button at the far left end of the SmartCenter. The drawer opens, displaying several folder tabs.

2. The first folder, Lotus Applications, should be open by default the first time you work with SmartCenter. The tab for the folder will appear "pushed up" to the top of the drawer. If it isn't, click its folder tab.

3. If the shortcut for the application you want to open isn't visible, click the down arrow at the bottom of the scroll bar at the right side of the folder as many times as needed to bring it into view.

4. When the shortcut for the application you want to start is visible (see Figure 1-2), double-click it to start the application.

There's one last way to open a SmartSuite application. You can click one of the SuiteStart buttons that appear at the right end of the taskbar, in an area called the *tray*, after you install SmartSuite. Simply click a particular SuiteStart button to launch the application it represents. Figure 1-3 shows the SuiteStart buttons.

Windows creates *associations* when you install an application and use it to create files. The association between the application and its files tells Windows what type of icon to use to represent each file in the Explorer. In addition, if you double-click a file in a Windows Explorer window, Windows launches the associated application (the application used to create the file), and then opens the file in the application. For example, if you double-click a 1-2-3 file in the Explorer, 1-2-3 opens and then the selected file opens. Each application assigns a three-character extension to the file name when you save the file, although you typically don't see the file name extension in recent Windows versions. Windows uses the extension to identify the file's association, so it knows which application to launch.

Click to open the folder.

Click to open the drawer.   Double-click to launch an application.

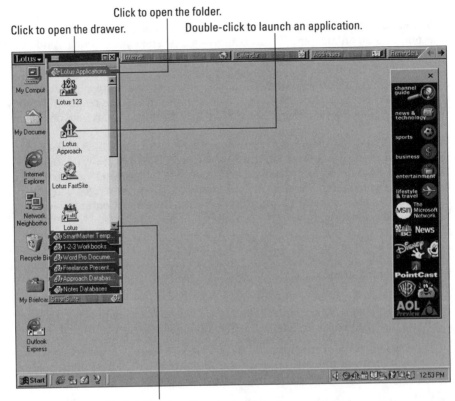

Click to scroll and display other shortcuts.

Figure 1-2: The first folder in the first drawer in SmartCenter contains shortcuts you can click to launch applications.

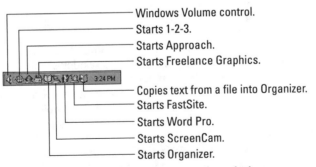

Windows Volume control.

Starts 1-2-3.

Starts Approach.

Starts Freelance Graphics.

Copies text from a file into Organizer.

Starts FastSite.

Starts Word Pro.

Starts ScreenCam.

Starts Organizer.

Figure 1-3: Click a SuiteStart button to launch the application it represents; this is the fastest way to open a SmartSuite application.

Note

Unless you work frequently with the SmartCenter, you may want to remove it from the screen to make more room for the application. (We'll hide the Windows taskbar in most figures after Chapter 2 as well.) To close the SmartCenter, select the Lotus button at its left end, and then choose Exit SmartCenter. In the rest of this chapter and the book, figures won't show SmartCenter unless it's being discussed in the accompanying text. If you do want to explore SmartCenter's capabilities, see Chapter 2, "Saving Time with SmartCenter," and Chapter 27, "Getting More from SmartCenter."

Common Screen Features

When Word Pro, 1-2-3, Freelance Graphics, or Approach first open, these applications display a Welcome dialog box, in which you need to specify whether you want to create a new document or open an existing one. Later chapters in the book explain how to work with the Welcome dialog boxes for individual applications. In Word Pro, for example, you can simply click Create a Plain Document to open a new, blank document.

Touring an Application Window

Once you've chosen to create a new file or open an existing file, the application window appears onscreen. Because each application offers different tools for performing different operations, naturally you'll see some differences between the windows for different applications. However, SmartSuite application windows also offer numerous similar features enabling you to use the same techniques to work with windows, choose commands, and so on. Figure 1-4 shows the Word Pro window, with key window features labeled. The application window in Figure 1-4 includes a blank document (file) window, too. The document appears fully enlarged, or *maximized*, by default. Document or file windows also offer consistent features you can use to control the window.

The window *title bar* identifies the application or document file. When the file window is maximized in an application, only one title bar appears, and it displays the application name, followed by the document name. Clicking a window's *Control menu box* displays a menu with commands for manipulating the window's size or closing the window. The application *menu bar* lists the names of pull-down menus that hold commands. When the file window is maximized, the application menu bar also holds buttons for the file window, such as the file window's Control menu box. The *Minimize, Restore,* and *Close buttons* for a window provide quick methods for working with the window's size; you'll learn about using these buttons next.

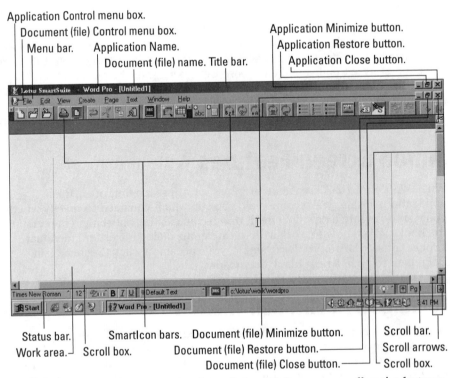

Application Control menu box.
Document (file) Control menu box.
Menu bar.   Application Name.
Document (file) name. Title bar.
Application Minimize button.
Application Restore button.
Application Close button.

Status bar.
Work area.   Scroll box.
SmartIcon bars.   Document (file) Minimize button.
Document (file) Restore button.
Document (file) Close button.
Scroll bar.
Scroll arrows.
Scroll box.

Figure 1-4: The application window in each SmartSuite program offers the features labeled here.

One or more *SmartIcon bars* appear below the application menu bar. Each SmartIcon bar holds a series of picture buttons called *SmartIcons*. Clicking a SmartIcon performs a command. The *work area* holds the contents of the currently open and active file, whether it's a Word Pro document, a 1-2-3 worksheet, or another type of file in another application. You enter, organize, and format information in the work area. After you've entered more than one screenful of information in a file, you can use the *scroll bars* to display different parts of the document. Click an arrow at the end of a scroll bar to scroll in the direction of the arrow, or drag a *scroll box* in the direction you'd like to scroll the display more quickly.

Most Windows applications offer a *status bar* providing information about the currently opened file, such as whether you're using a particular feature to work with it. In many SmartSuite applications, the status bar does even more, enabling you to apply formatting to a selection or navigate in the file.

Minimizing, Maximizing, and Restoring Windows

To navigate in Windows and SmartSuite applications, you need to master a few key window operations:

✦ **Minimizing a window.** Minimizing an application window reduces it to a button on the Windows taskbar. Minimizing a file window reduces it to a small title bar within the application window. Figure 1-5 shows both a minimized application and a minimized file window. The fastest way to minimize a window is to click its Minimize button, found at the right end of the window title bar, or at the right end of the menu bar for a maximized file window. If you prefer, click the Control menu box for the window, then click the Minimize option to select it.

✦ **Maximizing a window.** To return an application window to full-screen size or to make a file window fill the work area, maximize the window. To maximize an application window that's been reduced to a taskbar button, click its taskbar button. For an application window that's been minimized to a small title bar or any window that doesn't fill the available area for it, click the Maximize button at the right end of the window title bar. Alternately, click the window's Control menu box, and then choose Maximize in the Control menu.

Click the Control menu box to open the Control menu for a window.
    Maximize button.   This window is restored—neither maximized nor minimized.

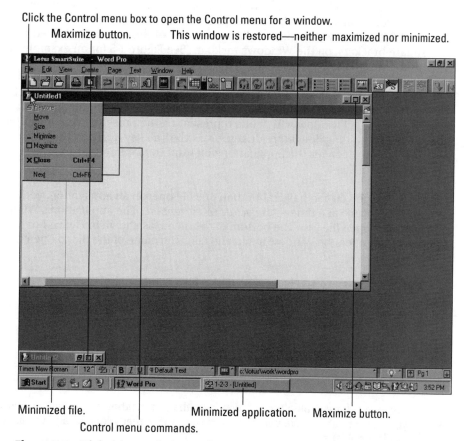

Minimized file.   Minimized application.   Maximize button.
       Control menu commands.

Figure 1-5: Minimizing a window reduces it to a button or small title bar, so you can focus on other work.

✦ **Restoring a window.** To specify an in-between size for a window, restore the window. Click the window's Restore button, or display the window Control menu and choose Restore. Then, you can drag any border of the window with the mouse, or drag the lower-right corner, to resize the window. You can drag the window title bar to move the window to another location onscreen.

Switching Between Applications and Files

During any given work session, you're likely to open a few different applications and even multiple files within any application. You need not close one application or file before opening another; you're free to open as many applications and files as your computer system can handle.

When you open an application, it becomes the *active* or *current application*. You can work only in the active application. To use the features in another application, you need to switch back to that application, or make it active. To use the mouse to switch to an application, click the application's button on the Windows taskbar. For example, if you started 1-2-3 earlier and want to make it the active application, click the 1-2-3 button, which also displays the name of the currently opened 1-2-3 file in square brackets, on the Windows taskbar. (See Figure 1-5 for an example of the 1-2-3 taskbar button.)

If it's more convenient for you, you can use the keyboard instead to select the active application. To do so, press and hold the Alt key, and then press Tab once to display a small window with icons representing the presently running applications. While still holding down the Alt key, press the Tab key as many times as needed to highlight the icon for the application you want to make active, and then release the Alt key.

Even though you can have more than one file open in an application, you can only work in one file at a time—the *active* or *current file*. The application's Window menu lists each open file near the bottom of the menu, as shown in Figure 1-6; to select the active file, open the Window menu and click the name of the file to open it.

Figure 1-6: Click a file's name on the bottom of the Window menu to make that file's window active.

When you have multiple open windows that are neither minimized or maximized, you can click any visible part of a window to make that window (and the application or file it holds) active.

Using Commands, Dialog Boxes, and InfoBoxes

This chapter has already described how to select a command from the Start menu or a Control menu. In the cases noted so far, selecting a command had a direct result. Other times, you'll need to provide additional details so the command has the result you intend. This section covers the ins and outs of selecting commands and specifying options for commands in SmartSuite. Even if you're not a computer novice, you should read through this section, because SmartSuite does offer a few unique twists on commands.

Choosing a Command

Commands perform actions in applications. Each pull-down menu on the menu bar groups related commands, to help you find the command you need, even if you're not sure of its name. For example, the Edit menu that's found in most of the SmartSuite applications offers four basic ways to select a command for working with the text or data you've entered in the application:

✦ **From a pull-down menu.** Click the menu's name in the menu bar to open the menu, and then click the command you want to select. To open a menu using the keyboard, press Alt plus the underlined letter (called the *selection letter*) in the menu name; or press F10 to activate the menu bar, press the right- and left-arrow keys as needed to select the menu name (the name will look "pressed" rather than highlighted), and then press Enter to open the menu. When a menu is open, press the underlined selection letter in the name of the command you want, or press the down-arrow key to highlight the command and press Enter to select it.

Note

This book uses shorthand expressions to tell you what menu and command to choose. An instruction like "Choose File ⇨ Open" means that you should open the File menu and then choose the Open command.

✦ **From a shortcut menu.** Before an application can perform some commands, you must select information or an object such as a graphic. Making a selection, however, also cues the application that you want to perform an action related to the selection. Right-click a selection and the SmartSuite application displays a *shortcut menu* with commands that apply to the selection, as shown in Figure 1-7. (Right-clicking means clicking with the right mouse button, rather than the left mouse button.) Click the command you want in the shortcut menu to select that command.

Hot Stuff

Press Esc twice to close an open pull-down menu. Press Esc once to close a shortcut menu. Alternately, click in the work area, away from the open menu, to close it.

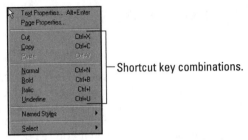

Figure 1-7: Right-clicking a selection displays a shortcut menu with commands that apply to the selection.

✦ **With a keyboard shortcut.** You can press the keyboard shortcut for the command, if available, to choose the command. For example, you can press Ctrl+O in any SmartSuite application to choose File ⇨ Open. The pull-down menus and shortcut menus list available keyboard shortcuts. Most keyboard shortcuts apply to commands for working with files, editing, or formatting a selection.

✦ **With a SmartIcon.** By default, SmartIcon bars appear below the menu bar at the top of the screen. Each SmartIcon represents a particular command. Simply click the SmartIcon to execute the command. To verify the SmartIcon's function before you click it, rest the mouse pointer on the SmartIcon. A yellow *Bubble Help* bubble appears to identify what the SmartIcon does, as shown in Figure 1-8.

Figure 1-8: To identify what a SmartIcon does, point to it with the mouse to display a yellow bubble with a description.

To display a particular SmartIcon bar, right-click any SmartIcon bar, then click the name of the SmartIcon bar to display.

You can move SmartIcon bars to other locations, as well as customize the contents of each SmartIcon bar. To learn more, see Chapter 28, "Working with SmartIcon Bars."

In addition to listing shortcut keys for commands, menus and shortcut menus include a few other special features, identified in Figure 1-9.

Divider lines separate related commands into groups. Check marks beside a command in a group indicate that command is selected or toggled on. Generally, only one command in a group can be selected at a time. Some commands have a triangle just to the right of the command name. The triangle indicates that the command displays a shortcut menu. You don't have to click the command to display the shortcut menu; instead, you can just drag the mouse down to highlight the command, called *pointing* to the command. When the shortcut menu appears, you can move the mouse to the right and down, then click the command of your choice in the shortcut menu. Finally, when a command name includes three dots (...), called *an ellipsis*, clicking the command displays a dialog box that you use to specify more options for completing the command, or an InfoBox that you use to specify *properties* (settings) for a selected object. The rest of this section explains how to work with dialog boxes and InfoBoxes.

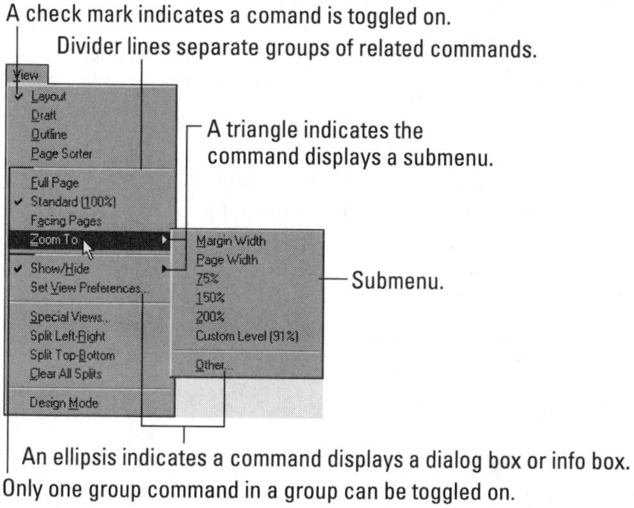

Figure 1-9: Menus provide cues that let you know when a particular command is enabled, or when you may need to provide additional information before the command executes.

Using a Dialog Box

Applications can't complete some commands if you don't provide more information. For example, you must specify a file name to complete the File ➪ Save As command, or choose a file to open after you use the File ➪ Open command. Other commands require that you choose from a group of available options, such as choosing which columns to sort by in a 1-2-3 worksheet. Dialog boxes offer numerous different ways to specify options, depending on what type of information the command needs. Dialog boxes can have any combination of these features (illustrated in Figures 1-10 and 1-11), sometimes called *controls*.

Drop-down list. ⌐ Title bar and Close button. ⌐

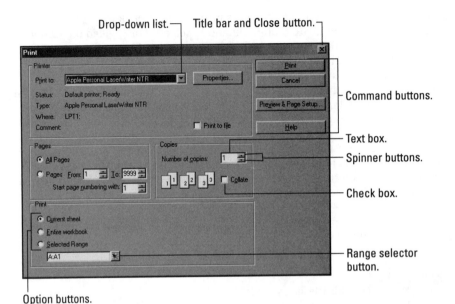

Command buttons.

Text box.

Spinner buttons.

Check box.

Range selector button.

Option buttons.

Figure 1-10: The Print dialog box for 1-2-3 contains many different ways to specify options for completing the File ⇨ Print command.

Scrolling list. Tabs.

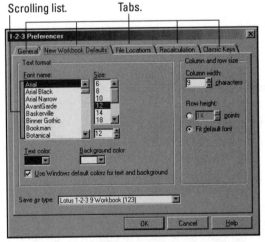

Figure 1-11: The 1-2-3 Preferences dialog box; the options a dialog box contains depends on the information the application needs to complete the command you chose.

✦ **Option buttons.** Option buttons (sometimes called *radio buttons*) appear in groups, telling you only one can be selected at a time. Click the option button you want to select it.

✦ **Check boxes.** Check boxes can be toggled on (enabled) or off (disabled). When you click to select the check box and toggle it on, a check mark appears in the box. Click the check box again to clear the check and disable the option.

✦ **Text boxes.** Click in a text box, and then enter the setting you'd like. Text boxes often appear in combination with a list box or drop-down list.

✦ **Drop-down lists.** When you see a down arrow at the right end of what looks like a text box, click the arrow to open a list of options. Click the option you want to select it.

✦ **Tabs.** Tabs or pages in a dialog box group related options, and help the dialog box offer more contents than could fit onscreen at once. Click the tab you want to bring to the front and display its options.

✦ **Scrolling lists.** Scrolling lists have a scroll bar beside them, as the name suggests. Use the scroll bar to view the options, clicking and holding one of the scroll bar arrows to scroll the list down or up. When you see the option you want in the list, click to select it.

✦ **Spinner buttons.** When a text box holds a numeric value, you may see a pair of up and down arrows at the right end of the text box. These arrows are spinner buttons. Click one of the arrows to increase (up arrow) or decrease (down arrow) the numeric value the text box holds.

✦ **Range selector buttons.** Some 1-2-3 dialog boxes contain a unique type of control called a *range selector button*. Clicking a range selector button collapses the dialog box so you can drag on the worksheet to select a range (contiguous block) of cells. After you select the range, the dialog box expands to its normal size, and the *address* identifying the selected range appears in the text box beside the range selector button.

✦ **Command buttons.** Command buttons perform actions when you click them. Virtually all dialog boxes contain an OK command button, which you click to accept your choices, close the dialog box, and finish the command. Dialog boxes also contain a Cancel button, which you click to close the dialog box without executing a command; and a Help button, which you can click to see Help onscreen. If a command button name includes an ellipsis (...), clicking that command button displays another dialog box.

✦ **Title bar and Close button.** The title bar for a dialog box displays the dialog box name. You can point to a dialog box title bar, and then press and hold the left mouse button and drag the dialog box to another location. Click the Close button at the right end of the dialog box title bar to close the dialog box without finishing the command or enabling your choices.

You can also use the keyboard to work with the options in a dialog box. When the dialog box opens, press the Tab key to move the highlighting (which sometimes looks like a dotted outline around an option name) to an individual control or group of option buttons. When the highlighting moves to controls like check boxes and command buttons, press the spacebar to select the control. When the highlighting moves to the contents of a text box, type a new entry to replace the existing one. For a highlighted scrolling list or drop-down list, press the down arrow to display or highlight other options in the list, until the option you want is highlighted. Similarly, when the highlighting moves to one of a group of option buttons, press the up or down arrow as needed to highlight the option you want.

Changing Settings with an InfoBox

An InfoBox collects numerous settings called *properties* that affect a selection or a certain part of a file. InfoBoxes gather settings that in previous versions of programs appeared in several different dialog boxes. For example, Figure 1-12 shows the InfoBox that holds text properties in Word Pro; the font settings and paragraph alignment settings it holds were in separate dialog boxes in older versions of Word Pro.

Figure 1-12: InfoBoxes do the work of several dialog boxes, and remain onscreen as long as you need them.

The controls contained in InfoBoxes work like those just described for dialog boxes. An InfoBox's behavior differentiates it from a dialog box. Once you select a command that opens an InfoBox, the InfoBox remains open until you click its Close button, enabling you to change the properties for numerous selections or objects in a file. So, for example, you could use the InfoBox shown in Figure 1-12 to change the properties for a text selection, make another selection and change its properties, and so on, before closing the InfoBox. (Your choices in a dialog box apply only to the current selection, in contrast.)

Press Esc to close a dialog box or InfoBox without applying any choices you made. Double-click the InfoBox title bar to collapse the InfoBox so it will take up less space onscreen. Click any tab in the InfoBox to expand it to full size.

How the Millennium Edition of SmartSuite Handles Dates

The Millennium Edition of SmartSuite comes fully prepared to deal with the turn of the century. The *Year 2000 problem* or *Y2K problem*, widely covered in the media, refers to the fact that most older programs assume all two-digit years you enter fall in this century, before the year 2000. In such a program, if you enter a date like 1/15/05, the program assumes you mean the year "1905," not "2005." Because we're moving forward in time, not back, programs need to be able to recognize dates after the year 1999.

The applications in SmartSuite Millennium Edition can correctly interpret two-digit year entries for this century and the next. Word Pro, 1-2-3, Freelance, and Approach all use the "80/20 rule" to interpret two-digit years. These applications assume that any two-digit year you enter falls either within the 80 years before the current year, or in the 20-year period that includes the current year and the 19 following years. So, if the current year is 1998, the application assumes a two-digit date entry falls somewhere between 1918 and 2017. If you enter 1/15/05, the application correctly treats that entry as January 15, 2005. If you enter 1/15/25, the application correctly treats that entry as January 15, 1925.

Organizer interprets two-digit dates similarly, but uses the 50/50 rule. It assumes a two-digit date entry falls either in the 50-year period that starts 49 years before the current year and includes the current year, or in the 50-year period after the current year. Again, if the current year is 1998 and you enter 1/15/05, Organizer correctly treats that entry as January 15, 2005. In contrast with the preceding 80/20 example, if you enter 1/15/25 in Organizer, it correctly treats that entry as January 15, 2025.

If you're dealing with historical data, such as creating a catalog of artifacts in Approach or a list of historical temperatures in 1-2-3, or if you otherwise want to override the 80/20 rule, enter years using all four digits, as in *1733* or *1899*.

If you want to learn more about how the SmartSuite applications deal with dates, choose Help Í Year 2000 if the application you're working in offers that command, or use the Index tab in the Help Topics dialog box to search for "2000." The "Getting Help" section later in this chapter explains how to work in online Help.

Mastering File Basics

If you've worked at all with a computer before, you know that applications create *files* or *documents* to hold information. You give each file a unique name that helps identify the type of information the file contains and helps you find the file again when you need to work with it, print it, and so on. This section covers crucial facts to help you work more effectively with the files you create in all the SmartSuite applications.

Navigating Drives and Folders in a File Dialog Box

The dialog boxes that you use to save, open, and otherwise work with files look very similar. Once you've learned to use a file dialog box in one application, you'll be able to use the same skills in other dialog boxes and other SmartSuite applications.

By default, a SmartSuite application saves the files you create in a subfolder on your computer's hard disk within the \lotus\ folder, the folder in which SmartSuite applications install by default. (A *folder* is a named storage area on a disk; each folder can hold files and other folders called *subfolders*.) So, when you try to save your first Word Pro file, Word Pro assumes you want to save it in the \lotus\work\wordpro folder, unless you specify otherwise. You may want to specify a different folder, for example, if you've created a folder to hold the files for each customer you serve or each project you manage. Or, you may want to save a file to a floppy disk instead of your hard disk (although that's not a great idea because hard disks generally provide more safety than saving to a floppy). All dialog boxes for working with files offer a drop-down list (called Save In, Look In, or something similar) that you can use to specify what disk to save a file to or open it from. Figure 1-13 shows the Word Pro Open dialog box, in which you use the Look In drop-down list to select a disk.

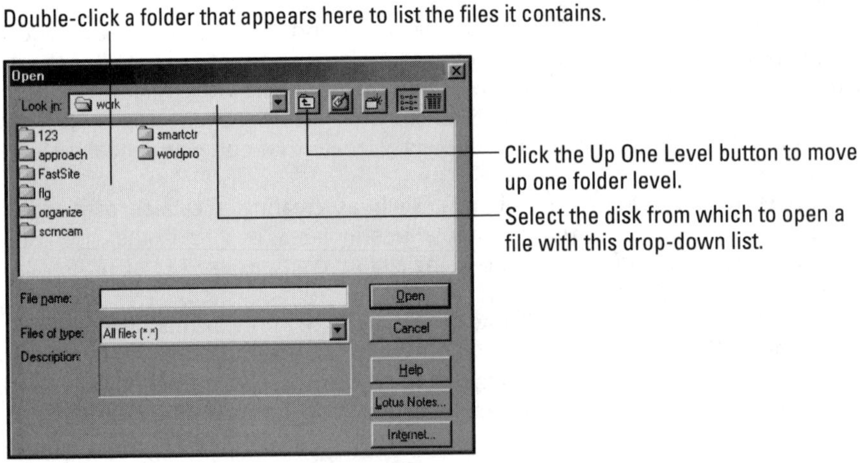

Double-click a folder that appears here to list the files it contains.

Click the Up One Level button to move up one folder level.

Select the disk from which to open a file with this drop-down list.

Figure 1-13: You must specify what disk and folder to save a file to or open in using the features in a file dialog box, such as this Open dialog box.

Click the arrow to open the drop-down list, and then click the disk you want. When a disk's folders (or the subfolders for a folder) appear in the list box below the Look In or Save In drop-down list, you can double-click the icon for a folder to display the files and subfolders it holds. For example, the dialog box in Figure 1-13 lists the subfolders within the \lotus\work\ folder. To display the files in \lotus\work\ wordpro in this example, double-click the wordpro folder in the list below the Look In list. On the other hand, to move up one folder level in a dialog box like this, click the Up One Level button on the dialog box toolbar. Continuing with the example in Figure 1-13, clicking the Up One Level button displays the contents of \lotus\.

If you want to create a new folder or subfolder while you're working in a file dialog box, right-click the area below the Look In or Save In list. Point to New on the shortcut menu, and then click Folder. An icon for the new folder appears. Type a name for the new folder and press Enter. You also can right-click a folder or file in a file dialog box to display a shortcut menu with commands for renaming, deleting, and performing other operations on the folder or file.

Saving, Closing, and Opening

Until you save your work in an application, that work exists only in your computer's working memory, called *Random Access Memory*, or *RAM*. Saving the work stores it in a file on a hard disk or floppy disk. When you save, you create a name for the file, and you use that name to later open the file and work with it again. No matter what SmartSuite application you're working with, use the following steps to save a file:

1. Choose File ➪ Save (Ctrl-S), or click the Save the Current Document SmartIcon on the Universal SmartIcon bar, which appears by default in the SmartSuite applications. (Note that this SmartIcon's name changes slightly from application to application.) The Save As dialog box appears. Figure 1-14 shows the Save As dialog box for Word Pro.

2. (Optional) Use the Save In drop-down list and the list below it to specify the disk and folder in which you want to store the file, as described previously in this section. If you don't change this setting, the application saves the file to the default folder it uses for files. Each application uses its own default folder. The Save In option enables you to organize your files however you want them on your hard disk, such as placing work-related files in a Work folder and personal files in a Home folder.

3. Click in the File Name text box (if the insertion point doesn't already appear in it) and type the name you want for the file.

Windows enables you to create file names with more than 200 characters, including spaces and special capitalization. So, try to make your file names as descriptive as possible. Include such information as the client's name, the type of document, and the date you created the file.

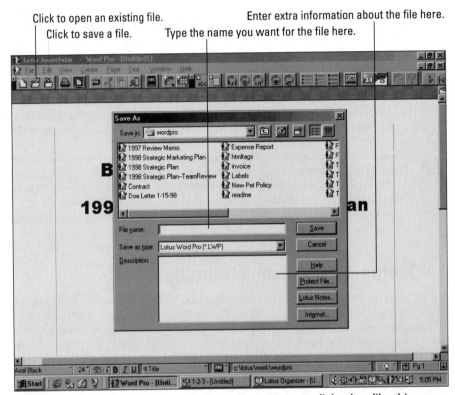

Click to open an existing file.

Click to save a file.

Enter extra information about the file here.

Type the name you want for the file here.

Figure 1-14: Each SmartSuite application offers a Save As dialog box like this one from Word Pro; use the Save As dialog box to give a file a name and to specify what disk and folder will hold the file.

4. (Optional) If you'd like to include additional information to help you distinguish the file from other files, click in the Description text box and enter that information.

5. Click the Save button to finish saving the file.

After you've saved and named a file, you should save it again periodically to ensure you don't lose any work. You also should save it before exiting or closing the application (described later in this chapter), to ensure all your changes are retained in the file. To save updates to a file you've already saved and named, choose File ➪ Save (Ctrl+S) or click again on the Save the Current Document SmartIcon. Rather than displaying the Save As dialog box again, the application simply saves your changes in the existing file, with its existing name.

Note

To save any file with a new name, choose File ➪ Save As. The Save As dialog box will reappear. Type a new name for the file in the File Name text box, and then click the Save button to finish saving the file under the new name, along with any changes you made to the file since you last saved it. The old file remains on the disk, under its old name.

Closing a file removes it from RAM and your screen, so you can no longer work on it. You should close a file whenever you've finished working in it to ensure you don't inadvertently make changes to it, and so that your computer can focus its resources on the files you do need to work with.

Each application offers a few different ways to close the current file. You can click the file window's Close button. The file window's Control menu, which you display by clicking its Control menu box, includes a Close command you can click to close the file. Pressing Ctrl+F4 invokes the Close command on the file window Control menu, closing the file. Finally, choose the application's File ➪ Close command to close the file. If the file contains changes that you haven't saved, a message box appears, giving you the opportunity to save those changes. Click Yes to do so, and the application closes the file.

After you've closed a file, you need to open it again to work with it. The SmartSuite applications provide a consistent method for opening files. Choose File ➪ Open or click the Open an Existing Document SmartIcon. The Open dialog box appears. Use the Look In list to navigate to the disk and folder holding the file you want to open. When the file you want appears in the dialog box list, click the icon for the file, and then click the Open button. The file opens in the application.

Printing

Each SmartSuite application offers different printing options (described in later chapters), but the overall printing process is the same. If you're already prepared to see a quick-and-dirty printout of a file, follow these steps:

1. Make sure you've turned on your printer and that it has paper.

2. Open the document to print, or select it to make it the current document.

3. Choose File ➪ Print (Ctrl+P) or click the Print SmartIcon. The Print dialog box appears. Figure 1-15 shows the Print dialog box for Word Pro.

4. If the printer you're using isn't listed in the Printer area near the top of the dialog box, open the Name drop-down list and select the name of your printer.

5. If you think you may need to adjust settings for the printer itself, click the Properties button beside the printer Name in the Printer area of the dialog box. A Properties dialog box appears, providing the options for your printer. Choose the settings you want, and then click OK to return to the Print dialog box.

6. Choose the other options you want in the Print dialog box. For example, you can increase the value in the Number of Copies text box in the Word Pro Print dialog box to print more than one copy of the document. The printing options vary depending on which SmartSuite application you're using, so if you're curious about the options for a particular application, refer to the chapter covering printing from that application.

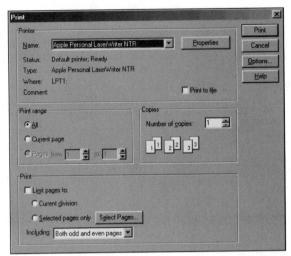

Figure 1-15: This Print dialog box holds the printing options for Word Pro; other SmartSuite applications offer different printing options.

7. Click the Print button to close the Print dialog box and send the file to the printer.

Getting Help

The Help menu in a SmartSuite application enables you to find the steps for completing a particular operation, definitions of key terms, and more. If you get stuck in an application, consult the Help Topics dialog box. To display the Help Topics dialog box, press F1 or choose Help ⇨ Help Topics. Figure 1-16 shows the Help Topics dialog box for Freelance Graphics. Each of the three tabs provides a particular type of help.

Click the Help command button in any dialog box to display a Help window describing how to use the dialog box to complete the operation at hand.

The first tab, Contents, lists Help topic areas within the help system. A book icon represents each topic area. Double-click a book icon to change it to an open book and list its contents — additional books and topics are represented by page icons. Double-click any topic to view it in its own Help window. To close a book, also double-click it. This tab is ideal for browsing through the available help.

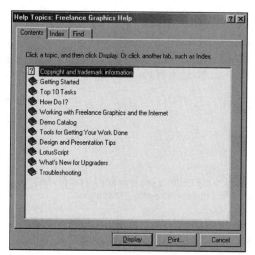

Figure 1-16: The Help Topics dialog box in any SmartSuite application offers three different types of help, each of which appears on a separate tab in the dialog box.

Use the second tab, Index, to search for a Help topic by name. Type the topic to search for in the top text box. Below, a list of topics scrolls to display the terms that match your entry. Double-click the Help topic you want in the lower list, or click it and then click the Display button. A Help window about the topic appears.

If you want help about a term, but can't find it via the Contents or Index tabs, try the Find tab. Follow these steps to use the Find tab:

1. The first time you click the Find tab, Help displays the Find Setup Wizard dialog box, so you can specify how many terms appear in the database the Find tab uses. Minimize Database Size (Recommended) is selected by default; you always can click the Rebuild button on the Find tab at a later time to choose another Find Setup Wizard option and build a larger database.

2. Click Next, and then Finish to build the minimal database. The Find tab becomes active.

3. Enter a word(s) to search for in the top text box and then click a word or phrase in the second box to narrow the list of Help topics displayed in the bottom scrolling list.

4. Click the topic you want in the bottom list to display a Help window about the topic.

The Help windows that hold information about a Help topic share common features to help you more easily navigate in Help. Figure 1-17 shows a Help window for Freelance Graphics, for example. Click the Help Topics button to return to the main Help topics dialog box for the application. Click Print to print the information in the window. Click Go Back to redisplay the last Help window you viewed, instead of the Help Topics dialog box.

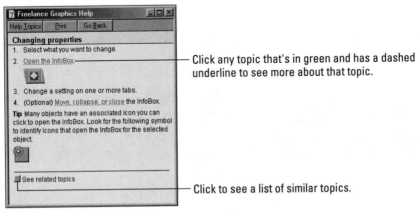

Click any topic that's in green and has a dashed underline to see more about that topic.

Click to see a list of similar topics.

Figure 1-17: Help windows like this one from Freelance Graphics work the same in all the SmartSuite applications.

Help provides more information about any topic in the window that's green and has a dashed underline; click the topic to display a pop-up box with more information or a definition, then click again to close the pop-up box. Finally, many Help windows include a See Related Topics button; click it to open a window listing other topics you can view information about in a Help window.

More Info   SmartSuite also offers Help about each application on the Lotus World Wide Web site. Later chapters explain how to access help on the Web in each SmartSuite application.

Two SmartSuite applications offer unique forms of Help on the Help menu:

✦ **Help ➪ Ask the Expert (Word Pro and 1-2-3).** This command (or clicking the status bar button with the light bulb on it) displays an Expert bar below the SmartIcon bars. The insertion point appears in a text box. Type a question in your own words or a topic to search for, and then click OK to display a Help window about the question or topic. A scrolling list at the right side of the Expert lists additional similar topics. Double-click a topic in that list to display a Help window about it. Click the Expert's Done button to close Ask the Expert.

✦ **Help ➪ Guide Me (Freelance Graphics).** This command displays a Guide Me window that lists operations you can perform from the current view or page (slide). Click the button beside the topic you want help with. Guide Me either displays a Help window with steps to follow or displays other windows with additional questions that you answer to proceed through the operation you want. Click the Cancel button or Close button to close the Guide Me window.

When you've finished working with Help, click the dialog box or the window's Close button to close any Help Topics dialog box or Help window and exit Help.

Closing a SmartSuite Application

When you've finished working with a file or application, you can close it (or exit the program) to free up system resources, such as memory, for other work you need to perform. As with closing a file, you can choose one of a few different methods to close any SmartSuite application:

✦ Click the application window's Close button.

✦ Right-click the application title bar to open its shortcut menu, and then click Close.

✦ Open the File menu for the application, and choose the Exit (Application Name) option.

✦ Press Alt+F4.

If you have any files open in an application you're closing, the application checks to ensure you've saved all your changes to those files. If you haven't, the application displays a dialog box asking whether you want to save your changes. Click Yes to do so, or No to close the files without saving your changes. In either case, the application closes.

✦   ✦   ✦

Saving Time with SmartCenter

Installing SmartSuite on your system makes a few cosmetic changes to the Windows desktop. By default, the Lotus SmartCenter appears at the top of the screen. In addition, the system tray area at the right end of the taskbar includes some new buttons — the SuiteStart buttons. This chapter explains how you can start using these desktop tools to access SmartSuite applications.

Navigating SmartCenter

Unless you specified otherwise when you installed SmartSuite on your system, SmartCenter loads automatically moments after the Windows desktop appears. As covered in Chapter 27, "Getting More from SmartCenter," if you've set up the SmartCenter to retrieve Internet information, it prompts you to connect to the Internet via the default Internet connection for your system. If you choose to connect, the SmartCenter appears at the top of the Windows desktop, as shown in Figure 2-1. (If you've set up your Windows taskbar to appear at the top of the screen, SmartCenter may appear at the bottom instead.) Rather than offering SmartIcons to click like the SmartIcon bars in other SmartSuite applications, the SmartCenter uses a drawer-and-folder design for organizing features that you'll want at your fingertips. Each drawer holds related items or features; for example, the SmartSuite drawer enables you to launch SmartSuite applications or open a particular file and simultaneously launch an application. Within most drawers, similar items are grouped into folders. For example, in the SmartSuite drawer, you find application startup shortcuts in the Lotus Applications folder; Word Pro documents in the Word Pro folder; and so on. So, anyone who has worked with files in a filing cabinet drawer will immediately feel comfortable with SmartCenter's layout.

Opens a menu for controlling SmartCenter.   Use to scroll the drawers.

Drawers.

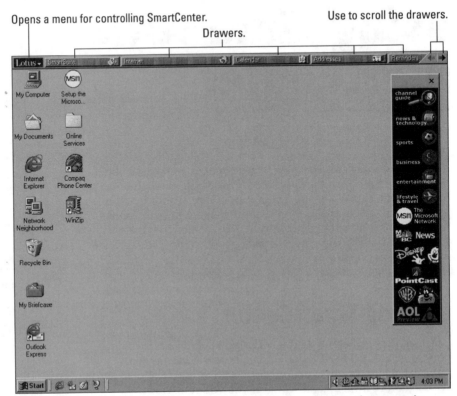

Figure 2-1: The SmartCenter provides folders you can use to launch SmartSuite programs, keep your calendar, and more.

Danger Zone

If you don't connect to the Internet when SmartCenter loads, you won't be able to work with the Internet drawer or some of the features in the Suite Help drawer (see "Scrolling the SmartCenter" below). On the other hand, if you connect to the Internet via a dial-up connection to an Internet Service Provider (ISP), which you'll learn more about in later chapters, you can't stay connected indefinitely without using the Internet in some way. After the connection is inactive for a certain period of time, the ISP may terminate it or at least prompt you to terminate it. In general, ISPs frown on users who leave a dial-up connection connected for hours on end, even for users with "unlimited access" accounts. Abusing your connect time could lead the ISP to ask you to take your business elsewhere. So, don't leave your connection to your ISP open. After giving SmartCenter a few minutes to update its Internet information, you can disconnect and then reconnect later as needed.

Scrolling the SmartCenter

On the SmartCenter, a drawer looks like a rectangular button. Each drawer button clearly displays the drawer's name at the left and a small icon-like picture at the right. The SmartCenter offers more drawers than can appear onscreen at once, and you have to be able to see a drawer to open it. When SmartCenter starts, you can see the SmartSuite, Internet, Calendar, Addresses, and Reminders drawers. You can use the arrows at the right end of the SmartCenter, which partially cover the Reminders drawer, to scroll right and left to change which folders appear. For example, if you click the right scroll arrow, the SmartCenter scrolls to the right to display three additional drawers: Reference, Business Productivity, and Suite Help. Click the left scroll arrow to scroll to the left and redisplay drawers hidden on that end of the SmartCenter. When you later add your own drawers to the SmartCenter (see Chapter 32, "Creating Web Documents with SmartSuite Applications"), you'll need to scroll to see those, too.

Save yourself the trouble of scrolling by changing the order of the drawers on the SmartCenter. To move a drawer, point to it with the mouse, press and hold the left mouse button, and drag the drawer over the drawer currently in the location you'd like for the drawer you're dragging. Release the mouse button and the drawer you dragged drops into the new position. The drawer that formerly held that position moves to the right.

Opening and Closing a Drawer

Just as you open a real file drawer to thumb through its folders, you open a SmartCenter drawer in order to select a folder and, subsequently, a file or feature within that folder. Click a drawer on the SmartCenter, and it opens downward to reveal folder tabs. You also can right-click a drawer and then click Open Drawer, but why use two clicks when one would do? Figure 2-2 shows the Internet folder open onscreen. To close the drawer, click again on its SmartCenter location (see the top of Figure 2-2), or click the bar holding the drawer's name at the bottom of the open drawer. To close the drawer, you also can click the button that appears near the top-right corner of the drawer to open a menu, and then click Close Drawer, though this process takes two steps rather than one.

Drawers remain open until you close them. In fact, you can have multiple drawers open at the same time, which enables you to move and copy some types of items — such as files — between folders that handle the same type of contents. If you launch or maximize a SmartSuite application or another application when a drawer is open, the application window covers the drawer. In that case, click the top of the drawer on the SmartCenter bar to close the drawer, and then click again to reopen the drawer over the application window.

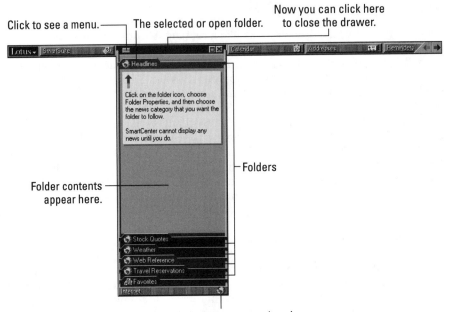

Click to see a menu. ── The selected or open folder.   Now you can click here to close the drawer.

Folder contents appear here. ──

── Folders

You can also click the drawer name to close it.

Figure 2-2: Clicking a drawer on the SmartCenter opens it to reveal its folders.

Selecting a Folder

Folders provide more specific groupings within drawers. Each folder holds a different type of feature you can use. When you open a drawer, the first folder in the drawer opens as well. This top folder in each drawer holds the features you're most likely to use from that drawer, but by no means all the features in the drawer. Other folders in the drawer group additional features. To select or open another folder, click the folder tab in the drawer. The folder tab slides up toward the top of the open drawer, and the contents of the folder appear in the central area of the drawer.

Selecting an Item Within a Folder

Chapter 1, "Getting Started with SmartSuite Applications," showed you how to launch a SmartSuite application using the SmartCenter. SmartCenter offers different types of folders, though, and each type of folder holds a different type of icon or feature. The "file" folder type works like a folder in Windows Explorer or My Computer. File folders hold application startup shortcuts, shortcuts for opening files, and files. To work with the icons in a SmartCenter file folder, use the same technique you'd use in Windows Explorer: double-click the icon or shortcut to launch a SmartSuite application and open a particular file, if applicable.

The following steps review how to launch an application and open a new file using a file folder in the SmartSuite drawer of the SmartCenter:

1. Click the SmartSuite drawer on the SmartCenter to open that drawer.

2. Click the SmartMaster Temp . . . (a truncated version of SmartMaster Templates) drawer to select it. This drawer holds shortcuts for creating new documents using SmartMasters, which hold formatting, starter text, and automated features to save you work in creating a new file of a particular type, such as a memo.

3. If you don't immediately see the icon for the item you want to select, look for a scroll bar at the right side of the folder. You can use the scroll bar to scroll down the folder display and reveal the icon you're seeking.

4. Double-click the icon or shortcut for the item you want to use. In this case, double-click the shortcut for the Word Pro Memo SmartMaster, as shown in Figure 2-3.

Figure 2-3: When a SmartCenter file folder holds shortcuts or file icons, you can double-click your selection.

When you select a shortcut or file icon in a file folder, the drawer and folder close, the application launches, and the specified file (if any) opens. For example, Figure 2-4 shows the new file created in Word Pro by selecting the Memo SmartMaster as illustrated in the preceding steps. You can work with the document as needed. The SmartCenter remains open onscreen, so you can use it later as needed.

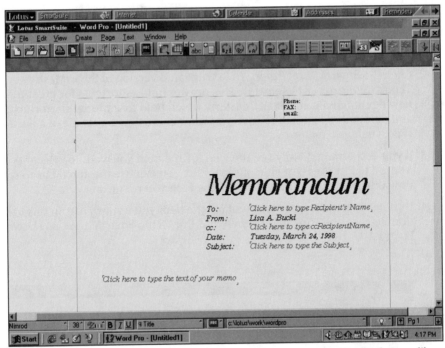

Figure 2-4: After you open an application and file from a SmartCenter drawer, like this new document based on the Word Pro Memo SmartMaster, you can edit, save, and otherwise work with the file.

Note

A SmartMaster contains formatting and starter contents like 1-2-3 formulas to help you save time in creating attractive, automated documents in SmartSuite. Later chapters explore the different SmartMasters offered in each of the SmartSuite applications.

Launching Help from SmartCenter

Even though a later chapter covers the ins and outs of working with the types of SmartCenter items you'll find in folders other than file folders, one additional feature you can access via SmartCenter merits mention here. You can use the SmartCenter to display some types of online Help for SmartSuite. The Help that you access via SmartCenter contains different contents than the Help you get from the individual applications, as described in Chapter 1, "Getting Started with SmartSuite Applications," even though you navigate the Help information in the same way. The Help you display from the SmartCenter covers overall SmartSuite features, such as using the SmartSuite applications together, rather than help about a particular SmartSuite application.

To learn more about using SmartCenter's numerous features, see Chapter 27, "Getting More from SmartCenter." That chapter reviews each of SmartCenter's default drawers and folders, and explains how you can create your own drawers and folders, store files and shortcuts in drawers, and more.

There are two ways to display the Help Topics: SmartSuite Help dialog box, shown in Figure 2-5:

✦ Click the Lotus button at the left end of the SmartCenter, and then click Help Topics.

✦ Scroll the SmartCenter to the right, then open the Suite Help drawer. If needed, select the Help folder, then double-click the SmartSuite Help shortcut.

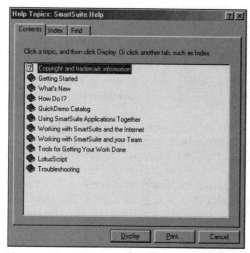

Figure 2-5: When you launch Help from the SmartCenter, the Help topics that appear apply to all of SmartSuite, not just a single application.

The Help Topics: SmartSuite Help dialog box offers three tabs that work just like the corresponding tabs in the Help Topics dialog box for an individual SmartSuite application. The *Contents* tab lists SmartSuite Help categories. A book icon represents each category, and you can double-click a book icon to open it and display the topics and subcategories it contains. Alternately, click the book icon and then click the Open button at the bottom of the dialog box. You can open a subcategory book icon to display the topics it holds. Once you see the topic you want in the Contents tab, double-click the topic or click it once and click the Display button. The Help topic appears in a Help window onscreen.

Rather than grouping Help in categories, the *Index* tab lists Help topics alphabetically. To use the Index tab to find Help, click the tab to select it, then type the topic or phrase you want in the top text box—Type the First Few Letters of the Word You're Looking For. The bottom list—Click the Index Entry You Want and then Click Display—scrolls to display the topics that match or most approximate the topic you typed. Double-click the topic you want in the bottom list, or click it once and click Display, to open the Help window for the topic.

Click the third tab, *Find,* when you want to see Help about a term or specific command that isn't listed as a specific Help topic, but may be covered within a Help topic. The first time you click the Find tab, the Find Setup Wizard dialog box appears, informing you that Help needs to build a search database of the words in Help. Leave the Minimize Database Size (Recommended) option button selected, click Next, and then click Finish to build the database.

Note

If the Find tab isn't displaying the terms you need Help about, you can adjust the Find database. To do so, click the Rebuild button on the Find tab to redisplay the Find Setup Wizard. To build the largest database possible, click the Maximize Search Capabilities option button, then Next and Finish. To fine-tune the database instead, click the Customize Search Capabilities option button in the Find Setup Wizard dialog box, then click Next. In the next five dialog boxes that appear, make your selections to adjust the terms in the database, then click Finish to rebuild the database.

With the Find tab selected, type the term, phrase, or command to search for in the Type the Word(s) You Want to Find text box. As you type, the lists at the center and bottom of the tab change to offer choices that approximate your entry. When you see a word or phrase that matches or approximates your entry in the Select Some Matching Words to Narrow Your Search List, click it in the list. The bottom list, Click a Topic, Then Click Display, changes to display topics that match or approximate your selection from the center list. When you see the topic that you think contains the word, phrase, or command you'd like help about, click it, and then click Display. The applicable Help window opens onscreen.

When you're working with a Help window, you can scroll to review the information it contains, if scroll bars appear. The Help windows for SmartSuite Help work just like those for individual applications, so review Chapter 1, "Getting Started with SmartSuite Applications," to learn more details. To return to the Help Topics: SmartSuite Help dialog box, click the Help Topics button near the top of the window. To close Help, click the Close button in the upper-right corner of an open Help window, or click the Cancel button in the Help Topics: SmartSuite Help window.

The Suite Help drawer on the SmartCenter offers three more drawers with different types of Help. (Some of the drawers may be empty, depending on how you installed SmartSuite). Open the Suite Help drawer and click the DocOnline folder to display shortcuts to several Help files in Adobe Acrobat format. Insert your SmartSuite CD-ROM in your CD-ROM drive, then double-click a shortcut to open the Acrobat document from the CD-ROM so you can read it. With the SmartSuite CD-ROM in the drive, you also can view interactive tours onscreen. The Lotus Online and SmartSuite Tips folders prompt you to connect to the Internet when you select them. After your system connects, the Lotus Online folder displays several hyperlinks to pages on the Lotus Web site. The SmartSuite Tips folder holds links to help about specific tasks, as shown in Figure 2-6. Click a link to launch your Web browser and display the Web information.

Figure 2-6: Click a hyperlink to display a Lotus Web page with a tip about SmartSuite.

Setting SmartCenter Properties

By changing a few easily accessible settings, you can adjust SmartCenter's position, look, and more to customize it for your taste and convenience. To customize the SmartCenter (as opposed to a drawer or folder in SmartCenter), choose the Lotus button at the left end of the SmartCenter, and then click SmartCenter Properties. The SmartCenter Properties dialog box appears, offering three tabs of settings that apply to the SmartCenter.

Figure 2-7 shows the first tab, Basics. The Display area near the top of the dialog box enables you to control two aspects of SmartCenter's appearance. Click to check Reserve Minimum Space for SmartCenter if you want SmartCenter to be available should you need it, but don't want it to take up much space onscreen. When the SmartCenter takes up minimum space only, it appears as a thin gray line above the title bar of a maximized application window. To display the SmartCenter, click that thin gray line. To resume working with the application, click anywhere in the application window. The Display area of the Basics tab also offers the Display Popup Help check box. With this check box enabled, SmartCenter displays a yellow Help label when you point to a drawer; as this label repeats the name of the drawer, most users will probably want to clear the Display Popup Help check box. The SmartCenter Position area of the dialog box enables you to control whether the SmartCenter appears at the Top of Screen or the Bottom of Screen. Click to choose the option button you want and reposition the SmartCenter.

Figure 2-7: Use the Basics tab options to control the display settings and position for the SmartCenter.

By now you've probably noticed that you hear a scraping sound effect whenever you open or close a SmartCenter drawer. Choose the Effects tab in the SmartCenter dialog box to display options for altering the sound and other effects for SmartCenter drawers. Figure 2-8 shows this tab. Open the Event drop-down list and use it to choose a drawer action, so you can adjust its sound effect. You can choose from six events: Open Drawer, Close Drawer, Delete Drawer, Add Drawer, Select Folder, and Add Folder. After selecting the event, you can use the Sound drop-down list to choose a different sound, but this list only offers the sounds already assigned to the delete, select, open, and add events. However, you should open the Sound drop-down list and choose (None) when you want to remove the current sound effect for the selected event. To assign another .WAV sound file that's stored on your hard disk to the selected event, click the Browse button on the Effects tab. The Browse for dialog box appears; the dialog box title bar includes the name of the event to which you're assigning the sound. This dialog box works like other dialog boxes for working with files, covered in Chapter 1, "Getting Started with SmartSuite Applications," so navigate to the folder that holds the sound you want. If needed, click a sound in the list of sound files, and then click the left button in the Preview area (see Figure 2-9) to listen to the sound. Double-click the sound you want to select it and close the Browse for dialog box. If the SmartCenter drawers open too slowly or quickly on your system, drag the slider bar in the Drawer Speed area of the Effects tab to make the drawer speed slower or faster.

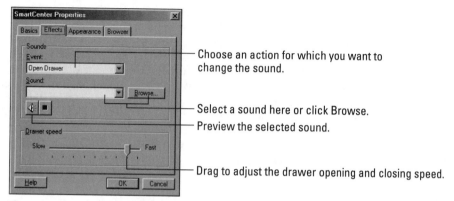

Choose an action for which you want to change the sound.

Select a sound here or click Browse.
Preview the selected sound.

Drag to adjust the drawer opening and closing speed.

Figure 2-8: Use this tab to select sounds for SmartCenter drawers and control how quickly drawers open and close.

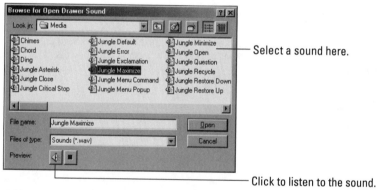

Select a sound here.

Click to listen to the sound.

Figure 2-9: You can browse for sounds to add to a SmartCenter folder event, such as opening a drawer.

Your Sound Source

Windows offers numerous sound files (see Figure 2-9), most of which are copied to your hard disk when you choose to install various sound schemes using the Windows setup program. Look in the \Windows\Media folder to see what sounds may be lurking in your current Windows installation. Alternately, use Start ⇨ Find ⇨ Files or Folders to search for additional .WAV files that may have been copied to your hard disk during the setup for other programs. You can, of course, also find and download sounds from the Internet, as long as those files are for your personal use only.

The Appearance tab gives you choices for applying a different design and color scheme to the drawers. Figure 2-10 shows the options in this dialog box. Lotus refers to the combination of color and design for the drawers as a "texture." To ensure you'll find a pleasing texture no matter what your system's display capabilities are, the Appearance tab offers textures optimized for different numbers of display colors. The first six textures look great on screens displaying 16 or 256 colors. The next several textures look best when used on a system that displays in High Color, also called 16-bit color. If you want a more generic appearance, or none of the others look right on your system, scroll to the bottom of the list of options to find None, which removes the current texture from the SmartCenter. Click the texture you want, then click OK to close the SmartCenter Properties dialog box.

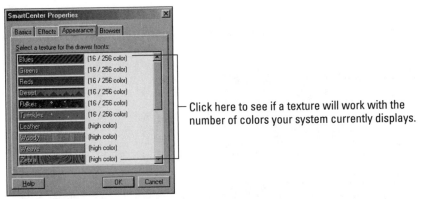

Click here to see if a texture will work with the
number of colors your system currently displays.

Figure 2-10: If you're not satisfied with how the SmartCenter
drawers look, choose a texture here to snazz them up.

The final tab, Browser, offers only two choices. Choose the System Default Browser option button if you want SmartSuite to open your default Internet browser when you click a link or call on another feature that requires your system to connect to the Internet. Choose SmartCenter Browser if you don't have a browser you prefer already installed on your system. Click OK to close the SmartCenter Properties dialog box to finish changing the settings in it, if needed.

You can change a couple of settings for SmartCenter without displaying the SmartCenter dialog box. To move the SmartCenter between the top and bottom of the screen, double-click a blank area on it — either between two drawers or at the far right end of the SmartCenter. To select a new texture for the drawers, click a blank area of the SmartCenter, and then press F8 repeatedly, until the texture you want appears on the drawers. When the color you want appears, click outside the SmartCenter or press Esc.

Closing and Launching SmartCenter

If your system has 16M or less of random access memory (RAM), you may need to be careful about how many applications you have open at any given time. If this describes your situation, or if you simply don't use the SmartCenter often, you may want to close the SmartCenter to remove it from your screen and free up the RAM it used for other uses.

You can close the SmartCenter at any time. To do so, choose the Lotus button at the left end of the SmartCenter, then click Exit SmartCenter.

Once you close SmartCenter, though, it isn't closed for good. If you alter your system so that SmartCenter doesn't load automatically (as described in the final section of this chapter, "Preventing SmartCenter or SuiteStart from Loading on Startup") or if you close the SmartCenter, you can use the Windows Start menu to reload SmartCenter. Choose Start ➪ Programs ➪ Lotus SmartSuite ➪ Lotus SmartCenter. The SmartCenter reopens, and prompts you to connect to the Internet if any SmartCenter drawers are set up to connect to the Internet. Connect if you wish, and resume your work as usual.

Working with SuiteStart Icons

The right end of the Windows taskbar contains an area called the *tray* that typically displays the current time (system clock); a volume icon you can use to control speaker volume and other sound settings for your system; a printer icon when you're printing; a connection icon when your computer is using your modem to connect to the Internet or an online service; and other icons, depending on the software and hardware installed for your system. If you perform the Typical installation for SmartSuite, the taskbar tray also offers several new icons called the *SuiteStart icons*.

The SuiteStart icons provide a one-click method for opening a SmartSuite application. Point to a SuiteStart icon to display a pop-up label telling you which application the icon starts. When you've identified the correct SuiteStart icon, click it to launch the application.

You may not need all of the SuiteStart icons to appear on your tray. For example, if you never use Lotus ScreenCam, you may want to remove that icon to reduce clutter and make it easier for you to click the icon you do need. To remove a SuiteStart icon from the tray, right-click the icon, and then click the Remove *X* Icon choice, where X is the name of the application icon to remove, as shown in Figure 2-11.

Figure 2-11: Right-click the SuiteStart icon and then click the Remove option if you no longer want the icon to appear on the tray.

At any later time, you can add a SuiteStart icon back to the tray. Right-click a SuiteStart icon in the tray, then choose Add File. The Add File dialog box that appears lists shortcuts for launching the SmartSuite applications. The shortcuts that appear in the folder shown in the Add File dialog box represent only the SuiteStart icons that currently appear on the tray; removing an icon earlier removed its shortcut from the folder. Use the Look In list to navigate to the folder that holds the startup command for the SmartSuite application for which you want to add an icon. For example, navigate to the \lotus\scrncam\ folder to display SCRNCAM.EXE, the startup file for ScreenCam. Click the startup file for the application you want, then click Open, or simply double-click the file. The SuiteStart icon for the selected application should reappear in the tray. If it doesn't, right-click a SuiteStart icon and click the Refresh command to refresh the SuiteStart contents.

Preventing SmartCenter or SuiteStart from Loading on Startup

You can use the Add/Remove Programs Properties icon in Control Panel to uninstall features within SmartSuite. This is covered in Appendix A, "Installing SmartSuite," because the simple process works the same (for the most part) as for other Windows applications. However, this method can be somewhat slow and tedious, and may require you to restart your system. Plus, if you use this method to remove SmartCenter from your system, you won't be able to use SmartCenter at all.

You can instead try a faster solution that leaves SmartCenter and SuiteStart installed on your system, but gives you the option of loading them only when you want to, sometime after you've started your system and begun working. Follow these steps to prevent the automatic loading of SmartCenter, SuiteStart, or both when you start Windows:

1. Right-click the Windows taskbar, then click Properties. The Taskbar Properties dialog box appears. (Alternately, choose Start ⇨ Settings ⇨ Taskbar & Start Menu.)

2. Choose the Start Menu Programs tab.

3. Click the Advanced button to display the Exploring-Startup Menu window. (Even though this window looks much like a Windows Explorer window, it's not, and the steps here won't work if you try to navigate through the Explorer rather than through Taskbar Properties.)

4. In the left pane of the window, click the plus sign beside the Programs folder icon. Its subfolders appear.

5. Double-click the Startup folder icon to display its contents in the Contents pane at the right side of the window.

6. In the right pane, click the shortcut for whichever startup application you want to remove, such as the Lotus SmartCenter shortcut. If you want to remove both applications from startup, press the Ctrl key and click the second shortcut.

7. Click the Cut button to remove the selected shortcuts from the Startup folder, open My Computer on the desktop, navigate to the drive and folder where you want to store the shortcuts, and click the Paste button. Alternately, you can move the shortcuts to the desktop by dragging them from the window and dropping them on the desktop; Figure 2-12 shows how both the Lotus SmartCenter and Lotus SuiteStart shortcuts appear when dragged and dropped onto the desktop.

8. Click the Close button for the Exploring-Startup window to close it, then click OK to close the Taskbar Properties dialog box and save your changes.

Once you've moved the shortcut(s) as just described, the next time you start or restart your system, the application(s) will no longer load. When you need SmartCenter or SuiteStart, you can double-click its shortcut in the location where you loaded it. That's why placing those shortcuts on the desktop will prove convenient. Alternately, you could place the startup shortcut for SuiteCenter into the Lotus Applications folder of the SmartSuite drawer on the SmartCenter, but this won't work for the SmartCenter startup (because you'd have to start SmartCenter to be able to access the shortcut for starting SmartCenter).

To temporarily unload all the SuiteStart icons from the tray, press Ctrl+Alt+Del at the Windows desktop to display the Close Program dialog box. Click Suitest in the list of open programs, then click End Task. To reload the SuiteStart icons, restart your system or double-click the Lotus SuiteStart shortcut if you've placed it on your desktop or in a folder on your hard disk or SmartCenter.

The shortcuts were dragged from here . . .

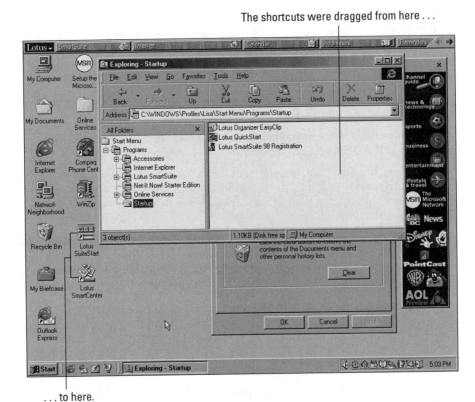

. . . to here.

Figure 2-12: Move the SmartCenter and SuiteStart shortcuts from the Startup folder to the desktop to prevent automatic program loading but still give you easy access.

✦   ✦   ✦

Word Pro

To learn how to use Word Pro to create impressive letters, memos, and other documents, rely on the chapters found in this part. You'll learn about the unique features of the Word Pro document window, and how to create a document after you start Word Pro. Explore the numerous techniques for entering and editing text, and then review how to polish that text by checking the spelling and grammar, changing words with the thesaurus, and tracking changes with revision marks. Then, apply the bells and whistles that make a document attractive, and then publish it on paper. We review the dozens of features available for changing the look of your text and explain how to use frames and tables to control text layout, and how to create master documents, divisions, and sections to bring together information with different formatting requirements.

You'll learn more advanced techniques such as how to automate your documents, how to create and use styles to quickly format text, and how to add Click Here blocks. You'll also find out how to record a script that performs a task, and how to create dozens (or hundreds) of individually addressed letters and envelopes by merging data into placeholders you specify in a document. Finally, we explore how to import information from other applications into a Word Pro document, or export Word Pro information for use in another program.

Creating and Working with Word Pro Documents

This chapter helps you accomplish your most mission-critical business tasks with Word Pro, SmartSuite's word processing program. Learn here how to start and move around in Word Pro, create a new document such as a letter, enter the document's contents, and save the document with the name you choose. The chapter also explains how to open and work with existing documents, use Word Pro's tools for reviewing and improving your text, and save and close documents when you've finished working with them.

Starting Word Pro and Making a New Document

To start the Word Pro program so that you can begin using it to create new documents, you can use any of the methods for launching SmartSuite applications presented in Chapter 1, "Getting Started with SmartSuite Applications":

✦ Choose Start ➪ Programs ➪ Lotus SmartSuite ➪ Lotus Word Pro.

✦ Open the SmartSuite drawer on the SmartCenter, then open the Lotus Applications drawer, if needed. Double-click the Lotus Word Pro shortcut.

✦ Click the Word Pro SuiteStart button on the right end of the taskbar.

Word Pro launches, displaying its Welcome to Lotus Word Pro dialog box, shown in Figure 3-1. (If you're prompted to enter information about yourself, as described next in this section, you'll have to do so before you see the dialog box.) The tabs in the dialog box list the choices you have for creating or opening a document. The remainder of this section explains how to create a new document. Later, the chapter teaches you how to open a document you've previously created.

Clicked here to list documents you've worked with recently.

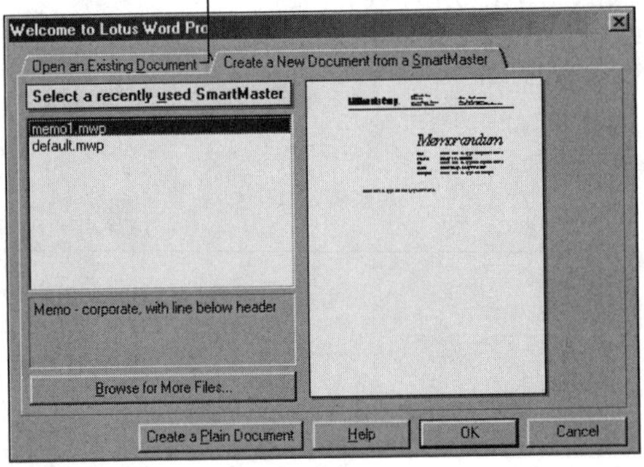

Figure 3-1: The Welcome to Word Pro dialog box prompts you to create a new file or open a file you've created earlier.

Entering Information About Yourself

The first time you start Word Pro, the program may prompt you to enter a variety of information about yourself, such as your title, company address, phone numbers, e-mail address, and more. You should take the time to enter this information, because Word Pro can then use the information you've entered when you create a document based on a SmartMaster (described later in this section), so you don't have to type that information in every document you create. You also can change the information you enter at any later time, using the same dialog box that Word Pro displays initially. To do so, choose File ⇨ User Setup ⇨ Word Pro Preferences, then click the Personal tab. Enter information or change the entries in the text boxes shown in Figure 3-2, then click OK.

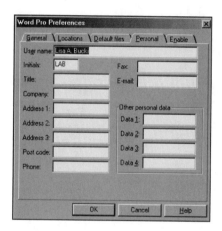

Figure 3-2: Word Pro uses the information you enter here to save you the trouble of retyping information about yourself in every document you create.

Making a Blank New Document

If you want to start with a completely blank page and build every aspect of your document, click the Create a Plain Document button in the lower-left corner of the Welcome to Lotus Word Pro dialog box (see Figure 3-1). Or, click the **Default.mwp** option in the Select a Recently Used SmartMaster list of the Create a New Document from a SmartMaster tab, and then click OK. Word Pro closes the Welcome screen and displays a new, blank document onscreen. As shown in Figure 3-3, Word Pro names the first document you create [Untitled 1], and sequentially numbers subsequent new documents you create as [Untitled2], [Untitled3], and so on. To give the document a unique name, save the new document as described later under "Saving and Naming a File."

Create a New Document SmartIcon.

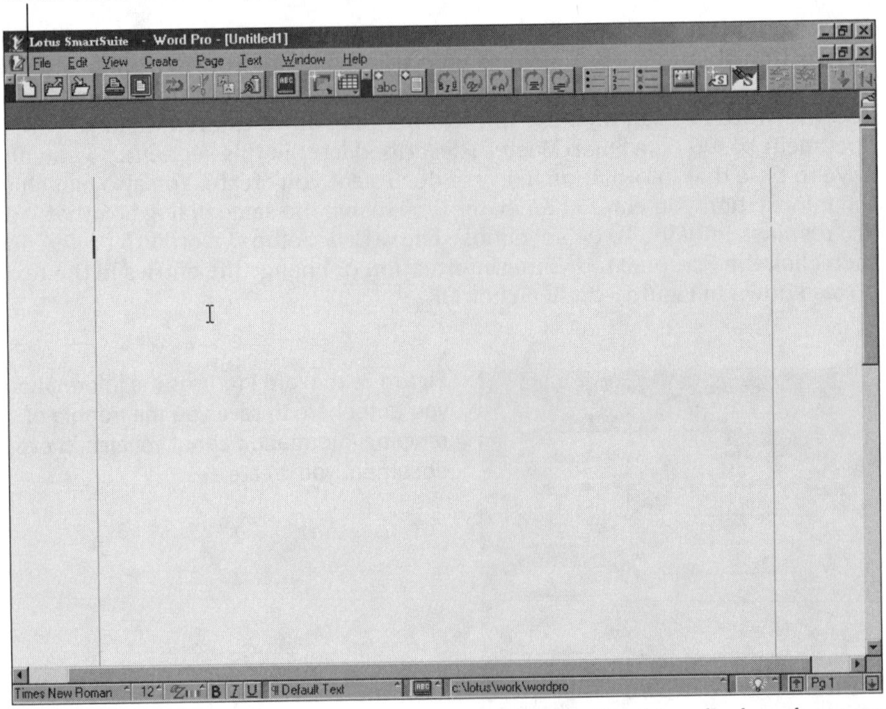

Figure 3-3: When you choose Create a New Document, Word Pro displays the empty first page for the document.

Using a SmartMaster to create a new document

SmartMasters provide the blueprint, or template, for various types of files, both in Word Pro and in other SmartSuite applications. For example, if you want to create a memo with standard information at the top (Title, Date:, To:, From:, and so on), you can choose a memo SmartMaster that will "type" that standard information for you in a new document. In addition, SmartMasters provide attractive formatting for the text. Everything you type in the document created from a SmartMaster adopts the same look as the starter text already in the SmartMaster, ensuring a polished look for your work. In some cases, SmartMasters include graphic images for your documents, too.

Follow these steps to use a SmartMaster to create a new Word Pro document:

1. Choose File ➪ New Document or click the Create a New Document SmartIcon to display the New Document dialog box, which looks somewhat like the Welcome to Lotus Word Pro dialog box.

2. Click the Create from Any SmartMaster tab to display the available SmartMasters, and then scroll the Select a Type of SmartMaster list to display the option that describes the type of document you'd like to create. When you see the option you want, click it once. For example, you could click the Memo option.

3. The tab changes to list the looks for the type of SmartMaster you selected in Step 2. For example, Figure 3-4 shows the 2. Select a Look options Word Pro presents if you select Memo in Step 2.

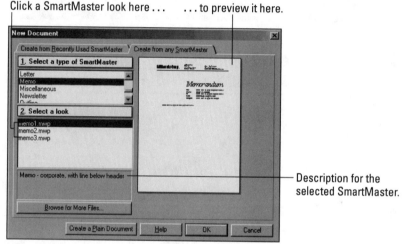

Click a SmartMaster look here . . .   . . . to preview it here.

Description for the selected SmartMaster.

Figure 3-4: Word Pro offers multiple SmartMasters for creating certain types of documents, like the memo choices shown here.

4. To preview one of the listed looks, click it. The example document to the right of the list changes to show you what a document based on the selected SmartMaster option would look like.

5. Once you've found the SmartMaster that has the look you want, double-click it in the list in the 2. Select a Look list, or click it once and click the OK button. Figure 3-5 shows an example memo created from a SmartMaster.

The document in Figure 3-5 illustrates some of the benefits a typical SmartMaster offers. If you use the Personal tab in the Word Pro Preferences dialog box (see Figure 3-2) to enter information about yourself, that information appears in special *fields* defined by the SmartMaster, so you don't have to type that information. Another field in the example enters the current date; the SmartMaster automatically updates the date each time you open the document. The different types of memo text, such as the company name and title, appear with attractive formatting specified by the

SmartMaster. Also note that red brackets set off several areas of italicized text, all of which begin with the phrase "Click here." These *Click Here blocks* prompt you to fill in other areas of text to make the document complete.

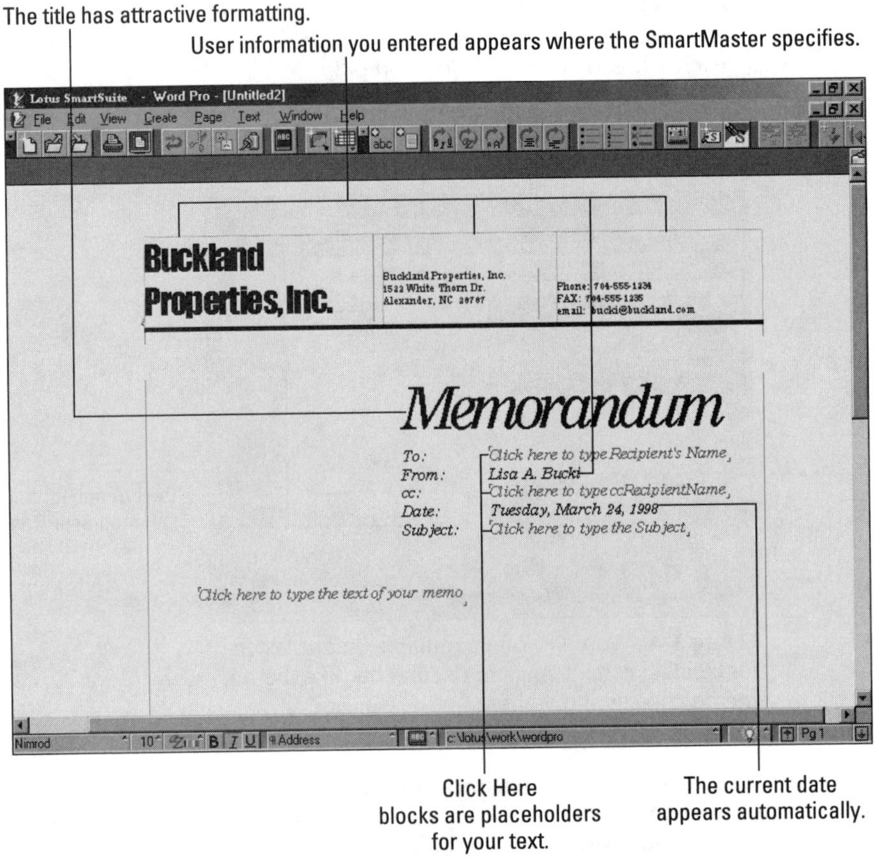

The title has attractive formatting.

User information you entered appears where the SmartMaster specifies.

Buckland Properties, Inc.

Buckland Properties, Inc.
1522 White Thorn Dr.
Alexander, NC 28787

Phone: 704-555-1234
FAX: 704-555-1235
email: buckl@buckland.com

Memorandum

To: ⌐Click here to type Recipient's Name,
From: Lisa A. Buckl
cc: ⌐Click here to type cc Recipient Name,
Date: Tuesday, March 24, 1998
Subject: ⌐Click here to type the Subject,

⌐Click here to type the text of your memo,

Click Here blocks are placeholders for your text.

The current date appears automatically.

Figure 3-5: This memo was created from a SmartMaster and contains basic information to help you address the memo and enter its subject matter.

More Info   Chapter 6, "Using SmartMasters, Styles, and Scripts for Control," teaches you how to create your own fields, Click Here blocks, SmartMasters, and more.

Exiting Word Pro

When you've finished working with Word Pro, you can close the program. To do so, click the Close button for the Word Pro window. Or, choose File ⇨ Exit Word Pro.

Reviewing the Word Pro Screen

Chapter 1, "Getting Started with SmartSuite Applications," introduced the screen features found in most SmartSuite applications. Word Pro's screen offers the same features, but some of them are more specific to Word Pro itself, as illustrated in Figure 3-6.

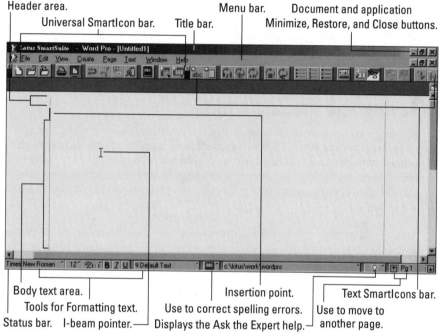

Figure 3-6: The Word Pro screen offers basic Windows and SmartSuite features, plus tools that are useful for developing documents.

Later chapters in this part discuss how to use the document-specific features of the Word Pro screen in more detail, but here's a brief introduction. The work area of the Word Pro screen holds a flashing vertical *insertion point* that indicates where the text you type next will appear. To reposition the insertion point within the document text, move the mouse so that the *I-beam pointer* appears at the location you want, then click. By default, the work area in a blank document displays two areas. Anything you enter in the *header* area near the top appears on every page of the document. The *body text* area holds the paragraph text, titles, and so on, for the document.

Two SmartIcon bars appear by default in Word Pro: the *Universal* SmartIcon bar that's a default in all SmartSuite applications, and the *Text* SmartIcon bar that offers tools for changing the appearance of text, such as adding bullets to a list. Likewise, you can use the first several buttons on the Status Bar to change the appearance of text. You can use the subsequent Status Bar buttons to correct a word's spelling, display document information, get Ask the Expert Help, and navigate in the document.

Saving, Closing, and Opening Documents

As explained in Chapter 1, "Getting Started with SmartSuite Applications," saving a file stores it on a hard disk or floppy disk (or a network drive, if you're connected to a network) until you're ready to make changes to it or print it. When you save a file for the first time, you give it a name to distinguish it from the other files you've saved. This section focuses on file naming and usage—saving, closing, and opening files.

Saving and naming a file

Although you can work as long as you'd like without saving a file, doing so is a risky proposition. If your system experiences a power fluctuation that causes it to reboot, you could lose a half-hour's or hour's worth of work. Not many of us can afford such a problem. So, even if you use a SmartMaster to create a new file, you should save it very early on in your creation process—even if you've only typed a few words.

As with other files in Windows applications, you can use more than 200 characters and spaces, and the capitalization you prefer, in saving a Word Pro file. Use the following steps to save a file for the first time and give it a new name:

1. Choose File ➪ Save (Ctrl+S), or click the Save the Current Document SmartIcon on the Universal SmartIcon bar, which appears by default in SmartSuite applications. The Save As dialog box appears.

2. (Optional) Use the Save In drop-down list and the list below it to specify the disk and folder where you want to store the file. Unless you change the folder, your Word Pro files are saved to the \lotus\work\wordpro folder on your hard disk.

3. Click in the File Name text box (if the insertion point doesn't already appear in it) and type the name you want for the file.

4. If you'd like to include additional information to help you distinguish the file from other files, click in the Description text box and enter that information. Figure 3-7 shows a File Name entry and a Description entered for a Word Pro file.

5. Click the Save button to finish saving the file.

After you make any changes to a file, you have to save it again. To do so, choose File ➪ Save, or press Ctrl+S, or click the Save the Current Document SmartIcon. Because you've previously named the file, you won't see the Save As dialog box. Word Pro simply saves the changes to the file.

Open an Existing Document SmartIcon.
Save the Current Document SmartIcon.

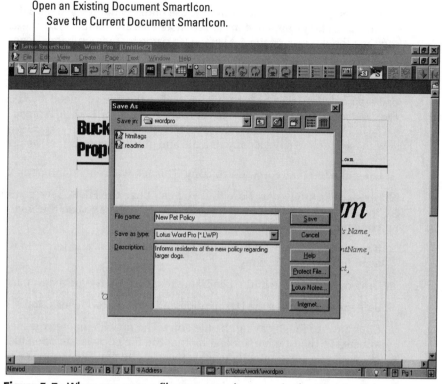

Figure 3-7: When you save a file, you enter its name in the Save As dialog box, as well as a description with more detail about the file, if you prefer.

When you save a file, you also can protect it using Word Pro's TeamSecurity feature by assigning it two passwords — one that controls who can open the file and one that controls who can edit the file. See Chapter 33, "Working with Communications and Team Editing Features," to learn how to use TeamSecurity in Word Pro.

Copying a file and giving it a new name

Saving gives you the option to name a file the first time, as well as to create a copy of an existing file. Let's say you create a weekly report file about ongoing projects. From week to week, some information remains relatively constant, such as the report title and the names of the projects. You wouldn't want to retype the constant information, which wastes time and can lead to mistakes, such as forgetting to type the name of one of the projects. A safer approach is to use the File ➪ Save As command to save a copy of the file each week, which you then can edit and update.

With the longer file names you can now use under Windows, you have the opportunity to name files in ways that make you more efficient in business. For example, you can (and should) include the date in the file name for memos, letters, reports, and so on. Then, you can easily scan to see which document you created most recently. Also consider including the recipient's initials in the file name for letters and memos. For example, you could simply name a proposal file *"Proposal."* But when you have several proposal files, you'll have better luck finding the one you need if you use names like *"Widget Proposal 7-15-98 MAC"* or *"Budget Proposal 12-2-98 J. Smith."*

Follow these steps to save a copy of a file and give the copy a new name:

1. Open the file that you want to copy. This file will remain intact on your disk.

2. Choose File ➪ Save As. Note that you can't use the File ➪ Save command or the Save the Current Document SmartIcon — you have to use the Save As command to redisplay the Save As dialog box.

3. If needed, use the Save In list to select another disk and folder in which you want to save the file copy.

4. Drag over the name in the File Name text box, then type a new name.

5. If needed, drag over the Description and type a new description.

6. Click Save to finish saving the file copy. The new file name you specified appears in the title bar, indicating that the file copy is the open file. Any changes you subsequently make appear in the new file copy. The original file closes, so if you need to make any changes to it, you must reopen it.

Closing a Document

When you've finished working with a document, you can close it to remove it from Word Pro. While most computers today have enough RAM to enable you to have multiple files and applications open at once, having too many files open at once will eventually slow your system down — not to mention the fact that you could accidentally make changes to the wrong file.

To close a file in Word Pro, click the file window's Close button or choose File ➪ Close. If you've made changes to the document but haven't saved them, a dialog box appears to remind you to save the file (see Figure 3-8). Click Yes to save the file and then close it, or No to simply close it.

Figure 3-8: Word Pro reminds you to save your changes before the file closes.

You also can use commands on the Window menu to close the current document or all open documents. Choose Window ⇨ Close Window to close the current document, or Window ⇨ Close All Windows to close all open files. If any of the files contain changes you haven't saved, Word Pro prompts you to save them, just as when you use the File ⇨ Close command.

Opening an existing file

When you want to work with a document you've previously saved and closed, you need to open it. You can then print, format, or otherwise make changes to the contents of the file. You can open as many files as you want; opening a file doesn't automatically close any other open files. The file you open becomes the *current file* or *active file*, meaning that changes and commands apply to that file until you switch to another file. Use these steps to open a file:

1. Choose File ⇨ Open (Ctrl+O) or click the Open an Existing Document SmartIcon. The Open dialog box appears.

2. Use the Look In list to navigate to the disk and folder that hold the file you want to open.

3. When you see the file you want in the Look In list, click the file name. Its description, if you entered one, and some statistics appear so you can verify that it's the file you want (see Figure 3-9).

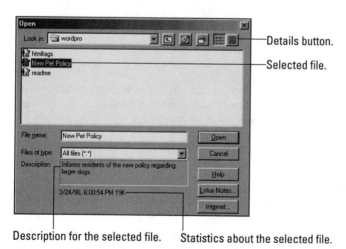

Details button.
Selected file.

Description for the selected file.   Statistics about the selected file.

Figure 3-9: Click a file to see the description you entered for it (if any) to verify it's the file you'd like to open.

Click the Details button in the Open dialog box to list the size, file type, and modification date beside each file in the Look In list.

4. When you find the file you'd like to open, click the Open button. Word Pro opens the file, and it appears onscreen.

By default, the bottom of the File menu lists the files you've worked with most recently. To open one of the files listed there, click its file name (see Figure 3-10).

Figure 3-10: Click a file name on the File menu to open that file.

You also can open a file from the Welcome to Lotus Word Pro dialog box if you just launched Word Pro, or if you want to see a lengthier list of recently used files along with a preview of the first page for the selected file:

1. Click the Open an Existing Document tab. The tab offers the Select a Document to Open list.

2. In the Select a Document to Open list, click the name of the file you'd like to open. A preview and description for the selected file appears, as shown in Figure 3-11.

3. When you're sure the file is the one you want, double-click it, or click the Open button to open it. If the file you want doesn't appear in the list, you can click the More Documents button below the list to display the Open dialog box and use it to select the file to open.

The selected file.   Click to display a list of recently used documents.

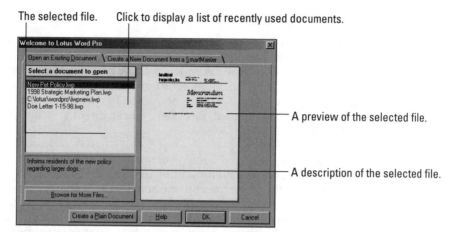

A preview of the selected file.

A description of the selected file.

Figure 3-11: You can open a file you've recently worked with from the Welcome screen.

Switching Between Documents

By default, each document you open appears maximized (at the full size), on top of other already opened documents, making the newly opened document the current document. If you want to work in a document you opened previously, you need to switch to that document and make it the current or active document. To switch to another document, open the Window menu, then click the name of the document you want at the bottom of the menu, as shown in Figure 3-12. You also can press Ctrl+Tab to move between open documents; repeat that key combination until the document you want appears.

Figure 3-12: To make a new document the current or active document, choose its name from the Window menu.

Entering Document Contents

Of course, a document isn't a document without a little text. Even though you may be familiar with your keyboard, Word Pro may have a few tricks to show you, as illustrated in this section.

Using a Click Here Block

If you used a SmartMaster to create a document, the document probably has one or more Click Here blocks, like the one identified in Figure 3-5. A Click Here block in a document prompts the user to type information. Many types of documents require specific information in a specific location; for example, tradition dictates that a memo offer a recipient line and subject line above the body of the memo. When you're creating or editing a document, Click Here blocks direct you to make entries in the correct location.

Click Here blocks provide the added benefits of reminding you not to forget key information and applying predefined formatting to the text you enter. For example, the Click Here blocks for the department name and article heading in a document created from one of the newsletter SmartMasters (see Figure 3-13) show specific formatting, which Word Pro applies to any text entered in those blocks. Word Pro identifies each Click Here block with a red bracket in the upper-left and lower-right corners. The Click Here block's placeholder text appears in a light green shade.

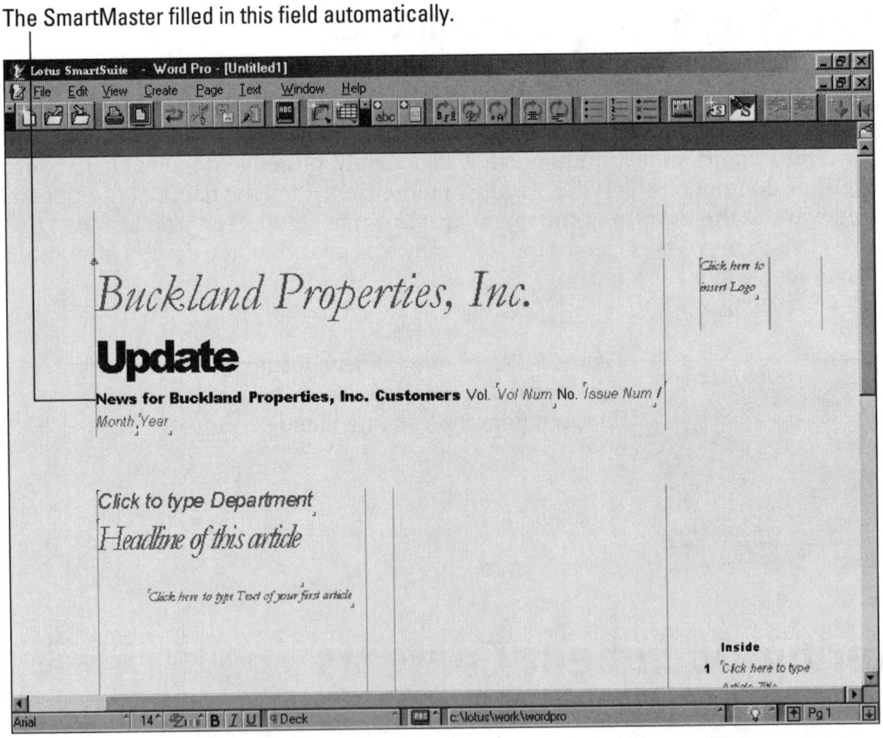

Figure 3-13: Click Here blocks prompt you for text and apply formatting.

To enter text in a Click Here block, click on the Click Here block with the I-beam pointer. As shown in Figure 3-14, a Bubble Help description appears to give you more detail about what to type in the Click Here block. Type your entry. As you type, it appears with the formatting defined by the Click Here block, as shown in Figure 3-15. You can use uppercase and lowercase as needed. Press the spacebar to insert a space between words, and press Enter to begin a new line of text. When you've finished making your entry for the Click Here block, click outside the area bounded by the red brackets to finish.

Word Pro also offers Click Here blocks for entering graphics and other special elements. Chapter 5, "Organizing and Highlighting Information," covers these other Click Here blocks. You also can create your own Click Here blocks to make your work easier or to create automated documents for other users. Chapter 6, "Using SmartMasters, Styles, and Scripts for Control," covers creating Click Here blocks.

Figure 3-14: Clicking the Click Here block displays Bubble Help with more details about what to enter.

Figure 3-15: Text you type in the Click Here block appears with the formatting specified by the block.

Typing

Whether or not you've typed with a typewriter, you'll find it easy to enter information in a Word Pro document. You use the same techniques to type text whether you're working in a Click Here block or the body of a blank document. Click to position the insertion point where you want to begin typing, and then use the keyboard. Characters you type appear to the left of the insertion point as it moves along the line. When you reach the end of the line, continue typing. Word Pro automatically *wraps* the text to the next line, creating what is called a *soft return* (automatic line break).

Even though Word Pro starts new lines automatically, you have to tell it when you want to start a new paragraph. To do so, press the Enter key. Word Pro inserts a *paragraph break*, which may include extra paragraph spacing to separate the new paragraph from the previous one. Pressing Enter to create a paragraph break positions the insertion point at the beginning of the new paragraph. Paragraph breaks are also called *hard returns*.

Note

In a default, blank document, and in the body text for many SmartMasters, Word Pro does not insert extra spacing between paragraphs. But extra spacing between paragraphs can make a document easier to read, by helping the eye punctuate the end of the block of text that covers a particular topic. Standard business documents typically use extra spacing between paragraphs. If you want extra spacing but don't want to change the default formatting for a document, press Enter twice at the end of each paragraph.

In some instances, you may want to start a new line, called a *manual line break* or *hard line break*, without starting a new paragraph. This technique makes it look as if you've started a new paragraph, but doesn't insert paragraph spacing. You might want to use this approach, for example, if you're creating a brief list of two or three items, but don't think that it needs any fancy formatting or spacing. (See Figure 3-16 for examples of a regular wrapped paragraph with soft returns, a hard return paragraph break, and manual line breaks.) Press Shift+Enter to insert a manual line break; Word Pro ends the line at the specified location and moves the insertion point to the beginning of the next line, without adding any paragraph spacing between the lines.

If you don't have much experience entering text in a word processing program, follow these guidelines to ensure your text has the most attractive appearance possible:

✦ Holding a key down repeats the character it types, just as with an electric typewriter. Keep a light touch on the keyboard. Doing so provides the added benefit of reducing keyboard wear; computer keyboards are less durable than typewriter keyboards were.

✦ Press the spacebar once, not twice, after each sentence. The character styles (called *fonts*) used by computers are optimized to provide the correct spacing between sentences both for display and printouts.

✦ Don't press Tab at the beginning of each paragraph to indent the paragraph; if you later decide to combine paragraphs, the document might contain tabs in unwanted locations. Instead use Word Pro's alignment capabilities, described in the next chapter, to create indentations.

Hard returns used to start new paragraphs.   Wrapped text, or soft returns.

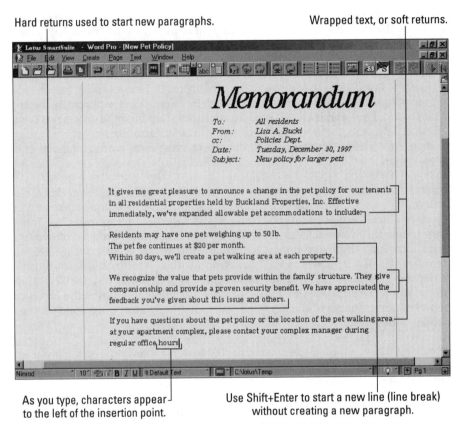

As you type, characters appear
to the left of the insertion point.

Use Shift+Enter to start a new line (line break)
without creating a new paragraph.

Figure 3-16: Word Pro automatically breaks lines at the right side of the document
(or column, if you've created columns) until you press Enter to create a new paragraph.

Getting SmartCorrect Help as You Type

Typing proficiency develops through habit. The more you type, the better you do it.
In some cases, your typing practice can work against you—in cases where you've
"learned" to type a word incorrectly. For example, many users often transpose
characters in particular words, typing "teh" instead of "the," or "ro" instead of "or."
Your personal bugaboo in this category might be that you don't press the Shift key
hard enough in many instances, meaning you fail to capitalize the first word in
a sentence.

Word Pro's SmartCorrect feature fixes common typos and misspelled words,
and makes needed formatting changes, as you type. When you type a word with
an error or type an entry that needs formatting and then press the spacebar,
SmartCorrect replaces the misspelled word or applies the formatting. SmartCorrect

is turned on by default and contains entries for dozens of misspelled words. In addition, SmartCorrect makes the following formatting corrections and changes to make text more legible, when needed:

✦ The fractions 1/2, 1/4, and 3/4 are formatted as stacked, "typeset" characters, as in: ½, ¼, and ¾.

✦ Straight quote marks (" "), also called *double primes*, are formatted as typeset curly quotes ("").

✦ Instances where you've capped two initial letters in a word (as in BUckland) by accidentally holding the Shift key too long are changed to a single initial cap (as in Buckland).

✦ Instances where you've failed to capitalize the first word in a sentence are corrected.

✦ Internet addresses you type in are changed to *hyperlinks* that you can click to display the document the hyperlink identifies.

SmartCorrect provides entries that correct the most common typos, but it may not necessarily correct the unique typos or tendencies that you've learned. You can create additional SmartCorrect entries to correct your most common typos. You also can turn off any of the automatic formatting features just listed.

You can create a SmartCorrect entry that acts as a typing shortcut, rather than a typo correction. For instance, you may need to type your company name dozens of times a week. Create a SmartCorrect entry that inserts the company name in place of a short entry you type; for example, you could create an entry that replaces *bpi* with *Buckland Properties, Inc.* Just ensure that the shortcut you use (as in *bpi*) isn't identical to another short word.

Follow these steps to create a SmartCorrect entry and specify which formatting corrections SmartCorrect makes:

1. Choose File ⇨ User Setup ⇨ SmartCorrect Setup to display the SmartCorrect dialog box.

2. If you're creating the document in a language other than U.S. English, select that language from the SmartCorrect Language drop-down list. If you don't take this step, SmartCorrect won't be able to fix typos you've made in another language, such as standard French. And, the SmartCorrect entries you create will be added into the list of entries for the wrong language.

3. Click the Add Entry button. The Add SmartCorrect Entry dialog box appears.

4. Type the misspelled word or shortcut that you want to have SmartCorrect replace in the SmartCorrect Entry text box. For example, enter **bpi** or **tecnique**. You don't need to worry about capitalization when you make your entry in this text box.

5. Press Tab or click to select the Replacement Text text box, and then enter the correction SmartCorrect should substitute for the entry you specified in Step 3. For example, you could enter **Buckland Properties, Inc.,** as the replacement for bpi, or **technique** as the replacement for tecnique. Figure 3-17 shows a new SmartCorrect entry being created with the Add SmartCorrect Entry dialog box. In this entry, capitalization does matter. You can specify that you want the replacement to appear with initial caps (capping the first letter in each word or words by default) or other special capitalization (such as capping one or more letters within a word). To do so, enter the capital letters (also called *uppercase letters*) where they need to appear, as in *Buckland Properties, Inc.* Otherwise, use all lowercase letters so you can specify the capping it should use when you type it.

Figure 3-17: When you type the entry from the top text box in a document and then press the spacebar, SmartCorrect replaces that entry with the contents of the bottom text box. In this case, you're telling SmartCorrect to enter *technique* to replace *tecnique*, a typo.

6. Click OK to close the Add SmartCorrect Entry dialog box. If the text you entered in the SmartCorrect Entry text box of the Add SmartCorrect Entry dialog box was identical to an existing SmartCorrect entry, you'll be asked to verify that you want to replace the existing entry. Click Yes to do so.

7. Repeat Steps 3 through 6 to create as many other SmartCorrect entries as you wish. SmartCorrect doesn't automatically correct different tenses of a verb or the plural form of a correction you enter, so you might need to create additional entries to correct all the forms of a word, such as acommodate (accommodate) and acommodates (accommodates), or tecnique (technique) and tecniques (techniques).

8. To view the correction that SmartCorrect will substitute for a particular typo or shortcut you type in a document, click the typo or shortcut in the SmartCorrect Entries list of the SmartCorrect dialog box. The correction appears in the Replacement Text for *X* area of the dialog box, where *X* is the name of the entry (see Figure 3-18).

9. The check boxes at the bottom of the dialog box control the formatting changes that SmartCorrect makes by default. Click a check box to deselect it, as follows:

   • **Change Straight Quotes to Smart Quotes.** Clearing this check box tells SmartCorrect to leave quotation marks you type as double primes rather than converting them to curly quotes. If you'll be having a document professionally typeset, the typesetter may request that you use double primes or straight quotes, in which case you want to make sure this feature is turned off.

- **Correct TWo INitial CApitals.** Clearing this check box tells SmartCorrect to leave the first two letters of a word in uppercase, if that's how you type it.

- **Start Sentences with Capital Letters.** When this option is turned on, SmartCorrect always capitalizes the first letter of the first word you type after typing a period. This feature becomes a problem, however, if your document contains numerous abbreviations such as etc., Inc., or Corp., because it can end up with a corresponding number of unwanted capitalized words. Clear the check box to turn off capitalization corrections for the first word in each sentence.

- **Change Internet Address to Hyperlink.** If you don't want Internet addresses you type to be converted to hyperlinks, clear this check box.

10. Click OK to finish making your entries and changes and close the SmartCorrect dialog box.

A new SmartCorrect entry becomes active immediately after you create it. Type the typo or shortcut you entered in Step 4, and then press the spacebar. SmartCorrect replaces the typo or shortcut text with the correction you specified in Step 5. Refer to the example presented in Figure 3-17; if you create that SmartCorrect entry and then type **tecnique** in a document and press the spacebar, SmartCorrect replaces *tecnique* with *technique.*

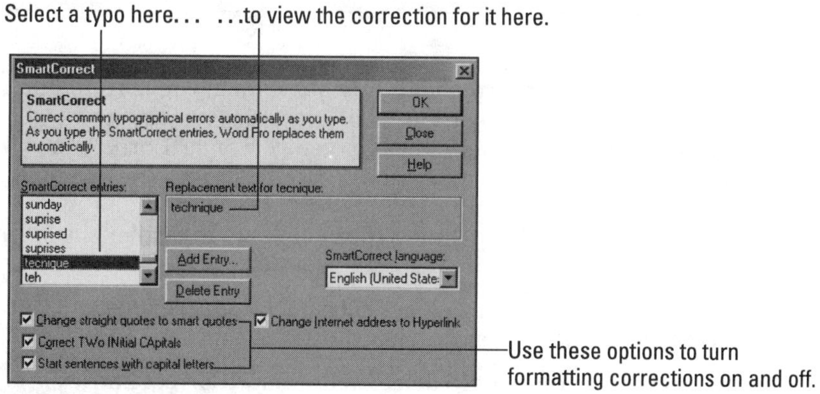

Select a typo here...   ...to view the correction for it here.

Use these options to turn formatting corrections on and off.

Figure 3-18: This dialog box enables you to create new SmartCorrect entries, view the correction for a typo, and control which formatting changes SmartCorrect makes.

You also can control the capitalization SmartCorrect uses for the replacement it inserts, assuming you entered that replacement (or all the words in the replacement phrase) with all lowercase letters in the Add SmartCorrect Entry dialog box, as described in Step 5 of the preceding steps. Table 3-1 illustrates how SmartCorrect handles capitalization when it replaces a typo or shortcut you type in a document, depending on how you use uppercase letters in the typo or shortcut. (SmartCorrect also caps the replacement if the entry is the first word in a sentence and you've left its Start Sentences with Capital Letters check box enabled.)

	Table 3-1 **How to Specify the Capitalization for SmartCorrect Replacements**	
How you type the entry	*How the replacement appears*	*Examples*
In all lowercase letters	In all lowercase letters	*tecnique* is replaced with *technique*
		bpi is replaced with *buckland properties, inc.*
Capitalize the first letter	With an initial cap	*Tecnique* is replaced with *Technique*
		Bpi is replaced with *Buckland properties, inc.*
In all uppercase letters	In all uppercase letters	*TECNIQUE* is replaced with *TECHNIQUE*
		BPI is replaced with *BUCKLAND PROPERTIES, INC.*

After you've used a SmartCorrect entry for some time, you may find that it no longer applies, becomes annoying, or conflicts with new jargon you've started using in your documents. Follow these steps to remove a SmartCorrect entry when you no longer need it:

1. Choose File ➪ User Setup ➪ SmartCorrect Setup to display the SmartCorrect dialog box.

2. If you created your SmartCorrect entry in a language other than U.S. English, select that language from the SmartCorrect Language drop-down list.

3. Click the entry you want to delete in the SmartCorrect Entries list.

Danger Zone

Word Pro doesn't prompt you to confirm that you want to delete a SmartCorrect entry, so proceed carefully and double-check to ensure you've selected the correct entry in the SmartCorrect Entries list. If you mistakenly delete an entry, in most cases you can easily add an identical new entry to replace it. However, if you delete the entry for ½, ¼, or ¾, you have to reinstall Word Pro to reinstate those SmartCorrect entries.

4. Click the Delete Entry button.

5. Repeat Steps 3 and 4 to delete other entries, as needed.

6. Click OK to close the SmartCorrect dialog box.

 See "Adjusting Word Pro's Preferences" in Chapter 6, "Using SmartMasters, Styles, and Scripts for Control," to learn how to turn off Word Pro features such as SmartCorrect.

Using Glossary Entries to Save Time

A *glossary* in a word processing program like Word Pro serves a different purpose than a glossary for a book, which lists and defines terms. In contrast, a Word Pro glossary file stores entries that you may want to use again. Each glossary file can store chunks of text, Word Pro frames that hold special elements like graphics or equations, or Word Pro tables. (See Chapter 5, "Organizing and Highlighting Information," to learn how to create frames and tables.) Rather than rewriting a paragraph or rebuilding a table from scratch each time you need it, you can save the paragraph or table as a glossary table, then later insert it in a document and edit it as needed.

Word Pro stores glossary entries in special glossary files. You can store all your glossary entries in a single file, or create multiple glossary files to organize glossary entries into logical groups. For example, let's say you're the head of your department and are responsible for interviewing and selecting candidates for new positions and promotions. You could create a glossary file to store your recruiting information, then add entries for various interview questions, job descriptions, key information about your department and workflows, and so on. To later prepare for an interview, you can review and select the glossary entries to build a list of interview questions, and a job and department description document that's customized for the job candidates. While you could draw such information from previously created documents, doing so would be more time-consuming, because you'd have to remember the name of each file you're looking for, open various documents, and copy information between documents. Inserting text and other elements that you've saved in a glossary file generally takes less time, and prevents you from making unwanted changes to older documents.

Creating the Glossary File and Glossary Entries

The first time you need to create a glossary entry, you also have to create your first glossary file to hold that entry and subsequent entries you create. Use the following steps to create a glossary entry and the new glossary file to hold it:

1. Enter the text (or create the frame or table) that you want to store as the glossary entry. Also apply the formatting that you want the entry to use; the next chapter describes how to format text. For example, you might enter the name and address of your company. If you press Enter after each line of the address to insert a hard return, the glossary entry also includes those hard returns.

2. Drag over the text with the mouse to select it. Or, click to position the insertion point at the beginning of the text, press and hold down the Shift key, and click at the end of the block of text to select it. (Chapter 5, "Organizing and Highlighting Information," describes how to select frames and tables; you can save selected frames and tables as glossary entries, too.)

3. Choose Edit ⇨ Glossary (Ctrl+K). A message box appears to tell you that the default glossary file, glossary.gls, does not exist.

4. Click Yes to create the glossary file and display the Glossary dialog box. By default, the insertion point appears in the Glossary Entry Name text box.

5. Type the name of the glossary entry. For example, if you're creating a glossary entry for your company address, type **Company Address**, as shown in Figure 3-19.

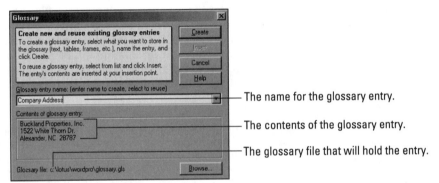

— The name for the glossary entry.

— The contents of the glossary entry.

— The glossary file that will hold the entry.

Figure 3-19: Use the Glossary dialog box to store glossary entries in a glossary file, or to choose a glossary entry to insert.

6. Click Create. Word Pro creates the glossary entry in the glossary file, and closes the Glossary dialog box.

After you create the first entry in the default glossary file, use a similar process to add subsequent glossary entries to the glossary file. Create the contents for the glossary entry, then select them in the document. Choose Edit ⇨ Glossary (Ctrl+K). In the Glossary Entry Name text box, type the name you want for the glossary entry, and then click Create to close the dialog box. If you try to give a new glossary entry a name that you've previously assigned to a glossary entry, a message box appears to tell you the name is already in use. Click OK to close the message box, then change the entry you've made in the Glossary Entry Name text box.

Making Other Glossary Files

If you want to store a glossary entry in a new glossary file that you create, you make that alternate glossary file using the Glossary dialog box. Follow these steps:

1. Create and select the text or element to save as the glossary entry.

2. Then choose Edit ⇨ Glossary to display the Glossary dialog box.

3. Click the Browse button near the bottom of the dialog box to display the Browse dialog box.

4. Use the Look In list to navigate to another disk or folder where you'd like to save the glossary file, and enter the name for the glossary file in the File Name text box, as shown in Figure 3-20. For example, if you're creating a glossary file to hold interview questions, job descriptions, and other hiring-related glossary entries, you could type **Interview** in the File Name text box. Glossary file names include the .GLS extension, but you don't need to type the extension in the File Name text box; Word Pro adds the extension for you.

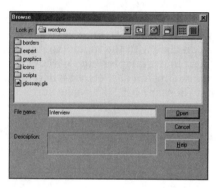

Figure 3-20: Display the Browse dialog box by clicking the Browse button in the Glossary dialog box, and then enter a file name to create a new glossary file.

5. Click Open. A message box informs you that the specified glossary file doesn't exist, and asks if you'd like to create it.

6. Click Yes to do so. A second dialog box tells you that the newly created file doesn't contain a glossary, and asks if you want to create one.

7. Click Yes to add the glossary to the file, making the file ready to select glossary entries. The Glossary dialog box reappears, and the name of the new glossary file appears at the bottom of the dialog box.

8. From there, you can continue creating the first glossary entry for the file. In the Glossary Entry Name text box, type the name you want for the glossary entry, and then click Create to close the dialog box.

Choosing a Glossary File

Once you have more than one glossary file to choose from, check the glossary file name at the bottom of the Glossary dialog box each time you display the dialog box. You need to make sure the glossary file that's listed is the one in which you want to store a new glossary entry you're creating or the one that holds the existing glossary entry you want to insert into a document.

If the wrong glossary file name appears, click the Browse button to display the Browse dialog box. Navigate to the disk and folder that hold the glossary file, if needed, using the Look In list. Click the name of the glossary file you want when it appears in the dialog box, then click Open. The name for the selected glossary file appears at the bottom of the Glossary dialog box.

You can then finish storing a new glossary entry in the selected glossary file, or select an existing glossary entry from the file to insert the glossary entry contents into your document, as described next.

Inserting a Glossary Entry into a Document

You can insert a glossary entry into any document. The glossary entry appears at the insertion point location. If the insertion point isn't at the location where you want to insert the glossary entry, you can click with the mouse to reposition it, or use one of the techniques described later in the chapter under "Moving the Insertion Point." When the insertion point appears at the spot where you want to insert the glossary entry, choose Edit ➪ Glossary (Ctrl+K). Make sure the correct glossary file name appears at the bottom of the dialog box; if not, browse to select the correct file, as just described. Then, open the Glossary Entry Name drop-down list, and click the name of the glossary entry to insert, as shown in Figure 3-21. Click the Insert button. The Glossary dialog box closes, and the glossary entry contents appear at the insertion point in your document.

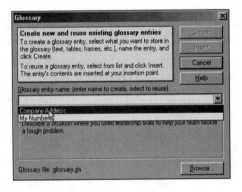

Figure 3-21: Use the Glossary Entry Name drop-down list in the Glossary dialog box to specify which glossary entry to insert.

Editing Your Text

None of us nails our document content from the first draft. In fact, it's pretty common to both enter and change—or *edit*—information as you go along. This section covers editing techniques, including basic survival skills like moving the insertion point, timesavers like copying information, and lifesavers like undoing a mistake.

Can You Edit the Entries in a Glossary File?

You can quickly create glossary entries, but it's not so easy to edit or delete an entry. In fact, Word Pro provides no automated method for changing or removing glossary entries. Once you've learned to edit text as described in the next section, and work with tables as described in Chapter 5, "Organizing and Highlighting Information," you'll have all the skills you need to edit a glossary manually. Each .GLS glossary file holds a Word Pro table. The left column of the table lists the names you gave to glossary entries as you created them, and the right column holds the corresponding contents for each glossary entry. To edit or delete entries in a particular glossary file, follow these steps:

1. First choose Edit ➪ Glossary, and then use the Browse button to select a glossary file that's *not* the one you want to edit. (Word Pro won't let you edit a glossary file that's currently selected.)

2. Then, open the glossary file to edit in Word Pro.

3. Choose File ➪ Open, and then select All Files (*.*) from the Files of Type drop-down list.

4. Navigate to the \lotus\wordpro folder, the default folder for glossary files, or the name of the folder in which you've stored the glossary to open.

5. Double-click the glossary file name to open it. Make your changes to individual glossary entries, or delete an entire row from the table to delete the glossary entry it holds.

6. Save and close the glossary file. When you next select that file using the Browse button in the Glossary dialog box, the glossary includes your changes.

Moving the Insertion Point

The insertion point enables you to pinpoint the location for your edits. You insert or delete text at the location of the insertion point, so you need to learn to control its location. You learned in the last section that in many cases the fastest way to move the insertion point is with the mouse. Point to the location where you want to place the insertion point, and then click the left mouse button once. This technique only saves time, however, if you're moving the insertion point within the same screenful of information, or if you've just been working with the mouse.

If you need to move a larger distance in the document, or if your hands are already on the keyboard typing, you may find it faster to use the keyboard to move the insertion point in the document. With the keyboard, you can move a line, paragraph, or page at a time. Table 3-2 covers the keystrokes you can use to move the insertion point within a document.

Table 3-2
Use These Keys and Key Combinations to Move the Insertion Point for Editing

Key/Key combination	Moves the insertion point . . .
Left arrow or right arrow	One character left or right
Up arrow or down arrow	One row up or down
PgUp or PgDn	One screen up or down
Home or End	To the beginning or end of the line that currently holds the insertion point
Ctrl+left arrow or Ctrl+right arrow	One word left or right
Ctrl+up arrow or Ctrl+down arrow	To the beginning or end of the paragraph that currently holds the insertion point
Ctrl+PgUp or Ctrl+PgDn	One page up or down
Ctrl+Home or Ctrl+End	To the beginning or end of the document
Ctrl+.	To the start of the sentence after the one that holds the insertion point
Ctrl+,	To the start of the sentence before the one that holds the insertion point

You can use the vertical scroll bar to display different areas of the document, but remember that you must then click with the mouse on the displayed portion of the document. Otherwise, the first time you press a key, the display will scroll back to the insertion point location. To change the display with the scroll bar, click the up or down scroll arrow to move by small increments. Click above or below the scroll box to scroll the display one screenful up or down, respectively, or drag the scroll bar to change the display more quickly. As you drag the scroll box, the Page Gauge indicator appears to tell you what page will display when you release the mouse.

You can't move the insertion point beyond the end of the document, even if you're clicking in an area that appears to be "wide open." If you want to leave some blank space between the current end of the document and new text you insert, click at the current end of the document and press Enter as many times as needed to insert the space.

Simple Deletions and Edits

You can handle a lot of your editing needs with a few simple keystrokes. Table 3-3 lists essential editing keystrokes that every user needs.

Table 3-3 Use These Keys and Key Combinations to Perform Common Edits	
Key/Key combination	**Result**
Backspace	Deletes one character left of the insertion point
Delete	Deletes one character right of the insertion point
Ctrl+Backspace	Deletes the word to the left of the insertion point, and also deletes one space to provide correct spacing between the remaining words
Ctrl+Delete	Deletes the word to the right of the insertion point, and also deletes one space to provide correct spacing between the remaining words
Alt+up arrow	Transposes the paragraph holding the insertion point with the paragraph above it
Alt+down arrow	Transposes the paragraph holding the insertion point with the paragraph below it

Using Insert and Type Over

By default, Word Pro works in *Insert mode*. In Insert mode, Word Pro inserts text you type at the insertion point. Any existing text to the right of the insertion point moves further right to make room for the inserted text. Consider the following sentence:

Profits for the fiscal quarter increased five percent.

The sentence would be more clear if it specified which fiscal quarter, such as the third quarter. To make that change in insert mode, click to position the insertion point just to the left of the "f" in "fiscal," and then type **third** and press the spacebar. All of the text to the right of "fiscal" moves further right to make room for the inserted word.

Word Pro offers a second typing mode called *Type Over mode*. In this mode, new characters you type replace characters to the right of the insertion point. Referring back to the example sentence, let's say that profits only increased four percent, so you want to replace the word "five" with "four." To do so in Type Over mode, click to position the insertion point just to the left of the "f" in "five," and then type **four**. Of course, if the words you're typing in Type Over mode don't have the same number of characters as the text being replaced, you'll have to delete or retype characters as needed to ensure the text reads correctly. Type Over mode also will type right through the end of a paragraph, overwriting the hard return that separates the paragraphs. You'll have to press Enter to reinstate the paragraph break. For these types of reasons, Type Over mode requires more concentration, and can lead to more errors. On the other hand, if you know you have to replace extensive blocks of text, or text contained within a table or frame, Type Over mode saves you the step of deleting existing text.

Danger Zone

Type Over mode can be very risky to use, especially if you're such a good typist that you don't watch your screen as you type. If you inadvertently misplace the insertion point and then begin typing in Type Over mode, before you know it, you'll have typed over essential text. Insert mode avoids such problems, and provides the added bene-fit of leaving text onscreen so you can choose what you want to delete at a later time.

To switch between Insert mode and Type Over mode, press the Insert key on your keyboard. If you want to verify the current typing mode, click the status bar area that provides information about the current document; this area lists the working folder by default. As shown in Figure 3-22, the list that pops up lists the typing mode. Click on the document outside the list to close it.

Figure 3-22: Click the status bar to see document information, including the current typing mode.

Selecting Text

Rather than deleting a character at a time, you may need to delete an entire word, sentence, paragraph, or other selected text block. Most actions you perform on text — including deleting, copying, moving, formatting, and so on — require that you *select* the text before you perform the action. For example, if you want to apply bold formatting to a word to call attention to it, you first select the word, and then apply the formatting. Because Word Pro identifies selected text with reverse black highlighting, selecting is also called *highlighting*. Figure 3-23 shows a selected sentence.

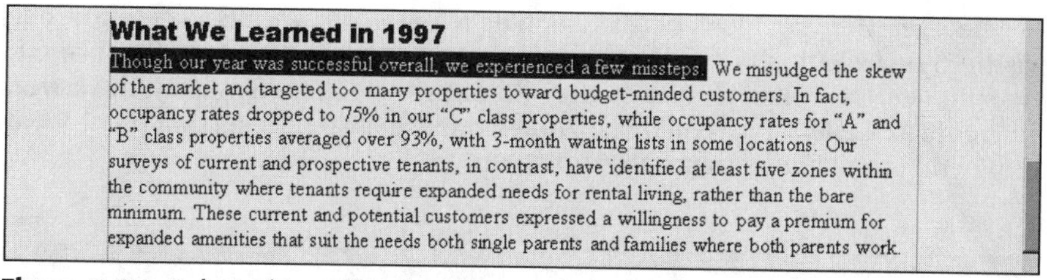

> **What We Learned in 1997**
>
> Though our year was successful overall, we experienced a few missteps. We misjudged the skew of the market and targeted too many properties toward budget-minded customers. In fact, occupancy rates dropped to 75% in our "C" class properties, while occupancy rates for "A" and "B" class properties averaged over 93%, with 3-month waiting lists in some locations. Our surveys of current and prospective tenants, in contrast, have identified at least five zones within the community where tenants require expanded needs for rental living, rather than the bare minimum. These current and potential customers expressed a willingness to pay a premium for expanded amenities that suit the needs both single parents and families where both parents work.

Figure 3-23: Selected text, like the first sentence on this page, appears in reverse highlighting. Select text to perform edits on it or apply formatting.

You can simply drag over text to select it, but this method can be imprecise and frustrating, because the screen can scroll unexpectedly while you drag over long blocks of text. Instead, you can use several techniques that use the mouse and the keyboard, usually in combination to make precise selections, as follows:

✦ **Words.** Double-click a single word to select it.

✦ **Sentences.** Press and hold Ctrl, then click anywhere in the sentence. (Press and hold Ctrl, and then drag to select multiple full sentences.)

✦ **Paragraphs.** Press and hold Ctrl, then double-click anywhere in the paragraph. (Press and hold Ctrl, and double-click and drag to select multiple paragraphs.)

You can use a menu command to select a word, sentence, paragraph, or the entire document. First, click the word, sentence, or paragraph to select; you don't have to specifically position the insertion point to select the whole document. Choose Text ⇨ Select or right-click and then click Select in the shortcut menu. The submenu that appears, shown in Figure 3-24, offers the commands for finishing your selection. Choose the command for the type of selection you want to make: Word, Sentence, Paragraph, or Entire Document.

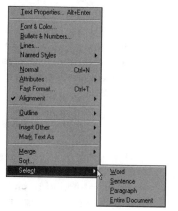

Figure 3-24: Choose a command from this submenu to select text in your document.

To select an irregular block of text, such as a few words within a sentence, click to position the insertion point where you want the selection to start. Press and hold the Shift key, then click to specify the end of the selection. Similarly, the keyboard shortcuts in Table 3-4 extend a selection from the current insertion point location to the end of the line, paragraph, and so on.

Table 3-4	
Use These Keys and Key Combinations to Extend a Selection	
Key/Key combination	**Extends the selection . . .**
Shift+up arrow or Shift+down arrow	From the insertion point up or down one line
Shift+PgUp or Shift+PgDn	From the insertion point up or down one screen
Shift+Home or Shift+End	From the insertion point to the start or end of the line
Shift+Ctrl+up arrow or Shift+Ctrl+down arrow	From the insertion point to the beginning or end of the paragraph
Shift+Ctrl+Home or Shift+Ctrl+End	From the insertion point to the beginning or end of the document

To remove selection highlighting so that you can work on another selection instead, click anywhere outside the selection in the document.

Danger Zone

After you make a selection, be careful with your hands. Typing a single character replaces the whole selection with the typed character, whether you're using Insert or Type Over mode. If you accidentally press a character and type over a selection, choose Edit ➪ Undo or press Ctrl+Z immediately.

Jumping to a Particular Point

If you're working on a basic document, the text you want to select might appear right in front of you. In contrast, if you're slogging through a 20-page document, finding the passage you want to change could be much more tedious. Before you learn more about larger-scale edits, in which you may be moving entire paragraphs from page to page, review this section to learn how to move the insertion point longer distances in documents.

Go To

Word Pro's Go To features enable you to move the insertion point to a specific page or element in a document. To move one page at a time, click either the up or down arrow button flanking the page number displayed at the far right end of the status bar. To move the insertion point to a location that's more than a page away or to jump to a particular element such as the next Click Here block, comment note, or page break in the document, follow these steps to use the Go To dialog box:

1. Choose Edit ➪ Go To (Ctrl+G), or click the page number displayed at the far right end of the status bar. The Go To dialog box appears.

2. Open the Type of Document Part to Go To drop-down list, and choose the type of element that you want to jump to, such as comment note or section. (The default selection is to jump to a particular page.) The dialog box changes to list the elements of that type found in the current document. In Figure 3-25, the Go To dialog box lists the pages in a particular document.

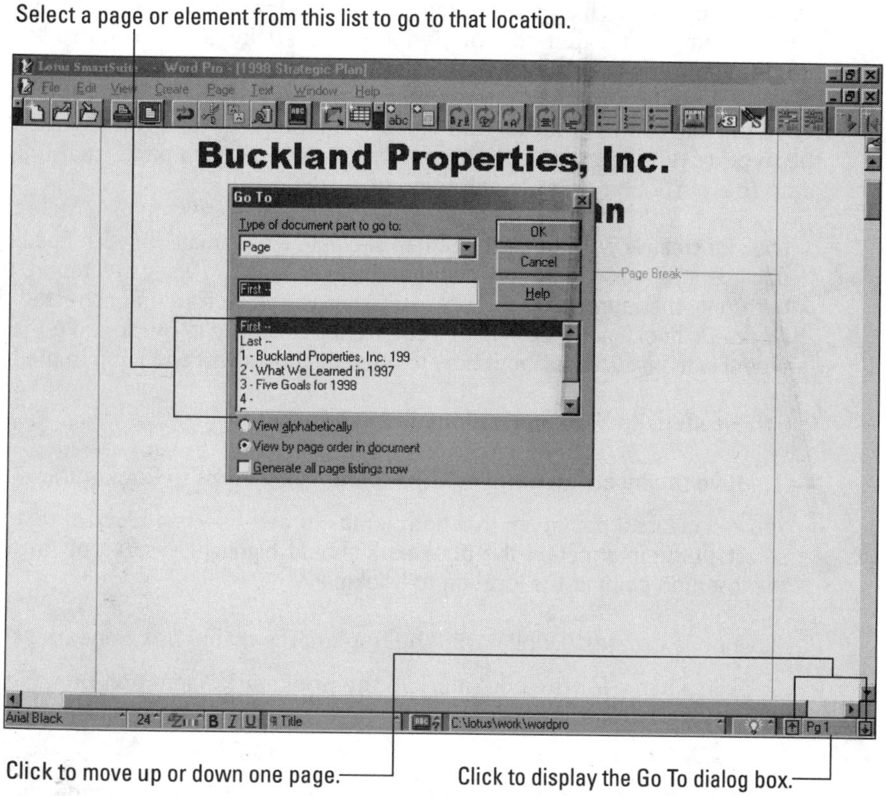

Select a page or element from this list to go to that location.

Click to move up or down one page.———   Click to display the Go To dialog box.——

Figure 3-25: The Go To dialog box enables you to move the insertion point to a particular page or other element in the document.

3. If you've left Page selected as the Type of Document Part to Go To and have recently added pages to the document, select the Generate All Page Listings Now check box to refresh the page listing.

4. If you want to change how the list in the dialog box organizes the entries you can go to, select either the View Alphabetically or View by Page Order in Document option button, as needed.

5. In the list of elements you can choose to go to, click the one you want. Often, these lists will include First and Last or Next and Previous choices, so you can go to the first or last or contiguous element in the document.

6. Click OK. Word Pro moves the insertion point to the location you specified. If you indicated that Word Pro should jump to a footnote, header, or similar element, Word Pro places the insertion point within that document part.

Bookmarks

If you're working with a paper document, you can mark a location by dog-earing the page, slipping on a paper clip, or slapping on a sticky note. Word Pro *bookmarks* provide the same benefits as those non-electronic tools. Each bookmark within a document marks a particular location, so that you can later select the bookmark to move the insertion point to it and display surrounding text. Bookmarks work like the hypertext links in online Help, or hyperlinks on a Web page, enabling you to jump to a particular point in a document.

Look for creative ways to use bookmarks. Create a bookmark for each heading in your document for easy navigation. If you have key statistics to verify in a report, bookmark each one, then remove each bookmark after you've verified and corrected the stat it marks. Or, bookmark a location that you want a colleague to check, and e-mail the document with instructions about how to open the document and jump to the bookmark.

Use these steps to bookmark a location in Word Pro:

1. Move the insertion point to the location you'd like to bookmark.

You can create a bookmark that both jumps to and selects a block of text. To do so, select all the information the bookmark should highlight, instead of simply placing the insertion point at the location to bookmark.

2. Choose Create ⇨ Bookmark. The Bookmarks dialog box appears.

3. Type a name for the bookmark in the Bookmark Name text box. Figure 3-26 shows an example.

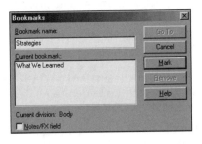

Figure 3-26: The Bookmarks dialog box enables you to assign a name to a particular document location so you can later jump to that location.

4. (Optional) If you're using Lotus Notes on your company network and may want to exchange information from the bookmark location with a Notes database, select the Notes/FX field check box.

5. Click Mark. Word Pro marks the bookmark and closes the Bookmarks dialog box.

You can use the Bookmarks dialog box to jump to or remove a bookmark. Choose Create ⇨ Bookmarks to redisplay the Bookmarks dialog box. Click the name of the bookmark to choose or delete in the Current Bookmark list. Then, click either the Go To button to jump to the bookmark in the document, or Remove to delete the bookmark. You also can use the Go To dialog box to jump to a particular bookmark; just choose Bookmark as the Type of Document Part to Go To, then select the bookmark to jump to, as just described in this section.

 You can display markers in your document that indicate the position of each bookmark. The section titled "Setting Your View Preferences" in Chapter 4, "Formatting and Printing a Document," shows you how to display visual cues like bookmarks in your documents.

Deleting, Copying, or Moving Text

Once you've found and selected a particular chunk of text, you can remove that text from the document, move it to another location, or copy it to reuse it. To permanently remove a selection from your document, press the Delete key.

The advantage of moving or copying text is obvious — you don't have to retype the information, and possibly introduce errors, to reposition or reuse that information. You use virtually the same steps to copy or move a selection. Word Pro uses the same mechanism to facilitate the operation — a holding area called the *Windows Clipboard*. To move text, you *cut* the text from its current location. To copy text, you *copy* the original selection. Word Pro moves the cut or copied selection to the Windows Clipboard, where it remains until you *paste* the selection to insert it into a new location.

Follow these steps to move (cut and paste) or copy (copy and paste) information:

1. Select the text you want to move or copy.

2. Choose the command for cutting or copying the selection.

   • **Cut.** Choose Edit ⇨ Cut (Ctrl+X), right-click the selection and click Cut in the shortcut menu, or click the Cut To Clipboard SmartIcon, as shown in Figure 3-27.

   • **Paste.** Choose Edit ⇨ Copy (Ctrl+C), right-click the selection and click Copy in the shortcut menu, or click the Copy to Clipboard SmartIcon.

3. Display the location where you want to insert the cut or copied information, and click to position the insertion point. This location can even be in another Word Pro document. Open or switch to that document, then position the insertion point.

4. Choose Edit ➪ Paste (Ctrl+V), right-click the insertion location and click Paste in the shortcut menu, or click the Paste Clipboard Contents SmartIcon.

You can replace a selection with other text that you've previously cut or copied to the Clipboard: Select the text to replace instead of clicking to position the insertion point at a paste location. Then, paste the Clipboard contents. You can also perform a special kind of paste operation to link the pasted information with the original information you copied it from. To learn more about this technique, refer to Chapter 35, "Sharing Information Between Documents."

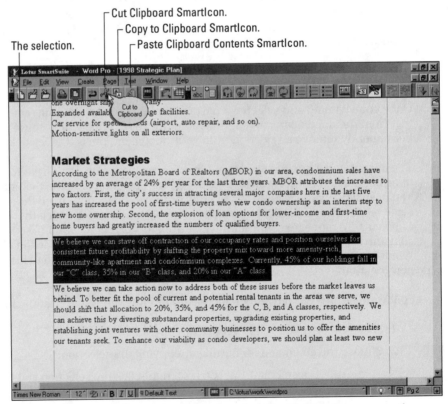

Figure 3-27: Cut or copy a selection to the Windows Clipboard so you can then paste it to a new location.

Using Drag-and-Drop Editing

Using cut, copy, and paste enables you to move or copy a selection of text within a document or between different documents. If you need to copy or move information within the same screenful or paragraph of information, you can employ a speedier technique. *Drag-and-drop editing* enables you to use the mouse to copy or move information over short distances. Using drag and drop editing requires fewer steps than a cut-and-paste or copy-and-paste operation.

Suppose you're creating letterhead from scratch. You enter your company name and address, and then below include your name and specific contact information. Later, you decide that your name and title should appear above the company address. You can accomplish such a change easily with drag and drop.

To use drag-and-drop to move or copy information, follow these steps:

1. First select the information to move or copy.

2. Point to the selection with the mouse, so that the mouse pointer changes to an open hand.

3. Press and hold the left mouse button to move the information; also press and hold the Ctrl key if you want to copy the information.

4. Drag the selection to the desired location. As you drag, the mouse pointer changes to a closed hand (including a plus sign if you're holding down the Ctrl key to copy the selection), and a red insertion point indicates the insertion position, as illustrated in Figure 3-28.

5. When the red insertion point reaches the spot where you want to place the moved or copied selection, release the mouse button to drop the selection into place.

No matter which technique you use to move and copy information, you may have to do a little preparation or cleanup to make the moved or copied text fit. For example, you may need to adjust the spacing before and after words, or between paragraphs. Or, you may have to press Enter to insert a new line after the last paragraph in a document before Word Pro enables you to move anything following that paragraph. Check carefully after every move or copy operation to ensure that spaces and paragraph breaks appear only where you need them.

The selection I'm moving.
The red insertion point indicates where the dropped selection appears.
The mouse pointer for moving a selection.

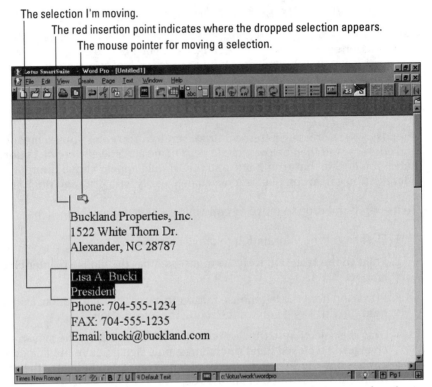

Figure 3-28: When you drag a selection to move or copy it to a new location, a special mouse pointer and insertion point appear.

Undoing a Change

If you mistakenly delete a letter or a word, fixing your error takes almost no time. You just retype what you nuked. In other cases, fixing a deletion or other error could be more of a problem. For example, if you delete a paragraph with statistical information that a colleague previously edited and you no longer have a hard copy of those edits, you could blow a lot of time retyping a paraphrase of the information and having the colleague check it again.

Like most applications today, Word Pro can bail you out of large and small jams. If you make a change or issue a command and then realize you've made a mistake, immediately choose Edit ➪ Undo (Action), press Ctrl+Z, or click Undo Last Command or Action SmartIcon. (The full name of the Edit ➪ Undo command changes depending on the action you last performed.) Word Pro undoes your mistake.

If you realize you've performed a couple of other operations since you made a mistake, you still can undo the mistake. You can click the Undo Last Command or Action SmartIcon multiple times, until the text returns to the state you want. For greater control, you can use another method. Once you undo one or more changes, you can redo them. You use the Undo/Redo dialog box to undo or redo previous operations, as follows:

1. Choose Edit ➪ Undo/Redo Special. The Undo/Redo dialog box appears. If you only want to redo a change, you can skip to Step 4.

2. To undo a previous change, click that change in the Edits You Can Undo list. The list organizes changes from most recent to least recent; if you click the second or third edit in the list, Word Pro highlights the above changes, too, as shown in Figure 3-29. That's because Word Pro must undo all the changes leading up to the change you're really interested in fixing.

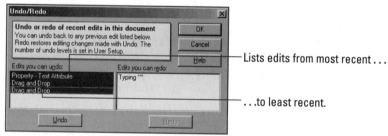

Figure 3-29: The Undo/Redo dialog box lists changes that you can undo or reinstate.

3. Click Undo. Word Pro reverses the selected changes, and the Undo/Redo dialog box remains open. If you don't need to redo a change, jump to step 6.

4. To redo a change you've previously undone, click that change in the Edits You Can Redo list. This list also organizes undone changes from most recent to least recent. Click the change to redo, which highlights that change and any above it in the list.

5. Click Redo. Word Pro reinstates the previously undone changes.

6. Click OK to close the dialog box.

More Info

The number of operations you want to be able to undo or redo is a matter of your skill and comfort. Chapter 6, "Using SmartMasters, Styles, and Scripts for Control" includes a section called "Adjusting Word Pro's Preferences" that explains how to control undo levels and other aspects of Word Pro.

Fine-Tuning Your Text

No one's going to stop you from reading your document over and over, and then making edits one by one. And no one's going to help you, either — except for Word Pro, that is. This section covers powerful automated editing features to help you improve and polish the content of your document. Most of these tools work and look the same, making it easy to get the most from them.

Finding Text Quickly

Earlier in the chapter, you learned how to go to a particular page or element in a document or a marked location called a bookmark. That's great, as long as you know what page holds the information you want or have taken the time to create bookmarks. If you know what text you want to find, but aren't sure what page it's on or haven't created a bookmark, you can use Quick Find to go to that text instead. Follow these steps to use Quick Find:

1. To begin the search from the top of the document, press Ctrl+Home.

2. Choose Edit ➪ Proofing Tools ➪ Quick Find (Ctrl+A). The Quick Find *bar* appears below the SmartIcon bar onscreen. (The Quick Find bar is a *modeless* bar that enables you to jump back and forth between the tools for a feature and the text in a document.)

3. Begin typing the word, number, or phrase to find in the Find text box. As you type, Word Pro scrolls through the document, highlighting the first instance of the term or phrase that matches your entry, as shown in Figure 3-30.

4. Continue typing until you make your full entry. The more complete your entry, the more accurate the match.

5. If the highlighted text in the document isn't the occurrence that you need to work with, click one of the direction buttons to indicate whether the search should look earlier or later in the document, then click Next. Repeat this step until you find the match occurrence that you want to work with.

6. You can then work with the highlighted match, editing or formatting it as needed.

Note   When you use any modeless bar, if you click in the document and make a correction, or click to move to another area of the document, a Continue button appears on the bar. Click that Continue button to have the modeless bar return to the operation at hand.

7. Repeat Steps 3 through 6 to find and work with other words and phrases.

8. Click Done to close the Quick Find modeless bar when you've finished finding terms.

Click for online help about the bar.
Quick Find bar.   Term to find.   Click to change the find direction.

Click to find the next matching
occurrence in the specified direction.

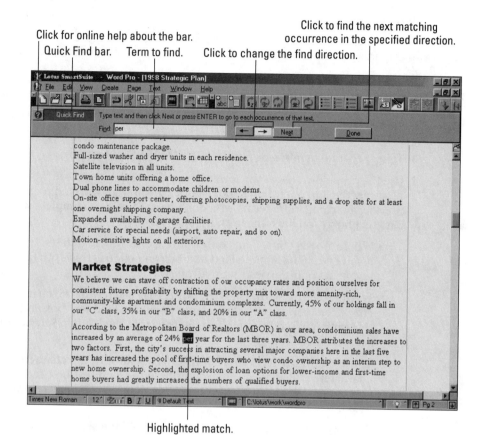

Highlighted match.

Figure 3-30: Display the Quick Find bar to search your document for a word or phrase.

Using Find & Replace

Quick Find leaves a little bit to be desired, in that it requires you to click in the document and make changes. If you want to find multiple occurrences of a term in a long document and also want to correct those occurrences, you should use Find & Replace instead. Find & Replace identifies each match of the word or phrase you specify and lets you choose whether or not to replace it with an alternate term or phrase you specify. For example, if you've created an extensive contract for a new vendor named *Smythe Company*, and realize that you've misspelled the company's name as *Smith* throughout the document, you can use Find & Replace to quickly make the replacements, with the added benefit that it catches mistakes you might miss (which could invalidate a contract or other legal document).

Making Replacements

When you need to find a term or phrase and replace one or more instances of that word or phrase with alternate text, follow these steps to perform the Find & Replace:

1. To begin the Find & Replace from the top of the document, press Ctrl+Home.

2. Choose Edit ⇨ Find & Replace Text (Ctrl+F). The Find & Replace bar appears below the SmartIcon bar onscreen.

3. Type the word, number, or phrase to find in the Find text box.

4. Use the drop-down list at the lower-left corner of the bar to tell Word Pro how precisely the find operation should work. (If you want the Find to be less precise, matching more terms, you don't have to enter a complete word in the Find text box.) You have these choices:

   • **Whole Words Only.** Finds only entire words that match the text to Find. If you enter **Smith** in the Find text box and choose this option, Word Pro highlights only entries that read *Smith*.

   • **Words Starting With.** Finds all words that begin with the character or characters you specify. If you enter **Sm** in the Find text box and choose this option, Word Pro highlights entries that read *Smith, Smythe, smoke, smart*, and so on.

   • **Words Ending With.** Finds all words that end with the character or characters you specify. If you enter **th** in the Find text box and choose this option, Word Pro highlights entries that read *Smith, math, path*, and so on.

   • **Words Containing.** Finds all words that hold the series of characters you specify. If you enter **th** in the Find text box and choose this option, Word Pro highlights entries that read *Smith, Smythe, the, math, path*, and so on.

5. Type the replacement word, number, or phrase in the Replace with text box.

6. If you need to change the direction of the search (if you skipped step 1), click one of the direction arrows to search backward or forward through the document.

7. You then have two options:

   • **Click the Replace All button.** Word Pro finds all entries that match the Find entry you specified, and replaces them with the Replace With text you specified.

   • **Click the Find button.** Word Pro finds the first match for the Find text you specified and highlights the match in the document, as shown in Figure 3-31. You can then click the Replace button to replace only the highlighted match; Word Pro does so and highlights the next match. If you don't want to replace a match Word Pro finds, click the Find button to skip it and instead go to the next match.

Use this drop-down list if you want to search for partial matches.

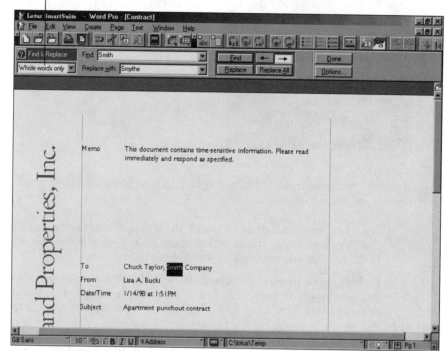

Figure 3-31: With Find & Replace, you can replace matches one at a time (shown here), or replace all matches simultaneously.

8. Repeat Steps 2–7 as needed to find and replace other entries.

9. Click Done to finish the Find & Replace and close the Find & Replace modeless bar.

Setting Find & Replace Options

As you become more proficient with Find & Replace, you may want even greater control over its features, such as limiting the parts of the document that Find & Replace searches through. You can set such options after you display the Find & Replace bar (Edit ⇨ Find & Replace Text). To do so, click the Options button on that bar, which displays the Find & Replace Text Options dialog box, shown in Figure 3-32.

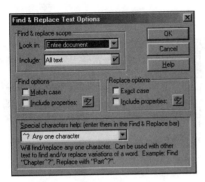

Figure 3-32: Find & Replace offers a number of options to control what document parts it searches, how it handles replacements, and more.

You can adjust one or all of the dialog box options to control the Find & Replace results you get, as follows:

✦ **Look In.** Choose whether to search the whole document or only the division that presently holds the insertion point. (You'll learn how to create divisions in Chapter 5, "Organizing and Highlighting Information.")

✦ **Include.** Choose what document parts Find & Replace searches through. The default choice, All Text, searches all parts of the documents. You can click one or more of the remaining choices to select them instead: Main Document Text, Headers & Footers, Tables, Frames, and Footnotes. When selected, each of these options displays a check; click it again to remove the check and deselect it. Click the check mark for this drop-down list box to close the list when you've finished making your selections.

✦ **Find Options.** Click the Match Case check box to tell Word Pro to only highlight entries that use exactly the same capitalization as the text you enter in the Find text box of the Find & Replace bar. If you want to find only entries that also match formatting you specify, select the Include Properties check box.

✦ **Replace Options.** Click the Exact Case check box to tell Word Pro to use exactly the same capitalization as the text you enter in the Replace With text box of the Find & Replace bar for all replacements it makes in the document. If you want to find text with particular properties, select the Include Properties check box.

Note

If you choose Include Properties under either Find Options or Replace Options, click the button beside the Include Properties check box in either location to display the Find & Replace Text Properties dialog box. On the Find tab, check the name of each formatting property (Font Name, Size, Text Color, and so on) that the text to find has, and then use the accompanying list to specify the formatting setting for each selected property. If you also want to replace the formatting on found selections with new formatting, click the Replace with tab, and then select which properties to replace and which replacement settings to use. Click OK when you've finished making your selections to return to the Find & Replace Text Options dialog box. See Chapter 4, "Formatting and Printing a Document," to learn more about text formatting.

✦ **Special Characters Help.** This drop-down list doesn't present options. Instead, when you select a choice from this drop-down list, the text below the drop-down list changes to explain the selected wildcard character. Wildcards are special codes that you can enter in the Find and Replace With text boxes to find special characters or to replace parts of terms. For example, you could enter ^t^t in the Find text box and ^t in the Replace With text box to replace instances of two tabs with a single tab. Refer to this list to learn how to use the wildcards.

After you set the options you want in the Find & Replace Text Options dialog box, click OK to finalize those settings and close the dialog box. If you then perform a Find & Replace, it follows the new settings.

Checking Spelling

Iff you doant spel or tipe vere wel, let Wird Prau chek yowr techst. Misspellings not only hinder understanding, they also make you look unprofessional and reduce your credibility. Top-of-the-line word processors like Word Pro have offered spell checking capabilities for years now. This section covers how to benefit from spell checking.

Performing a Spell Check

Typos can prevent clear communication. If you're in a profession in which you publish information — annual reports, contracts, Web documents, and so on — your boss or customers will have a "zero tolerance" policy regarding typos. Use the following steps to spell check information in every Word Pro document you create, before you subject it to critical eyes:

1. To begin the spell check from the top of the document, press Ctrl+Home.

2. Choose Edit ➪ Check Spelling (Ctrl+F2) or click the Check Spelling SmartIcon. The Spell Check bar appears below the SmartIcon bar onscreen, and Word Pro highlights the first word that doesn't match the entries in the dictionary spell check uses. Figure 3-33 shows that spell check has highlighted a proper name; most proper names aren't found in the dictionary.

Note

Spell check actually highlights all misspelled words whenever the Spell Check bar appears onscreen. The word you're currently working with appears in heavy, reverse red highlighting. Other words that may be misspelled appear with lighter background highlighting (light blue by default).

3. If the word is spelled correctly, like the proper name shown in Figure 3-33, you can click the Skip All button to tell Spell Check to ignore all occurrences of the word in the document. Click Skip to skip only the occurrence that's presently highlighted. If you'll be using the proper name or unique word often, click the Add to User Dictionary button; this inserts the word into Spell Check's dictionary, so that it won't highlight it as a misspelled word in future spell checks.

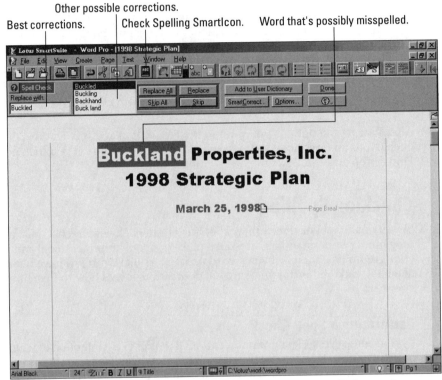

Figure 3-33: Spell check highlights each word not found in its dictionary; it suggests replacements and gives you numerous correction options.

4. If the word is spelled wrong, first review the correction suggested in the Replace With text box. If that correction isn't the one you need, you can click an alternative correction in the list of other possible corrections, or edit the entry in the Replace With text box. Once the Replace With text box contains the correction you want, use one of the following techniques to tell Spell Check how to handle the correction:

- **SmartCorrect.** Click this button to display the Add SmartCorrect entry dialog box, then click OK. SmartCorrect now fixes the misspelling as you type it, reducing potential typos in the event that you don't spell check a document. (You must use this option before you choose either of the choices described next.)

- **Replace All.** Click this button to tell Spell Check to replace all instances of the misspelled word in the document, using the text from the Replace with Text box.

- **Replace.** Click this button to tell Spell Check to replace only the highlighted instance of the misspelled word, then continue the spell check.

5. After you perform Step 3 or 4, Spell Check highlights the next word not found in the dictionary, so you can address whether and how to correct the word. Repeat Steps 3 and 4 as often as needed to reach the end of the document.

6. Click Done to close the Spell Check modeless bar.

You also can make quick spelling corrections as you type, without taking the extra time to display the Spell Check bar. The status bar offers a button that cues you when the word that holds the insertion point may be misspelled. That button, near the center of the status bar, resembles the Check Spelling SmartIcon. If the word holding the insertion point may be misspelled, a question mark appears at the right side of the spelling button on the status bar. Click the button to display a list of options for correcting the word, as shown in Figure 3-34. Click one of the suggested replacements to fix the misspelling, or click one of the commands telling Word Pro to skip the word or simply add it to the dictionary.

These choices work like those on the Spell Check bar.

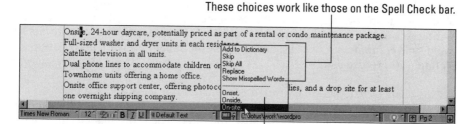

You can click a replacement word instead.

Figure 3-34: The button near the center of the status bar cues you when a word may be misspelled. Click the button to display options for correcting the typo.

Setting Spell Check Options

You can control more than simply what words Spell Check finds and replaces. For starters, if you click the "globe" button on the Spell Check bar, you can select a different language for Spell Check to use (assuming you installed the dictionaries you need when you installed SmartSuite). Click the Options button to display the dialog box for setting Spell Check options, as shown in Figure 3-35.

The first three check boxes (Check for Repeated Words, Check Words with Numbers, and Check Words with Initial Caps) turn spell checking on and off for the specified feature. The Include User Dictionary Alternatives check box ensures that alternative spellings you add for a term in any dictionary (also called a *user dictionary*) appear in the list of possible corrections in the Spell Check bar. If you want Spell Check to highlight unrecognized words with a different color, choose a new color from the Color for Unrecognized Words drop-down palette. If you've previously told Spell Check to skip particular words (such as proper names) during a spell check, click the Clear Skipped Words button to have Spell Check return to highlighting the words as unrecognized words rather than skipping them.

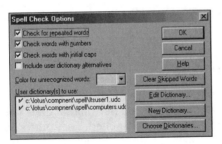

Figure 3-35: You can tell Spell Check which dictionary to use, which words to check, and choose other options in this dialog box.

If you've created one or more user dictionaries, you can choose which dictionaries Spell Check compares words to during the next spell check. Selecting fewer dictionaries may reduce the number of unrecognized words Spell Check highlights, thus streamlining the spell check. Select each dictionary to use in the User Dictionary(s) to Use list; a check appears beside any dictionary Spell Check currently uses. To create a new dictionary, choose New Dictionary. The New User Dictionary dialog box appears. Enter the name for the dictionary in the New File Name text box; for example, if you're creating a dictionary of computer terms, you could type **computers**. Click OK, and the new dictionary appears in the User Dictionary(s) to Use list.

Making changes to a dictionary requires a lengthier process and is a bit counterintuitive. When you make entries to a user dictionary, you tell the dictionary which misspellings to highlight (because you often type those misspellings) and what correction to suggest for each misspelled term. Start by choosing Edit Dictionary. The Edit User Dictionary dialog box appears. Choose the Dictionary to Edit using the drop-down list of that name; your choice here specifies where to save your special terms and suggested corrections. To create an entry for a misspelling, type the term in the Word to Edit text box. In the Word Options area of the dialog box, select Always Mark Word as Misspelled to ensure that Spell Check highlights the misspelling. Type the preferred correction for the misspelling in the Replacement Option text box (see Figure 3-36); this entry appears in the Replace With text box of the Spell Check bar when you're correcting the misspelling. If the term can only be hyphenated in a certain way for line breaks, type the term with the correct hyphenation in the Special Hyphenation text box. Click Add to add the misspelling (and its suggested correction) to the dictionary.

To remove a misspelling you've included in a dictionary, click it in the list below the Word to Edit text box, then click the Remove button. You also can edit a misspelling, rather than remove it. Click the term in the list below the Word to Edit text box, make the changes you want in the Word Options area of the dialog box, then click Add.

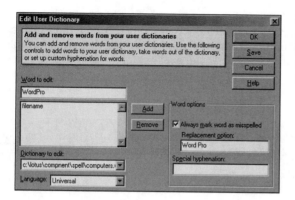

Figure 3-36: Use the Word to Edit and Word Options text boxes to identify a misspelling and its correction, then click Add to add them to the selected dictionary.

Before you close the Edit User dialog box, click the Save button to save all your changes. Then click OK to return to the Spell Check Options dialog box. Click OK in that dialog box to finish your selections, close the dialog box, and continue working with Spell Check.

The Choose Dictionaries button displays the Word Pro Preferences dialog box so that you can select which dictionaries appear in the Dictionaries to Use list. Refer to Chapter 6, "Using SmartMasters, Styles, and Scripts for Control" to learn more about using the Word Pro Preferences dialog box.

Checking Grammar

Grammar Check reviews your text for blatant grammatical mistakes or tricky matters of style and suggests corrections where it can.

Word Pro's grammar checking program does not install by default. You need to perform a custom installation, as described in the Appendix, "Installing SmartSuite," to reinstall Word Pro with the grammar checker.

Follow these steps to check the grammar in the current document:

1. To begin the Grammar Check from the top of the document, press Ctrl+Home.

2. Choose Edit ➪ Proofing Tools ➪ Check Grammar. The Grammar Check modeless bar appears below the SmartIcon bar onscreen. Grammar Check highlights the first word, phrase, clause, or sentence that presents a grammatical problem, and suggests a correction, if possible.

3. Review the scrolling explanation for why the error was highlighted. Grammar check uses a number of *rules* to guide it in identifying errors. If the explanation isn't clear, choose Explain to learn more about the underlying grammar rule, as shown in Figure 3-37. Click OK to close the explanation after you've reviewed it.

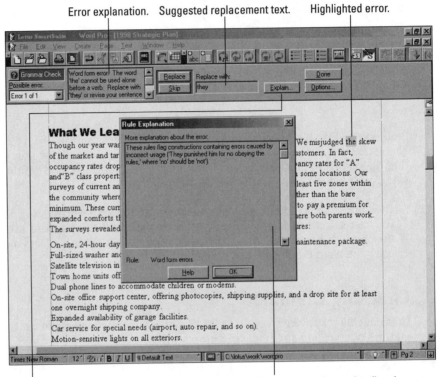

Figure 3-37: Grammar Check highlights a grammatical problem, explains what's wrong, and suggests replacement text when it can.

4. If the sentence has more than one grammatical error and you want to correct one of the other errors, instead, select the error to correct from the Possible Error drop-down list.

5. Handle the error:

   • Click in the document, correct the error, then press continue.

   • Choose Replace to correct the error using the Replace With contents.

   • If the text is OK as is, choose Skip.

6. Repeat Steps 4 and 5 to handle all the grammatical errors in the document.

7. Click Done. The Readability Statistics dialog box appears, providing information about the total number of words and paragraphs checked, the average words per sentence and paragraph, and your text's score on several different readability scales.

8. Click Close to close the Readability Statistics dialog box.

If you've used the grammar check a few times and find that it flags too many or too few errors, you can adjust its options to smooth the process. Display the Grammar Check bar (Edit ⇨ Proofing Tools ⇨ Check Grammar) and then click the Options button. The Grammar Options dialog box appears. The first tab, Rules, enables you to choose how many rules Grammar Check applies. You can select a Quick Proof or Full Proof from the Grammar Check Level list; a full proof applies all the rules, and a quick proof does not. Choose whether Grammar Check should use Informal, Standard, or Formal language from the Formality drop-down list. Use the Rule Type list to see what each rule means, and to select which rules apply. Figure 3-38 shows the description for a rule. Click to check or clear the check beside rules as needed; Grammar Check applies only the rules with checks beside them.

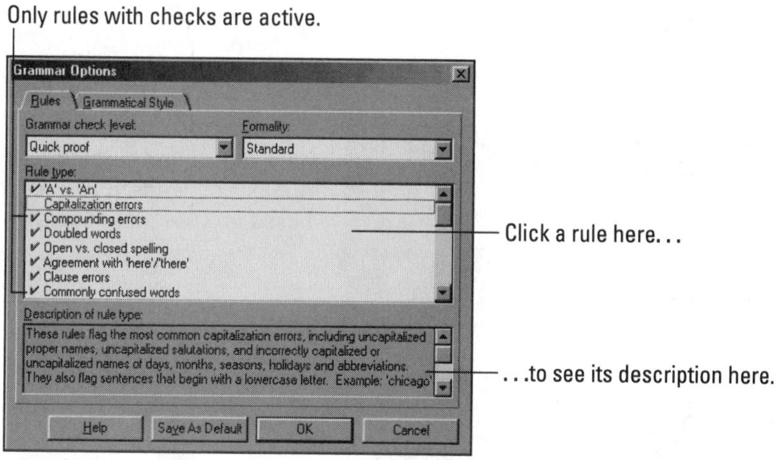

Figure 3-38: Choose whether Grammar Check applies many rules or only a few on the Rules tab.

Click the Grammatical Style tab (see Figure 3-39) to set its options next. The choices you make on this tab, described as follows, control style details that you want Grammar Check to flag for you, so you can consider whether to correct them:

✦ **Maximum Number of Words Per Sentence.** Flags any sentence with more words than you specify here as a possible error.

✦ **Number of Spaces Between Sentences.** Flags an instance where there are more spaces between sentences than you specify.

✦ **Flag Consecutive Prepositional Phrases.** Tells Grammar Check never to flag multiple prepositional phrases, or to only flag when there are three, four, or five in a row.

✦ **Flag consecutive nouns.** Tells Grammar Check never to flag multiple nouns in a sentence, or to only flag when there are three, four, or five in a row.

✦ **Flag split infinitives.** Tells Grammar Check to never or always flag split infinitives, or to only flag when at least two, three, or four words intervene.

Note

A quick grammar lesson. . . . An infinitive is the verb form that begins with "to," as in "to work." According to formal grammar rules, you should never insert a modifying word within an infinitive phrase, as in "to really work." Yet in this example, moving that modifying word to the preferred location, as in "to work really," destroys the meaning. For that reason, you may want to lighten up a bit on correcting split infinitives if you're creating an informal document.

✦ **Maximum Number of Identical Sentence Openers.** Starting every sentence with "The" or "There is" leads to boring writing. The numbers you enter here tell Grammar Check to alert you if you use the same opener the designated number of times for a given number of consecutive sentences or within ten sentences.

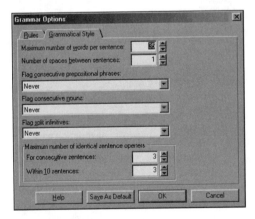

Figure 3-39: Grammar Check can help you control such issues as the number of words in each sentence, based on your preferences set here.

Once you've established all your Grammar Check preferences, you might want to make them the default that Word Pro uses so you don't have to choose them again the next time you perform a grammar check. To do so, click the Save As Default button. Then choose OK to close the Grammar Options dialog box. You can then perform a grammar check or close the Grammar Check bar.

Using the Thesaurus to Improve a Word Choice

Most of us fall back into a comfort zone as we create a document. We make the same typos and grammatical errors, and frequently use the same words over and over — especially at the end of the day when we're burnt out and anxious to bail out of the office. To kick the word choice blahs without eating up too much of your time, try the thesaurus. The thesaurus suggests synonyms for a word you select. You can use one of those synonyms, presumably a livelier relation, to replace your original word. To use the thesaurus, first select the word that you want to replace. Choose Edit ➪ Proofing Tools ➪ Check Thesaurus.

If Word Pro doesn't recognize the selected word, the Can't Find Word in Thesaurus dialog box appears. If the selected word is misspelled, click a correction in the Replace With list, then click OK; otherwise click Cancel. In the latter case, you won't be able to use the thesaurus to replace the word.

When the thesaurus recognizes your word, the Thesaurus dialog box appears, as shown in Figure 3-40. In the Meanings For list, click the general meaning that most closely matches how you used your original word in the document. For example, because the example text discusses amenities for rental property, clicking **Facilities** in the Meanings For list would yield the best possible synonyms. In the Synonyms For list, click the synonym that's most appealing. (If that synonym isn't quite right, you can click the Lookup button to see further synonyms for it.) Click Replace to close the dialog box and replace the original word with the synonym you selected.

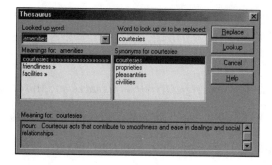

Figure 3-40: Use the Thesaurus dialog box to choose a more lively replacement for a word you've selected.

Checking Word Count

Most of us have too little time to wade through a magnum opus memo when a few paragraphs would do. If you're writing for a professional publication or other restricted setting, you may face a requirement that's more quantifiable than your audience's attention span — a word count restriction. You may need to submit an article of 500 words or less, for example.

Word Pro can count the number of characters and words in a selection or the entire document. If you need a word count for a selection in addition to the whole document, select the block of text. Then, choose Edit ➪ Proofing Tools ➪ Word Count. A message box appears (see Figure 3-41) to give you the word and character counts for the document and selection. Click OK when you've finished reviewing these statistics.

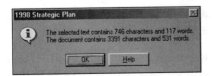

Figure 3-41: Word Pro can count the words and characters in a selection or the entire document, so you can learn whether you need to tighten up your writing.

Marking and Reviewing Revisions, Highlighting, and Comment Notes

As noted earlier, the undo/redo special feature can track a number of changes you've made to a document. Undo/redo special has a few limitations, however. First, it doesn't show you prior changes onscreen and its notes about specific changes in its dialog box are a little sketchy. Second, if you need to undo or redo a change, you may be forced to undo or redo several changes to get to the one you want. Finally, the undo/redo options remain available only during the current Word Pro session. Once you exit Word Pro, there's no record of what you can undo or redo.

Revision marks, in contrast, highlight all the edits made in a document. Further, you can select each edit (in any order) and specify whether Word Pro should accept it (finalize the change) or reject it (undo the change). The revision marks remain active in the document until you physically remove them,

A special SmartIcon bar offers tools for working with revision marks and the other highlighting tools — highlighting and comment notes — covered in this section. Right-click a displayed SmartIcon bar, and then click Review/Comment Tools to display the Review/Comment tools SmartIcon bar. Figure 3-42 shows this SmartIcon bar and identifies each of its buttons.

Create Comment Note.
Toggle Highlighter On/Off.
Highlight and Create a Comment Note.
Previous Comment Note.
Next Comment Note.
Open All Comment Notes.
Close All Comment Notes.

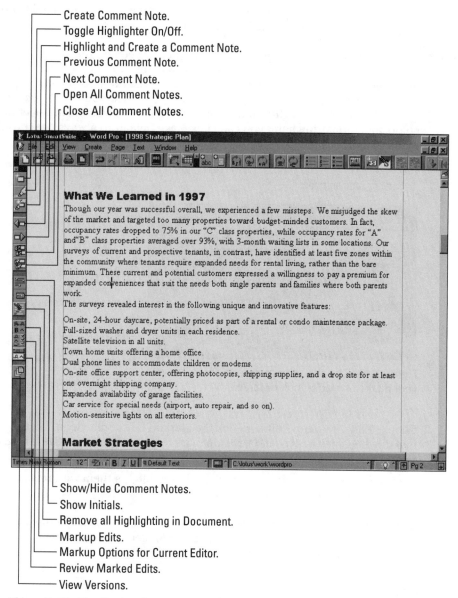

Show/Hide Comment Notes.
Show Initials.
Remove all Highlighting in Document.
Markup Edits.
Markup Options for Current Editor.
Review Marked Edits.
View Versions.

Figure 3-42: The Review/Comment Tools SmartIcon bar provides tools for marking revisions, highlighting text, and more.

Marking Edits

If you're developing a document over multiple days or are routing it to others for comment, you should use revision marks (called *Markup Edits* in Word Pro) to keep a record of all the changes. Follow these steps to record edits in a document you've created or a document you're reviewing for a colleague:

1. Click the Markup Options for Current Editor SmartIcon on the Review/Comment Tools SmartIcon bar. The Markup Options For (Your Name) dialog box appears, as shown in Figure 3-43. Use the drop-down lists to specify how Word Pro should mark your *insertions* (text you insert), *deletions* (text you delete), highlights, and comment notes. After you finish selecting colors and formatting here, you can click Make Default to always use those settings. Click OK to close the dialog box.

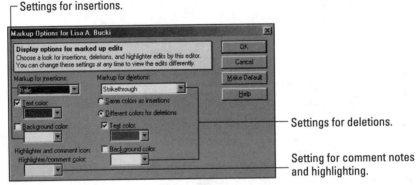

Figure 3-43: Use the settings here to control how your marked-up edits look onscreen.

2. Choose Edit ⇨ Markup Edits or click the Markup Edits SmartIcon. Revision marking becomes active, and revision mark symbols appear on the insertion point.

3. Make your edits in the document. Word Pro highlights them with revision marking, as illustrated in Figure 3-44.

You can turn the markup edits feature off by choosing Edit ⇨ Markup Edits or clicking the Markup Edits SmartIcon. Word Pro no longer marks your revisions, but the marks for your previous changes remain visible.

Reviewing Edits

To finalize your document, you want to decide whether to keep or discard each revision that's been made. Press Ctrl+Home to move the insertion point to the top of the document. Then, choose Edit ⇨ Review Marked Edits or click the Review Marked Edits SmartIcon. Click Next Edit to move to the first marked revision in the document, as shown in Figure 3-45.

Insertions.   Deletions.

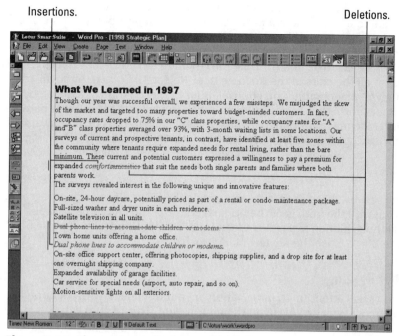

Figure 3-44: The markup edits feature highlights your insertions and deletions.

Choose how to handle this edit.

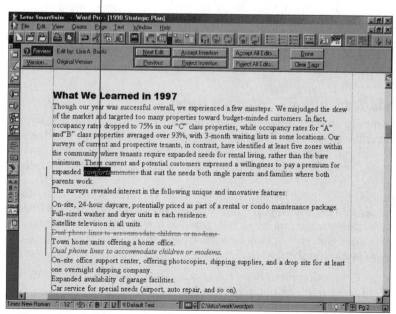

Figure 3-45: Use the Review modeless bar to specify which changes to accept or reject.

To skip an edit without making a decision, click Next Edit. You can click Previous, when needed, to move back to a previous edit without accepting or rejecting the presently highlighted one. Click Accept Insertion or Accept Deletion (the name changes depending on the nature of the highlighted change) to implement the change. Click Reject Insertion (or Deletion) to undo the edit. Click Accept All Edits to implement all the edits in the document, or Reject All Edits to undo all edits made in the document; after you choose either of these buttons, a dialog box appears. Specify whether to accept or reject all the edits in the current paragraph or the entire document, or only the edits you've made to the current paragraph or document (leaving changes by other editors intact), then click OK. A dialog box informs you of how many edits were accepted or rejected. Click OK to close the dialog box.

Behind the scenes, Word Pro tracks who made the first edit to each paragraph. It assigns a tag with the initials of the original editor of the edited paragraph. To remove all those hidden tags, click Clear Tags. Choose Done when you've finished reviewing edits to close the Review modeless bar.

Using Highlighting

If you need to call attention to information in your document without applying formatting per se, you can *highlight* the information. This feature works just like highlighting a text book with a marker. You turn on highlighting, then drag over the text to highlight.

To turn on highlighting, click the Toggle Highlighter On/Off SmartIcon on the Review/Comment Tools SmartIcon bar. Drag in the document to highlight one or more words, phrases, or chunks of text (see Figure 3-46). The highlighter remains on until you turn if off again. When you've finished highlighting, click the Toggle Highlighter On/Off SmartIcon. To clear highlighting from a file, click the Remove All Highlighting in Document SmartIcon on the Review/Comment Tools SmartIcon bar.

Adding and Working with Comment Notes

Comment notes enable an editor to make a note about a spot in the text without inserting an edit into the text. You can add a comment note by itself, or highlight nearby text and add a comment note. Follow these steps to use various SmartIcons on the Review/Comment Tools SmartIcon bar to add comment notes to a document:

1. (Optional) Click the Show Initials SmartIcon. This tells Word Pro to display your user initials, which you entered when you first started Word Pro. You can also change your user name as described in the Word Pro Preferences coverage in Chapter 6, "Using SmartMasters, Styles, and Scripts for Control" in the note marker in the document.

2. Click the Create Comment Note (or choose Create ➪ Comment Note) or Highlight and Create a Comment Note SmartIcon.

3. Click to position a comment note by itself at the desired location in the document, or drag to apply the highlighting where needed and place the comment note. The comment note window opens onscreen.

4. Type your note text. Figure 3-47 shows a new note. In this case, it was created with highlighting.

5. Click the Close button on the note window to close and finish the note.

Highlighted text.

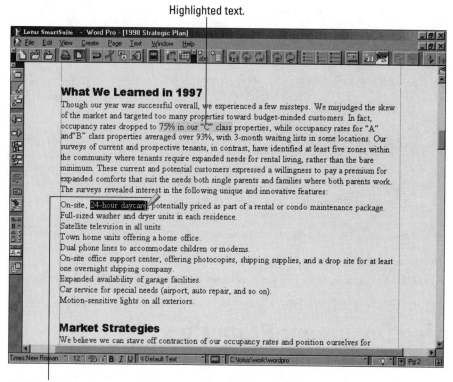

Highlighted pointer.

Figure 3-46: When highlighting is toggled on, drag to highlight text.

To redisplay a note, double-click its marker. Use the Previous Comment Note and Next Comment Note SmartIcons to move from marker to marker in the document. Use the Open All Comment Notes or Close All Comment Notes SmartIcons to open or close all the note windows. To remove a comment note, right-click its marker, then click Delete in the shortcut menu. Or, to hide comment note markers without removing the notes, click the Show/Hide Comment Notes SmartIcon; click that SmartIcon again when you need to redisplay the markers.

The marker for another note.

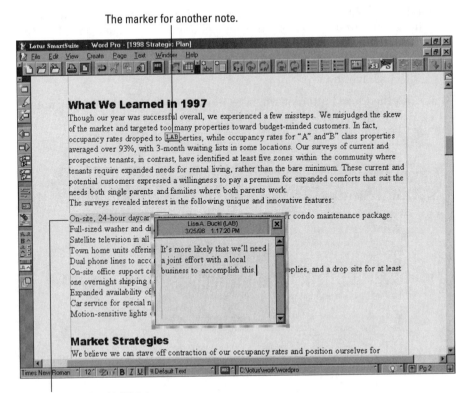

This note includes highlighting.

Figure 3-47: Add a note to give your two cent's worth about text in a document.

Setting Document Properties

Document properties include statistics about a file, information that describes a file, and options that control text hyphenation, comments, and filler pages. To work with document properties, choose File ➪ Document Properties ➪ Document. The Document Properties dialog box appears.

The first tab, *General,* offers a number of statistics about the document (and the document version, if you've saved multiple versions of a document) near the top of the dialog box. (Document versions are discussed in Chapter 33, "Working with Communications and Team Editing Features.") The statistics presented include the total editing time, last editing date, and last editor. If you want to assign a category to identify the document—such as form, newsletter, or resume—select the category from the Document Category drop-down list, or type a new category in the Document Category text box. You also can assign a category to any division in a document. Choose the division name from the Division to Categorize drop-down list, and then use the Category option to choose or type a category. Enter a Description and Keywords for the file in the text boxes of those names. Then, if you use Windows to search for the file, you can search for it by specifying all or part of the Description or Keyword comments you created.

Clicking the *Fields* tab displays document information that you can insert into a document by creating a *power field.* Power fields display information that is calculated or tracked by Word Pro behind the scenes, such as the creation date, number of words, and more. (See Chapter 6, "Using SmartMasters, Styles, and Scripts for Control," to learn how to create and use power fields.)

You can scroll through the list of field names at the top of the dialog box to see what field information Word Pro routinely captures. You can also create your own field of "behind-the-scenes" information. For example, let's say you want to track a department code, but don't necessarily want to type it into the document. Instead, create a field for it. To do so, choose the Fields button. Word Pro inserts a new field, and activates the Field Name and Contents text boxes. Enter the Field Name, such as **Department**, and the Contents, which in this case would be the department code, such as **1311**.

If you want to be able to export the field to a Notes database, leave the Export As Notes/FX Field Data check box selected. Click New to finish the field entry; because this simultaneously adds another new field, click Delete to delete that field and Yes to confirm the deletion.

The two options at the bottom of the dialog box control how power fields and Click Here blocks display in the document. Check Show Power Field Formulas in Text if you want to display the formula code for power fields, rather than the displayed result. If you fill in all the Click Here blocks you care to use in a document and no longer want to see the prompts for other Click Here blocks you didn't use, clear the check beside Show Unfilled Click Here Block Prompts.

Click the final tab, *Options,* to see the mother lode of document properties settings. Figure 3-48 shows this tab. The Typographic & Language Options section of the dialog box offers numerous settings:

✦ **Options For.** Choose a division to set the options for that division.

✦ **Auto Hyphenation.** Turn on this option to have Word Pro hyphenate words at the right margin as you type, so more text (potentially) fits on each line. Note that hyphenation only kicks in for words of a certain length: "Revolutionaries," if large chunks of it can be made to appear on each line, is likely to be automatically hyphenated. On the other hand, "before," even though it is a two-syllable word that could technically be hyphenated, almost never will be.

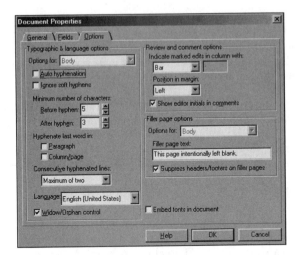

Figure 3-48: The Options tab in the Document Properties dialog box offers settings that affect how hyphenation, comments, and filler pages work.

✦ **Ignore Soft Hyphens.** If you've manually entered a soft hyphen (which you can do by pressing Ctrl+hyphen), selecting this option ignores those hyphens and displays the text without them.

✦ **Minimum Number of Characters.** When you've turned on auto hyphenation, use the Before Hyphen and After Hyphen entries to specify how many characters need to appear before and after the hyphen. These choices affect where the hyphen appears in each word, or prevent Word Pro from adding a hyphen if there's no breaking point that accommodates these settings.

✦ **Hyphenate Last Word In:** If you want to enable Word Pro to hyphenate the last word in a Paragraph or Column/Page, choose the applicable text box. Usually, you'll want to leave these options off, because they can lead to single syllables dangling alone on a line.

✦ **Consecutive Hyphenated Lines.** When the same word or a hyphen lines up at the right margin, typesetters call it a *stack*. Because stacks are unattractive, you should prevent them where possible. To control how much of a hyphen stack you'll allow at the right margin, choose Only One, Maximum of Two, or No Maximum from this drop-down list.

✦ **Language.** Choose the language the document uses by default for typing, spell checking, SmartCorrect, and other editing features. (Note that you have to install the right language files when you install SmartSuite.)

✦ **Widow/Orphan Control.** When this option is checked it prevents the last line of a paragraph from appearing or printing at the top of a new page or column, and prevents the first line of a paragraph from appearing or printing alone at the bottom of a page or column.

The Review and Comment Options area of the tab lets you control revision bars, which appear in the margins beside marked-up edits, and the initials in comment note markers. Use the Indicate Marked Edits in Column With drop-down list to choose whether to mark the edits with a vertical Bar (the default), None (nothing), or a specified Character. If you choose Character, type the character in the text box beside the drop-down list. Choose where the marks should appear in the margin — Left, Right, or Outside — from the Position in Margin drop-down list. To make sure editor initials appear in the marker for the comment note, select Show Editor Initials in Comments.

Use the Filler Page Options settings to control how a filler page looks when the document contains one. Choose the division to which the filler page options apply from the Options For drop-down list. Edit or enter the wording that you want to appear on the filler page in the Filler Page Text text box. To ensure the filler page remains completely blank, check the Suppress Headers/Footers on Filler Pages check box.

If a document contains a number of unusual fonts that likely aren't installed with Windows or SmartSuite by default, check Embed Fonts in Document. This tells Word Pro to save fonts with the document. If the document is opened on another system that doesn't have a needed font, Word Pro installs the font from the document to the user's system.

When you've finished setting all the properties, click OK to close the Document Properties dialog box.

✦　　✦　　✦

Formatting and Printing a Document

While the documents you write must have substance to be effective, style also sets them apart from the flood of other documents your readers deal with daily. *Formatting*—the letter style, borders, margins, and other bells and whistles you apply to make a document attractive— can attract a reader's eye and help with understanding. For example, when you box an important paragraph or set off a list with bullets, you make information more attractive and more accessible. This chapter shows you how to apply different formatting to text, paragraphs, and pages. It also covers how to work with different views to help you better select which formatting changes to make, and how to print a finished document.

Using Views to Better See Your Work

Dressing and grooming yourself for an important occasion requires some effort. You try on different garments and color combinations until you find the look you like, and carefully brush your teeth, shave or put on makeup, and comb your hair. Your household mirrors play an important part in your preparation, enabling you to look at the results of your efforts. For example, a full-length mirror gives you the best overall picture of your garment selections, while you rely on your bathroom mirror for a close-up look at your makeup or teeth.

Just as you use different mirrors to groom yourself and check out your appearance, you use different *views* in Word Pro as you build and format your document. The selected view controls how many pages of a document appear onscreen at once and whether the document text appears at its normal size or an enlarged or reduced size. For example, some views work much like a full-length mirror, letting you see the effects of a layout change on a full page or several pages. Other views better display specific formatting selections, much like a makeup mirror uses special lighting to highlight facial features.

This section explains how you can select and work in the different views as you create and format your document.

Basic Views

You can select the four most crucial views from the top of the View menu, shown in Figure 4-1. A check mark appears beside the currently selected view. These four commands are set off by a group divider line on the menu, telling you that only one of the options in the group can be checked (selected) at a time.

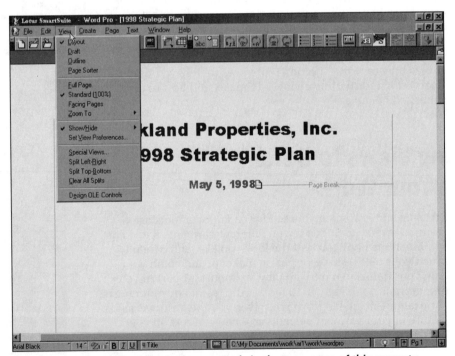

Figure 4-1: Select one of the four commands in the top group of this menu to change the current view. Only one view can be selected (checked) at a time—in this case, it's layout view.

Figure 4-1 shows *Layout* view, the default view for Word Pro shown in the figures throughout Chapter 3, "Creating and Working with Documents." Layout view shows the document at actual (100%) size, and margins—the white space at the edge of the page—at actual width, so you can see how each line of text wraps. Headers or footers (see "Creating a Header or Footer" later in the chapter) appear on the pages where you inserted them. Use Layout view to best see the results of the page layout changes you make and the actual position of special elements you insert into the document, such as frames. Choose View ⇨ Layout to display the document in Layout view.

If you want to focus on the text of the document rather than the page appearance, choose View ⇨ Draft to change to the *Draft* view. This view (see Figure 4-2) displays top and side margins at a reduced size so that more text fits onscreen. This view hides any special elements such as headers, footers, and frames—again providing more room for text onscreen but also enabling the screen to scroll more quickly as you move from page to page in the document. Consider selecting this view for entering and proofing text, then switch to the Layout view to format the text and page.

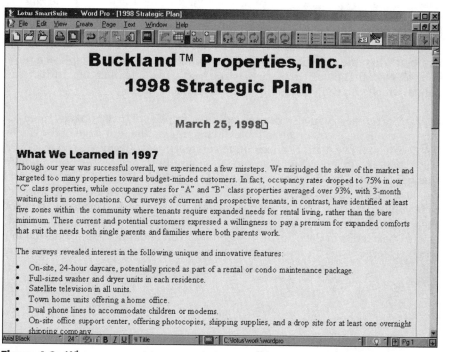

Figure 4-2: When you want to concentrate on editing text, use the Draft view.

Outlining helps you establish a logical framework for your document, enabling readers to better follow your text to a conclusion or find details pertinent to a particular topic. With outlining, you create headings to set off topics within a document and assign each heading to a particular level, thus building a hierarchy that cues the reader about the relative importance of, and relationship between, topics. Word Pro provides a special view for working with outlining, called *Outline* view. Outline view indents text at the various heading levels, among other things, to give visual cues about the outline structure of the document. It also displays the Outline bar with tools for viewing and working with the outline. To change to the Outline view, choose View ➪ Outline.

More Info

The section called "Outlining" in Chapter 5, "Organizing and Highlighting Information," explains how to work with the Outline view and how to set up outlining in your own documents.

Note

To navigate in Layout, Draft, and Outline views, use the keyboard shortcuts and mouse techniques you learned in the previous chapter. You don't need any special navigation techniques to work in these views.

If you want a "big picture" view of the current document, switch to the *Page Sorter* view by choosing View ➪ Page Sorter. As shown in Figure 4-3, Page Sorter view can display multiple pages at once so you can look over the layout and overall progression of the pages. Each displayed page includes a gray bar with the page number. When the gray bar for a page lists multiple pages and displays a plus sign, you can click that plus sign to display the next page. The plus then turns to a minus, which you can click to hide the subsequent page.

In Page Sorter view, you also can move an entire page of text. You may need to do this, for example, if you create a table of contents on the first page of the document, but decide to move it after an executive summary page. To move a page, point to the gray bar at its top. Press and hold the left mouse button until the mouse pointer changes to a four-headed arrow with a page attached, and drag. When the vertical red insertion mark between the pages appears at the new location you want for the page you're dragging, release the mouse button to drop the page at the new location. Technically, you can click to position the insertion point, drag to highlight text, and type to make edits in Page Sorter view; unless you're editing text formatted in a relatively large size, you won't be able to see your changes, so edit text sparingly in this view.

Drag by this gray bar to move a page. ┌── Click a plus to display the subsequent page.

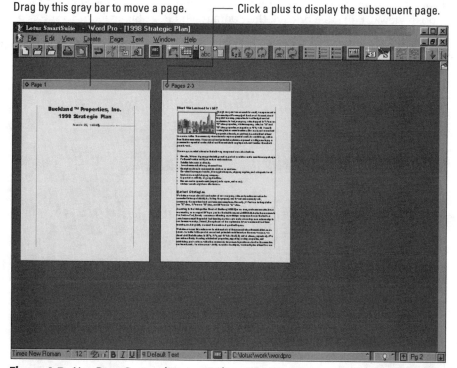

Figure 4-3: Use Page Sorter view to see how pages progress and to move entire pages in the document.

Zooming In for a Close-up

The next group of commands on the View menu controls *zooming*, or how large the document appears onscreen. By default, documents appear at 100% size (the same size that the document prints at). You can *zoom out* to full-page size or another size that's less than 100% to see the effect of page layout changes such as changes you make to margin sizes. Or, you can *zoom in* to a percentage that's greater than 100% to handle close-up tasks, such as precisely positioning a frame.

Note

The zoom percentage you specify works with the Layout, Draft, and Outline views. For example, if you're working in Draft view and decide to zoom out, Word Pro displays a zoomed-out version of the Draft view, with minimized margins and elements like headers and frames hidden. Not all of the zooming options are available within Draft view. A check mark appears in the View menu beside the selected zoom choice: Full Page, Standard (100%), Facing Pages, or Zoom To (when you select one of the options on that submenu).

If you want to see the entire current page onscreen at once (see Figure 4-4), you can choose View ➪ Full Page or click the Zoom to Full Page SmartIcon. To see two pages onscreen at once, choose View ➪ Facing Pages. You also can zoom to another preset size using choices on the Zoom To submenu of the View menu. After you choose View ➪ Zoom To, the zoom sizes you can choose include the following:

Zoom to Full Page SmartIcon.

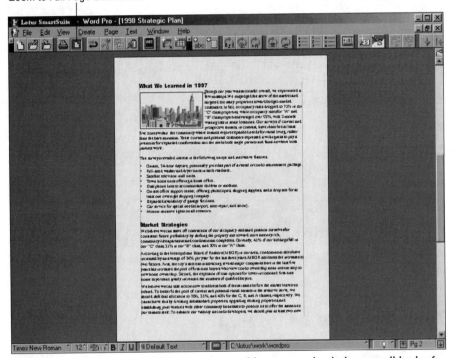

Figure 4-4: Zooming out to full-page size enables you to check the overall look of the page.

✦ **Margin Width.** Zooms the document to a size that places the left and right margins nearly at the edge of the screen, so margin space doesn't occupy the screen.

✦ **Page Width.** Zooms the document so the left and right sides of the page fit within the display area. You might want to choose this setting when you're formatting a document that's wider than it is tall (called *landscape* orientation), so that you can see how the formatting looks and still be able to edit the text.

✦ **75%, 150%, or 200%.** Zooms the document in or out to the designated percentage. For example, you might choose 150% if it's near the end of the day and your eyes are tired.

✦ **Custom Level (%).** This choice zooms the document to the percentage specified within the parentheses. You change the Custom Level percentage using the Other option, listed next.

✦ **Other.** This option displays the Zoom tab of the View Preferences dialog box (see Figure 4-5), which offers settings for choosing a zoom layout. Check the Show Draft check box to display the document in Draft view as well as the zoom setting you specify. Then, you can choose the Zoom Level check box, and select a zoom from the accompanying drop-down list (which offers choices such as Facing Pages and Page Width, in addition to percentages) or by using the Custom Level text box to create a custom percentage. To zoom by selecting how many pages to display across the document window instead, choose the View to Show Multiple Pages option button, and then use the Pages Across Screen text box to specify how many pages to show. Figure 4-6 shows three pages displayed across the screen, for example. To make the settings you specified on the Zoom tab the default for all documents, select the Make Default check box. Click OK to close the dialog box and apply your zoom settings.

Choose this option button and specify how many pages to display.

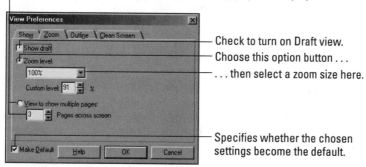

— Check to turn on Draft view.
— Choose this option button . . .
— . . . then select a zoom size here.

— Specifies whether the chosen settings become the default.

Figure 4-5: This tab in the View Preferences dialog box enables you to choose a custom zoom setting, or the default Word Pro uses.

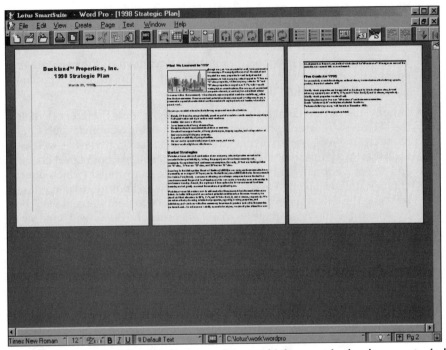

Figure 4-6: You can zoom the display to show multiple pages in the document window.

You can return to the default 100% view at any time by choosing View ⇨ Standard (100%).

Working with Splits

Splitting a document view means creating multiple panes for the document onscreen, so you can simultaneously display different pages of the same document. Choose View ⇨ Split Left-Right to add a vertical split bar that divides the document window into left and right panes. Choose View ⇨ Split Top-Bottom to add a horizontal split bar that divides the document window into top and bottom panes (see Figure 4-7). Word Pro displays a scroll bar for each pane that you can use to change the area displayed in that pane.

To work with the page shown in one of the panes, click in the document in that pane to make it the active or current pane. You also can then switch the view displayed within the selected pane. For example, if you split a document that's in Layout view, you can click in the document in one of the panes and choose View ⇨ Draft to change the selected pane to Draft view.

Horizontal split bar.

Drag to move the split bar.

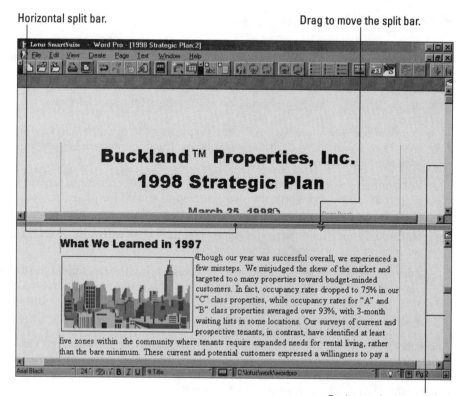

Each pane has a scroll bar.

Figure 4-7: Add a split to the document window to view different parts of the document at the same time.

You can use the View ➪ Split Left-Right or View ➪ Split Top-Bottom command to split the current pane into even smaller panes. For example, you could split the bottom pane in a top-bottom arrangement into smaller left and right panes.

When you split a document window, Word Pro splits it equally. You can move the split by dragging it if you want one pane to be smaller. Point to the split bar until you see the double-headed split pointer, then drag the split bar to the desired location. You also can eliminate the split bar by dragging it offscreen—that is, to the right for a vertical split bar or to the bottom for a horizontal split bar. You also can choose View ➪ Clear All Splits to remove a split; this method will likely be faster if you've inserted multiple splits in the current document window.

Working with Special Views

Special views combine the basic views, zoom settings, and splits to create views that simultaneously give you at least one close-up view pane for editing and one or more panes for navigating or checking the layout and outline of your document. You could set up your screen to duplicate any special view, but choosing the special view saves you steps and time. Word Pro offers four special views:

✦ **PageWalker** view includes a left pane displaying the document in Layout view with 100% zoom and a right pane displaying the document in Layout view with full-page zoom.

✦ **Panorama** view includes a top pane displaying the document in Layout view with 100% zoom and a bottom pane zoomed to show four pages across.

✦ **DocSkimmer** view includes a left pane displaying the document in Draft view with 100% zoom, an upper-right pane in Outline view with 100% zoom, and a bottom-right pane zoomed to show three pages across.

✦ **Zoomer** view includes an upper-left pane displaying the document in Draft view with 100% zoom, an upper-right pane displaying the document in Layout view zoomed to margin width, and a bottom pane zoomed to show three pages across.

To display a document in one of the special views, choose View ➪ Special Views. The Special Views dialog box appears (see Figure 4-8). Click the name of the view you want under Special View; a description for the selected view appears in a box to the right. Click OK to apply the view you want.

Figure 4-8: Use this dialog box to display a special view. When you select an option button for a view, its description appears to the right.

To remove a special view, first click in the document in the pane that shows the view settings you want to work with next. Then, choose View ➪ Special Views. In the Special Views dialog box, select Clear All Splits and Special Views, then click OK. (Instead of redisplaying the Special Views dialog box, you can usually get away with choosing View ➪ Clear All Splits.)

Controlling Onscreen Elements

The Word Pro application offers a number of different tools and visual cues to help make your work — particularly your formatting work — proceed much more smoothly. Every tool has its purpose, though, and you will certainly encounter times when you'd prefer not to have a particular tool or cue onscreen and distracting you from your work. Word Pro offers you a great deal of flexibility in specifying which items appear onscreen, as described next.

Showing and Hiding Features

The View ⇨ Show/Hide command displays a submenu that you can use to display or hide a particular screen element. When a check mark appears beside an item on the submenu, it means that item is currently displayed. Clicking a checked item on the submenu removes that item from the screen. Clicking an unchecked submenu item redisplays that element onscreen. After you choose View ⇨ Show/Hide, you can choose whether to hide or display the following items by clicking to check (select) or uncheck (deselect) an item as needed:

- ✦ **SmartIcons (Ctrl+Q).** Hides or displays the Universal and Text SmartIcon bars that appear just under the menu bar by default.

- ✦ **Ruler.** Hides or displays a *horizontal ruler* that appears just below the default SmartIcon bars. You can use this ruler to set and move tab stops, among other operations.

- ✦ **Headers & Footers.** Controls whether headers and footers (or empty placeholder boxes for them) appear onscreen in Layout view.

- ✦ **Clean Screen.** Displays the Word Pro Clean Screen (see Figure 4-9), which hides most parts of the document window so that you see more of the current document. Try the Clean Screen if you're using a 14-inch monitor to get a better look at your work.

- ✦ **Review/Comment Tools.** Hides or displays the Review/Comment Tools SmartIcon bar.

- ✦ **Internet Tools.** Hides or displays the Internet Tools SmartIcon bar.

- ✦ **Misspelled Words.** When checked, displays colored highlighting behind words that aren't recognized by Spell Check, even when the Spell Check bar isn't onscreen.

- ✦ **Power Field Formulas.** When checked, displays the formula that tells Word Pro what information a power field displays. When not checked, displays the information (calculated or referenced by the formula) the power field holds.

- ✦ **Click Here Prompts.** When checked, displays the prompt text and brackets for Click Here blocks. When not checked, completely hides the brackets and prompts.

Click to redisplay the parts of the Word Pro window.

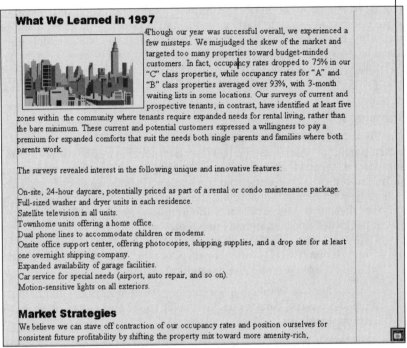

Figure 4-9: Clean Screen hides elements of the Word Pro window so you see more of the document.

The choices you make in the View ⇨ Show/Hide submenu apply to all open documents, until you change those settings.

Setting Your View Preferences

You can use the View Preferences dialog box to provide even more specific direction to Word Pro about what tools, cues, and other features to display onscreen. To display the View Preferences dialog box, choose View ⇨ Set View Preferences. The View Preferences dialog box appears, with the Show tab displayed, as shown in Figure 4-10.

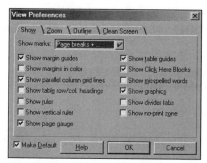

Figure 4-10: Clear the check beside any option shown here to remove it from display.

Use the options on the Show tab to control the display of specific features of the screen, creating helpful guides and highlights for the reader. The Show Marks drop-down list enumerates the *nonprinting marks* that appear in a document, such as tabs, spaces, and page breaks. If you need to see these marks in the current document to check for errors such as double spaces, click to open the Show Marks drop-down list, click to place a check beside each type of nonprinting character to display (or clear the check beside each type of nonprinting character to hide it), and then click the check mark at the right end of the drop-down list to close the list. To turn off display of all nonprinting characters without using the Show Marks drop-down list, click to check the Ignore Settings check box beside the drop-down list. When you next need to reactivate your choices on the Show Marks drop-down list, clear the Ignore Settings check box.

Each of the other check boxes on the Show tab, when checked, displays a particular feature as part of the Word Pro window or a particular type of highlighting or guideline in documents. For example, check Show Ruler to display the ruler or Show Misspelled Words to turn on highlighting for words not found in the Spell Check dictionary.

If you need a detailed description of all the items on the Show Marks drop-down list and the rest of the Show tab, click the Help button, and then click the See Details button under Step 3 in the Help window.

Each tab of the View Preferences dialog box includes a Make Default check box. If you want the changes you make on a particular tab to apply to the current document only, clear the Make Default check box on that tab. When Make Default is checked on a tab and you click OK to close the View Preferences dialog box, your choices on that tab become the defaults used by Word Pro.

The Zoom tab settings work just as described earlier under "Zooming In for a Close-up." You can make your setting share the default for Word Pro by checking the Make Default check box.

Figure 4-11 shows the third tab in the View Preferences dialog box, Outline. Select the Show Outline check box to display the Outline view. Use the check boxes in the Outline Options area of the dialog box to control features of the outline display; check a feature to turn it on.

✦ Show Outline Buttons determines whether outline buttons appear at the left side of the document.

✦ Show Level Indents specifies whether Word Pro indents each paragraph of text in the document to reflect the paragraph's outline level.

✦ Show Outline Button for Headings Only controls whether outline buttons for all document styles appear, or only outline buttons for headings.

✦ Show Only Headings When Collapsed to Level tells Word Pro that text under headings should be hidden when you collapse the outline to the top level.

✦ Wrap within Window specifies that text should be rewrapped to display within the document window, even when indented to the appropriate outline level, so you can read all the document text.

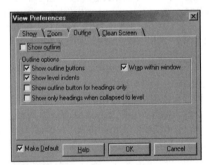

Figure 4-11: Use the Outline tab to control which tools appear in the Outline view.

To determine what elements Word Pro includes on the Clean Screen view, select the Clean Screen tab in the View Preferences dialog box. Click to check each element that you want to appear onscreen in the Clean Screen view, such as the Menu Bar.

When you've finished making your selections on the tabs in the View Preferences dialog box, click OK to close the dialog box and apply those choices.

Formatting Text

Text formatting includes the letter design (*font*); *attributes* such as boldface, italics, and colors; and paragraph settings such as alignment and line spacing. The formatting you apply to the words and paragraphs in your document serves two important functions. First and foremost, good formatting choices help make a document more readable, enabling the reader's eye to travel smoothly through the text or identify areas of emphasis. Second, it sets a mood or tone for the publication, subtly emphasizing the purpose of your communication with the reader, be it businesslike, motivational, or fun. This section shows you how to choose the formatting for the words and paragraphs in your documents, and clues you in about design tips and traps.

Setting Individual Fonts, Styles, and Attributes

To apply formatting to a word, sentence, or paragraph, start by selecting the text you want to format. Word Pro provides a few different methods for formatting the selection.

First, you can use the pop-up lists on the status bar; click one of the first seven buttons on the status bar to apply a particular type of formatting. Clicking the first button displays the list shown in Figure 4-12, which enables you to select a new font for the text; the available fonts depend on which fonts have been installed with Windows on your system. Click a font to close the list and apply the font to the selection. The second button displays a list of font sizes, in *points* (a point is $\frac{1}{72}$ of an inch); click a size to apply it and close the list. The third button displays a palette of colors you can apply to the selected text; click a color to apply it and close the list. Click the fourth, fifth, or sixth button to apply or remove **boldface**, *italics*, or underlining. Clicking the seventh button displays a list of the *styles* offered by the SmartMaster for the document. (A style applies predefined formatting, including a particular font, size, and color.) Click a style to apply it to the paragraph holding the selection.

Cycle Through Font Size Options SmartIcon.
Cycle Through Typeface Options SmartIcon.
Cycle Through Atrribute Options SmartIcon.
Text Properties SmartIcon.
Text in another font.
Text with other colors (besides black).

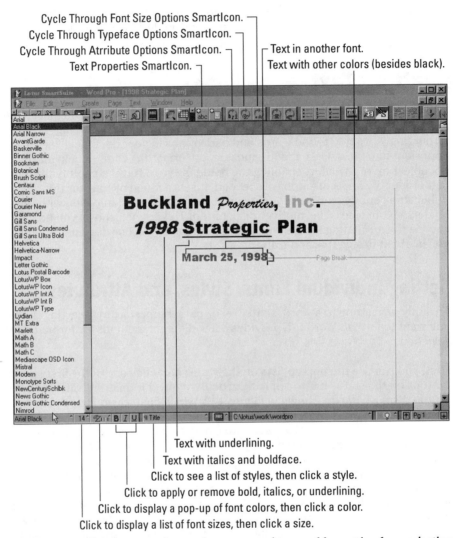

Text with underlining.
Text with italics and boldface.
Click to see a list of styles, then click a style.
Click to apply or remove bold, italics, or underlining.
Click to display a pop-up of font colors, then click a color.
Click to display a list of font sizes, then click a size.

Figure 4-12: Click the status bar to choose several types of formatting for a selection, such as using the font list shown here.

More Info

See "Using Styles" in Chapter 6, "Using SmartMasters, Styles, and Scripts for Control," to learn more about using and creating styles in Word Pro.

You also can work with the bold, italic, and underlining attributes; font color; and font size, using CycleKeys and SmartIcons for those CycleKeys on the Text SmartIcon bar. A *CycleKey* does what its name suggests; clicking the CycleKey SmartIcon *cycles* through particular formatting for the text. For example, clicking the Cycle Through Attribute Options SmartIcon applies bold, then italics, then bold and italics, then underlining, then no attributes to the selection. Figure 4-12 identifies the CycleKey SmartIcons for basic formatting. If you want to set up particular function keys (F keys) to act as CycleKeys, choose File ➪ User Setup ➪ Function Key Setup. In the Customize Function Keys dialog box, click the Assign Function Keys to CycleKeys option button, then click the option button for each CycleKey to turn on (Style, Font, Attributes, and so on). Click OK to finish assigning the CycleKeys.

One tried-and-true rule for selecting the right font is to use a *serif* font (one that has small cross-strokes at the ends of the letters, such as Courier, Times New Roman, Garamond, Palatino, or Bookman) for large blocks of text and a *sans serif* font (such as Arial, Helvetica, or AvantGarde) for headings. Serifs help the eye to travel along the letters, making the text more readable. To further help the reader, use a larger body font for wider columns. For example, use at least 12-point lettering for paragraphs that span margin-to-margin in an 8.5×11-inch document.

The Text menu provides an obvious avenue to commands for formatting text. Choose Text ➪ Normal to remove all attributes you've previously applied to selected text to return it to the default formatting for its paragraph style. Choose Text ➪ Attributes to display a submenu with commands for applying attributes and sizing:

✦ Bold (Ctrl+B) applies or removes boldface.

✦ Italic (Ctrl+I) applies or removes italics.

✦ Underline (Ctrl+U) applies or removes underlining.

✦ Enlarge Text (F4) increases the selection to the next largest font size.

✦ Reduce Text (Shift+F4) reduces the selection to the next smallest font size.

The final way to specify basic text formatting settings for a selection is to use the Font, Attribute, and Color tab in the Text InfoBox. You can display this InfoBox in a number of ways: click the Text Properties SmartIcon; choose Text ➪ Text Properties; choose Text ➪ Font & Color; choose Text ➪ Attributes ➪ Other; or press Alt+Enter. Figure 4-13 shows the Text InfoBox with the Font, Attribute, and Color tab selected.

Use to display properties for the page, instead.

Figure 4-13: The first tab in the Text InfoBox enables you to apply formatting to selected words.

Click the desired font for the text in the Font Name list. Click the correct size for the font in the Size list, or enter a precise size (or specify it with the accompanying spinner buttons) in the box below the Size list. Click your choices in the Attributes list to apply the Bold, Italic, or Underline attributes to the text, as well as Word Underline (underlining each word, but not spaces between words), Dbl Underline (double underlines), Superscript, Subscript, Strikethrough, Small Caps, Upper Case, Hidden (marks text as hidden for use with TeamSecurity, described in Chapter 33, "Working with Communications and Team Editing Features"), Protected (marks text as protected for use with TeamSecurity; see Chapter 33), and No Hyphenation (turns off hyphenation for text). Any changes you select in the Properties InfoBox apply immediately. After you finish making changes on the Font, Attribute, and Color tab, you can work with other tabs in the InfoBox, or click its Close button in the upper-right corner to close it.

Note

The Text InfoBox remains open until you close it. You can apply InfoBox settings to one selection, select text in the document and change InfoBox settings for it, and so on. When you finish working with the InfoBox, click its Close button to close it. You can right-click a tab in any InfoBox for Bubble Help identifying the tab; this book uses the Bubble Help descriptions to identify tabs that don't have a text name on them.

Hot Stuff

To underline the words in a selection but not the spaces between the words, press Ctrl+W.

Putting Fast Format to Work

If you've created a specific look for a selection that includes a particular font, font color, and attributes, you can copy that collection of settings to other text using Fast Format. Fast Format copies the formatting used by the word holding the insertion point, so that you can "paint" that formatting to any additional locations you choose. To use Fast Format, click in the word that holds the formatting to copy. Choose Text ➪ Fast Format (Ctrl+T). In the Fast Format dialog box, click The Look of the Text at the Insertion Point under Load the Mouse Pointer with, then click OK. Fast Format copies the look of the text at the insertion point, and the mouse pointer changes to a paintbrush. Drag over other selections in the document to apply the formatting (see Figure 4-14). To turn off Fast Format, choose Text ➪ Fast Format (Ctrl+T).

Text with the copied formatting.   Text formatted with Fast Format.

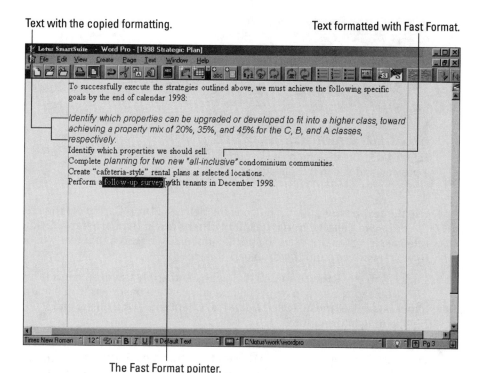

The Fast Format pointer.

Figure 4-14: Use Fast Format to copy the formatting you've applied to text.

Adding a Drop Cap

Professional document designers often format the first character of the first page of a document with a large, fancy font. Then, designers align the character so it's flush with the top of the paragraph and other text wraps around it. Designers refer to this kind of treatment as a *drop cap*. You could combine a number of different formatting techniques in Word Pro to create a drop cap, but you don't have to. Word Pro provides an automatic method for creating a drop cap, using these steps:

1. Select the letter that you'd like to format as a drop cap.

2. Choose Create ➪ Drop Cap. The Drop Cap dialog box appears (see Figure 4-15).

3. Under Place Drop Cap, choose the option button for the drop cap location you prefer. Below First Line (Dropped) aligns the drop cap with the top of the paragraph and wraps subsequent lines around the letter. Above First Line (Raised) aligns the base of the drop cap with the bases of the other letters on the first line. Beside Paragraph (Dropped) aligns the drop cap with the top of the paragraph but indents all lines in the paragraph. The preview box to the right of the Place Drop Cap option buttons shows you the result of your placement selection.

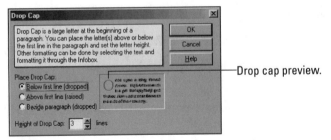

Drop cap preview.

Figure 4-15: Create a drop cap by simply specifying a position and size in this dialog box.

4. Use the text box or spinner buttons for Height of Drop Cap to set the size for the drop cap, relative to the height of other lines in the paragraph. Using relative sizing (as opposed to specific font sizes) ensures that text will be able to wrap neatly around the drop cap, if needed.

5. Click OK to close the Drop Cap dialog box and apply the drop cap settings. The drop cap appears in a special box you can see onscreen. You'll learn more about boxes like these, called *frames*, in Chapter 5, "Organizing and Highlighting Information."

6. (Optional) While the frame still appears, you can drag over the drop cap within it, then apply an alternative font or attributes to the drop cap. Be careful not to choose a font that makes the cap too large for its frame, or the drop cap may appear "cut off" at one or more edges.

7. Click outside the drop cap to finish working with it and deselect its frame. Figure 4-16 shows an example drop cap.

Consider formatting the drop cap in the same font used for the heading in the document. Doing so lends a cohesive look to your design and avoids the "ransom note" appearance that can arise when a document includes too many different fonts.

> **What We Learned in 1997**
>
> **T**hough our year was successful overall, we experienced a few missteps. We misjudged the skew of the market and targeted too many properties toward budget-minded customers. In fact, occupancy rates dropped to 75% in our "C" class properties, while occupancy rates for "A" and "B" class properties averaged over 93%, with 3-month waiting lists in some locations. Our surveys of current and prospective tenants, in contrast, have identified at least five zones within the community where tenants require expanded needs for rental living, rather than the bare minimum. These current and potential customers expressed a willingness to pay a premium for expanded comforts that suit the needs both single parents and families where both parents work.

Figure 14-16: A drop cap like this one draws attention to the beginning of a paragraph.

Inserting Special Symbols

Some documents require special characters you can't normally create using a keyboard, such as trademark, register mark, and copyright symbols, currency symbols, or specially accented letters for foreign languages. Most computer fonts offer such special characters, so that you can insert them into a document in Word Pro with the Insert Symbol bar.

To display the Insert Symbol bar, choose Text ➪ Insert Other ➪ Symbol. Then, click in the document to position the insertion point where you'd like to add a special symbol. Open the Font drop-down list and select the font that you want the inserted symbol to use. The large scrolling list at the center of the bar displays the symbols available in the selected font. Click the symbol you want, then click the Insert button on the Insert Symbol bar. The symbol appears in the document. Figure 4-17 shows the Insert Symbol bar and a trademark symbol inserted into a document. You can insert other symbols as needed, then click the Done button to close the Insert Symbol bar.

Select a font.   Select a symbol to be inserted.   Inserted symbol.

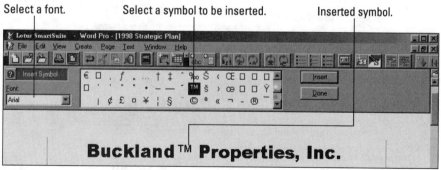

Figure 4-17: Insert special characters with the Insert Symbol bar.

Setting Alignment, Indentations, and Paragraph Spacing

Certain formatting settings control the look of the paragraph, such as how the paragraph text lines up in relation to the margins (called *alignment*). The paragraph formatting selections you make apply to the paragraph that holds the insertion point, or multiple paragraphs, if you previously selected them.

You can make several paragraph formatting changes on the Alignment tab of the Text InfoBox (see Figure 4-18). To display the InfoBox, choose Text ➪ Text Properties (Alt+Enter) or click the Text Properties SmartIcon. Then, click the second tab of the Text InfoBox, which is the Alignment tab.

To change the alignment for the selected paragraph(s), click one of the Alignment buttons in the InfoBox. The first three buttons align the paragraph along the left margin, center text between margins, and align the text along the right margin, respectively. The fourth button *justifies* the text, inserting spacing between letters so the text aligns flush with both the left and right margins. The final button left-aligns text but aligns numeric entries according to the Numeric Alignment option you choose on the Misc. tab. If you prefer not to display the InfoBox, you can cycle through the alignment choices by clicking the Cycle Through Alignment Options SmartIcon. Finally, you can choose an alignment from the Text ➪ Alignment submenu, which offers Left (Ctrl+L), Center (Ctrl+E), Right (Ctrl+R), and Full Justify (Ctrl+J) alignments.

Cycle Through Alignment Options SmartIcon.   Cycle Through Indent Options SmartIcon.

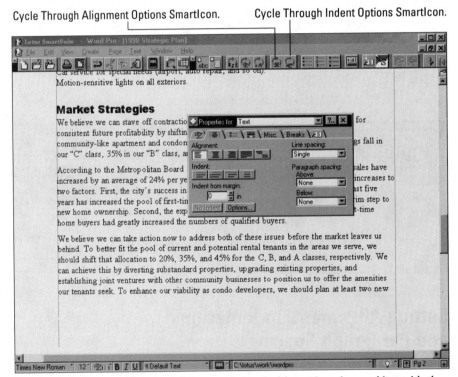

Figure 4-18: The second tab of the Text InfoBox holds settings for working with the alignment, spacing, and indention for paragraphs.

When you *indent* text, you're inserting extra spacing between the margin and one or more lines of the paragraph. For example, you may see the first line of each paragraph indented in a document, to cue the reader about where each new paragraph starts. You can click one of the four Indent buttons in the Text InfoBox to indent all lines in the paragraph by 0.5 inches at the left, indent only the first line at the left by 0.5 inches, indent all lines but the first line by 0.5 inches (called a hanging indent), or indent both sides of the paragraph by 0.5 inches. To indent all of the lines in the paragraph by a measure other than 0.5 inches, change the Indent from Margin setting; a negative value for this setting outdents the left margin, aligning text to the left of the left margin. To remove indention from a paragraph, click the No Indent button.

You also can cycle through the different types of indentations by clicking the Cycle Through Indent Options SmartIcon. Two commands on the Text menu also help you work with indentation. Choose Text ➪ Alignment ➪ Indent to indent the current paragraph at the left by 0.5 inches, or Text ➪ Alignment ➪ Outdent to remove 0.5 inches of indention.

If you want more precise control over the indention settings, click the Options button on the Alignment tab of the Text InfoBox. The Indent Options dialog box appears (see Figure 4-19).

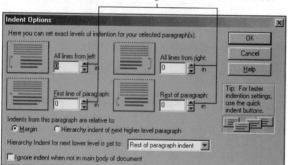

Figure 4-19: Control indentation measurements in this dialog box.

Use the text box (or its spinner buttons) beside the preview for the type of indention that you want to specify. Negative values outdent the text. If you want the indention you specified to position the paragraph relative to the outline indention for the paragraph (above it) in the next highest outline level, choose Hierarchy Indent of Next Higher Level Paragraph under Indents from This Paragraph Are Relative To. Then, to control the indention for paragraphs at the next lower outline level, choose a setting from the Hierarchy Indent for Next Lower Level Is Set To drop-down list. If you want Word Pro not to apply the indention in divisions that are not part of the main body of the document, check the Ignore Indent When Not in Main Body of Document. (See Chapter 5, "Organizing and Highlighting Information," for more on divisions.) Click OK to finish and apply the custom indention settings.

You also can use the ruler to add indention to paragraphs. Display the ruler by choosing View ➪ Show/Hide ➪ Ruler or by clicking the Show/Hide Ruler SmartIcon. The ruler includes indent indicators for the left and right sides of the text. Position the insertion point in the paragraph you want to set indention for, then drag the applicable indicator to the desired position on the ruler.

As shown in Figure 4-20, when you point to an indicator, the mouse pointer changes to show that dragging will move that particular indicator. Dragging the first line indent indicator (a down-pointing triangle) indents the first line of the paragraph from the left. Dragging the hanging indent indicator (an up-pointing triangle) indents all but the first line of the paragraph at the left. Dragging the indent indicator for the left side (a rectangle) or right side (an up-pointing triangle) of the paragraph indents all lines in the paragraph from the left or right margin. Choose View ➪ Show/Hide ➪ Ruler or click the Show/Hide Ruler SmartIcon to remove the ruler from the screen when you've finished using it to indent text.

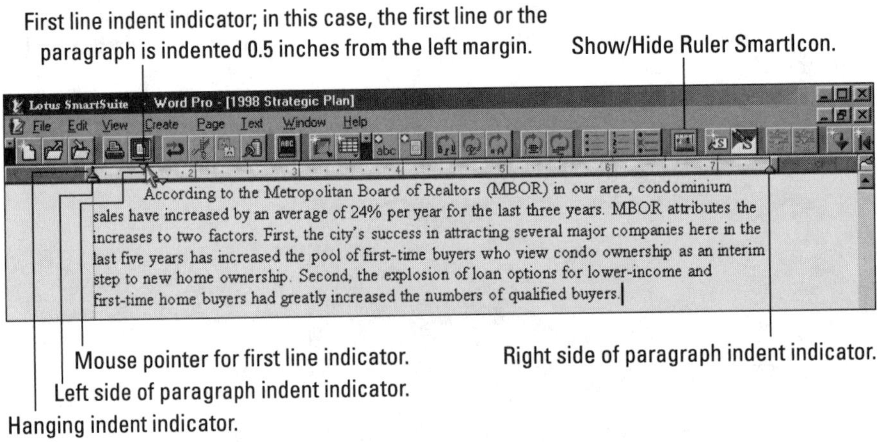

First line indent indicator; in this case, the first line or the
paragraph is indented 0.5 inches from the left margin.   Show/Hide Ruler SmartIcon.

Mouse pointer for first line indicator.   Right side of paragraph indent indicator.
Left side of paragraph indent indicator.
Hanging indent indicator.

Figure 4-20: Drag indent indicators on the ruler to change indention.

Finally, the Alignment tab of the Text InfoBox (refer back to Figure 4-18) also offers settings for controlling the spacing between lines and paragraphs. When you open the Line Spacing drop-down list, you can choose one of several spacing options for the lines within a paragraph:

✦ **Single.** Doesn't insert extra spacing between lines, using the default line height for each line. The default line height generally is the font size plus a bit of *leading*, extra spacing that ensures the ascenders (the top parts of tall letters like t, d, and h) and descenders (the bottom parts of letters like p, y, and g) don't touch between lines.

✦ **½.** Actually eliminates spacing so that each line of text only has half the default height. This setting generally causes lines of text to overlap.

✦ **1½.** Inserts an extra half line of spacing between each line of text.

✦ **Double.** Inserts a full line of extra spacing between each line of text.

✦ **Multiple.** Displays the Spacing Multiple dialog box, in which you use the Multiple text box to indicate how many extra lines of spacing to insert between lines of text. For example, you could insert three lines of spacing between lines of text in a paragraph. Click OK to finish making your setting and close the dialog box.

✦ **Leading.** Displays the Spacing Leading dialog box, so you can enter a precise leading measurement to control the space between paragraphs. You would use this method, for example, when you want to add less than a half line of spacing between lines in a paragraph. First use the Spacing Units drop-down list to determine whether you want to indicate spacing in inches, centimeters, picas (⅛" increments), or points (1/72" increments). Then, use the Leading text box to specify the amount of leading and click OK.

✦ **Custom.** Displays the Spacing Custom dialog box, which you use to specify a particular line height. Choose the type of measure to use from the Spacing Units drop-down list, enter the Custom Spacing measurement, then click OK.

Note

The net effect of changing the leading versus setting a custom line height is really the same: you have more or less white space between lines of text in the document. The technique you choose depends on your other design needs for the document. For example, if you're more concerned with "stretching" text to fill a particular space in a newsletter document, you might find it easier to work with the leading. In contrast, if the document will include a number of special elements like frames and you want to be able to carefully coordinate frame height with line height, you might want to choose a line height that's easy to multiply, like 1.5 picas or 0.2 inch. Then, you can easily format the frame height to be 10 lines (15 picas or 2 inches) high. (See Chapter 5, "Organizing and Highlighting Information," for more on frames.)

Many of the Word Pro templates do not include spacing between paragraphs. You can press Enter an extra time to include needed spacing between paragraphs, but doing so inserts a full line of blank space—more than you may want. Instead, you can use the Above and Below drop-down lists under Paragraph Spacing in the Alignment tab of the Text InfoBox to add a precise amount of spacing before or after the paragraph holding the insertion point.

It's typical to include extra spacing before paragraph headings, creating a clean break. It's also common to add extra spacing after each paragraph of text, to set off the beginning of each new paragraph. The Above and Below drop-down lists each contain commands that work just like those described for line spacing: ½ line, One line, 1 ½ lines, Two lines, Multiple, and Custom. In addition, the Above and Below drop-down lists each include a None choice, which removes any spacing before or after the selected paragraph. After you finish working with the Alignment tab, you can work with other tabs in the InfoBox or click its Close button to close it.

Working with Bullets and Numbering

You can use bullets or numbering to set off each item in a list. Using automatic bullets or numbering saves you quite a bit of time. You don't have to insert each bullet character individually or worry about setting indents. And, if you delete an item from a numbered list, you don't have to renumber subsequent items—Word Pro handles that for you. To apply the default bullet or number style to a list, first make sure you used a hard return (pressed Enter) to end each item. Next, select the entire list. Then, click the Insert Default Bullet or Insert Default Number SmartIcon. Word Pro adds the bullets or numbers to the list. Click outside the list to deselect it and better see the bullets or numbering, as shown in Figure 4-21. To remove the bullets or numbering from a list, select the list and click the SmartIcon again.

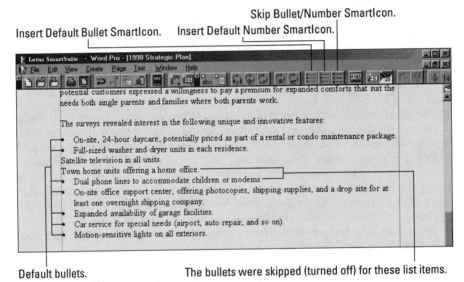

Insert Default Bullet SmartIcon.   Insert Default Number SmartIcon.   Skip Bullet/Number SmartIcon.

Default bullets.   The bullets were skipped (turned off) for these list items.

Figure 4-21: Click a SmartIcon to add bullets or numbers to the items in a list.

Alternately, you can apply bullets or numbering as you enter the items for a list. Press Enter to start the first item of the list, then click the SmartIcon for bullets or numbering. Type each list item, pressing Enter to finish each item and start a new one. After you create the last list item and press Enter, click the appropriate SmartIcon again to turn off the bullets or numbering.

There may be instances in which you want to use the indention settings for a bulleted or numbered list, but don't want to include a bullet or number. For example, let's say you have a numbered list item that's two short paragraphs long. You need to turn off the numbering for that second paragraph, but you want it to be indented, and you want the numbering to resume in order for the list item following that second paragraph. To turn off the bullet or numbering for a list item (or text you want to include as a second paragraph below the list item), click in the list item or paragraph, then click the Skip Bullet/Number SmartIcon. You can turn the bullets or numbering back on for one or more items by clicking that SmartIcon again.

You can change the bullet or numbering style used for selected list items by using the Bullet and Number tab (the third tab) in the Text InfoBox. After selecting the list items to change, display the InfoBox by clicking the Text Properties SmartIcon, then click the third tab to display its options (see Figure 4-22). You also can display this tab by choosing Text ➪ Bullets & Numbers. To change the bullet type for a bullet list, click a Bullet Style button. Or, click the Font button and choose the font that holds the bullet you want to use from the Font for Bullet Characters list in the Bullet Font dialog box, then click OK. Once you've specified a new bullet font, click the Other drop-down list button, then click the bullet to use in the pop-up list that appears. To change the numbering used for a numbered list, click a Number Style button. Or, click the Custom choice to display the Custom Numbering dialog box, which offers two tabs you can use to specify the following: text that should appear before or after each number (as in *Chapter* 1, *Chapter* 2); the starting number for the list; whether the division or section number should be included in the numbering; whether numbering should be contingent on outline position or a particular document element if numbering is stopped and restarted; or that the list should use an engineering or legal outline numbering sequence. Click OK to close the Custom Numbering dialog box after you've made your choices.

Figure 4-22: Use this tab in the Text InfoBox to choose a new bullet or numbering style.

To use a graphic such as your company logo as a bullet, use the Edit on Page check box on the Bullet and Number tab. Chapter 5, "Organizing and Highlighting Information," provides more detail about this technique.

Further, you can change the indenting and wrapping style for the bullet or numbered list on the Bullet and Number tab. Use the Indent from Margin text box to specify how much space should appear between the bullet or number and the left margin. Use the Space Before Text text box to indicate how much spacing to include between the bullet or number and the text for the item. Click an Indent Type button to choose whether all the lines of the bullet or numbered item should indent or only the first line should indent, so that subsequent lines wrap back to the left margin.

To skip a bullet or number for the selected list item(s), check Skip Bullet/Number. If a numbered list uses multidigit numbers (as in 1.a.1), choose Right Align to line up the right sides of those numbers so that the space between each number and its accompanying text remains constant.

After you finish working with custom bullet and numbering settings, you can work with other tabs in the Text InfoBox or click its Close button to close it.

Using Lines and Shading with Paragraphs

One of the fastest ways to call attention to a paragraph is to add a line or some background shading to set it off. To add lines or shading to the current paragraph, use the fourth tab (Color and Line Style) in the Text InfoBox. You can open the InfoBox and click that tab, or choose Text ➪ Lines. Figure 4-23 shows this tab in the InfoBox, along with lines and shading applied to text.

This paragraph has a line below it.

These two paragraphs have a background color (shading) and pattern applied.

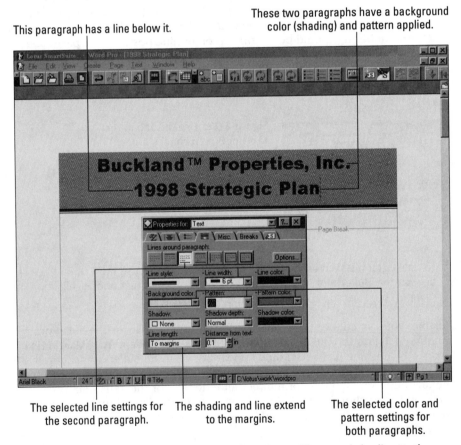

The selected line settings for the second paragraph.

The shading and line extend to the margins.

The selected color and pattern settings for both paragraphs.

Figure 4-23: You can apply numerous combinations of lines and shading to the current paragraph.

To apply a line to the current paragraph, click the Lines Around Paragraph button. The first button specifies that no line should appear. Then, use the Line Style, Line Width, and Line Color drop-down lists to specify the appearance for the line. You can add a unique combination of lines, such as a line to the left of and below the current paragraph. You also can format each line around a paragraph, such as the line above and the line below, with a different appearance. To accomplish either of these feats, click the Options button beside the Lines Around Paragraph choices to display the Line & Shadow Options dialog box. Click the check box beside each type of line that should appear, then use the drop-down lists for that line to select its Style, Width, Color, Distance From Text, and Line Length/Position. You also can specify Shadow Options at the bottom of the dialog box. Click OK to finish adding the custom lines.

To add shading behind the current paragraph, choose a color from the Background Color drop-down list. Choose a Pattern and a Pattern Color to apply those, as well. If you box or shade the paragraph and want to include a drop-shadow, use the Shadow, Shadow Depth, and Shadow Color drop-down list options to create the shadow.

Danger Zone

Lines and shading surround the current paragraph only. If you have extra spacing between paragraphs, background shading you apply won't cover that spacing; remove the spacing, if possible, to fix the problem. You can then press Enter, instead, to insert spacing that will be shaded; adjust the font size of the paragraph mark (display it with View Preferences as described earlier in the chapter) to change the amount of spacing. If you try to box a bulleted list, Word Pro places a box around each item or paragraph in the list. To fix this problem, you need to create the bulleted list in a frame, and then format the frame outline. Chapter 5, "Organizing and Highlighting Information," describes how to create and work with frames.

Finally, you can control the width for the line(s) or shading using the Line Length drop-down list options. You can have the line(s) or shading extend to the margins or only to the width (length) of the paragraph. Or, click Custom, enter the desired Line Length in the Line Length dialog box, then click OK. Use the Distance From Text text box to specify how close line(s) should be to the text, or how much shading should extend beyond the edges of the paragraph.

After you finish working with lines and shading, you can work with other tabs in the Text InfoBox or click its Close button to close it.

Setting Tabs

Tabs enable you to line up entries in a list with columns. (If your list contains lengthier entries, use a table instead. Chapter 5, "Organizing and Highlighting Information," explains how to create tables in Word Pro.) By default, there's a left tab stop every 0.5 inches, so you can simply press Tab to move to each tab stop and type. However, if some of your entries are lengthier than 0.5 inches, you need to create your own tab stops to align the text as you choose. Custom tabs you create override the default tab stops. In addition, you can create tabs that align differently than the default left tab stops. Here's a rundown of the available tab stop types:

- ✦ **Left.** The left side of the text you type aligns at the tab stop.

- ✦ **Right.** The right side of the text you type aligns at the tab stop.

- ✦ **Center.** Text you type centers itself at the tab stop.

- ✦ **Numeric.** For numeric entries that include decimal points, the decimal points (or the position where it would appear) aligns at the tab stop; the right side of text aligns at the tab stop.

The ruler provides the most speed and flexibility for setting tabs, because you can click to position a tab exactly where you need it. Display the ruler by choosing View ➪ Show/Hide ➪ Ruler or clicking the Show/Hide Ruler SmartIcon. Select *all* the lines of text for which you want to set tabs; if you miss a line or two, you'll have to go back and apply tabs for them individually.

Then, click either the Insert a Quick Center Tab or Insert a Quick Right Tab SmartIcon, and click on the ruler to create the center tab stop or right tab stop. To choose another type of tab, right-click the ruler to display its shortcut menu, then click one of the commands for selecting a tab type: Create Left Tabs, Create Right Tabs, Create Centered Tabs, or Create Numeric Tabs. You can then click on the ruler to set one or more tabs; the tab type you specified remains selected until you choose another tab type. Figure 4-24 shows some tab stops on the ruler, and how they look when applied to a list.

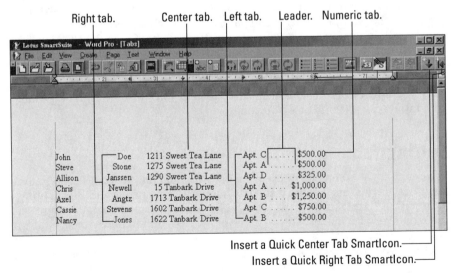

Figure 4-24: Use the ruler to set tab stops, the locations where text aligns when you press Tab to insert a tab character.

To make changes to tab stops using the ruler, first make sure you select all the paragraphs to which you want to apply the tab changes. To move a tab, drag it to a new location on the ruler. To delete a single tab, drag it off the ruler. To delete all tabs, right-click the ruler, then click Clear All Tabs. Word Pro removes your custom tabs and reinstates the default left tabs set at 0.5-inch increments.

To remove the ruler from the screen, right-click it, and then click Hide Ruler.

You also can use the ruler to set a tab at a precise measurement or include a *leader*, a repeating character that helps the eye travel between tab stops on a line. Right-click the ruler, then click Set Tabs. The Set Tabs on Ruler dialog box appears (see Figure 4-25). With (New Tab) selected under Tab to Set, use the Tab Type and Leader drop-down lists to specify what kind of tab and leader to use.

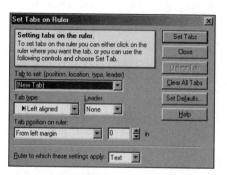

Figure 4-25: Create a tab stop at a precise measurement or include a leader for it using this dialog box.

Creating a tab is easy if you follow the guidelines that follow. When you've finished entering the settings for each tab, click Set Tabs to set the tab.

✦ To simply set the tab a particular distance from the left margin, specify a value using the Tab Position on Ruler text box.

✦ To create a tab based on a particular distance from the right margin, open the Tab Position on Ruler drop-down list and click From Right Margin, then use the text box to enter a measurement. The On Center Between Margins option in the Tab Position on Ruler drop-down list centers the tab; you don't have to enter a measurement.

✦ To create multiple tabs at specific distances, choose Evenly Spaced Every from the Tab Position on Ruler drop-down list, then enter the distance between tab stops in the accompanying text box. By default, Word Pro inserts the tab stop you're creating in the selected text.

✦ The Ruler to Which These Settings Apply drop-down list offers a couple of alternative places to apply the new tab. You can insert it into the ruler for the current layout only (see "Starting a New Page Layout" later in this chapter to learn how to insert layouts) or add it in any paragraph formatted with the same style as the selected paragraph.

You can continue using the Set Tabs on Ruler dialog box to add more tabs or remove others. To remove a tab, choose it from the Tab to Set drop-down list, then click Delete Tab. To remove all tabs, click the Clear All Tabs button. Click Close when you've finished working with the Set Tabs on Ruler dialog box.

The Text InfoBox also provides a means for setting tabs. Display the InfoBox by clicking the Text Properties SmartIcon or choosing Text ➪ Text Properties (Alt+Enter), and click the fifth tab, labeled Misc. You can click the Set Tabs button to display the Set Tabs on Ruler dialog box. Or, open the Tab Settings drop-down list to choose one or more tabs to set. You can choose Evenly Spaced Every to set multiple, evenly spaced tabs. Choose From Left Edge or From Right Edge to set a single tab relative to the left or right margin. The Custom choice displays the Set Tabs on Ruler dialog box. Remove Local Tabs deletes any tab(s) you previously set with the Text InfoBox. After you choose a Tab Settings drop-down list option, use the text box below that drop-down list to specify the space between multiple tabs or between the new tab and the applicable margin. Click the Close button for the InfoBox if you've finished using it.

Working with Other Miscellaneous Settings

In addition to the Tab Settings just discussed, the Misc. tab in the Text InfoBox offers a number of other options for formatting paragraphs and the document (see Figure 4-26). Use the Language drop-down list to choose the default language for the document. The Outline Settings area of the dialog box enables you to tell Word Pro how to identify text at the various outline levels in the document. If you want to specify the outline level paragraph-by-paragraph in the document, clear the check beside Use Smart Level. Then, you must use the Document Level text box to specify an outline level for each and every paragraph in the document. If you instead leave Use Smart Level checked, Smart Level automatically specifies outline levels based on the styles in the document.

Figure 4-26: Use the Misc. tab to set up other aspects of text formatting in the document.

If you enable the Heading Paragraph check box, Word Pro starts each numbered list following a paragraph with a heading style with 1, unless you manually specify otherwise. Use the Numeric Alignment drop-down list to specify whether numbers containing decimals should align a particular distance From the Right Margin or From the Left Margin, enter the needed distance in the text box below the drop-down list, and then click the fifth Alignment button on the Alignment tab to activate your Numeric Alignment settings.

Advanced Options

Click the Advanced Options button on the Misc. tab to display the Advanced Options dialog box, which contains special formatting settings you can apply to selected text. If you want to apply an overstrike character to selected text in the document, enter the character to use in the Overstrike Character text box. To adjust the spacing between letters (called *kerning*) in the words in the selection, specify a Kerning percentage using that text box or its accompanying spinner buttons. To adjust how the selected text aligns vertically (compared with other text on the same line), specify the Vertical Character Alignment to use, in points. Click OK to apply your Advanced Options settings.

Paragraph Breaks

The next tab in the Text InfoBox, the Breaks tab shown in Figure 4-27, offers you some control over how paragraphs break along with a page break or column break. If the current paragraph must appear with other paragraphs on the same page or in the same column, check Keep Paragraph, then use the accompanying drop-down list to specify whether the current paragraph must appear With Next Paragraph, With Previous Paragraph, or with the Next and Previous paragraphs on a page or in a column. If you don't want the paragraph to break along with a page break, check Keep Entire Paragraph on Same Page.

Figure 4-27: Use this tab to determine how paragraph breaks react with page and column breaks.

To insert a page or column break before or after the selected paragraph, check either Before Paragraph or After Paragraph, and then use the accompanying drop-down list to specify whether the inserted break should be a page break or a column break. (Both page and column breaks are covered more fully later in this chapter.) When the selected paragraph or its style includes spacing before or after the paragraph, use the Add Paragraph Spacing drop-down list to determine whether that spacing should always appear or whether it should appear only When Not at Break (when the paragraph isn't at a page or column break). If the paragraph following the current paragraph needs to use a particular style, check Style to Use for Next Paragraph, and choose a style from the accompanying drop-down list.

The final tab in the Text InfoBox provides options for working with styles in the document; Chapter 6, "Using SmartMasters, Styles, and Scripts for Control," covers this topic in more detail. If you've finished working in the Text InfoBox, you can click its Close button to remove it from the screen.

Using Page Formatting

Page formatting settings apply to the bigger picture—the overall appearance of your page. You usually won't need to adjust page settings when you create basic documents, especially if you create a document based on a SmartMaster. However, once you start creating longer, more complex documents or highly specialized documents like mailing labels or greeting cards, you'll need to take control over the size, margin, and other parts of the page.

To control page formatting, use the Page InfoBox, shown in Figure 4-28. To display the Page InfoBox, choose Page ⇨ Page Properties or click the Page Properties SmartIcon. You also can choose Page ⇨ Page Size, Page ⇨ Margins, or Page ⇨ Orientation to display the Page InfoBox with the first tab, Size and Margin, selected. The rest of this section covers the various settings in this InfoBox. Once you open the InfoBox, you can move from page to page in the document and from tab to tab in the InfoBox. The InfoBox remains open until you close it by clicking its Close button.

Page Properties SmartIcon.

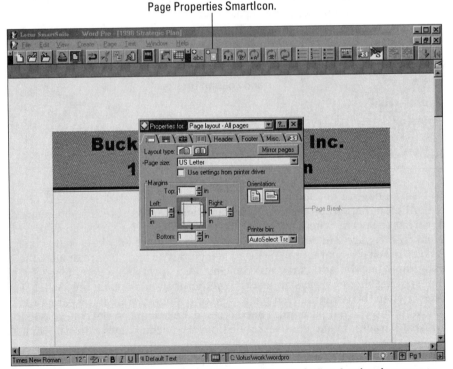

Figure 4-28: Use this InfoBox to format the overall page layout for the document.

The settings you specify in the Page InfoBox apply to every page in the document. This could be a problem if you want to include a background color or lines around one page, such as a title page, but don't want to include those elements on subsequent pages. You can use two different techniques to fix this problem. You can insert a new page layout to change the formatting for subsequent pages. "Starting a New Page Layout," later in this chapter, covers this technique. Or, you can create new divisions in the document, and then use the Page InfoBox to change the page layout for the selected division. Chapter 5, "Organizing and Highlighting Information," explains how to create divisions.

Setting Page Size and Margins

The first tab in the Page InfoBox is the Size and Margin tab, shown in Figure 4-28. It enables you to indicate the overall area that's available to hold text and other elements in a document, as well as the orientation for the document.

Click one of the Layout type buttons at the top of the tab to determine whether every page looks the same (the left button), or left and right pages use different layout settings (the right button). If you choose the second layout type, the drop-down list at the top of the dialog box changes to say Page Layout – Right Pages if the current page is an odd-numbered page, or Page Layout – Left Pages if the current page is an even-numbered page. From then on, choose an odd-numbered page in the document to create layout settings for right-hand pages, and choose an even-numbered page to create layout settings for left-hand pages in the document. Use the Page Size drop-down list to choose the page (paper) size to use for the document. The available sizes vary depending on the printer Word Pro's currently set up to use. If you want the settings in the Print dialog box (including options set for the printer, such as paper orientation) to override corresponding settings you choose in the Page InfoBox, check Use Settings from Printer Driver. Clear that check box to have the Page InfoBox take precedence. If your printer offers more than one method for feeding paper, choose the feeding source to use from the Printer Bin drop-down list.

Click an Orientation button to determine the general width for the page, based on the selected Paper Size. The left Orientation button chooses the *portrait orientation*, making pages taller than they are wide. The right Orientation button chooses the *landscape orientation*, making the pages wider than they are tall.

You also use this tab to determine how wide the blank space around the page contents, called the *margin*, should be. Use the text box or spinner buttons to change the Top, Bottom, Left, and Right margin widths. The preview between those margin settings shows you the effects your changes have on the document layout. If you've set up the document to use left and right pages and have entered asymmetrical margin settings, click the Mirror Pages button to set up left and right pages to use the opposite margin settings. This is called creating *facing pages*. You should use this technique if you plan to print or copy the document on both sides of the paper and then bind it or insert it in a three-ring binder.

Note You also can display the first tab of the Page InfoBox from the ruler. Right-click the ruler, then click Set Indents. The ruler includes vertical margin indicators for the left and right margins. You can drag the left or right margin indicator to change the width of the margin it represents.

Working with Page Background Features

The Page InfoBox offers the Color, Pattern, and Line Style tab next. Like the tab for adding lines and shading to a paragraph, described earlier in the chapter, this tab enables you to add lines, shading, and patterns to the whole page.

Click one of the Lines Around Page buttons to add a box around each page, at the margin. If you select one of these buttons, you can use the Line Style, Line Width, and Line Color drop-down lists to format the line. You also can use the Shadow, Shadow Depth, and Shadow Color drop-down lists to add or format the shadow for the page's box.

For a fancier look, open the Designer Borders drop-down list. You can then click one of the available borders, or click Other to display more borders in the Designer Borders dialog box. Click a border in the Designer Borders list and then click Select. If the border you want doesn't appear in the Designer Borders list, click a blank rectangle in the list, then click the Browse button; in the Browse dialog box, double-click a border file to add that border to the Designer Borders list. You can then click the border and click Select to apply it. The border appears around the page. Figure 4-29 shows the Color, Pattern, and Line Style tab of the Page InfoBox, and a designer border applied around the page.

If you don't want to box the page, open the Show Lines drop-down list, then click to check which side(s) of the page the line or designer border should appear on. For example, to have the line appear at the top and bottom of the page only, click Top and Bottom. Then click the check mark at the right side of the drop-down list to close the list. Use the Line Placement drop-down list to choose whether the line or border you've added appears On Margin, in the Middle between the margin and the edge of the page, or on the Page Edge. If you click Other in the Line Placement drop-down list, the Line Placement dialog box appears. You can enter a measurement to specify a precise Line Placement from Edge, then click OK to move the line to that location. Use the Corners drop-down list to specify how rounded the box corners should be.

Figure 4-29: This page has a girder-style designer border applied.

Whether or not you apply a line or border, you can fill the page with a color or pattern. Word Pro fills each page all the way to its edges. Use the Background Color, Pattern, and Pattern Color drop-down lists to choose a fill color, pattern, or both.

Note

Whenever a drop-down list in a Page InfoBox tab offers a None choice, such as the Pattern or Designer Borders drop-down lists on the Color, Pattern, and Line Style tab, choosing None removes the formatting normally applied by that list.

Danger Zone

Most printers can't print in the *nonprinting area* around the edge of a default-sized page. For example, many laser and Inkjet printers must leave about 0.25-inch blank around an 8.5×11-inch page. So, if you choose to place the page line on the Page Edge, it may be cut off or not print at all. In that case, place the line in the Middle or use the Other option to specify how far away from the edge of the page the line or designer border should print. Alternately, choose a smaller page, then trim the pages after you print them; this approach also ensures you won't have white space around pages to which you've added a background or pattern.

Adding a Watermark

When expensive paper has an attractive image such as a logo subtly imprinted into the grain of the paper, that imprint is called a *watermark*. While Word Pro can't enable you to create paper, it does enable you to create a printed watermark that emulates the elegance of a traditional watermark. It can also provide security, because it sends a message about how widely a document should be distributed, if at all.

When you insert a watermark using the Page InfoBox, Word Pro places the watermark on each page of the document. The watermark is really a graphic that Word Pro places in a special "layer" so that text can flow over it. You can use a graphic file in a number of different formats — including Word Pro Draw (.sdw), Windows Bitmap (.bmp), JPEG (.jpg), Paintbrush (.pcx), and TIFF (.tif) — as a watermark. Chapter 5, "Organizing and Highlighting Information," provides more information about the graphic file formats you can work with in Word Pro. Some graphic files work better as a watermark than others, so you might have to experiment or even edit the file you want to use to achieve the best effect. For example, if you want to use a logo with dark colors as a watermark, it might be better to use a graphics program to edit the logo file so that it uses paler shades and text printing over it will be readable. Printed watermarks can be as subtle as those created with paper fibers.

The third tab in the Page InfoBox is the Watermark Options tab. Follow these steps to use that tab to add a watermark to the pages in your document:

1. Select the watermark to insert from the Watermark drop-down list. (Choosing None removes a watermark you inserted previously.) If you want to insert a graphic file that doesn't appear on the drop-down list, click the Other option to display the Select Watermark dialog box. Navigate to the drive and folder that holds the graphic file to use as a watermark, click the file in the Look In list, and click Open.

2. Select a size for the watermark from the Scaling drop-down list:

   • The default choice, Fit To, displays the graphic at the largest size possible that still enables it to fit within the page.

   • Original Size displays the graphic without any size adjustments, so it appears in the size specified for it when it was created in a graphics program.

   • The Percentage choice enables you to increase or decrease the graphic to display at a percentage of its original size; after you choose Percentage, use the Percentage text box and spinner buttons that appear to indicate a sizing percentage.

- The Custom choice enables you to size the graphic to specific dimensions. After choosing Custom, decide whether you want the graphic to retain its original height-width ratio using the Scale Proportionately check box. When you leave Scale Proportionately checked, you only have to change the Width or Height text box setting; Word Pro calculates the other setting for you. If you clear the Scale Proportionately check box, you can change the settings in both the Width and Height text boxes. Be aware that the latter method might distort the watermark's appearance.

3. Use the Placement drop-down list to indicate where on the page the watermark should appear. Centered centers the watermark vertically and horizontally. Automatic places the watermark in the upper-left corner of the page, or as close as possible given the size you specified for the graphic. Tiled repeats the watermark graphic as many times as needed to fill the page.

If you can't place a watermark where you'd like it to appear on the page, you can place one in a header, footer, table cell, frame, or parallel column. Click where you want to position the watermark, then right-click and click the command that displays the InfoBox for the selected location, such as Header Properties, if you right-clicked in a Header. Then use the Graphic and Watermark Options tab in the InfoBox that appears to insert and format the watermark. You have the most control if you insert the watermark in a frame. You can place it in a number of page locations, or specify whether the frame and its watermark should appear on every page or only the current page. The section called "Adding Frames" in Chapter 5, "Organizing and Highlighting Information," provides a detailed overview of working with frames, including how to create one that repeats on every page.

4. Depending on the type of graphic you inserted as the watermark, you may be able to rotate it to a different angle. If the Rotate Image drop-down list is enabled, use it to specify the rotation you want.

5. If you added a background fill and/or pattern to the page and you want it to show through the watermark, click the Transparent check box.

When you finish with the Watermark Options tab settings, the watermark appears in the document location you specified. Figure 4-30 shows a watermark inserted in a document, and the Watermark Options tab settings in the Page InfoBox used to create it.

If you print your document and your watermark prints as a black and white blob, you can use image processing to fix it. See "Troubleshooting Graphics Printing" in Chapter 5, "Organizing and Highlighting Information."

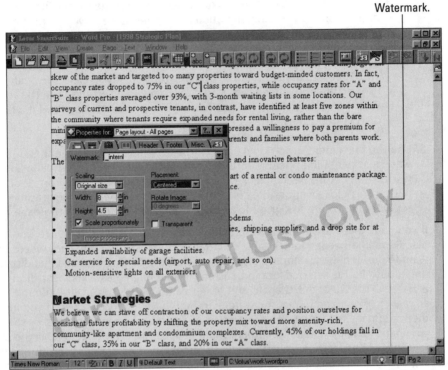

Watermark.

Figure 4-30: A watermark provides a subtle method for communicating additional information to your reader or enhancing the document's appearance.

Creating a Serious Background

You can use the watermark feature to use a graphic as the page background (or as the background for a table cell, header, frame, or other element), rather than simply adding a color and pattern as a background. In fact, many of the choices on the Watermark drop-down list are intended to be used as a background. (Big clue—the names for many of these choices begin with *bkgnd*, an abbreviation for *background*.) Choose a background graphic choice from the Watermark drop-down list, leave it scaled to its original size, and choose Tiled from the Placement drop-down list. You'll love the dramatic effect, like the example illustrated in Figure 4-31. Just remember to reformat your text, if needed, to ensure that it's readable over the background.

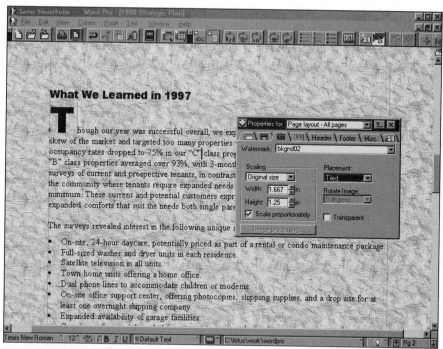

Figure 4-31: Also use the Watermark Options tab in the Page InfoBox to create a page background, shown here.

Creating Columns

You can format a document into multiple vertical columns, called *newspaper columns*, to make the text easier to read or to create a document in a format that traditionally employs columns, such as a newsletter. For example, you might need to use fairly small text in your resume to fit it on one page; formatting the resume text in two columns makes the small text more readable, because it leads to fewer words per line. Use the fourth tab in the Page InfoBox, the Newspaper Columns tab, to create newspaper columns. This tab has a few straightforward options:

- ◆ **Number of Newspaper Columns.** Use this text box and its accompanying spinner buttons to indicate how many columns you'd like. Change the setting back to 1 to return the text to full-page width.

- ◆ **Space Between Columns.** The *gutter* space separates columns to make them easy to read. If you'd like to increase the gutter for design reasons or decrease it to squeeze more text onto the page, adjust the value in this text box.

- ◆ **Vertical Line Between Columns.** This area of the dialog box offers Line Style, Line Width, and Line Color drop-down lists so that you can insert a vertical line in the center of the gutter to further set off the columns.

✦ **Column Balance.** Turn on this check box to ensure that Word Pro includes equal amounts of text in all columns on the page, leading to an attractive appearance.

Figure 4-32 shows example newspaper columns and the settings used to create them.

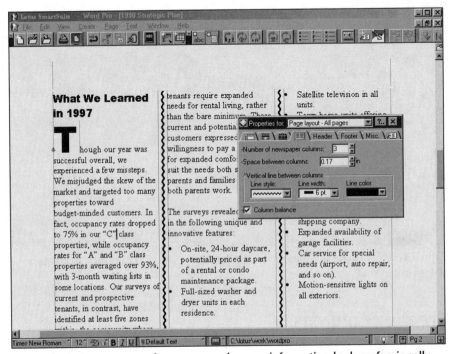

Figure 4-32: Newspaper columns can make your information look professionally published, as shown here.

The Newspaper Columns tab settings tell Word Pro to automatically create new columns and wrap text where it best fits. There may be instances where you instead want to create a column break at a particular location, such as before a particular heading paragraph or the lead-in paragraph for a bulleted list. To insert a column break at a particular location, first create the newspaper columns in the document. Then, click to position the insertion point at the beginning of the paragraph where you'd like to insert a column break. Choose Page ➪ Insert Column Break. Or, choose Text from the Properties For drop-down list in the title bar of the Page InfoBox or click the Text Properties SmartIcon to display the Text InfoBox. Click the Breaks tab. Select the Before Paragraph or After Paragraph check box to indicate where you'd like to position the break, and then choose Break Column from the accompanying drop-down list.

To remove a manual column break added before a paragraph, click to position the insertion point at the start of the paragraph (which should be at the top of a new column), press Backspace, and then press Enter. Removing a column break inserted after a paragraph is a bit more tricky. Click in the paragraph, redisplay the Breaks tab in the Text InfoBox, then clear the check beside After Paragraph.

There's one last way to insert a column break after you create newspaper columns. Click to position the insertion point exactly where you want the column break to appear. Choose Text ➪ Insert Other ➪ Column Break. Word Pro inserts the column break, and displays a column break mark to show exactly where you placed the column break. To remove the column break, drag over the column break mark to select it, then press Delete.

Creating a Header or Footer

Header and *footer* information repeats at the top or bottom, respectively, of the pages of your document. The header or footer can contain such information as the document title, the date it was created, or the page number to help the reader better identify the significance and timeliness of the document. The Page Layout view of a document shows the header and footer area at the top or bottom of each page. There are really three separate operations involved in creating a header and footer: setting up the header or footer area, entering information in the header or footer area, and fine-tuning the formatting for the header or footer.

The options for setting up the header or footer area appear on the Header and Footer tabs of the Page InfoBox. Because these tabs have virtually identical options, once you learn how to use the Header tab as described here you'll know how to use the Footer tab as well. Figure 4-33 shows the Header tab in the Page InfoBox.

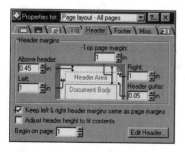

Figure 4-33: Set up the boundaries for page headers on this tab of the Page InfoBox.

The preview area at the top of the tab does a good job of clarifying what each measurement means. The Top Page Margin setting (the same as the margin setting for the top of the page from the first tab in the Page InfoBox) indicates how wide the top page margin, which encompasses the header area, is. The Above Header setting controls the distance between the top edge of the page and the top boundary of the header area. The Left and Right settings control the left and right margins for the header area, which you may or may not want to match the side page margins. The Header Gutter measurement indicates the spacing between the bottom of the header area and the top of the document body area.

You can change any of the settings to increase, decrease, or reposition the header area. If you've changed the Left or Right header area margin settings but want to return to the same settings used for the page, check Keep Left & Right Header Margins Same As Page. If you want the header area to expand to fully display all the contents you enter, such as a graphic or large text, check Adjust Header Height to Fit Contents; when the header area expands, it pushes the document body area down, so text doesn't overlap. If you want the header to begin on a page other than the first page of the document, as when you leave the heading off a title page, change the Begin on Page text box setting.

After you've tweaked the boundaries for your header or footer, you can create the actual contents for the header or footer. To create or edit header or footer text, click the Edit Header button on the Header tab of the Page InfoBox (or Edit Footer on the Footer tab). Alternatively, click in the header or footer area in Page Layout view. Or, choose Page ⇨ Header or Page ⇨ Footer. The Header/Footer bar appears. Again, this bar works the same for creating a header or footer. This section describes how to create a header, you can use identical techniques to create a footer.

Choose a Layout Type button to determine whether you want all pages to use the same Header (the left button) or different headers for left and right pages (the right button). If you choose the latter button, you'll need to enter the needed header information on both an even- and odd-numbered page. Click a Cursor Position button to indicate where you want to type text or display text from a *field*. Fields contain information that Word Pro calculates, stores, or updates, such as the date, file name, or page number. After you select a Cursor Position, type the text you want, or click the Insert Field button, and then click a field to insert in the Click Field to be Inserted list that appears (see Figure 4-34). For example, click the Page Number option to insert the page number for each page. You also can click the Insert the Current Date SmartIcon to include the Today's Date (System) field in the header.

You can insert frames and other elements into the header, too, using techniques described elsewhere in this book. Clicking the Header Properties button on the bar redisplays the Page InfoBox with the Header tab selected, so that you can work with its margins as previously described. If your document contains multiple divisions and you want your header or footer (new or edited) to appear in all other divisions, click Update Divisions.

The Today's Date (System) field inserted in the header.

Insert Page Number SmartIcon.

Insert Date/Time SmartIcon.

Insert the Current Date SmartIcon.

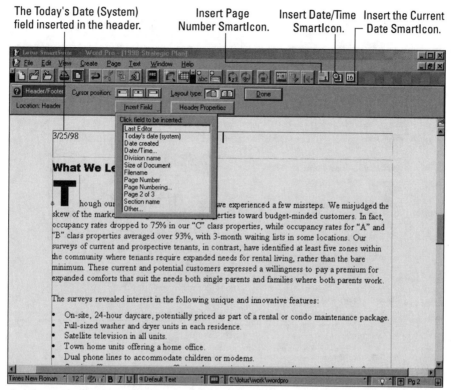

Figure 4-34: When you insert a field into the header or footer, Word Pro updates its information (if needed) each time you open and print the document.

Note

The Date/Time and Page Numbering options in the Click Field to be Inserted work like the Insert Page Number and Insert Date/Time SmartIcons identified in Figure 4-34. These list options and SmartIcons display dialog boxes for formatting the inserted page numbering or date/time. See "Inserting a Page Number" or "Inserting the Date and Time" later in this chapter to learn more about setting up fancier page numbering or a date and time.

You can format the text and fields in a header or footer by selecting it and applying fonts and attributes as described earlier in this chapter. You also can use an InfoBox to change a number of formatting settings for the header. When the insertion point is within the header, choose Page ⇨ Header/Footer Properties or click the Header Properties SmartIcon to display the Header or Footer InfoBox. The settings in this InfoBox work just like corresponding settings in the Page InfoBox. Figure 4-35 shows example formatting applied to header text, and a line added to the bottom of the header area via the Header InfoBox.

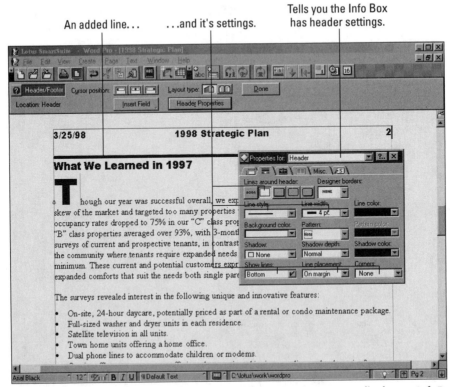

Figure 4-35: When you're working in the header or footer, you can display an InfoBox with settings for formatting the header or footer.

When you finish working with the header or footer contents or formatting the header or footer area, click outside the header or footer area or click Done to close the Header/Footer bar.

Adding Tabs, Grids, and Other Miscellaneous Formatting

The seventh tab in the Page InfoBox, the Misc. tab, enables you to change a number of default page settings for the document. Figure 4-36 shows this InfoBox.

Use the Tab Settings area of the Misc. tab to create tabs that apply to all the text in the document, not just a selection. Open the Tab Settings drop-down list to choose one or more tabs to set. You can choose Evenly Spaced Every to set multiple, evenly spaced tabs. Choose From Left Edge or From Right Edge to set a single tab relative to the left or right margin. The Custom option displays the Set Tabs on Ruler dialog box.

Figure 4-36: Create other default document settings on this tab.

After you choose a Tab Settings drop-down list choice, use the text box below that drop-down list to specify the space between multiple tabs or between the new tab and the applicable margin. You also can click the Set Tabs button to display the Set Tabs on Ruler dialog box. You can use this dialog box to create specific tabs for the document, using the same techniques described earlier under "Setting Tabs." If you want to add or alter the evenly spaced default tabs for the document, click the Set Defaults button to display the Set Default Tabs dialog box. If needed, select the Division for which you want to create default tabs from the drop-down list of that name. Then, enter the distance between tab stops in the Set Default Tab Stops Every (X) Inches text box and click Set Tabs. Click Close to close the Set Tabs on Ruler dialog box when you've finished working with it.

The Grid Settings area of the Misc. tab enables you to display a nonprinting grid that you can use to align frames in a document. Click one of the Grid Settings buttons to choose an appearance for the grid, then specify the spacing between gridlines using the accompanying text box and its spinner buttons. If you want Word Pro to help you ensure that frames align to the grid, check Snap Frames to Grid.

Click a Vertical Alignment button to specify how text should align between the top and bottom margins of the document: top, centered, or bottom. You can click a Text Direction button to specify how text runs in the document (this setting is available within frames, headers, and footers, too). So, for example, the header can run from left to right as normal, but the body text can run bottom to top, as if the page were turned on its side. To specify a new default style for all new paragraphs in the document, choose the style you want from the Initial Paragraph Style dialog box. To enable Word Pro to link the file to a Notes database, check Notes/FX Field, then enter a name for the notes field in the Name text box.

The final tab in the Page InfoBox provides options for working with styles in the document; Chapter 6, "Using SmartMasters, Styles, and Scripts for Control," covers this topic in more detail. If you've finished working in the Page InfoBox, you can click its Close button to remove it from the screen.

Inserting a Page Number

You can insert a field that displays the current page number anywhere in the body text of a document, in a frame, or in a header or footer. Follow these steps to insert and format page numbers:

1. Click to position the insertion point where you want the page number to appear. If you insert the page number in a header or footer, or a frame formatted to repeat on every page, the correct page number displays for each page.

2. Choose Page ⇨ Insert Page Number. The Insert Page Number dialog box appears.

3. Enter text to appear before or after (or both) the number in the Text Before or Text After text boxes. For example, if you want your page numbers to read *Page 1*, *Page 2*, and so on, enter **Page** and press the spacebar in the Text Before text box. Check the preview in the Example area at the bottom of the dialog box to ensure that spaces appear where you need them. Figure 4-37 shows some leading text added for a page number.

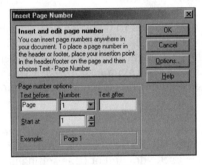

Figure 4-37: You can include text with page numbers, as illustrated in the Example area near the bottom of the dialog box.

4. Choose a Number Style from the Number drop-down list. For example, if you want to use letters rather than numbers to identify pages, choose the "A" or another letter style.

5. If you want to start with a number other than page 1, such as if you've divided a report document into multiple files, change the Start At setting. For example, if you specify **5** here, the first page number that appears will be 5.

6. Click Options. The Page Number Options dialog box appears.

7. Use the Reset Page Number drop-down list to tell Word Pro if you want to restart page numbering (restarting at page 1, for example) On Each New Section, On Each New Division, or Never (Continuous in Document).

8. You can use the Begin Numbering On Page Setting to control which page in the document displays the first page number. For example, if you're inserting the page number in a header and you entered 5 as the Start At setting described in Step 5, you could enter 2 as the Begin Numbering On Page Setting; this combination tells Word Pro to display the first page number (5) in the header for the second page.

9. You can include the section or division name along with the number. If you use this technique rather than typing the name as Text Before or Text After, Word Pro can automatically update the page numbering if you change the section or division name. To include the section or division name, check the Include in Number Style check box, then choose Section Name or Division Name from the accompanying drop-down list. Then click the Before Number or After Number option button to specify the position for the name.

10. Click OK to close the Page Number Options dialog box, and OK again to close the Insert Page Number dialog box.

11. If you inserted the page number into existing header or footer text, a dialog box asks whether you'd like to update the page numbering to the new settings in the entire document. Click Yes to do so and insert the page number field. What you see onscreen is the displayed page numbers generated by the field, not the field itself.

To redisplay the Insert Page Number dialog box to edit the page number, drag to select the inserted page number, then choose Page ⇨ Edit Page Number.

Note

Drag over the displayed page number, date, or time for an inserted field to select it and format it, move it, or delete it. For example, to delete the selected field, press the Delete key.

Inserting the Date and Time

You can insert a date/time field that displays a date and/or time anywhere in the body text of a document, in a frame, or in a header or footer. The date/time field calculates the display based on the date and time kept by your computer's system clock. Follow these steps to insert and format a date/time field:

1. Click to position the insertion point where you want the date/time to appear. If you insert the date or time in a header or footer, or a frame formatted to repeat on every page, the date or time displays on each page.

2. Choose Text ⇨ Insert Other ⇨ Date/Time. The Insert Date/Time dialog box appears (see Figure 4-38).

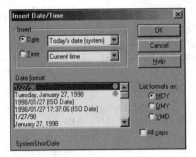

Figure 4-38: Insert a field displaying a particular date or time anywhere in the document using this dialog box.

3. In the Insert area of the dialog box, choose the Date or Time option button to determine whether the field should display an inserted date or time. Then, use the accompanying drop-down list to tell Word Pro exactly what date or time the field should display. For example, if you chose Date, it can display Yesterday's Date, the Date of Last Save, or other dates. If you chose Time, it can display the Time Created or Time of Last Save instead of the Current Time.

4. If you chose Date in Step 3, you can choose an option button to determine how Word Pro sorts the choices in the Date Format list under List Formats As. You also can check All Caps if you want to format dates and months in the inserted date using all capital letters.

5. In the Date Format (if you chose Date in Step 3) or Time Format (if you chose Time in Step 3) list, click the display format you want. Note that some of the Date Format options can display a precise time of day as well.

6. Click OK to insert the field and close the dialog box. The specified date or time displays onscreen.

To redisplay the Insert Date/Time dialog box to edit the inserted date or time, drag to select the inserted date or time, then choose Text ➪ Insert Other ➪ Date/Time.

Inserting a Page Break

In addition to inserting a column break at a particular location, you can insert a manual page break to start a new page wherever one is needed. Some guidelines for good page design call for inserted page breaks, for example. You should never start a new page just after a heading or a heading plus a couple of lines of text; better to start the page just before the heading. Similarly, if you can avoid breaking a numbered or bulleted list across pages, your reader can more easily take in the list and won't miss any list items that fall on the preceding or following page.

To insert a page break, click to position the insertion point exactly where the page break should appear. Choose Page ➪ Insert Page Break (Ctrl+Enter). Word Pro starts the new page, and inserts a page break mark (see Figure 4-39). To delete a manual page break, you can click to the left of the first line of the paragraph just after the page break, then press Backspace. You can click just to the left of the page break mark, then choose Page ⇨ Delete Page Break. Or, you can drag to select the page break mark, then press Delete.

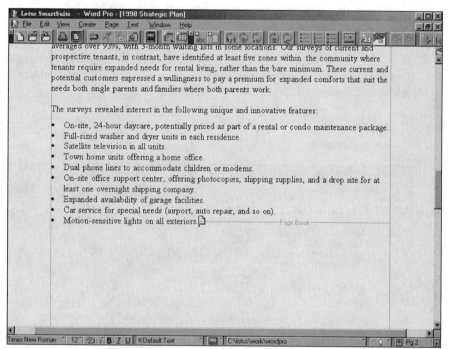

Figure 4-39: The page break mark at the end of the text on this page shows you where a manual page break has been inserted.

Starting a New Page Layout

Creating a new page layout enables you to specify different — but similar — page formatting for the pages following the inserted layout. For example, you might want the title page of a document to include a watermark but not the subsequent pages, even if you want all the other page formatting settings to be the same. You can accomplish this by inserting and formatting the new layout, using these steps:

1. Click to position the insertion point where you want the new layout to begin.

2. Choose Page ⇨ Insert Page Layout. The Insert Page Layout dialog box appears.

3. If multiple page styles appear in the Insert Page Layout with Page Style list, click the page style to use.

4. Use the Start Page Layout drop-down list to tell Word Pro where to begin the new page layout. For example, you can choose On Next Page if you want to insert a page break to create a new page on which to start the new layout, or

Within Page if you want the new layout to begin at the insertion point, but don't want to insert a page break.

5. If you don't want to create a new header and footer for the new layout, be sure the Use Header Text from Previous Page Layout and/or Use Footer Text from Previous Page Layout check boxes stay checked.

6. Click Insert & Edit. Word Pro inserts the page layout (and a page break if necessary), and displays the Page InfoBox so you can create the format for the new page layout. A page layout mark indicates the beginning of the new layout (see Figure 4-40).

Page layout mark.

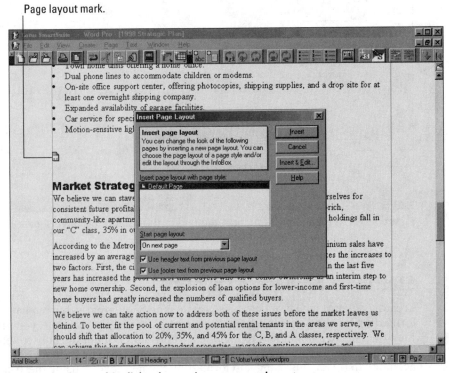

Figure 4-40: Use this dialog box to insert a page layout.

To remove the inserted page layout, drag over the page layout mark, then press Delete. If the page layout mark appears "behind" the first letter in a paragraph, click to the left of that letter, then press Enter once or twice. You then can drag over the page layout mark to select it.

Printing

And the drumroll, please. . . . In most instances, the ultimate outcome of all your typing, editing, and formatting has to be a clean printed copy for each person who needs one. Follow these steps to print the current document:

1. Save the document. If you want to print a particular page, click to position the insertion point on that page.

2. Choose File ➪ Print or click the Print SmartIcon. The Print dialog box appears (see Figure 4-41).

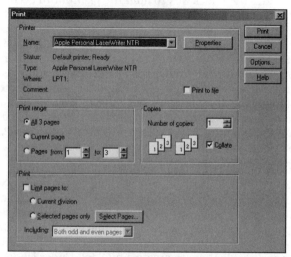

Figure 4-41: Select a printer and pages to print in this dialog box.

3. If you've installed more than one printer under Windows and need to select the proper one to use, open the Name drop-down list in the Printer area of the dialog box, then click the printer to use. If you want to print the file to a disk file that you can later send to the printer, click to check Print to File. If you need to change any of the settings for the printer, click the Properties button. The Properties dialog box for the selected printer appears; this dialog box offers unique options for each type of printer, but you may be able to specify such settings as how many pages print on each sheet of paper, paper size, the size of unprintable areas at the edge of the page, and more. Click OK after you've finished setting printer properties.

Note   If you choose Net-It Now! SE from the Name drop-down list when you click the Print button, the demonstration version of the Net-It Now! program included with SmartSuite opens, so you can convert the document to a Web page.

4. In the Print Range area of the dialog box, choose which pages in the document to print. Choose All (X) Pages to print the whole document. Choose Current

Page to print only the page that holds the insertion point. To print a selected ranges of pages in the document, choose the Pages option button, then enter the first page in the range to print in the From text box and the last page in the range to print in the To text box.

5. In the Copies area of the dialog box, use the Number of Copies text box to indicate how many copies of the document should print. To group all the printed copies for each page (rather than printing the whole first copy, printing the whole second copy, and so on), select the Collate check box.

6. If the Print Range settings don't provide the flexibility you need in specifying what pages Word Pro prints, you can use the options in the Print area of the Print dialog box. When you check the Limit Pages To check box, you can use the other choices under the check box to limit the printout to certain pages. First, click an option button to indicate whether to print the Current Division or Selected Pages Only. If you choose Selected Pages Only, click Select Pages to display the Select Pages dialog box. To print a List of Pages, leave the option button of that name selected, then enter the page numbers in the List the Pages text box, inserting commas between page numbers and using a hyphen to indicate a range of pages. Or, click Whole Divisions, then click the name of each division to print in the Divisions to Print list. Click OK to close the Select Pages dialog box. Back in the Print area of the Print dialog box, use the Including drop-down list to choose whether to print only Even Pages, only Odd Pages, or Both Odd and Even Pages.

7. Click the Options button in the Print dialog box to display the Print Options dialog box (see Figure 4-42). This dialog box enables you to control whether special elements print and how other automated features are handled during printing. For example, you can click the Without Pictures check box under Print Options to print the document without printing graphics, for faster printing. Or, you can click As Booklet to print the pages in such a way that you can fold the pages and staple them to create a booklet. Under Update, click any of the check boxes to tell Word Pro to update the selected element (such as Fields) before printing, ensuring the timeliness and accuracy of the printed document. (To learn more about any of the options in the Print Options dialog box, click the Help button, then click the See Details button under Step 4 or Step 5). After you make your choices in the Print Options dialog box, click OK to close it and apply your settings.

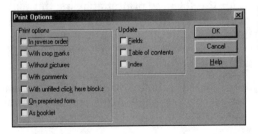

Figure 4-42: Choose how to handle special elements for printing here.

8. Click Print to finish the print job and send the document to the printer.

How Do I Preview a Printout?

Many word processing applications, and those from other applications such as spreadsheets, offer a special *print preview* view that enables you to check the margins, page breaks, and headers and footers in a document before you print it. Word Pro, in contrast, doesn't offer a special print preview. You can use other views to get an approximate preview of a document's printed appearance, instead. Choose the Page Sorter view (View ➪ Page Sorter) for a bird's-eye view of how several pages look. To "preview" the current page only, first switch to the Layout view (View ➪ Layout), then click the Zoom to Full Page SmartIcon to see how the single page looks.

Printout Problems?

Some printers, especially older laser printers, have trouble printing shades of gray or printing "reverse" treatments—white text on a dark background—in Word Pro. If you're having either problem when you try to print a document in which you've used shading and patterns, try the following solutions:

✦ Change the text printing setting for your printer before printing. Choose File ➪ Print, click the Properties button beside the printer, then check the Print TrueType as Graphics or TrueType Fonts As Graphics options, which are probably found on the Graphics tab. Click OK, and then Print, to print the document.

✦ If you've placed shading or a pattern behind two separate paragraphs and the second paragraph doesn't print at all, combine the paragraphs into a single paragraph. For some reason, this works.

✦ Choose a different background pattern or colors. Some of the patterns are so small and intricate that they simply blend into a shaded blob on a black and white printer. Or, if the color of the text is too close to the color of the background or pattern, changing the text or background color keeps the text from blending in.

✦   ✦   ✦

Organizing and Highlighting Information

Using the same words and phrases over and over in a document can bore readers and sometimes cause them to skim right past an important point. Similarly, plain vanilla formatting throughout a document can cause readers to miss, or at the very least have trouble identifying, key information. Word Pro offers a number of features you can use to better highlight and organize information in a document. When you apply the techniques described in this chapter, you help your readers more easily navigate a document and understand its topics. You can set off a quote in a frame or add a graphic to illustrate a point. You can insert columns of related data in a table, and then sort the rows into the most useful order for your reader. To ensure you've organized your document logically, use outlining. When you need to use a new layout or page numbering for a certain portion of the information in a document, break it into divisions or sections. Finally, create a table of contents, index, footnotes, and other "professional" features to help your reader find and understand the resources for topics in a document.

Adding Frames

When you add a *frame* to a Word Pro document, you drag to define a rectangular holding area for text, a graphic, a chart, a drawing, or an equation. Placing such objects in a frame provides a number of benefits. You can easily move or resize the object. You can control how other text in the document is positioned relative to a frame, even placing a frame in the center of a wide paragraph, so that text flows on both sides of it. And, you can add formatting to a frame, such as a nice border, to call attention to the frame contents. Word Pro offers two methods you can use to insert a frame in the current document. This section explains how to use either method to insert frames to add variety and interest to a document.

Inserting a Frame

The first method for inserting a frame enables you to create a frame by entering exact dimensions for it. For example, if you're creating an annual report document that includes photos of corporate officers, each photo may need to be 2" × 2". Use the following steps to create a frame with a precise size:

1. Choose View ➪ Layout to change to the Page Layout view. You can only create, see, and work with frames in Page Layout view.

2. Click to position the insertion point at the approximate location where you want to insert the frame. For example, to have the frame appear at the left side of a particular paragraph, click just to the left of the first word in the paragraph.

3. Choose Create ➪ Frame. The Create Frame dialog box appears (Figure 5-1).

Figure 5-1: You can use the Create Frame dialog box to specify precise dimensions for a new frame.

4. (Optional) Use the Frame Style drop-down list to select the style to use for the frame. The frame style controls the appearance of the frame and its contents; so, if you change the settings for a frame style, those settings change for all frames using that frame style. Most SmartMasters only offer one or two frame styles by default: Default Frame and Default Graphic/OLE.

More Info

To learn how to select or create a frame style, see "Using Styles" in Chapter 6, "Using SmartMasters, Styles, and Scripts for Control."

5. Use the Width and Height text boxes (or their spinner buttons) to specify the dimensions for the frame.

6. Click OK. Word Pro places the empty frame in the document, with its upper-left corner located just beneath the insertion point you selected.

Figure 5-2 shows an example frame added at the right side of a paragraph. By default, an insertion point appears in the frame, to accept text you type. The Default Frame style also includes a thin, black line around the frame, which you can see just inside the frame border in Figure 5-2. The Frame menu and Text in a Frame SmartIcon bar also appear automatically. The menu and the SmartIcons enable you to insert an element other than text (a graphic, chart, or drawing) in the frame or format the frame and frame contents.

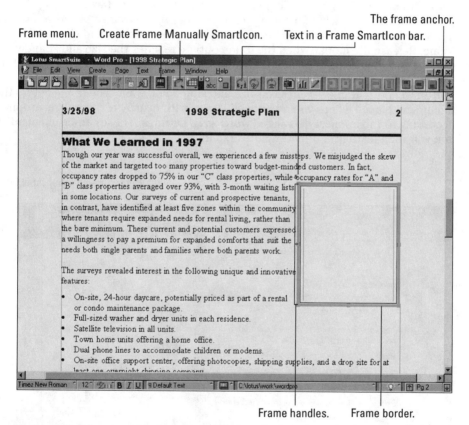

Figure 5-2: A frame can hold text, graphics, and other elements. Special tools for working with the frame appear on the Text in a Frame SmartIcon bar.

An anchor for the frame also appears near its upper-left corner. (If the anchor doesn't appear, select View ➪ Set View Preferences and click the Show tab. Next, click the check mark located beside the Show Marks list box. Locate and select Anchors to place a check mark beside it, and then click OK to close the dialog box.) The anchor helps you to manage the frame's position relative to that anchor point. For example, if a graphic must follow a sentence that references the graphic, the sentence holds the anchor for the frame holding the graphic. If you add text above that sentence, the sentence could be bumped to the next page. You could then use the anchor settings to move the frame automatically to the next page, near the sentence that references it. You'll learn more about using anchoring later in this section.

If you want to insert the frame at a specific position, which is the second method for adding a frame, you can create the frame by dragging. To do so, choose Create ⇨ Frame, make a choice from the Frame Style drop-down list, and then click Size & Place Frame Manually. The mouse pointer turns red and includes crosshairs along with a frame box. Drag in the document to create the frame; start dragging at the precise location you want for the upper-left corner of the frame. As shown in Figure 5-3, a frame outline and pop-up box shows you the orientation and size for the frame. Release the mouse when the frame outline reaches the size and shape you want. If you want to drag to create a frame that uses Default Frame style, click the Create Frame Manually SmartIcon, drag in the document, and release the mouse button when the frame reaches the size and shape you want. The frame enters the document, placed where you positioned it, and with nearby text scrolling around it according to the frame style's saved word wrap settings. These can be changed, as you will soon learn in "Formatting the Frame."

Current frame dimensions.

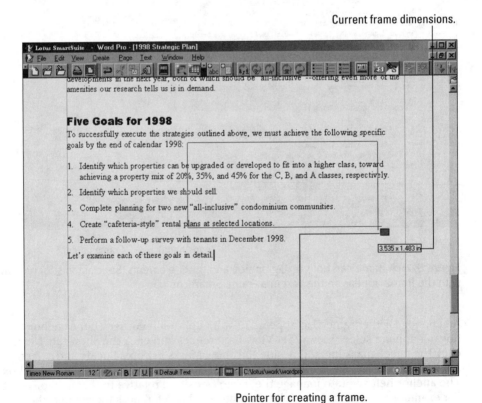

Pointer for creating a frame.

Figure 5-3: Word Pro displays a special pointer when you're dragging to create a frame.

Selecting a Frame

A frame's behavior varies slightly depending on the contents you insert in it. Immediately after you add a frame to your document, a light-gray border with handles appears to define the frame. The light-gray border indicates that the frame is *active* and ready to receive the contents you specify. You can create the contents for the frame, and then click outside the frame to deactivate it.

When you want to edit or format the contents of a frame that holds text, click inside the frame to reactivate it and redisplay the light-gray border. If you want to reactivate a frame that holds a Word Pro drawing you've created, a chart, or an equation, double-click the frame contents to redisplay the light-gray border, so you can then make the edits you want to the frame contents. However, when you want to perform certain operations on any frame, rather than its contents — such as moving it or resizing it — you have to *select* the frame instead. You also can think of this as selecting the frame border. To select a frame when it's inactive, point to the frame border and click. To select an active text frame, point to the frame border (or the area where it would be if there's not a line displayed around the frame border) until the mouse pointer changes to a hand, and then click. Or, right-click any frame, and then choose Select ⇨ Frame from the shortcut menu that appears. When you use either method to select the frame, the frame border darkens and the frame handles turn black. If a frame holds a graphic (also called a *picture*) that you've inserted, click the frame border or its contents. The dark selection border and black handles appear.

To select multiple frames, click the first frame's border, and then press and hold the Shift key and click additional frames to select.

To select text within a frame, right-click the frame, choose Select from the shortcut menu, and then choose a command from the submenu that appears. To deselect a selected or active frame, click outside the frame.

Adding Text to a Frame

Inserting text into a frame enables you to position the frame and the text within it wherever you want in a document. You aren't limited to living with Word Pro's wrapping, column breaks, or page breaks. Additionally, you can apply special formatting to the frame and the text within it to call attention to that text. For example, you can use a frame to create a *pull quote*, an enlarged and highlighted quotation from the main body of the document. Newspapers and magazines commonly use pull quotes to highlight important text and motivate readers to read particular stories.

Each brand-new frame you create automatically holds the insertion point. If an empty frame isn't active, click it once to display the insertion point. Then, type the text that you want, just as if you were typing in a document. Press Enter to start a new paragraph within the frame, and use the Shift key to create capital letters. You can insert symbols, or use the Bullets & Numbers command on the Text menu to create a bulleted or numbered list. Drag over text to select it within the frame. You can use the same techniques to edit text in a frame that you use to edit text in the body of the document.

The text you enter uses the Default Text style. Select the text in the active frame. Then, use the status bar or the formatting commands on the Text menu to apply the desired formatting, included a different text style. In addition, you can use the Text in a Frame SmartIcons shown in Figure 5-4 to apply formatting or align the text vertically within the frame.

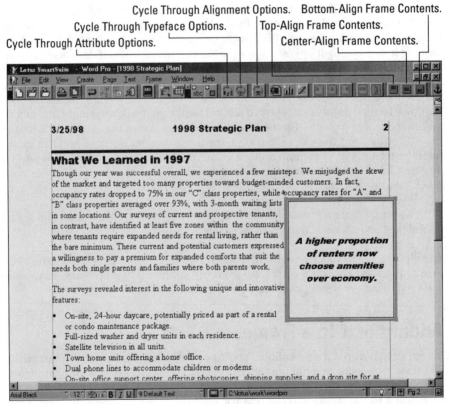

Figure 5-4: The text in the frame on this page is centered both vertically and horizontally. Italics and a new sans serif font also have been applied.

Inserting a Graphic

After you create a frame in your document, you can insert a graphic (also called a *picture*) into the frame. Table 5-1 lists the different types of graphic files you can insert into a frame. The table lists the file name extensions, even though you might not always see those extensions under recent versions of Windows and Windows NT.

Table 5-1	
Types of Graphics (Pictures) You Can Insert into a Frame	
Format	*File Name Extension*
Computer Graphics Metafile	.CGM
CorelDRAW 3	.CDR
DrawPerfect 1 and 2	.WPG
Encapsulated PostScript	.EPS
Word Pro Equation	.TEX
Freelance Graphics Drawing	.DRW
Graphics Interchange Format	.GIF
Hewlett-Packard Graphics Language (HPGL)	.PLT
Joint Photographic Experts Group (JPEG)	.JPG
Kodak Photo CD	.PCD
LotusPIC	.PIC
Paintbrush	.PCX
PNG	.PNG
Tagged Image File Format (TIFF)	.TIF
Windows Bitmap	.BMP
Windows Metafiles	.WMF, .EMF
Word Pro Draw	.SDW

Note

To be able to include a graphic of a particular format in a document, the filter for that type of graphic needs to be installed in Word Pro (and the file name must be using the extension that matches the filter). Not all graphics filters install with a QuickInstall or automatic install. To install additional graphics filters, perform a custom install as explained in the Appendix, "Installing SmartSuite."

To insert a graphic into a frame you just created or an empty frame you've selected, follow these steps:

1. Choose File ➪ Import Picture or click the Import a Picture SmartIcon on the Text in a Frame SmartIcon bar. The Import Picture dialog box appears.

2. If needed, choose a particular graphic file format from the Files of Type drop-down list.

3. If the file you want doesn't appear in the dialog box, use the Look In list to navigate to the disk and folder holding the graphic you want to insert.

4. Click the graphic file in the list. To verify that it's the correct graphic, check the Preview check box. A preview for the graphic appears in the lower-left corner of the dialog box (Figure 5-5).

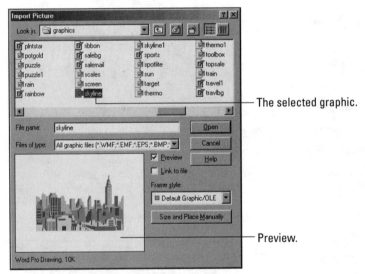

Figure 5-5: Select the graphic file to insert using this dialog box.

5. (Optional) By default, Word Pro inserts a copy of the selected graphic file in the frame. If you want to link the inserted graphic to the original (source) graphic file, select the Link to File check box. When you re-open a document that includes a linked graphic, Word Pro checks the source graphic file for changes and updates the copied graphic in the document to display those changes.

6. (Optional) Use the Frame Style list to change the style for the selected frame, if you wish.

7. Click Open. Word Pro closes the Add Picture dialog box and inserts the graphic into the frame.

Note If you decide to insert the selected graphic in a location other than the selected frame, click the Size and Place Manually button, and then drag in the document to create another frame.

In a New Frame

If you haven't already added a frame to the document, you can create a frame and insert a graphic into it in a single operation. Choose File ➪ Import Picture. The Import Picture dialog box appears. Select the graphic file to insert, and indicate a Frame Style and whether you want Link to File to be active. Click Open. Word Pro inserts a new frame with the graphic placed inside it and sizes the frame based on the default size for the graphic file.

Using a Click Here Block

Some of the Word Pro SmartMasters include Click Here blocks for inserting a graphic into a predrawn frame in a document. For example, the *news1* newsletter SmartMaster includes a Click Here block that reads *Click Here to Insert Picture*. To insert a graphic file for a Click Here block designed to hold a picture, click the prompt for the Click Here block. Word Pro activates the frame holding the Click Here block and displays the Import Picture dialog box. Use it to select, preview, and open the graphic file you want to insert into the frame holding the Click Here block.

Adding a Graphic for a Bullet

You can use a graphic file you've created as a bullet in a bulleted list. For example, if your business manufactures small fasteners like nails and screws, you might already have a small picture file for each type of fastener. You could use each picture as the bullet for the bulleted list item describing the pictured fastener. To use a graphic as a bullet, click in the bulleted list item for which you'd like to use the graphic. Choose Text ➪ Bullets & Numbers, click the Bullet and Number tab of the Text InfoBox, and then check the Edit on Page check box. Drag over the bullet that you want to replace with a graphic, and choose File ➪ Import Picture. The Import Picture dialog box appears. Use it to select the graphic file to display as a bullet, as described earlier in this section. Once the graphic is inserted as a bullet, you can resize or move its frame before clicking back into the text.

Inserting a Chart

Word Pro can automatically generate a chart to illustrate relative discrete values, proportions, and trends in data you enter. For example, you can create a *bar chart*, *stacked bar chart*, or *100% stacked bar chart* to emphasize the difference between discrete values. You can create a *line chart* or *area chart* to show how data changes over time, or a *pie chart* to illustrate how the individual values contribute to the whole. Word Pro also enables you to create a *high/low/close/open chart* for illustrating daily stock prices or an *x-y (scatter) chart* to plot how two different sets of values overlap.

To create a chart, follow these steps:

1. (Optional) Create a frame to hold the chart or click the empty frame that you want to hold the chart.

2. Choose Create ⇨ Chart or click the Create Chart SmartIcon (it's available only if you've selected a frame). The Create Chart dialog box appears.

3. Click the kind of chart you want in the Select a Chart Type list (see Figure 5-6). The buttons beside the list change to show the available variations for the selected chart type. Click the variation you want to use.

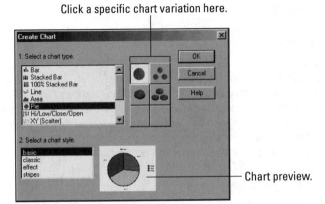

Click a specific chart variation here.

Chart preview.

Figure 5-6: In this dialog box, choose the type of chart that best illustrates your data.

4. To select an attractive appearance for the chart, choose the look you want from the Select a Chart Style list. The preview area in the dialog box changes to show how the chart will look based on your selection.

5. Click OK. The Edit Data dialog box appears. It includes a spreadsheet-like grid you can use to enter chart data values or labels (optional on the tab holding this grid). Notice the text labeled and arrowed cells in the upper-left corner of this grid. They direct the entry location for, and entry direction of, your labels.

6. Enter the data that Word Pro should chart by clicking cells in the Data tab and typing the entries. You can press Tab or an arrow key to move between cells. Each specific group of data is called a *series*. By default, Word Pro assumes you're entering each series of values in a single column. Choose the Series by Row option button if you want to enter each series in a row instead. Figure 5-7 shows data entered for a single pie chart. You can use the Cut, Copy, and Paste buttons in the Edit Data dialog box to copy and move data between

cells. If you type a number in one cell, you can drag to select adjoining cells, and then click the Fill by Example button to have Word Pro fill the selected cells with incremented values based on the first value. If the data you want to chart exists as a 1-2-3 file, click the Import Data button, and then use the Open dialog box that appears to specify the name of the file to open. Enter series labels here or click the Text Labels tab to do so; Step 7 explains label entries.

Slice titles. Chart title. Values.

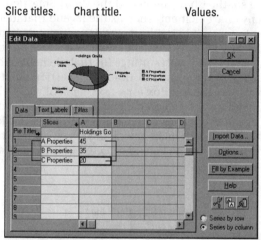

Figure 5-7: This Edit Data dialog box shows data for a single pie chart; the preview area shows how the charted data looks.

If you have a long list of data to chart, you can add more display room in the Edit Data dialog box by removing the chart preview. To do so, click the Options button, clear the check beside Show Chart Preview, and then click OK.

7. If you didn't label each series in Step 6, label them now. Click the Text Labels tab and make the entries or changes you want. Look for cells with arrows in the upper-left corner of the grid. The arrows indicate the direction (across the row or down the column) in which you need to enter the labels. To enter a series label for all but the x-y (scatter) chart, look for the cell that reads "Slices" or "Labels" and notice the direction its arrow points. For the x-y (scatter) chart, look for the cell that reads "Legend" and notice the direction its arrow points. Follow the direction of the arrow and begin making label entries in the first nongray cell you see. Continue entering labels in the next cell, moving away from the arrow. Click the Data tab again to see the labels you entered placed next to their series of values. If it is easier for you, use the Data tab to enter both label entries and series values so that you can see them located beside each other.

8. To add a chart title and/or subtitle and a note about the chart, click the Titles tab and make the entries you want.

9. Click OK. The Edit Data dialog box closes and the chart appears in the frame. (If you didn't create or select a frame for the chart in Step 1, Word Pro inserts a frame for the chart.)

You double-click a frame that holds a chart to activate the chart and make changes to its contents. When you do so, the Chart menu and the Chart SmartIcon bar appear. You can then click any chart element, such as the legend that identifies each series, and then drag it to move it in the frame or drag one of its handles to resize it. You can double-click any nontext element (such as a series bar or pie slice) in the chart to display an InfoBox with settings for that element. When you double-click a text element such as the legend or title, the insertion point appears so you can edit the text. To display the InfoBox for a text element, right-click it, choose the Properties command for the selected element from the shortcut menu that appears (such as the Legend Properties command if you selected a legend), and then use the InfoBox that appears to make the changes you want to the chart element. For example, Figure 5-8 shows the legend selected in the chart, along with the InfoBox for the legend.

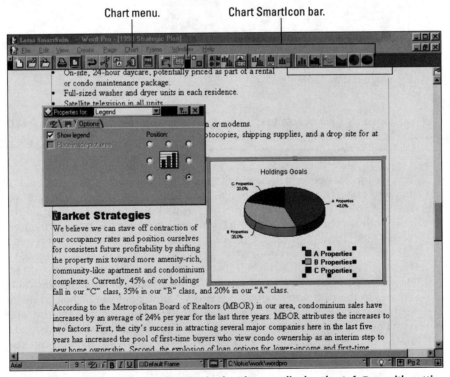

Figure 5-8: Double-click any element in the chart to display the InfoBox with settings for formatting it.

The Chart menu also contains commands that display the InfoBox for a particular chart element, such as the Legend or Plot area. It also offers the Chart Type and Chart Style commands for changing the chart type or style. To redisplay the Edit Data dialog box so you can edit chart data, double-click the chart, and then choose Chart ➪ Edit Data. The Edit Data dialog box appears. Make the changes you want, and then click OK.

Inserting a Drawing

You can create a basic drawing in a frame in Word Pro. Word Pro's drawing tools aren't very sophisticated, but you can use them to create interesting effects, such as text layered over a basic shape like an oval or polygon. To insert a drawing, create a frame and then click the Create Drawing SmartIcon to display the Drawing Tools SmartIcon bar, or choose Create ➪ Drawing to create the frame and display the Drawing Tools SmartIcon bar and the Drawing Actions SmartIcon bar; the latter appears along the right side of the screen by default. The Draw a Line, Draw a Rectangle, Draw a Rounded Rectangle, Draw an Oval, and Draw an Arc SmartIcons on the Drawing Tools SmartIcon bar work the same: click the SmartIcon, and then drag in the frame to draw the shape to the size you want. The Draw a PolyLine and Draw a Polygon SmartIcons work a bit differently: click the SmartIcon, drag to draw each segment and click to finish it, and double-click to finish the shape, which closes the polygon. To add text to the drawing, click the Create a Draw Text Object SmartIcon on the Drawing Tools SmartIcon bar, click in the frame, and then type the text.

To select an object you've drawn in the frame, double-click the frame to display the Drawing Tools SmartIcons first, if needed. Click the Select Draw Objects SmartIcon on the Drawing Tools SmartIcon bar, and then click the object in the drawing frame; press and hold Shift and click to select additional objects. Drag a selected object to move it, or drag one of its handles to resize it. Or, you can group and ungroup the objects using some of the SmartIcons on the Drawing Actions SmartIcon bar. Grouping drawn objects works just like grouping frames, described later under "Grouping and Ungrouping Frames." To format a drawn object, select it, and then click the Draw Properties SmartIcon to display the InfoBox with settings for formatting that object (see Figure 5-9). You can open the Draw menu and use its commands or click a SmartIcon on the Drawing Actions SmartIcon bar to work with the selected drawn object, too.

If you double-click an object you've drawn in the frame, special handles appear. For a draw text object, drag one of the handles to rotate the text. For other types of objects, drag one of the handles to change the shape of the object to some irregular shape.

To reactivate a drawing in a frame and redisplay the Draw menu and the SmartIcon bars with drawing tools, double-click inside the frame holding the drawing.

Figure 5-9: Select an object and then click the Draw Properties SmartIcon to display the InfoBox for formatting the object.

Adding Equations

Equations use a variety of mathematical symbols that you can't re-create with a keyboard, in particular because equations require that you precisely place numbers and letters in and around the mathematical symbols. You can use Word Pro's Equation Editor to build an equation in a new or existing frame.

Danger Zone

It is important to note that scientific and mathematical equations created in Word Pro are used for graphical display in your documents; functions within the equations are not performed.

Note The Word Pro Equation Editor doesn't install during a QuickInstall or automatic install. If you need to build equations, perform a custom install as explained in Appendix A, "Installing SmartSuite," to ensure that you install the Equation Editor.

To insert an equation, create a frame, and then choose Create ⇨ Equation to create the frame and change to Equation mode. The Equation menu, Equation SmartIcon bar, and the Equation Symbols SmartIcon palette appear onscreen. The insertion point appears next to the equation frame's anchor, ready for you to begin entering the elements of an equation. Click one of the SmartIcons offered on the Equation SmartIcon bar or palette to add its symbol or math form. Use the keyboard to enter numbers and text to an equation frame. Choose Equation ⇨ Insert Symbol to display a submenu of symbol palettes. Once a palette is selected and appears onscreen, click one of its displayed symbols to enter it in the equation frame. Select Equation ⇨ Insert Math Form to view its submenu. Select one of the first four items on this menu to place the math form of the item into your equation. If you select one of this drop-down menu's remaining items, the Insert Math Form dialog box opens. This dialog box enables you to configure a variety of math forms. (Math forms are the parts of an equation: operators, mathematical functions, brackets, spaces, and so on.) Click a tab in this dialog box, Customize a Math Form, and then click the Insert button accessed by the tab. Word Pro places the math form in your equation. Click Cancel when you are finished using this dialog box.

Fill in the grayed entry box areas of math forms by clicking in them. Revise equation elements by double-clicking them. When you do so, a Revise dialog box specific to the element opens onscreen. Make the revision you want, and then click the Revise button to accept it. Toggle between a Math or Text entering mode while working on equations by choosing Equation ⇨ Text Mode or Equation ⇨ Math Mode. Highlight an equation element and press Ctrl+C to copy it, or press the Delete key to remove it. A copied equation item can be repasted in the equation frame by positioning the insertion point and pressing Ctrl+V. Change the point size of most equation elements at once by first highlighting one of its elements, and then selecting another point size (the status bar is helpful for this). Click in different positions in your equation frame, or use all four arrow keys on your keyboard to move through any elements included within it, to make equation entries. At times, within an equation frame, it is difficult to see the exact location of the insertion point. If you enter an element in error because of this, click the Undo SmartIcon and reposition the insertion point.

You can change the look of an equation by customizing its Global Settings. Select Equation ⇨ Global Settings to open the Scientific Equations Global Settings dialog box to view your options. Choose Equation ⇨ View Preferences to make further changes to the way elements in an equation appear. When your equation work is complete, click outside of the equation frame to resume working with the rest of your document. To select an equation frame so that you can edit its contents, click once within the frame. The Equation SmartIcon bar and Equation Symbols palette, as well as the Equation menu, appear onscreen, ready and accessible.

You can use several tricks to make entering numerous equation frames a faster process. The first is to create one equation Click Here block, and then copy and paste it throughout a document. Read how to create, copy, and paste a Click Here block in Chapter 6 under "Cueing a User with Click Here Blocks." Then, to fill in an equation Click Here block, simply click the block to activate Equation mode and display the equation tools. The second is to customize an ever-present SmartIcon bar, such as the Universal bar, for instance. Select File ➪ User Setup ➪ SmartIcons Setup, and then select Universal from the Bar Name list of the SmartIcons Setup dialog box. Scroll down the Available Icons list to locate and point to the Create Equation SmartIcon. Next, drag and drop the SmartIcon onto the Universal bar's preview at the top of the dialog box, and then drag and drop several of the gray spacers off the bar. Click OK to close the dialog box and place the new SmartIcon.

Moving and Removing the Frame

You can move both a frame with its contents and the frame's anchor. Moving the frame repositions the frame contents and rewraps the text around the frame, but leaves the frame anchor in place. Moving the frame anchor doesn't move the frame, but moves the reference point that you can use to control the frame's position.

To move a frame, click its border to select the frame, so that dark selection handles appear around the frame. Point to the frame border so that the mouse pointer changes to an open hand. Press and hold the left mouse button, which changes the mouse pointer to a closed hand, and then drag the frame to the new position you want and release the mouse button.

To move an equation frame, you must reformat its default Place Frame setting before you can select it. See "Formatting the Frame" later in this chapter to learn how to adjust frame settings. To select and move a frame inserted as a bullet, click the bulleted item. Next, select Text ➪ Bullets & Numbers, click the Bullet and Number tab, and check the Edit on Page box. Then, click the bullet frame once to activate and move it as described above.

You also can copy and move a selected frame (and its contents) using commands, which gives you more control for moving a frame to another page of the document. To copy the frame, select it and then choose Edit ➪ Cut (Ctrl+X) or click the Cut to Clipboard SmartIcon. Click to position the insertion point at the new location for the frame's anchor, and then choose Edit ➪ Paste (Ctrl+V) or click the Paste Clipboard Contents SmartIcon. To move the frame, select it and then choose Edit ➪ Copy (Ctrl+C) or click the Copy to Clipboard SmartIcon. Then paste the frame into the new position.

Drag one of the handles on the selected frame to change the size and shape of the frame.

When you click the frame border to select the frame, you select the frame's anchor, too. A white box appears around the selected anchor. To move the anchor, point to it so that the mouse pointer includes a small anchor. Press and hold the left mouse button so the mouse pointer changes to a hand holding the anchor, and then drag the anchor and drop it into a new position, as shown in Figure 5-10. If you can't see the anchor when you select the frame, click the Show/Hide Frame Anchors SmartIcon to toggle anchor display back on.

To remove a frame from the document, delete it just as you would delete text. Click the frame's border so its black selection handles appear. Press Delete to remove the frame from the document. Alternately, right-click the selected frame or open the Frame menu, and then choose Delete Frame.

Word Pro does not display a warning or prompt you to confirm that you want to delete a frame. If you mistakenly delete a frame, click the Undo Last Command or Action SmartIcon to return the frame to the document.

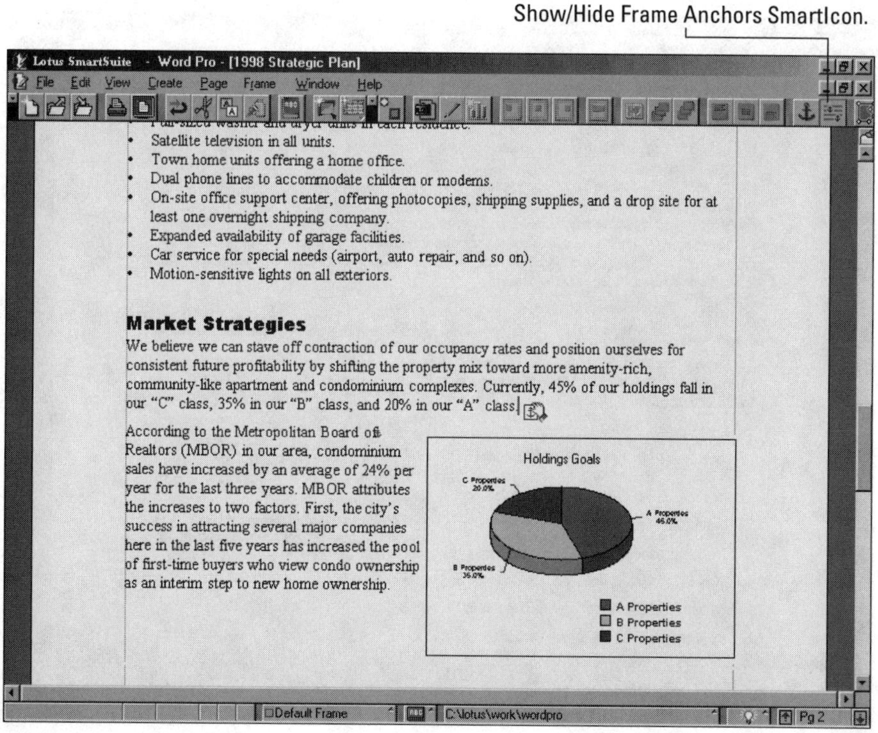

Show/Hide Frame Anchors SmartIcon.

Figure 5-10: The anchor for the frame shown here is being dragged to a new position at the end of the paragraph above the frame.

Grouping and Ungrouping Frames

When you group two or more frames together, Word Pro begins treating them as a single unit. You can then drag the group to a new location, which repositions all the frames in the group. Any formatting changes you make apply to all the frames in the group.

To group the frames, start by selecting all the frames to group. Click the border for the first frame, press and hold the Shift key, and then click the border for each of the other frames that you want to include in the group. Figure 5-11 shows some frames selected for grouping.

After you've selected all the frames to group, choose Frame ➪ Group or click the Toggle Frames to Group/Ungroup SmartIcon. Word Pro groups the frames, placing a larger border around the border for the grouped frames. The anchor for the group is moved by default to the upper-left corner of the group. To ungroup the frames, click the group, and then choose Frame ➪ Ungroup or click the Toggle Frames to Group/Ungroup SmartIcon.

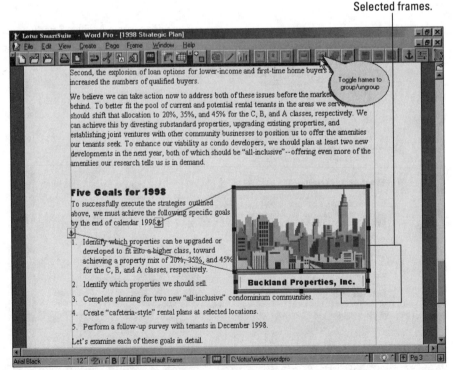

Figure 5-11: You can select frames and then group them to have Word Pro treat them as a single unit.

You can select and move individual frames within the border for the frame group. To do so, click the group so that you can see the light-gray border for the group. Then, within the group, click the individual frame that you want to work with so that its border appears with black selection handles. You can then drag the frame within the group (the group border expands automatically, if needed) or format the individual frame within the group.

Formatting the Frame

Just as you use an InfoBox to format a text selection or page, an InfoBox provides most of the settings for formatting frames. To display the Frame InfoBox for the selected frame, choose Frame ➪ Frame Properties or click the Frame Properties SmartIcon. The Frame InfoBox appears. The tabs and options in this InfoBox are nearly identical to those in the Page InfoBox, described in "Using Page Formatting" in Chapter 4, "Formatting and Printing a Document."

The first tab of the Frame InfoBox is the Color, Pattern, and Line Style tab, which is identical to the tab of the same name in the Page InfoBox. (You also can display the first tab in the Frame InfoBox by choosing Frame ➪ Lines Around Frame or Frame ➪ Background Color.) The tab enables you to format the frame border, and apply a background color, pattern, or shadow to the frame. For example, you can use the Designer Borders drop-down list to add a designer border around a frame.

Like the Page InfoBox, the Frame InfoBox offers a Graphic and Watermark Options tab, which is second in the InfoBox. (Display this tab directly by choosing Frame ➪ Graphics Scaling.) Use the Watermark option button and accompanying drop-down list to insert a watermark within the frame. Choosing a background graphic from the Watermark drop-down list and then choosing Tiled from the Placement drop-down list creates an attractive background in the frame, as shown in Figure 5-12.

You can change the size for a graphic in a frame using the settings in the Scaling area of the dialog box. Choose a Placement for the watermark or graphic using the drop-down list of that name, or use the Rotate Image drop-down list to specify an angle for the frame's graphic. You also can make the graphics in some frames transparent by changing the Pattern drop-down list setting on the Color, Pattern, and Line Style tab to None, and then enabling the Transparent check box on the Graphic and Watermark Options tab. Finally, you can use the Image Processing button when it's offered to adjust the print quality for certain types of graphics; see "Troubleshooting Graphics Printing" below for more about working with image processing.

The next tab in the Frame InfoBox is the Size and Margin tab (see Figure 5-13). You can use the Frame Width and Frame Height text boxes to adjust the frame to a precise size. Use the Margin All Sides text box to change the space between the text or graphic in the frame and the frame border. Use the All Sides text box under Padding Around Border to specify how much space should appear between the frame border and any text that wraps around the frame. If you don't want the frame margins or padding to be equal on all sides, click the Margin Options button. Choose Inside of Border or Outside of Border from the Margins drop-down list; change the needed entries in the Top, Bottom, Left, or Right text boxes; and then click OK. Finally, if you want the frame to resize itself to fit its contents, choose a setting from the Automatic Frame Sizing to Fit Contents drop-down list.

Scaling settings
for the selected frame.

This frame has a tiled watermark
and drop shadow.

Selected frame.

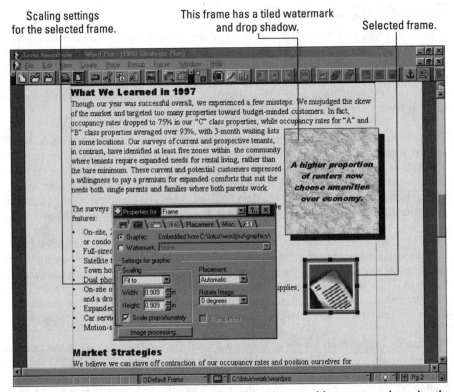

Figure 5-12: The Watermark Options tab enables you to add a watermark or size the graphic in a frame.

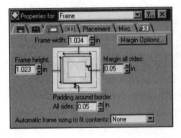

Figure 5-13: Fine-tune the frame size and set up the margin inside and outside the frame border using this tab in the Frame InfoBox.

Note

You have another option for fine-tuning the graphic inserted in a frame. When you select a frame that holds a graphic file, a special menu for the graphic type appears to the left of the Frame menu. This menu might be named Draw, GIF, JPEG, or Bitmap, depending on the format of the graphic in the selected frame. Select the Crop option from the graphic menu to display the Crop Image dialog box, drag a handle in the image preview to crop out a portion of the image, and then click OK.

The next tab in the Frame InfoBox is the Newspaper Columns tab. Its settings work just like those in the Newspaper Columns tab of the Page InfoBox, described in Chapter 4, "Formatting and Printing a Document." Basically, you use the Newspaper Columns tab to format the text within a frame into multiple columns. The settings on the Misc. tab of the Frame InfoBox also work like those described for the Misc. tab of the Page InfoBox in Chapter 4, with a few slight exceptions. On the Misc. tab of the Frame InfoBox, use the Name, Link Frame Contents To, and Other Options settings on this tab to name a frame, link its contents to another named frame, or protect a frame, in that order. To link frame contents to other frames using this option, both frames must have names and the same or very similar Place Frame settings, such as "On Current Page." These settings are discussed in the text that immediately follows. Another frame linking option is explained in this chapter's section entitled "Linking Frames."

The fifth tab, the Placement tab, offers settings for controlling the frame's position in the document and in relation to its anchor, as well as how body text wraps around the frame. You can display this tab by clicking the Frame Anchoring Options SmartIcon. Use the Place Frame drop-down list to specify where in the document the frame should appear:

✦ **On All Pages.** Tells Word Pro to repeat the frame and its contents on every page of the document.

✦ **On Left/Right Pages.** Tells Word Pro to repeat the frame on all left or right pages, depending on whether the selected frame is on a left or right page, and if you've set up the document to use different page formatting for left and right pages.

✦ **In Text.** Anchors the frame to a specify character, so that if you insert or delete text before the character, the frame moves with it.

✦ **With Paragraph Above.** Anchors the frame to the paragraph above its current position.

✦ **Same Page As Text.** This option is the default for a new frame, and it tells Word Pro to always place the frame on the same page as its anchor.

✦ **On Current Page.** Anchors the frame to a particular point on the page. If the text around the frame changes, the frame does not move.

✦ **In Text – Vertical.** Anchors the frame to a particular character, but only enables the frame to move vertically when you add or delete text before the anchor point.

✦ **In Frame or In Cell.** If you've inserted the frame in a table cell or another frame, these choices keep it anchored there.

The choice you make in the Place Frame drop-down list determines what options Word Pro offers for aligning the frame within the page and layering the frame. If you choose In Text, Same Page As Text, or In Text – Vertical, you can't change the alignment for the frame; that's because Word Pro determines the alignment based on the position of the text to which the frame is anchored. If you choose another placement—such as On Current Page—the Placement tab Quick Alignment buttons, the SmartIcons for aligning the frame, and Frame ⇨ Alignment submenu commands appear, as shown in Figure 5-14.

You can also choose an alignment to move the frame to the correct position relative to the margins. If you have two or more frames that you want to layer, choose On All Pages, On Left/Right Pages, or On Current Page from the Place Frame drop-down list in the Frame InfoBox for each frame. You can then select one of the frames and use the Frame ⇨ Priorities submenu choices or Bring Frame to Front and Send Frame to Back SmartIcons to determine the layering order for the frames.

For some of the Place Frame settings, you can specify the frame's position relative to its anchor point by changing the Vertical and Horizontal settings under Offset from Anchor Point to Frame. You can click the Clear button to reset those measurements to 0. Click the Placement and Anchoring button to display the Placement Options dialog box, which offers additional settings for controlling the anchor point and frame placement. This dialog box also offers a Place Frame drop-down list. Under it are two settings that you can use to control where the anchor point appears on a page and how the anchor point attaches to the frame. Click the page under Anchor Point to move the anchor point to the desired location, such as the upper-right margin or corner of the page instead of the upper-left margin or corner. Under Tie Anchor to Frame, click the example frame to choose which grid point on the corner or side of the frame aligns to the anchor point. You can then use the options under Offset from Anchor Point to Frame to change the distance between the frame and anchor point. Click Done to close the Placement Options dialog box and accept your settings there.

Create a Look with Layers

You may need to layer frames to achieve the look that you want. For example, you can create a "picture frame" effect by creating a frame with a background color or pattern, or a watermark background. Insert the graphic you want to "frame" in a slightly smaller frame, and then drag it over the frame that holds the background you created.

Aligns the frame to the left margin, center, or right margin.   Expands the frame so it spans between the left and right margins.   Frame Anchoring Options SmartIcon.

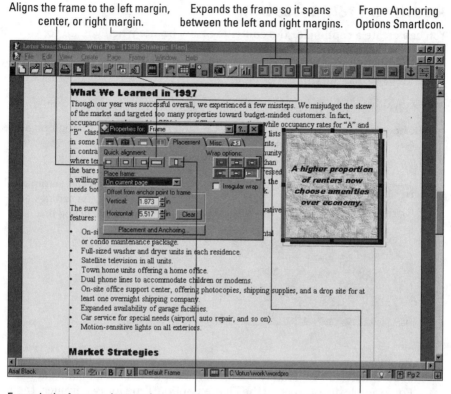

Expands the frame so it spans between the top and bottom margins.   Text wrapping choices.

Figure 5-14: For some frame placements, you can choose how the frame aligns relative to the margins.

The final choice to make on the Placement tab is how the body text in the document wraps around or behind the frame. The available Wrap Options also change based on the Place Frame option you've selected. Click the Wrap Options button that illustrates the type of wrapping you want. For frames that hold irregularly shaped graphics or drawings, such as one of the arrow graphics that comes with Word Pro, the Irregular Wrap check box may become active when you select other wrap options; checking the Irregular Wrap option enables text to wrap within the frame, up to the edge of the graphic within the frame. So, if you inserted the arrow5.sdw drawing from the \lotus\wordpro\graphics folder in a frame, choosing a wrap option and then enabling Irregular Wrap causes the text to wrap right up to the edge of the circle of arrows in that drawing.

The final tab in the Frame InfoBox is the Named Style tab. You can use it to create and apply frame styles. Chapter 6, "Using SmartMasters, Styles, and Scripts for Control," explains how to work with styles in Word Pro.

Adding a Frame Caption

You can create a caption for the contents of any frame. When you do so, Word Pro inserts the new caption in a small frame within the frame that holds the chart, graphic, equation, or other item that you want to identify with the caption. Follow these steps to insert a caption for a frame:

1. Select the frame for which you want to add the caption.

2. Choose Frame ➪ New Caption. The Create Frame Caption dialog box appears (see Figure 5-15), with its Caption tab displayed.

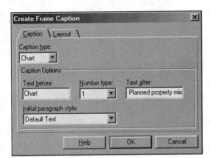

Figure 5-15: Word Pro can automatically insert a caption using the settings and text you specify in this dialog box.

3. Choose a caption type from the Caption Type drop-down list. Word Pro sequentially and separately numbers the captions based on the caption type. For example, if you specify the Figure Caption Type for two frames, the first caption is numbered 1 and the second is numbered 2. If you specify the Chart Caption Type for the next two frames, they are also numbered 1 and 2, due to the change in caption type.

4. To change the text that appears before the caption number (as in *Figure 1*, *Chart 1*, or *Table 1*), you can edit the contents of the Text Before text box under Caption Options.

5. Choose the style of number to use for numbering the captions from the Number Type drop-down list under Caption Options.

6. To include specific descriptive text after the caption, enter it in the Text After text box under Caption Options.

Danger Zone Be sure to press the spacebar to start your entry in the Text After text box, to ensure there will be a space to separate the caption number and the text that follows it.

7. If you want to use a particular text style for the caption, select the Style from the Initial Paragraph Style drop-down list.

8. Click the Layout tab, and then choose the desired Caption Position, Line Around Caption, and Caption Text Alignment.

9. Click OK to finish the caption.

Word Pro inserts the caption within the frame that holds the object to which you've added the caption. You can resize the caption's frame, or click within the caption to edit its text. Figure 5-16 shows an example of a caption frame with the insertion point in it. Select the caption frame and press Delete to delete the caption.

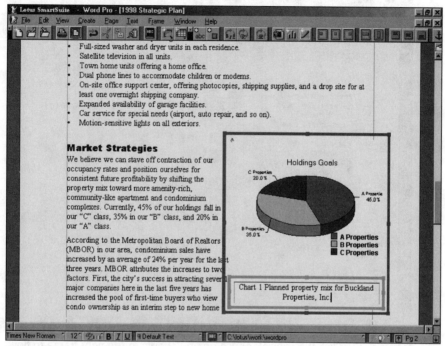

Figure 5-16: A caption appears as a frame within a frame.

Linking Frames

Linking two or more frames tells Word Pro to flow text from the first frame into the second frame. Then, when you adjust the frame sizes, Word Pro automatically readjusts how the text "breaks" between frames. To link text between frames, use these steps:

1. Create the first frame and insert the text you want to appear in it, even if it's more text than can display in the frame at its current size.

2. Create the second frame.

3. Make sure you select the same Place Frame drop-down list setting for both frames on the Placement tab in the Frame InfoBox.

4. Select or activate the first frame, which holds the text.

5. Choose Frame ⇨ Link Frame Contents.

6. Point to the second frame, so that you see the special mouse pointer for placing the linked frame contents, as shown in Figure 5-17.

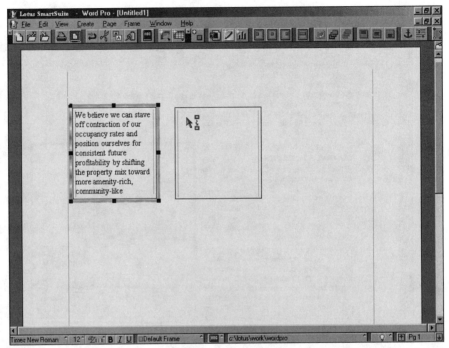

Figure 5-17: Click the special mouse pointer shown in the right frame to flow text from the left frame into the right frame, thus linking the frame contents.

7. Click the second frame to flow the text into it and create the link.

If you're linking more than two frames, you would create the third frame, and then select or activate the second frame, choose Frame ⇨ Link Frame Contents, and click the third frame. Repeat the process for subsequent linked frames.

When you select one of the linked frames, a small link indicator appears in the lower-right corner (for the first linked frame) or the upper-left corner (for subsequent frames). The link indicator looks like a small green squiggle.

To remove the link between frames, select or activate the first frame (or the next-to-last frame when you've linked more than two frames). Then, choose Frame ⇨ Unlink.

Troubleshooting Graphics Printing

Graphics printing can be a bit hit-or-miss, especially if you're printing a color graphic using a black-and-white printer. Often, the color gradations in the graphic "overwhelm" the printer, so it prints the image in black and white without any gradations at all (called *posterizing* the image), making it look like a blob. You can use Word Pro's image processing capabilities to help correct such printing problems, both for black-and-white and color printers.

Word Pro can only perform image processing on certain types of graphics, called *bitmap graphics.* Graphics in the .PCX or .BMP formats are bitmap graphics. If the graphic or watermark you've inserted into a frame is a *vector graphic*, which includes the Word Pro Draw (.SDW), JPEG, and .GIF formats, you can first convert the graphic to a bitmap graphic in Word Pro, and then use image processing to help the printing. To convert the graphic, select the frame that holds it. Then, open the menu for the graphic type (Draw, GIF, or JPEG, for example) that appears to the left of the Frame menu, and choose Convert. The Convert dialog box appears. In the Object Type list, click Bitmap, and then click OK.

You can then use the image processing features. To do so, display the Frame InfoBox for the frame that holds the bitmap and click the Image Processing button on the Graphic and Watermark Options tab. Alternately, double-click the bitmap image in the frame to activate the frame, and then choose Bitmap ⇨ Image Processing. The Image Processing dialog box appears (see Figure 5-18). Use the Brightness, Contrast, Edge Enhancement, or Smoothing sliders or text boxes to change the various tones and values of the graphic. Check Invert Image to change black tones to white and vice versa. Or, check Auto Contrast to have Word Pro automatically select the best image processing settings based on the default printer selected under Windows. Click the Apply button to test out any of the settings you make without closing the dialog box, or Revert to undo the settings. Click OK to finish making your image processing settings.

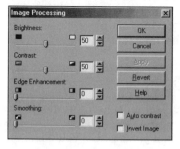

Figure 5-18: Work with the Image Processing settings to improve printing for a bitmap graphic.

Note

Double-clicking the bitmap image to activate it changes the options on the Bitmap menu.

After you close the Image Processing dialog box, you can activate the bitmap and choose Bitmap ➪ Revert to remove the image processing changes. If you've inserted one bitmap into the document, you can activate it and then choose Bitmap ➪ AutoContrast on Import to toggle that option on, so that Word Pro automatically adjusts the image processing settings for other bitmaps you insert or convert in the document. Finally, you can use the options on the Bitmap ➪ Halftone Printing submenu (Fastest Printing, Best Quality, Automatic, Use Printer Driver, and Posterize), to adjust how Word Pro prints *halftone* images — images that have gradations of color and light and dark.

Note

To turn on Auto Contrast by default, you can edit the Windows Registry. Click the Start button and choose Run. Enter **regedit** in the Open text box and click OK. The Registry Editor opens. Use the Registry ➪ Export Registry File option to make a backup copy of your Registry information, which you should always do before you make any changes. Navigate to the \HKEY_CURRENT_USER\Software\Lotus\Wordpro\98.0\ lwpimage.ini\ScreenOptions key using the tree in the left pane of the Registry Editor, and then double-click the Auto Contrast value in the right pane. Change the Value Data entry to **TRUE**, click OK, and choose Registry ➪ Exit to close the Registry Editor. Restart your system so that your change takes effect, and then restart Word Pro.

Using Tables for Organization

Tables enable you to organize information in neat rows and columns. Even though you can create rows and columns of information using tab settings, a table can make the job easier because it divides data into discrete *cells*. Each cell is the box formed by the intersection of a row and column. If an entry in a particular column is too wide for the column, it can wrap within the cell so that it doesn't lap over into the next column to the right. In addition, tables provide formatting options not possible when you use tabs. You can add lines between rows and columns, add a background color to one or more cells, or insert the table in a frame. This section covers the key points for creating and formatting a table in Word Pro.

Hot Stuff

You can create a table inside a frame to enable you to easily move the table within the document, or enhance the table with additional formatting.

Creating a Table and Entering Data

Follow these steps to insert a table into the document and enter information into it:

1. Click in the document to position the insertion point where you'd like the table to appear. To insert the table in a frame, create the frame.

2. Use one of two methods to insert the table cells:

- Choose Create ⇨ Table. Choose a table style from the Table Style drop-down list. Use the Number of Columns and Number of Rows text boxes to specify how many rows and columns the table should have. Click OK to insert the table. (If you didn't create a frame in Step 1, you could click Size & Place Table Manually, and then drag in the document to create the table in a frame.)

- Click the Create Table Grid SmartIcon, and then drag on the grid to specify how many columns and rows the table should have (see Figure 5-19). Release the mouse to insert the table of that size in the document.

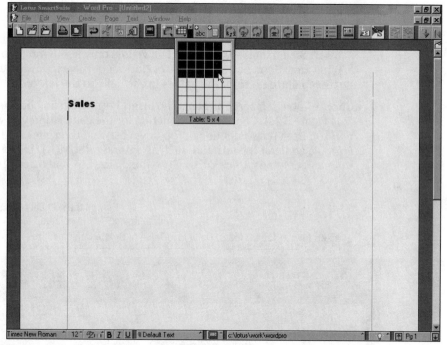

Figure 5-19: Use the Create Table Grid SmartIcon to indicate how many rows and columns the table should have.

3. The insertion point appears in the first table cell. If you want the table to include a row of column headings, enter them in the top row of the table. To make each entry, type the text (pressing Enter to wrap the text to multiple lines in the cell, if needed), and then press Tab to move to the next cell. Shift+Tab moves the insertion point to the previous cell.

4. Optionally, you can either copy a numeric or text entry from one cell to other cells, or fill a series of numbers by entering the first two and then dragging to enter other numbers using the same increment. For example, if you enter 2 and 4, you can fill subsequent entries in the series, such as 6, 8, and 10. Or, enter a day of the week or month to fill cells with similar entries. Select the cell(s) that holds the first entry or entries for the fill (click a single cell to select it or drag over multiple cells). Point to the lower-right corner to display the fill pointer, which includes small green arrowheads. Drag the fill pointer over the cells to fill and release the mouse button.

5. You can use a formula to total numeric entries in the cells above a column or the cells to the left in a row:

- Click the cell to hold the total, and then click the Insert SmartSum of Column SmartIcon (Table ➪ Insert SmartSum ➪ Column) to total the values in the cells above it or Insert SmartSum of Row SmartIcon (Table ➪ Insert SmartSum ➪ Row), which is visible only if you move the Text in a Table SmartIcon bar to the side or bottom of the window or to its own floating palette, to total the values in the cells to the left of it.

- Choose Table ➪ Insert Formula. The Insert Formula dialog box appears (see Figure 5-20). Choose the @Function for the calculation you want to perform from the @Functions drop-down list, and then click Add to Formula and edit the formula, such as entering @SUM(A1..E5) to total both rows and columns. Click OK to close the dialog box and insert the formula.

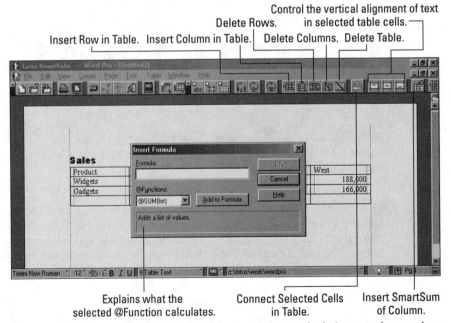

Figure 5-20: You can create basic formulas to perform calculations on the numbers entered into a table row or column.

If you enter **Total** in the far left cell in a row or the upper-right cell in the table and then press Tab, Word Pro automatically enters SmartSum formulas for the Total row or column.

6. To change the entry in a cell, click to simultaneously select the cell and position the insertion point within it, and then make the changes you want to the entry. To edit a cell that holds a formula, right-click the cell, and then click Edit Formula to redisplay the Insert Formula dialog box so you can make your changes.

Use the Create ➪ Parallel Columns command to set up a table-like column block with one, two, or three columns. Then, enter information in each "cell" of the column block, just as you'd enter text in table cells.

Table Formatting

You can insert and remove rows and columns within a table. First, click a cell in the position where you want to insert a row or column, and then click the Insert Row in Table or Insert Column in Table SmartIcon, or choose one of the Table ➪ Insert submenu choices. To delete a row or column, click a cell in the row or column to delete (or drag to select several), and then click the Delete Rows or Delete Columns SmartIcon, or choose one of the commands on the Table ➪ Delete submenu. You can click any cell in a table and click the Delete Table SmartIcon.

Table rows increase in height automatically to accommodate the amount of text or the font size you specify for text in the row. To change a column's width, point to the right border for the column until the mouse pointer changes to a double-headed arrow, and then drag to change the width of the column.

To apply formatting to the contents of a cell, column, or row, you must select it first. You click a cell to select it, or drag over contiguous cells to select or highlight them. You can click a cell in the table, and then use the options on the Table ➪ Select submenu to select the Row Contents (whole row), Column Contents (whole column), or Entire Table. When the insertion point is inside any table cell, you also can move the mouse pointer just to the left of the row you want to select or just above the column you want to select until you see a yellow arrow pointer; then click to select the row or column the arrow is pointing to. You can then use the status bar and the Text menu choices to format the table cell contents.

To format the appearance of the selected table cells, click the Table Cell Properties SmartIcon or choose Table ➪ Cell Properties to display the Table Cell InfoBox. The settings for most tabs in this dialog box resemble those you've seen in the Page and Frame InfoBoxes. A few differences are worth noting, however. The Size and Margin tab, third in the InfoBox, contains settings for specific Row Dimensions and Column Dimensions, and enables you to set Left, Right, Top, and Bottom margins inside the selected cells to provide for more or less white space between the text and lines defining the table cells. The fourth tab is the Number Format tab. This tab enables you to specify how numeric entries in selected cells appear. For example, Figure

5-21 shows how to format numbers as currency. Choose a Format Category and Current Format from the lists of those names. To display more or fewer decimal places, change the Decimal Places text box entry. To add the Current Format selection to the Frequently Used option under Format Category, click the Frequently Used check box.

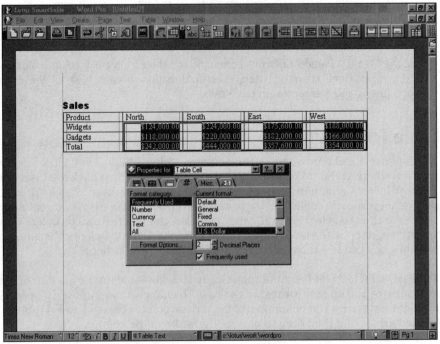

Figure 5-21: The selected cells have been formatted as currency using the Number Format tab in the Table Cell InfoBox.

To make further changes to the selected Current Format, click the Format Options button to display the Edit Format dialog box. Use the Condition to Edit drop-down list to specify whether the change should apply to Any Number, or only Negative Numbers or Zero values formatted with the current format. Then, make your choices from the Text Before and Text After drop-down lists (or make a custom entry in those text boxes). To specify a particular color for the format, click the Number Color check box, and then use the drop-down list beside it to choose a color. Click Reset to return the format to its original defaults, or OK to close the dialog box and accept your changes. One other noteworthy setting: Check the Protect Cell check box on the Misc. tab to add protection for the selected table cells.

To apply formatting for the entire table, such as a line around the border for the whole table, margins inside and outside the table border, table placement, and more, use the Table InfoBox. To display that InfoBox, click any cell in the table, and then click the Table Properties SmartIcon or choose Table ➪ Table Properties. Again, most of the settings in this InfoBox resemble those you've seen for other elements, such as the Wrap Options on the Placement tab, the margin options on the Size and Margins tab, and so on.

The Misc. tab has a few settings that are unique to tables. Check Prevent Editing of Protected Cells to "lock" the entries for any cells you protected with the Protect Cell check box of the Misc. tab in the Table Cell InfoBox. Check Protect Entire Table to add protection for all table cells. If you're using outlining in the document, turn on the Restart Paragraph Numbers on Each Column to change how Word Pro numbers the table cells. Finally, if you plan to export the table to a Notes database, enter a name for the table object in the Name text box.

After you create and format a table, you can save it as a glossary entry and insert it into other documents.

Sorting a Selection

Use Word Pro's *sorting* capabilities to rearrange rows of information in a table, or information divided into columns via tab stops or another delimiter. Word Pro treats each column in the table or tabular material as a *field* of discrete information, and each table row or text paragraph as a *record*. For text that hasn't been separated with tabs, Word Pro treats each paragraph as a single field; so, if you have a list of two- or three-word entries and you pressed Enter after each, you can sort that list, too. You can sort according to the contents of a single field, or up to three fields. Follow these steps to perform a sort:

1. Select the rows of information to sort in the table or text.

2. Choose Text ➪ Sort. The Sort dialog box appears (see Figure 5-22).

3. In the First Sort By row of options, choose the first field to sort by using the Field/Col. Text box. Use the Type column to specify whether the sort is alphanumeric (for columns that contain text or text with numbers), or purely numeric. Choose Ascending or Descending from the Order drop-down list. If the entries in the selected field contain multiple words and you want to sort by a word other than the first word in the field, choose the word to sort by from the Word drop-down list.

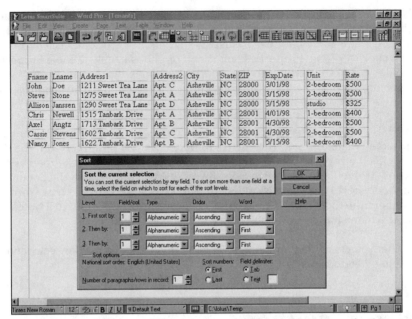

Figure 5-22: Use the Sort dialog box to rearrange the rows in a selection, such as the rows selected in the table in this figure.

4. If you want to specify secondary and tertiary fields to sort by, make your selections in the second and third Then By rows. Suppose you chose to sort a list by a last name field as the First Sort By field. If you know some of the rows have the same entries in the last name field, you could then choose to sort by the first name as the second Then By sort field, to ensure Word Pro would use the first name entries to "break the tie" and choose how to order rows with the same last name entries.

5. If each record in the selected text actually is entered as more than one table row or paragraph, use the Number of Paragraphs/Rows in Record setting to indicate how many paragraphs or rows each entry contains. For example, if you have a list in which each first name appears on a separate row or paragraph, followed by each last name on a separate row or paragraph, change the Number of Paragraphs/Rows in Record setting to 2.

6. For alphanumeric sorts, specify whether to Sort Numbers First (before sorting the text in the specified fields) or Last.

7. Tell Word Pro what Field Delimiter separates the fields in the selected text. Leave Tab selected if you've used tabs to separate the text. If the text uses another character as a delimiter, click the Text option button, and then enter the delimiter character(s) the text uses in the accompanying text box.

8. Click OK to perform the sort according to the settings you specified. If the sort doesn't work as you expected, immediately click the Undo Last Command or Action SmartIcon to undo the sort.

Outlining

Behind the scenes, Word Pro outlines your document as you create it. When you need to, you can display the outline so you can see how the topics in your document flow, and make choices about rearranging topics.

To display the outline for your document, choose View ➪ Outline. The Outline bar appears onscreen, and Word Pro indents the text in the document according to its outline level (see Figure 5-23). You can use the buttons on the outline bar or the corresponding commands on the Text ➪ Outline submenu to work with the outline level for a selection, or to collapse or expand outline levels.

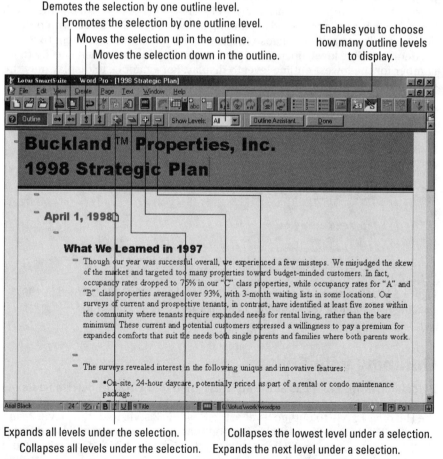

Demotes the selection by one outline level.
Promotes the selection by one outline level.
Moves the selection up in the outline.
Moves the selection down in the outline.

Enables you to choose how many outline levels to display.

Expands all levels under the selection.
Collapses all levels under the selection.
Collapses the lowest level under a selection.
Expands the next level under a selection.

Figure 5-23: Changing to the Outline view displays tools for working with the outlining levels of your text.

In an outline, the "selection" is the paragraph that currently holds the insertion point. The contents for the selection include all the body text and headings at lower outline levels that follow it, up to the next paragraph that's at the same outline level as the selection. So, if the selection is a heading that's followed by some body text, you can collapse the body text to hide it under the heading. You can then move the heading in the outline using one of the Outline buttons for moving the selection, and the collapsed body text travels with it. Or, if there are headings at lower outline levels within the selection, promoting or demoting the selection also promotes or demotes the paragraphs at other outline levels within the selection.

To collapse or expand all the contents within a selection at a particular outline level, click the Outline bar button for expanding or collapsing all the text and entries at lower outline levels within it. When a selection contains information collapsed within it, a plus sign appears just above and to the left of it to tell you there's hidden information, as shown in Figure 5-24. You also can use the Outline bar buttons for collapsing and expanding individual outline levels within the document. To expand or collapse the outline for the whole document to a particular outline level, open the Show Levels drop-down list and specify the number for the lowest outline level to display. For example, to display only the first three outline levels, choose 3. To redisplay all the document text, choose All.

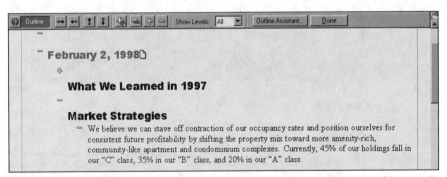

Figure 5-24: The plus sign above and to the left of the "What We Learned in 1997" heading tells you that text and other headings are collapsed under it.

Outlining with Styles

By default, Word Pro looks at the style assigned to the text to determine its outline level. (The next chapter teaches how to apply and create styles.) Word Pro assigns the Heading 1 style to outline level 1, the Heading 2 style to outline level 2, and the Heading 3 style to outline level 3. Beyond that, it's up to you to tell Word Pro what outline level to apply to different styles in the document. You can use the Outline Assistant to assign outline levels to styles. To open the Outline Assistant, click the Outline Assistant button on the Outline bar or choose Create ➪ Outline.

Click the Next button to select the Step 2. Select the Style tab. This tab presents several different sets of preformatted heading styles (with outline levels) that you can apply to a document. Each set of heading styles specifies nine outline levels. Depending on the set you select, the styles also might add bullets, numbering, or indention to each heading level. Click the preview for the set of headings and outline levels you want to use in the document, and then click Done to close the Outline Assistant. You can then apply those heading levels (and the corresponding outline levels) to the text in your document.

If you open the Outline Assistant and click Next twice, the Step 3 (Optional) Modify the Style tab appears (see Figure 5-25). You also can choose Text ⇨ Outline ⇨ Outline Styles to display these options directly. You can use this tab to change the formatting and outline level for a style; any text formatted with that style then displays those changes in the outline and the document.

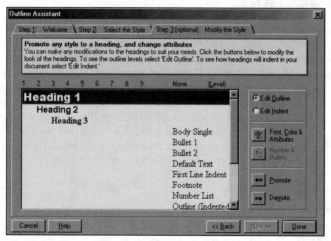

Figure 5-25: Modify the outline level for each particular style here.

In the list of document styles, click the style for which you want to change the formatting and outline level. Leave the Edit Outline option button selected, and then use either the Font, Color, & Attributes or Number & Bullets button to display a dialog box you can use to change the style's formatting. Click either the Promote or Demote button to move the style to the outline level you want; the outline levels appear across the top of the list of styles. Click the Edit Indent option button to display text boxes for changing the style's indention in the outline, in other views, and in printouts. Make an entry in the All Lines text box to set the indention for all lines of paragraphs using that style, or specify separate First Line or Rest of Lines indents using those text boxes. Click Done to finish your outline style changes and close the Outline Assistant dialog box.

Outlining with Document Levels

You can select an outline level for each individual paragraph in the document using the Misc. tab of the Text InfoBox. Click in the paragraph for which you'd like to change the outline level, and then click the Text Properties SmartIcon to display the Text InfoBox. Click the Misc. tab. under Outline Settings, and change the Document Level text box entry to specify the outline level the paragraph should use. To designate the paragraph as a heading, click the Heading Paragraph check box. To clear a headline level you've applied manually and return the selected paragraph to the default outline level determined by Word Pro, click the Use Smart Level check box.

Breaking a Document into Divisions and Sections

Divisions and sections break your document into discrete portions, enabling you to establish different page formats, header and footer numbering, and so on, for different groups of pages in the document. This section shows you how to insert divisions and sections in a document to better manage and format document contents. You can think of a *division* as the real "document" within a Word Pro file. When you create a Word Pro document, even a blank one, it contains at least one division, usually called *body*. You can display that body division at any time by clicking the icon that looks like overlapping file folder tabs at the top of the vertical scroll bar. A tab for the division appears at the top of the document. Each section is a portion of a division; section tabs are grouped within the division tab that holds them.

Creating a Division or Section

Suppose you need to print most of the text in a report using the normal portrait page orientation, while select pages holding budget information and charts may need to print in landscape format. If the budget and chart pages appear in separate divisions, you can include those pages within the document to print the whole thing at once. Without divisions, you'd have to create and print one document for the portrait pages and one document for the landscape pages, and then collate the printed pages together.

When you create a new division, you can either insert the contents of an existing file as the division, or create a blank division and then enter its contents. Follow these steps to insert a new division into the document:

1. Position the insertion point at the location where the new division should begin.

2. Choose Create ➪ Division. The Create Division dialog box appears (see Figure 5-26).

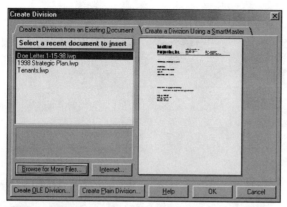

Figure 5-26: You can use this dialog box to create a division using an existing file or SmartMaster.

3. Select how to create the division:

   - On the Create a Division from an Existing Document tab, click one of the listed documents or use the Browse for More Files button to select another file to insert as the division. Then click OK.

   - On the Create a Division Using a SmartMaster tab, click one of the listed SmartMasters or use the Browse for More Files button to create a division based on a SmartMaster. After you click Browse for More Files, click the Create From Any SmartMaster tab and make a selection from the Select a Type of SmartMaster list, and then click your choice in the Choose a Look list. Click OK when you have chosen a SmartMaster.

   - Click the Create Plain Division button to add a division based on the default, blank SmartMaster.

4. In the Insert Division dialog box that appears, specify where to insert the new division by clicking the appropriate option button: After Current Division, Before Current Division, or At Insertion Point (if you positioned the insertion point for the start of a new division in Step 1). If you're inserting an existing document, you also need to specify how to insert the file. Click Inserted Into Current Document to copy the original file contents and place them in the new division. Click Linked to External File to tell Word Pro to check the original (source) file for changes each time you open the document holding the division based on that source file, and to update the opened document to include the source file changes.

5. Click OK to close the Insert Division dialog box and insert the division. Word Pro inserts the new tab for the division (see Figure 5-27). To display the division tabs, if needed, click the icon at the top of the vertical scroll bar. Linked documents insert as a division with a double division tab, which shows the file name with a body tab within it. This is the same type of tab you will see when you group divisions together.

A new division.   Click to display or hide division tabs.

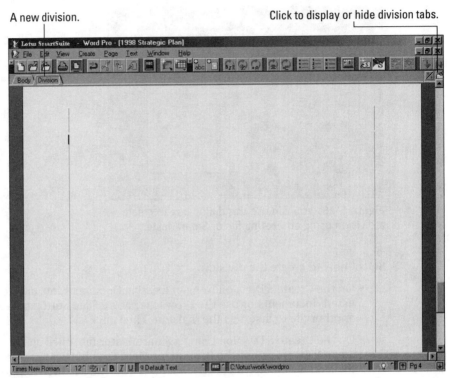

Figure 5-27: Inserting a new division breaks the document into parts that you can format and number separately.

To insert a new section within a division, position the insertion point where you'd like the new section to begin, and then choose Create ➪ Section. The Create Section dialog box appears (see Figure 5-28).

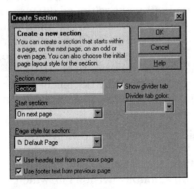

Figure 5-28: Inserting a section primarily entails giving the section a name using this dialog box.

The settings in this dialog box really are self-explanatory. Type a Section Name, use the Start Section drop-down list to designate the start of the section, or choose a page style for the section (if you've previously saved a page style) from the Page Style for Section drop-down list. Use the Show Divider Tab check box to control whether or not a tab for the section appears within the division tab for the division holding the section. Use the Divider Tab Color drop-down list to choose a display color for the divider tab. If you want the header or footer from the previous page in the division to be used in the new section, leave the Use Header Text from Previous Page or Use Footer Text from Previous Page check boxes selected. Click OK to finish inserting the new section.

Within the text of the document, section marks identify the beginning of each new section. You can add text before and after a section mark, just as you would add and delete text before and after page breaks you've inserted.

A *master document* consolidates several files into a single document. Each of the files you insert into a master document appears as a division in that document. To create a master document, open or create the file you'd like to use as the master document. Choose Create ➪ Master Document. Click the Add button, select the document to add in the Browse dialog box, and click Open to add each document to the list of Top Level Divisions in Master Document. Click OK to add all the files into the master document, and then save the master document file.

To select the division or section to work in, click the tab for the division or section, and then click in the text that displays onscreen to begin working. When a division holds multiple sections, its tab displays a minus sign. You can click that minus sign to hide the section tabs in the division; the minus sign in the division tab changes to a plus. Click that plus to redisplay the section tabs.

Formatting a Division or Section

You can work with the tabs for the divisions or sections, performing such operations as changing the name for a section or division or displaying color for its tab. You can delete divisions or sections (thus deleting their contents) or combine and split divisions or sections. To access these commands for working with divisions or sections, right-click the division or section tab to display a shortcut menu like the one shown in Figure 5-29. The Division Properties or Section Properties command displays a dialog box with choices for changing the division or section name, changing the tab color, or even saving the selected division as a new document. The other commands enable you to perform such operations as combining or deleting divisions and sections.

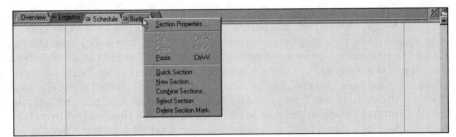

Figure 5-29: Right-click the division or section tab to display commands for altering the division or section.

In addition to formatting the division tab or deleting or otherwise working with the divisions, you can set up the page layout for each division or section. For example, if you have a division that contains two sections, you can change the page layout settings for text within the division itself (before the start of the first section) and for each of the sections. To change the page layout for a division or section, click the tab for the division or section to select it. Then, choose Page ➪ Page Properties or click the Page Properties SmartIcon. The Page InfoBox appears. Any setting changes you make in the Page InfoBox apply only to the currently selected division or section. After you finish making the page formatting changes for one division or section, click the tab for another division or section and change its Page InfoBox settings, and so on.

Creating Professional Document Features

Many professions have standards for document preparation. Some of these standards help make a document more usable, while others enhance credibility by identifying the sources of information in the document. This section highlights the Word Pro features you can use to make a document more useful for all readers and to help the document fulfill the requirements for your profession.

Turning on Line Numbering

Traditionally, legal documents use line numbering along the left margin to facilitate discussions about particular portions of the text. To turn on line numbering in a document or section, choose Page ➪ Line Numbering. The Line Numbering dialog box appears. Figure 5-30 shows line numbering settings and the resulting numbers displayed.

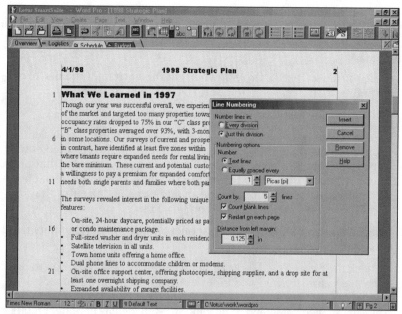

Figure 5-30: For legal documents, you may need to add line numbering, as shown here.

Under Number Lines In, choose whether to display the line numbers in the Entire Document or Just This Division (for the division holding the insertion point). Then choose the Numbering Options. To have Word Pro count the lines of text, choose Text Lines. Or, to create evenly spaced numbers, choose the Equally Spaced Every option button, and enter the distance between numbers using the options below that button.

Use the Count By setting to control the increment for the displayed numbers; for example, enter 5 to display a number beside every fifth line (line 5, line 10, line 15, and so on). Click the appropriate check boxes if you want Word Pro to Count Blank Lines or Restart on Each Page. Also, use the Distance from Left Margin text box to specify how close to the left margin the page numbers appear and print. Click Insert to finish and apply your line numbering settings, or Remove to remove line numbering from the document or division.

Adding a Table of Contents or Index

If you're creating documentation to help your customers use your products, or any lengthy document that you want to help the reader navigate, you can generate a table of contents (TOC) or index. Follow these general steps to create a table of contents or index:

1. First, you need to mark the entries that Word Pro will compile as the TOC or index. Choose Text ⇨ Mark Text As to display a submenu, and then choose TOC Entry or Index Entry to display the Mark Text bar (see Figure 5-31). Use it as follows:

   • Use the Mark Text As drop-down list at the bottom of the bar to choose whether to mark a selection as a TOC Entry or Index Entry.

   • Drag over the text to mark in the document.

   • For a TOC entry, use the TOC Level text box to specify an indention level for the selection in the TOC. For an index entry, the selected entry appears in the Primary text box. To create a sub-entry for that primary entry, type the sub-entry text in the Secondary text box. Also click And Vice Versa if you want to include an additional index entry that transposes the Primary and Secondary Entry.

   • Click Mark, and then select subsequent entries in the document and mark them, too.

   • Check the Show TOC Marks or Show Index Marks check box to display the marks for the TOC and index entries within the document.

Note

If you've already applied paragraph or heading styles to identify important topics in a document and you want to compile a table of contents, you can skip Step 1. Word Pro can compile the table of contents based on the style, instead, as described in Step 6.

2. Click Done to close the Mark Text bar after you've marked all the entries you want.

3. Choose Create ⇨ Other Document Part to display a submenu, and then choose Table of Contents or Index. The Table of Contents Assistant or Index Assistant dialog box appears.

4. Both dialog boxes have a Step 1: Look tab. Use the options on this tab to choose a SmartMaster to format the TOC or index and any other formatting settings, such as alignment and page numbering, that you want to adjust.

5. Both dialog boxes have a Step 2: Scope and Placement tab. Click it to display its options. The top drop-down list enables you to choose whether to generate the TOC or index for the Entire Document, Current Division, or Other Document Part. The second drop-down list enables you to choose where to insert the TOC or index: At Beginning of Document, At Beginning of Division, At Beginning of Group, or At Insertion Point. If you want, clear the Place in Separate Division check box to insert the TOC or index within the text, rather than in a new division.

Click to select the next or previous marked entry.   Click to unmark all entries.

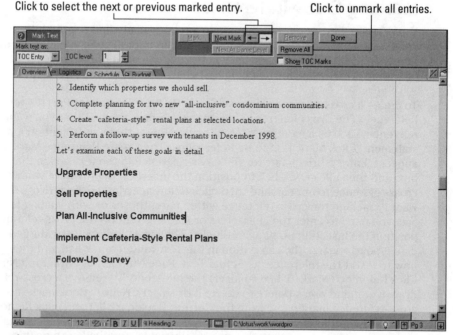

Figure 5-31: Use this bar to mark information to be compiled into a table of contents or index.

6. The Table of Contents Assistant dialog box offers a third tab, Step 3: Contents. Click it to tell Word Pro which styles of text to include in the TOC at a particular TOC level. Click the style in the list, and then use the left and right arrow buttons to the right of the list to promote or demote the style to a particular TOC level, indicated by the numbers above the list. To exclude text from the TOC, demote it until it moves to the right under None. All text formatted with a given style appears in the table of contents at the specified level.

7. Click Done. Word Pro compiles the table of contents or index, calculates the page number for each entry, and inserts the table of contents or index at the specified location in the document.

Note   Word Pro offers Index, Outline, and Table of Contents SmartMasters that you can use to insert new divisions set up to compile a specific type of information in a document.

Marking Cross-References

You can insert cross-references to help a reader easily find related information in a document. For example, if you're suggesting an overall goal, you might cross-reference the specific heading later in the document that introduces the text providing the timeline for reaching that goal.

To create a cross-reference, choose Create ⇨ Other Document Part ⇨ Cross Reference. The Cross Reference bar appears. Select the text that you want to cross-reference, such as a location later in the document that sheds light on a particular statement. Click Mark Text to Be Referenced. The Create Reference Mark dialog box appears. Enter a brief name for the cross-reference in the text box in that dialog box, and then click OK. Click to position the insertion point where you want the cross-reference to appear, and then click Reference Marked Text. (Note that if you want to include the cross-reference within parentheses or with leading text such as *See,* you need to enter the characters or lead-in to set off the cross-reference and position the insertion point accordingly.) The Insert Reference to Marked Text dialog box appears. Click an option in the Text to Reference list, and then choose how to insert the reference: as Actual Text, Page Number, or Paragraph Number. Click Reference Marked Text to insert the reference. To remove a cross-reference, drag over it and press Delete to delete it or select Create ⇨ Bookmark and select the cross-reference mark name from the Current Bookmark list and click Remove. Marked cross-references are actually bookmarked text. The references that reflect the content of those bookmarks are actually fields, and fields can be updated as their bookmarked inclusions are edited. Read more about how to update or delete a field easily in Chapter 6 under "Updating or Removing a Power Field."

Using Footnotes and Endnotes

Academic writing requires footnotes and/or endnotes, which identify the source of quoted or heavily referenced material. In fact, if you don't properly credit your sources, you could face legal consequences. Footnotes appear at the bottom of each page that includes a footnote number; endnotes appear as one long list compiled at the end of the document or division. Use the following steps to add a footnote or endnote:

1. Click to position the insertion point after the text for which you want to include a footnote or endnote citation.

2. Choose Create ⇨ Footnote/Endnote. The Create Footnote dialog box appears. Leave the Create Footnote check box selected.

3. Open the Place Footnote At drop-down list, and choose a location for the footnote or endnote, such as End of Document or End of Division.

4. If you choose a Place Footnote location other than Bottom of Page, you can check the Place in Separate Division check box to create a separate division to hold all the citations, which would be endnotes in such a case.

5. (Optional) Click the Options button to display the Footnote and Endnote Options dialog box, which contains three tabs of options for formatting the

citations in a document. For example, you can include text before or after footnote/endnote numbers, add lines to separate citations, and so on. Choose the formatting you want, and click OK to close the dialog box.

6. Click OK to insert the number for the footnote at the designated citation within the text, and move the insertion point to the corresponding location for the actual citation.

7. Enter the information for the footnote or endnote citation, as shown in Figure 5-32. You can apply the formatting you want to the footnote or endnote text you enter.

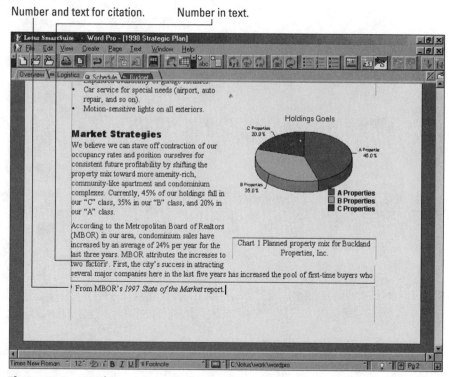

Figure 5-32: Word Pro automatically numbers and formats footnotes or endnotes you type.

8. Repeat Steps 1–7 (omitting Step 5) to create other footnotes or endnotes in the document.

9. To delete a footnote or endnote, drag over the footnote or endnote number in the body text, and then press Delete. Word Pro renumbers the remaining footnotes or endnotes to reflect the change.

✦　　✦　　✦

Using SmartMasters, Styles, and Scripts for Control

E ven though Word Pro offers literally hundreds of commands and options for creating and formatting documents, and dozens of SmartMasters to launch documents for you, it can't anticipate the look and content you'll need for all situations. On the other hand, you don't want to have to build each document from the ground up, performing similar formatting and text entry over and over. This chapter focuses on tools you can use to save time when you create a document. You learn how to apply styles and SmartMasters to change the look of the document and how to save your own styles and SmartMasters. The chapter also covers features that enable you to automate text entry or preformat text, so that you or anyone else using a document can just fill in the blanks. In addition, you learn how to save a series of steps as a script that you can rerun, and how to change some aspects of how Word Pro operates.

Using Styles

The earlier chapters covering Word Pro refer to styles in a number of instances. Each style stores formatting settings for a particular document part under a particular style name in the SmartMaster used for the document. Once formatting settings are saved as a style, you simply apply the style to a selection to apply all the formatting settings stored in the style. This section uncovers key style operations: applying a style, creating a style, and managing the styles in a SmartMaster.

Applying a Style to a Selection

Each Word Pro SmartMaster contains one or more styles for the each of the following document objects: paragraph, page, header, footer, frame, caption, table, table cell, and drop cap. You also can create a text style to apply font settings and attributes to a selected word, without changing the paragraph formatting. To apply a style to an object, select that object. For example, click in a paragraph to choose a paragraph format, click in the header area to choose a header format, and so on. Word Pro offers a few different techniques you can use to apply a different style to the selected object.

First, you can click the status bar button listing the name of the style that's currently applied to the document object. Word Pro displays a pop-up list of the styles available for the selected type of object (see Figure 6-1). Click the style you want to apply to the selection and close the pop-up list.

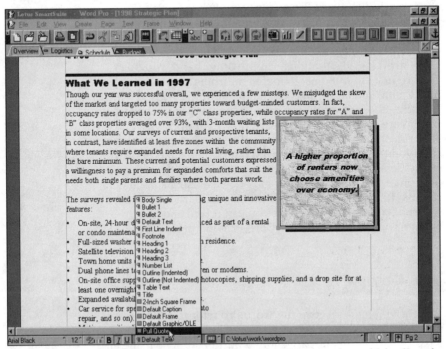

Figure 6-1: You can apply a style to a selection using the status bar, which offers the styles available for the selected type of object. The selected frame in this example uses a custom style named Pull Quote.

You can use the Fast Format feature to copy the paragraph style used by one paragraph to other paragraphs in the document. To do so, click to position the insertion point in the paragraph formatted with the paragraph style you want to re-use. Choose Text ⇨ Fast Format (Ctrl+T). In the Fast Format dialog box that appears, click The Paragraph's Named Style Only (Advanced) under Load the Mouse Pointer With. Click OK. The mouse pointer changes to the Fast Format pointer. In the document, click in each paragraph to which you want to apply the copied format. When you've finished copying the format, choose Text ⇨ Fast Format (Ctrl+T) to turn off the Fast Format pointer.

You can even use Fast Format to copy a style from one document to another. Select the paragraph with the style to copy, and then turn on Fast Format as just described. Use the Window menu to switch to the document into which you want to copy the style, click a paragraph to apply the copied style, and then choose Text ⇨ Fast Format to turn off Fast Format.

To review how to use Fast Format to copy attributes, rather than a style, see "Putting Fast Format to Work" in Chapter 4, "Formatting and Printing a Document."

You can also use the Named Style tab, the last tab in any InfoBox, to choose a new style for the selected object in the document. All the InfoBoxes — Text, Page, Header, Footer, Frame, and so on — include a Named Style tab. Select the object to which you want to apply a style, then right-click and select the Properties command for the object, such as Frame Properties if you've selected a frame. (Or, you can use the appropriate menu command or SmartIcon for displaying the InfoBox.) Click the last tab in the InfoBox, which is the Style tab. Figure 6-2 shows the Style tab for a selected frame. To use a different style for the selected objected, click the style you want in the Style list in the InfoBox. Word Pro immediately changes the selected object to display the formatting for the newly selected style.

If you apply a style to a particular element in a document and then change a formatting setting or two, those formatting settings *override* the settings used by the applied style. If you then apply a different style, the formatting choices you made still override the style. You could go back and try to remove the formatting changes you made, but you may not remember exactly what they were. Instead, you can reset the selection to the default for a particular style using the Named Style tab in the InfoBox. To do so, click the style to use in the Style list, and then click the Reset to Style button. For most elements, that finishes the process.

However, if you're trying to reset a text selection to the paragraph style, the Reset to Style dialog box appears so you can specify exactly what settings to remove from the selection: Remove All Overrides to the Paragraph Settings, Remove Only Overrides to the Character Settings, or Remove Only Character Style. (The last option only appears if you've created and applied a character style to the selection.) Click the option button you want, and then click OK to finish resetting the text to the paragraph style.

Here's a description for the selected style.   Select a style here.

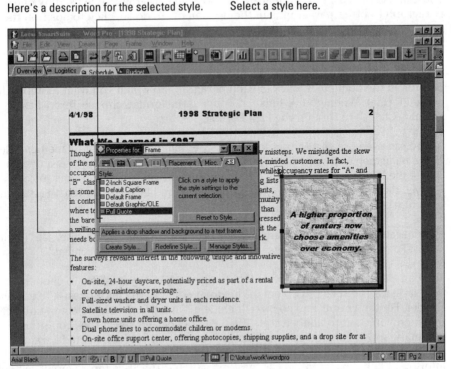

Figure 6-2: Use the Style tab, the last tab in any InfoBox, to apply a style to the selected text or document object.

Note

The menu bar menu for many selected objects also offers a submenu of commands for applying, resetting, creating, redefining, and managing styles. For example, if you select text in the document, you can choose Text ➪ Named Styles to display commands for working with styles. If you select a frame, choose Frame ➪ Named Styles to find the style commands.

Danger Zone

Applying a new style doesn't always work perfectly. For example, in some cases, if you apply to a frame a style that includes a watermark, and then apply a different style that doesn't include a watermark, Word Pro sometimes "forgets" to remove the watermark. In cases like this, you need to use the InfoBox to apply or remove a particular setting manually.

Creating Your Own Styles

When you hit on a combination of formatting settings that you find appealing, you can save those formatting settings as a style. Then, rather than remembering and selecting each individual setting, you can simply apply the style you created, saving a great deal of time and effort.

When you create a style, Word Pro saves it in the current document. You can save the style within the current division only, or save it so that you can apply it to an object in any division of the document. You can create styles for characters, paragraphs, entire pages, frames, headers, footers, frames holding captions, and so on. You can use the InfoBox for any displayed object to create a style you can apply to similar objects.

Note Styles save a good deal of time, but there may be instances when the style settings don't all work automatically when you apply the style to text or an object. For example, the style may not override manual formatting settings you've applied to text or a frame. In such cases, you can manually tweak the formatting that the style application didn't handle for you.

To create a style, you must first select the object that will serve as the example for the style, and then apply all the individual formatting settings that you intend to save as the style. For example, say you want to create a frame style that inserts a particular graphic in your document and formats the frame. Create the first frame and insert a graphic file into it, and then select the frame and display its InfoBox. Select the frame size and line or designer border, a color for the border, and any other settings you want in the InfoBox. Then click the Named Style tab. Click the Create Style button on that tab. The Create Style dialog box appears.

Type a name for your new style in the Style Name text box, and use the Description text box to store a lengthier label for the style. Figure 6-3 shows the name and description for a new frame style. Use the Style Type drop-down list to choose the type of style you're creating, if you're creating a style that applies to a text selection; you can choose to create either a Character style (applies font and attribute changes to the selected word or phrase only) or a Paragraph style. If you want to include the new style in all divisions of the current document, make sure the Create In All Divisions check box is checked.

Next, you need to determine what settings for the style Word Pro stores within the style definition itself, and what settings remain linked to the default or original style for the selected object. (All objects use a default style when you create them; or you can apply a style and then make changes to it to save steps in creating the new style.) When you leave style settings linked to the default or original style, changing those settings in the default or original style also changes them in the new style. So, if you want the new style to remain as independent as possible of other styles in the document, avoiding unexpected changes, click the Hierarchy button to display the Style Hierarchy Definition dialog box (see Figure 6-4).

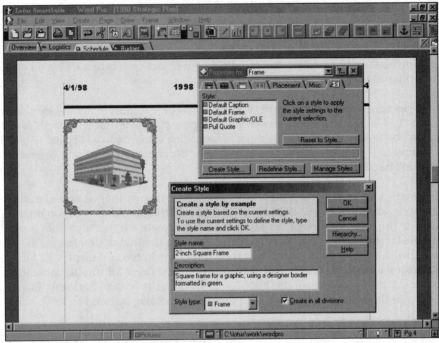

Figure 6-3: Enter a name and description for the new style in the Create Style dialog box.

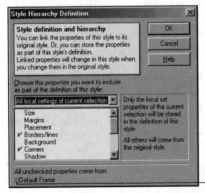

The default or original style
the new style is based on.

Figure 6-4: Check properties in the list to store them
with the definition for the new style you're creating.

First use the drop-down list above the list of styles to specify, generally, which
properties to store in the new style definition: All Properties, All Local Settings
of Current Selection (that is, the specific formatting selections you made in the
InfoBox), or Specific Properties (local settings plus others you select). After you
make a selection from the drop-down list, you can fine-tune the list of properties to
store with the style by clicking to check or uncheck properties in the scrolling list

below the drop-down list. Place a check beside any property to include in the style definition, or clear the check beside any property to link to the default or original style. Click OK to save your settings in the Style Hierarchy Definition dialog box, and OK again in the Create Style dialog box to finish creating the style. The new style then appears in the Style list of the Named Style tab of the InfoBox, so you can apply it to other selections. Be sure to save the document in order to save your new style.

You can save formatting changes to any style, a process called *redefining* the style. To redefine a style, first apply it to a selection, and then use the InfoBox for the selection to make the formatting changes for the style. Click the Named Style tab, and then click the Redefine Style button. The Redefine Style dialog box appears. Edit the description for the style in the Description text box. If you want the formatting changes for the style to apply in all divisions of the document, leave the Redefine in All Divisions check box checked. Further, you can control which properties Word Pro stores in the redefined style definition. To do so, click the Hierarchy button to display the Style Hierarchy Definition dialog box. Use it as described earlier for choosing which properties Word Pro saves with the style definition. Click OK to save your changes in the Style Hierarchy Definition dialog box, and OK again to save your changes to the style and close the Redefine Style dialog box. Then, save the open document in order to save your style changes.

Note   You can create a style for pages in the Page InfoBox, and then apply that page style to any division or section in the document. To apply a style to a division or section, click the division or section tab, and then click the Page Properties SmartIcon to display the Page InfoBox. Click the Named Style tab, and then click a new style for the division or section in the Style list, which displays available page styles.

Managing Styles in the Current File

Word Pro saves the styles you create in the current file. SmartMasters also contain styles, so that any document based on a SmartMaster uses the styles stored in that SmartMaster. To add styles to the document that's currently open, you can copy styles from another document or SmartMaster into the current document. In addition, you can rename a style, delete a style, or assign a function key (for applying the style) in the current document. You can use the Manage Styles button on the Named Style tab in any InfoBox of the document to manage styles. (Alternately, open the menu for the selected object, point to Named Styles, and choose Manage.) The Manage Styles dialog box that appears lists the styles in the document in the Style Name list. Click a specific style in that list to work with it. Use the following options to work with styles in a document in the Manage Styles dialog box:

✦ **Renaming a style.** Click a style in the Style Name list, and then click the Rename button. In the Rename Style dialog box that appears, edit the To and Description text box entries. If you want the new name and description to apply to all the divisions in the document, click the Rename This Style in All Divisions in This Document check box. Click OK to finish making the name change.

✦ **Deleting a style.** Click a style in the Style Name list, and then click the Delete button. If you want to delete the style from all divisions in the document, check the Delete This Style from All Divisions in This Document check box; to delete the style from the current division only, leave the check box unchecked. Then, click Yes to finish deleting the style.

✦ **Copying a style.** To copy a style from the current document or another document or SmartMaster file into the current document, click the Copy From button. Under the first step, choose the Current Document option button to copy a style from the current document. Or, leave the Another File option button selected, click the Browse button, and then use the Browse dialog box to select the Word Pro file or SmartMaster file that holds the style to copy. Under Select the Styles to Copy, click each style to copy by placing a check mark beside the style name (see Figure 6-5). Each name includes an icon, the name of the division that holds the style, and the style name. To add the selected style(s) to all divisions of the current document, check the Paste This Style in All Divisions in This Document check box. Click the Copy button to finish copying the selected style(s) into the current document.

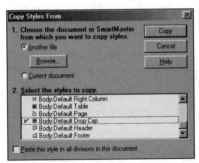

Figure 6-5: Click to check the name of each style to copy into the current document.

✦ **Selecting function keys to apply styles.** If you want to be able to press a particular function key to apply a particular style, click the Function Keys button in the Manage Styles dialog box to display the Function Key Setup dialog box. Use the drop-down list beside each function key (F2 through F12) to select a style; this tells Word Pro to apply the designated style to the current selection when you press the function key to which you've assigned the style. Click the OK button when you've finished assigning styles to particular function keys.

After you've made all the changes you want in the Manage Styles dialog box, click the Close button to finish making your changes to the style in the current document.

Choosing a New SmartMaster for a File or Section

While copying styles between files does enable you to re-use those styles, there's no need to copy every style from one document into another one. Choosing another SmartMaster with the styles you need provides a more efficient approach to updating all the styles in a document or section.

Danger Zone

Applying a new SmartMaster to a document changes the styles available in the document, but it doesn't change the contents or overall page design established by the first SmartMaster. Suppose you create a letter document using a SmartMaster that inserts your company name, address, and other contact information in a frame at the top of the letter, with a heavy line underscoring that information. It also may include Click Here blocks at particular points in the document. When you apply another letter SmartMaster, it leaves the company contact information frame, decorative line, and Click Here blocks in place. The new SmartMaster's styles do apply to the text, though, changing the look for most or all of the text.

To choose a new SmartMaster, first select the division to which you want to apply the SmartMaster. Choose File ➪ Choose Another SmartMaster. The Choose Another SmartMaster dialog box appears, offering two tabs. Its first tab, Change to Recently Used SmartMaster, lists SmartMasters you selected for documents you recently created. Click the SmartMaster you want in the list to see a preview of it at the right. If the SmartMaster you want isn't listed, click the Change to Any SmartMaster tab. In the Select a Type of SmartMaster list, choose a SmartMaster category to display SmartMasters of that type in the Select a Look list. Click a SmartMaster to see a preview of it at the right, as shown in Figure 6-6. If Word Pro doesn't list the SmartMaster you want on either tab, click the Browse for More Files button to find and select the SmartMaster you want.

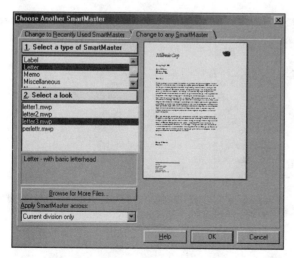

Figure 6-6: You can select a new SmartMaster from any of the SmartMaster categories.

After you select the SmartMaster you want, then use the Apply SmartMaster Across drop-down list (it appears on both tabs) to determine whether to apply the new SmartMaster to the Current Division Only, All Divisions at Same Level & Below, or the Entire Document. Click OK to finish applying the new SmartMaster.

Cueing a User with Click Here Blocks

You've seen how many SmartMasters include Click Here blocks that prompt you to insert text or a graphic at a particular location in a document. If you're creating a document that you intend to re-use often, share with others in your organization, or save as a SmartMaster (see "Saving and Editing SmartMasters" later in this chapter), you can include your own Click Here blocks. This section shows you how to add or edit a Click Here block.

Adding a Click Here Block

Word Pro offers a number of different types of Click Here blocks that you can add into a document. For example, you can create a Click Here block that prompts the user to insert a table, a symbol, or the date and time. You can even create a Click Here block that stores a list of options (called *keywords*), so the reader can just select the option to insert in the block. Use the following steps to insert a Click Here block in a document:

1. Create the text leading up to the Click Here block. To insert the Click Here block in a table cell or frame, create the table cell or frame and position the insertion point in it.

2. Choose Create ➪ Click Here Block. The Create Click Here Block dialog box appears (see Figure 6-7), with its Click Here Block tab displayed.

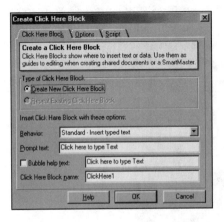

Figure 6-7: Use this dialog box to create and set up a Click Here block.

3. Under Type of Click Here Block, leave Create New Click Here Block selected. (If you instead choose Repeat Existing Click Here Block, you can then choose to copy another Click Here block that's already in the document; choose it from the Existing Blocks drop-down list that appears, make any needed changes in the rest of the dialog box, and then click OK.)

4. Under Insert Click Here Block with These Options, open the Behavior drop-down list and choose the action that you want the Click Here block to perform. For example, to create a basic Click Here block that prompts the user to enter text, choose Standard – Insert Typed Text. Choose Insert Table to create a Click Here Block that displays the Create Table dialog box. Choose Insert Glossary Text to create a Click Here block that displays the Glossary dialog box. If you want to create a Click Here block that displays a list of options (keywords) for the reader, such as a list of product ID numbers for an invoice, choose Display Keyword List.

5. If you chose Display Keyword List in Step 4, click the Keywords button to display the Design Keyword Format dialog box. In the Allowable Keywords list, enter each item that you want the user to be able to choose, pressing Enter after each item. Figure 6-8 shows an example list of products and ID numbers for a framing shop invoice document. If you want to give the user the flexibility to make an entry that's not on the list, check Allow Values Not in List. If you want the user to be able to choose more than one value from the list, check Allow Multi-Values. To sort the Allowable Keywords list entries (by the first word or number in each entry), click the Sort button. Click OK to finish the list and close the dialog box.

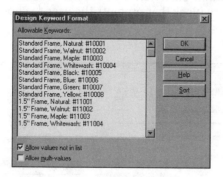

Figure 6-8: Create a list of keywords, so a Click Here block displays a list of options for the user.

6. In the Prompt Text text box, enter the text that you want the Click Here block to display before the user fills it in, such as **Click here to choose an item number**.

7. If the Bubble Help Text option is available, click its check box to enable Bubble Help for the Click Here block, and then enter the help text to display in the Bubble Help Text text box.

8. By default, Word Pro names each new Click Here block in the document using sequential numbering, as in ClickHere1, ClickHere2, and so on. If you want to specify a more unique name for your Click Here block, so you can use Go To to find it more quickly or clearly identify it if you want to repeat it elsewhere in the document (see Step 3), enter the name you want in the Click Here Block Name text box. For example, you could enter **Invoice Items** if your Click Here block displays a list of products and their ID numbers.

9. Click the Options tab in the dialog box. Under Navigation Behavior, specify an Order When Tabbing Between Blocks value to tell Word Pro how many times the user needs to press Tab to select the new Click Here block when the user is pressing Tab to move between blocks. If you want to enable the user to press Enter or Tab within the Click Here block, check Allow Tabs to Be Inserted as Data in This Block and Allow Returns to Be Inserted as Data in This Block. Under Advanced Properties, check the options you want to apply. Fill-In Required prevents the user from saving or exporting the document if the field isn't filled in. Select SmartCollect to have the Click Here block used with SmartCollect, which will automatically prompt users of the SmartMaster holding the Click Here block to enter data in any new document based on the SmartMaster. This feature can only be used with the Standard Click Here block. Skip Block When Tabbing tells Word Pro to skip the new block if the user is pressing Tab to move between Click Here blocks. Select the Notes/FX Field to enable the data in the Click Here block to be shared with Lotus Notes.

10. (Optional). Use the Script tab to add a script to the Click Here block. See "Adding a Script to a Click Here Block" later in this chapter to learn more.

11. Click OK. Word Pro inserts the new Click Here block in the document. Figure 6-9 shows an example Click Here block that prompts the user to choose an item number in an invoice.

Description	Quantity	Price	Amount
Click here to choose an item number			$0.00
			$0.00
			$0.00
			$0.00
			$0.00
		Subtotal	$0.00
		Shipping	$0.00
		Tax	0.00%
		TOTAL	$0.00

Figure 6-9: The "Click here to choose an item number" Click Here block prompts the user to fill in a table cell on an invoice.

To choose text formatting for the Click Here block and its entered contents, select the paragraph holding the Click Here block, and then choose a paragraph style from the status bar.

Copying and pasting an oft-used Click Here block can save time, but copying it without activating it can be a trick. To do this the easiest way, create a blank line in your document, then click at the beginning of the line and enter only two spaces with the spacebar. Position your insertion point between the spaces and create the Click Here block there. As soon as it is created, press the right arrow key one time to grab the space to the right of the Click Here block, and then press Shift+Home to highlight the Click Here block and grab the space before it as well. Click the Copy icon and you are ready to paste the Click Here block throughout your document, with a pre-made one space buffer zone on each side of it.

Using a Click Here block

As you learned in Chapter 3, "Creating and Working with Documents," in order to fill in a Click Here block, start by clicking the block prompt in the document. For a Click Here block that prompts you to enter text, the insertion point appears so you can begin typing. When you click another type of Click Here block, a dialog box appears to prompt you to create the object designated by the Click Here block. For example, if the behavior for the Click Here block is Insert Table, clicking the block displays the Create Table dialog box. Use the dialog box that appears to create the contents that fill in the Click Here block in the document. For a Click Here block designated to display a Keywords list, the Keywords list you created appears in the Select Keyword dialog box. Figure 6-10 shows items for an invoice in the Keywords list. You or the user can click an option in the Keywords list, or type a custom entry in the New Keyword text box, if it's available. Click OK to finish.

To deselect a Click Here block without filling it in, click the Cancel button in any dialog box that appears, and then click outside the Click Here block in the document.

Changing a Click Here Block

Because Click Here blocks offer a number of different options, you can change those options as your document requires. To edit a Click Here block, right-click it, then click Edit Click Here Block. The Click Here Block Properties dialog box appears. The options in this dialog box are identical to those in the Create Click Here Block dialog box shown in Figure 6-7. Make the changes you want, then click OK to close the dialog box.

To remove a Click Here block from the document, right-click the Click Here block, then click Delete Click Here Block in the shortcut menu.

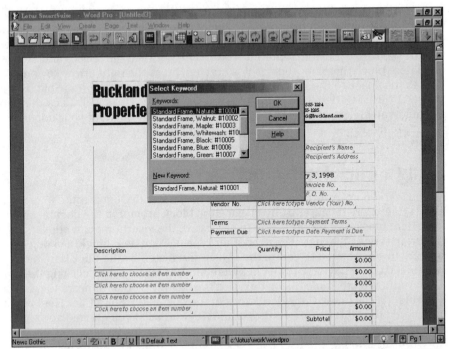

Figure 6-10: Many types of Click Here blocks prompt you to take an action; here, select or type a keyword to enter in the Click Here block location in the document.

Using Fields

Fields automatically display or capture information in a document. As with Click Here blocks, fields help automate a document, ensuring that the right information appears in the right location. This section covers the three types of fields you can include in a document.

Creating and Using Text Entry Fields

Text entry fields enable you to create familiar fill-in-the-blanks documents such as registration forms or order forms. You may have created such forms in the past by typing a label such as Name and then pressing the Shift+underscore key as many times as needed to create an underlined blank. If so, you're familiar with the drawbacks of this approach. It's hard to get all the blanks to line up evenly. And you can't fill in the blanks onscreen; typing either overtypes the underlining or pushes it to the right so you then must delete it.

Text entry fields in Word Pro overcome these two drawbacks. Each text entry field is actually a blank Click Here block within a small frame with a line under it. So, you can make your entries onscreen without disturbing the "blank" for it, and print a nice, neat form. Also, Word Pro makes it easy to size each text entry field "blank." Use the following steps to create and use text entry blanks in a document:

1. Choose Create ➪ Text Entry Field. The Text Entry Field bar appears.

2. Create the label or lead-in text for the text entry field in your document. Position the insertion point exactly where you want the "blank" to begin.

3. If you want the field to be a precise length, specify that length in the Field Width text box. Also choose a Line Style, Line Width, and Line Color from the drop-down lists of those names.

4. Click Create Field. Word Pro inserts the text entry field frame into the document.

5. Repeat Steps 2–4 to create as many other text entry fields as needed in your document.

6. To delete a text entry field, with the Text Entry Field bar still displayed, click the text entry field and then click Delete Field.

7. To size a text entry field to the full column width (a good technique to use to line up all the fields), click the field and then click to check the Maximize Field Length check box. The top two fields in Figure 6-11 have been maximized.

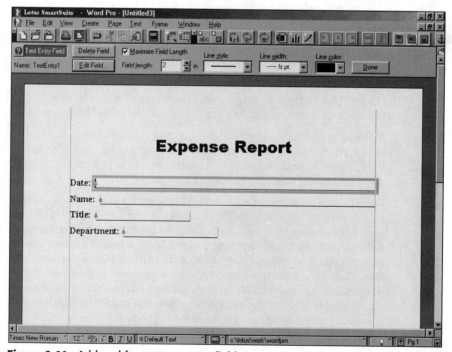

Figure 6-11: Add and format text entry fields to create neat forms that you can fill in onscreen.

8. To set up a Click Here block within a text entry field, click the field and then click Edit Field. The Click Here Block Properties dialog box appears. Choose the settings you want, then click OK.

9. Click Done to close the Text Entry Field bar and save the document.

10. To use a text entry field, click it. The insertion point appears within it. Type the information you want, and then click elsewhere in the document to finish.

Adding a Power Field or Document Field

Two other types of fields enter information automatically for the reader. *Power fields* gather and display information each time you open the document, such as the current date, the user name for the person opening the file, and so on. *Document fields* display statistics about the document, such as its size and the total editing time. For the most part, a power field or document field spares the user the trouble of entering information. These fields also ensure the accuracy and completeness of the document.

Use the following steps to insert a power field or document field in the document:

1. Click to position the insertion point at the location where you want to insert the field.

You can insert power fields and document fields within frames, table cells, or text entry fields.

2. Choose Text ➪ Insert Other ➪ Power/Doc. Field. The Document Fields dialog box appears.

3. Under Type of Field to Insert, click Document Field or Power Field. The rest of the options in the dialog box change, depending on the selected field type.

4. If you're inserting a document field, scroll through the list of Field Names to insert, then click to select the field you want to use. If you're inserting a power field, click the field to use in the Field Name list. The Instructions, Description, and Options for the field appear (see Figure 6-12).

5. For a power field, choose the look you want for the displayed field contents by clicking an option in the Options list. If you need to edit the field instructions (see the field Description to learn how the instructions for each field should read), edit the entry in the Instructions text box. If you want to prevent the field from updating once its contents are calculated, check Lock. If you want the field to update each time you open the document that holds it, check Auto Run. If the field appears in a document you will save as a SmartMaster, check Convert on New to tell Word Pro to update the field when the document is new, and then convert it to regular text. This latter option in essence creates a field that only calculates or gathers information once.

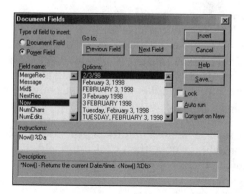

Figure 6-12: Insert a document field or power field using this dialog box.

6. Click Insert. Word Pro inserts the document field or power field into the document.

Really Powerful Power Fields

Some power fields perform calculations or display a dialog box so the user can make a selection. To set up such power fields, you have to edit the instructions for the selected field in the Document Fields dialog box. Look at the Description under the instructions to learn how to work with each field's instructions. While there isn't room in this book to describe all the power fields in Word Pro, here are a couple of cool examples:

✦ To display a dialog box that asks the reader a specific question or tells the reader how to fill in the field and includes a text box for making the field entry, use the Query$ power field. For example, click the Query$ field in the Field Name list and edit the Instructions to read **Query$("Make your request at least a week in advance")**. Enclosing text in quotation marks tells the field instructions to display that text either in the prompt or the result, depending on the nature of the field. Insert the field. When you the select or update the field, a dialog box that reads Make Your Request at Least a Week in Advance appears. Make your entry in the dialog box text box, and click OK to insert that entry into the field.

✦ To insert a bookmarked selection into another spot in the document, click the Bookmark field in the Field Name list, and then click the bookmark to insert from the Options list. Click Insert, and the new field displays the bookmark text.

✦ Use the Decide field to display a dialog box that asks the user to click Yes or No; the field then displays Yes or No depending on which button the user clicked. Select the Decide field in the Field Name list, and then edit the Instructions to read as follows: **IF decide("Choose Yes or No") "Yes" ELSE "No" ENDIF %Db**. Notice that this field requires a few special characters to finish the instructions. Click Insert to insert the field.

Editing and Saving a Power Field

By default, the field displays the information it gathers or calculates, not the instructions (formula) for the field. For example, the Now power field shown in Figure 6-12 displays the current date. To turn the field formula display on and off, choose View ➪ Show/Hide ➪ Power Field Formulas. Or, right-click any field and choose Show Power Field Formulas to display or subsequently hide the formulas.

To change how a power field works, you need to edit its instructions. To edit a power field, right-click the field or field formula, then click Edit Field. The Document Fields dialog box appears, displaying the selected field and its instructions. Edit the instructions as needed, then click Apply.

If you create a power field with relatively unique instructions and would like to use that power field again, you can save the field instructions under a new power field name. Display the Document Fields dialog box and choose Power Field as the Type of Field to Insert. Click the Field Name, then edit the instructions and choose an option as needed. Click Save. The Save Power Field dialog box appears. Enter a name for the field in the Field Name text box and a Description, as shown in Figure 6-13. Click OK. Word Pro adds the new power field name to the Field Name list in the Document Fields dialog box.

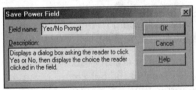

Figure 6-13: You can save a unique power field under a new name in order to re-use it later.

Note   When you create a power field, you can use it in all Word Pro documents. A document field you create is available only within the document for which you created it.

Creating a Document Field

You create document fields for the current file in another dialog box—the Document Properties dialog box. The "Setting Document Properties" section in Chapter 3, "Creating and Working with Word Pro Documents," explains how to create a document field, but here's a review. Choose File ➪ Document Properties ➪ Document. Click the Fields tab and click New. Enter the Field Name and the Contents the field will display when inserted into a document, and then click OK.

Updating or Removing a Power Field

To update a power field so it recalculates the information it displays or prompts you to make a new entry, right-click the field display or field formula and click Update Field. If needed, the field prompts you for entries. If you right-click a field and click Update All Fields, Word Pro updates the fields one by one, displaying dialog boxes to prompt you for input, if needed.

You can either remove a power field from the document or convert its contents to regular text. To remove a power field, right-click any power field and choose Show Power Field Formulas to display the formulas. Then, right-click the field you want to delete and choose Delete Field. To convert a power field to text, be sure to hide the field formulas by right-clicking any field and choosing Hide Power Field Formulas. Then right-click the field to convert and click Delete Field.

Using Scripts to Automate Tasks

A *script* stores a series of commands or actions you perform so that you can *play back* those actions at a later time. (Scripts were called *macros* in Ami Pro, Word Pro's predecessor. You can still run many of those old macros under Word Pro.) In essence, a script condenses multiple commands and selections into a single command. For example, you could create a script that opens the Print dialog box, selects a printer, selects a number of print options, and then prints the document. This section looks at the basic scripting skills you need in Word Pro.

Several helpful books that teach script writing are *LotusScript For Dummies* and *Teach Yourself LotusScript*, both available from IDG Books.

Recording and Running a Basic Script

Recording a script resembles turning a tape recorder on and off, and it is just about that easy. Everything you do in-between turning it on and turning it off appears in the script. A recorded script does not have to be saved, so save any changes to your document before recording, and close the document without saving to rid it of unwanted scripts. Or . . . experiment with recording scripts liberally, beginning with a plain test document.

Scripts can be stored in one of two file types: within a Word Pro document (.lwp) file or within an .lss script file. There are intricate reasons why you might select one type over the other, but for now, consider saving a script in an .lwp file when you want quick access to it while the file is open. Consider saving a script to an .lss file for easy script editing using a text editing program, as explained shortly.

Use one .lwp file as a tidy and easily accessible holding tank for many scripts. Open a blank document and create a script within it. Save and name the file as your main script file. When creating scripts in the future, choose to save them into another file, selecting the main script file's name as their storage spot. If scripts placed within this file are not machine-specific (that is, if the script doesn't access private drives or files), the script file can be shared across a network.

Saving a Script to a Word Pro .lwp File

The following steps create a sample script and save it into an .lwp file. Once saved, the sample script can be replayed to print out a document in duplicate. Use these same steps to create longer and more complex scripts:

1. Prepare for your recording session. For example, if you're creating a script that prints two copies of the current document, preparations include creating a short document (a paragraph long), saving it, and turning on your printer.

2. Choose Edit ➪ Script & Macros ➪ Record Script. The Record Script dialog box appears (see Figure 6-14).

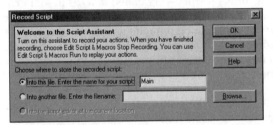

Figure 6-14: Before you record the script's steps, name the script and specify where to save it using this dialog box.

3. Select the current file or another .lwp document file to store the script by name:

   • To save the macro in the current file, leave the Into This File option button selected, then enter a name for the script in the text box beside that option button. For the example covered here, you could enter the script name: **Dotwo**.

   • (Optional) To save the script in another document file, click the Into Another File option button to select another file in which to store the script. Type the file path and name in the accompanying text box or click the Browse button to find the file and select it. The file and its path are placed in the text box. Position the insertion point to the immediate right of the file name and type in the script name. Separate it from the file name using only an exclamation point; for example: **c:\myfiles\myscript.lwp!Dotwo**. The exclamation point helps Word Pro keep track of a number of subs (scripts) placed in one file.

Danger Zone You can't include spaces in a script name. If you do, Word Pro won't use the script name you've entered, and instead saves the script under the default name, Main. If you need to separate words in a script name, use the underscore character.

4. Click OK. The status bar informs you that Recording... is in progress.

5. Perform the actions you want to record in your script. For the sample script that prints two copies of the document, you would select File ⇨ Print, enter 2 in the Number of Copies text box, and then click Print.

6. Choose Edit ⇨ Script & Macros ⇨ Stop Recording to turn off the recorder. The Script Editor window opens and displays the contents of the script Word Pro wrote. If you selected Into Another File in Step 3, the file you selected opens when the Script Editor does. Test the script. Select Script ⇨ Run Current Sub in the Script Editor or press the F5 key. If the script runs satisfactorily, continue with the next step. If not, choose File ⇨ Close in the Script Editor window, and begin recording again.

7. Choose File ⇨ Save Scripts in the Script Editor. A Save Scripts dialog box opens to tell you that saving the script also saves the document. That's what you want, so click OK.

8. Choose File ⇨ Close Script Editor in the Script Editor window to close that window and return to your document.

To play back and perform a script's steps after you have closed the Script Editor, choose Edit ⇨ Script & Macros ⇨ Run. The Run Script dialog box appears. If you stored the script in the current file, click Run Script Saved in the Current File, and then select the script you want to run from the drop-down list below it (see Figure 6-15). If the script is stored in another file, select the Run Script Saved in Another File option button, use the Browse button to select the file, and then enter an exclamation point and the script name after the file name. (Refer to Step 3 for an example of how this path, file, and !script name looks.) Click OK to run the script.

Figure 6-15: You can run a script you've saved in the current document or another document.

Script recording is very literal, because Word Pro records your exact selections. For example, say you want to record a script that hops from one division to the next. The insertion point is positioned in division two when you begin recording. You click on the division three tab, which is the next division. When you play back your script, if the insertion point is located in division one, instead of the script taking you to division two, it goes to what you literally selected while recording—division three. If you want to record a script that moves from one object to the next of its kind, don't record mouse clicks. Instead, record the use of the Go To feature.

Saving a Script to a Script Source .lss File

LotusScript source files have the .lss extension. They are basically a text file and so are easily edited using a text editor. Providing an easy means to learn and use script editing, they can also be used to hold complex or multiple scripts (subs). Follow these steps to create a sample script that types your name:

1. Open a plain document.

2. Click Edit ➪ Script & Macros ➪ Record Script. Make no entries in the Record Script dialog box, and click OK to begin recording.

3. Type your name into the document, then click Edit ➪ Script & Macros ➪ Stop Recording.

4. When the Script Editor opens after you record Step 3, the contents of the code window look something like this:

   Sub Main

   Type "YourFirstName YourLastName"

   End Sub

5. Using the editor menus, select File ➪ Export Script. When the Export Script dialog box opens, locate and select the Lotus\Wordpro\Scripts folder.

6. Select the File of Type Script Source (*.lss) and enter a script name in the File Name box. For this example you could enter **myname.lss**.

7. Click Save to save the file and close the Export Script dialog box.

You can run a script stored in an .lss file by selecting Edit ➪ Script & Macros ➪ Run. Choose Run Script Saved in Another File and then click the Browse button to open the Lotus Word Pro – Choose Script or 3.0 Macros dialog box. Select Script Source (*.lss) from the Files of Type drop-down list, and then locate and select the .lss file. Click Open to insert the path and file name of the .lss script in the Run Script Saved in Another File text box of the Run Script dialog box. Click OK to run the script.

The myname.lss file, or any other .lss file, can be easily attached to a custom SmartIcon and placed on one of your ever-present SmartIcon bars. Clicking the SmartIcon runs the attached script. See "Creating a Custom SmartIcon with a Script" in Chapter 28 to learn how to customize a SmartIcon with an attached script and place it on a SmartIcon bar.

You can easily edit an .lss script in a text editor like Notepad. If you want, the myname.lss file could be opened and edited to type other names. For example, edit

> Type "YourFirstName YourLastName"

to read

> Type "Benjamin Franklin"

or

> Type "William H. Harrison"

Once edited, save the file as a text file using another name with the .lss extension and place it in either the Lotus\Wordpro\Scripts folder or another where it can be easily found and selected. Edited .lss files can be shared across a network unless they refer to specific file or directory names or other items not available to other network users.

Adding a Script to a Click Here Block

You can add a script that runs automatically when you use a particular Click Here block. For example, you can create a script that runs when you first click the Click Here block (Enterclickhere) or after you finish using the Click Here block (Exitclickhere). For example, if the Click Here block appears in a table cell, you can create a script that changes the background color of that table cell after you finish filling in the Click Here block (Exitclickhere). The fastest way to add a basic script for a Click Here block is to record it, as follows:

1. Right-click the Click Here block, then click Edit Click Here Block.

2. Click the Script tab, and then click the Script button on that tab. The Script Editor opens.

3. Select the subroutine (Enterclickhere, Exitclickhere, Initialize, or Terminate) into which you want to record the script from the Script drop-down list near the upper-right corner of the Script Editor window. For example, choose Exitclickhere to record a script that executes after you fill in the Click Here block and press Tab or an arrow key, to move out of the block.

4. The insertion point appears before the Sub line in the code window for the script. Choose Script ➪ Record at Cursor from the Script Editor menu to begin recording.

5. Perform the actions you want to record in Word Pro.

6. Choose Edit ⇨ Script & Macros ⇨ Stop Recording from the Word Pro menu to finish recording the script. The recorded script code commands appear in the Script Editor window (see Figure 6-16).

Recorded script.

The Sub line that starts the script.

Choose the subroutine.

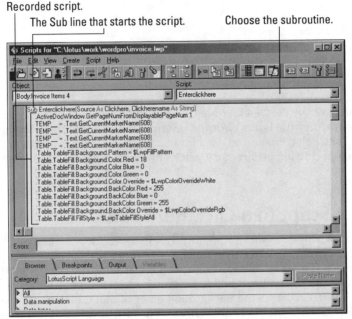

Figure 6-16: The script recorded for a Click Here block appears in the Script Editor.

7. Choose File ⇨ Save Scripts. At the dialog box that tells you that saving the script also saves the document, click OK.

8. Choose File ⇨ Close Script Editor in the Script Editor window to close that window and return to your document.

Then, you can use the Click Here block to run the script you recorded for it.

Setting a Startup Script

Save steps by creating a script that is run automatically when you open Word Pro. A startup script is useful when you find yourself performing the same tasks on a daily basis. For example, perhaps each day's work starts by creating a new memo and fax, followed by logging your work into a diary document. Instead of opening the memo and fax SmartMasters and your diary document daily, let Word Pro do it for you when it opens, by creating the example startup script described next.

1. Close all documents in Word Pro, then select File ➪ New and create a plain document. Next, create the script that will start each time you open Word Pro. Follow Steps 1–4 in this chapter under "Saving a Script to a Word Pro .lwp File," selecting your script to be saved Into This File in Step 3. When you get to Step 5 in which you perform actions, record the three actions you want to occur on startup: two instances of opening a SmartMaster (first one, then the other, and leave the documents open onscreen after opening them), and one instance of opening a file. Continue with Steps 6 and 7. In Step 7, save your script with a name you'll remember and into a folder location that stays static; Word Pro will look for the script file there each time it opens. Finish with Step 8 and then follow these steps to set up the startup script: Select Edit ➪ Scripts & Macros ➪ Set Startup Scripts to open the Startup Scripts dialog box.

2. Click the Browse button to view the Lotus Word Pro – Choose Script or Macro 3.0 dialog box. Locate and select the script file you just saved. Click Open to finish selecting the script and insert the path name and file of your script into the Scripts to Run on Startup of Word Pro list.

3. Click OK to close this dialog box and test the script. Close Word Pro and reopen it. Once it is open, select Window from the Word Pro menus to see your opened documents listed.

Your fax and memo documents list as Untitled 1 and Untitled 2; your daily log file lists by name. Select whichever of these documents you want to work in first, by selecting it from this menu. Save your documents and work with them as you always do. When you want to work with another of these documents, again select the Window menu item and make your selection.

Saving and Editing SmartMasters

Once you've added all the automatic features you want to a document, you can save that document as a SmartMaster, so you and your colleagues can use the SmartMaster to create new documents. When you save a document as a SmartMaster, the SmartMaster contains all the styles, contents (frames, graphics, fields, tables, and so on), and scripts you created in the original document. Follow these steps to save a file as a SmartMaster:

1. Create or open the file that holds the features and contents to save as a SmartMaster, then choose File ➪ Save As. The Save As dialog box appears.

2. Choose Lotus Word Pro SmartMaster (*.MWP) from the Save As Type drop-down list.

3. Navigate to the drive and folder in which you'd like to store the SmartMaster file. If you want to store it in the same folder as the SmartMasters that come with Word Pro, choose the \lotus\smasters\wordpro folder. Doing this will make the SmartMaster available from the selections available when you select File ➪ New and click the Create from Any SmartMaster tab.

4. Enter a name for the SmartMaster in the File Name text box.

5. Click Save. The Save As SmartMaster Options dialog box appears (see Figure 6-17).

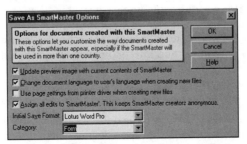

Figure 6-17: Use the options here to select how the SmartMaster should behave when someone uses it to create a new document.

6. Select the options for the SmartMaster:

- **Update Preview Image with Current Contents of SmartMaster.** Use this option when you want the preview of the SmartMaster you're saving updated. If selected, when you choose File ➪ New, the preview of this SmartMaster will show in its updated form in this panel's view.

- **Change Document Language to User's Language When Creating New Files.** This switches the document's language to that selected in the Control Panel of the SmartMaster user's window. If not selected, the language used in this SmartMaster will be the one it was created in.

- **Use Page Settings from the Printer When Creating New Files.** Check this option to have the SmartMaster adapt new files based on it to use the default page settings for the printer currently selected under Windows.

- **Assign All Edits to "SmartMaster."** Tells Word Pro not to identify you as the creator of the SmartMaster.

- **Initial Save Format.** Tells Word Pro what format to use the first time you save a new file created from the SmartMaster.

- **Category.** Tells Word Pro what type of SmartMaster you've created.

7. Click OK. Word Pro saves the SmartMaster. The document you based the SmartMaster on stays open. You can save it as a regular document and close it.

To edit a SmartMaster, choose File ➪ Open. In the Open dialog box, choose All Files or Lotus Word Pro SmartMaster (*.MWP) from the Files of Type drop-down list. Navigate to the disk and folder holding the SmartMaster file, then double-click the file name. Make the changes you want in the SmartMaster, then choose File ➪ Save As. Choose Lotus Word Pro SmartMaster (*.MWP) from the Save as Type drop-down list, and make sure the File Name text box entry is the same as the SmartMaster's original file name. Click Save. A dialog box informs you that a file with the specified name already exists. Click Yes to overwrite the existing file. The Save As SmartMaster Options dialog box appears. Choose options in the dialog box as described under Step 6, and then click OK. Word Pro closes the SmartMaster itself, but displays a document based on the SmartMaster.

Adjusting Word Pro's Preferences

Customizing some of Word Pro's general preferences can make your word processing more convenient. You can change such settings as those Word Pro uses to find files (such as your SmartMasters), insert information about you into power fields, or perform routine document operations.

To set Word Pro preferences, choose File ➪ User Setup ➪ Word Pro Preferences. The Word Pro Preferences dialog box appears (see Figure 6-18).

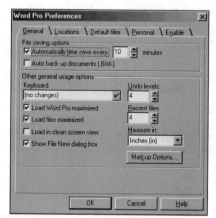

Figure 6-18: Preferences help Word Pro operate more smoothly and track information about you.

Here's what you can control with each Word Pro Preferences tab:

✦ **General.** Under File Saving Options, you can check either check box to have Word Pro Automatically Time Save Every (X) Minutes to save your file for you so you don't lose work, or Auto Back Up Documents, which means that Word Pro creates a copy of your file with the .BAK extension each time you save. Use the Keyboard drop-down list to specify how Word Pro treats the keyboard layout; click any option on the list that applies. The four check boxes below the Keyboard drop-down list enable you to tell Word Pro what size it should use for loading its window and file windows, and whether to show Clean Screen or the New File dialog box on loading. Use the Undo Levels text box to designate how many preceding operations you can undo. The Recent Files setting controls how many file names appear on the File menu. Measure In sets the default measurement unit in all documents. Click Markup Options to display a dialog box that lets you choose colors, and so on, if you choose to mark up edits in a document.

✦ **Locations.** Use the text boxes on this tab to tell Word Pro which disk and folder to use as the default location for saving Documents, SmartMasters, User Dictionaries, and other types of files.

✦ **Default Files.** Use the text boxes on this tab to choose default files Word Pro should use for plain documents (a SmartMaster), the user dictionary, the default glossary, and more.

✦ **Personal.** Fill in the text boxes with the requested information, such as your Title and Company. Word Pro stores this information, and you can insert the information into documents via power fields. So, if you change your User Name (because you got married, for example) all documents that use a power field to display your user name will update automatically to use the correct name.

✦ **Disable.** Use this tab to turn various Word Pro features on and off, depending on which features you really need and how efficient your computer is. If your computer operates too slowly, disabling more features may help. In either the General Usage or Performance lists, click to place a check beside any feature you want to turn on (enable) or click to clear the check beside any feature you want to turn off (disable).

✦   ✦   ✦

Merging, Importing, and Exporting Information

Computers save tremendous amounts of time by enabling you to reuse information. This started with the concept of saving and copying files, and has evolved into capabilities that enable you to share information between files and even different programs. This chapter covers some of the most useful features that enable you to reuse and integrate different types of information: *merging*, *importing*, and *exporting*. Merging enables you to insert information from an address list (or other list of information) into a boilerplate document to create individualized copies of the document. Importing enables you to open files from other applications to use their contents in Word Pro. Exporting, the opposite of importing, saves a Word Pro document so that its contents can be opened and edited in another application.

Adding an Envelope to a Document

Most documents you create only need to be distributed to one or two individuals, so before you read about using merging to create large mailings, learn here how to create envelopes one at a time.

When you create an individual envelope, Word Pro inserts it into the current document, in a new division named *Envelope* by default. In a new, blank document, the envelope division becomes the only division. If the current document includes an address that looks like a recipient address, Word Pro automatically suggests that address as the Send To (recipient) address.

Follow these steps to create and print an envelope for a document:

1. Open or create the file that you want to hold the envelope. This document does not have to be a letter. If you've previously saved one or more envelopes in the document, make sure the insertion point is in a division that's *not* an envelope division.

2. Choose Create ⇨ Envelope. Word Pro creates the Envelope division and displays the Envelope bar (see Figure 7-1). If you inserted the envelope into a document with text that Word Pro guesses is the recipient's address (called the Send To address), that address appears in the frame for the Send To address on the envelope, as shown in Figure 7-1.

New envelope division.   Send To address frame.   SmartIcons for frames on the Text

Envelope bar.   Return address frame.   in Frame SmartIcon bar.

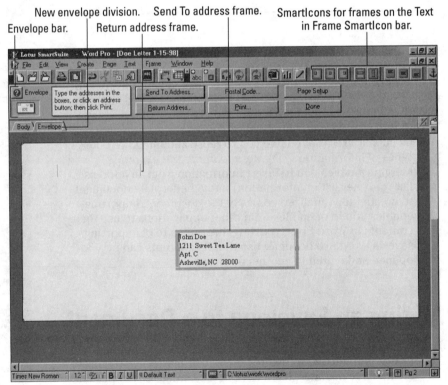

Figure 7-1: The Create ⇨ Envelope command does most of the work. It sets up the envelope and adds frames to hold the Send To address and Return address.

3. You can use one of two methods to enter or edit the Send To address:

   • Click in the frame and type or edit the entry.

- Click Send To Address on the Envelope bar. The Send Address dialog box appears (see Figure 7-2). Type or edit the address in the Current Send Addresses text box, then click Add to List to add it to the list of Available Send Addresses. (This drop-down list actually displays Word Pro's list of commonly used addresses that you can use for recipient and return addresses.) If you previously saved the needed recipient address, select it from the Available Send Addresses drop-down list. In addition, to add a postal bar code that aids the postal service in delivering your letter, check the Envelope Bar Code check box. Click OK when you've finished specifying the Send To address.

Figure 7-2: Use this dialog box to enter and save a recipient address.

Note

To delete or update an address from Word Pro's behind-the-scenes list using the Send Address or Return Address dialog box, select the address from the drop-down list at the top of the dialog box. To delete the address, click the Delete from List button. To change the saved address, edit it in the text box at the center of the dialog box, then click Update List. To save the selected address to a Lotus Notes database, click Notes Data.

4. You can use one of two methods to enter or edit the return address:

- Click in the frame and type or edit the entry.

- Click Return Address on the Envelope bar. The Return Address Dialog box appears; it looks and works like the Send Address dialog box in Figure 7-2. Type or edit the address in the Current Return Address text box, then click Add to List to add it to the list of Available Return Addresses. If you previously saved the needed return address, select it from the Available Return Addresses drop-down list. If you don't want to print a return address, instead check the No Return Address check box. Click OK when you've finished specifying the return address.

5. (Optional) Click Page Setup to display the Properties InfoBox for the envelope division. You can change property settings such as margins to make sure the envelope prints correctly.

6. Perform any other formatting you like. You may need to adjust the frame for either the Send To or return address, making it wider so the address displays without unwanted line wraps. You can change the formatting of the Send To and return addresses. Both of these use the Default Text style for the document by default. You also can insert a graphic such as a company logo on the envelope, or create a frame that holds a watermark reading *Final Notice* or *Confidential*. Just remember not to obscure the Send To address. Figure 7-3 shows an envelope with some of the property settings mentioned in this step and the last.

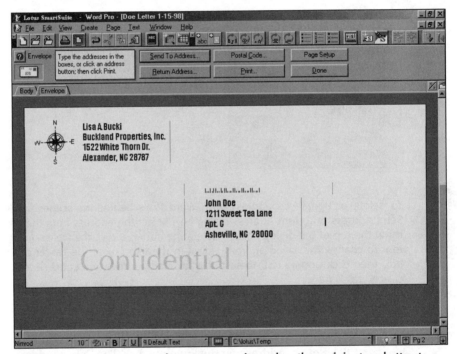

Figure 7-3: Format your envelope to ensure it reaches the recipient and attracts attention.

7. If you forgot to add an envelope bar code but need one, click Postal Code to display the Bar Codes dialog box. If you're working in a language other than U.S. English, choose the bar code type from the Bar Codes drop-down list. Click OK.

8. Prepare your printer to print an envelope, then click Print. The Print dialog box appears. Its default settings will do for most printouts, but you can change the Number of Copies setting to print extras. Click Print to close the Print dialog box and send the envelope to the printer.

9. Click Done to close the Envelope bar.

10. Save the document file that holds the envelope. You then can open that document, select the Envelope division, and print the envelope whenever you need a copy. Note that you may need to consult your printer manual to verify how to feed envelopes and to find out if your printer requires any other special steps for envelope printing.

Try This if Your Envelopes Don't Print

Some printers work more effectively at printing envelopes than others. When your printer and Word Pro don't see eye-to-eye, the text may print too low on the envelope, the return address may get cut off at the left, or the envelope might not print at all. Try the following techniques to resolve the problem, or to figure out how to print an irregularly sized envelope:

✦ Cut some scrap paper to the size of the envelope to use for test prints. You don't want to waste preprinted company or personal envelopes.

✦ Make notes about the changes that work, so you can make the same changes the next time you add an envelope to a document.

✦ Try rotating the envelope in the feeder for the printer. For some printers, you might have to flip the envelope in the opposite direction, with the flap toward the right instead of left or vice versa because the printer driver (the file in Windows that runs the printer) transposes the printout.

✦ Click Page Setup on the Envelope bar, then increase the size of the left margin (or other margin where envelope text runs off the page). Then either drag the address frame(s) within the new margins, or click the frame to realign and then click one of the SmartIcons for frames on the Text in a Frame SmartIcon bar that appears anytime the Envelope bar displays.

✦ If the margins seem OK, but the position is off for either address, drag its frame to a better position.

✦ Click Page Setup on the Envelope bar, and experiment with different page sizes. By default, Word Pro creates a standard #10 business envelope, which it calls the Env Comm10 4⅛ × 9½ inch size, or something similar, depending on the printer you're using. If you're printing an envelope that's an irregular size (such as those for note cards), create a custom page size that matches the size of the envelope.

✦ The last-ditch option is to install a driver for a similar printer, perhaps a model that's slightly different from yours but from the same manufacturer, and select that printer in Windows before you create the envelope. Look for a model that uses the same toner or ink cartridges as yours (check out a catalog that sells cartridges). Such a printer's printer driver may work with your printer, because they probably use similar internal hardware. Believe it or not, my old Apple Personal LaserWriter NTR prints envelopes better when I install and select the driver for the HP LaserJet IIIP PostScript+, a model that uses the same toner cartridge as my Apple. To learn more about installing and selecting printer drivers, consult online Help in Windows.

After you've saved an envelope in a document, you can redisplay the Envelope bar at any time to adjust or print the envelope. To do so, go to the division for the envelope to change by clicking its division tab. Click the icon at the top of the vertical scroll bar to display the division tabs first, if needed. When you've selected the correct division, choose Create ⇨ Envelope to redisplay the Envelope bar. Do what you will with the envelope, but make sure you save any changes.

Danger Zone

Word Pro gives the same name — Envelope — to the division for each envelope you insert. If you add more than one envelope to a document file, you should give each envelope division a new, unique name. To change a division name, double-click the division tab, edit the division name, and press Enter.

An Overview of Merging

Most people receive enough junk mail to have seen an example of *merging* — a letter that appears to be a form letter, but has your name and address at the top and in the text. Does something like this look familiar?

> ***Lisa Bucki of 1234 Main Street, Bucklawn, OH, you're our $1,000,000 winner!***

While you may be a bit annoyed to be on the receiving end of one of these gems, Word Pro's merging capabilities can be a boon for you if you use it tastefully. You can use merging to send personalized letters to a mailing list of prospective or existing customers. For example, if your boss tells you to mail a letter about a rate change to 100 customers and you have to finish the task today, you likely won't finish the job unless you use merging. (And who wants to spend a whole day manually changing addresses and printing 100 letters, anyway?)

The merge process involves the following steps:

1. Create or select the *merge data file*, which holds the individualized information to merge, such as names and addresses. Each individual set of information, like the full name and address for one recipient, is called a *record*. Each individual item of information within a record, such as the last name, is a *field*. The data source file must divide information into records and fields (more on this shortly), or else merge won't be able to work with the data.

2. Create the *merge document*, which holds the boilerplate text that's repeated in each copy of the document resulting from the merge. Also insert the *merge field* codes in the merge document. Each merge field code corresponds to a field in the data file. For example, if your merge data file contains a Title field, the Title entry from each record appears where you insert the <TITLE> merge field code in the merge document.

3. Set *conditions* to control how many of the records Word Pro actually merges into individual new documents, then merge the data file with the merge document. You can send each merged copy directly to the printer, or double-check each merged copy and then print it.

Urge to Merge

Exploit merging as much as you can, whether you're using SmartSuite in business or personally. Creative business uses for merging include name tags for seminars or large meetings, customized rate sheets for clients, envelopes (or clear address labels) for holiday cards, small quantities of business cards, floppy disk labels, and so on. In the home, you can merge to create placecards for parties, holiday card envelopes, invitation envelopes (don't laugh; one of us merged our wedding invitations using a font that matched the invitation text), PTA or club mailings, postcards announcing a change of address, return address labels, and the like.

Just keep in mind that it might take a bit of experimentation on your part to set up a document to print on mailing labels or perforated sheets for business or note cards, for example. Despite the work, the results can be attractive and much less expensive than going to a quick-print shop. Remember, you can apply attractive formatting to the merged information, insert graphics, and so on, to jazz up the result.

The Mail Merge Assistant walks you through the process of merging a letter, envelopes, or mailing labels. Before discussing how to perform each of those types of merges, however, let's look at how to prepare the merge data file—perhaps the most complicated and time-consuming aspect of merging.

Working with Data Sources

You can display the Mail Merge Assistant dialog box at any time. To do so, choose Text ⇨ Merge ⇨ Letter or Text ⇨ Merge ⇨ Envelope. Figure 7-4 shows the Mail Merge Assistant dialog box for merging a letter.

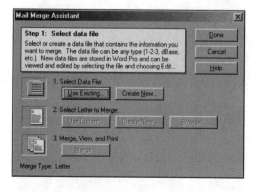

Figure 7-4: The Mail Merge Assistant walks you through the merge steps. First you must select or create the merge data file.

The first step in the merge process is to select or create the merge data file. Each of these actions requires a bit of detailed discussion, provided next.

Merging Data Files from Other Sources

You can use a file from a number of different applications as the merge data file for a Word Pro mail merge. The merge data file needs to organize the information in records and fields, so that Word Pro can recognize each piece of information and insert it in the proper place in the merge document.

Some applications, such as Lotus Organizer, organize data in records and fields by default. In other applications, such as word processors and spreadsheet programs, you have to set up the data in a special way to use it for a merge. For example, in a word processor, you have to include field names on the top row of a file (usually), and then enter each record on a single line. You must separate all fields and records consistently by typing a delimiter between them. A *delimiter* is a keypress or character such as a Tab or comma. In a spreadsheet program, the data must reside in a database table, with the top row holding the field names and each subsequent row holding a single record. The database table must start on row 1 of the worksheet; inserting a title or other text before the database table prevents Mail Merge Assistant from recognizing the merge data. Figure 7-5 shows a database table in 1-2-3.

Field names appear in the top row.

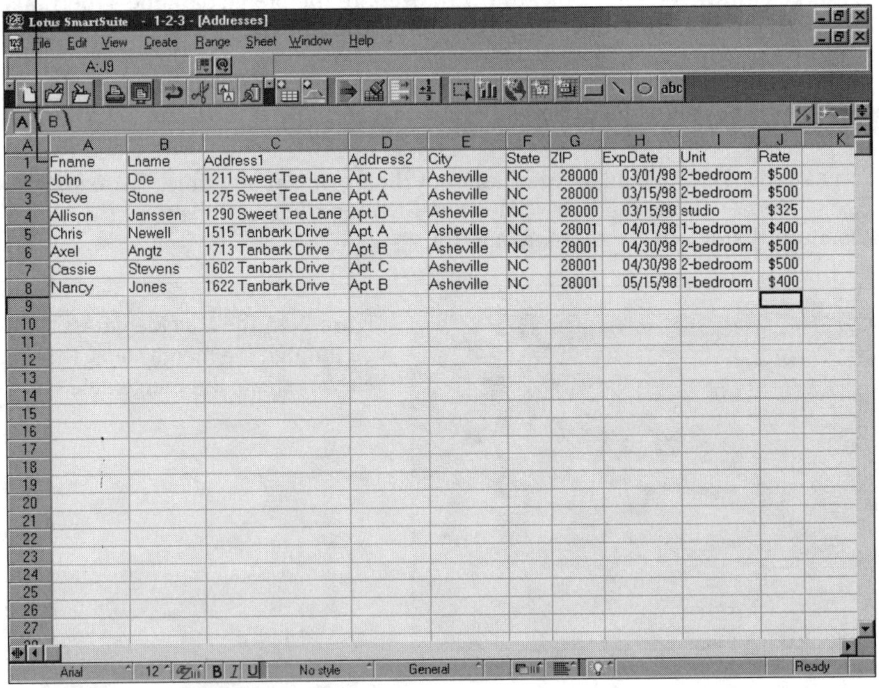

Figure 7-5: You merge information from a 1-2-3 database table, like this partial list of tenants, into a Word Pro document.

When you click the Use Existing button under Select Data File in the Mail Merge Assistant dialog box, the Browse dialog box appears. Use the Files of Type drop-down list to select the type of file to import; you'll find more than 50 options in this list, which appears in Figure 7-6. (Scroll through the Files of Type drop-down list to review the formats you can use for merge data files.) Then, use the Look In list to navigate to the disk and folder that holds the file with the merge data. When you see the file, select it and then choose Open.

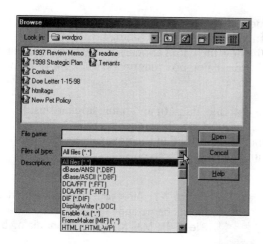

Figure 7-6: The Files of Type drop-down list shows you which kinds of files you can use as a merge data file.

If Mail Merge Assistant doesn't immediately recognize the file type for the selected file, it displays the File Type dialog box; select the type to use in the Please Choose the Type list, then click OK. After you select the merge file to use, Mail Merge Assistant operates as described in the following paragraphs.

Depending on the type of file you selected, the Mail Merge Assistant may display an additional dialog box. For example, if you're using a 1-2-3 file, the 1-2-3 Choose Range dialog box appears. Use its options to specify whether you want to merge the Entire File, a selected Worksheet, or a selected Range; if you choose Worksheet or Range, use the combo text/drop-down list below the option button to type or select the worksheet or range to use. Then click OK.

Danger Zone

In order for the Mail Merge Assistant to be able to use a file of a particular type, the filter for importing and exporting that type of file must be installed in Word Pro. For example, you can use Lotus Organizer files as merge data files; but the filter for Organizer files doesn't install with a quick or automatic install. If your Word Pro installation doesn't have the filter it needs to use the type of file you've selected, a message box appears to tell you that you must install the filter. Click OK to close the message box. Then, close Word Pro and any other open SmartSuite application, and perform a Custom install as described in Appendix A, "Installing SmartSuite," to install the filter. You can find different tabs of filters in the Customize dialog box for Word Pro in the Lotus Install program.

For many file types, the Mail Merge Assistant subsequently displays the Merge Data File Fields dialog box. You use the two option buttons in this dialog box to specify where the merge field names are located: either in the first record (row) of the data file or in a separate description file that you can select using the accompanying Browse button. If the merge data file doesn't contain field names and there isn't a description file, click the Create New Description file button. In the Create Data File dialog box that appears, include each field name by typing its name in the Field Name text box or selecting it from the Commonly Used Fields list, then clicking Add.

After you've added all the field names, click OK, and then Yes in the dialog box that asks whether you want to save changes. In the Save As dialog box that appears, enter a File Name and click Save. The new file name appears in the Description File text box when the Merge Data File Fields dialog box reappears. Click OK to finish making your choices in the dialog box.

After you've successfully selected a data file, its path and name appear beside Select Data File in the Mail Merge Assistant dialog box (see Figure 7-7). You can then complete the rest of the merge steps, as described in the next three sections that cover merging letters, envelopes, and labels, respectively.

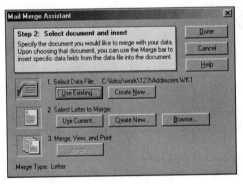

Figure 7-7: After you select a merge data file, its name appears beside Select Data File in the Mail Merge Assistant dialog box.

If you want the records in a merge data file to appear in a particular order, sort those records in the source application and save the data file before you choose it in the Mail Merge Assistant dialog box.

Word Pro Merge Data Files

Mail Merge Assistant also can work with merge data files created in Word Pro itself, for those of you who prefer to work in a single application. You can use an existing Word Pro file that contains the data in the right format, or create a new data file using the Mail Merge Assistant.

To use an existing Word Pro file as a merge data file, the file must hold the data in a Word Pro table. (Chapter 5, "Organizing and Highlighting Information," explains how to create tables.) The table should include the field names in the first row and each record in a single row. In addition, the table must appear alone in the document and must appear at the very top of the document, as shown in Figure 7-8; inserting a title or other text before the table prevents Mail Merge Assistant from recognizing the merge data in the table. Save and close the Word Pro file that holds the database. Display the Mail Merge Assistant (Text ⇨ Merge ⇨ Letter or Text ⇨ Merge ⇨ Envelope) and use the Use Existing button under Select Data File to select the Word Pro merge data file, using the process described earlier for selecting data files of other types.

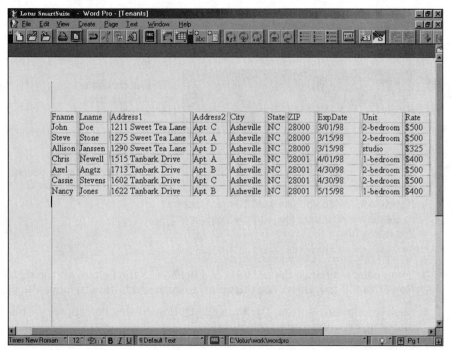

Figure 7-8: In a Word Pro merge data file, place the field names in the first row of the table and position the table at the top of the first page (but not in the header area).

Alternately, you can use the Mail Merge Assistant to create a Word Pro file holding merge data. This process enters each record as delimited text, and has a couple of drawbacks. First, you may not be able to use the delimited text for other purposes, unlike data stored in a Word Pro table, a more readable format. Second, using this method to create the data file can take more time than using another application, especially if you're entering a long list of names. On the other hand, you may want to use Mail Merge Assistant to create the merge data file if you're only merging a few records or are merging data you may not reuse frequently.

Use the following steps to use the Mail Merge Assistant to create a delimited Word Pro merge data file:

1. Choose the Create New button under Select Data File in the Mail Merge Assistant dialog box. The Create Data File dialog box appears.

2. To create each field name, either click the field name you want in the Commonly Used Fields list or type it in the Field Name text box, then click the Add button. Figure 7-9 shows several fields already added using this technique.

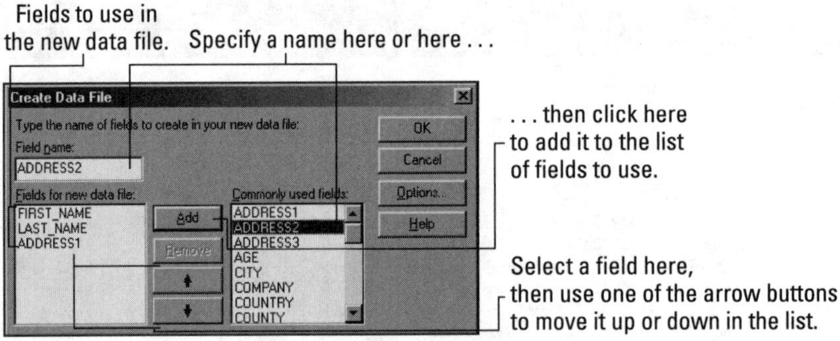

Figure 7-9: When you use Mail Merge Assistant to create a merge data file, add the fields using this dialog box.

3. If you need to change the position of a field, click the field in the Fields for New Data File list, then click the up or down arrow button to move the field.

4. Click the Options button. The Data File Options dialog box appears. This dialog box enables you to select the delimiter characters to use — one to separate fields and one to separate records.

5. By default, the data file will use the tilde (~) to separate files, and the pipe symbol (|) to separate records. Use the Field Delimiter and Record Delimiter drop-down lists to specify alternate delimiters, if needed, then click OK.

6. Click OK again to close the Create Data File dialog box. The Edit Data File dialog box appears. You use this dialog box to enter the records for the data file.

7. To enter each record, fill in the field text boxes (see Figure 7-10), then click Add Record. The dialog box displays a tab for each added record, with the first field's contents appearing on the tab.

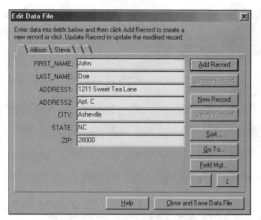

Figure 7-10: After you identify the field names, just fill in the blanks and click Add Record to create each record.

If you want each tab to display the contents of another field or to add or remove fields, click Field Mgt, make the field changes you want, and click OK.

8. To edit or delete any record, select the record by clicking its tab. If the tab isn't visible because it scrolled offscreen as you added records, use one of the arrow buttons below the Field Mgt button to redisplay it or click Go To. In the Go To Record dialog box, you can choose First Record or Last Record to go to one of those records in the list. Or, click Specific Record, choose a field name from the drop-down list, and type the contents in that field for the record you want to display. Click OK to go to the specified record. Then, make changes to the displayed record and click Update Record, or click Delete Record to remove the record from the merge data list.

9. When an existing record is selected, click New Record to display a blank tab and add a new record.

10. If you entered the records in no particular order and want to sort them according to the contents of one of the fields, click Sort. In the Sort Records dialog box that appears, choose Sort by Field. Then, choose a Sort Type (Alphanumeric or Numeric) or Sort Order (Ascending or Descending). Click OK to finish the sort.

11. After you've made all the needed entries and changes to the data file, click Close and Save Data File. A dialog box asks you whether to save changes to the current data file. Click Yes. In the Save As dialog box that appears, specify a File Name and folder to save the data file to, then click Save.

After you save the data file, its name appears in the Mail Merge Assistant dialog box beside Select Data File (see Figure 7-11). Notice that the dialog box contains an extra button, Edit, beneath the merge data file name (refer back to Figure 7-7 for comparison). You can click this button any time during the merge process to redisplay the Edit Data File dialog box and make changes to the data file.

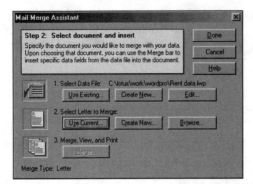

Figure 7-11: The new data file appears in the Mail Merge Assistant dialog box, so you can finish the merge.

Merging Letters or Other Documents

Now that you've explored all your options for setting up or creating a merge data file, it's time to zoom back out to the big picture of completing the merge. Use the following steps to create a merge document such as a letter, merge the merge data file records, and print the merged documents:

1. Open an existing document into which you want to merge information, or create a new document. For example, you can create a new document using a letter SmartMaster. (Or, you can wait to create a new document or open another document as instructed in Step 4.)

2. Choose Text ⇨ Merge ⇨ Letter. The Mail Merge Assistant dialog box appears.

3. Select or create the merge data file. If needed, refer back to the section "Working with Data Sources" for details.

4. The next step is to tell the Mail Merge Assistant which document to use as the merge document—the file holding the boilerplate text that will appear in all the merge documents and the codes that identify where the fields from each record will be inserted. Use one of the buttons under Select Letter to Merge to do so:

   • **Use Current.** Enables you to begin inserting the merge fields and working with the text in the document you created or opened in Step 1.

   • **Create New.** Displays the Browse dialog box so you can select a SmartMaster to use to create a new file, into which you can then begin to insert merge fields and text.

   • **Browse.** Displays the Browse dialog box so you can select an existing file to open, if you've previously created one that holds the boilerplate text you want to merge information into. You can then insert the merge fields.

5. After you select the merge document, the Mail Merge Assistant dialog box closes, and the Merge bar appears onscreen. It lists the fields from the merge data file. To insert each field where you want its contents to appear in the document, click in the document to specify the location for the field, click the field name in the list on the Merge bar, then click Insert Field. You also can

double-click the field name in the list to insert it. Figure 7-12 shows some fields inserted into a letter document; a field code in brackets (<>) identifies where each field's contents will appear. Use the following guidelines to ensure you set up the fields correctly:

- Make sure you use proper punctuation, such as spaces, commas, and hard returns between field codes. For example, if you forget to include a space between the <FNAME> and <LNAME> fields, the contents of those fields run together in the merged documents (*JaneSmith* instead of *Jane Smith*.)

- You can insert merge fields in Click Here blocks. Click the block, then insert and punctuate the fields as needed.

- If you insert the wrong field by mistake, select it and delete it like any other text. You also can move a field to another location.

- When the Merge bar is onscreen, you can also enter and format other text to develop the full document contents. For example, to enter a letter greeting, you can type **Dear**, press the spacebar, insert the <FNAME> field, and press comma.

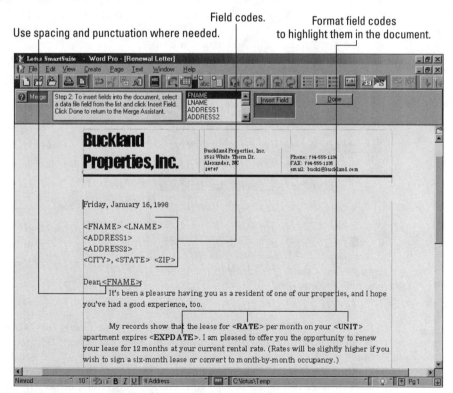

Figure 7-12: A code in brackets indicates the insertion location for each field, such as the <FNAME> and <LNAME> fields.

You also can format the field codes themselves to control the appearance of the merged text. For example, in the letter in Figure 7-12, boldfacing fields will help call the recipient's attention to important merged information.

6. When you've entered all the fields and text, click Done. The Merge bar closes and the Mail Merge Assistant dialog box reappears.

7. Click the Merge button under Merge, View, and Print. The Merge, View and Print dialog box appears.

8. (Optional) If you want to print only certain records in the data file, click Set Conditions to display the Merge Records dialog box and specify conditions used to select which records to merge. For each condition, specify the Field Name, Operator, and matching Value; use the Exact Case check box if the capitalization for the merge field contents needs to match the capping used in the Value entry. Click And or Or between multiple entries to specify whether the records must match all the conditions (And) or any of the conditions (Or). Figure 7-13 shows two conditions; if a record does not match both conditions, that record will not be merged. To remove a condition, select it in the Conditions list and click Delete Condition. To edit a selected condition, just change the Field Name, Operator, and Value entries. When you've finished creating conditions, click OK to close the dialog box. The Merge, View, and Print dialog box reappears with the Selected Records option chosen under Merge.

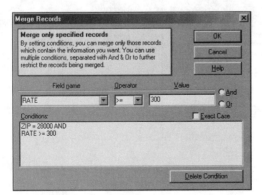

Figure 7-13: Create conditions to merge the matching records only.

9. In the View and Print Merged Documents area of the dialog box, specify how to complete the merge. The default option, View On Screen Before Printing, enables you to review each merged document for accuracy before sending it to the printer. If you choose this option, continue to Step 10. Send Directly to Printer prints each merged copy of the document, finishing the merge. Print to File displays the Save As dialog box so you can save the merged document copies in a new file, also finishing the merge. Use this option if you need to print multiple copies of the merged documents or if you set complicated

conditions and don't want to reconstruct them later. After you've made your selection, click OK.

10. If you opted to review the merged documents, the Merge toolbar reappears, along with the document for the first merged record (see Figure 7-14). To print only the displayed copy, click Print and View Next. When the document displays a record you didn't intend to merge, click Skip and View Next. You can continue using those buttons until you've viewed and printed or skipped all the documents; or, if you decide that the merge worked smoothly and just want to print the remaining document copies, click Print All. If you check and print the first few document copies and then want to stop checking and simply print the rest of them, click Print Rest. To stop viewing and printing the merged documents, click Done.

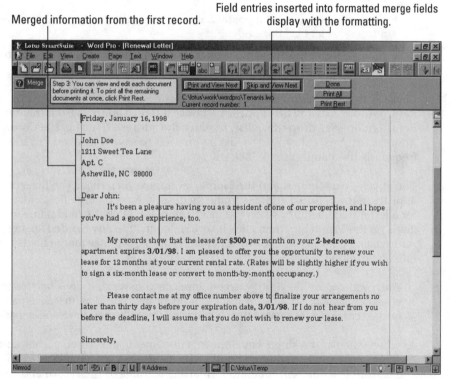

Figure 7-14: The Merge bar reappears to enable you to review and print the merged documents.

11. After you've finished viewing and printing all the merged copies, the Merge bar and Mail Merge Assistant dialog box both close. At this point, save the merge document so that you can open it and remerge the records any time you'd like.

Merging Envelopes

You use the same overall process to merge and print envelopes that you use to merge and print other types of documents, just described. The process starts out a bit differently — choose Text ⇨ Merge ⇨ Envelope. Use the Mail Merge Assistant dialog box to select or create the merge data file. Then, click the Setup button under Setup Envelope. The Envelope Setup Options dialog box appears, offering a few simple options:

✦ **Envelope Size.** Choose an envelope size other than the default #10 business envelope (called Env Comm10 4⅛ × 9½ inch, or something similar, depending on the printer you're using) if needed.

✦ **Bin.** Choose the paper tray your printer uses to feed envelopes from this drop-down list.

✦ **Bar Code.** If you want a postal delivery bar code to appear above the Send To address, select US Bar Code.

✦ **Include Return Address.** Check this option when you want your return address to appear on each merged envelope.

Click OK to finish your settings in the Envelope Setup Options dialog box. The Return Address dialog box appears. Choose a return address from the Available Return Addresses drop-down list, or enter the address to use in the Current Return Address text box. (Click Add to List if you want to save it in Word Pro's list of frequently used addresses.) Click OK.

The envelope document and the Merge bar appear onscreen. The insertion point appears in the Send To address frame by default. Insert merge fields just as you did for a letter document. Position the insertion point, click the field name in the list of fields on the Merge bar, then click Insert Field. Include any needed spaces, hard returns, and punctuation between fields. Figure 7-15 shows merge fields inserted into an envelope.

Danger Zone

When you choose the Text ⇨ Merge ⇨ Envelope command, it does *not* create a new envelope division. So, open a blank document and use it as the document file for merged envelopes, or create a new division and create the new envelope in that division.

As when you insert a single envelope in a document (described earlier under "Adding an Envelope to a Document"), you can format the envelope as you wish. You can apply a different font and formatting settings to the return and Send To addresses, insert a frame with a graphic or watermark, and so on. When you've finished inserting the merge fields and applying the desired formatting, click Done to close the Merge bar and redisplay the Mail Merge Assistant dialog box.

Under Merge, View, and Print, click Merge. The Merge, View, and Print dialog box appears. You can use this dialog box and the Merge bar to review and print your envelopes, just as described in Steps 8–10 in the previous section, "Merging Letters or Other Documents." After you view and print the envelopes, save the envelope merge document for later use.

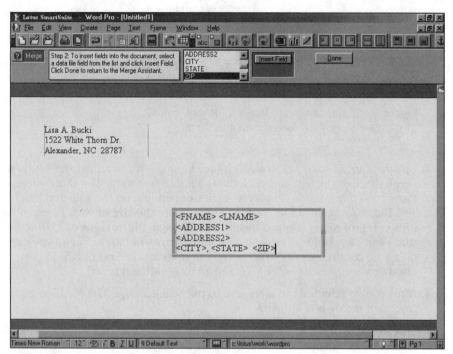

Figure 7-15: Insert the merge fields for merged envelopes within the Send To address frame.

Creating and Merging Labels

You can create and print mailing labels in Word Pro, and even use merging to create address labels for recipient names stored in a data source file. Or, for event name tags, include only name, company, and title fields on the merged labels. Word Pro enables you to set up labels in the sizes offered by Avery, which have become the standard in label sizing. You also can create labels in popular international sizes.

You can build and merge labels as follows:

1. Click the Create a New Document SmartIcon, then click Create from Any SmartMaster.

2. Click Label in the Select a Type of SmartMaster list, then double-click label.mwp in the Select a Look list. The Create Labels dialog box appears, as shown in Figure 7-16.

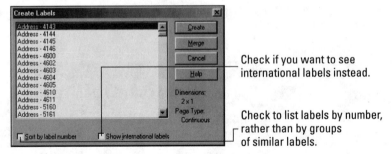

Check if you want to see
international labels instead.

Check to list labels by number,
rather than by groups
of similar labels.

Figure 7-16: You can create labels in dozens
of standard sizes, then merge data into them.

3. Use the check boxes below the list (see Figure 7-16) to adjust the list display, scroll through the list, and click the label size you want. The Dimensions and Page Type information displayed varies depending on the selected label type. The Dimensions information does not indicate the size of each label; rather, it tells you how many labels appear on each page. Dimensions of 3×10 indicate that each page holds three columns and 10 rows of labels. Page Type can either be continuous (for tractor-fed dot-matrix printers) or 8.5×11 (or another sheet size if you've selected an international label).

4. After you've selected the label size to use, click Merge. The Mail Merge Assistant dialog box appears.

Note

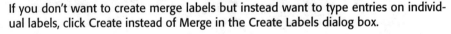

If you don't want to create merge labels but instead want to type entries on individual labels, click Create instead of Merge in the Create Labels dialog box.

5. Under Select Data File, choose or create the merge data file to use. If you need a refresher, consult the earlier section called "Working with Data Sources."

6. Choose Use Current under Select Letter to Merge. The Merge bar appears, along with the layout for a single label on the Master Label division that Word Pro inserts in the file. The same layout will be duplicated for all the labels in the Label Sheet division, after you set up the label on the Master Label division.

7. Choose View ➪ Standard (100%) to better see the master label, if you wish, then insert merge fields just as for a merged letter or envelope. Position the insertion point, click the field name in the list of fields on the Merge bar, then click Insert Field. Include any needed spaces, hard returns, and punctuation between fields.

8. Format the merge fields and make any other design changes you'd like. For example, in the label shown in Figure 7-17, a frame holds the merge fields, to make it easier to align them. The text uses a smaller size of a decorative font. And, the label has a graphic inserted at its left side.

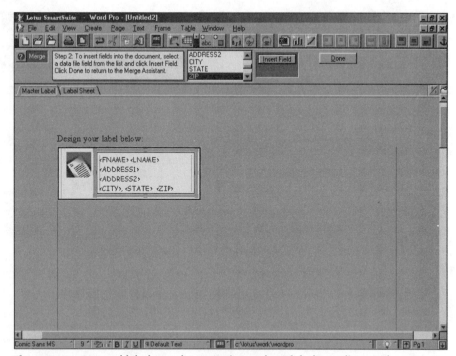

Figure 7-17: Merged labels can be attractive and useful, depending on the formatting you apply to the inserted merge fields and remaining space on the label.

9. Click Done when you've finished inserting merge fields and formatting the label.

10. Under Merge, View, and Print, click Merge. The Merge, View, and Print dialog box appears. You can use this dialog box and the Merge bar to review and print your labels, just as described in Steps 8–10 in the earlier section, "Merging Letters or Other Documents." Figure 7-18 shows some merged labels, which appear in the Label Sheet division.

11. After you view and print the labels, save the label merge document for later use. Note that the Master Label division disappears, so you cannot further edit the label layout.

You have to shell out a surprising amount of cash to buy mailing labels for printing. So, if your merge data list isn't long enough to use all the labels on the sheet, be creative in reusing the rest of the labels. If they're totally blank, just turn the sheet around and print from the other end the next time you print labels. If they have a graphic, as shown in Figure 7-18, save them to hand-write labels when you need one or two at a time.

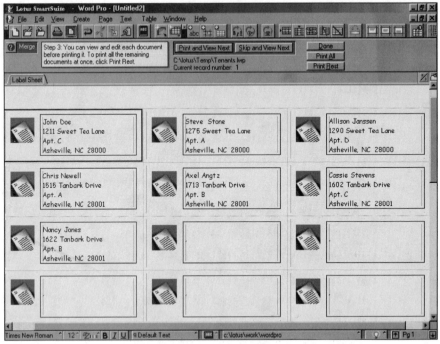

Figure 7-18: Here's how a short list of merged labels might look before you print them.

Reusing or Updating a Merge Document

You can open a document that contains merge fields and rerun or modify the merge at any time. For example, if you add new records to the merge data file, you may need to remerge the document to make copies for the new records. After opening the document, choose Text ⇨ Merge ⇨ Letter (for letters, labels, and other documents) or Text ⇨ Merge ⇨ Envelope. The Mail Merge Assistant dialog box appears. You can then perform either or both of the following actions:

✦ Use the buttons under Select Data File to either select or create a different merge data file, to merge a new set of data with the existing letter or document text.

✦ Choose Edit Fields under Select Letter to Merge to redisplay the Merge bar so you can add and remove fields, or edit the document's text and formatting. Click Done to close the Merge bar when you've finished.

After you've adjusted the merge data file or merge document, click Merge under Merge, View, and Print. The Merge, View, and Print dialog box appears. You can use this dialog box and the Merge bar to review and print your merged documents, just as described in Steps 8–10 in the earlier section, "Merging Letters or Other Documents." When you finish, be sure to save your changes to the merge document.

Importing Existing Information

A program's *file format* refers to the specific way that it codes information. Sometimes file formats for different programs are relatively similar; for example, the Windows WordPad program can work with files from Word for Windows 6.0. More often, though, wildly disparate file formats result because each word processor handles formatting coding differently, or a spreadsheet program has to divide information differently than a word processor does. Companies make huge investments to *standardize* on a particular type of software to ensure that coworkers can share information. This takes care of many file format issues. However, if you're dealing with a customer or consultant, you may need to use files from another word processor. Or, if information you need for a document happens to be in a 1-2-3 file, you have a hurdle to overcome. Word Pro enables you to *import* information from other applications in situations like these, so you can reuse the information without retyping it.

You can import files in more than 50 different formats into Word Pro, either into a current document or as a brand-new document. To import a file of a particular type, the filter for importing and exporting that type of file must be installed in Word Pro. If your Word Pro installation doesn't have the filter it needs to use the type of file you've selected during the import process (described next), a message box appears to tell you that you must install the filter. Click OK to close the message box. Then, close Word Pro and any other open SmartSuite application, and perform a Custom install as described in Appendix A, "Installing SmartSuite," to install the filter. There are a few different tabs of filters in the Customize dialog box for Word Pro in the Lotus Install program.

Follow these steps to import Word Pro information:

1. Choose File ➪ Import/Export. The Import or Export dialog box appears (see Figure 7-19). Leave Import Data from Another Application (or Word Pro File) selected under the first step.

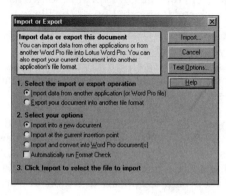

Figure 7-19: Follow the steps in this dialog box to import information from another application into Word Pro.

2. Under Select Your Options, specify where the imported information should be placed:

   - **Import into a New Document.** Lets you enter a file name to save the imported data in a new Word Pro file.

   - **Import at the Current Insertion Point.** Inserts the information into the current document.

   - **Import and Convert into Word Pro Documents.** To import multiple files, choose this option. Then, select multiple files from the Open dialog box (see Step 6); use Ctrl+click to select the multiple files in the dialog box. Word Pro converts each of the files (leaving the original intact) into a Word Pro file, placing the converted files in the same disk and folder as the originals.

3. If you want the Format Check to examine the open file and correct common formatting and typing errors, select the Automatically Run Format Check check box.

4. If you're importing a word processing file or other text file (such as a file exported from a spreadsheet program into plain-text format), click the Text Options button to display the Text File Options dialog box. Use this dialog box to help correct formatting errors as the information is imported. For example, if the file being imported has a hard return at the end of each line (instead of each paragraph, as usual) and you'd like to better group paragraphs, choose the Carriage Return and Line Feed After Each Line option button under Text File Options; otherwise, leave the default option button selected. If the imported document contains style names you want to preserve, select the Keep Style Names check box. If the document you're importing uses a unique character set, choose it from the Character Set drop-down list. Click OK to close the dialog box.

5. Click Import. The Open dialog box appears.

6. Select the type of file to import from the Files of Type drop-down list. Use the Look In list to navigate to the disk and folder that holds the file to import. When it appears in the dialog box, click it, and then click Open.

7. Depending on the type of file you selected, Word Pro may display an additional dialog box. For example, if you're importing a 1-2-3 file, the 1-2-3 Choose Range dialog box appears. Use its options to specify whether you want to merge the Entire File, a selected Worksheet, or a selected Range; if you choose Worksheet or Range, use the combo text/drop-down list below the option button to type or select the worksheet or range to use. Then click OK. The imported information appears onscreen, either at the insertion point or in a new document, depending on the selection you made in Step 2. The format for the imported data varies depending on its original file types. For example, data imported from most spreadsheet programs appears as a table in Word Pro.

In addition to importing 1-2-3 data, you can copy a 1-2-3 range and paste it into Word Pro as a table. Select the range to copy in 1-2-3, then click Copy to Clipboard. Switch to Word Pro, and click to place the insertion point in the document where you want the table to appear. Choose Edit ⇨ Paste Special. In the Paste Special dialog box, choose Rich Text Format in the As list, then click OK. The table appears in the Word Pro document; each cell from the 1-2-3 range appears as a cell in the Word Pro table.

The File ⇨ Import Picture command displays the Add Picture dialog box. Use this dialog box to select a file to place in the document; it works just like other dialog boxes for selecting files. (Word Pro doesn't insert the picture into a frame unless you first create and select it before displaying the Add Picture dialog box.) If the proper graphics filter for the file hasn't been installed, perform a Custom installation (see the Appendix, "Installing SmartSuite") of Word Pro to install the filter.

Exporting Document Contents

Suppose a Word Pro document contains some contents that you or a colleague needs to work with, such as a table of information. The catch is, you need to use that information in another word processor or another type of application. In such a situation, you can *export* the information from Word Pro to save it in another file format.

Although you can import data from applications of different categories, such as spreadsheets, you can only export Word Pro data into other word processing formats.

Follow these steps to export the current Word Pro file:

1. Choose File ⇨ Import/Export. The Import or Export dialog box appears (Figure 7-19).

2. Under the first step, Select the Import or Export Operation, choose Export Your Document Into Another File Format. The Import or Export dialog box changes to display a list of export formats, as shown in Figure 7-20.

3. Click the Text Options button to display the Text File Options dialog box. Use this dialog box to specify a formatting change as the information is exported. To insert a hard return at the end of each line (instead of each paragraph, as usual) in the exported file, choose the Carriage Return and Line Feed After Each Line option button under Text File Options; otherwise, leave the default option button selected. If you want to export style names into the exported file, select the Keep Style Names check box. If you want to use a unique character set in the exported file, choose it from the Character Set drop-down list. Click OK to close the dialog box.

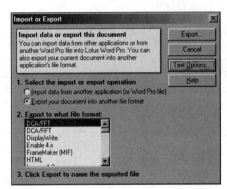

Figure 7-20: The export format options appear in the Import or Export dialog box during an export operation.

4. Under Export to What File Format, select the file format for the exported file.

5. Click Export.

6. If the format for the exported file doesn't support some of the formatting or data features in Word Pro — such as frames, tables, or graphics — a dialog box warns you that some data or formatting could be lost. Click Yes to continue the export information.

7. In the Save As dialog box, specify the File Name for the new file, as well as the disk and folder to save it to. Click Save. Word Pro finishes the export and saves the file. You then can open it in the specified word processor.

✦   ✦   ✦

1-2-3

The 1-2-3 program has long been a favorite spreadsheet for organizing and calculating numerical information. This part enumerates all the 1-2-3 features that you can put to work. You'll learn how to get started with 1-2-3 workbook files, how to create and protect a file, move around the cells in the file, and enter text, numbers, and dates and times. We then give you details on the core power of 1-2-3 — calculations. Learn how to work with ranges of cells, refer to cells by address, and copy and move information. Then we lead you through all the techniques for improving the appearance of your worksheet files. You'll find out how to use graphics to reinforce the message your worksheet data conveys — how to draw on a worksheet or insert a picture created in another program. You'll also learn how to chart your data and alter the chart design. Finally, we cover features for power users, such as how to transpose the entries in a range and to parse long cell entries into multiple cells. We also describe how to use 1-2-3 SmartMasters, perform what-if analysis, find a solution with Backsolver, work with distribution and regression, and more complex statistical analysis features.

Working with Worksheet Files

SmartSuite's 1-2-3 application falls into the spreadsheet category of software; you'll notice, as you work through this chapter, that the gridlike appearance of the work area in 1-2-3 emulates the green columnar paper used by accounting professionals when they prepare spreadsheets of information. As you might expect, using 1-2-3 helps you "do math." Using a spreadsheet program makes repetitive math tasks and "what-if analysis" very easy. 1-2-3 remembers lists of numbers that you enter and allows you to change those numbers to quickly see the effect. For example, you'll find it easy to predict the effect on your net profit of a 10 percent increase in the cost of producing your products, or a 5 percent decrease in the price of your products. Budgeting is a breeze with a spreadsheet.

Starting 1-2-3

When you work in 1-2-3, you enter and change data on a *worksheet; worksheet* is the term 1-2-3 uses to describe what you see onscreen. You can think of a worksheet as a single page in a book or an individual piece of green columnar paper containing spreadsheet data. *Workbooks* are the files in which you save your work. A workbook can contain a single worksheet, or it can contain several worksheets.

To start 1-2-3, follow these steps:

1. Click the Start button.

2. Select Programs ➪ Lotus SmartSuite ➪ Lotus 1-2-3 Release 9.

3. When you first start 1-2-3, you see the Welcome to 1-2-3 dialog box shown in Figure 8-1. You can choose a SmartMaster template on which to base your workbook. SmartMasters contain text, formulas, formatting, macros, and scripts to help you perform common tasks. To follow along in this chapter, choose Blank Workbook (No SmartMaster).

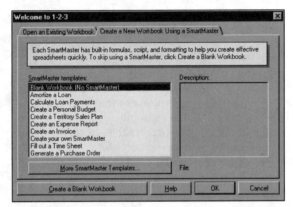

Figure 8-1: From the opening dialog box in 1-2-3, you can choose to use a SmartMaster or create a blank workbook.

See Chapter 14, "Saving Time with Power 1-2-3 Features," for more information on SmartMasters.

Understanding the 1-2-3 Screen

The row/column format of a worksheet makes the worksheet look like the spreadsheets accounting professionals create using columnar pads (see Figure 8-2). Unlike a columnar pad, however, you'll also see tools onscreen that help you work with your electronic spreadsheet. For example, the menus on the menu bar contain commands to perform various actions in 1-2-3, and the SmartIcons are shortcuts for commands you'll use frequently. Clicking a SmartIcon is the same as opening a menu and choosing a command.

Sheet tab. Navigator. ┌@Function Selector. ┌Contents box.   Horizontal splitter.
Selection Indicator.   Title bar. Menu bar. ┌SmartIcon bar. Sheet tab scroll arrows.

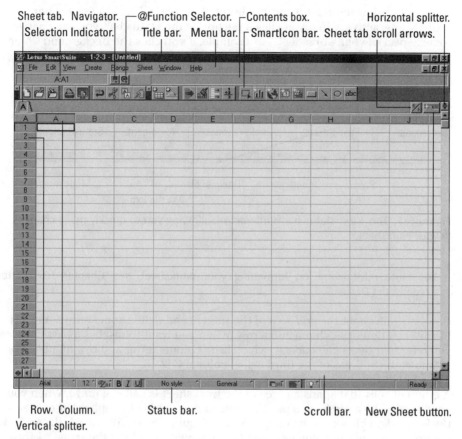

Row. Column.   Status bar.   Scroll bar. New Sheet button.
Vertical splitter.

Figure 8-2: The 1-2-3 screen contains rows and columns in which you enter data and provides tools to help you make entries.

In the Sheet Tab area, you see the sheets contained in the workbook; by default, each workbook begins with only one sheet, Sheet A. Other screen elements, such as the Selection Indicator and the Contents box, are discussed later in this chapter. We'll talk about other elements, such as the Navigator and the @Function Selector, in other chapters.

More Info

For more information on the Navigator and the @Function Selector, see Chapter 9, "Working with Ranges, Formulas, and Functions."

You'll notice that the 1-2-3 status bar is split into parts. The 1-2-3 status bar is actually interactive; when you click a portion of the status bar, you can change some aspect of your worksheet. For example, if you click the Background Color button on the status bar, you can choose a different color for the background of the worksheet. Figure 8-3 shows the status bar.

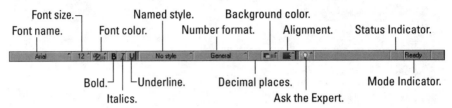

Figure 8-3: The 1-2-3 status bar is interactive, allowing you to quickly make changes to your worksheet.

 For more information on formatting your worksheet, see Chapter 10, "Better Spreadsheet Design."

Now let's talk about the *grid* area of the screen, and define some terms. A *cell* is the intersection of a column and a row. When you want to discuss a particular cell, you refer to it by its cell *address*, which is its column letter and row number. For example, the address of the third cell in column C is C3.

A group of cells that spans an area of the worksheet is called a *range*. When you need to identify a range, you use the cells that appear in the upper-left corner and the lower-right corner of the range. To talk about cells A1, A2, A3, B1, B2, and B3, the first three cells in columns A and B, you would talk about the range A1 through B3. When you write (or type) this expression, you use the cell addresses of the upper-left and lower-right corners of the range and separate them with a colon (:) or a period (.). You would write A1 through B3 as A1:B3, A1.B3, or A1..B3. 1-2-3 converts the colon or single period to two periods, but you can use any of these entry methods.

In Figure 8-2, you can see only 27 rows and 10 columns (A–J). In actuality, each 1-2-3 worksheet contains 65,536 rows and 256 columns. Column names run A–Z, then begin again with AA for column 27, AB for column 28, and so forth. After Column AZ, you'll find Columns BA, BB, BC, and so forth. The 256th column in a 1-2-3 worksheet is IV.

Selecting Cells

Much of the work you'll do in a 1-2-3 worksheet involves selecting cells; you select cells to format text or numbers, to change text or background colors, or to move or copy information. In fact, you'll probably spend more time selecting cells in 1-2-3 than any other single action. Take some time to master efficient techniques for selecting cells to speed up your work in 1-2-3.

You select individual cells by clicking them or pressing the arrow keys on your keyboard. You can identify the selected cell because its border appears outlined; 1-2-3 calls this outlined border the *cell pointer* because it indicates the location of the selected cell. In Figure 8-3, the selected cell is A1. At any time while you work in 1-2-3, at least one cell is selected — the cell surrounded by the cell pointer.

You can select an entire row or column by clicking the row number or the column letter. In Figure 8-4, Column E is selected. To cancel a selection, select any cell in the worksheet; effectively, you cancel a selection by making a new selection. You can also cancel a selection by pressing Esc.

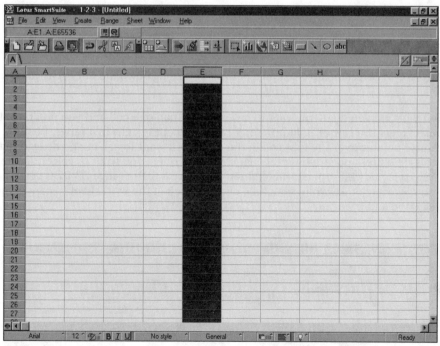

Figure 8-4: Select a column by clicking the column letter.

You also can use Windows selection techniques to select multiple rows or columns. To select a contiguous set of rows, click the row number of the first row you want to select; then, press and hold the Shift key as you click the last row you want to select.

You can drag across row numbers or column letters to select contiguous rows or columns.

In Figure 8-5, both Row 5 and Row 7 are selected. To select noncontiguous rows and columns, click the row number or column letter of the first row or column you want to select. Then, press and hold the Ctrl key as you click the next row or column you want to select.

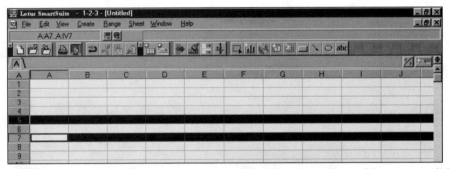

Figure 8-5: Select multiple columns or rows by holding down the Ctrl key as you click.

But what do you do if you want to select more than one cell and you don't want to select an entire row or column? You drag to select the cells in a range. Position the mouse pointer over the first cell in the range you want to select and drag until the mouse pointer appears over the last cell in the range you want to select. As you drag, selected cells appear highlighted. In Figure 8-6, the range B3:D7 is selected. If you make a mistake while selecting, click any cell in the worksheet to cancel the selection and try again.

Figure 8-6: Select a range of cells by dragging the mouse pointer over them.

And, just as you suspected, you can select noncontiguous cells and ranges using the Ctrl key as you select. 1-2-3 calls this type of selection a *collection*. You might want to select a collection to clear out old data while leaving formula cells untouched, or to apply a specific number format to a group of cells without changing the format of all the cells in a range.

Note　You can release the Ctrl key when you are not dragging and press it again to add more cells to a collection. If you make a mistake while selecting cells in a collection, simply hold the Ctrl key and click over the incorrect portion of the collection to cancel that portion of the selection. Then, hold the Ctrl key and select the correct cells.

Moving Around a Worksheet

After selecting cells, moving around a worksheet is probably the most common task in 1-2-3. Typically, you use the directional keys on your keyboard to move around a worksheet. In Table 8-1, you see the most commonly used keys and their resulting actions. Whenever you see a plus sign (+) separating key names in Table 8-1, hold down the first key while pressing the second key. Whenever you see a space separating key names in Table 8-1, press and release the first key before you press and release the second key.

Note　Some of the keys listed in Table 8-1 can function differently if you change your 1-2-3 preferences. See Chapter 14, "Saving Time with Power 1-2-3 Features," for more information on changing 1-2-3's behavior.

Table 8-1 Navigation Keys in 1-2-3	
Press These Keys	*To Take This Action*
Left or Right Arrow	Move the cell pointer left or right one column
Up or Down Arrow	Move the cell pointer up or down one row
Ctrl+Left, Right Arrow or Tab, Shift+Tab	Move the cell pointer left or right by the number of columns currently visible in the window
Page Up or Page Down	Move the cell pointer up or down by the number of rows currently visible in the window
Home	Move the cell pointer to cell A1 in the current sheet

(continued)

Table 8-1 *(continued)*

Press These Keys	To Take This Action
End Home	Move the cell pointer to the last cell in the lower-right corner of the worksheet that contains information
End Left Arrow or End Right Arrow	Move the cell pointer left or right in the current row to the next cell that contains data and appears next to a blank cell. Use this key combination and the next key combination to move quickly past cells containing information.
End Up Arrow or End Down Arrow	Move the cell pointer up or down in the current column to the next cell that contains data and appears next to a blank cell. Use this key combination and the previous key combination to move quickly past cells containing information.

Hot Stuff

Notice what happens to the Selection indicator when you move the cell pointer: The current location of the cell pointer appears. By checking the Selection Indicator, you can always locate the cell pointer.

In addition to using the directional keys on your keyboard, you can use 1-2-3's Go To command to specify the cell to which you want to move the cell pointer. The Go To dialog box is particularly useful when you need to move the cell pointer a large distance.

Press F5 to display the Go To dialog box (see Figure 8-7). Type the address of the cell to which you want to move the cell pointer in the text box that appears below the Type of Object list box; then choose OK. 1-2-3 will move the cell pointer to select the cell you specify.

Figure 8-7: Use the Go To dialog box to move the cell pointer to a specific cell address.

Entering Information into a Worksheet

You can enter four basic types of information into a 1-2-3 worksheet cell:

✦ Text

✦ Numbers

✦ Dates and times

✦ Mathematical formulas

Entering Text

1-2-3 refers to text entries as *labels*. This name is logical when you consider that most text entries serve to identify some other entry. To enter a label into a cell, select that cell and begin typing. As you type, the letters you type appear in the cell. When you finish typing your label, press Enter. 1-2-3 leaves the cell pointer in the original cell and stores your entry, the label, in the selected cell.

You also can press an arrow key to have 1-2-3 simultaneously store a cell entry and move the cell pointer to the next cell in the direction of the arrow key. And, you can change your preferences so that pressing Enter functions the same as pressing the down arrow key.

While the cell is selected, you also see the contents of the cell in the Contents box (see Figure 8-8).

Contents box.

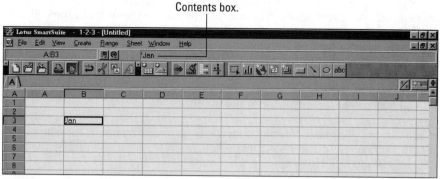

Figure 8-8: When you select a cell containing information, the information appears in both the cell and the Contents box.

Notice that the Contents box shows an apostrophe (') preceding the label in the cell. I didn't type that apostrophe; 1-2-3 inserted it. The apostrophe indicates that the label is aligned at the left edge of the cell. By preceding a label with a carat (^), you tell 1-2-3 to align the label in the center of the cell. To align a label with the right edge of a cell, type a quotation mark (") as the first character of the label. In Figure 8-9, the entry in B3 is left-aligned, the entry in C3 is centered, and the entry in D3 is right-aligned.

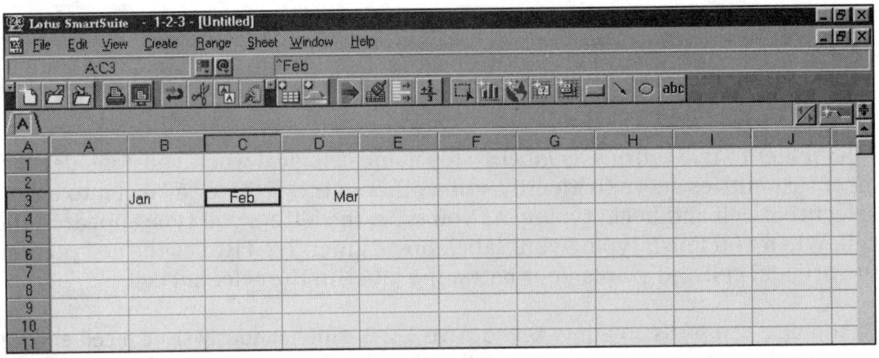

Figure 8-9: Notice the alignment of information cells B3, C3, and D3.

Entering Numbers

As you just saw, 1-2-3 aligns labels at the left edge of the cell by default. As you would expect, 1-2-3 aligns numbers at the right edge of the cell by default so columns of numbers will align properly. To enter a number in a specific cell, select the cell and type the number. As you type, the number appears in the cell. After you press Enter, the number appears both in the cell and in the Contents box, just as a label appeared in both the cell and the Contents box. Notice, however, that 1-2-3 does *not* precede numbers with alignment characters. This fact is *very* important if you expect to use the numbers that you enter in mathematical calculations, as you'll see later in this chapter. 1-2-3 understands that a number is a number *only* *if* no alignment character precedes the number.

Note   You can, but don't need to, enter punctuation to format numbers. For example, if you type 1,000 and include the comma when you type, 1-2-3 will display the number exactly as you typed it — including the comma.

If your number entry is larger than the width of the cell, or your number includes punctuation that makes the number too wide to fit in the cell, you will see asterisks in the cell instead of the number you typed, as shown in cell B4 of Figure 8-10. You can correct this problem by making the column wider, as shown in cell C4.

This number is too large to fit in B4.

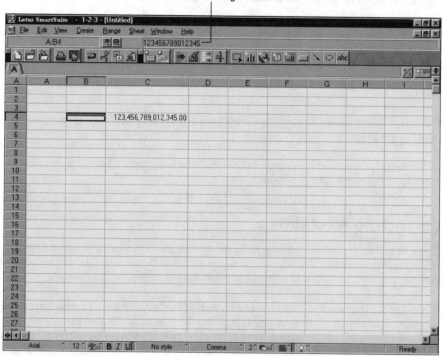

Figure 8-10: When a number is too large to fit in a cell, 1-2-3 displays asterisks instead.

See Chapter 10, "Better Spreadsheet Design," for more information on changing column widths.

Entering Dates and Times

Date entries in a worksheet are numbers that appear in the familiar mm/dd/yy format. To enter a date, select the cell in which you want the date to appear, and then type the entry in mm/dd/yy format. For example, to enter the date January 15, 1998, click a cell, type **01/15/98**, and press Enter.

1-2-3 can store the time of day as well as the date. To enter a time, select a cell and then type an entry using the time format HH:MM:SS. The parameter for seconds, SS, is optional.

For more information on making dates and times appear in formats other than the default, see Chapter 10, "Better Spreadsheet Design."

Entering Mathematical Formulas

Formula entries cause 1-2-3 to do some real work by performing calculations on your data. For example, if you want to calculate the sum of a set of numbers, you would use a mathematical formula. 1-2-3 can work with many different types of formulas, from very simple ones like +A1 to show the current value in cell A1, to very complex formulas such as you might use to calculate accrued interest on bonds.

You enter formulas by beginning your entry with a plus sign (+), an equals sign (=), or an at sign (@).

For more information on using mathematical formulas, see Chapter 9, "Working with Ranges, Formulas, and Functions."

Correcting Mistakes

If you discover a mistake after you have made a cell entry, erase the entry by selecting the cell and pressing the Del key on your keyboard. Or, simply type over the existing entry; 1-2-3 will replace the existing entry with the new entry.

If you are typing in a cell and discover your mistake before you press Enter, you can cancel the entire entry by pressing Esc. Or, you can edit the entry by pressing F2. If you press F2 while typing the entry, 1-2-3 will allow you to use the left and right arrows to move around within the entry you are typing, and the Del and Backspace keys to delete characters to the right and left of the insertion point, respectively. When you type, 1-2-3 will insert whatever you type without overwriting existing text.

Use 1-2-3's Undo SmartIcon to reverse the effects of the last action you took. If you accidentally type over the contents of a cell, click Undo to restore the original contents.

But suppose you discover your mistake *after* you press Enter to store an entry. If you don't want to retype the entire entry, you can edit the cell entry by selecting the cell and pressing F2. Again, 1-2-3 will let you press the left arrow (and the right arrow key, as needed) to move around within the cell entry, use the Del and Backspace keys to delete the character to the right and left of the insertion point, and insert characters as needed.

Saving and Naming a Workbook

After you put in some information, you're going to want to save your workbooks. If your workbook is new and you've never saved it before, the first time you save it you'll need to supply a name. To save a workbook and supply a name, choose File ⇨ Save or click the Save SmartIcon. The Save As dialog box appears (see Figure 8-11).

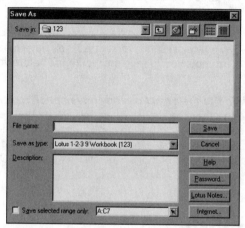

Figure 8-11: Use this dialog box to provide a name for a new workbook.

To save the workbook, type a name in the File Name box — don't supply an extension, because 1-2-3 will automatically assign 123 as the extension — and click the Save button. 1-2-3 saves the workbook using the name you provided. That name will appear in the title bar, replacing "Untitled."

By checking the title bar, you can tell if your workbook is new and has never been saved. 1-2-3 assigns the name "Untitled" to each unsaved workbook. If you have more than one new workbook open, 1-2-3 adds a numeric character to the name — the second unsaved workbook will be named Untitled1, the third unsaved workbook will be named Untitled 2, and so on.

Some Commonly Asked Questions

What will happen if I've already saved a workbook and I click the Save SmartIcon? 1-2-3 will save the workbook using the same name without displaying the Save As dialog box.

How can I save a workbook using a different name? Choose File ⇨ Save As. The Save As dialog box will appear and suggest, in the File Name box, the same name you supplied originally. Simply change that name and click Save.

How can I close a workbook I no longer need? Choose File ⇨ Close. If you have made no changes since the last time you saved, 1-2-3 simply closes the workbook. If you have made changes since the last time you saved, 1-2-3 prompts you to save the workbook before you close it.

How can I start a new workbook in addition to the ones I already have open? You can start a new workbook at any time, even with other workbooks open, by clicking the New SmartIcon or choosing File New. 1-2-3 displays the New Workbook dialog box, which closely resembles the Welcome to 1-2-3 dialog box you saw in the beginning of this chapter — and you use it the same way. Select a Blank Workbook or a SmartMaster and click OK.

Setting Workbook Properties

Workbook properties are preferences you can set that apply to just the workbook in which you are working. The Workbook Properties dialog box has five tabs: the View tab (see Figure 8-12), the General tab (see Figure 8-13), the Statistics tab (see Figure 8-14), the Notes/FX Fields tab (see Figure 8-15), and the Security tab (see Figure 8-16). Some of these tabs are informational only, while others contain settings you can use to set preferences for your workbook. Select File ⇨ Workbook Properties to display the Workbook Properties dialog box.

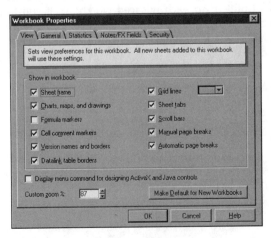

Figure 8-12: From the View tab of the Workbook Properties dialog box, you can choose screen elements to view or hide.

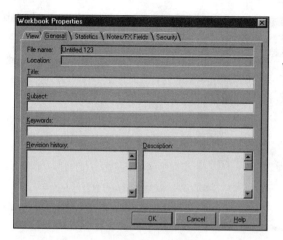

Figure 8-13: On the General tab, you can set a title and subject for your workbook, and keywords that 1-2-3 can use to find your workbook when you search for it.

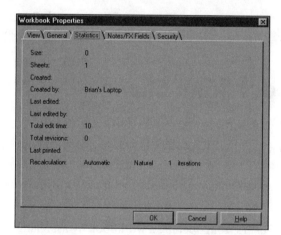

Figure 8-14: You don't make changes on the Statistics tab; instead, 1-2-3 provides you with information that describes your workbook.

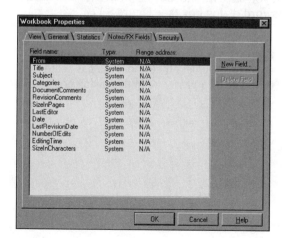

Figure 8-15: The Notes/FX Fields tab lists named ranges in your workbook that you can use to exchange information between 1-2-3 and Lotus Notes.

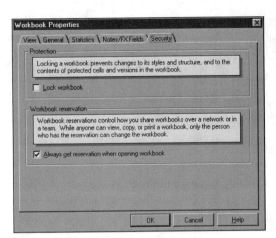

Figure 8-16: From the Security tab, you can lock a workbook to prevent changes; and you can establish, in a network, your right to change the workbook.

More Info

You'll learn about ranges and named ranges in Chapter 9, "Working with Ranges, Formulas, and Functions"; you learn about protecting workbooks in the next section.

Protecting a Workbook from Changes

In 1-2-3, you can provide security for your workbooks at two different levels:

✦ You can prevent users from opening the workbook unless they know the password.

✦ You can let users open the workbook, but not modify it unless they provide the password.

In the first case, you can prevent users from opening a workbook by assigning a password to the workbook when you save it. Choose File ➪ Save As and click Password to display the Set Password dialog box (see Figure 8-17).

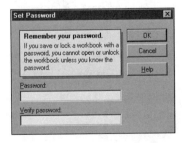

Figure 8-17: Prevent others from opening a workbook unless they know the password by assigning a password in this dialog box.

In the second case, you *lock* the workbook; other users can open and view a locked workbook and even make changes, but they can't save the changes unless they can supply the password. You lock workbooks from the Security tab of the Workbook Properties dialog box by placing a check in the Lock Workbook check box.

Locking works in conjunction with another 1-2-3 feature: protecting cells. By default, when you lock a workbook, 1-2-3 locks all cells in the workbook, which means that no changes can be made to the workbook unless the user knows the password. You can, however, protect part of a workbook instead of the entire workbook. That way, a user can change the unprotected portion of the workbook without knowing the password, but that same user cannot save any changes made to protected areas of the workbook.

To protect only part of a workbook, select the range or collection that you want to leave unprotected. Choose Range ➪ Range Properties to display the Range Properties InfoBox. Then, click the Security tab and remove the check from the Protect Cell Contents from Changes check box.

After you have identified the protected and unprotected cells in the workbook, lock the workbook in the Workbook Properties dialog box to enable the protection. Any user who tries to change a protected cell in a locked workbook will be prompted for a password.

Working with Existing Workbook Files

Once you have saved a file and closed it, you can reopen it to edit it by clicking the Open SmartIcon or by choosing File ➪ Open. The Open dialog box (see Figure 8-18) appears. Select the file you want to open and choose Open. If you don't see the file you want to open, use the Look In list box to navigate to the drive and folder containing the file.

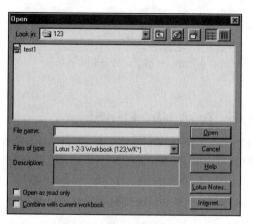

Figure 8-18: Use the Open dialog box to reopen a file that was saved previously.

When you first start 1-2-3 after you have saved workbooks, 1-2-3 displays the Welcome to 1-2-3 dialog box. The first tab of the dialog box contains a list of your "recently opened" workbooks, making it easy for you to open a workbook you've used lately.

You can open several workbooks at the same time using this process; each workbook will appear in its own window that fills the screen. To switch between open workbooks, open the Window menu (notice how 1-2-3 shows the purpose of a menu in the title bar when you open a menu). At the bottom of the menu (see Figure 8-19), you'll see all the open workbooks listed. The one you're currently viewing has a check mark next to it. Simply select the one you want to view.

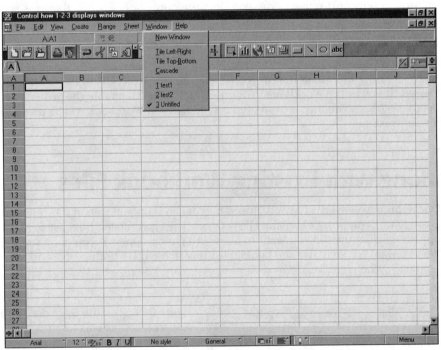

Figure 8-19: All open workbooks appear at the bottom of the Window menu.

Combining Information in Two Workbooks

Occasionally, you may find that you have stored some information in one workbook and you need the information in another workbook. If you combine the workbooks, you can

✦ Replace information in one workbook with information from the other.

✦ Add the information in one workbook to the same cells in the other workbook.

✦ Subtract the information in one workbook from the same cells in the other workbook.

Because combining data can overwrite existing data, always save the workbook you're viewing before you start the following process. To combine two workbooks, follow these steps:

1. Open the workbook in which you ultimately want the data.

2. Select the cell into which you want to begin combining data. Any data that comes in from the other workbook will be combined starting at the cell you select in this step.

3. Select the workbook containing the information that you want to combine.

4. Place a check in the Combine with Current Workbook check box. The Open button in the dialog box changes to the Combine button.

5. Click the Combine button. The Combine 1-2-3 File dialog box appears (see Figure 8-20).

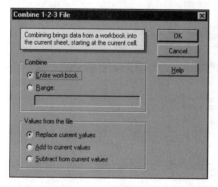

Figure 8-20: Set the options for combining files in this dialog box.

6. Choose the correct option button to combine either the entire workbook or just a specified range.

7. Choose the correct option button to replace current values in existing cells, add to current values in existing cells, or subtract from current values in existing cells.

8. Click OK. 1-2-3 combines the data in the workbook stored on disk with the data in the workbook you are viewing. Depending on the options you chose, the data in the workbook on disk will either replace, be added to, or be subtracted from, the data in the workbook you are viewing onscreen.

Combining two or more workbooks isn't the only way to use information from another workbook. You can also use formulas to refer to the data in another workbook. Often this is a better way to consolidate information from several workbooks — especially if you need to use formulas to calculate results, such as average sales from each of your company's branches.

Saving a Workbook in Another Format

You may need, on occasion, to save a 1-2-3 workbook into a different file type. Typically, this need arises if you share data with others who are not using the same version of 1-2-3 that you are using.

To save a 1-2-3 workbook to a different file type, open the file. Then, choose File ➪ Save As to display the Save As dialog box. Open the Save as type list box and choose the correct file type (see Figure 8-21). Then, supply a name in the File Name box and click the Save button.

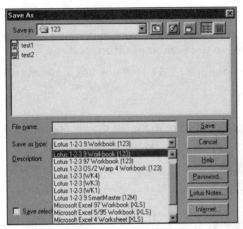

Figure 8-21: Choose a file type for your workbook.

Understanding Sheets

Sheets are synonymous with *worksheets*; a sheet is one page of a workbook. A workbook can contain up to 256 individual sheets. Typically, you use separate sheets in a workbook to help you organize information. Suppose, for example, that you were in charge of the budget for a division made up of several departments. You might consider creating each department's budget on a separate sheet in the same workbook. The top sheet in the workbook might be a consolidated sheet that shows the budget for the entire division — and draws information from other sheets in the workbook.

Adding a Sheet

When you add a new sheet to a workbook, you can choose whether to add the new sheet before or after the current sheet.

If you know you want to add a new sheet *after* the current sheet, simply click the New Sheet button. To create a new sheet and choose whether to place it before or after the current sheet, choose Create ➪ Sheet. 1-2-3 displays the Create Sheet dialog box.

Specify the number of sheets you want to add and the placement of the new sheets in relation to the current sheet. Then choose OK. 1-2-3 adds the sheets to the workbook. The first new sheet will be the current sheet (see Figure 8-22).

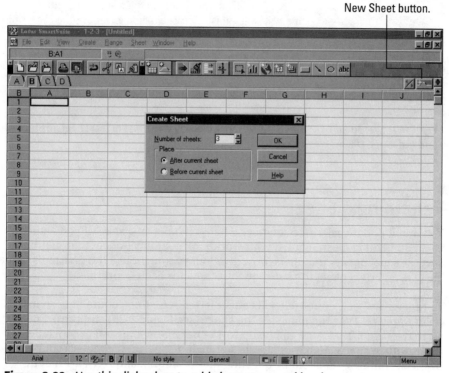

Figure 8-22: Use this dialog box to add sheets to a workbook.

When you work with more than one sheet in a workbook, you must distinguish between cell A1 in the first sheet and cell A1 in the second sheet. 1-2-3 makes this distinction by adding the sheet letter to the cell's address. Therefore, the address of cell A1 in Sheet A is A:A1. In Sheet B, cell A1's address is B:A1.

Switching Between Sheets

To work on a sheet, you must bring it to the front of the screen, making it the current sheet. You can simply click the sheet tab to switch sheets, or you can use the following keys on the keyboard to move between sheets in the current workbook.

Key Combinations	Cell Pointer Movement
Ctrl+Home	To cell A:A1. If you have hidden the first sheet or frozen titles in the first sheet, this key combination will move the cell pointer to the top left cell in the first sheet.
Ctrl+Page Up and Ctrl+Page Down	To the last active cell in the previous or next sheet.
End Ctrl+Home	To the bottom right corner of the active area in the last sheet containing information.
End Ctrl+Page Up and End Ctrl+Page Down	To the corresponding cell in the first or last sheet, respectively.

Renaming a Sheet

You might find it easier to remember what you have on a sheet if you name the sheet something meaningful. If your workbook contains budget information for several departments that make up a division, you might use the division's name for Sheet A and then name the subsequent sheets for each department.

To rename a sheet, double-click its sheet letter. A text box containing an insertion point appears. Type the name for the sheet (see Figure 8-23) and press Enter to store the name. The name can be up to 15 characters long and can include, but not begin with, a space. Also, you should not include special characters such as periods, commas, semicolons, question marks, ampersands (&), arithmetic operators (+, −, *, /, >, <), curly braces ({}), the at sign (@), or the pound sign (#), because these characters will confuse 1-2-3 when you create formulas.

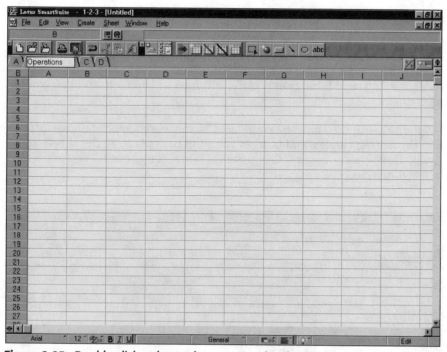

Figure 8-23: Double-click a sheet tab to rename the sheet.

Avoid sheet names that look like cell addresses, use the names of keys on your keyboard (such as Home or Ctrl), or begin with numbers. Do not name a sheet with a letter that could actually be a sheet that 1-2-3 would create. For example, don't name a sheet AA.

Deleting, Hiding, and Redisplaying Sheets

Right-click the sheet name to display a shortcut menu (see Figure 8-24). Choose Delete Sheet to delete a sheet, or Hide to hide a sheet.

Figure 8-24: You can delete, hide, and show sheets from the shortcut menu.

If you choose to hide a sheet, you can redisplay it by choosing Unhide from the shortcut menu. The Unhide dialog box, which lists all hidden sheets, appears. Select the sheet you want to redisplay from the list and click OK.

Grouping and Ungrouping Sheets

Often, when you use multiple sheets in a workbook, several sheets may have similar settings or formats that you want to apply. It would be very tedious to set up each sheet individually; if you group the sheets, however, you can apply the styles, settings, and formats only once, and 1-2-3 will apply them to all grouped sheets.

To group sheets, they must be contiguous in the workbook. Set up one of the sheets with the settings, styles, and formats you want to apply to all the sheets in the group. Then, choose Sheet ➪ Group Sheets. The Group Sheet dialog box appears (see Figure 8-25).

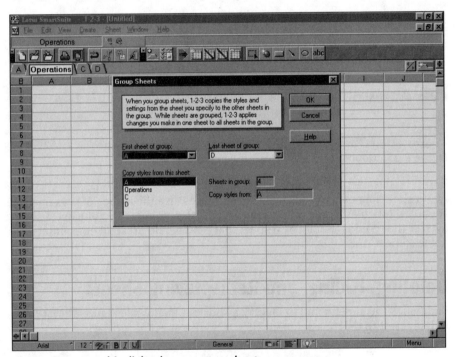

Figure 8-25: Use this dialog box to group sheets.

Select the first and last sheets to include in the group and choose the sheet containing the settings, formats, and styles you want to apply to the entire group. Then, choose OK.

While you work with grouped sheets, any formatting, style, or settings change that you make to one of the sheets applies to all the sheets. On the positive side, you can take a single action to format cells in all grouped sheets as bold; on the negative side, if you delete a column in one sheet of a group, you delete that column in all the grouped sheets. Therefore, you may want to group sheets only long enough to apply common settings. Then, consider ungrouping the sheets.

To ungroup sheets, select a sheet that is a member of the group. Then, choose Sheet ➪ Clear Sheet Group. The group will no longer exist.

When you clear a sheet group, you simply cancel the link between the sheets in the group that made them all function collectively. You *do not* remove the sheets or any data in them. Also, you cannot remove a single sheet from a group; instead, you must create a new group that doesn't include the sheet. Remember, though, that sheet groups must be contiguous — you can't create a group that doesn't include one of the sheets that would be in the middle of the group.

✦   ✦   ✦

Working with Ranges, Formulas, and Functions

Ranges, formulas, and functions are among the most powerful features in 1-2-3. Using ranges, you can specify groups of cells to copy, move, delete, or reference in formulas and functions. Formulas in 1-2-3 help you perform basic math operations, such as addition, subtraction, multiplication, and division. Functions in 1-2-3 serve a special purpose: They abbreviate long, complex mathematical operations. For example, 1-2-3 contains a function to calculate the net present value of a set of numbers.

If you master the information in this chapter, you'll be on your way to becoming a 1-2-3 power user.

Copying and Moving Cell Entries

The ability to copy and move information in a workbook will save you more time than any other technique you'll use while working with a spreadsheet. The real power of copying and moving becomes apparent when you copy or move cells that contain formulas or functions — a subject you'll learn about later in this chapter.

Copying reproduces information found at one location and places it in another location. The content of the original cells remains unchanged. When you *move* information, you empty the original cells containing the information and relocate that information to a new place in the workbook.

Whether you move or copy information, you must identify two locations during the process:

✦ The location that contains the information you want to move or copy — some people call this the *source* or *original* location

✦ The location where you want the information to appear when you complete the process — also called the *target* or *destination* location.

The major difference between copying and moving is the effect of the action on the original cells containing the information. But both operations have the same effect on the cells that receive information: Any information that may have existed at the destination location *is replaced* by the information you copy or move. It's important to understand that both copying and moving destroy any information that appears at the destination location.

Perhaps the most confusing aspect of moving or copying information in 1-2-3 involves understanding what to select at the original location and what to select at the destination location. Follow these rules of thumb and you won't go wrong:

✦ Always select *all* the cells containing information you want to copy or move.

✦ When you select a cell to receive the information, select the *upper-left corner* of the block where you want the new information to appear. You *don't* need to select multiple cells to complete the moving or copying process; 1-2-3 will automatically fill up additional cells to accommodate the number of cells you move or copy.

In 1-2-3, you can use two different methods to copy or move information:

✦ Drag and drop
✦ Cut (or copy) and paste

Both of these methods are discussed below.

Dragging and Dropping Information

If you want to move or copy information a short distance in the same worksheet, dragging and dropping will probably be the most efficient method for you to use.

Note   If you need to move or copy information a fairly large distance within the same worksheet — from an original location that you can see to a destination location that you can't see at the same time — consider using the cut (or copy) and paste method described later in this chapter; you may find it easier than the drag and drop method.

The drag and drop method works the same way whether you are moving or copying information. Follow these steps:

1. Select the cell or cells containing the information you want to move or copy.

2. Slide the mouse pointer (drag it) over the edge of the selected cell or range until you see the mouse pointer change to a hand.

3. To copy the information, press and hold the Ctrl key.

4. Drag the information to the cell that represents the upper-left corner of the destination location. If you are holding Ctrl, you'll see a plus sign (+) attached to the mouse pointer shaped like a hand; otherwise, you'll see just a hand. As you move the information, you'll see a dotted outline that indicates where the information will appear if you drop it (see Figure 9-1).

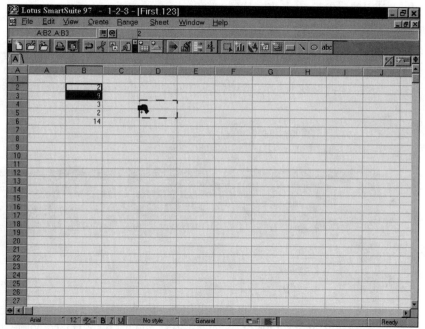

Figure 9-1: The mouse pointer looks like a hand grabbing something as you move or copy information.

5. Release the mouse button (if you're copying, release the mouse button *before* you release the Ctrl key). The new information appears in the destination location. If you copied information, it still appears in the original location; if you moved information, the cells at the original location appear blank.

Cutting (or Copying) and Pasting Information

This technique is particularly useful under three different sets of circumstances:

✦ If you need to move or copy information between worksheets or workbooks.

✦ If you need to move or copy information a long distance on the same worksheet.

✦ If you need to copy the same information several times.

There is one important distinction between the drag and drop method discussed above and the cut or copy and paste method: When you drag and drop, 1-2-3 *does not* store information on the Windows Clipboard. For this reason, you should not use the drag and drop method if you intend to copy the same information several times.

You use the Cut SmartIcon to move information or the Copy SmartIcon to copy information. To do so, follow these steps:

1. Select the cell(s) you want to move or copy.

2. Click the Cut SmartIcon to move the information; click the Copy SmartIcon to copy the information. The title bar changes to remind you of your next step (see Figure 9-2); if you cut the information, it disappears from the selected cells.

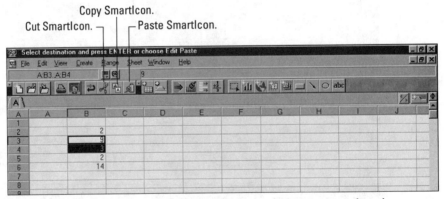

Figure 9-2: After cutting or copying, 1-2-3's title bar helps you complete the process.

3. Select the cell that represents the upper-left corner of the destination location and press Enter or click the Paste SmartIcon. 1-2-3 places the information you cut or copied in the new location.

At this point, if you want the information to appear anywhere else in the workbook, repeat the last step, clicking the Paste SmartIcon instead of pressing Enter.

Understanding Referencing

Referencing is a term 1-2-3 uses to describe using a cell address. In the last chapter, you learned that you can enter text, numbers, dates, and times into cells. You also can enter cell addresses into cells. For example, suppose your workbook contains some numbers, like the one shown in Figure 9-3. Suppose further, that you want to repeat the number shown in B3 in D7. You could just type the number, or you could type the cell address that contains the number you want to repeat.

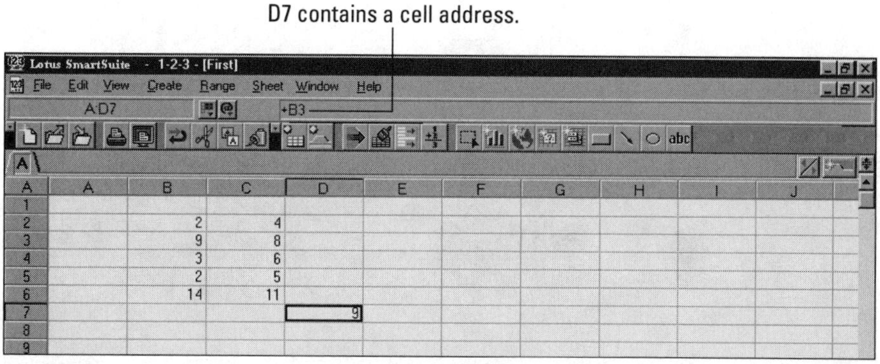

D7 contains a cell address.

Figure 9-3: You can type cell addresses into cells.

Note

As you might recall from Chapter 8, "Working with Worksheet Files," when you type numbers in 1-2-3, they align at the right edge of the cell. You can control the alignment of text entries by using the apostrophe, carat, and quotation alignment characters. To type a cell address, you must also use a special character to precede it; otherwise, 1-2-3 assumes you're entering a label, because the first character of every cell address is text. To tell 1-2-3 that you're entering a cell address instead of a label, precede the cell address with a plus sign (+) or an equal sign (=).

The beauty of using a cell address in D7 instead of retyping the value in B3 becomes clear when you change the value in B3. Every time you change B3, D7 will also change.

OK, so now you know how to reference a cell — type its address. References become a very powerful tool when you include them in formulas, as you'll learn in the next section. 1-2-3 recognizes three different kinds of cell references:

✦ Relative references

✦ Absolute references

✦ Mixed references

Each of these are discussed below.

Relative Referencing

If you simply type a cell address, such as +B3, you are typing a *relative reference*. When you use a relative reference, 1-2-3 doesn't look at the actual location you typed; instead it looks at the location *in relation to* the current location of the cell pointer. The relative reference B3 in cell D7 actually means that 1-2-3 should use the value from the cell two columns to the left and four rows above the current cell. If you copy this relative reference to another cell, say E7, 1-2-3 will then adjust the reference so it points to the cell two columns to the left and four rows above the new cell. In this case the cell two columns to the left and four rows above E7 would be C3, as shown in Figure 9-4.

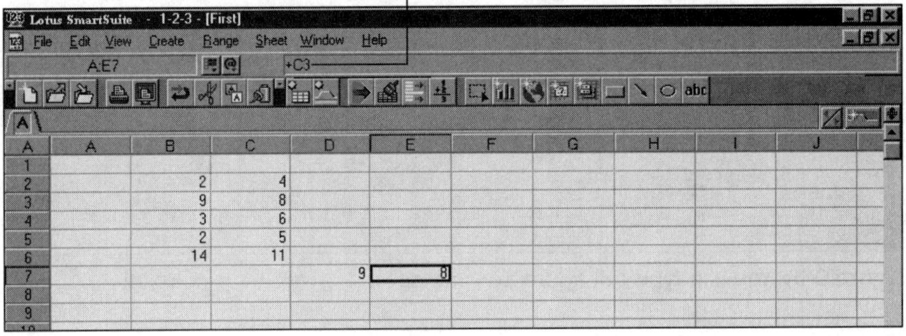

Figure 9-4: When you copy a cell containing a relative cell reference, 1-2-3 adjusts the cell reference.

In most cases, you're going to use relative cell references because you're going to want 1-2-3 to adjust the references when you copy the cells. Suppose you have three columns of numbers; Column A contains January sales figures, Column B contains February sales figures, and Column C contains March sales figures. At the bottom of Column A, you enter the formula to sum the January sales figures. Instead of reentering that formula for February and March, you can copy the formula. If you use relative references when you sum Column A and copy the formula to Columns B and C, 1-2-3 will adjust the formula to sum Columns B and C, respectively.

Absolute Referencing

There will be occasions, however, when you don't want 1-2-3 to adjust a cell reference when you copy the cell. Suppose, for example, that you've built a worksheet similar to the one in Figure 9-5 that contains product sales information. Your products are listed in Column A, and Columns B through D contain monthly sales data for the first quarter. In Column E, you sum each product's total sales for the quarter. In Column F, you calculate each product's total sales divided by the total for all products, using the following formula:

Product's Total Sales / All Sales

The formula in F2 should be E2/E6 — the total of the hotdog sales divided by the total of all sales. The formula in F3 should be E3/E6. The formula in F4 should be E4/E6. The formula in F5 should be E5/E6. Last, the formula in F6 should be E6/E6.

Notice that E2, E3, E4, and E5 each need to be divided by E6—the total of all sales. In other words, you want each of the formulas to absolutely refer to cell E6. To make a reference absolute you add a dollar sign ($) before the column letter and the row number, as in E6. When you use an absolute reference, 1-2-3 always refers to the same cell, even when you copy the reference to a different worksheet cell.

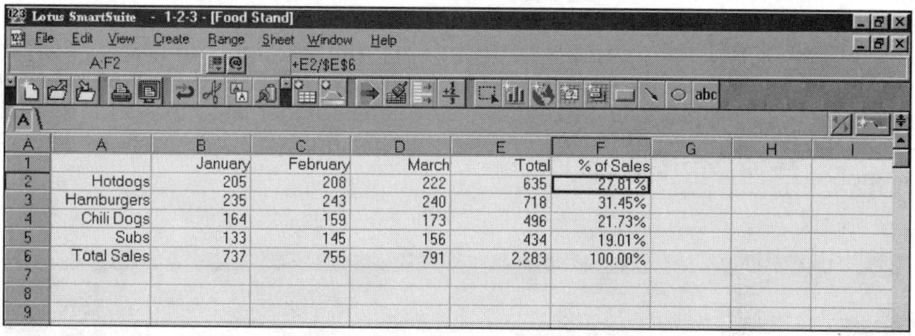

	A	B	C	D	E	F	G	H	I
1		January	February	March	Total	% of Sales			
2	Hotdogs	205	208	222	635	27.81%			
3	Hamburgers	235	243	240	718	31.45%			
4	Chili Dogs	164	159	173	496	21.73%			
5	Subs	133	145	156	434	19.01%			
6	Total Sales	737	755	791	2,283	100.00%			

Figure 9-5: When you calculate a percentage of the whole and need to copy the formula, the reference in the formula to the total sales must be absolute.

If you use an absolute reference to E6 when you create the formula in F2, you'll be able to copy the formula from F2 to F3, F4, F5, and F6. 1-2-3 will adjust the first part of the formula but not the absolute reference to E6. When you use absolute references, 1-2-3 looks at the cell you specify; it *does not* take its position into consideration.

You can quickly change a cell reference from relative to absolute. Select the cell containing the reference you want to change and press F2 to edit that cell. Use the left arrow key to place the insertion point anywhere in the cell reference you want to change. Then, press F4. 1-2-3 will add the dollar signs for you.

Mixed References

On occasion, you may want part of a reference to be absolute and part to be relative; that is, you may want to create a reference that you can copy in which 1-2-3 will hold part of the reference constant while changing the other portion. For example, you may want to increment the row number without changing the column letter.

You can make create a "mixed reference" by including the dollar sign before either the column letter or the row number, as appropriate. If you copied the reference $F6, 1-2-3 would hold the column constant but change the row number as appropriate. Similarly, if you copied the reference F$6, 1-2-3 would change the column letter as appropriate but hold the row number constant.

As an example, consider the worksheet shown in Figure 9-6. In this case you use 1-2-3 to calculate the monthly payments for a number of different auto loans in order to see how much you can afford when you're shopping for a new car. The formula in cell B2 is @PMT($A2,B$1/12,60). The @PMT function takes three arguments — principal, interest rate, and term, respectively. Because you want to compare several different loan amounts and interest rates, you need a formula that references the correct column (A) for the principal, and the correct row (1) for the interest rate (because interest is normally quoted as an annual rate, you need to divide the rate by 12 to obtain the monthly rate). The formula in B2 uses $A2 to make certain the principal always references column A, but adjusts for the proper row. Likewise, B$1 always refers to the interest rate row, but adjusts for the proper column. When you copy the formula from cell B2 to B2..H17, the mixed references enable 1-2-3 to properly calculate the entire range of loan amounts and interest rates. For more information on formulas that use built-in 1-2-3 functions, see "Functions," later in this chapter.

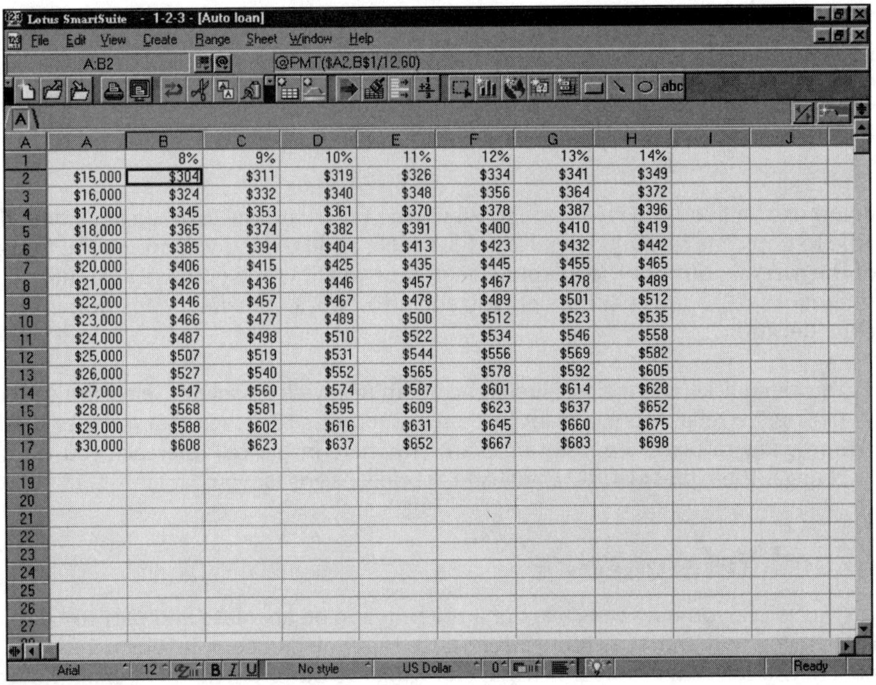

	A	B	C	D	E	F	G	H	I	J
1		8%	9%	10%	11%	12%	13%	14%		
2	$15,000	$304	$311	$319	$326	$334	$341	$349		
3	$16,000	$324	$332	$340	$348	$356	$364	$372		
4	$17,000	$345	$353	$361	$370	$378	$387	$396		
5	$18,000	$365	$374	$382	$391	$400	$410	$419		
6	$19,000	$385	$394	$404	$413	$423	$432	$442		
7	$20,000	$406	$415	$425	$435	$445	$455	$465		
8	$21,000	$426	$436	$446	$457	$467	$478	$489		
9	$22,000	$446	$457	$467	$478	$489	$501	$512		
10	$23,000	$466	$477	$489	$500	$512	$523	$535		
11	$24,000	$487	$498	$510	$522	$534	$546	$558		
12	$25,000	$507	$519	$531	$544	$556	$569	$582		
13	$26,000	$527	$540	$552	$565	$578	$592	$605		
14	$27,000	$547	$560	$574	$587	$601	$614	$628		
15	$28,000	$568	$581	$595	$609	$623	$637	$652		
16	$29,000	$588	$602	$616	$631	$645	$660	$675		
17	$30,000	$608	$623	$637	$652	$667	$683	$698		

Figure 9-6: Use mixed references when you need part of the reference absolute and part of the reference relative.

Formulas, Mathematical Operators, and Calculations in 1-2-3

Formulas are just what you think they are: numbers combined with mathematical operators to produce a result. 1-2-3 recognizes and uses some standard mathematical operators as well as some Boolean operators, both of which are discussed in the next section.

1-2-3 and Mathematical Operators

Mathematical operators are the symbols you use to represent operations such as addition and subtraction. In 1-2-3, use the operators shown in Table 9-1 to represent their corresponding functions.

Table 9-1	
Mathematical Operators	
Symbol	**Function**
+	Add numbers
–	Subtract numbers
*	Multiply numbers
/	Divide numbers
^	Raise numbers to a power, or multiply a number by itself a specified number of times. The number of times is called an *exponent*.

In addition to these mathematical operators, 1-2-3 also supports logical operators such as those used in Boolean algebra. In Boolean algebra, a formula's result can be either true or false; 1 is used to represent a "true" outcome, while 0 is used to represent a "false" outcome. In 1-2-3, you can formulate Boolean questions about worksheet information. For example, you might use a Boolean expression to ask "Were last year's sales higher than this year's sales?" or "Did the Rochester plant produce more than the Erie plant last year?" 1-2-3 recognizes the logical operators listed in Table 9-2.

Table 9-2	
Logical Operators	
Operator	**Description**
>	Greater than
<	Less than
=	Equals

(continued)

Table 9-2 (continued)	
Operator	**Description**
<>	Does not equal
>=	Greater than or equal to
<=	Less than or equal to
#NOT#	Logical NOT, which is used in conditional statements; when you use the logical NOT, 1-2-3 returns false when the condition is actually true and true when the condition is actually false
#AND#	Logical AND, which is used in complex statements that contain multiple conditions; when you use the logical AND, all the conditions must meet the criteria
#OR#	Logical OR, which is used in complex statements that contain multiple conditions; when you use the logical OR, only one of the conditions must meet the criteria

For example, if you want to know if the value in cell A1 is greater than 100, you could use the Boolean formula +A1>100. If the value in A1 is greater than 100, the formula result will be 1 (one). If the value in A1 is 100 or less, the formula result will be 0 (zero). You might use this type of formula to determine whether to pay a sales bonus, for example.

Creating a Formula

A formula might be 2+6-3*2 and you can type such a formula in a single cell; 1-2-3 will display what you typed in the Contents box and the result of the formula in the selected cell. This formula is a valid formula, however, if you use cell addresses instead of actual values; you begin to take advantage of the power 1-2-3 provides when you create a formula. Let's look at an example. Suppose the numbers in cells B2..B5 and cell B6 contained a formula that used the cell addresses of the numbers in the formula instead of the actual numbers. The formula in B6 would then be B2+B3–B4*B5. The result would be the same and it would appear in B6, but the Contents box would show the formula (see Figure 9-7).

If you start typing B2+B3–B4*B5, 1-2-3 will assume you're entering a label, because the first character you type, B, is text. To tell 1-2-3 that you're entering a formula instead of a label, make sure you precede the first entry of the formula with a plus sign (+) or an equal sign (=).

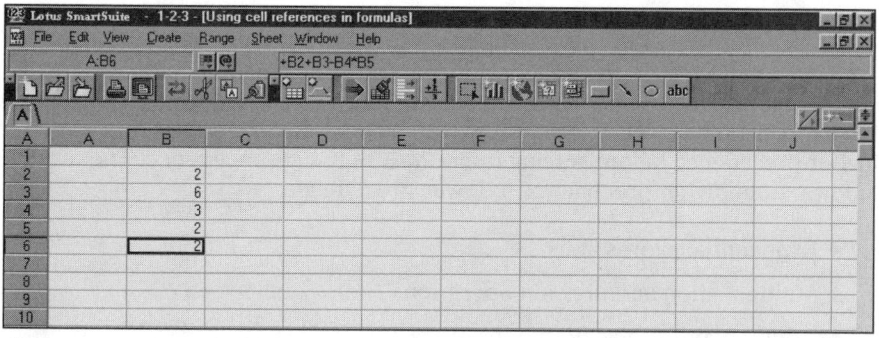

Figure 9-7: A formula that uses cell addresses instead of actual values.

Why is this powerful? If you change the contents of cell B2, B3, B4, or B5, 1-2-3 will automatically update the value that appears in B6 — without changing the formula stored in B6 — to reflect the change (see Figure 9-8). If, however, you had used the numbers in the formula, rather than cell references, you would have to modify the formula itself to change the result. The moral: Use cell addresses instead of numbers in formulas whenever possible.

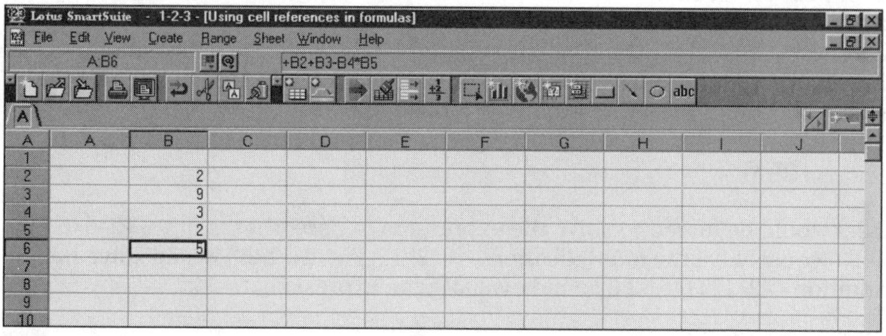

Figure 9-8: The formula in B6 makes the value that appears in B6 change to reflect the change made to B3.

Typing Numbers That Aren't Really Numbers

You *must* include an alignment character (', ^, or ") when you enter a number that really is a label; for example, you don't typically use phone numbers in math calculations. To correctly enter a phone number in 1-2-3, precede the phone number with an alignment character. If you don't use an alignment character, 1-2-3 will attempt to subtract the second portion of the phone number from the first portion. That is, if you type 985-7023 *with* an alignment character, then the number will appear in your worksheet as a typical phone number. However, if you type the same number *without* including an alignment character, 1-2-3 will display –6038 in the cell containing 985-7023.

Controlling How 1-2-3 Calculates

1-2-3 uses the order of precedence you learned in high school math when solving a complex formula. That is, 1-2-3 solves a formula one expression at a time and reads the expression from left to right; however, by default, 1-2-3 solves operations of higher precedence before solving operations of lower precedence. The order is as follows, from higher precedence to lower precedence:

✦ Exponential expressions

✦ Multiplication and division operations

✦ Addition and subtraction operations

✦ Logical operations

In high school math, you learned that you could change the order of calculation by using parentheses. 1-2-3 also uses parentheses to change the order of calculation. The rule is simple: Any expression that appears in parentheses is evaluated before any expression not in parentheses. That way, you can force 1-2-3 to add before it multiplies. Let's take a look at the effect of using parentheses with some actual numbers.

In our earlier example, we let 1-2-3 evaluate the expression 2+9–3*2. 1-2-3 produced the result of 5. 1-2-3 solved the multiplication first — 3*2=6 — and then solved the addition — 2+9=11. Last in this expression, 1-2-3 solved the subtraction — 11–6=5. However, suppose we rewrote the expression to include parentheses around the subtraction, and the expression now looked like this:

2+(9–3)*2

1-2-3 would be forced to solve the expression in parentheses first — 9–3=6. Then, 1-2-3 would solve the multiplication — 6*2=12. Finally, 1-2-3 would solve the addition — 2+12=14. 1-2-3 would evaluate the expression to 14.

Now that you've seen the math with real numbers, let's use cell addresses instead (as recommended earlier) and add the parentheses. As you can see in Figure 9-9, 1-2-3 evaluates the expression and returns a result of 14.

Linking Sheets with Formulas

Another powerful feature in 1-2-3 is the ability to use formulas to perform mathematical calculations across sheets in a workbook. Suppose, for example, that you have a workbook containing expense information for three departments that make up a division. Suppose, further, that the workbook contains four sheets — one for each of the three departments and one "totals" sheet for the division. A department's sheet might look like the one in the top half of Figure 9-10, while the "totals" sheet might look like the one in the bottom half of Figure 9-10.

Parentheses change the order of calculation.

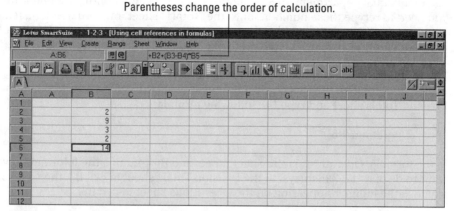

Figure 9-9: Using parentheses changes the order in which 1-2-3 performs calculations — and affects the result 1-2-3 displays.

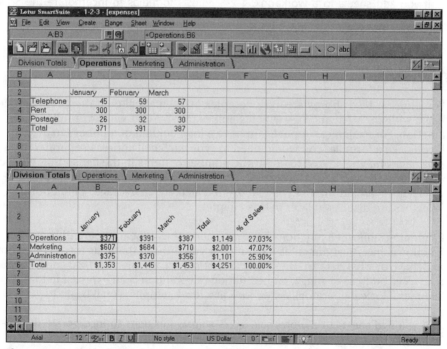

Figure 9-10: An individual department's sheet (shown at the top), and the sheet containing totals for all departments (shown at the bottom).

Each individual department sheet contains totals for each month. You might think you need to retype these numbers onto the "totals" sheet, but you don't. Instead, you can use a formula to link the sheets together, displaying on the totals sheet the information previously calculated on the individual department's sheet.

The total for the Operations Department's January expenses appears in B6. To display that total on the Division Totals sheet, place the cell pointer in B3 on the Division Totals sheet and type the following formula:

+Operations:B6

In the formula, Operations is the Sheet name, and B6 contains the information you want to display. 1-2-3 displays, in the Division Totals sheet in cell B3, the value 371, which is the number appearing on the Operations sheet in cell B6.

Each of the cells on the Division Totals sheet that displays a value actually contains a formula that draws the value from some other sheet in the workbook.

If you add sheets to a workbook, 1-2-3 adjusts formulas to incorporate the Sheet name.

Functions

Functions in 1-2-3 abbreviate long, complex mathematical operations. All functions begin with an "at" sign (@) — which signifies to 1-2-3 that whatever follows is a function. For example, suppose you have a long column of numbers to average. If you used a formula, you would need to type each cell address separated by a plus sign, *and* you'd need to count the number of items in the list so that you could divide the sum by the correct value. That would be a long and tedious process. 1-2-3 has an @AVG function you can use to calculate an average. @Functions Selectors are discussed later in this chapter.

In addition, almost all functions have *arguments* that appear in parentheses after the function name. An argument is a parameter you provide that tells the function how to behave or what data to use when calculating. An argument in 1-2-3 can be a value, text, a cell address or range, or a condition (a condition is an expression that includes a logical operator). As we look at a few functions, you'll begin to get the idea.

If you add sheets to a workbook, 1-2-3 adjusts functions to incorporate the Sheet name.

Adding Columns of Numbers

Because the most common mathematical operation that people perform in 1-2-3 is to add a column or row of numbers, 1-2-3 contains a function that helps you add long lists of numbers: the @SUM function.

To make things even easier, 1-2-3 has a SmartIcon you can use to instantly add a column or row of numbers. Consider the worksheet in Figure 9-11. In this worksheet, you might want to sum columns B, C, and D. To quickly sum column B, select cell B6 and click the Sum SmartIcon. 1-2-3 places the @SUM function in B6. The argument for the @SUM function is the range of cells to sum, so 1-2-3 includes the range B1:B5 in parentheses (1-2-3 doesn't know whether you might replace the label in B1 with a numerical value, so it includes the entire contiguous range from B1 through B5).

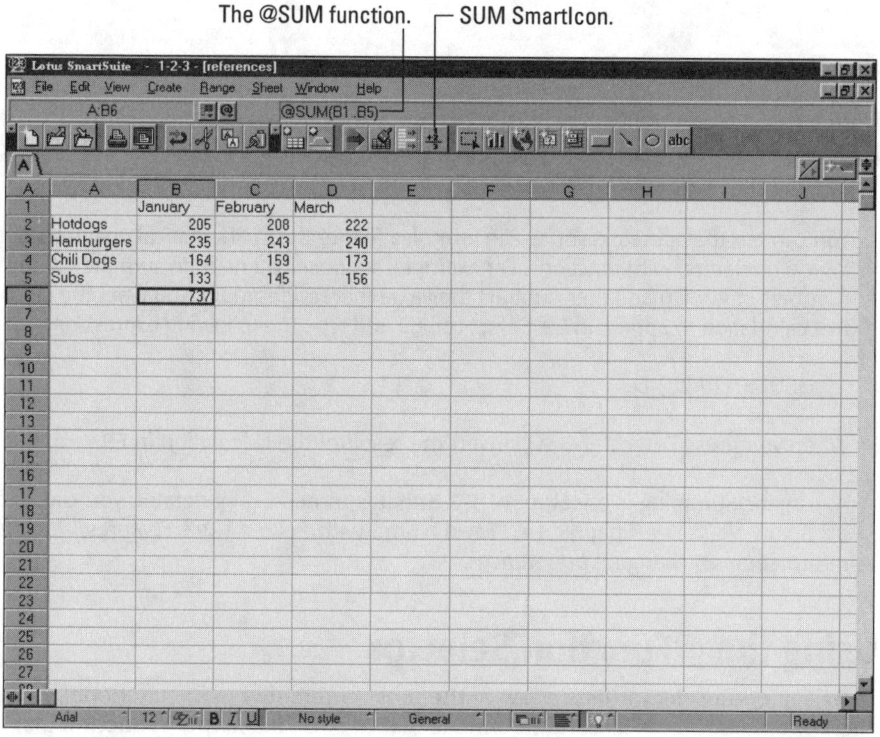

The @SUM function. ─ SUM SmartIcon.

	A	B	C	D	E	F	G	H	I	J
1		January	February	March						
2	Hotdogs	205	208	222						
3	Hamburgers	235	243	240						
4	Chili Dogs	164	159	173						
5	Subs	133	145	156						
6		737								

Figure 9-11: Use the Sum SmartIcon to quickly add a column or row of numbers.

You can, just as easily, add numbers across a row. To add row 2, place the cell pointer in E2 and click the Sum SmartIcon. Better yet, select the entire range of numbers plus an extra row and column to apply both row and column totals in one step. For example, select the range B2..E6 before you click the Sum SmartIcon to add the row and column totals for B2..D5. Just make certain there are no existing entries in the totals row or column before you select the range.

A Trick for Adding Numbers

1-2-3 has a built-in shortcut that's really clever. If you type the word "Total" or "Totals" as the heading label for the row or column you want to sum, 1-2-3 will automatically sum the rows below the label or the columns next to the label. Only two rules apply to use this trick:

1. You *cannot* include an alignment character with the label. Just type the word and press Enter or an arrow key.

2. The cells in the rows below or the columns next to the word Total or Totals must be empty when you type.

Notice that 1-2-3 actually enters the formula with two periods separating the cells in the range. You can type B2:B6 and 1-2-3 will convert that to B2..B6. If you prefer, you can type ranges separated by two periods.

Note

You can mix the operators you use in formulas (either the mathematical operators or the logical operators) with functions. For example, suppose you need to sum the column of numbers in A2:A20 and then subtract the value that resides in D7. You want the result of this calculation to appear in E9. Select cell E9 and type the following expression:

@SUM(A2:A20)-D7

When you press Enter, 1-2-3 will insert the result of the calculation in E9.

More Info

Automatic Summing is a feature of 1-2-3 that is turned on by default; you can turn it off if you want. See Chapter 14, "Saving Time with Power 1-2-3 Features," for more information on changing preferences.

Using the @Function Selector

The @Function Selector lists a few of the most commonly used functions. If you click the @Function Selector and choose List All, you'll see the @Function List dialog box (see Figure 9-12).

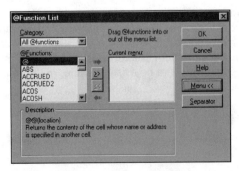

Figure 9-12: Easily insert one of the commonly used functions in your worksheet by selecting it from this list.

Following are descriptions of some of the @Functions:

✦ **@SUM** adds long lists of numbers.

✦ **@AVG** calculates the average of a list of numbers.

✦ **@ROUND** rounds decimal values to whole numbers.

✦ **@IF** allows you to evaluate a condition and determine whether it is true or false.

✦ **@TODAY** inserts today's date in the selected cell; this date will change as the year progresses.

✦ **@NPV** calculates the net present value of a range.

Let's see how the @Function Selector works. Suppose you want to calculate the average sales for January. Place the cell pointer in the cell where you want the average to appear. Click the @Function Selector and choose AVG. 1-2-3 inserts the function in the cell and provides you with a hint for the argument (see Figure 9-13).

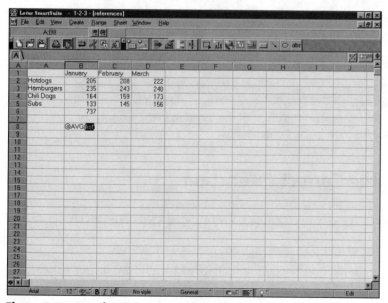

Figure 9-13: Use the @Function Selector to insert functions with hints for the arguments.

Because the hint, *list*, is already selected, anything you supply will replace it. To average January sales, select the range B2:B5.

Selecting a range, rather than typing it, helps ensure that you don't introduce any typing mistakes.

When you press Enter, 1-2-3 will calculate the average of the range. You'll see the result in the cell, and the function in the Contents box (see Figure 9-14). If you're the untrusting sort, sum your list and divide by the number of items in the list.

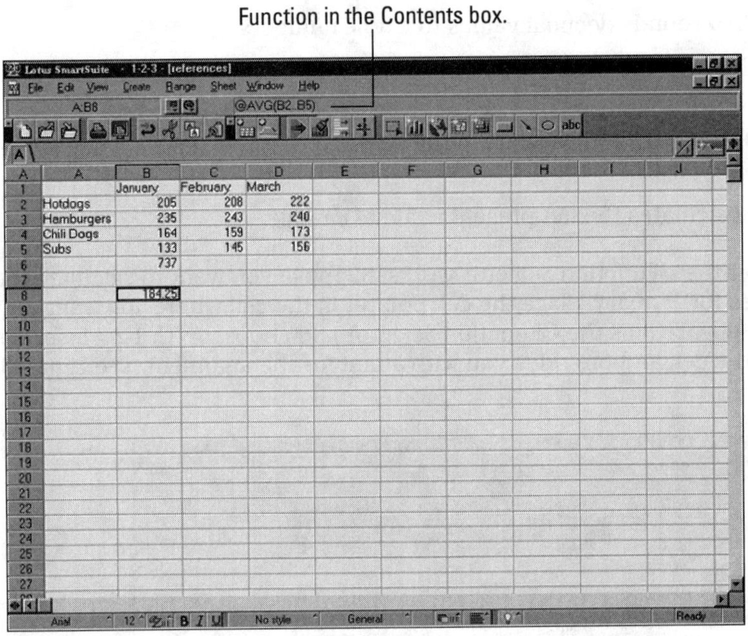

Function in the Contents box.

Figure 9-14: 1-2-3 displays the result of the function in the worksheet, and the actual function in the Contents box.

Finding the Correct @Function

Suppose you have no clue what function 1-2-3 uses to calculate the task you need to accomplish. Try viewing the functions by category. Follow these steps:

1. Select the cell into which you want to place a function.

2. Click the @Function Selector and choose List All. 1-2-3 displays the @Function List dialog box.

3. Initially, all functions are listed in alphabetical order. Open the Category list box to select a category to narrow your search (see Figure 9-15).

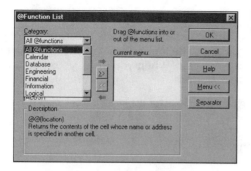

Figure 9-15: The Category list lets you view functions of a specific type.

4. After you choose a category, only the @Functions in that category appear in the list below — again, in alphabetical order. Notice that when you highlight a particular function, 1-2-3 displays an explanation of its purpose in the Description box below the list (see Figure 9-16).

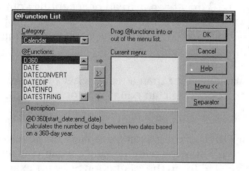

Figure 9-16: When you highlight a function, an explanation of its purpose appears in the Description box.

5. When you find the function you need, highlight it and click OK. 1-2-3 will insert the function in the selected cell along with the argument hint(s) in parentheses.

6. Supply the arguments and press Enter.

Adding an @Function to the @Function Menu

Now that you found the function, you may not want to hunt for it the next time you need it. Or, if you find yourself using, on a regular basis, a particular function that doesn't appear when you click the @Function Selector, you may want to add it to the @Function Selector list. Follow these steps:

1. Click the @Function Selector and choose List All to display the @Function List dialog box.

2. Find the function you want to add to the list. Type the first letter of the function's name to move to that letter in the alphabetical list. Or, use the Category list to narrow the search.

3. Click the Menu button.

4. To add a function to the list, drag the function to the location where you want it to appear in the list. As you drag, the mouse pointer changes to a hand with a plus sign, indicating you are copying. When you drop, your function appears in the list.

To remove a function from the @Function Selector list, drag it from the list on the right to the list on the left. While you drag, the mouse pointer will look like a trash can.

5. Click OK to save your changes.

What to Do When a Formula or Function Doesn't Work

When you enter a formula or function, you may see the text of your formula or the function, or you may see ERR, or 1-2-3 may beep instead of accepting your formula or function. This indicates that there is an error preventing 1-2-3 from properly evaluating the formula. To correct the problem you'll first have to determine just what is wrong. Here are some things to look for:

✦ If you see the text of the formula rather than a result, check to make certain you started the formula with a plus sign, an equal sign, or an at sign.

✦ If you see ERR, check to make certain you haven't told 1-2-3 to divide by zero.

✦ Another possible cause for ERR is if you haven't supplied all the necessary arguments. You may want to try starting over, making certain you actually provide all the information called for in the @Function Selector example.

✦ If 1-2-3 seems to refuse to accept the arguments, make certain you haven't accidentally added a space to the formula. You may think that spaces between the arguments make the formula easier to read, but 1-2-3 doesn't recognize extra spaces.

✦ If the status indicator says "Circ" you've created a circular reference — a formula that ultimately refers to itself. For example, if you include the formula cell in an @SUM formula, there is no "correct" answer because every time 1-2-3 recalculates the worksheet the sum will increase.

Occasionally a circular reference may actually be justified. The classic example of this is the case in which sales bonuses are based on net profit. But because commissions and bonuses are a part of the cost of sales, it is necessary to create a circular reference to calculate the sales bonus. Fortunately this situation is the exception, rather than the rule, and most circular references should be considered errors to be eliminated.

Using Range Names for Efficiency

Suppose you've got a range of numbers in your worksheet that you continually reference as you work in the sheet. You might find yourself getting tired of continually typing B4:B23. And, each time you type the range, you introduce the possibility of additional data entry errors due to typographical errors. *Range names* are an excellent solution. Create an English-language name for the range and use that instead of the cell addresses when you need to reference the range.

If you add sheets to a workbook, 1-2-3 adjusts named ranges to include the Sheet name.

Naming a Range

Range names, because they look like words, are often easier to use while you work. You can name a single cell or a group of cells.

When you choose a range name, keep the following rules in mind:

✦ It cannot be more than 15 characters long.

✦ You can include spaces in the name, but don't start the name with a space, an exclamation point (!), or a number.

✦ Don't include any of the following characters in a range name: comma, semicolon, period, plus or minus sign, asterisk, question mark, ampersand (&), curly braces ({}), slash, less than or greater than signs, the "at" sign, or the pound sign.

✦ Don't use a cell address, a function name, or a key such as Backspace, as a range name.

Follow these steps to name a range:

1. Select the cell or cells you want to name.

2. Choose Range ➪ Name. The Name dialog box appears (see Figure 9-17).

Figure 9-17: Use this dialog box to create a range name.

3. Type a name for the range and click OK.

Once you name a range, if you select the range, the range name will appear in the Selection Indicator instead of the cell address (see Figure 9-18).

The Selection Indicator contains the range name.

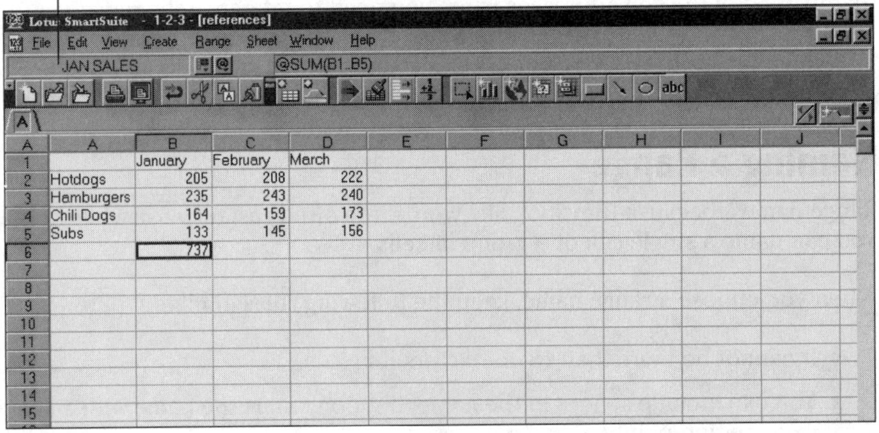

Figure 9-18: 1-2-3 uses the range name instead of the cell address in the Selection Indicator.

Note   If the named range consists of more than one cell, you must select all the cells in the range to see the range name in the Selection Indicator.

Selecting a Named Range

Use the Navigator to easily select a named range. Just click the Navigator to display a list of available named ranges (see Figure 9-19). Then, click the range you want to select. 1-2-3 selects that range.

Navigator.

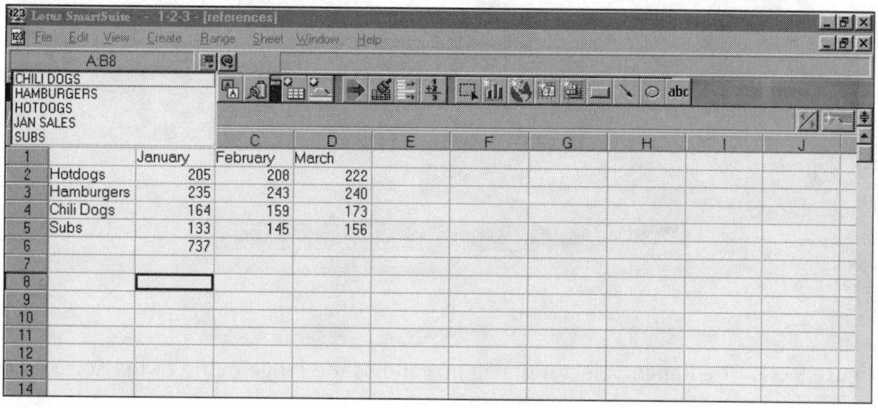

Figure 9-19: Use the Navigator to view and select a named range.

You also can select a range name using the Go To dialog box. Press F5 to display the dialog box (see Figure 9-20).

Figure 9-20: You can "go to" a named range.

Select the range name and choose OK. 1-2-3 selects the named range.

Changing a Range Name

You can change a range name in one of two ways: You can change the label you used or you can change the cells included in the range. You make both changes from the Name dialog box. Choose Range ⇨ Name.

To change the cells included in an existing range, highlight that range name in the Name dialog box. Then, click the Range Selector. 1-2-3 hides the Name dialog box and displays the Range Selector dialog box and selects the cells currently included in the named range (see Figure 9-21).

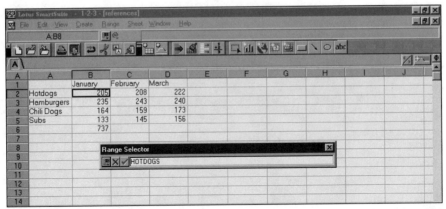

Figure 9-21: The Range Selector dialog box shows the range name of the selected cells.

Drag to select all the cells you want to include in the named range, even cells that were previously included. When you release the mouse button, 1-2-3 redisplays the Name dialog box, and the new range you selected appears at the bottom of the box. Click Add and 1-2-3 redefines the cells included in the named range and continues to display the Name dialog box. If you prefer, you can click OK instead of Add; in this case, 1-2-3 will still redefine the range name, but the Name dialog box will close.

To change the name of an existing range, highlight the existing name in the Name dialog box. Then, change the Name and click Add. You'll see both the old name and the new name in the list. Click the old name to select it and then click Delete to delete it.

Note

To delete any range name, choose Range ⇨ Name; highlight the range name; and click Delete. Deleting the range name *does not* affect the contents of the cells included in the range name. You simply can no longer refer to that cell or group of cells by name; instead, you must use cell addresses.

Using a Range Name in a Formula or Function

If you name a range, you can use either the cell address *or* the range name in formulas or functions. For example, suppose you want to average the sales of hotdogs for the quarter. Your formula would be @AVG(hotdogs). You can even choose HOTDOGS from the Navigator. Follow these steps to get an idea of how the process would work.

1. Place the cell pointer in the cell where you want the average to appear.

2. Click the @Function Selector and choose AVG. 1-2-3 fills the cell with the @AVG function and includes the argument hint.

3. Click the Navigator to select a range name as the argument of the function. 1-2-3 replaces the argument hint with the range name.

4. Press Enter. 1-2-3 makes the calculation. The cell displays the result, and the Contents box displays the function that includes a range name as an argument.

Filling a Range

1-2-3 allows you to fill a range of cells automatically with numbers, dates, times, or text using either the Fill dialog box or your mouse. Each method offers certain advantages.

Using the Fill Dialog Box

Filling a range by using the mouse (as described in the next section) is generally faster when you want to fill a relatively small range, such as the cells you can see on one screen. Filling a larger range using the Fill dialog box may be a little easier, especially if you want to use a specific ending value, because you won't have to determine how many cells need to be filled—your ending value will automatically determine the fill range.

Note

To fill a range by example—that is, to fill the range using a set of values that match a pattern you provide—you must type information in at least the first two cells that you select before you open the Fill dialog box. See the following section for an easier approach to filling a range by example.

Select a range of cells to fill and choose Range ▷ Fill. 1-2-3 displays the Fill dialog box (see Figure 9-22).

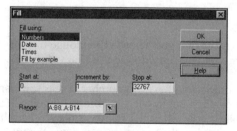

Figure 9-22: Use the Fill dialog box to fill a selected range with numbers, dates, times, or text.

Hot Stuff

You don't need to figure out exactly how many cells to select; you'll be able to tell 1-2-3 to stop filling cells even if you selected more than you need.

Choose whether to fill the range with numbers, dates, times or by example. Fill in the Start At, Increment By, and Stop At boxes. For example, to a fill a range of 10 cells with the numbers 1, 3, 5, 7, 9, and so on, type 1 in the Start At box, type 2 in the Increment By box. Type 19 (the last odd number you want in the range) in the Stop At box. Click OK. 1-2-3 fills the cells as you specified.

Using the Mouse to Fill a Range

As an alternate method, you can use the mouse and fill by example. Let's use the preceding example once again. You want to fill a range of cells with odd numbers. In the first and second cells of the range you want to fill, type the first two numbers of the sequence you want: 1 and 3 in our example.

Note   You need to fill enough cells so that 1-2-3 can identify the pattern you want to use when filling cells; you need a minimum of two cells, but in some cases you may need more.

Then, select those two cells. Move the mouse pointer to the lower-right corner of the selected range. When you point correctly at an edge of the selected range, the mouse pointer changes to the shape you see in Figure 9-23.

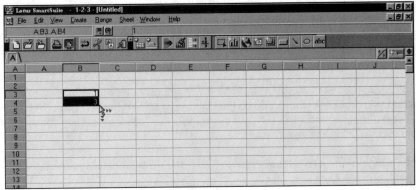

Figure 9-23: When you see a mouse pointer like the one in this figure, you can drag to fill the range.

Drag to select all the cells you want to fill. When you release the mouse button, 1-2-3 fills the selected cells using the model you provided in the first two cells.

Note   When you fill by example, you need to drag across the exact number of cells you want to fill or 1-2-3 will behave like the Energizer Bunny — it just "keeps on going." For example, if you want 1-2-3 to stop filling cells when the numbers reach 17 in the worksheet shown in Figure 9-23, you must drag the mouse pointer down to row 11. That's why it's often easier to use the Fill dialog box when you want to fill a range with a specific set of numbers — you don't have to figure out how many cells will be needed.

Using SmartFill

1-2-3's SmartFill feature makes it easy for you to fill a range with text. How many times have you needed to use the months of the year as column headings? Take advantage of SmartFill. In the first cell you want to fill, type the first month you want listed. Then, use the mouse to fill by example (see Figure 9-24).

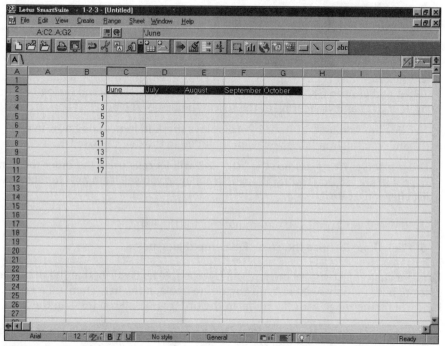

Figure 9-24: Typing June into C2 and then dragging to fill the rest of the selected cells created this list.

Creating and Modifying a Custom Fill List

1-2-3 comes with predefined lists containing the months of the year and the days of the week, but you can create your own custom fill lists. Suppose your company has divisions in a variety of cities around the country: New York, Chicago, Denver, San Francisco, San Diego, Las Vegas, Dallas, and Tampa. You probably find yourself typing these cities over and over in 1-2-3 workbooks. Create a custom fill list to save yourself time using the following steps:

1. Choose File ⇨ User Setup. From the submenu that appears, choose SmartFill Setup. 1-2-3 displays the SmartFill Setup dialog box (see Figure 9-25).

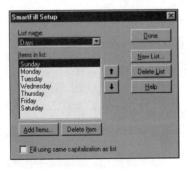

Figure 9-25: Use the SmartFill Setup dialog box to create lists of labels you use frequently.

2. Click New List. 1-2-3 displays a dialog box in which you type a name for the list and choose OK; 1-2-3 then redisplays the SmartFill Setup dialog box with your list name appearing at the top in the List Name box.

3. Click the Add Item button. 1-2-3 displays the Add Item dialog box, in which you type the first label you want included in the list. Choose OK.

Note

Order matters. When you use the list, 1-2-3 will fill cells using the order the items appear in the list. Don't worry, though. In a minute you will learn how to reorder the list after you create it.

4. Repeat Step 3 until you enter all items for the list.

5. Click Done to close the SmartFill Setup dialog box.

To use a custom list you've created, fill by example as described in the previous section, but you only need to type one of the items in the list. Then, fill a range. 1-2-3 will fill the range with the items in the order you entered them in the list.

Note

You don't need to type the first city in the list to use the custom fill list. 1-2-3 will fill the range with the items in the custom list starting with the item you enter as the example and continuing with subsequent items in the order they appear in the list. In the example of cities cited above, if you start by typing San Diego, the next city 1-2-3 will enter in the list is Las Vegas.

Some additional notes about using SmartFill:

✦ If you select a range that is larger than the number of items in the list, 1-2-3 will repeat the list.

✦ You can add items to the list by using the SmartFill Setup dialog box. Select the list and click Add. Follow the preceding steps to complete the process.

✦ You can delete items from the list by using the SmartFill dialog box. Select the list, highlight the item, and click Delete.

✦ You can reorder items in a list by using the SmartFill dialog box. Select the list, highlight the item, and drag it to a new location in the list.

✦   ✦   ✦

Better Spreadsheet Design

At this point, you know enough to "get by" and make use of 1-2-3. Now let's "get efficient" and "get fancy." In this chapter, you'll learn how to change the structure of your worksheet by adding and deleting rows, columns, and cells. The techniques you learn will help you efficiently add new data to your worksheet and remove data you no longer need.

You'll also learn how to improve the appearance of your worksheet using formatting, such as color, font attributes, and alignment for both text and numbers. Using styles, you can store formatting you use regularly — so that you can apply it in one stroke instead of several.

Restructuring a Worksheet

When you start using the worksheet, it's a nice set of rows and columns—and you fly along entering information. At some point, you're going to realize that you left something out—and it belongs between rows 15 and 16 of a worksheet in which you have entered data all the way down to row 52. No, you don't need to retype everything; you can add a row to the worksheet. Similarly, you can add columns or ranges of cells. And, if you find that you have included information that you no longer need, you can delete rows, columns, and ranges of cells.

Inserting and Deleting Rows and Columns

It never fails to happen: You enter a lot of information and then discover one more line you needed to add—right in the middle of all the information you just entered. No problem: add a row. Consider Figure 10-1. To add a row for Finance between Operations and Marketing, click in the worksheet frame, on row 4—the row number that you want to appear *below* the row you add. With the row selected, choose Range ➪ Insert Rows. 1-2-3 inserts a blank row above the row you selected.

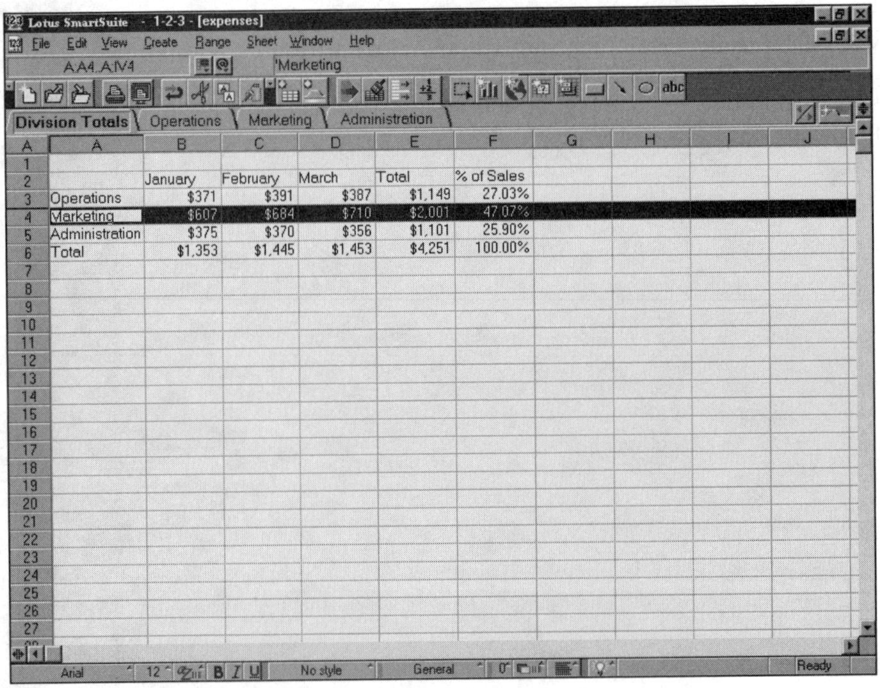

Figure 10-1: 1-2-3 inserts new rows *above* the selected row.

Keep the following significant points in mind:

✦ 1-2-3 inserts rows only when you first select a row. Later in this chapter, you'll learn how to insert cells.

✦ You can insert more than one row by selecting the number of rows you want to insert. 1-2-3 will insert new rows above the first row you select.

✦ After you insert a row, 1-2-3 cancels the selection and places the cell pointer in column A of the first row you added.

✦ When you insert a row at the bottom edge of a selection, the inserted row assumes the formatting of the row above it.

These same points apply to columns, and you use the same technique to add a column, keeping in mind that 1-2-3 will insert new columns *to the left* of the column you select. And, if you insert a column at the right edge of a selection, the inserted column will assume the formatting of the column to its left. To insert a column between the March column and the Totals column in Figure 10-1, select column E in the worksheet frame. Then, choose Range ➪ Insert Columns.

1-2-3's Range menu is context-sensitive. When you select a row, you'll see commands related to rows on the menu; however, when you select a column, you'll see commands related to columns on the menu.

To delete a row or column *and all data contained in that row or column*, use the same technique: select the row(s) or column(s) you want to delete. Then, open the Range menu and choose the appropriate command—Delete Rows or Delete Columns.

As you'll learn later in this chapter, inserting and deleting rows, columns, or cells can affect formulas that refer to the deleted rows, columns, or cells; and you may need to adjust formulas.

Inserting and Deleting a Range of Cells

Suppose you've entered information into A1:D9 and into F1:G8. Now suppose that you find you need to add two rows, but only to the information in range A1:D9. This is a case where you don't add entire rows (or columns, if the situation warrants). Instead, you add cells.

Adding or deleting cells changes the structure of a selected area of your worksheet. You can create a very strange-looking worksheet if you add or delete cells. Remember that you can undo your last action.

When you add cells, you change the structure of a selected portion of your worksheet. To add two rows to the range A1:D9, select the cells you want to appear below the new cells you add. In Figure 10-2, we're adding two rows of cells above A6:D7.

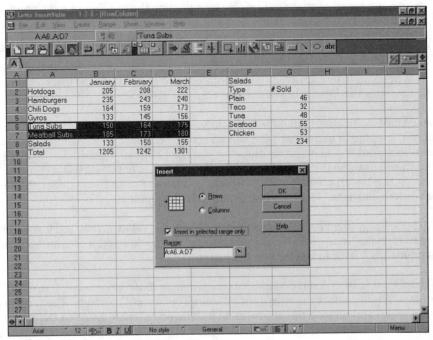

Figure 10-2: Adding cells to a worksheet.

After selecting the cell(s) above which you want to add cells, choose Range ➪ Insert to display the Insert dialog box. To add cells in a row, select the Rows option button and place a check in the Insert in Selected Range Only check box.

When you choose OK, 1-2-3 adds cells above the selected cells. Notice, in Figure 10-3, that adding cells did not affect the information in F1:G8.

As you can see in the Insert dialog box shown in Figure 10-2, you also can add cells in a columnar fashion by choosing the Columns option button and placing a check in the Insert in Selected Range Only check box. Cells added in a columnar fashion will appear to the left of the selection.

You can delete cells using the same technique. Select the cells you want to delete and choose Range ➪ Delete. The Delete dialog box, which closely resembles the Insert dialog box, appears, with the same options. Choose either the Rows or Columns option button and place a check in the Delete in Selected Range Only check box.

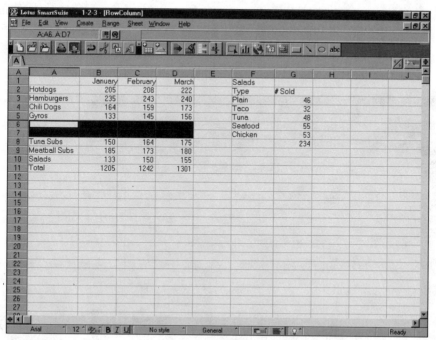

Figure 10-3: When you add cells, you affect only that portion of the worksheet that you selected.

Formulas and Worksheet Structural Changes

Adding or deleting rows, columns, or cells to areas of a worksheet that contain formulas can affect those formulas. Keep in mind the following rule of thumb when you make changes to the structure of your worksheet: If you insert or delete a cell, a row, or a column in the middle of a range that is included in a formula, 1-2-3 will adjust the formula to account for the insertion or deletion. However, if you insert or delete a cell, row, or column *at the edge* of a range that is included in a formula, 1-2-3 will *not* adjust the formula to accommodate the insertion or deletion.

Compare the ranges A11..D20 and F11..I20 in Figure 10-4 to understand this distinction. In columns A through D, a row was added below row 18 and then numbers were entered in columns B, C, and D. Notice that 1-2-3 did not change the values that appear in the Total row. Now compare columns F through I. The new row added in this range appears in the middle of the range — and 1-2-3 adjusted the Total row.

To summarize, you will create inaccuracies in your formulas if you add or delete rows, columns, or cells to which those formulas specifically refer. That's not to say, "Don't delete rows, columns, or cells to which formulas refer," because sometimes that action is unavoidable. Just be aware that you will need to adjust the formulas that refer to added or deleted rows, columns, or cells.

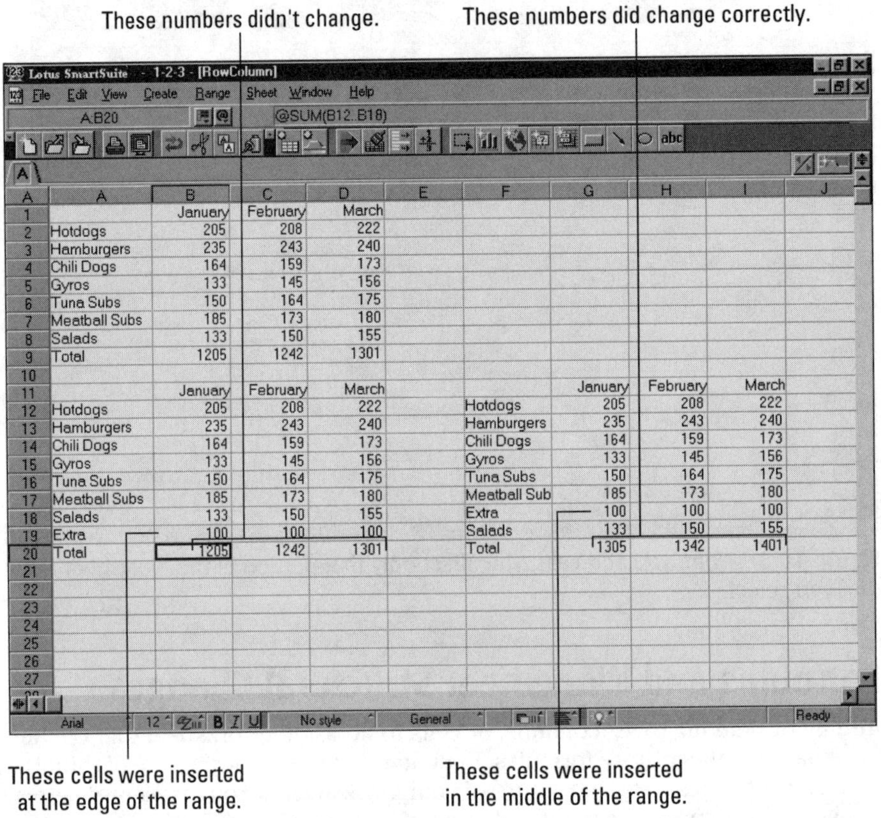

These numbers didn't change.   These numbers did change correctly.

	A	B	C	D	E	F	G	H	I	J
1		January	February	March						
2	Hotdogs	205	208	222						
3	Hamburgers	235	243	240						
4	Chili Dogs	164	159	173						
5	Gyros	133	145	156						
6	Tuna Subs	150	164	175						
7	Meatball Subs	185	173	180						
8	Salads	133	150	155						
9	Total	1205	1242	1301						
10										
11		January	February	March			January	February	March	
12	Hotdogs	205	208	222		Hotdogs	205	208	222	
13	Hamburgers	235	243	240		Hamburgers	235	243	240	
14	Chili Dogs	164	159	173		Chili Dogs	164	159	173	
15	Gyros	133	145	156		Gyros	133	145	156	
16	Tuna Subs	150	164	175		Tuna Subs	150	164	175	
17	Meatball Subs	185	173	180		Meatball Sub	185	173	180	
18	Salads	133	150	155		Extra	100	100	100	
19	Extra	100	100	100		Salads	133	150	155	
20	Total	1205	1242	1301		Total	1305	1342	1401	
21										
22										
23										
24										
25										
26										
27										

These cells were inserted   These cells were inserted
at the edge of the range.   in the middle of the range.

Figure 10-4: You must add cells in the middle of a range if you want 1-2-3 to correctly adjust the formulas.

Formatting Text in Cells

Reading worksheet data — typically columns of numbers with one row and one column of text labels — can easily become boring. You can improve the appearance (and the readability) of your worksheet using formatting.

More Info

On the following pages, you're going to learn about several different formatting techniques that you can apply. If you format one cell with several different attributes, you can copy that cell's formatting to other cells in your worksheet. See "Fast Formatting: A Formatting Shortcut" later in this chapter for details.

Changing the Font and Font Size

By default, 1-2-3 uses a 12-point Arial font for all text and numbers you type. But you can use a large selection of fonts and font sizes available to you. And, 1-2-3's interactive status bar makes changing the font or font size as easy as selecting the cells you want to change and then selecting a new font or font size from the available lists. Figure 10-5 shows the font selector that appears when you click the font name on the status bar. If you click the font size button you can select from the available font sizes.

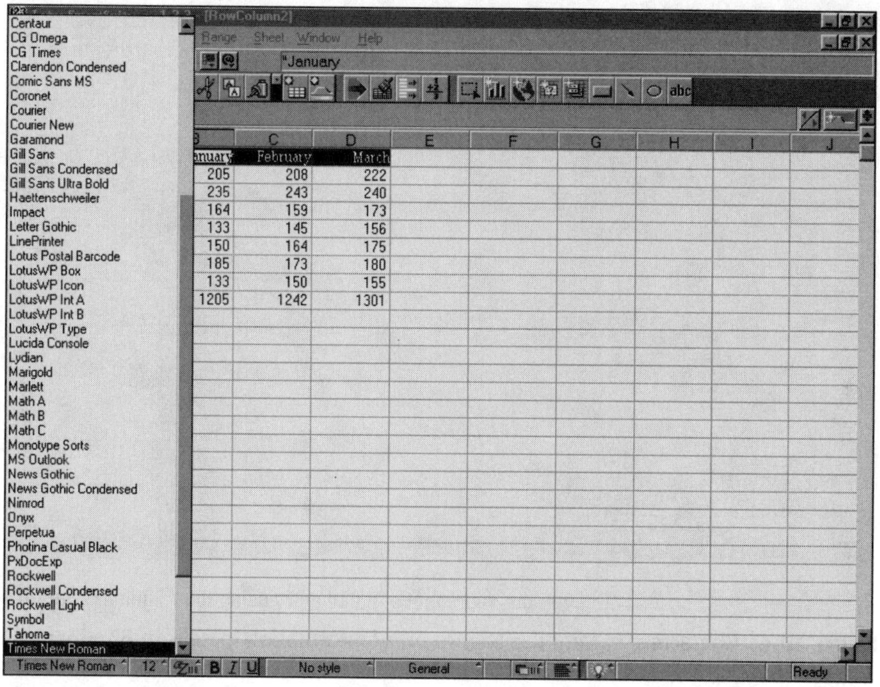

Figure 10-5: Select a font from a large number of options.

Aligning Text Horizontally Within Cells

In Chapter 8, "Working with Worksheet Files," you learned how to use keyboard characters to align text within cells. By simply typing a label, you tell 1-2-3 to align the text in the cell at the left edge of the cell—and 1-2-3 automatically inserts an apostrophe (') in the cell at the beginning of the label. By preceding a label you type with a carat (^), you tell 1-2-3 to align the label in the center of the cell. To align a label with the right edge of a cell, type a quotation mark (") as the first character of the label. In Figure 10-6, the entry in B3 is left-aligned, the entry in C3 is centered, and the entry in D3 is right-aligned. Suppose, however, that you decide you want a different alignment for an entry *after* you type it. To change a cell entry's alignment, use the Alignment button on the status bar.

Centering character.

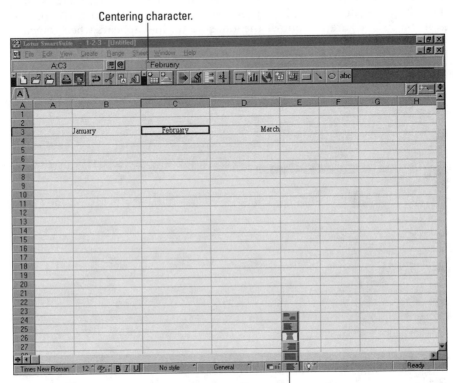

Change the alignment of a cell entry using the Alignment button.

Figure 10-6: Characters control the alignment of information in cells in B3, C3, and D3.

Aligning Text Vertically Within Cells

You can also align text vertically within a cell. In Figure 10-7, the text in B2 is aligned at the top of the cell; the text in C2 is aligned in the center of the cell; and the text in D2 is aligned at the bottom of the cell. Use the Vertical Alignment buttons on the Alignment tab of the Range Properties InfoBox to set vertical alignment (choose Range ➪ Range Properties or click the Range Properties SmartIcon).

More Info

Later in this chapter, you'll learn how to adjust row height so that you can take advantage of vertical alignment.

Range Properties SmartIcon.　　　Vertical Alignment buttons.

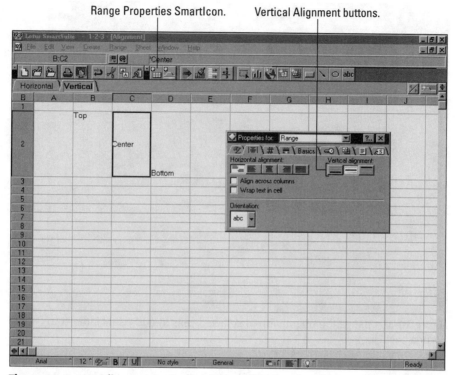

Figure 10-7: You align text vertically within cells using the Alignment tab of the Range Properties InfoBox.

Note

You don't need to close the Range Properties InfoBox to format other cells that you didn't select when you opened the InfoBox. Simply click in the worksheet; the title bar of the InfoBox will turn gray. Select the new group of cells you want to format and click again in the InfoBox. To shrink the size of an InfoBox so that you can see more of the worksheet, double-click its title bar. To redisplay the InfoBox, double-click its title bar again.

Orienting Text Within a Cell

By default, text is oriented horizontally across a cell; you can, however, change the orientation of text within a cell. Use different text orientations to both add interest and save space in a worksheet. Change the orientation of selected cells from the Alignment tab of the Range Properties InfoBox (see Figure 10-8).

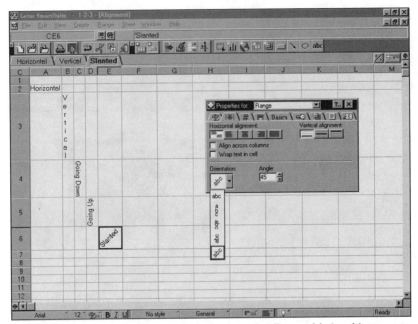

Figure 10-8: Change the orientation of selected cells to add visual interest to a worksheet.

Aligning Text Across Cells to Create a Title

Suppose you decide to include a title row for your data, and you want to center the title across columns A–D. Follow these steps:

1. Type your title in cell A1 and select A1:D1.

2. Click the Range Properties SmartIcon or right-click to display a shortcut menu and choose Range Properties to display the Range Properties InfoBox.

3. Click the Alignment tab.

4. Place a check in the Align Across Columns check box.

5. Choose the alignment you want for the text — in our example, we centered the text. 1-2-3 merges the selected cells into one cell and aligns the information as you specified (see Figure 10-9).

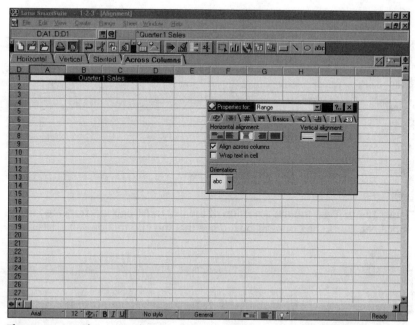

Figure 10-9: When you align text across cells, 1-2-3 merges the selected cells into one cell.

Handling Long Cell Entries

Occasionally, you'll type text into a cell and notice that the text seems to extend beyond the cell into adjacent cells. All of the text is all stored in the original cell even though it appears as if some of the text is stored in adjacent cells. For example, if you place a long entry in A1 and then try typing in B1, a portion of the text in A1 will seem to be replaced by the entry in B1 (see Figure 10-10).

Using the Wrap Text feature, you can expand the height of the cell containing the long label so that all the text in that cell appears to be contained in a single cell. To wrap text, place a check in the Wrap Text in Cell check box on the Alignment tab of the Range Properties InfoBox (see Figure 10-11).

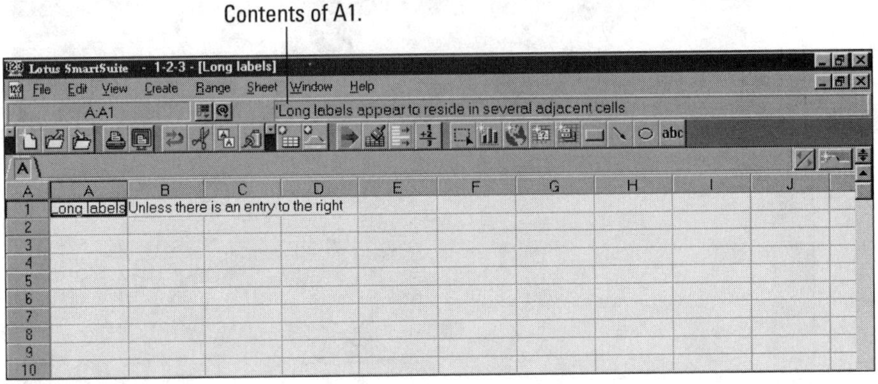

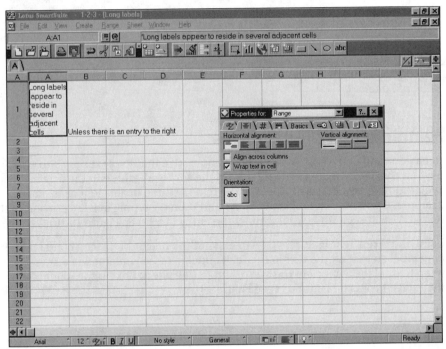

Figure 10-10: Even though a portion of the text in A1 appears truncated in the worksheet, check the Contents box to see that the information still exists.

Figure 10-11: Because the text in A1 is wrapped, the text in B1 no longer hides any portion of A1's long label.

Enhancing Text

To truly strengthen the presentation of your worksheet information, try using text enhancements such as boldface text, italics, and underlining. In Figure 10-12, underlining and boldface were added to the title in A1 and italics were applied to B2:B4 by selecting cells and using the buttons on the status bar.

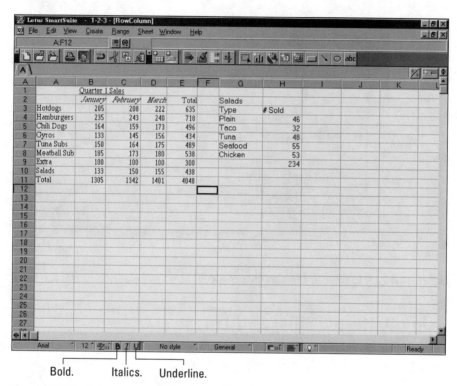

Bold.   Italics.   Underline.

Figure 10-12: Enhance text using the Bold, Italics, and Underline buttons on the status bar.

Changing Text Color

If you're planning to display your worksheet data on a color monitor or print it to a color printer, make use of color to enhance the appearance of your worksheet. Select the cell(s) to which you want to add color and use the Text Color button on the status bar to apply a color to the contents in the cell (see Figure 10-13).

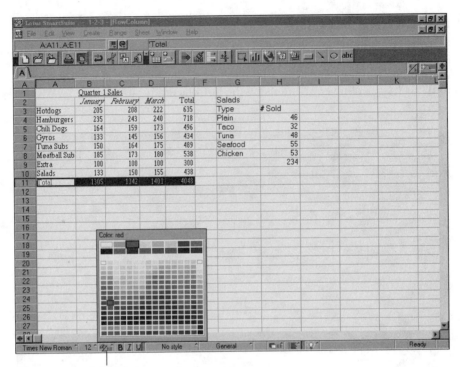

Text Color button.

Figure 10-13: Add color to the contents of a cell.

Using Patterns, Fills, and Lines

Use lines, patterns, and fill colors to add interest to your worksheet. When you add these features, you affect the *background* of the cell, not the contents.

First, consider the effects of patterns. In Figure 10-14, you see a background pattern in cells B2:B5. You apply patterns and fill colors to selected cells from the Color, Pattern, and Line Style tab of the Range Properties InfoBox (choose Range ➪ Range Properties or click the Range Properties SmartIcon).

Notice that a pattern can easily obscure cell contents. You might apply a pattern to the blank cells surrounding the cells to which you want to draw attention.

You can also fill the background of a cell with color. If you add color and then print using a black-and-white printer, the color will print as a shade of gray, although the correct color will appear if you print using a color printer.

In Figure 10-15, you see border lines applied to cells B8:C12. To apply lines to cells, you choose a border pattern and a line style from the Color, Pattern, and Line Style tab of the Range Properties InfoBox. Notice that you can also choose a color for the lines.

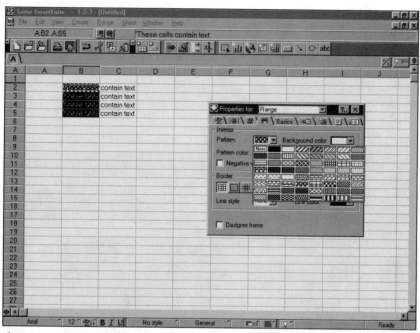

Figure 10-14: Apply patterns carefully; they can obscure cell contents.

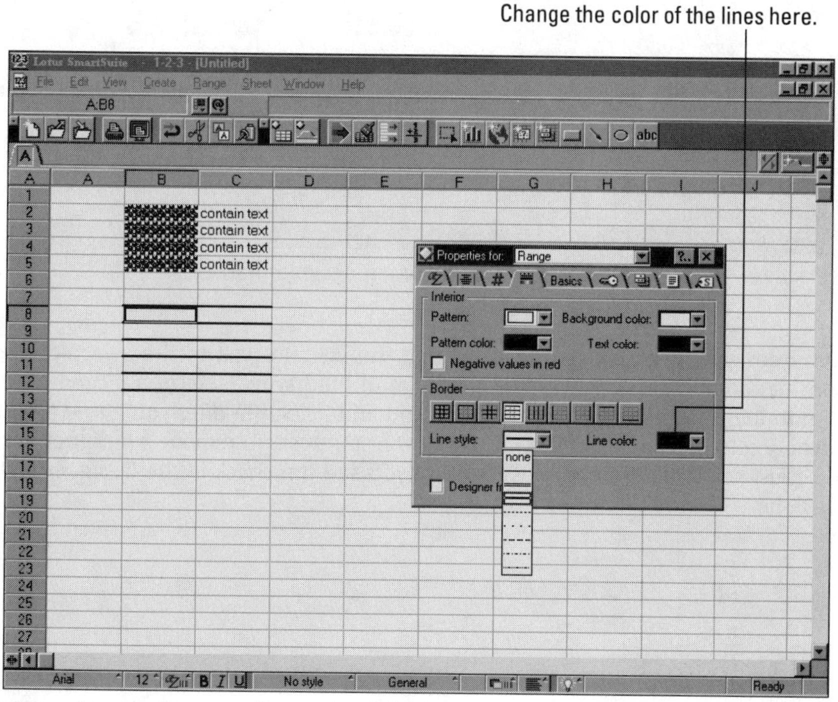

Change the color of the lines here.

Figure 10-15: Choose a line style and a border pattern to outline cells.

Adding Designer Frames

Call special attention to a set of cells in 1-2-3 by outlining the cells with a designer frame. In Figure 10-16, you see B3:F13 outlined in a designer frame. You add a designer frame by selecting cells and placing a check in the Designer Frame check box on the Color, Pattern, and Line Style tab of the Range Properties InfoBox. Once you check the box, two list boxes appear. Choose a frame style from one and a frame color from the other.

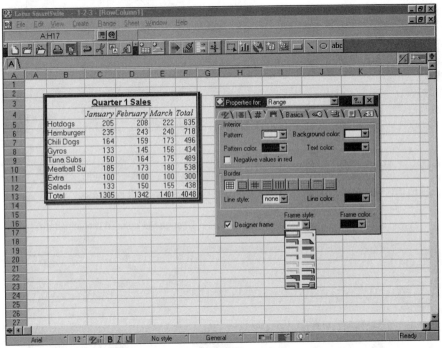

Figure 10-16: Spruce up a worksheet by adding a designer frame.

Note   Some designer frames can "run over" into the column next to the selected range. Consider adding a column at the right edge of the framed selection if the next column to the right contains information. If you add a column *after* you frame a range, the new column will be framed, defeating your purpose. To remove a designer frame, you must select the framed range so that you see the check in the Designer Frame check box.

Formatting Numbers, Dates, and Times

Some numbers, dates, and times provide more meaning than others because they have a recognizable format that tells you something about the values. You recognize a monetary figure immediately when you see a number preceded by a dollar sign. You also know that dates and times can appear in different formats. Think of formats as punctuation you apply to numbers, dates, and times to make them more easily recognizable.

 More Info

Using 1-2-3's Fast Formatting feature, you can copy number formats the same way you copy text formats. See "Fast Formatting: A Formatting Shortcut" later in this chapter for details.

Applying a Number Format

You use the same technique to apply a number format, a date format, or a time format, so we'll focus on applying a number format. In Figure 10-17, the numbers in B3:E6 appear as dollars, while the numbers in column F appear as percentages. You can enter a number with a dollar format in 1-2-3 by simply typing each number as you want it to look. Typing number formats can mean a lot of additional keystrokes. Save time and effort by entering numbers and applying number formats independently. To apply a format, select the cell to which you want to apply the format. Then, click the Number Format button on the status bar and choose a format.

The Number Format button on the status bar uses a default format; for example, when you choose US Dollar, the number will be formatted to display a dollar sign, commas if appropriate, and two decimal places. If you want more control over the format you select — that is, suppose you don't want to display decimal places — use the Number Format tab of the Range Properties InfoBox (see Figure 10-18). You'll also need to use the Number Format tab of the Range Properties InfoBox if you wish to use one of the available formats that is not shown in the list displayed by clicking the Number Format button.

To apply a format to the selected cells, choose the format from the Current Format list box. Use the Category list on the left side of the InfoBox to control the formats that appear in the Current Format list box. For example, if you select the Frequently Used category from the Category list, 1-2-3 displays the most commonly used formats in the Current Format list. To see all possible date formats, however, you need to select Date in the Category list.

Use the Parentheses check box to place parentheses around the entries, but be aware that negative numbers will appear in two sets of parentheses if you apply parentheses this way.

Now that you've seen how to apply formats, let's examine some of the common number formats you can apply in 1-2-3. There are many other available number formats, but you'll probably use these options most of the time.

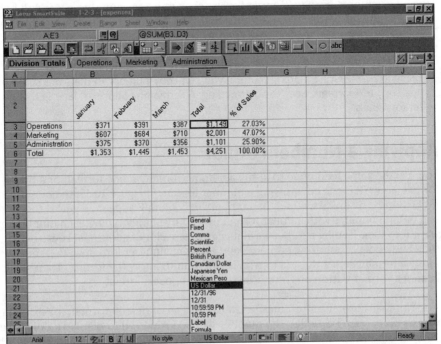

Figure 10-17: The formatting applied to numbers makes them easily recognizable.

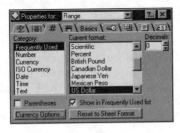

Figure 10-18: Use the Number Format tab of the Range Properties InfoBox to control the appearance of a format.

General Format

1-2-3 automatically uses the General format when you type a number without including any punctuation in the entry except a decimal point. The General format fits as much of a number as possible within the space allowed by a cell's width. If you type the entry 12345.6789 into a cell with General format, 1-2-3 shows the entry as you've typed it — or in scientific notation (discussed shortly) if the cell is too narrow to hold all the digits.

You can control the number of digits that appear after the decimal point for all number formats except the General format.

Percent Format

When you apply the Percent format, 1-2-3 displays numbers as percentages. Since 100% equals 1, be sure you apply the Percent format only to decimal values; otherwise, your numbers make look strange. If you format the number .03 as a percent, it will appear as 3%. Similarly, the Percent format of .3 would be 30%. However, the percent format of 3 would be 300%.

You can specify the number of digits that 1-2-3 should display after the decimal point for percentages (and for numbers using a Currency, Fixed, or Comma format) by using the Decimals counter control on the Number Format tab of the Range Properties InfoBox. You should understand, however, how 1-2-3 handles rounding when you specify decimal places.

Even though 1-2-3 rounds the numbers onscreen, 1-2-3 still uses all digits of the number in calculations. Consequently, the sum 1-2-3 returns for a column of Fixed formatted numbers may not be the same as the sum you get if you add the column of numbers with a hand-held calculator. To correct addition errors like this one, use 1-2-3's @ROUND function to truly round the numbers when you set up the formula to sum numbers. See Chapter 9, "Working with Ranges, Formulas, and Functions," for details on working with @Functions.

Fixed Format

By default, the Fixed format includes two decimal places in the number format, but no other punctuation appears in the number. The Fixed format is particularly appropriate to use when your data contains a series of numbers with varying numbers of digits appearing after the decimal. Applying a Fixed format makes the columns neater and the numbers easier to read, because 1-2-3 automatically rounds numbers using standard rounding techniques — if the digit to be rounded is less than 5, 1-2-3 rounds the digit down; otherwise, 1-2-3 rounds the digit up.

Comma Format

The Comma format is similar to the Fixed format decimal places in that 1-2-3 assigns a number of digits to appear after the decimal point. However, the Comma format differs from the Fixed format because it also includes commas to represent the thousands place markers in a number.

A cell may appear filled with asterisks after you assign a number format. The asterisks signify that the entry, including its formatting, is too long to fit within the assigned column width. Either adjust the column's width using techniques you'll learn later in this chapter, or use a different format.

Scientific Format

Scientific notation commonly expresses numbers as powers of 10, typically annotated as 10^2 for 100 or 10^3 for 1000. In 1-2-3, when you apply the Scientific format, 1-2-3 uses the letter E and a plus or minus sign (+ or –) powers of 10. So the familiar 5.67×10^3 becomes 5.67E+03 in a worksheet cell with Scientific format.

Currency Formats

1-2-3 offers a broad range of currency formats that cover most of the world's major currencies. In fact, you can choose from 90 different currency formats if you count both the standard and ISO variations. The ISO currency formats use a standard abbreviation, rather than a currency symbol, to identify the currency. For example, in US Dollar format one hundred dollars would appear as $100.00 while in ISO US Dollar format it would appear as USD 100.00.

Formatting Dates and Times

In 1-2-3, a date entry is a number to which you apply a special format. 1-2-3 treats dates as consecutive integers that represent how many days have passed since December 31, 1899. When you type a date in the mm/dd/yy format, 1-2-3 internally converts it to a serial number. You can, therefore, use formulas to calculate the number of days that have passed between two dates. In fact, 1-2-3 has a whole series of functions specifically intended to work with dates.

Note   Although 1-2-3 can use dates between January 1, 1900 and December 31, 9999, there is an error in the way 1-2-3 calculates dates prior to March 1, 1900. If you format the number 60 using a date format, 1-2-3 will happily tell you that the date is February 29, 1900. However, since the year 1900 was not a leap year, that date did not exist.

You can see the other date formats available to you in the Range Properties InfoBox. Display the Number Format tab and choose Date from the Category list (see Figure 10-19).

1-2-3 treats a time entry the same way it treats a date entry — 1-2-3 considers a time entry to be a number that you format. You can type a time entry into 1-2-3 using a standard time format, such as HH:MM:SS. Again, the time entry actually is a decimal value that represents what percentage of a day has passed since midnight. That means that 1-2-3 treats your entry of 6:00 A.M. as the value .25. As with dates, you can calculate the amount of time that has passed between two time entries.

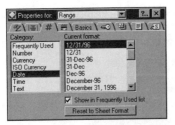

Figure 10-19: View all the available date formats from the Number Format tab of the Range Properties InfoBox.

To display the available time formats, open the Range Properties InfoBox, choose the Number Format tab, and choose Times from the Category list.

Using the Text Format

Sometimes, particularly when you have a problem in your worksheet, you want to see, in the cells, the actual formulas you've entered, rather than the results of the formulas. If you assign a text format to a cell that contains a formula, the formula appears in both the Contents box and in the cell (see Figure 10-20).

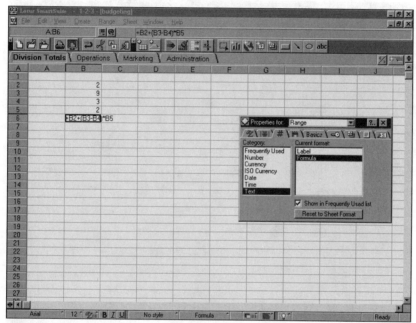

Figure 10-20: Cell B6 contains a formula; by formatting B6 as text, you see the formula in the worksheet and in the Contents box.

Fast Formatting: A Formatting Shortcut

On the preceding pages, you learned how to apply several different types of formatting. Here's a shortcut: You can apply the same formats to several different cells by copying formatting from one cell to another using 1-2-3's Fast Formatting feature.

Select the cell containing the formatting you want to copy and click the Fast Format SmartIcon or choose Range ➪ Fast Format. When you slide the mouse onto the worksheet area, the pointer changes to a paintbrush (see Figure 10-21).

Click the cell to which you want to copy formatting. 1-2-3 automatically applies the formatting of the first cell to the second cell. Fast formatting remains in effect until you "turn it off"; to stop copying formatting, click the Fast Format SmartIcon again or choose Range ➪ Fast Format again.

You can copy formatting to a range of cells by selecting a range instead of a single cell.

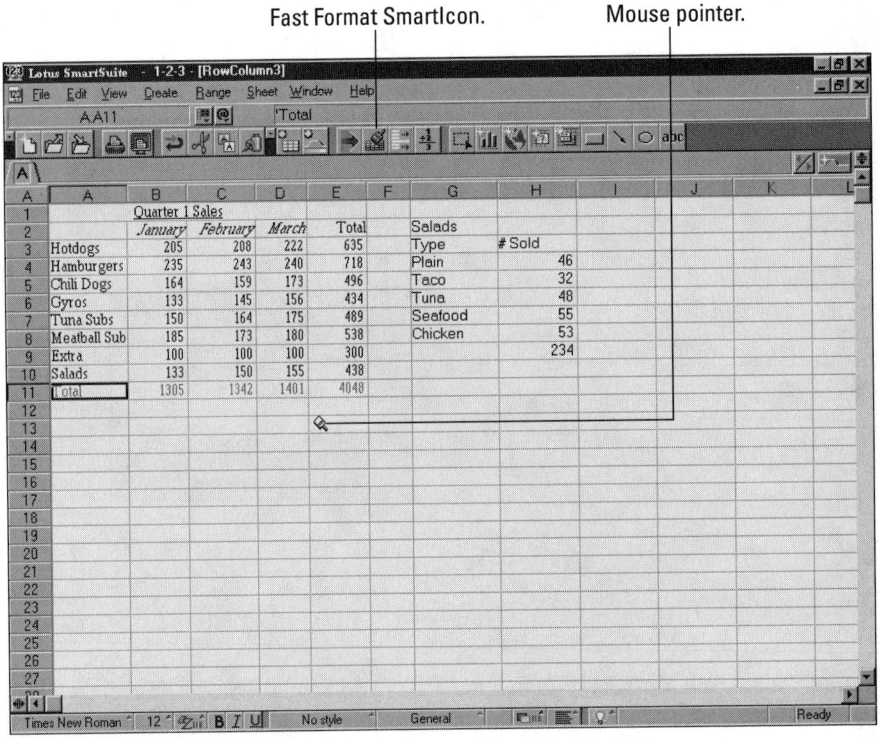

Fast Format SmartIcon.   Mouse pointer.

	A	B	C	D	E	F	G	H	I	J	K	L
1		Quarter 1 Sales										
2		January	February	March	Total		Salads					
3	Hotdogs	205	208	222	635		Type	# Sold				
4	Hamburgers	235	243	240	718		Plain	46				
5	Chili Dogs	164	159	173	496		Taco	32				
6	Gyros	133	145	156	434		Tuna	48				
7	Tuna Subs	150	164	175	489		Seafood	55				
8	Meatball Sub	185	173	180	538		Chicken	53				
9	Extra	100	100	100	300			234				
10	Salads	133	150	155	438							
11	Total	1305	1342	1401	4048							

Figure 10-21: You can copy formatting from one cell to another.

Working with Styles

Perhaps you find yourself applying the same styles to many different cells. Suppose you often create a title row, make the text in that row bold, italicized, and underlined, change the font to Arial and the font size to 18. In addition, you always format the numbers in your worksheet as fixed with two decimals and use Times Roman, 14-point type as the font for numbers.

These are situations that lend themselves well to creating and using *named styles*. You store, in a named style, a set of attributes that you want to apply to a cell. Then, instead of applying each attribute separately to a cell, you apply the style—which applies *all* the attributes in one step.

You can store, in a named style, font, point size, number format, bold, italics, underlining, patterns, colors, and alignment settings. This feature is discussed next.

Creating a style

1-2-3 creates named styles "by example"; that is, 1-2-3 stores the formatting applied to the selected cell. So, to create a named style, first apply the formatting you want to save in the named style to a cell. Then, select the formatted cell and choose Range Properties. Click the Named Style tab of the Range Properties InfoBox. Click the Create Style button and type a name for the style. Choose OK, and the name you typed will appear in the Style Name list (see Figure 10-22).

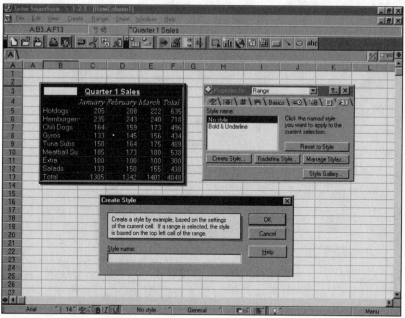

Figure 10-22: Creating a named style.

Applying a Style

Applying a style is easy. Select the cell(s) to which you want to apply the style. Then, use the Named Style button on the status bar to select the style you want to apply.

To remove a named style from a cell, click the Named Style button on the status bar and choose No Style. To rename or delete a named style, reopen the Range Properties InfoBox and, from the Named Style tab, click Manage Styles. To redefine a named style, create a cell containing the new attributes you want to store. Select the formatted cell and open the Named Style tab of the Range Properties InfoBox. Highlight the style you want to redefine and click the Redefine Style button.

1-2-3 comes with a set of predefined, named styles that you can apply to selected cells from the Style Gallery. When you click the Style Gallery button on the Named Style tab of the Range Properties InfoBox, you see the Style Gallery dialog box (see Figure 10-23). Select a style from the Style Templates list and choose OK.

Style Gallery button.

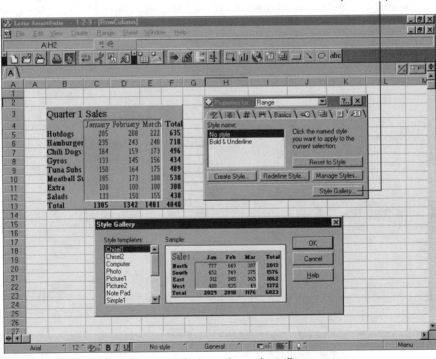

Figure 10-23: Use a predefined style from the Style Gallery.

Applying a style from the Style Gallery will override any styles you applied to the selected cells. To remove a style you applied from the Style Gallery, select the cells from which you want to remove Style Gallery formatting and, from the Named Style tab of the Range Properties InfoBox, click the Reset to Style button. 1-2-3 will return the selected cells to the default settings for the worksheet.

Setting Worksheet Defaults

Speaking of default settings for the worksheet, 1-2-3 has standard default settings for every new workbook you create. To view sheet defaults, open the Sheet Properties InfoBox by clicking the Sheet Properties SmartIcon or choosing Sheet ➪ Sheet Properties. The Sheet Properties InfoBox contains seven tabs; you set various defaults for the current worksheet from these tabs. Following is a list of the settings you can make with the Sheet Properties InfoBox:

✦ Use the Font, Attribute, and Color tab to change the default font, font size, or text color.

✦ Use the Alignment tab to set the default alignment.

✦ Use the Number Format tab to set the default number format.

✦ Use the Color, Pattern and Line Style tab to set the default colors, pattern and line style, and to specify if negative numbers should appear in red.

✦ Use the Basis tab to set the sheet name, tab color, and default row and column settings.

✦ Use the View tab to control which worksheet elements (such as grid lines) will appear.

✦ Use the Outline tab to control whether 1-2-3 will use the worksheet outlining features.

More Info

Most of the Sheet Properties InfoBox settings simply set the default values for cells you haven't specifically formatted. Worksheet outlining, however, is one feature that does not have an equivalent range setting. See Chapter 13, "Using Data Management and Analysis Tools," for information on outlining.

Sizing Rows and Columns

Occasionally, you may need to change column widths and row heights. Sometimes a one- or two-character adjustment can make the difference between fitting all your data on one display or having to move the cell pointer to the right or left to shift the display. Sizing options are discussed in the following section.

Automatically Sizing Rows and Columns

In many cases, you need to adjust a column's width to be wide enough to display all of each entry in the column. You can quickly adjust a column's width to fit its widest entry. Slide the mouse pointer into the worksheet frame to the right edge of a column whose width you want to change. The pointer changes into a two-headed arrow, as shown in Figure 10-24. Double-click. 1-2-3 automatically enlarges the column so that it accommodates the largest entry in it.

To "fit" several columns at once, select all the columns that you want to change. Slide the mouse into the worksheet frame at the right edge of *any* selected column. When the mouse pointer changes to a two-headed arrow, double-click. Each selected column snaps to a width that fits its own widest entry.

Mouse pointer.

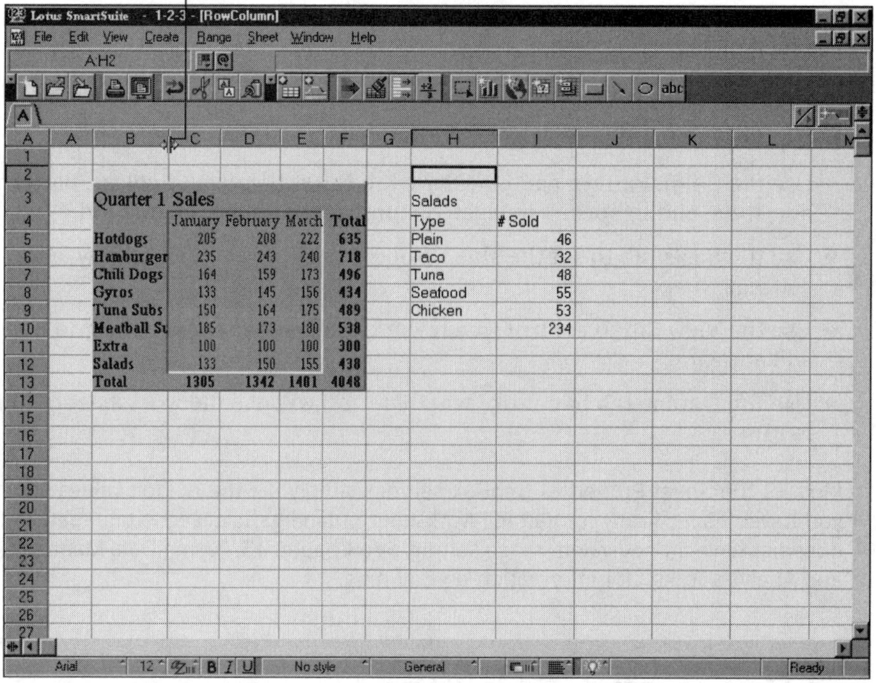

Figure 10-24: When you slide the mouse to the edge of a column in the worksheet frame, the pointer changes to a two-headed arrow.

You can also adjust row heights to fit the tallest entry in the row by double-clicking the bottom of the row, but remember that 1-2-3 *automatically* adjusts a row's height to fit the tallest entry. You only need to double-click the bottom of rows whose heights you have changed manually—which you'll learn how to do in the next section.

Manually Adjusting Row or Column Size

If you want to control the width of a column or row instead of letting 1-2-3 adjust the column or row size to fit the largest entry, you can drag to adjust column width or row height. Move the mouse in the worksheet frame to the right edge of the column you want to adjust. Then, drag right to widen the column, or left to narrow the column.

When you adjust a column's width and you press the mouse button to drag, a dotted line appears down the worksheet. In addition, you'll see a small box that indicates the number of characters the column can currently hold (see Figure 10-25).

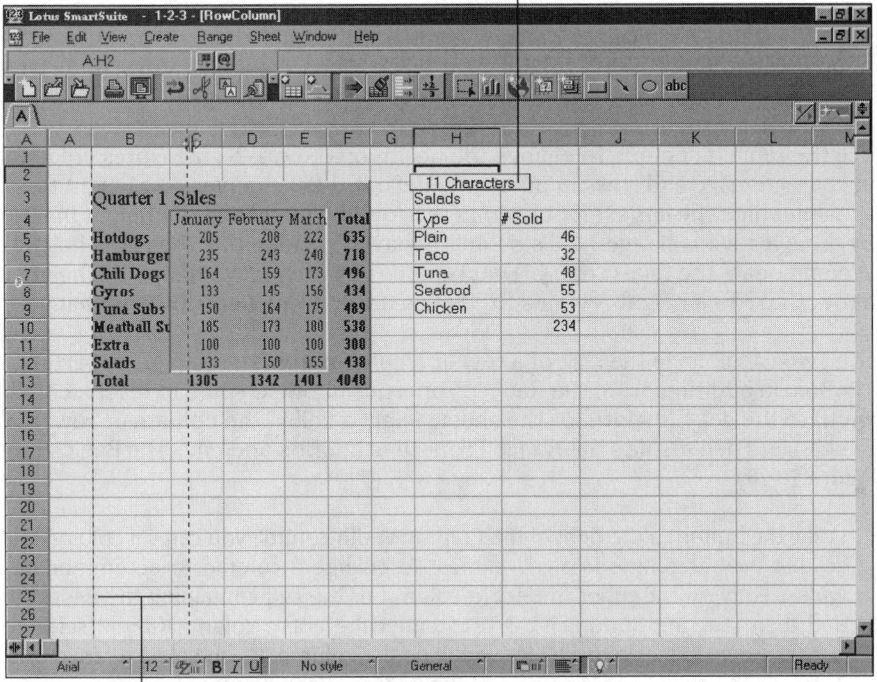

Character measurement.

Dotted lines.

Figure 10-25: While dragging to change a column's width, you'll see dotted lines around the column, and a character measurement.

This is an unusual measurement because a character's width changes, depending on the font and font size you selected. Each font's character width is fixed by a default setting, typically 12 points per character, that you can't change. When you release the mouse button, 1-2-3 sets the column width to the closest width allowed based on the number of characters you see when you release the mouse button. Therefore, dragging the line 18 points may result in a change of only 12 points when you release the mouse pointer.

To change the widths of several adjacent columns uniformly at once, select all the columns you want to change. To select several adjacent columns at once, select the first column, then press and hold the Shift key and click the last column.

To select several nonadjacent columns or rows, hold down the Ctrl key and click each one.

Then, move the mouse pointer within the frame to the right border of one of the selected columns until the pointer changes. Drag to change the column's width. Release the mouse button when you reach the desired column width. The width of all selected columns will change.

You may find it difficult to determine when the pointer changes, because both the pointer and the selected columns are black. When the white arrow (the standard mouse pointer) disappears, you'll know the pointer has changed.

Use the same technique to change the height of a row. 1-2-3 measures columns in character size and rows in points; by default, 1-2-3 changes row height to accommodate the largest font used in the row. If you change the height of a row by dragging, you change 1-2-3's default behavior of adjusting the row's height to accommodate the tallest entry. That is, once you manually change the height of a row, that row's height remains fixed even if the sizes of entries in it change.

You also can change the size of a row or a column from the Range Properties InfoBox; in addition, from the Range Properties InfoBox, you can reset a column's width to the default width for the sheet. Select a cell in the column or row you want to change. Then display the Range Properties InfoBox and click the Basics tab (see Figure 10-26).

Using the button to the right of the Column Width control, you can set column widths so that they accommodate cell entries. To enlarge a column to accommodate the widest entry, select either the entire column or the cell containing the widest entry and then click the button. 1-2-3 uses either the entire column (if you selected it) or the current cell as a model for widening the column. If you select a range of cells, 1-2-3 fits the column to the width of the widest selected entry.

Clearing Cell Contents and Cell Formatting

In 1-2-3, you have the option to remove the contents of a cell, its formatting, or both. For example, you may need to remove the data from a range, but leave the range's styles and formats in place so future entries assume the characteristics of the current ones. To clear the data from a range, but leave the formats and styles in place, select the range. Then, choose Edit ➪ Clear. 1-2-3 displays the Clear dialog box (see Figure 10-27).

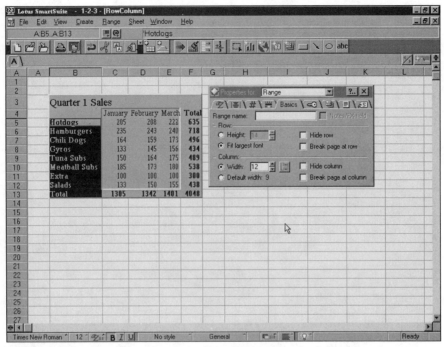

Figure 10-26: Set row or column size from the Basics tab of the Range Properties InfoBox.

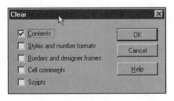

Figure 10-27: Use the Clear dialog box to selectively delete data, formatting, or both.

Danger Zone

When you choose Edit ➪ Clear to erase data, 1-2-3 does not store the deleted entries on the Windows Clipboard.

Hot Stuff

If you want to clear the styles and formatting you applied to the range, you don't need to display the Clear dialog box. Select the range to clear and choose Edit ➪ Clear Styles. 1-2-3 removes formatting from the selected cells, but leaves content.

✦   ✦   ✦

Picture This — Using Graphics in Worksheets

◆　◆　◆　◆

In This Chapter

Using graphic images in 1-2-3

Creating charts using worksheet information

Working with maps in 1-2-3

◆　◆　◆　◆

You use 1-2-3, which is primarily spreadsheet software, to manipulate numbers. However, that's not *all* 1-2-3 can do. In this day and age, most people would agree that a picture is worth a thousand words — and often you'll find that expressing your point with a picture is more effective than using numbers.

In this chapter, you'll learn how to use 1-2-3 to visually present your information in varying ways.

Adding Graphics

Sometimes, all you need to make a point is a graphic image. Suppose, for example, that you want to point out a particular number. You could format the cell so that the number stands out, as you learned in the last chapter, or you could simply draw an arrow to point at the number.

1-2-3 lets you use three different kinds of graphic images in a worksheet:

◆ Lines and shapes

◆ Blocks of text

◆ Pictures

1-2-3 calls each of these a *graphic object*. In this book, they may simply be referred to as objects.

Drawing Lines and Shapes

Consider our preceding example: You want to draw an arrow to point out a particular number. You would follow these steps to do so:

1. Click the Arrow SmartIcon. When you move the mouse pointer into the worksheet area, the mouse pointer shape will be a plus sign.

2. Position the mouse pointer where you want the portion of the arrow *without* the arrowhead to appear.

3. Drag the mouse to the location where you want the arrowhead to appear. As you drag, you'll see a dotted line that represents the arrow (see Figure 11-1).

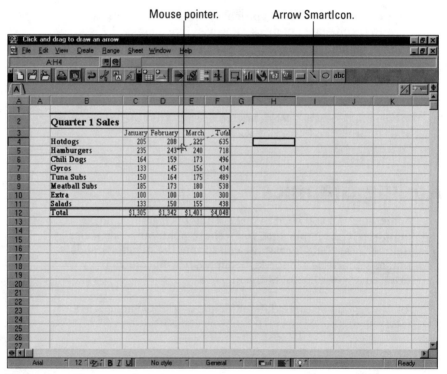

Figure 11-1: It's easy to draw an arrow.

4. Release the mouse button. An arrow will appear; the black boxes you see at each end of the arrow, called *handles*, indicate that the graphic object is selected.

5. Click anywhere in the worksheet to cancel the selection.

You can draw objects of many different shapes. To see all the shapes you can draw, choose Create ➪ Drawing. The shapes you can draw appear on the Drawing submenu (see Figure 11-2).

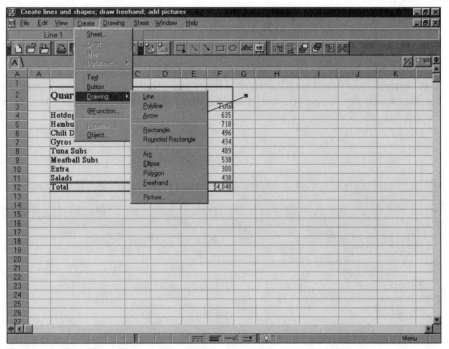

Figure 11-2: Use the Drawing submenu to choose from a list of shapes you can draw in a 1-2-3 worksheet.

Adding a Text Block

Text blocks are also graphic objects; instead of being images, however, they are rectangles into which you can type text. You create the block and then type the text.

A text block operates like a word processor, in that words *wrap* as you reach the outer edge of the block, so you don't need to press Enter to start a new line.

To insert a text block, click the Text Block SmartIcon. Again, the mouse pointer will change to a plus sign when you move it into the worksheet area. Position the mouse pointer where you want the upper-left edge of the text block to appear and click. A text block will appear.

You can control the size of the text block by dragging instead of clicking. Drag down and to the right, estimating the size of the text block. Release the mouse button when you reach the location where you want the lower-right corner of the text block to appear. As you drag, you'll see a dotted box that represents the outline of the text block.

The flashing insertion point indicates that 1-2-3 is waiting for you to type text into the block, and as you slide the mouse pointer over the text block, the pointer shape will change to an I-beam—like the one you see when you work in a word processing program. Type as you would in a word processing program—don't press Enter when you reach the right edge of the block. 1-2-3 will wrap words for you automatically. When you finish typing, click anywhere outside the text block in the worksheet. Handles will surround the text block (see Figure 11-3).

Text Block SmartIcon.

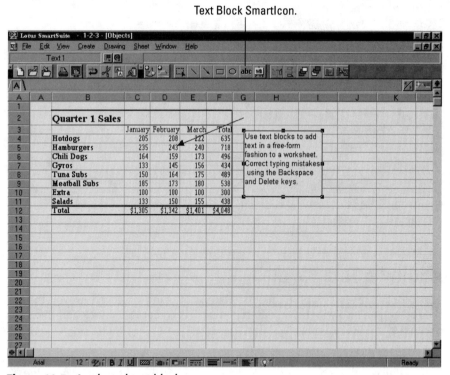

Figure 11-3: A selected text block.

Note

After you type in the block, you'll discover that it is, in all likelihood, either too big or too small. Don't worry about the size of the block; you'll learn how to resize graphic objects later in this chapter.

If you find a mistake in a text block after you finish typing and click elsewhere in the worksheet, you can go back and edit the block. To do so, double-click in the text block and the insertion point will reappear.

Inserting a Picture

You can also include graphic images in worksheets. 1-2-3 will let you import pictures you obtain from other sources; for example, Lotus Development Corporation markets a product called *SmartPics,* which contains professionally drawn images of people, buildings, machines, etc.

You can import any picture file stored in a BMP, WMF, GIF, JPG, CGM, or PIC format. These are simply different file formats used by many different programs to save image files. For example, BMP files are commonly used as Windows wallpaper, while both GIF and JPG files are very common on the Internet.

To import a picture file, follow these steps:

1. Choose Create ➪ Drawing ➪ Picture. The Picture dialog box appears.
2. Open the File of Type list box and choose the type of graphic file you wish to open.
3. Locate and select the desired image file.
4. Click the Open button to close the dialog box.
5. Drag the mouse pointer to create a box the size you would like for the image. 1-2-3 imports the image as a graphic object into the worksheet.

In addition to importing a graphic file, you can copy and paste images from other Windows applications to 1-2-3. Simply open the image in any other Windows program, copy it to the Windows Clipboard, switch to 1-2-3, and click the Paste SmartIcon.

Working with Graphic Objects

Once you have a graphic object in your worksheet, you can manipulate it in many ways. You can move or copy it, resize it, or rotate it. You can modify its appearance using attributes such as color or line width. You can group several objects together so that actions you take for one affect the entire group. You can place objects on top of one another, layering them; and then select the object you want on top.

Selecting Objects

Before you can do anything to an object, you must select it. You'll know when an object is selected because you'll see handles surrounding the object. To select any object, move the mouse pointer over the object and click.

You can select more than one object at a time. Select the first object by clicking, but for each subsequent object you want to select, press and hold the Ctrl key as you click.

Copying and Moving Objects

You copy an object the same way you copy cells. Select the object and click the Copy SmartIcon. Then, click the cell where you want the object to appear and click the Paste SmartIcon.

To move an object, drag and drop it. Click first to make sure it is selected. Then, drag it to a new location. Make sure that you position the mouse pointer over the object and not over a handle surrounding the object. As you drag the object, you'll see a dotted outline representing the current location of the object, and the mouse pointer will change to the hand you typically see when moving a cell (see Figure 11-4). When you reach the desired location, release the mouse button.

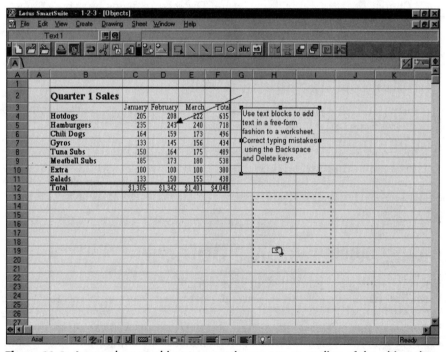

Figure 11-4: As you drag an object to move it, you see an outline of the object that represents the object's current location.

Resizing an Object

You can easily change the size of an object. Click the object to select it. Then, slide the mouse over one of the handles. The pointer changes to a four-headed arrow (see Figure 11-5).

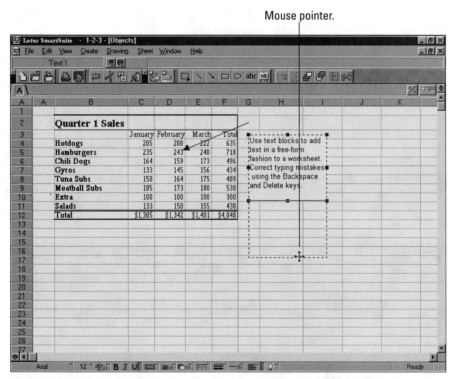

Figure 11-5: When you drag a handle, you change the size of an object.

Drag the handle outward to make the object larger, or inward to make the object smaller. As you drag, you'll see the dotted outline representing the object's boundaries. Release the mouse button when the object appears to be the size you want.

Setting the Properties of an Object

You set the properties of an object in much the same way you set the properties of a range or a cell — use either the buttons on the status bar or the tabs of the Draw Properties InfoBox. Click the object to select it. Notice the buttons that appear on the status bar — they change depending on the type of object you select, and they are interactive, as they were when you selected a cell or a range.

If you prefer, use the Draw Object Properties InfoBox. After selecting an object, right-click the mouse to display a shortcut menu. From that shortcut menu, choose Drawing Properties to display the Draw Object Properties InfoBox. You can also display the Draw Object Properties InfoBox by clicking the Change Drawing Properties SmartIcon — which replaces the Range Properties SmartIcon when a drawing object is selected. The tabs you see in this InfoBox vary, depending on the object you selected when you opened it. For a text object, the Draw Object Properties InfoBox contains four tabs: the Basics tab, the Font tab, the Alignment tab, and the Color, Pattern, and Line Style tab.

In the Basics tab (Figure 11-6), *fastening* determines what happens to the object's size and placement when you move the cells underneath the object. *Hiding* an object does exactly what its name implies — it makes the graphic invisible in the worksheet. If you *lock* an object, it cannot be manipulated in any way; for example, you can't move it or change its size. In the figure you can see examples of how fastening objects can affect those objects. All three text boxes started out the same size and at the same vertical position. After the text boxes were created, row 2 was resized as shown in the figure. The leftmost box was fastened top-left and right-bottom, so it grew in size and moved down as row 2 was expanded. The middle text box was fastened top-left, so it moved down but didn't change size. The rightmost text box wasn't fastened, so it was unaffected by changes in the worksheet.

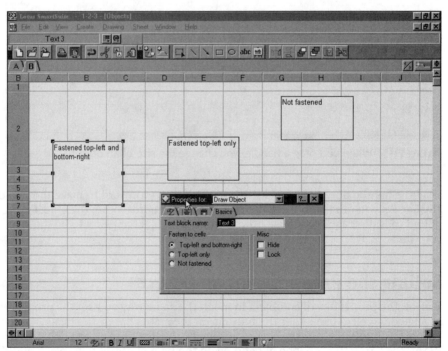

Figure 11-6: From the Basics tab, you set options for fastening, hiding, or locking objects.

As you would expect, the Font tab (Figure 11-7) appears only for text blocks. Using the Font tab, you can apply text attributes to all text in a text block. Select the block so that you see handles surrounding it; then, use the Font tab and apply attributes.

Figure 11-7: From the Font tab, control the font, font size, and font attributes of a text block.

The Alignment tab (Figure 11-8) appears only for text blocks, and you use it to control the alignment of the entire text block. Click the block so that you see handles. Then, apply an alignment or rotate the text within the block.

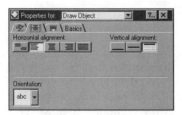

Figure 11-8: From the Alignment tab, you can control the alignment and orientation of a graphic object.

Use the choices on the Color, Pattern, and Line Style tab (Figure 11-9) to set a background color and patterns (for text objects and shapes such as rectangles and circles) and a line color and patterns for lines and the edges of other shapes. You can also get fancy by adding a designer frame. See "Adding Background Color, Colored Borders, and Designer Frames to Charts" later in this chapter for more information on using designer frames.

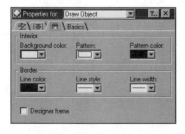

Figure 11-9: From the Color, Pattern, and Line Style tab, set background and line colors and patterns.

Grouping and Ungrouping Objects

Grouping objects can be useful if you want to perform the same set of actions on several different objects. By grouping them, you can perform the actions only once, and all objects in the group will be affected. For example, if you want to set the same colors and line styles for several objects, group them before making the settings. When you do make the settings, those settings will apply to all objects in the group. If you move a grouped object, all objects in the group move together.

To group objects, select each object you want to include in the group. Right-click the selected objects and choose Group from the shortcut menu that appears. Once you group objects, handles no longer appear around individual objects; instead, they appear around the outside edges of the grouped objects.

When you no longer want to group objects — for example, if you want to move some of the objects but not the whole group, select the group by clicking any object included in the group. Then, right-click the group and choose Ungroup from the submenu that appears.

Layering Objects

Layering objects can be effective when objects overlap. Suppose, for example, that you draw a rectangle and give it a background color (or even make it white) so that you can't see the lines of the cells behind it. Then, you decide you want a label in the center of the rectangle. When you add a text object containing the label, you won't be able to see it because it will be hidden by the rectangle. If, however, you layer the objects so that the text object appears "on top" of the rectangle, you'll be able to see both objects.

To layer objects, select one of the objects and right-click to display a shortcut menu. From the menu (see Figure 11-10), select the command to layer the objects effectively: Send to Back or Bring to Front.

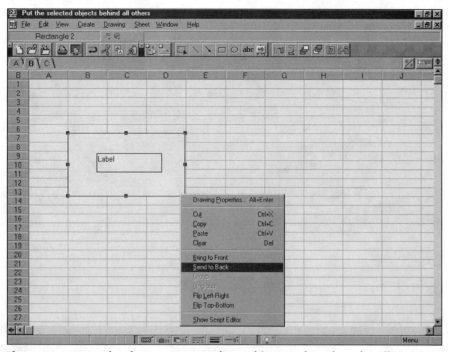

Figure 11-10: Use the shortcut menu to layer objects and produce the effect you need.

Adding a Chart to a Worksheet

Drawing can be fun, but using worksheet data to produce charts really helps you make your point. In 1-2-3, you can create a variety of different types of charts; you also can change easily from one chart type to another. Because charts are based on worksheet data, they update dynamically when you change the data in the worksheet that you used to create the chart.

You also have control over some of the visual aspects of a chart. For example, you can change lines, colors, and patterns that appear in the chart area, add and modify a legend, and add text notes.

To add a chart to a worksheet, select the worksheet data you want to chart (see Figure 11-11). Include the title row and column, but don't include rows or columns that contain totals of data you wish to chart—these rows and columns would skew your data and make your chart less meaningful.

Chart SmartIcon.

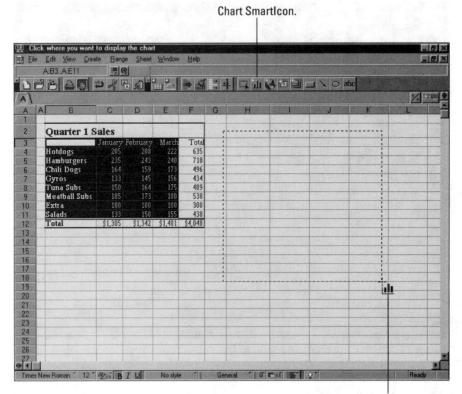

Mouse pointer as a small chart.

Figure 11-11: When you select data to chart, include title rows and columns, but don't include rows or columns that contain totals of the data you wish to chart.

If you don't select any data before choosing to create a chart, 1-2-3 will display the Chart Assistant, which will prompt you to select a range to chart.

Choose Create ➪ Chart. 1-2-3 changes the shape of the mouse pointer to a small chart. Draw a rectangle in your worksheet to contain the chart. Start at the location where you want the upper-left corner of the chart to appear. Then, drag down and to the right, releasing the mouse button when the pointer reaches the location where you want the lower-right corner of the chart to appear. 1-2-3 displays a bar chart of the selected data (see Figure 11-12).

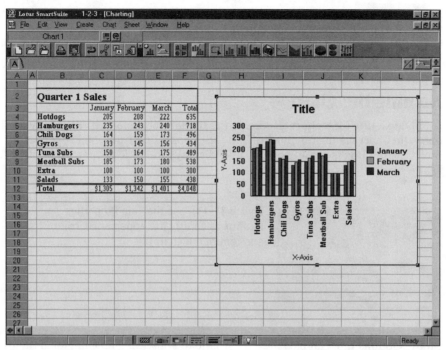

Figure 11-12: 1-2-3 places the chart in your worksheet, surrounded by selection handles.

Well, you've got a chart — but it needs some help. For example, naming the chart and identifying the information on the X and Y axes would probably help the reader better understand the chart. In the following section, you'll learn about the changes that you can make to enhance your chart's meaning.

Sprucing Up Your Chart

You can modify the entire chart or elements of the chart. When you select some portion of a chart, 1-2-3 displays the Chart menu in place of the Range menu in the menu bar. The commands on the Chart menu help you make changes to your chart.

You will always see one context-driven command on the Chart menu that will open a Properties InfoBox related to the chart. Because the command is context-driven, the command you see on the menu, and the InfoBox that opens when you choose that command, depends on the portion of the chart you select before you open the menu. Save some time and just click the Change Chart Properties SmartIcon that replaces the Range Properties SmartIcon when any part of a chart is selected.

Approach making changes to a chart by focusing on various elements on the chart. Click the object on the chart before you open the InfoBox; or if you've already opened the InfoBox, choose the chart object from the drop-down Properties for List Box at the top of the InfoBox.

Naming the Chart

Supplying a title for a chart also helps the reader understand it. To supply a title, open the Chart menu and choose Title (or choose Title from the Properties for List Box if the InfoBox is already open). 1-2-3 displays the Title Properties InfoBox (see Figure 11-13).

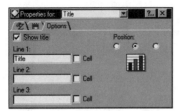

Figure 11-13: Use the Title Properties InfoBox to control the appearance, color, and font of the chart title.

On the Options tab, change Line 1 from Title to something meaningful. If the title you want to use appears in a cell in the worksheet, click the Cell check box and use the Range Selector button to identify the cell. Use Lines 2 and 3 to supply subtitles for the chart. Align the titles at either the center or the left or right edge of the chart.

When you use the Color, Pattern, and Line Style tab (see Figure 11-14), imagine a box surrounding the title. The patterns, colors, and lines you choose will appear in that box.

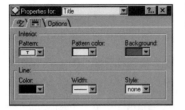

Figure 11-14: Use this tab to draw and fill a box around the chart title.

From the Font, Attribute, and Color tab, change the font, font size, font style, and font color of the title's text (see Figure 11-15).

Figure 11-15: Use the Font, Attribute, and Color tab to control the appearance of the title's text.

Identifying the Axes

Changing x-axis and y-axis to something more meaningful would definitely help your reader. If an InfoBox is open, simply click the appropriate axis to display the InfoBox for that axis. If you have closed the InfoBox, choose Chart ⇨ Axes & Grids.

The InfoBox will change to display the information for the selected axis. Simply select the other axis to view its settings.

The Titles tab for the axes looks very similar to the Options tab for the chart title. Create a meaningful title for the axis the same way you created a meaningful title for the chart. Use the Font tab to control the appearance of the axis title. Use the Ticks tab (see Figure 11-16) to display tick marks.

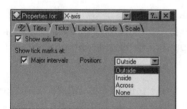

Figure 11-16: Use this tab to display tick marks on the x-axis.

Use the Labels tab to hide or display the labels that appear along the x-axis. Use the Grids tab to control whether gridlines appear on the axis; by default, 1-2-3 shows gridlines for the y-axis but not for the x-axis. Use the Scale tab to control the scale that appears along the axis. On the x-axis, you can control the direction (ascending or descending) in which 1-2-3 displays the values (1-2-3 uses the order in which you entered the information in the worksheet). On the y-axis, you can control the minimum and maximum scale values as well as the direction (ascending or descending) of the values.

Adjusting the Chart Type

Different types of charts help convey different types of messages — and some chart types explain certain types of information more effectively than other chart types. In 1-2-3, you can create several different types of charts, including bar, line, area, pie, and so on. You can further refine your chart's appearance by selecting a variation for the chart.

To change from one chart type to another, choose Chart ➪ Chart Type. 1-2-3 displays the Type tab of the Chart Properties InfoBox (see Figure 11-17).

Figure 11-17: Switch the chart type from the Type tab of the Chart Properties InfoBox.

As you select a type from the Chart Type list, the buttons that appear at the right change to display the variations, such as three-dimensional, available for the chart type you selected.

Bar charts track data over a period of time, with an emphasis on individual data points. In 1-2-3, the default chart you've seen so far is a simple bar chart. Notice the visual effects when you switch the chart type to a three-dimensional chart (see Figure 11-18).

Stacked bar charts and 100% stacked bar charts are similar to standard bar charts, but with an important difference — all of the data is graphed in a single bar. In a stacked bar chart each data element contributes to the overall height of the bar, so if your data consisted of three items with values of 10, 20, and 30, the overall bar would be 60 units high. This type of chart enables you to compare the overall performance of a product line, such as the overall sales at your food stand month by month. A 100% stacked bar chart also graphs all data in a single bar, but shows each data segment as a percentage of the total.

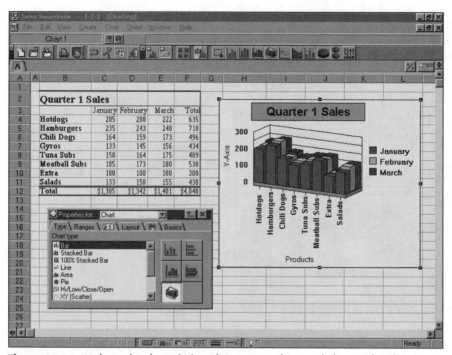

Figure 11-18: Make a simple variation change to a chart and change the chart's appearance completely.

Line charts, like area charts (covered next), help you see trends. They are most effective when you have many related data points; by connecting the points with a line, you see a general trend.

Area charts (see Figure 11-19), like bar charts, also show data over time, but an area chart helps you see data as broad trends, rather than individual data points. Area charts stack the data much like a stacked bar chart so you can see the overall trend.

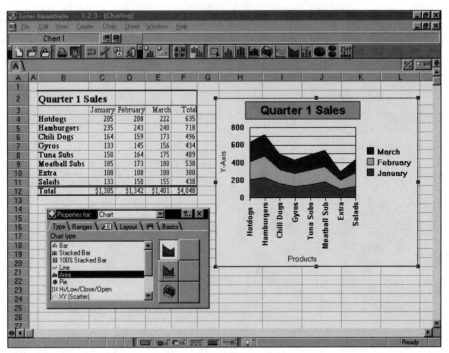

Figure 11-19: An area chart of the same data you've been viewing.

Pie charts effectively show the relationship of a part to the whole. Pie charts are effective when you're trying to show, for example, the percentage of total sales for which the Midwest region is responsible.

An HLCO (Hi/Low/Close/Open) chart is often used for stock market reports. This chart type is very effective to display data that fluctuates over time.

People with a statistical background often use a scatter chart, also called an XY chart, to determine whether there is a correlation between two variables. Both axes on a scatter chart are numeric, and the axes can be linear or logarithmic.

Use a radar chart when you want to compare data series that consist of several different variables. Each data series on a radar chart has its own axis that "radiates" from the center of the chart—hence the name radar chart. A line connects each point in the series. Typically, you'll see more than one data series on a radar chart, because they are intended to be comparison charts; however, don't include too many series on a radar chart or it will become difficult, if not impossible, to read.

If you choose 1-2-3's Mixed Chart type, you can combine a bar and a line chart, a 3-D bar and line chart, or a 3-D line and area chart.

Number grid charts look just like a spreadsheet of the data you selected to create the chart. You can include row and column totals in a number grid chart even if you don't have the totals shown in the worksheet.

Doughnut charts are useful for those times when you'd like to use a pie chart but would rather have something a little less filling. Actually, the only difference between a doughnut chart and a pie chart is that the doughnut chart has a hole in the middle.

Changing the Chart Data

When you change the data in the range you used to create a chart, 1-2-3 automatically updates the chart. For example, if you change the value for Chili Dogs in February from 159 to 600, the chart will change to reflect the new data.

If you don't want to change chart data, but you would like to change chart colors quickly, use the Named Style tab of the Chart Properties InfoBox. You can create your own set of chart colors from that tab.

Adding Notes to Charts

You can add notes to charts to point out items of particular interest — and you can draw lines from the notes to some point on the chart. To add a note, choose Chart ⇨ Note. 1-2-3 displays the Note Properties InfoBox (see Figure 11-20). Type your note in Lines 1, 2 and 3 — each line you fill adds a line to your note. If you prefer, use a cell address to identify the location of the text you want to include in the note. Like a chart title, the note is stored in a box that, by default, you don't see. If, however, you use the Color, Pattern, and Line Style tab to add those attributes to the background of the note box, you'll see a rectangular shape behind the note text. Use the Font box to control the note's font attributes.

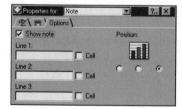

Figure 11-20: Add a note to a chart.

Using the techniques you learned earlier in this chapter, you can draw an arrow from a note to some chart element.

Adding Background Color, Colored Borders, and Designer Frames to Charts

From the Color, Pattern, and Line Style tab of the Chart Properties InfoBox, you can add background color to the entire chart object or change the color of the line that surrounds the chart's outside border. To add a designer frame to your chart, place a check in the Designer Frame check box and choose the frame style and color. A designer frame can greatly improve the appearance of your chart (see Figure 11-21).

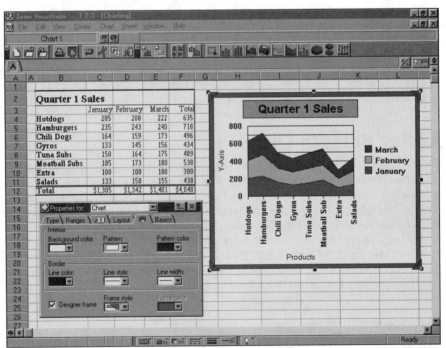

Figure 11-21: Add a designer frame to the edge of a chart to create a polished effect.

Adding a Map

You can present worksheet data on maps. This feature is particular effectively when the data you want to present relates to geographic areas. Using 1-2-3's mapping feature, you can present data on any of the built-in maps, or you can purchase additional maps from Lotus Corporation. Before you consider purchasing additional maps, however, you should note that 1-2-3 includes a large number of maps that are not automatically installed if you used the default installation settings. If you need a map that doesn't appear to be available, your first step should be to check to see if the map is available on the SmartSuite CD-ROM when you use the Custom install option.

In the next section, you'll learn about the details involved in creating and using maps.

Creating the Map

Creating a map is very similar to creating a chart in 1-2-3. You need, at a minimum, two columns of data. One column should contain the name of the geographic area for which you are mapping information, and the other column should contain the values you want to map.

Suppose, for example, that you are mapping sales data for part of the United States, as shown in Figure 11-22. At a minimum, column A should contain the abbreviations of the states for which you are creating a map, and column B should contain the sales data for each of those states. You can, optionally, include a third column of data that contains region names for your data.

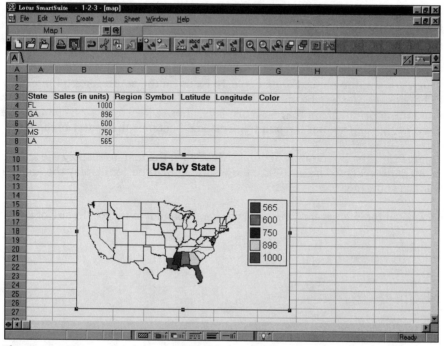

Figure 11-22: A map and the data used to create it.

You may also want to use four additional columns to store information 1-2-3 needs in order to position text or symbols within the chart. Using Figure 11-22 as an example, column D should contain the text or symbols you want 1-2-3 to place in the chart. Columns E and F should contain the latitude and longitude of the point where you want the text or symbol to appear. You may need to do some research to find out the latitudes and longitudes you need, but if you don't need exact measurements, you can use a trick we'll show you later in this chapter. Finally, column G should contain a code that selects a color for the text or symbol. These last four columns are entirely optional.

Figure 11-22 also shows a map containing data for a hypothetical company that does business only in the Southeast portion of the United States. To create a map, select the map data. Then, choose Create ➪ Map (or click the Create a Map SmartIcon). The mouse pointer shape changes to a plus sign with a globe attached. Drag from the upper-left corner to the lower-right corner of the location where you want the map to appear. The map in Figure 11-22 was created using the range A4:B8.

You can resize the map using the techniques you learned earlier in this chapter to resize a graphic object. Drag a corner of the map's border.

Focusing a Map on a Specific Geographic Area

While 1-2-3 produces a map showing the entire United States, you may want to focus only on a small portion of that map. You can easily refocus the map viewer's attention by recentering and zooming.

To recenter the map, click the mouse in the approximate center of the area on which you want to focus. For example, to focus on the southeastern United States, right-click the western border of Georgia about 1/3 of the way down the border. From the shortcut menu that 1-2-3 displays, choose Recenter. 1-2-3 changes the focus of the map so that the point you clicked becomes the center of the map.

Enlarge the area by zooming in. Again, right-click the map to display the shortcut menu and choose Zoom In. 1-2-3 enlarges the map to better display the area you want to show (see Figure 11-23).

You can zoom in several times, and you can zoom out to reduce the size of the map.

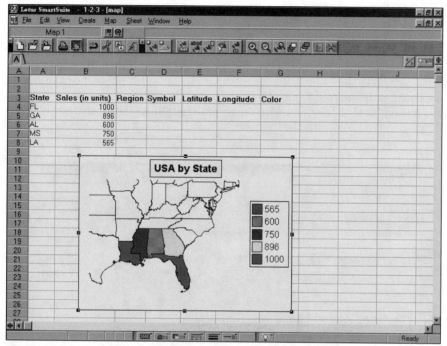

Figure 11-23: Zoom in to enlarge the visible portion of the map.

Naming the Map

Change the title of the map to something that will be more meaningful to the person who reads it. Click anywhere on the map to select. When you select the map, you'll see a Map command on the menu bar. Like the Chart command, the Map command is context-sensitive and appears only when you select some element of a map. Open the Map menu and choose Title (or click the Change Map Properties SmartIcon that replaces the Range Properties SmartIcon when a map is selected). 1-2-3 displays the Title Properties InfoBox (see Figure 11-24).

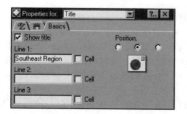

Figure 11-24: Change a map's title to make it more meaningful from the Basics tab of the Title Properties InfoBox.

On the Basics tab, change the text that appears in Line 1 to the title you want for your map. If you want additional lines in the map title, complete Line 2 and Line 3.

Finding Latitude and Longitude

If you need an exact location on your map, you'll have to do some research to determine that location's latitude and longitude. However, if the general vicinity is close enough, use this trick to obtain latitude and longitude coordinates for placing text or symbols. Right-click the approximate location for the text or symbol. From the shortcut menu (see Figure 11-25), choose Copy Coordinates. The coordinates that appear next to the command represent the latitude and longitude of the location you clicked with the mouse.

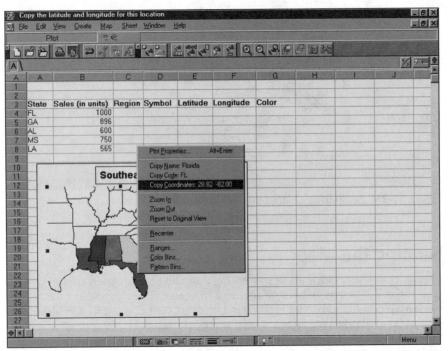

Figure 11-25: Get the latitude and longitude for any spot you right-click on the map from this shortcut menu.

1-2-3 stores the coordinates on the Windows Clipboard. Simply paste the coordinates in your worksheet map data. Then, supply text or a symbol in the appropriate column in the same row as the latitude and longitude. This might be some text like "Headquarters" or a symbol from one of the icon fonts like Wingdings or LotusWPIcon. If you want to use a symbol, you may find the Windows Character Map accessory handy for finding the correct symbol. For example, try inserting a semicolon (;) and formatting it with the LotusWPIcon font. When you redefine the data range for the map, as you will in the next section, 1-2-3 will add the text or symbol to your map at the specified location.

Changing the Data Used to Create a Map

When you add map data to the worksheet, you need to change the range 1-2-3 is using to draw the map. Click the map and choose Map ⇨ Map Properties. The Ranges tab of the Map Properties InfoBox shows the original ranges you selected when you drew the map.

Add the ranges for the additional information you want to map. To include information for patterns, add the range information to the Data to Map with Patterns text box. To incorporate the symbol, latitude and longitude, add the range to the Pin Characters, Latitude and Longitude text box (see Figure 11-26). Notice how 1-2-3 places any text you entered in the symbol column at the map location specified by the latitude and longitude entries.

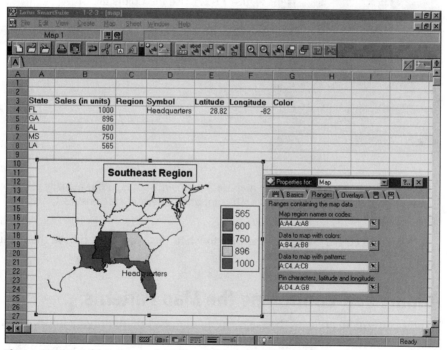

Figure 11-26: Add ranges to include additional information on the map.

Note

To add range information for text or a symbol, the range you add *must* be at least three columns wide and include the text or symbol, the latitude, and the longitude.

The text or symbol appears on the map using the font and font size set for the cell in which the information is stored. Adjust the size of the text or symbol on the map by adjusting the font size of the range in which it is stored.

Controlling Map Colors

Suppose you don't like the colors 1-2-3 chooses for the ranges on your map. You can change them from the Colors tab of the Map Properties InfoBox. Click the outside border of the map and choose Map ➪ Map Properties. Then, click the Colors tab (see Figure 11-27). Change the Colors from Default to Manual. Then, use the list box arrows that appear next to each bin to select a new color for that range.

Figure 11-27: Use the Colors tab of the Map Properties InfoBox to control the colors 1-2-3 assigns to each range of your map.

1-2-3 refers to each row in your map data as a *bin*. That is, a bin actually refers to a row of your map data. A bin has both color and pattern characteristics.

To eliminate colors, change all the bins to white (first you must choose the manual option in the Colors drop-down list box).

Adding and Controlling the Map Patterns

To add patterns to areas of the map, enter some sort of identifying information in the third column of data for the map. 1-2-3 will assign the same pattern to each map element that contains the same label in this column (see Figure 11-28).

You can control the patterns that 1-2-3 uses from the Patterns tab of the Map Properties InfoBox (refer to Figure 11-28). Change patterns the same way you changed colors — change the Patterns list box to Manual so that you have access to each bin's list box button. Then, click a bin's list box button to select a pattern for that bin.

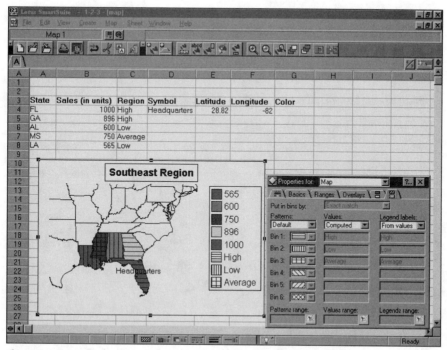

Figure 11-28: Notice that Florida and Georgia have the same map pattern because their label in the third column of map data is the same.

Manipulating the Legend

By default, the map legend shows both colors and patterns. Colors refer to each data point, while patterns refer to each text or symbol you supply in the third column of map data. However, you can control the legend's appearance. From the Basics tab of the Legend Properties InfoBox (see Figure 11-29), you can control whether the legend appears by removing the checks from the Show Color Legend *and* the Show Pattern Legend check boxes. Remember to click the map legend to see the Legend Properties InfoBox. To display either the color legend or the pattern legend, check *only* that check box.

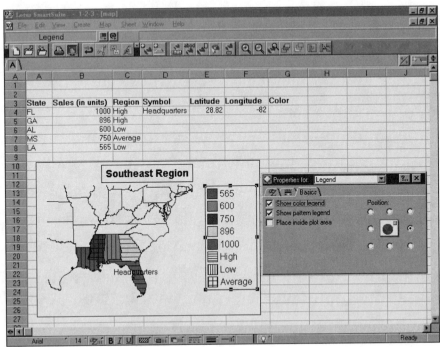

Figure 11-29: Use the Legend InfoBox to control the appearance of a map legend.

✦   ✦   ✦

Previewing and Printing a Worksheet

After doing all that work, eventually you're going to want to show it to someone. You could hand them the file—but you will probably want to print your workbook.

1-2-3 offers you significant control over the appearance of your printed output. In addition to learning how to print in this chapter, you'll learn how to change margins and the orientation of information on the page.

How Will It Look?

Before you print, it's always a good idea to see what your printed page will look like before you print it. That way, if things aren't quite the way you want them, you can make adjustments before you print.

Previewing is a simple matter. Open the workbook you want to print and click the Preview SmartIcon. 1-2-3 divides your screen in half—on the left, you see the workbook; and on the right, you see a preview of the workbook as it will appear when it prints (see Figure 12-1).

Preview SmartIcon.   Maximize button.

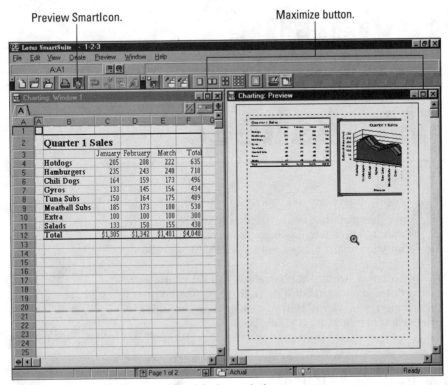

Figure 12-1: Previewing a workbook before printing.

Note   1-2-3 also displays the Preview and Page Setup InfoBox when you click the Preview SmartIcon; the InfoBox is closed in Figure 12-1 so you can focus on the preview and the worksheet.

If you maximize the worksheet, as shown in Figure 12-2, you'll notice a gray dotted line surrounding the area of the worksheet that 1-2-3 displayed in the preview. The gray dotted line represents the area 1-2-3 will print.

Note   To redisplay the preview, click the Restore button.

Hot Stuff   Notice that the shape of the mouse pointer in Figure 12-1 is a magnifying glass. You can zoom in on an area of the preview by clicking that area. If you click again, the picture will be even larger. Click a third time and 1-2-3 redisplays the preview in its original size.

If 1-2-3 determines that your worksheet will produce more than one printed page, you can scroll the pages in the Preview window. When the Preview window is the active window, you'll see the SmartIcons shown in Table 12-1; these SmartIcons help you "maneuver" through the Preview window.

Restore button.

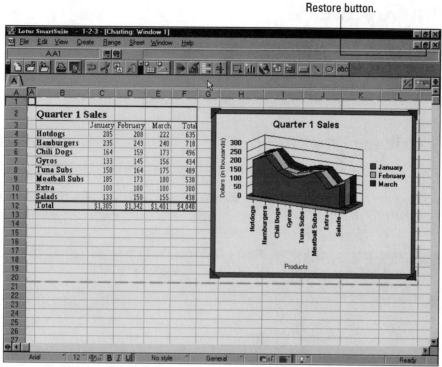

Figure 12-2: The gray dotted line surrounding data in the worksheet represents the information 1-2-3 will print.

Table 12-1
SmartIcons for Previewing

Icon	Description
	Opens the Preview & Page Setup InfoBox
	Moves to the next page in the Preview window
	Moves to the previous page in the Preview window
	Displays a single page in the Preview window
	Displays two facing pages in the Preview window
	Displays four pages in the Preview window
	Displays nine pages in the Preview window
	Prints the current selection
	Closes the Preview window

Setting Up the Page

Rarely do you see in the Preview window exactly what you want to print — which is exactly why you chose to preview before printing. For example, in our sample, the chart is cut off so that a portion will print on a different page. On the following pages, you'll learn various techniques to change the Preview window so that 1-2-3 prints what you want to print exactly the way you want to print it.

Specifying What to Print

In Figure 12-2, you saw the gray outline that signifies what 1-2-3 will print. You can change the print range using the Preview & Page Setup InfoBox. Click the Change Page Setup Properties SmartIcon to display the box and then click the Include tab (see Figure 12-3).

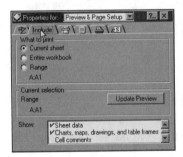

Figure 12-3: Use the Include tab to specify what you want to print.

You can, for example, choose to print only some pages in the workbook. Or, you can choose not to print charts with worksheets. Or you can change the range 1-2-3 prints by clicking the Range option button. Then, select a different range in the worksheet; when you select a range in the worksheet, 1-2-3 switches from the Preview & Page Setup InfoBox to the Range Properties InfoBox. Click the Preview window to redisplay the Preview & Page Setup InfoBox, click the Include tab, and then click the Update Preview button.

Selecting a Paper Size

By default, 1-2-3 will print to letter-size paper — which is generally an 8½ × 11-inch sheet of paper in North America. You can, however, change the paper size from the Printer, Paper Size, and Pages tab of the Preview & Page Setup InfoBox (see Figure 12-4).

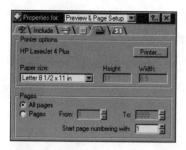

Figure 12-4: Use this tab to select a different paper size or a different printer.

Adjusting Page Breaks

Perhaps you don't like the page breaks 1-2-3 chose. You can change them by inserting page breaks prior to the ones 1-2-3 inserted. In the worksheet, select a cell in the row *below* or the column *to the right* of the location where you want the page break to appear. Then, click the Range Properties SmartIcon and display the Basics tab (see Figure 12-5). Place checks in one or both of the Break check boxes — Break Page at Row or Break Page at Column. 1-2-3 inserts a page break above or to the left of the currently selected cell.

Figure 12-5: Use the Basics tab of the Range Properties InfoBox to manually set page breaks.

Setting Page Layout

By default, 1-2-3 leaves a half-inch margin on all sides of the page. You can change the margins on the Margins, Orientation, and Placement tab of the Preview & Page Setup InfoBox (see Figure 12-6).

Use the spinner box buttons to change the Left, Right, Top, or Bottom margins. For a problem like the one we have in Figure 12-1, in which part of the chart is cut off, change the page orientation from the default, portrait, to landscape. And improve the visual appearance of information by centering it on the page.

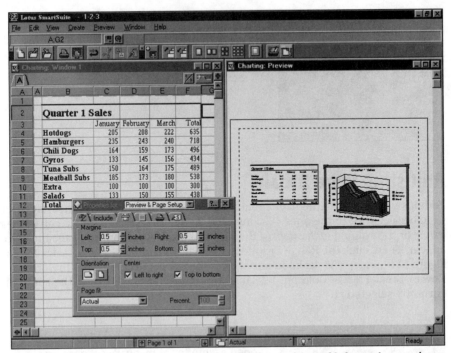

Figure 12-6: Change margins, orientation, and the position of information on the page from this tab of the Preview & Page Setup InfoBox.

Using the Page Fit list box, you can tell 1-2-3 to shrink information that spills onto two pages so that it will fit on one page. Remember, though, that 1-2-3 will reduce the font size (possibly making the information difficult to read) to fit the information on one page.

Adding and Formatting Headers or Footers

Headers and footers are particularly appropriate when you are printing a worksheet that spans many pages. Using headers and footers, you can help your reader identify the page of the report, the report name, or even the date the report was prepared.

Use the Header and Footer tab of the Preview & Page Setup InfoBox to create headers and footers for your worksheets. Either type in the header and footer boxes on the tab or use the buttons below the header and footer boxes to insert information in the header or footer. You can insert the current date, time, page number, total number of pages in the report, file name of the workbook, or the contents of the cell currently selected in the worksheet. When you use the buttons,

1-2-3 inserts symbols in the InfoBox that represent the information you want. The information appears in the preview and when you print the worksheet. In Figure 12-7, buttons were used for the header, and information was typed in for a left-aligned footer. You may also want to adjust the font settings for improved readability.

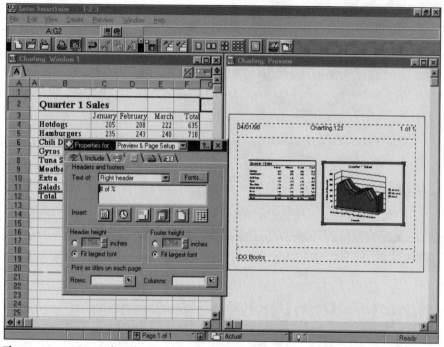

Figure 12-7: Create headers and footers that contain standardized information or type your own information.

Saving Customized Print Settings

When you create customized print settings, you can save them in a *named style*. That way, you only need to create them once. Then, you can copy them to other workbooks and apply them whenever you need them.

To create a named style for printing, choose the settings you want in the style using the Preview & Page Setup InfoBox. Then, click the Named Style tab and click Create Style. In the Create Style dialog box (see Figure 12-8), name and describe the style so that you know what it contains for future reference. Note that you can choose to include or exclude the selection as part of the style.

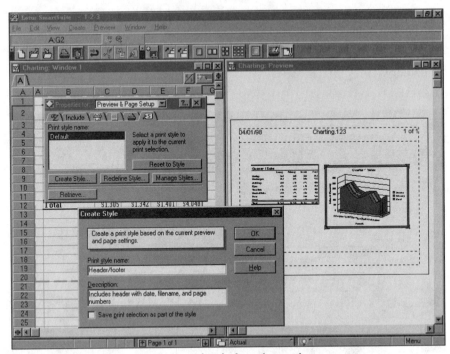

Figure 12-8: You can create a named style for print settings.

Sending the Print Job to the Printer

Now that you've got the worksheet set up the way you want it, all you need to do is print it. Click the Print SmartIcon and your job is off to the printer.

If you need to change the printer, you can use the Printer tab of the Preview & Page Setup tab or the Print dialog box. Just choose the printer you need from the list box.

✦   ✦   ✦

Using Data Management and Analysis Tools

You can analyze and manage information in 1-2-3 by
taking advantage of two powerful features: outlining
and database lists. When you outline worksheet information,
you organize your information to quickly and easily display
summary information, usually labeled "Totals," and the details
that comprise that summary information. With database lists,
you can quickly arrange and find information.

Outlining

Outlining provides you with a way to highlight the summary
information in a worksheet — or, just as quickly, display the
details that make up the summary information. Consider a
worksheet like the one in shown Figure 13-1.

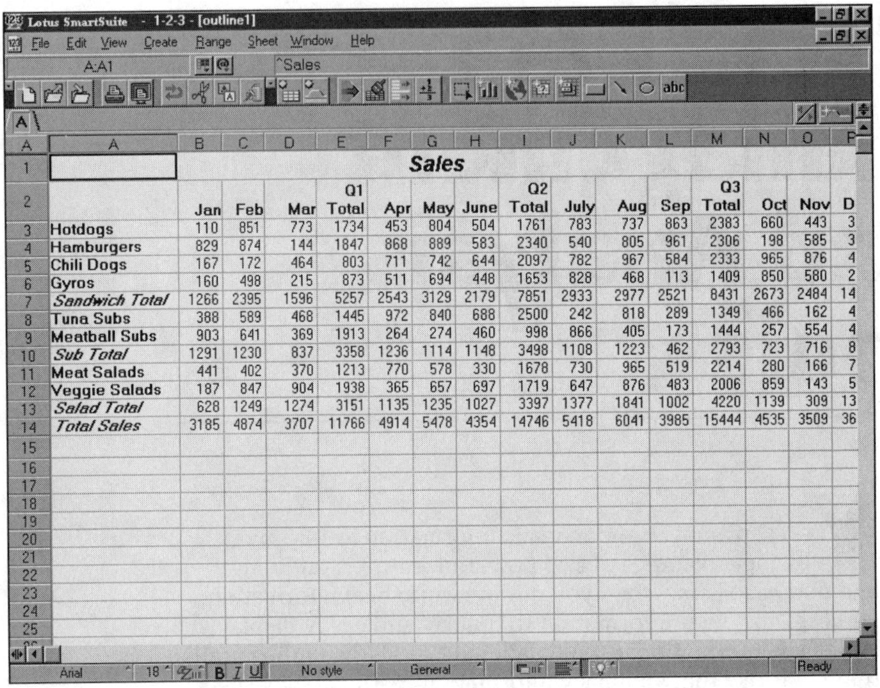

	Jan	Feb	Mar	Q1 Total	Apr	May	June	Q2 Total	July	Aug	Sep	Q3 Total	Oct	Nov	D
Hotdogs	110	851	773	1734	453	804	504	1761	783	737	863	2383	660	443	3
Hamburgers	829	874	144	1847	868	889	583	2340	540	805	961	2306	198	585	3
Chili Dogs	167	172	464	803	711	742	644	2097	782	967	584	2333	965	876	4
Gyros	160	498	215	873	511	694	448	1653	828	468	113	1409	850	580	2
Sandwich Total	1266	2395	1596	5257	2543	3129	2179	7851	2933	2977	2521	8431	2673	2484	14
Tuna Subs	388	589	468	1445	972	840	688	2500	242	818	289	1349	466	162	4
Meatball Subs	903	641	369	1913	264	274	460	998	866	405	173	1444	257	554	4
Sub Total	1291	1230	837	3358	1236	1114	1148	3498	1108	1223	462	2793	723	716	8
Meat Salads	441	402	370	1213	770	578	330	1678	730	965	519	2214	280	166	7
Veggie Salads	187	847	904	1938	365	657	697	1719	647	876	483	2006	859	143	5
Salad Total	628	1249	1274	3151	1135	1235	1027	3397	1377	1841	1002	4220	1139	309	13
Total Sales	3185	4874	3707	11766	4914	5478	4354	14746	5418	6041	3985	15444	4535	3509	36

Figure 13-1: A candidate worksheet for outlining.

From this worksheet, in which all the detail is visible, it's difficult to focus on and read either the quarterly totals or the totals for each category of sandwich. But if you use outlining, you can quickly and easily view or print just those totals (see Figure 13-2). In the next section you'll learn how to use the 1-2-3 outlining feature in your worksheets.

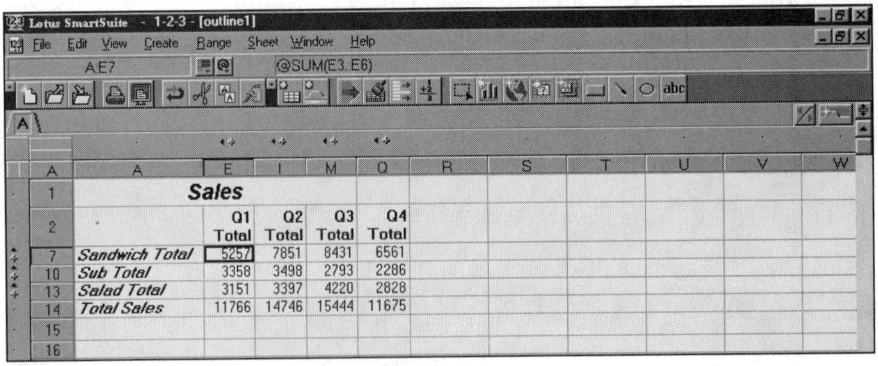

	Q1 Total	Q2 Total	Q3 Total	Q4 Total
Sandwich Total	5257	7851	8431	6561
Sub Total	3358	3498	2793	2286
Salad Total	3151	3397	4220	2828
Total Sales	11766	14746	15444	11675

Figure 13-2: The worksheet after outlining.

Setting Up Outlining

To set up outlining and have it work effectively, you need to analyze your worksheet, looking for summary rows and columns. Determine where the summary information appears in relation to the detail, because 1-2-3 will want to know if summary rows appear above or below details and whether summary columns appear to the left or right of details.

You use the Outline tab of the Sheet Properties InfoBox (see Figure 13-3) to set outlining properties for the entire worksheet. Click the Sheet Properties SmartIcon or choose Sheet ➪ Sheet Properties. Then, click the Outline tab.

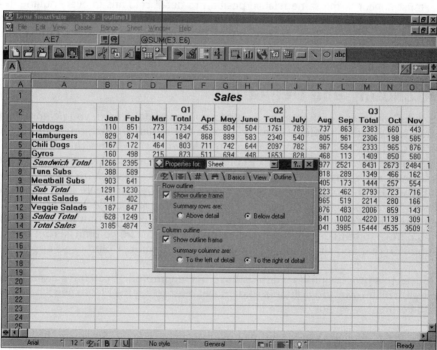

Figure 13-3: Set outline properties for a worksheet in the Sheet Properties InfoBox.

Place checks in the Show Outline Frame check boxes for the row outline and the column outline, if both are appropriate. (In the sample worksheet shown in Figure 13-1, the worksheet contains both row and column summary totals. These results are reflected in Figure 13-2.) Then, choose the appropriate option button(s) to define whether summary rows appear above or below detail rows. If appropriate, also choose the appropriate option button(s) to describe whether summary columns appear to the left or right of detail columns. In our sample worksheet, summary rows appear below details, and summary columns appear to the right of details.

As you make these selections, notice that 1-2-3 displays small dots in the worksheet frame to the left of the row numbers and above the column numbers. These dots let you know that you are in Outlining mode. You can now close the Sheet Properties InfoBox.

Danger Zone

Because outline properties apply to the entire sheet, all outlines within a worksheet must function the same way; that is, summary rows must appear in the same relative position to detail rows in every outline in the worksheet. Similarly, summary columns must appear in the same relative position to detail columns in every outline in the worksheet. If your worksheet contains a mixture of outline settings, move information for some of the outlines to another worksheet to make all outlines function consistently within the same worksheet.

Promoting and Demoting

To take advantage of the outline settings you just established, you *demote* detail rows and columns to view the worksheet in a summarized fashion. Demoting a row or a column moves the row or column to a lower outline level. This allows you to selectively hide the detail rows or columns, as you can choose which outline levels you want to display. For example, in Figure 13-4, rows 8 and 9 are the detail rows for row 10 — the total sales for Subs. If necessary you can create even more outline levels by demoting rows or columns more than one level. Select a set of details and choose Sheet ⇨ Outline (be sure to select the entire row or column — otherwise, you'll have to tell 1-2-3 whether to demote the row or the column). From the submenu that appears, choose Demote Rows or Demote Columns as appropriate.

Repeat this process until all details have been demoted. If you have a question about which rows and columns to demote, refer to Figure 13-2 to see which rows and columns were not demoted.

Hot Stuff

To make outlining easier you may want to right-click the SmartIcon bar and add a check to the Outlining SmartIcon bar.

Note

If you need to promote rows or columns you previously demoted, select the rows or columns and choose Sheet ⇨ Outline ⇨ Promote.

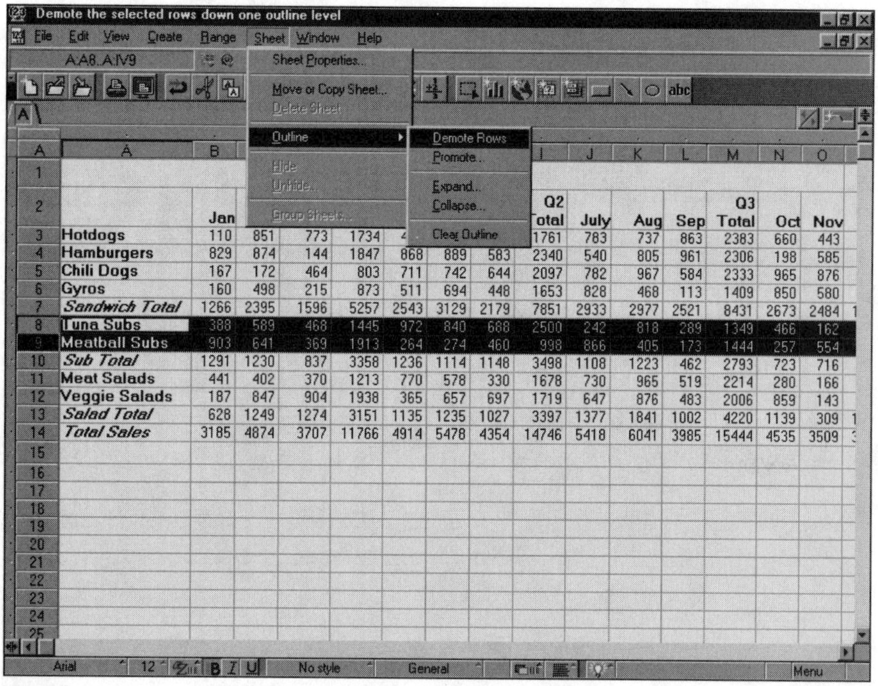

Figure 13-4: You can demote details in your worksheet.

Expanding and Collapsing the Outline

When you expand and collapse an outline, you see the functionality of the outlining feature. You collapse an outline to show less detail, and you expand an outline to show more detail.

Now that you have demoted rows and columns, notice that the worksheet frame contains, in addition to the outline dots, symbols that look like carats. When the outline is fully expanded, a minus sign appears underneath or to the right of the carat. If you click the minus sign near any of the symbols, 1-2-3 changes the minus sign to a plus sign, which indicates that a portion of the worksheet is summarized and collapsed. Figure 13-5 shows some sections of the outline expanded and some collapsed.

Minus sign indicates this — Plus sign indicates this —
section is fully expanded.   section is collapsed.   Outlining SmartIcon bar.

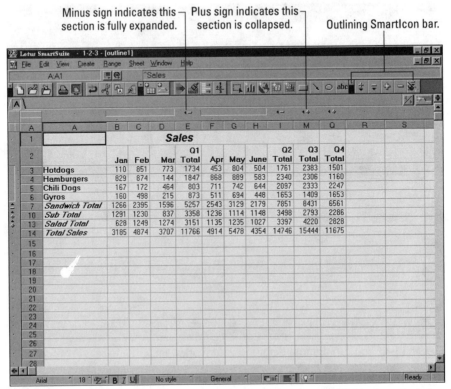

Figure 13-5: After demoting rows and columns, 1-2-3 places additional symbols in the worksheet frame.

And, of course, if you repeat this process for the entire worksheet, you'll see only summary information. The easiest way to collapse your entire outline is to select all of the summary rows and columns, click the Collapse Columns or Rows in the Selected Range SmartIcon (on the Outlining SmartIcon bar), choose Both, and click OK.

You cannot use the Go To dialog box to move to a cell in a collapsed range because the collapsed columns and rows are hidden. To move to one of these cells you must first expand the outline so the cell is visible.

Expand sections by clicking the plus sign to redisplay information.

Clearing the Outline

When you don't want to use outlining in a worksheet any longer, you can clear outlining. By clearing the outline, you *do not* affect any data in the worksheet. Select any cell within the outlined portion of the worksheet. Then, choose Sheet ➪ Outline ➪ Clear Outline.

Developing a 1-2-3 Database Table

A *database* is a collection of related information. In a worksheet, the information is organized into rows and columns, so 1-2-3 refers to the database as a database table. In a *database table*, all the information about one database item appears on one row of the worksheet — and each row is called a *record*. In order to function as a database table, the worksheet must include a row of unique labels that identify each piece of information you're collecting about a record; each piece of information is called a *field*.

Danger Zone

Do not separate the row of labels from the first row of information in a database table. That is, don't try to include a blank row between the labels and the data, because 1-2-3 will treat the empty row as a blank record.

In Figure 13-6, you see a database table showing sales for each sales representative of Christmas lights. The company sells two product numbers that represent two different sizes of lights. In addition, each size comes in four different colors. Each row represents one sale, and each column represents some piece of information about that sale.

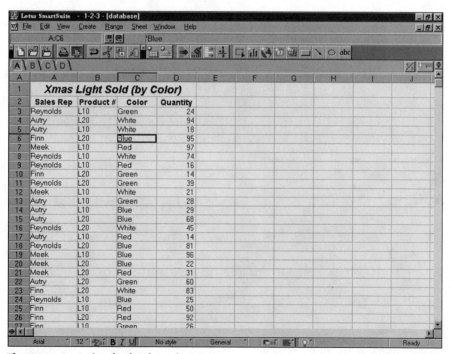

Figure 13-6: A simple database in 1-2-3.

Notice that the information does not appear in any special order. That's one of the advantages of using a database table; you don't need to worry about the order in which you enter information because you can sort the information later. Sorting information is covered next.

You may find it useful to create a range name for the database table; that way, when you need to refer to the database table, you can simply supply the range name. Make sure you include the labels when you define the range for the range name — that way you'll be able to use the database table name in database @Functions.

Sorting Data

You can sort any range of rows in 1-2-3, so you can sort the information in your database table by any column.

Always save your worksheet before sorting — so that you can simply close it and reopen it if you make a mistake. Indeed, you may prefer *not* to sort a database table, because you can accidentally overwrite information. Instead, you may prefer to build a query table from the database table and sort the information in the query table. See the next section to learn how to build and sort a query table.

Select the database. Then choose Range ➪ Sort. The Sort dialog box appears (see Figure 13-7).

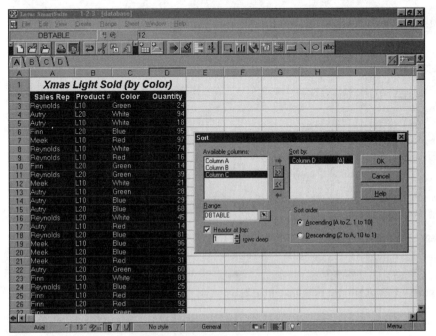

Figure 13-7: Use the Sort dialog box to sort any range in 1-2-3.

Click the column by which you want to sort the selected information and then click the arrow in the center of the box to make that column appear in the Sort By box. Then, select a sort order option. If you wish to sort by more than one column — perhaps to sort first by product number and then color — choose the additional columns and sort orders. Last — and this is most important — make sure that a check appears in the Header at Top check box. A check in this box means that your selection includes, as its first row, the labels you provided as field names. You *don't* want 1-2-3 to sort that row as part of the data, and the check mark tells 1-2-3 *not* to include the first row as part of the data it sorts. Click OK, and 1-2-3 reorganizes your database table information in the way that you indicated.

If you don't like the results of the sort, either click the Undo SmartIcon or close the workbook and reopen it.

Using Approach Features to Analyze Data

To perform most common database analysis functions, 1-2-3 works with Approach, the database software included in Lotus SmartSuite. In Part V of this book, you'll learn about Approach. In this chapter, we're going to cover some basic database analysis tools you can use with 1-2-3.

Working with Query Tables

A *query table* is a Lotus Approach object that is embedded in a 1-2-3 worksheet. In many ways, a query table is like other objects, in that you can move and size it. In one way, though, a query table differs from other objects: If you double-click a query table, you open both 1-2-3 and Approach, and you can use both programs to edit, sort, and query the database.

The query table is linked to the source table. A query table contains a copy of the records found in a database table in 1-2-3, and you create a query table to sort or find records in a database table. You can send information from a query table to an output range. In the output range, you can format the information for printing or use the data for calculating or to create charts or maps.

To create a query table, follow these steps:

1. Click in any cell in the database table for which you want to create a query table.

2. Choose Create ⇨ Database ⇨ Query Table. The Query Table Assistant dialog box appears (see Figure 13-8).

3. Identify the database table that will supply information to the query table.

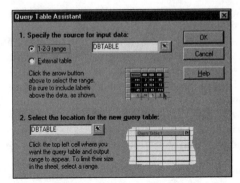

Figure 13-8: Use the Query Table Assistant
dialog box to create a query table.

4. Select the location for the query table. Click the range selector next to the
second list box and then click the top left cell of a blank range where you want
the query table to appear.

5. After a few moments, the Worksheet Assistant appears, asking you to select
the fields you want to include in the query table (see Figure 13-9).

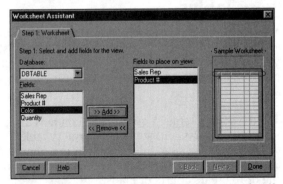

Figure 13-9: Use the Worksheet Assistant to identify
fields to include in the query table.

6. Click each field you want to include in the query table and then click the Add
button.

Note You *do not* need to include all fields of a database table in a query table; if your
database table is very wide (includes many columns), you may want to create several
query tables and include only a small subset of columns in each.

7. Click Done. The query table appears in your worksheet with handles
surrounding it, indicating 1-2-3 has selected it (see Figure 13-10).

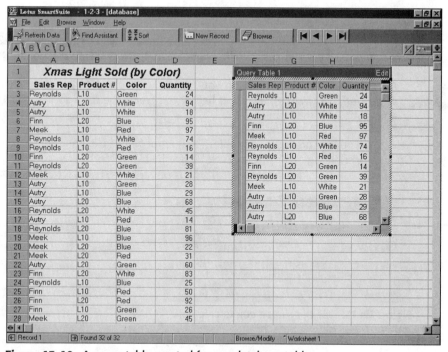

Figure 13-10: A query table created from a database table.

Once you create a query table, you can find database records in it or sort the records in the query table. With the query table selected, 1-2-3 activates the table, making some changes to the window, as shown in Figure 13-10.

To sort, click in the column by which you want to sort. Then, open the Browse menu and choose the Sort command. From the submenu that appears, choose Ascending or Descending. The sorted data appears in the query table but the database table is not affected. You can also use the Sort button to sort the query table.

Hot Stuff

Use the Define command to open a dialog box and set up a more complicated sort.

If you suspect that the original database table has been changed, click the Refresh Data button to update the query table. Use the Find Assistant button to locate specific records, the New Record button to add a record, and the Browse button to review or edit the data.

Hot Stuff

You can delete a query table at any time without affecting any data in the database table. Select the query table (make sure you see handles around it) and press the Del key on your keyboard.

Creating a Form

You can create a form to help you enter, edit, and view information in a 1-2-3 database table. 1-2-3 works with Approach to help you create this form.

A form is a full-screen object, so you may want to place it in another sheet in the same workbook. Add a new sheet before you create the form so that you'll have an empty sheet for the form.

Select any cell in the database table. Then, choose Create ⇨ Database ⇨ Form. The Create Form dialog box appears (see Figure 13-11).

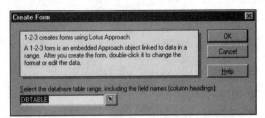

Figure 13-11: Use this dialog box to create a form in 1-2-3 using Approach.

Make sure that the correct range appears selected for the database table and choose OK. You'll see the mouse pointer change shape — it will look like a database form — and you'll see a message telling you to click where you want the form to appear. After a few moments, you'll see the Form Assistant dialog box (see Figure 13-12).

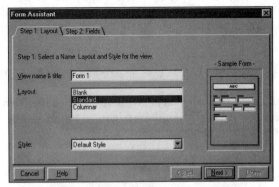

Figure 13-12: In this dialog box, choose the layout you want to use and the fields you want to appear on the form.

Danger Zone

Be sure to use the mouse to navigate to the location (even another sheet tab) where you want to place the form; if you use the keyboard, you will stop the creation of the form.

From the Layout tab, choose the appearance you want for the form. Use the View Name & Title box to supply a title for the form that will appear after you create the form. Click each layout to see a sample form to help you choose. Once you've selected a layout, click the drop-down Style list box to choose an appearance option. From the Fields tab, select the fields you want to include on the form and click the Add button for each field. Choose Done, and the form appears in your workbook (see Figure 13-13). If you cannot see all of the fields, drag the form selection handles to make the form larger.

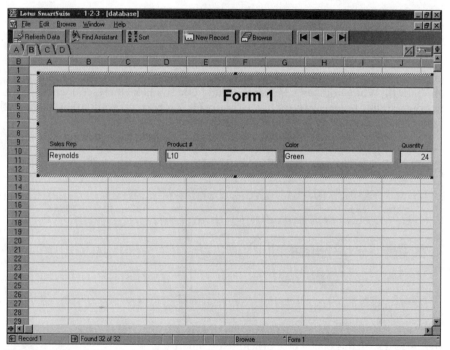

Figure 13-13: A form created for entering and editing data in a database table.

More Info

For information on using a form for data entry and editing in Approach, see Chapter 21, "Creating a Database and Entering Information." For more information on creating additional forms for a database in Approach, see Chapter 23, "Viewing, Summarizing, and Automating Data."

Creating a Report

You create a report of database information in much the same way you created a query table and a form. Click in any cell of the database table for which you want to create a report. Then, choose Create ➪ Database ➪ Report. The Create Report dialog box appears (see Figure 13-14).

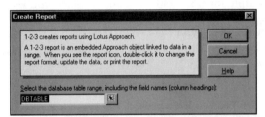

Figure 13-14: Use this dialog box to create a report in 1-2-3 using Approach.

Make sure that the correct range appears selected for the database table and choose OK. When you see a message telling you to click where you want the report to appear, click an empty spot in a worksheet. After a few moments, you'll see the Report Assistant dialog box (see Figure 13-15).

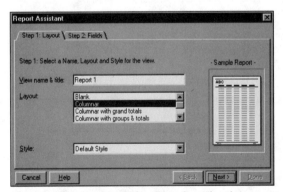

Figure 13-15: In this dialog box, describe the report you want to create.

Danger Zone

Be sure to use the mouse to navigate to the location (even another sheet tab) where you want to place the report; if you use the keyboard, you will stop the creation of the report.

From the Layout tab, choose the appearance you want for the report. Use the View Name & Title box to supply a title for the report, which will appear after you create the report. Click each layout to see a sample report to help you choose. Once you've picked a layout, use the options in the drop-down Style list box to choose a style for the report.

Note

The number of tabs in the Report Assistant dialog box varies, depending on the layout you choose. You need to supply information on each tab that appears.

From the Fields tab, select the fields you want to include on the report and click the Add button for each field. Choose Done. An embedded object representing the report appears in your worksheet, and the report appears in an Approach window. (see Figure 13-16).

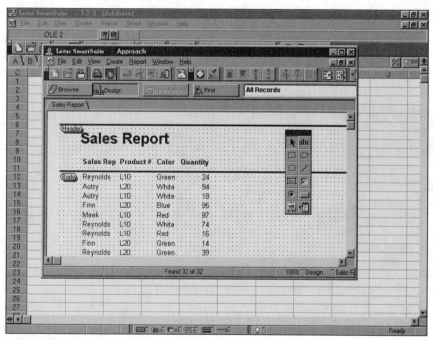

Figure 13-16: A report of a database table.

More Info

For information on creating and working with reports for a database in Approach, see Chapter 23, "Viewing, Summarizing, and Automating Data."

Creating a Dynamic Crosstab

A *crosstab* is an analysis tool you can use to help you categorize and summarize database records for a database that contains at least three fields. In our example database, the names of the sales reps appear several times in the first column, and the product number and color each appear several times in their respective columns. If you wanted to summarize your database information for any one of these three elements, you could create a *dynamic crosstab*.

A crosstab is a full-screen object, so you may want to place it in another sheet in the same workbook. Add a new sheet before you create the crosstab so you'll have an empty worksheet you can dedicate to the crosstab.

You create a crosstab of database information in much the same way you created a query table, a form, and a report. Click in any cell of the database table for which you want to create a crosstab. Then, choose Create ➪ Database ➪ Dynamic Crosstab. The Dynamic Crosstab dialog box appears, which looks very similar to the Create Report dialog box and the Create Form dialog box. Make sure that the correct range appears selected for the database table and choose OK. Click where you want the report to appear. After a few moments, you'll see the Crosstab Assistant dialog box, which contains three tabs.

From the Rows tab (see Figure 13-17), highlight each field you want to include as a row in the crosstab and click the Add button. If you wanted to summarize results by sales rep you would choose the Sales Rep field as a row in the crosstab.

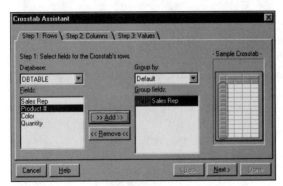

Figure 13-17: Select the rows to include in the crosstab.

From the Columns tab, highlight each field you want to include as a column in the crosstab and click the Add button. In this case you might choose the Color field to view the results by color.

Use the Values tab to identify the fields on which you want to summarize. Generally you'll want to select a field that includes numeric values. Also identify the action you want the crosstab to perform using the Calculate The list box. For example, to see total sales choose Sum.

Choose Done. The crosstab appears in your worksheet (see Figure 13-18). If you can't see the entire crosstab, drag the selection handles to resize the crosstab so you can see all the fields.

For information on creating and working with crosstabs in Approach, see Chapter 23, "Viewing, Summarizing, and Automating Data."

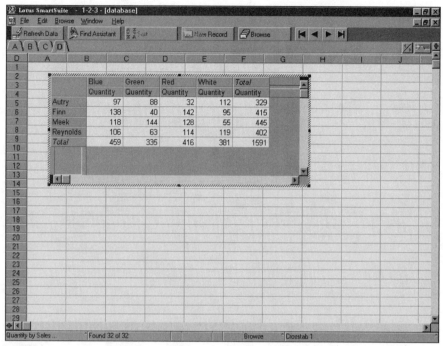

Figure 13-18: A dynamic crosstab.

Creating Mailing Labels and Form Letters

If your database contains name and address information, you can create both mailing labels and form letters from your database. The basic process is the same in 1-2-3 as it was to create a form, a report, and a query table. Click in any cell of the database table for which you want to create mailing labels or form letters. Then, choose Create ⇨ Database. From the submenu that appears, choose either Mailing Labels or Form Letter. The appropriate dialog box appears, looking very similar to the Create Report dialog box and the Create Form dialog box. Make sure that the correct range appears selected for the database table and choose OK. Click where you want the report to appear. After a few moments, you'll see the appropriate Assistant dialog box.

Use the Assistant dialog box to help you create your mailing labels or form letters.

More Info For information on creating and working with form letters and mailing labels in Approach, see Chapter 24, "Performing a Mail Merge in Approach."

✦   ✦   ✦

Saving Time with Power 1-2-3 Features

In This Chapter

Changing 1-2-3 preferences

Advanced work with ranges and cells

Using SmartMasters

Analyzing data

Using add-in applications

Basic scripting

In each of the preceding chapters on 1-2-3, you've learned about specific topics that focus on day-to-day actions you take in 1-2-3. In this last chapter on 1-2-3, you'll be introduced to some of the power features in 1-2-3 that can help you save time and create more meaningful workbooks.

Adjusting 1-2-3 Preferences

Using the 1-2-3 Preferences dialog box, you can control the general behavior of 1-2-3, as well as properties of all new workbooks. To display the dialog box, choose File ⇨ User Setup ⇨ 1-2-3 Preferences. You'll see the General tab of the dialog box initially (see Figure 14-1); from this tab, you can control 1-2-3's general behavior. For example, if you don't want to see the Welcome dialog box when you start 1-2-3, you can remove the check from Show Welcome Dialog.

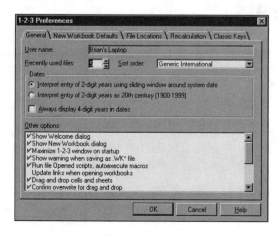

Figure 14-1: Use the 1-2-3 Preferences dialog box to control the behavior of 1-2-3.

Other tabs on the 1-2-3 Preferences dialog box are also quite useful:

✦ Use the New Workbook Defaults tab to control properties such as font and point size for all new workbooks you create from this point forward. Suppose, for example, that you don't want to use 1-2-3's default font of Arial 12-point for all new workbooks. You can use this tab to change the default font.

✦ Use the File Locations tab to change the default locations where 1-2-3 stores workbooks, SmartMasters, automatically opened files, and add-ins. For example, you might want to change the default location for storing workbook files if your company has a network file server to which someone backs up user files on a scheduled basis.

✦ Use the Recalculation tab to control the way 1-2-3 recalculates workbooks. Automatic recalculation works well in smaller workbooks, but when workbooks contain a lot of formulas, you may want to set recalculation to manual. Then, 1-2-3 will only update the formulas in your workbook when you press F9. You also can change the order in which 1-2-3 calculates the formulas in your workbook. When 1-2-3 recalculates using the default, Natural, formulas are recalculated based on dependency; that is, if one formula uses the results of a second formula, 1-2-3 recalculates the second formula before recalculating the first formula.

✦ Use the Classic Keys tab to control how 1-2-3 responds to the 1-2-3 for DOS command keys. If you memorized all those commands that appeared when you pressed the slash key (/) and could just whip right through an operation, the Classic Keys tab helps you operate as if you were using 1-2-3 for DOS.

Note   Note that 1-2-3 for Windows contains commands that were not available in 1-2-3 for DOS, and those commands will not appear on the "Slash menu." Also remember that certain features in the DOS product simply are not available in the Windows version; those commands may appear, but nothing will happen when you select them.

Adding Cell Comments

We've all been there—there's a number in the workbook that you need to explain. You can try putting notes at the bottom of the sheet, but directing the reader's eye from the bottom of the sheet to the appropriate cell is difficult at best. The solution: *cell comments*. You can attach a cell comment to a cell in your workbook.

To create a cell comment, select the cell on which you want to comment. Then, open the Range Properties InfoBox and click the Cell Comment tab (see Figure 14-2).

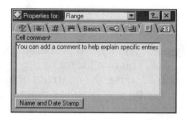

Figure 14-2: Type your cell comment here.

If you click the Name and Date Stamp button, 1-2-3 inserts for you your name and the date you created the comment.

When you finish typing, collapse or close the InfoBox. When you move the cell pointer to another cell, you'll notice a tiny red dot in the upper-left corner of the cell. This is the cell comment marker.

If you don't see the cell comment marker, choose File ⇨ Workbook Properties, and, on the View tab, place a check in the Cell Comment Markers check box.

To see a cell comment, select the cell containing the comment and choose Range ⇨ Cell Comment. To include cell comments when you print, choose File ⇨ Preview and Page Setup to open the Preview and Page Setup InfoBox. Click the Include tab (see Figure 14-3) and place a check next to Cell Comments.

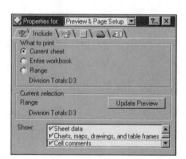

Figure 14-3: Including cell comments when you print a worksheet.

1-2-3 will print cell comments on a separate page and identify the cell address containing the comment on the printed page.

Parsing

It happens. We hate it, but it happens. Somebody places, in a word processing file, information that *should* have appeared in a workbook. You don't want to retype the entire thing, but what else can you do? Try letting 1-2-3 parse the contents of the file for you — you may be able to save yourself a lot of typing. *Parsing* simply means reading or examining some text to try to determine the contents of the text. For example, you might look at a text file and determine that it contains names, addresses, and phone numbers. When 1-2-3 parses, it divides information that wasn't created in columns into a columnar format for you.

To use 1-2-3's parsing feature, you must start with some sort of standard text file such as ASCII, text, or comma-delimited. This shouldn't be a problem, because most of today's popular word processing packages can save a file as a text file.

Choose File ⇨ Open. In the Open dialog box, choose Text from the Files of Type list box (see Figure 14-4). Notice that 1-2-3 recognizes several different types of text files.

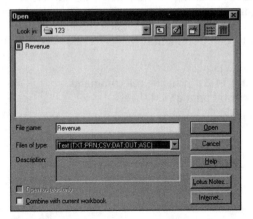

Figure 14-4: Choose Text as the file type.

Select the file from the Look In list and click the Open button. 1-2-3 displays the dialog box you see in Figure 14-5.

Figure 14-5: Use the Text File Options dialog box to set your parsing options.

The options you choose in this dialog box depend on the format of the text file. If tabs separated the data in the text file, try selecting the first option. You can also choose, from the list box in the first option, comma, semicolon, space, or other character(s). If the first option doesn't work for you, simply reopen the file and try the other options until you find the best fit for your file.

Using Range Versions

There you are, working on the budget, and you want to change some of the numbers to see the effect on the whole. But, you really don't want to lose the original numbers you entered — and you don't want to spend time writing down the cell addresses you changed and the changes you made. You are in the perfect situation to use 1-2-3's Version feature.

Creating a Version

In 1-2-3, *versions* are different sets of information for the same range. You create a version name for the range, and then make changes as needed. 1-2-3 tracks the name, date, and time the version was created, as well as who created or modified the version.

Versions work best if you create them before you start changing information. You can, optionally, assign a range name to the range for which you intend to create versions. Select the range and choose Range ➪ Name. In the Name dialog, type a name for the range.

To create a version for the range, select the range and choose Range ➪ Version ➪ New Version. The New Version dialog box appears (see Figure 14-6). If you forget to select the range before choosing the command, you'll see the Version Assistant dialog box in place of the New Version dialog box. Just select the correct range and you can continue.

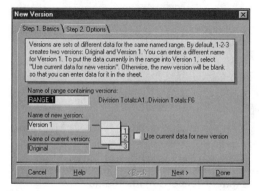

Figure 14-6: Use this dialog box to create a version.

On the Step 1. Basics tab, supply a name for the version — for example, you might be creating versions for the Best Case, Most Likely Case, and the Worst Case — or you can use Version 1, which 1-2-3 supplies by default. To include data you've already entered in the version, place a check in the Use Current Data for New Version check box.

Danger Zone

If you *don't* place a check in the Use Current Data for New Version check box, the cells in the version you are creating will be blank.

Use the Step 2. Options tab to enter a comment about the version and to set other options about the range. If you want to protect a version, use the Protection list box on the Step 2. Options tab. Protecting a version prevents changes, and may be a good idea for your original version. Click Done to finish creating the version. Now, make any changes that you want to appear in this version of the information.

Switching Between Versions

To switch between versions, click the button in the version frame to display the available versions and select a version (see Figure 14-7).

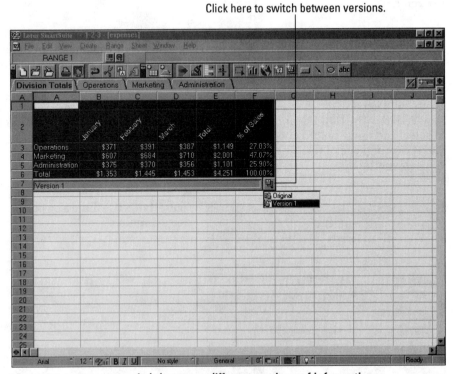

Figure 14-7: You can switch between different versions of information.

Any changes you make to the range will be stored in the version you are currently viewing. You may want to create several different versions so you can quickly switch between multiple scenarios.

Reporting on Versions

You can create a report that contains selected versions and allows you to compare the versions. Place the cell pointer in any cell in the range on which you want to report and choose Range ⇨ Version ⇨ Report. 1-2-3 displays the Version Report dialog box you see in Figure 14-8.

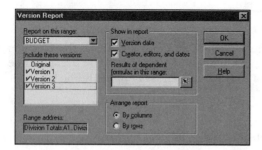

Figure 14-8: In this dialog box, select the versions you want to include in the report.

After you select the versions and the options you want to include in the report, click OK. If you wish to know how the various versions affect the results of formulas that are not contained within the version ranges, be sure to specify the formula range in the Results of Dependent Formulas in This Range text box. 1-2-3 creates the version report in a separate worksheet file named Report1 (if Report1.123 already exists, 1-2-3 increments the report number as necessary).

Using Version Groups

A *version group* is a collection of versions you have created for different ranges. Suppose you have four different ranges in the same worksheet for which you are creating versions, and you are creating a Best Case, Most Likely Case, and Worst Case set of scenarios. Your end goal is to be able to display the correct version for all four ranges at the same time. In a case like this one, you can create a *version group* that includes all four ranges for all three versions.

First, create versions for each range individually, as described in the preceding sections. Then, display on the worksheet the correct numbers for the first version for all ranges. Choose Range ⇨ Version ⇨ Version Group. In the Version Groups dialog box that appears, click New Group. The New Version Group dialog box appears (see Figure 14-9).

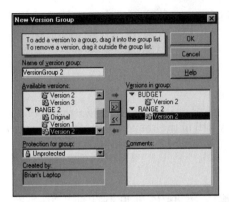

Figure 14-9: The New Version Group dialog box.

Supply a name for the version group, such as Best Case, and select the versions you want to include in the version group by highlighting the version in the Available Versions list and clicking the button to make the version appear in the Versions In Group box.

Note

In a version group, you cannot include versions from the same range. A version group must consist of versions from different ranges.

Click OK to redisplay the Version Groups dialog box, which will show the results of your selections. Anytime you want to view a version group, simply reopen the Version Groups dialog box and click Display Group.

Transposing a Range

One common mistake is to set up the rows as the columns and the columns as the rows — and, of course, realize it *after* entering a significant amount of data. For example, you may wish to use the Approach database features to analyze some data, but accidentally forgot that you must use rows for records and columns for the fields.

All is not lost in this situation, however. You can use 1-2-3's Transpose feature to switch things around — making the rows columns and the columns rows.

Danger Zone

Transposing can cause data loss, because you are copying information and can accidentally overwrite data. Save your workbook before you begin.

Consider Figure 14-10. Suppose you decide that you really want the months to appear down the side of the worksheet instead of appearing across the top, as shown in A1.F5. Select the entire range you want to transpose — in the example worksheet, select A1:F5. Choose Range ➪ Transpose to display the Transpose dialog box.

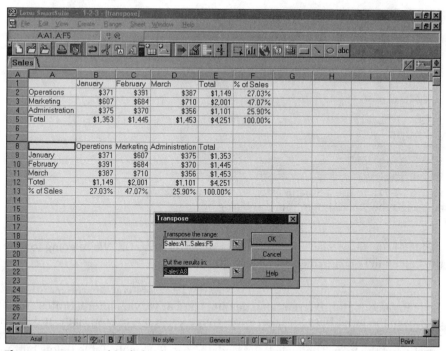

Figure 14-10: Use this dialog box to specify the range to transpose and the location to place it.

Because you will be overwriting data when you transpose, we suggest that you place the new transposed information in a *different location* than the original location, as we specified in the dialog box in Figure 14-10. Click OK, and 1-2-3 copies the information to the new location, switching rows and columns as shown in the lower portion of the figure.

Working with 1-2-3's SmartMasters

SmartMasters are templates that help you perform business and financial tasks. Lotus Development Corporation supplies a series of SmartMasters for you, and each contains sample data and instructions that show you how to use the template. You enter you own data into the SmartMaster and let it do the work for you. If you click the New SmartIcon, 1-2-3 shows you the available SmartMasters in the New Workbook dialog box (see Figure 14-11). You can create your own SmartMasters or use a SmartMaster created by someone else — you aren't limited to the SmartMasters provided with 1-2-3.

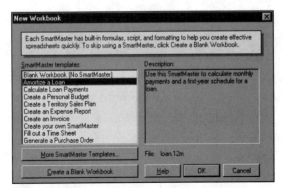

Figure 14-11: To use a SmartMaster, start a new workbook and select the SmartMaster from this dialog box.

Highlight the SmartMaster you want to use and choose OK. We're going to look at the Calculate Loan Payments SmartMaster.

As you can see from Figure 14-12, this SmartMaster lets you see the monthly payment amount for different loan amounts and at varying interest rates. You supply, in the Input Data for Loan Table range version, the Low, High, and Increment amounts for the Loan Principal and Annual Interest Rate, and you also provide the duration of the loan. Then, click the Update Loan Payments Table Below button, and 1-2-3 recalculates the amounts, based on the values you provide.

If you decide to save the work you do in a SmartMaster, you must save the file just as you would save any other workbook. Choose the Save SmartIcon and the Save As dialog box will appear.

You'll probably want to try out some of the other SmartMasters that Lotus Development Corporation provides. As you do, notice that both the Personal Budget SmartMaster and the Sales Territory Plan SmartMaster make use of multiple sheets in the workbook that add up to the numbers that will appear on the first sheet of the workbook. In this case, you must complete the other sheets in the SmartMasters, and 1-2-3 provides the results on the first sheet.

If none of the existing SmartMasters meet your needs, you can create your own SmartMaster template. Use the Create Your Own SmartMaster option to display the SmartMaster Shell (see Figure 14-13), which you can use as the foundation to create your own SmartMasters. As the figure shows, you can even create your own pop-up help icons, which users can click to get help using your SmartMaster. You may want to see "Creating a SmartMaster template" in the 1-2-3 online Help system for more information on creating your own SmartMasters. When you save a workbook as a SmartMaster, you give it a .12M extension.

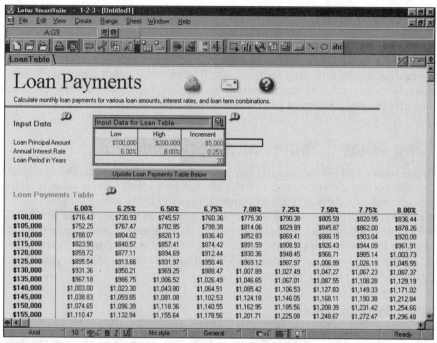

Figure 14-12: The Calculate Loan Payments SmartMaster.

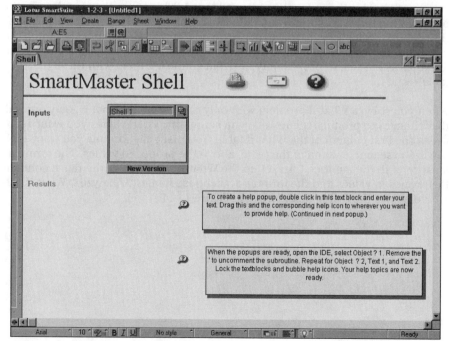

Figure 14-13: The SmartMaster Shell lets you build your own SmartMaster.

Analyzing Data

Now that you've got all the information in a worksheet, take advantage of 1-2-3's real power by using one of various methods 1-2-3 provides to analyze the information. In the following sections you'll learn more about using the What-if tables, Backsolver, frequency distribution analysis, regression analysis, and matrix manipulation capabilities of 1-2-3 to analyze your data.

Using What-if Tables and Backsolver

What-if tables and Backsolver are two different ways you can answer questions involving formulas. Suppose, for example, that you want to know what the effect on your profit would be if your expenses increased by 10%. In a What-if table, you substitute different values for variables that appear in formulas, and 1-2-3 recalculates the results for you. When you use Backsolver, you specify the value you want for the formula's results, and 1-2-3 calculates the different values for variables in the formula. To use both What-if tables and Backsolver, you must set up the table in a specific format.

Using a What-if Table

Suppose you're trying to determine a product's price based on its cost and its markup. You could use a What-if table to help you. Set up a worksheet similar to the one shown in Figure 14-14. Cell B2 contains the value for the cost, which is a fixed amount. Cell B3 is the *input cell*—the cell that 1-2-3 uses for the sample values it places in the formula as the What-if table is calculated. C6 contains the formula (B2*B3)+B2, which is used to calculate the retail price. Because B3 is empty, the formula shows the equivalent of no markup. You may want to format your What-if formulas as hidden, to prevent anyone from confusing them with the actual What-if table results.

When you solve a What-if problem with only one variable—that is, only one value that changes to produce the results, you set up proposed values you want 1-2-3 to use in the first column of the What-if table. You place the formula you want 1-2-3 to use in the second column of the table, above the proposed values. The formula must refer to the input cell. To set up the What-if table, select the range containing the proposed values and the formula and choose Range ➪ Analyze ➪ What-if Table. 1-2-3 displays the dialog box you see in Figure 14-14.

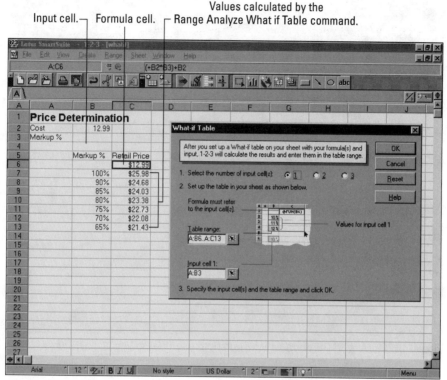

Input cell. — Formula cell. — Values calculated by the Range Analyze What if Table command.

Figure 14-14: A worksheet set up to solve a What-if problem for one variable.

Make sure you select the number of input cells; a one-variable What-if table contains only one input cell. Specify the table range as the selected range. The input cell represents the variable you want 1-2-3 to change while solving, and *is not* part of the table. When you complete this dialog box, choose OK. 1-2-3 calculates the formula based on the values you proposed. In Figure 14-14, 1-2-3 has supplied proposed prices for each proposed markup level.

Using Backsolver

Backsolver lets you specify the result you want, and then 1-2-3 calculates changes to variables you specify. For example, you might decide that you can afford a $500-per-month car payment and you'd like to know how much you can borrow. To use Backsolver, your worksheet needs at least one formula; the rest of the cells can contain values. In Figure 14-15, B6 contains the formula to calculate a loan payment; all the other numbers in column B are values.

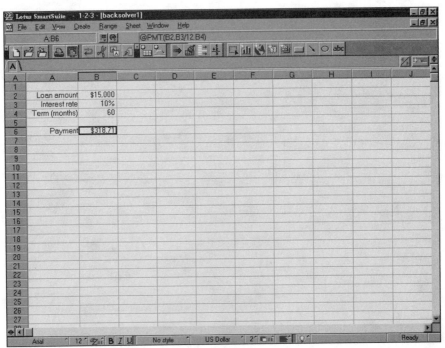

Figure 14-15: A worksheet on which you could use Backsolver.

To use Backsolver, select the cell containing the formula and choose Range ⇨ Analyze ⇨ Backsolver. 1-2-3 displays the dialog box you see in Figure 14-16.

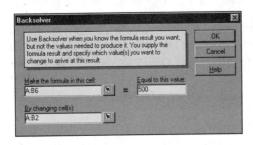

Figure 14-16: When backsolving, specify the formula's expected result and the cells 1-2-3 can change to achieve the result.

Because you started by selecting the cell containing the formula you want to solve, set the value for the formula in the Equal to This Value box. Identify the cell or range of cells 1-2-3 should change to achieve the formula result you specified. When you choose OK, 1-2-3 adjusts the specified cells (see Figure 14-17).

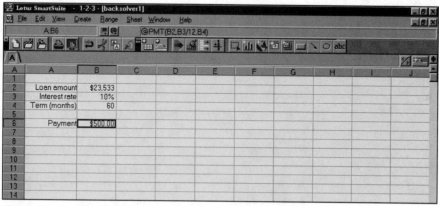

Figure 14-17: The changes 1-2-3 makes after backsolving.

Calculating a Frequency Distribution

When you have a list of numbers, you can use a frequency distribution to determine how many values in the group fall between two specified numbers. Teachers use frequency distributions when establishing grade curves by determining the number of students' scores that fall between intervals on the curve.

In 1-2-3, each set of numbers that form the intervals is called a *bin*. On the worksheet that contains the list of numbers for which you want to calculate a frequency distribution, set up bin values from smallest to largest, with no text or blank cells in the bin range. Each bin value represents the high end of the range, because 1-2-3 counts the number of values in your list that are equal to or less than the bin value. In the worksheet in Figure 14-18, the bin values appear in D3:D9; notice that the range immediately to the right of the bin range is blank. 1-2-3 will place the results of the frequency distribution in E3:E9.

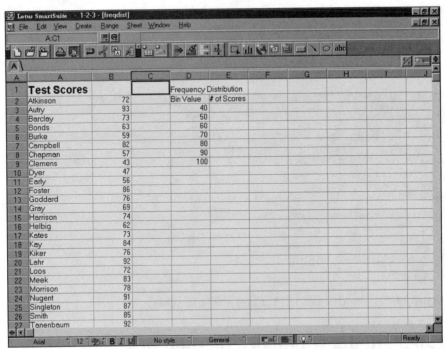

Figure 14-18: A worksheet set up to calculate a frequency distribution.

To calculate the frequency distribution, select the list of numbers you wish to analyze. Then choose Range ⇨ Analyze ⇨ Distribution. 1-2-3 displays the Frequency Distribution dialog box (see Figure 14-19).

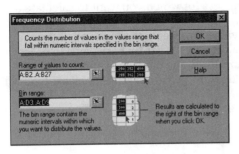

Figure 14-19: In the Frequency Distribution dialog box, define the location of the list of numbers and the bin range.

The address for the range of the list of numbers should appear in the Range of Values to Count box. Use the range selector at the right side of the Bin Range text box to specify the bin range, and choose OK. 1-2-3 counts the values in the list and places the count in the bin range. In Figure 14-20, no scores in the list equal 40 or less, and 8 scores fall between 70 and 80. Notice that cell E10 shows zero, which indicates that none of the values were above the highest value in the bin range.

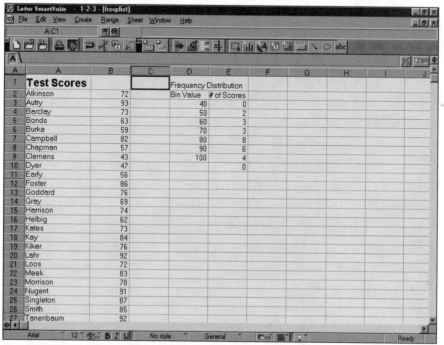

Figure 14-20: After calculating the frequency distribution, the bin range shows the number of values in the list that are equal to or less than the bin value.

Performing Regression Analysis

You can use *regression analysis* to determine whether one set of independent values has any relation to another set of dependent values. For example, you might use regression analysis to attempt to determine the factors that affect the sales of your products. If you determine that the two data sets are indeed related, then you can make predictions; your predictions will be more likely to occur if the two data sets are closely related.

For example, suppose you sell beer at the ballpark, and you believe that the temperature, the sales of hot dogs and pretzels, and the number of ticket-holders affect your beer sales. You can collect information and perform a regression analysis to determine if you are correct. In a 1-2-3 regression analysis, you place the data you collect for the dependent variable in one column, and 1-2-3 refers to the data in that column as the X-range. In this example, the quantity of beer that you sell is the dependent variable because it depends on the other four variables, which are independent variables. In a 1-2-3 regression analysis, you can have up to 75 independent variables. The values for each independent variable must appear in separate, contiguous columns in the worksheet, and 1-2-3 refers to the columns containing the data for the independent variables as the Y-range. If you collected data in this test for ten days, your worksheet might look like the one shown in Figure 14-21.

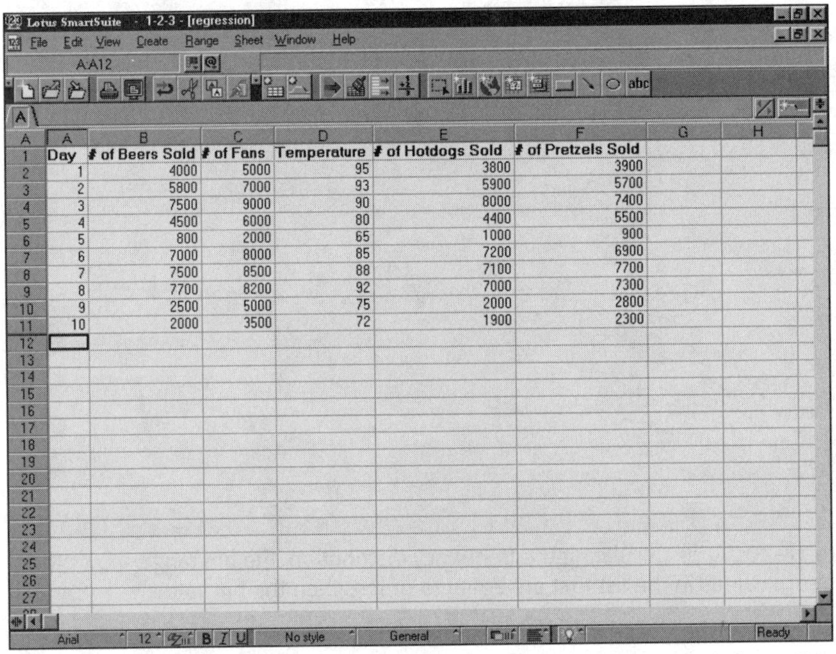

Day	# of Beers Sold	# of Fans	Temperature	# of Hotdogs Sold	# of Pretzels Sold
1	4000	5000	95	3800	3900
2	5800	7000	93	5900	5700
3	7500	9000	90	8000	7400
4	4500	6000	80	4400	5500
5	800	2000	65	1000	900
6	7000	8000	85	7200	6900
7	7500	8500	88	7100	7700
8	7700	8200	92	7000	7300
9	2500	5000	75	2000	2800
10	2000	3500	72	1900	2300

Figure 14-21: In this worksheet, the dependent variable appears in column B, while the independent variables appear in columns C, D, E, and F.

Note   You must have the same number of data points for each of the independent variables as you have for the dependent variable.

When you perform the regression, 1-2-3 will need a place to enter the results, so make sure you identify a range where you can place the regression results. You'll always need 9 rows (regardless of the number of variables) and the same number of columns as you have independent variables for to store the regression results. To perform the regression, select the values for the independent variable and choose Range ➪ Analyze ➪ Regression. 1-2-3 displays the Regression dialog box you see in Figure 14-22. Make certain the correct ranges are specified in each of the text boxes. Generally you will want to allow 1-2-3 to compute the y-intercept (trend line) value. Forcing the y-intercept to zero may skew your results. After you complete the dialog box, choose OK.

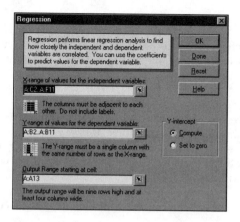

Figure 14-22: In the Regression dialog box, identify the X-range, the Y-range, and the starting cell of the output range.

1-2-3 displays the results of the analysis at the location you indicated (see Figure 14-23). The R Squared value (shown in this figure), also called the *correlation coefficient,* tells you how closely related the dependent and independent variables are. R Squared should be a number between 0 and 1; when R Squared is close to 1, the relationship between the dependent variable and the independent variables is quite strong, and variations in the dependent variable can, most likely, be explained by variations in the independent variable.

Lotus SmartSuite - 1-2-3 - [regression]							
A:A13							

	A	B	C	D	E	F	G	H
1	Day	# of Beers Sold	# of Fans	Temperature	# of Hotdogs Sold	# of Pretzels Sold		
2	1	4000	5000	95	3800	3900		
3	2	5800	7000	93	5900	5700		
4	3	7500	9000	90	8000	7400		
5	4	4500	6000	80	4400	5500		
6	5	800	2000	65	1000	900		
7	6	7000	8000	85	7200	6900		
8	7	7500	8500	88	7100	7700		
9	8	7700	8200	92	7000	7300		
10	9	2500	5000	75	2000	2800		
11	10	2000	3500	72	1900	2300		
12								
13		Regression Output:						
14	Constant			-1427.8180059				
15	Std Err of Y Est			306.343048567				
16	R Squared			0.99198184725				
17	No. of Observations			10				
18	Degrees of Freedom			5				
19								
20	X Coefficient(s)		0.1096075	16.5522696454	0.429220332205404	0.440637062573416		
21	Std Err of Coef.		0.2405332	16.0963913766	0.208404593833336	0.265568270064142		
22								

Figure 14-23: In regression results, the R Squared value helps you determine whether you were correct in assuming a relationship between the variables.

Working with Matrixes

In 1-2-3, a *matrix* is a range of cells, each of which contains a value. The range can be in one sheet or across sheets. Each value in the matrix represents a constant or the coefficient for a variable in a formula.

Problems with several variables often require solving simultaneous equations. When faced with problems that involve several variables, you may be able to use matrix calculations to help solve the simultaneous equations. *Matrix analysis* finds the relationship between at least two sets of variables in one or more formulas. You use the results of matrix analysis to determine which combination of numbers will produce the result you want for the formulas.

You can invert a matrix or multiply matrixes. Both of these options are discussed in the following section.

Inverting a Matrix

You can invert a matrix only if the matrix is *square* — that is, the matrix must have the same number of rows and columns. Once you invert the matrix, the new matrix will be the same size as the original matrix. To invert a matrix, select the range containing the matrix and choose Range ➪ Analyze ➪ Invert Matrix. 1-2-3 displays the Invert Matrix dialog box. Specify the location for the inverted matrix. Choose OK, and 1-2-3 places the results of the matrix inversion at the location you specified. Figure 14-24 shows the original matrix, the inverted matrix, and the Invert Matrix dialog box.

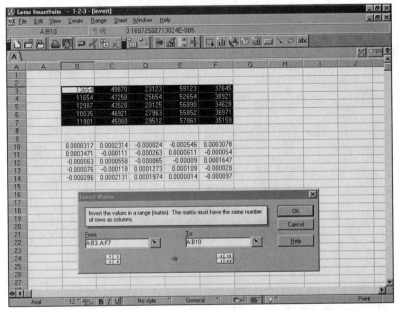

Figure 14-24: When you invert a matrix in 1-2-3, any data in the To range will be overwritten.

Multiplying Matrixes

To multiply matrixes, the number of columns in the first matrix must equal the number of rows in the second matrix. And, the order in which you multiply the matrixes will affect the results.

When you multiply two matrixes, the resulting matrix will have the same number of rows as the first matrix and the same number of columns as the second matrix. To multiply matrixes, select the range containing the first matrix and choose Range ➪ Analyze ➪ Multiply Matrix. 1-2-3 displays the Multiply Matrix dialog box. Specify the three ranges and choose OK. 1-2-3 multiplies the matrixes and displays the result at the specified location. Figure 14-25 shows the Multiply Matrix dialog box and the completed matrix multiplication.

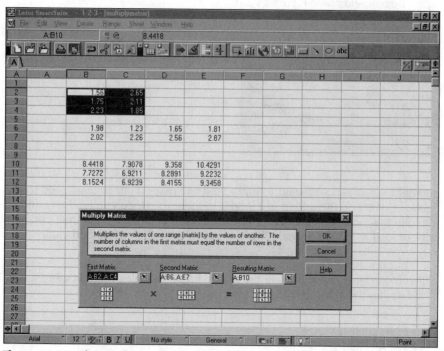

Figure 14-25: The resulting matrix contains the same number of rows as the first matrix, and the same number of columns as the second matrix.

Adding Features with Add-Ins

Add-ins are special 1-2-3 files that are created by Lotus Development Corporation or by other software developers. Add-ins work with 1-2-3 to extend its capabilities; to the end user, the capabilities of the add-in appear to be built into 1-2-3. In fact, unless you are a developer, you will be more likely to use an add-in that someone else provides for you.

Add-ins consist of applications or @Functions. The add-in applications are composed of compiled scripts in a workbook and perform some specific task in 1-2-3. Add-in @Functions behave like other 1-2-3 @Functions and are used in formulas.

To load an add-in, choose File ➪ Add-Ins ➪ Manage Add-Ins. The Manage Add-Ins dialog box appears (see Figure 14-26).

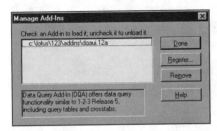

Figure 14-26: Use this dialog box to select add-ins to load.

Highlight the add-in you want to load; 1-2-3 will place a check mark next to it. Choose Done, and the add-in will load into memory. Once you load an add-in, 1-2-3 will load that add-in into memory in each subsequent 1-2-3 session. If you don't want to load an add-in, reopen the Manage Add-Ins dialog box and click the add-in to remove the check beside it.

Hot Stuff   If you don't see any add-ins in the Manage Add-Ins dialog box, click Register. 1-2-3 will display the available add-ins.

Scripting in 1-2-3

A *script* is a series of program statements that automate tasks. You write scripts in a language called *LotusScript,* and this language is actually used in all SmartSuite products.

You can write scripts directly using scripting commands or you can let 1-2-3 record your keystrokes. In this section you'll learn about the recording method, which works for many common tasks in 1-2-3.

Recording a Script

When you record a script, 1-2-3 keeps track of the keystrokes you use and creates the appropriate scripting statements. Once you record a script, you can look at it to get an idea of how the scripting language works — and even use basic scripts to help teach yourself more about scripting.

To keep the example simple, we're going to create a script to print the worksheet. You wouldn't need to create this script because you can click the Print SmartIcon, but the example will help you understand how to record a script and view the script statements. While you're learning, creating a script for an action with which you're familiar can help you understand the script statements 1-2-3 will generate. Follow these steps to create the sample script:

1. Choose Edit ➪ Scripts & Macros ➪ Record Script. 1-2-3 displays the Record Script dialog box (see Figure 14-27).

Figure 14-27: Use the Record Script dialog box to supply a script name and file in which to save the script.

2. Supply a name for the script and optionally the name of the open workbook in which you wish 1-2-3 to place the script. Then click Record. 1-2-3 displays a pair of buttons onscreen; the one on the left stops recording, while the one on the right pauses or restarts recording (see Figure 14-28).

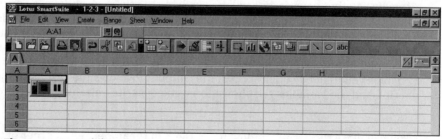

Figure 14-28: While recording a script, you'll see a stop button and a pause button onscreen.

Don't name scripts with words that 1-2-3 might use for commands. For example, you'll get an error if you name this script "Print" instead of "Printing."

3. Work as you usually would to perform the action you want stored in the script. In our example, Choose File ➪ Print, make the appropriate settings in the Print dialog box, and click the Print button.

4. Click the Stop button that appeared when you started recording the script. The recording toolbar disappears, and 1-2-3 displays the Script Editor window with the script statements you just recorded (see Figure 14-29).

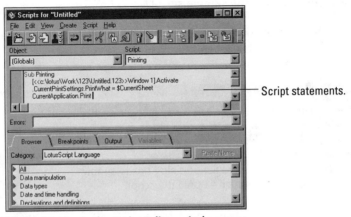

Script statements.

Figure 14-29: In the Script Editor window, you see the script statements you just recorded.

The Script Editor window has several tools to help you refine your scripts. In addition to the script window there is an Object list box, which enables you to specify whether your scripts will be available to other workbooks; a Script list box that enables you to choose which script you wish to edit; and an Errors list box to help you solve problems you may encounter when you create scripts. The lower section of the Script Editor window has a Browser tab where you can view examples of the script language and its various elements. The Breakpoints tab enables you to debug your scripts, the Output tab shows the results of running a script, and the Variables tab shows the value of script variables as you step through a script.

You can close the Script window using the X in the upper-right corner of the window. When you save your worksheet, 1-2-3 will save the script as well. You can go back to look at the script again in the Script Editor, and even make changes to refine the script as you learn more about LotusScript. Choose Edit ➪ Scripts & Macros ➪ Show Script Editor. In the Script Editor window, choose View ➪ Previous Script.

Running a Script

What's the point of creating a script if you can't use it? The obvious way to run a script you've created is to choose Edit ➪ Scripts & Macros ➪ Run. 1-2-3 displays the Run Scripts & Macros dialog box. Highlight the script you want to run and click the Run button.

Note 1-2-3 can run both scripts and macros, but it is highly recommended that you only use scripts to automate your work. The macro capabilities are largely available to allow you to run existing macros in workbooks created in older versions of 1-2-3. In fact, the 1-2-3 online Help system no longer even lists the individual macro commands.

You also can run scripts by attaching them to buttons or SmartIcons, by assigning keyboard shortcuts to them or by placing them on the Actions menu. These options are discussed below.

Creating a Script Button on a Worksheet

You can add a graphic button to your workbook to which you can assign a script. Then, when you click the button, 1-2-3 will run the script.

Hot Stuff If you want to attach an existing script to a button, you need to copy all the script's statements *except* the first and last statement to the Clipboard. That is, copy everything except the Sub and End Sub lines.

To create a button, choose Create ➪ Button. The mouse pointer turns into a plus sign. To create a default size button, click the mouse on the worksheet where you want the button to appear. If you want to control the button's size, drag to draw the button instead of clicking. 1-2-3 displays a graphic icon on your worksheet called Button 1, and also opens the Script Editor window (see Figure 14-30).

Enter the script statements that you want the button to perform when you click it. (You may want to refer to Figure 14-29 for this.) If you copied existing script statements (the easiest way to do this is to click Globals in the Object list box, copy the statements, and click Button 1 in the list box to return to the script for Button 1), paste them at the location where the insertion point appears by default—on the blank line between the first and last statements. You can change the button name to something more meaningful than Button 1. Right-click the button graphic and choose Drawing Properties. The Draw Properties InfoBox appears. Change the verbiage that appears in the text box from Button 1 to whatever you want.

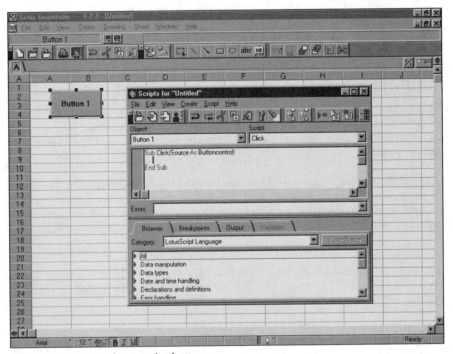

Figure 14-30: Creating a script button.

Close the Draw Object InfoBox and the Script Editor. Then, click anywhere in the worksheet to cancel the selection of the button. When you next click the button, the script will run.

Attaching a Script to a SmartIcon button

Perhaps you don't want the button on the worksheet; instead, you'd like to attach the script to a SmartIcon that you can click to run the script. Follow these steps:

1. Choose File ➪ UserSetup ➪ SmartIcons Setup. 1-2-3 displays the SmartIcons Setup dialog box.

2. Open the Bar Name list box and select the SmartIcon bar on which you want to place the SmartIcon you will attach to your script.

3. Click the Edit Icon button to display the Edit SmartIcons dialog box (see Figure 14-31).

4. Create a new SmartIcon picture by drawing on the blank SmartIcon or simply choose an existing SmartIcon. If you select one of the default SmartIcons, you won't be able to change its picture, but you can attach your script to the button.

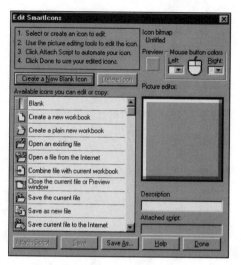

Figure 14-31: Use this dialog box to attach a script to a SmartIcon.

5. In the Description box below the icon you selected, type a phrase that 1-2-3 can display as Bubble Help for this SmartIcon.

6. Click the Save As button and type a name for the button picture. 1-2-3 will save the button as a .BMP image file.

7. Click the Attach Script button, which became available when you saved the button image. 1-2-3 displays the Attach Script dialog box.

8. Choose the script you want to run when you click this SmartIcon and click Attach.

9. Click Save and then Done to return to the SmartIcons Setup dialog box.

10. Scroll to the bottom of the SmartIcons Setup dialog box, where you'll see the SmartIcon you created.

11. Drag your SmartIcon onto the SmartIcon bar at the top of the dialog box. When you drop the SmartIcon, it will be added to that SmartIcon bar.

12. Click the OK button.

Note

You may need to hide and display the SmartIcon bar set to which you added your SmartIcon in order for it to appear on-screen.

✦　　✦　　✦

Freelance Graphics

◆ ◆ ◆ ◆

This part of the book presents everything you need to create great slide shows with Freelance Graphics. You'll learn how to create a new presentation, and how to add new pages (slides) of information. Then, we show you how to build your message by entering text, using the Outline view to enter text and review the overall flow of information, and editing, copying, deleting, and reorganizing pages. Learn how to add a chart to a page, and create an organization chart.

Don't forget the importance of how your presentation looks. You learn how to choose a new page layout or to change the look of the whole presentation, how to draw on a slide, and how to insert a graphic or clip art. Then, find out how to run your presentation as a Screen Show on a computer by creating transitions between slides, adding sounds for transitions, creating effects, and running the onscreen show. Finally, you'll learn how to set up and print your presentation pages on paper or as 35mm slides.

◆ ◆ ◆ ◆

Starting, Saving, and Opening Presentations

As notebook computer prices dropped over the last few years, making it easier to deliver an onscreen presentation while on the road, customers and audiences have increasingly expected more than accurate information. Color, graphics, and interactivity now provide the impact that closes the sale, inspires the troops, or teaches the skills. People in all professions have learned to use presentation graphics programs like SmartSuite's Freelance Graphics to develop attractive, compelling presentations. This chapter can be your first step in building career-enhancing presentations. Learn here how to start and move around in Freelance Graphics and create a new presentation by choosing a predefined look or starter contents. The chapter also covers saving and working with presentation files, adding new pages to the presentation, and changing your view of the presentation. Finally, learn to work with preferences that dictate how your presentation file and Freelance behave.

Starting Freelance Graphics and Making a Presentation

To start the Freelance Graphics program so that you can begin using it to create new documents, you can use any of the methods for launching SmartSuite applications presented in Chapter 1, "Getting Started with SmartSuite Applications":

✦ Choose Start ➪ Programs ➪ Lotus SmartSuite ➪ Lotus Freelance Graphics.

✦ Open the SmartSuite drawer on the SmartCenter, then open the Lotus Applications drawer, if needed. Double-click the Lotus Freelance shortcut.

✦ Click the Lotus Freelance Graphics SuiteStart button on the right end of the taskbar.

Freelance Graphics launches, displaying its Welcome to Lotus Freelance Graphics window. If it isn't selected, click the Create a New Presentation Using a SmartMaster tab, shown in Figure 15-1. This tab of the Welcome window lists the options you have for creating a new presentation. The remainder of this section explains how to create a new presentation. Later, you learn how to open an existing presentation file.

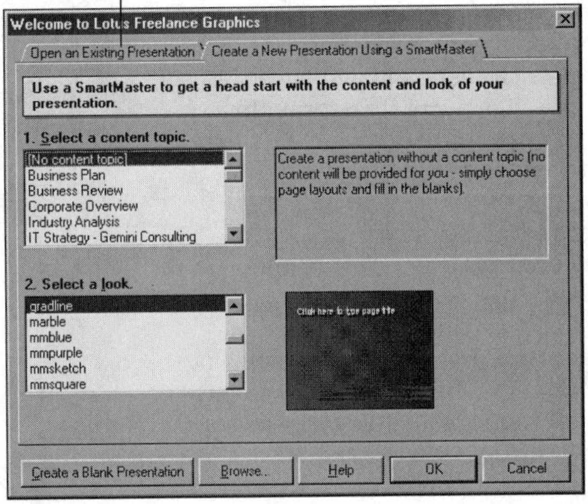

Click this tab to list documents you've worked with recently.

Figure 15-1: The Welcome to Lotus Freelance Graphics window prompts you to create a new presentation.

In a presentation graphics program, the *presentation* is the file you create. In Freelance Graphics, you add pages to the presentation file, with each page covering a single topic area. Because each file in the page is discrete, you can choose a different design for each page, as called for by the subject matter the page covers. After you create the presentation file, you can use it in a number of ways. You can run the presentation on your computer as a *screen show*, displaying each page on the screen in turn as you discuss its contents. Or, you can print the presentation in a variety of formats, with each page in the presentation typically occupying a single page in the printout. You can print your presentation pages to transparency film, so you can use them as overheads. And finally, you can send your presentation file to a special print shop or service bureau to have each presentation page printed as a 35mm slide, so you can present a traditional slide show.

Creating a Presentation with Starter Content and a Look

The Create New Presentation Using a SmartMaster tab offers two lists you can use to tell Freelance Graphics to do part of the work of creating a new presentation for you. The top list, Select a Content Topic, lists Freelance content topics that not only provide a look for the presentation text and pages, but also include suggestions for the overall flow of topics for a presentation. For example, you could click the Meeting – Standard choice to create a presentation with Click Here blocks (placeholders) that suggest agenda topics for a team meeting. Scroll through the Select a Content Topic list, and click the presentation topic that best reflects the purpose of the new presentation you're building. A description of the currently selected contents appears beside the list. Or, to create all the presentation content from scratch, click [No Content Topic].

If you choose a content topic from the Select a Content list, Freelance automatically selects Look Stored with Content Topic in the bottom list, Select a Look. That's because each of the SmartMasters holding suggested presentation content also offers a suggested presentation look (see Figure 15-2). The sample page to the right of the list of looks previews the currently selected look. If you chose [No Content Topic] from the top list, or if you want to use a look other than the one included with the content topic, scroll through the Select a Look list and click the look you want. The Select a Look list offers the SmartMasters you can choose for a Freelance presentation. Each SmartMaster defines the formatting used by the text, background, pages, and other elements on the presentation pages. To create a presentation with a completely blank background, choose [No Look-Blank Background] from the Select a Look list.

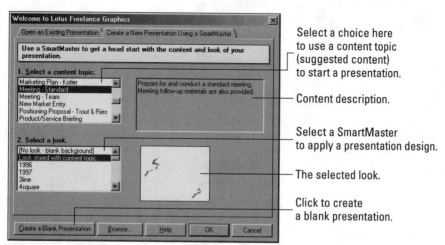

Figure 15-2: Choose the content and look you want for your new presentation.

After you choose content and a look for the new presentation, click OK. If the content topic or SmartMaster you select for a new presentation includes scripts and you have security features enabled, a dialog box appears to warn you about the scripts. Click Yes to allow the script to run, or No to open the content topic or SmartMaster without the scripts. If you selected a content topic, it may display a Welcome dialog box that explains the overall content structure of the presentation. Review the information, then click OK. The New Page dialog box appears, so that you can create the first *page* for the new presentation.

The appearance of the New Page dialog box varies, depending on whether or not you selected a content topic for the presentation. If you did choose a content topic, the New Page dialog box displays two tabs. The first tab, Content Pages, lists pages of suggested topics for the presentation content (see Figure 15-3). You can click the page that you want to serve as the first page in your presentation. A preview and description of the selected page appears beside the list. Or, to add multiple pages at once, click the Choose Multiple Content Pages button to display the New Page – Choose Multiple Content Pages dialog box, press and hold Ctrl and click each page to add to the presentation, then click OK. If you don't want to choose a page with a suggested topic as the first page, click the Page Layouts tab, then click the page layout you want in the list on the tab. After you choose the page to add from either tab, click OK to add the page to your presentation.

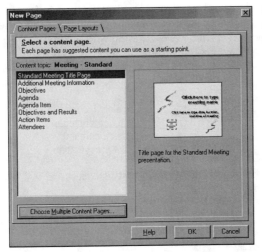

Figure 15-3: Add a page with suggested text to the presentation using this dialog box tab.

If you only selected a SmartMaster look (and no content topic) for the presentation in the Create New Presentation Using a SmartMaster tab of the Welcome to Lotus Freelance Graphics window, the New Page dialog box contains only a list of page layouts (see Figure 15-4). The layout options listed are the same as those that you'd see if you clicked the Page Layouts tab in the New Page dialog box shown in Figure 15-3. Click the page layout you want. A preview and description of the selected page layout appears beside the list. After you choose the page to add, click OK to add the page to your presentation.

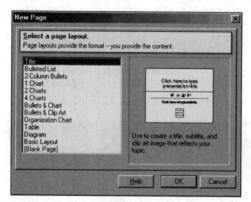

Figure 15-4: If you opted to create your own presentation content, choose the page layout for your first slide here.

Creating a Blank Presentation

You may have noticed that the Welcome to Lotus Freelance Graphics window shown in Figure 15-1 includes a button in its lower-left corner called Create a Blank Presentation. Click this button to create a presentation that has no content topic or SmartMaster, and therefore no suggested content or formatting. If you've already used the Welcome to Lotus Freelance Graphics window to create a presentation, you'll need to instead click the Create a New Presentation SmartIcon (it's the first one on the SmartIcon bar). In the New Presentation dialog box, choose [No Content Topic] from the Select a Content Topic list, choose [No Look – Blank Background] from the Select a Look list, and then click OK.

When you choose to create a blank presentation, a blank title page slide appears by default. Freelance doesn't give you the option of selecting a page layout for the first slide.

Exiting Freelance Graphics

When you've finished working with Freelance Graphics, you can close the program. To do so, click the Close button for the Freelance Graphics window. Or, choose File ⇨ Exit Freelance Graphics (Alt+F4). If you have a presentation that's open and you haven't saved your changes to it, Freelance displays a message box asking you if you want to save your changes. Click Yes to do so and finish closing Freelance Graphics.

Reviewing the Freelance Screen

After you create the presentation and select the first slide for it, the new presentation opens in the Freelance Graphics application window. Chapter 1, "Getting Started with SmartSuite Applications," introduced the screen features found in most SmartSuite applications. Freelance Graphics offers the same features, but some of them are more specific to Freelance itself, as illustrated in Figure 15-5.

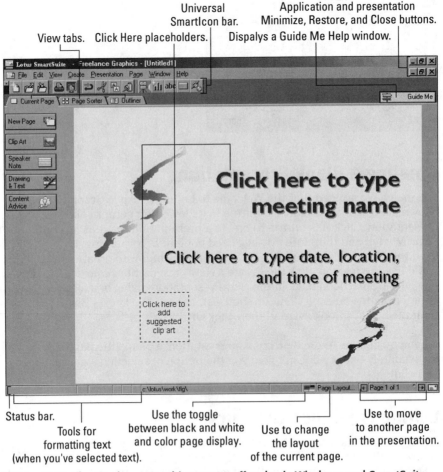

Figure 15-5: The Freelance Graphics screen offers basic Windows and SmartSuite features, plus tools that are useful for developing presentations. This is the default view, Current Page view.

Later chapters in Part IV discuss how to use the document-specific features of the Freelance Graphics screen in more detail, but here's a brief introduction. The work area of the Freelance screen holds *view tabs* for selecting different ways to look at the pages in the presentation. By default, the presentation appears in the Current Page tab, so that tab is selected. Each page includes *Click Here* placeholders (like those in Word Pro) for adding text, clip art, and other elements to the page. If you need help about how to proceed with your work on the current page, click the Guide Me button near the upper-right corner of the page to open a Help window listing different tasks, then click the button for the task about which you need guidance.

The *Universal* SmartIcon bar appears by default in Freelance. In addition, the Current Page View tab includes several command buttons at the left for working with the presentation and the contents of the currently displayed page. If you've selected text in a text Click Here placeholder, the first several buttons on the status bar become active so you can use them to change the appearance of text. You can use the subsequent status bar buttons to display document information, choose whether to display the presentation in black-and-white or color, choose a new layout for the current page, and navigate in the presentation.

Managing Presentation Files

Saving a presentation file stores it on a hard disk or floppy disk until you're ready to make changes to it or print it. As in the other SmartSuite applications, when you save a presentation file for the first time in Freelance Graphics, you give it a name to distinguish it from the other files you've saved. Then, you can find and open the file you want. This section focuses on file naming and usage—saving, closing, and opening files.

Setting Properties for the Current Presentation

Freelance automatically tracks certain properties for each presentation file—such as the number of pages, file size, and number of revisions—behind the scenes. You can include a few other pieces of information with the presentation file before you save it to your hard disk or network drive, so that you can use that information to identify the file when you're trying to open it or find it under Windows.

To view, enter, and edit properties for the open presentation file, choose File ➪ Presentation Properties. The Presentation Properties dialog box appears. The top of the dialog box lists the statistics Freelance tracks about the open presentation file. Below that, the dialog box lists two text boxes. Enter a description for the file in the Description text box; you can later view the description in the Open dialog box to verify that you're opening the correct file. Use the Keywords text box to enter important topics in the presentation; you can use these keywords to find the file later under Windows. Figure 15-6 shows a Description and Keywords entered for a file.

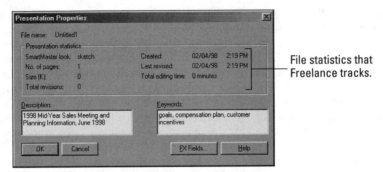

File statistics that
Freelance tracks.

Figure 15-6: You can review file statistics or enter
descriptive information about the presentation in
this Presentation Properties dialog box.

If you'll be exporting the presentation to a Lotus Notes database, click the FX Fields
button. The FX Fields dialog box lists eight field text boxes for fields named Field1,
Field2, and so on. (To rename fields, click the Rename Fields button, enter the new
name for each field in the text box beside its current field name in the Rename
Fields dialog box, and then click OK.) Enter the information to export for each field
in the text box beside the field name; the information you enter for each field name
appears under the field name when exported to Notes. Click OK to finish entering
the Notes information.

Click OK to close the Presentation Properties dialog box. You should then save your
document to save its properties with it.

Saving and Naming a Presentation

You can't hear too often that you should save your work every ten minutes or so. If
your computer shuts down or spontaneously reboots due to a power fluctuation,
you lose all work you haven't saved. And you don't have to use 1-2-3 to calculate
that it's easier to rebuild ten minutes' worth of work than a couple hours' worth.

When you save a Freelance Graphics presentation file for the first time, you give it a
name. You can use more than 200 characters and spaces, and the capitalization you
prefer. Use the following steps to save a presentation file for the first time and give
it a new name:

1. Choose File ⇨ Save (Ctrl+S), or click the Save the Current Presentation SmartIcon
   on the SmartIcon bar. If you have only one page in the presentation, Freelance
   may display a message box informing you that you can add more pages before
   saving. Click OK to bypass this message box. The Save As dialog box appears.

2. (Optional) Use the Save In drop-down list and the list below it to specify the
   disk and folder in which you want to store the file. Unless you change the
   folder, your Freelance Graphics files are saved to the \lotus\work\flg folder
   on your hard disk.

3. Click in the File Name text box (if the insertion point doesn't already appear in it) and type the name you want for the file.

4. If you didn't enter a description for the file in the Presentation Properties dialog box, you can enter one in the Description text box of the Save As dialog box. Figure 15-7 shows a File Name entry and a description entered for a presentation file.

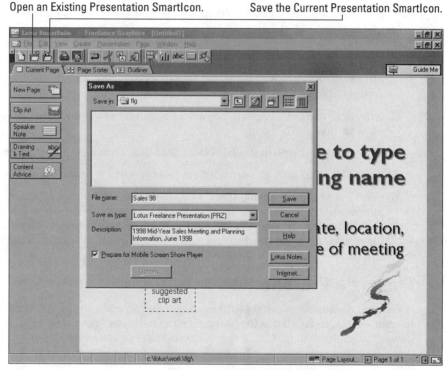

Figure 15-7: When you save a file, you enter its name in the Save As dialog box, as well as a description with more detail about the file, if you prefer.

5. If you may be running the presentation using the Mobile Screen Show Player, a separate program that runs presentations as a screen show without requiring the full Freelance Graphics program, make sure the Prepare for Mobile Screen Show Player check box is checked. Otherwise, you can clear this check box.

6. Click the Save button to finish saving the file.

After you make any changes to a file, you have to save it again. To do so, choose File ⇨ Save, press Ctrl+S, or click the Save the Current Presentation SmartIcon. Because you've previously named the file, you won't see the Save As dialog box. Freelance Graphics simply saves the changes to the file.

Copying a Presentation Under a New Name

If you create a presentation that works well, you may want to reuse the bulk of its contents for subsequent presentations. For example, suppose you create a sales presentation that really impresses a customer. You can copy the presentation under a new name and customize the copied presentation so that it appeals to the next customer you meet with. Use the File ➪ Save As command to save a copy of a presentation file under a new name, so you can then edit and update the presentation.

Use the following steps to save a copy of a file and give the copy a new name:

1. Open the file that you want to copy. This file will remain intact on your disk.

2. Choose File ➪ Save As. Note that you can't use the File ➪ Save command or the Save the Current Presentation SmartIcon — you have to use the Save As command to redisplay the Save As dialog box.

3. If needed, use the Save In list to select another disk and folder in which you want to save the file copy.

4. Drag over the name in the File Name text box, then type a new name.

5. If needed, drag over the description and type a new description.

6. Click Save to finish saving the file copy. The new file name you specified appears in the title bar, indicating that the file copy is the open file. Any changes you subsequently make appear in the new file copy. The original file closes, so if you need to make any changes to it, you must reopen it.

Closing a Presentation

When you've finished working with or displaying a presentation, you can close it to remove it from Freelance Graphics. Closing a file ensures that you won't make unwanted changes to it. Also, if a presentation file contains sensitive information, you should always close that file before leaving your office to ensure that others don't see information not intended for them.

To close a file in Freelance Graphics, click the file window's Close button or choose File ➪ Close (Ctrl+W). If you've made changes to the document but haven't saved them, a dialog box appears to remind you to save the file (see Figure 15-8). Click Yes to save the file and then close it, or No to simply close it.

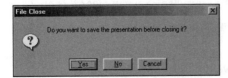

Figure 15-8: Freelance reminds you to save your changes before the file closes.

Opening an Existing Presentation

Opening a presentation file that you've previously saved and closed makes it the *current file* or *active file*, meaning that changes and commands apply to that file until you switch to another file. You can then print, format, or otherwise make changes to the contents of the file. You can open as many files as you want, and all remain open; that is, opening a file doesn't automatically close any other open files. Use the following steps to open a presentation file:

1. Choose File ⇨ Open (Ctrl+O) or click the Open an Existing Presentation SmartIcon. The Open dialog box appears.

2. Use the Look In list to navigate to the disk and folder that holds the file you want to open.

3. When you see the file you want in the Look In list, click the file name. Its description, if you entered one, and a preview of the first page, appears so you can verify that it's the file you want (see Figure 15-9).

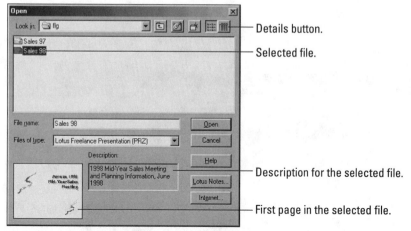

Figure 15-9: Click a file to see the description you entered for it (if any) to verify it's the file you'd like to open.

Click the Details button in the Open dialog box to list the size, file type, and modification date beside each file in the Look In list.

4. When you find the file you'd like to open, click the Open button. Freelance Graphics opens the file, and it appears onscreen.

Note

If the content topic or SmartMaster used to create the file you're opening contains scripts, a warning message about those scripts appears. These messages can become a bit tedious if you work with Freelance often. Click to check the Don't Display This Message Again check box before clicking Yes or No to prevent Freelance from displaying such warning messages.

By default, the bottom of the File menu lists the files you've worked with most recently. To open one of the files listed on the File menu, click its file name.

You also can open a file from the Welcome to Lotus Freelance Graphics window if you just launched Freelance Graphics. To do so, use the following steps:

1. Click the Open an Existing Presentation tab in the Welcome to Lotus Freelance Graphics window.

2. In the list of presentations, click the name of the file you'd like to open. A preview and description for the selected file appears to the right of the list, as shown in Figure 15-10.

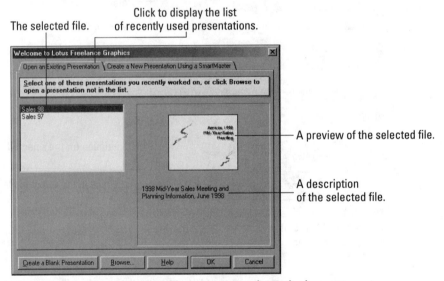

Figure 15-10: You can open a file you've recently worked with from the Welcome to Lotus Freelance Graphics Window.

3. When you're sure the file is the one you want, double-click it, or click the OK button to open it. If the file you want doesn't appear in the list, you can click the Browse button below the list to display the Open dialog box and use it to select the file to open.

Starting a New Presentation

You can create a brand-new presentation at any time after you start Freelance Graphics. Choose File ⇨ New Presentation or click the Create a New Presentation SmartIcon to display the New Presentation dialog box (see Figure 15-11). The New Presentation dialog box offers virtually the same options as the Create New Presentation Using a SmartMaster tab of the Welcome to Lotus Freelance Graphics window. Under Select a Content Topic, choose a content topic for your presentation or [No Content Topic] to create your own presentation topics. Under Select a Look, choose the SmartMaster presentation design you want to use, if the default choice doesn't suit your needs. To create a presentation with a completely blank background, choose [No Look-Blank Background] from the Select a Look list. Click OK to finish creating the new presentation.

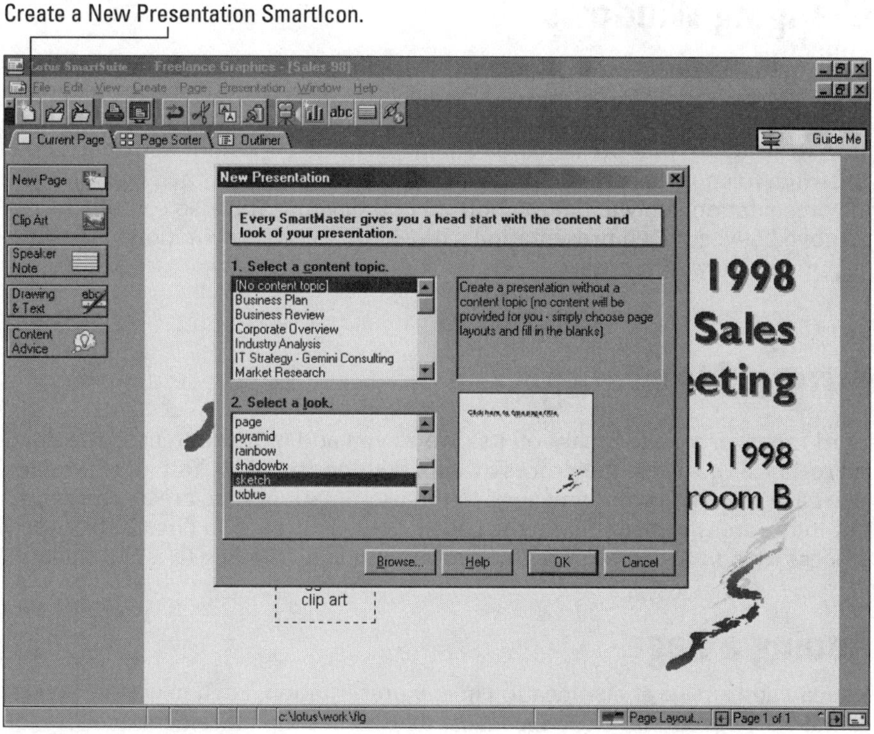

Create a New Presentation SmartIcon.

Figure 15-11: The File ⇨ New Presentation command displays this dialog box, so you can create a new presentation any time you're working in Freelance.

The Golden Rule of Presentation Looks

Over time, a number of different organizations have studied questions such as "What makes text more readable?" and "What makes an audience fall asleep?" Mining these veins has yielded nuggets of document and presentation design wisdom. In choosing a look for your presentation, you need to consider how you will ultimately share it. If you're planning to print the pages of your presentation only, choose a look that offers dark text on a light background. This treatment is most readable for document hard copies, even color print-outs. For a presentation you'll be providing onscreen, perhaps in a dimmed or darkened room, choose light text on a dark background. Light, glowing letters tend to be easier to read onscreen, especially if your audience is a bit tired.

Changing Windows

By default, each presentation you open or create appears maximized (at the full size), on top of other already opened files, making the newly opened presentation the current presentation. If you want to work in another open presentation, you need to switch to that presentation and make it the current or active presentation. To switch to another presentation, open the Window menu, then click the name of the presentation you want at the bottom of the menu. You also can press Ctrl+Tab to move between open presentations; repeat that key combination until the document you want appears.

Adding a New Page

Word Pro inserts page breaks on its own as you add more content to the document. In Freelance Graphics, the process works the opposite way. You must first add a new page with the layout you need to the presentation, then create the content within the areas designated by the page layout. This section covers the overall process for adding a new page to a presentation and moving to a particular page.

Adding a Page

You can add a page at any location in any presentation. Each new page you add contains a *page layout*. The *page layout* determines the placement and size for elements such as the page title, other page text like a subtitle or bulleted list, clip art, a diagram, a table, or charts. So, when you add a new page to your presentation, you choose the page layout that reflects the contents you want the new page to hold. For example, if you want to discuss a list of key points when discussing the new page, choose the Bulleted List page layout.

Follow these steps to insert a new page, using any view, in the current presentation:

1. Choose the page after which you want to insert the new page. (The next subsection explains how to select a particular page in the presentation.) If the presentation contains only a single page or you've selected the last page of the presentation, the new page you add becomes the last page in the presentation.

2. Choose Page ➪ New Page. Or, if the Current Page view tab is selected, click the New Page button at the left side of the tab. The New Page dialog box appears.

If you don't see the Page menu in Current Page view, that means an item such as a text or clip art placeholder is selected (rather than the page itself). In such a case, click the New Page button or choose Create ➪ Page (F7) to add a new page.

3. As described earlier in this chapter under "Creating a Presentation with Starter Content and a Look," the appearance of the New Page dialog box varies, depending on whether or not you selected a content topic when you created the presentation. If you did, the New Page dialog box displays the Content Pages and Page Layouts tabs (see Figure 15-3). You can select a page suggesting particular content and a layout by clicking a page topic option on the Content Pages tab. If you want to choose a page by layout only, click the Page Layouts tab, then click the page layout you want in the list on the tab. After you choose the page to add from either tab, click OK. If you chose a SmartMaster but not a content topic, the New Page dialog box lists only page layouts (see Figure 15-4). Click the page layout to use, then click OK. Freelance inserts the new page in the current view.

To add multiple content pages at once if you used a content topic for the presentation, click the Choose Multiple Content Pages button on the Content Pages tab of the New Page dialog box to display the New Page – Choose Multiple Content Pages dialog box, press and hold Ctrl, and click each page to add to the presentation, then click OK.

Moving to a Particular Page

You have to select a particular page in the presentation to edit its text, change its page layout, or otherwise work with it. While each of Freelance Graphics' three views (discussed next) provides various methods for moving from page to page, three methods work in every view: using Go To Page, using the Page menu, and using the status bar. When you move to a page, it becomes the current or active page.

The Go To Page dialog box lists the *title* for each slide in the presentation. (Freelance uses the text you enter in the title Click Here placeholder on the slide layout as the slide title.) To display the Go To Page dialog box, choose Edit ➪ Go To (Ctrl+G) or Page ➪ Go To Page. The Go To Page dialog box appears. Click the page to go to in the list (see Figure 15-12), and then click OK.

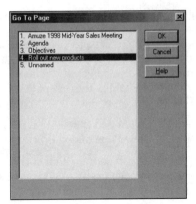

Figure 15-12: Select the page you want to work with from the Go To Page dialog box.

The Page menu offers other options for displaying a particular page. Choose Page ↪ Next Page to display the next page in the presentation, or Page ↪ Previous Page to display the preceding page in the presentation.

Danger Zone

If the Outliner view tab is selected, you first have to select a whole page by clicking the page thumbnail at the left, then choose Page ↪ Go To Page, Page ↪ Next Page, or Page ↪ Previous Page.

You also can use the buttons near the far right end of the Freelance Graphics status bar to display a particular page in the presentation. You can click the left or right arrow buttons to move to the previous or next page in the presentation. To go to a particular page in the presentation, click the status bar button that displays the current page number. A list of pages in the presentation pops up. Click the page you want to display in the list.

Working with View Options

You can click one of the View tabs near the top of the Freelance Graphics window to display the current presentation in one of three views: Current Page view, Page Sorter view, and Outliner view. Each of these views helps you work with the presentation in a particular way. In addition to offering various views, Freelance enables you to control different aspects of each view's appearance. This section covers how to use the View menu to choose and control a view.

Note

The options offered on the View menu vary depending on the currently selected view. Current Page view offers the most options on the View menu, Page Sorter view the fewest. This section points out the most critical View menu differences.

More Info

Chapter 16, "Developing the Presentation Content," provides details about entering text and other slide information in each Freelance view.

Reviewing Current Page View

Figure 15-13 shows the Current Page view. Use this view to focus on the design of each slide in the presentation. When you use this view to apply formatting to text and graphics or move those elements around on the page, you can easily see the effect of each change.

To display the presentation you're working with in Current Page view, click the Current Page view tab, or choose View ➪ Current Page. The left side of the Current Page view offers convenient buttons for working with pages and page elements. The presentation displays the page you were working with in Current Page view; so if page 5 was selected before you changed to Current Page view, page 5 appears when you switch to the Current Page view. In addition to choosing a page as described earlier, you can press PgUp and PgDn to display the previous and next page in Current Page view.

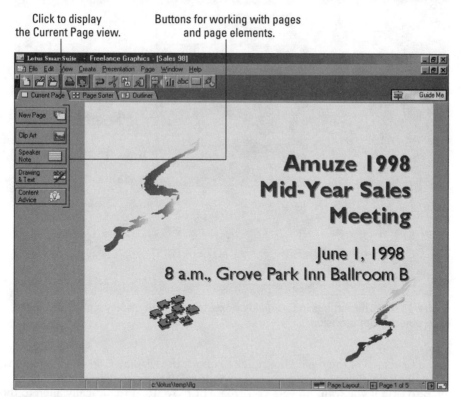

Figure 15-13: Use the Current Page view to design the appearance of each slide.

Because Current Page view is intended for close-up work, it provides two View menu choices that display view features to help you position objects more carefully: Set Units & Grid and Set View Preferences. Both of these options are discussed in the sections that follow.

Adjusting the Layout Grid

If you choose View ⇨ Set Units & Grid in the Current Page view, you can display a
nonprinting grid to help you align graphics, charts, and other objects you add to a
page. Figure 15-14 shows the Set Units & Grid dialog box with grid settings turned
on, and the resulting grid on the page. Under Units, click an option button to select
the overall unit of measure you want to use to set up the grid spacing. (The Units
option you select also determines the measurement units Freelance uses for rulers
and other alignment settings.)

Grid dots.

Figure 15-14: The settings in this dialog box enable you to display a grid so you can
align objects with precision.

In the Grid area of the dialog box, click to check the Display Grid check box to turn
on the grid display; clear this check box to turn off the grid display. Click to check
Snap to Grid if you want objects you create or move to automatically align to the
nearest horizontal and vertical grid positions. In the Horizontal Space and Vertical
Space text boxes, enter the actual spacing you want between grid dots. If you
choose Inches (System) under Units, then enter **.25** as the Horizontal Space and
Vertical Space; grid dots are .25 inches apart, so every fourth grid dot marks an
inch. Click OK to finish making your settings and close the dialog box.

Adjusting View Preferences

Choosing View ➪ Set View Preferences displays the Set View Preferences dialog box, which offers additional settings to help you choose the correct positioning for objects and text on the page. Figure 15-15 shows this dialog box and some of its settings in action. Under Show Page Borders, you can click the Recommended Drawing Area and Printable Area options to display a border that delineates some white space around the page, so you can avoid placing objects there. Click the None option to remove page border display. The check boxes in the Display area enable you to turn specific view features on and off. The Coordinates option displays coordinates for the mouse pointer position in the status bar. Drawing Ruler displays horizontal and vertical page rulers that help you position objects as you drag them. Text Block Ruler displays a ruler in any open text block, so you can gauge the width of the text block and the text it contains. Under Cursor Size, choose an option to determine the size the mouse pointer assumes when you select a drawing tool to draw an object on the page. Click OK to finish choosing your settings in the Set View Preferences dialog box and close the dialog box.

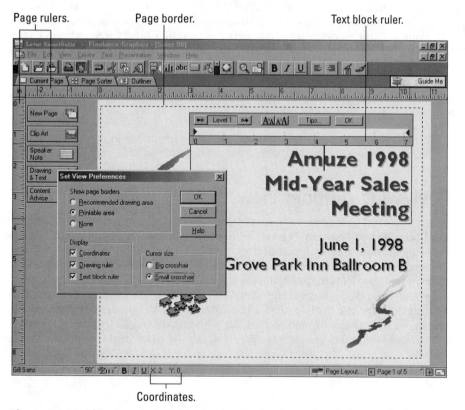

Figure 15-15: The view preferences for the Current Page view help you display a page border, rulers, and drawing coordinates.

You can press Shift+F7 to turn the Snap to Grid feature on and off without displaying the Set Units & Grid dialog box.

You can add a number of SmartIcons for working with view features, including grid display and grid snapping, to any SmartIcon bar. See Chapter 28, "Working with SmartIcon Bars," to learn how to add a SmartIcon to a SmartIcon bar.

Reviewing Page Sorter View

Click the Page Sorter view tab or choose View ➪ Page Sorter to display your presentation in the Page Sorter view (see Figure 15-16). In this view, each page appears at a thumbnail size, with the page title below the page, so that you can check how the topics in your presentation progress. A heavy black border appears around the selected page. To select another page, you can click it, press PgUp or PgDn, or use one of the techniques described in the preceding section. To move the selected page to a new location in the presentation, point to the page, press and hold the left mouse button, drag the page to the new location you want, and release the mouse button. As you drag the page, a dark gray bar will appear to show when you have reached a location where the page can be placed. In addition, the Page–Sorter SmartIcon bar appears next to the Universal SmartIcon bar, offering tools for working with slide pages, such as the Add a New Page SmartIcon, which displays the New Page dialog box.

To change from Page Sorter view to Current Page view, double-click the slide you want to display in Current Page view.

You can click the Undo Last Command or Action SmartIcon in Freelance Graphics to undo a change you don't like, such as returning a moved slide to its previous position.

Reviewing Outliner View

When you want to focus on the text in your presentation, click the Outliner view tab or choose View ➪ Outliner. Figure 15-17 shows a presentation in the Outliner view. Entering and working with text in the Outliner view is much like outlining text in Word Pro; you can promote and demote text to organize the hierarchy of information. By default, the Outliner view includes a picture of each page beside the page contents. (If the page stores its contents in a table or graphic, those contents are not listed on the outline itself.) The icons above the pictures enable you to display or hide them, or change their size. You also can use the View ➪ Show Pictures of Pages and View ➪ Page Size commands to control the picture display.

To select an entire slide in the Outliner view, in case you want to move or delete it, click the page picture. A heavy black border appears around the picture and the slide text.

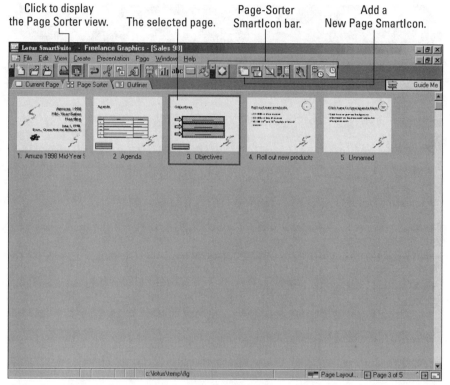

Figure 15-16: Use the Page Sorter view to review the order of slides in the presentation.

To work with the outline text itself, click in the text, or drag over text to select and format it. The Text – Outliner SmartIcon bar offers SmartIcons you can click to apply an attribute such as boldface or underlining to a selection. You can use other icons above the outline to hide or show the text formatting in the outline, expand or collapse the displayed outline text, or promote or demote the current line in the outline. The View ➪ Show Text Attributes command also toggles formatting display on and off. The Expand All, Collapse All, Expand, and Collapse commands on the View menu enable you to expand or collapse the displayed text.

Displays or hides pictures of pages.

Displays or hides text attributes.

Expand or collapse text in the outline.

Use to promte or demote text.

Change the display size of the page pictures.

Click to display the Outliner view.

Text-Outliner SmartIcon bar.

Adds a new page.

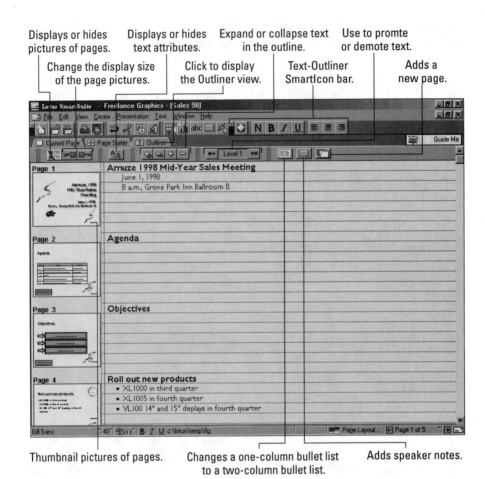

Thumbnail pictures of pages.

Changes a one-column bullet list to a two-column bullet list.

Adds speaker notes.

Figure 15-17: If you prefer to enter text and then focus on the content, work in Outliner view.

Other View Menu Options

The View menu offers additional options for determining how the presentation looks onscreen and what Freelance features appear. This subsection reviews them, but keep in mind that the available View menu selections vary substantially depending on the presentation view you're using.

Zooming In and Out

You can *zoom in* to display the page or pages in a larger size to better see a detail, or *zoom out* to a smaller size to check the overall page appearance or the appearance of certain elements relative to each other.

In the Current Page and Page Sorter views, you can choose View ➪ Zoom to Full Page to return the page view to the default size for the view. Current Page view means that the page fills the available space on the View tab; Page Sorter view can fit about five of its full-size pages on each row. In both those views, you can zoom in and out by increments of about 25%. Choose View ➪ Zoom, then choose the In, Out, or Last command from the submenu to zoom by increments.

In Current Page view, you also can zoom to the *output size* — the actual printout size based on the printer and the page size it's using. To see the printout size, choose View ➪ Zoom to Output Size.

Redrawing the Screen

If you make a change to an onscreen element and that change doesn't immediately appear or the page seems stuck, you can *redraw* the screen. Freelance Graphics offers screen redraw in the Current Page and Page Sorter views. To redraw the screen, choose View ➪ Redraw or press F9.

Hiding and Showing Screen Features

The View menu (see Figure 15-18) also offers commands that enable you to toggle certain display features on and off.

Figure 15-18: The View menu (shown here in Current Page view), enables you to toggle a number of screen features, such as rulers, on and off.

All of the following options appear in Current Page view, and some appear in the other views, too:

✦ **Show Ruler.** Toggles the horizontal and vertical page rulers on and off.

✦ **Show SmartIcons.** Shows or hides all SmartIcon bars.

✦ **Show Internet Tools.** Shows or hides the Internet Tools SmartIcon bar.

Note

The three options just listed are the ones that appear in the Page Sorter and Outliner views in addition to Current Page view.

✦ **Show in Color (Alt+F9).** Toggles between color and black-and-white display.

✦ **Show OLE Objects and Design OLE Controls.** Enables you to display or hide embedded objects and use tools for adding OLE controls (interactive elements such as option buttons) that you embed from other sources.

✦ **Reviewing Tools.** Enables you to add (Reviewer) or review (Author) comment notes about a presentation.

Setting Freelance Preferences

Preferences enable you to change certain defaults in Freelance Graphics, to save you time and spare you the aggravation of turning off or undoing features you don't want. Choose File ➪ User Setup ➪ Freelance Preferences. The Freelance Graphics Preferences dialog box appears (see Figure 15-19).

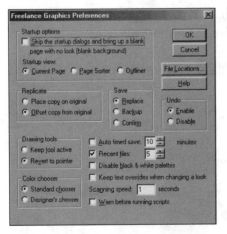

Figure 15-19: Control basic Freelance operations using this dialog box.

In the Startup Options area of the dialog box, you can check the Skip the Startup Dialogs and Bring Up a Blank if you want Freelance to display a blank presentation. Also click the option button (under Startup View) for the view you want Freelance to use when it starts up.

A few areas in the dialog box pertain to graphics and drawing. The choice you make in the Replicate area tells Freelance where to place the pasted copy of an object. Offset Copy from Original makes it easier to select and move the copy. Your choice under Drawing Tools affects how the mouse pointer behaves after you draw an object with the drawing tool; Revert to Pointer changes the pointer back to the regular mouse pointer, and Keep Tool Active leaves the selected tool on, so you can draw additional objects. The Color Chooser option affects which color palettes are available for drawing and formatting objects. Standard Chooser offers 16- and 256-color palettes, while Designer's Chooser includes additional palettes.

Choose a file saving option under Save. Replace, the default, simply saves the latest changes to the current file. Backup saves the changes, but also saves a version of the file without the changes using the .BAK file extension. Confirm tells Freelance to display a dialog box asking you to confirm every save operation.

You can turn Freelance's Undo capability on or off by choosing Enable or Disable under Undo. You can have Freelance automatically save the current file (so you don't lose any work in the event of a power fluctuation, by checking Auto Timed Save and entering a saving interval. If you want Freelance to display files you've recently worked with at the bottom of the File menu so you can easily open any of those files, check Recent Files and use the accompanying text box to specify how many files (from 0 to 5) to display.

Check Disable Black & White Palettes if you don't need the option to display the presentation onscreen in black-and-white. Check Keep Text Overrides When Changing a Look if you want to keep the formatting and attributes you've applied to individual words even if you change the SmartMaster the presentation uses. Check Warn Before Running Scripts to have Freelance display a warning dialog box any time you choose a SmartMaster or open a file that includes scripts, so you can specify whether or not the scripts should be active.

Some dialog boxes, such as the Choose a Look for Your Presentation dialog box (displayed by selecting Presentation ➪ Choose a Different SmartMaster Look), offer a *scan button* that previews the options, one by one, so that you don't have to repeatedly click to preview each option. To change the scanning speed, in seconds, change the Scanning Speed (X) Seconds text box entry to a value between .1 and 100.

Finally, click the File Locations button to display the File locations dialog box. Use the text boxes in this dialog box to specify the folders in which Freelance saves and looks for Presentations; SmartMaster looks, palettes & clip art; and Backup files by default. Click OK to accept your folder changes.

After you finish making all you preferences selections, click OK to close the Freelance Graphics Preferences dialog box.

✦   ✦   ✦

Developing the Presentation Content

Your message is the most important part of any presentation. No matter how many graphics, charts, drawings, or special effects a presentation includes, if the text isn't well-written and logically organized, the bells and whistles are only "perfume on a pig." Fancy formatting won't cover up the fact that the presentation jumps around between topics, includes typos, lacks topics you intended to include, and generally doesn't communicate your message well. This chapter keys in on entering and organizing the text for your presentation; you can worry about changing the design elements later. This chapter explains how to enter text for the presentation in both Current Page and Outliner view. Learn how to copy pages of information from other presentations, how to delete pages that no longer work in the presentation, and how to change the order of pages. Directions for editing text and checking its spelling also appear here.

Entering Text in Current Page View

Current Page view provides a page-by-page perspective of your presentation. Many users feel most comfortable adding presentation information in this view, because it enables them to enter text for each page at a time, choosing the right page layout and seeing exactly how text fits on that page layout. In addition, in Current Page view, you can see the helpful placeholders that each page offers, such as Click Here placeholders, text blocks, bulleted lists, and tables. This section explores how to add text to those placeholders in Current Page view.

Adding Content to a Click Here Block

A Click Here block placeholder on a presentation page prompts you to type information. Many Freelance Graphics page layouts require specific information in a specific location; for example, virtually every layout offers a Click Here block for entering the title of the page, which identifies the topic of the page. When you're entering the text for a presentation, Click Here blocks direct you to make entries in the correct location and also apply predefined SmartMaster formatting to the text you enter. In Freelance Graphics, each Click Here placeholder begins with the words "Click Here," followed by a description of the type of entry you should make in the Click Here block

Note   A Click Here block is really a *text block* with a predefined prompt. Freelance stores any type of text—whether it's a title, bulleted list, or paragraph—in a text block. All text blocks offer the same features.

To enter text in a Click Here block placeholder on a page, select the Click Here block by clicking it with the mouse. As shown in Figure 16-1, the Click Here text block opens, with the insertion point inside it. The Text SmartIcon bar appears, with SmartIcons for formatting the text. In addition, the text formatting choices on the status bar become active, and the Text menu appears on the menu bar.

If you don't want to use the default SmartMaster and page layout formatting for your text, you can select new fonts, attributes, and so on, before you begin typing. Then type your entry. As you type, the entry appears with the Click Here block's predefined formatting (unless you otherwise changed the formatting), as shown in Figure 16-2. You can use uppercase and lowercase as needed. Press the spacebar to insert a space between words, and press Enter to begin a new line of text.

More Info   The section called "Formatting Text" in Chapter 18, "Working with Graphics and Design" delves into the specific options for changing text formatting in Freelance Graphics.

When you've finished making your entry for the Click Here block, you can click outside the text block to finish working with it and deselect it completely. The Text menu disappears from the menu bar, and the Page menu reappears.

You can also click OK on the bar at the top of the open text block to close the block, but leave it selected (with black selection handles around it). This leaves the Text menu onscreen so you can use it to change the selected block. Or, if the page includes another Click Here block that you want to fill in, press the down arrow key to finish the entry in the first block and move the insertion point to the next block, which opens for your entry.

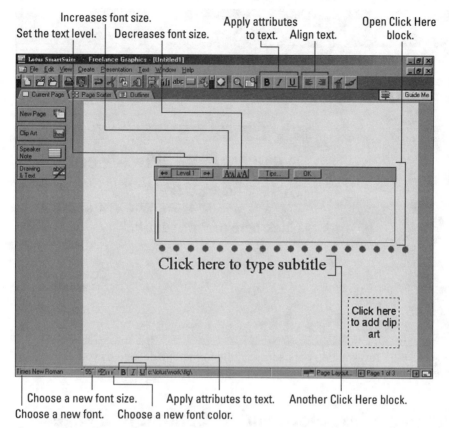

Figure 16-1: When you click a Click Here placeholder, its text block opens onscreen and text formatting tools appear.

If you select a Click Here block and decide not to enter text in it, simply click outside the block to close it. Its prompt remains intact, ready for you to use it at any time. Similarly, if you later delete the text from a Click Here block, its prompt returns. (This does not happen when you delete the text from a text block you've added to a page; in that case, the text block disappears altogether.)

If you choose not to fill in a Click Here block, its prompt does not print out or display if you run the presentation as a screen show. So, you do not have to delete an unfilled Click Here block. You can leave it in place should you later need to use it in the presentation.

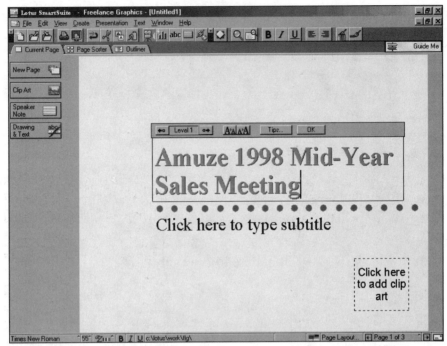

Figure 16-2: Text you enter appears with the formatting defined by you or the presentation's SmartMaster and the page layout.

Adding a Text Block and Its Content to a Page

If the page layout you choose doesn't offer a Click Here block to position text where you need it, or if you want to create a completely free-form page design, you can add your own text block to any page. For example, if you add a page using the Basic Layout option, that option offers only the SmartMaster background and graphics and a page title Click Here block. In the area below, you can add any text blocks, graphics, charts, or other page elements that you want. On another page, you might want to add a text block to serve as sort of a "footnote" identifying the source for a statistic.

Danger Zone

When you create your own text block on a page, the contents you enter in that text block don't appear in the outline for your presentation. This prevents you from effectively using the Outliner view to rearrange the information in your presentation. So, to ensure that your entries appear in the outline, either limit yourself to filling in the Click Here blocks provided by the page layout, or add the text in the Outliner view.

Follow these steps to add a text block and enter its content:

1. Display the page to which you want to add the text block.

2. Choose Create ➪ Text or click the Create a Text Block SmartIcon.

3. Drag on the page to define the text box boundary, as shown in Figure 16-3.

Create a Text Block SmartIcon.

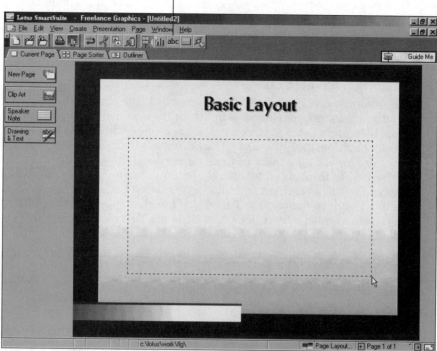

Figure 16-3: After you choose Create ➪ Text, drag to place the text box.

4. When the dotted guideline reaches the size and shape you want for the text block, release the mouse button. The open text block appears, with the insertion point in it (refer to Figure 16-1).

5. Enter the text for the text block. The new text uses default formatting defined for its level in the SmartMaster. See "Working with Bulleted Lists and Text Levels" (covered next) to learn more about what text levels are and what they mean to your presentation.

6. When you finish entering text in the text block, click outside it to finish working with it, or click OK on the bar at the top of the text box to finish the entry but leave the text block selected.

Working with Bulleted Lists and Text Levels

A few different page layouts include a Click Here block that prompts you to "Click Here to Type Bulleted Text." These bulleted text Click Here blocks make it easy to create lists of information. For each listed item, the Click Here block adds a nicely formatted bullet.

All text blocks offer you the opportunity to assign different text levels (indentations) to text. When you change text levels within a bulleted list, the Click Here block assigns different bullets to the text at different levels.

Because bulleted lists and text levels work so well together, they're discussed next.

Entering a Bulleted List

When you click a bulleted text Click Here block, the text block opens, and the insertion point appears beside a bullet for the first item in the list. Type the list item, then press Enter to start a new item. If a bulleted item is fairly lengthy, Freelance automatically wraps it to one or more lines as needed. If you want to create a new line for a bulleted item, rather than letting it wrap on its own, press Ctrl+Enter. To learn about techniques for entering the bulleted list (which also apply to text in any other text block or text-based Click Here block), click the Tips button. Figure 16-4 shows the Tips dialog box that appears, along with a few items entered in a bulleted list. Click OK to close the Tips dialog box.

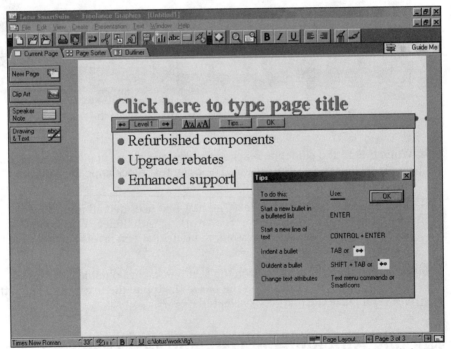

Figure 16-4: Press Enter to start each new bulleted item in a bulleted list Click Here block or click Tips to see helpful information.

Applying Text Levels

Freelance offers five different text levels, each of which applies a particular indention and in some cases particular formatting, that you can apply to the regular text or bulleted list in a text block. When you enter text into any bulleted list text block or any other text block that holds plain text, Freelance automatically applies the Level 1 text level to it. However, you may want to *indent* bulleted items under a Level 1 bulleted item. You can do this by pressing Tab when you start the new bulleted item or clicking the indent button on the bar above the text block to indent that item to Level 2. Freelance indents the line and applies the Level 2 bullet for it. When you press Enter, Freelance automatically formats the next item as a Level 2, and continues using Level 2 until you *outdent* a line to Level 1. To outdent the line, press Shift+Tab or click the outdent button on the bar above the text block.

Figure 16-5 shows text levels and indention applied to a bulleted list on a page. When you indent or outdent text to a different level, the level change applies only to the current bulleted item or paragraph; entries under that level aren't changed, unless you change them as well.

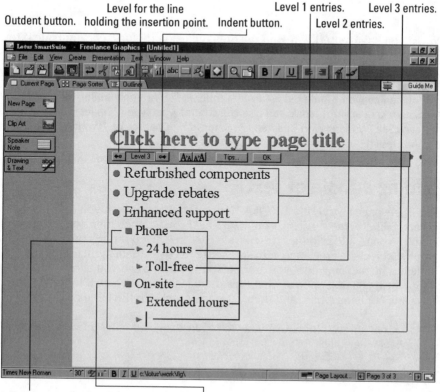

Figure 16-5: Use text levels to indent and outdent the text or bulleted list in a text block.

Driving Your Message Home

Professional speechwriters and public speakers employ tricks of the trade to help a presentation both communicate effectively and hold the reader's attention.

People generally need to hear a message a few times before it really sticks, so in a presentation you should: Tell them what you're going to tell them, tell them, and then tell them what you told them. This means that early in your presentation you should include at least one page outlining the key points or agenda for your discussion, perhaps in a bulleted list. Then, there should be at least one page for each key point or agenda item to elaborate on that topic or item. Finally, a page near the end of the presentation should summarize or restate the key topics the presentation covered, again in a bulleted list.

To avoid packing a page with too much information so that your audience can better grasp each "sound byte," you should limit any bulleted list on a page to about three items if each is a sentence in length, or five or so items if each item is one or two words. If you include 20 items on a page and spend a minute or two discussing each one, you risk overwhelming and boring your audience members, who will have to stare at that same onscreen page or handout for 20-plus minutes.

When you finish entering text in the bulleted list text block, click outside it to finish working with it, or click OK on the bar at the top of the text box to finish the list but leave the text block selected.

You can convert a bulleted list to a numbered list, or apply bullets or numbering to plain text in any text block. You also can control what type of bullet is used at any text level. See "Working with Bulleted List Settings" in Chapter 18, "Working with Graphics and Design," to learn how to control your lists.

Adding a Table of Text

The Table page layout offers a Click Here block that prompts you to "Click Here to Create Table." A *table* organizes text into neat rows and columns on a page, and even enables you to add gridlines to separate each cell. Even though tables are really graphic objects in Freelance, it makes sense to cover them in this section, because a table has no meaning until you enter text into it. So, when you click a table Click Here block, you first choose what type of table to create (how it looks and how many rows and columns it has) and then enter your text into the table cells.

As for text in text blocks that you create, anything you enter into a table does not appear in the outline for your presentation.

Follow these steps to insert a table in a table Click Here block:

1. Click the block, which reads Click Here to Create Table. The Table Gallery dialog box appears (see Figure 16-6).

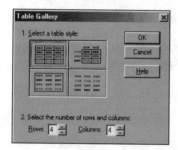

Figure 16-6: Choose a table style and size in the Table Gallery dialog box.

2. Under Select a Table Style, click the thumbnail that uses the gridline format you want for the table.

3. Under Select the Numbers of Rows and Columns, change the Rows and Columns text box entries to designate the size of the table. (Don't forget to include a column for "row labels" and a row for "column labels" to identify the table contents, if needed.)

4. Click OK. The table appears on the page, with black selection handles around it.

5. Click in the first table cell to position the insertion point in it, then type the entry for that cell.

6. Press Tab to move the insertion point to the next cell in the table.

7. Repeat Steps 5 and 6 to make additional table entries. You can press Shift+Tab to move back one cell in the table, or click in a particular cell to work with it. Figure 16-7 shows table entries in progress.

Note   Freelance automatically aligns text and alphanumeric entries to the left side of a table cell; and numeric entries to the right.

8. Click outside the table when you finish making your entries.

You can add a table to any page in the presentation. Display the page to which you want to add the table, then choose Create ➪ Table. The Table Gallery dialog box appears. Make your choices there (refer to Figure 16-6), then click OK. The table appears on the page, with black selection handles around it. Drag to move the table to a new position, if needed, then enter text in the table as just described. When you're working with a table, the Table SmartIcon bar appears onscreen. You can use its SmartIcons to format and work with table rows and columns, described in "Formatting a Table" in Chapter 18, "Working with Graphics and Design."

Table SmartIcon bar.

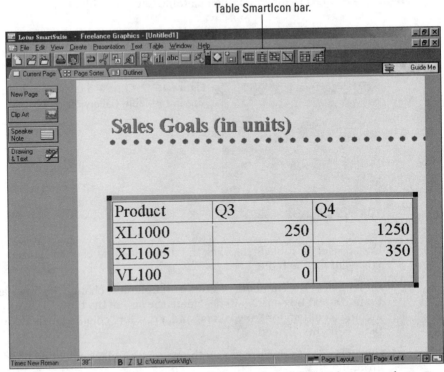

Figure 16-7: Type text in each table cell. Press Tab and Shift+Tab to move between cells, or click to select a table cell.

Entering Text in Outliner View

Chapter 15, "Starting, Saving, and Opening Presentations," noted that the Outliner view provides advantages for entering and organizing the text in your presentation. For instance, you can see the text of multiple pages onscreen at once, so you can check the order of topics in the presentation. You can view the text without the pages, and collapse or hide text detail to build the outline one level at a time. And you can easily move text around, even from one page to another. This section shows you how to create the text for your presentation in the Outliner view.

Adding Text and Working with Text Levels

Generally, you'll have at least one page in your presentation when you change to the Outliner view, because you can't create a new presentation without adding the first page. If you didn't add a title or any other text for the page, you see blank lines beside the first page picture. To enter the title for the first page, type it and press

Enter. Freelance moves the insertion point to the next line, which it automatically designates with the Level 1 text level. (Freelance assigns a new level, the Title level, to the title for each page.) If the page layout is for a Title page, the second line of text becomes the subtitle for the page. Therefore, it includes no bullet. If you enter the title for any page that contains a bulleted list and press Enter, Freelance designates the new line as Level 1 and adds a bullet for it.

To add additional lines of text to any page, press Enter and type each line. If you're working in a bulleted list, the needed bullet automatically appears. You can use the same techniques as you would in a text block to promote or demote each line (whether it has a bullet or not). Press Tab or click the indent button on the Outliner view tab to demote the text to the next lowest level. Press Shift+Tab or click the outdent button on the Outliner view tab to promote the text to the next highest level.

You can paste text from a Word Pro document into the Outliner view in Freelance Graphics. Select the text in Word Pro, then click the Copy to Clipboard SmartIcon. Click the Freelance Graphics button on the Windows taskbar, then create the presentation you want to insert the outline into and click the Outliner view tab. Click the Paste Clipboard Contents SmartIcon or choose Edit ⇨ Paste. The text appears in the presentation outline. You can then edit and change text levels as needed.

When you're working in Outliner view, you can only add new pages using the Bulleted List layout to the presentation. A new page you add appears immediately after the page that holds the insertion point. Outliner view offers a few methods for adding a bulleted list page. You can click the new page button on the Outliner view tab. You can choose Create ⇨ Page. Or, if you've already entered the title for the new page on a line, outdent the bulleted text to the Title text level, which converts it to a new page. Figure 16-8 shows a new page added to the outline, as well as some previously entered outline text.

If you find the text formatting applied by the SmartMaster difficult to read, click the button on the Outliner view tab that hides and displays formatting (refer to Figure 16-8). When you "hide" the formatting, the Outliner view uses a plainer font and hides attributes such as boldfacing, so you can more easily read the text. If you need more room to enter and edit the outlined text, click the button on the tab that hides or displays the page pictures. If you have a lengthy bulleted list and want to reformat it into two columns, click to position the insertion point in the bulleted item that should start the new column, then click the button on the tab that toggles a bulleted list between one and two columns. Figure 16-9 shows a bulleted list divided into two columns. To return to a single column, click the row that starts the second column, then click the Undo Last Command or Action SmartIcon.

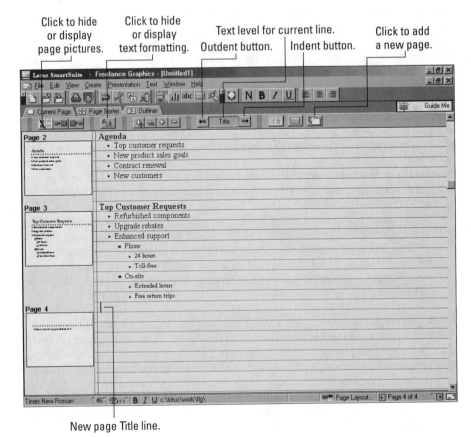

Click to hide or display page pictures.

Click to hide or display text formatting.

Text level for current line. Outdent button.

Indent button.

Click to add a new page.

New page Title line.

Figure 16-8: You can add a new page in Outliner view.

Hiding and Displaying Text in the Outline

You can collapse (hide) the text for a single page or all the pages in the presentation. You might want to do this to help you move pages to a different position in the presentation. When you hide the text for a page in the Outliner view, then move the page to a new location, all the page contents move, even though you can't see them. Use the following steps to collapse and expand page text in the Outliner view:

1. First, hide the page pictures at the left side of the page. This closes up any blank lines that the outline displays simply to accommodate the depth of each picture.

Marker for the start of the first column.   Click to start the second column of the bulleted list.

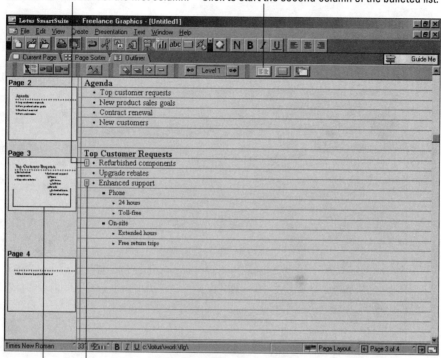

Preview of the two columns.   Marker for the start of the second column.

Figure 16-9: You can divide a bulleted list into two columns.

When you've hidden page pictures in Outliner view, click the icon that appears beside the page number at the left to select the entire page.

2. To collapse (hide) the contents of a single page, click anywhere in the page text, then click the button for collapsing a single page's contents on the Outliner view tab. Freelance hides the page text, displaying only its title. See Page 2 in Figure 16-10. A plus (+) sign appears beside the page number to tell you the page contains hidden topics.

3. To expand (display) the contents of a single page, click anywhere in the page text, then click the button for expanding a single page's contents on the tab. Freelance redisplays the page text.

4. To collapse the text for all the pages, click the Outliner view tab button that collapses text for all pages. The outline lists only the page titles.

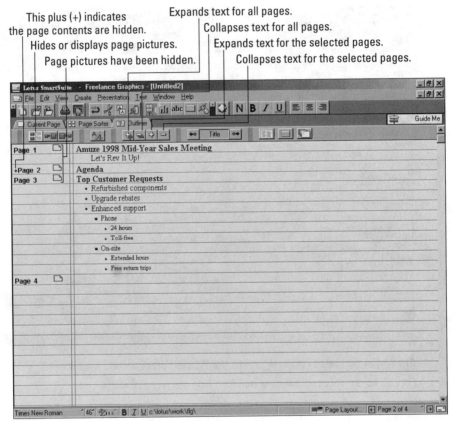

Figure 16-10: You can collapse the text for one or more pages in the Outliner view.

5. To redisplay the text for all the pages, click the Outliner view tab button that expands text for all pages.

6. Redisplay the page pictures, if you wish.

Copying a Page

You can save yourself time in developing a presentation by copying an existing page. Copying a page saves you the trouble of choosing a layout, entering text, adding and formatting elements such as tables or charts, or making any of the other changes you made to the original page. Duplicating a page can reduce a lengthy series of operations to a couple of easy steps, as you learn in this section.

Note

Page Sorter view might be your best bet when you want to copy or reorganize pages, because that view displays the Page Sorter SmartIcon bar to the right of the Universal SmartIcon bar. This SmartIcon bar offers the Add a New Page, Duplicate Pages, Delete Pages, and Copy Pages from Other Presentations SmartIcons, which you can use to add, copy (from the current presentation or another one), and delete pages.

Duplicating a Page in the Current Presentation

Duplicating a page creates a copy of the page and inserts the copy after the original page in the presentation. You can duplicate a page in any view in Freelance Graphics. In the view, select the page to duplicate; to do so, use the buttons at the right end of the status bar or another method to display the page in Current Page view, or click the page picture or page icon for the page to copy in the Page Sorter view or the Outliner view. Choose Page ⇨ Duplicate Page (Alt+F7). Or, right-click the selected page and click Duplicate Page. Freelance inserts the new page into the presentation. Figure 16-11 shows a duplicated page.

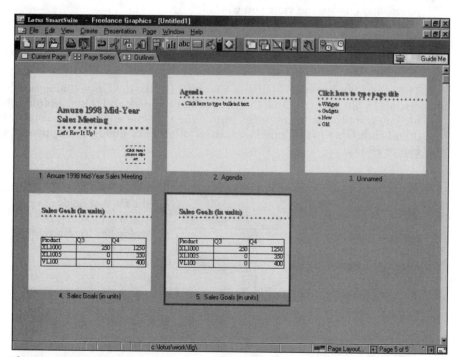

Figure 16-11: In this zoomed-in look at Page Sorter view, Page 5 is a duplicate of Page 4.

Note   When you select a page in the Outliner view, a heavy black outline appears around the page picture and the outlined text.

Danger Zone   If the Page menu isn't available in the Current Page view, click on the page background to ensure another element isn't selected. The Page menu should then appear.

Using Pages from Another Presentation

If the page you want to duplicate appears in another presentation, no problem. With Freelance, you can duplicate one or more pages from another presentation and insert those duplicates into the current presentation. The duplicated pages contain all their original contents, but take on the appearance of the SmartMaster for the presentation into which you insert them. Use the following steps to duplicate and insert one or more pages from another presentation:

1. Open or create the presentation into which you want to insert the duplicated pages, and choose the view you want.

2. Select the page before or after which you want to insert the duplicated page(s).

3. Choose Page ⇨ Copy Pages from Other Files. The Select Presentation dialog box appears.

4. The Select Presentation dialog box works just like the Open dialog box for opening a file. Use the Look In list to select the disk and folder holding the file you want to duplicate pages from. When the file appears in the list, click it and click Open. The Copy Pages from Other Files dialog box appears (see Figure 16-12).

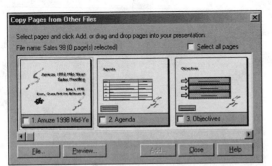

Figure 16-12: After you select the file that holds the pages you want to copy, use this dialog box to select which pages to copy.

5. You can then use one of two methods to copy pages to the current presentation:

- If you're working in Page Sorter or Outliner views, you can drag one or more pages from the Copy Pages from Other files dialog box to the desired position in the presentation and drop it into place.

- If you want to simply insert one or more pages in any view, click to check the check box beside the number and title of each page to insert, or check the Select All Pages check box to select them all, then click Add. In the Add Page(s) dialog box that appears, click the option button to determine where to insert the duplicated page (After Current Page, Before Current Page, or At End of Presentation), then click OK.

6. Click Close to close the dialog box after you've inserted all the pages you want.

Note

After you insert pages from another file into the current presentation, if you choose Page ➪ Copy Pages from Other Files again, the pages for the file you previously inserted pages from still appear in the Copy Pages from Other Files dialog box. Click the File button to select another file from which you'd like to duplicate files.

Deleting and Reorganizing Pages

Deleting a page cuts the page entirely from the presentation, not just the page contents. You should only delete a page if you're sure that you don't need any of its contents in the presentation.

You can delete a page in any view. Select the page to delete; to do so, use the buttons at the right end of the status bar or another method to display the page in Current Page view, or click the page picture or page icon for the page to delete in the Page Sorter view or the Outliner view. Choose Page ➪ Delete Page.

Or, right-click the selected page and click Delete Page. If the page you're deleting contains a graphic object such as a chart or table, the Deleting Page dialog box appears to warn you that the deletion will remove a graphic (that may take more time to recreate). Click OK to verify the deletion.

Note

If you mistakenly delete a page, click the Undo Last Command or Action SmartIcon to reinstate it.

You can change the order of pages in the presentation only using the Page Sorter view or the Outliner view. That's because these views include more than one page. You can use one of two techniques to move a page to a new position:

✦ Select the page to move, then drag it and release the mouse button to drop it into a new location, which is indicated by a dark gray bar appearing to the right of the new location in Page Sorter view, or below it in Outliner view.

✦ Select the page to move, then choose Edit ⇨ Cut (Ctrl+X) or click the Cut to the Clipboard SmartIcon. Select the page after which you want to insert the cut page (even it it's in another open presentation file that you first choose from the Window menu), then choose Edit ⇨ Paste (Ctrl+V) or click the Paste Clipboard Contents SmartIcon.

You can select more than one page at a time in Page Sorter or Outliner view. In Page Sorter view, click the picture for the first page to select it, then press and hold the Shift key and click additional contiguous or noncontiguous pages to select them as well. In Outliner view, you can only select contiguous pages. Click the picture or icon for the first page to select it, then press and hold the Shift key and click the next page to add to the selection, the next page, and so on. After you select more than one page in either view, you can delete or move all the selected pages.

You also can copy and paste to duplicate a page within or between presentation files. Choose Edit ⇨ Copy (Ctrl+C) or click the Copy to the Clipboard SmartIcon, select the page after which you want to insert the copied page (changing to another open presentation with the Window menu first, if needed), then choose Edit ⇨ Paste (Ctrl+V) or click the Paste Clipboard Contents SmartIcon.

Editing Text

The text editing techniques you use in Freelance Graphics greatly resemble those you use in both Word Pro and 1-2-3. To edit text in Freelance, you need to be able to move the insertion point, select text, and perform the edits you want. This section covers those techniques.

You cannot edit page text in the Page Sorter view.

Moving the Insertion Point and Editing and Selecting Text

You can edit text in both the Current Page and Outliner views. In Current Page view, you first have to display the insertion point in a text block in order to edit the text. To display the insertion point in a text block, first click the text block to select it, then click again to position the insertion point in the location you want. In the Outliner view, click to position the insertion point in any location you want. You also can use the techniques outlined in Table 16-1 to move the insertion point around.

Table 16-1
Moving the Insertion Point in a Selected Text Block in Current Page View or Outliner View

Pressing This . . .	Moves the Insertion Point . . .
Arrow keys	One character or row in the direction of the arrow.
Ctrl+left arrow	To the beginning of the word holding the insertion point or the previous word.
Ctrl+right arrow	To the end of the word holding the insertion point or the following word.
Home	To the beginning of the line holding the insertion point.
End	To the end of the line holding the insertion point.
Ctrl+Home	To the beginning of the text block (Current Page view) or the beginning of the presentation (Outliner view).
Ctrl+End	To the end of the text block (Current Page view) or the end of the presentation (Outliner view).

After you position the insertion point, type any text to insert in the text block or page. Freelance inserts the new text. Press the Backspace key to delete the character to the left of the insertion point, or press the Delete key to delete the character to the right of the insertion point. (Pressing Backspace or Delete also deletes any text you've selected.) If you're working in a text block in Current Page view, you also can press the Insert key to toggle between Insert and Overtype modes. In Overtype mode, text you type replaces the text to the right.

Note   To edit text in a table, double-click the table, then click in the table cell that holds the contents you'd like to edit.

In either a text block in Current Page view (in the default Overtype mode) or a line in Outliner view, you can select a word or more. Then, anything you type replaces the selection. To select a single word, double-click it. To select more, drag over it. In the Outliner view, click to the left of the bullet to select the whole row. Or press the Shift key and then use one of the arrow keys to extend the selection; pressing and holding Shift and Control, then using an arrow key also extends the selection. After you select some text, type the text that you want to replace the selected text.

Danger Zone   If you switch to the Outliner view and add text in addition to the page title to a page with a page layout that includes a table or chart, that text is inserted in a new text block on the page layout. You'll have to use the Current Page view to move the text block to the desired location on the page.

Copying, Moving, and Clearing Text

You can copy, move, or clear (delete) text you added to a presentation. You start each of these operations by selecting the text that you want to copy, move, or delete. Then, do one of the following:

✦ **Copy to another location.** Choose Edit ➪ Copy (Ctrl+C), right-click and choose Copy, or click the Copy to the Clipboard SmartIcon. Position the insertion point in the location to copy to, then choose Edit ➪ Paste (Ctrl+V), right-click and choose Paste, or click the Paste Clipboard Contents SmartIcon.

✦ **Move to another location.** Choose Edit ➪ Cut (Ctrl+X), right-click and choose Cut, or click the Cut to the Clipboard SmartIcon. Position the insertion point in the location to move the selection to, then choose Edit ➪ Paste (Ctrl+V), right-click and choose Paste, or click the Paste Clipboard Contents SmartIcon.

✦ **Clear (delete) the selected text.** Clearing (deleting) text removes it from the presentation; you can't paste it to another location. To delete or clear the selected text, choose Edit ➪ Delete, right-click and choose Delete, or press the Delete key.

Using the Undo Feature

Just as you can undo page operations by choosing Edit ➪ Undo or clicking the Undo Last Command or Action SmartIcon, you can choose the same command or click the same SmartIcon to undo an editing change.

Checking Your Spelling

The final barrier to audience understanding may be your spelling or your typing capabilities. As they learn typing, most users also tend to develop a tendency to make certain typographical errors, such as "teh" instead of "the," or leaving the "s" or "g" off the end of a plural word or a word ending in "ing."

To check the spelling in your presentation, follow these steps:

1. Choose Edit ➪ Check Spelling (Ctrl+F2). The Spell Check dialog box appears (see Figure 16-13).

2. Under Check Spelling Of, choose whether to check the spelling of the Current Page or the Entire Presentation. Or, if you selected text or a text block in Current Page view before displaying the Spell Check dialog box, Selected Word(s) will be checked by default, telling Spell Check to check only your selection.

3. If your presentation includes pages with charts or speaker notes, be sure to check the check boxes under Include to ensure Freelance checks the spelling in those elements as well.

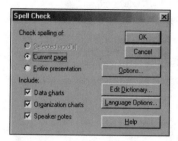

Figure 16-13: Specify the Spell Check options you want in this dialog box.

4. If you created the presentation using a language other than American English, click the Language Options button, choose the proper language in the Language list of the Spell Check Language dialog box, then click OK. This ensures Freelance correctly checks non-American English words in the spell check.

5. Click the Options button to display the Spell Check Options dialog box (see Figure 16-14). Check to enable or disable one of the top four check boxes as needed if you want the spelling check to stop on repeated words, words with numbers or initial caps, or words not contained in the listed dictionary alternatives (User Dictionary to Use). Click OK.

Figure 16-14: Determine how thorough the Spell Check is using this dialog box.

6. To add new, unique words to the dictionary, so Spell Check doesn't assume those words are errors, click the Edit Dictionary button in the Spell Check dialog box to display the Spell Check User's Dictionary dialog box. In the New Word dialog box, type a new word for the dictionary, then click Add; repeat the process to add additional words to the dictionary. Click OK to close the dialog box.

7. Click OK back at the Spell Check dialog box to begin the spell check.

8. When Spell Check finds a word it doesn't recognize in its dictionary, it stops and identifies the word that it doesn't recognize (according to the contents of the user dictionary). Figure 16-15 shows an example.

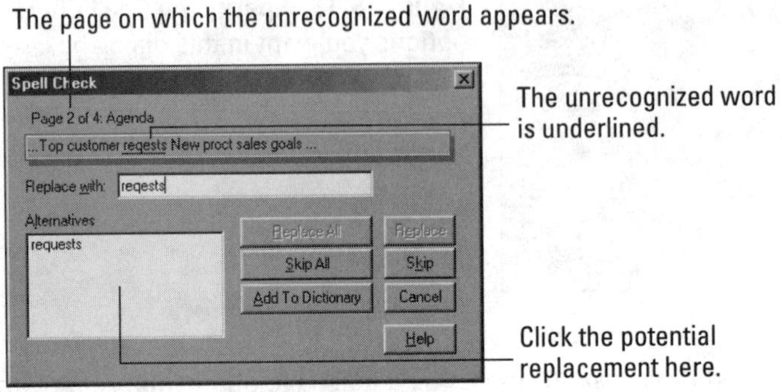

The page on which the unrecognized word appears.

The unrecognized word is underlined.

Click the potential replacement here.

Figure 16-15: Spell Check informs you when it doesn't recognize a word, offering options for handling it.

9. Tell Freelance how to handle the potentially misspelled word, as follows:

   • To add the unrecognized word to the user dictionary so that Freelance doesn't stop on it as an unrecognized word, click Add to Dictionary.

   • To skip the word without changing it, or skip all occurrences of the word, click Skip or Skip All.

   • If you want to correct the unrecognized word, click the replacement to use in the Alternatives list or enter the replacement you want in the Replace With text box. Then, click Replace to replace the currently found instance of the misspelled word, or Replace All to replace all instances of the misspelled word.

10. Continue to select the replacement options described in Step 9 to handle each misspelling that Spell Check identifies.

11. When Spell Check finds no more typos or words it doesn't recognize, it displays a message box telling you the spell check is complete. Click OK to close the message box and end the spell check.

✦   ✦   ✦

Adding and Working with Charts

Sales results. Quality improvement statistics. Market share goals. Numeric data of all types drives decision-making in business. When you're including numeric information that supports a key point in your presentation, you need a format to make that information clear and useful to the audience. A *chart* presents data in a meaningful graphic format.

In this chapter you learn how to create a chart on a presentation page — from choosing the chart type, to entering the data, to formatting the chart and chart elements. The chapter explains how organization charts differ from regular charts, and helps you create and format organization (org) charts, too. Finally, the chapter shows you how to move and delete charts on the page.

Adding a Chart to a Presentation Page

You go through three overall steps when you add a chart to a page in a presentation. First, you determine what type of chart will best fit the data. Next, you choose a page layout that includes a chart placeholder. Finally, you select the chart type and enter the data for the chart. This section walks you through those operations for creating a chart.

Freelance Chart Types

Each chart type in Freelance Graphics best depicts a particular type of data. If you choose the wrong type of chart for your data, the chart may do more to confuse your audience than to communicate key facts. The chart you choose depends on how many *data series* you want to chart and what the series represent. Each data series includes all the related points of data to chart. For example, the sales by quarter for your business North territory is one series, sales for the South region is a second series, and so on. Each discrete value in a series also is called a *data point*. For example, the Q1 sales value for your business' North territory is one data point, the Q2 sales is the next data point, and so on. Most charts include an x-axis, the horizontal axis along the bottom of the chart that usually shows the series or the time; and a y-axis, the vertical line at the left of the chart that shows the scale of values for the chart.

Table 17-1 identifies the types of charts you can create in Freelance Graphics and provides a bit of guidance for choosing each.

Table 17-1
Charts You Can Create in Freelance Graphics

Chart type	Purpose
Bar	Compares discrete values at one or more specific points in time.
Stacked Bar	Compares discrete values, stacking the series to illustrate a total.
100% Stacked Bar	Stacks the series, displaying each value as a percentage of the total illustrated by the bar.
Line	Compares the values in a series with one another via trendlines between each datapoint in the series; highlights the trend in each series.
Area	Compares the values in a series with one another via trendlines with the solid area below indicating volume.
Pie	Plots one series of data, showing each value as a percentage of the total illustrated by the pie.
Hi/Low/Close/Open	Compares values that change during a given time period, such as stock prices (which have an opening, high, low, and closing price each day) or temperatures; for each charted time period, the vertical bar illustrates the span between the high and low values, the left hash mark shows the opening value, and the right hash mark shows the closing value.
Scatter	Plots pairs of values according to the numeric scale on the x-axis and axis to show concentration or correlation. For example, you could plot the height and weight of each student in a class; the largest cluster of points then indicates the most typical height/weight for the class members.
Radar	Shows how multiple series of data compare to multiple axes; for example, plot the number of schools, hospitals, and parks a number of different cities have.

Chart type	Purpose
Mixed	Includes a bar chart and a line chart to display both discrete values and trends in the same chart; Freelance charts series A and B as bars, and series C and D as lines.
Number Grid	Displays data in a table with rows, columns, and cells. This chart is virtually the same as the text tables you learned to create in Chapter 15, "Starting, Saving, and Opening Presentations"; the difference is that selecting a number grid chart displays charting SmartIcons, while selecting a text table displays text SmartIcons.
Doughnut	Creates a pie chart with a hole in the middle. Doughnut charts display one series and illustrate what percentage of the series total each value represents.

In addition to selecting the basic chart type, you can display some charts in 3-D. In some cases, the 3-D effects make each charted value more clear. For example, when you select the 3-D look for a bar chart that displays multiple series, the rotation helps you see each data point more clearly. For some types of charts, you can choose whether or not to stack the series. For instance, you can choose to stack the series in an area chart to illustrate total volume in addition to the volume for each series. For the pie and doughnut charts, you can choose to add a second or third pie or doughnut to chart additional series.

Creating the Chart

No matter what type of chart you're creating, you use the same overall steps to finish the process: Add a presentation page to hold the chart, select the chart Click Here placeholder, tell Freelance which type of chart you want, then enter the data for it. Note that you can only work with charts in the Current Page view. You can't edit page elements at all in the Page Sorter view, and chart data doesn't appear at all in Outliner view. Follow these specific steps to add a chart:

1. In the Current Page view, select the page after which you want to insert the new chart, then choose Page ➪ New Page (F7) or click the New Page button at the left side of the View tab to display the New Page dialog box. Select the 1 Chart, 2 Charts, or 4 Charts page layout to create a slide with a Click Here placeholder for one, two, or four charts. Click OK.

2. Add the title for the page in the Click Here to Type Page Title Click Here block.

3. Click the Click Here to Create Chart Click Here block. The Create Chart dialog box appears (see Figure 17-1).

Click a specific chart variation here.   Chart preview.   Click a Click Here block on the page layout to insert the chart.

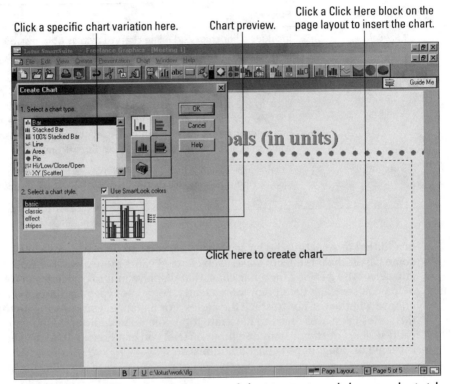

Figure 17-1: You tell Freelance what type of chart to create and choose a chart style using the Create Chart dialog box.

4. Click the kind of chart you want in the Select a Chart Type list. The buttons beside the list change to show the available variations for the selected chart type. Click the variation you want to use.

5. To select an attractive appearance for the chart, choose the look you want from the Select a Chart Style list. The preview area in the dialog box changes to show how the chart will look based on your selection.

6. If you want the chart to use colors derived from the SmartMaster look for the presentation, make sure the Use SmartLook Colors check box remains checked. Clearing the check box tells Freelance to use the colors defined in the selected chart style, rather than the SmartMaster colors.

7. Click OK. The Edit Data dialog box appears (see Figure 17-2). It includes a spreadsheet-like grid you can use to enter the labels and values for the chart data.

8. Enter the data that Freelance should chart on the Data tab. Click a cell, type the entry for it, then press Enter or an arrow key to finish the cell entry.

Choose the Series by Row or Series by Column option button to specify whether you want to enter each series in a row or column. Freelance identifies each series alphabetically, starting with the letter A. If you're entering the series in rows, the row heading letters identify each series; if you're entering the series in columns, the letters appear in the column headings instead. Figure 17-2 shows data entered for a bar chart. You can use the Cut, Copy, and Paste buttons in the Edit Data dialog box to copy and move data between cells. You also can fill entries by example or import the data to chart; see the next two sections, "Using Fill by Example" and "Importing Chart Data," to learn more about these techniques.

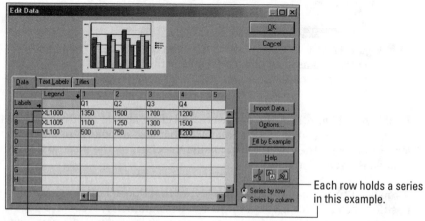

Each row holds a series in this example.

Figure 17-2: This Edit Data dialog box shows data for a bar chart; the preview area shows how the charted data looks.

If you have a long list of data to chart, you can add more display room in the Edit Data dialog box by removing the chart preview. To do so, click the Options button, clear the check beside Show Chart Preview, then click OK.

9. To make changes to the labels for each series or value, click the Text Labels tab and make the entries or changes you want. In addition, you can add a text label for a particular data point by typing the text you want to appear in the cell corresponding to the cell for that data point on the Data tab. For example, suppose you enter the highest value in cell C3 on the Data tab, and you want to add a label highlighting that amount. To do so, you would enter the label you want, such as **We're counting on this peak!**, in cell C3 of the Text Labels tab.

10. To add a chart title, a note about the chart, or labels for the axes, click the Titles tab and make the entries you want. Figure 17-3 shows example entries on the Titles tab.

11. Click OK. The Edit Data dialog box closes and the chart appears on the page.

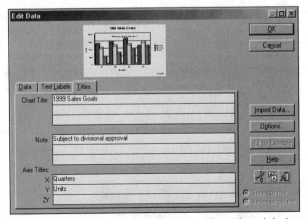

Figure 17-3: Use the options on the Titles tab to label the chart and its axes, or to add a note in the lower-right corner of the chart.

As shown in Figure 17-4, the newly created chart appears with selection handles. The Chart menu and the Chart SmartIcon bar also appear, providing you with tools for working with the chart. Click outside the chart on the page to deselect it and remove the selection handles.

If you want to add a chart to a page layout that doesn't offer a Click Here block to position the chart, or if you want to create a completely free-form page design, you can add your own chart to any page. For example, if you add a page using the Basic Layout option, that option offers only the SmartMaster background and graphics and a slide title Click Here block. In the area below, you can add any text blocks, graphics, charts, or other page elements that you want.

Use the following steps to add a chart to a page:

1. Display the page to which you want to add the chart in the Current Page view.

2. Add the title for the page, if needed.

3. Choose Create ⇨ Chart or click the Create a Chart SmartIcon. The Create Chart dialog box appears.

4. Follow Steps 4–11 above to select the chart type and enter the data and labels for the chart. After you click OK to close the Edit Data dialog box, the chart appears in a default position on the page. You can then move or resize the chart and adjust the position you want, as described later in this chapter.

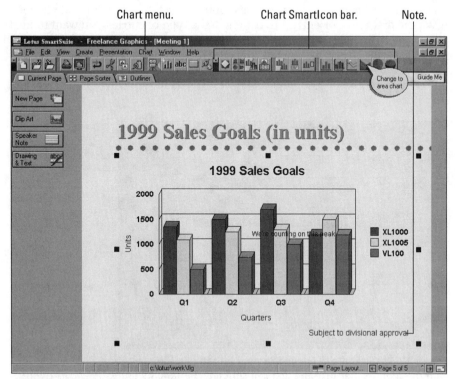

Figure 17-4: The new chart appears on the page, along with tools for working with the chart.

Using Fill By Example

Freelance Graphics offers some built-in intelligence to help you make certain types of entries for a chart on the Data tab of the Edit Data dialog box. The Fill By Example feature will fill in a list of similar entries in a selection of contiguous cells. You can fill the following type of entries, among others, with Fill By Example:

✦ **Months.** You can enter **January** in one cell, then fill subsequent months (February, March, and so on) in adjoining cells.

✦ **Quarter abbreviations.** You can enter **Q1** in the first cell, then fill adjoining cells with Q2, Q3, and Q4.

✦ **Numbers.** You can enter the first two numbers to establish the increment between values, such as **5** and **10**, and then fill adjoining cells with more incremented values (15, 20, 25, and so on). If you enter only a starting value (meaning you don't make two entries to specify an increment), Freelance increments values by 1, basing the filled entries on the starting value. For example, you can enter **1996** (for the year), then fill 1997, 1998, and subsequent years.

To use Fill By Example to make entries on the Data tab of the Edit Data dialog box, make the first entry or entries to establish the type of entries you want to fill. Drag over the initial entry (or entries), and down the column or across the row to select the cells to fill. Then click the Fill By Example button to have Freelance fill the selected cells with entries or incremented values based on the first entry or entries you made. For example, Figure 17-5 shows months filled in a selection.

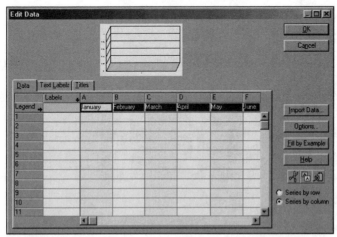

Figure 17-5: Clicking the Fill By Example button filled the selection with the months, because the first cell contains the January entry.

If you need more room in the Edit Data dialog box to see more rows or columns to fill or edit, drag a dialog box border to resize the dialog box, or click the Options button and remove the check from Show Chart Preview.

Importing Chart Data

If the data you want to chart exists in a 1-2-3 file, you don't have to reenter it in Freelance Graphics. Instead, you can use the Import Data button in the Edit Data dialog box as you're creating the chart to import the data from the 1-2-3 file.

Follow these steps to import the data:

1. Create the page to hold the chart, select the chart Click Here placeholder, then make your choices in the Create Chart dialog box and click OK.

2. In the Edit Data dialog box, click the Import Data button. The Open dialog box appears.

3. Use the Look In list to navigate to and select the 1-2-3 file that holds the data to chart. After you select the file, Freelance displays the Edit Links dialog box (see Figure 17-6), which you use to specify which parts of the data to chart.

Note

You also can import data from files of other types, such as Excel Worksheets, dBase database files, and ASCII text files. Select the type of file you want to import from the Files of Type drop-down list, then navigate to and select the file to open. You can then use Steps 4 through 9 to finish the import operation.

4. Select either the Series by Row or Series by Column option button to clarify whether each series of data to chart appears in a worksheet row or column.

5. Use the Worksheet drop-down list to choose which worksheet in the file holds the chart data or label(s), then use the Range Names drop-down list or drag on the worksheet display to select the information to add to the chart.

6. Then, at the left side of the dialog box, click the button beside the text box for the chart element that the selected information represents. For example, if you selected the cell holding a label to use as the chart title, click the button beside the Title text box to enter the cell address(es) in that text box.

7. Repeat Steps 5 and 6 to add other ranges of worksheet information to the appropriate part of the chart. Figure 17-6 shows worksheet information selected for various parts of the chart.

Danger Zone

When you specify the Data for the chart, select the range of cells that holds the values to chart only; do not include the row and/or column labels identifying that data. Instead, specify the range holding the series labels (which will be row labels at the left if the series are in rows, or column labels otherwise) as the Legend entry. Specify the range holding the value labels (which will be column labels at the top if the series are in rows, or row labels otherwise) as the X Axis Labels entry.

8. To link the charted data to the data in the 1-2-3 file (so Freelance checks the 1-2-3 file and updates the chart with any changes you've made to that file), click to check the Keep File Links check box.

Note

If you need to instead select the data to chart for each individual chart part (such as if the data for each series is on a different worksheet in the workbook), click the Individual button before performing Steps 4–7. Then, use the scrolling list below Choose the Specific Chart Part to Import at the left side of the dialog box to select the chart part for which you want to choose data. Select the worksheet holding the data to chart from the Worksheet drop-down list. Drag on the worksheet display or use the Range Names dialog box to select the data or labels for that chart part. Then, click the Apply button under the third step at the left side of the dialog box to apply the selection to the chart part. Repeat as needed for other chart parts, and choose to link the chart data, if needed.

Select each cell or range to chart here . . .

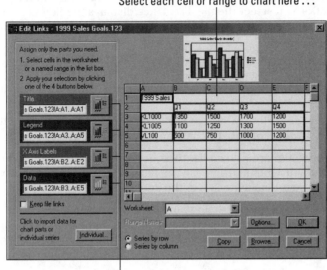

... then click a button here to assign that information to a chart part.

Figure 17-6: Select the 1-2-3 data to chart in the Edit Links dialog box.

9. Click OK. Freelance inserts the imported data into the Data tab of the Edit Data dialog box. You can use the other tabs in the dialog box to finish entering chart labels and titles, then click OK to add the chart to the presentation page.

If you've already charted the data and formatted the chart in 1-2-3, you can copy the entire chart onto a Freelance page. (It's best to create a new page using the Basic Layout page layout, which includes only a title Click Here block. This way, you don't have to worry about deleting other Click Here blocks.) To do so, start 1-2-3 and open the 1-2-3 file that holds the chart. Click the chart to select it, then choose Edit ➪ Copy (Ctrl+C) or click the Copy to Clipboard SmartIcon. Open or switch to Freelance Graphics, then open or create the presentation file into which you want to copy the chart. In the Current Page view, select or add the page onto which you want to place the copied chart, then choose Edit ➪ Paste (Ctrl+V) or click the Paste Clipboard Contents SmartIcon. The chart appears on the presentation page. You can then select and work with the chart using the techniques described throughout this chapter.

Selecting, Resizing, Moving, or Deleting a Chart

You must select a chart to make any changes you'd like to it. You can select the chart at any time and redisplay the selection handles by clicking the chart background area. (Don't click on a specific element such as one of the series; doing so selects that individual object, rather than the whole chart, in which case selection handles appear around the object only.)

Once the selection handles appear, you can drag any selection handle to resize the chart. As you drag, a dashed outline shows you the changing chart dimensions. Release the mouse button when the chart dimensions reach the size and shape you want.

To move the chart, select it, point to it, and press and hold the left mouse button. Drag to move the chart; as you drag, a dashed outline shows you the changing chart position. Release the mouse button when the chart reaches the destination you want.

To delete the selected chart, press the Delete key. Freelance removes the chart from the page. If you created the chart via a Click Here placeholder, the placeholder remains on the page. You can click it again to create an entirely new chart.

Note You can cut (Edit ➪ Cut) or copy (Edit ➪ Copy) a selected chart, then paste it (Edit ➪ Paste) onto another slide. You also can access the Cut, Copy, and Paste commands, as well as the Clear command, by right-clicking the chart to display its shortcut menu.

Formatting the Chart

Use the Chart InfoBox in Freelance Graphics to change the look and feel for the selected chart. There are a number of ways to display the InfoBox. For example, after you've selected the chart, you can click the Change Properties of Selected Object SmartIcon or choose Chart ➪ Chart Properties. You also can right-click the chart and choose Chart Properties or double-click on the chart background. The InfoBox appears, as shown in Figure 17-7. You also can display a particular tab in the InfoBox by choosing the Chart menu command or SmartIcon that corresponds to the function for the tab. For example, choosing Chart ➪ Chart Style ➪ Apply opens the Chart InfoBox and displays its third tab, the Named Style tab.

More Info The Screen Show tab is the last tab in the Chart InfoBox. This tab enables you to apply transition effects for the chart if you'll play the presentation as an onscreen show. See Chapter 19, "Creating and Running an Onscreen Show," to learn how to work with screen show effects.

After you display the Chart InfoBox, select the tab that holds the settings you want, then make your selections. The rest of this section covers your options for formatting the chart and using those tabs. You can close the Chart InfoBox when you've finished using it by clicking the Close button in the upper-right corner of the InfoBox.

Change Properties of Selected Object SmartIcons.

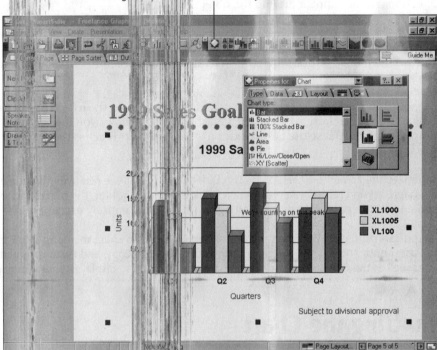

Figure 17-7: The Chart InfoBox offers settings for working with the appearance of the selected chart.

Changing the Chart Type

The first tab in the Chart InfoBox is the Type tab (see Figure 17-8). You can click this tab to select it if you've already opened the Chart InfoBox. Or, you can both open the InfoBox and display the tab by choosing Chart ⇨ Chart Type, right-clicking the chart and clicking Chart Type, or clicking the Set Chart Type SmartIcon. Once you've displayed the Type tab, scroll through the Chart Type list and click the new chart type to apply. Then, click one of the buttons beside the Chart Type list to choose which chart type variation to apply, such as the 3-D version of the selected chart type.

You also can use the six SmartIcons at the right end of the Chart SmartIcon bar to directly apply a new chart type. Simply click one of the SmartIcons to apply the new chart type—vertical bar, vertical bar with depth (3-D), line, area, pie, or 3-D pie—directly to the selected chart. Figure 17-8 identifies these SmartIcons.

Note

If you choose a new chart type, your old data may or may not work effectively with the new chart type. For example, if you switch from a bar chart to a pie or doughnut chart, the new chart only displays the first series from the bar chart. If you switch from a bar chart to a scatter chart, the new chart will be empty. If you find that the new chart type you select doesn't display the data in the way you wish, you can simply change the chart back to the original chart type you selected. Your chart data reappears, because Freelance Graphics doesn't discard data when you change chart types.

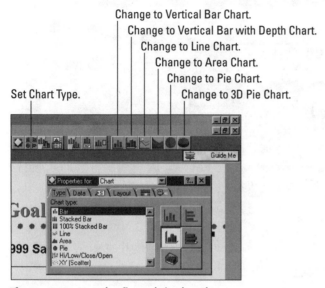

Figure 17-8: Use the first tab in the Chart InfoBox to select a different chart type.

Changing the Charted Data

You have to redisplay the Edit Data dialog box in order to edit the data for the selected chart. You may need to edit chart data if you find you've made a typo or if you need to change an estimated figure. Freelance offers a few different ways to redisplay the Edit Data dialog box. You can choose Chart ⇨ Edit Data, right-click the chart and click Edit Data, click the Edit Data button on the Data tab of the Chart InfoBox, or click the Show/Edit Chart Data SmartIcon. The Edit Data dialog box appears (see Figure 17-9).

To change the entry in a cell on the Data tab, click the cell, type the new entry, then press Enter to finish the entry. Alternately, you can double-click a cell to place the insertion point in it, edit the entry, then press Enter or an arrow key. You also can edit your entries on the Text Labels and Titles tabs by clicking the tab and then changing cell entries as needed. After you've made all the changes you want to the data, labels, and titles, click OK to close the Edit Data dialog box. Freelance automatically updates the chart to display the new data, labels, and titles.

This button also displays the Edit Data dialog box. ┌ Show/Edit Chart Data SmartIcon.

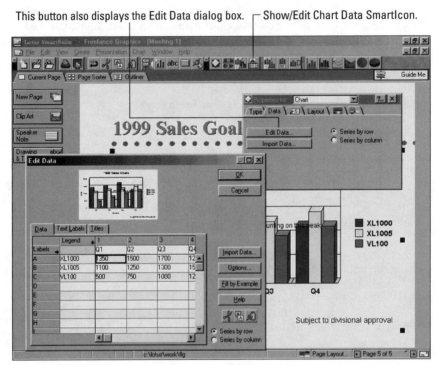

Figure 17-9: Redisplay the Edit Data dialog box to change the charted data.

Note

If you want to change the data you imported and charted to a whole new set of data, you can click the Import Data button on the Data tab of the Chart InfoBox or choose Chart ➪ Import Data to choose another file and other data to import. You have to repeat the full import process described earlier under "Importing Chart Data." Importing all new data or re-importing previous data can be faster than editing the chart data in Freelance and can ensure the data's accuracy if you edited the original data (in its source application) and want to make sure all your changes appear in Freelance.

Using Another Chart Style

The chart style determines the formatting for the chart area and all the elements within a chart, such as the colors and fills used for the series, the border used for the chart area, and so on. Therefore, you can radically and quickly change your chart's appearance by choosing another style for the chart. Freelance offers four different styles that you can apply to charts on the Named Style tab (see Figure 17-10), the third tab of the Chart InfoBox. You can display that tab by clicking it in the InfoBox. Or, you can choose Chart ➪ Chart Style ➪ Apply or the Set Default Chart Type and Style SmartIcon. Click the style you want from the list of styles on the left side of the tab. If you want to use the colors from the selected style, rather than the SmartMaster used for the presentation file, clear the check beside Use SmartLook Colors. Click Apply to apply the selected style to the chart.

Select a style here.   Set Default Chart Type and Style SmartIcon.

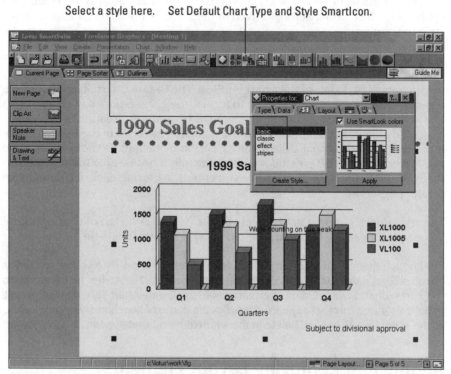

Figure 17-10: The Named Style tab of the Chart InfoBox, shown here, lists the available chart styles at the left.

Setting the Default Chart Style

You can set up Freelance to suggest a default chart type and style each time you display the Create Chart dialog box by clicking a chart placeholder or using the Create ⇨ Chart command in any presentation file. Freelance refers to this as the *default chart style*, even though it really includes both the chart type and the chart style. To specify the default chart style, choose Chart ⇨ Chart Style ⇨ Set Default Chart. The Set Default Chart dialog box appears. Choose the chart type Freelance will suggest by default from the Select a Chart Type list. Click one of the buttons beside the list to choose the chart type variation that Freelance will suggest by default. Then, choose the chart style Freelance will suggest by default from the Select a Chart Style list. Click OK to finish your default selections. The next time you create a chart, the Create Chart dialog box appears with the default chart type, variation, and style you indicated. You can either change to other selections for those settings, or click OK to continue and apply the defaults to the new chart.

Saving a Chart Style

After you've applied all the formatting you want to the chart and the elements on the chart (as described later under "Formatting Specific Chart Elements," you can save your formatting as a new style, with the name that you specify. Then, you can apply all the formatting settings saved in the style to any chart by applying the style to the chart.

When you've formatted the chart and its elements with the settings you'd like to save as a style, choose Chart ➪ Chart Style ➪ Create or click the Create Style button on the Named Style tab of the Chart InfoBox. The Create Chart Style dialog box that appears reminds you that you need to format the chart before saving the formatting as a style. If you've already done so, click OK to continue creating the style. In the Save As dialog box that appears, enter a name for the style in the File Name text box. Freelance adds the .CL file name extension by default. Do not change the disk and folder to save to; if you did so, Freelance might not be able to find your file so that you can apply it to charts. After you enter the file name, click OK to finish creating the style.

The style doesn't appear immediately on the Named Style tab of the Chart InfoBox. You need to close the InfoBox, then redisplay it so that it lists the new style.

Although there's not a command for deleting an old chart style you've created, you can still get it deleted. (Don't delete any of the default chart styles, however.) Choose Chart ➪ Chart Style ➪ Create, then click OK in the Create Chart Style dialog box. In the Save As dialog box that appears, right-click the name of the chart style file to delete in the list of files, then click Delete in the shortcut menu that appears.

Adding and Removing Layout Elements

The Layout tab of the Chart InfoBox enables you to specify whether certain chart elements appear on the chart. Click the Layout tab in the InfoBox to display its options (see Figure 17-11). When you check the Show Title, Show Note, and Show Legend check boxes, those layout elements appear on the chart; removing the check beside a layout element hides that element. To specify where in the chart area a displayed layout element appears, use the drop-down list to the right of the check box for that layout element. For example, to place the legend at the top of the chart, you have to choose North from the list, because Freelance uses the compass directions to describe layout element locations. You also can hide the note or legend by clicking either the Hide Chart Note or Hide Chart Legend SmartIcon. If the note or legend is already hidden, those SmartIcons change to Show Chart Note and Show Chart Legend, so you can click to redisplay the specified layout element.

The *plot area* appears within the whole chart area and defines the boundaries for the charted data. Layout elements normally appear outside the plot area. You can place the *legend* that identifies each series on top of the plot area, making it easier to match up the legend information with each series. To do so, click to check the

Place Legend Inside Plot check box. If you've moved or resized the plot area, click the Restore Plot Size button to return it to its original size and position. Finally, if you don't want the horizontal grid to appear in the plot area, click the Turn Horizontal Grid On/Off SmartIcon to hide it.

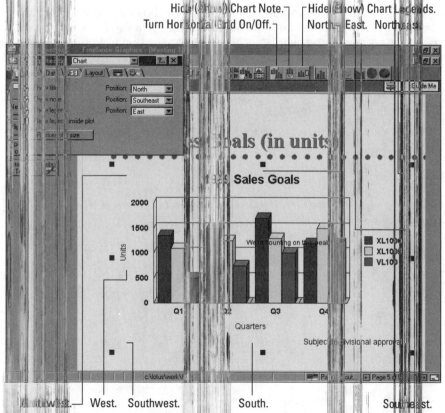

Figure 17-11: Control which layout elements appear and where they appear using the Layout tab.

Adding Borders and Patterns

Click the fifth tab in the Chart InfoBox—the Color, Pattern, and Line Style tab—to display options for adding borders around the chart area and fills within the chart area. In the Border area, choose options from the Style, Width, and Color drop-down lists to add a border around the chart area. Under Interior, use the Pattern, Pattern Color, and Background drop-down lists to insert a fill within the chart area. Check the Same Color as Border check box if you want the Pattern Color selection to change automatically if you change the Color drop-down list selection under Border.

Note   If your presentation includes an attractive backdrop (background) and you want the
backdrop to show through the chart, make sure you select the option that looks like
a squat "T" (for transparent) from the Pattern drop-down list in the Interior area of the
Color, Pattern, and Line Style tab.

If you want to include a drop-down shadow for the box around the chart area,
choose a shadow position from the Shadow drop-down list. Also, if you want to
round the corners of the chart area box, make a selection from the Rounding drop-
down list. Figure 17-12 shows a border and interior fill pattern added to a chart.

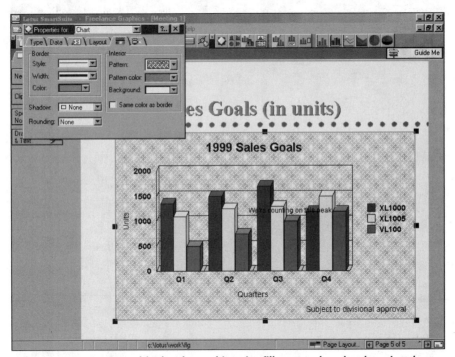

Figure 17-12: You can add a border and interior fill to any chart by changing the
settings on the chart InfoBox tab shown here.

Formatting Specific Chart Elements

Whether or not you've selected the chart itself, you can click any chart part (or
element or *object*), such as the legend that identifies each series, and then drag it to
move it or drag one of its handles to resize it. You can click the Change Properties
of Selected Object SmartIcon to display an InfoBox with settings for the selected
element. For example, Figure 17-13 shows the InfoBox for the legend, with the
Options tab of the InfoBox selected.

Handles appear around the selected element.

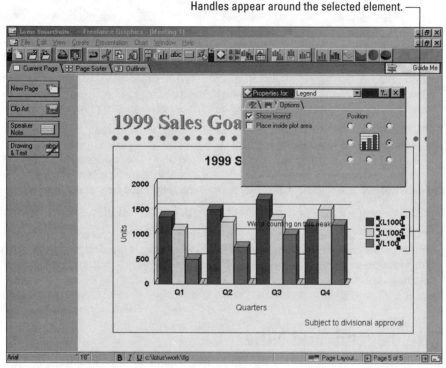

Figure 17-13: You can display an InfoBox presenting formatting choices for the selected element or part of the chart.

Note

You also can double-click some chart elements to display the InfoBox with formatting options. However, if you double-click any text on the chart (including the title, note, legend text, X-axis title, or Y-axis title), Freelance instead places the insertion point inside the text element so that you can edit the text.

The Chart menu also contains commands that display the InfoBox for a particular chart element, such as the Legend or Plot area. Choose the corresponding Chart menu command when you want to display the InfoBox for a particular element. For example, choose Chart ➪ Legend to display the InfoBox shown in Figure 17-13. The available Chart menu commands vary depending on the chart type for the selected chart, but in general, they correspond. For instance, the Chart menu offers Series and Series Labels commands for a bar chart, or Slice and Slice Labels commands for a pie chart. In general, the commands for any chart type are analogous to those described in this section.

Given the number of elements on each chart, there are several different InfoBoxes for chart elements, each of which has two to seven tabs, with a varying number of options. The available options in any InfoBox vary depending on the chart type. This section covers your options for formatting chart elements, focusing on the most common bar, line, and pie charts.

Good Charts, Bad Charts

Clear charts hammer your point home. Confusing charts mislead your audience. The choices you make in creating and formatting the chart determine its effectiveness:

✦ **Less is more.** Don't try to show too much data in a single chart. For example, if each series has 100 values (data points), and you're charting four series in a bar chart, your audience will have to discern the difference between 400 points. Better to chart a more limited number of values per series.

✦ **Leave well enough alone.** Don't radically resize the chart or change the scale for either axis, because doing so can skew the chart and make values appear inflated or deflated, or flatten or exaggerate trends. For example, making a line chart radically taller without resizing the width exaggerates the difference between values.

✦ **GIGO (garbage in, garbage out).** Double-check your figures before you enter them.

✦ **KISS (keep it simple, stupid).** You're better off emphasizing one series in a chart than you are trying to emphasize all of them. For example, applying a pattern to the bars for one series clearly emphasizes that series; applying a pattern to all the series creates a mishmash.

Title, Legend, and Note

You can display the InfoBox for the chart title, legend, or note by choosing Title, Legend, or Note from the Chart menu. The InfoBox for the chart title, legend, note, or any other selected text object generally offers three different tabs of options. The first tab (Font, Attribute, and Color) offers options for formatting the text itself. Use the Font Name list to choose another font, the Size list to choose a different size for the text, and the Style list to choose a different attribute (such as bold or italic). To change the text color, choose a new color from the Text Color drop-down list.

The Color, Pattern, and Line Style tab (second in the InfoBox) offers choices for adding a border to the box holding the text element and/or a fill for that box. Use the Pattern, Pattern Color, and Background drop-down lists under Interior to specify the fill to appear behind the text. Under line, choose new settings from the Color, Width, and Style drop-down lists to specify what kind of line appears around the text box.

The Options tab appears last, offering choices that are a bit more specific to the selected text element. In all cases, there's a Show (Object) check box, such as the Show Legend check box for a legend. Clearing this check box hides the selected element. The tab also offers a chart picture in the Position area; click the option button that indicates the position in which you'd like the selected element to appear. For the chart legend, the tab offers the Place Inside Plot Area check box; select it to move the legend over the plot area for the chart. For the chart title and note, the Options tab includes the Line 1, Line 2, and Line 3 text boxes. You can use those text boxes to add or edit one or more lines of text for the title or note.

X-axis and Y-axis

For charts with an x-axis and a y-axis, you can display the InfoBox for a chart axis by choosing a command from the Chart ➪ Axes & Grids submenu, or by clicking the axis or one of its labels and then clicking the Change Properties of Selected Object SmartIcon. The first tabs in the InfoBox vary depending on whether you've selected the axis line itself, or the labels for the axis.

When you're selecting elements in a chart, the mouse pointer changes slightly to help you click with precision on the element you want. Over text, the mouse pointer includes a small A. Over a line (like an axis), the mouse point includes a small L. Over another element, like a bar for a bar chart, the mouse pointer includes a small shape resembling the shape of the object it's over.

The Color, Pattern, and Line Style Tab

If you've selected the axis line, the first tab in the InfoBox for the chart axis is the Color, Pattern, and Line Style tab. It offers the Line Color, Line Width, and Line Style drop-down lists. Your choices from those drop-down lists change the appearance of the axis line itself. If you selected the axis labels, the first tab (Font, Attribute, and Color) offers options for formatting the text itself. Use the Font Name list to choose another font, the Size list to choose a different size for the text, and the Style list to choose a different attribute (such as bold or italic). To change the text color, choose a new color from the Text Color drop-down list.

The Number Format Tab

The second tab in the InfoBox for the chart axis, the Number Format tab, enables you to choose a number format for numeric axis labels. Choose a number format from the Format Type list. If you choose Currency or ISO Currency from the Format Type list, you also can choose the currency format for the correct country from the Current Format list. If you want to include parentheses around the values, check the Parentheses check box. To alter the number of decimal places each numeric value includes, change the Decimal Places text box entry. Figure 17-14 shows the Number format tab, with the Comma format (set with 0 Decimal Places) applied to the selected y-axis values.

The remaining tabs in the InfoBox are the same whether you've selected the axis or the axis labels.

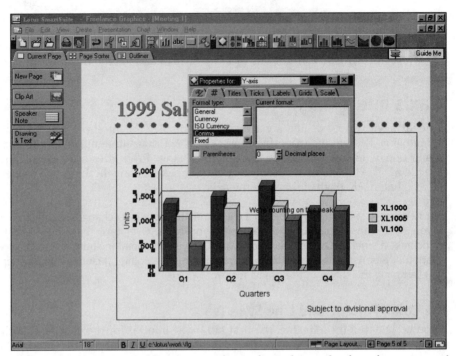

Figure 17-14: Use the Number Format tab to select a format for the values on an axis.

The Titles Tab

The Titles tab in the InfoBox for the chart axis enables you to hide or display the title and subtitle for the axis. To show either one, click to check the Show Title or Show Subtitle check box, then enter the title or subtitle to show in the text box below the check box. Or, for the Show Subtitle check box, you can click the Based on Scale option button to generate the subtitle based on your choice from the Units drop-down list on the Scale tab (more about it shortly). Use the Subtitle Position drop-down list to specify whether or not the subtitle appears on the same line as the title. Finally, use the Orientation drop-down list to choose whether the title (and subtitle) appear horizontally, bottom-to-top, or top-to-bottom.

The Ticks Tab

The Ticks tab in the InfoBox for the chart axis controls whether tick marks appear on the axis to clarify value increments. Make sure a check appears beside the Show Axis Line check box so that the axis line itself displays. Under Show Tick Marks At, check Major Intervals to add tick marks to the value intervals Freelance automatically places on the axis, and check Minor Intervals to add tick marks between the major intervals. Then, choose a location for each set of tick marks from the accompanying Position drop-down list. Choosing Outside places the tick marks outside the axis and plot area. Choosing Inside places the tick marks inside the axis, over the plot area. Across places the tick marks across the axis, so it spans both outside and inside the plot area.

The Labels Tab

The Labels tab in the InfoBox for the chart axis enables you to control the display of the scale labels, the numeric labels Freelance generates for the axis, based on the charted series. Check the Show Scale Labels Every check box, then edit the accompanying Ticks text box to display labels and determine whether they appear for every major tick mark (1), every other major tick mark (2), and so on. If you display extra gridlines using the Grids tab (discussed next), you can add numeric labels for those gridlines by checking the Show Scale Labels for Extra Grid Lines check box.

The Grids Tab

The Grids tab in the InfoBox for the chart axis controls whether horizontal grid lines appear for the y-axis values on the plot area, or (if you've selected an x-axis) whether vertical gridlines for the x-axis intervals appear on the plot area. Under Show Grid Lines At, check Major Intervals to show gridlines at the major value intervals that Freelance calculates, and Minor Intervals to include a gridline for each minor interval Freelance calculates between the major intervals. Figure 17-15 shows gridlines displayed for the major and minor intervals.

For the y-axis, you also can include one or more extra gridlines to mark a specific value. For example, if major and minor gridlines appear at increments of 250 for the y-axis and you want to add a gridline to mark 1,100, the average of the charted values, you can do so. First, check the Show (x) Extra Grid Lines check box, then enter the number of extra gridlines in the text box. Then, for each extra gridline to display, choose its Line Number (with 1 being the first extra gridline), and specify the Line Value for that Line Number (such as 1,100 to display the gridline at 1,100 on the plot area). Choose a Line Number of 2 for the next extra gridline, enter its Line Value, and so on.

The Scale Tab

The final tab in the InfoBox for the chart axis is the Scale tab. It enables you to override the axis scale that Freelance Graphics calculates, also affecting where your choices on the Ticks, Labels, and Grids tabs appear. For example, in Figure 17-15, the scale has a *minimum value* of 0 and a *maximum value* of 2,000. Major ticks mark every increment of 500, and minor ticks mark every increment of 250.

To override the axis Maximum, Minimum, Major Ticks, or Minor Ticks value, check the appropriate check box under Scale Manually on the Scale tab, then enter the value or increment you want in the accompanying text box. When the Intercept check box is available, click it to override the value at which the x-axis and y-axis intercept, and then enter the new Intercept value in the text box.

Includes major interval tick marks outside the axis.

Major interval gridline.

Minor interval gridline.

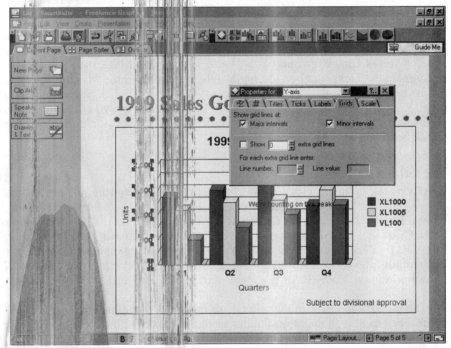

Figure 17-15: Gridlines on a bar chart help the viewer identify the value each bar represents.

Use the Direction drop-down list to indicate whether the axis values appear in Ascending or Descending order. If the Position drop-down list is active, choose a position for the axis labels from that list. The Type drop-down list options determine how Freelance calculates the axis values: Linear values, Log (logarithmic) values, or 100% (percentage) values.

Finally, use the Units drop-down list to specify what units the values on the selected axis represent, such as Thousands or Millions; if you choose Other, you can enter a unit scale value in the text box beside the Units drop-down list.

Series and Series Labels

You can display an InfoBox for formatting one or more chart series, or labels you've entered for the series. Choose Chart ➪ Series or double-click one of the series to display the InfoBox for editing the series. (Note that you also can select individual pie slices in a pie chart and change slice attributes as described here.) In this InfoBox, you may prefer to use the second tab (Options) first. Use the top, unnamed drop-down list on the tab to select the series for which you want to adjust the bars or lines or other series marker. (You can select one series from the drop-down list, change all its InfoBox settings, select the next series and change its settings, and so on.)

To hide the selected series from the chart, clear the Show Series check box. To add a second y-axis to plot the selected series against, click to check the Plot Against 2nd Y-Axis check box. If you want to change the series marker used for the selected series, such as displaying it as a line, rather than a bar, choose the series marker you want from the Mixed Type drop-down list. Finally, if you want to change the name displayed for the series in the legend, edit the Legend Label text box entry.

To change the pattern and fill for the selected series, click the first tab in the InfoBox — the Color, Pattern, and Line Style tab. Under Interior (available for bar, area, and series for similar chart types), use the Pattern, Pattern Color, and Background drop-down lists to change the fill for the selected series. In the Border area, choose options from the Color, Width, and Style drop-down lists to adjust the border that defines the series. Figure 17-16 shows a diagonal pattern applied to the first series in a bar chart.

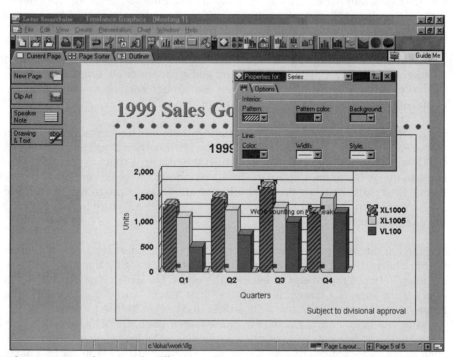

Figure 17-16: Changing the fill pattern for a series helps that series stand out.

If you've added labels to one or more individual series values in the selected chart, choose Chart ⇨ Series Labels to display the InfoBox for formatting the labels. Again, use the drop-down list at the top of the Options tab to indicate which series labels to format. Check the Show Value Labels, Show Percent Labels, or Show Text Labels to enable display for any or all of those label types.

Use the Position drop-down list to indicate a position for the labels, and the Orientation drop-down list to display the labels horizontally, vertically, or diagonally. The first tab (Font, Attribute, and Color) offers the options for formatting the label text itself. Use the Font Name list to choose another font, the Size list to choose a different size for the text, and the Style list to choose a different attribute (such as bold or italic). To change the text color, choose a new color from the Text Color drop-down list.

Plot Area

To change the appearance of the plot area for the selected chart, choose Chart ⇨ Plot. The InfoBox that appears will vary quite a bit depending on the chart type. For bar, line, and area charts, the first tab is the Color, Pattern, and Line Style tab. If the chart is a 3-D chart, you can format only one part of the plot area (side, back, or bottom) by clicking a button beside Plot Section. Under Interior, use the Pattern, Pattern Color, and Background drop-down lists to change the fill for the selected plot section. In the Border area, choose options from the Color, Width, and Style drop-down lists to adjust the border that defines the plot area.

Danger Zone

Don't have too much going on in your plot area. If you use numerous gridlines, consider not including a pattern or fill. If you add a pattern or fill, simplify your gridline choices or eliminate gridlines altogether. Remember, keeping it simple helps your audience better understand the chart information.

For most charts, the Plot InfoBox offers an Options tab. If you want to resize the plot area, choose the Custom Settings option button, then drag the plot area; click the Default Settings option button to return the plot area to its original size. You can copy an image file to the Clipboard (from a Windows image editing program such as Paint), then click the Paste Picture button on the Options tab to use the picture as the backdrop for the chart information. Click the Delete Picture button to remove the pasted picture.

The Layout tab options vary widely depending on the chart type. For example, for bar charts, the tab offers only a Gap % text box. Changing this value adjusts the distance between the groups of bars on the chart. For a pie chart, the Layout tab offers more options. Change the Explode Slices % text box setting to insert space between the pie slices. Choose a Slice Direction option button to determine whether Freelance charts the data in clockwise or counterclockwise order. Edit the Start Angle text box entry to specify what position the first slice occupies. Finally, click to check Sort Slices by Size if you want Freelance to sort the values charted in the pie.

Displaying a Data Table

For some chart types, you can include a table of the charted data, so your audience members can see the actual values along with the graphical chart. To display the table for the selected chart, choose Chart ➪ Table, then click the Show Data table check box on the Options tab of the Table InfoBox that appears. As shown in Figure 17-17, you also can use the Show Row Headers and Show Column Headers check boxes to include or hide headers in the table. To have Freelance total the values in each column and display those totals, check Show Column Totals, then enter a label for the total row in the Column Totals Label text box. Figure 17-17 shows "Total Units" entered as the label for the total row, which appears at the bottom of the table. At the bottom of the tab, a drop-down list includes the chart series. You can select a series from this drop-down list, then use the Show Series in Table and Show Series in Chart check boxes to control whether the selected series appears in the chart, the table, or both.

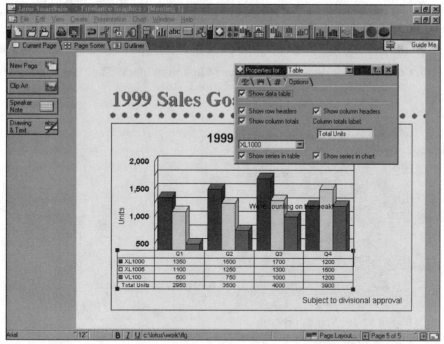

Figure 17-17: You can display a table of the charted values within the chart.

The other three tabs (Font, Attribute, and Color; Color, Pattern, and Line Style; and Number Format) work as described for other chart elements earlier in this section. The only difference exists on the Color, Pattern, and Line Style tab. On that tab, you can click a button in the Line area to control where Freelance includes lines to separate table cells.

Creating an Organization Chart

Organization (org) charts show relationships. You can use an organization chart to show relationships between departments, individual positions, tasks, topics, or any other dependencies you need to clarify. This section explains how to add and format an organization chart in your presentation.

Adding the Org Chart

Although an organization chart differs somewhat from other chart types, the process for adding one to your presentation should seem familiar if you've worked with other chart types. You add a presentation page with the Organization chart layout, select the chart placeholder, choose a style, and then enter the chart data. Follow these steps to include a page with an organization chart in your presentation:

1. In the Current Page view, select the page after which you want to insert the new chart, then choose Page ➪ New Page (F7) to display the New Page dialog box. Select the Organization Chart page layout. Click OK.

2. Add the title for the page in the Click Here to Type Page Title Click Here block.

3. Click the Click Here to Create Chart Click Here block. The Organization Chart Gallery dialog box appears (see Figure 17-18).

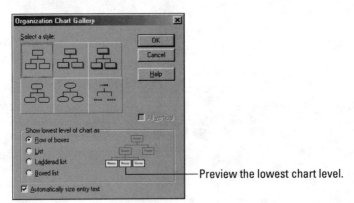

Figure 17-18: You can choose an organization chart style using the Organization Chart Gallery dialog box.

4. Click the button illustrating the style of chart you want under Select a Style.

5. Under Show Lowest Level of Chart As, click the option button that describes the appearance you want for those positions. The preview in that area of the dialog box changes to show you how the selected option looks. If you choose either List, Laddered List, or Boxed List, you also can check All Vertical to confine the listed positions to a vertical column.

6. To specify that Freelance should determine the text size for each box or listing on the chart, in order to ensure that all the information squeezes onto the chart, leave Automatically Size Entry Text checked. If you clear this check box, Freelance uses the default size defined by the chart style and SmartMaster, meaning that you may need to manually resize some entries.

7. Click OK. The Organization Chart Entry List dialog box appears (see Figure 17-19). It includes an Outliner style lined page you can use to enter the position to chart.

8. For each box or listing, enter the name on one line, the title on the next line, and any comment on the next line. Press Enter to start each new line, or to skip a line without making an entry for it.

9. When you finish the first (top) entry, pressing Enter automatically creates a subordinate below the top entry. After you finish that first subordinate entry, you have to indicate the level for subsequent entries. To demote an entry to make it a subordinate of the entry preceding it, press Tab or choose Edit ⇨ Demote from the dialog box menu bar. To promote an entry to the next highest level, press Shift+Tab or choose Edit ⇨ Promote. As you make the entries, Freelance uses indentation and different bullets to help you distinguish which entries appear at each level.

10. To create or edit a staff position for the top entry, choose Edit ⇨ Staff from the dialog box menu bar. In the Organization Chart Staff dialog box that appears, define the position by making entries in the Name, Title, and Comment text boxes, then click OK. Or, click Remove in the dialog box to remove a staff position you previously included. Note that the staff position does not appear on the entry list, even though it does appear in the finished chart.

11. You can use the View menu in the dialog box to restrict how many lines for each entry appear in the entry list. Choose Names Only, Names and Titles, or All, from the View menu to adjust the view accordingly. For example, Figure 17-19 illustrates how the list appears when it includes names and titles only.

12. To check the chart appearance, click Preview. If the chart doesn't include all the positions in the correct location, click Change in the Preview dialog box to return to the Organization Chart Entry List and make your changes.

13. Click OK to finish the chart entries. The chart appears on the page, as shown in Figure 17-20.

Press Tab to denote an entry.   Subordinates for the top level.

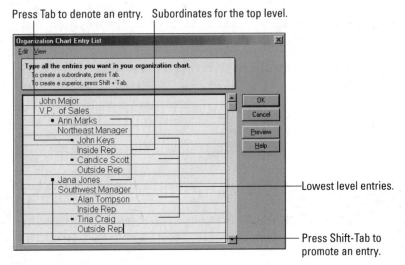

Figure 17-19: You can view only the names and titles you enter in your list.

Edit Organization Chart Data SmartIcon.   Staff position.

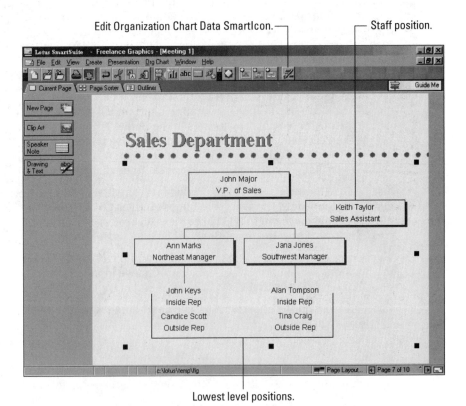

Lowest level positions.

Figure 17-20: Here's the organization chart for the entry list illustrated in Figure 17-19.

Note Click the organization chart on the page, then choose Org Chart ➪ Edit Data or click the Edit Organization Chart Data SmartIcon to redisplay the Organization Chart Entry List dialog box. Make the changes you want to the previously entered positions, then click OK.

Formatting the Org Chart

As for other chart types, you can click the chart to select the organization chart itself, or click the box for any position (whether there's an actual outline around the box or not) to select that box. Then, you can click the Change Properties of Selected Object SmartIcon or use one of the commands on the Org Chart menu that appears to display an InfoBox for the chart or the box.

Choose Org Chart ➪ Org Chart Properties to display the InfoBox for the chart itself. In addition, you can choose Org Chart ➪ Connecting Lines to display an InfoBox for changing the lines between positions. You also can make a selection from the Org Chart ➪ Box Properties submenu, active only when you've selected a box, to make your InfoBox changes apply to the Current Box & Peers (all boxes at the same level as the selected box) or the Current Box & Subordinates (all boxes at the same level and the next level below the selected box).

Many of the tabs in the InfoBoxes for Org Charts resemble those described in the previous two sections for other charts. The Font, Attribute, and Color tab appears in the InfoBox for the organization chart or a selected box. It works just as described earlier, offering Font Name, Size, Attributes, and Text Color settings. In addition, you can click an option button at the top of the tab to apply the font changes to only one line of text, such as the Name or Title. The InfoBox for the organization chart, the chart frame, the connecting lines, or any selected box offers a Color, Pattern, and Line Style tab, which you can use to adjust lines and fill patterns, as described earlier for other chart types.

Note When you change the Font, Attribute, and Color tab or Color, Pattern, and Line Style tab settings in the InfoBox for the full organization chart, the settings apply to each box in the chart, not the chart itself. To add a border around the organization chart itself, choose Org Chart ➪ Frame, and then make your changes in the InfoBox that appears.

The InfoBox for the overall organization chart or a selected box includes an Alignment tab. On that tab, click the Horizontal alignment button that illustrates the alignment you want the text in all the boxes or the selected box to follow.

Finally, the InfoBox for the organization chart offers an Organization Chart Layout tab and a Screen Show tab. (Chapter 19, "Creating and Running an Onscreen Show," covers the Screen Show tab.) The Organization Chart Layout tab enables you to change the organization chart style. To do so, click the down arrow for the chart sample shown under Layout, then click the new layout style to use in the pop-up palette of choices. Under Lowest Level, choose an option button to change the display style for the lowest level. You can enable or clear the Automatically Size Entry Text and All Vertical check boxes, described earlier in the steps for creating an organization chart. Lastly, you can click the Edit Data button to change the entries you've made for the selected organization chart.

✦   ✦   ✦

Working with Graphics and Design

As rich and varied as the Freelance Graphics SmartMasters are, you don't have to be a designer to create a professional-looking presentation. On the other hand, you may need to adjust some aspects of your presentation's appearance to ensure it presents information in the needed format and looks as attractive as possible. Read on to learn how to make changes to the look of individual pages and whole presentations. This chapter spans the full range of design topics — from selecting a different page layout to creating a new page layout, from drawing to adding an existing graphic, and from formatting text to copying that formatting.

Changing the Page Layout

Often, you may find you need to add more elements to a page in your presentation. For example, a page may include only a bulleted list, and you might want to add clip art. Or, your page may include one chart, and you may want to add another. While you could manually add, move, and resize elements to achieve the look you want for a page, you can accomplish your objective much more quickly by choosing another page layout. If you change from the Bulleted List page layout to the Bullets & Clip Art page layout, Freelance Graphics keeps the previous title and bulleted list text you added, resizing the bulleted list to make room for a new clip art Click Here block. If you've created and formatted a chart on a page using the 1 Chart page layout, you can preserve that chart and add a placeholder for a second chart by switching to the 2 Charts page layout.

Follow these steps to choose another page layout for a slide page:

1. In Current Page view, display the page for which you want to change the layout. In Page Sorter or Outliner view, click the picture for the page with the layout that you want to change.

2. Choose Page ⇨ Switch Page Layout. The Switch Page Layout dialog box appears.

3. In the list of page layouts, choose the new page layout to use. For example, if the page originally used the Bulleted List page layout, you might choose the Bullets & Clip Art layout.

4. Click OK. The Switch Page Layout dialog box closes, and the selected page displays the new page layout.

As you can see in the example in Figure 18-1, any contents you created in the original page layout remains on the page. That is, if the new layout you select has elements that correspond to the elements in the original page layout, such as when each layout has a bulleted list, Freelance simply shifts the page contents to the new location called for by the new page layout.

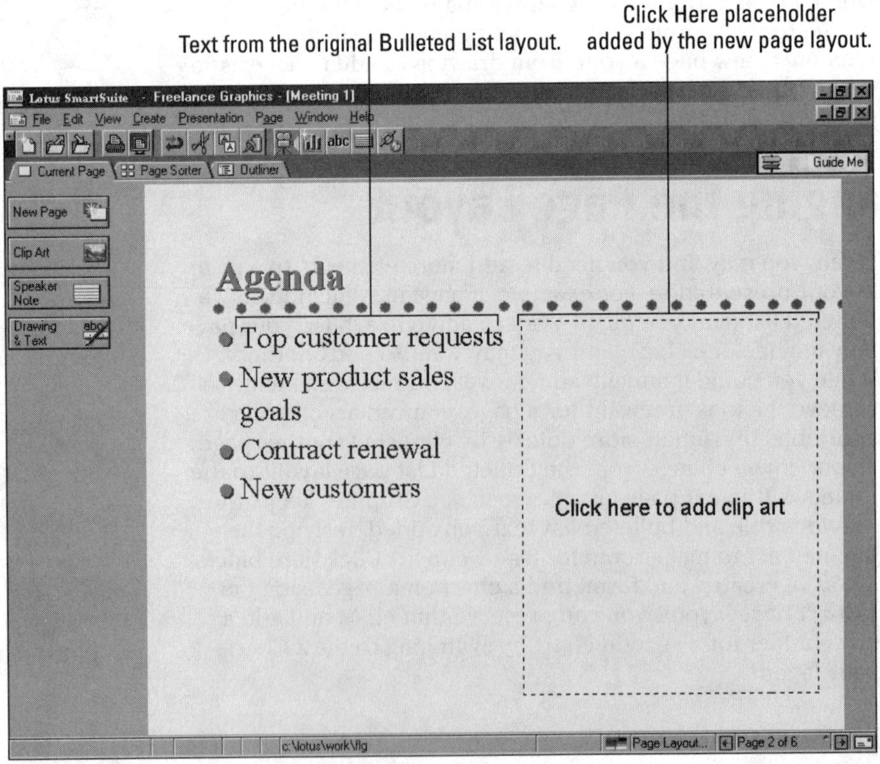

Figure 18-1: Applying a new page layout rearranges, adds, and removes page elements.

If you choose a new page layout that's wildly dissimilar from the original page layout, such as if you change from the Bulleted List page layout to the 1 Chart layout, the old elements and their contents remain in their original locations, and the new layout elements appear. So, if your page had a Bulleted List layout and you had already entered text into it, changing to the 1 Chart page layout leaves the bulleted text in place and adds a Click Here block for adding a chart over the bulleted text. Or, suppose the old page layout had more elements than the new one and you had already filled all the placeholders in. For example, you might have used the Bullets & Clip Art layout, then added the bulleted list text and selected some clip art. If you then switch the page to the Bulleted List layout, the clip art remains but the bulleted list changes to a wider shape and may run over the clip art; if the clip art Click Here block is empty, switching to the simpler page layout removes that empty Click Here block.

In addition to switching to a new page layout, you may want to remove the page layout from a slide to give yourself total flexibility in redesigning the slide. Called *unlinking the page layout*, this technique ensures the page remains as it currently looks, even if you edit a particular page layout (see "Creating a Custom Page Layout and Editing Click Here Blocks" later in this chapter). Unlinking the page layout also unlinks the page from the page formatting supplied by the SmartMaster. Then, choosing a new look for the presentation does not change the page for which you unlinked the page layout. To unlink the page layout, display or select the page to unlink from its layout. Choose Page ⇨ Unlink Page Layout. The Page Unlink dialog box that appears warns you about the consequences of unlinking the page layout. Click OK to proceed and unlink the page layout.

Note   If you're not satisfied with the new page layout you select or mistakenly unlink the page layout, immediately click the Undo Last Command or Action SmartIcon.

Changing the SmartMaster or Content Topic

Chapter 15, "Starting, Saving, and Opening Presentations," illustrates how you can create a new presentation by choosing a SmartMaster (template) that contains a look (design) for the presentation, or by choosing a content topic (suggested pages) for the presentation along with a SmartMaster look. Later, you may find that you want to change the look or content topic for a presentation, as described in this section.

Choosing a New Look

The look you should choose for a presentation depends on how you plan to share it with your audience. If you'll be outputting the presentation as 35mm slides or displaying it with an LCD projector, you can choose a look with a colorful background and light text. If you'll be printing the presentation, especially on a black-and-white printer, the most effective looks offer lighter backgrounds and dark text. In some instances, you may need to accommodate both scenarios, generating printed output before delivering the presentation in a live setting. In such a case, you'll need to start with one SmartMaster look, then select another.

Choosing a new look for the presentation changes the background appearance (backdrop) for all the slides, and applies the formatting for text and other elements as defined by the SmartMaster and each page layout. For example, some SmartMasters might left-align page titles, while others center page titles. When you choose a new SmartMaster, it applies the new alignment to all the page titles. To choose another look for the current presentation, follow these steps:

1. Choose Presentation ➪ Choose a Different SmartMaster Look. The Choose a Look for Your Presentation dialog box appears, as shown in Figure 18-2. The dialog box includes a preview of the currently selected SmartMaster look. It lists all the SmartMasters stored in the default SmartMaster folder for Freelance Graphics, /lotus/smasters/flg.

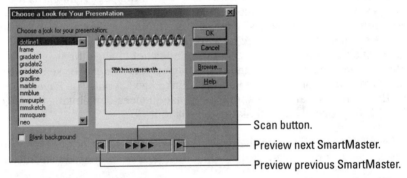

Figure 18-2: Use this dialog box to choose a new SmartMaster and update the look for your presentation.

2. You can use one of three methods to move through and preview the SmartMaster looks:

   • Press the up arrow key or down arrow key or use the mouse to move through the selections in the Choose a Look for Your Presentation list.

   • Click either the left-pointing or right-pointing arrow button below the preview to display the previous or next SmartMaster, respectively.

   • Click the Scan button (it has four right-pointing arrows on it) below the preview. Freelance automatically displays each SmartMaster preview, pausing briefly before advancing to the next one. The Scan button changes to a Stop button with a square on it. Click the Stop button at any time to stop the scan display.

3. Select the SmartMaster you want in the Choose a Look for Your Presentation list. If the SmartMaster you'd like to use isn't in the default SmartMaster folder, click the Browse button, use the Look In list to browse to the disk and folder that holds the SmartMaster you want to use, then select the file and click Open. Or, if you don't want to use a SmartMaster look with all the bells and whistles, check the Blank Background check box.

4. Click OK. Freelance applies the new SmartMaster to the presentation. For example, Figure 18-3 shows a new SmartMaster applied to the page shown in Figure 18-2.

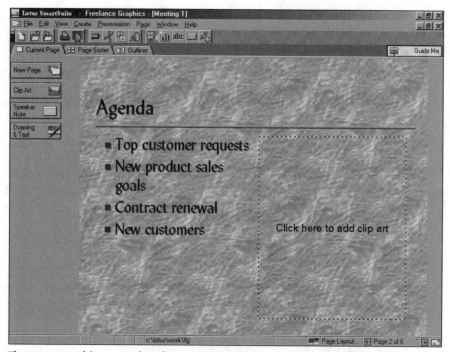

Figure 18-3: This page, also shown in Figure 18-2, displays a newly applied SmartMaster.

You can't undo a SmartMaster change. You have to redisplay the Choose a Look for Your Presentation dialog box, and choose the SmartMaster the presentation used previously. So, if needed, keep notes about which SmartMasters you apply to a particular presentation file for particular purposes.

Choosing a New Content Topic

A content topic not only suggests an overall structure for your presentation, but also suggests topics for particular pages and includes a SmartMaster look. If you didn't select a content topic when you started creating your presentation, you can apply it to the presentation at any later time, enabling you to begin incorporating the content by adding new pages to the presentation. Use the following steps to start using a content topic for the current presentation:

1. Choose Presentation ⇨ SmartMaster Content ⇨ Select a Topic. The Select a Topic & Look dialog box appears (see Figure 18-4).

2. Scroll the Select a Content Topic list and select the content topic you want to begin using.

3. The Select a Look list automatically changes to the Look Stored with Content Topic choice. If you don't want to change the SmartMaster look, scroll through the list and click the SmartMaster the presentation currently uses. Or, click the Browse button, use the Look In list to browse to the disk and folder that holds the SmartMaster you want to use, select the file, and click Open.

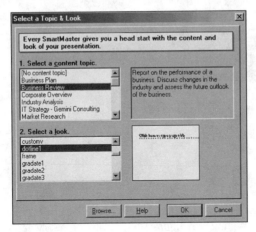

Figure 18-4: Begin using a content topic in your presentation by selecting the topic you want from the top list in this dialog box.

4. Click OK to close the dialog box and apply the content topic and SmartMaster look.

5. If the content topic includes scripts, the LotusScript Security Warning dialog box appears. Click Yes to confirm that you want the scripts to run, and close the dialog box. The content topic information immediately becomes available in the presentation.

6. The New Page dialog box appears, with its Content Pages tab selected. You can click one of the listed pages and click OK to add it to the presentation, or click Cancel.

When the content topic is active for the presentation, any time you display the New Page dialog box (with Page ➪ New Page or F7), it offers the Content Pages tab so that you can select a page displaying a suggested topic (or topics) and layout. If you no longer want to use the selected content topic, choose Presentation ➪ SmartMaster Content ➪ Stop Using. From that point, the New Page dialog box no longer suggests content pages. If needed, you can repeat the preceding steps to choose another content topic so you can incorporate its suggestions into your presentation.

Inserting Clip Art or a Graphic

Although you can create your own drawings directly on any page using the drawing tools offered in Freelance Graphics, for most of us nonartists, using premade artwork saves time and yields more pleasing and professional results. This section explains how to add existing artwork to any page in your presentation.

Note Whenever you work with graphics, drawing, and even the formatting for the text in your presentation, use the Current Page view. Not only does Current Page view provide the only means for working with many of the features described in the remainder of this chapter, but it also provides the only adequate way to view the results of your changes.

Adding Clip Art

Freelance Graphics offers a number of *clip art* images — predrawn artwork you can add to any page to make it more attractive. One page layout, Bullets & Clip Art, includes a Click Here placeholder you can use to add a piece of clip art to a defined location on the page. However, you also can insert a clip art image anywhere on any page, and then move it into position. The steps for inserting clip art you use in either case are about the same:

1. Add a new page using the Bullets & Clip Art page layout, then click the Click Here to Add Clip Art placeholder. Or, to insert the clip art on any other page, choose Create ➪ Add Clip Art or click the Clip Art button at the left on the Current Page view tab. The Add Clip Art or Diagram to the Page dialog box appears (see Figure 18-5).

Click here to add clip art to any page.　　　　The number of images in the category.

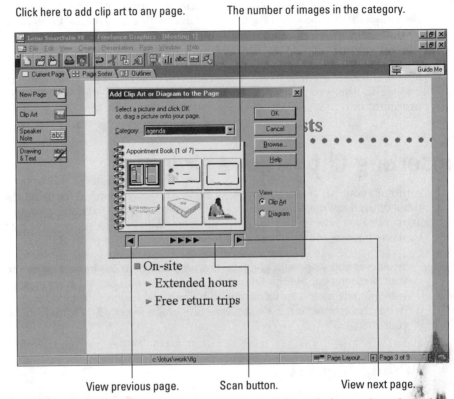

View previous page.　　　Scan button.　　　View next page.

Figure 18-5: Choose a clip art category, then scroll through the preview pictures to find the picture you want to add to the page.

2. Click the Clip Art option button in the View area of the dialog box, if needed.

3. Use the Category drop-down list to jump to the group of images that reflects the subject matter of the page. Then, click either the left-pointing or right-pointing arrow button below the page of images to display more pages in the category, or to move to the next category of images. Optionally, click the Scan button (it has four right-pointing arrows on it) below the page of images. Freelance automatically displays each page preview, pausing briefly before advancing to the next one. The Scan button changes to a Stop button with a square on it. Click the Stop button at any time to stop the scan display.

4. Click the image you want to insert on the page of images. A description for the selected image appears at the top of the page of images.

5. Click OK. If you added the clip art to a page with a Click Here placeholder, Freelance inserts the clip art in the appropriate location. Click outside the image to finish. Otherwise, go on to Step 6.

6. If the clip art image appears in the wrong location, drag it into place. If it's the wrong size, drag one of its black selection handles to resize it. When you finish, click outside the image. Figure 18-6 shows clip art inserted on a page.

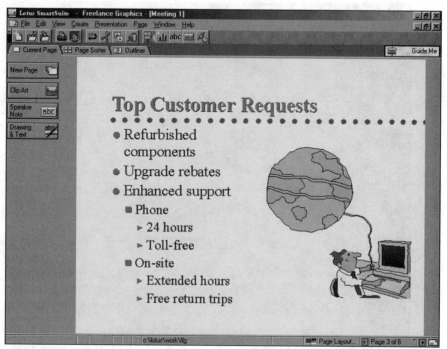

Figure 18-6: You can add a clip art image such as the one shown here to any page.

Adding a Diagram

Freelance also offers a number of predrawn diagram formats that you can use to graphically illustrate how ideas or departments relate, or to create a flow chart for a process. Diagrams resemble the organization charts discussed in Chapter 17, "Adding and Working with Charts," but the dozens of diagrams in Freelance provide you with more options to present your information in the most accurate, attractive way possible.

The process for adding a diagram to a presentation page is nearly identical to the just-described process for adding clip art. Click a Click Here to Add Clip Art placeholder or the Clip Art button on the Current Page view tab to display the Add Clip Art or Diagram to the Page dialog box. (Alternately, you can choose Create ⊏➢ Drawing/Diagram, select the Use a Ready-Made Diagram option button, then click OK.) Click the Diagram option in the View area of the dialog box, if needed. Browse through the diagram options, click the style of diagram to insert, then click OK.

The diagram, when it appears, includes several placeholders for text that read Type Text. Click the placeholder to fill in, then type your text, as shown in Figure 18-7. After you fill in each placeholder, click outside the diagram to finish.

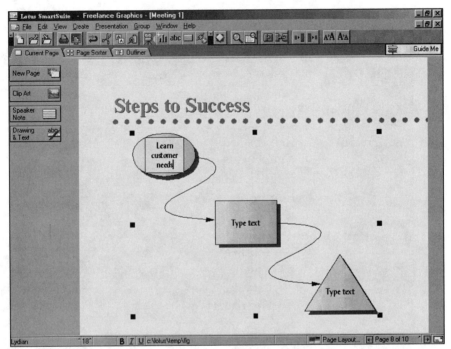

Figure 18-7: To create an attractive diagram, choose the look you want, then fill in the text placeholders.

Inserting a Graphic

Finally, you may have access to other graphic files that you may want to insert in your presentation. For example, most companies have the company logo available as a graphic file. You also may have scanned pictures of your company's products or other such material to include in a presentation file. Freelance Graphics enables you to insert graphics in most common formats (.BMP, .PCX, .JPG, .TIF, and .GIF) on a page in a presentation.

Danger Zone

The graphic file you insert will have a rectangular shape. Unlike clip art images you insert, you can't format the graphic file background. So, you might end up with a "rectangle" around the graphic that doesn't match the page backdrop. To cope with this issue, either change the presentation SmartMaster look to a background that matches the graphic's background; change the backdrop for the page that holds the graphic (described later in this chapter); or edit the graphic file to give it the correct background color in a graphic editing program such as Windows Paint.

Use the following steps to insert an existing graphic file on a page in your presentation:

1. In the Current Page view, choose Create ⇨ Add Picture. The Add a Picture dialog box appears.

2. If needed, use the Files of Type drop-down list to select the type of graphic file to insert.

3. Use the Look In list to navigate to the disk and folder that holds the graphic file to insert.

4. Click the file in the list, then click Open. The Embed a Copy of the Image File? dialog box appears. It asks you whether or not you want to link the inserted graphic to the original graphic file, or simply embed a copy of the graphic.

5. Click Yes to embed the graphic. (Linking the graphic creates difficulty if you later want to display the presentation as a mobile screen show.) The graphic appears with selection handles on the current page, like the logo shown in the upper-left corner of Figure 18-8. You can move or resize the graphic, as described later in this chapter, or click outside it to deselect it.

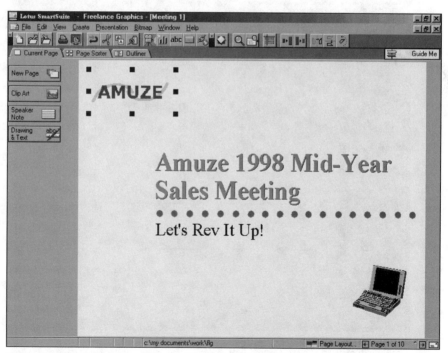

Figure 18-8: When you add a graphic to a presentation page, it appears with selection handles.

Adding a Drawing

If the image you want to include on your slide doesn't exist as clip art or you only need to create a basic line, shape, or arrow to adorn a page, you can open the Drawing & Text Palette and use its tools to draw on the page. This section explains how to use the tools on the Drawing & Text Palette, which you work with in the Current Page view.

To display the Drawing & Text Palette, click the Drawing & Text button on the Current Page view tab, or choose Create ⇨ Drawing/Diagram, select the Make Your Own Diagram with Elements from the Drawing & Text Palette option button, and then click OK. The palette opens below the Drawing & Text button on the Current View tab, as shown in Figure 18-9.

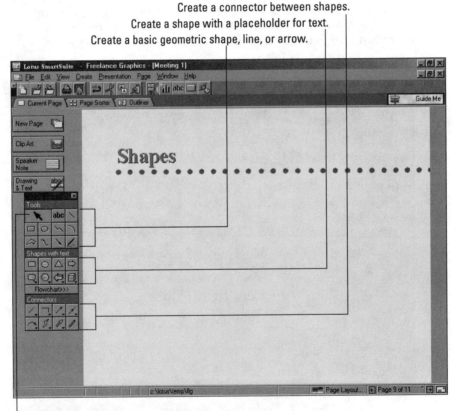

Figure 18-9: Click a tool on the Drawing & Text Palette, then drag on the page to create a shape.

The palette groups its tools in three areas: Tools, Shapes with Text, and Connectors. Use the tools in the Tools area of the palette to draw basic geometric shapes such as rectangles, ovals, and lines; each tool creates the shape pictured on it. Click the upper-left tool, which has a large arrow on it, then click to select an object you've already drawn. The tool with the letters "abc" on it adds a text box, into which you can then add text. The tool with the pencil on it creates a free-form line. To use most of these tools, click the tool, drag on the worksheet to create the shape, then release the mouse button when the shape reaches the size you want. For the angled line, polygon, and curve tools, click to create the first point (or apex), click to create subsequent points, then double-click to finish the shape.

The Shapes with Text area of the palette offers several shapes that include a text placeholder. These are called *text shapes*. You can click one of the top four tools, then drag on the page to draw the shape. Or, you can click one of the tools in the second row or click the Flowchart button to display a pop-up palette of additional options, click the option you want, and then drag on the page to draw the shape. Once you've drawn the shape, click in it to display the insertion point, type the text to include in the shape, and then click OK on the bar that appears above the text block.

You don't have to fill in the text placeholder, so you also can use these tools as an easy way to generate a more complicated shape or polygon, with or without 3-D rendering.

The Connectors area of the palette offers tools you can use to draw attractive lines and arrows between the shapes you draw, so you can create your own, free-form flow charts. Click one of the tools, and if it displays a pop-up palette, click the look you want. Then drag on the page to draw the shape.

Figure 18-10 illustrates shapes added to a presentation page. While this book can't possibly illustrate all the drawing possibilities, keep in mind that you should feel free to experiment with layering and arranging different shapes to achieve the effect you want.

Click this tool . . .   . . . click at every apex, then double-click to finish.

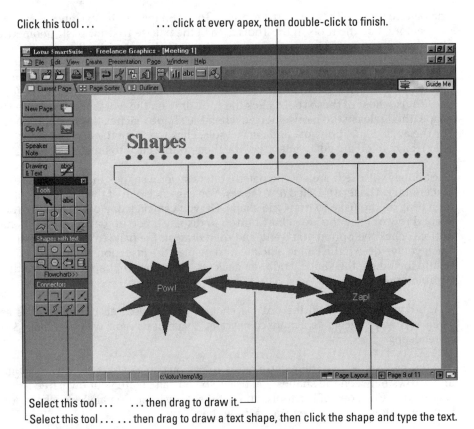

Select this tool . . .   . . . then drag to draw it.
Select this tool . . . . . . then drag to draw a text shape, then click the shape and type the text.

Figure 18-10: These are basic examples of how to draw shapes.

Selecting and Adjusting Objects

You must select a clip art image, graphic, drawing, or text shape object in order to make any changes you'd like to it. You can select the object at any time and redisplay the selection handles by clicking the drawing on the page. To select multiple objects, click the first one, press and hold the Shift key, and click any other objects you want to select.

Once the selection handles appear, you can drag any selection handle to resize the object. As you drag, a dashed outline shows you the changing object dimensions. Release the mouse button when the object reaches the size and shape you want.

Note To resize any Click Here or text block, click it once to display selection handles. Then, drag a selection handle to resize it.

When you select one or more drawings or text shapes, the Drawing or Text Shape menu appears. When you select multiple objects of different types, the Collection menu appears. When you select a clip art object, the Group menu appears (because Freelance clip art objects are built with multiple individually drawn objects); and when you select an inserted graphic, the Bitmap menu appears. No matter what its name, you can open this menu and choose one of the commands on the Object Size submenu to change the size for the selected object(s)

Finally, the SmartIcon bar that appears when you select most objects includes SmartIcons for Make Selected Object Larger, Make Selected Object Smaller, and Make Selected Objects the Same Size, which you can click to change the object sizing by 20% in either direction or to make a number of selected objects the same size.

To move any type of object, select it, point to it, and press and hold the left mouse button. Drag to move the object; as you drag, a dashed outline shows you the changing object position. Release the mouse button when the object reaches the destination you want. If you've selected multiple objects, you can align them all by choosing the Align command from the menu for the selected object(s). In the Align Objects dialog box that appears, choose one of the alignment option buttons (such as Align Right Sides, to align the right sides of all the selected objects), then click OK.

To move, add, or eliminate particular points on a polygon, angled line, or curve, you need to change to Points mode. To do so, choose Edit ⇨ Points Mode (Shift+F6), then select the object to reshape. Markers appear on the various points for the object, and the mouse pointer changes to include a dot within it. Click any point on the shape to select it, then drag it to a new position or choose Edit ⇨ Edit Points ⇨ Delete Points to remove it. Or, choose Edit ⇨ Edit Points ⇨ Add Point, then click the shape to add another point that you can then move. To turn off Points mode, choose Edit ⇨ Points Mode (Shift+F6).

To rotate the selected object, choose the Rotate command from the Menu bar menu (Drawing, Text Shape, or Collection) that appears for the object. The mouse pointer changes to an arc with arrows at each end and a plus sign in the middle. Point to one of the selection handles, drag to rotate the object, and release the mouse button. You also can flip a selected object. Choose the Flip command from the menu, then choose Left-Right or Top-Bottom from the submenu that appears to choose the flip direction.

To delete the selected object, press the Delete key. Freelance removes the selected object from the page.

Replicating Objects

You can copy and paste drawing objects between pages in a presentation. To do so, select the object, choose Edit ➪ Copy (Ctrl+C) or click the Copy to the Clipboard SmartIcon. Display the page to which you want to copy the object, then choose Edit ➪ Paste (Ctrl+V) or click the Paste Clipboard Contents SmartIcon.

If you want to create an exact copy of a selected object on the same page, choose Edit ➪ Replicate (Ctrl+F3). An exact copy of the object appears, so you can drag it to the desired position.

Setting Priority

Setting priority means controlling where a particular object appears when you "stack" or "layer" multiple objects to create a particular effect. For example, you can create a rectangle with a desired pattern or fill, and then layer a clip art image or inserted graphic over it so that the rectangle creates a patterned frame around the graphic. Or, you can layer a number of circles to create a bulls-eye appearance. To control where a selected object appears in the stack, open the menu that appears for the selected object, then choose Priority. In the submenu that appears, choose Bring to Front or Send to Back to move the object to the top or bottom of the stack. To move the object forward or back one layer only, choose Bring Forward One (Shift+F8) or Send Back One (F8).

Grouping and Ungrouping

Grouping a number of objects temporarily "welds" them together into a single object that you can move or resize. For example, if you layer a graphic over a rectangle, you can group them to move them both together, rather than moving them one at a time. To create a group, click the first object, then press and hold the Shift key and click the other objects to group. Choose Collection ➪ Group. From that point, changes you make apply to the whole group, as if it were a single object. If you want to format an individual object from the group, you have to ungroup the object. To do so, click the grouped object, then Choose Group ➪ Ungroup.

Formatting Clip Art, Graphics, and Drawn Objects

You can double-click most clip art images, graphics, or drawings you've added to a presentation page to display an InfoBox with settings for formatting that object. The only object you can't double-click is a text shape; double-clicking one of these displays the text block and insertion point for the shape, rather than the InfoBox. To display the InfoBox for a selected text shape, choose Text Shape ➪ Text Shape Properties. You also can display the InfoBox for other selected objects by choosing the (Object) Properties option from the menu for the selected object. For example, choose Group ➪ Group Properties to display the InfoBox for a selected clip art object. Finally, you can select any object and then click the Change Properties of Selected Object SmartIcon to display the InfoBox.

The InfoBox that appears offers different tabs and formatting options, depending on the type of object you're formatting. All the InfoBoxes include a Screen Show tab, which you use to control the object's display when you play the presentation onscreen. Chapter 19, "Creating and Running an Onscreen Show," explains how to work with the Screen Show tab for graphics and other types of selected objects.

The InfoBox for bitmaps (inserted graphic files) offers only one additional tab, the Image tab. You can increase or decrease the values in the Contrast, Sharpness, and Brightness text boxes to adjust the image's overall appearance. When it's available, you can check the Make Image Transparent check box to enable the slide backdrop to show through the image, so the image blends in on the slide in a bit more pleasing fashion.

Click the Invert Colors check box to reverse the colors in the image (lights to darks and vice versa) to dramatically alter the object's appearance. Likewise, the InfoBox for a selected clip art object (group) typically includes only one additional tab — the Color, Pattern, and Line Style tab. It provides options for adding borders around, and fills in, the grouped drawing objects (not the "box" holding the clip art). In the Border area, choose options from the Style, Width, and Color drop-down lists to adjust the border around all the grouped objects. Under Interior, use the Pattern, Pattern Color, and Background drop-down lists to change the color of the fill within the grouped objects.

Check the Same Color as Border check box if you want the Pattern Color selection to change automatically if you change the Color drop-down list selection under Border. Use the Shadow drop-down list to display a shadow for each grouped object and choose a shadow position.

To add a border around the entire clip art object, draw a rectangle and set its priority to send it to the back. Then, format the rectangle with a transparent pattern and the border style, color, and width you want.

The InfoBox for simple drawing objects also includes the Color, Pattern, and Line Style tab. Depending on what type of object you selected, the options it offers will be identical to those just described for the group, or may vary slightly. For example, if you're formatting a rectangle, the tab offers all the options just described, plus a Rounding drop-down list you can use to specify whether or not the rectangle should have rounded corners. For a selected line object, the tab substitutes Arrowhead settings for Interior settings. You can choose an arrowhead Position and Size, as well as choose what type of Marker to display at each end of the line. For a selected connector you've drawn, the InfoBox also adds an Offset tab. Change the Space Between Connector and Object text box setting to increase or decrease the spacing between each end of the connector and the connector's original end points. (This is less complicated than it sounds. Your setting simply changes the length of the connector.)

The InfoBox for a selected text shape object (or a group that includes text shapes) includes the greatest number of tabs (see Figure 18-11), because it offers settings for adjusting both the object and the text within it. The first three tabs (Font, Attribute, and Color; Alignment; and Bullets) offer settings that affect text, as does the last tab (Named Style). The next section, "Formatting Text," describes how to use these tabs in any InfoBox in which they appear. The Color, Pattern, and Line Style tab works as already described for other objects.

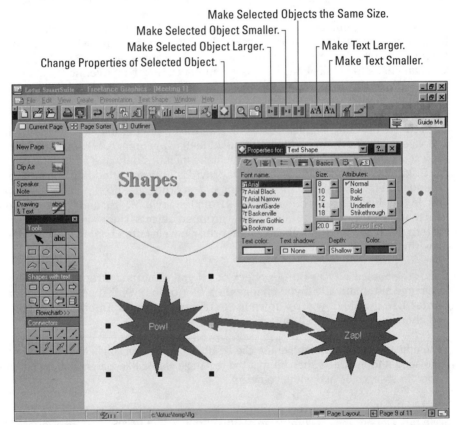

Figure 18-11: The InfoBox for a selected text shape offers a number of tabs for formatting both the object and the text it holds.

The unique tab in the InfoBox for a selected text shape object is the Basics tab, which is best used before you enter the text for the selected shape. On it, click the Shrink Text to Fit Shape text box to ensure that Freelance automatically sets the font size depending on the size of the text shape and the amount of text you type for it. If you want the text shape to include a prompt for typing text (like those you saw in an added diagram), check Display Prompt Text, then edit the prompt in the text box below it.

Note   The Text Shape menu that appears when you select a text shape also includes a number of commands for formatting the shape and its text.

Formatting Text

Text formatting includes the letter design (*font*); *attributes* such as boldface, italics, and colors; and paragraph settings such as alignment and line spacing. The SmartMaster applies default formatting to the text blocks in your presentation. This section shows you how to override the SmartMaster text formatting to choose the text formatting you want.

Changing the Font for the Entire Presentation

Although the rest of this section describes how to make changes to text you've selected on individual pages, fiddling too much with the look of the text on each page destroys the design consistency lent by the SmartMaster. If the font on every page differs from that on the previous page or if you use multiple fonts on every page, the audience can become distracted by the ever-changing look of your presentation. If you want to change text but still maintain some consistency, you can change the font for all the text in the presentation — in every text block on every page, as well as in charts, tables, and organization charts.

To change the font used by the text in your presentation, choose Presentation ➪ Change Typeface Globally. The Change Typeface Globally dialog box appears (see Figure 18-12). Choose the font (typeface) you want to use from the scrolling list of fonts. The preview box below the list changes to display the look of the selected font. If you want to apply the selected font to other elements in the current presentation, check the Data Charts, Tables, and Organization Charts check boxes as needed to apply the new font to all elements of each selected type in the presentation. Click OK to close the dialog box and apply the new font.

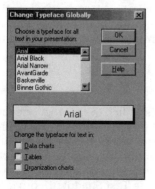

Figure 18-12: Use this dialog box to choose a new font for all the pages in the presentation.

Selecting Text

You can use two different techniques to select text in Freelance Graphics. You can simply click once on any text block to display selection handles around it and make the SmartIcons and other tools for formatting text become available. Bear in mind, though, that when you use this method to select text, the formatting changes you make apply to all the text in the text block. To change only part of the text within a text box, you need to select that text within the text block. To do so, double-click the text block, then drag over the text to select.

You can drag a selection handle for a text block to resize the block. You also can point to the text block border and drag it to a new location on the page.

Choosing Font, Size, and Attributes

Freelance provides a few different methods for changing the font, size, and attributes for the selection. First, you can use the pop-up lists on the status bar; click one of the first six buttons on the status bar to apply a particular type of formatting. Clicking the first button displays a list of fonts. Click a font to close the list and apply the font to the selection. The second button displays a list of font sizes, in *points* (a point is 1/72 of an inch); click a size to apply it and close the list. The third button displays a palette of colors you can apply to the selected text; click a color to apply it and close the list. Click the fourth, fifth, or sixth button to apply or remove **boldface**, *italics*, or <u>underlining</u>. The Text SmartIcon bar also offers icons for applying boldface, italics, or underlining.

The Text menu provides numerous commands for formatting text. Choose Text ➪ Normal (Ctrl+N) to remove all attributes you've previously applied to selected text, returning it to the default formatting defined by the SmartMaster. Choose Text ➪ Attributes to display a submenu with commands for applying attributes and sizing. Bold (Ctrl+B) applies or removes boldface. Italic (Ctrl+I) applies or removes italics. Underline (Ctrl+U) applies or removes underlining. Enlarge Text increases the selection to the next largest font size. Reduce Text reduces the selection to the next smallest font size.

The final way to specify basic text formatting settings for a selection is to use the Font, Attribute, and Color tab in the All Text Levels InfoBox. You can display this InfoBox in a number of ways: click the Change the Properties of the Selected Object SmartIcon, choose Text ➪ Text Properties, choose Text ➪ Font & Color, choose Text ➪ Attributes ➪ Other, or press Alt+Enter. Figure 18-13 shows the All Text Levels InfoBox with the Font, Attribute, and Color tab selected.

Click the desired font for the text in the Font Name list. Click the correct size for the font in the Size list, or enter a precise size in the text box below the Size list. Click your choices in the Attributes list. Clicking the Curved Text button enables you to apply curvature to the text, described later in this section. Use the Text Color drop-down list to change the color of the selected text. Or, to add a shadow for each letter in the selection, choose shadow settings from the Text Shadow, Depth, and Color drop-down lists.

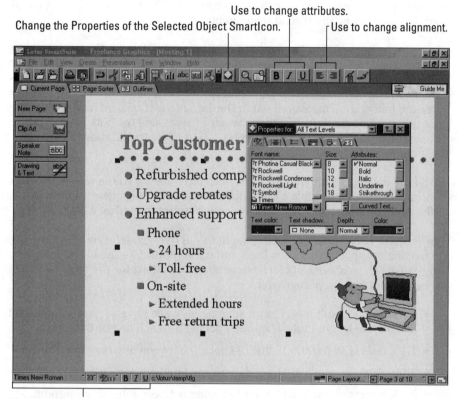

Figure 18-13: The first tab in the All Text Levels InfoBox enables you to apply formatting to selected text blocks or words.

Adjusting Alignment

You can control how the text lines up in relation to the text block boundaries (called *alignment*). You can also control the spacing between each line or paragraph of text. Each time you press Enter within a text block, you create a new paragraph in the text block. The Alignment tab, which is the second tab and appears only in the InfoBox for an entire text block you've selected, includes alignment and spacing settings that apply to all the text in the selected text block.

To change the alignment for the text block, click one of the Alignment buttons in the InfoBox. In the Horizontal row, the first three buttons align the paragraph along the left side of the text block; center text in the text block; and align the text along the right boundary of the text block, respectively. The fourth button *justifies* the text, inserting spacing between letters so the text aligns flush with both the left and right margins. The buttons in the Vertical row align the text at the top, center, or bottom of the text block, respectively. You also can choose an alignment from the

Text ➪ Alignment submenu, which offers the Left (Ctrl+L), Center (Ctrl+E), Right (Ctrl+R), and Full Justify (Ctrl+J) alignments.

When you *indent* text, you're inserting extra spacing between the left boundary of the text block and one or more lines of each paragraph. For example, you often see the first line of each paragraph indented, to cue readers about where each new paragraph starts. To indent only the first line of each paragraph in the text block, enter the indentation measurement in the 1st Line text box. To indent all of the lines in each paragraph from either the left or right side (or both), enter the needed measurement in the Left or Right text box. To remove indentation, change any of the indentation entries to 0.

Note   You can indent and outdent text by 0.5-inch increments if you've selected an individual paragraph of text within a text block. Choose Text ➪ Alignment ➪ Indent to indent the current paragraph, or Text ➪ Alignment ➪ Outdent to outdent it.

The Space Between area of the Alignment tab in the Text InfoBox offers settings for controlling the spacing between lines and paragraphs. Use the Lines or Paragraphs drop-down list, to choose one of several spacing options for the lines within a paragraph or between paragraphs:

✦ **1 (single).** Doesn't insert extra spacing between lines or paragraphs, using the default line height and paragraph spacing for each line or paragraph.

✦ **1.15.** Inserts an extra 0.15 line of spacing between lines or paragraphs.

✦ **2 (double).** Inserts a full line of extra spacing between lines or paragraphs.

✦ **2.15.** Inserts an extra 1.15 line of spacing between lines or paragraphs.

✦ **3.00.** Inserts two extra lines of spacing between lines or paragraphs.

The Wrap Text check box, when checked, automatically wraps text to a new line within the current size for the text block. When you clear the Wrap Text check box, Freelance expands the size of the text block to accommodate longer lines.

Working with Bulleted List Settings

Bullets or numbering set off each item in a list. Using a Click Here block placeholder for a bulleted list saves you quite a bit of time, because you don't have to insert each bullet character individually or worry about setting indents. You can change the bullet style or select numbering instead. Rather than working with the whole text block, double-click the text block to select it, then select each paragraph (bulleted item) that has a bullet for which you'd like to change the appearance. Then, choose Text ➪ Bullets & Numbers to display the Bullets tab of the Text InfoBox.

To change the bullet type or choose numbering instead, open the Style drop-down list under Bullet Attributes, then click a bullet or numbering style in the pop-up palette that appears. (Click None to remove the bullet, or click Clip Art to display the Choose Clip Art for Bullet dialog box, selecting an image to use as the bullet.) Choose a color and size for the bullet or number using the drop-down lists of those names.

Figure 18-14 illustrates a new bullet, with a new size and color as well. If you chose a numbering or lettering style of "bullet" for the selected paragraph(s), enter the number or letter to use for the first numbered item in the Start Number text box.

The adjusted bullet.

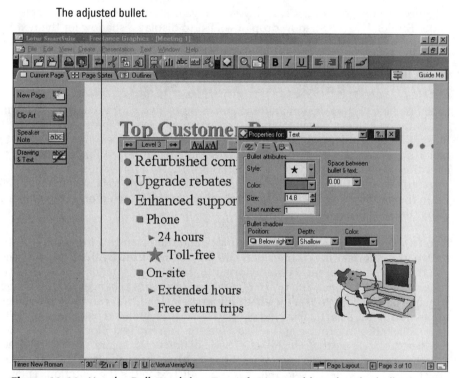

Figure 18-14: Use the Bullets tab in a Text InfoBox to add or alter the bullet for one or more paragraphs.

Further, you can change the spacing between the bullet or number and the text. To do so, choose a spacing measurement from the Space Between Bullet & Text drop-down list. In the Bullet Shadow area of the tab, choose a Position, Depth, and Color option to add a shadow for the bullet for the selected paragraph(s).

Note

You can create your own bulleted or numbered list by formatting the whole text block. Each paragraph within the text block becomes a bulleted or numbered item. To do so, click the text block once to select it, then choose Text ⇨ Bullets & Numbers to display the Bullets tab of the Text InfoBox.

Adding Borders and Patterns

If you click the entire text block to select it and then choose Text ⇨ Text Properties, the fourth tab in the dialog box is the Color, Pattern, and Line Style tab. It provides options for adding a border and fill pattern to the whole text block. In the Border area, choose options from the Style, Width, and Color drop-down lists to adjust the border around the selected text block. Under Interior, use the Pattern, Pattern Color, and Background drop-down lists to change the color of the fill within the text block. Check the Same Color as Border check box if you want the Pattern Color selection to change automatically if you change the Color drop-down list selection under Border. Use the Shadow drop-down list to display a shadow for the text block and choose a shadow position.

Applying, Creating, and Saving Styles

Each Freelance SmartMaster contains one or more styles for each of the following presentation objects: page title, bulleted text, numbered list, presentation title, presentation subtitle, and label text. You can change the style only for a whole text block. To do so, click the text block to select it, choose Text ⇨ Text Properties, then click the Named Style tab (last in the InfoBox). To use a different style for the selected text box, click the style you want in the Text Style for Current Text Block list in the InfoBox. Freelance immediately changes the selected object to display the formatting for the newly selected style.

If you apply a style to a particular text block and then change a formatting setting or two, those formatting settings *override* the settings used by the applied style. If you then apply a different style, the formatting choices you made still override the style. You could go back and try to remove the formatting changes you made, but you may not remember exactly what they were. Instead, you can reset the selection to the default for a particular type of text block (title, bulleted list, and so on). To do so, click the style to use in the Text Style for Current Text Block list, then click the Reset to Style button. The Reset to Style dialog box appears so you can specify exactly what settings to remove from the selection. Under the first step, choose how to reset the style: as Selected Text or as All Text in the Presentation. Then, under the second step, indicate whether to remove only Character Overrides (font and attribute settings) or Level Overrides (changes to bullets and indentation, and so on). Click the option buttons you want, then click OK to finish resetting the text to the style.

Note   You can choose Text ⇨ Named Styles to display commands for working with styles.

You also can save your own styles in Freelance Graphics. First, format the contents of a text box with the settings you'd like to use for the new style. Note that you should apply the formatting you want for each level in the text block, especially if you're creating a style that you'll used for bulleted lists using multiple levels of indentation. Then, select the text block, choose Text ⇨ Text Properties, and click the Create Style button on the Named Style tab. In the Create Text Style dialog box, enter a style name in the top text box, then click OK. The new style becomes available immediately.

To delete a style you've created, click the Manage Style button on the Named Style tab, click the name of the style to delete in the Manage Styles dialog box, then click Delete. If you've applied the style to a text box in your presentation, a dialog box appears to warn you that the style is in use.

Curving Text

You can curve the text in a selected text block. Curving doesn't curve individual letters, but instead aligns the words along a curving or bent baseline. To start the process, choose Text ➪ Curved Text or click the Curved Text button on the first tab of the Text InfoBox. The Curved Text dialog box appears. Scroll through the available curve and angle shapes, click the shape you want to use, then click OK. The dialog box closes, and Freelance curves the text, expanding the text block as needed to accommodate the shaped text. Figure 18-15 shows text curved to a quarter-round shape.

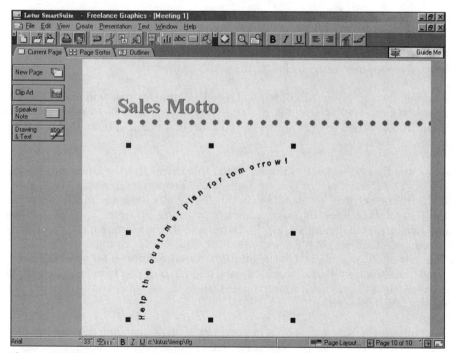

Figure 18-15: Curving text places it along a shaped baseline.

Danger Zone   Don't go overboard with using curved text, because it can be difficult to read. Also, avoid curving the title text for a page. Your best bet is to used curved text to create a small logo or emphasize a short phrase.

Formatting a Table

Just as you can select a text block or drawn object to change its formatting, you can click a table once to select it, displaying the Table menu with various commands for working with tables. Then click again to work with individual cells, rows, or columns in the table.

You can insert and remove rows and columns within the table. First, click a cell in the position where you want to insert a row or column, then click the Insert a Row or Insert a Column SmartIcon, or choose one of the Table ⇨ Insert submenu choices. To delete a row or column, click a cell in the row or column to delete, then click the Delete Rows or Columns SmartIcon, or choose one of the commands on the Table ⇨ Delete submenu. You can click any cell in a table and click the Delete Table SmartIcon.

Table rows increase in height automatically to accommodate the amount of text or the font size you specify for text in the row. To change a column's width, point to the right border for the column until the mouse pointer changes to a double-headed arrow, then drag to change the width of the column.

To apply formatting to the contents of a cell, column, or row, you must select it first. You click a cell to select it, or drag over contiguous cells to select or highlight them. You can then use the status bar and the Text menu options to format the table cell contents.

To format the appearance of the selected table cells, click the Open InfoBox for Selected Cell SmartIcon or choose Table ⇨ Cell Properties to display the Table Cell InfoBox. The settings for most tabs in this dialog box resemble those you've seen in the Text InfoBox. A few differences are worth noting, however. The Color, Pattern, and Line Style tab includes Apply To buttons in the Border area; click a button to specify which side(s) of the selected table cell(s) border changes apply to. The Columns and Rows tab, last in the InfoBox, contains settings for specific Row Height and Column Width measurements, and enables you to enter a Cell Margin measurement to provide for more or less white space between the text and lines defining the table cells.

To change formatting for all cells in the table, such as changing the font for all table cells, use the Table InfoBox. To display that InfoBox, click the table, then click the Change Properties of Selected Object SmartIcon or choose Table ⇨ Table Properties. Again, most of the settings in this InfoBox resemble those you've seen for other elements. The Color Pattern and Line Style tab includes the Apply To buttons (see Figure 18-16), and the InfoBox includes a Columns and Rows tab. It also offers one additional tab, Table Layout, sixth in the InfoBox. Click the button for the Layout choice on this tab, then click a layout choice from the pop-up palette that appears to change basic table formatting (border positions, mostly), with a single selection.

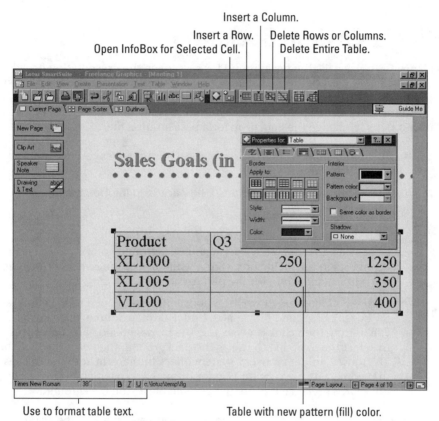

Figure 18-16: Click an Apply To button, unique for tables, to apply border changes to only certain sides of each cell.

Using Fast Format

If you've created a specific look for a text block or text in a table, a drawing object, or a text shape, you can copy the same settings to another object using Fast Format. Fast Format copies the formatting used by the selected object, so that you can apply that formatting to any additional objects you choose. To use Fast Format, select the object using the formatting to copy. Then, open the menu for the selected object: Text, Drawing, Text Shape, or Connector. Open the Fast Format submenu, then click Pick Up Attributes. Fast Format copies the formatting for the selected object. Select the object to copy the formatting to, open its menu, then open the Fast Format submenu and choose Apply Attributes; repeat the process to apply the selected formatting to any other objects you want to change.

You can use Fast Format to copy formatting between dissimilar objects, such as a text shape and connector, or a text block and a text shape.

Creating a Custom Backdrop

Freelance Graphics calls the background for each page the presentation *backdrop*. You can change the presentation backdrop, which overrides the backdrop provided by the SmartMaster for the presentation and changes the appearance for every page (unless you've changed the page layout for a particular type of page). Use the following steps to change the backdrop for a presentation file:

1. Choose Presentation ➪ Edit Backdrop. Freelance changes to Presentation Backdrop Editing view.

2. Choose Backdrop ➪ Page Properties. The Backdrop InfoBox that appears offers only one tab.

3. Use one of these techniques to specify the fill for the page:

   - Choose a pattern, pattern color, and background color from the drop-down lists in the dialog box. (For a white background, choose solid for the pattern and white for the pattern color.)

   - On the Pattern drop-down list, choose Bitmap to open the Use Bitmap for Page Background dialog box. Under Bitmap Source, click the From File button, then click Browse. Use the Browse dialog box that appears to select the .bmp file to use as the background, then click Open. (The \Windows\ folder on every system offers bitmaps in addition to those that come with SmartSuite.) Under Bitmap Arrangement, choose Tile. Click OK. Freelance repeats the graphic file as the background.

If you're not satisfied with the backdrop look (you can't preview the backdrop), repeat Steps 2 and 3 to select another backdrop. To change from one bitmap to another, though, you need to first select a pattern from the Pattern drop-down list, then open the Pattern drop-down list again and click Bitmap to reopen the Use Bitmap for Page Background dialog box.

4. Add any clip art, drawings, or graphics (such as your company logo) that you want to appear on every page of the presentation. Figure 18-17 shows a graphic fill and logo added to a presentation backdrop.

A logo that will appear on every presentation page.

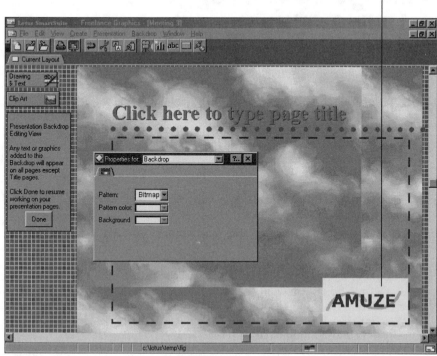

Figure 18-17: The Backdrop InfoBox shows the page using a bitmap file for its fill pattern.

5. Make any changes you want to page title text. These changes will also apply to every page.

6. Click Done. Freelance returns to Current Page view, and the presentation pages immediately display the new backdrop. Be sure to save the presentation to save your changes.

Note

To add a logo to every page in your presentation, you customize the backdrop. Start the process by choosing Presentation ⇨ Add a Logo to Every Page or Presentation ⇨ Edit Backdrop. Then, insert or draw the logo and click Done.

Creating a Custom Page Layout and Editing Click Here Blocks

You can create or edit a page layout so that all elements on all pages using that page layout adopt the sizing, positioning, and other formatting supplied by the page layout. For example, you can create a page layout that includes a table and a graphic, or alter another page layout to change the size of its elements. Working with page layouts involves, to a large degree, creating and changing Click Here blocks. Follow these steps to create a custom page layout in a presentation file:

1. Choose Presentation ⇨ Edit Page Layouts. The Edit Page Layout dialog box appears.

2. Click Create. The Create New Page Layout dialog box appears.

Note

To edit an existing page layout instead of creating a new one, select the page layout to edit and then click Edit in Step 2. From there, edit, add, and delete page elements, then click Done.

3. Enter a Page Name in the text box of that name. Check the Use Backdrop check box if you want the page layout to use the presentation backdrop. Change the Number of Click Here Blocks setting to determine how many Click Here blocks to include below the page title, then click OK. The page appears in Layout Editing view.

4. To change a Click Here block, click it to display selection handles around it. Then, you can drag the selection handles to resize the block, or drag to move the whole block. Or, press Delete to remove the block from the page layout.

5. Choose "Click Here" ⇨ "Click Here" Properties. The InfoBox for the Click Here block appears. You can display this InfoBox for any Click Here block while creating or editing a page layout — whether you're creating or changing it. Click the Basics tab, which is the most important tab in the InfoBox.

6. Use the Type of Block drop-down list to select what type of element Freelance will create (and prompt for) when you click the Click Here block on a page using the new page layout. Figure 18-18 shows a Click Here block that's designated to create a table.

7. If you want to create a custom prompt for the Click Here block, open the Use Standard Prompt drop-down list and click Custom Prompt. Then, click in the Click Here block and edit the prompt text. When you finish, reselect the block itself to redisplay the InfoBox settings for the block.

Note

A few other options on the Basics tab for a Click Here block tell the SmartMaster how to position and format elements created with that Click Here block. You shouldn't change these settings unless you've spent a great deal of time learning how to create page layouts and SmartMasters.

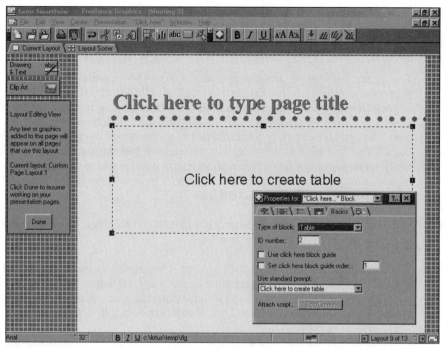

Figure 18-18: Select the type of Click Here block to create from the Type of Block drop-down list.

8. Use any other tabs as needed to set the default formatting for a user's entries into the Click Here block. For example, if you created a text Click Here block and want it to be a bulleted list, use the Bullets tab to specify default bullets. Make sure to alter the Use Standard Prompt option to prompt the user to enter a bulleted list in such a case.

9. Repeat Steps 4–8 to alter other Click Here blocks. To add a new Click Here block anywhere on the layout, choose Create ➪ "Click Here" Block, then drag on the page to create the block.

10. Edit any other aspects of the page design you want. For example, you could include a drawing or graphic on the page layout.

11. Click Done. Freelance returns to the Current Page view. The next time you add a page to the presentation, your new page layout appears among the options. Save the file to save the new page layout.

Saving Your Own SmartMaster Look or Content Topic

The styles, backdrops, and custom page layouts you create are available only in the presentation in which you created them. If you find that you're making a particular change in every presentation you create, such as adding the logo for the backdrop, you can edit the SmartMaster to include the logo in the backdrop. Or, you can add a custom page layout to any SmartMaster file; change its backdrop; or change a page layout, its Click Here block prompts, and default formatting for any of its Click Here blocks. For a content topic SmartMaster, you also can save particular pages of information you use over and over, such as a page with an organization chart of your department, with the content topic.

Note   You can perform a custom SmartSuite installation to install more SmartMasters for Freelance Graphics, Word Pro, and 1-2-3.

You can edit either a SmartMaster look or a SmartMaster content topic, then save your changes to a new file to create a custom SmartMaster. In fact, this is probably wiser than simply saving over the default SmartMasters that Freelance provides. To create a new SmartMaster based on an existing one, follow these steps:

1. Choose File ➪ Open or click the Open an Existing Presentation SmartIcon. The Open dialog box appears.

2. Choose Lotus Freelance SmartMaster Look (MAS) or Lotus Freelance SmartMaster Content (SMC) from the Files of Type list, depending on which type of SmartMaster you want to edit.

3. Navigate to the drive and folder holding the SmartMaster to edit. The default folder for Freelance Graphics SmartMasters is \lotus\smasters\flg.

4. Select the SmartMaster file to open, then click Open. If you opened a SmartMaster look, the SmartMaster appears in Layout Editing view. On each page layout, make the changes you want to the layout, the Click Here blocks, and so on. If you opened a content topic SmartMaster, the title bar serves as perhaps your only clue that you're editing a SmartMaster, because it includes [Editing Content SmartMaster] along with the file name. You also see the Layout menu instead of the Page menu; use it to add new pages of content. You can add new page layouts, click any Click Here block and change the prompt it displays (these prompts supply the "content topic" for the SmartMaster), or make any other design changes you'd like.

5. When you've finished making your changes, choose File ➪ Save As. The Save As dialog box appears.

6. The correct file format should already be selected in the Save as Type drop-down list. Enter a new File Name, use the Save In list to navigate to the location where you'd like to save the file, then click Save.

7. You can then close the SmartMaster file.

Note

You can save any presentation file as a SmartMaster, but in the long run, it may not save much time because you may end up deleting as much text as you actually keep and reuse. However, to save a presentation file as a SmartMaster, choose File ⇨ Save As. Choose Lotus Freelance SmartMaster Look (MAS) or Lotus Freelance SmartMaster Content (SMC) from the Save as Type list. Enter a File Name, specify the location to save to, then click Save.

✦   ✦   ✦

Creating and Running an Onscreen Show

◆   ◆   ◆   ◆

In This Chapter

Changing overall
screen show settings

Choosing a transition
and other screen
show options for
a page

Creating a special
effect with text or
another object

Inserting a movie to
enhance the action

Rehearsing the
screen show

Running and
controlling a
screen show

◆   ◆   ◆   ◆

After you invest your time in developing presentation content, charting your data, and designing the appearance of each page, you're nearly ready for the big payoff — impressing your audience with a stunning onscreen show. In this chapter, you learn how to add the touches that make your screen show an entertaining and informative multimedia experience. You can add transitions and other effects to control how and when pages and other elements appear onscreen. You can include sounds and animations to make the presentation more lively. Rehearse the show to nail down your timing and double-check the results of the effects you've added, and then play the show for your audience.

Setting Up the Screen Show

You can display any Freelance Graphics presentation file onscreen as a *screen show*. When you run the screen show, the Freelance application window itself is hidden, so that the screen displays only a single presentation page at a time, at the largest size possible given the size of your screen. You can tell Freelance when to advance from one page to the next, or you can set up the show to play automatically. You also can specify what type of *transition effect* Freelance uses when it moves from one page to the next. For example, Freelance can wipe the old page off from the left to the right, revealing the new page.

This section explains how to choose screen show effects that apply to every page in the screen show, how to display tools for controlling the screen show, and how to add some basic automation to the screen show. Even though you can adjust the behavior of individual pages and options, the basics you specify here go a long way toward presenting a polished, professional show.

To work with screen show options for the current presentation file, choose Presentation ➪ Set Up Screen Show. The Set Up Screen Show dialog box appears. It includes three tabs of options, described next. Make the choices you want from each tab, click OK to apply the selections to the presentation, and save the presentation file.

Adding Page Effects

The Page Effects tab appears first in the Set Up Screen Show dialog box (see Figure 19-1). At the top of the tab, choose an option button beside Apply To. Click All Existing Pages to use the transition to display all the pages in the presentation or New Pages Only to apply the selected transition only to pages you subsequently add into the presentation. Then, in the Transition list, click to select the transition you want to use for all the pages or new pages, depending on your Apply To selection. Freelance offers more than two dozen different transitions. You need to run or rehearse the show to see how your selected transition looks, but the name for each one does a great job of suggesting how the transition will look.

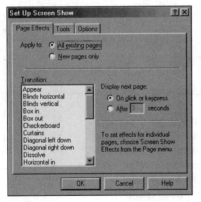

Figure 19-1: Choose transitions between presentation pages on the Page Effects tab of the Set Up Screen Show dialog box.

Note   The Appear transition displays the page all at once. Choose Appear to remove any other transition you've selected.

The option you choose under Display Next Page tells Freelance whether you want to control exactly when each page displays, or whether you want Freelance to display each page automatically when you run the screen show. To retain control of when each page displays, leave the On Click or Keypress option button selected. To set up the screen show to display automatically, click the After (X) Seconds option button. Then, enter the length of time, in seconds, that Freelance should display each page during the screen show in the text box. For example, entering 5 seconds will cause Freelance to display each page for 5 seconds before displaying the next page.

Even if you set the pages to advance after a designated number of seconds, you can still advance to the next page more quickly, if needed, when you run the screen show. The section called "Running Your Screen Show" at the end of the chapter explains how to move between pages in a screen show.

Using Screen Show Tools

Click the Tools tab (see Figure 19-2) in the Set Up Screen Show dialog box to control whether or not you can use certain tools while the screen show runs. Under Control Panel, select the Display Control Panel check box to display the control panel pictured in the dialog box onscreen during the screen show. The control panel offers buttons you can click to display the next or previous page, to jump to a particular page, or to stop the screen show. If you're most comfortable working with the mouse or may need to jump around between the pages in a presentation, rather than proceeding from start to finish, you should display the control panel. After you check the Display Control Panel check box, make a choice from the Position drop-down list to specify where onscreen the control panel appears during the screen show.

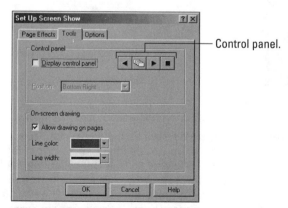

Figure 19-2: Display a control panel for running the screen show or enable onscreen drawing using the options on this tab.

If you want, you can use the mouse to draw onscreen during a presentation. For example, you might want to circle a particular value or underline a key phrase as you speak. When you check the Allow Drawing On Pages check box under On-Screen Drawing, you can use the mouse to draw on any page while running the screen show. Then, choose Line Color and Line Width from the drop-down lists of those names. Keep in mind that if your presentation pages use a dark background with light text, you should choose a light line color, and vice versa.

If you're not an experienced speaker and want to add liveliness to your presentation without using gestures that look too forced, plan on drawing on one or two pages, and rehearse the presentation to practice.

Setting Screen Show Control Options

The final tab in the Set Up Screen Show dialog box, the Options tab (see Figure 19-3), enables you to turn a number of screen show options on or off. Under Cue for Displaying Next Page, check Sound a Tone to have Freelance play a simple tone each time it displays a new page. If you don't want to display the whole control panel but would like to display a button you can click to display the next page, check Display an Arrow.

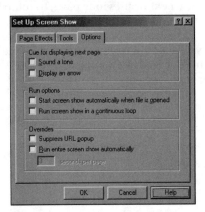

Figure 19-3: Use the Options tab to turn on certain options, such as setting up the screen show to run continuously.

The Run Options settings enable you to automate the screen show. Check Start Screen Show Automatically When File Is Opened to tell Freelance to run the screen show each time you open the presentation file. You could check this option, for example, if you wanted to e-mail the file to a colleague so that the colleague could run the screen show by double-clicking the file in the Windows Explorer or a My Computer window. (To interrupt the show and remove the automatic run feature, press Esc and then click Quit Screen Show. Choose Presentation ➪ Set Up Screen Show, click the Options tab, and remove the check beside Start Screen Show Automatically When File Is Opened. Click OK, then save the file to save the change.)

The Screen Show As a Training Tool

Setting up a screen show to run automatically provides you with a fantastic way to conduct employee orientation or training. Set up Freelance on a computer system in a designated training room, then create the presentation content. After creating and saving the file, set the screen show effects. On the Page Effects tab of the Set Up Screen Show dialog box, click the After (X) Seconds option button under Display Next Page, then enter a value from 5 to 10 in the text box for the option button. Then, on the Options tab, check Run Screen Show in a Continuous Loop under Run Options. Then, you can save the presentation, start the screen show, and let it run. Employees can come and go as needed to review the screen show in the training room. This saves the time needed to both create complicated training schedules and to teach employees how to work with Freelance. Similarly, you can run a presentation automatically at trade shows, open houses, or any other setting in which audience members need the flexibility to come and go.

To set up the screen show to run repeatedly once you start it, check Run Screen Show in a Continuous Loop. Use this feature to create a show that runs unattended, or if you want to use a screen show more as a backdrop than as the focal point for your presentation.

The Overrides area enables you to override two features you specify for particular objects and pages. You should use the Overrides settings to temporarily change how the show runs, rather than going back and undoing your settings for individual pages. In the first case, you can specify that clicking a particular object during a screen show displays a designated Web page; by default, pointing to such an object during the screen show displays the URL (Web address) for the page that displays if you click the object. Checking Suppress URL Popup hides the Web address when you point to the object, although clicking the object still displays the designated Web page. If you set up different display timing for particular pages, you can temporarily change the setup so that all pages display for the same length of time by checking Run Entire Screen Show Automatically, then entering the display time in the Seconds Per Page text box.

Working with Page Transitions

Most screen shows call for something other than a one-size-fits-all approach to transitions and effects. For example, using the same transition over and over gets a bit repetitious. Or, you may want to play a sound when a particular page with important information displays during the screen show, or even prevent a page from displaying during the show. Follow these steps to specify the screen show display effects for a particular page in the presentation:

1. In Current Page view, display the page for which you want to specify screen show effects. In Page Sorter or Outliner view, click the picture for the page to set effects for.

2. Choose Page ➪ Page Properties. The Page InfoBox appears.

3. Click the second tab, the Screen Show tab (see Figure 19-4).

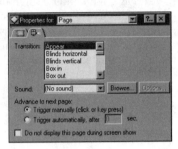

Figure 19-4: The Screen Show tab in the Page InfoBox enables you to set screen show options for the selected page.

4. Choose from the Transition list the transition that Freelance uses to display the selected page.

5. To play a sound when the screen show displays the selected page, click the Browse button beside the Sound text box. (If you've previously navigated to a folder holding sound files, you can open the Sound drop-down list directly and select one of the files.) In the Attaching Sounds To dialog box, use the Look In list to navigate to a folder that holds sound files. From the Files of Type drop-down list, choose whether you want to list Wave Files (WAV) or MIDI Clips (MID). Click a sound in the Look In List, then click Play to preview it. Under Store in Presentation, choose between using An Embedded Copy of the Sound File or creating A Link to the Sound File. Then, click Open to apply the sound to the transition.

Windows comes with a number of WAV and MIDI sound files. Look for them in the \Windows\Media folder.

If you plan to e-mail a presentation file to a colleague or use it as a mobile screen show, do not link the transition sound to its source sound file.

6. (Optional) After you select a sound file, click the Options button to specify additional details about how the sound plays in the Options for (Selected Sound) dialog box. Choose whether the sound should Start Playing During Transition (as the page first appears) or After Transition (after the page fully displays). If you select After Transition, other dialog box options become available (see Figure 19-5). Under Play Sound, choose Play Continuously to play the sound over and over after it starts; only enable this choice for lengthier sound clips. Otherwise, enter the number of times to play the sound in the Play (X) Time(s) text box. If you want the sound to stop when the next automatic event occurs (such as the next page displaying), check the Finish Sound Before Next Automatic Event check box. If the Store in Presentation

options are available, choose to use An Embedded Copy of the Sound File or to create A Link to the Sound File. Click OK when you finish setting sound options.

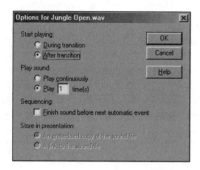

Figure 19-5: If you include a sound with a transition, you can control how and when the sound plays in this Options dialog box.

7. Under Advance to Next Page, choose Trigger Manually (Click or Key Press) to indicate that you or the viewer must specify when to display the page. If you want the screen show to display the selected page for a designated length of time before displaying the next page, select Trigger Automatically, After (X) Sec., and then enter the number of seconds to display the page in the text box for that option.

8. To hide the page so that it does not display at all during the screen show, select Do Not Display This Page During Screen Show. For example, you may have a page with background information that you want to print but not display during the show.

9. Leave the Page InfoBox onscreen. Select each additional page for which you want to alter the screen show settings, then repeat Steps 4–8.

10. Close the Page InfoBox and save the presentation file to save your settings.

Creating Special Effects with Text, Charts, and Graphics

By default, the screen show displays all the elements on a page at once, using any transition you specify. However, you can adjust exactly when and how each particular text block or object (chart, drawing object, or inserted graphic) appears. This gives you the finest level of control over how the screen show plays.

Controlling the Transition

You use the Screen Show tab in the InfoBox for a selected text block or object to determine how the selected object behaves during an onscreen show. Use the following steps to set Screen Show properties for an object on a page:

1. Click the text block or object to select it.

2. Click the Change the Properties of Selected Object SmartIcon. The InfoBox for the selected object appears.

3. Click the Screen Show tab, which is next to last in the dialog box.

4. In the Timing area at the top of the dialog box, choose Display Page First, Then Display Text (or Object, if you selected an object). This option enables the other settings in the dialog box (see Figure 19-6), so that you can control when and how the text block or object appears. You can then choose to display the text block or object On Click (when you click the displayed page) or After (X) Seconds (the designated number of seconds after the page appears). If you choose After (X) Seconds, enter the number of seconds to wait before displaying the text block or object. (You can click the Sequence button to sequence objects on the current page, as described next under "Sequencing Objects."

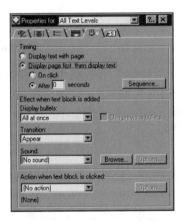

Figure 19-6: Choose to display the text block or object after the page to enable the other dialog box settings for the object.

5. Choose the settings you want under Effect When Text Block Is Added:

- **Display Bullets.** If you selected a text block that holds a bulleted list, you can specify whether the bullets appear All at Once or One at a Time. If you choose One at a Time, the screen show uses a "build effect" to display the bullets one by one. Each bullet will display when you click or after a designated number of seconds, depending on your choices in the Timing area at the top of the dialog box. You can click the Dim Previous Bullets check box to have the screen show dim out bullets it already displayed, highlighting the current bullet.

- **Transition.** Select an effect the screen show should use to display the selected text block or object.

- **Sound.** To play a sound when the screen show displays the selected text block or object, click the Browse button beside the Sound text box. (If you've previously navigated to a folder holding sound files, you can open the Sound drop-down list directly and select one of the files.) In the Attaching Sounds To dialog box, navigate to a folder that holds sound files, and use the Files of Type drop-down list to choose what type of sound to use. Click a sound in the Look In List, then click Play to preview it. Under Store in Presentation, choose whether to use An Embedded Copy of the Sound File or to create A Link to the Sound File. Then, click Open to apply the sound to the transition. After you select a sound file, you can click the Options button to specify additional details about how the sound plays. See Step 6 under "Working with Page Transitions" to learn how to set sound options.

6. You can use the Action When Text Block Is Clicked area of the dialog box to turn the text block or object into a "button" that you can click to perform a particular action. (The mouse pointer changes to a pointing hand when it's over any object set up as a "button.") Open the drop-down list to select what kind of action the screen show will perform when you click the object:

   • **Go to an Internet Location.** Choose this option to display the Go To URL dialog box. In the text box, enter the Web address (URL) for the Internet page you want and click OK. Then, if you click the text block or object while running the screen show, your Web browser launches; your system connects to the Internet, if needed; and the specified page appears.

   • **Go To Another File.** Choose this option to display the Browse dialog box, select another presentation file, and click Open. Then, if you click the text block or object while running the screen show, the designated file opens.

   • **Go To Another Page.** Choose this option to display the Go To Page dialog box (see Figure 19-7), click a choice in the Choose a Page to Jump To list, then click OK. Note that you also can choose to have the "button" Quit Screen Show, Pause/Resume the show, or List the pages in the show so you can click the page you want to display. If you click the text block or object while running the screen show, the designated page appears or the designated action occurs.

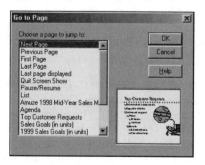

Figure 19-7: Choose a page in this dialog box to set up a "button" that you can click to display the selected page.

- **Run application.** This option displays the Launch Application dialog box. Enter the Application Command Line in the text box of that name, or use the Browse button to locate the startup command for the application you want to run. Click OK. Then, if you click the text block or object while running the screen show, the designated program starts. For example, you could enter the startup command for 1-2-3 (\lotus\123\123w.exe), to launch 1-2-3 so you could open a spreadsheet file to provide more detail about a topic.

- **Play Sound.** This option displays the Play Sound dialog box. Select a sound file, then click Open. Then, when you click the text block or object while running the screen show, the designated sound plays.

- **Play Movie.** This option displays the Play Movie dialog box. Select an Add Impact Movies (AIM) file to run, then click Open. (See the later section titled "Adding a Movie File to a Page" to learn more about movies.) Then, when you click the text block or object while running the screen show, the designated movie file plays.

Note

If you select Play Sound or Play Movie, the Options button becomes active. Click it to designate whether the selection should play continuously or a designated number of times. For a movie file, you also can designate the Speed and onscreen Location at which the movie plays.

7. Leave the object InfoBox open. Select each additional text block or object for which you want to alter the screen show settings, then repeat Steps 4–6.

8. Close the Page InfoBox and save the presentation file in order to save your settings.

Sequencing Objects

If a page includes multiple text blocks and objects (as most pages do), you can control the order in which the objects appear after the page displays. First, select the page that holds the objects to sequence. Then, select the first object to sequence, click the Change Properties of Selected Object SmartIcon, and click the Screen Show tab in the InfoBox that appears. Make sure you click Display Page First, Then Display Object; otherwise, the object won't appear in the list of objects for which you can change the sequence. For each object that you want to sequence, be sure to select Display Page First, Then Display Object on the Screen Show tab of the object's InfoBox.

Choose Presentation ⇨ Sequence Objects on Page, or click the Sequence button on the Screen Show tab in the InfoBox for a selected object. The Screen Show Sequence Overview dialog box appears (see Figure 19-8). The objects display in the order shown in the Sequence list at the left. To change the display order for an object, drag it to a new position in the Sequence list. When you click an object in that list, a preview for the object appears at the right of the dialog box. The Screen Show settings for the selected object appear in the Current Object area at the bottom of the dialog box. By default, Freelance names each text block or object based on the order in which you added it to the page. You can click in the Object Name text box and edit the name for the selected object, if needed. After you've made all the sequence changes you want, click OK to close the dialog box.

The object's Screen Show properties.

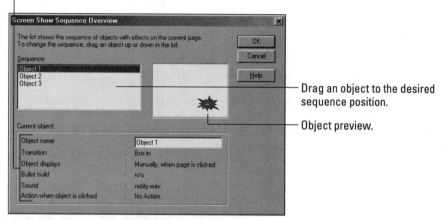

Drag an object to the desired sequence position.

Object preview.

Figure 19-8: You can control the order in which objects on a page appear using this dialog box.

Adding a Movie File to a Page

Freelance Graphics enables you to add a movie file to any page in a presentation. Then, when you run the presentation as a screen show and display the page holding the movie, the movie file runs using the timing you designate.

Freelance Graphics also enables you to add different types of movie files. Generally speaking, *movie files* include both cartoon-like animations and video clips. Animations are saved in the Add Impact Movies (AIM) and Animation Works Movies (AWM) formats, and video clips are saved in the Windows Movie (AVI) and QuickTime Movies (MOV) formats. For example, your company might have an animated logo file. Or, you may have digitized a video about how a product works. Adding a movie to the presentation creates motion and interest.

Movie files, especially digitized video, can be very large. If you intend to e-mail a presentation file or have an older system with less than 16M of RAM, you should limit the number of movie files you add to your presentation.

Use the following steps to add a movie file to the current page of the presentation:

1. Choose Create ➪ Add Movie. The Add a Movie dialog box appears.

2. From the Files of Type drop-down list, choose which type of movie file to insert.

3. Use the Look In list to navigate to the disk and folder that holds the movie file to insert. (If you left the default file type, Add Impact Movies (AIM) selected, you should see the movie files stored in Freelance's default movie folder, \lotus\flg\media.)

4. Click the name of the movie file you want, and click the Preview button to see how it looks, if needed.

5. Under Store in Presentation options, choose to use An Embedded Copy of the Movie File or to create A Link to the Movie File.

6. Click Open. Freelance inserts the movie file on the page, displaying it as an icon in the Current Page view.

Once the movie icon appears on a presentation page, you can click the Play a Movie SmartIcon to play the movie at any time. You can click the icon for the movie once to select it. Then, click the Change Properties of Selected Object SmartIcon to display the InfoBox for the movie (see Figure 19-9).

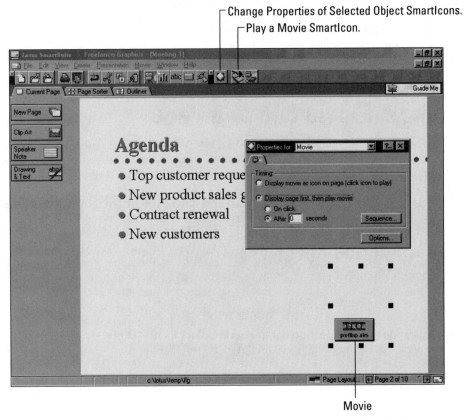

Figure 19-9: When you add a movie file to a page, it appears as an icon in the Current Page view, but plays when you run the screen show.

Under Timing, click Display Movie as Icon On Page if you don't want the movie to appear or play on its own during the screen show, but instead want to click the movie icon to play the movie. If you instead select Display Page First, Then Movie, you don't see any icon for the movie during the screen show.

You can choose On Click to specify that you have to click on the page to start the movie, or After (X) Seconds (enter the number of seconds in the text box) to have the movie play automatically after the designated number of seconds.

Click the Options button to display an Options For dialog box that enables you to choose whether the movie should Play Continuously or Play (X) Time(s). Check Hold Last Frame to have the screen show display the last frame of the movie when it finishes playing. Also choose a Speed for the movie. Then click OK to close the Options For dialog box. You also can click the Sequence button to change the sequence for the movie and the other objects on the page, as described at the end of the previous section.

Rehearsing the Show

In addition to the other benefits of Freelance extolled throughout this part of the book, the program enables you to practice for your big moment at the podium. You can *rehearse* the screen show to see how long you really spend discussing each page and to gauge the overall length of your presentation. Not only does this enable you to practice your delivery, but it also gives you the opportunity to go back and set up pages to advance automatically at intervals you specify so that you can automate the show (totally) and concentrate on your delivery.

To rehearse the show, choose Presentation ➪ Rehearse ➪ Start. (If you've previously rehearsed, a Warning dialog box appears. Leave Clear Page Times selected if you weren't satisfied with a previous rehearsal, and click OK to begin a new rehearsal. If you opt to Keep Page Times, then you need to click the Continue button when the rehearse screen appears.) The rehearse screen appears, as shown in Figure 19-10.

Go through the presentation, clicking the mouse to advance through the pages as needed. Click the Speaker Note button to display the window for adding a speaker note for the page. Click Pause to pause the rehearsal; after you click Pause, it toggles to the Continue button, so you can click Continue to restart the rehearsal. The rehearse screen displays how much time you've spent on the current page and the whole presentation. If you need to restart the rehearsal, click the Restart button next to the current page time at the bottom left of the rehearse screen. When you've finished the rehearsal, click the Done button.

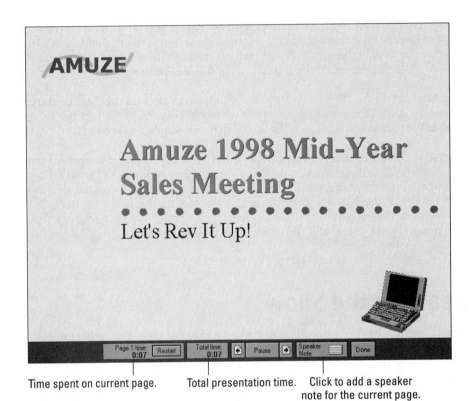

Time spent on current page.   Total presentation time.   Click to add a speaker
note for the current page.

Figure 19-10: Use this screen to track how much time you need to discuss each page in your presentation.

After you click the Done button, the Rehearse Summary dialog box appears (see Figure 19-11) to show you how much time you spent discussing each page and the total duration of your presentation. Click OK to close the Rehearse Summary dialog box. You can redisplay it at any time by choosing Presentation ➪ Rehearse ➪ Summary.

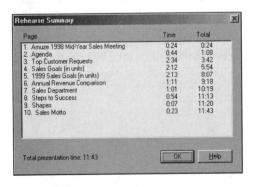

Figure 19-11: After you finish rehearsing, Freelance displays statistics about your performance.

Note

After you've set all the screen show options you need and have rehearsed the show, make sure you save the presentation file to save all the settings and rehearsal information.

Running Your Screen Show

When the big moment arrives, you can use a few different methods to start the screen show and control how the pages progress onscreen.

Start out by opening the presentation file to display as an onscreen show. Choose Presentation ➪ Run Screen Show ➪ From Beginning (Alt+F10) or click the Run Screen Show from Beginning SmartIcon. The elements of the Freelance Graphics window disappear from the screen, and the first page of the screen show appears at full-screen size.

Hot Stuff

If you want to start the show from a particular page, select that page in the current view. Then choose Presentation ➪ Run Screen Show ➪ From Current Page (Alt+F11).

From there, you can use a few different techniques to control the show (unless you set it up to run automatically). Click a blank area of the page with the mouse or press Enter or PgDn to display the next page or object. (PgUp displays the previous page or object.) Keep in mind that if a page includes multiple objects to display, you need to click the mouse or press a key multiple times to display all the page objects. For example, Figure 19-12 shows a bulleted list being "built" onscreen.

If you displayed the control panel for the presentation, you can click the control panel button with a right-pointing arrow to display the next page, the button with a left-pointing arrow to display the previous page, or the button with the box to stop the screen show.

Finally, right-click the current page to display a shortcut menu and choose the Next or Previous command to display a different page. (Note: You can display or hide the control panel by right-clicking the page, clicking the Control Panel command, and then clicking an option in the shortcut menu that appears.)

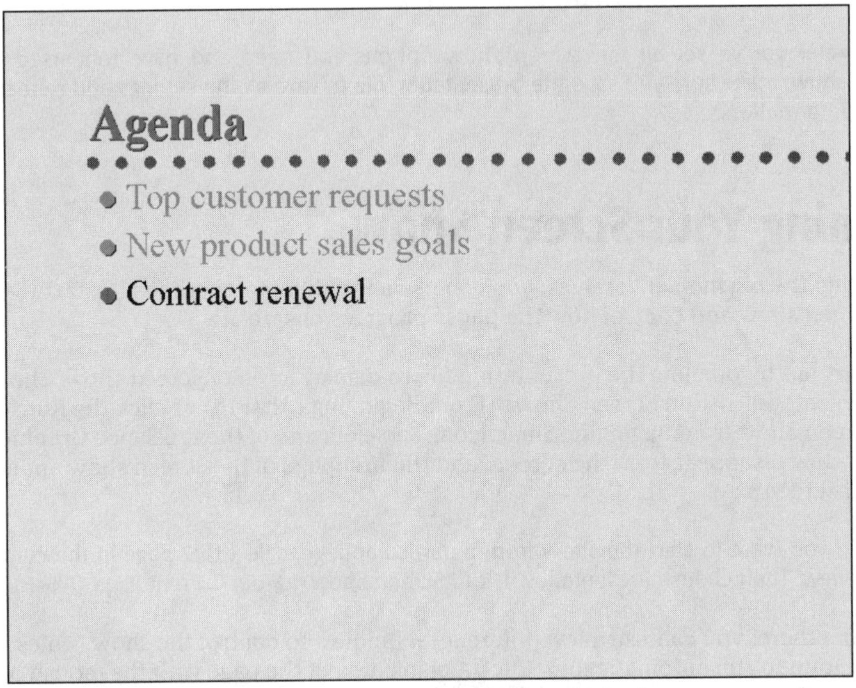

Figure 19-12: Click or press Enter or PgDn to display objects in sequence on a page.

To jump to a particular page in the show, right-click the current page and click Go To or click the Go To button (it has stacked pages) on the screen show Control Panel. The Screen Show Pages dialog box appears (see Figure 19-13). Click the page you want in the Page to Go To list, then click Go To Page. Alternately, you can just click Resume Screen Show to return to the current page, or Quit Screen Show to end the screen show and resume your work in Freelance.

You also can end the screen show by pressing Esc, or by right-clicking and then clicking End Screen Show in the shortcut menu.

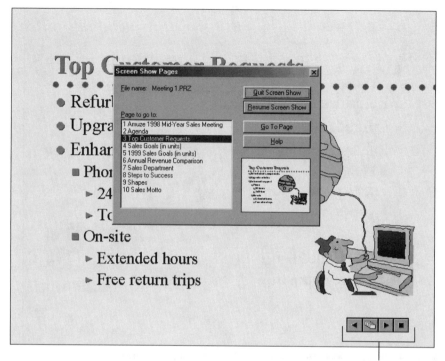

Screen Show control panel.

Figure 19-13: This dialog box lists the presentation pages, so you can jump to any page you'd like.

Drawing During the Show

As noted earlier, you can draw on the presentation to annotate a page and emphasize your comments. If you didn't turn on drawing when you specified your settings for the screen show, you can right-click the current page, then click Allow Drawing in the shortcut menu. When drawing is enabled, simply press the right mouse button and then draw on the screen, as shown in Figure 19-14. The changes you make don't stay permanently on the page; they just appear as long as the current page displays during the screen show.

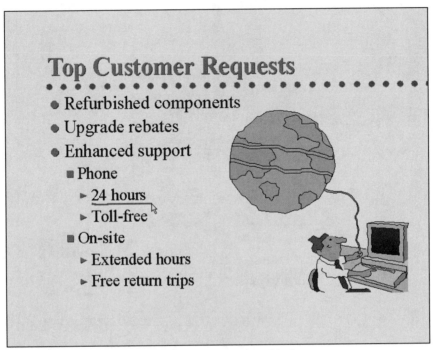

Figure 19-14: You can draw on the current page with the mouse.

Mobile Screen Show Player

The Mobile Screen Show Player enables you and other users to run a screen show file without installing the Freelance Graphics program. The Mobile Screen Show Player doesn't install by default. You need to perform a custom installation as described in Appendix A, "Installing SmartSuite," to install the Mobile Screen Show Player. The Mobile Screen Show Player is actually a single file named Mobiless.exe that SmartSuite installs to the \lotus\flg folder on your hard disk.

Provide a copy of Mobiless.exe to anyone who needs to run a presentation without the full Freelance program. You or any user can install the Mobile Screen Show Player by double-clicking the Mobiless.exe file in any Windows Explorer or My Computer window, or by using Start ➪ Run to run the exe file. The Mobile Screen Show Installation dialog box appears. Specify the folder in which to install the player and screen show file in the Install To text box, and then click OK. The Add a Presentation dialog box appears. Once Mobile Screen Show player is installed, you (or another user) can reopen it and the Add a Presentation dialog box by choosing Start ➪ Programs ➪ Lotus SmartSuite ➪ Freelance Mobile Screen Show Player or by double-clicking the Ltmobn11.exe file in the folder to which you installed the Mobile Screen Show Player (\lotus\compnent\player by default).

In the Add a Presentation dialog box, select the presentation file to display as a self-running show, then click Open. Then, click the file in the list of files in the Lotus Mobile Screen Show Player dialog box (see Figure 19-15), and click Run Show. You can then use the techniques described earlier in this section to move through the pages and end the show.

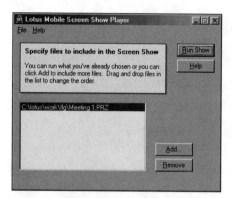

Figure 19-15: Use the Lotus Mobile Screen Show Player dialog box to display a presentation as an onscreen show without installing Freelance.

Do not link any sounds, movies, or graphics files you add to a presentation to their source files if you plan to distribute a presentation to be run on another computer or as a Mobile Screen Show. Instead, embed a copy of the sound, movie, or graphic to ensure that it plays correctly in your screen show.

Equipment Considerations

It's increasingly common to play screen shows by hooking up a notebook or desktop computer to an LCD Projector. Prices for these units start at about $2,000, so you might check out renting one to hook up your system to, especially if you'll be traveling to another city to give your presentation. (Check out sites on the Web like www.ysite.com/sunset/service.htm to find out about renting such equipment.) However, a word of caution is in order.

Always make sure you display your screen show on the actual equipment you'll be using. This precaution can save you time and trouble in a couple of ways. It ensures that the equipment works and that you can work effectively with it. It also ensures that your audience will be able to see all elements of your screen show, clearly and easily. If the screen show looks too dark or murky, you can go back and change the look to make the show more readable and attractive.

✦　　　✦　　　✦

Generating Printouts, Handouts, and Notes

Once you expend the effort to create a presentation, you'll probably use the information it contains in a variety of ways and on a variety of occasions. You can display the presentation as a screen show when you need to share and discuss it with multiple colleagues. Or, you can print the presentation so that you and your audience have a record of the presentation or notes about it. This chapter covers just that topic—creating printed output of your presentation and choosing options to control the appearance of that printout.

Adding and Editing Speaker Notes for a Page

Chapter 16, "Developing the Presentation Content," discussed creating page content. That chapter also advised you to keep the content of individual presentation pages as streamlined as possible to avoid overwhelming or confusing your audience members. But if you're the one discussing the pages in a presentation, a modest number of bulleted points doesn't give you much to go on. Unless you're delivering a talk you've given many times before, chances are good you need to have some notes elaborating on the background information, statistics, and details supporting each point you list on a presentation page. To capture such information so that you can refer to it during your presentation, add a *speaker note* to each page for which you need such information at hand.

Adding and Formatting Speaker Notes

Use the following steps to add and format speaker notes:

1. In any view, select the page for which you want to add a speaker note.
2. Choose Page ➪ Create Speaker Note or click the Add or Edit Speaker Notes SmartIcon. In Current Page view, you also can right-click the page and click Create Speaker Note in the submenu. The Speaker Note dialog box for that page appears.
3. Type your notes in the scrolling text area in the dialog box. Press Enter to start each new paragraph. By default, Freelance formats all speaker note text in a 20-point font, including a bulleted point for each paragraph. Figure 20-1 shows a couple of bulleted points entered into the Speaker Note dialog box for a slide.

Add or Edit Speaker Notes SmartIcon.

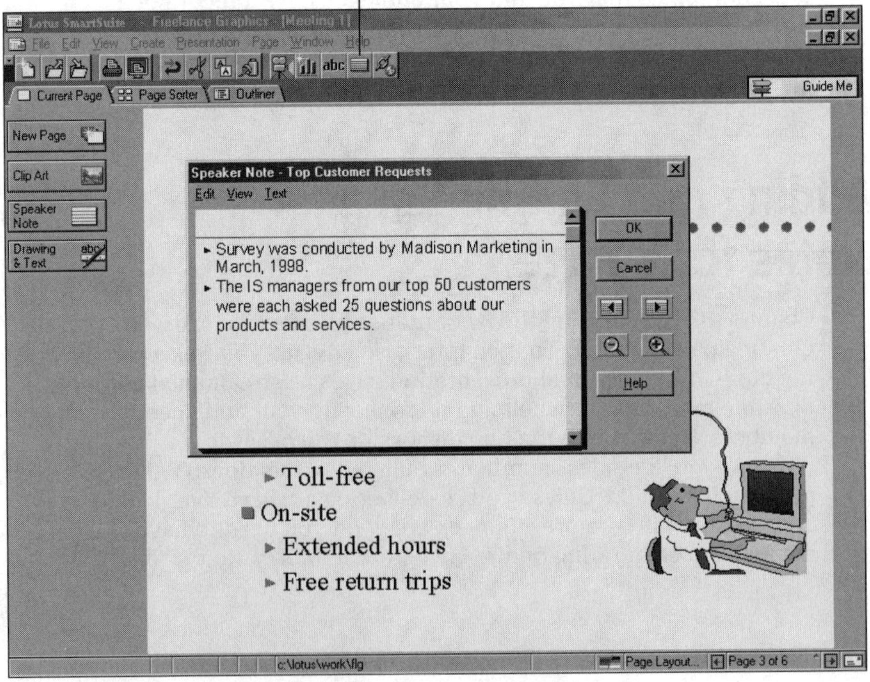

Figure 20-1: Create a speaker note to make available information you may need to share with your audience as you give your presentation.

4. You can drag over text in the text area, and then change its formatting using the commands on the Text menu of the Speaker Note dialog box:

- **Attributes.** Choose a command from this submenu to apply the Bold (Ctrl+B), Italic (Ctrl+I), or Underline (Ctrl+U) attribute to the selection.

- **Normal (Ctrl+N).** Removes attributes you've previously applied.

- **Text Properties (or Font or Bullets & Numbers).** Each of these commands displays the Text Properties for Speaker Note dialog box. Use the Font, Size, and Attributes lists to choose the new formatting you want for the text. Open the Bullet drop-down list to choose another bullet for the selected paragraph or paragraphs. A check mark appears beside the currently selected bullet. Click the alternate bullet you want, as shown in Figure 20-2. Click None to remove bullets, or one of the number or letter options to itemize the selected paragraphs. Check the Apply to All Speaker Notes check box if you want the new formatting selections to be applied to all speaker notes in the current presentation and any speaker notes you add from then on in other presentations. (Clear this check box at a later time if you want to revert to the note formatting settings determined by the SmartMaster.) Click OK to close the dialog box.

- **Reset to Default.** Removes any formatting you've applied to the selection that isn't part of the default style or the styling you've created in the Text Properties for Speaker Note dialog box.

- **Apply Style to All Speaker Notes.** Functions just like the Apply to All Speaker Notes check box in the Text Properties for Speaker Note dialog box. Enable this check box to apply the formatting for the current selection to all other speaker notes.

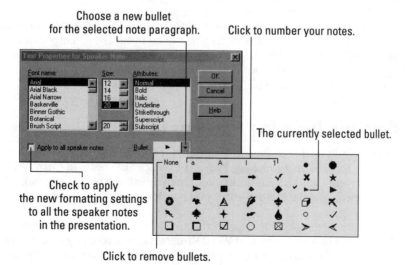

Figure 20-2: The formatting settings you choose here apply to the selected text in the Speaker Note dialog box.

5. You can zoom in or out on the speaker notes to inspect the results of your formatting. Open the View menu, and choose one of its commands for zooming. Zoom to Full Page displays the note at 100% size, the size it prints at. Zoom to Custom displays a submenu listing zoom percentages; click a percentage to zoom to that percentage. The Zoom submenu enables you to zoom in or out by 25%. You also can click one of the zooming buttons at the right side of the Speaker Note dialog box (see Figure 20-3).

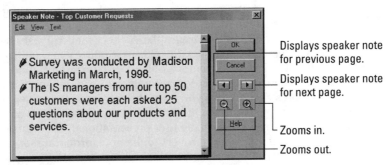

Figure 20-3: The text in this speaker note is zoomed to Full-Page (100%) size, the size it will print at.

6. To create each subsequent speaker note, choose View ➪ Next or click the button at the right side of the dialog box that displays the next note. Repeat Steps 3–5 to create each new note.

7. Click OK to close the Speaker Note dialog box.

After you finish adding a speaker note to a page in the presentation, the Add or Edit Speaker Notes SmartIcon (which looks like a lined notecard) changes to the Open Speaker Note SmartIcon (which looks like a lined notecard with the letters **abc**). In the Page Sorter view and the Outliner view, a small, lined notecard icon appears beside the title of every page for which you've added a speaker note.

Editing and Deleting Speaker Notes

If you want to edit or delete the speaker note for the current page, click the Open Speaker Note SmartIcon, or choose Page ➪ Open Speaker note. In Current Page view, you also can right-click the page and click Open Speaker Note. The Speaker Note dialog box opens, displaying the notes you previously entered for the selected page.

To move the insertion point around in the speaker note text, use the same techniques used in text boxes and Word Pro. Press an arrow key to move one character in any direction. Ctrl plus left arrow or right arrow moves the insertion point one word left or right. Press PgDn and PgUp to move down and up in the text. Or, click to position the insertion point at any location you want.

Editing works similarly, too. Press Backspace to delete the character to the left of the insertion point, and Delete to delete the character to the right of the insertion point. If you select text by dragging over it, you can press Backspace or Delete to delete the whole selection, or type to replace it.

Press the Insert key to toggle between Insert mode (in which text to the right of text you type moves to the right to make room) and Overtype mode (in which text you type replaces text to the right).

You can cut the selection with Edit ➪ Cut (Ctrl+X) on the Speaker Note dialog box menu bar, or copy the selection with Edit ➪ Copy (Ctrl+C). Position the insertion point in another location, then choose Edit ➪ Paste to insert the cut or copied text at a new location. When you finish making the changes you want to the note text, you can edit the speaker note for the next or previous page (choose View ➪ Previous, View ➪ Next, or one of the view buttons). Click OK when you finish using the Speaker Note dialog box.

You also can delete the entire speaker note for any page. To do so, display the page that has the speaker note to delete, then choose Page ➪ Delete Speaker Note. In Current Page view, you can right-click the page and click Delete Speaker Note. The Delete Speaker Note dialog box appears (see Figure 20-4). Choose the option button that specifies whether to delete the notes for the Selected Page(s) or All Pages, then click OK to delete the speaker notes.

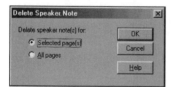

Figure 20-4: You can delete speaker notes for a single page or all pages in the presentation.

You can select multiple pages in Page Sorter view, then delete the speaker notes for all those pages. Click the first page, then press and hold Shift and click additional pages. Then choose Page ➪ Delete Speaker Note, click the Selected Page(s) option button, and click OK.

Using Page Setup

The Page Setup dialog box enables you to change some aspects of the page layout for a presentation prior to printing. You can use the Page Setup dialog box to add a header or a footer to print on all the presentation pages. The dialog box also enables you to choose the orientation — portrait or landscape — for the printout. To display the Page Setup dialog box, choose File ➪ Page Setup.

You also can click the Page Setup button in the Print dialog box to display the Page Setup dialog box.

Creating a Header or Footer

A *header* prints along the top of each page, and a *footer* prints along the bottom. The header or footer can number the printed pages, identify the file name for the presentation, display the printout date and time, or include any other information audience members may need to know about the presentation, such as its title or your name and contact information. Use the Headers & Footers area of the Page Setup dialog box to create and format the header or footer information you enter.

The Headers & Footers area includes a row of three text boxes each (Left, Right, and Center) for the header or footer. Enter the header or footer text in the appropriate text box to specify where that text aligns — Left to left-align it, and so on. Click in the text box you want, and type your entry. You can press Enter in any text box to wrap text to the next line. You also can insert a formatted field to have Freelance print the Page number, File Name, Date, or Time in the header or footer. Click the icon that inserts the formatted field you want. Figure 20-5 shows some typed text and formatted fields entered in a footer.

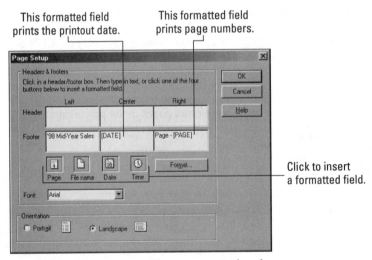

Figure 20-5: The text area where you enter header or footer information determines its alignment.

To choose a printout format for a Date or Time formatted field you've inserted, click the Format button beside the icons for the formatted fields to display the Format dialog box (see Figure 20-6). Finally, if you want the header or footer to print in another font, choose the Font to use from the Font drop-down list.

Note You need to save your document after adding a header or footer and closing the Page Setup dialog box to ensure that Freelance saves the header or footer with the document.

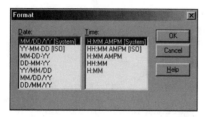

Figure 20-6: Click an option in the Date or Time list to specify formatting for a date or time you've included in a header or footer.

Choosing the Page Orientation

The bottom section of the Page Setup dialog box, Orientation, offers two option buttons. Choosing the Portrait option button tells Freelance to display and print each page so it's taller than it is wide—called *portrait* orientation. The Landscape option button instead selects *landscape* orientation, in which each page is wider than it is tall. In most cases, you don't need to change the page orientation for your presentation. The SmartMaster chooses the correct orientation for you.

If you use the Page Setup dialog box to change the orientation of the pages to an orientation other than the default for the presentation, and then try to change it back, you may find that some of the default formatting changes. For example, Freelance might apply a smaller font to each page title. You can't undo this change. So, after you change the orientation the first time, close the file without saving it and then reopen it to restore its original orientation.

Previewing a Page Printout

You may have designed your presentation to display it onscreen, but that doesn't mean you'll never print it out. Your presentation pages may look very different in hard copy form, especially if you're printing to a black-and-white printer; if you used very similar colors for text and a background or overlapping objects, they could unexpectedly blend into a big gray blob on the printout. Or, a header or footer you've added may overlap with existing text or a graphic on the presentation. To check for such problems before you zip through a tree's worth of paper, you should preview the printout.

You can only preview full-page printouts. You can't preview the handout, speaker notes, or audience notes printout formats discussed later in this chapter.

To preview the printout, you can start from any view in Freelance. Choose File ➪ Print Preview or click the Preview SmartIcon shown in Figure 20-7. In the Print Preview dialog box that appears, choose an option button to specify whether you want to begin with previewing the First Page or the Current Page of the presentation. Click OK to close the dialog box and begin the preview.

Print SmartIcon.   Print Preview SmartIcon.

Figure 20-7: You can click the Print Preview SmartIcon to review how each printed page appears.

As shown in Figure 20-8, one page appears onscreen at a time. You can use the Previous and Next buttons to display other pages in the preview. If you're satisfied with all the pages, you can click the Print button to display the Print dialog box and print out the document, as described in the next section. If you don't want to print immediately or want to make some changes before printing, click the Quit button to return to the view you were previously using.

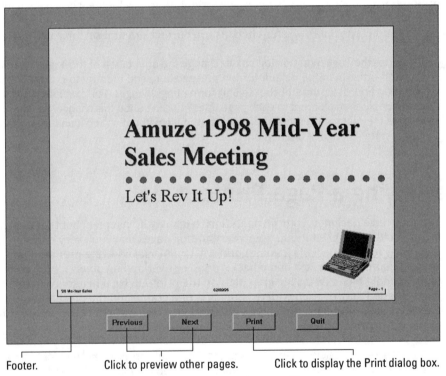

Footer.   Click to preview other pages.   Click to display the Print dialog box.

Figure 20-8: The preview shows how a printed page will appear.

You also can click the Preview button in the Print dialog box to preview the presentation page printouts.

Setting Print Options and Printing

After you've created speaker notes, added a header or footer, and have previewed your printout, you can use the Print dialog box to set remaining print options and print one or more pages in the presentation. Use the following steps to print the current presentation:

1. Save the presentation. If you want to print a particular page, select that page in the view you're using.

2. Choose File ➪ Print or click the Print SmartIcon. The Print dialog box appears (see Figure 20-9).

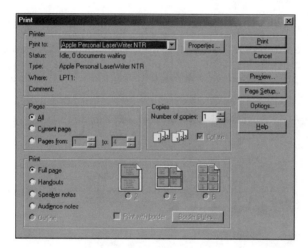

Figure 20-9: Select a printer and pages to print in this dialog box.

3. If you've installed more than one printer under Windows and need to select the proper one to use, open the Print To drop-down list in the Printer area of the dialog box, then click the printer to use. If you want to print the file to a disk file that you can later send to the printer, click to check Print to File.

4. If you need to change any of the settings for the printer, click the Properties button. The Properties dialog box for the selected printer appears; this dialog box offers unique options for each type of printer, but you may be able to specify such settings as how many pages print on each sheet of paper, paper size, the size of unprintable areas at the edge of the page, and more. Click OK after you've finished setting printer properties.

5. In the Pages area of the dialog box, choose which pages in the document to print. Choose All to print the whole document. Choose Current Page to print only the page that holds the insertion point. To print a selected range of pages in the document, choose the Pages option button, then enter the first page in the range to print in the From text box and the last page in the range to print in the To text box.

6. In the Copies area of the dialog box, use the Number of Copies text box to indicate how many copies of the document should print. To group all the printed copies for each page (rather than printing the entire first copy, printing the entire second copy, and so on), select the Collate check box.

7. To specify what type of pages to print, choose one of the following option buttons in the Print area of the Print dialog box:

   • **Full Page.** Prints each presentation page as a full-size page, as if it were a single slide.

   • **Handouts.** Prints pictures of two, four, or six presentation pages per printed page. You can give printed handouts to your audience at the conclusion of your presentation, so audience members have a hard copy of the presentation contents.

   • **Speaker Notes.** Prints a picture of one, two, or three presentation pages per printed page, and also prints the speaker notes you entered for each page. As the samples in Figure 20-10 show, the speaker notes print below the page picture or beside it. Print speaker notes pages before you deliver the presentation, so you can use your notes at that time.

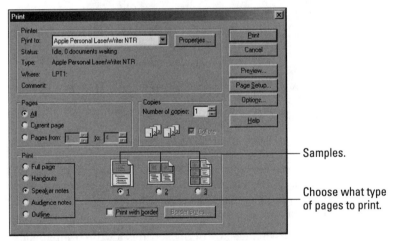

Figure 20-10: Specify what type of printed pages you want in the Print dialog box.

   • **Audience Notes.** Prints a picture of one, two, or three presentation pages per printed page, and also includes an area for audience members to make their own notes about each page. Distribute audience notes pages before your presentation, so audience members can follow along and record any notes they wish about each page.

- **Outline.** If you display the Print dialog box from the Outliner view, the Outline option button becomes enabled under Print. Click the Outline option if you want to print the outline for one or more presentation pages, without graphics. Note that this option disables the other options in the Print area of the Print dialog box.

8. If you choose Handouts, Speaker Notes, or Audience Notes in Step 6, choose how many presentation pages to include per printed page by clicking the option button for the appropriate number of pages. Each option button appears below the sample showing how the pages appear in the printout.

9. If you choose Handouts, Speaker Notes, or Audience Notes in Step 6, you can add a border around each page in the printout. To do so, check the Print with Border check box, then click the Border Styles button beside it. In the Select Print Border Style dialog box, select the border style to use (see Figure 20-11), and then click OK.

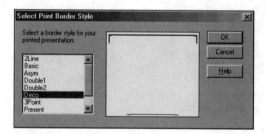

Figure 20-11: Select a border to add to printed notes or handouts pages in this dialog box.

10. Click the Options button in the Print dialog box to display the Options dialog box (see Figure 20-12), which enables you to control the print quality and speed, to some degree. Check the Adjust Output Library for Printing option to help your printer better handle the color choices used in the presentation. If enabling this setting makes the printout worse, turn this check box off. Check Print Graduated Fills as Solids if your printer is taking too long or is crashing when you try to print a presentation with many graduated fills and objects. Graduations consume a lot of printer memory, so most printers print faster if you opt to print the graduations as solid. For fastest printing, check Print with Blank Background (No Look). This prints without the SmartMaster background, for a clean-looking, fast printout. Make sure the presentation text uses a dark enough color to print without its background. After you make your selections in the Options dialog box, click OK to close it and apply your settings.

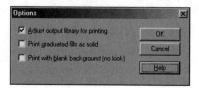

Figure 20-12: The options shown here help you improve or speed up printing.

11. Click Print to finish the print job and send the document to the printer.

12. If you're printing speaker notes pages and your notes are too lengthy to fit on one or more pages of the printout, the Print – Speaker Notes dialog box appears (see Figure 20-13). This dialog box asks whether you want to *scale* the font size of the too-large speaker notes to make them fit on the printout. Choose Scale All Speaker Notes Uniformly to scale the size of all speaker notes you've added into the presentation. Choose Scale Oversized Pages Only to have Freelance fix only those speaker notes that are too large, leaving other speaker notes with the size you originally specified. Choose Don't Scale Any Pages if you don't want to scale the speaker notes. Click Print after making your selection to finish the printout.

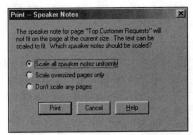

Figure 20-13: Choose to scale the speaker notes for one or more pages so that those notes fit.

Special Printer Options: Faxing and Screen Show

If you open the Print To drop-down list in the Print dialog box, you may notice a couple of unusual options. First, you may see an option like "Compaq Fax," "Microsoft Fax," or another communications package. Such an option appears if you have a FAX/modem and faxing software set up on your system. Choosing this fax or communications driver enables you to fax the current presentation. After you choose the fax or communications driver from the Print To drop-down list, you should make your other selections in the Print dialog box as usual, then click Print. The faxing software for your system opens. Choose the fax recipients and whether or not to include a cover sheet (see Figure 20-14), and then click Send to fax the presentation from your computer without printing a hard copy. This is a handy method to use if a colleague needs to preview your presentation but doesn't have Freelance Graphics.

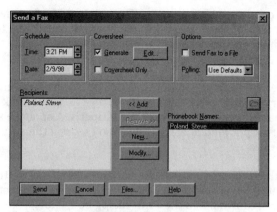

Figure 20-14: With a FAX/modem and faxing software, you can fax the presentation without printing out a hard copy.

The Screen Show option on the Print To drop-down list in the Print dialog box (refer back to Figure 20-9) scales the contents of each page in the presentation to come as close to the edge of the screen as possible. You should choose this option only if you plan to display your presentation solely onscreen. If you do need to go back and print the presentation, you can choose a printer from the Print To drop-down list to change the scaling, but this may have unpredictable results.

To avoid the scaling problem, use the File ⇨ Save As command to copy the final presentation file, then scale one copy and print the other.

Creating 35mm Slides

Chances are, your company doesn't have the film rendering equipment used to generate 35mm slides of your presentation for you to use with 35mm projection equipment. (And, with the increasing availability of large LCD display screens for computers, buying that equipment would be a bad investment at this point.) So, if you need to have 35mm slides of your presentation printed, you need to find a *service bureau* to create the slides for you.

You can find a number of service bureaus by searching the World Wide Web, and can save turnaround time and shipping dollars by e-mailing the Freelance file directly to the service bureau. A brief search yielded the following Web sites for slide output services: www.ezslides.com, www.totalchrome.com, and www.ysite.com/sunset/ service.htm. You also can use a service bureau to make color printouts for you (from any SmartSuite application), or to print your Freelance pages as overheads, if you can't do so with your own printer.

Most larger cities have at least one source for creating 35mm slides. Check under Slides, Slides & Film Strips, Printing, or even Imaging in your yellow pages, and look for a company that provides 35mm output or digital graphic services.

Most service bureaus can work directly with Freelance Graphics .PRZ files. However, each company may require that you choose particular margin sizes and other settings. So, before you try to drop off or send a file in, make sure you ask about any necessary setting changes and prepare your file properly. Also make sure you're delivering the file on the proper media. A Zip drive won't work if the service bureau can only handle floppy disks.

Some service bureaus require that you select a particular printer as part of setting up the file. To install a new printer driver under Windows, so that you can select that printer from the Print To drop-down list in the Print dialog box, choose Start ➪ Settings ➪ Printers, to open the Printers window in Windows. Double-click the Add a Printer icon, then follow the onscreen instructions to install the printer driver. After you finish the installation process, you can then select the printer as directed by your service bureau. If you can't find the printer driver file you need to install on your Windows CD-ROM, ask the service bureau to provide the needed file or to suggest an online location from which you can download it.

✦   ✦   ✦

Approach

Database management can intimidate even hardy computer users. The chapters in this part reveal how straightforward and indispensable the Approach database program really is. We step you through the process of creating and managing database files. You'll learn what *fields* and *records* are, and how to create the fields in a database. You'll review the different views, and learn how to use a form to enter data more quickly. You'll soon be able to find, sort, and duplicate records, and even join databases so you can access their data simultaneously. We then provide more detail about the different types of fields and how to define them. Learn about how to use forms, reports, worksheets, crosstabs, and charts — all different formats for displaying data. Then, use contact information you've captured in Approach to perform a mass mailing.

Creating
a Database
and Entering
Information

When it comes to storing and retrieving your valuable
data easily, Approach has no equal. Approach is a
"database" — an application that enables you to:

✦ Decide what kind of data you want to store. Approach
supports many powerful types of fields, including fields
that calculate values, automatically enter certain types
of data, and check your entries for validity.

✦ Create attractive forms for inputting your data. You can
customize the field background, use colors and fonts to
draw the user's eye to important features, choose the
format to present data in, and decide how the user will
enter the data into various fields.

✦ Create reports, worksheets, charts, form letters, and
mailing labels for presenting your data.

✦ Create automated macros without programming. You can
activate these macros from a button or menu selection,
or even automatically when you run the Approach
application.

✦ Easily find information that matches specific criteria.
You can find the records you are looking for through
successive searches, and even extract the records you
find into a new database — or delete them altogether.

Planning Your Database

Databases can be exciting and powerful, and there is a definite temptation to just "jump in" and start working on your database application. However, a little planning goes a long way toward making your work easier.

Approach makes it easy to add all the fields in the database to a form or report when you create it. Thus, it is a good idea to analyze the data that you will need to store in fields beforehand. This will save you from having to add a lot of fields to the database later, and then manually add those fields to forms and reports.

You also need to understand how you are going to use your data, and a little advance planning helps you do that. For example, you could easily create a single large field for someone's first, middle, and last names. However, if you later discover that you will need to search for records by last name only, you have a problem—the last name is buried in a field and not easily accessible. Although there are workarounds for problems like this, it is best to avoid the problem altogether by storing data in a way that will make it easy to use.

In addition to creating databases "from scratch," you can use the powerful SmartMasters that come with Approach to quickly create complex database applications. Approach comes with a large number of commonly used database applications, such as a wine list, a music list, expense forms, stocks and bonds, a household inventory, and many others.

This chapter looks at all the central functions of Approach. By the time you get done reading the chapter, you'll be able to create a database, add fields to the database, enter data into a form, find and spell check your information, use the built-in SmartMasters to create complex database applications easily, and set your Approach preferences. Later chapters explore these functions in greater detail, so you may want to refer to them for more information about the topics covered here.

Starting Approach and Creating a Blank Database

One of the first things you will want to do is to create a new, blank Approach database and start working with it. This section gets you started.

Creating and Naming the File

To create a new database, use the following steps:

1. Choose New Database from the File menu. Approach displays the New dialog box (see Figure 21-1).

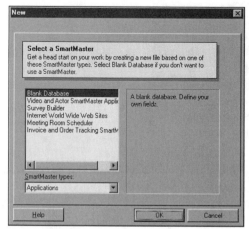

Figure 21-1: Use the New dialog box to create a new database.

Note

Depending on how you have your preferences set (discussed later in this chapter), you may see the "Welcome to Lotus Approach" dialog box when you first run Approach. Except for the heading, this dialog box works just like the New dialog box, and you can follow these instructions to create a new database using the Welcome to Lotus Approach dialog box.

2. Select the Blank Database selection from the list box on the left side of the New dialog box and click OK.

3. Approach displays a second version of the New dialog box (see Figure 21-2). Enter the name of the database in the File Name text field. If necessary, use the Create drop-down list to select the folder in which you want to create the file.

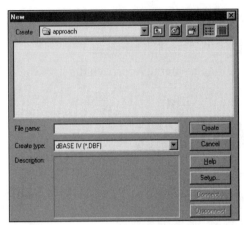

Figure 21-2: Enter the name and type of the database into the New dialog box.

4. Choose the type of database you want to create from the Create type drop-down list. You can choose from a wide variety of database types, including dBase IV, dBase III+, Microsoft Access, Paradox, SQL Server, Oracle, and FoxPro.

Note If you aren't sure what type of database to use, dBase IV is a good, general-purpose choice. It doesn't require a mandatory key column (as Access and Paradox do), and most other types of database applications can read and write dBase IV files.

5. Click the Create button. Approach creates the new database file and presents you with a dialog box to enter the fields for the database.

Adding Fields to a Database

Once you have created a blank database and named it, you must define the fields that you will use to store your data. To create the fields, you use the Creating New Database dialog box (see Figure 21-3), which Approach presents automatically after you name the database file (Step 5 above).

To define a field in the Creating New Database dialog box, you must at least define the Field Name and Data Type. The field name is not only the name of the field in the database, but also the default label for the field on forms and reports. Thus, you may initially want to choose a field name that lends itself to being used on a form (although you can change the field label on the form or report).

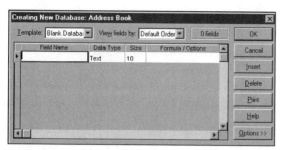

Figure 21-3: Define the fields in your database using the Creating New Database dialog box.

As you may be aware, various databases have rules about how fields can be named. For example, dBase III+ and dBase IV limit a field name to ten characters, and spaces are not allowed in field names. You don't need to worry about that because Approach allows you to use long field names with spaces. However, if you ever open your database in dBase IV, you might be surprised at the field names — they would not match your Approach field names. Instead, you would see the field names Approach constructs to obey the rules for the type of database you are creating.

The Data Type is a drop-down list of the different types of data that Approach supports. The various data types are covered in more detail in Chapter 22, "Working with Field Types," along with the various choices for Field Size and the options you can set for each type of field. Fill in the Data Type, Size, and Options.

When you have finished defining the database fields, click the OK button. Approach creates the database, creates a default form, and you are ready to input data!

Make sure you save your work whenever you create a new Approach file or make changes to the layout of any of your Views (forms, reports, charts, form letters, and so on) in Approach. Although your data is saved automatically when you input it, changes to Views are *not* saved automatically; you must choose Save Approach File from the File menu to save your work.

Rearranging the Database Fields

You can change the order in which the fields are displayed in the Creating New Database dialog box. To change the order, make a selection from the View Fields By drop-down list. You can choose to display the fields sorted by Field Name, Data Type, or Custom Order. If you select Custom Order, you can arrange the fields in the dialog box by using the following steps:

1. Click in the small box (perhaps containing a triangle) at the left end of the field you want to move. Don't forget to release the button.

2. Click and hold with the mouse pointer still located over the small box at the left end of the field. The mouse pointer turns into a hand.

3. Click and drag the box up or down. A rectangle appears alongside the mouse pointer. As you move the rectangle up and down, a dark line appears between the fields in which the selected field will appear. Release the mouse button when the selected field is positioned correctly.

Inserting and Deleting Fields

You can insert and delete fields in the Creating New Database dialog box. To insert a field, click on the field above which you want the new field. Click the Insert button and Approach opens up a new row in the dialog box. Enter the field name and other information.

If you need to delete a row, simply click anywhere in the row and click the Delete button. Approach deletes the row.

Note

> If you try to delete a row (and thus the database field) for which you have entered data in the database, Approach will ask you to confirm that you want to delete the row (field) and all the data in the database for that field.

Reviewing the Approach Screen

There is a lot of information on the Approach screen, and you must understand the various screen elements in order to use Approach effectively. Exactly what information is present on the screen depends on whether you are simply entering data or creating new Views (forms, reports, form letters, charts, etc.). This section discusses the Approach screen elements, as shown in Figure 21-4, which displays an Approach screen in "Design" mode.

The Title Bar

The title bar stretches across the top of the Approach window. The text in the title bar specifies the name of the Approach file in use as well as the name of the current view displayed on the screen. The title bar also shows you an explanation of the function of any menu or menu item that you select with either the mouse or the keyboard equivalents.

Menu bar.   Action bar.   View tabs.   Title bar.   SmartIcon bar.   Tool palette.

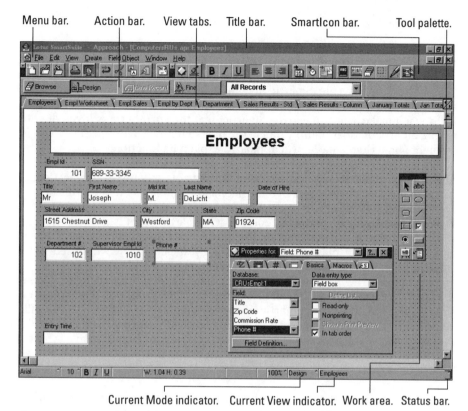

Current Mode indicator.   Current View indicator.   Work area.   Status bar.

Figure 21-4: An Approach screen in Design mode

The Menu Bar

Just below the title bar is the menu bar. The menu bar contains all the Approach menus, including the File, Edit, Window, and Help menus present in all Windows applications. The rest of the menu items vary depending on which mode you are in and the type of view (form, report, worksheet, form letter, chart, etc.) you are working with. Available menu commands are displayed in black letters, while unavailable menu commands are "grayed out" and can't be chosen.

Note

The menu title alongside the "Window" menu reflects exactly what you have selected in the view. Because its title varies according to the context, this particular menu title is referred to as the "context-sensitive menu."

The SmartIcon Bar

Below the menu bar is the SmartIcon bar. The SmartIcon bar displays small rectangular boxes, known as "SmartIcons." Clicking a SmartIcon activates a function. For example, clicking the SmartIcon that shows a blue arrow leaving a yellow folder opens a file. SmartIcons duplicate commands that are also available from the menus. Just like a menu, a SmartIcon can be "grayed out" and unavailable if it doesn't make sense to use the SmartIcon at the current time. If you are unsure what a SmartIcon does, simply pause the mouse pointer over the SmartIcon for a moment and a Help balloon will appear to explain its function.

Although the SmartIcon bar looks like it consists of just one set of SmartIcons, you can actually view several sets of SmartIcons in the SmartIcon bar at the same time. For example, in Figure 21-4, you can see the Default SmartIcon set and the Default Browse SmartIcon set. At the left end of each SmartIcon set is a small blue box and a tiny down arrow. You can click on the down-arrow (or right-click anywhere in the SmartIcon bar) to display a menu from which you can choose which sets of SmartIcons you wish to view. SmartIcon sets that are visible in the SmartIcon bar are displayed in the menu with a check mark next to them. Select a SmartIcon set in the menu to toggle the setting on or off. You can also choose to Hide this bar of SmartIcons (hide the set of SmartIcons whose menu you selected) or Hide All SmartIcons. The SmartIcon sets change automatically when you change modes or the type of view you are displaying. For example, if you change from a form to a worksheet, the Default Browse SmartIcon set changes to the Default Worksheet SmartIcon set.

Each set of SmartIcons can be attached (docked) to any edge of the screen, or float in its own window on the screen. To relocate a set of SmartIcons, move the mouse pointer over the small blue box at the left edge of the screen. Click and hold down the left mouse button, and drag the SmartIcon set away from the SmartIcon bar. If you drag the set of SmartIcons near any edge of the screen, the set will locate against that edge. If you drag the set of SmartIcons anywhere else on the screen, it will float in its own window. Like any other window, you can click and drag an edge of the SmartIcon window to resize it.

If you drag all the SmartIcon sets off the SmartIcon bar, the SmartIcon bar will disappear from the screen. To retrieve it, simply drag a SmartIcon set back to a position just under the menu bar.

To display or hide the SmartIcon bar, choose Show SmartIcons from the View menu.

The Action Bar

Just below the SmartIcon bar is the Action bar. The Action bar contains buttons that help you perform common functions quickly. Most of the time, these buttons enable you to easily switch between Browse and Design mode, create a new database record, or search for a record in Find mode. Additionally, the drop-down list enables you to switch to a saved sort order or find a set of records for the database, according to criteria you set.

The Action bar changes its appearance and content when you change modes. In Design mode (used for building and modifying views), the New Record button is grayed out and not available. In Find mode (used for finding records), the entire Action bar contents are replaced with buttons to define a new find condition, clear all the find conditions, or call for the help of the Find Assistant.

Similar to the SmartIcon bar, you can click and drag the Action bar anywhere you want on the screen. When you move the Action bar in this manner, it remains in the shape of a bar, stretching most of the way across the screen. You can also relocate the Action bar by right-clicking between the buttons and choosing the location: Top, Left, Right, Bottom, or Float. For any selection except Float, the Action bar relocates to the appropriate edge of the screen. If you choose the Float option, the Action "bar" becomes a small window containing the Action bar buttons. You can drag the window to any location on the screen, but you cannot resize the window as you can with the SmartIcon bar.

To display or hide the Action bar, choose Show Action Bar from the View menu.

The View Tabs

Just below the Action bar are the View tabs. Approach displays a View tab for each view present in the database application. The name of the view is displayed on the tab. Approach creates a default name such as Form 1 when you create a view, but you can change the names of the views (and the text on the View tab).

To change to a particular view, simply click on the View tab for the view you want. If the View tabs extend past the edges of the screen, you may need to scroll the View tabs left or right until you can see the View tab you want. To scroll the View tabs, click on the triangular arrow buttons that appear at the right edge of the tabs.

In Design mode, you can change the text on a View tab in two ways:

✦ Directly change the name of the View. To do so, select the first item (Properties) from the menu that corresponds to the type of View. For example, to change the properties of a form, choose Form Properties from the Form menu. Then, change the name of the View in the Basics tab of the dialog box.

✦ Change the text of the View tab. To modify the View tab text, double-click on the View tab. Approach highlights the View tab text. Simply type in the new text.

To display or hide the View tabs, choose Show View Tabs from the View menu, or choose the Show/Hide View Tabs SmartIcon.

The Tool Palette

The tool palette is a floating palette of tools that you use for designing views in Design mode. As you build a view, you choose the tools you need from the tool palette. The palette includes the following types of tools:

✦ Various graphic shapes you can use to draw on the screen. These shapes include a rectangle, oval, rounded rectangle, and line.

✦ Field types for entering data on the screen. You can choose from text data entry fields, check boxes, and radio buttons.

✦ A button tool so that you can add automated functions to your view. These functions usually consist of a set of automated commands that you create using Approach's macros.

✦ A text block tool to add text headings, tips, labels, and instructions, to the screen.

✦ A PicturePlus tool to place graphics, sound, and OLE objects in your database.

The tool palette is only visible in Design mode. To display or hide the tool palette, select Show Tool Palette from the View menu or choose the Show/Hide Tool Palette SmartIcon.

The Work Area

The large area in the middle of the screen displays a view that shows the data in your database in a format that you define. Approach has quite a few different kinds of views: forms, reports, worksheets, crosstabs, charts, form letters, mailing labels, and envelopes. Each view may show only some of the your data, or format your data in a special way (such as mailing labels).

The Status Bar

At the bottom of the work area is the status bar. The status bar contains a considerable amount of information, some of which varies depending on what mode you are in. For example, in Design mode, the status bar displays a set of screen coordinates, the percentage magnification (from 25% to 200%), the current mode and the current view. Click on the current mode indicator to pop up a list of modes so that you can select a different mode. Click on the current view indicator to pop up a list of views so that you can select a different view. In addition, if you select a field or text label, the left end of the status bar displays the current font, size, and three "effects" buttons (**Bold**, *Italics*, and <u>Underline</u>). The effects buttons act as toggles — click a button once to "depress" it and activate the effect; click it again to turn off the effect. If you click the current font indicator, a list of fonts pops up so that you can choose a different font. If you click the current size, a list of sizes pops up so that you can choose a different size.

Note

The screen coordinates section of the status bar displays the coordinates of the mouse when nothing is selected. If you select an object on the screen, Approach shows either the width and height of the object (W: and H:) or the left and top coordinates of the object (L: and T:).

In Browse mode (used for entering and modifying data), the status bar displays the current record number, buttons to move back and forth through the records, the current number of active records, the current mode indicator (with its pop-up list to change modes), and the current view indicator (with its pop-up list to change views).

In Print Preview mode (used for previewing how a view will print), the status bar displays the current record number, buttons to move back and forth between pages, the number of active records, the percentage magnification, the current mode indicator (with its pop-up list to change modes), and the current view indicator (with its pop-up list to change views).

Note

While in Print Preview mode, the mouse pointer becomes a magnifying glass. To zoom in on the view, press the left mouse button. To zoom out, press the right mouse button.

The Infobox

The Infobox is a special dialog box that is available only in Design mode (see Figure 21-5). With the Infobox, you can set all the properties for any object on the screen: text, fields, buttons, and even the properties of the view itself (such as margins, style, background color and font, and so forth). The Infobox provides all the tools for customizing the look of a screen object. You can set the font, size, and effects of text in a field or text box as well as the display format of data in a field. You can also set the background color, frame style and color, borders, and shadow color for many types of objects. Finally, you can connect macros to an object. For example, you can specify a macro that will execute when you tab into or out of a field, or whenever the data value in the field changes.

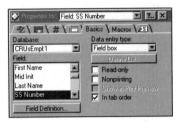

Figure 21-5: An Infobox provides you with the tools to customize properties of a screen object.

To display the Infobox for an object, double-click on the object, or right-click on the object and choose Properties from the pop-up menu. You can also click on the Change the Properties SmartIcon or choose the Properties item from the context-sensitive menu. For example, to display the Infobox for a field, you can right-click on the field and select Field Properties from the pop-up menu. Alternatively, you can click on the field and choose Field Properties from the Field Object menu.

You can leave the Infobox visible on the screen as you work in Design mode, and it will change to display the properties of the currently selected object. The Infobox is separated into many panels, each with its own tab. To move to a different property panel, click the panel's tab.

Note   To access the Infobox for a view, click anywhere in the view where there are no other objects. Or, you can click the Properties For drop-down list in the title bar of any Infobox and choose the view from the list.

Note   If you want to clear the screen of all distractions so that you can focus on your data, choose Clean Screen from the View menu. This option removes the SmartIcon bar, Action bar, View tabs, and status bar from the screen. However, once you have chosen the Clean Screen option, you can't easily reverse it. Instead, you must put back the various missing elements one at a time. To do so, choose the various "Show" options (such as Show SmartIcons) one by one from the View menu.

Managing Files

Although you may not realize it, each time you work with Approach you are working with multiple files on your hard drive or network. A set of files that are managed together are often referred to as an *application*. When you create a database and build views, you are constructing an application. An application built in Approach has two kinds of files:

✦ **Database files.** Database files contain the actual data that you enter on a form and view in a report, chart, form letter, etc. When you define the field names, data types and size (as described earlier in this chapter), you are creating the structure of the database file that you will then fill with data.

✦ **Approach file.** The Approach file contains all the information about your application *except* for the structure of the database and the data itself. This includes all the information about your views, special field properties that are not supported by the database native formats, passwords and security details, relationships between database files, and the names of all the database files that your application uses.

Although it is common for a set of database files to be used by only one Approach file, this is not a necessity. Several Approach files (perhaps with different views or security) can all access the same database files.

You don't ever have to save the contents of a database file because, once created, the database files are updated automatically as you enter data. However, you must save your Approach file any time you make changes to any of the views (e.g., when you rearrange fields, add graphics or text, or change the background color); otherwise, your changes will be lost. You must also save your Approach file when you add or modify any calculated fields, as these too are stored in the Approach file.

Setting Properties for the Current File

Each Approach file has a set of properties that you can set. To access the current Approach file's properties, choose Approach File Properties from the File menu. Approach displays the Approach File Properties dialog box (see Figure 21-6).

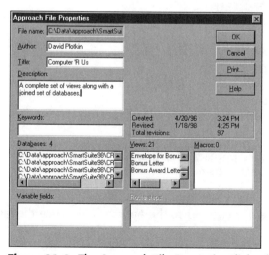

Figure 21-6: The Approach File Properties dialog box.

Some of the information in the dialog box is display-only. For example, you can only view the list of databases, variable fields, views, and macros. But you can change the value of the Author, Title, Description, and Keywords for the Approach file. The keywords help to identify what the database application does, but they are most helpful when you use Lotus Notes. When an Approach database is embedded in a Notes/FX document, the keywords become a field in the document. You can then create a view that shows the fields, sort by keywords, and search for the keywords of interest.

Saving and Naming an Approach File

As mentioned earlier, you must save your Approach file to preserve the details of your application. To save your Approach file, choose Save Approach File from the File menu. The first time you save the Approach file, Approach opens the Save Approach File As dialog box (see Figure 21-7). Specify the name for the file in the File Name field and choose the location for the file from the Save In drop-down list.

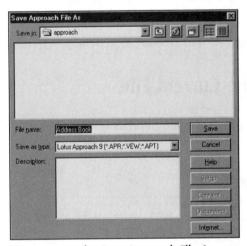

Figure 21-7: The Save Approach File As dialog box enables you to name your Approach file.

Thereafter, whenever you save your Approach file, Approach uses the same file name so you don't have to respecify the name.

Note   If the Save Approach File item in the File menu is unavailable (grayed out), it means that you have not made any changes to the Approach file since the last time you saved it.

Saving an Approach File with a New Name

You can spend a considerable amount of time creating an Approach file that contains all the details of your application. Approach enables you to create a copy of your Approach file so that you can create a similar application without building it from scratch.

Note

Remember that your Approach application must be linked to at least one database file. Thus, when you copy an Approach file, you must either connect the Approach file to an existing database or ask Approach to make copies of existing databases and connect the new Approach file to the database copies.

To create a copy of your Approach file with a new name, use the following steps:

1. Open the Approach file you want to copy by choosing Open from the File menu, selecting the Approach file, and clicking Open.

2. Choose Save As from the File menu. Approach opens the Save Approach File As dialog box (see Figure 21-7).

3. Type the name of the new Approach file into the File Name field and use the Save In drop-down list to navigate to the folder in which you want to save the file.

4. If you just want to copy the Approach file, click in the Save APR File Only check box. Once you click the Save button, Approach will copy just the Approach file and connect it to the same database(s) as the original Approach file. Otherwise:

   Approach opens the Save Table As dialog box once for each table (database file) that the Approach file is connected to (see Figure 21-8).

5. Choose an option from the set of radio buttons in the Save section of the dialog box. There are three options:

   • **Exact copy:** This option saves an exact copy of the database file, complete with all the data in the database.

   • **Blank copy:** This option duplicates the structure of the database so that you can enter new data. None of the data in the existing database file is copied into the new database file.

   • **Same database:** This option links the new Approach file to the same database as the original Approach file. This is useful if you are creating a new application that uses one or more of the same databases as the original application, but also needs some new or blank copies of some of the original databases.

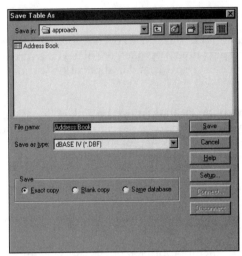

Figure 21-8: Use the Save Table As dialog box to save a copy of each database file (table).

6. Click the Save button to save the Approach file and any new database files.

Note   Choosing Cancel in any of the Save Table As dialog boxes cancels the entire operation — neither the new Approach file nor any of the database files are saved with new file names.

Opening a Database File

Besides opening Approach files (as described earlier in this chapter), Approach can directly open database files, including dBase III+ and IV, FoxPro, Paradox, SQL Server, Oracle7, and Microsoft Access.

Note   Always open database files created in Approach by opening the Approach file. Opening the Approach file automatically opens the database file, as well as presenting you with the rest of the application information. If the database doesn't have an Approach file (because it was created in another application or you forgot to save the Approach file) then you must open the database file directly in Approach. Approach creates a new Approach file of the same name. Customize the new Approach file any way you like, and then save it. From then on, you can simply open the Approach file to get to your application.

To open a database file directly in Approach, use the following steps:

1. Choose Open from the File menu. The Open dialog box appears (see Figure 21-9).

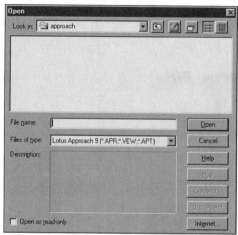

Figure 21-9: Use the Open dialog box to open a file in Approach.

2. Choose the type of database you want to open from the Files of Type drop-down list.

3. Navigate to the file location using the Look In drop-down list.

4. Choose the file you want to open and click Open. Approach opens the file and presents you with a default input form that displays one form field for each field in the database. Don't forget to save the Approach file when you are done.

Deleting a File

You can delete an Approach file or a database file from within Approach. As with any other file delete procedure, you should be very careful about which files you get rid of! When you delete an Approach file or a database file, it is gone — Approach does not move it to the Recycle bin. So be careful!

Danger Zone

If you delete a database file that is referenced by an Approach file, the Approach file will become unusable because it can't find the database file. Again, be careful when deleting!

To delete a file, use the following steps:

1. Make sure that the Approach file you want to delete or any Approach file that references the database file you want to delete is closed. You can't delete a file that is open. The easiest way to ensure that the file is closed is to close all the Approach files prior to starting the delete operation.

2. Select Delete Approach File from the File menu. Approach opens the Delete File dialog box (see Figure 21-10).

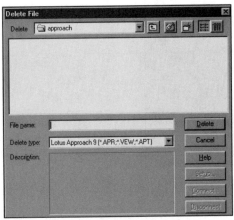

Figure 21-10: Use the Delete File dialog box to delete Approach or database files.

3. Select the type of file you want to delete from the Delete Type drop-down list.

4. Use the Delete In drop-down list to navigate to the location of the file you want to delete.

5. Select the file you want to delete and click the Delete button. Approach asks if you are sure you want to delete the file. Click Yes if you are sure, or click No if you change your mind.

6. If you are deleting an Approach file, Approach asks if you are sure you want to delete each associated database file. For each query, click Yes to remove the database file, or click No to keep a particular database file.

Using Modes

As mentioned earlier, Approach provides several different modes for working with your views:

✦ **Browse mode.** Browse is the mode in which you enter and edit your data. You can add new records, delete records, and add and change the data in fields.

✦ **Design mode.** Design is the mode in which you create and modify views. You can create new forms, reports, worksheets, and other types of views (discussed in more detail in Chapter 23, "Viewing, Summarizing, and Automating Data"). You can also add and rearrange fields on views, add text blocks, graphics, and buttons. Remember to save your Approach file (choose Save Approach File from the File menu) if you make any changes in Design mode.

✦ **Print Preview mode.** Print Preview is the mode that displays a sample of what your data will look like when printed. This mode is especially useful with reports and mailing labels, as you often set properties that make these types of views print well—but you can't see the results of setting these properties until you either print the view or view it in Print Preview mode.

✦ **Find mode.** Find is the mode in which you can search for records that match the search criteria you specify. This mode is especially important for large databases, in which you want to find a specific record (such as someone with a certain last name) or a set of records (such as the people who sent you Christmas cards last year).

Entering and Editing Data with a Form

The main purpose of creating a database application is to store your data in it. Approach makes this very easy—once you create the database structure you want to use (discussed earlier in this chapter), you can start entering data on the default form that Approach provides (an example of a default form is displayed in Figure 21-11). Of course, you can customize the form or create new forms if you wish (see Chapter 23, "Viewing, Summarizing, and Automating Data," for more information).

Creating a New Record

The first step in entering information is to create a new record. There are quite a number of ways to do this in Browse mode:

✦ Click the New Record button in the Action bar.

✦ Select New Record from the Browse menu (or use the keyboard shortcut Ctrl+N).

✦ Click on the New Record SmartIcon.

Regardless of how you create the new record, the view you are working with clears and you are ready to enter data.

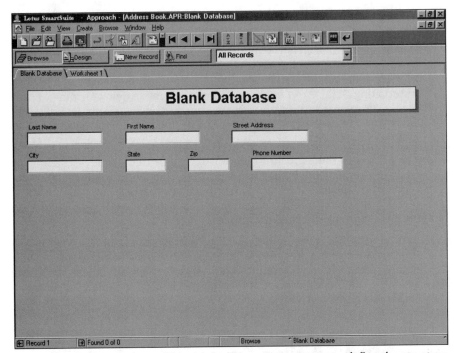

Figure 21-11: Approach provides a default form as soon as you define the structure of a database.

Note   Once you have created a record, you can duplicate the record by choosing Duplicate Record from the Browse, Chart, Worksheet, Crosstab, or Report menu.

Entering the Data

Entering data into a field is straightforward. However, the data you can enter depends on the type of data that the field is designed to hold (e.g., numeric, text, date, time, etc.) and the format of the field in the view (e.g., text, drop-down list, radio button, etc.).

More Info   For more information on data types and formats, see Chapter 22, "Working with Field Types."

It is important to understand the difference between the field *type* and the field *format*. The type is set when you create the database. The format is set when you build the form. For example, you can create a text field type, which is designed to hold alphanumeric characters (e.g., the state in an address book application). When you place the State field on the form, however, you could choose to use a text format field object, or you could choose to use a drop-down list. If you choose a text format object, you would type the state into the field on the form. However, if you choose a drop-down list, then you must configure the drop-down list with the 50 states — clicking the drop-down list and picking the state you want.

More Info Chapter 22, "Working with Field Types," discusses ways you can set special formats for form fields. For example, you can format a text field to display ALL CAPITALIZED.

What you see when you enter data onto a form depends on the setting of the Show Data Entry Format check box in the field's Infobox. If the check box is checked, Approach will dynamically format your data as you enter it. If the check box is not checked, Approach will format your data when you move to the next field.

Figure 21-12 displays a form that contains all the different formats of field objects that you can use. This should help you understand the following discussion on data entry.

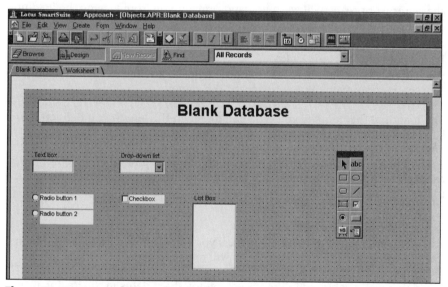

Figure 21-12: A sample form that displays all the different formats of data input objects.

Typing Data into Text Format Fields

A text-format field on a view is represented as a box into which you can type text. Editing text works pretty much like any other Windows application. The blinking insertion point indicates where the next character you type will appear. You can move the insertion point by using the arrow keys or clicking in the field with the mouse. To select the text to be edited, you can use one of two methods:

✦ Click and drag the mouse pointer over the text you want to edit.

✦ Place the insertion point just to the left or right of the text to be selected. Then, hold down the Shift key and use the arrow keys to move the insertion point, selecting the text.

Once you have selected the text, you can delete it by pressing the Delete or Backspace keys, or choosing Clear from the Edit menu. You can also place selected text into the Windows Clipboard by choosing Cut or Copy from the Edit menu. Finally, you can replace selected text with the contents of the Clipboard by choosing Paste from the Edit menu.

Approach has specific rules that limit what information you can enter into a text-format field in a view. These rules vary depending on which data type (text, numeric, date, time, memo, and so on) you assigned to the field when you created the database.

Typing Data into Text Fields

The size of a text type field is limited to the size that you specified in the Field Definition dialog box when you created the database. If you try to type in too many characters, Approach will warn you and prevent you from leaving the field until you reduce the number of characters in the field.

Typing Data into Numeric Fields

You can only enter numbers into numeric fields. If you try to enter non-numeric characters, Approach refuses to accept the value.

The length of the number you type can't exceed the length you defined in the Field Definition dialog box when you created database. Also, the portion of the number to the left and right of the decimal point must not exceed the length defined in the database. For example, if you defined a number as length 7.2, you cannot use more than seven digits to the left of the decimal point and two digits to the right of the decimal point.

Typing Data into Date Fields

You must enter a date into a Date field. If you try to enter data that Approach doesn't recognize as a date, Approach will refuse to accept the value.

The date must be entered in the format set for short dates in the Regional section of the Control Panel. If you used the default U.S. short date format (DD/MM/YYYY), you can enter up to ten digits in a date field, including a four-digit year and the slashes. If you have the Show Data Entry Format check box (in the field's Infobox) checked, you won't need to type in the slashes — Approach types them in for you.

You don't have to enter the whole date under all circumstances. For example, if you want to use the current month and year, just type in the day. If you want to use the current year, you can just type in the day and month. And if you want the default century (19), you can just type in the last two digits of the year.

Typing Data into Time Fields

You must enter a time into a Time field. If you try to enter data that Approach doesn't recognize as a time, Approach will refuse to accept the value.

A time field can be up to 11 characters. You can type two digits for the hours, minutes, and seconds, separating them with colons (HH:MM:SS). If you type in tenths-of-a-second or hundredths-of-a-second, separate them with decimal points (HH:MM:SS.00). You can enter as much or little detail as you like; for example, you could just type in the hours (HH).

You don't have to type the colons in a time field if you have the Show Data Entry check box (in the field's Infobox) checked.

You can also type in "am" or "pm" after the time, and Approach will reformat a 12-hour time into a 24-hour time if you have set your Control Panel time format to use 24-hour time (otherwise, Approach will just leave the am or pm as you typed it). You can also type in a 24-hour time and Approach will reformat it to a 12-hour time (with am or pm) if you configured your Control Panel time format for 12-hour time.

Typing Data into Memo Fields

To enter data into a Memo field, type it in. There are no length constraints on a memo field. You can insert a blank line by pressing the Enter key. If you type more data into a memo field than Approach can display on the screen, Approach automatically provides a horizontal scroll bar so that you can scroll through the text.

Typing Data into Boolean Fields

A Boolean field accepts a very limited set of values that indicate either Yes or No:

   ✦ **Yes:** Approach accepts Yes, Y, or 1

   ✦ **No:** Approach accepts No, N, or 0

Any other value you type in is interpreted as Yes. Approach reformats the contents of the field to display Yes or No, depending on your entry.

Because valid Boolean values are so limited, it is usually best to provide the user with a better method of data entry than having to type in one of the valid values. A check box (checked for yes, unchecked for no) works well to capture Boolean values.

Typing Data into Calculated Fields

Because a calculated field displays the results of a calculation, you can't change the data displayed in the calculated field manually. Instead, you have to change the formula that defines the results displayed in a calculated field.

For more information on creating calculated fields, see Chapter 22, "Working with Field Types."

Entering Data into Drop-Down Lists

A drop-down list in a view (usually a form) provides a list of values to choose from. To choose a value, click the arrow to the right of the field and select a value from the list that appears.

Entering Data into a Field Box and List

A Field Box and List in a view (usually a form) enables you to choose from a list of predefined values or to enter a new value in the field. To choose a predefined value from the list, click the arrow to the right of the field and select a value from the list that appears. To enter a new value (one that isn't in the list), type the value into the field.

Entering Data into a List Box

A list box in a view (usually a form) provides a list of values to choose from. Unlike a drop-down list, a list box shows as many values as will fit in the field—if there are more values than can be displayed in the field, you can use the double-headed arrow to the right of the list box to scroll through the values one entry at a time. To choose a value, click the value in the list box.

Entering Data into a Check Box

A check box in a view provides only two possible values: checked and unchecked. It is a great way to capture data when that data can have only two values (e.g., Yes or No, True or False, Right or Left, etc.). Clicking a check box toggles its condition—if it was off, clicking the check box turns it on (storing the value associated with the on condition); and if it was on, clicking the check box turns it off (storing the value associated with the off condition).

Entering Data into a PicturePlus Field

A PicturePlus field is a special Approach field that enables you to insert graphics and OLE (Object Linking and Embedding) objects into an Approach database application. Because OLE objects can be sounds, charts, word processing documents, animations, and many other kinds of objects, a PicturePlus field enables you to store a considerable variety of items in a database.

 See Chapter 35 , "Sharing Information Between Documents," for more information on OLE.

Approach provides a large number of ways to bring information into a PicturePlus field. You can import a graphic, drag and drop a file, choose Object from the Create menu, choose Paste from the Edit menu, and choose Paste Special from the Edit menu. Here are the details:

✦ To bring a graphic (picture) into a PicturePlus field, you can select the Import submenu from the Picture item in the Edit menu. Approach displays the Import Picture dialog box, in which you can select the graphic you want to import. Approach directly imports BMP, WMF, TIF, PCX, GIF, TGA, EPS, and JPEG files.

✦ You can embed any file as an OLE object using drag and drop. To do so, you must have Windows Explorer open on your desktop. Click a file and drag it to the PicturePlus field on the Approach form (see Figure 21-13).

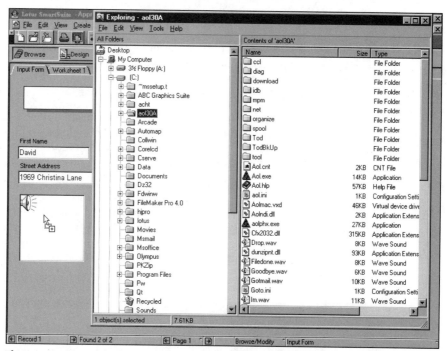

Figure 21-13: Drag a file from Windows Explorer and drop it in the PicturePlus field in Approach (notice the mouse pointer in the square on the left side of the SmartSuite window).

✦ You can embed or link an object to a PicturePlus field by choosing Object from the Create menu. Approach opens the Insert Object dialog box (see Figure 21-14) from which you can either create a new object to embed or select a file to be embedded or linked. More details on embedding and linking are provided in Chapter 35, "Sharing Information Between Documents."

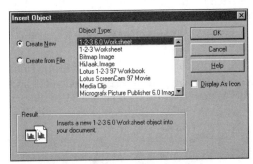

Figure 21-14: The Insert Object dialog box enables you to embed a new object or embed or link an existing file as an object.

✦ You can embed an object into a PicturePlus field by first copying the object from its originating application (e.g., selecting and copying a graphic in Microsoft Paint), switching to Approach, selecting the PicturePlus field, and choosing Paste from the Edit menu.

✦ The final way to embed an object into a PicturePlus field is to use Paste Special from the Edit menu. As with the previous method, you copy an object from the originating application, switch to Approach, select the PicturePlus field, and choose Paste Special from the Edit menu. Approach displays the Paste Special dialog box (see Figure 21-15). There, you can choose how you want to paste the object into the Approach PicturePlus field.

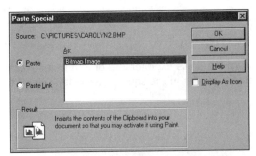

Figure 21-15: The Paste Special dialog box enables you to choose the format for pasting the object into Approach.

Editing Data in a PicturePlus Field

Editing the data in most fields in a view is pretty straightforward—just tab to the field (or click it) and change the entry. However, PicturePlus fields are a little more complicated because editing the data in a PicturePlus field requires rerunning the application (called the *server application*) that created the OLE object or graphic in the first place. A further complication is that double-clicking a PicturePlus field produces different results, depending on the type of OLE object in the field. Here is the rule: If the object in the PicturePlus field is an animation or a sound, double-clicking the PicturePlus field will play the animation or sound. Otherwise, double-clicking the PicturePlus field opens the server application for editing.

The cleanest way to always ensure you will edit the object in the PicturePlus field is to use the following series of steps for editing the object:

1. Click the PicturePlus field containing the object you want to edit.

2. Open the PicturePlus menu and choose the entry for the type of object you want to edit. For example, if you are editing a sound, choose Wave Sound Object from the PicturePlus menu. Approach displays a submenu with two items—Play and Edit.

3. Choose Edit from the submenu. Approach opens the server application that created the OLE object.

4. Make the changes you want in the server application.

5. If the Save menu item is available in the File menu of the Server application, choose it. A few server applications have an Update item in their File menu; if Update is provided, choose that instead. Otherwise, simply move on to Step 6.

6. Choose Exit from the menu in the server application. You are returned to Approach.

Note   If the OLE object in the PicturePlus field is linked and the link type is automatic (see Chapter 35, "Sharing Information between Documents"), the object is updated immediately. If the link type is manual, you'll have to use the Links dialog box to update the PicturePlus field.

Moving Through the Fields

On a form or other view with editable fields, the field that is available for data entry has the "focus." Different types of fields show the focus in different ways:

✦ In text fields, Approach displays the focus with a blinking insertion point in the field.

✦ In a drop-down list (or Field Box and List), the single visible entry is highlighted when the field has the focus.

✦ For radio buttons and check boxes, a faint dotted line appears around the field when the field has the list.

✦ For PicturePlus fields, the border of the field is highlighted when the field has the focus.

✦ A list box does not show any visible indication when it has the focus.

To move the focus from one field to another, you can use the following methods:

✦ Press Tab to move to the next field in the tabbing order (see Chapter 22, "Working with Field Types," for more information on setting tabbing order). Pressing Shift+Tab moves to the previous field in the tabbing order.

✦ Move the mouse pointer to the field you want to use and click in it.

✦ If the Use Enter Key to Move Between Fields check box is checked in the General panel of Approach Preferences, you can press Enter to move to the next field in the tabbing order. Pressing Shift+Enter moves to the previous field in the tabbing order.

Moving Between Records

Once you have more than one record in your database application, you'll need a way to move between the records. Approach provides a number of ways to switch between records:

✦ To advance to the next record, choose the Next Record SmartIcon. To return to the previous record, choose the Previous Record SmartIcon.

✦ To move to the first record in the database, choose the First Record SmartIcon. To move to the last record in the database, choose the Last Record SmartIcon.

✦ The status bar (at the bottom of the screen) also provides a way to navigate to the next record or the previous record. At the far left end of the status bar is a small icon that displays a page with a left-facing arrow. Click this icon to move to the previous record. Slightly to the right of this icon is another icon that features a page with a right-facing arrow. Click this icon to move to the next record.

✦ If you know which record you want to move to, you can navigate there directly from the status bar. Between the two icons mentioned in the previous bullet is a button labeled with the record number that you are currently viewing (e.g., if you are looking at record 2, the button reads "Record 2). Click this button. Approach displays the Go to Record dialog box (see Figure 21-16). Enter the number of the record and click OK.

Figure 21-16: The Go To Record dialog box enables you to navigate directly to a particular record.

Joining Databases

Approach is a relational database—that is, you can work with more than one database at a time in an application, provided that there is some relationship established between each of the databases. Why would you want to do this? Let's look at an example.

Suppose you own a mail-order business, selling magazine subscriptions to customers. Each time a customer calls in to order a new subscription, you create a subscription order that includes the customer's name, address, telephone number, and a list of the magazine subscriptions that the customer is ordering (see Figure 21-17).

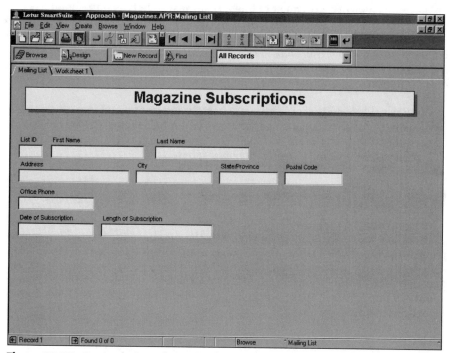

Figure 21-17: A sample form for a magazine subscription business.

Suppose one of your best customers has ordered hundreds of subscriptions over the years, so the customer's address is on quite a few subscription orders, many of which are current (that is, the subscriptions are still running). Because you use the information on the subscription order to contact the customer about any problems with the subscription, the information must be accurate.

Now suppose this customer calls in to say that they are moving and changing their address and phone number. Do you have a problem? You bet you do. The customer's address and phone number is now wrong in *hundreds* of places, and your only option is to find each record and correct it manually. Wouldn't it be better if the customer's address were recorded in just one place, so you could change it once and it would change everywhere it was used (like on all those subscription orders)?

This is exactly the type of problem that a relational database is designed to solve. When you have a set of data that appears multiple times (known as a *repeating group*), you can store it in its own database and create a link (a *relationship*) between that database and any other database that needs the information. In the previous example, you could create a customer database that includes the name, address, and phone number of the customer, and another database (the subscription database) that records the customer's subscriptions.

To make this all work, you must define a relationship between the databases that tells Approach which records in the subscription database belong to which record in the customer database. This relationship is defined by one or more fields in each database that contain the same information. These fields are called *join fields*. The two databases joined via the join fields are referred to as the *main* database and the *detail* database.

While not strictly necessary, it is usually best for the join field(s) in each database to be named the same. It is then easier to see which fields represent the link between databases. For example, a field called "Customer ID" could be the link between the Customer database and the Subscription database.

Understanding the Main and Detail Databases

When you join two databases, it is important to decide which one of them will be the main database. Typically, this would be the database that contains a single record that has multiple matching records in the other database. In our customer/subscription example, the main database would be the Customer database, because each customer has multiple subscriptions. The Subscription database is known as the detail database because it provides multiple details about each of the records in the main database.

Understanding Types of Joins

You can create a number of different types of joins in an Approach database application. The steps you use in creating the joins depends on their types. The three most common types of joins are one-to-many, many-to-many, and Alias.

One-to-Many Joins

In the example we have been using, each customer record in the Customer database has multiple matching records in the Subscription database. This is the most common type of join, known as a *one-to-many*. Figure 21-18 illustrates a one-to-many join.

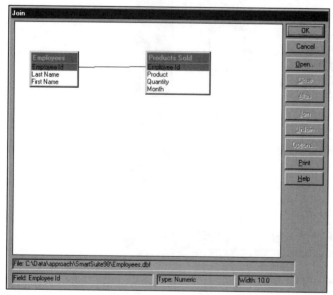

Figure 21-18: A one-to-many join in Approach's Join dialog box.

Many-to-Many Joins

In some circumstances each record in the detail database matches more than one record in the main database. This type of relationship is called a *many-to-many* because each record in the main database matches many records in the detail database, and each record in the detail database matches many records in the main database. An example of this could be Purchase Orders and Products. Each Purchase Order is for multiple Products, and each Product is ordered on many Purchase Orders. Relational databases cannot handle a many-to-many join directly.

To create a many-to-many join, you must create another database, called an *intermediate* database. This database, at a minimum, contains the join fields from the two databases you were trying to join. For example, say the Purchase Order database had a join field called Order Number, and the Product database had a join field called Product Number. The intermediate database would have at least two columns, Order Number and Product Number. This is called "resolving the many to many." What is happening here is that each of the original databases (Purchase Order and Product) now have a one-to-many relationship with the intermediate database (perhaps called "Line Item"). Figure 21-19 illustrates how a many-to-many join would be implemented in Approach.

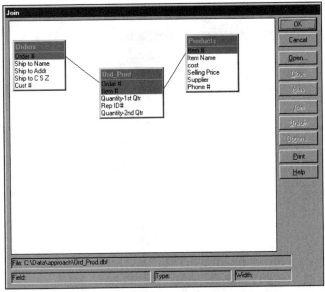

Figure 21-19: Creating a many-to-many join by using an intermediate database.

The intermediate database is an excellent place to put data that is related to the connection between the two other databases. For example, the quantity of each product ordered on each purchase order would be located in the intermediate database.

Alias Joins

An alias join refers to a situation in which a database refers back to itself. The classic example is an employee database, in which each employee has a supervisor. However, because the supervisor is also an employee, the link from employee to supervisor is really a link back to the same (Employees) database. Approach does not directly allow you to connect a database back to itself; instead, you create an *alias*. An alias is not a copy of the database, but simply a second representation of the same database. After creating the alias, you can join the original database (Employees, in this example) to the alias (Approach will name the alias Employee:2) via the join fields. In Figure 21-20, the Supervisor EmplId in the CRUsEmpl:1 database joins to the EmplId field in the CRUsEmpl:2 alias. Thus, for each Employee record, you can retrieve information from the Employees database about that employee's supervisor.

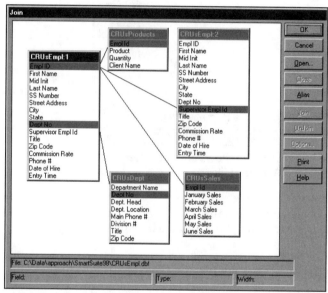

Figure 21-20: An Alias join enables you to join a database to itself ("self join").

Creating the Join

To create a join between one or more databases, use the following steps:

1. Open the Approach file that uses the database that will be the main database.

2. Choose Join from the Create menu. Approach opens the Join dialog box (see Figure 21-21). The database associated with the Approach file is displayed in the working area of the Join dialog box, along with a listing of the fields.

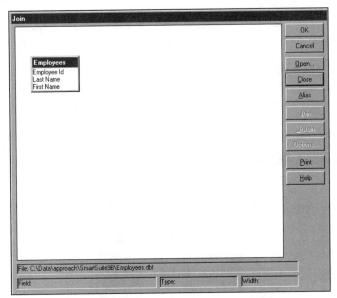

Figure 21-21: The Join dialog box shows any databases associated with the open Approach file.

3. Choose Open to open another database to join to any of the databases already visible in the Join dialog box. Approach displays the Open dialog box.

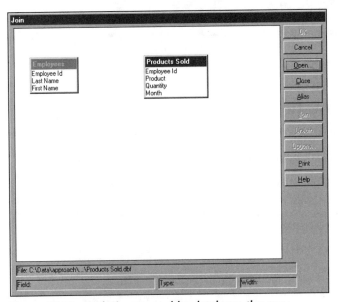

Figure 21-22: Each time you add a database, the new database becomes visible in the Join dialog box.

Note To create an alias of a database already visible in the Join dialog box, click that database and choose the Alias button. You can then join the Alias just like any other database.

4. Pick the database you want to add to the Join dialog box from the Open dialog box and click Open. The database you picked is now visible in the Join dialog box (see Figure 21-22).

5. Create a link between the databases by clicking the join field in one database and clicking the join field in the other database. Then click the Join button. Approach connects the two fields with a join line, as displayed in Figure 21-23.

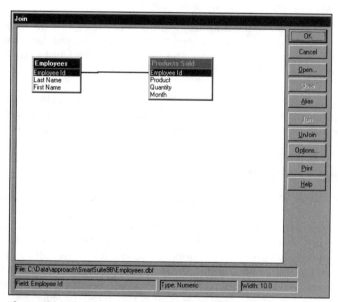

Figure 21-23: Approach displays a join line between the fields in the two joined databases.

6. If you want to add more databases to the joins, repeat Steps 3–5 for each database.

7. Choose OK to complete the Join operation. When you save the Approach file, all the join information will be saved as well. The next time you open the Approach file, all the joined databases will also be opened and ready for you to use.

Note To unjoin two databases, click the join line and choose Unjoin.

Joins That Don't Work

Although there is no limit to the number of databases you can add to the Join dialog box, there are several things that Approach will not allow you to do:

✦ You cannot create a string of joined databases that form a loop. For example, if you join database A to database B, and database B to database C, you cannot join database A to database C, because this string of joined databases forms a loop. If you try to create this type of join structure, the OK button in the Join dialog box is grayed out (unavailable).

✦ You cannot leave any of the databases in the Join dialog box unconnected. That is, you can't open a database and then not create a join line from that database to some other database in the Join dialog box. Until you create a join line, the OK button in the Join dialog is grayed out (unavailable).

Hot Stuff Although you can't create a loop of joined databases, you can avoid this limitation by using aliases. Instead of joining database A to database C (see the first bullet above), you could join database A to an alias of database C—achieving the same result.

Setting Join Options

When you create a join line between two databases, you have the opportunity to set some options about that join. To set the options, click the Options button in the Join dialog box. Approach opens the Relational Options dialog box (see Figure 21-24). The options are broken into two main sections—options that apply to the main database, and options that apply to the detail database. The two options above the line determine what occurs in the detail database when you add or delete a record in the main database. The two options below the line determine what occurs in the main database when you add or delete a record in the detail database.

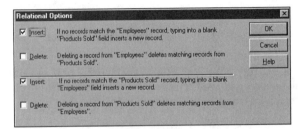

Figure 21-24: The Relational Options dialog box enables you to set options for the relational link.

The options are as follows:

✦ **Insert:** For a form based on the main database that also has fields from the detail database, choose the Insert option from above the line to automatically add a record to the detail database when you add a record to the main database. The record added to the detail database automatically has the *same* value for the join field, so that the two records (one in the main database, one in the detail database) are joined. This way, you can simply enter values on the form for the fields in the detail database. If you don't set this option, you would have to go to a form based on the detail database to add a record (including the join value).

✦ For a form based on the detail database that also has fields from the main database, choose the Insert option from below the line to automatically add a record to the main database when you add a record to the detail database that has a value in the join field that does not match any record in the main database.

✦ **Delete:** For a form based on the main database, choose the Delete option above the line to automatically delete any records in the Detail database when the linked record in the main database is deleted. This is called a *cascading delete* in database parlance. If you don't use this option, the records in the detail database become "orphans" — leaving you, for example, with subscription records for customers who don't exist anymore!

✦ For a form based on the detail database, choose the Delete option from below the line to automatically delete the linking record in the main database when a record is deleted in the detail database.

Danger Zone

It is very rare that you would want to use the second Delete option. You normally don't want to delete a record from the main ("one") database when you delete a record in the detail ("many") database. This is because the record in the main database is linked to multiple records in the detail database — and deleting the main record when you delete one detail record leaves orphans behind in the detail database.

Managing Your Records

Once you begin to really use Approach to store your information, you will find that you need to effectively manage your records. Otherwise, your Approach application becomes the equivalent of a huge filing cabinet full of paper — you know something is in there, but you can't find it. Approach provides functions to find your records, delete the ones you don't need, duplicate records so you don't have to build them from scratch, sort the records in any order, and save a find or sort so you can re-use it later.

Finding Records

Approach contains a powerful set of capabilities for finding information based on criteria that you specify. Executing a search through the database is called *performing a find*. Approach can perform a find based on the contents of any field, compare your search criteria against complex formulas or the contents of other fields, and even use multiple search criteria to find just the data you are looking for. You have the option of entering your search criteria into any of your views using special notation, or using the Find Assistant, which will walk you through the process of creating the find criteria. Either way, you have the option of naming the results of your find so that you can easily use the find again.

Once Approach returns the results of your find (called a *found set*) you can work with just the records in the found set. You can hide the found set, change the contents of a field, or even delete all the records in the found set.

Finding Information with an Approach View

To perform a find using an Approach View, use the following steps:

1. Switch to the view you want to use. The view must include any fields for which you want to specify find criteria.

2. Switch to Find mode. When Approach switches to Find mode, your data disappears from the selected view (so that you can type in your find criteria). Approach also displays the Find SmartIcon bar and replaces the Action bar buttons with a new set of buttons that assist in performing a find (see Figure 21-25). Approach provides a number of ways to switch to Find mode:

   • Click the mode area of the Status bar (which reads "Browse" when in Browse mode). Choose Find from the pop-up list.

   • Click on the Find button in the Action bar.

   • Click on the Find a Set of Records SmartIcon.

   • Choose Find Using Form from the context-sensitive menu to the left of the Window menu. All the context-sensitive menus have the Find Using Form option.

3. Type in the find criteria (as detailed in the next few sections), including any of the special find operators you need to use. You can also add the find operators to a field by clicking on the SmartIcon for the operator

4. When you have completely entered the search criteria for all the fields you want to include, press Enter and click OK in the Action bar, or click the Enter SmartIcon. Approach processes the find request and displays only the records that meet the find criteria (the found set).

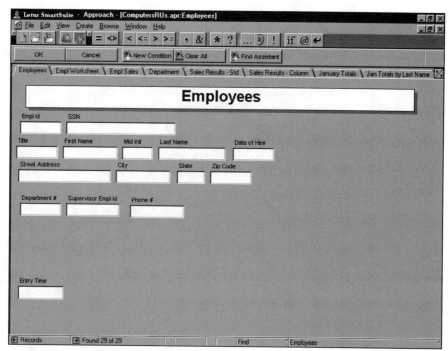

Figure 21-25: When in Find mode, the Find SmartIcons are displayed, and new buttons appear on the Action bar.

Specifying the Find Criteria

To specify the find criteria (including formulas and values in other fields), you must specify exactly what Approach is to look for. This specification can take the form of matching text; specifying the desired condition of radio buttons, check boxes, or value lists; and the use of special "find operators" that further define how Approach is to perform the search.

For example, if you wanted to find all the employees with a Last Name beginning with "Mar," you could simply type "Mar" into the Last Name field. However, if you wanted to find all employees with a last name of "Mar," you'd have to type "=Mar" into the Last Name field, where the "=" is the find operator that specifies an exact match on the find criteria. If you wanted to find all employees with a hire date later than 01/01/95, then you could just type ">01/01/95" into the Hire Date field, where the greater than symbol ">" is another of Approach's find operators.

Table 21-1 provides descriptions of the Find Operators and the matching SmartIcon for the operator.

Table 21-1
The Approach Find Operators and SmartIcons

Operator	Description	SmartIcon
=	Finds an exact match to the criteria. By itself, this symbol finds blank fields. **Example:** =*Martin* in the Last Name field finds all records in which the Last Name field contains only "Martin."	=
<>	Finds when the contents of the field doesn't match the criteria. By itself, finds nonblank fields. **Example:** <>*Martin* in the Last Name field finds all records in which the Last Name field does *not* contain "Martin."	<>
<	Returns a match when the contents of the field are less than the criteria. For text strings, the string is alphabetically less (AA<AB); for dates and times, the date or time is earlier than that specified. **Example:** <*M* in the Last Name field finds all records in which the Last Name begins with A through L. **Example:** <*01/01/95* in the Hire Date field finds all records in which the Hire date was before 1995.	<
<=	Returns a match when the contents of the field are less than or equal to the criteria. **Example:** <=*01/01/95* in the Hire Date field finds all records in which the Hire date was before 1995 or on Jan. 1, 1995.	<=
>	Returns a match when the contents of the field are greater than the criteria. For text strings, the string is alphabetically more (AB>AA); for dates and times, the date or time is later than that specified. **Example:** >*M* in the Last Name field finds all records in which the Last Name begins with Ma through Z. **Example:** >*01/01/95* in the Hire Date field finds all records in which the Hire date was between 01/02/95 and the present.	>
>=	Returns a match when the contents of the field are greater than or equal to the criteria. **Example:** >= *01/01/95* in the Hire Date field finds all records from 1995 to the present.	>=
, (comma)	Separates multiple criteria typed into a single field. Records are returned when the contents of the field match any of the comma-separated criteria (an OR match). See "Specifying Multiple Criteria in a Single Field," later in this chapter. **Example:** *Martin,Johnson* in the Last Name field finds all records in which the Last Name begins with "Martin" or "Johnson."	,

Operator	Description	SmartIcon
&	Separates multiple criteria typed into a single field. Records are returned when the contents of the field match all of the criteria (an AND match). See "Specifying Multiple Criteria in a Single field," later in this chapter. **Example:** *>01/01/92&<01/01/95* in the Hire Date field finds all records in which the Hire date was in 1992, 1993, or 1994.	&
*	A "wild card" that substitutes for any number of characters in a find criteria. **Example:** *=M*n* in the Last Name field finds all records in which the Last Name field contains any name that begins with "M" and ends with "n" — and has any collection of letters in between.	*
?	A "wild card" that substitutes for a single character in a find criteria. **Example:** *=D?ve* in the First Name field finds all records in which the first name is Dave, Dive, Dove, etc. — that is, in which the second character is any letter.	?
...	Specifies a range of values. You must specify the beginning and end points of the range, with the lower end of the range to the left of the "..." and the higher end of the range to the right. The ends of the range are included in the find. **Example:** 01/01/92...01/01/96 in the Hire Date field finds all records in which the hire date is between 01/01/92 and 01/01/96.	...
~	Returns a match when the contents of the field "sound like" the criteria you typed in. This is handy when you aren't sure how to spell what you are looking for. **Example:** *~Jon* in the First Name field finds all records in which the first name is Jon or John.	
!	Specifies that the text find will be case-sensitive. Normally, find criteria ignores any case information. For example, a find criteria of Martin would find Martin, martin, mArTiN, martinowsky, and so on. By using the case-sensitive operator, only records that match the case of the criteria are found. **Example:** *!Martin* in the Last Name field finds all records in which the last name begins with Martin (and not martin, mArTiN, etc.).	!

(continued)

Table 21-1 *(continued)*

Operator	Description	SmartIcon
IF	Enables the use of a conditional formula in a find. Approach returns a match for all records in which the formula evaluates as true. See "Using the IF Function in a Find," later in this chapter. **Example:** *IF("Hire Date"-Today ()<=90)* typed into any field returns a list of all employees who have been hired in the last 90 days.	if
@	Enables a find in which the contents of a field is compared to the formula following the "@". Everything after the "@" is considered to be a formula, and you can use most of the functions available for making calculations in Approach. **Example:** If the Full Name field contains the first and last name separated by a space, then the following find criteria, typed into the Last Name field, will return a set of records in which the contents of the Last Name field match the last-name portion of the Full Name field: *@Right("Full Name", Length("Full Name") – Position("Full Name"),' ',1))*	@
Enter	Performs the find	↵

Entering Values in Radio Button, Check Box, or Value List Fields

Radio button, Check box, and value list fields don't allow you to type in values, even when you are in Find mode. To enter find criteria for these types of fields, you must enter the value just as you would when using them in Browse mode:

✦ For radio buttons, click the button that represents the value you want to search for.

✦ For check boxes, click the check box to specify that you want to search for all instances in which the check box is checked. To search for all instances in which the check box is not checked, you must click the check box (so the check mark appears) and then click it again to remove the check mark. If you don't follow this procedure, the contents (or noncontents) of the check box are not used as part of the find criteria.

✦ For a value list, click the list and select the value you want to search for. If the field is a Field Box and List, you can also type in the value, just as you would with a text field. Once you have included a drop-down list value in the find criteria, there is no way to remove it from the find criteria without canceling the find and starting over.

Note

Because you can't type values into check boxes, value lists, or radio buttons, you can't use any of the find operators. So, for example, you can't search for multiple valid values for a value list or radio buttons. To use find operators with these fields, you can either create a special find form in which these fields are represented as text format fields, use an IF find, or use the Find Assistant.

Specifying Multiple Criteria in a Single Field

You can specify multiple find criteria in a single field. Depending on how you specify the criteria, the find can work in one of two ways:

✦ AND finds cause Approach to return the records that meet *all* the specified find criteria. The records returned meet the first find criteria AND the second find criteria AND the third find criteria, and so on.

✦ OR finds cause Approach to return the records that meet *any* of the specified find criteria. The records returned meet either the first find criteria OR the second find criteria OR the third find criteria, and so on.

Each part of the compound criteria can (and must) form a complete, standalone find criteria.

To construct an AND find in a single field, type in the first find criteria, type an & (ampersand), and type the next find criteria. For example, to return all records in which the Hire Date field contains a date between 01/01/95 and 01/01/96, type the following into the Hire Date field: >=01/01/95&<=01/01/96.

To construct an OR find in a single field, type in the first find criteria, type a , (comma), and type in the next find criteria. For example, to return all records in which the Last Name field contains names beginning with A or M, type the following into the Last Name field: **A,M**.

Using AND Finds to Specify Multiple Criteria in Multiple Fields

In order to find the records you need, you may need to enter find criteria into more than a single field. For example, you might want to find all records in which the Hire date was later than 01/01/95 and the salary was greater than $65,000. This type of multiple-field find is again called an *AND find* because only records that match all the find criteria will be returned.

To create a multiple-field AND find, type the first find criteria into a field (e.g., >01/01/95 into the Hire Date field). Then type the next find criteria into the next field (e.g., >65000 into the Salary field). Continue adding find criteria into fields until you have fully specified the find. Execute the find and Approach will return all records for which all the find criteria have been satisfied.

Note Each of the criteria must form a complete, standalone find criteria. You can use any of the options and find operators you would normally use in a find criteria, including multiple criteria in a single field. For example, you could return all records in which the last name begins with A or M and the salary is greater than $65,000 by typing A,M in the Last Name field and >65000 in the Salary field.

Using OR Finds to Specify Multiple Criteria in Multiple Fields

You can create multiple-field OR criteria—that is, finds that return records if the records match any of the specified find criteria. For example, you can create a find to look for anyone with a hire date after 01/01/95 or a salary greater than $65,000.

When you use a view to create a multiple-field OR find, Approach uses multiple copies of the view so that you can specify each set of find criteria. Each copy of the view is called a *find request*. You can fill out each find request using any of the techniques discussed in this section, including multiple-field AND criteria and single-field OR criteria. Approach returns a record in the found set if the conditions on the first request (a copy of the view) are satisfied OR the conditions on the second request are satisfied OR the conditions on the third request are satisfied, and so on.

To create a multiple criteria OR find in multiple fields, use the following steps:

1. Switch to Find mode and select the view that you want to use.

2. Type the first set of find criteria into the fields on the find request.

3. From the Browse menu, choose Find and then choose Find More. A new blank form appears.

4. Type the next set of find criteria into the fields on the find request.

5. Continue repeating Steps 3 and 4 until you have specified all the OR find requests you want.

6. Execute the find. Approach returns the records that match any of the find requests.

Using a Formula in a Find

The simplest type of find criteria consists of a string of characters (a *find string*) and any find operators, as detailed in the examples in Table 21-1. However, you can also enter formulas as find criteria, providing the formula is preceded by the ampersand (@). Using a formula enables you to construct powerful finds. The information you can type into a find criteria formula can include the following:

✦ **Field Names**. A formula can reference other fields (including fields that are not visible in the current form), making it possible to compare the contents of one field to the contents of another. Using a variable (see Chapter 22, "Working with Field Types") to capture what the user wants to search for, you can then create a macro that performs the find by comparing the contents of the specified field to the value that the user typed into the variable field. If the field name includes a space, you must enclose the field name in double quotes (" ").

✦ **Approach Functions.** You can include many of Approach's functions in formulas. Table 21-1 listed some of the common functions that make sense to use in find criteria. These include text-parsing functions (Left, Right, Position, etc.), conversion functions (date to text, number to text, etc.), Date/Time functions, and Logical functions (Is blank, and so on).

✦ **Arithmetic Operators.** You can use three of the four common arithmetic operators (add, subtract, divide). You can't use the multiply (*) operator because it is also a find operator.

Note

Except for the special cases of (,) and (&), Approach does not allow a find criteria to include more than a single find operator. That is why you can't use the multiply operator in a find formula: The formula already includes the find operator (@) that identifies the text as a formula.

Hot Stuff

To use a formula in a find that includes a multiplication operation, compare the contents of the find field to a calculated field that contains the formula.

✦ **Constants.** You can include constants (values that don't change) as part of a formula as well. To enter constants into the formula, you must follow these rules:

- Text constants must be enclosed in single quotation marks (for example, 'Fred').

- Date constants must be typed as month/day/year, separated by slashes (for example, 05/22/54).

- Time constants must be typed as hours, minutes, and seconds, followed by fractions of seconds. Separate the hours, minutes and seconds with a colon (:), and separate seconds and fractions of seconds with a decimal point (for example, 11:55:00.30).

- Boolean constants must be typed as either 'Yes' or 'No' (enclosed in single quotes). You can also use the numbers 1 (for Yes) or 0 (for No).

- Numeric constants can simply be entered as numbers, but you can't use scientific notation.

Using the IF Function in a Find

The If function is a powerful way to retrieve records in Approach. It returns all records in which the expression in the If( ) statement evaluates as true. You can type the If( ) statement into any field on the form that accepts typed input during a find. The statement need not have anything whatsoever to do with the field into which it is typed. For example, you could type the statement If("Last Name">="M") into the First Name field.

The If function makes it possible to specify find criteria that can't be performed any other way. You can accomplish the following with the If function:

✦ You can specify typed find criteria for radio buttons, drop-down lists, and check boxes. Without the If function, you can select a single value for a drop-down list or radio button. However, you can't normally specify multiple-criteria finds for these type of fields. With the If function, however, you can type a find criteria for these types of fields, just like any other. For example, you could specify a find criteria for a drop-down list of states in which you wanted Ca, Wa, or Or: If(State='Ca' OR State='Wa' OR State='Or').

✦ You can compare the contents of two fields. For example, you could check to see if an employee's salary for this year (stored in the field Salary) is greater than the salary for last year (stored in the field Last Salary) by specifying the criteria as If(Salary>"Last Salary").

✦ You can evaluate virtually any formula. For example, to find all records in which the Hire date is within 90 days of the current date, use the formula If("Hire Date"–Today()<=90).

✦ You can specify find criteria for fields that don't appear on the current form. This can be handy when you want to specify multiple-field find criteria for a set of fields that don't all appear on a single form. Rather than creating a special form, just specify the find criteria for the fields that do appear in the "normal" way, and use the If function (typed into any unused fields) for the fields that don't appear on the form.

Saving and Naming the Find

Although Approach makes it relatively easy to re-create a find, once you have built a find you like using a view, you can easily save it for re-use later. To name and save the find, use the following steps:

1. Create and execute the find. Approach displays the view with the first record in the found set visible (see Figure 21-26).

2. To the right of the buttons in the Action bar is a drop-down list. Immediately after a find, this list reads "<Current Find/Sort>". Click once in the text section of the drop-down list to highlight the text.

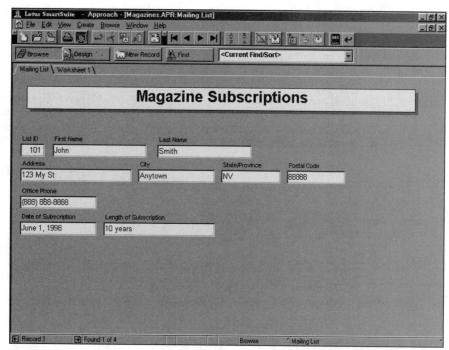

Figure 21-26: After a find, Approach displays the view with the first found record visible.

3. Type in the new name of the find. From then on, you can re-execute the find by clicking the drop-down list and selecting the named find. For more information on managing Named Finds and Sorts, see "Using a Named Find or Sort," later in this chapter.

Because the drop-down list includes both Finds and Sorts, it is a good idea to use the words "Find" or "Sort" (depending on what you are naming) in the name. That way, you can tell from the name whether you are about to re-execute a Find or a Sort.

Finding Information with the Find Assistant

Creating a find using an Approach view is very powerful; however, it can also be quite confusing. You have to type in the various find criteria and remember what functions the find operators perform. You also have to remember when to include quotes and how to format constants. Approach provides another option, the Find Assistant.

The Find Assistant provides a dialog box for creating several common types of finds. In the dialog box, you can pick the fields and operators and type in values to specify find criteria. The Find Assistant takes care of the formatting of the find, and makes it much easier to create more complex finds, such as multiple criteria in multiple field finds.

The first step in creating a find using the Find Assistant is to choose the view on which you will want to see the results of the find. Then, choose Find Assistant from the Find item in the context-sensitive menu (which reads Browse if you are using a Form). Approach opens the Find/Sort Assistant dialog box (see Figure 21-27).

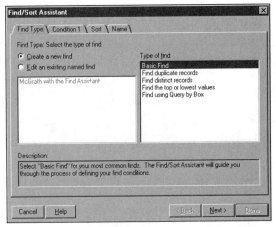

Figure 21-27: The Find/Sort Assistant dialog box assists you in specifying a find.

The Find Assistant enables you to create five different types of finds. All of them provide the capability to specify the sort order for the results of the find, and to name the find so it can be retrieved later. The following five types of finds appear on the Find Type tab:

✦ **Basic Find**. This find duplicates most of the functions of the find by form. You can specify fields, an operator, and a comparison string. You can create finds based on multiple fields.

✦ **Duplicate Records.** This find finds records with duplicate values in one or more fields that you specify.

✦ **Distinct Records.** This find finds records with distinct or unique values in one or more fields that you specify.

✦ **Top or Lowest Values.** This find finds the records with the highest or lowest values in a numeric or calculated field. You can specify the actual number of highest/lowest records to return, or specify the top/bottom percentage of the records.

✦ **Query by Box.** This find enables you to graphically construct the find, picking the database, field, operator, and comparison criteria—and string multiple criteria together with AND and OR statements.

Creating a Basic Find

To create a Basic find using the Find Assistant, use the following steps:

1. Choose Basic Find and click the Next button.

2. In the Condition tab, choose the database and field for which you want to specify the find criteria (see Figure 21-28).

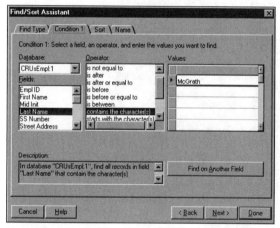

Figure 21-28: The Condition tab of the Find Assistant enables you to pick a database, field, and find criteria.

3. Choose the Operator from the list of operators, and type the comparison criteria in the Values list. You can type multiple values in the Values list, and Approach will treat them as "OR" comparisons—that is, a record will be returned when any of the values are matched.

Note As you build the find criteria in the Find Assistant, the Description field displays a English-like translation of your complete criteria.

4. If you want to add another field to the find criteria, click the Find on Another Field button. This action adds a new Condition tab to the dialog box, in which you can specify the additional criteria just as you did in Step 3. However, an additional set of radio buttons allows you to specify whether the new condition is added to the previous one with an AND (both must be satisfied) or an OR (either may be satisfied).

5. Once you've added all the conditions to the find, click Next to add any sort conditions (see "Creating a Sort Order for the Results of a Find," later in this chapter).

6. Click Next again to move to the Name tab. If you wish, check the Named Find/Sort check box and enter the name of the find (see Figure 21-29).

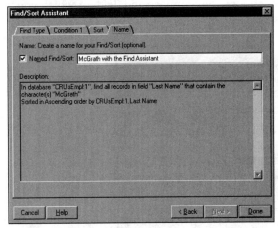

Figure 21-29: The Name tab of the Find Assistant enables you to pick a name, and displays the full find criteria.

Note

Notice on the Name tab that the entire textual description of the find is displayed. This is a good time to make sure that the find actually reflects the criteria you want.

7. Click Done to execute the find. If you chose to name the find, the name of the find now appears in the drop-down list at the right end of the Action bar.

Duplicate Records

To create a Duplicate Records find using the Find Assistant, use the following steps:

1. Choose Find Duplicate Records and click the Next button.

2. In the Find Duplicates tab, choose the field(s) that will be checked for duplicate values (see Figure 21-30). Click the >>Add>> button to move the fields from the Fields list to the Fields to Search list.

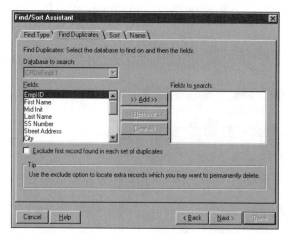

Figure 21-30: Specify the fields to check for duplicate values in the Find Assistant.

3. If you wish, check the Exclude First Record Found in Each Set of Duplicates check box. This leaves the first record in each set of duplicates out of the found set, making it easy to discard the duplicates by choosing Delete Found Set from the Browse menu.

4. Click Next and optionally set the sort options and name the find, and click Done to execute the find.

Distinct Records

To create a Distinct Records find using the Find Assistant, use the following steps:

1. Choose Find Distinct Records and click the Next button.

2. Choose the field(s) that define whether the record is considered unique. Click the >>Add>> button to move the fields from the Fields list to the Fields to Search list. If the values in the selected fields are identical, then the records are not considered distinct.

3. Click Next and optionally set the sort options and name the find, and click Done to execute the find.

Top or Lowest Values

To create a Top or Lowest values find using the Find Assistant, use the following steps:

1. Choose Find the Top or Lowest value and click the Next button.

2. From the Find Top/Lowest tab, choose the option you want from the drop-down list. You can choose either the top/bottom number of records or the top/lowest percentage values (see Figure 21-31). Choose the actual value (number or percentage) from the number spinner.

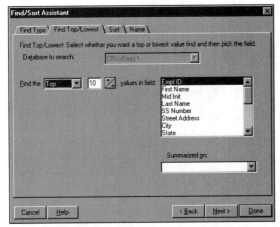

Figure 21-31: Choose the type of top/bottom value filtering in the Top/Lowest tab.

3. Select the field containing the number used to determine whether the record meets the find criteria.

4. Click Next and optionally set the sort options and name the find, and click Done to execute the find.

Query by Box

To create a Query by Box find using the Find Assistant, use the following steps:

1. Choose Find Using Query Box and click the Next button.

2. In the Query by Box tab (see Figure 21-32), choose the table (database), field, and operator from the drop-down lists. Type the comparison value into the Value text box.

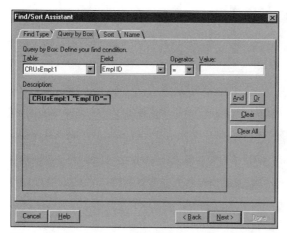

Figure 21-32: Build multiple find criteria graphically with the Query by Box portion of the Find Assistant.

3. To add another find criteria, click either the And button or the Or button. Repeat Steps 2 and 3 to add as many find criteria as you need.

4. Click Next and optionally set the sort options and name the find, and click Done to execute the find.

Creating a Sort Order for the Results of the Find

When you create a find with the Find Assistant, you can specify the order in which you want the returned records (the found set) displayed by using the Sort tab in the Find Assistant (see Figure 21-33). To sort on a particular field, select the field in the Fields list and click the >Add> button to move it to the Sort Order list. If you want, add additional fields the same way. If you add a second field, Approach will sort the records first based on the first field, and for all records with the same value in the first field, it will sort those records based on the second field, and so on.

Note

If your database includes any summary fields, you can sort based on one of those fields by selecting it from the Summary fields list. If you have created summary reports (see Chapter 23, "Viewing, Summarizing, and Automating Data"), you can choose any of the summary reports that summarize based on the sorted field by selecting the report from the Summarized On drop-down list.

Modifying Your Last Find

It can take a fair amount of effort to build a complex find, and the results may not always be what you expect. The good news is that Approach doesn't make you redefine your last find from scratch. If you run the find and discover that the results aren't what you expected, simply select Find Again from the Find item in the Browse menu. If you used a view for the last find, Approach displays the view again with the find criteria. You can edit the find criteria and execute the find again.

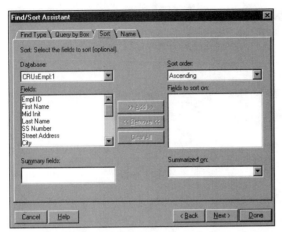

Figure 21-33: Use the Find Assistant's Sort tab to set the sort order for the find.

If the last find you used was done with the Find Assistant, selecting Find Again reopens the Find Assistant. As you step through the tabs, you'll find that the specifications from your last find are available in the Find Assistant. You can edit the find information and execute the find again.

If you saved and named a find in the Find Assistant, you can also edit the find at any time. Use the following steps:

1. Choose Find Assistant from the Find item in the context-sensitive menu, and click the Edit an Existing Named Find radio button.

2. Choose the find you want to edit from the list of finds.

3. Select the type of find you want to create from the Types of Find list. Notice that you can use one type of find to create a completely different type of find.

4. Step through the rest of the Find Assistant tabs, specifying the find criteria as discussed earlier. The information from the saved find is available as the default in each tab. Click Done to re-execute the find.

Deleting Records

Occasionally, you'll find that you no longer need certain records in your database. There are two ways to delete records: individually and after a find.

To delete individual records, you must select the record(s) for deletion. For views that display just a single record (such as forms), you can display the record you want to delete on the screen. For views that display multiple records (worksheets, reports, mailing labels, etc.), select the row(s) representing the record(s). To select multiple, non-adjacent records, select the first record, hold down the Ctrl key, and click the additional records.

Once you have displayed/selected the records, choose Delete Record from the Browse menu. Approach confirms that you want to delete the records, and if you click the Yes button, deletes the records.

Deleting a record cannot be undone, so make sure you really don't need the record any longer.

You can delete the records returned by a find (the found set) as well. After executing the find, choose Delete Found Set from the Browse menu. Approach confirms that you want to delete the found set, and if you click the Yes button, deletes all the records in the found set.

Sorting Records

Approach normally displays records in the order in which you enter them. If you would like to view your records in some other order, you'll need to rearrange them by defining a different sort order. There are two kinds of sort orders: default and temporary. The default sort order is used whenever there are no temporary sort orders in force. For information on setting the default sort order, see "Setting Approach Preferences," later in this chapter.

Temporary sort orders are just that: temporary. If you perform a find, choose Show All after a find, or close and reopen the Approach file, the sort order reverts to the default.

To create a temporary sort order, use the following steps:

1. Choose Define from the Sort item in the Browse menu. Approach displays the Sort dialog box (see Figure 21-34).

2. Select a field from the Fields list and click the >Add> button to move it to the Fields to Sort On list. Choose the sort order (Ascending or Descending) from the Sort Order drop-down list.

3. Repeat Step 2 for any other fields you want to sort on. If you choose more than a single sort field, Approach sorts the records first by the topmost sort field. For any records that have the same value in that sort field, Approach sorts those records by the second sort field, and so on.

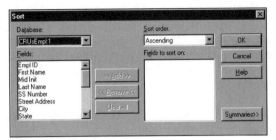

Figure 21-34: The Sort dialog box enables you to define a temporary sort order.

4. When you have set the sort order the way you want, click OK to execute the sort.

There is a quick way to sort the records on one field: Click the field you want to use for your sort field, and then choose either Ascending or Descending from the Sort item in the Browse menu. You can also click the Ascending or Descending SmartIcon.

Using a Named Find or Sort

As mentioned earlier, you can name a find that you perform using a view, and name a find/sort that you create using the Find Assistant. You can work directly with any named finds or named find/sorts by choosing Named Find/Sort from the Create menu. When you do, Approach opens the Named Find/Sort dialog box (see Figure 21-35).

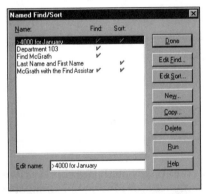

Figure 21-35: The Named Find/Sort dialog box enables you to work with finds and sorts.

When you open the Named Find/Sort dialog box, it displays all previously created named finds and sorts. The two check mark columns (Find and Sort) indicate whether the listed item is a find or a sort. Notice that if you specified a sort order in finds you created with the Find Assistant, both columns display a check mark. With the Named Find/Sort dialog box, you can do the following:

✦ **Give the current sort or find a name.** If you open the dialog box when a sort or find is active, you can give the current find or sort a name by typing it into the Edit Name text box. Note that this is the only way to save and name a temporary find or sort.

✦ **Edit a find.** Click any item that has a check mark in the Find column and then click the Edit Find button. If the find was created using a view, the view reappears, and you can edit the find criteria. The new find criteria is saved as part of the find. If the find was created with the Find Assistant, the Find Assistant reappears, and you can step through the tabs, redefining the find criteria (and the sort order, if you wish).

✦ **Edit a sort.** Click any item and then click the Edit Sort button. The Sort dialog box appears, and you can define a sort order. You can redefine the sort order for finds created with the Find Assistant this way, and the new sort order will be visible in the Sort tab of the Find Assistant the next time you open the find for editing. You can also add a sort order to finds created using a view.

✦ **Create a new find.** Clicking the New button brings up a dialog box giving you the option to create a new find using either the current view or the Find Assistant. Make your choice and then go about defining the find as previously outlined. If you choose to define the find using the current view, Approach will request the name for the find when you are done defining it (press Enter or click OK in the Action bar).

✦ **Copy an existing find or sort.** Clicking the Copy button displays a dialog box requesting the name of the find or sort. Approach then creates an exact copy of the selected find or sort with the new name so that you can edit it.

✦ **Delete an existing find or sort.** Clicking the Delete button displays a dialog box requesting confirmation that you want to delete the find or sort. Clicking Yes deletes the find or sort.

✦ **Run a find or sort.** Clicking the Run button executes the find or sort, displaying the results on the current form.

Creating a New Database with a SmartMaster

Once you've been building database applications for a while, you'll begin to notice that the same sort of databases and database applications keep showing up over and over: customer lists, wine lists, art collections, employees, event lists, and so on. If you need to build one of these common types of databases, wouldn't it be nice to start from a pre-built version and then just customize it for your own needs?

Approach provides just this capability with SmartMasters. There are two flavors of SmartMasters: templates and applications. Templates are single databases that provide the fields you'll need. Applications are entire database applications that include databases, views, macros and scripts, and even joins between databases to define the entire application.

To create a new database using a SmartMaster, use the following steps:

1. Choose New Database from the File menu. Approach displays the New dialog box (see Figure 21-36). If the Welcome dialog option in the Display tab of Approach Preferences is checked, then closing all open databases or starting Approach displays the Welcome to Approach dialog box. This dialog box has a tabbed panel labeled Create a New File Using a SmartMaster. This tabbed panel displays the same information as the New dialog box.

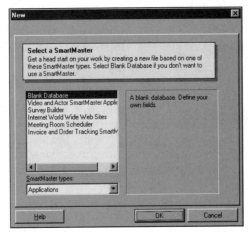

Figure 21-36: The New dialog box enables you to pick a SmartMaster for creating a new database application.

2. Choose the type of SmartMaster you want from the SmartMaster Types drop-down list.

3. Choose the template or application from the list above the SmartMaster Types drop-down list. Notice that Blank Database appears in both the Template list and the Application list. A description of the selected template or application appears in the text box on the right side of the dialog box.

4. Click OK to create the template or application. Approach creates the template or application (an application can take a few minutes to create) and displays the first view in the application.

Setting Approach Preferences

You can customize the way Approach works in quite a few ways. To access the Approach preferences, choose Approach Preferences from the User Setup item in the File menu. Approach opens the Approach Preferences dialog box (see Figure 21-37).

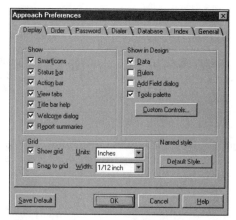

Figure 21-37: Set the Approach Preferences to customize the way Approach works.

The Display Tab

The Display tab enables you to set the following options:

✦ The check marks in the Show section set what you want to see on the screen.

✦ The check marks in the Show in Design section set what you want to see on the screen specifically in Design mode. If you click the Custom Controls button, you can pick from a list of specialized controls that you can add to the toolbox. The options you have depend on the applications you have installed on your machine.

✦ The controls in the Grid section set the units and width of the grid, as well as whether to view the grid and "snap to" the grid. Snapping to the grid locates control points (text box corners/edges, field edges, and so on) only on grid points. This helps with aligning objects in a view.

✦ Clicking the Default Style button enables you to define the style that will be used when no other named style is specified or the Infobox is not used to modify an object's style. The default style includes the font (typeface, effects, size, text relief, alignment, and color), lines and colors (borders, line styles, colors, frame, and shadow), label specifications (same as font choices), picture specifications (crop or shrink if the field is too small, enlarge if the field is too large), and the background specifications (same options as lines and colors).

The Order Tab

The Order tab enables you to set the default sort order for the database. This dialog box looks just like the Sort dialog box — and you specify the default sort order the same way as any other sort order: Pick the fields, click >Add> to move the field from the Fields list to the Fields to Sort On list, and choose the sort direction from the Sort Order drop-down list.

The Password Tab

The Password tab provides you with options for both setting a password to protect your database and setting up various categories to limit access to the application.

The Dialer Tab

Use the Dialer tab to configure Approach to use your modem for phone dialing. You must supply information about your modem, such as the port, speed, AT codes, and so on.

The Database Tab

The Database tab enables you to set all the fields in the database as read-only, choose a character set, and compress a dBase or FoxPro database. Compression is necessary because when you delete a record from one of these types of databases, the record is not actually deleted, but simply made invisible to the normal user. Compression removes the deleted records and regains the disk space.

The Index Tab

The Index tab enables you to create indices for a database. However, Approach cannot create indices this way for most types of databases, nor is there usually any reason to create indices this way — Approach will create any indices that it needs to find records quickly automatically when you create a find.

The General Tab

The General tab enables you to set the following options:

✦ The check boxes in the Show section provide some miscellaneous options, such as whether to show calculated fields in the Join dialog box (you can use calculated fields for joining), whether to display a dialog box that enables you to cancel a macro when running macros, and whether to display a special dialog box called the Add Field dialog whenever you add a field to the database. The Add Field dialog box makes it easy to drag the new field onto a view, making sure that you have a place to input or display the contents of the new field.

✦ The check boxes in the Navigation section let you choose whether to use the Enter key to move between records and whether to expand drop-down lists automatically when the drop-down list has the focus.

✦ The check boxes in the Data section enable you to choose whether to download the latest data from the network before printing (this can take time) and whether to use optimistic record locking. Optimistic record locking means that two users can have the record open for editing at the same time, and Approach will manage any conflicts between the edited data.

✦ The Default Directories button enables you to set the default directories to look in for Approach files and custom SmartIcon bars.

✦   ✦   ✦

CHAPTER 22

Working with Field Types

In This Chapter

- Understanding different types of fields
- Defining a new field
- Adding a field to a view
- Adjusting the properties of a field in a view

Now that you've gotten a good introduction to what Approach can do, it's time to focus on some of the specifics. Working with field types is an important part of using Approach. You need to understand the limits of the different types of fields, how to specify the default value and validation options, how to build formulas, and how to add fields to a view and set the field properties on a view. Before you can do any of this, however, you first need to know how to define a new field.

Defining a New Field

Before you can use fields, you must define them as part of a database. You specify the field information in one of two dialog boxes:

- ✦ For new databases, you create the field definitions in the Creating New Database dialog box (you'll see this later in Figure 21-3).
- ✦ To add fields to an existing database, or modify the definition of an existing field, you use the Field Definition dialog box (see Figure 22-1).

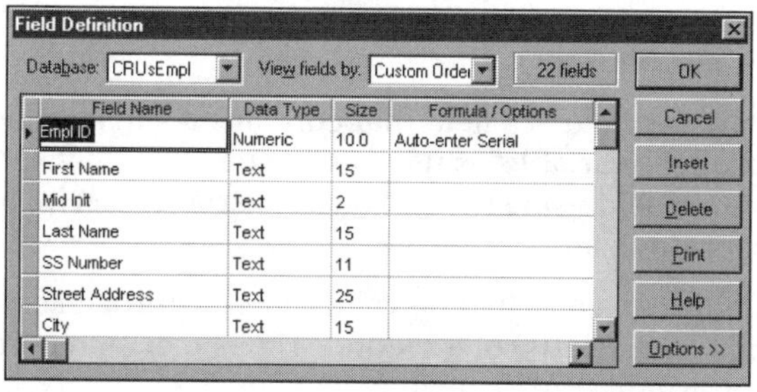

Figure 22-1: Define the fields and field types in the Field Definition dialog box.

Specifying the Basics

For each field, you must specify three basic pieces of information: the name, the type, and the size or length of the field.

Specifying the Field Name

Unlike the limits in the underlying databases (e.g., dBase only lets you use ten characters for a field name), Approach lets you use 32 characters for a field name. You can use mixed case and spaces in the Approach field names as well (which are often not permitted in the other databases). You type the field name into the Field Name column of the dialog box.

Specifying the Field Type

Next, you must specify the data type for the field from the Data Type drop-down list. Approach provides nine different types of fields, each of which has its uses and limitations:

✦ **Boolean Fields.** Boolean fields can contain only two possible values: Yes or No. However, Approach can recognize four distinct values: Y and 1 (which mean "Yes"); and N and 0 (which mean "No").

✦ **Date Fields.** A date field can contain only a valid date.

✦ **Memo Fields.** Memo fields can contain an unlimited amount of text. These fields are ideal for recording comments, text of articles, or research papers.

✦ **Numeric Fields.** Numeric fields can contain only numbers.

✦ **Text Fields.** Text fields can hold text strings up to 255 characters long (254 in dBase III+, dBase IV, and FoxPro). You can enter any type of text characters (including numbers).

✦ **Calculated Fields.** A calculated field holds the result of a calculation. The calculation (defined when you initially define the field) can return a text string, number, date, time, or even a Boolean value.

✦ **PicturePlus Fields.** A PicturePlus field contains either a graphic or an OLE object. As discussed in Chapter 35, "Sharing Information Between Documents" you can either embed or link the OLE object in the PicturePlus field. The types of OLE objects you can use depend on what other applications (OLE Servers) are installed on your machine.

✦ **Variable Fields.** A variable field is a field that contains a single value for the entire database. Although "variable" is used as a type, you must set the actual data type of the variable field using the options. A variable can be text, numeric, date, time, or Boolean.

✦ **Time Fields.** Time fields can contain only valid times. Approach enables you to record time to the nearest 1/100 of a second. Times can be recorded in either 24-hour format or A.M./P.M. format.

Specifying the Field Size

The size of the field specifies how much information the user will able to type into the field once it appears in a view. For each field, you specify the size in the Size column. Only Text and Numeric fields have a size:

✦ **Text.** Type in any length between 1 and 255 (254 for dBase files).

✦ **Numeric.** Type in the number of digits to the left of the decimal point, the decimal point, and the number of digits to the right of the decimal point. For example, if you want ten digits to the left of the decimal point and three digits to the right, type in 10.3. If you only need an integer, you can leave out the decimal point and the second number. You can have up to 19 digits on the left of the decimal point and 15 digits on the right, but the total length of the number can't exceed 19 digits.

Specifying Field Options

You can set options for all of the different field types permitted by Approach. Any options you set are displayed in the Formula/Options column of the Create New Database/Field Definition dialog boxes. However, you can't type anything into this column. Instead, you set the options (and formula for a calculated field) by clicking the Options button to display two additional panels below the main dialog box. Under most circumstances, these panels enable you to set default values and validation criteria for the fields.

Setting Default Field Values

Click the Default Value tab to display the Default Value panel. The information you enter in this panel provides a default value for a field when you first create a record — but you can override this value in the field during data entry. The Default values are available for all field types except Calculated, PicturePlus, and Variable fields.

The following options are available in the Default Field Value panel:

✦ **Nothing.** This is the default. If this radio button is selected, Approach does not enter any information by default in the field when you create a new record. You can select this option when modifying an earlier default option to clear the previous choice.

✦ **Previous Record.** Choosing this option enters the data from the same record in the previously entered record. This is a useful option if you are creating many new records that have the same data in a particular field.

✦ **Creation Date.** This option is available only if the selected field is a date field or a text field long enough to hold a date. The creation date is the date on which the record was created. This is handy for tracking when a record was first entered.

✦ **Modification Date.** This option is available only if the selected field is a date field or a text field long enough to hold a date. The modification date is the date on which the record was last modified. This date is the same as the creation date when the record is first created. This is handy for tracking when a record was last changed.

✦ **Creation Time.** This option is available only if the selected field is a time field or a text field long enough to hold a time. The creation time is the time when the record was created.

✦ **Modification Time.** This option is available only if the selected field is a time field or a text field long enough to hold a time. The modification time is the time when the record was last modified.

✦ **Data.** This option enters a particular piece of data into a field each time a record is created. Enter the data you want in the text box alongside the Data option.

✦ **Serial Number.** This option is available for text and numeric fields only. Approach enters a sequential number into the field whenever you create a new record. Specify the starting number by typing the number into the Serial Number Starting At text box. Specify the increment between the numbers by typing the number into the Increment By text box. The Serial Number option is handy where arbitrary numbers (such as Employee ID) are used.

✦ **Creation Formula.** This option tells Approach to enter the result of the formula into the field when you create the record. The formula is entered into the field only when the record is created, so if you modify the data in the field, Approach will not re-evaluate the formula and refresh the result. You can either type the formula into the text box, or click the Formula button to open the Formula dialog box. Once the Formula dialog box is displayed, use its capabilities to build the formula.

Note   The first time you specify a default value that is a creation formula or modification formula, Approach automatically opens the Formula dialog box.

✦ **Modification Formula.** This option tells Approach to enter the result of the formula into the field whenever you modify the record. Although you can place your own data value in the field, Approach will re-evaluate the formula whenever any field in the record is modified, overriding your data. You can either type the formula into the text box or click the Formula button to open the Formula dialog box and create the formula.

Validating User Entries

Click on the Validation tab to display the Validate panel. The information you enter in this panel validates the data entered into a field. Validated values are available for all field types except Calculated, PicturePlus, and Variable fields.

The following options are available in the Validate panel:

✦ **Unique.** This option ensures that once a value has been entered into a field, it cannot be entered into this field in any other record in the database. This is handy when you must ensure that the value never appears more than once; for example, with an identifier. When entering data, if you try to enter a non-unique value in the field, Approach displays an error message requiring a unique value.

✦ **From.** This option ensures that the value entered into this field falls between the values specified. Type the range into the two text boxes: The low end of the range goes into the left text box, and the high end of the range goes into the right text box. You can enter both numbers and letters into the text boxes. When entering data, if you try to enter a value outside the acceptable range, Approach displays an error message reminding you of the valid range.

✦ **Filled In.** This option ensures that some value is entered in the field. If you try to leave the field blank, Approach displays an error message reminding you to enter a value.

✦ **One of.** This option ensures that the value entered into a field is one of those you entered into the list at the right side of the check box. This option is handy when you need to limit the values to a predetermined list.

To add values to the list, type the value into the text box and click the Add button. To remove an item from the list, click the item you want to remove and click the Remove button.

When you use the One Of validation option, Approach automatically provides a drop-down list for the field in any view. The list provides only the valid options you specified.

✦ **Formula is true.** This option enables you to supply a formula that validates the value typed into the field. The value is accepted only if it makes the formula evaluate as true. You must use the name of the field in the formula; for example, LastName>='A' AND LastName<='Z' ensures that the data in the Last Name field begins with an alphabetic character.

You can either type the formula into the text box or click the Formula button to open the Formula dialog box. Once the Formula dialog box is displayed, use its capabilities to build the formula.

Although Approach will allow it, validation formulas should *not* separate references to values in different fields with Boolean operators (AND and OR). If you build such a formula, any portion of the formula (clause) that doesn't include the field being validated is ignored. For example, if you build a validation formula for the Last Name field that reads "Last Name"> 'A' AND "Hire Date">'05/22/54', the reference to Hire Date is ignored.

Note

During data entry, if you enter a value in a field that doesn't make the formula true, Approach will only let you edit the validated field OR any field that is referenced in the validation formula. You can't edit any other fields in the view. For example, if the validation formula for Hire Date reads "Hire Date">"Birth Date", Approach will only allow access to the Hire Date and Birth Date fields.

✦ **In Field.** This option ensures that the value entered during data entry is a value already present in another field (called a *validation field*) in this or another (joined) database.

When you use the In Field option, Approach automatically provides a drop-down list for the field in any view. The list provides only the valid values from the validation field.

Specifying Formulas for Calculated Fields

When you choose a calculated field type, you must define the calculation that Approach will perform to populate the contents of the field. As soon as you choose Calculated from the Data Type column in the Create New Database/Field Definition dialog boxes, Approach expands the bottom of the dialog box to display two tabs: Define Formula (see Figure 22-2), and Define Summary.

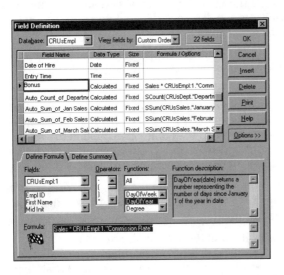

Figure 22-2: Use the Define Formula tab to create or modify the formula that Approach uses in a calculated field.

In the Define Formula panel, choose selections from the Fields, Operators, and Functions lists to define the calculation that defines the contents of the calculated field.

If you wish to define a summary for the calculated field, click on the Define Summary tab to switch to that panel. Choose the type of summary you want from the Summarize On drop-down list. If you want the summary to be a running summary (recalculated after each record), click the Make Calculation a Running Summary check box.

Note

As you choose functions, Approach displays a brief description of the function in the Function Description box at the right side of the panel. Also, the flag in the Formula area is displayed with a red "X" through it until the formula is syntactically correct. Approach will not allow you to exit the Define Formula panel until the formula is correct and the red "X" disappears.

For more information on using Formulas, see "Working With Formulas," later in this chapter.

Specifying Options for a PicturePlus Field

PicturePlus fields can contain two major types of information: graphics in several standard formats and OLE (object linking and embedding) objects. When you choose PicturePlus as the Data Type in the Create New Database/Field Definition dialog boxes, you can use the PicturePlus Options panel (see Figure 22-3) to determine whether to allow OLE objects (check the Allow OLE Objects check box if you want to allow OLE objects) and to choose the default OLE object type for the PicturePlus field (pick from the list).

Figure 22-3: Use the PicturePlus Options panel to set whether the PicturePlus fields can contain OLE objects.

Note

Note that your list of available OLE objects will be different from the one in the figure, depending on what OLE-aware applications you have installed on your computer.

Specifying Options for a Variable Field

A variable field contains a value that is the same for every record in the database, and is usually used for temporary storage of a value so that you can reference it in a formula or as part of a find criteria. When you choose Variable as the Data Type in the Create New Database/Field Definition dialog boxes, you can use the Variable Options panel (see Figure 22-4) to set the actual data type of the variable and the optional default value. The data type of the variable can be either numeric, text, Boolean, date, or time. If you enter a default value, it must match the data type you chose for the variable. Otherwise, Approach displays an error message.

Figure 22-4: The Variable Options panel enables you to pick a data type and default value for a variable field.

Working with Formulas

Formulas play a very important role in Approach. You can build validation formulas, define the formulas for calculated fields, and create formulas for summarizing information in reports. You build formulas from four kinds of items:

✦ References to the contents of fields

✦ Constant values ("constants")

✦ Operators (arithmetic, comparison, and Boolean operators)

✦ Approach's functions

References to Contents of Fields

To include the contents of a particular field in a formula, you can choose the field name from a list, or type the field name into the formula. If the field name contains spaces, however, you must enclose the field name in quotation marks ("").

Note

A validation formula *must* refer to the name of the field it is validating. You can also refer to the names of other fields.

Constant Values

Constants (or constant values) are values that don't change from one record to another. Constants can be strings, dates, times, numbers, or Booleans. Use the following rules when entering a constant into a formula:

✦ **Strings.** Enclose the text string in single quotes ('Computer').

✦ **Dates.** Type date constants as mm/dd/yy or mm/dd/yyyy, separated by slashes and enclosed in single quotes ('05/22/54').

✦ **Times.** Type time constants as hh:mm:ss.HH, separating the main portion of the time with colons and the seconds from the fraction-of-seconds with a decimal point. Also, enclose the time in single quotes ('06:30:00.30').

✦ **Numbers.** Type numeric constants normally, using a standard decimal point to separate the whole number from the fractional part of the number (45.36). Do *not* use scientific notation to represent the number.

Operators

Approach recognizes three kinds of operators: Arithmetic operators, Comparison operators, and Boolean operators. You can add any of these operators to a formula by choosing it from the Operator list or typing it into the formula.

Arithmetic Operators

You can use the following arithmetic operators:

+	Addition
–	Subtraction
/	Division
*	Multiplication
%	Percentage
NOT	Negation

Approach evaluates arithmetic operators in a specific order:

✦ Multiplication (*) and Division (/) are evaluated first.

✦ Addition (+) and Subtraction (–) are evaluated next.

✦ The percent operation (%) is evaluated next.

✦ The negation (NOT) is evaluated last.

✦ If any operators are on the same evaluation level (such as multiplication and division), they are evaluated from left to right in the formula.

✦ To modify the normal evaluation order, use parentheses. Approach evaluates the contents of parentheses before evaluating other parts of the formula. Within a set of parentheses, the evaluation order is as described above.

Comparison Operators

You use comparison operators to compare two quantities. The result of each comparison is either true or false. Following are the comparison operators:

=	equal to
>	greater than
<	less than
<>	not equal to
>=	greater than or equal to
<=	less than or equal to

For example, to ensure that the Hire Date is within 90 days of today's date, you could use the following validation formula:

"Hire Date">=Today()-90

Boolean Operators

The Boolean operators AND and OR are used to connect parts or clauses of a formula. These operators work as follows:

✦ AND. A clause containing the AND operator evaluates as true only when both of the parts connected by the AND evaluate as true.

✦ OR. A clause containing the OR operator evaluates as true so long as either of the parts connected by the OR evaluate as true.

Approach evaluates multiple AND and OR clauses from left to right, unless you use parentheses to change the evaluation order (Approach always evaluates the contents of parentheses first).

Approach's Functions

Approach supports a large number of functions that can perform various operations on text and numeric values. The functions are grouped into types, including Conversion, Date&Time, Financial, Logical, Mathematical, Statistical, Summary, and Text. Most functions operate on one or more values (called *arguments*); and these can be references to fields or constants. If the function uses multiple arguments, you must separate the arguments with commas (or whatever the delimiter is set to in the Regional Settings of the Windows Control Panel).

Adding a Field to a View

When you define a new field in the Field Definition dialog box (as discussed earlier in this chapter), there are two ways you can add the field to a view. If you set your Approach preferences to display the Add Field dialog box (using the General panel in the Approach Preferences dialog box), then whenever you exit the Field Definition dialog box after creating a new field, Approach displays the Add Field dialog box with the new fields in it (see Figure 22-5).

Figure 22-5: The Add Field dialog box displays new fields that you can add to a view.

To add a field to the view from the Add Field dialog box, simply click on the field and drag it onto the view. You can then adjust the field properties as detailed later in this chapter.

Note   You can also display the Add Field dialog box by choosing Add Field from the context-sensitive menu (for example, Form, Report, Worksheet, and so on). In this case, the Add Field dialog box displays all the fields in the database, and you can drag any of the fields onto the view.

The other way to add a field to the form is to use the tools in the Tool Palette. The Tool Palette provides tools for adding text fields, radio buttons, check boxes, value lists, and PicturePlus fields. See Chapter 21, "Creating a Database and Entering Information," for additional information about the Tool Palette.

More Info

You can also add various graphics objects using the Tool Palette, including lines, rectangles, circles, and buttons. See the section, "Adding Graphics with the Tool Palette" in Chapter 23, "Viewing, Summarizing, and Automating Data."

Adding a Text Field to the View

To add a text field to the view, use the following steps:

1. Click on the Draw Field tool in the Tool Palette. The mouse pointer turns into a copy of the tool.

2. Click and drag the mouse pointer to define the dimensions of the field in the view. When you release the mouse pointer, Approach draws the new field and displays the Infobox.

3. From the Field list in the Infobox, choose the field in the database that will supply the data for the text box.

4. From the Data Entry Type list in the Infobox, choose Field Box format.

Adding a Radio Button to the View

To add radio buttons to the view, use the following steps:

1. Click on the Draw Radio button tool in the Tool Palette. The mouse pointer turns into a copy of the tool.

2. Click and drag the mouse pointer to define the dimensions of the field in the view. These dimensions are for the entire collection of radio buttons as a group.

Note

You can also use Steps 1–3 under the section "Adding a Text Field to the View," and then choose Radio Button from the Data Entry Type list in the Infobox. This technique is also ideal for converting another data entry type field to a set of radio buttons.

3. Approach opens the Define Radio Buttons dialog box (see Figure 22-6).

4. From the Field list, choose the field in the database that will supply the data for this set of radio buttons.

5. For each radio button in the set, enter a clicked value and a button label. The clicked value is the value that Approach stores in the database when you select the radio button. If the database field is of type text, the clicked value

can contain any value up to the maximum length of the field. If the database field is a Boolean type field, the clicked value must be either Yes or No. Finally, if the database field is numeric, the clicked value must be numeric and conform to the format (number of decimal places and overall length) specified in the field definition.

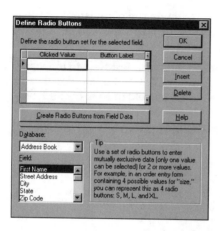

Figure 22-6: The Define Radio Buttons dialog box enables you to define the values for a set of radio buttons.

6. To rearrange the order of the radio buttons, click in the small box at the left end of the row (clicked value and button label) you want to move. Approach displays a right-facing arrow in the box. Click in the box again and drag the row to its new position. You can also use the Insert button to insert a blank line for a new clicked value/button label, or use the Delete button to remove a line.

Note

If you've already entered values in a field, you can use the Create Radio Buttons from Field Data button (located near the bottom of the Define Radio Buttons dialog box). When you click this button, Approach creates a clicked value and button label (identical to the clicked value) for each unique data entry for that field. If the field was a drop-down list prior to converting it to a set of radio buttons, Approach creates a clicked value and button label for each value you placed in the list, regardless of whether you had used the value in a record.

7. Click OK to place the set of radio buttons in the view.

More Info

Although Approach displays the individual button labels next to each button, Approach does *not* automatically label the *set* of radio buttons for you. You will most likely want to add a text object to the view adjacent to the set of radio buttons to identify what the radio buttons are for. See the section, "Adding Graphics with the Tool Palette," in Chapter 23, "Viewing, Summarizing, and Automating Data," for instructions on how to add a text label to the view and group it with the set of radio buttons.

Adding a Check Box to the View

To add a check box to the view, use the following steps:

1. Click on the Draw Checkbox button tool in the Tool Palette. The mouse pointer turns into a copy of the tool.

2. Click and drag the mouse pointer to define the dimensions of the field in the view. These dimensions are for the entire collection of check boxes (if there are more than one).

Note

You can also use Steps 1–3 in the section "Adding a Text Field to the View," and then choose Check Boxes from the Data Entry Type list in the Infobox. This technique is also ideal for converting another data entry type field to a set of check boxes.

3. Approach opens the Define Check Box dialog box (see Figure 22-7).

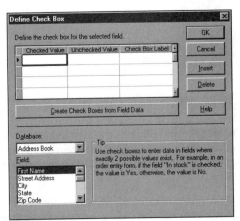

Figure 22-7: Use the Define Check Box dialog box to define the values stored when a check box is selected.

4. From the Field list, choose the field in the database that will supply the data for this set of check boxes.

5. If there is only one check box in the set, enter a checked value, an unchecked value, and a check box label. If you are going to use more than one check box, enter only a checked value and the check box label. When there are multiple check boxes in a set, the check boxes work like radio buttons, and the unchecked value is ignored.

The checked value is the value stored in the database when the check box is checked; the unchecked value is the value stored in the database when the check box is left unchecked. If the database field is of type text, these values can contain any value up to the maximum length of the field. If the database field is a Boolean type field, these values must be either Yes or No. Finally, if the database field is numeric, these values must be numeric and conform to the format (number of decimal places and overall length) specified in the field definition.

6. To rearrange the order of multiple check boxes, click in the small box at the left end of the row (clicked value and button label) you want to move. Approach displays a right-facing arrow in the box. Click in the box again and drag the row to its new position. You can also use the Insert button to insert a blank line for a new checked value/unchecked value/check box label, or use the Delete button to remove a line.

Note

If you've already entered values in a field, you can use the Create Check Boxes from Field Data button. When you click this button, Approach creates a checked value and check box label (identical to the checked value) for each unique data entry for that field. If the field was a drop-down list prior to converting it to a set of check boxes, Approach creates a checked value and check box label for each value you placed in the list, regardless of whether you had used the value in a record.

7. Click OK to place the set of check boxes in the view.

Note

As with radio buttons, Approach does *not* automatically label the *set* of check boxes for you, so you'll probably want to add a text object to label them.

Adding a Value List to the View

Approach provides three different controls that can use valid lists of values: the drop-down list, the field box and list, and the list box. (See the section "Entering the Data" in Chapter 21, "Creating a Database and Entering Information," for details of how they work.) Although these three list-type controls look and work differently you set them up the same way:

1. Click on the Draw Field tool in the Tool Palette. The mouse pointer turns into a copy of the tool.

2. Click and drag the mouse pointer to define the dimensions of the field in the view. When you release the mouse pointer, Approach draws the new field and displays the Infobox.

3. From the Field list in the Infobox, choose the field in the database that will supply the data for the List field.

4. From the Data Entry Type list in the Infobox, choose Drop-down list, Field box and List, or List box. Approach opens the appropriate Define List dialog box (see Figure 22-8). Except for the heading, the three dialog boxes are almost identical.

Note

For a Drop-down List and Field Box, there is an additional check box, Show Drop-down arrow. Unless you check this box, the drop-down arrow to the right of the field is not visible until you tab into the field.

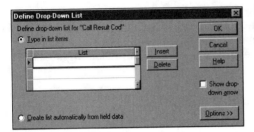

Figure 22-8: The Define List dialog box enables you to select the valid values for the three list-type controls.

5. Specify the valid list of values as detailed in the following section and click OK to place the list control in the view.

Typing in a Valid List of Values

If you are going to type in a valid list of values, enter one value on each line in the Define List dialog box. As with radio buttons and check boxes, you can rearrange the order of the items in the list by dragging the rows in the dialog box. You can also use the Insert and Delete buttons to insert and delete rows in the dialog box.

Using Another Field to Supply a Valid List of Values

If you want to create the data in the list automatically from data already present in the database, click the Create List Automatically from Field Data radio button. By default, Approach populates the list with any data already present in the field that the list control represents. However, you can click on the Options button (see Figure 22-9) to specify far more information about where the list comes from.

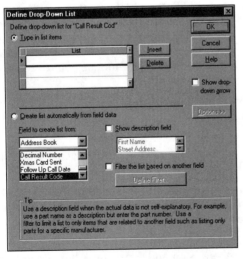

Figure 22-9: The list options enable you to specify more information about where the valid values originate.

Following are the options you can use to populate a list of valid values:

✦ **Populate the list from another field.** To create the list of valid values from contents of a different field, choose the field from the Field to Create List From list. The field can be in another database if the database is joined to the database containing the current field.

✦ **Show Description Field.** Sometimes, the value you want to store in the database doesn't have any readily apparent meaning. For example, you might want to store just a number or code (such as M or F for gender) whose particular meaning isn't obvious to the user who has to pick the value from a list. Checking the Show Description Field enables you to pick another field that contains a description of the number or code, and it is this description (for example, Male or Female) that Approach displays in the list.

✦ **Filter the List Based on Another Field.** By default, when you create a list automatically from field data, the list includes all the previously entered data in the field. However, if you check the Filter the List Based on Another Field check box, Approach enables you to filter the set of values — using only values that meet the criteria you set in the Define Filter dialog box (see Figure 22-10). First, you choose the field to filter by from the Select Field to Filter By list. The values from the filter by field are used in the valid value list when the other criteria are met. Next, you pick the match field from the Using the Current Value In list. For any record, when the contents of the match field are the same as the contents of the match field in the current record (current when you defined the filter), the filter by field value is available in the list.

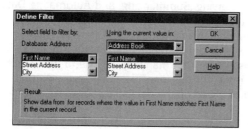

Figure 22-10: Filtering the available values in the list enables you to limit the values by criteria you set.

Adding a PicturePlus Field to the View

To add a PicturePlus field to a view, use the following steps:

1. Click on the Draw PicturePlus Field tool in the Tool Palette. The mouse pointer turns into a copy of the tool.

2. Click and drag the mouse pointer to define the dimensions of the field in the view. When you release the mouse pointer, Approach draws the new field and displays the Infobox.

3. From the Field list in the Infobox, choose the field in the database that will supply the data for the PicturePlus field. Only PicturePlus type fields are listed, so if the Field list is empty, you'll have to define a new field that is of type PicturePlus by clicking the Field Definition button in the Infobox to open the Field Definition dialog box.

Adding a Repeating Panel to the View

As mentioned earlier, you can place fields from any joined database onto a view by dragging them from the Add Field dialog box or by using the Tool Palette. This works fine as long as there is only one record in the detail database that is related to the view's main database. But adding individual fields doesn't work when (as is usually the case) a record in the view's main database is related to multiple records in the detail database. For example, a purchase order (main) has many line items (detail).

Note

As you will see in Chapter 23, "Viewing, Summarizing, and Automating Data," each form has a main database. The main database is, by default, the database from which you add the first field to the form. To use a repeating panel, the main database for the form *must* be the "one" database in a one-to-many relationship. The repeating panel represents fields from a database that is the "many" in the one-to-many relationship. If the main database for the form is not the "one" database, you will not be able to add a repeating panel to the form based on the database you want.

In order to add multiple records from the detail database to a form (it doesn't make sense to add repeating panels to other types of views), you must use a *repeating panel*. A repeating panel looks like a multi-row table. Each row in the table represents one record in the detail database, and each column represents a field from that database or databases joined to that database. Thus, in our purchase order example, the main information in the form would be the purchase order information, and the repeating panel displays the line item information from the joined database. When you design a repeating panel, you specify which joined database to get the data from, which fields from that database to display, and how many rows of data to show at one time in the repeating panel. If there are more matching records than there are rows in the repeating panel, Approach provides a scroll bar so you can scroll through the extra records.

Note When specifying the fields in a repeating panel, *do not* place the join field in the repeating panel. When you create a new record in the repeating panel, Approach automatically fills in the value in the join field in the detail database that matches the value in the main database. Placing the join field in the repeating panel just wastes precious space (space is usually tight in the repeating panel) and you *never* want to change the value in the join field.

To add a repeating panel to a form, use the following steps:

1. In Design mode, choose Repeating Panel from the Create menu. Approach displays the Add Repeating Panel dialog box (see Figure 22-11).

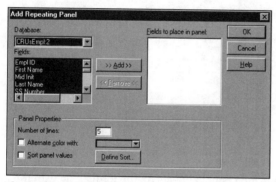

Figure 22-11: The Add Repeating Panel dialog box lets you add records from the detail database to a form based on the main database.

2. From the Database drop-down list, choose the database whose fields will appear in the Repeating Panel. Only databases that are joined to the form's main database will appear in the list.

3. Select the fields you want to appear in the repeating panel from the Fields list, and click the >>Add>> button to move them to the Fields to Place in Panel list.

4. Type the number of lines you want to appear in the repeating panel into the Number of Lines text box.

5. If you want to alternate the background color of each row, click the Alternate Colors With check box and choose the color from the drop-down list. Using alternating colors helps to make the records stand out.

6. If you want to sort the records that appear in the repeating panel, check the Sort Panel Values check box, click the Define Sort button, and specify the sort order.

7. Click OK to place the repeating panel on the form (see Figure 22-12).

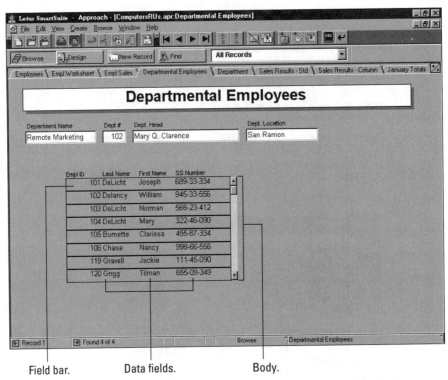

Field bar.   Data fields.   Body.

Figure 22-12: The repeating panel appears on the form along with the fields you added to it.

The Parts of a Repeating Panel

You can customize a repeating panel in many ways, but first you need to understand the parts of the panel. As you can see in Figure 22-12, there are three main parts to the panel:

✦ **The field bar.** This is the first line of the repeating panel, which contains the data fields (see next bullet). Any data field you want to appear in each line of the repeating panel must be fully contained within the field bar.

✦ **The data fields.** These are the fields from the related detail database — the ones you pick when you build the repeating panel, or add later.

✦ **The body.** The balance of the repeating panel is the *body*. The body indicates the size of the repeating panel on the form. The entire body is filled with rows of records, each row being the size of the field bar.

Modifying a Repeating Panel

Once you create a repeating panel, you can customize it. You can change its size, relocate the panel on the form, add and delete fields, and modify the column headings of the repeating panel.

Changing the size of a repeating panel

Changing the overall size of a repeating panel can be very handy if you need to display more fields than will initially fit in the field bar. To change the size of the repeating panel, you must change the size of the field bar. When you change the length of the field bar, the whole repeating panel changes its width to match. And if you change the height of the repeating panel, the repeating panel changes its height so that it contains the same number of the wider rows.

To change the size of the repeating panel, select the repeating panel by clicking in it. Approach displays the field bar with a heavy gray border. Move the mouse cursor over any border of the field bar and it will turn into a two-headed arrow. Click and drag the border to resize. Dragging a size border modifies the panel width, while dragging the top or bottom border modifies the panel height.

Moving a repeating panel

To move a repeating panel, simply click the body portion of the panel and drag the entire panel to its new location.

Adding and deleting fields

To delete a field from the field bar, simply click the field and press the Delete key.

Adding a field is a little more involved. First, you must make sure there is room for the new field in the field bar. If there isn't, resize the field bar. Next, either drag a field from the Add Field dialog box (as detailed earlier in this chapter) or use a tool in the Tool palette to draw a new field in the field bar.

Adding text headings

When you create a repeating panel with fields, Approach automatically adds headings at the top of each column. Approach also performs this service when you add fields to the field bar. However, the column headings are, by default, the field names, which may not be as descriptive as you'd like. To modify the column heading for a field, right-click the field and choose Properties to open the Infobox. Choose the Font, Attribute, and Color tab, and click the Label radio button. Change the Label Text box to reflect the column heading you want.

Setting the Tab Order in a View

When you are using a form to enter data, you can move from field to field by pressing the Tab key. When you first create a form, Approach automatically sets this "tabbing order" from left to right, top to bottom.

If you modify the form by moving fields around (as we'll discuss in the next section), however, Approach does not re-order the fields to reflect the new layout. Thus, your cursor could end up bouncing to fields scattered all over the screen if you did a significant amount of rearranging.

To set the tabbing order for the field in an Approach view, use the following steps:

1. In Design mode, select Show Tab Order from the View menu. Approach displays the view with a small numbered box alongside each field. This box indicates the tabbing order (see Figure 22-13). The Action bar displays some new buttons, including Revert (return to the old tabbing order) and Clear Tabs (erases all the numbers so you can enter them from scratch).

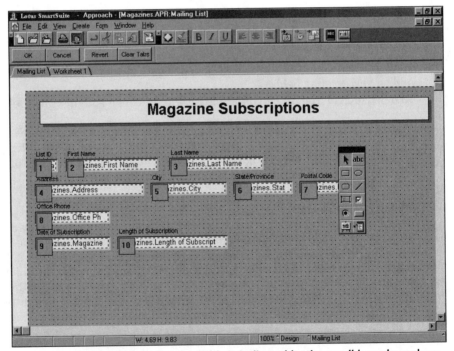

Figure 22-13: The tab order for the fields is indicated by the small boxed numbers to the left of each field.

2. To adjust the tabbing order for a field, click a numbered square, delete the number, and type a new number. The other numbers adjust if you use a number

already in use. You can also click the Clear Tabs button in the Action bar to erase all the numbers, then click in each square and type in a new number.

3. Choose OK from the Action bar or turn off the Show Tab Order check mark in the View menu.

Moving and Sizing a Field in a View

You can move objects around in an Approach view or resize objects. To move an object, you must first select the object. You can select the object by simply clicking it. You can see that an object is selected because it has four small black squares (called *sizing handles*) — one in each corner of the rectangle that surrounds the object. Once the object is selected, you can move it by dragging it to its new location.

You can select multiple objects before moving them. To select multiple objects, click the first object. Then, hold down the Shift key and click the other objects you want. If you accidentally click an object you don't want, simply click it again (with the Shift key still held down).

To resize an object, select it and then click one of the sizing handles. Hold down the mouse button and drag the handle to adjust the size of the object.

Adjusting the Settings for an Existing Field

One of the best features to come along in a while is Lotus' Infobox. In Approach you can adjust almost any property of a field or other screen object using the object's Infobox. The Infobox (see Figure 22-14) is divided into multiple panels. You can set different sets of properties on each panel. The tab for each panel carries a symbol, but because it is hard to refer to the panel by its symbol (especially as some are graphics), we'll use the names that appear in the tooltip when you pause the mouse over the symbol.

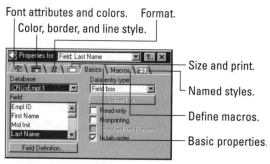

Figure 22-14: The Infobox enables you to set the properties of any field — and the view, too.

Next, we will discuss the options that the Infobox provides for setting properties for fields on views. Other options offered by the Infobox for views and view objects other than fields are discussed in Chapter 23, "Viewing, Summarizing, and Automating Data."

The Basic Properties Panel

The Basic Properties panel enables you to choose general information about the field you have selected. You can modify the database and database field that the view field is bound to, as well as the data entry type (field box, drop-down list, check box, etc.). If you choose a data entry type that requires a list, you can also modify the list elements by clicking the Define List button. Finally, you can make the field read-only, nonprinting (doesn't appear in a view printout), and determine whether it is included in the tab order.

The Font, Attribute, and Color Panel

This panel enables you to set the options for the typeface of both the data in a field and the label for the field. You can set the font, style, size, alignment, relief, and color. For a field label, you can additionally change the text of the label and label position in relation to the data (above, below, left, right, or No Label).

The Color, Border, and Line Style Panel

This panel enables you to change the properties of the background and border. You can change the fill color for the field, as well as the frame style (3-D, dotted, raised, and so on). In addition, you can change the shadow color and which sides (if any) you want a border line drawn on. You can also change the color of the border line, the border width, and whether to include the label within the borders.

Note   If the style of the field is 3-D (either indented or raised), the Border Width drop-down list is grayed out and unavailable. This is because the 3-D effect takes precedence. If you want to be able to set the border width, you'll have to choose a style that isn't 3-D.

The Size and Print Panel

This panel provides spacing and size information about the field. You can set the exact width and height, as well as the coordinates of the top left corner of the field (you can also set these quantities as discussed in "Moving and Sizing a Field in a View"). You can also use the check boxes in the When Printing Slide section to instruct Approach to move fields up and left to close up holes left by partially filled fields or fields that are empty. This last set of options is especially useful when using mailing labels, where space is at a premium.

The Define Macros Panel

This panel enables you to attach macros, which are automated procedures (see Chapter 23, "Viewing, Summarizing, and Automating Data") to the field. You can assign a macro to specific actions:

✦ **On Tab Into.** When you tab into the field during data entry, the identified macro executes. Macros that execute On Tab Into are useful for validating that all necessary conditions are satisfied prior to entry of data into the field.

✦ **On Tab Out Of.** When you tab out of the field during data entry, the identified macro executes. Macros that execute On Tab Out Of are useful for ensuring that the data that was entered meets any specified validation criteria.

✦ **On Data Change.** When you change the data in a field during data entry, the identified macro executes. Macros that execute On Data Change are useful to ensure that entered data meets any specified validation criteria.

The Object Alignment Panel

The Object Alignment panel enables you to align multiple objects on the screen. You can align objects horizontally or vertically, and align their edges or center lines. For more information on aligning objects, see "Aligning and Grouping Objects" in Chapter 23, "Viewing, Summarizing, and Automating Data."

The Named Style Panel

The Named Style panel enables you to create named "styles." A style is a collection of information that defines how an onscreen object will look and behave. A style lets you define fonts, colors, border, and background information. To work with styles, click the Manage Styles button in the Named Style panel. Approach opens the Named Styles dialog box (see Figure 22-15).

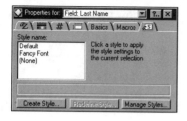

Figure 22-15: The Named Styles dialog box enables you to create new styles and modify existing styles.

To modify an existing style, select the style from the list and click Edit. Or, you can create a new style by clicking New. Either way, you can access the following options using the tabs in the Define Style dialog box (see Figure 22-16):

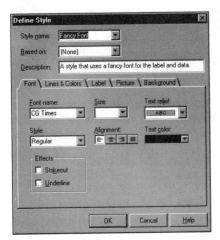

Figure 22-16: Set the properties of a named style in the Define Style dialog box.

✦ **Main Panel.** In the main panel (accessible regardless of which other panels are selected), you can specify or change the name of a style, specify which other style the new style is based on, and provide a brief description. If you base one style on another, all properties of the new style will be same as the "based on" style, except where you change them.

✦ **Font.** The Font panel enables you to specify the font, size, effects, style, alignment, text relief effect, and color. This information is used for the data in fields and the text in text objects (see Chapter 23, "Viewing, Summarizing, and Automating Data").

✦ **Lines & Colors.** This panel enables you to set the border width, which side(s) of the object have a border line, and a frame style for the object. You can also set the color for the border, the fill, and the shadow for the field. Finally, you can allow the border to enclose the field label.

✦ **Label.** The Label panel enables you to set the same information listed in Font, as well as set the position of the label relative to the field.

✦ **Picture.** The Picture panel enables you to specify how pictures are handled when they don't fit exactly into a field. You can choose to stretch the picture if the field is too large, or shrink or crop the picture if the field is too small. You can also allow drawing in the picture. If you do allow drawing, then you can use a few colors and pen styles to mark-up a picture.

✦ **Background.** The Background panel enables you to set the same properties as those listed in Lines & Colors (except for allowing the border to enclose the label) for view backgrounds.

The Format Panel

Approach can display the data in your database either exactly the way you entered it, or in a series of user-configurable display formats. You can change the display format for a field from Design mode at any time using this panel of the Infobox (see Figure 22-17).

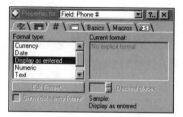

Figure 22-17: The Format panel gives you greater control over how your data is displayed in an Approach view.

Note   Depending on the data type of the field you selected, not all of the following formats are available. For example, if you choose a numeric field, only Display as Listed, Currency, and Numeric are available.

The formats you can set are as follows:

✦ **Display as Entered.** This option displays the data you entered exactly as you entered it. This is the default option, and you can also use it to return to looking at your data in the format in which you typed it in.

✦ **Currency.** When you choose to display your data as currency, you can choose the national currency symbol you want, and the number of decimal places. You can also click the Edit Format button and edit the exact format using the numeric editing symbols discussed in the "Numeric" section.

✦ **Date.** When you choose to display your data as a date, you can choose from a wide variety of date formats, including formats that spell out the day of the week, display month, day, and year in various orders, and formats that just display the quarter and year.

You can also edit the date format directly by clicking the Edit Format button. Approach provides the Edit Format dialog box, in which you can type in special characters that define the format of the date. Table 22-1 illustrates the characters you can use in creating a date format.

Table 22-1
Date Format Characters

Character	Description	Example
N, NN, NNN	Where N is the number 1, 2, 3, or 4. The digit represents the quarter of the year. For example, 1 represents the first quarter. If you use a single digit, the date format is simply the number; if you use two digits, the number is represented as 1st, 2nd, 3rd, or 4th. If you use three digits, the abbreviation is spelled out (First, Second, Third, or Fourth).	1: 1 22: 2nd 333: Third
d, dd, ddd, dddd	Where d represents the day of the month. A single d represents the day using the minimum number of digits. dd displays the day always using two digits, including the leading zero where necessary. ddd displays the day as the three-letter day abbreviation (for example, Thu). dddd displays the day as the fully-spelled out day of the week (Thursday).	d: 1 dd: 03 ddd: Thu dddd: Thursday
m, mm, mmm, mmmm	Where m represents the month. A single m displays the month number using the minimum number of digits. mm displays the month number always using two digits, including a leading zero where necessary. mmm displays the three-letter month abbreviation (for example, Mar). mmmm displays the month by its fully-spelled out name (March).	m: 4 mm: 04 mmm: Mar mmmm: March
yy, yyyy	Where y represents the year. yy displays the year as two digits (no century), while yyyy displays the year as four digits (with the century).	yy: 97 yyyy: 1997

✦ **Text.** You can choose the textual format for the display of your data. You can choose to have the text displayed as ALL CAPITALS, all lowercase, first capitalized (first letter of each word capitalized) and Lead Capitalized (first letter of the first word in the text capitalized).

✦ **Time.** If you choose to display your data in a time format, you can choose from a wide variety of 12-hour and 24-hour time formats, with precision varying from just the hour to hundredths of a second.

If you want, you can edit the time format by clicking the Edit Format button. In the Edit Format dialog box, you can choose between 12- and 24-hour time formats, select the A.M. and P.M. notation, and choose a delimiter (the default is a colon [:]).

✦ **Numeric.** If you choose to display your data in numeric format, you can choose from a list of numeric formats, including scientific notation, percent, fixed decimal, zip code, social security number, and telephone number. Where appropriate, you can choose the number of decimal places to display.

You can create your very own numeric format using special symbols (much like creating a date format). Table 22-2 illustrates the characters you can use to create a numeric format.

<table>
<tr><th colspan="3">Table 22-2
Numeric Format Characters</th></tr>
<tr><th>Character</th><th>Description</th><th>Example</th></tr>
<tr><td>Zero (0)</td><td>Zeroes specify the number of decimal places to the right of the decimal point and the minimum number of digits to the left of the decimal point. If there are any unused digits to the left or right of the decimal point, they are displayed as zeroes in the formatted result.</td><td>Number: 7
Format: 000
Result: 007.</td></tr>
<tr><td>Pound Sign (#)</td><td>Pound signs also specify the number of digits to the left and right of the decimal point. Unlike a zero, however, unused digits are left blank in the formatted result.</td><td>Number: 5.6
Format: ##.##
Result: 5.6</td></tr>
<tr><td>Decimal Point (.)</td><td>The decimal point specifies the location of the decimal in the formatted result.</td><td>Number: 4
Format: 00.0#
Result: 04.0</td></tr>
<tr><td>Semicolon (;)</td><td>The semicolon splits the display format into two separate parts. The portion to the left of the semicolon is the format for positive numbers; the portion to the right of the semicolon is the format for negative numbers.</td><td>Number: −3.4
Format:
##.##;(##.##)
Result: (3.4)</td></tr>
<tr><td>Percent (%)</td><td>The percent symbol indicates that the number entered is to be multiplied by 100. The number is displayed with a percent sign to its right.</td><td>Number: .80
Format: ##.#%
Result: 80%</td></tr>
<tr><td>Comparison Operators (>, <, =)</td><td>The comparison operators enable you to specify a display format that is sensitive to the number of digits in the result. Each operator, when used, must be followed by a number, a space, and the numeric format to be used. For example, if you wanted to specify a seven-digit phone number format, you could use =7 000-0000. However, if the phone number were ten digits (the area code was included), you could use =10 (000)000-0000. You can combine these into a format that varies depending on whether the phone number is seven digits or ten digits (the two parts are separated by a "pipe" (|)): =7 000-0000|= 10 (000)000-0000</td><td></td></tr>
</table>

✦ ✦ ✦

Viewing, Summarizing, and Automating Data

To get the most out of Approach, you need to learn to build your own views: forms, reports, worksheets, crosstabs, and charts. Each of these views serves a unique purpose, displaying data in different ways. By learning to build these different types of views, you will be able to create applications that present your data any way you need to.

You also need to learn how to place objects other than fields on views, using the layout tools that Approach provides to make the job easier. These objects could include graphics, the date and time, and buttons. These objects not only "dress up" the views, but provide additional information that make the views more informative.

Approach also provides ways to automate tasks that you need to perform repetitively. Macros enable you to record or specify a sequence of actions (such as menu options executed in a certain order), while scripts are actual programs you can write using a simple, somewhat limited built-in language called *LotusScript*. See "What Are Macros and Scripts?" later in this chapter for details. In this chapter, you'll learn to build macros.

Data comes from many sources, many of which are *not* Approach database applications. You will learn to import data from other data sources, such as text files, spreadsheets, and other database formats. You will also learn to export data to other formats. Sometimes, you'll need to export portions of an Approach database to another Approach database application.

Finally, printing your data is very important, because even in this day of widespread computer usage, many people expect to see their data on paper, perhaps even looking like the pre-computer forms they were used to. Approach can not only print virtually anything you can see on the screen, but provides many options for customizing the printouts, and even previewing what the printout will look like on the screen, enabling you to adjust the print settings without wasting paper.

Creating and Modifying Forms

Probably the most-often used type of view in Approach is the *form*. A form is not the only type of view into which you can enter data. However, because a form is based on a single record in a database (or a single record in the main database and the joined records in the detail database), it is the easiest to use for entering data, performing finds, and doing quick reviews of the information in a single record.

As we mentioned in Chapter 21 ("Creating a Database and Entering Information") Approach creates a default form from the fields you define in the database, and you can rearrange the fields on that form (or any other view), and add fields using the Tool palette or the Add Field dialog box. However, eventually you will want to create additional forms. Reasons for creating these additional forms might include the following:

✦ Having someone enter just a subset of the information in the database. For example, you might record employee salary in the database, but this classified information might not appear on the normal employee information input form.

✦ Using special forms for performing finds. Approach enables you to type the information you are looking for into a form, so you might want to create a special "find form" for just such a purpose.

✦ Creating a form that is more convenient to use than the default form.

Note   Because all view (form, report, worksheet, and so on) definitions are stored in the .APR (Approach) file, you must make sure you save your Approach file whenever you change a view definition—otherwise, your changes will not be saved. To save the Approach file, choose Save Approach File from the File menu.

Adding a New Form

To add a new form, you must be in Design mode. Use the following steps:

1. Choose Form from the Create menu. Approach opens the Form Assistant dialog box (see Figure 23-1).

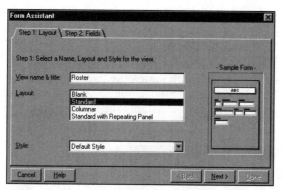

Figure 23-1: Use the Form Assistant dialog box to create new forms in Approach.

2. Type the name of the form into the View Name & Title text box.

3. Choose a layout for the form from the list of layouts. The blank form provides no default field layout. The Standard layout arranges the fields horizontally across the page, dropping down to the next line when there is no more room on the page. The fields are arranged in the order they were created. A columnar layout arranges the fields vertically in columns. Finally, if you have a database joined to the main database for the new form, you have the option to pick the layout Standard with Repeating Panel. This uses the field layout for Standard layout and adds a repeating panel to the form for you.

4. Select a named style from the Style drop-down list. A style gives the form a set of specific properties, such as background color, text attributes, and line width/style/color. Approach comes with a set of predefined styles.

5. Click the Step 2: Fields tab or click the Next button to move to the Fields panel of the Form Assistant (see Figure 23-2). Or, if you chose the Blank layout, click Done.

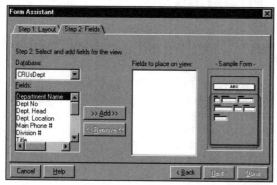

Figure 23-2: The Fields panel of the Form Assistant enables you to pick the fields to display on the form.

6. The Field page contains two lists. The Fields list displays all the available fields in the currently selected database (which you can change from the Database drop-down list). To add the field to the form, select the field and click the >>Add>> button to move the field to the Fields to Place on View list.

7. If you didn't choose the Standard with Repeating Panel layout, click Done to create the form. Otherwise, click the Step 3: Panel tab or the Next button to move to the Panel page of the Form Assistant (see Figure 23-3).

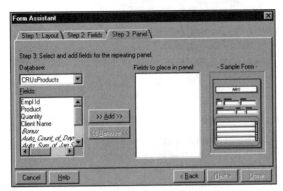

Figure 23-3: The Panel page of the Form Assistant enables you to specify the forms from the detail database to display in the repeating panel.

8. Choose a linked database from the Database drop-down list (all linked databases are available in the list). Choose the fields to display in the repeating panel from the Fields to Place in Panel list, and click the >>Add>> button to move the fields to the Fields to Place on View list.

9. Choose Done to create the form.

Setting the Form Properties

You can change all the properties of a form once you have created it. To change the properties, choose Form Properties from the Form menu. Approach displays the form's Infobox. The Infobox enables you to change the following properties:

✦ **Basic Properties.** From the Basic Properties panel, you can change the name of the form, assign a name to the current page of the form (you'll see shortly how to add pages), change the main database for the form, hide the form in Browse mode, and choose which menu bar to display in Browse mode. The Short menu option hides the Create and Browse menus, significantly limiting what the user can do with the form.

✦ **Color, Border and Line Style.** From this panel, you can choose the style (including 3-D styles) for the form, the background fill color, the color and width of any form border, and which sides of the form to enclose with a border.

✦ **Define and/or Attach Macros.** From this panel, you can define the macros that will execute when you switch to or from the form.

You can also check the Show Form As dialog check box. Use this check box when you want to create a customized dialog box for use in your database application. You build the form as usual, using fields, buttons, and graphic objects. However, the form is not available in Browse mode, and there is no tab for it (nor can you select it from the view list in the status bar). You switch to this form with a macro or script (use the View macro command and pick the form name). When you do, Approach displays the form as a dialog box. The form is cropped to a size just large enough to display the form's contents, and Approach uses a title bar and Close box style consistent with a dialog box. Approach does not create OK or Cancel buttons, so you'll need to create Macro buttons (see "Macros and Scripts," later in this chapter) to perform these functions.

✦ **Margins for Current View.** Use this panel to set the top, bottom, left, and right margins. You can set wide margins to shrink or enlarge the active size of the form.

✦ **Named Style.** Use this panel to choose a named style for the form, or to create and manage named styles for the database applications.

Other Form Operations

You can duplicate forms, add and delete pages to forms, and delete forms when you don't need them anymore.

To duplicate a form, switch to the form you want to duplicate and choose Duplicate Form from the Form menu. Approach creates an exact copy of the form, with the name constructed by preceding the original name of the form with the words "Copy of."

To delete a form, switch to the form you want to delete and choose Delete Form from the Form menu. After confirming that you actually want to delete the form, Approach discards it.

Danger Zone

Deleting a form (or any View) cannot be undone, so be sure!

Forms can have multiple pages, so you can essentially add an unlimited amount of information to a single form. To add a page to a form, switch to the form you want to add the page to, and choose Add Page from the Form menu. Approach creates a new, blank page for the form. You can switch between the multiple pages in a form by clicking the Page area of the status bar. A list of pages pops up (see Figure 23-4), and you just choose the page you want to move to. From the Basics tab of the Form Infobox, you can create a name for each page in the Page Name text box.

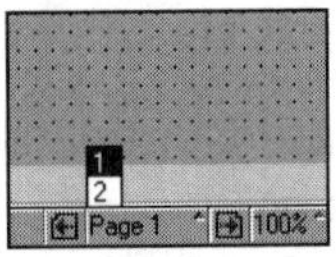

Figure 23-4: Use the Page area of the status bar to switch pages in a multipage form.

If you no longer need a page, you can delete the page by switching to the page and choosing Delete Page from the Form menu. After confirming that you actually want to delete the page, Approach removes the page from the form.

Note

Because you can't delete the last page of a form (delete the form instead), the Delete Page item is grayed out when there is only one page in the form.

Creating and Modifying Reports

Although getting your data into Approach and viewing it one record at a time is important, it is not the only analysis function. Sometimes, you need to be able to view multiple records on one page, format and print out eye-catching output, and summarize your data over many records. Approach provides all these functions with its reports. Building reports is much like building forms — you can create a report from a multitude of layouts, and once you have created the report, you can customize it by adding graphics, moving and sizing fields, and changing the properties of anything in the report.

Approach Report Layouts

Unlike forms, which have just a few simple layouts available, reports have a considerable number of layout options. Table 23-1 describes Approach's report options.

Table 23-1
Approach Report Options

Option	Description
Standard Layout	A Standard layout displays only database information — you can't use summaries or calculations based on database data. The Standard layout displays each record in a single row. Each field in the record is placed in the row (adjacent to the previous field), and displays the field label and the field contents.
Columnar Layout	Like a Standard layout, the Columnar layout displays only database information. Each record is one row, but unlike the Standard layout, the fields are arranged in columns, with a column heading at the top of each column.
Columnar with Groups and Total	The Columnar with Groups and Total layout enables you to choose a set of fields, and group the fields based on a field. You can choose to display the grouped field above a set of records (leading group) or below the set of records (trailing group). You can also summarize any of the displayed fields, using a summary function. For example, you can choose to sum a numeric field such as "Sales." The summary can be displayed above a set of records (leading summary) or below the set of records (trailing summary).
Columnar with Grand Total	Lists the fields you choose in columns, and will calculate a grand total for any specified columns. You can place the grand total either above the set of records (leading grand total) or below the set of records (trailing grand total). As with other summarized reports, Approach will automatically create the summary calculated fields for you.
Summary Only	A Summary Only report doesn't show any detail records. Instead, you select only a grouping field and any fields you want summarized. Approach creates a report with a total of the summary field for each value of the grouping field — and a grand total at the end.
Repeating Panel	The Repeating Panel layout is just a shorthand way of creating a Columnar with Groups and Totals report with a leading group and a trailing summary.

Note You don't have to define a calculated field in the database to summarize the data in the report; Approach will create the summary field(s) automatically.

Creating Reports with the Report Assistant

Approach provides you with all the help you'll need to create your reports. The Report Assistant walks you through a series of panels in which you can pick and choose your options. Exactly which panels you'll see depends on the type of report you pick, but we'll discuss them all. To create a report using the Report Assistant, use the following steps:

1. In Design mode, choose Create from the Report menu. Approach opens the Report Assistant (see Figure 23-5).

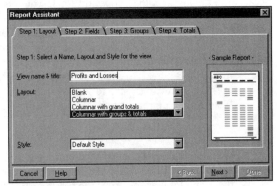

Figure 23-5: Use Approach's Report Assistant to build your reports.

2. Type the name of the report into the View Name & Title text box.

3. Choose the layout you want (as described in the previous sections) from the Layout list. The tabs you see at the top of the Report Assistant will change depending on which layout you pick. Once you pick a layout, Approach displays a miniature sample of the report at the right side of the Report Assistant.

4. Choose a report style from the Style drop-down list. Approach comes with a wide variety of predefined styles. These styles customize the look of your report.

5. If you picked a blank report, click Done, or choose Next to proceed to the next panel.

6. For all report layouts except Repeating Panel, Step 2 is entitled Fields. In the Step 2: Fields tab, pick the fields from the Fields list and click the >>Add>> button to move the fields to the Fields to Place on View list. You can pick fields from multiple databases, but the default main database for the report is the first database you pick fields from.

   In the Repeating Panel layout, Step 2 is entitled Groups. Choose a field to group on from the Fields list.

7. If you picked a Columnar or Standard layout, click Done, or choose Next to advance to the next panel.

8. The next panel is Step 3. The contents of the Step 3 panel depends on the layout you picked. Following are the possibilities:

   • **Columnar with grand totals.** Step 3 is entitled Grand Totals. Choose the fields on which you want to summarize by clicking the fields in the Fields list and selecting the >>Add>> button to move the fields to the Summary Fields list. For each field, choose a summary function from the Calculate The drop-down list.

   • **Columnar with groups and totals.** Step 3 is entitled Groups. Choose the fields on which to group by clicking the fields in the Fields list and selecting the >>Add>> button to move the fields to the Group Field list. Choose how you want to group the records from the Group By drop-down list. The options depend on the type of field you choose to group.

   • **Summary only.** Step 3 is entitled Summary. Choose the fields on which to summarize from the Fields list, and click the >>Add>> button to move them to the Summary Fields list. For each field, choose a summary function from the Calculate The drop-down list.

   • **Repeating panel.** Step 3 is entitled Repeating Fields. Choose the fields you want to display in the body of the report by clicking them in the Fields list, and selecting the >>Add>> button to move them to the Fields to Repeat list.

9. If you chose Columnar with Grand Totals or Summary Only, choose Done, or Choose Next to proceed to the next panel.

10. Only two of the layouts have a fourth panel.

    For the Columnar with Groups and Totals layout, the fourth panel is entitled Totals. Choose the fields you want to total on from the Fields list and click the >>Add>> button to move the fields to the Summary Fields list. Choose the totaling function from the Calculate The drop-down list for each field.

    For the Repeating Panel layout, the fourth panel is entitled Summary. Choose the fields you want to summarize on from the Fields list and click the >>Add>> button to move the fields to the Summary Fields list. Choose the summarizing function from the Calculate The drop-down list for each field.

11. Click Done to create the report.

Working with Columns

Most Approach reports include columns, and adjusting the columns is an important method for making your reports more readable. You can move columns, adjust their width, and change the text of the column heading. You can also adjust many other properties of columns using the Infobox.

Danger Zone

Before making any adjustments to columns, make sure the Turn on Columns option is checked in the Report menu, and the Show Data option is checked in the View menu. With these options checked, you can see your data even in Design mode, and you can operate on the entire column (including the heading) as one object.

To move a column, click anywhere in the data of the column. Approach highlights the whole column (see Figure 23-6). Drag the column to its new location. If you are using a trailing summary for the column, you'll have to relocate the summary information, as it will no longer be under the column.

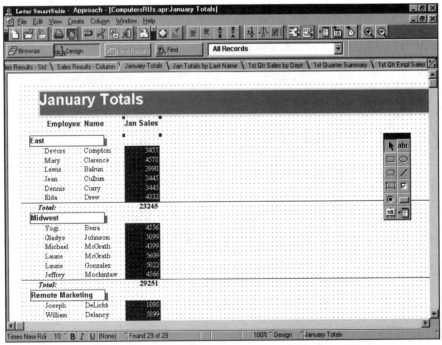

Figure 23-6: Click a column to highlight the entire column.

To change the width of a column, select the column. Click on one of the rectangular sizing handles, and drag.

To change the text of the column heading, click on the column and choose Column Properties from the Column menu. Approach displays the Infobox. On the Font, Attribute, and Color panel, click the Label radio button, and change the Label text.

Working with Headers and Footers

By default, Approach provides both a header and footer for any report you create. The header is the area at the top of the report that contains the report title as well as the column headings. The footer is the area at the bottom of the report that is often used for recording the date and page number of the report.

Adjusting the Header

You can change the report title text in the heading, the text of the column headings (as described in the last section), and the overall dimensions of the header. You can also use the graphics tools in the Tool palette (see "Adding Graphics with the Tool Palette," later in this chapter) to place text and graphics in the header.

To change the report title text, click twice on the title (click once, pause, click again). This puts you into Text Editing mode. Now you can highlight the text you want to change and type in the new text.

You can click the heading text object once and use the Infobox to change many other properties of the heading text as well (see "Adjusting the Properties of Items on a Report," later in this chapter).

To provide more room at the top of the report, you can click in an empty spot of the heading area (choose an area just below the text heading). Approach surrounds the heading with a heavy border (see Figure 23-7). Move the mouse over the lower border and drag it to change the height of the heading.

Note

To turn off the header altogether, uncheck the Add Header item in the Report menu. To turn the header back on again, reselect the Add Header item.

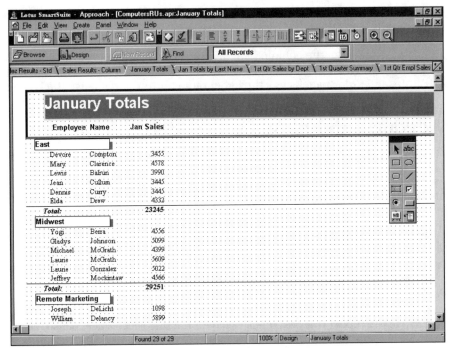

Figure 23-7: Click in an empty area of the header to place the sizing border around the header.

Adjusting the Footer

Approach automatically places the date and page number for the report in the footer. You can relocate these items and adjust the height of the footer to provide more room at the bottom of the report. You can also use the graphics tools in the Tool palette (see "Adding Graphics with the Tool Palette," later in this chapter) to place text and graphics in the footer.

To relocate the date or page number fields, click on either one to display the sizing handles for the field. Then drag the field to its new location. Be careful not to move the field out of the footer or it will not appear on every page.

To adjust the height of the footer, click in an empty area of the footer. Approach surrounds the footer with a heavy border. Move the mouse over the upper border and drag it to change the height of the footer.

Note   To turn off the footer altogether, uncheck the Add Footer item in the Report menu. To turn the footer back on again, reselect the Add Footer item.

Adding a Title Page

A title page is the unique first page of the report. This page has a special header and/or footer that is independent of the header or footer on the pages of the rest of the report.

To add a title page, choose Add Title Page from the Report menu. The displayed report immediately changes to show the title page, and if you had the header and/or footer options turned on, the regular header and footer disappear, to be replaced by the title page header and footer (see Figure 23-8).

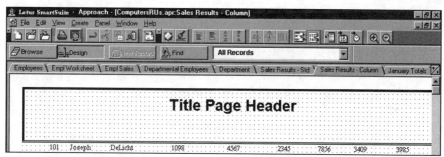

Figure 23-8: The first page of the report has a unique header and/or footer when you turn on the Title Page option.

Once you add the title page, you can add or remove the header or footer from the title page by toggling the Add Header or Add Footer items in the Report menu. You can also customize the header and footer using the Tool palette (see "Adding Graphics with the Tool Palette," later in this chapter).

Note   It is important to understand that the condition (on or off) of the header and footer in the title page is completely independent of the condition of the header and footer in the pages of the balance of the report.

Switching between the title page and the rest of the pages in the report is simple — just toggle the Add Title Page item on (to use the title page) or off (to use the other report pages). Toggling the Add Title Page item off does not erase any customizing you have done to the title page.

One of the more common things to do with a title page is to stretch the height of the header so that no records are displayed on the title page — the title page is then just the "cover page" of the report. This is an attractive option because, unlike the normal report header, the title page header does *not* include the column headings. This means that if you want to display records on the title page, you'll have to add the column headings to the title page header.

Working with Summary Panels

When you choose a layout that uses grouping, summary, or grand totals, the summarized fields are placed in an area of the report known as a *summary panel* (see Figure 23-9). To adjust the look of your report, you can adjust the height of a summary panel, change the grouping, and make the summary panel either a leading panel (above the set of records) or a trailing panel (below the set of records).

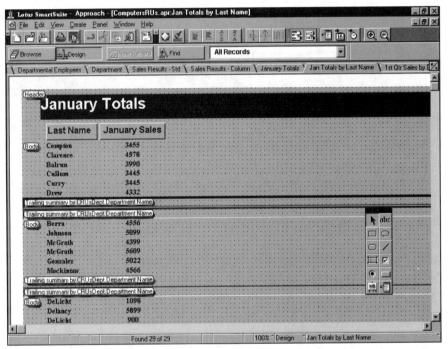

Figure 23-9: Summary panels hold summarized fields on a report.

To adjust the height of a summary panel, click in a blank area of the summary panel. Approach surrounds the summary panel with a heavy border. To modify the height of a leading summary panel, click the *lower* border and drag it. To modify the height of a trailing summary panel, click the *upper* border and drag it.

To change the grouping on which the summary panel is based, click the panel and choose Panel Properties from the Panel menu. In the resulting Infobox, make a grouping selection from the Basics panel:

✦ **Every X records.** This option groups the records in the order they were entered, but creates a summary every "X" records, where X is the value for the number of records on which you want to summarize.

✦ **All records.** This option creates a single group for all the records in the database, and calculates any summarized fields over the whole database.

✦ **Records grouped by.** From this list of fields, you can pick the field upon which to group. If the database is not already sorted so that all records with the same value in the group field occur together, Approach will ask you if you want to sort them that way. Respond Yes unless you want a useless jumble of records and summaries.

Duplicating or Deleting a Report

Even with the Report Assistant, creating a new report is a fair amount of work. If you find that you need a report that looks a lot like an existing report, you can create a duplicate report and modify the duplicate. To create the duplicate, choose Duplicate Report from the Report menu. Approach creates an exact copy of the report; the name of the new report adds "Copy of" to the name of report from which it was duplicated.

If you find that you no longer need a report, you can delete it by choosing Delete Report from the Report menu. After confirming that you truly want to delete the report, Approach makes the deletion.

Adjusting the Properties of Items on a Report

Up to now, we've discussed setting special properties of items on reports (such as the grouping for summary panels and column headings). However, you can adjust many other properties of objects on a report using the Infobox. Most of the options for objects on a report are identical to the options for objects on a form (discussed previously in Chapter 22, "Working with Field Types"), so here we'll just discuss the special properties for reports.

A report has three special properties that you won't find on forms:

✦ **Keep records together.** If you select this option in the Basics panel of the report's Infobox, Approach won't break a record across a page boundary (unless a record is more than a page long). This makes the report a lot more readable.

✦ **Number of columns.** If you have lots of records to print, but each record doesn't have many fields, you can choose this option from the Basics panel of the report's Infobox. If you choose to print multiple columns in the report (see Figure 23-10), Approach prints the specified report layout down the page, and then continues the report layout in the next column, snaking from the bottom of one column to the top of the next column.

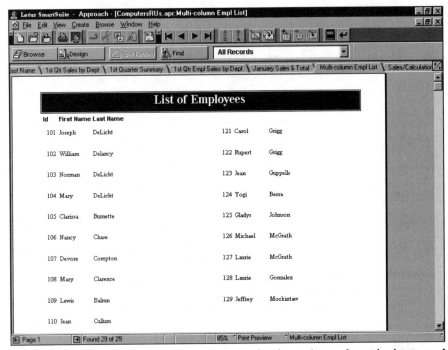

Figure 23-10: A multicolumn report continues the data printout from the bottom of one column to the top of the next.

✦ **Enable outer join.** This option is available from the Options panel of the report's Infobox. As discussed earlier, each record in the main database may have no, one, or many matching records in the detail database. However, by default, if a main record does *not* have any detail records attached (for example, a department has no employees), that main record does not show up in a report. If you want to see all the main database records in the report, regardless of whether they have matching detail records attached or not, you must choose the Enable Outer Join option.

Creating and Modifying Worksheets

On occasion, you want to see many records all at once — and perhaps make changes to those records. Forms don't serve this purpose well because they show you only one record at a time. However, worksheets are ideal.

A worksheet looks much like a spreadsheet — it is essentially a table in which fields are represented as columns, and records are represented as rows (see Figure 23-11). With the exception of performing columnar arithmetic, you can perform the same operations on a worksheet as you can on a form or report, including entry of new data, editing of existing data, finds, and sorting. You can rearrange the fields (columns) in a worksheet, and even use drop-down lists for data input. Worksheets are also easy to use and customize. In fact, Approach automatically creates a default worksheet for you when you create a new database.

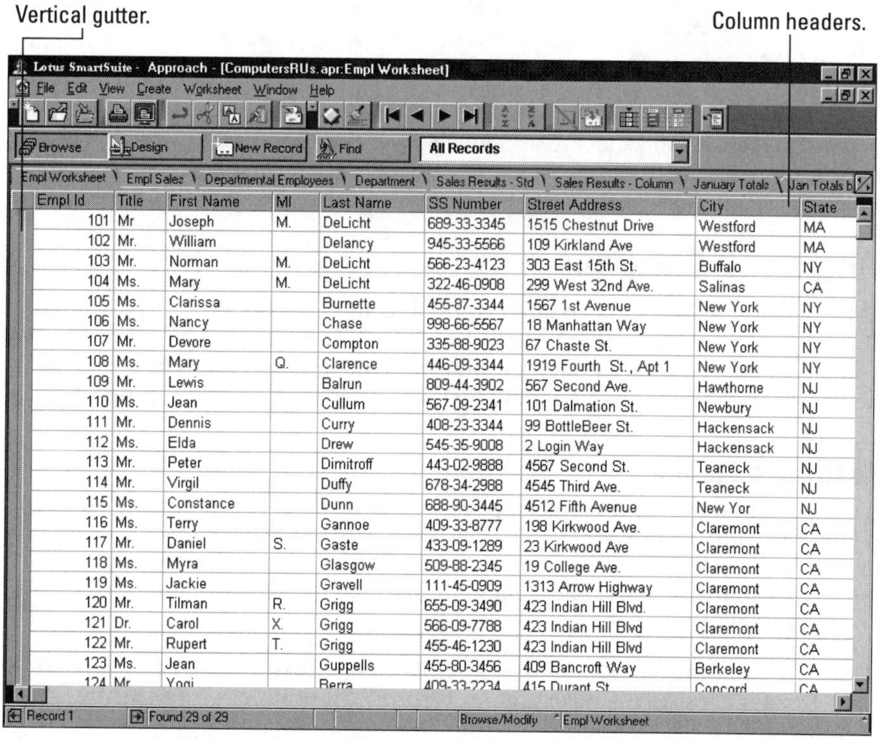

Vertical gutter.   Column headers.

Figure 23-11: A worksheet represents your Approach data in a table.

Creating Worksheets with the Worksheet Assistant

As with all the other types of views, Approach provides an assistant to help you create worksheets. However, building a worksheet with the assistant is very simple. Just choose Worksheet from the Create menu, and pick the fields you want on the worksheet from the single panel in the Worksheet Assistant dialog box (see Figure 23-12). Once you click OK, you can see your worksheet.

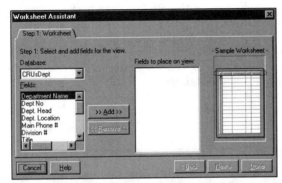

Figure 23-12: The Worksheet Assistant helps you build worksheets.

Adjusting Columns

Most of the changes you can make to the layout of a worksheet involve adjusting the columns. To customize the layout of the worksheet, you can resize or relocate columns, add a field or a column to the worksheet, delete a column, change the row height, change the column heading text, and change the column properties.

Resizing a Column

If the column takes up too much space, or looks too crowded for the data, you can adjust the width of the column. To do so, use the following steps:

1. Click in the heading of the column to select the entire column (see Figure 23-13).

2. Move the mouse pointer over the right edge of the selected column in the header area. The mouse pointer turns into a double-headed arrow.

3. Click and drag the border to adjust the width of the column.

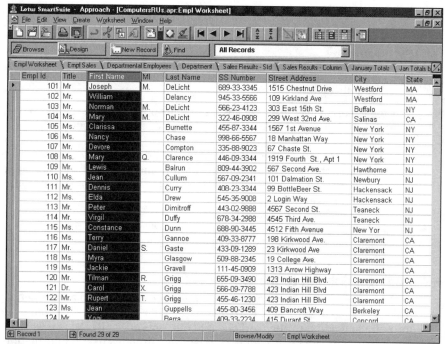

Figure 23-13: To select a column prior to moving or resizing it, click in the header to highlight the whole column.

Changing the Location of a Column

When you use the Worksheet Assistant to create a worksheet, Approach places the columns in the worksheet in the order that you picked the fields. However, this might not be the best order, or you might add or delete columns (see the next two sections) and need to rearrange the columns.

To relocate a column in the worksheet, click in the heading of the column to select the entire column. Click again in the header, hold the mouse button down, and drag the column to its new location. As you drag the column, the mouse pointer indicates the name (header text) of the column you are moving, and a heavy black line appears between existing columns to indicate where the column will be located if you release the mouse button.

Adding a Database Field to a Worksheet

When you add a database field to a worksheet, you are actually physically adding a column to the worksheet, because fields are represented as columns. However, Approach provides two ways to perform this operation: adding a field to a worksheet and adding a column to the worksheet. The Add Column option is discussed in the next section.

To add a field to a worksheet, use the following steps:

1. Choose Add Field from the Worksheet menu. Approach displays the Add Field dialog box.

2. Select the field you want to add to the worksheet by clicking it in the Add Field dialog box.

Note If you choose a field that contains a summary operation, the resulting column in the worksheet will be empty. However, Approach does not prevent you from doing so.

3. Drag the field into the worksheet. As you drag the field, the mouse pointer indicates the field name you are adding, and a heavy black line appears between existing columns to indicate where the column's field will be located if you release the mouse button.

Note The default column header name is the field name. See "Changing the Column Heading Text," for instructions on changing the heading.

Adding a Column to the Worksheet

Adding a column to the worksheet is one of the more useful adjustments you can make, because it enables you to create a calculated field (a field that evaluates a formula) and add it to the worksheet in one operation. Because a worksheet looks much like a spreadsheet, adding calculations provides useful information (such as a calculation that adds up several numeric fields). Unfortunately, Approach does not allow you to perform summary calculations (such as the sum of all the values in a column) in a worksheet.

To add a column to the worksheet, use the following steps:

1. Select the column to the right of which you want the new column.

2. Choose Add Column from the Worksheet menu, or click the Insert a Column SmartIcon. Approach opens the Formula dialog box (see Figure 23-14).

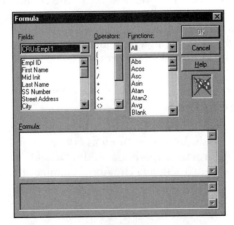

Figure 23-14: The Formula dialog box enables you to build formulas for insertion into a worksheet column.

3. Define the formula (including just adding a single field) using the Formula dialog box. For more information on defining a formula for a calculated field, see "Specifying Formulas for Calculated Fields" in Chapter 22, "Working with Field Types."

4. Click OK to add the column to the worksheet. The contents of the column display the results of performing the calculation on each record in the worksheet.

Note   Although Approach will not prohibit you from including summary functions in the formula, the column will be empty if you do. Further, if you had previously defined calculated fields using summary functions, you can include these in the formula (or even make one the entire formula), but the column will be empty in the worksheet.

Deleting a Column

To delete a column from the worksheet, select the entire column by clicking in the header. Press the Delete key or choose Clear from the Edit menu. Alternately, after you select the column, click in the header and begin to drag the column toward the top of the screen. At some point the mouse pointer turns into a trashcan, and you can release the mouse button to delete the column.

Danger Zone   Approach does *not* ask you to confirm the column deletion. If you accidentally delete a column, immediately press Ctrl+Z or choose Undo from the Edit menu to return the column to the worksheet.

Adjusting the Row Height

Normally, Approach sizes the row height to show the data with some surrounding white space, making the text easier to read. However, you can adjust the row height to add more white space or jam in more data on each screen.

To adjust the row height, click the right-facing arrow at the far left side of the screen (known as a *vertical gutter*), highlighting the entire row (see Figure 23-15). Move the mouse pointer over the lower border of the selected row *in the gutter*. When the mouse pointer becomes a two-headed arrow, click and drag the border to adjust the row height (which affects all the rows in the worksheet).

Empl Id	Title	First Name	MI	Last Name	SS Number	Street Address	City	State
101	Mr.	Joseph	M.	DeLicht	689-33-3345	1515 Chestnut Drive	Westford	MA
102	Mr.	William		Delancy	945-33-5566	109 Kirkland Ave	Westford	MA
103	Mr.	Norman	M.	DeLicht	566-23-4123	303 East 15th St.	Buffalo	NY
104	Ms.	Mary	M.	DeLicht	322-46-0908	299 West 32nd Ave.	Salinas	CA
105	Ms.	Clarissa		Burnette	455-87-3344	1567 1st Avenue	New York	NY
106	Ms.	Nancy		Chase	998-66-5567	18 Manhattan Way	New York	NY

Figure 23-15: Select the entire row by clicking the arrow at the left side of the screen. Then you can adjust the height of the rows.

Changing Column Heading Text

By default, Approach titles each column with the corresponding field name. However, you can change the text of the heading to make it more descriptive. To change the column heading text, double-click the heading, which selects just the heading. Pause, and click the heading again. This puts you in Text-Edit mode. You can then simply type in the new heading text.

Changing Column Properties

As with virtually every other object that appears on a view, you can modify the properties of an entire column by selecting the entire column (click in the header) and choosing Worksheet Properties from the shortcut menu or the Worksheet menu.

Note   Normally, when you select an object in a view, the context-sensitive menu changes to reflect what was selected. However, columns in a worksheet are an exception. Even though you have selected a column prior to requesting the column properties Infobox, the context-sensitive menu still reads "Worksheet Properties." However, when the Infobox appears, it is actually ready to adjust the column properties.

For columns, you can change the font, size, attributes, color, alignment, the background fill color; the display format, and the field and data entry type for the column. However, unlike fields on forms (for which you can specify six different data entry type formats), you have only three options for the data entry type of a column on a worksheet: Field box, drop-down list, and Field box and list.

Working with Records in a Worksheet

As explained earlier, you can change the data in your database using the worksheet as an editing mechanism. You can directly edit the data, set all the data in a column to the same value ("filling" the field), and add or delete records just as you would with a form.

Editing Your Data

To edit the data in a worksheet, move the mouse pointer into any cell (the intersection of a row and column) in the worksheet and double-click. If the field is a field box, Approach places you in Text-Edit mode, and you can type in the new value. If the field is a drop-down list, click the arrow and choose a new value from the list. Finally, if the field is Field box and list, you can choose either input method.

Filling a Field with a Value

It can be helpful to place the same value or a value that results from evaluating a formula into either all the records in the database or just the records that result from a find (perform the find prior to performing the fill field operation). This is called *filling* a field.

To fill a field, use the following steps:

1. If you want, choose the field (column) or a cell in the column that you want to fill.

2. Choose Fill Field from the Worksheet menu. Approach displays the Fill Field dialog box (see Figure 23-16).

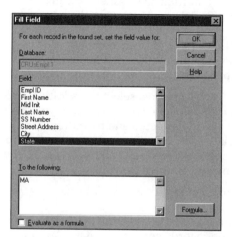

Figure 23-16: The Fill Field dialog box enables you to define the field you want to fill.

3. Choose the field you want to fill from the Field list. The default is the field that you selected prior to beginning the fill operation (if any).

4. Type in the value you want to fill the field with (the default is the contents of the cell you selected prior to beginning the fill, if any). Alternately, click the Formula button and define the formula that Approach will evaluate to provide the contents of the field. Click OK in the Formula dialog box to return to the Fill Field dialog box.

5. Choose OK to fill the field with the value.

Adding Records

A worksheet offers a handy view of your data, so you may want to use it for adding and deleting records. You can quickly move through your records, seeing multiple records on a single screen.

To add one or more new records, choose New from the Records item in the Worksheet menu. Approach inserts a new row at the bottom of the worksheet and places the text cursor in the first (leftmost) field. Enter data in each cell, and tab to the next cell.

Note If you enter data into a new record and press Tab from the last (rightmost) field, Approach automatically adds another new record (which takes the form of a row in the worksheet).

Deleting Records

Deleting records is especially convenient from a worksheet because it is easy to select multiple records for deletion. To delete records, use the following steps:

1. Move the mouse pointer to the left side of the screen and click in the gutter (the space between the leftmost field and the edge of the form) alongside the record you want to select. Approach highlights the entire record.

2. If you want to delete other adjacent records, select the additional records. You can select additional records in one of two ways. First, you can click in the gutter for the record you already selected and then drag up or down. Or, you can hold down the Shift key and click in the gutter of another record. Approach selects the newly chosen records *and* all the records between the newly selected record and one you selected previously.

Note You cannot delete multiple, non-adjacent records in a worksheet.

3. Click the Worksheet menu and choose Delete. From the Delete submenu, choose Selected Records. If the records contain any data, Approach deletes the selected records after you confirm the deletion. If the records are empty, Approach does not ask for confirmation before deleting the records.

Duplicating Records

The multiple records available in a worksheet also make it an ideal place to duplicate records. Simply select the record or records you want to duplicate (as detailed in Steps 1 and 2 of the previous section) and choose Duplicate from the Records item in the Worksheet menu.

Hiding Records

You can temporarily hide records so that you can see just the records you are interested in. To hide one or more records, select the records (as detailed in Steps 1 and 2 of Deleting Records) and choose Hide from the Records item in the Worksheet menu.

To see all your records again, choose Find All from the Find item in the Worksheet menu.

Rearranging the Records

You can change the order in which Approach displays the records in the database by sorting on the contents of one or more adjacent columns (fields). As with other kinds of sorting, you are not actually changing the order in which the records are stored — just the order in which they are displayed. To change the order of the records in the worksheet, use the following steps:

1. Click in the header area of the column on which you wish to sort. Approach highlights the entire column.

2. If you want to select secondary sort columns, drag the mouse pointer into the header of any adjacent columns. Each additional column is used to distinguish between records that have the same value in the first selected field. For example, if you click in the Last Name field first, then the records will be sorted by last name. If you then drag into the First Name field (selecting it), then all the records with the same last name will be sorted by first name, and so on.

3. Choose Ascending or Descending from the Sort item in the Worksheet menu, or select one of the Sort SmartIcons. Approach sorts the contents of the worksheet based on the selected columns.

Creating and Modifying Crosstabs

Crosstabs look much like worksheets, but instead of displaying individual records from the database, a crosstab summarizes the information in the database according to relationships that you define. In a classic crosstab, you specify a field that provides the contents of the leftmost column (for example, the Last Name field). You also specify a field to provide the contents of the column headings.

Finally, you specify how you want to summarize each cell in the crosstab. Approach automatically adds a summary column at the far right and a summary row at the bottom of the crosstab, but you can change the summary function used or delete the summary row or column. Figure 23-17 illustrates sales of products by employee, summing the total of each product for each employee.

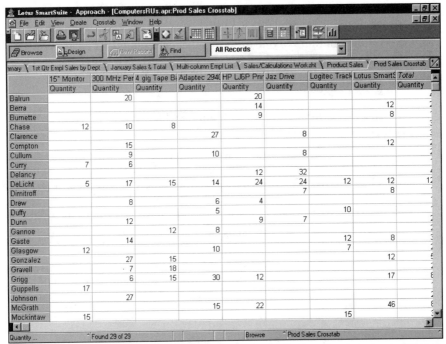

Figure 23-17: A sample crosstab of product sales by the employees who made them.

Note

Although adding up quantities (summing) is the most common operation for the body cells in a crosstab, Approach can perform other operations, including Count, Average, Maximum, and Minimum.

Creating a Crosstab

To create a crosstab, use the following steps:

1. Choose Crosstab from the Create menu. Approach opens the Crosstab Assistant dialog box (see Figure 23-18).

2. In the Step 1: Rows panel, choose the field you want to use for the rows. The field you pick here will supply the values that go in the leftmost column of the crosstab. Choose the field in the Fields list, and click the >>Add>> button to move the field to the Group Fields list. Choose how you want to group the records from the Group By drop-down list. The options depend on the type of field you choose to group. When you are through, click Next to move to the next panel.

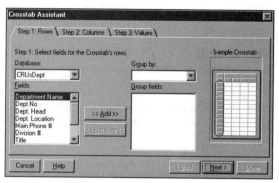

Figure 23-18: The Crosstab Assistant guides you through the steps to create a crosstab.

Note

Although Approach will let you pick multiple fields, the results of doing so are quite confusing. Essentially, if you pick multiple fields, Approach nests the fields and provides a total for each nesting. For example, if you pick Last Name and then First Name, the leftmost column will contain values of each last name. The next column will list the first name (with multiple records where employees have the same last name) and summarize the count on each first name. If all you want is the full name of the employee in the crosstab, create a calculated field that contains the employee's full name.

3. In the Step 2: Columns panel, choose the field you want to use for the columns. The field you pick here will supply the values that appear in the topmost row of the crosstab. Choose the field you want from the Fields list, and click >>Add>> to move the field to the Group Fields list. Click Next to move to the next panel.

Note

The column field should contain the categories that you want to view your data by. In our example, we want to see the number (quantity) of products that was sold by an employee, so the employee identifier (last name or employee #) goes in the row, and the product field is used for the column, because you want one column for each product sold.

4. In the Step 3: Values panel, choose the field you want to summarize on and the calculation you want to perform. The results of the calculation appear in each cell. In our example, the quantity (sum of the field Quantity) of each product sold by each employee is displayed. Choose the field to summarize on from the Field list and click the >>Add>> button to move the field to the Summary Fields list.

5. Choose the calculation you want to make from the Calculate The drop-down list. Then choose Done to create the crosstab.

Note   The value field you select in Step 4 is normally a numeric field (such as Quantity in our example). If you select a field that is not numeric, the only operation you can choose from the Calculate The drop-down list is Count.

6. If you are working with joined databases and have placed fields from more than one database in the crosstab, Approach opens a dialog box requesting the main database. Choose the database from the drop-down list and click OK.

Once you are through creating a crosstab, Approach displays the crosstab in Browse mode, with a summary column at the far right and a summary row at the bottom.

Working with Summary Fields

Because the purpose of a crosstab is to summarize your data, there tend to be quite a few summary calculations present in a crosstab. These summary calculations include the summary row and summary column that Approach provides when you build the crosstab, as well as any summary fields you add to the crosstab. You can change the summary field calculations for the default row and column, as well as add new summary calculations to the crosstab.

Changing the Summary Field Calculations

You can change the calculation formula for the summary column (the right side of the crosstab) and the summary row (the bottom of the crosstab). To change the calculation for the summary column, use the following steps:

1. Click in the header area of the summary column. Approach selects the entire column.

2. Choose Crosstab Properties from the Crosstab menu.

3. In the Infobox for the column, click the Formula tab (see Figure 23-19), and choose the formula you want to use.

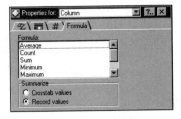

Figure 23-19: The Formula panel in a summary field Infobox enables you to choose the calculation you want to perform.

To change the calculation for the summary row, select the row "header" at the left side of the summary row, and follow Steps 2 and 3.

Adding Summary Fields to a Crosstab

Although Approach automatically provides a single summary column at the right side of the crosstab, and a single summary row at the bottom of the crosstab, you may wish to add more. To add a new summary column at the right side of the crosstab, use the following steps:

1. Choose Summarize Rows from the Crosstab menu. This may seem a little strange, but each cell in the new summary column is actually summarizing the row that the cell is in.

2. Approach displays a new summary column. Choose Crosstab Properties from the Crosstab menu to display the Infobox.

3. From the Formula panel in the Infobox, choose the formula you want to use for the new summary column.

To add a new summary row at the bottom of the crosstab, use the following steps:

1. Choose Summarize Columns from the Crosstab menu.

2. Approach displays a new summary row. Choose Crosstab Properties from the Crosstab menu to display the Infobox.

3. From the Formula panel in the Infobox, choose the formula you want to use for the new summary row.

Adding Fields to a Crosstab

Once you have built a crosstab, you can add fields to one of three areas of the crosstab: rows, columns, and summaries. The technique is the same for all three areas. Simply choose Add Field from the Crosstab menu, and Approach displays the Add Field dialog box. Click the field you want to add and drag it to the appropriate area of the crosstab. You can perform the following operations:

✦ **Add a Field to the Row.** To add a field (column) to the left side of the crosstab, drag the field from the Add Field dialog box toward the left side of the crosstab. Continue dragging until a heavy border appears to the right of the leftmost column. Release the mouse button, and Approach will nest the added field as a lower-level crosstab row. If you keep dragging until the heavy border appears to the left of the column, the field you added becomes the higher-level row, and the existing field becomes the lower-level crosstab row.

✦ **Add a Field to the Column.** To add a field (row) to the top of the crosstab, drag the field from the Add Field dialog box toward the top of the screen. Continue dragging until a heavy border appears just below the topmost row. Release the mouse button and Approach will nest the added field as a lower-level crosstab column. If you keep dragging until the heavy border appears above the row, the field you added becomes the higher-level column, and the existing field becomes the lower-level crosstab column.

✦ **Add a Field to the Summary.** To add a field to the cell area of the crosstab, drag the field from the Add Field dialog box into the cell area. A heavy rectangle appears around the cell area of the crosstab. When you release the mouse button, Approach adds another column for each category across the top of the screen. This column performs the calculation you specify on the added field.

To specify the calculation, select the column and choose Crosstab Properties from the Crosstab menu. Click the formula tab of the Infobox, and choose the formula to use from the list.

Drilling Down to the Data

The data that Approach displays in the cells of a crosstab is calculated from the records in your database. You can request to see the records from which a particular cell value was calculated, a process called *drilling down*. To do this, click the cell and choose Drill Down to Data from the Crosstab menu. Approach brings up a view that displays just the records used in calculating the cell.

You can set the view that Approach uses to display the records by choosing it from the Drill Down View drop-down list in the Basics tab of the Crosstab's Infobox. To return to viewing all records, choose Find All from the Find item in the context-sensitive menu (for example, Worksheet, Form, Report, and so on).

Because a calculation normally includes multiple records, it is best to choose a worksheet for displaying the source records, as a worksheet can display multiple records without having to page through them.

Comparing Crosstabs to Worksheets

Crosstabs are very similar to worksheets, and you can modify the format of a crosstab in many of the same ways you can modify the format of a worksheet. For example, you can:

✦ Adjust the font, alignment, color, size, and attributes of header text and cell text.

✦ Change the fill color for columns and rows in the worksheet.

✦ Adjust the width of individual columns and the height of all rows.

✦ Delete columns by selecting the entire column (click in the header) and pressing the Delete key.

✦ Edit the text of some column headings.

✦ Change the name, printing parameters, and macros for a crosstab.

✦ Create up to four panes for viewing different parts of the crosstab.

However, some unique properties of a crosstab make it different from a worksheet. These differences include the following:

✦ You cannot edit column labels that represent actual data in the database. For example, you can't edit the column headings that correspond to products.

✦ You cannot rearrange the columns in a crosstab, nor can you move the summary columns or rows from their default positions.

✦ You cannot edit the values in the body (cells) of the crosstab, because they are calculated values.

Converting a Worksheet into a Crosstab

Because worksheets and crosstabs are similar, it is relatively simple to create a crosstab from an existing worksheet. First, you must decide which field you want to use to create the summary row (leftmost column) from. If that field is already present in the worksheet, click in the header for that column and drag the field to the left edge of the worksheet until the left gutter (where the row arrow is) shows a heavy blue border. Release the mouse button to create the crosstab. If the summary row field is not in the worksheet, you can drag it from the Add Field dialog box. Figure 23-20 shows an example of what happens after dragging the department name into the left gutter to create a crosstab.

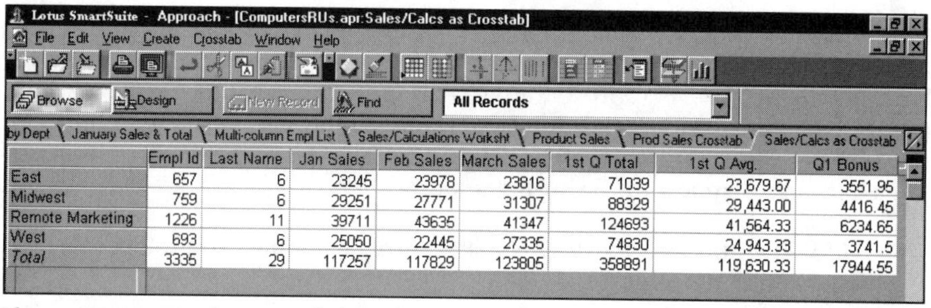

Figure 23-20: Turning a worksheet into a crosstab can sometimes lead to unexpected results.

Notice that in Figure 23-20, there are some strange entries in some numeric fields (such as Empl Id) and in some text fields (like Last Name). This is because, when you create a crosstab from a worksheet, Approach summarizes all the cells by the summary row (in this case, Department Name). Where the data is numeric (Empl Id), Approach sums all the results. This makes sense for some kinds of number (Sales results) and not for others (Empl Id). Where the data is textual, Approach counts the number of records, leading to results like numeric Last Name. You can remove these nonsensical columns if you wish.

When you create a crosstab from a worksheet, Approach does *not* automatically add a summary row at the bottom of the crosstab. However, you can add one by choosing Summarize Columns from the Crosstab menu. You can't add a summary column at the right side of this crosstab.

Creating and Modifying Charts

Although worksheets and reports lend themselves to viewing lots of data in a numeric format, it is often difficult to understand large quantities of data or spot trends when viewing data this way. Charts are a powerful way to summarize data in graphical format, usually making it easier to understand the information.

Except for a pie chart, Approach's charts represent data plotted against an x-axis (horizontal axis) and a y-axis (vertical axis). The x-axis usually contains categories, such as products, time, geographic areas, or other ways of grouping your data. The y-axis displays the scale that the data values are plotted against (plotted against the x-axis categories).

Browse mode is not available for charts, because you can't directly enter data into a chart. Browse does not appear in the mode pop-up list of the status bar, and the Browse button is unavailable in the Action bar.

Figure 23-21 shows a typical bar chart — the quantity of products sold is on the y-axis; the product names are on the x-axis. For each category, there are a series of bars, one for each sales representative. This grouping is called a *series*. A series is an effective way of adding an additional level of information to a bar chart.

The chart also displays the following important areas:

✦ **Title.** The title identifies the chart. Approach enables you to specify the title while building the chart.

✦ **Y-axis title.** This title identifies what is being displayed (typically the field name) along the y-axis (vertical axis).

✦ **X-axis title.** This title identifies what is being displayed along the x-axis (horizontal axis).

✦ **Plotted area.** The rectangular area inside the axes is where the data is plotted. The plotted area can display a grid of lines to help you see the data more clearly.

✦ **Legend.** If you use a series, you need something to tell you what the various data representations (lines, points, bars, pie slices, and so on) mean. The legend does just that.

Y-axis title.   Title.   Legend.

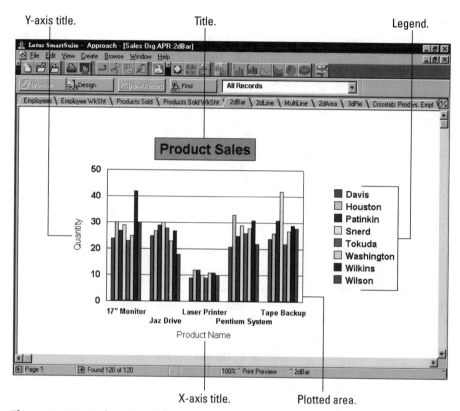

X-axis title.   Plotted area.

Figure 23-21: A chart that shows the various areas of importance.

Understanding the Different Chart Types

Approach enables you to define many different kinds of charts. These charts fall into several major types. The following sections show you some of the more common types. Which type you choose will depend on the type of data you want to represent.

Note

Within each chart type, there are many different options you can choose to customize the chart. For example, for a bar chart, you can choose a vertical bar chart (bar length is measured on the y-axis) or a horizontal bar chart (bar length is measured on the x-axis). And, you can choose from many different styles of charts, such as 3-D chart styles.

Bar Charts

Bar charts are the most often-used chart, especially in business. Each bar either represents one item (defined by the series, if there is one) of a group of items, or one category as listed on the x-axis. The height of the bar indicates the value of the item in relation to the values listed on the y-axis.

Line Charts

A line chart displays one or more lines, with each line connecting a series of dots; the dot represents a category listed on the x-axis. The height of the dot represents the value of the measured category in relationship to the values listed on the y-axis (see Figure 23-22). If you use the series feature for a line chart, you end up with multiple points in each category — and multiple lines to connect the dots — one for each value in the series (see Figure 23-23).

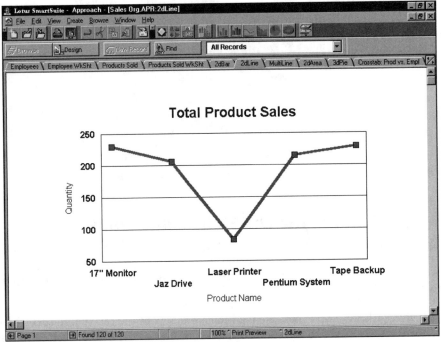

Figure 23-22: A line chart that does not use series — and thus displays only a single line.

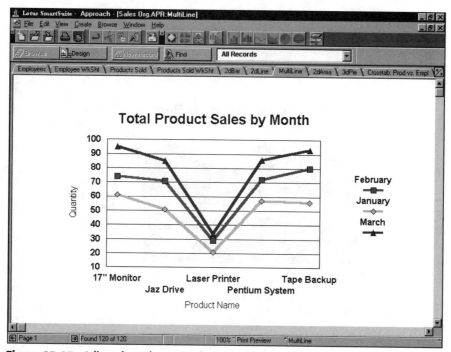

Figure 23-23: A line chart that uses the series feature (grouping by month). There is one line for each value in the series.

Area Charts

Area charts are best for showing trends of data over time. They display much the same kind of data as line charts, but "fill in" the area under the line, emphasizing how the area under the line has changed. If the area chart employs series, then multiple lines with areas are filled in (as in Figure 23-24).

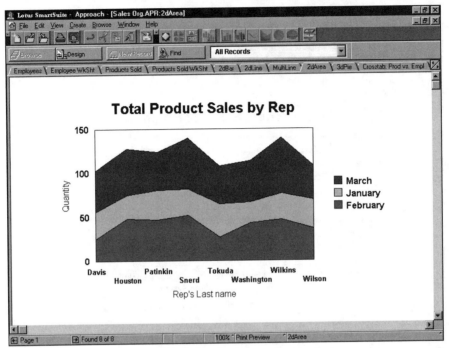

Figure 23-24: An area chart with series shows trends over time.

Pie Charts

A pie chart shows the relative contribution of each part to the whole. Pie charts are popular in illustrating things like market share, percent of product sales, and other quantities where the percentage contribution is important (see Figure 23-25).

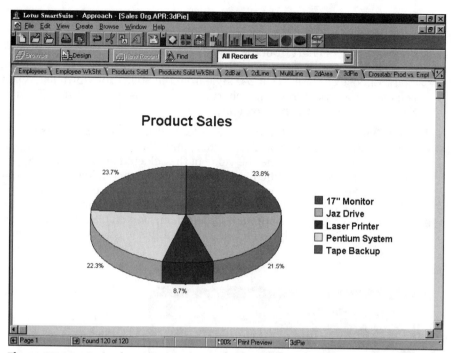

Figure 23-25: A pie chart displays how much each part contributes. The legend identifies what each part means.

Creating a Chart with the Chart Assistant

To create a chart using the Chart Assistant, use the following steps:

1. Choose Chart from the Create menu. Approach opens the Chart Assistant dialog box (see Figure 23-26).

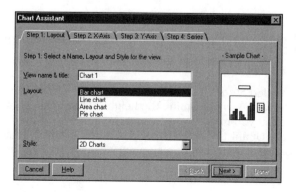

Figure 23-26: The Chart Assistant guides you through creating a chart.

2. In the Step 1: Layout panel, choose a name for the chart and type it into the View Name & Title field.

3. Choose a type of chart from the Layout list. As you click a particular chart type, the diagram to the right of the list changes to display a sample of the chart. Choose either a 2-D or 3-D style from the Style drop-down list. Again, as you choose a style, the sample chart changes to display a sample. Then click Next to advance to the next panel.

4. If the chart is a pie chart, the next panel is entitled Step 2: Pie fields (see Figure 23-27). There are two lists in this panel. Pick a field from the Show a New Slice For list. Each time the value of the selected field changes, Approach will create a new slice in the pie. Next, pick a summary calculation from the Each Slice Shows The drop-down list. This calculation is performed on the values for the field you pick from the Of Field list. The results of the summary calculation are used by Approach to determine and display the relative sizes of the slices. Once you have picked the quantities in this panel, click Done to view the chart.

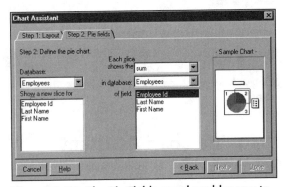

Figure 23-27: The Pie Fields panel enables you to specify the field Approach uses for creating new slices, and the calculation and field used to determine the slice size.

5. If the chart is any type other than a pie, the next panel is entitled Step 2: X-Axis (see Figure 23-26). Choose the x-axis field from the list. Click Next to advance to the next panel.

6. The next panel is entitled Step 3: Y-Axis. Choose the field whose values you want to use in a calculation to determine the height of the lines, bars, dots, and so on. For example, you might want to sum the quantity of products sold, so you would pick the Quantity field in this panel. Click >>Add>> to add the field to the Of Fields list. Then, choose a summary calculation.

Note You can choose multiple fields in Step 6. However, the results are confusing and the potential usefulness is questionable.

7. Click Done if you are finished, or click Next if you want to add a series. If you choose Done and you used more than one database from a joined set of databases, Approach asks you to pick the main database for the chart.

8. In the Step 4: Series panel, choose the field for each value for which you want to have a new series.

9. Click Done to display the chart. If you used more than one database from a joined set of databases, Approach asks you to pick the main database for the chart.

Creating a Chart from a Crosstab

Because crosstabs also summarize data (but in a tabular format), it is easy to convert a crosstab to a chart (which summarizes data graphically). To do so, simply open the crosstab you want to convert to a chart, and choose Chart This Crosstab from the Crosstab menu. Approach creates the chart.

When you convert a crosstab to a chart, the crosstab rows become points along the x-axis. The crosstab groups (column headings) become the series for the items listed below the x-axis. The values along the y-axis are automatically scaled from the values in the body cells.

Duplicating and Deleting Charts

Building a chart involves a lot of decisions, but you can duplicate an existing chart if you need a chart that is similar to one you've already built. To duplicate a chart, choose Duplicate Chart from the Chart menu.

If you are done with a chart and don't need it anymore, you can delete the chart by choosing Delete Chart from the Chart menu.

Enhancing Your Data in Design Mode

You have a lot of power over the design of your data. Approach allows you a lot of flexibility over the placement of fields and their properties (as well as the properties of the view). Approach also enables you to customize your view. You can insert system-derived values, add graphics, and use various tools to help get the layout just right.

Inserting the Date, Time, or Page Number

It is often helpful to insert the current date, time, or page number into a form or report. Some of these quantities are automatically inserted into report headers and footers when you create a report, but you can add them to any view.

To add the current date, choose Today's Date from the Insert item in the context-sensitive menu. Approach places a field on the view that is automatically updated to show the current date. When Show Data is checked in the View menu, the date is visible until you double-click the date field (see Figure 23-28). If you double-click the date field, (or Show Data is not checked), the date is represented on the view as <<DATE>>.

Once you double-click the date (or any of the other items discussed in this section), you can edit the text. However, if you do, the field will show just the edited text — it will no longer display the date.

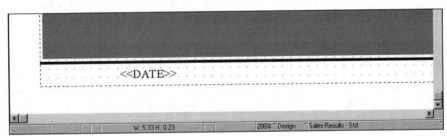

Figure 23-28: The current date is represented in double braces when you don't have Show Data checked, or you double-click the Date in Design mode.

To add the current time, choose Current Time from the Insert item in the context-sensitive menu. Approach places a field on the view that is automatically updated to show the current time. When Show Data is checked in the View menu, the time is visible until you double-click the time field. If you double-click the time field (or Show Data is not checked), the time is represented as <<TIME>>.

To add the page number (especially useful in report headers and footers), choose Page Number from the Insert item in the context-sensitive menu. Approach places a field on the view that is automatically updated to show the current page number. When Show Data is checked in the View menu, the page number is visible until you double-click the page number field. If you double-click the Page Number field (or Show Data is not checked), the page number is represented as <<#>>.

Adding Graphics with the Tool Palette

One of the more useful ways to design a form or report is to make it look like the paper version that people are used to. However, paper forms and reports have more than just fields on them — they have fancy titles, boxes, text, and so forth.

Fortunately, Approach has tools that enable you to duplicate the look of existing forms and reports (and any other types of you view you want). You can add text, lines, rectangles, ellipses, and rounded rectangles to a view—including the header or footer.

To add text to a form, choose the Text tool from the Tool palette, or select Text from the Drawing item in the Create menu. The mouse cursor turns into the text-drawing cursor. Click the view where you want the upper-left corner of the text box to be, and then drag to the lower-right corner. Approach creates a text box of the size you specified (see Figure 23-29). The text insertion point is located at the upper-left corner of the box, ready for you to type in the text.

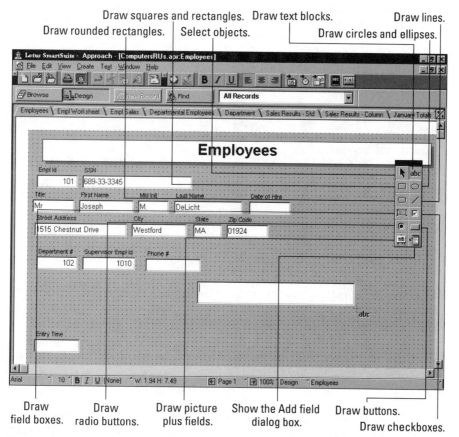

Figure 23-29: Once you click and drag the text rectangle, Approach creates it with the text insertion point, ready for you to type the text. (You can add and manipulate text and graphics using the tools identified in the Tool palette.)

Type in the text you want. You can change the properties of either the text or the text box using the Infobox.

To add a graphic to a form, choose the graphic tool you want from the Tool palette (rectangle, ellipse, rounded rectangle, or line) or from the Drawing item in the Create menu. As with the text box, click the view where you want the upper-left corner located (or starting point of the line) and drag to the lower-right corner (or end of the line). Approach creates the selected graphic in the size you specified. You can adjust all of the standard properties using the object's Infobox.

Inserting a Field Value

Once you create a text box, you can insert the value of any field in the database into the text box. One reason you might want to do this is to display the data in the field —but not allow the user to edit the contents. A field value in a text box is *not* editable by the user in Browse mode. Another reason might be to add explanatory text along with the field value (see Figure 23-30). The text you type in is still displayed, along with the inserted field value.

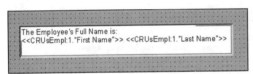

The Employee's Full Name is:
<<CRUsEmpl:1."First Name">> <<CRUsEmpl:1."Last Name">>

Figure 23-30: Inserting a field value enables you to display the value (without allowing editing), or embed it in other text.

To insert a field value into a text box, use the following steps:

1. Click the text box, pause, and then click again to enter Text-Edit mode.

2. Type any text you want in the text box.

3. Place the cursor where you want the field value inserted, and choose Field Value from the Insert item in the context-sensitive menu. Approach displays a list of fields available for you to insert in the Insert Field dialog box.

4. Choose the field and click OK. Approach inserts the field into the text box. While still editing the text, the field name is represented in braces <<>>. The contents of the field are displayed in Browse mode or if you tab out of the field and Show Data is checked in the View menu.

Note   You can also insert the time, date, or page number into a text block. In Step 3, choose Current Time, Today's Date, or Page Number from the Insert item in the context-sensitive menu.

Setting Properties for Graphics

As with fields, you can set the properties of text and graphics objects that you have added to a view. The properties you can set are as follows:

✦ Text font, size, color, relief, attributes, alignment and line spacing (for text objects only).

✦ Border style, fill color, shadow color, which sides have a border, the border color, and width.

✦ Size and location, and whether to slide the object up or left when printing.

✦ Macros to execute when tabbing into or out of a graphic, or when you click the graphic. As we'll see later in this chapter, being able to execute a macro when you click a graphic enables you to build graphical buttons in your applications.

✦ Define and connect a named style to a graphic object.

Using the Rulers and Grid

Approach provides some tools to help you lay out your view. In Design mode, Approach can display a set of rulers along the top and down the side of the form. As you move the mouse cursor, a pair of thin lines move along the rulers, providing a measure of how far the mouse cursor is from the left side of the view and the top of the view. To turn the rulers on or off, select Show Rulers from the View menu.

If you enter Text Edit mode for the text object (see the preceding section on "Adding Graphics with the Tool Palette"), the ruler displays the left margin (a right-facing black arrow), the right margin (a left-facing black arrow), and any tabs (blue arrows). You can remove tabs by dragging them off the ruler, and add new tabs by clicking the ruler.

Another helpful tool is the *grid*, a set of equally spaced dots (see Figure 23-31). Not only do the dots help you line up items in the view, but you can also have Approach automatically "snap to" the grid. That is, whenever you drag an item on the view, it automatically locates itself so that its upper-left corner is on a grid point. To show or hide the grid, select Show Grid from the View menu. To toggle the Snap to Grid feature, choose Snap to Grid from the View menu.

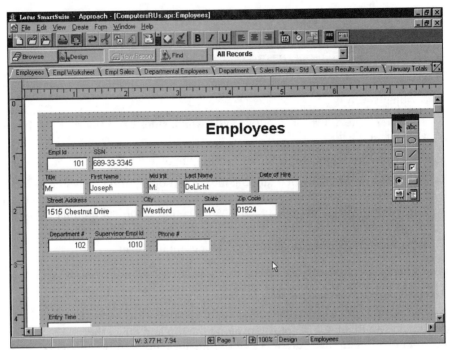

Figure 23-31: Rulers and the grid help you lay out your view.

Zooming In and Out for a Better View

Approach normally displays a view as close to the size that it will print as possible. However, you can zoom in closer (for detail work) or zoom out (for an overall view). In fact you can zoom from 25% (very small) all the way up to 200% (very large). There are several ways to change the zoom level:

✦ From the View menu, choose Zoom In to increase the magnification (up to 200%) or Zoom Out to reduce the magnification (down to 25%). Each time you choose Zoom In or Zoom Out, the magnification changes one step. The steps are 25, 50, 75, 85, 100, and 200.

✦ Choose Zoom To from the View menu. A fly-out menu displays all the zoom options (listed in the last bullet). Select one from the menu list.

✦ Click the Zoom percentage in the status bar (alongside the mode). A pop-up menu displays all the zoom options. Select one from the menu list.

Note Some operations automatically change the zoom setting. For example, Print Preview sets the zoom to 85%. When you exit Print Preview (back to Design or Browse), the zoom does *not* automatically return to its previous setting.

Aligning and Grouping Objects

It can often be helpful to line up objects precisely, or group a set of objects so you can drag them or resize them as a single object. Approach provides tools to perform these operations.

To align two or more objects, select the objects by either dragging a rectangle around the objects or clicking the first object, and then shift-clicking additional objects. Once you have objects selected, choose Align from the Multiple Objects menu. Approach opens the Infobox for the multiple objects and displays a new panel: the Object Alignment panel (see Figure 23-32).

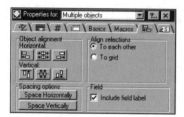

Figure 23-32: The Object Alignment panel enables you to align objects to each other or to the grid.

Your horizontal alignment options are as follows:

✦ **Left.** Approach aligns the left edge of all objects with the left edge of the object that is farthest to the left.

✦ **Center.** Approach aligns all objects so that their left-right centers are lined up.

✦ **Right.** Approach aligns the right edge of all objects with the right edge of the object that is farthest to the right.

✦ **Space Horizontally.** Approach distributes the location of all objects evenly between the object that is farthest to the left and the object that is farthest to the right.

Your vertical alignment options are as follows:

✦ **Top.** Approach aligns all objects so that their top edges align with the top edge of the object that is highest.

✦ **Center.** Approach aligns all objects so that their top-bottom centers are lined up.

✦ **Bottom.** Approach aligns all objects so that their bottom edges align with the bottom edge of the object that is lowest.

✦ **Space Vertically.** Approach distributes the location of all objects evenly between the highest and the lowest objects.

You can have two other options for alignment. The first is to align the objects to each other. This is the default. The other option is align the objects to the grid. This is handy if you had previously turned off Snap to Grid, and now want the objects to realign to the grid.

Arranging Objects

Approach provides you with the ability to place objects on top of one another; in effect, stacking the objects. Each object is in its own layer, with more recently added objects being closer to the "top" layer. As you add objects on top of other objects, they obscure the objects beneath them. For example, if you add a large rectangle to a form (perhaps to provide a color fill), it will hide the fields (or other objects) underneath.

You can, however, adjust this stacking order to change the layering of objects. To do so, choose Arrange from the context-sensitive menu. You have four options in the menu that appears when you choose Arrange:

✦ **Bring to Front.** This option moves the selected object(s) to the top layer, hiding anything beneath them.

✦ **Send to Back.** This option moves the selected objects(s) to the bottom layer, and anything on top of them becomes visible.

✦ **Bring Forward.** This option brings the selected object(s) one layer forward. You may not notice any change, but this command gives you very fine control over stacking order.

✦ **Send Backward.** This option sends the selected object(s) one layer back. Again, you may not notice any visible changes.

Applying a Style

As discussed earlier in this book, you can define styles that set the format for objects, including fonts, size, alignment, color, line width, border location, and so on. To apply a style to an object, select the object and open the object's Infobox. Choose the Named Style panel, and select the style you want from the Style Name list.

Note If you want to use a painstakingly created object style to define a new style, click the object, and choose the Named Style panel in the object's Infobox. Click the New Style button and simply give the style a name and a description. By default, the new style will use all the attributes of the selected object.

Using Fast Format

Once you have the formatting options set just right for an object, you can use Approach's fast formatting option to immediately copy the style to another object. To do so, click the object that you want to use as a style template, and choose Fast Format from the context-sensitive menu (or choose the Apply Format SmartIcon). The mouse turns into a paintbrush. Click any other objects that you want to adopt the chosen style.

Note To exit the Fast Format mode, press the Esc key or reselect Fast Format from the context-sensitive menu.

Building Macros and Scripts

After you use Approach for a while, there is very little you can't make it do for you in Browse mode. You can enter records, sort them, print reports, execute finds, and so on. But what about the people who have to use the application you built? They might not be familiar with how Approach works, or they might only use your application infrequently. It is important to make the application easy to use and easy for someone to refamiliarize themselves with. For example, wouldn't it be nice for a user to just push one button on the screen to have a report come up, sort the records according to a predetermined order, and then print out? Or, perhaps a user could switch to a special "find form," and Approach would automatically request the find criteria—and then execute the find.

Approach provides two very different mechanisms for adding such automation: *macros* and *scripts*. Although macros and scripts are a little work to learn, it is better for the application developer to build as much automation into the application as possible, because the application developer knows Approach better than the casual user.

What Are Macros and Scripts?

A macro is a sequence of instructions for Approach to follow. For example, you might want Approach to apply a sorting order and then print a set of records. You could construct a macro that specifies these instructions. Each "step" in a macro is an instruction, and many steps have optional parameters that further specify information about the step. For example, one common step is "View," indicating that you want Approach to switch to a particular view. The further information you need is which view to switch to. Almost any series of actions you can perform with Approach can be automated with a macro, either by directly creating the macro or by recording the macro as you perform the steps.

Sometimes you want more control over how Approach executes than you can specify in a macro. For example, you may want to test for certain conditions and execute actions based on those conditions. This isn't something you can do with a macro. Approach comes with a complete programming language called *LotusScript*. Using LotusScript, you can write scripts, which are programs that control every aspect of Approach execution. However, it is much more difficult to write a script than to use a macro!

Recording Macros and Scripts

You can record both macros and scripts by performing the exact series of steps that you want recorded. You can then later go back and edit the resulting macro or script to make any changes.

The steps for recording a macro or script are very similar. First, you must "turn on" the recorder by selecting Record Transcript from the Edit menu. Approach displays the Record Transcript dialog box (see Figure 23-33).

Figure 23-33: The first step in recording a macro or script is to decide which one you want to record.

Choose what you want to record by picking one of three radio buttons:

✦ **As macro.** Your recorded actions will be translated into a macro. Pick the existing macro or type a new macro name in the drop-down list to the right of the As Macro radio button.

✦ **As script.** Your recorded actions will be translated into a script. Pick the existing script or type a new script name in the drop-down list to the right of the As Script radio button.

✦ **At script cursor.** Your recorded actions will be translated into a script "fragment" that is inserted at the current location of the text cursor in an existing script. You must ensure that the text cursor is located in the appropriate place in the Script Editor (discussed later in this chapter).

Note   It is no more complicated to record a macro than to record a script. However, if you intend to later modify the result of the recording, it is easier to modify a recorded macro—if you need to modify a recorded script, you will need to use LotusScript.

Choose Record to initiate the recording, and perform the steps you want to record. When you are done, choose Stop Recording from the Edit menu. Approach displays either the Define Macro dialog box or the Script Editor. You can make any changes you want to the macro or script.

Building a Macro Using the Define Macro Editor

Building your own macros (rather than recording them) gives you a great degree of control over what you want the macro to do. To build your own macro, use the following steps:

1. Choose Macros from the Edit menu. Approach displays the Macros dialog box (see Figure 23-34).

Figure 23-34: From the Macros dialog box, you can create, copy, edit, run, and delete macros. You can also convert a macro to a script.

2. Choose the New button to create a new macro, or select a macro and choose Edit to edit an existing macro. Approach displays the Define Macro dialog box (see Figure 23-35).

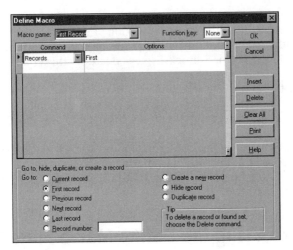

Figure 23-35: Use the Define Macro dialog box to set the steps in the macro, and the options for each step.

3. If this is a new macro, type the name for the macro into the Macro Name drop-down list. You can also select an existing macro for editing by choosing it from the list. If you want to assign the macro to a function key (the macro executes when you press the function key in Browse mode), choose the key from the Function Key drop-down list.

4. Choose a command from the Command drop-down list. Approach opens a list of commands so you can pick one (see Figure 23-36).

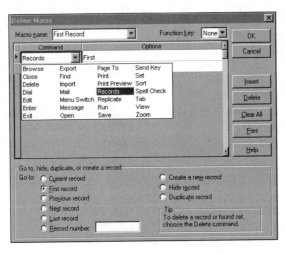

Figure 23-36: The drop-down list in the Define Macro dialog box displays all the available macro commands. For each command, the options appear at the bottom of the dialog box.

5. If the chosen command has any options, choose the appropriate option from the list at the bottom of the dialog box.

6. Continue adding commands and options to define the macro. If you need to insert a command between two other commands in the macro, use the Insert button. You can also use the Delete button to delete a command/option pair.

7. Choose OK to complete defining the macro. Approach returns to the Macros dialog box.

8. If you want the macro to appear in the Run Macro item at the bottom of the Edit menu, check the Show in Menu check box.

Building a Script Using the Script Editor

To create a script, choose Show Script Editor from the Edit menu (see Figure 23-37). Create the script by following these steps:

1. Choosing the View or Approach object that the script is attached to from the Object drop-down list.

2. Choosing the Event that the script executes on from the Script list. For example, the script might execute when you switch to a particular form. In addition to events, the Script list also contains general script categories, such as Options and Declarations.

3. Writing the script using the main window to type commands, and using the lower window to pick LotusScript commands, classes, constants, prebuilt subroutines and functions, variables, and OLE classes. Pick a category from the Category drop-down list, a command from the hierarchical list of available options, and choose Paste Name to place the command at the text cursor.

4. Testing your script using the tools provided, such as setting Breakpoints.

Note

For more information on programming in LotusScript, see the publication *LotusScript Language Reference* (included in SmartSuite 98).

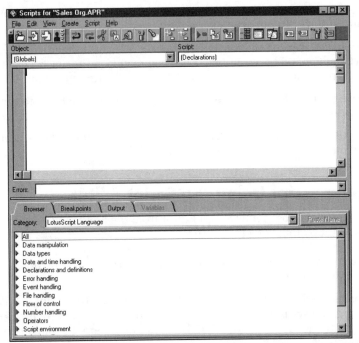

Figure 23-37: The Script Editor enables you to build and edit scripts, and attach those scripts to views.

Running Macros

You can run a macro in quite a few ways:

✦ Press the function key (if any) that you assigned to the macro.

✦ Open the Edit menu, choose Run Macro, and select the macro from the macro list that appears. Only macros for which you checked the Show in Menu check box in the Macros dialog box appear in this menu.

✦ Click the name of the Macro in the Macros dialog box and then click the Run button.

✦ Run a macro automatically when you open an Approach file or close an Approach file. To run a macro automatically when you open an Approach file, create the macro and name it "Open." To run a macro automatically when you close an Approach file, create the macro and name it "Close."

You can also run a macro automatically when certain events occur, such as tabbing into a field. To assign a macro to run when an event occurs, you use the Macros panel of the object's Infobox. The events and their corresponding Infobox entries are as follows:

✦ When you tab into or out of a particular field or graphic object. Choose the macro from the appropriate drop-down list: On Tab Into or On tab Out Of.

✦ When you click a graphic object or a button (see "Adding a Macro Button to a View"). For a graphic object, select the macro from the On Selected drop-down list. For a button, select the macro from the On Clicked drop-down list.

✦ When you change the value of a field. Select the macro from the On Data Change drop-down list.

✦ When you switch into or out of a particular view. To execute a macro automatically when you switch to a view, select the macro from the On Switch To drop-down list. To execute a macro automatically when you leave a view, select the macro from the On Switch Out drop-down list.

Adding a Macro Button to a View

One of the handiest ways to execute a macro is to click a button. Users are used to doing this, and you can create a set of buttons that execute common functions. For example, instead of requiring your users to remember which menu option or SmartIcon advances to the next record, you can simply add a button to the form that reads "Next Record."

To add a macro button to a view, use the following steps:

1. Choose the Draw Button tool from the Tool palette.

2. Click in the view where you want the upper-left corner of the button, and drag to the lower-right corner. Approach displays a button with the default label "Button" and opens the Infobox for the button (see Figure 23-38).

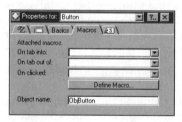

Figure 23-38: A macro button is convenient for triggering execution of macros.

3. In the Basics panel of the Infobox, you can change the text that appears on the button by modifying the text in the Button text field.

4. In the Macros panel, select a macro (if desired) for the On Tab Into, On Tab Out Of, and On Clicked drop-down lists.

Importing and Exporting Data

It is very common to need to share data with other applications. Data is often available only in a text file or a spreadsheet, or perhaps another database format, and you'd like to have that data in an Approach database. The process of bringing the data into Approach is called *importing*.

Another possibility is that you need to share your data with someone who needs it in another format, perhaps for use in a spreadsheet or word processor. You might even want to use part of the contents of one Approach database application in another Approach database application. The process of sending your data to another format or to another Approach application is called *exporting*. Both importing and exporting are easy to do, but you must understand the types of files involved, and map the fields from one file format to another. These concepts are all explained in the next few sections.

Importing Data

When you do an import, there are two files of interest: the source data file (outside of Approach), and the target data file, which is a database in Approach. To set the target database, simply open the Approach file that contains it and switch to a view in which the target database is the main database for the view. The next step is to pick the source file, which is covered next.

Understanding the Types of Source Files

There are three types of source files that you can import:

✦ **Import from another database.** Importing from another database is the most straightforward type of import. This is because you can (as you'll see shortly) easily map the fields in the source database to the fields in the Approach target database.

✦ **Import from a spreadsheet.** Lots of people use spreadsheets to hold data because most spreadsheets have rudimentary database capabilities. When you import from a spreadsheet, each column in the spreadsheet maps to a field in the Approach database. If the first row of the spreadsheet contains the column headers (that identify the data in the column), you can use these column headers to help you in the mapping process. If the spreadsheet does not contain column headers in the first row, you must map the columns (designated A, B, C, and so on) to the fields in the database.

✦ **Import from a text file.** Although not much data is stored in raw text files anymore, most applications have the ability to export to text files, so a text file may have to serve as an intermediary file between the application that contains the source data and Approach. Most text files are "delimited"—there is a special character (usually a comma) between each value on a line in the text file. Each line is imported into a record in Approach, and the values are imported into the fields. If the first line has "field names" in it, you can use them to help you with the mapping process. Otherwise, you'll have to map "Field1," "Field2", and so on from the text file to Approach.

A fixed-length text file does not use a delimiter between field values. You specify a fixed length for each field (for example, the last name value field is 30 characters long; the first name value field is 20 characters long; and so on). Each value takes up the entire specified length — spaces are used to pad the fields to ensure that the length is always exactly the same. When mapping from a fixed-length text file, you must specify how long each field is.

Performing the Import

To actually perform an import, use the following steps:

1. Open the Approach file and move to a view that uses the target database as its main database. You will have the opportunity to change to another (linked) database if you want, but it is easier to choose the right view first.

2. In Browse mode, choose Import Data from the File menu. Approach displays the Import Data dialog box from which you pick the file from which you want to import data (see Figure 23-39). Choose the file and click Import.

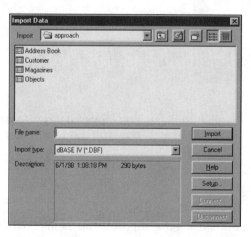

Figure 23-39: Pick the file and type of import you want to do from the Import Data dialog box.

3. If the file selected is a spreadsheet file, Approach displays the Field Names dialog box. It has only a single check box for you to choose whether the first row contains field names.

If the file selected is a delimited text file, Approach displays the Text File Options dialog box (see Figure 23-40). Choose the delimiter from either the predefined radio buttons or specify the delimiter. You can also choose whether the first row contains field names.

If the file selected is a fixed-length text file, Approach displays the Fixed Length Text File Setup dialog box (see Figure 23-41). Here, you can enter the field names, their type, the start position in each row, and the width of the field. You can also specify if the first row contains field names.

Figure 23-40: The Text File Options dialog box enables you to choose the delimiter for a delimited text file.

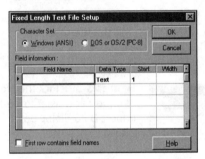

Figure 23-41: The Fixed Length Text File Setup dialog box enables you to specify the fields and their lengths.

4. Approach displays the Import Setup dialog box (covered next). Use the options in the dialog box to specify exactly how you want the import to proceed.

5. Choose OK to perform the import.

Understanding the Import Setup Dialog Box

The heart of performing an import is using the Import Setup dialog box. This dialog box (see Figure 23-42) is used to map fields from the source file to the Approach database that receives the data.

Figure 23-42: The Import Setup dialog box helps you map fields from source to target — and even view the contents of the source field.

The main window in the Import Setup dialog box is split into three sections. The left section contains the information from the source file. The right section contains the Approach database name (in the Fields In drop-down list) and its fields. You can select a different database in the Approach file from the drop-down list. To link a field on the left side with a field on the right side, click in the center section to add a blue arrow. Clicking the blue arrow a second time removes it.

Prior to linking the fields, you must rearrange them so that the fields on the left and the right line up correctly. You can only modify the order of the right-hand (Approach) fields. To do so, click a field name and drag it to a new position in the list.

The buttons in the lower-left corner (with the black triangles on them) enable you to view records in the source data file. Clicking the right-facing arrow button advances one record, while clicking the left-facing arrow button goes back one record. This feature is very handy for text and spreadsheet files that do not have field names in the first row. You can preview the data to help you decide how to map the fields.

The Import Options drop-down list at the bottom of the dialog box enables you to choose how you want to import your records. The three options in the list are only available if you are performing a database-to-database import:

✦ **Add imported data as new records.** This option creates new records from the imported data and appends them to the end of the database.

✦ **Use imported data to update existing records.** This option does *not* create any new records. Instead, it uses the criteria you specify to identify records that refer to the same basic data (for example, the same customer or purchase order) and updates just the existing records.

> ✦ **Use imported data to update and add to existing records.** This option
> updates existing records (identified by the criteria you set) and, if it does find
> a matching record, adds a new record by appending it to the end of the
> database.

If you choose an import option that updates existing records, the Import Setup
dialog box changes to add a fourth column (see Figure 23-43) so that you can
specify the criteria for matches. Click in the new column alongside the fields that
must contain identical values in order for Approach to identify the records as
equivalent (and thus update Approach from the imported record). The fields
should contain unique information, such as a customer number, or a combination
of first name, last name, and phone number.

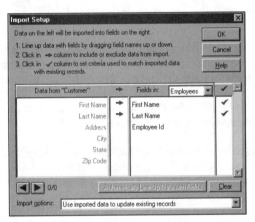

Figure 23-43: If you merge (update) fields
from two databases, you must identify the
record-matching criteria in the new column
of the Import Setup dialog box.

You can't use the update options for spreadsheet or text file import. However, you
can import the text or spreadsheet into a new database first, and then use the update
options when importing from this intermediate database to Approach.

Exporting Data

Using Approach's export function, you can export data to other database formats,
another Approach database, a text file, or a spreadsheet. And, because you can sort
your data; perform a find to limit the records exported; or choose only certain
fields for export; an export gives you the capability to rearrange your data in a new
file or export a subset of data for use in other ways. For example, you could export
the subset of your customers who have made purchases in the last year.

As with importing, exporting uses the concept of a source file and a target file.
However, with exporting, the source file is the Approach database, and the target file
is the file into which you will export the Approach data.

To perform an export, use the following steps:

1. If you don't want to export all records in the database, perform a find to limit the records to the found set.

2. If you want to rearrange the records in the target database, perform a sort in the source database file.

3. Choose Export from the File menu. Approach displays the Export Data dialog box (see Figure 23-44).

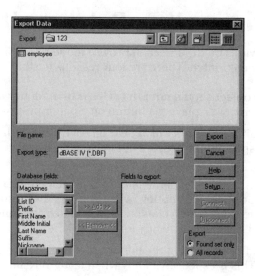

Figure 23-44: The Export Data dialog box enables you to choose the type of export file, the fields to export, and whether to export just the found set.

4. From the Export Type drop-down list, choose the type of file you want to export to. A variety of database formats, text formats, and spreadsheet formats are available. Enter the file name for the export file in the File Name text box.

5. In the Database Fields list, choose the fields you want to export and click the >>Add>> to move the fields to the Fields to Export list. Until you select a field, the >>Add>> button is unavailable.

6. If you performed a find prior to starting the export, choose one of the radio buttons in the Export section in the lower-right corner. You may export either just the found set (the default) or All records.

7. Press the Export button. If you chose a database format, Approach exports the records to the new database. If you chose a spreadsheet format, Approach displays the Field Names dialog box. Check the First Row Contains Field Names check box if you want the field names to appear in the first row of the exported spreadsheet file.

If you selected a delimited text file, Approach displays the Text File Options dialog box (refer back to Figure 23-40) for you to specify the delimiter and whether the first row should contain the field names. Make the appropriate choices and click OK.

If you selected a fixed-length text file, Approach displays the Fixed Length Text File Setup dialog box (refer back to Figure 23-41) for you to specify the widths of each field. Specify the fields and click OK.

Previewing and Printing Your Database View

The views that Approach provides on the screen in Browse mode may not resemble what the view will look like when printed. There are four reasons for this:

✦ You may specify that an object should not print. This is often done with buttons — what is the point of displaying a button on a paper printout?

✦ You may specify that multiple records will appear on each page of the printout. And, you may specify that a record not be split across pages when you print.

✦ You may use the Size and Print panel of the Infobox to specify that an object slides up and left when printing. This option, when combined with the Reduce Boundaries option (in the same panel) eliminates blank lines and unfilled fields when printing, and is especially handy for mailing labels.

✦ You may use the Size and Print panel of the Infobox to specify that an object expand its boundaries. This is especially handy when using scrolling text fields in which the field contents exceed the height of the text field in the view. With this option on, the next line of fields (or the next record, if this field is on the last line) will move down out of the way to allow enough room to print the entire field contents.

✦ You may use summary fields that summarize data across multiple records in the database. These summary fields do not display their values in Browse mode.

For all of these reasons, it is important to have a method of seeing what your printout will look like prior to potentially wasting a lot of paper printing out something you don't want. To preview your printout, switch Approach to Print Preview mode by choosing Print Preview from the mode area of the status bar, clicking the Print Preview SmartIcon, or choosing Print Preview from the File menu. In all cases, Approach switches into Print Preview mode and shows you what your printout will look like (see Figure 23-45).

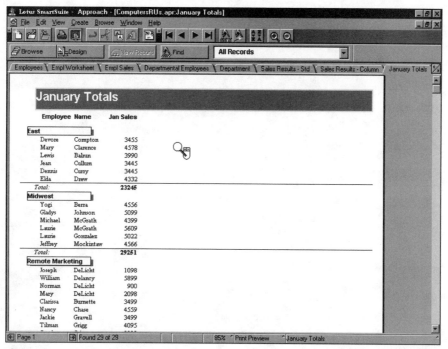

Figure 23-45: Print Preview mode shows you how your printout will look on paper.

While you are in Print Preview mode, the mouse cursor becomes a mouse with a magnifying glass. You can zoom in (up to 200% magnification) on the print preview by clicking the left mouse button, and zoom out (down to 25% magnification) by clicking the right mouse button.

When you are done with Print preview, you have the following options:

✦ Print the view by choosing the Print SmartIcon or choosing Print from the File menu. You can, of course, also print a view without previewing it first.

✦ Return to the last mode you were in by turning off the check mark next to Print Preview in the File menu.

✦ Switch to any mode by choosing it from the mode area of the status bar.

✦　　　✦　　　✦

Performing a Mail Merge in Approach

✦   ✦   ✦   ✦

In This Chapter

Creating a form letter

Creating an envelope
for a form letter

Creating mailing
labels

✦   ✦   ✦   ✦

In addition to the types of views we've discussed so far, Approach provides still other ways for you to use your data—form letters and mailing labels. When you generate the form letters or mailing labels, you can use your whole database, or just a found set, as a source. You can also generate envelopes for mailing your form letters. If your printer can handle printing directly on envelopes, you can save yourself the step of creating mailing labels and then affixing them to envelopes.

Working with Form Letters

A form letter is a customized letter that uses data from your database to "personalize" the information in the letter. You've undoubtedly gotten such letters, which use your name, address, and any other information the sender has to make the letter seem that it was prepared for you, personally. Using Approach, you can create your own form letters using the Form Letter Assistant.

Form letters come in four basic layouts:

✦ **Block.** Everything in the letter is aligned to the left margin.

✦ **Letterhead.** This style leaves out the return address at the top of the letter, assuming that the letter will be printed on letterhead paper, which already has the return address printed on it. It also aligns the closing to the right margin.

✦ **Modified Block.** Everything is aligned to the left margin except for the return address and the closing, which are aligned to the right margin.

✦ **Personal.** Omits the return address and inside (send-to) address, and right aligns the closing.

To use the Form Assistant, you need to understand the various parts of the form letter (see Figure 24-1). There are also special SmartIcons that help you modify a form letter after you create it.

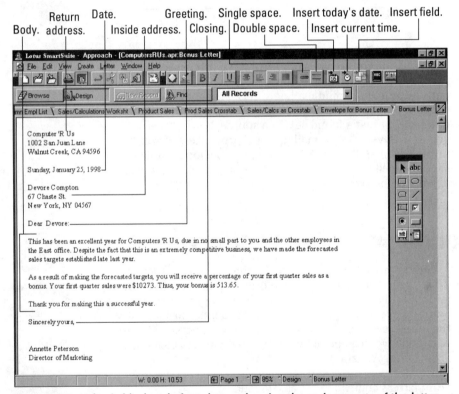

Figure 24-1: A basic block-style form letter, showing the various parts of the letter.

Creating a Form Letter

To create a form letter, use the following steps:

1. Choose Form Letter from the Create menu. Approach displays the Form Letter Assistant (see Figure 24-2).

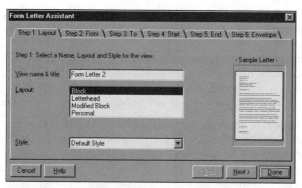

Figure 24-2: The Form Letter Assistant walks you through the process of building a form letter.

2. In the Step 1: Layout panel, give the form letter a name by typing it into the View Name & Title text box. Choose a layout from the Layout list, and select a style from the Style drop-down list. The styles vary the font. Click Next to move to the next panel.

3. If you chose the Block or Modified Block layout, the next panel is Step 2: From. Fill in the return address in the text box, or click the None radio button to forego a return address. Click Next to move to the next panel.

4. If you chose Block, Modified Block, or Letterhead, the next panel (To:) is where you enter the inside address of the recipient (see Figure 24-3). Choose the address layout you want to use from the Address Layout drop-down list. This list varies the address from three-line addresses to various special international addresses.

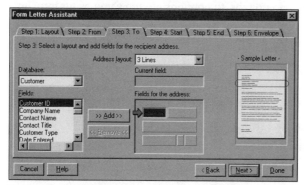

Figure 24-3: The Step 3: To panel of the Form Letter Assistant enables you to specify an address format and add fields to the address template.

5. From the Fields list, click the field you want to go into the first empty space in the address template, and click >>Add>> to move the field to the template (Fields for the Address area). Repeat this step, adding fields to completely specify the address. The red arrow that indicates where the next field will be placed in the template moves through the fields in the address template automatically, but you can click any field in the template to respecify the field that goes there. When you are through, click Next to move to the next panel.

6. The next panel, Start, is available for all the letter layouts. It enables you to specify the salutation for the letter, or click the None radio button to dispense with the salutation. Type the greeting (such as "Dear," "My Dearest," or whatever) into the first text box. Then select up to two fields (such as First Name and Last Name) to make up the rest of the salutation from the two field lists. Both lists have a None option, so you can use just one field (Dear Jerry) if you wish. Finally, type in the character that ends the salutation line (the default is a colon). When you are finished, click Next to move to the next panel.

7. The next panel, End, is available for all letter layouts. It enables you to specify the close of the letter (the default is "Sincerely yours") or to click the None radio button to dispense with the ending. When you are done specifying the ending, click either Done (for Personal layout) or Next to move to the Envelope panel.

8. You can have Approach generate an envelope for each form letter using the Envelope panel. If you want the return address printed on the envelope, click the Print return address check box. Select the envelope size from the Envelope Size drop-down list, or choose the dimensions of the envelope if you are not using a standard envelope. Finally, choose whether the envelopes are to print in landscape mode (horizontal) or portrait mode (vertical). Click Done to create the form letter (see Figure 24-4).

Note   You can create envelopes directly by choosing Envelopes from the Create menu. Except for the Start and End tabs, the options are the same as for form letters.

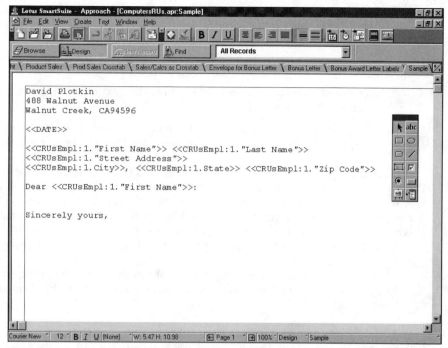

Figure 24-4: The form letter as it comes out of the Form Letter Assistant. You still need to add the body of the text.

Customizing the Form Letter

Of course, the form letter is not done yet! The body of the letter is missing. The form letter is actually a large text object. When you click in the form letter in Design mode, a blue frame surrounds the text object, and you can see the fields from the database and any other fields (such as the date) you inserted using the Form Letter Assistant. If you click outside the blue frame, and you have Show Data checked in the View menu, you can see the actual data that will appear when you print the form letter.

To add text to the body of the form letter, simply click in the text object to place the insertion point where you want to start typing, and add the text you want. You can edit the text block just like any other text — cutting, copying, and pasting. You can also select any of the text and change the attributes of the text with the Infobox (which reads "Text editing" in the Properties For drop-down list. You can change the font, color, relief, attributes, alignment, and line spacing from the appropriate tabs in the Infobox.

You can add fields to the text of the form letter, and Approach will fill in the field values when you print, just as with the fields inserted using the Form Letter Assistant. To add fields to the text, use the following steps:

1. Place the text insertion point where you want to insert the field.

2. Choose Field Value from the Insert item in the Text menu. Approach displays the Insert Field dialog box.

3. Choose the field you want to insert from the list and click OK. Approach adds the field at the insertion point, complete with the <<>> braces surrounding it.

You can move fields in the text using the standard techniques of copy, cut, and paste. However, be sure to include the surrounding braces (<<>>), or you will move only part of the field (and leave part behind), and Approach will no longer recognize it as a field. Similarly, if you highlight a field to change the format properties of the text, make sure you highlight the entire field, including the braces. If you miss even one brace, Approach will ignore the format change.

Danger Zone

You cannot undo text editing changes you make to the form letter or the embedded fields. If you make a mistake, you'll have to recreate the text or the bracketed fields by hand.

You can add the time or date to a form letter by choosing Current Time or Today's Date from the Insert item in the Text menu. You can also add a page number to the form by clicking the Page Number SmartIcon.

Note

If the form letter is more than one page long, you must use the status bar to navigate to other pages. The fourth section from the right is labeled with the page number and small arrows facing left and right. You can click the page number section and input the page you want to jump to, or click the left arrow (previous page) or the right arrow (next page).

Printing the Form Letter

The primary purpose of creating a form letter is to print it, so when you are ready to print, choose Print from the File menu. In the Print dialog box, you can choose from the following options:

✦ **Current Record.** This prints just the currently selected record. This option is handy for looking at a sample letter without printing all the letters.

✦ **All Records.** This prints either all the records in the database (if no find is in effect) or just the found set (if a find is in effect).

✦ **Record.** You can print just a range of records by choosing this radio button and specifying the record number range. You may wish to sort the records in order to group records of interest together.

You can also choose which pages of a multipage form letter to print. This can be especially helpful if only the first page has "personalized" data on it, and the rest of the pages can be simply duplicated with a copy machine.

Working with Mailing Labels

Mailing labels are another handy use for your data. Once you create a letter (either using Approach or a word processor such as Word Pro), you can generate mailing labels for virtually all the standard sizes of labels sold — or create a custom label.

Creating Mailing Labels

To create mailing labels, use the following steps:

1. Choose Mailing Label from the Create menu. Approach displays the Basics tab of the Mailing Label Assistant (see Figure 24-5).

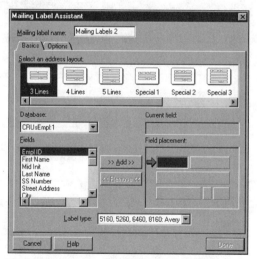

Figure 24-5: Use the Mailing Label Assistant to create mailing labels from your Approach data.

2. Enter the name for the mailing label view in the Mailing Label Name field.

3. Select an address layout from the graphics in the layout list. Each of the layouts supports a different field configuration. When you pick a layout, the field configuration appears under the Field placement label in the lower-right corner of the dialog box.

4. In the Field placement section, click the rectangular field placeholder where you want the next field to go. A red arrow indicates the placeholder that will receive the next field.

5. From the Fields list, choose a field and click the >>Add>> button. Approach moves the field to the placeholder you selected in Step 4.

6. Repeat Steps 4 and 5 for each field. The red arrow moves through the placeholders automatically as you insert fields.

7. Choose the type of label you want to use from the Label Type drop-down list. Most of the Avery product line is available in this list, and most other label manufacturers state the equivalent Avery label number on their packaging. If the label you want to use is not available in this list, proceed to the Options panel (see the next section, "Configuring the Label Options").

8. Choose Done to create the labels. Approach creates the labels and shows you a preview of what the labels will look like (see Figure 24-6).

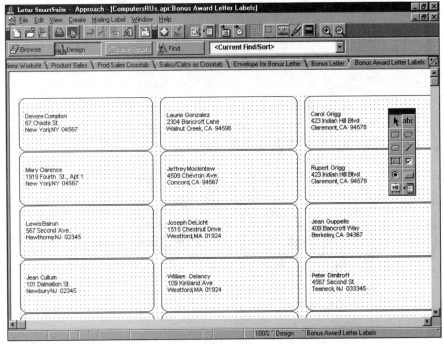

Figure 24-6: When you are done with the Mailing Label Assistant, you can see what your Mailing Labels will look like.

Configuring the Label Options

It doesn't happen very often, but occasionally you may need to create mailing labels that don't correspond to the list of Avery products at the bottom of the Mailing Label Assistant. If this situation occurs, you can click the Options panel in the Mailing Label Assistant (see Figure 24-7).

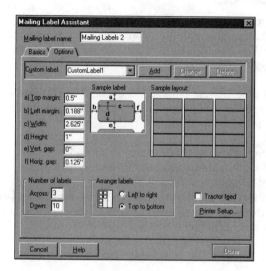

Figure 24-7: The Mailing Label Assistant Options panel enables you to set the margins, size, and layout of a custom mailing label.

With the Options panel, you can customize the following label properties:

✦ **Layout Name.** Enter the name in the Custom Label field box and list. You can then pick the name from this list to re-use the layout for another set of mailing labels.

✦ **Margins.** You can specify the top and left margins in the (a) and (b) text boxes. You can also specify the vertical and horizontal gaps between labels in the (e) and (f) text boxes.

✦ **Label size.** You can specify the width and height of the label in the (c) and (d) text boxes.

✦ **Number of labels.** You can specify the number of labels across and down in the Number of Labels section.

✦ **How the labels will be printed.** In the Arrange Labels section, you can specify whether the labels will be printed left to right by row (leaving unused labels near the bottom of the sheet) or top to bottom by column (leaving unused labels near the right edge of the sheet).

Note You can access the Mailing Label Options panel by opening the Infobox for the Mailing Labels, switching to the Basics panel, and choosing the Edit Label Options button.

Customizing Mailing Labels

You can modify all the standard properties of a mailing label using the Infobox, including the name, main database, margins, attached macros, fill color, and border placement, width, color, and style. You can also modify the properties of the fields on a mailing label using the Infobox.

Hot Stuff It is much easier to select a field on a mailing label if you uncheck the Show Data option in the View menu. With the Show Data option on, it is hard to see the boundaries of the field, and thus harder to select the field.

By default, the When printing, slide options in the Size and Print panel are checked. This is especially important with mailing labels, as space is usually at a premium on a mailing label, and you don't want to waste any space displaying unused field length or blank lines. The most important thing to remember when modifying fields on a mailing label is that these options fail to work properly if all the fields on a line are not aligned. If you suddenly find that the fields are not sliding up and left when you are in Print Preview mode, select all the fields on the errant line and use the Align function to align them to one another.

Note The effects of the Slide Up and Slide Left options are not visible when you are in Browse mode. You must switch to Print Preview mode or Design mode (with Show Data checked) to see a preview of the fields as they will look when you print.

✦   ✦   ✦

Organizing Your Life

This part explains how to use Organizer to organize yourself, and how to use the SmartCenter and SmartIcon bars to organize SmartSuite. Learn how to create a file and work with sections in the file. Find out how to build your contacts list, and then use it to make calls and perform a mail merge. You'll learn what's in each default drawer in SmartCenter, how to use drawer information, and how to create your own drawers and folders. Then, find out how to hide, display, and customize a SmartIcon bar in any SmartSuite application.

Using Organizer to Track Appointments, Notes, and To Do Lists

The Lotus Organizer application serves as your Personal Information Manager (PIM). Professionals of all types have exploited Organizer's robust features for years, boosting it to the top of the PIM market. In return, Organizer provides professionals like you with numerous tools to manage your schedules, upcoming tasks, contact lists, and more. This chapter and the next introduce you to the key features in Organizer. In this chapter, you learn how to navigate between sections in Organizer, and how to set up each section to suit your needs. You also learn to create and track appointments and to do lists, take notes, find entries, and print a section when your computer can't travel with you.

Starting and Touring Organizer

To start the Lotus Organizer program so that you can begin using it to track your schedule and upcoming tasks, you can use any of the methods for launching SmartSuite applications presented in Chapter 1, "Getting Started with SmartSuite Applications":

> ◆ Choose Start ➪ Programs ➪ Lotus SmartSuite ➪ Lotus Organizer.

✦ Open the SmartSuite drawer on the SmartCenter, then open the Lotus Applications drawer, if needed. Double-click the Lotus Organizer shortcut.

✦ Click the Lotus Organizer SuiteStart button on the right end of the taskbar.

The Lotus Organizer application opens, showing a calendar with the current date in the Calendar selected by default. The Organizer screen resembles a date planner book and offers seven different *sections*, each identified by a tab with the section name. Sections can include multiple pages of information. You move between pages using the lower outside page corners. In addition to the SmartIcon bar, Organizer offers a toolbox with icons for working in the currently selected section at the left side. Icons for changing the view in the current section also appear below the toolbox.

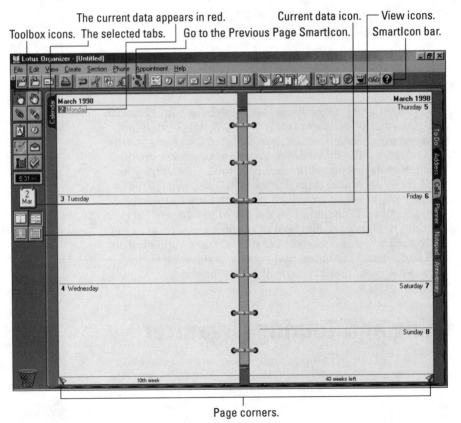

Figure 25-1: Organizer presents information in a date-book format, with a tab identifying each section of information.

To select a section, click its tab or choose Section ⇨ Turn To and click the section to display in the submenu that appears. The section tab turns to the left side of the screen; the tab for the selected section becomes the bottom tab at the left. Some sections display subtabs within them when they're open. For example, the Address tab includes a tab for each letter in the alphabet, to separate names and dresses alphabetically, as in a paper address book. Click a subtab to open it to the left.

Some sections include multiple pages within them. To display the next page, click the lower corner of the right page. To move to the previous page, click the lower corner of the left page. You also can press the PgDn and PgUp keys to move forward and back through the pages, or click the Go to the Previous Page SmartIcon to move back one page.

Adjusting the View and Setting Preferences in a Section

The View icons at the left side of the screen vary depending on the currently selected section. For example, when you select the To Do tab, the View by Priority, View by Status, View by Start Date, and View by Category icons appear. Depending on the section, clicking a View icon either sorts the section information or adjusts the view so it displays more or less detail (such as showing a single day per page or a full week per page in the Calendar section). To learn what each View icon does in the current section, point to the icon so that its Bubble Help description appears. The View menu options also vary depending on which section you've selected. The commands at the top of the View menu correspond with the View icons. You can choose one of the commands instead of using the View icons.

Danger Zone

When you redisplay the Calendar section after working in another section, the section displays the calendar for the full year, and Organizer hides the View icons. (It also includes subtabs for other years; you can click one to display the calendar for that year.) To display the Work Week view for the calendar and redisplay the View icons, you can click the Current Date icon at the left. Or, to display the work week that holds a date other than the current date, double-click the date in the yearly calendar.

In addition to choosing a View to adjust each section's contents, you can select various preferences that affect how the section looks and functions. To display the dialog box for setting preferences in the current section, choose View ⇨ (Section Name) Preferences, the bottom command on the View menu. For example, choose View ⇨ To Do Preferences in the To Do section to display the dialog box shown in Figure 25-2.

Choose the view.   Select how much or little information to display.

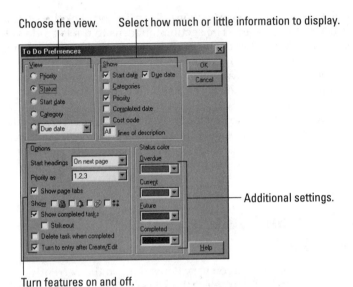

Additional settings.

Turn features on and off.

Figure 25-2: You can display a Preferences dialog box for each section to set up how it works.

The preferences vary quite a bit from one section to another, but in general they cover four different areas: choosing the view, controlling how much information displays, turning features in the section on and off, and additional settings such as color preferences. (To learn more about the options in each section's Preferences dialog box, click the Help button in the dialog box, then click the word Options where it appears in green and with a dashed underline.) After you make your choices in a Preferences dialog box, click OK to close the dialog box and apply them.

Note

You also can set preferences for Organizer itself. To do so, choose File ➪ User Setup ➪ Organizer Preferences.

Exiting from Organizer

When you've finished working with Lotus Organizer, you can close the program. To do so, click the Close button for the Lotus Organizer window. Or, choose File ➪ Exit Freelance Graphics (Alt+F4). If you have a file that's open and you haven't saved your changes to it, Organizer displays a message box asking you if you want to save your changes. Click Yes to do so and finish closing Organizer.

Saving, Copying, and Opening Organizer Files

You have to save the information in a Lotus Organizer file to ensure you can work with it again. In addition, you can copy an Organizer file to other computers, so you can have access to your appointment, to do, and contact information anywhere: on your desktop system at work, on the laptop computer you use during business travel, and on your home computer.

When you save an Organizer file for the first time, you name it and can also assign one or more passwords to limit who can enter and view information in the file.

Saving an Organizer File

Use the following steps to save your Organizer information in a file:

1. Choose File ⇨ Save (Ctrl+S), or click the Save the Current File SmartIcon on the SmartIcon bar. The Save As dialog box appears.

2. Use the Save As Type drop-down list to specify whether to save the file as a Single-User Access Organizer file, if you're creating a file for your personal use; or a Multi-User Access Organizer file, if you're creating a file to track information for a workgroup and will be saving the file on a shared network disk drive.

3. Use the Save In drop-down list and the list below it to specify the disk and folder where you want to store the file. Unless you change the folder, your Organizer files are saved to the \lotus\work\organize folder on your local hard disk. If you chose to create a multi-user access file in Step 2, make sure you select the appropriate folder on a shared network disk drive.

4. Type the name you want for the file in the File Name text box.

5. (Optional) If you want to restrict who can make changes to and view the Organizer file, click the Passwords button. The Passwords dialog box appears. It offers three text boxes for specifying up to three different passwords for different access levels. (After you enter a password in the top text box, the other text boxes become enabled, as shown in Figure 25-3.) The following list describes what type of access each password you enter allows:

   - **Owner.** Provides full access, so you can see and edit both entries and preferences for the file. You must have owner access to change or set the other passwords.

   - **Assistant.** Anyone who enters this password to open the file can see and edit all entries, except those marked as confidential.

   - **Reader.** Anyone who enters this password to open the file can only see nonconfidential entries. Reader access does not allow the user to edit any entries.

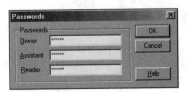

Figure 25-3: Enter up to three different passwords when you save an Organizer file.

6. Enter the Owner password, then the Assistant password, then the Reader password. Click OK. The Verify Passwords dialog box appears.

Note

To change the password(s) for a file, choose File ➪ Save As. Click the Passwords button, then enter the new password(s). Click OK, then reenter the password to confirm it, and click OK. Click OK to finish changing the password(s).

7. Reenter the password(s) to verify them, then click OK.

8. Click the Save button to finish saving the file.

After you make any changes to a file, you have to save it again. To do so, choose File ➪ Save; press Ctrl+S; or click the Save the Current Presentation SmartIcon. Because you've previously named the file, you won't see the Save As dialog box. Freelance Graphics simply saves the changes to the file.

Copying an Organizer File

If you want to create a copy of an Organizer file, choose the File ➪ Save As command, specify a new File Name, and click OK. For example, you may want to create new appointments in a file, but may not want to reenter all your contact information in the Address section. In such a case, copy the file with File ➪ Save As, and then change the information in the sections where needed.

Opening an Organizer File

When you start Organizer, by default each section is blank. You have to open the Organizer file that holds your schedule and contact information to regain access to that information. You can then make changes to the contents of the file, or print the file.

Danger Zone

Unlike other SmartSuite applications, Organizer has only one file open at a time. So, if you use multiple Organizer files, always check to ensure that the correct file is open before you make a change.

Use the following steps to open an Organizer file so you can work with its information again:

1. Choose File ➪ Open (Ctrl+O) or click the Open an Existing File SmartIcon. The Open dialog box appears.

2. Use the Look In list to navigate to the disk and folder that holds the file you want to open.

3. When you see the file you want in the Look In list, click the file name.

4. Click the Open button. If you assigned one or more passwords to the file, a dialog box prompts you to enter the password(s). You can enter the password for any of the access levels: Owner, Assistant, or Reader.

5. Enter the password in the Password text box, then click OK. The file opens.

You can skip Steps 1 through 4 and open a recently used Organizer file by choosing the file from the bottom of the File menu.

Danger Zone   If you forget the Owner password you've created, you won't have full access to your Organizer file. Be sure to record the Owner password in a safe location, especially if you tend to forget file passwords.

Creating Categories and Codes to Capture Essential Details

One of the most common ways to evaluate your contribution to a company or to establish how much to charge a client is to multiply an hourly rate by the number of hours you spend. In Organizer, you can create *categories* to identify how much time or which task is related to a particular activity. Or, to have even finer control, you can create *customer codes* and *cost codes* to assign to particular appointments and tasks. Make sure you create the categories and codes in the Organizer file in which you want to use them. (That is, open the file before you create the categories and codes, and then save the file after you add them.) Typically, you should create your categories and codes before you start entering information in the Organizer file, so you can accurately categorize and code entries like appointments and to do tasks from the get go.

Creating Categories

Organizer offers several predefined categories, such as Calls, Meetings, Follow Up, and so on. In addition, you can create your own categories, such as "Planning," "Project Management," or "Billing." To view the available categories or create a category, choose Create ⇨ Categories. The Categories dialog box appears. You can scroll through the Categories list to see the existing categories. To create a new category, type the category name in the Name text box, select a symbol for the category from the Symbol drop-down list (see Figure 25-4), then click Add. To rename a category, click it in the Categories list, click the Rename button, change the Entry in the New Name text box of the dialog box that appears, then click OK. To delete a category, click it in the Categories list, click the Delete button, then click Yes to confirm the deletion. After you finish working with categories, click OK to close the Categories dialog box.

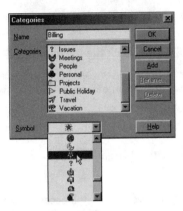

Figure 25-4: Create and use categories to group your activities. Enter a category name, then choose the symbol, as shown here.

Creating Codes

Cost codes and customer codes provide even finer control than categories do. In addition to assigning a category, assigning both a customer code and a cost code identifies the particular customer and job for which you performed the category activity. For example, let's say you've created the *101: First Bank* customer code, and the *003: Consulting, Advertising* cost code. If you set up an appointment for a consulting meeting with that client, you can identify the appointment by assigning the Meetings category, the customer code, and cost code. Then, you'll know the correct billing rate to charge for the appointment.

Note   Customer codes can be either alphabetical or numeric. If you have no problem remembering numeric billing and cost codes your company already uses, then use the same numbers when you create customer and cost codes. If you have trouble remembering numbers, use the names instead or use a combination like *101: First Bank*.

To create cost and customer codes, choose Create ➪ Cost Codes. The Cost Codes dialog box appears. In the Customer area at the top of the dialog box, enter a new code name in the Code text box, then click Add. Repeat to create other customer codes. You also can select a code in the list, edit the Code entry, then click Rename. Or, click the Delete button to remove the selected code from the list. The Cost Codes area at the bottom of the dialog box works the same. Enter the name or number for the cost code in the Cost Codes text box, then click Add. You also can use the Rename or Delete entries to work with the cost codes. Figure 25-5 shows example customer and cost codes in the Cost Codes dialog box. When you finish creating and working with the codes, click OK to close the Cost Codes dialog box.

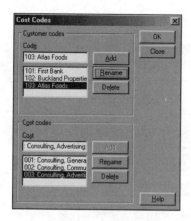

Figure 25-5: Create customer and cost codes to better track how you spend your time, so you can generate more accurate records and billing.

Creating Appointments

If you want to ensure that your colleagues and customers continue to be impressed by your professionalism, then you need to ensure that you honor all your appointments and commitments. Nothing drains your credibility cache faster than missed meetings and deadlines. You can use the Calendar section in Organizer to schedule appointments, turn on an alarm to alert you about an appointment, assign a category and cost codes, and more.

Note   An appointment you make in the Calendar is also called an *entry*. Anything you enter in any section is called an entry, such as a To Do task or a Note.

Use the following steps to create an appointment in the calendar:

1. Open the Organizer file that you want to hold your appointments. Select the Calendar section and the view you want.

2. Move to the page that holds the date on which you want to schedule the appointment.

3. Choose Create ⇨ Appointment (Insert), double-click the date on which you want to schedule the appointment, click the Create an Entry toolbox icon, or click the Create an Appointment SmartIcon. No matter which method you used, the Create Appointment dialog box appears.

4. Use the Date and Time drop-down lists to specify the date and starting time for the appointment. When you open the Date drop-down list, a calendar appears. Click the date for the appointment. When you open the Time drop-down list, a 24-hour timescale appears (see Figure 25-6). Click the appointment start time you want on the timescale. The start time below the top clock face displays the appointment start time you set, and the middle bar indicates the current scheduled duration. Drag the bottom clock face to the finishing time for the appointment, thus changing the duration. Click the drop-down list arrow to close the Time drop-down list.

Create an Entry icon.   Create an Appointment SmartIcon.   Use to scroll the time scale.

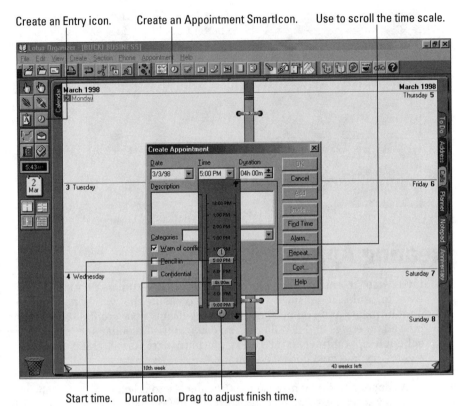

Start time.   Duration.   Drag to adjust finish time.

Figure 25-6: Drag the bottom clock face on the time scale to set the appointment finish time.

5. If you didn't use the Time drop-down list to specify the duration, click the plus (+) and minus (–) buttons beside the Duration text box to increase or decrease the length of time Organizer should schedule for the appointment. Organizer shows time in the 00h 00 (hours, minutes) format. Don't neglect to adjust this setting. If you allow too much time, you miss the opportunity to squeeze in other appointments. Allow too little time, and you'll be overbooked.

6. Enter a name or description for the appointment in the Description text box.

7. Open the Categories drop-down list and choose one or more categories to assign to the appointment. Click each category you want to assign. Click the drop-down list arrow to close the list after you select the category.

8. Click the Cost button, select the codes to assign to the appointment from the Customer Code and Cost Code drop-down lists, then click OK.

9. To play an alarm tune and display an alarm message before or after the appointment, click the Alarm button to display the Alarm dialog box (see Figure 25-7). Change the default Date and Time for the alarm. By default, the selected On option button means the alarm plays at the exact appointment time. To play the alarm earlier or later, click the Before or After option button, then adjust the time in the text box beside it. Play the alarm after the appointment if you only want a reminder should you be running late. Select the alarm sound to play from the Tune drop-down list, then use the Message text box to enter any alarm message to display. Keep the Display Alarm check box checked to ensure your alarm message displays. Figure 25-7 shows the Alarm dialog box with settings for an appointment alarm. Click OK to close the dialog box and finish setting the alarm.

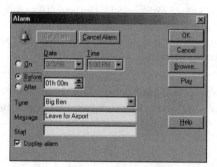

Figure 25-7: Use this dialog box to set when an alarm plays, what tune it plays, and what message it displays.

10. Back in the Create Appointment dialog box, leave the Warn of Conflicts check box checked to ensure that Organizer warns you if you try to set up an appointment at a date and time when you've already scheduled another appointment.

11. To tentatively set the appointment, select the Pencil In check box.

12. To mark the appointment as Confidential, click to check the check box with that name.

Note

If your calendar is very full and you think you might have a scheduling conflict with the Date, Time, and Duration you've specified, enter all the information for the appointment as directed through Step 12, then click the Find Time button. Organizer automatically changes the appointment Date and Time to the next available (later) date and time in your calendar that can accommodate the full duration for the appointment. That is, if you try to schedule a two-hour appointment at a date and time when you only have one free hour (as determined by other appointments you've already entered for that date), click Find Time to have Organizer change the Date and Time entries to the next date and time at which you have two hours available.

13. (Optional) If the appointment will recur at regular intervals and you want to schedule several of those regular appointments, click the Repeat button. Choose your settings in the Repeat dialog box that appears (see Figure 25-8), then click OK to finish setting up the recurring appointments:

   • In the Repeats area, select the overall interval between appointments (such as Weekly or Monthly) from the top drop-down list, then fine-tune the interval using the options that appear in the drop-down list and list box below the top drop-down list. The options in these other two lists vary depending on your selection in the top drop-down list.

   • If you choose Custom from the top drop-down list in the Repeats area, instead use the Custom Dates drop-down list, then click Add to add particular appointment dates.

   • Then, in the Duration area, select either an Until date (to specify the end of a project, which eliminates the need for status meetings about the project) or click the For option button, and use the plus and minus buttons beside the first text box to indicate how many future appointments to schedule.

   • When the At Weekends drop-down list becomes enabled, select an option from that list to tell Organizer how to move an appointment that mistakenly falls on the weekend.

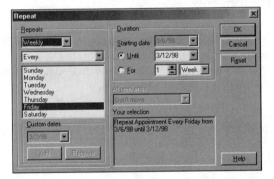

Figure 25-8: You can set up regular appointments by changing the settings in this dialog box.

14. Click the Add button to add the appointment to your calendar.

15. Repeat Steps 4 through 14 to create additional appointments, as needed.

16. Click Close to close the Create Appointment dialog box.

17. Save the Organizer file to save your appointment information.

After you finish creating appointments, they appear immediately on your calendar. Most Calendar views identify the appointment by its start time and description. Depending on the preferences you set for the Calendar section, the view also may include small indicator icons to give you more information about the appointment, as illustrated in Figure 25-9. So, to check your appointments for an upcoming date or to review past appointments to document your work, display the calendar page that holds the date you want to look at.

Indicator for a penciled-in appointment.   Alarm indicator.   Category symbols.

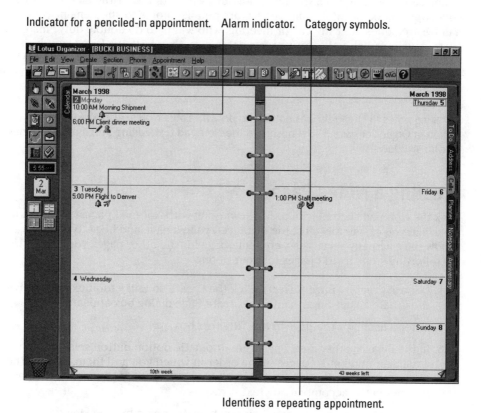

Identifies a repeating appointment.

Figure 25-9: The Calendar displays an onscreen datebook of your appointments.

Note

You can use the Anniversary section to mark anniversaries, and the Planner tab for scheduling future work. You can make entries in these sections using techniques similar to those for creating an appointment entry in the Calendar or creating Notes or To Do entries. Then, you can show the Anniversary and Planner information in the Calendar section. To learn how to do so, see "Using Show Through," later in this chapter.

Taking Notes About an Appointment or Other Event

Given the number of responsibilities—both personal and professional—each of us has, it pays to keep notes about decisions, details, and delegations for every conversation and task. Most of us make a habit of taking notes during a meeting or phone call, but sometimes we can't read our own writing after the fact. While you could open a document file and enter more detailed notes to supplement your handwritten ones after the call or meeting, who wants to do double duty? Instead, try to develop a habit of entering your notes directly into Lotus Organizer during a conversation (on your desktop system) or meeting (on your notebook or hand-held system). You enter notes on note pages in the Notepad section, as described in this section.

Danger Zone   Taking notes in Organizer has nothing to do with Lotus Notes. Also, the Notepad section in Organizer has no relationship to the Notepad text-editing program that comes with Windows.

Creating a Notes Page

Click the Notepad section icon to begin working with Notepad pages. Although it looks like you can simply click the displayed yellow page and begin typing, the yellow page actually serves as a contents page for the other pages you create. Use the following steps to add pages for your notes:

1. Choose Create ➪ Page (Insert), click the Create an Entry toolbox icon, or click the Create a Page SmartIcon. The Create Page dialog box appears.

2. Enter a name for the page in the Title text box.

3. In the Page Number area, leave the Automatic option button selected to have Organizer number all pages in the order in which you add them, or click the Manual option button and enter an alphanumeric entry to serve as the page number in the accompanying text box.

4. In the Style Area, specify what kind of page to create by checking the appropriate check box(es). Check Start a Chapter if you want to create a page that starts a chapter of related notes, such as all the project notes for a particular client. Check Links Page if you want to link entries from other sections to the links page in the Notepad section. If you want the new page to be a page that you can open to twice the normal width, check Folded. In addition, choose a Color for the page from the drop-down list of that name.

Hot Stuff   Set up the first page in a chapter as a links page, too, and then add links from other notes pages in that chapter to the title/links page. Then, the first page in the chapter serves as a table of contents for the chapter.

More Info See "Linking Related Entries" later in this chapter to learn how to create and use links.

5. Choose one or more categories for the page from the Categories drop-down list. In the list, click each category to assign, then click the drop-down arrow for the list to close it. Figure 25-10 shows options for a typical new page.

Create an Entry icon.   Create a Page SmartIcon.

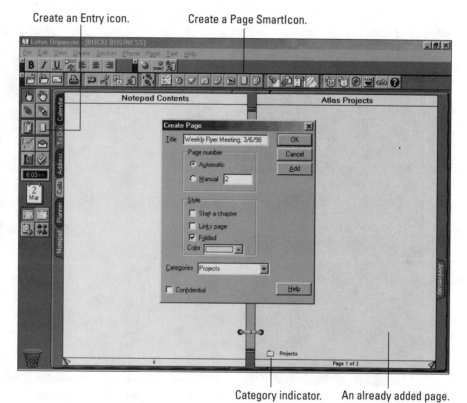

Category indicator.   An already added page.

Figure 25-10: Add new pages to the Notepad section, then type your notes on the appropriate page.

6. To designate the new page as confidential, limiting who can see it, check the Confidential check box.

7. Click Add to add the page to the Notepad section.

8. Repeat Steps 2–7 to create other pages in the Notepad section.

9. Click Close to close the Create Page dialog box.

Selecting a Notes Page

After you've created the notes pages you need, you need to select the page on which you'd like to type your notes. You can click the lower page corners to display the previous or next page, or press the PgUp or PgDn key. Or, if you just turned to the Notepad section, the Notepad Contents page appears, listing the pages you've added (see Figure 25-11). To jump directly to a page you want to read or edit, double-click the page.

Figure 25-11: The Notepad Contents page lists the pages you've added to the Notepad section, by title and page number.

Making and Editing Entries

To enter text on a Notepad page, turn to that page, then click inside the body area for the page so that the blinking insertion point appears. Type your text as you would in Word Pro, pressing Enter to start each new paragraph. For example, Figure 25-12 shows some text entered into a Notepad page. You can drag over the text to select it, and press Delete or use other editing techniques to make changes. Further, you can use the Text SmartIcons that appear to change the style, font, or alignment for selected text. To finish entering text on the page, press F2. To edit the text on any page, select the page and then click in the body area. Make the needed changes, then press F2 to verify them. Save your Organizer file in order to save your new Notepad pages and notes information.

Use these SmartIcons to format the note text.   Click to expand the folded page.

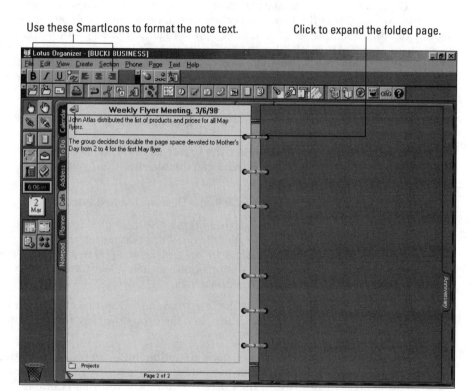

Figure 25-12: Type your notes in the body of the note page.

Adjusting the Page

If you click a page on the Notepad Contents page or click the page title on the page, you can choose Edit ➪ Edit Page (Ctrl+E) to display the Edit Page dialog box, which offers the same settings as the Create Page dialog box. Make the changes you want, then click OK. To change just the page style, click the page on the Notepad Contents page or click the page title, and then choose Page ➪ Page. Change the Style settings in the Page dialog box, then click OK. Alternately, you can click a page listing or page title, then click either the Edit Page or Page command to display the needed dialog box and adjust the page.

Working with the To Do List

The To Do section in Organizer enables you to enter a list of tasks, each of which you can check off when you complete it. By adding a Start Date and Due Date for the task, Organizer can play an alarm sound and display a visual alert to remind you of the task, or divide the tasks into categories to help you stay organized. You may say that this sounds a lot like creating appointments. The steps for doing so are similar, but unlike the Calendar, the To Do list doesn't lock you into precise time periods for your activities. In fact, you don't have to specify deadlines at all in the To Do section, making it an ideal place to list the ongoing and routine tasks that you work in around scheduled activities.

Start by clicking the To Do section tab. Then, follow these steps:

1. Choose Create ➪ Task (Insert), click the Create an Entry toolbox icon, or click the Create a Task SmartIcon. You also can double-click the To Do section page. The Create Task dialog box appears.

2. Enter the nature or name of the task in the Description text box.

3. In the Date section, leave the No Date option button selected for any ongoing task or task for which there's no specific deadline. (Organizer always considers such tasks current tasks.) Or, for a task you need to start and finish on specific dates, click the Start options button, then select the necessary dates from the Start and Due drop-down lists.

4. Select one or more categories for the task from the Categories drop-down list by clicking the categories to use, then click the drop-down list arrow to close the list.

5. Assign a priority for the task by clicking an option button in the priority area. (When you assign priorities, you can then use the View ➪ By Priority to divide the list of tasks by priority on the Current, Future, Overdue, and Completed subtabs). Figure 25-13 shows basic settings entered for a new task.

6. To mark the task as Confidential to restrict who has access to the task information, click to check the check box with that name.

7. Click the Cost button, select the codes to assign to the appointment from the Customer Code and Cost Code drop-down lists, then click OK.

8. If you want Organizer to play an alarm tune and display an alarm message before or after the task, click the Alarm button to display the Alarm dialog box. Specify a Date and Time for the Alarm; by default, Organizer suggests the Start date for the Date setting. To adjust when the alarm plays/displays relative to the specified time, click the Before or After option button, then adjust the time in the text box beside it. Select the alarm sound to play from the Tune drop-down list, then use the Message text box to enter any alarm message to display. Keep the Display Alarm check box checked to ensure your alarm message displays. Click OK to close the dialog box and finish setting the alarm.

Create an Entry icon.   Create Task SmartIcon.   Subtabs.

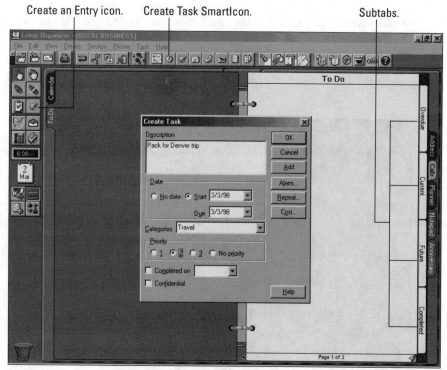

Figure 25-13: Specify information about a new task in this dialog box.

9. If the task will recur at regular intervals and you want to schedule several more, click the Repeat button. The Repeat dialog box appears. This dialog box works just like the Repeat dialog box for setting appointments. Refer to Step 13 under "Creating Appointments," to learn how to work with options for setting up either recurring tasks or appointments. Click OK to finish setting up the recurring task.

10. Click Add to add the new task to the To Do list.

11. Repeat Steps 2–10 to add more tasks to the To Do list.

12. Click the Close button (which was the OK button before you added the first task) to close the Create Task dialog box, then save the Organizer file.

After you finish creating tasks, they appear immediately in the To Do section. By default, tasks scheduled to start on the current date or on no particular date appear on the Current subtab. Tasks scheduled to start at a later date appear on the Future subtab. Tasks that you should have completed by a particular date but which you haven't yet marked as completed appear on the Overdue subtab. Tasks you've checked off as finished appear on the Completed subtab. (Organizer uses different subtabs if you choose a command other than View ⇨ By Priority.) Organizer automatically moves tasks between subtabs based on the date and your updates to the To Do list. Depending on the preferences you set for the To Do section, the list also may include small indicator icons to give you more information about the task, such as whether you've set an alarm for it or what category you've assigned. In addition, the To Do list includes a circle with any priority you've set for the task, and displays any Start and Due dates you've entered. Figure 25-14 shows examples of indicators and priority settings.

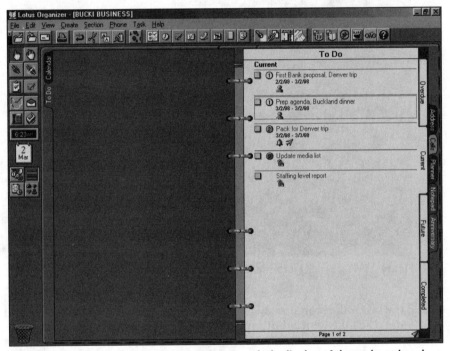

Figure 25-14: The To Do section provides an orderly display of the tasks at hand, with information about each task such as its priority, start date, and due date.

To check your To Do list, turn to the To Do section, and click the subtab to review. The tasks on the subtab appear. If you have numerous tasks, you can use the PgDn and PgUp keys to move between pages in the To Do section. When you finish a task, you literally check it off in the list. Click the check box beside the task to check it. Organizer moves the task to the Completed subtab, as shown in Figure 25-15. Organizer also records the date on which you marked the task as completed, in case you need to review that information later.

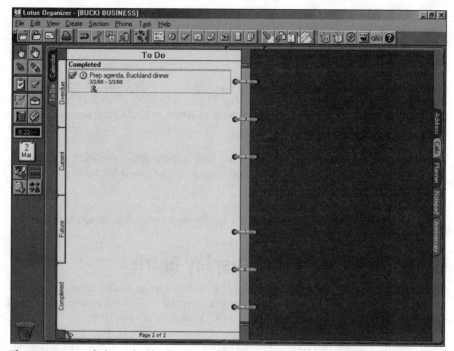

Figure 25-15: Click to check off a completed task and move that task to the Completed subtab.

Selecting and Working with Entries

In most sections in Organizer, you use the same general techniques to select and make changes to entries. (The Notepad section functions a bit differently than most, however.) While the particular options may differ slightly from section to section, the steps described in this section should provide you with a comfortable roadmap to changing and working with entries.

Selecting and Editing an Entry

To select an entry so you can make changes to it, select the section and then the page that holds the entry. Click the Focus, Select, and Drag and Drop icon on the toolbox (it's the upper-left one on the toolbox). Click the entry, such as a Calendar appointment or To Do task, to select it. An outline appears around the selected entry, and a menu appears with commands for working with the entry. In the Calendar section, you see the Appointment entry, and in the To Do section, the Task menu appears. You can use the commands on the entry menu to change specific settings with regard to the entry. For example, use the Categorize command to change the category you've assigned to the entry. Or, use Appointment ➪ Pencil In to mark a Calendar entry as penciled in, or to toggle off the Pencil In status after you've firmed up the appointment.

To display an Edit dialog box that you can use to change multiple settings for the selected entry, choose Edit ➪ Edit (Entry Type). The Edit (Entry Type) dialog box appears, offering you all the options you had when you created the entry. Make the needed changes, then click OK.

Note   In some sections and views, scroll arrows may appear when you click on a particular page or date. Use the scroll arrows to display more or less information.

Hot Stuff   You also can right-click a selected entry to display commands for working with it.

Using Go To or Find to Display Entries

If you're not sure where a particular entry is, don't want to flip through multiple sections or pages, or want to see numerous entries of a particular type without missing one, you can use the Go To or Find features to save time.

Go To enables you to go to a particular area within a section, such as a particular Calendar date, a particular To Do subtab, or a particular Notepad page. To use Go To, choose Edit ➪ Go To (Ctrl+G). The Go To dialog box appears. Choose the section that contains the information to go to from the Section drop-down list. Then, using the list or text box that appears below the Section drop-down list, choose what element in that section to display. Click the OK button to turn to the specified section and page and close the Go To dialog box.

The Find feature enables you to look for a specific entry or all entries containing particular text that you specify. To use Find to go to one or more entries, choose Edit ➪ Find (Ctrl+F) or click the Find Text SmartIcon. The Find dialog box appears. Enter the word or phrase to find in the Find text box. In the Options area, check Case Sensitive to have Find display only entries with capitalization matching the capitalization you used in the Find text box. Click Whole Word to ensure exact matches, rather than partial matches.

To limit the find operation to a single section, click the Section option button and select the section from the accompanying drop-down list. Otherwise, leave the All Sections option button selected. Click Find Next to display the next entry that matches the Find text, then click Close to close the dialog box. Or, click Find All to list all matching entries, then double-click the entry you want to review in the Occurrences list. Organizer displays that entry (see Figure 25-16), so you can review it. If it holds the information you want, click Close to close the Find dialog box.

Focus, Select, and Drag and Drop icons.   Find Text SmartIcon.

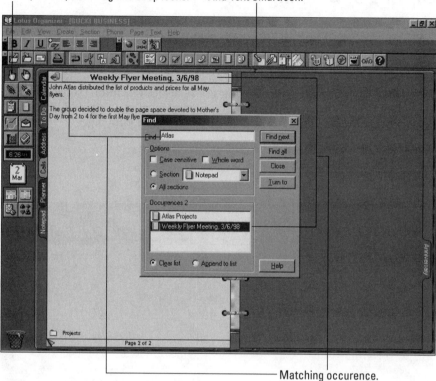

Matching occurence.

Figure 25-16: You can find entries that match text you specify, as shown here.

Moving an Entry

To move an entry, in particular a Calendar entry on the same page, you can easily drag and drop the entry. To do so, click the Move an Entry icon on the upper-right corner of the toolbox. Click the entry to move, so that the mouse pointer changes to a hand holding a page (the page has a clock in it if you're moving a Calendar entry). Then click the date (moving to the appropriate page first) or other location to which you want to move the entry. Organizer moves the entry to the new location.

Note

If you want to reschedule a Calendar appointment on the current day in any view other than the Day Per Page view (View ➪ Day Per Page), do not click the Move an Entry icon. Instead, click the appointment and then click in it again to display a timescale at the right. You can drag the start time, finish time, or both, to change the appointment schedule. Then, click the appointment again to finish.

Copying or Deleting an Entry

The toolbox provides a special tool you can use to copy an entry to as many
locations as you'd like. Click the Focus, Select, and Drag and Drop icon on the
toolbox, click the entry to copy, then drag and drop it onto the toolbox icon that
has a clipboard on it (it has a lengthy name). The clipboard changes to show that it
holds a copied item. Then, display the page or date to which you want to copy the
entry and drag from the clipboard icon to the desired location (see Figure 25-17).
You can drag the entry from the icon to as many locations as you'd like, or drag it
to the trashcan icon so that it's no longer available for copying.

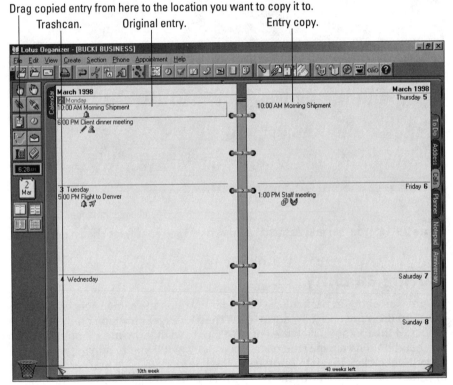

Drag copied entry from here to the location you want to copy it to.
Trashcan.   Original entry.   Entry copy.

Figure 25-17: You can copy an entry by dragging and dropping.

You can remove any entry from the current page. To do so, click the Focus, Select,
and Drag and Drop icon on the toolbox, and click on the entry to delete. Then, you
can either drag the entry and drop it into the trashcan icon at the lower-left corner
of the screen, or right-click the entry and then click Clear.

You can copy or move an entry between sections, and Organizer automatically changes the entry type. For example, if you want to block out time for a task on your schedule for the day, copy the task entry to the current date in the Calendar, then adjust the schedule for the new appointment as needed. Or, to turn an upcoming appointment into a To Do task, copy the appointment from the Calendar section to the To Do section.

Handling Alarms

When you set an alarm for an appointment or task and opt to display the alarm, Organizer displays the Alarm dialog box at the appointed time, as shown in Figure 25-18. To have the alarm replay at a slightly later time, specify the time interval using the Snooze For text box, then click Snooze. Or, to display the appointment or task for which you set the alarm, click Turn To. Otherwise, click OK to close the Alarm dialog box.

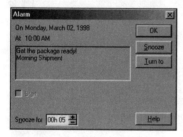

Figure 25-18: Organizer plays a sound and displays the Alarm dialog box to remind you of an appointment or task (or warn you if you're running late).

The Organizer program has to be open in order for it to play and display alarms.

Linking Related Entries

When you link related entries, you can easily move back and forth between them in the Organizer file. For example, you might want to link your Notepad notes about a phone call or meeting appointment to the appointment entry in the Calendar.

To link two entries, click the Create Links toolbox icon. Then, click the first entry to link, so that the mouse pointer changes to a hand with a chain link extending from either side. Then, display the entry to which you want to link the first entry (even if it's in another section), and click that entry. A link symbol appears in the upper-right corner of each linked entry. To use the link, click the link symbol, then click the linked task to go to in the pop-up list that appears, as shown in Figure 25-19.

Create Links icon.
Break Links icon.

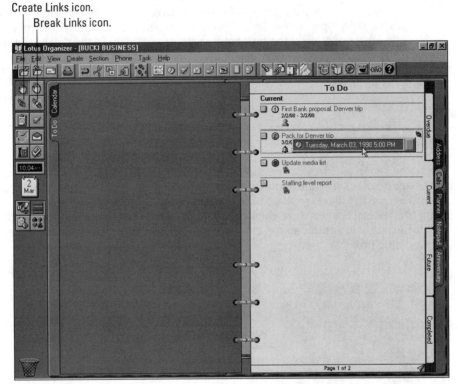

Figure 25-19: To follow the link, click the link symbol, then click the task to go to.

To remove a link, click the Break Links icon on the toolbox, then click the link symbol for either linked entry. In the list of links that appears for that entry, click the entry link that you want to remove.

Using Show Through

The Show Through feature enables you to show the entries from other sections in either the Calendar Section or the Planner section. For example, you can also display the To Do, Calls, Planner, and Anniversary section entries in the Calendar. Why would you want to do this? To limit the amount of time you spend flipping between sections, and to minimize the likelihood that you'll miss an important task or anniversary, for example.

To use Show Through in the Calendar section, display the Calendar section, then choose Section ➪ Show Through. Leave Calendar selected in the Show Into drop-down list (unless you're working in the Planner), then click each other section for which you want to show entries in the From list. Click the Preferences button to display the Calendar Show Through Preferences dialog box. In the Preferences area, choose either the Above Appointments or Below Appointments dialog box to specify where to display the show through information.

To limit the show through to a single line of information for each entry, check the First Line Only check box under Show. Click OK, then click OK again to close the Show Through dialog box and display the Show Through information, as shown in Figure 25-20.

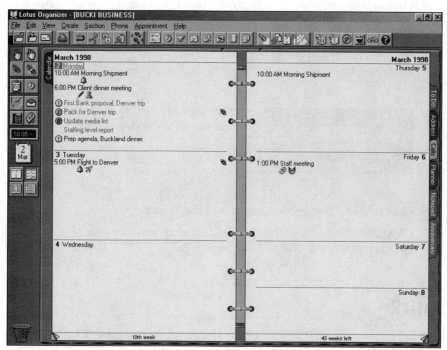

Figure 25-20: In this example, March 2 shows To Do section tasks in addition to the appointments for the day.

To turn off Show Through, choose Section ➪ Show Through in the Calendar (or Planner) section. Click each highlighted section in the From list, then click OK.

Creating a Section

You can add a section of a particular type anywhere within an Organizer file. For example, in addition to the default To Do section in which you include your professional To Do list, you may want to add a personal To Do section. To create a section, follow these steps:

1. Choose Section ➪ Customize. The Customize dialog box appears.

2. In the Tabs list of the Sections tab, click the section after which you want to insert the new section.

3. Click Add. The Add New Section dialog box appears.

4. Choose the kind of section to create from the Section Type drop-down list. Specifying a section type tells Organizer what types of entries you want the new section to contain, and how it should behave.

5. Type the name you want to appear on the new section's tab in the Section Name text box, as shown in Figure 25-21.

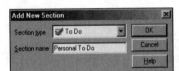

Figure 25-21: Specify a section type and name for the new section.

6. Click OK. The new section appears in the Tabs list.

7. Click OK again to close the Customize dialog box. The new section appears in the current Organizer file.

Printing

If you're fortunate, you'll be able to use Organizer on a notebook computer or even a hand-held system, so you can "go paperless." Many of us still need to work with printed output from an Organizer file, unfortunately. You may not have a notebook or hand-held system, in which case you may need a printout of your Calendar or To Do list to place in your day-planner binder. Or, you might need to share Notepad notes or address contact information with a colleague. In any instance when you need to, you can print a section of Organizer information.

Use the following steps to print in Organizer:

1. Open your Organizer file, make any needed updates, and then save the file.

2. Choose File ➪ Print or click the Print SmartIcon. The Print dialog box appears.

3. Click the Setup button to display the Print Setup dialog box. Choose the printer to print to from the Name drop-down list. You can choose another paper size using the Size drop-down list, but it's not likely that your printer will support the particular style of planner pages you use if you plan to print directly to pages for your planner. You may have to experiment with the paper size you choose, or even click the Properties button and then choose Paper Size, Layout, and Orientation options; however, experiment with some scrap paper and the other settings in the Print dialog box before you work with printer properties. Click OK to close the printer Properties dialog box (if you displayed it), and click OK again to close the Print Setup dialog box.

4. Open the Section drop-down list, and then choose which section to print.

5. Open the Layout drop-down list, and then choose a layout for the printout. The layout determines not only how much information appears in the printout, but also whether any special design elements appear on the printout.

If you want to preview what a layout looks like, click the Layouts button to display the Layouts dialog box. (You also can display it directly in Organizer by choosing Edit ➪ Layouts.) Then, select the layout you want to see from the Layout drop-down list. A sample in the dialog box changes to show you the general look of the selected layout. Once you become proficient with Organizer, you can use the Layouts dialog box options to fine-tune a layout, using the Preferences choices, the Styles button (which displays a dialog box for designing layout elements), and the Paper button (which displays a dialog box for adjusting the paper size). Click OK to finish using the Layouts dialog box.

6. If you've added your own custom section to the current file and the selected layout uses a section of that type, the Sections button becomes enabled to ensure that the printout includes the correct section. For example, if you chose the Daily Calendar/To Do list and have two To Do sections in your Organizer file, click the Sections button. Make sure To Do is selected in the For Part of Layout list, then click the To Do section to use in the Use Information From list, as shown in Figure 25-22. Click OK to close the Sections dialog box and return to the Print dialog box.

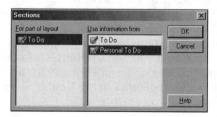

Figure 25-22: When you have more than one section of the same type, choose the correct section to include in the printout using this dialog box.

7. Choose the type of paper to print to from the Paper drop-down list. For example, you can choose a Day Runner, Day-Timer, Filofax, Franklin Day Planner, or Time Manager format in addition to more traditional paper sizes. If you choose to print an address section, you instead might want to choose an Avery label paper format. Figure 25-23 shows a paper selection.

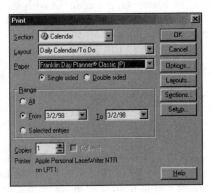

Figure 25-23: The Paper drop-down list offers sizes for popular day planner formats.

8. Choose an option button to indicate whether the paper is single-sided or double-sided. You'll have to print pages and then turn them over when prompted if you choose double-sided.

9. In the Range area, choose All to print all the information in the selected section(s), use the From and To settings (which vary depending on the section type) to print a limited range of entries, or click the Selected option button if you selected a group of entries prior to printing.

10. To print multiple copies, increase the entry in the Copies text box. This enables the Collated check box, which you can check to specify that Organizer should collate pages for you.

11. Click the Options button to display the Print Options dialog box and display a few last printing options. In the Preferences area, check the check boxes as needed to Skip Blank Entries or Print in Black & White. In the Print Order area, active if you're printing an address section, click an option button to specify whether to print Across then Down or Down then Across. In the Labels area, also active if you're printing addresses, adjust the Print Each Label (X) Times text box entry to specify whether to print multiple label copies, and also adjust the Starting Label text box entry if you don't want the printout to start from the first label. Finally, if you choose double-sided paper in the Print dialog box, choose Full Page or Perforated Paper in the Double Sided area to more completely describe the paper you're using. Click OK.

12. Click OK to send the print job to the printer you specified and close the Print dialog box.

✦ ✦ ✦

Tracking Contacts and Calls in Organizer

As you learned in the last chapter, you can use Organizer
to manage all your commitments. In addition, you can
use it to track and keep in touch with people. In the Address
section, you can enter home and business contact information
for anyone you need to be in touch with in the near or distant
future. Then, you can display the address, phone, and e-mail
information you've entered about a person, and even use
Organizer to dial-up that person using your modem. This
chapter explains how to accomplish these feats.

Entering Addresses for Contacts

You use the Address section in Organizer to keep an address-
book style list of names and addresses. But, naturally, the
Address section enables you to capture a much more rich
collection of information, including e-mail addresses, the name
of a contact's assistant, notes, and more. You also can assign a
category for each contact, which defines how that contact fits
into the scheme of your work and other relationships.

If you're a sales professional, you already understand that the
more you know about the person you're selling to, the better
you can adjust your appeal to meet that person's interests,
increasing your odds of developing a successful relationship.
The truth is, the personal approach pays off in all fields,
especially some growing ones like customer service, project
management, and any other small business or service
business you can think of.

Use the following steps to enter a list of contacts in Organizer, so you can start to shine:

1. Open the Organizer file into which you want to add the list of contact information.

2. Click the Address section tab. The Address section opens, displaying a subtab for numeric letters and each alphabetical entry, as shown in Figure 26-1.

Create an Entry icon.   Create an Address Record SmartIcon.   Subtabs.

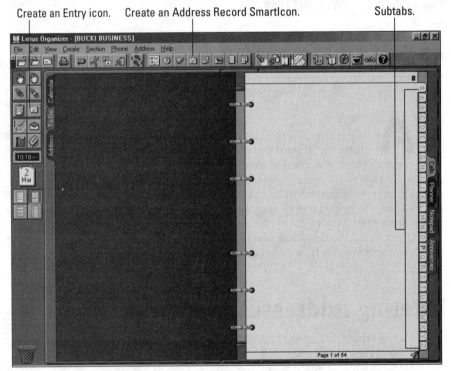

Figure 26-1: The Address section looks like a paper address book and offers subtabs to help you access the alphabetized entries.

3. Choose Create ➪ Address (Insert), click the Create an Entry toolbox icon, or click the Create an Address Record SmartIcon. You also can double-click a blank area in any Address section subtab. The Create Address dialog box appears.

You actually can create an entry in any section no matter what section is currently displayed. To do so, choose Create ➪ Entry In, and then choose the type of entry to create in the submenu that appears.

4. Select a personal or professional title such as Ms. or Dr. from the Title drop-down list. Then enter the contact's First Name and Last Name in the text boxes provided. (You can also refer to each text box as a *field* of information.)

5. Next, fill in the text boxes on the Business tab in the dialog box, choose a category from the Categories drop-down list, and click the Confidential check box if you want to limit access to the contact information based on the password a user enters to open the file. As shown in the example in Figure 26-2, most of the entries are self-explanatory. You can use the Ext text box to enter a phone extension, the Tel 2 number to enter an alternate business phone number, such as a mobile phone number, and the Assistant text box to enter the name of the contact's workplace assistant.

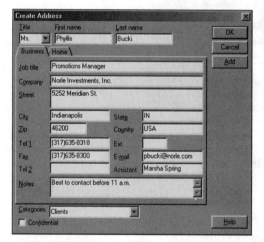

Figure 26-2: Enter information about how to contact someone at his or her job on the Business tab.

If you plan to use Organizer to dial phone calls using the contact information you enter in the Address section, you must use parentheses around the area code of each phone number, as shown in Figure 26-2. If you use a hyphen or slash, Organizer won't be able to dial your calls correctly. You don't have to enter a country code, however. You can select that code from the Dial dialog box, as described later under "Dialing the Call with QuickDial."

The quickest way you can move around in the Create Address dialog box is by pressing Tab to move from text box to text box.

6. Click the Home tab, and enter personal information about the contact in its text boxes. Figure 26-3 shows example entries. Again, most of the entries on this tab are self-explanatory, but the tab does include two fields for "extras," [Unused1] and [Unused2]. You can enter miscellaneous information of any type in these text boxes.

7. Click Add to add the entry to the appropriate alphabetical subtab in the Address section. You don't have to select the correct tab. Organizer alphabetizes the entries for you.

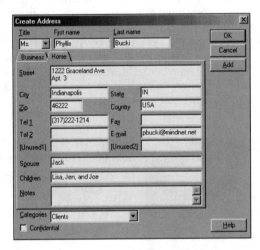

Figure 26-3: Enter more personal information about the contact on the Home tab.

8. Repeat Steps 4–7 to add as many other contact entries as needed. As Organizer adds the addresses to various subtabs, it turns the letter on the subtab black to tell you the subtab contains entries.

9. Click Close when you finish adding entries to the Address section.

10. Choose File ➪ Save or click the Save the Current File SmartIcon to save the address information you've entered.

Working Together

The section titled "Merge Data Files from Other Sources" in Chapter 7 explains how to use the contact list you enter into the Address section in a Word Pro mail merge to create customized letters and address labels for the contacts you specify. Enter your contact information, then save and close your Organizer file prior to performing the mail merge. Using information you've already captured in Organizer saves you the work of creating a new merge data file in Word Pro.

Displaying and Editing an Address

Of course, the whole point in keeping an address book is to be able to view and use the address book information when you need it. Lotus Organizer offers you significant advantages in viewing and updating address information. For starters, you can control how much or how little information Organizer displays at any given time, so you can choose the display format that's most convenient for you. In addition, an Organizer address list remains considerably more tidy than a paper address book, because you don't have to erase mistakes or changes, or use liquid paper to cover them. You can simply reprint the information you need. In this section, you'll learn how to change the detail display, and select, and edit your address entries.

More Info

The section called "Printing" in Chapter 25, "Using Organizer to Track Appointments, Notes, and To Do Lists," explains the process for printing information from Organizer. When you display the Print dialog box and select Address as the Section to print, you can choose print layouts that include different address cards, contact cards, envelopes, labels, or phone lists.

Selecting and Editing an Address

To use or edit an address, you first must display the needed address. To do so, click the subtab that holds the contact. If the letter marked by the subtab includes multiple pages, click the lower page corners or press PgDn or PgUp to display the page that holds the contact you want. The contact appears on the Address page in alphabetical order, as shown in Figure 26-4. Click to select the entry you want.

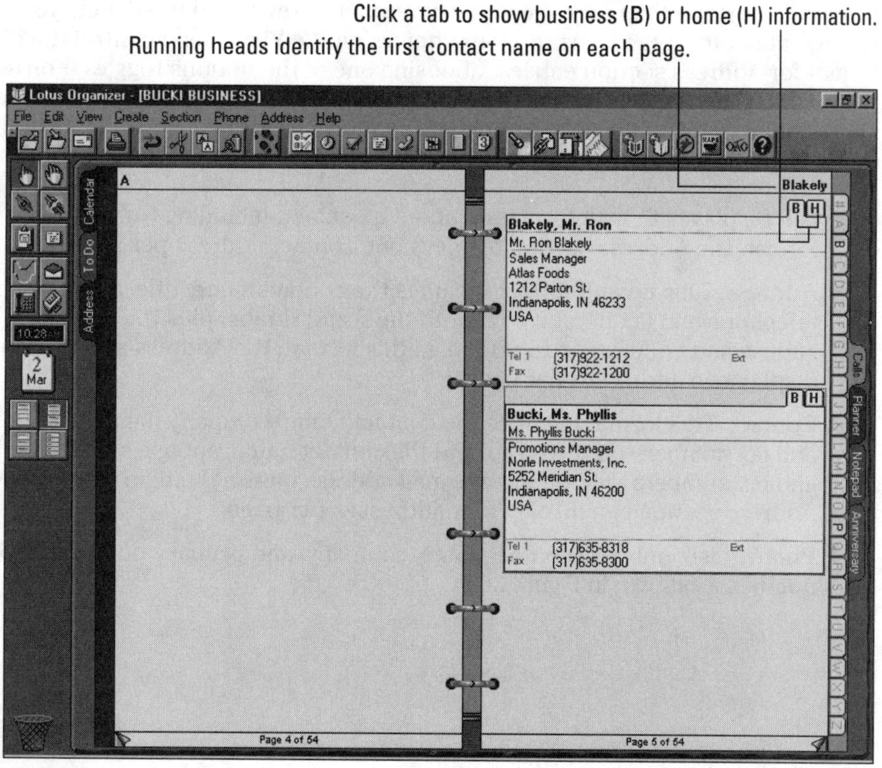

Click a tab to show business (B) or home (H) information.
Running heads identify the first contact name on each page.

Figure 26-4: Each contact appears in alphabetical order on the subtab page.

To go directly to a contact, choose Edit ➪ Go To (Ctrl+G). In the Go To dialog box, make sure Address is selected in the Section drop-down list. The bottom drop-down list varies, depending on how you've organized the listings in the Address section, as described later under "Controlling How the Address Section Organizes Entries." By default, the Address section organizes listings by last name, so you can select the name of the contact to display from the Last Name drop-down list. If you've organized the entries by company, choose the company name from the Company drop-down list. After you select the entry to go to from the bottom drop-down list, click OK.

To edit the selected entry, choose Edit ➪ Edit Address or double-click the address entry. The Edit Address dialog box appears. It offers identical text boxes to the Create Address dialog box. Change the entries as needed, then click OK. Save your Organizer file to save your address information.

Controlling How Much Information Appears

By default, the Address section displays each entry in its Address card format. You can change the display so that each listing includes more information, or less. For example, you may only need to see contact phone numbers to make most calls, but before an important conversation, you may want to review all the details you've entered about a contact. The top four choices on the View menu control the display format for Address section entries. Choosing one of the options toggles it on, and the previously selected option off. You can choose one of the following four View menu commands to select how much information the address book displays about each entry:

✦ **All.** Displays all the information about a contact, including Notes. In this format, the Address section displays one contact address per page.

✦ **Address.** This default format includes the contact name, title, address, and telephone and fax numbers on both the B and H tabs, plus the contact's spouse and children on the H tab. In this format, the Address section can display two addresses per page.

✦ **Contact.** This format includes the contact name, company name, telephone and fax numbers on the B tab, and the contact name, spouse name, telephone and fax numbers, and personal e-mail address on the H tab. In this format, the Address section can display four addresses per page.

✦ **Phone.** Lists only the contact name, company, and primary business phone number, as shown in Figure 26-5.

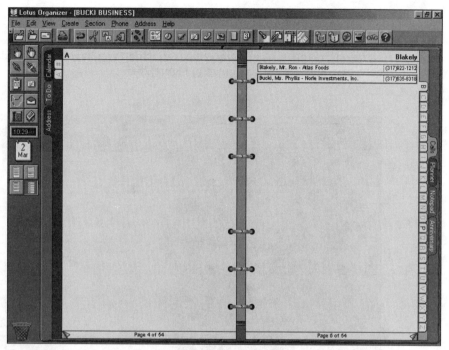

Figure 26-5: Choosing View ⇨ Phone displays minimal contact information.

Controlling How the Address Section Organizes Entries

The second group of four commands on the View menu enable you to specify how Organizer sorts your entries and places them on the alphabetical subtabs in the Address section. As with the first four View menu commands, choosing one of the sorting commands toggles it on, and the other commands off. Choose one of the following View commands to adjust how Organizer sorts the Address section entries:

✦ **By Last Name.** The default choice, this commands sorts the entries according to last name, and places the entries on the subtabs according to last name. For example, all entries with a last name that begins with A appear on the A subtab.

✦ **By Company.** This command sorts the entries alphabetically according to company name. All the entries with a company name that starts with R appear on the R subtab, for example, no matter what the contact person's name is.

✦ **By ZIP.** This command sorts the entries according to the business zip code you entered. It moves all the entries to the # subtab, and organizes them in ascending order by zip code number.

✦ **Category.** This command sorts the entries according to the category you've assigned for them. For example, it places all the entries to which you've assigned the Clients category on the C subtab, then alphabetizes them by last name on the tab. It places any entries to which you haven't assigned a category on the # tab, as shown in Figure 26-6.

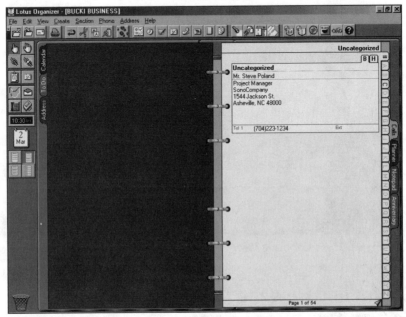

Figure 26-6: When you sort entries by Category, Organizer places uncategorized entries on the # subtab.

Sending and Receiving Calls

You can use your modem to make phone calls if you have your phone connected to your modem. You use software to specify the number to dial, and pick up your handset and talk. Most modems come with software you can use to send faxes, make calls, or connect to the Internet. In this case, however, you'll use Organizer, along with the contact information you've already entered, to place calls with your modem. Using your contact information means you won't have to manually type or press the number to dial, and ensures that you dial the correct number every time.

Note

This section assumes your modem has been properly installed and configured, and connected to a handset phone. If you've been using the modem for other purposes and to dial calls from other software, it is probably correctly installed and configured. To connect your modem to your phone once you've installed the modem hardware, plug the phone cord from the phone into the jack labeled PHONE on the modem; then plug one end of a second phone cord into the jack labeled TELCO or something similar, and the other end into your phone jack on the wall. You'll also need to install modem driver software to make Windows recognize the modem. If you need help installing or setting up the modem, consult online Help in Windows or the documentation that came with the modem.

Dialing the Call with QuickDial

The QuickDial feature enables you to place a call while using the Address book section. To use QuickDial to make a call, follow these steps:

1. Select the entry for the person you want to call.

2. Choose Phone ➪ Quick Dial (Ctrl+Q). Alternately, you can drag the entry to call from the Address section and drop it on the Drag an Entry Here to Dial toolbox icon. The Dial dialog box appears, as shown in Figure 26-7.

Drop the entry for the person to call on this toolbox icon.

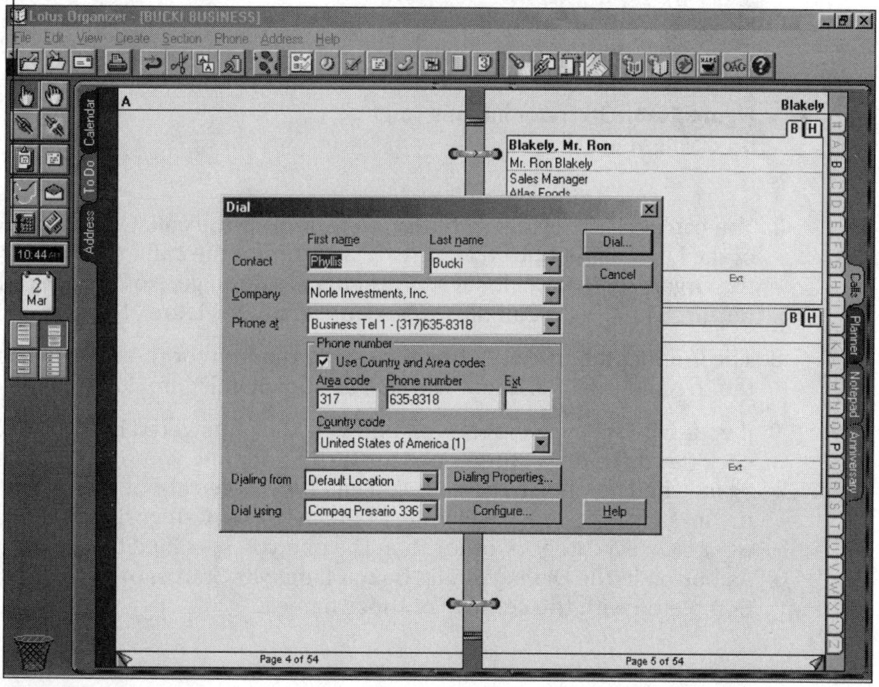

Figure 26-7: You can dial a number for any contact you've entered in the Address section.

3. Verify that the dialog box identifies the correct person to call. If it doesn't, use the Last Name or Company drop-down list to choose a different person or company to call.

4. By default, Organizer assumes you want to call the contact's primary business phone number. To call another number, such as the person's home number, select the number to call from the Phone At drop-down list.

5. If you don't need to dial the area code with the number, clear the Use Country and Area Codes check box.

6. Click Dial. The Dialing dialog box appears (see Figure 26-8), and you can hear your modem dial the call. You should pick up the handset after you hear the modem dial.

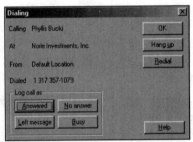

Figure 26-8: Organizer informs you that it's dialing your call.

7. You can click the Hang Up button to terminate the call. Or, you can click one of the Log Call As buttons to create a record of the call in the calls section of the Organizer file. Click the Answered, Left Message, No Answer or Busy button. The Create Call dialog box appears (see Figure 26-9).

8. The Contact tab presents the dialing information for the call. Click the Notes tab to review details about the call, as shown in Figure 26-9.

9. If your contact answers the call and you click Answered in the Dial dialog box, click the stopwatch at the right to start it and time your call; double-click it again when you finish the call. You can type Notes about the conversation or the message you left, assign one of the available Categories to the call (if you want to use a category other than the one you specified by clicking a Log Call As button in the Dialing dialog box), change its Status, or mark it as Completed with the settings of those names.

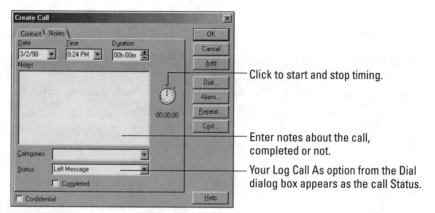

Figure 26-9: Use the Notes tab to track
the true history of the call.

10. To finish an answered call, hang up the phone.

11. Click the Add button to add a record of the call to the Calls section in
Organizer.

12. Click OK to Close the Create Call dialog box.

Creating and Using a Calls Section Entry

If you click the Calls section tab, it displays a record of each call you've made or still
need to make, alphabetizing the calls by your call recipient's last name, as shown in
Figure 26-10. You can click a subtab to display the calls it holds, then double-click
any entry to display it in the Edit Calls dialog box, which offers the same options as
the Create Calls dialog box. You can update any information on the Contact or Notes
tab, or click the Dial button to display the Dial dialog box and redial the call. When
you finish the call, update the information in the dialog box, especially marking the
call as Completed, then click OK to finish making your changes.

Note

When you open the Edit Call dialog box for a call you're previously made or created,
the dialog box includes a Follow Up button. Click that button to display the Create a
Follow Up Call dialog box, then change the Date and Time settings to schedule the
follow-up call. Leave the Link To check box checked at the bottom of the dialog box
to link the follow-up call to the original call entry from which you generated it, then
click OK.

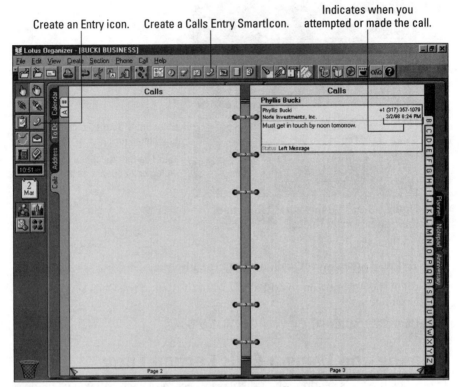

Figure 26-10: Track calls and calling status in the Calls section.

Rather than using QuickDial to dial a call from the Address section, you can create an entry in the Calls section and use it to dial the person you're calling. This technique is useful if you want to create a recurring call entry (for a regular conference call, for example) or set an alarm for a call you need to make in the future. To create a call entry in the Calls section, use the following steps:

1. Open the Organizer file into which you want to add the call entry.

2. Click the Calls section tab. The Calls section opens, displaying a subtab for numeric letters and each alphabetical call entry.

3. Choose Create ➪ Call (Insert), click the Create an Entry toolbox icon, or click the Create a Calls Entry SmartIcon. You also can double-click a blank area in any Calls section subtab. The Create Call dialog box appears.

4. On the Contact tab, enter the First Name, Last Name, and Company for the person to call. Or, if you've already entered the person's contact information

in the Address section, choose the person to call using either the Last Name or Company drop-down list.

5. Select the number to call from the Phone At drop-down list, then change the settings in the Phone Number area if needed.

6. Check the Confidential check box at the bottom of the dialog box to restrict access to the call depending on the password used to open the file, if needed.

7. Click the Notes tab, then specify options on it. Use the Date, Time, and Duration options to schedule the timing for the call. You can type Notes about the upcoming conversation, assign one of the available Categories to the call, change its Status, or mark it as Completed with the settings of those names.

8. If you want Organizer to play an alarm tune and display an alarm message before or after the call, click the Alarm button to display the Alarm dialog box. Specify a Date and Time for the Alarm; by default, Organizer suggests the call date for the Date setting. To adjust when the alarm plays/displays relative to the specified time, click the Before or After option button, then adjust the time in the text box beside it. Select the alarm sound to play from the Tune drop-down list, then use the Message text box to enter any alarm message to display. Keep the Display Alarm check box checked to ensure that your alarm message displays. Click OK to close the dialog box and finish setting the alarm.

9. If the call will recur at regular intervals and you want to schedule several more, click the Repeat button. The Repeat dialog box appears. In the Repeats area, select the overall interval between calls (such as Weekly or Monthly) from the top drop-down list, then fine-tune the interval using the options that appear in the drop-down list and list box below the top drop-down list. The options in these other two lists vary depending on your selection in the top drop-down list. Then, in the Duration area, select either an Until date or click the For option button, and use the plus and minus buttons beside the first text box to indicate how many future calls to schedule. (If you choose Custom from the top drop-down list in the Repeats area, instead use the Custom Dates drop-down list, then click Add to add particular call dates.) When the At Weekends drop-down list becomes enabled, select an option from that list to tell Organizer how to move a call that mistakenly falls on the weekend. Click OK to finish setting up the recurring calls.

10. Click the Cost button, select the codes to assign to the call entry from the Customer Code and Cost Code drop-down lists, then click OK.

11. Click Add to add the call to your Calls section.

12. Repeat Steps 4–10 to schedule other calls.

13. Click Close to close the dialog box, then save the Organizer file.

14. When you later need to dial a call from a call entry you've created, double-click the call entry in the Calls section to display the Edit Call dialog box. Click Dial, record your changes to the call information, then click OK.

Getting an Incoming Call

In addition to tracking outgoing calls in the Calls section, you can track incoming calls so that you can both record the discussion and plan any follow-up action you have to take as a result of the call. When you receive a call, open the Calls section, then choose Phone ⇨ Incoming Call. The Answer Call dialog box appears. Its options also are identical to those in the Create Call dialog box, as shown in Figure 26-11. Enter information about the caller on the Contact tab; use the Notes tab to include information about the call's duration, category, status, and so on; and use the command buttons to adjust settings for the call if it will be repeated, for instance. Double-click the stopwatch when you conclude the call, tidy up your notes about the call, then click the Add button to log the call entry in, and then click Close to close the Answer Call dialog box.

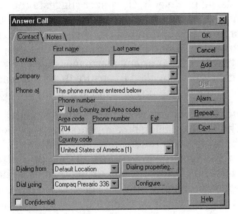

Figure 26-11: Record information about an incoming call in this dialog box to add a Calls section entry for the call.

✦   ✦   ✦

Getting More from SmartCenter

C hapter 2, "Saving Time with SmartCenter," introduced you to SmartCenter, which appears at the top of your screen and adds features you can use from the Windows desktop or while you're working with a SmartSuite application. This chapter takes a closer look at SmartCenter, teaching you how to set the properties for drawers and their contents, customize folders and drawers, and work with the features offered in each of the drawers.

What's in SmartCenter

SmartCenter by default includes eight drawers, each providing unique features. Folders within drawers organize those features into logical groups as described in the following list:

+ **SmartSuite.** The first folder in this drawer holds shortcuts for launching SmartSuite applications, as you learned in Chapter 2. The remaining folders hold different types of shortcuts and files, such as shortcuts to SmartMaster templates and SmartSuite application files you've stored in the default application folder. These folders enable you to easily find and work with SmartMasters and files.

+ **Internet.** You can set up the folders in this drawer to retrieve news headlines, stock quotes, weather reports, travel reservation information, and reference information. In addition, a folder displays the contents of your Favorites folder (a subfolder of the \Windows\ folder on your system), so you can double-click a shortcut or icon to display a Web page or file.

✦ **Calendar.** Enter appointments for the current date, two days, or up to the next week, and tell SmartCenter how far in advance to remind you of the appointment.

✦ **Addresses.** Enter a contact list of names and addresses in this drawer, or even display and use an address list you created in Lotus Organizer.

✦ **Reminders.** Create two task checklists: one for Home and one for Business. As you complete tasks, check them in the appropriate folder.

✦ **Reference.** Type a word to look up its meaning or synonyms using the Dictionary or Thesaurus folder, respectively.

✦ **Business Productivity.** This drawer organizes the SmartMasters from all the SmartSuite applications by use, such as business management or marketing, rather than by application.

✦ **Help.** Use this drawer to access online Help about SmartSuite or to display specialized Help, such as a tour of a SmartSuite application. See the section titled "Launching Help from SmartCenter" to learn how to work with this drawer and its folders.

For simplicity, you can think of each feature held within a drawer as an item. SmartCenter's drawers collect features that otherwise would be scattered throughout Windows, SmartSuite, and other applications. For example, you can set up a folder in the Internet drawer to retrieve current quotes for your favorite stocks. SmartCenter doesn't provide the power to replace other applications such as a full-featured Web browser, but it does provide faster, more convenient access to certain types of information. Later, this chapter covers in detail how to work with each of the eight drawers in SmartCenter.

Working with Drawers and Folders

By now you know that you can open and close a SmartCenter drawer by clicking the drawer (a rectangular button with the drawer's name) on the SmartCenter. Click the right arrow button at the far end of SmartCenter to scroll right and display more drawer names, or click the left arrow button to scroll SmartCenter back to the left. Inside a drawer, a folder tab identifies each folder. The folder tab displays the folder name. Click a folder tab to select or open that folder, sliding its tab up and pushing the tabs above it up as well (see Figure 27-1).

The rest of this section covers general procedures for working with and setting up drawers and folders. However, because each drawer offers different kinds of contents, refer to the latter sections in this chapter to learn more about working with specific folder properties and items (features) in each drawer.

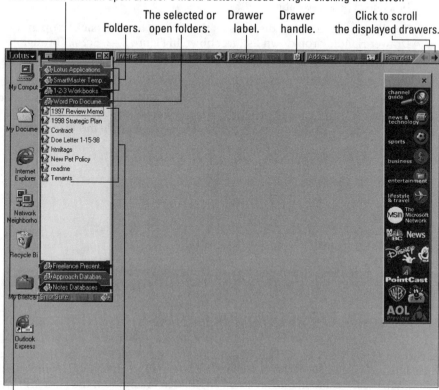

You also can click an open drawer's menu button instead of right-clicking the drawer.

The selected or   Drawer   Drawer   Click to scroll
Folders.   open folders.   label.   handle.   the displayed drawers.

Folder contents, called "items"; in this case, the folder holds Word Pro files.
Click here or here, or press Esc to close the drawer.

Figure 27-1: The SmartCenter provides folders you can use to launch SmartSuite programs, keep your calendar, and more.

Finding the Properties for a Drawer

Each SmartCenter drawer has only two properties (settings) that you can change. You can specify a new drawer label, or drawer name. You also can choose a different icon, called the drawer *handle,* to appear on the right side of the drawer on SmartCenter. Refer back to Figure 27-1, which identifies both of these items for a drawer. To change the properties for any drawer, use the following steps:

1. Right-click the drawer on SmartCenter (or click the drawer menu button), then click Drawer Properties. The Drawer Properties dialog box appears. It has only one tab, Basics.

2. To change the drawer's name, double-click the entry in the Drawer Label text box and type a new label.

3. To change the icon that displays as the drawer handle, click to open the Drawer Handle drop-down list, as shown in Figure 27-2. Scroll through the list and click the icon you'd prefer.

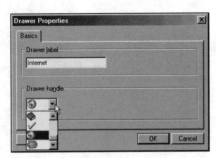

Figure 27-2: Change the name and icon that identify any SmartCenter drawer with the two settings in this dialog box.

4. Click OK to close the dialog box and finalize your changes.

Finding the Properties for a Folder

Like the Drawer Properties dialog box, the Folder Properties dialog box that you use to set properties for any SmartSuite folder has a Basics tab, and its options are the same for every folder. You can use the Basics tab to change the name (folder label), tab color, and icon displayed on any folder. In addition, the Folder Properties dialog box offers one or more additional tabs with specific options for customizing the folder and the types of items it contains. The latter sections of this chapter that deal with each drawer explain how to deal with the properties that apply to specific folders in specific drawers. You can jump ahead to the section that applies if you're ready to set up and work with folders in a particular drawer.

Use the following steps to change the properties on the Basics tab only:

1. Open the drawer that holds the folder for which you want to set properties, then click the folder to select it.

2. Right-click the folder tab, then click Folder Properties. The Folder Properties dialog box appears. The Basics tab appears on top by default, as shown in Figure 27-3.

3. To change the folder's name, double-click the entry in the Folder Label text box and type a new label.

Changes you make here . . .

. . . apply to this folder.

One or more additional tabs
provide properties for setting up
or customizing each particular type of folder.

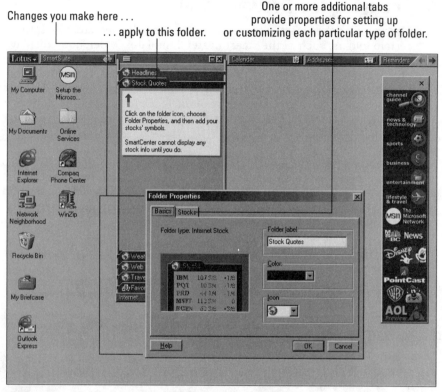

Figure 27-3: Right-click a folder tab and click Folder Properties to display this dialog box for adjusting the folder's settings.

4. To select the display color for the folder tab, click the drop-down arrow beside the Color option, and click a color in the palette that appears.

5. To change the icon that displays on the folder tab, open the Icon drop-down list, scroll through the list, and click the icon you'd prefer.

6. Click OK to close the dialog box and finalize your changes.

Note

Because the folders in each drawer have different characteristics and hold different types of items, the folder shortcut menu (which appears when you right-click a folder tab) offers different options in each drawer. For example, because SmartSuite's drawer folders hold shortcuts and files, the folder shortcut menu for that drawer includes options for arranging the shortcut and file icons, moving the drawer to the Windows desktop, and more.

Changing the Drawer Width

After opening the SmartSuite drawer you can see immediately that the names for certain folders, such as the SmartMaster Templates folder, don't display completely. When a folder name doesn't fit on the folder tab, the name appears cut off and trails with an ellipsis (three dots). In other cases, the information within a folder can't display completely and appears cut off at the right side, or you may simply want to be able to view more of the icons (or other information) within the folder simultaneously. This is where changing the width of a drawer comes in handy.

You can drag with the mouse to change the width of any drawer. To do so, open the drawer, then point to the right border of the drawer until you see the double-headed arrow, as shown in Figure 27-4. Press and hold the left mouse button, then drag left to make the drawer narrower, or right to make the drawer wider. Release the mouse button when the drawer reaches the width you prefer. After you resize the drawer, you can close it or work with its folders as needed.

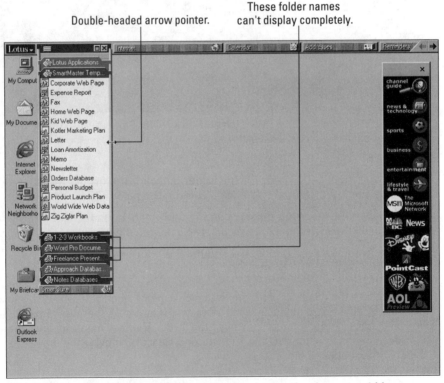

Figure 27-4: Drag a drawer's right boundary to change the drawer's width.

Adding and Removing Drawers and Folders

One universal rule applies to any number of aspects of computing: No matter how much of something you have, you always want more. The same is true in regard to drawers and folders. While SmartSuite offers more drawers than can display onscreen at once, you might prefer to create your own custom drawer to make it easier to access SmartCenter features. For example, you can create a single drawer that holds folders for files, Internet information, and your calendar, so you can perform your favorite operations from a single drawer, rather than multiple drawers.

To add a drawer to SmartCenter, click the Lotus button at the left end of SmartCenter, then click New Drawer. The New Drawer dialog box appears. It offers a single tab, Basics, and the same two options as the Drawer Properties dialog box shown in Figure 27-2. To name the new drawer, drag over the entry in the Drawer Label text box and type a new label. Click to open the Drawer Handle drop-down list, scroll through the list, and click the icon you'd prefer. Click OK to close the dialog box and finish creating the new drawer.

To add a folder to a drawer, use the following steps:

1. Right-click the drawer and choose New Folder. The New Folder dialog box appears. Initially, this dialog box displays a single tab labeled Step 1: Type. The Folder Type list enables you to choose what kind of folder to add to the drawer. The folders listed here offer the same features as the corresponding folders found elsewhere in SmartCenter; for example, the Calendar folder type creates a new Calendar folder that works just like the one found in the default Calendar drawer.

2. Select the folder type from the Folder Type list. The dialog box changes to display additional tabs, like the example shown in Figure 27-5. These tabs enable you to set the initial properties for the folder.

3. Click Next or click the Step 2: Basics tab to display its options.

Additional tabs appear to let you
set properties for the new folder.

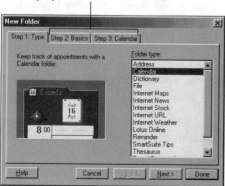

Figure 27-5: SmartCenter offers several folder types; select the type of new folder you want to determine what contents that folder will hold.

4. The Step 2: Basics tab appears for all folder types, and displays the same options as the Basics tab of the Folder Properties dialog box (refer to Figure 27-3). Use the options on the tab to specify the Folder Label, Color, and Icon.

5. Click the Step 3 tab (its name varies depending on the folder type), or click Next. The next tab of properties appears. Make any changes needed to the default settings shown on the tab. Those properties will vary depending on the folder type; the latter sections of the chapter describe the properties for various types of folders.

6. If a Step 4 tab appears, click it or click Next, then change settings as needed on it, too.

7. Click Done to finish adding the folder to the drawer.

If the drawer was closed when you right-clicked it to add the folder, open the drawer to see the new folder. Figure 27-6 shows a custom drawer, with two custom folders added within it.

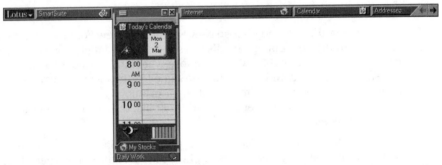

Figure 27-6: The custom folder called Daily Work holds two folders, added after the drawer was created.

By default, a new drawer you add to SmartCenter appears at the far right end of SmartCenter, and a new folder you add into a drawer appears at the bottom of the list of folders. You can move both folders and drawers to other locations. To move a drawer, drag it right or left until it's over the drawer located where you want the moved drawer to appear, then release the mouse. To move a folder, drag its tab up or down. Release the mouse when the tab appears in the correct position: above the tab for the folder that you want to appear below the moved folder if you're dragging up, or below the tab for the folder you want to appear above the moved folder if you're dragging down.

You can remove any drawer from SmartCenter, but you should avoid removing its default drawers. You'd have to remove, then reinstall, SmartCenter to get the default drawer back, or rebuild the drawer and all its folders from scratch. You also can delete any folder from a drawer. To remove a drawer or folder from SmartCenter, right-click the drawer or folder, then choose Delete Drawer or Delete Folder. The Delete Drawer or Delete Folder dialog box appears, asking you to verify that you want to delete the drawer or folder. Click Yes to do so, or No to cancel the deletion.

Organize and Launch Files with the SmartSuite Drawer

The folders in the SmartSuite drawers hold shortcuts to the SmartSuite programs and SmartSuite files. Double-clicking a shortcut launches the application, and opens the file if the shortcut was for a file. The first three folders in the drawer hold shortcuts. The Lotus Applications folder holds shortcuts for launching SmartSuite applications. The SuiteMasters folder holds shortcuts for SuiteMasters, SmartMaster templates that help you accomplish a business task using more than one SmartSuite application. SuiteMasters don't install by default; you have to rerun the Install program and perform a custom installation to install them. The SmartMaster Templates folder holds a shortcut for each SmartMaster template; double-click a shortcut to launch the associated application and create a new, blank document based on the selected SmartMaster.

The next four folders display the files saved in the \lotus\work\ subfolders on your system, as listed in Table 27-1:

Table 27-1	
SmartSuite Drawer Subfolders	
SmartSuite Drawer Folder	*Folder On Your Hard Disk*
1-2-3 Workbooks	\lotus\work\123
Word Pro Documents	\lotus\work\wordpro
Freelance Graphics Presentations	\lotus\work\flg
Approach Databases	\lotus\work\approach

Double-click a file in one of these folders to launch the associated application, and open the file in that application. The final folder, Notes Databases, holds shortcuts to databases if you're working in a Notes environment.

If you want to run a Freelance Graphics presentation screen show directly from the file icon or shortcut in a SmartCenter file folder, right-click the file or shortcut, then click Screen Show.

Setting Up a SmartSuite Drawer Folder

When you right-click a default folder in the SmartSuite drawer and choose Folder Properties, the Folder Properties dialog box that appears offers two tabs: the Basics tab and the Display tab. You learned earlier how to use the Basics tab in any Folder Properties dialog box to change the name, color, and icon for any folder. Click the Display tab, which also appears in the Folder Properties dialog box for any folder of the File type, to display settings controlling how the shortcuts and icons within the folder are arranged. (These settings work just like those for a Windows My Computer or Explorer window.) Click either the Large Icons or Small Icons option button to specify the size for the icons in the folder. Click to open the Arrange By drop-down list and then click your choice to specify whether the folder should sort the icons in order by Name, Type, Size, or Date the file was last saved.

You also can right-click a folder tab, display the View or Arrange Icons submenus from the shortcut menu, and click a view or sorting option to change the display for a folder's file icons and shortcuts.

When you create a new folder of the File type (by choosing File in the Folder Type list of the Step 1: Type tab of the New Folder dialog box), the New Folder dialog box changes to display three more tabs: Step 2: Basics, Step 3: Display (which offers the options just described for choosing an icon size and arranging icons), and Step 4: Location. Make your selections in the first three tabs, then display the Step 4: Location tab, shown in Figure 27-7.

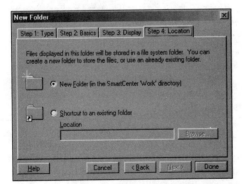

Figure 27-7: When you create a new File folder, use the fourth tab to create or choose the hard disk folder that will store the files.

The Step 4: Location tab enables you to create or choose the *real folder* on your hard disk that will store the files displayed in the SmartCenter File folder. The top option button creates a new folder as a subfolder within the hard disk folder that holds information for the current drawer. Each SmartCenter drawer has a subfolder within the \lotus\work\smartctr\ folder. For example, the hard disk folder for the SmartSuite drawer is \lotus\work\smartctr\SmartSuite\. If you leave the top option button on the fourth tab selected, SmartCenter uses the Folder Label entry from the Step 2: Basics tab as the name for the new hard disk folder. For example, if you enter **My Files** as the Folder Label and are creating the new File folder in the SmartSuite drawer, the hard disk folder SmartCenter creates for the new folder is \lotus\work\smartctr\SmartSuite\My Files\.

In contrast, if you want the new File folder in the SmartCenter drawer to display files from an existing folder on your hard disk, choose the Shortcut to an Existing Folder option button. Then type the folder path in the Location text box, or click the Browse button and use the Browse dialog box that appears to select the appropriate hard disk folder. Once you've specified a hard disk location for the file folder's files, click Done to finish setting the properties for the new File folder.

Danger Zone

Once you create a File folder for a SmartCenter drawer and specify the hard disk folder that will hold its files, you cannot change that hard disk folder setting. Instead, you need to delete the File folder from the drawer and create a new one that points to the correct folder.

Working with Shortcuts and Files

Once you've created a new File folder, any files you save to the hard disk folder for that File folder appear in the File folder in the SmartCenter drawer. Alternately, copy or move files from a Windows My Computer or Explorer window to the open folder in the SmartCenter drawer; or create a shortcut in the drawer for the file. To do so, open the My Computer or Explorer window for the folder that holds the file you want to include in your SmartCenter file folder. Then, open the SmartCenter drawer and folder that you want to hold the file or shortcut. Point to the file icon in the My Computer or Explorer window, then press and hold the right mouse button. Drag the file from the window to the selected File folder, then release the mouse button. In the shortcut menu that appears (see Figure 27-8), click Copy Here to copy the file, or Create Shortcut(s) Here to create a shortcut icon for the file.

Once the file copy or shortcut appears in the SmartCenter File folder, you can double-click the file or shortcut to launch the associated application and open the file. And, just as you can right-click a file or shortcut in a My Computer or Explorer window to display a shortcut menu with commands for working with the file or shortcut, you can do the same in a SmartCenter file folder. Commands included on the shortcut menu include the Rename command for renaming the file or shortcut, and the Delete command for deleting the file or shortcut. The Move to Desktop command on a file or folder shortcut menu moves that file or folder to the Windows desktop, where you can open it by double-clicking it.

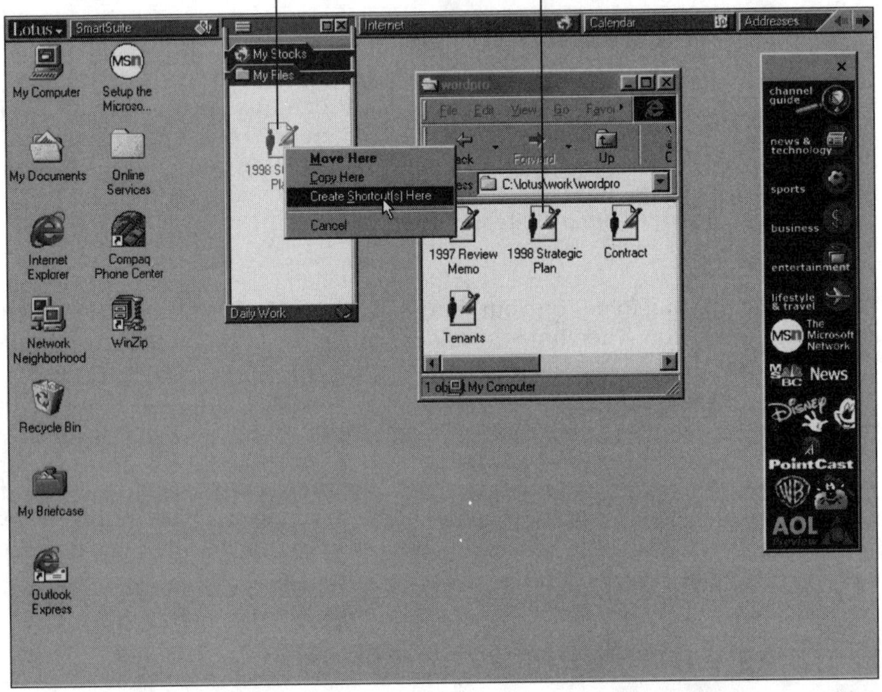

You can create a file copy or shortcut in a File folder.

The original file in the My Computer window.

Figure 27-8: You can copy a file from a My Computer or Explorer window to a File folder by dragging with the right mouse button, then clicking your shortcut menu choice.

Keep in mind that renaming or deleting a file in a File folder renames or deletes the file in the hard disk folder that really stores it. However, if you delete a file or shortcut from a SmartCenter File folder, you can restore it using the Windows Recycle Bin.

Finding Online Information with the Internet Drawer

The SmartCenter Internet drawer offers five folders, each of which helps you access different types of information on the Internet: Headlines, Stock Quotes, Weather, Web Reference, Travel Reservations, and Favorites (or Bookmarks if you use Netscape Navigator, rather than Internet Explorer). Basically, each of the folders offers links or shortcuts to—or information from—particular Web sites published by Lotus, Yahoo (an online Internet search and information service), and others. The first three folders, however, don't display any information until you set the folder properties to reflect what information you want them to hold. Right-click one of those folders, and then click the second tab (named News for the Headlines folder, Stocks for the Stock Quotes folder, and Weather for the Weather folder). Figure 27-9 shows each of these tabs.

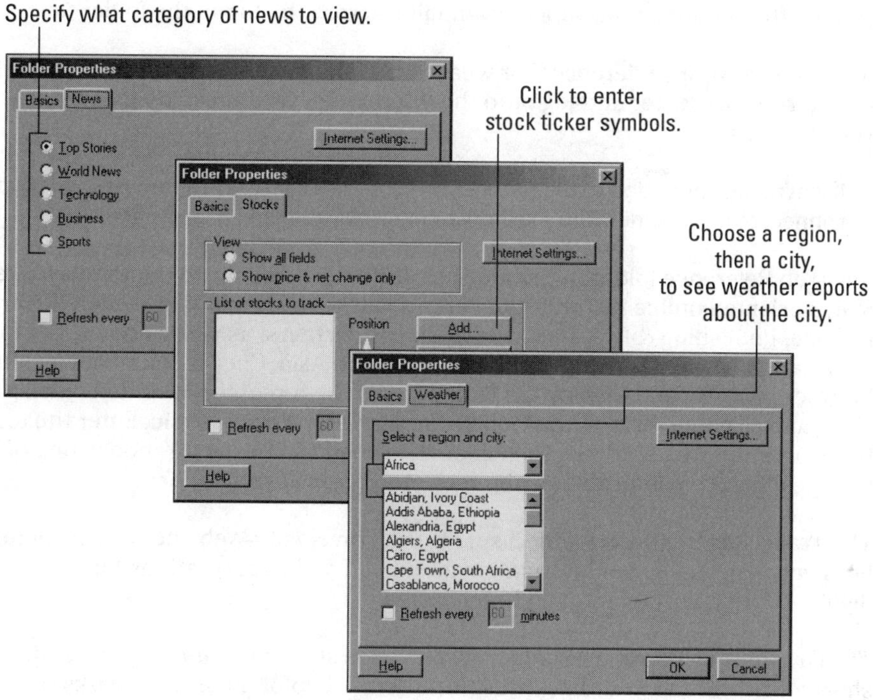

Specify what category of news to view.

Click to enter
stock ticker symbols.

Choose a region,
then a city,
to see weather reports
about the city.

Figure 27-9: Use the Headlines, Stock Quotes, and Weather folders to find up-to-date information on the Internet.

Note

After you set up any of the folders in the Internet drawer to retrieve information, any time you start SmartCenter, it prompts you to connect to the Internet if you access it via a dial-up connection. If SmartCenter loads automatically when you start up your system, it also prompts you to connect to the Internet at that time.

As Figure 27-9 illustrates, you don't need to be an Internet wizard to use the options on the tabs. On the News tab for the Headlines folder, click an option button for a news category. On the Stocks tab for the Stock Quotes folder, click the Add button, enter a ticker symbol in the Add Stock Symbol dialog box, and click OK; in the View area of the Stocks tab, click an option button to Show All Fields or Show Price & Net Change Only. If you don't know the stock ticker symbol you need, click the Symbol Guide button; SmartCenter will prompt you to connect you to the Internet if you're not already connected, then display a list of symbols. In the Weather tab for the Weather Folder Properties, select a region from the upper drop-down list and a specific city from the scrolling list below.

Each of the tabs also offers a Refresh Every . . . Minutes setting; check this check box and enter a minutes setting to specify how often the information in the Internet drawer folders should be updated (while you're connected to the Internet). If you don't enter a Refresh Every . . . Minutes setting, you can right-click a folder name and click Refresh to update the folder or turn off folder refreshing (which is on as long as you see the shooting range ducks swimming across the top of the folder tab).

After you set your preferences for what these folders should display the next time you start SmartCenter and log onto the Internet, each will display the information you specified.

Danger Zone

If you're not connected to the Internet and you click a link, you'll be asked whether to connect to the Internet. You must do so to display the linked Web page.

The Web Reference folder in the Internet drawer holds links to numerous United States-oriented online resources in various categories, including General Reference, Finance, Publishing & Graphics, and Business Partners, as well as resources for information in various categories for Europe and Asia. Click a link to open your Web browser program and display the linked page. The top of the Web Reference page also enables you to search the Web for information about a topic. Enter the topic in the Search the Web text box, then click the Go button to see a Yahoo listing of links to pages that have information about the topic you searched for.

The Travel Reservations folder displays the Travelocity Web site, which contains links you can click to get information about and make reservations for airline flights, car rentals, cruises, and hotel rooms.

The Favorites or Bookmarks folder displays the shortcuts, and folders holding shortcuts, stored as your Favorites (for Internet Explorer) or Bookmarks (for Netscape Navigator) in your Web browser. Double-click a shortcut here to launch your Web browser and display the favorite or bookmarked Web page.

You can add four types of Internet folders to any drawer. When you right-click a drawer and click New Folder, these types are listed in the Folder Type list of the Step 1: Type tab. The Internet News, Internet Stock, and Internet Weather options are identical to the default Headlines, Stock Quotes, and Weather folders in the Internet drawer, just covered in this section. After you select one of these folder types, you enter its Basics information, then choose the headline types, stock tickers, or city.

In addition, you can create an Internet Page folder, which displays the Web page you specify. (Of course, you'll need to make the folder much wider to see the page.) After you select Internet Page from the Folder Type list of the Step 1: Type tab in the New Folder dialog box, you can enter the Step 2: Basics tab information, then click the Step 3: URL tab. Enter the address for the Web page to display in the Internet Location text box; for example, enter **http://www.idgbooks.com** (one of our personal favorites).

What to Do If Your Internet Drawer and Folders Come Up Empty

If you connect to the Internet via a dial-up connection to an Internet Service Provider (ISP), you can't stay online all day long. On the other hand, if you don't connect when SmartCenter loads, the Internet drawer won't contain current information. You can connect later and refresh the information; to do so, right-click the folder and click the Refresh command, an option on the shortcut menu. If that doesn't work, your best bet is to log on to the Internet when you start your system and SmartCenter prompts you to do so, stay connected briefly to enable the Internet drawer to refresh (and check your e-mail while you're at it), then disconnect. To disconnect, double-click the icon for your connection in the tray area at the right end of the Windows taskbar, then click Disconnect.

If you select a SmartCenter folder item that requires you to reconnect to the Internet, a dialog box automatically prompts you to do so. If you choose not to log on to the Internet when SmartCenter loads the first time, but you later need updated Internet information, exit SmartCenter, restart SmartCenter, and log on to your Internet connection. If you access the Internet via a proxy server and don't get your Internet information, you may need to check your settings. To do so, display the Folder Properties dialog box for any folder in the Internet drawer, click the second tab (its name varies, depending on the drawer name), and click the Internet Settings button. Check your settings in the Internet Settings dialog box that appears, make any changes needed to establish your proxy settings, and click OK. Click OK at the Folder Properties dialog box, then exit and restart SmartCenter.

If you want to ensure that SmartCenter (and SmartSuite) uses your system's default Web browser, click the Lotus button at the left end of the SmartCenter, then click SmartCenter Properties. Select the Browser tab, click the System Default Browser option button, then click OK.

Track Appointments with the Calendar Drawer

The Lotus Organizer application in SmartSuite provides powerful features for managing your schedule, contacts, and to do list. If your time and contact management needs are more modest or you don't want to take the time to launch and navigate through Organizer, you can use a few of the SmartCenter drawers for time and contact management instead.

The Calendar drawer enables you to enter appointments, and specify how far in advance of appointments the drawer should open, reminding you of the appointment. The Calendar folder in the Calendar drawer divides your schedule into 15-minute increments, and can display appointments for one day, two days, and so on, up to seven days. Use the following steps to add an appointment in Calendar:

1. Open the Calendar drawer.

2. If the Calendar folder tells you that you need to specify a calendar data file, right-click the folder tab and click Folder Properties. Click the Calendar tab, choose Text File from the File Type drop-down list, and click OK.

2. If needed, click one of the vertical sections on the Days to Display bar to display more of the calendar. For example, if you want to set an appointment that's more than a week away, you'll need to click on the second vertical section of the Days to Display bar to display another seven days in the calendar, so you can enter your appointment in the next week.

Hot Stuff

If you click one of the calendar pages near the top of the Calendar folder, a pop-up calendar that you can use to display earlier or later dates appears. So, if you need to set an appointment that's a month away, you can display that date, set the appointment, and redisplay the current date.

3. Scroll to display the appointment time. To scroll to an earlier time (each day starts at 12 A.M., midnight), click the up-arrow icon with the sun on it near the top, left corner of the Calendar folder. To scroll to a later time, click the down-arrow icon with the moon on it near the lower-left corner of the Calendar folder.

4. Click on the time for the appointment. The Create Appointment dialog box appears.

5. As shown in Figure 27-10, type the name for, and any pertinent information about, the appointment; then click OK to add the appointment at the scheduled time.

6. To specify when SmartCenter should notify you of the appointment (by opening the Calendar drawer and playing an alert sound), right-click the Calendar folder tab and choose Folder Properties. Click the Calendar tab to display its options. Under Appointment Alerts, click to check the Open Drawer . . . Minutes Before Appointments check box. If needed, edit the text box entry beside the check box to specify how much advance warning you want about each appointment. Click OK.

Danger Zone

If you do not enable the Open Drawer . . . Minutes Before Appointments check box, SmartCenter won't alert you about appointments.

7. You can repeat Steps 2–6 to set additional appointments, then close the Calendar drawer when you've finished.

The current time.   Click to scroll to an earlier time.

An appointment on the schedule;
point to its black border
and drag to move the appointment.

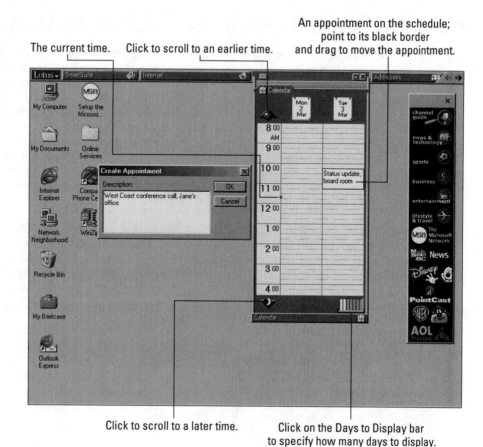

Click to scroll to a later time.   Click on the Days to Display bar
to specify how many days to display.

Figure 27-10: Use the Calendar folder to enter and view appointments, and to have SmartCenter remind you of each upcoming appointment.

After you've added an appointment, you can move it on the Calendar tab by pointing to the black border around the appointment box (the mouse pointer changes to a grabber hand) and dragging the appointment to a new time. To view or edit appointment information, right-click the appointment and click Appointment Properties, or double-click the appointment. Change the entry in the Description text box of the Appointment Properties dialog box, then click OK. To delete an appointment, right-click it and click Delete Appointment. Click Yes in the Delete Appointment dialog box to verify that you want to delete the appointment.

Keeping Contacts with the Addresses Drawer

The Addresses drawer enables you to enter contact information and display it quickly. Not only is it more convenient to work with contact information onscreen, but Address Book also offers other advantages. You can enter information more quickly (most people can type more quickly than they can write by hand). And, you can store more detailed contact information than in a traditional address book, because most paper address books limit entries to a few lines.

To set up the Addresses folder in the Addresses drawer, if the folder has a message telling you that no file is specified, open the drawer and right-click the Addresses folder. Click Folder Properties, then click the Names & Addresses tab. Select Text File from the File Type drop-down list, then click OK.

To enter information about a contact in the Addresses drawer, open the drawer, then click the tab for the first letter in the contact's last name. Click the next available line on the tab, which displays Add Name . . . in dim gray text. An address entry dialog box pops up. Enter Business and Home contact information (see Figure 27-11) and click OK to finish the entry. At that point, the contact entry remains onscreen in a pop-up dialog box so that you can use it to send a message or place a call. Click the entry's Close button to close the entry.

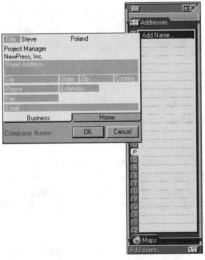

Figure 27-11: To enter contact information in the dialog box, click a field and type your entry; you also can press Tab to move between fields.

Displaying Lotus Organizer Information in the Calendar or Addresses Folder

If you've already saved appointment and contact information in a Lotus Organizer file, you can display that information in the default Calendar or Addresses folders. To do so, right-click the folder tab and click Folder Properties. Click the second Tab in the Folder Properties dialog box (named Calendar for the Calendar folder, and Name & Address for the Addresses folder). Open the File Type drop-down list and choose Lotus Organizer File. Enter the full path name in the Name of Lotus Organizer File text box or use the Browse button beside the text box to display a dialog box for selecting the file. If that Organizer file contains more than one calendar or address section, select the section you want from the Section drop-down list. Click OK to close the dialog box and display the Organizer information in the folder. If the Organizer file you selected included passwords that you don't want to use with the SmartCenter folders, right-click the folder displaying the Organizer information, and choose Clear Passwords. Click Yes at the message box that appears to verify that you'd like to clear the passwords.

The amount of contact information you enter determines how many tasks you can perform directly from the dialog box for that contact. To view and use the contact information, open the Addresses drawer, click the tab for the first letter in the contact's last name, and click the contact name. Figure 27-12 shows the types of operations you can perform with the contact information.

Following is a description of each operation:

✦ **Write a Letter.** Click the Write a Letter button beside the address to use a Word Pro SmartMaster to create a letter addressed to the contact. After you click this button, the Word Pro SmartMaster dialog box appears. Enter the full path and file name for the SmartMaster to use in the Name of Word Pro SmartMaster text box, or use the Browse button beside the text box to select a SmartMaster. Then, click OK to close the Word Pro SmartMaster dialog box, launch Word Pro, and create and address the letter.

✦ **Call.** Click the Call button beside the contact phone number to launch the Windows Phone Dialer accessory and dial the contact's phone number with your modem. If your computer has a voice-capable modem, you can then talk to your contact over the modem and phone line.

✦ **Fax.** Click the Fax button to launch your faxing software (usually Microsoft Fax) to create and send a fax to the contact.

✦ **Send Mail.** Click the Send Mail button to create and send a TeamMail message to the contact. TeamMail is described in Chapter 33, "Working with Communications and Team Editing Features."

Click to use a SmartMaster to create a letter for the contact.

Click to edit the contact information.

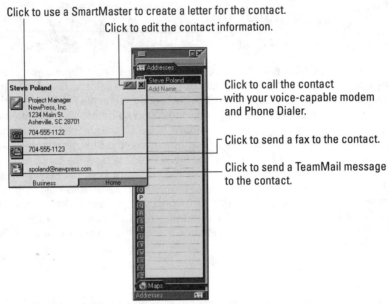

Click to call the contact with your voice-capable modem and Phone Dialer.

Click to send a fax to the contact.

Click to send a TeamMail message to the contact.

Figure 27-12: Click a contact name to display the contact information; click a button in the dialog box to choose a method for communicating with the contact.

To edit the contact information, click the contact to display its information, then click the button with the pencil, next to the Close button. Edit the information, then click OK. You can then work with the contact information, or close the contact dialog box by clicking its Close button. To delete a contact, right-click the contact name in the appropriate tab of the Addresses folder, then click Delete Name & Address.

You can make two more properties changes, in addition to those discussed earlier, for any Addresses folder. In the Addresses drawer, right-click the Addresses folder, then click Folder Properties. Click the third tab, the Options tab. To change the first property, click one of the two option buttons in the Display Names area near the top of the tab to select a display order for the contact names in the folder: Standard Order or Last Name First. The second property you can change is whether or not to choose a SmartMaster to appear by default in the Name of Word Pro SmartMaster text box of the Word Pro SmartMaster dialog box when you click the Write a Letter button for a contact. Under Write a Letter in the tab, type the full path and file name for the default SmartMaster in the Name of Word Pro SmartMaster text box, or use the Browse button beside the text box to specify the SmartMaster. After you finish making selections on the Options tab, click OK to close the Folder Properties dialog box.

The Addresses drawer also contains a Maps folder. Clicking it connects to the Internet, if needed, then displays the search tools from the Mapquest Web site. You can then search for address information. For example, you can enter a zip code in the Zip Code field, and then click the Search button to have Mapquest tell you what city and state that zip code represents. So, the Maps folder can help you flesh out address information as needed.

Using Reminders to Keep Yourself on Track

Use the Reminders drawer to create a to do list and check off tasks as you complete them. The drawer offers folders for two to do lists: Home and Business. Open the drawer and click one of the tabs to display tasks it holds, or to add and remove tasks. To add a task, click in the placeholder for the next task (a blank rectangle), then type the task and press Enter. Figure 27-13 shows existing tasks and a completed one that's been checked off. To delete a reminder, right-click it and then click Delete Reminder. Or, if a folder contains a number of completed reminders, you can right-click the folder tab and then click Delete Completed Reminders to remove them simultaneously.

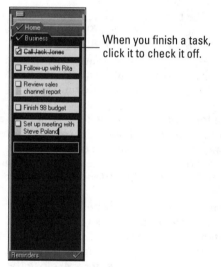

When you finish a task, click it to check it off.

Figure 27-13: Create one or more to do lists in the Reminders drawer.

You can perform a number of task operations by dragging task reminders with the mouse. For example, to create a reminder, you can select text in a Word Pro document, open the Reminders drawer and folder you want, then drag the text from the document onto the reminders folder. You can drag reminder tasks between Reminder folders. You also can place the reminder on the desktop, like a sticky note, to remind you of the urgency of the task. To do so, drag the reminder onto the desktop. When the task reminder appears on the desktop, you can click to check it once you've completed the task. In addition, you can right-click the reminder (see Figure 27-14), then click Move Back to Folder to return the task reminder to its previous location;, or Delete Reminder to remove the reminder altogether. The Desktop Reminders Always on Top option on the shortcut menu controls whether a task reminder displays on top off all open applications (checked) or on top of the Windows desktop, but under other open applications (not checked).

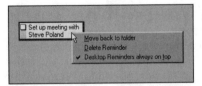

Figure 27-14: Putting a task reminder on the desktop keeps it "in your face" until you finish the task. Right-click to display a submenu for moving or removing the reminder.

SmartCenter saves task reminders in a text file behind the scenes. At any time, you can create a new reminder file, or open an older one. For example, you might want to create a new reminder text file every week to keep a record of tasks you've accomplished and to document your job performance. The default task reminder text file for the Home folder in the Reminders drawer is \lotus\work\smartctr\ Reminde1.txt; the Business folder uses \lotus\work\smartctr\Reminde2.txt.

To create or specify another reminder file for a folder, right-click the folder tab and choose Folder Properties. Click the Reminder tab in the Folder Properties dialog box. Edit the file name portion of the Name of Text File text box entry to create a new reminder file. Make sure you include a .txt extension, so the new file path and name might read something like **\lotus\work\smartctr\06-01rem.txt**.

To select another existing reminder file, or to choose a folder before entering the name for a new reminder text file, use the Browse button. Click OK to close the dialog box, and display reminder file contents, if any, in the folder. (Note that if you don't want reminders that you drag to the desktop to stay on top by default, click to clear the Desktop Reminders Always on Top check box before you close the Folder Properties dialog box.)

Getting Dictionary and Thesaurus Help with Reference

When you need a definition or synonym for a word, you can use reference information from the Lotus SmartSuite CD-ROM to find it. Insert the CD-ROM in your computer's CD-ROM drive, click to open the Reference drawer, then click either the Dictionary or Thesaurus tab. Choose the Dictionary tab when you need to find a word's meaning, and the Thesaurus tab when you need to find a synonym (a word with a similar meaning) for a word. In the text box near the top of either folder, type the word to define or find synonyms for, then press Enter. The folder displays the definition or list of synonyms. Figure 27-15 shows a definition in the Dictionary folder.

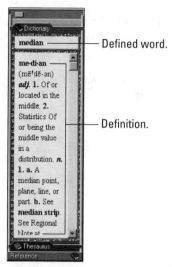

Figure 27-15: The Dictionary folder defines the word specified near the top of the tab.

If you forget to insert the Lotus CD-ROM before entering a term in the text box on the Dictionary or Thesaurus folder, a message box appears to remind you to insert the CD-ROM. Do so, then click the Retry button. The Reference drawer and its folders offer only the Basics properties that are universal for all drawers and folders, so you don't have to worry about customizing this drawer or choosing particular dictionary files.

Launching a File from the Business Productivity Drawer

The Business Productivity drawer is as straightforward as the Reference drawer. This drawer contains shortcuts for all the SmartMaster templates, giving you another easy way to find and launch those templates. File folders in the drawer organize the SmartMasters by topic or purpose, rather than by SmartSuite application file type. (Incidentally, these file folders work like and have the same properties as SmartSuite drawer file folders or any custom File folders you create, as described earlier in the chapter.)

The File folders in the drawer are Business Management, Finance & Accounting, Account Management, Sales, Marketing, and Internet. To launch an application and create a document based on a particular SmartMaster, open the Business Productivity drawer, select a tab, and double-click the shortcut for the SmartMaster you want.

If you want to verify that you're selecting the right Word Pro SmartMaster shortcut, right-click the shortcut and click Preview. Click OK to close the preview when you've finished reviewing it.

For information on working with the Suite Help folder, see "Launching Help from SmartCenter" in Chapter 2, "Saving Time with SmartCenter."

✦   ✦   ✦

Working with SmartIcon Bars

SmartIcons embody a simple concept: point and click to choose a command. In creating each version of SmartSuite over the last several years, Lotus has evaluated and refined the SmartIcon selection offered in each application. Despite such an effort, no software program or set of tools meets every user's specific needs. To make the SmartIcons meet your needs, you can customize them. This chapter explains how to control which SmartIcon bars display and where they appear onscreen, and how to set other SmartIcon bar features. If a particular SmartIcon bar has icons that you don't need or you don't like the order of the icons, the chapter describes how to add, delete, and move icons as needed, and then save your changes. Finally, if you've created a handy script, you'll see how to create a SmartIcon that makes it a click away.

Hiding and Displaying SmartIcon Bars

The SmartIcon bars in SmartSuite applications provide context-sensitive tools. Many of the SmartIcon bars display onscreen by default when you choose a command that requires a particular set of tools. For example, when you begin recording a script, the Record SmartIcon bar appears. You can display any other SmartIcon bar, such as the Internet Tools SmartIcon bar, whenever you need it. When you finish working with a particular SmartIcon bar, you can hide it so it doesn't obscure important information onscreen. To have a really clear screen in instances when you're focusing on data entry and don't really need any SmartIcons, you can hide all the SmartIcon bars or reposition one or more of them to a less intrusive onscreen location.

Each SmartSuite application offers a shortcut menu or Control menu you use to toggle the display of individual SmartIcon bars on and off. To display the shortcut menu, right-click anywhere on a SmartIcon bar. To display the Control menu, which looks and works just like the shortcut menu, click the Control menu button at the left end of the bar (it has a small down-arrow on it). Figure 28-1 shows the Control menu for a SmartIcon bar in 1-2-3. The top of the menu lists three commands (Hide This Bar of SmartIcons, Hide All SmartIcons, and SmartIcons Setup); the menu lists each of the available SmartIcon bars below the SmartIcons Setup command. A check mark appears beside the name of any currently displayed SmartIcon bar to tell you the bar is toggled on. SmartIcon bars without check marks don't currently appear onscreen.

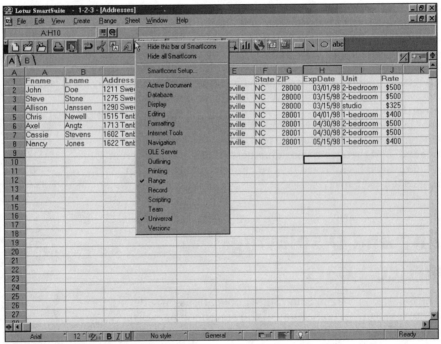

Figure 28-1: Right-click any SmartIcon bar or click the Control menu button at its left end as shown here to display the shortcut menu for managing SmartIcons.

After you display the shortcut menu or Control menu for a SmartIcon bar, click any SmartIcon bar name to toggle the display of that bar on or off and close the shortcut menu. When a SmartIcon bar name doesn't have a check, clicking that name adds the check and displays the SmartIcon bar. The reverse happens when you click a SmartIcon bar that has a check beside it in the shortcut menu; the application removes the check and hides the SmartIcon bar.

If you want to hide the SmartIcon bar from which you displayed the menu (that is, you right-clicked it or clicked its Control menu button), you can choose the Hide This Bar of SmartIcons command at the very top of the menu. Just be sure you know which bar you're hiding.

To really clean up the screen, you can put away all the SmartIcon bars. To do so, choose View ⇨ Hide SmartIcons, or display the shortcut or Control menu from any bar, then choose Hide All SmartIcons. The application removes the SmartIcon bars from the screen.

You have only one method for redisplaying them: choose View ⇨ Show SmartIcons. You may have noticed in your travels that SmartIcon bars appear in predetermined locations onscreen by default. For example, the Internet Tools SmartIcon bar appears along the left side of the window. You can reposition a SmartIcon bar to any location you want: top (below the formula bar), left, right, bottom, or floating bar. Figure 28-2 shows SmartIcon bars in each of these positions.

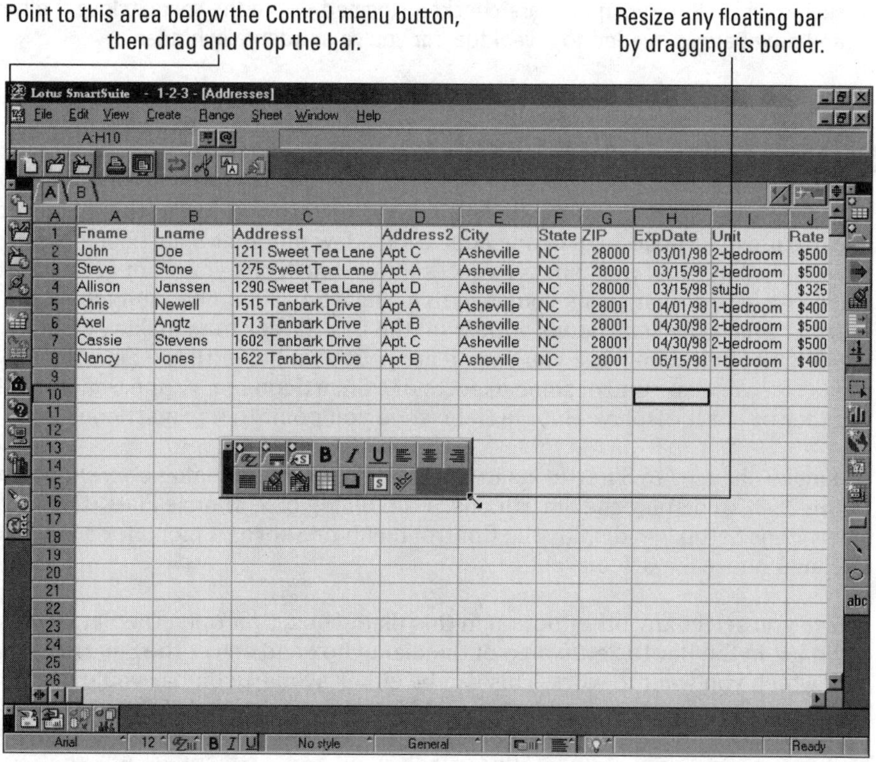

Figure 28-2: Drag a SmartIcon bar to any side of the screen, or into its own floating bar.

To move a SmartIcon bar, point to the solid area below the Control menu button until the mouse pointer changes to a hand; press and hold the left mouse button; and drag to the position you want and release the mouse. As you drag, a dotted outline indicates the shape and position of the SmartIcon bar. When you approach any edge of the screen, that outline snaps to the correct orientation (vertical or horizontal), to cue you that you can release the mouse and let the bar snap or dock in the correct position at the side, top, or bottom of the window. When you release the mouse to drop a bar over the center of the window, you can then point to one of the floating bar's borders until you see the two-headed mouse pointer, then drag to resize the bar.

Danger Zone

The SmartSuite applications don't prevent you from dropping one SmartIcon bar on top of another one, obscuring part of the bottom bar's buttons. Sometimes when this happens, however, the Control menu button (at the left end) for each bar remains visible, cueing you that you've covered part of a bar. You can then drag either bar to another position to have all the tools you need. In other cases, a larger bar may completely cover a smaller bar and its Control menu button. To verify which SmartIcon bars are currently displayed, open the Control menu for a bar that you can see; after seeing which SmartIcon bars are checked (toggled on) in the menu, close the menu and drag bars as needed to reveal the bar you've accidentally hidden.

Customizing a SmartIcon Bar

The more you use SmartSuite, the better handle you develop on which SmartIcons you use most. If those SmartIcons appear on a few different SmartIcons bars, you have to display all of those bars to access the SmartIcons you want to use. Instead, you can add the SmartIcons you need to a single SmartIcon bar and adjust the order in which the SmartIcons appear on the bar. Rather than making changes to the default SmartIcon bars, you can create your own bar with the SmartIcons you want. You can also control some aspects of a SmartIcon bar's appearance, such as whether or not it displays Bubble Help when you point to its SmartIcons.

You make changes to SmartIcons in the SmartIcons Setup dialog box, shown in Figure 28-3. To display the SmartIcons Setup dialog box, choose File ➪ User Setup ➪ SmartIcons Setup. Or, display the Control menu or Shortcut menu for a SmartIcon bar and choose SmartIcons Setup.

Before you select any other option in this dialog box, first open the Bar Name drop-down list in the Bar to Setup area of the dialog box and select the SmartIcon bar with which you want to work. This can be either a SmartIcon bar you'd like to make changes to, or any other bar that you'd like to use as the basis for the new bar. For example, if the Formatting SmartIcon bar in 1-2-3 contains many of the SmartIcons you'd like to include in a custom SmartIcon bar, choose the Formatting SmartIcon bar from the Bar Name drop-down list. After you've selected the correct bar, use the techniques described in the rest of this section to make the SmartIcon display changes you want.

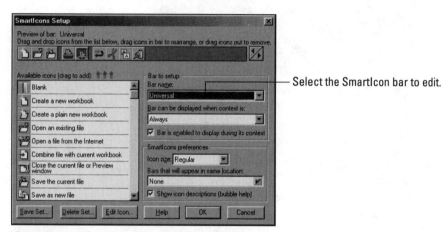

Select the SmartIcon bar to edit.

Figure 28-3: The SmartIcons Setup dialog box enables you to change the SmartIcons displayed on the selected SmartIcon bar.

Moving, Adding, and Removing Icons

When you've chosen the SmartIcon bar to edit in the Bar Name drop-down list of the SmartIcons Setup dialog box, a preview of that bar appears along the top of the dialog box. You drag and drop SmartIcons on the bar preview to change the icon order and to add and remove icons and spacers, as follows:

✦ **Moving a SmartIcon.** Point to the icon, press and hold the left mouse button, and drag the icon. When the icon is over the icon or spacer that currently holds the spot to which you want to move the icon you're dragging (see Figure 28-4), release the mouse button. The icon drops into place, and the icon that formerly held the spot moves right.

✦ **Removing a SmartIcon.** Drag the SmartIcon to remove from the preview bar to the blank gray area below the bar (or in another direction away from the bar), then release the mouse button.

✦ **Adding a SmartIcon.** Scroll through the Available Icons (Drag to Add) list to display the SmartIcon you'd like to add to the bar. Drag the icon from the list (see Figure 28-5) and drop it into the desired position on the preview bar.

Preview bar.   SmartIcon being dragged.

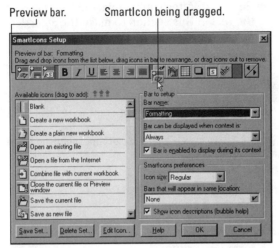

Figure 28-4: Drag SmartIcons on the preview bar
to change their positions.

Icons added to the bar.   Icons moved from the left end of the bar.

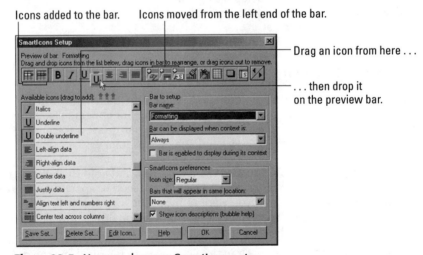

Drag an icon from here . . .

. . . then drop it
on the preview bar.

Figure 28-5: You can drag any SmartIcon onto
the preview bar from the scrolling list below.

Repeat each of these techniques as needed until the preview bar holds the
SmartIcons you want. Before you close the dialog box, however, you may want to
adjust a few other settings for the bar and then save your changes to the current
bar or as a new bar. Both of these details are described next.

Changing Other Bar Settings

The SmartIcons Setup dialog box offers other options for controlling the display capabilities of the SmartIcon bar you're editing or creating. You can first specify whether you want the SmartIcon bar to appear automatically when you select or create a particular item, such as a range or drawing. Setting up a bar for such automatic display requires that you change two options. First, select *any option except* Always from the Bar Can Be Displayed When Context Is drop-down list. Then, click to check the Bar Is Enabled to Display During Its Context check box. For example, if you're editing the Formatting toolbar or creating your own custom toolbar, you would select A Range from the Bar Can Be Displayed When Context Is drop-down list. Then, click to check the Bar Is Enabled to Display During Its Context check box. If you want the SmartIcon bar to appear only when you select it from a SmartIcon bar Control menu, clear the check box beside Bar Is Enabled to Display During Its Context.

The SmartIcons Preferences area of the SmartIcons Setup dialog box provides a few additional settings you can tweak to specify how all SmartIcon bars should appear onscreen. Make a selection from the Icon Size drop-down list to specify whether icons should display in Regular or Large size. Figure 28-6 shows what SmartIcons look like when set to the large size, with the Windows screen resolution set to 800×600.

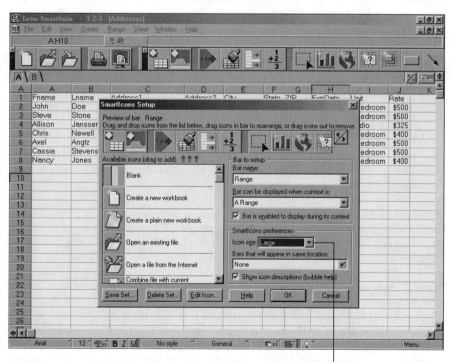

Select an icon size.

Figure 28-6: Display icons in a large size if you're having trouble distinguishing icons or clicking the correct icon.

Even at 800 × 600, large-sized SmartIcons fill a lot of screen real estate. But at resolutions of 1024 × 768 or higher, they actually don't look so large and can be easier to read. To check what resolution you're using, right-click the Window desktop, choose Properties, and then click the Settings tab. The Screen Area portion of the dialog box tells you what the current resolution is and offers a slider for adjusting that resolution.

You can enable SmartSuite to overlap several open SmartIcon bars when they display to save room onscreen. To do so, open the Bars That Will Appear in Same Location drop-down list, click to place a check beside each bar that you want to overlap in the same location, then click the check mark at the right side of the drop-down list to close the list. When the selected bars appear onscreen, you can see each bar's Control menu button, so that you can move bars as needed. Use this feature with caution, however. If someone else also uses your computer, that person might have trouble finding needed SmartIcons. Also, unless you have a stellar memory, you could easily forget the positions of particular SmartIcons, in which case having the SmartIcons available doesn't really save you any time, because you have too many of them open and too many to look through for the SmartIcon you want.

To control the display of the Bubble Help that appears when you point to a SmartIcon, use the Show Icon Descriptions (Bubble Help) check box. Clear the check box if you no longer want the Bubble Help to display, or check it if you do need Bubble Help.

Turning off Bubble Help for SmartIcons also turns off Bubble Help for InfoBox tabs. So, if you need that help in InfoBoxes, redisplay the SmartIcons Setup dialog box and click to check the Show Icon Descriptions (Bubble Help) check box.

Saving Changes to the Current Bar or a New Bar

Unless you save your changes to the SmartIcon bar you chose using the Bar Name drop-down list or to a new SmartIcon bar, you'll lose those changes when you close the SmartIcons Setup dialog box.

To save your changes, click the Save Set button in the SmartIcons Setup dialog box. The Save As SmartIcons File dialog box appears. To save the changes to the current set only, click the Overwrite button. Click OK again to close the SmartIcons Setup dialog box.

To save the changes as a brand-new SmartIcon bar, choose Save As New from the Save As SmartIcons File dialog box. The Save As New SmartIcons File dialog box appears. Enter the name you want to use for the SmartIcons bar on the SmartIcons Control menu in the SmartIcons Bar Name text box. Then, enter a name for the disk file that holds the SmartIcon bar in the SmartIcons File Name text box. Figure 28-7 shows example entries for a bar that offers formatting tools. Click OK to accept the names you entered, then click OK again to close the SmartIcons Setup dialog box.

Figure 28-7: Enter the display name and file name for the SmartIcon bar when prompted by this dialog box.

Danger Zone

SmartSuite assigns the .SMI file name extension to SmartIcon bar files. Deleting an .SMI file from your hard disk, therefore, results in the permanent deletion of the SmartIcon bar it held.

Deleting a Bar

Use caution when deleting SmartIcon bars. If you mistakenly delete one of the SmartIcon bars that comes with SmartSuite, you have to reinstall SmartSuite to get that icon bar back. If you're sure you want delete a SmartIcon bar, use the SmartIcons Setup dialog box and follow these steps:

1. Choose File ➪ User Setup ➪ SmartIcons Setup. Or, display the Control menu or Shortcut menu for a SmartIcon bar and choose SmartIcons Setup. The SmartIcons Setup dialog box appears.

2. Click Delete Set. The Delete Set dialog box appears.

3. Click the name of each set you want to delete in the Bar(s) of SmartIcons to Delete list (see Figure 28-8). If you mistakenly select a bar for deletion, click its name again to deselect it.

Figure 28-8: Click the name of each SmartIcon bar to delete; you can select more than one bar if needed.

4. Click OK. The Warning dialog box appears, asking you to verify that you want to delete the selected set.

5. Click Yes. The selected SmartIcon bar(s) are deleted.

6. Click OK to close the SmartIcons Setup dialog box.

The following folders hold the SmartIcon bar files in SmartSuite applications:

Application	Folder
SmartSuite	\lotus\compnent
Word Pro	\lotus\wordpro\icons
1-2-3	\lotus\123\icons
Freelance Graphics	\lotus\flg\icons
Approach	\lotus\approach\icons
Organizer	\lotus\organize\icons

If you use a backup program, you can restore .SMI files to try to recover a SmartIcon bar you deleted by mistake, which may be faster than reinstalling.

Creating a Custom SmartIcon with a Script

SmartIcons execute commands and selections. Scripts store commands and selections. So, it makes sense that SmartSuite applications enable you to create a custom SmartIcon that runs a script (called a *macro* in some instances, such as in Approach) you've previously recorded or written. Otherwise, you need to display the Run Scripts & Macros dialog box (or create some other type of onscreen button) to run the script.

Approach doesn't enable you to create custom icons. However, it does enable you to assign scripts to other objects in an Approach file.

The current versions of Word Pro and 1-2-3 primarily enable you to create scripts. However, if you're working with files from much earlier versions of the programs, they may contain macros, older relatives of scripts. For example, older 1-2-3 versions stored macros on a worksheet and those macros only worked in the file containing that worksheet, whereas scripts are always captured behind the scenes and are available to any 1-2-3 file. The current version of Approach enables you to create both macros and scripts.

You can use the SmartIcons Setup dialog box to create a custom SmartIcon for a script, using these steps:

1. Choose File ➪ User Setup ➪ SmartIcons Setup. Or, display the Control menu or Shortcut menu for a SmartIcon bar and choose SmartIcons Setup. The SmartIcons Setup dialog box appears.

2. Choose Edit Icon. The Edit SmartIcons dialog box appears.

3. By default, it displays a new, blank icon in the Picture Editor portion of the dialog box. If you want to edit the image from an existing icon to speed up your creation process, scroll the Available Icons You Can Edit or Copy list, then click the icon to edit. If you select one of the icons that comes with SmartSuite, a dialog box appears to inform you that you can only use the icon image as a starting point for a new icon. Click OK. Figure 28-9 shows an icon selected for editing.

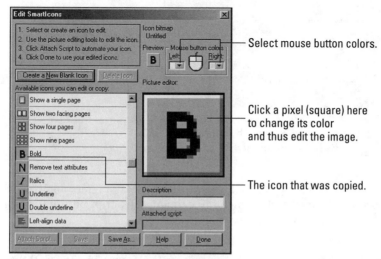

Figure 28-9: You can choose an existing SmartIcon to use its image as the basis for a new SmartIcon.

4. You click or right-click on the image in the Picture Editor preview to edit that image. Each time you click or right-click, you change the color of the pixel (small square) you selected in the image. Use the Left and Right drop-down palettes to choose the color that each mouse button applies to the selected pixel when you click that mouse button. (You also can drag while holding the left or right mouse button to work a bit more quickly). Figure 28-10 shows a nearly completed icon image. The icon that will be attached to this icon applies bold, red formatting, so it has a red B and a red border, but still looks similar to the default SmartIcon on which it was based.

5. Click the Save As button, or Save if you started from a blank icon. The Save As dialog box appears.

6. Specify a File Name for the icon's bitmap (.bmp) image file. If needed, use the Save In list to specify a different disk and folder to save the icon to. Click Save.

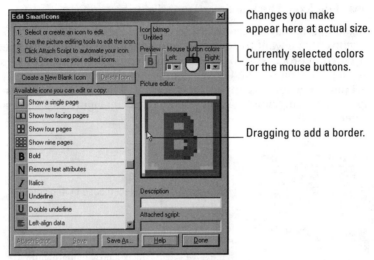

Changes you make
appear here at actual size.

Currently selected colors
for the mouse buttons.

Dragging to add a border.

Figure 28-10: You can make any changes
you wish to the icon image by clicking and
dragging with the left and right mouse buttons.

7. When the Edit SmartIcons dialog box reappears, it offers an Attach Script
button in its lower-left corner. Click the Attach Script button to display the
Attach Script dialog box (see Figure 28-11).

Figure 28-11: Select the script or
macro to attach to the icon you
created by selecting it from the
Script Name list.

8. Choose whether you want to attach a Script or Macro.

9. If you have multiple files open, choose the file that holds the script or macro
to attach using the From drop-down list.

10. Click the script or macro to attach in the Script Name (Macro Name) list, then
click Attach to close the Attach Script dialog box. The Edit SmartIcons dialog
box now displays the script name under Attached Script.

11. (Optional) If you want to include a Bubble Help description for your
SmartIcon, type it in the Description text box, as shown in Figure 28-12.

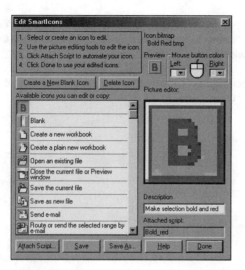

Figure 28-12: Enter Bubble Help for the new icon in the Description text box to make your SmartIcon as easy to use as possible.

12. Click Done. A message box informs you that the new icon has been modified and asks if you want to save the changes. Click Yes to do so.

13. You can then use the SmartIcons Setup dialog box to add the new SmartIcon to any toolbar. Find the new SmartIcon at the bottom of the Available Icons (Drag to Add) list, as shown in Figure 28-13. Click Save Set to save the added SmartIcon with the SmartIcon bar.

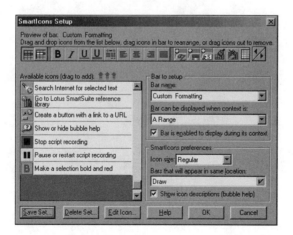

Figure 28-13: Make sure you scroll to the bottom of the listed icons to find your new SmartIcon.

14. Repeat Steps 2–14 to create and use other SmartIcons.

15. Click OK to close the SmartIcons Setup dialog box and apply your changes.

For information on creating scripts and editing scripts that you can assign to custom SmartIcons, consult Chapter 6, "Using SmartMasters, Styles, and Scripts for Control," and Chapter 14, "Saving Time with Power 1-2-3 Features."

To learn advanced scripting techniques, consult *Teach Yourself LotusScript 3.2 for Notes/Domino 4.5* (by Rocky Oliver and Bill Kreisle), published by IDG Books Worldwide.

✦   ✦   ✦

SmartSuite Online

◆ ◆ ◆ ◆

SmartSuite offers more online features for connecting with other users than ever before—and this part details those features. You'll learn how to use FastSite, the new Web-building application added to SmartSuite, including how to create a Web site, choose its look, add content, create hyperlinks, save, and post your site. We then lead you through features for editing a site.

We connect you with features you can use to get help from the Lotus Web site, create hyperlinks in your SmartSuite documents, and access an FTP site to save and open documents. Next, we show you how to convert content from a SmartSuite document into a Web page. Finally, we cover the features that let you safely share information and documents with other users.

◆ ◆ ◆ ◆

Using FastSite to Create a Web Site

FastSite is the Lotus solution for those of you who have wanted to place a Web site online, but have not had the means to do so swiftly, easily, and cost-effectively. Using the point and click features present in FastSite, new or old documents created in Lotus and other products can be pulled together into a neatly organized, link navigated, online page presentation. Those who have not had the time or skill to use Web page building and editing software can now easily construct an Internet or network-accessible site and you don't need to learn a whole new computer language to do so.

This chapter introduces you to the FastSite workplace and all the site-building tools you'll need to create a Web site. It also walks you through building, previewing and posting a site online to its public audience.

An Internet, Intranet, Extranet, and Online Overview

A Web site's files are eventually transmitted to a server computer via an online connection to the Internet or a network, such as an intranet or extranet (an *extranet* denotes two or more connected networks.) There, they become available for their intended viewers. Prior to building and publishing your site, it is important to understand and consider online communications, how a Web site fits into them, and which type of server computer will act as a file repository for your site's files. The following overview will assist you in this effort.

Online connections provide a means of communicating with others through the gathering and sharing of information held in computer files and deposited on server computers. In order to access these servers, a dial-up or cable connection must be made. Both the server computer and the computer connecting to it must have particular software installed on board in order to interpret certain commands and files, turning them into graphical displays. Server computers use server software, such as the Lotus Domino product, for this purpose. The computers connecting to them use either a client software such as Lotus Notes, or a browser such as Netscape Navigator or Internet Explorer.

Almost anyone can transmit and present documents online, and one of the primary ways to do this is through a vehicle known as a Web site. A Web site is somewhat like a file page package, similar to a book, that can be opened and read on a computer screen. Hyperlinks within a virtual book's pages are a type of mouse-clicked push button that propels a reader through them or to other Web sites. Links are generally highly noticeable and commonly visible as either graphics or underlined contrasting text. Using FastSite you can both build a Web site filled with pages and hyperlinks, and transmit it online to its host server computer.

Online with the Internet

The most typical online connection is through the Internet by using an Internet Service Provider (ISP). Local, privately run companies, as well as others — including CompuServe, America Online, IBM Internet Services, and MCI Web Services — can provide this type of service. Once established with an ISP, you will have a user ID, a password, and often, provision on their server computer for the deposit of your Web site files. If you decide to use an Internet connection to transmit your site's files, FastSite gives you the means to post them to an Internet server.

Online with an Intranet or Extranet

An intranet is a string of computers connected into a private network. Using similar current Web technology as the Internet, these computers make use of file-storing server computers and browsers. Access to information provided by the intranet's server is made available only to those who are both connected and authorized. While these computers may be able to contact and use, or be contacted and used by, another network of computers, such as the Internet or an extranet, their private information is available only to their enabled users. In order to use FastSite to post to a network server, you will need to check with your server administrator for availability of space and write privileges to access the drive.

An extranet is similar to an intranet in that it is private, it is also similar to the Internet in that it connects multiple networks together. In fact, an extranet can be connected to the Internet. As a secured network, an extranet is accessed by invitation only, a password or certificate being the key to opening its door. If your site's intended availability is for extranet access, you'll need to ask your network administrator which type of server you will post your site to when that time comes.

Before Building a Web Site

FastSite enables you to post a site to a local drive or network server, an Internet server, or a Domino server. Prior to beginning your site, you may want to contact your server administrator and inquire about several issues, taking notes. Following, are a few of the questions you might want to ask sooner rather than later:

✦ Are you entitled to place a Web site on the server?

✦ How many megabytes of storage space are provided for your site?

✦ May you acquire or purchase more site space if needed?

✦ Are there any other site requirements or charges?

✦ Is your server a Domino server?

✦ Who do you contact for assistance in configuring the FTP connection?

A full explanation of online connections is worthy of a manual in itself. The preceding information gives you just a panoramic overview; if you find yourself hungry for more information, refer to the following books published by IDG Books Worldwide: *Teach Yourself the Internet and the World Wide Web Visually*, *Internet Bible*, and *The Internet For Dummies, 5th Edition*.

The FastSite Staging Area

The process of building a Web site involves organization and layout, gathering of files, printing (converting files to Web-viewable pages), review, and finally presentation. FastSite provides the desktop and tools to work through this process, while you provide the files that will be gathered. Document files, such as those created in Lotus and other applications, including word processed documents, spreadsheets, databases, screen presentations and graphic files, can be pulled together for this purpose. As you nail sites together using FastSite, folders and more files will mysteriously be created and deposited into a workbasket known as the *staging area*.

The staging area is merely a compartmentalized file directory/test area located on your computer's disk. As a holding tank for your newly formed folders and files, the staging area is used by FastSite to shape your Web site package as you work. When your site is complete and satisfactorily presentable, FastSite will dish files up from this area and ship them to the server computer you specify.

By default, Lotus establishes the main *staging directory* in a folder called FastSite and places it in this path: lotus\work\fastsite. Figure 29-1 reveals a staging area typical of one that might form on your drive, in this directory, as you create a number of sites using FastSite. When you create sites, the folders and files that form in this area are named after their site and its contents. The highlighted folder name you see in the left side of the Explorer window shown in Figure 29-1 denotes a site's main folder created by FastSite. The folder and files you see in the left side of this Explorer window are those created by FastSite to hold and organize the site's contents.

This part of the staging area shows folders and files within an open site folder.
This part of the staging area shows sites you create.

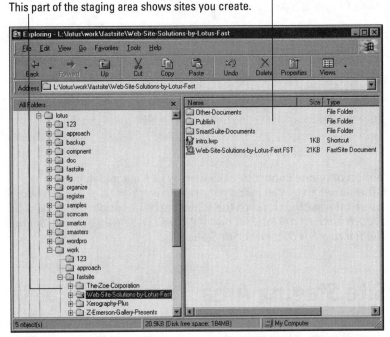

Figure 29-1: The Windows Explorer reveals the FastSite staging area.

Staging area file and folder development begins by using FastSite. In order to get started, you'll need to know how to start the application. Of course, it follows that you will also need to know how to exit it when your site work session is complete.

Starting and exiting FastSite, as with other Lotus SmartSuite applications, can be accomplished in several ways. Following are a few of the ways to do each.

To start FastSite, use one of the following three methods:

✦ If you have SmartCenter installed, open the SmartSuite drawer, open the Lotus Application's folder and locate the Lotus FastSite icon. Double-click the icon.

✦ If you prefer to use menus, select Start ⇨ Programs ⇨ Lotus SmartSuite ⇨ Lotus FastSite to open FastSite.

✦ Click the Lotus FastSite SuiteStart icon, as shown in Figure 29-2.

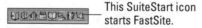
This SuiteStart icon starts FastSite.

Figure 29-2: Clicking the FastSite SuiteStart icon located on your Window's taskbar is the quickest way to start FastSite.

Once FastSite is open, it has a very comfortable Window's application face. Menu items will be much like those you have seen elsewhere, and exiting techniques will be the Window's standard. Following are four ways to exit FastSite:

✦ Double-click the FastSite icon in the upper-left corner of the FastSite window.

✦ Click the "X" in the upper-right corner of the FastSite window.

✦ Select File ⇨ Exit FastSite.

✦ Press and hold down the Alt key, then press the F4 key.

Understanding the FastSite Screen

Introducing yourself to the FastSite screen introduces you to its site building tools and paned workspace areas. Using one of the methods mentioned in "Starting and Exiting FastSite," start FastSite. Menu items like the ones shown in Figure 29-3 will appear across the top of the screen. Many of the menu items you see as you open each particular menu will be familiar; most all that are not will become that way as you digest the following text. If you are the type of person that prefers to keep your hands on the keyboard, rather than reaching for a mouse, you might pay special attention to some of the keyboard shortcuts listed next to the menu items as you look them over.

Hot Stuff

To print a list of keyboard shortcuts select Help ⇨ Help Topics and click the Index tab. Type the letter **K** into box 1. Look in box 2 and select Keys, Keyboard Shortcuts. Click the Display button, and when the FastSite Help for Keyboard Shortcuts displays onscreen, click the Print button.

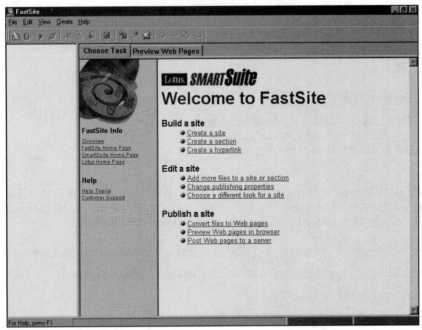

Figure 29-3: Your first view of the FastSite workspace will look similar to the one you see here.

The FastSite Icon Bar

Located under the main FastSite menu items, at the top of the screen, is the icon bar. When you first open FastSite, many of these icons will appear grayed out and will not function with a mouse click. They will take on their colors and be ready for action as soon as you perform a task that makes them useful. Figure 29-4 shows how pointing your mouse at an icon and letting it hover for a moment, pops up text revealing the task that the icon will begin executing if clicked. As you look at the tasks each icon executes, you will realize that you can perform many of these tasks using selections from the FastSite drop-down menus as an alternative.

Figure 29-4: One click on a FastSite icon is all it takes to begin performing a FastSite task.

Perhaps you prefer to work from the menus or with keystrokes and would rather have more real estate onscreen to view your work. If this is the case, select View ➪ Show ➪ Icon Bar to remove the check mark next to this menu item. The icon bar will disappear from the screen. To reverse this process, again select View ➪ Show ➪ Icon bar, replacing the check mark next to the menu item and placing the bar back onscreen.

The FastSite icon bar can be relocated on the screen. To move the icon bar from its original position, point your mouse at the double barred area of the icon bar, as shown in Figure 29-5.

Figure 29-5: Using drag and drop methods, you can point to and grab the double upright bar located on the FastSite icon bar to move it into another screen position.

With your mouse pointer located over the FastSite icon bar's double bar as shown in Figure 29-5, press and hold down the left mouse button as you drag the bar to any position onscreen. As you do this, you will see an outline of the bar moving with your mouse pointer. Release the mouse button when the outline of the bar is situated where you want it. If you deposit the bar near the side or bottom edges of the FastSite window, it will cling to them in a parallel fashion. Depositing them away from the window edges, or further into them, allows an icon bar to reside as an icon palette. Reshape icon palettes as you might a window. Place your mouse pointer over the palette's side edges until it turns into a double arrow; when it does, press and hold down your left mouse button and drag up, down, right or left. Click the "X" located in an icon palette's upper-right corner to remove it from the screen view, and select View ⇨ Show ⇨ Icon bar to bring it back into view.

If your experimentation with moving the icon bar is unsatisfactory, you can place it back in its original position. First locate your mouse pointer over the double lines on the icon bar (as shown in Figure 29-5) or, if the bar exists in palette style, over the title bar of the icon palette, as shown in Figure 29-6.

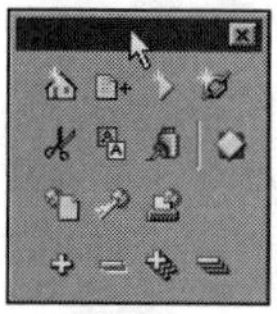

Figure 29-6: Move an icon palette by placing the mouse pointer over its title bar. Grab, drag, and drop it elsewhere.

With your mouse pointer in this position, grab and drag the icon bar just beneath the menu items. When you see the outline of your bar snap into a bar shape as you drag it there, release the left mouse button. You can move this bar farther right or left according to your taste.

The FastSite Workspace

Directly under the default location of the icon bar are the two, paned portions of the FastSite workspace. To the left is the *site pane* and to the right is the *tabbed pane*. You can increase or decrease the size of these panes by moving their dividing line right or left. Place your mouse pointer over this line until it turns into a double-barred, double arrow that looks like the one shown in Figure 29-7. When your mouse pointer turns into this double arrow, drag right or left to customize the viewing area of your FastSite workspace panes.

When your mouse pointer looks like this,
you can drag right or left to increase or decrease the view in a FastSite pane.

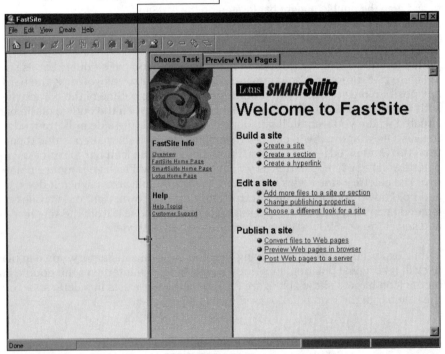

Figure 29-7: Customize the size of the FastSite panes by increasing or decreasing their width according to your viewing needs.

The Site Pane

When you newly open FastSite, your site pane, on the left of the screen, will be empty. This pane provides your site's layout, organization, and information-gathering area. It is simply an area in which you will create your site outline. Similar to the outlines you created in school before tackling a writing project, site outlines show title, heading, and subheading levels just as any other outline. Using point, click, and type, or drag-and-drop procedures, you will construct a site outline that includes a title (home page), headings (which could be files or a FastSite section) and subheadings (more files or sections). As your site outline takes shape, your site will come into being, with FastSite working behind the scenes to make sure. You can preview how a site outline entitled "Web Site Solutions by Lotus FastSite" shapes up in the site pane shown in Figure 29-8. To the right of the site pane is the tabbed pane, which you will read more about shortly.

Site pane.

Tabbed pane.

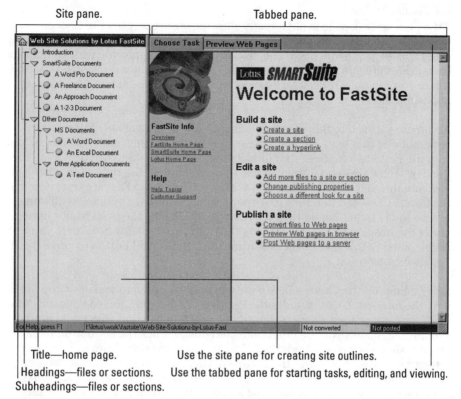

Title—home page.

Headings—files or sections.
Subheadings—files or sections.

Use the site pane for creating site outlines.

Use the tabbed pane for starting tasks, editing, and viewing.

Figure 29-8: The site pane displays an outline form of your site as it takes shape.

The first step in forming a site outline is to create a new site. This new site (or site item) serves a dual purpose. In FastSite it acts as the site's home page, or site outline title, and it also acts as a folder container for other outline items dropped within it. Growing sites appear in the site pane with a tree-like, or outline, structure. This structure, filled with sites and its contained items, is referred to as the *site hierarchy*. Looking at the site hierarchy, you are able to see how travel through your site is being mapped, creating what is known as a *site map*. Prior to filling in the site pane with your site outline, give some thought to how you want visitors routed through your site. Sometimes even a scruffy handwritten sketch is helpful.

The Tabbed Pane

The tabbed pane, located to the right of the site pane, has two visible tabs that show just under the icon bar. Think of this paned area of the desktop as a two-tabbed multipurpose notebook; the tabs lead you to viewing the pages, or in this case, the panes. Whereas the site pane provides the organizational and layout zone for your final product, the tabbed pane supplies a dual-purpose service center. This service center assists you in accomplishing FastSite tasks, and provides you with a print shop and review room for your site, so to speak. Click either the Choose Task tab or the Preview Web Pages tab to bring its pane into view.

The Choose Task tab

If the Choose Task pane is not already showing onscreen, click the Choose Task tab to bring it into view. This pane presents the FastSite main service center, looking like a tidy and elegant home page. The links on this page supply you with an information center (FastSite Info), a help center (Help) and a tool center (Welcome to FastSite), where you can quickly click task-executing links useful to building, editing, or publishing sites.

Acclimate yourself to this pane by clicking a few of its available hyperlinks, remembering that links are often presented as contrasting, underlined text. Start with the FastSite Info, Overview link. Its overview of FastSite will display in the Preview Web Pages pane. You can use the scroll bar, to the right of this pane, to navigate through its text. When you are done reading the FastSite Overview, click the Choose Task tab to return to its pane view. Familiarize yourself with immediate access to the Lotus Online Help for FastSite by clicking the Help Topics hyperlink under the heading Help, which opens the Help Topics dialog box. After you become accustomed to this quick-access feature, click the Cancel button to close the Help Topics dialog box.

Several links on the Choose Task pane will only be useful to you after you are online with the Internet. Looking under the FastSite Info heading and clicking any "Home Page" link brings up a dialog box notifying you that a connection could not be established, unless you are first connected online. Click the OK button to close this box if it shows onscreen. Under the Help heading, clicking Customer Support will attempt to connect you with the Lotus Internet support site. This works nicely if you are online with the Internet first; if you are not, your browser will probably show onscreen with notification that a connection could not be established.

The Preview Web Pages tab

The right tab of the tabbed pane, the Preview Web Pages tab, is appropriately named. Think of this as your print review area. Here you will exercise judgment about whether or not your site goals are met as you preview and test your site pages in this tabbed pane. Does your site look and work the way you want it to and in an organized fashion? If not, you will want to back up a few steps and regroup, making necessary additions, deletions, and adjustments to your site before previewing it again and deciding to publish it. This tabbed pane can also be used as either a Web browser or a file manager.

The initial pane view seen by clicking the Preview Web Pages tab is that of the FastSite Overview. After you begin constructing sites, this pane view will display selected site pages in preconverted or converted form. Figure 29-9 shows how a preconverted home page displays in this pane. Notice that the Convert button implanted in the middle of the page invites you to convert it and view your handiwork in converted form instantaneously.

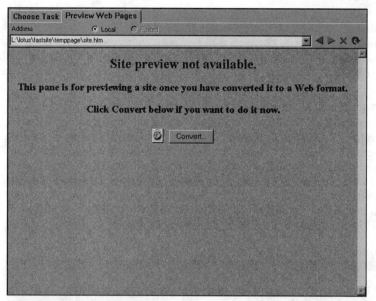

Figure 29-9: An unconverted home page, section, or document page viewed in the Preview Web Pages pane will look similar to the one you see in this graphic.

Notice the radio buttons, Local and Posted, just under the Preview Web Pages tab. These buttons give you the opportunity to switch between a site that resides unposted in your site pane and its posted version. Helpful when comparing the contents of the two sites, use these radio buttons to assist you in keeping sites updated. The sidebar at the end of this chapter exercises this feature.

The Browser feature

Although the Preview Web Pages pane is fundamentally for viewing your site work, it also functions as a Web browser. If you have FastSite opened, this pane visible, and a connection to your online service established, you can type a URL ("Uniform Resource Locator" or online address such as http://www.host.com) into the Address box that shows, press Enter, and you will tunnel to the address. If you type the address in wrong, FastSite will notify you, informing you that it couldn't establish a connection. In that case, check the address you entered, and with your cursor in the Address box, again press Enter. Click the downward pointing arrow, to the right of the Address box, to access a drop-down list of online sites or drive directories you have visited in the past. Click an address in this list to select it and go to the location again.

Note

When viewing a site page, you can navigate through it in several ways. Click within the page and use the up- or down-arrow keys, Page Up or Page Down keys, or the slider bar to the right of the Preview Web Pages pane. Pressing the Home key rapidly takes you to the top of the page, while pressing the End key takes you to the bottom.

The File Manager feature

Do you have a particular hard drive directory that holds most of your work files? These may be the files you want to plant into the new Web site you create with FastSite. Type the full path location of this directory into the Address box, and with your cursor located within or at the end of the address, press Enter to see a screen view of this directory in the Preview Web Pages pane. If you right-click, either in a blank spot or on a file or folder name in this pane's view, you will have the Window's management menus at your command. Figure 29-10 shows the Preview Web Pages pane acting as a file manager.

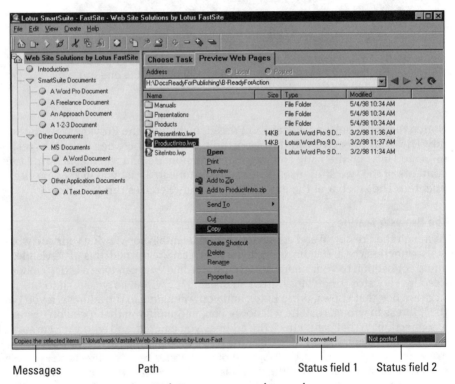

Figure 29-10: The Preview Web Pages pane can be used as a file manager

Hot Stuff

When a file directory is visible in the Preview Web Pages pane, you can drag and drop files from it to a Web site visible in the site pane. The Ctrl+click and the Shift+click options are available to you for selecting files, just as they are in Windows Explorer.

The Browser Control Buttons

Located to the far right of the Address box are the four FastSite browser control buttons (refer to Figure 29-10). Clicking the left-pointing arrow button propels you backward through pages you've visited, while clicking the right-pointing arrow button propels you forward through them. If some of the pages no longer exist, or are URLs and you are not connected online, you will be informed.

When browsing online, there may be times in which you type in a URL and begin to download a site into view. Second thoughts, or a slow-loading site, might make you wish you hadn't. Simply click the X-shaped navigational button to stop the downloading process. The circular-shaped arrow button is used to reload a page. This comes in handy when you are online and have placed a message in an Internet site page similar to one of the user support sites that Lotus offers. After doing so, you can double-check to see if the message successfully made it into the message base by clicking the reload button and reviewing the reloaded message base page. This button is also useful for quickly reloading an HTML document you have freshly edited while in FastSite.

The Status Bar

Look again at the status bar that stripes the bottom of the FastSite window shown in Figure 29-10. A four-part display, the status bar reveals information about the site, site item or FastSite component that holds the current focus.

While performing varied tasks around FastSite, the leftmost display of the status bar displays messages to assist or inform you. With the focus in a FastSite dialog box, this area reminds you "For Help, press F1." Point your mouse pointer at an icon or drop-down menu item and the message you see here offers a bit of extended explanation about the icon or menu item. If a Web page holding links is visible in the Preview Web Pages pane, place your mouse pointer over any of the links and the message in the status bar shows where the link is directed. When busy at work with FastSite as a browser, this portion of the status bar reveals activity. For example, if the browser is making its way to a Web site online or offline, the text you see here might read "Connecting to," "Loading from" or "Opening picture."

Reading from left to right across the status bar, the next display shows the full path of the site or file highlighted in the site hierarchy. Continuing right is Status field 1. Its purpose is to inform you if a highlighted local site or file is up-to-date and in converted, Web-ready form. If it is, Status field 1 reads, "Local: Up to date." Otherwise, it reads "Not converted" or "Out of Date." Approaching the far right of the status bar is Status field 2. It announces the state of a server version of a site and its files. The message for a freshly converted and posted site reads "Posted: Up to date." If a site has not been posted, the message states "Not Posted." Notifying you that a posted site was edited after its last posting, Status field 2 reads "Posted: Out of date." Republishing the site to the server brings the posted site back up-to-date.

Before You Create a Site

You can customize the location of the directory in which your future staging area files and folders will be kept before you create your first site. Select File ➪ User Preferences and then click the File Locations tab to open the User Preferences dialog box shown in Figure 29-11. Click in the Staging Directory text box and type in a new directory path if you want to change this. If you need to peruse your drive first, click the Browse button to locate another folder, and then click it while in the Browse for Folder dialog box. Click OK when it is selected, and its path will be inserted into the Staging Directory text box. When you click OK in the User Preferences dialog box, you will have established a new staging area location.

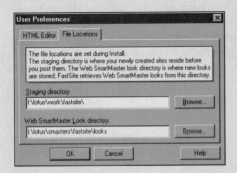

Figure 29-11: The User Preferences dialog box gives you the option to change the location of your site's staging directory.

Before you click OK or Cancel to close the User Preferences dialog box, notice that you can change where Web SmartMaster Looks will be kept on the drive. This is covered in Chapter 30, "Fine-Tuning Your Web Site," under "Customizing a Look for a Section or Site." Next, click the HTML Editor tab and then click the drop-down list available in this panel. The HTML-savvy can select their choice of editor, if they wish to ply HTML editing skills from within FastSite. When you are finished looking over the User Preferences dialog box, click OK to accept any edits you may have made, or Cancel to leave all settings as they were.

There are guidelines for editing FastSite Web pages with a Web editor. Prior to doing so, please read the section in Chapter 30 entitled "Editing Outline Items."

Setting Up the Web Site

In previous sections you have learned about the site hierarchy as the outline and organizational area for your Web site. This is where you will begin seeing your site take shape. The first decision you will make about your site is how you want it titled and subtitled.

You can begin your site creation in one of several ways:

✦ From the Choose Task pane, under the Build a Site heading click Create a Site.

✦ From the icon bar, select the home-shaped icon.

✦ From the menu, select Create ➪ Site.

When you select to create a site, the Create Site – Basics dialog box appears onscreen. Figure 29-12 shows this dialog box with a site name and description already entered. It also shows the new Staging Directory path where the site will be kept.

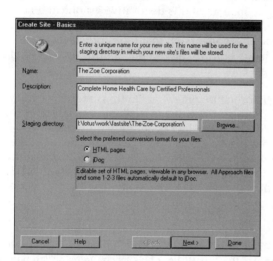

Figure 29-12: The Name box in the Create Site – Basics dialog box holds the title to your Web site. The Description box holds your site's subtitle.

Titling Your Site

With the Create Site – Basics dialog box in view, type a title for your site into the Name box and a subtitle for your site into the Description box. A subtitle is optional. These bits of text will be the introductory words the public will see on your home page. Eventually, once your site is created, the title (name) that you give your site will also be its file folder name in the staging area. Windows limits the length of long file or folder names, so you may want to limit the length of your site title. Doing so will also present the most elegant result in the site's page layout. The Create Site – Basics dialog box gives you an opportunity to Browse and locate another staging directory to hold your site's newly forming files and folders, if you desire. Leaving the path shown in the Staging Directory text box will plant the site and its contents in this path's directory. The last directory in the path will be named after the site being created.

Selecting a File Conversion Format

Radio buttons in the Create Site – Basics dialog box permit you to select a preferred conversion format for your files. HTML is selected as the default setting. HTML (HyperText Markup Language) is used to create WWW pages, which can include images, hyperlinks, and text formatting. HTML text formatting can be somewhat limiting. It permits heading styles, bold or italicized text, numbered and indented lists among other things, while it may not permit the use of certain font types. Whether certain font types read well after conversion into an HTML format is also dependent on the browser reading the document. As an example, Word Pro offers a lovely graphical font named "Botanical." If you were to use this font in a document you convert using the HTML format, instead of this decorative graphical text displaying after conversion, alphabetical and numeric text would appear. The jDoc file format was designed to produce file conversion that looks precisely the same as your documents were created; it is readable by Java-enabled browsers. Most of the newer generation browsers are Java-enabled.

Although publishing a site in HTML format is somewhat limiting in terms of fancy formatting, using this format may produce a site that is available to a larger audience, because many people are still using older-generation browsers. If you don't know which conversion format to select, it is best to leave the default. Later experimentation with your particular file types, the document formatting used within them, and the different conversion means used will help you discern whether HTML or jDoc better suits your document conversions. Additionally, if neither conversion format suits your document well, changing the formatting of a document a bit and then reconverting is surely easier than learning HTML or Java document coding.

More Info The section called "Updating Pages" in Chapter 30, "Fine-Tuning Your Web Site," explains how to change the way FastSite converts your files by changing a Web page's file properties. Prior to converting your documents, in many cases, you will be able to change your mind about the conversion method FastSite will use.

After inputting information and making decisions in the Create Site – Basics dialog box, you can select Done and a home page will be created. An option to Cancel is also provided, however; if you make the mistake of selecting Done, don't worry. Deleting a page is even easier than creating one, and is covered later in this chapter. Select Next to step to another dialog box.

Select a Web SmartMaster Look

FastSite offers several different "looks" for your site. The Web SmartMaster Look you select dictates the background and text formats seen on your site's home and section pages. When you select a look, the navigational sets that will be placed throughout your site, as well as the bullets that will show next to the page links showing on the site's pages, come along with it. Click the Next button on the Create Site – Basics dialog box to view the Create Site – Web SmartMaster Look dialog box. Figure 29-13 shows an example of a Web SmartMaster Look selected from the scrolling list of available looks offered in this dialog box.

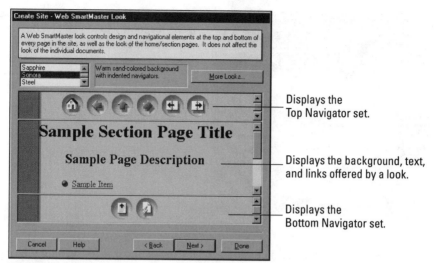

Figure 29-13: Select from one of many Web SmartMaster Looks using the Create Site – Web SmartMaster Look dialog box.

Scroll down the list of options in the upper-left corner of this dialog box to see the various looks present for use. When you click a look name, its description shows in the indented box just to the right of the list. Its overall appearance is presented in the other scrolling frames of this dialog box. The Top Navigator set that comes with a Web SmartMaster Look is visible in the upper frame. These navigators will appear at the top of a site page to help visitors navigate their way through. The page background, text, and links a look provides is viewed in the middle frame. Bottom Navigator sets show in the bottom frame of this dialog box. These navigators will be placed at the bottom of site pages to assist site viewers in navigating the site map. After selecting a look that meets your needs, you can click Done, creating your home page immediately; however, there are more options for you to enjoy if you click Next and continue.

Adding or Removing Files

Click the Next button on the Create Site – Web SmartMaster Look dialog box and the Create Site – Content dialog box appears for more decision-making. This dialog box is a provision for filling your site with documents right from the start. FastSite lets you add or remove files during any part of the Web site–building process or you can do so at this point. (See the section, "Adding, Moving, and Removing Pages" in Chapter 30 for details.) When you click the Add Files button, you can dip into your present file folders and select documents that you wish to produce as Web pages. One or many files can be added at a time. Ctrl+click, or Shift+click methods can be used to select a group of files to add all at once. Figure 29-14 shows the Add Files dialog box with a number of files selected for addition to a site during creation.

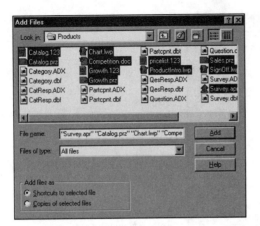

Figure 29-14: The Add Files dialog box is the location where you first have an opportunity to add files to your site.

At the bottom, left corner of this dialog box are radio buttons for adding files as either shortcuts or copies. After selecting the file or file names to be added to a site, decide how you want the files added. Selecting to add a file as either a shortcut or a copy has different advantages; make your selection according to your particular site's needs. The following sections describe each option.

Adding a File as a Shortcut

When you add a file as a shortcut, a Window's shortcut link file, pointing to the actual location of the source file, is placed in the staging area of a site. Following are the advantages and disadvantages:

Advantages:

✦ Site pages formed from files added as shortcuts automatically and immediately receive modifications each time their source files are saved with modifications, and without user effort.

✦ Graphics located next to a site's shortcut-added files reflect changes made to their source files as soon as they are made. This reminds you that the files must be reconverted.

✦ Site pages formed from the contents of a linked file will be posted to the site showing their modifications, if they have been converted, and upon the site's next posting.

Disadvantages:

✦ The page contents formed from files added to a site as a shortcut will not remain static if their source files are edited and saved and the page is converted.

✦ If a source file's edits are only partially finished, the shortcut-added file's pages could be posted to a site before they are ready.

✦ Sites can be shared with other network users as template sites, via a site import. If an imported site contains shortcut-added files, their links may point to source files located on disks or in directories inaccessible to other users. Shortcuts pointing to files in inaccessible locations will not form site pages.

Adding a File as a Copy

When you add a document file to a site as a copy, a copy of the file is placed in the staging area of the site. Two copies of the file will be on disk, the source file remaining in its directory. Following are the advantages and disadvantages:

Advantages:

✦ Edits made to source files will not be reflected in the copy file's site pages until you are ready and replace the copy file with its source file.

✦ There is less chance that a semi-edited page will be posted to a site than if the file were added as a shortcut.

✦ Files added to sites as copies move with the site when the site is imported for the use of others.

Disadvantages:

✦ File copies added to a site do not change as source file edits are made; sites that must be kept updated with all file edits should be added as shortcuts.

✦ When you want the edits of a copy-added file's source file to show in FastSite, and thus in the file's Web pages, you must replace the file copy in its staging area location with the edited source file. The copy added to the site must then be reconverted into a Web page before posting.

✦ If you make edits to the file copy in its staging area location using File ➪ Open Document or by right-clicking the file and selecting Edit Document, and you make edits to the file copy's original source file in its location, you may end up with two separate, differently edited files. This could confuse the editing intended for the file and, thus, its Web page contents.

✦ Files unnecessarily added to a site as copies bloat the staging file area's used disk space.

However you add a file to a site, whether as a shortcut or a copy, will not affect the performance of how the file posts to a server later. They both post equally well.

Once all decisions in the Add Files dialog box are made, click Add and file selections will be visibly listed in the Create Site – Content dialog box. Look across the top of the file listing area in Figure 29-15 to see the headings Hyperlink Name, Filename, and Shortcut/Copy. A file's default hyperlink name is the name of its corresponding file minus its file extension. For example, the file ProductIntro.lwp becomes a hyperlink named "ProductIntro" unless you change it. Because the name of a hyperlink is what a site viewer will click to read a file page, you might want to change the name accordingly. Change a hyperlink name by clicking it, pausing, and clicking again. As soon as you click the second time, you can type in a new name. Toggle to decide whether to add your file as a shortcut or copy, by clicking the selection you made originally. Look to the right of a file name in the list, and under the heading Shortcut/Copy, to see this selection.

Click here to edit the name of a hyperlink.

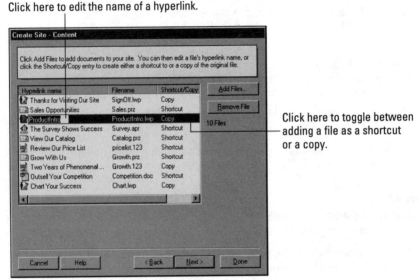

Click here to toggle between adding a file as a shortcut or a copy.

Figure 29-15: While in the Create Site – Content dialog box, you can edit a file's hyperlink name and whether it will be added as a shortcut or copy.

What if you have added files to your site that you decide you really don't want to add after all? Within the list of files you see showing in the Create Site – Content dialog box, click the file name you want to remove, Ctrl+click more than one file to remove. Next, click the Remove File button. Doing this removes the file or files from the list, but not from their source location. When you are satisfied with the list of files you have chosen to add to your site, you can select the Done button to create your site immediately, with these files included. In the event that you would like to continue through the site-creation dialog boxes to their end, click Next to open a final congratulatory dialog box called Create Site – Next Steps. You will be reminded of tasks you can perform "next" and you will be given a Back button to review or change decisions you have made throughout this process. Furthermore, a Cancel button lets you escape the process, a Help button lets you clear up any questions, and a Done button lets you finish the job. Click Done when you are ready to view your new site in the site pane.

"Zipped" files can be added to a site, just like any other document file. When you add a zip file, its converted Web page will offer a clickable link including either the zip file name or the descriptive text you give the link. A link for a zip file might say "Try my new shareware" or "Product Line Spec Sheets." A clicked zip link offers the zip file as a download from your site.

The First Fruits of Site Creation

After working through all the new site dialog boxes and clicking the Done button, a small, yellow home-shaped graphic will be dropped into the site pane. Your new home page will be created and its site item name will appear to the right of this graphic. Yellow orb-shaped (or spherical) graphics show to the left of the file hyperlink names representing file pages you have added to the site. Each home or orb-shaped graphic changes color noticeably after its representative page has been converted. Again, they will change back to their unconverted color as soon as you make a change that requires a reconversion of the page beside which they are placed. A reconversion becomes necessary for any number of reasons, two of which are changing the look of a site or editing the contents of a file within the site. The graphic's changing color is a reminder to reconvert the page prior to publishing it.

A "plus" located to the left of a home graphic generally means that a site's contents are not in full view in the site map. The exception to this is a new site created adding no files; it also has a plus sign. Click a site item name to highlight it, and then click the item's plus sign to Expand it into full view. When a "minus" sign shows next to a home page, it indicates you can Collapse the site to remove clutter from your view and tuck all Web pages under their site name. Click a site item's name to highlight it, and then click the minus sign to collapse the site. When a particular site name is highlighted, clicking either the Expand or Collapse icon will perform the same task as clicking the plus or minus sign. If your site map ever includes more than one Web site, click the Expand All or Collapse All icon to expand or collapse all site outlines at once.

Use the scroll bar at the bottom of the site pane to bring long site names into view, or with your cursor focus in the site map, press Ctrl+right arrow or Ctrl+left arrow to do the same. Press the up and down arrow keys to navigate up and down a site map. Press the right or left arrow keys to expand or collapse a site when its name is highlighted.

Deleting or Removing a Site

You can delete a site. Right-click its name in the site hierarchy to view the drop-down menu. When you do, you will see a drop-down menu that looks like the one shown in Figure 29-16.

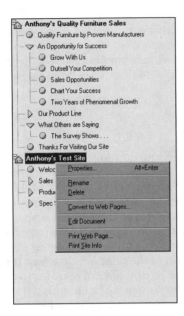

Figure 29-16: Right-click a site hierarchy item when you want to use this menu to initiate the removal or deletion of a site.

Quickly look over the options presented on this menu to introduce yourself to them, then select Delete. When you do, you will see the Remove Confirmation dialog box shown in Figure 29-17.

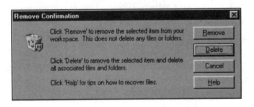

Figure 29-17: Click Delete to delete a site item along with its staging area files and folders.

Clicking Remove deletes a site from the site pane but permits the current staging area files of the site to remain where they are, uninhibited. If you later decide you want to try working with this site again, you can bring it back into the site pane by using the FastSite import feature. If, instead, you decide to press the Delete button, the site, along with all of its folders and files, will be deleted from both the site map and the staging area. It will become a trash heap, without form, lost in the Window's recycle bin.

Defining Sections

A section is a subset page within a site. After a section is created and titled, you can drop documents or other outline items into it. When your site is converted, links to the items held within a section's sublevel outline are placed on the section page.

To create a section in your site, first click its site item name in the hierarchical view. Next, do any one of the following:

✦ With the Choose Task pane onscreen, click Create a Section under the Build a Site heading.

✦ Click the Create a Section icon on the icon bar.

✦ Select Create ➪ Section from the menu items.

When you do one of the above, a section item will immediately be dropped into your site map awaiting its new title. A yellow graphical section marker will point to the highlighted words New Section and the cursor will be flashing in their midst. Type in a title for your section. On conversion, a section's title displays as a text heading across the Web page, so type what you want viewers to see. Press Enter or click in a blank area of the screen to set the section's title in the site map. Automatically, a new staging area folder titled after the section is placed within the site's folder. Once a section is created, you can place files, other sections, or hyperlinks within it. Doing this will increase the levels of the site outline showing in the site hierarchy. Look at Figure 29-18 to see how sections shape up under a home page and one another. Notice the direction the section markers point. If a section item has contents, you can click it to highlight it, and then click its right-pointing section marker to expand it and reveal them. Highlight a section item and click its downward pointing marker to collapse it, tucking its contents neatly out of view. After converting a section into a Web page, its yellow section marker will change color.

Danger Zone

When a converted section's name is highlighted in the site map, Status field 1 reads Local: Up to date. Even though this may be the case, be cautious before sending the section online. If you have added outline items to the section after having converted it, its links may not be updated. Convert the section again if you have any doubts about its up-to-date status.

A section takes the look of its parent page (the one that it was placed within), unless at a later point you change its particular look. Read how to do this in Chapter 30, "Fine-Tuning Your Web Site," under "Choosing Another Look."

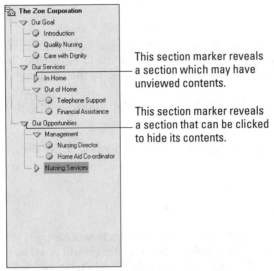

This section marker reveals a section which may have unviewed contents.

This section marker reveals a section that can be clicked to hide its contents.

Figure 29-18: View this figure's site hierarchy to see how a site outline holding sections and subsections shapes up.

Adding Hyperlinks to Link Content

Only a home or section page can hold a hyperlink; file pages cannot. Hyperlinks provide passage between Web pages in your site, or between your site and another. While most hyperlinks will form on your site's pages as a result of additions to their outline and converting them, you can create additional links. To create a link on a page, first click the page's title in the site hierarchy. Next, launch your link creation in one of the following ways:

✦ With the Choose Task pane onscreen, click Create a Hyperlink under the Build a Site heading.

✦ Click the Create Hyperlink icon on the icon bar.

✦ Select Create ⇨ Hyperlink from the menu items.

After you select to create a hyperlink, the Create Hyperlink dialog box will open. If you click to drop down the Action list in this box, as shown in Figure 29-19, you will see that you are given a choice between two types of links to create. Decide whether you want a link to point traffic to another Internet location or to another section or file page of your site. Figure 29-19 illustrates the creation of a hyperlink that will jump site viewers from a home page to another site page that may be more the focus of their interest. A viewer could leisurely navigate through a site map to get to the same page, but a quick link to a high-traffic page offers respite to a hurried visitor.

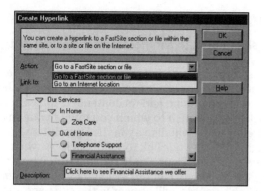

Figure 29-19: The Action list in the Create Hyperlink dialog box provides a creative means to route site traffic.

Linking to Another Site

You can create a link to send site traffic to another Internet location. To do so, click a site or section item in the site hierarchy to highlight it. Next, click the Create Hyperlink icon to open the Create Hyperlink dialog box. Dropping the Action box list, select Go to an Internet Location. Type the URL address to which you wish your link to connect in the Link To box. In the Description box, you can replace the link's URL address with the text you prefer viewers read when they see the link on your site's page. If you are currently connected online while creating a link, clicking the Browse button will open a Web Navigator, permitting you to navigate to this or other URLs. Clicking the Browse button while you are offline will promptly open the Web Navigator and inform you that a connection could not be established. If you have previously created URL links, clicking the "Link to" list in the Create Hyperlink dialog box will display the ten most recent addresses to which you linked. Select OK to create the new hyperlink, which will show on its parent page upon its conversion. Figure 29-20 demonstrates how a hyperlink is set up to route traffic to the IDG Books Web site.

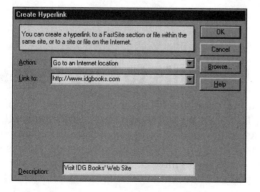

Figure 29-20: Create a link that takes site viewers to another Internet location.

Linking to Another Page in a Site

What if you don't want your public shuffling off to another Internet location, but would like them to revisit a page in your site? Click a site or section item in your site to create a new page link in it. Next, select Create ➪ Hyperlink to open the Create Hyperlink dialog box. "Go to a FastSite Section or File" is selected by default in the Action box and a representation of your site outline and its contents displays in the Link To box. Within this outline, click the page item to which you intend your link to connect. After you do, the page item's name will display in the Description box. Retype the description if it isn't what you want your link to read. Click OK when you are ready to set the link in your site's page. Figure 29-19 demonstrated how a hyperlink is set up to link two site pages together. Figure 29-21 shows how this link, along with its accompanying "chain link" graphic, will appear in the site pane after it is created. Upon conversion, the link will be viewable on its parent page.

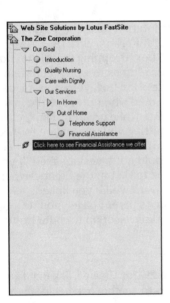

Figure 29-21: Created hyperlinks show in the site pane with a chainlink graphic appearing to their left.

Converting the Site's Contents to Web Pages

Once you have filled in your site outline, dropping files, sections, and links into it, you are ready to convert your site. The results you receive upon conversion will vary depending on what type of documents, and which type of formatting, you have positioned. It would be a wonderful, perfect world if format conversions always did what we expected, but don't feel dejected if you have to do some touch-up work to documents or around the site after you've converted it. Doing this is often quick and dirty. Additionally, there is the huge possibility that things will fly together so brilliantly you will want to tackle dressing up your site even more. You can do that because FastSite is amazingly flexible.

As you know, a site can contain non-SmartSuite files; however, how they convert will depend on the application in which the file was created. Documents created using the Microsoft Office product Word will be converted (published) as HTML-formatted documents. Excel, Access, and PowerPoint files will publish as a plain white site page including a hyperlink, just as will many other odd document types. In other words, upon conversion you won't see a readable version of the file on the file's site page. Instead, a link to the file and the text, "Click the link to view this file or to download it," will appear on the page. If this type file presentation disconcerts you in any way, consider a tangible solution. Lotus products offer file filters for opening different application documents. Once a Lotus filter opens a document of this nature, it can be edited and saved into a Lotus, or other application, file format. Consider changing site files either into a Lotus file format or one that FastSite supports and converts easily into readable pages (.doc, .htm, and .html are several).

SmartSuite files, including those made in 1-2-3, Approach, Freelance Graphics, and Word Pro, can be formatted as jDoc, but other file types cannot. If you intend to include non-SmartSuite files in a site that you plan to format as jDoc, either reconsider including these files in your site as such, or remember to format them as HTML for the best conversion results. For an explanation of how to use varying conversion formats for files included in your site, read "Updating Pages," in Chapter 30, "Fine-Tuning Your Web Site."

Click your site's title and select one of the following methods to initiate conversion of your site to Web pages (you will see the Convert to Web Pages dialog box shown in Figure 29-22):

✦ With the Choose Task pane onscreen, click Convert Files to Web Pages under the Publish a Site heading.

✦ Click the Convert to Web Pages icon on the icon bar.

✦ Select File ⇨ Convert to Web Pages from the menu items.

✦ Right-click a site's name and select Convert to Web Pages from the drop-down menu.

When the dialog box opens on screen, an outline of the site you chose to convert is present in the Convert to Web Pages dialog box window. Site items that you highlight will be converted for publishing when you click the Convert button. You can highlight site items in a number of ways; when you do, the Convert button becomes active. Clicking the All button highlights all site items for conversion. Clicking the Out of Date button highlights only newly added site items or those that have been edited since the site's previous conversion. If you prefer to select and highlight one or several items for conversion, use the click, Ctrl+click or Shift+click method. If you err in highlighting items, click None to clear it from the site outline.

When you click Convert, the site publishing process will begin with your pages being converted into Web-ready format. If, for some reason, you decide you want to bail out of this dialog box and rework your site a tad more before converting it, select Cancel; although no harm will be done by proceeding. When your pages are converted, you can play with your site, reviewing its pages in the Preview Web Pages pane.

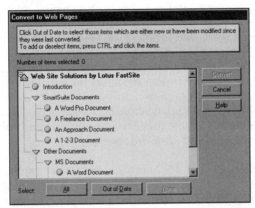

Figure 29-22: Select the items in a site you wish to convert to Web pages using the Convert to Web Pages dialog box.

Note   If at any point in time you want to convert one particular Web page, you can click the Convert button presented on the unconverted page. Highlight the page's item showing in the site hierarchy, then click the Preview Web Pages tab to see the page in its unconverted form. The Convert button will be there, present, and at your disposal.

Scrutinize your site map. Notice how the graphics next to each part of your site have changed color. Click your home page item in the site pane, then click the Preview Web Pages tab to preview how it looks in this pane. If the look and navigational sets aren't quite what you had hoped for, don't abandon your work; this can be changed with a few mouse clicks, as you will see in "Choosing Another Look" in Chapter 30, "Fine-Tuning Your Web Site." Figure 29-23 shows a view of the site you saw in Figure 29-8 after it has been converted into Web pages for the first time. Site map graphics have changed colors and the home page is now ready for its public with no muss or fuss. However, with a little fuss, editing, and a few additions, it can take on a whole different look. See Chapter 30 for more details.

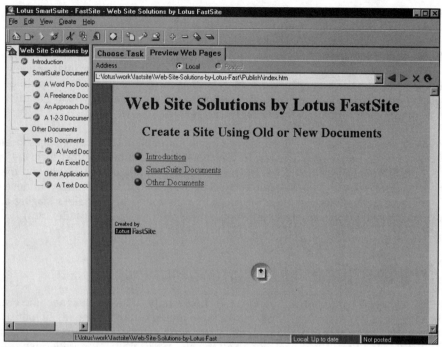

Figure 29-23: A converted site.

Reviewing How the Site Looks and Works

Prior to publishing a site, you'll want to make sure that all links are functioning and all pages look as you wish. The best way to do this is to preview your site in the type of browser your public will use. All browsers are not created equally, and all Web pages do not appear the same in each browser, so if you have several browsers on your machine, you might want to preview the site in each. If some Web pages don't meet your standards, you can edit, save, and reconvert them. If your home or section page links need revamping, see Chapter 30, "Fine-Tuning Your Web Site."

Highlight the site you want to preview in the site hierarchy, and then click the tab to bring the Choose Task pane into view. Under the heading Publish a Site, select Preview Web Pages in Browser. This task can also be initiated by selecting View ➪ Preview in Browser. After you do this, your Browser will open and your home page will come into view onscreen. Navigate through your site's document links. Make an Internet connection and check to see that URL hyperlinks react as intended. Click the navigational buttons of your site to make sure that they are working as designed, flipping a viewer through the pages of a site as intended. If all is well, you are nearly ready to publish your site to a server. Ah, yes, remember you can also browse your site in the Preview Web Pages pane. This is a sleek way for a midway review of your site while working on it; however, don't base your final preview "OK" here. Test your site using the browser type that the better part of your public will use. When everything checks out according to your standards, you are ready to save and post your site to its server location.

Note   Most browsers offer a File ➪ Open Page menu item option for viewing pages located on your hard drive or otherwise. To view your site in a browser other than the one FastSite opens by default, look for this menu item in any other browser you might have installed. When you select it, you will be given an option to search your drive for a file to open. Select to open the index.htm file found in your site's staging area Publish folder (for example, lotus\work\fastsite\sitefolder\publish\index.htm).

Saving the Site

Have you ever worked on a document for hours only to have your machine crash in a fiery blaze of "unglory?" Some folks have pulled out whole heads of hair over losing their work this way. Though most site work will save to the staging directory on the fly, don't take chances. Saving all the sites in FastSite simultaneously couldn't be easier. Select File ➪ Save from your menu items, or Ctrl+S, to save your sites in their current state. A Saving All Sites dialog box will pop up on your screen to notify you that your sites have been successfully saved. Click OK or press the Escape key to close the dialog box.

Posting the Site

Put, pass, push, publish or post—however you want to term the uploading of site files to a server, the whole point of stepping through all the site-building hoops is to present your site face to the public. With your Web site built and previewed for functionality and appearance, it's time to throw it on stage before its audience. Regardless of whether you intend to post your site to an Internet server, a local drive or network server, or a Domino server (covered next), you must first perform a few basic steps. These steps are discussed in the following sections.

First Steps – Before Posting to a Server

If you have not read the sidebar "Before Building a Web Site," earlier in this chapter, you might want to return to it before continuing. You will need to feed pertinent information into a few dialog boxes before you can complete the posting procedure. In the site pane, highlight the site you wish to publish to a server, and then select one of the following options to open the Post to Server dialog box shown in Figure 29-24:

✦ With the Choose Task pane onscreen, click Post Web Pages to a Server, which is listed under the Publish a Site heading.

✦ Click the Post Web Pages to Server icon on the icon bar.

✦ Select File ➪ Post Web Pages to Server from the menu items.

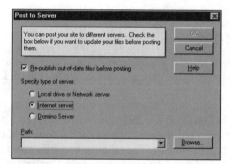

Figure 29-24: Your selections in the Post to Server dialog box depend on which server type will receive your posted Web site.

The first decision to make in the Post to Server dialog box is if you want to have FastSite republish (reconvert) the out-of-date files it has found in your site, before it shoots them online. If so, make sure the Re-publish Out-of-date Files Before Posting box is checked to check it. This box will be grayed-out if there were no out-of-date items found in your site when the Post to Server dialog box opened.

With pertinent information in hand and first steps complete, hone in on the following section that refers to your particular server type in order to carry on with posting your site. If you are feeling a little uneasy, you might want to publish your site to a local drive first.

Publishing to a Local Drive or Network

A painless exercise way to ready yourself for posting a site to a server is to first post it to your local hard drive. If you are the least bit nervous about taking the posting plunge, publishing your site in this way should provide a little relief. Make sure that you have write privileges before you attempt to post to either a local or a network server's (for example, intranet) drive. Read over and follow the "First Steps" found at the beginning of the "Posting the Site" section. With the Post to Server dialog box open, click the Local Drive or Network Server radio button to post to one of these options. In the Path box, type in the location of the drive folder to which you desire to post. If you prefer, click Browse to open the Browse for Folder dialog box. Locate and select the folder on disk and then click OK to insert its path in the Post to Server dialog box. Once back in this dialog box, double-check the path reading in the Path box and then click OK to start the posting procedure. A Posting to Server dialog box, ablaze with flying files, will appear onscreen, letting you know that your site is being posted. If there are files present in the folder you selected to post within, a pop-up dialog box will ask if you wish to delete the files and directories present there. Click your choice to continue.

For a little entertainment after posting a site to a local drive, compare its staging and posting area folders and files using the Windows Explorer. The posted site will contain fewer files and take up less disk space. If your already pounding heart can stand any more excitement, open the index.htm file found in the newly posted site with your browser, and check to see that all is in order. Often, double-clicking a file name in Explorer will open the file in its application. You might try this with your index.htm file.

Publishing to the Internet

Read over and follow the "First Steps" found at the beginning of the "Posting the Site" section and then connect to the Internet using a dial-up connection. Let the connection run in the background as you continue. With your Post to Server dialog box open, click the Internet server radio button and then click Browse. A Browse for Directory dialog box will open; when it does, click the Setup button. The first time you post a site to the Internet, you will be welcomed by a dialog box that introduces itself as the Internet Setup Assistant. This dialog box informs you that you have a few vital steps to take. You'll need to configure your server and proxy settings and connect to the Internet. Click Next to view the Internet Setup Assistant dialog box shown in Figure 29-25. You may have to check with your server administrator before filling-in the options that apply to you.

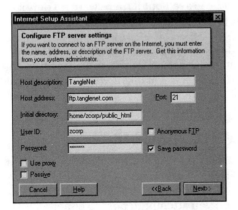

Figure 29-25: Use the Internet Setup Assistant dialog box to configure your FTP server settings.

To configure your FTP server settings, fill-in the boxes with the information you've gathered from your server administrator. Type your server's name into the Host description text box and their FTP address into the Host address text box. This address generally looks similar to a WWW address. Your server's WWW address may be www.hostname.com, while their FTP address may be ftp.hostname.com. Enter the name of the directory to which you've been instructed to post, in the Initial Directory text box. If instructed, include the directory's path along with it. For example, your initial directory may be named "public_html." With a directory path, your entry in the Initial Directory text box may be "home/yourIDname/public_html." Move on by clicking in the Anonymous FTP box to remove the check mark, or leave this box checked if the FTP host supports posting without a user ID. Type your User name in the User ID box noting that the entry of uppercase or lowercase letters can influence the success of your connection. Type your password into the Password box—carefully, because asterisks entered in lieu of text make proofreading impossible. If posting anonymously, enter your e-mail address in the password box. Click Use Proxy or Passive if you've been instructed to do so and then you're ready to click Next. When you do, the Internet Setup Assistant appears onscreen to receive your proxy information. If this applies to you, fill in the boxes and click Next. If it doesn't, click Next to continue.

Advanced Proxy settings can be made using the Internet Setup dialog box. Select File ➪ Internet Setup and the Proxies tab. Click to mark the Connect Through a Proxy Server box, and then click the Advanced button.

Red check marks are visible in front of the configuration steps you've completed when the Internet Server Assistant dialog box again surfaces onscreen. Click Save to register your FTP server's configurations. The last step in the dialog box encourages you to choose Connect to continue. If you didn't make your online connection with the Internet before configuring the FTP server, it is time to do so now, before clicking the Connect button. After your online connection is established, click Connect. If a dialog box shows that you are unable to connect, click OK and the Back buttons to retrace your steps and correct your settings. Reroute back to the Connect button by clicking the Next buttons. Again, click Connect. When the connection goes well, A Browse for Directory dialog box makes its appearance. Your server's name shows in the FTP Servers text box, with the word "Connected" to the box's right side. The Save In text box reads with the name of the initial directory you entered, its path showing in the Current Path text box. With everything in order, click OK to close that dialog box and return to the Post to Server dialog box. There you'll see the full path of your FTP connection showing in the Path text box, where it will be stored in the drop-down list ready for future connections using less setup time.

With all in order, you are ready to post your site. Click the Post to Server dialog box OK button. A Posting to Server dialog box will appear, letting you know that the site is posting. If, instead of seeing this dialog box, you see a FastSite dialog box, it will note that FastSite has found files or folders in the directory where your site is heading. Read the instructions in the box and then click Yes to have the files deleted, or No to post to the directory as is. After you do, your site posting process begins.

When all files have been published to the server, FastSite marks the Preview Web Pages tab's Posted radio button. Its browser then attempts to connect to and open the directory where the site was posted. If a dialog box appears onscreen letting you know that the attempt failed, click OK to close the dialog box. It is likely the browser will succeed when an appropriate HTTP address (rather than an FTP address) is inserted in the browser's Address box. It's now time to go have a look at your site on the Internet! What address should you use to access your site for viewing? Different servers require different addresses. Inquire of your server, if one of the following suggestions doesn't work for you. First, establish a connection with the Internet and open your browser. Within the Address or Location text box, type in either **http://www.yourservername.com/yourID** or **http://www.yourservername.com/~yourID** and press Enter. If your site doesn't come into view, insert "/index.html" at the end of either of these addresses, and press Enter again. The file names "index.htm," "default.htm," or "default.html" can be exchanged for "index.html" if your site still is not in view.

By now your site "should" be showing in your browser and ready for last-minute testing. There are any number of possibilities why it wouldn't be. One of these possibilities is that the site's initial file name (such as index.html or default.htm) may need renaming. Of course, there may be other reasons for the setback. Again, your server administrator becomes your best source of help in this situation.

Hot Stuff

The first posting of a site to an Internet server takes the longest, because you must configure the server's FTP settings. The next posting is a speedy five-step process. First connect to the Internet. Next, click the Post Web Pages to Server icon and then the Internet server radio button found in the Post to Server dialog box. Select your server's name from the Path drop-down list. Finally, click OK to begin posting.

After the initial server setup in FastSite, other new setups are a bit different. Select File ⇨ Internet Setup and click each tab of the Internet Options dialog box to fill in the information boxes presented on the panels. Save your changes and click OK when you finish. To post a site to this server, click the Post Web Pages to Server icon and then click Browse in the Post to Server dialog box. In the Browse for Directory dialog box, select the server's name from the FTP Servers drop-down list. Click Connect and, if all information is correct in the next Browse for Directory dialog box in which you see yourself connected, click OK. Back to the Post to Server dialog box, and you are again ready to click OK to post the site.

Publishing to Domino

Domino is software used to convert a normal computer into one that functions as a server computer. Prior to using FastSite with a Domino server, you must know about and do a few things. First, because each site you post to a Domino server must have its own Notes database file, you must make sure that the Notes database file that ships with FastSite was installed on your machine. Notes databases are signified by their .nsf extension; the FastSite database is fittingly named fastsite.nsf. If it is on disk, it will be found in the lotus\fastsite directory. If you did not perform a custom install of FastSite, selecting to install this Domino database, you must rerun the install and do so. Once this file is installed on your machine, you will need to provide it to your server administrator to install on the Domino server. A document entitled "About This Database" is included within the database, detailing setup instructions for the server administrator. When the preparations are completed, you can continue with posting your site.

Read over and follow the "First Steps" found at the beginning of the "Posting the Site" section. If your Domino server connection is established via the Internet, connect to the Internet and allow the connection to run in the background. With the Post to

Server dialog box open click the Domino Server radio button. If you know the path to your Domino server, including the database name, type it into the Path text box. An example of how this might look is `http://servername/directoryname/ fastsite.nsf`, though not all servers will use a directory name. Click OK to connect and begin the posting process. If you don't know the database name (*.nsf) to which you will post, select Browse to view the Select Database dialog box shown in Figure 29-26.

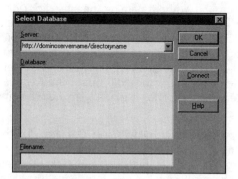

Figure 29-26: The Select Database dialog box is used for posting Domino sites.

With the Select Database dialog box onscreen, type the Domino server's address into the Server text box. Include any directory name that may apply. If you've previously posted to the server to which you are now posting, instead select the server's address from the Server drop-down list. Click Connect when the server's address (with directory, if applicable) is correctly entered. After connection, a list of databases stored on the server are visible in the Database text box. From within the list, select the fastsite.nsf file or, if your server has renamed that file, select the renamed .nsf file. Click OK and your site begins its posting process.

When viewing your newly situated Domino site, don't be surprised if you see a new link on the home page. Domino supplies a full-text search capability such that, when viewers of your site click this link, it will invoke the Domino search engine, which will then go rummaging through the HTML code in your site, finding what was hunted for. In addition to this unique feature offered in a Domino site, all the documents in a site are completely contained in the site's .nsf file, so site files can be safely copied and replicated. Moreover, one does not need a Notes client to browse to a FastSite Web site on a Domino server.

Publishing to an Extranet

An extranet-accessible site can require posting to either of the server options available when you click the Post Web Pages to Server icon and view the Post to Server dialog box. Consult with your network administrator for advice about which server type you should use to post your site. To post your site, skim over the "Posting the Site" section, follow the "First Steps," and then focus on the section appropriate to publishing your site.

Compare Your Local and Posted Sites

After you are comfortable with FastSite, building and posting several sites, test how the Local and Posted radio buttons work by stepping through the following rapid-fire instructions. First you will create a site in the site pane, then you will post it to a local drive (as if you were posting it to a server), and finally you will edit the site in the site pane and compare it to its posted version.

First, create a new site; click the New Site icon and, without naming the site, click Done. Add three files to the site; click the Add File icon, locate a directory filled with document files, Ctrl+click three files to add them to the File Name text box, and then click the Add button. Next, convert the entire new site; select File ⇨ Convert to Web Pages to open the Convert to Web Pages dialog box, click the All button, and then click Convert. Immediately, the Preview Web Pages tab appears onscreen with the Local radio button marked. Left mouse click your newly converted site's name, which reads "My New Site," in the site pane. Note that the site's home page contains three links to files.

Continuing, select an empty directory on your drive to which you'll post that site; click the Post Web Pages to Server icon to open the Post to Server dialog box, select the Local drive or Network server radio button, and click Browse. Browse your drive and click an empty directory to select it, then click OK. Once you have selected the directory, its path reads in the Path text box of the Post to Server dialog box. Click OK to post the site to your drive, just as if it were going online. After the site posts to the local drive, the Posted radio button on the Preview Web Pages tab is marked and the posted site's home page shows onscreen. Click the Local radio button. In the site map, left mouse click to highlight one of the three files in the newly posted site's outline, and delete it; press the Delete key and click Delete. Reconvert the whole site again: click the Convert to Web Pages icon to open its namesake dialog box, click the All button and then the Convert button. Again, look at the local site's home page. Click it in the site hierarchy if it is not already highlighted and preview it in the Preview Web Pages tab. There are now two file links on the page.

Finally, with the site item still highlighted in the site hierarchy, click the Posted radio button in the Preview Web Pages tab. The posted site still has three file links, just as you posted it. The local, edited site has two. Click between the Local and Posted radio buttons to compare the two sites. It is easy to see how these radio buttons can be used to assist you in keeping sites updated. One more time, click the Local button, and repost your site to the local drive, updating it. You will see a dialog box asking you if you want to delete files present in the local directory to which you intend to post. Click Yes. After the site posts again, notice that clicking between the Local and Posted radio buttons again shows identical home pages.

✦   ✦   ✦

Fine-Tuning Your Web Site

Building a Web site is both an organizational and creative effort. As with most efforts of this nature, the work evolves. When it does, focal points often need to be reworked and shifted into a different order so that the final creative presentation brings about the effect you desire. This chapter updates you on the FastSite outlining features available for changing a Web site's focal points and contents. It also shows you how to change the look of a home or section page, and print site pages or information.

Working with the Outlining Features

Chapter 29, "Using FastSite to Create a Web Site," introduced you to the ease with which you can create a Web site using the FastSite tools, and files that you've created. That chapter acquainted you with the dual-paned look of the workspace and the purpose of each pane. With the site pane noted as the location where site construction begins, you learned how to use it, creating your first FastSite outline. Once a site is underway, it is just as easy to rearrange and fine-tune as it was to create it. The FastSite outlining features make that possible.

The first step in creating a Web site is a mental one, and that's where the outlining feature can be a great help. Ask yourself what you want to accomplish. Think about which documents you want to add to your Web site. If you are short on files to experiment with, create a few new ones. Open a SmartMaster in each Lotus application and save them to file names in an easy-to-locate folder. Have fun playing with the FastSite outlining features, and remember that it is when you update your site by converting its pages to HTML or jDoc format that your fine-tuning actually translates to the Web site's pages.

Open FastSite and form three new sites within the site pane. To create the first site, click the New Site icon and name the site **Web Site Solutions by Lotus FastSite**. Press the tab key to move to the Description box and type in **Form a Site with Already Created Documents**. Leave the default settings as they are and click Done.

To create the second site, again click the New Site icon and name the site **SmartSuite Documents**, and then click Done. Create the third site by pressing Ctrl+N. This time, do not name the site, merely click the Done button immediately. This site appears in the hierarchical view, with the default name "My New Site." Use these sites for experimentation as you read this chapter.

Please note that references to "site hierarchy items," "hierarchy items," "site map items," and so on, indicate a graphic or named object present in the hierarchical view seen in the site pane. A site, section, file, and link are examples of site hierarchy items.

Changing Site Item Properties

Two site properties are quickly changed using outlining features. A site's name (its title) and its description (its subtitle) are both editable.

Point at a site name visible in the site hierarchy and click once. Pause and click again to change a site's name property. The cursor flashes in the name box of the current site, ready for you to change or edit the current name. Begin typing to delete the old name and type in a new one, or press the Home or left arrow keys to reposition the cursor and edit the name. When the cursor is flashing in a name box, the left-click can also be used to reposition the cursor and begin editing. Press Enter or click in a blank space of the site pane to accept the new site name.

To change the name or description properties of a site, right-click the site's name in the hierarchical view and select Properties from the drop-down menu. The Site Properties dialog box shown in Figure 30-1 appears onscreen with the site name highlighted. To open the Site Properties dialog box using keystrokes, highlight the site name in the site hierarchy and press Alt+Enter.

Begin typing to delete the old name of the site and enter a new one. Edit the name by repositioning the cursor first. Use the Home or arrow keys, or click the mouse to place the cursor where you want to begin editing the name. Press the Tab key to move the cursor focus into the Description box. Edit the description applying the same techniques used to edit the site name. Click directly into the Description box text, if you prefer to begin your editing that way. Click OK to accept edits in the Site Property dialog box, or click Cancel to remove the edits made. Converting the site places the new site name and description on the site's page, as its new title and subtitle. If you are anxious to see how your site property changes affected your home page, jump ahead and read "Updating Pages," later in this chapter.

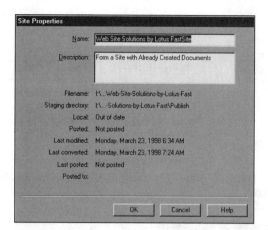

Figure 30-1: Open the Site Properties dialog box to edit the name or description properties of a site.

Each outline item, site, section, file, and hyperlink, has unique properties. Change the name property, visible in the site map, just as you changed the name of a site item. Click the item name, pause, and then click the name again to edit it. Right-click any site hierarchy item and select Properties from the drop-down menu to open the item's Properties dialog box, or press Alt+Enter while an outline name is highlighted, to do the same. Use the same techniques you learned in editing the Site Properties dialog box to edit any item's properties.

Making Multiple-Line Titles in FastSite

Carriage returns, within names and descriptions, are not possible in the FastSite Properties dialog box. As a result, it appears that you are relegated to one-liners for the titles and subtitles placed on home and section pages. But what if you would like a multiline title, or a listed subtitle? FastSite seems to readily take at least a little HTML code placed within the text of a site or section name or description. The HTML element for a line break is **
**. To enter multiline titles or subtitles on site or section pages, insert **
** into the text of the name or description, wherever you want a line break to occur. Figure 30-2 shows how a little HTML code, typed into the following name and description boxes of a site, translates into a customized multilined title and subtitle on a home page:

Type the following in the Site Name box:

```
Z Emerson Gallery<br>
```

(continued)

(continued)

Type the following in the Site Description box:

```
<i>presents</i><br>_____<br><br>
Original Oils from the 18th Century<br><i>and</i><br>Bronze by
Rolet<br>_____
```

As shown above (using 32 underscore characters), be sure to type in enough underscores so the result looks pleasing after you convert the page (look at the results in Figure 30-2). If you know or learn small bits of HTML code, such as surrounding text with <i> and </i> to italicize it, you can experiment with inserting code into names and descriptions to enhance titling and subtitling site and section pages.

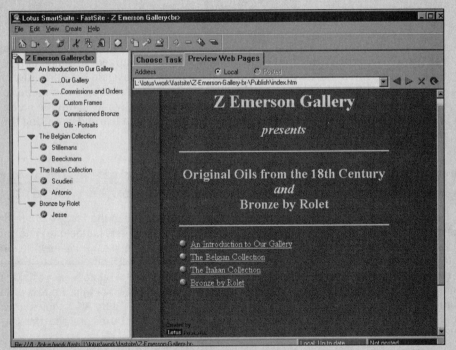

Figure 30-2: Site names and descriptions can be enhanced by inserting a little HTML code within them.

Cutting and Pasting Outline Items

Click any item you see in the hierarchical view and select Edit ➪ Cut to remove it from the site map. FastSite places cut items into the Window's Clipboard. If you cut any hierarchical item other than a site item you can put it back where it was in the site hierarchy. Click the name of the site hierarchy item that originally contained the cut item, and immediately select Edit ➪ Paste. Why immediately? Because the

Window's Clipboard holds only one cut item at a time, so paste back cut items you want returned to the site hierarchy before cutting anywhere else in your computing. Cut a site hierarchy item, rather than deleting it, if there is a chance you may want it back. When you paste a site hierarchy item, every outline item contained within it goes along with the paste. You can view what a hierarchical item contains by looking at the sublevel site map attached to it, as well as its sublevel outline.

If you cut a site item in error, it will not paste back into its former site pane position as a Web site. It must paste back into a site hierarchy container, such as another site or section item. Site and section items can receive items dropped into them, whereas link and file items cannot; thus, site and section items are containers. So, to paste back a cut site item, quickly create a new site item container in the site pane. With the new site's name highlighted in the site hierarchy, select Edit ⇨ Paste or the Paste icon. The cut site item returns to the site hierarchy as a new section in the newly created site. Use the drag-and-drop techniques explained in "Moving Outline Items," to move this new section back into the site pane as a site item. When it is moved back, its contents will go along with it.

There may come a time when you are working on several site outlines at once, toying with a "best look" for your site. With an elaborate section item built in one site, you might decide it would best be placed in the other site. Don't redo your work. You can move that elaborate section using cut-and-paste techniques. First, cut the section item you want to move, then paste it where you want it to go. Cut site, section, or file items can be safely pasted into other site or section items. Cut the hierarchical item you want to move from the site hierarchy, and click the name of the hierarchical item due to receive its paste. Press Ctrl+V or the Paste icon to complete the paste. Cutting removes an item from the site map but not from its staging area directory. As hierarchical items paste elsewhere, their files and folders travel with them, becoming a part of their new site's staging area.

Cutting and pasting between prototype sites is a great way to save time when site-building. After all, you've already stepped through the creation of the link once, and it works great. Why do the same work twice when you can just cut and paste the link? You can cut hyperlinks that refer to URLs, safely pasting them into other site or section pages of their own or other site outlines. Beware, however, when pasting hyperlinks that were created to refer to other pages in "their" own site. This type of hyperlink neatly pastes back into its "original" site outline, but pasting into "another" site's outline is risky business.

Pasted hyperlinks do not appear to carry the files they are linked with to "other" site outlines. So, if in the midst of your work, you miss a little cut-and-paste action, like making sure a link's referral file is brought along to a new site, your link won't work. You should test all links after you convert and preview your site. To cut and paste a link, first highlight the link item in the site hierarchy by clicking it. If it is a URL link, you will probably get a dialog box warning that the link could not be connected to; click OK to escape out of the dialog box. Click the Cut icon to cut the link. To paste the hyperlink, click the site or section item that will receive the paste. Click the Paste icon or select Edit ⇨ Paste to paste the link. After conversion, don't forget to test your results.

To test the cut-and-paste of a URL-based hyperlink, click one of the sites you created earlier in this chapter. Click the Create Hyperlink icon. In the Action box of the Create Hyperlink dialog box, select Go to an Internet location. In the Link to box, type **http://www.idgbooks.com** and in the Description box type **Go to IDG Books' Home Page**. Click OK. If you get a warning dialog box saying a connection couldn't be established, click OK again to close the box. The new link will be in the site map and highlighted. Now, with the link highlighted, click the Cut icon and then click another site item in the site map. Click the Paste icon to paste the link (if the connection dialog box shows again, click OK to exit it). One more thing, have a look at the new link's properties. The newly pasted link should be highlighted in the site map, if it isn't, highlight it. Then, press Alt+Enter to have a look at the Hyperlink Properties dialog box and what it offers. Click OK to exit the dialog box.

Copying and Pasting Outline Items

Copying and pasting hierarchical items into other site outline positions works much like cutting and pasting them. Click a site item, then press Ctrl+C or click the Copy icon to copy it. Click another site item and press Ctrl+V or the Paste icon to paste the copied item into its new outline position. When you copy and paste any hierarchical item, the outline items contained within the copied item go along with the paste (refer back to "Cutting and Pasting Outline Items" for more details).

The properties of a copied site hierarchy item can be pasted along with it. Click a site item in the site pane, then click the Copy icon. Highlight another site item and select Edit ➪ Paste Special to view the Paste Special dialog box shown in Figure 30-3. Paste using the FastSite native format when you want the properties set for a site item to travel with its paste.

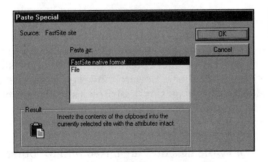

Figure 30-3: Select Edit ➪ Paste Special to open the Paste Special dialog box.

Deleting or Removing Outline Items

To delete most outline items from the site map, click the item and select Edit ➪ Clear and then click Delete, or press the key. Delete hyperlinks in the same way, but select Remove, or press the R key. If you delete a "file" item from the site map, it does not delete the original file from the drive. Deleting a section or site item also results in the deletion of any site hierarchy items contained within it. When any hierarchical item is deleted from the site map, its resulting staging area files or folders are also deleted from the disk. Deleted site items are not retrievable as such; they have to be recreated if you want them back.

Highlight any site map item and select Edit ➪ Clear, and then click the Remove button to remove it from view in the site map, while not deleting any folders or files. You get an extra benefit when removing a site item: Even though a site has been removed from the site map, it and its whole site outline can be imported back into the site pane as a copy. A deleted site does not have this benefit; it would have to be rebuilt. How one imports sites back is explained in this chapter's section, "Inserting Other Sites."

Moving Outline Items

As mentioned earlier, using the cut and paste outlining feature is a wonderful time-saver in site-building, and it is a practical way to move items around sites. The copy-and-paste feature works just as well. However, you also have other ways to move outline items, and certain effects will occur with the item and the site when they are moved. This section addresses these issues and explains how to move site hierarchy items using drag-and-drop features.

What happens when a hierarchical item moves around the site hierarchy, or into another hierarchical item, depends on what item is being moved, to it is being moved, and how it is being moved. FastSite's multifaceted means of moving site items around the site hierarchy offers so many possibilities and site outline reactions, they are best placed in a list. Refer to the list at the end of this section to learn which hierarchical items can be moved, where they can be moved, and what will happen when they are moved. Move several site hierarchy items to get a feel for the FastSite drag-and-drop feature.

When you move items, the position they take within the links on the page into which they are placed is dictated by where they are placed in the outline. Only one hierarchical item can be selected and moved at any time. You cannot Ctrl+click to select a number of hierarchical items to move at one time; however, any contents in a hierarchical item moves with the item when it moves.

Using techniques learned in the last several sections, copy the "My New Site" item and paste it into the "SmartSuite Documents" item. It becomes a new section, by the same name, in the "SmartSuite Documents" site. Rename the original "My New Site" item. Copy it and again paste it into the "SmartSuite Documents" site. Voilà! Two sections created from site items.

One more time, rename the original "My New Site" site item. This time, and with your site map fully expanded in view, point at the newly named site item. Press and hold the left mouse button and drag the item a little to the right and then slowly in the direction of the two newly formed sections. As you drag, watch for a blue, horizontal line to travel with the item, through the outline. This line shows where an item will be placed when the mouse button is released. When the blue line is in-between the two sections you formed, release the mouse button to view a dialog box which queries "Do you want to inherit this section's Web SmartMaster Look from its new parent?" Click Yes if you want a site and its section to have a uniform look. If you want the newly forming section to retain its Web SmartMaster Look, click No. Dragging a site item into another site item gives you the option to make choices about a Web SmartMaster Look, whereas pasting it did not. What happens when this site of three sections is converted? The three sections formed will list, in their outline order, as links on the converted site page. Moving a site item into a different site map priority can be a little tricky. The best way to do this is to collapse all site outlines first. Click the Collapse All icon, then drag and drop the site item using the technique just learned. If you accidentally drop one site into another site, forming a new section, just drag the section back into the site pane, carefully watching for the blue line to let you know where it can be released. No harm will be done to the site as it moves around; its contents will travel with it.

To move one hierarchical item into another empty item, click the item you wish to move. Press and hold the left mouse button and drag the item over the top of the other item until its name is highlighted. Release the mouse button to complete the move.

The following list of terms and explanations describe which hierarchical items can be moved, where they can be moved, and what happens when they are moved.

✦ **File item:** the graphic or title representing a file (document) placed in the site hierarchy. A file item becomes a Web site viewable page or a page containing a link to its document upon conversion. File item documents or their representative shortcut files are placed within their parent site or section staging area folders. File items can be moved into any site or section item; they cannot be moved into a blank space of the site hierarchy. When they are moved, their new parent site or section page will reflect them as a link upon conversion, making them available for viewing.

✦ **Hyperlink or link item:** the graphic or title representing a hyperlink placed in the site hierarchy. Hyperlinks appear as underlined and clickable text or graphics on their site or section parent page. When clicked, they direct site traffic to another page within the contents of their parent site, or to another site's URL. Link items can be moved to other site or section items within the contents of their parent site. URL link items can be moved within other sites and their sections. Upon conversion, a link's parent page will reflect them as a link.

✦ **Parent or Parent item:** any site hierarchy item that contains another site item, represented by its graphic, title, or associated Web page. The item placed within the parent item is referred to as the child.

✦ **Section item:** the graphic or title representing a section page placed in the site hierarchy, whether placed directly in a site item, or as a subsection within another section item. Section items have staging area folders named after them, which hold their component item's files. Section folders in the staging area reside inside their parent item's folders. Section items can contain other section, file, and link items. Items within a section item show as links on the section's page upon conversion and if they are connected to it by the site map. Links are listed according to their priority in the site outline. Any hierarchy item can be moved within a section item. When site or section items move within a section item, they reflect as sections (subsections) in the section item's outline; their own outline follows them. Section items can be moved into other site or section items. They can also be moved away from their parent page and into the site hierarchy as freestanding site items. When they are moved, their contents follow them.

✦ **Site hierarchy or hierarchical item:** any site, section, file, or hyperlink item placed anywhere within the site pane.

✦ **Site item:** the graphic or title representing the main entry home page of a Web site placed in the site hierarchy. Site items are sometimes referred to as the site, because they are the main Web site container. Sites have staging area folders named after them. Their folders contain their files, as well as all section folders and their component item's files. Site items can contain section, file, and link items. Items within a site item show as links on the home page upon conversion and if they are connected to it by the site map. Links are listed according to their priority in the site outline. Any hierarchy item can be moved within a site item. When site or section items move within a site item, they appear as sections in the site's outline, and their contents follow them. Sites can be moved into other site or section items. They can also be moved up or down the site list within the site hierarchy. When they are moved, their contents follows them.

Note that each time you move an item of any type, its new position shows in the outline where it moves. Conversion will reestablish all links as they have been edited. Upon conversion, sites become functionally navigable either by a converted link or a navigator button. Site visitors, handy at maneuvering site maps, will be able to see every page. Consider how easily a visitor might navigate through your site map as you build your site.

Danger Zone

At times, the graphic for a site map item may appear with a red X on it. This X indicates that something concerning that item is either inaccessible or unavailable. If the item refers to a document file added to a site as a copy, the X indicates the copy has been detected as missing. If the item refers to a document file added as a shortcut, the X indicates that either the shortcut file, or the file to which it points, has been detected as missing. In the case that a site, section or link item graphic appears with a red X, files or folders to which that item refers have been detected as either inaccessible or missing. As you might expect, an X'd item is not functional. Correct the problem that caused the X, or remake the site map item, before converting and moving your site online.

Editing Outline Items

One of FastSite's many advantages is that you can place already created documents, such as file items, into site maps; and have them converted into Web pages for viewing. Of course, some older documents don't convert as viewable pages. Instead, they get placed into site pages as links. Your site visitors can then click those links to download the files or open them, assuming they have the file's associated application on board. Either way, documents are easily slipped into FastSite outlines so that your public can get their hands on information you want to share. But what if you want to edit a document you've placed in FastSite before it is converted? Ah, now this is a slick FastSite trick.

Click any outline file item created using one of the applications you have installed on your machine. Now, double-click the file item name, and the file and its associated application will open, ready for you to edit the document. Some older Windows programs, those not designed for Windows 95 and newer, might act a little strange when you do this. They may appear to open and then disappear from the screen view. If this occurs, look on the Windows Taskbar for their representational button. Click their buttons to bring them and the document into view. You can also open documents you wish to edit in other ways. Highlight the document's file item name in the site map. Right-click the item name and select Edit Document from the drop-down menu or select Edit ➪ Open Document. In order to open a file item document for editing in this way, you must have an application installed on your machine that will read and perform edits to it.

Though the ability to open and edit documents placed in site outlines is swift, it won't be such a neat trick if you don't remember to convert the edited documents again before placing them online. Converted (updated) files that have been edited after conversion, must be reconverted to get them in a Web-ready estate.

And what if you want to do a little HTML editing on site or section pages? You can do this, but there are restrictions regarding what you can and cannot edit. For those who are familiar with HTML and want to brave a little coding in and around FastSite pages, the FastSite "Help" pages, about HTML and editing, are recommended reading. There are tags, objects, and other bits of HTML code that FastSite does and does not support. These are listed in the FastSite Help screens. Refer to the Hot Info icon under "Choosing Another Look" in this chapter to learn more.

Navigating the Outline

Click any hierarchy item or into a site pane blank space. With your cursor focus in this pane, use the up- or down-arrow to travel through the site map, an item at a time. Press the PgUp or PgDn keys to flip up or down through pages of forming outlines. Press the Home or End keys to jump from the top of the site map to the bottom, and vice versa. If you prefer to use mouse clicks to travel the site hierarchy, click any hierarchy item name, or graphic, to bring it into FastSite's purview, making it ready for action.

Controlling the Outline View

The site map can become unwieldy and cluttered at times. To collapse a lengthy section, use arrow keys to navigate to it in the site map or click the section item to highlight it. With the focus on the section item, click the downward pointing triangular graphic to its left. To expand a section, highlight it and click either the Expand icon or the section's right-pointing triangular graphic. To collapse a site item, first highlight it, then click the minus sign located to the left of the site item. To expand a site, highlight it and select View ➪ Expand or the Expand icon. Collapse or Expand all sites at once by using the View ➪ Collapse All or View ➪ Expand All menu items or their associated icons.

Adding, Moving, and Removing Pages

Web site pages are created by adding site, section, and file items to an outline. When these items are converted, they become Web pages. Create a new site (site item), to add a home page to your site. And while you are creating that new site, continue on navigating through the Create Site dialog boxes until you get to the Create Site – Content dialog box. This dialog box permits you to add one or many file items (pages) to your site, right from the start.

After an initial site creation, you have a home page and file pages, if you added files to the site in your first effort. If you continue working on the site, dropping section items within it, you add section pages to it. (Refer to the following section "Adding, Moving and Removing Sections" to learn more about adding section pages.) But how do you add even more pages to your site later? Most of your site pages will form from files you place within it. This being the case, this section focuses on adding file pages.

Files can be added to either a site or section item. Click the item and press Ctrl+A or click the Add File icon to open the Add Files dialog box. Figure 30-4 shows a number of random files highlighted using Ctrl+click. In this case, the files have been selected to add to a "Depot" site in the site hierarchy, so that they can be disbursed into several different sections of another working site using drag and drop. Selecting files as a group, you can add a number of files to a site or a section item at once.

Use the Look In drop-down list of the Add Files dialog box to navigate to the folder holding files you want to add to your outline. Click one file name or Ctrl+click a number of files to insert their names in the File Name text box. After selecting files, click either the Shortcuts to Selected Files or Copies of Selected Files radio button to add files as either shortcuts or copies. Click Add to add the file or files to your site map.

Add files to an outline using Windows Explorer. With FastSite onscreen, right-click the Windows Start button. Select Explore from the drop-down menu to open Windows Explorer.

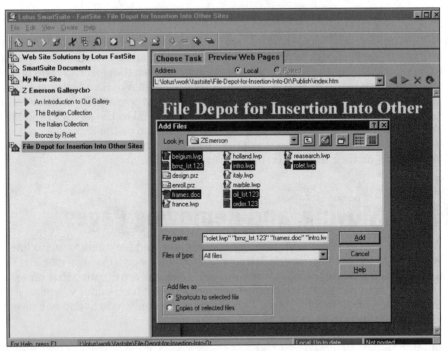

Figure 30-4: Files can be added to a site or section, singularly or in mass.

Navigate through the Explorer to open a folder holding files you want to add to your site. Add a consecutive list of files to a site or section item by clicking the top file name of the list to highlight it. Press and hold the Shift key and click the file name at the bottom of the list. The whole list will be highlighted. Press Ctrl+C to copy the list or click the Explorer's Copy icon. Press the FastSite button on the Windows taskbar or use the Alt+Tab toggle to take you back to FastSite. Click a site or section item that you want to contain these files. Press Ctrl+V or the FastSite Paste icon to place these files within the hierarchical item.

A very convenient way to add files to site map items — whether a site, section, or subsection item — is by using the Preview Web Pages pane as a file manager. Try the following steps to see how this works. First, click the Preview Web Pages tab to view this pane. Click within the Address text box and type the full path of one of your disk folders containing files you want to add to a site or section item. Perhaps the path might look like this: C:\Lotus\Work\Wordpro. With your cursor in the Address text box next to your entry, press Enter. The files in the folder will appear in the pane's viewing area. Change the way the files appear in the pane by right-clicking in a blank spot of the pane. When you do, a drop-down menu shows onscreen. Point at the View menu item until its drop-down menu presents itself. Slide your mouse pointer over to this menu and click to select your file viewing preference. The view of the files in the Preview Web Pages pane will change according to your selection. Note that each time you add a new path name into the Address text box, pressing Enter afterwards, the path you entered is added as a selection available from the Address drop-down list. This list can then be navigated for quick access to files all over your disk by using the Back or Forward navigator buttons to the right of the Address text box. When files you want to add to your site outline appear in the Preview Web Pages pane, Ctrl+click to select and highlight them. Next, point at one of the highlighted files, then press and hold the left mouse button and drag the files over the site hierarchy. When your mouse pointer points at and highlights the name of the hierarchical item into which you want to drop the files, release the mouse button. With both the FastSite and Windows Explorer windows layered on your screen, drag-and-drop methods, just like this, can also be used to move files from Windows Explorer into a site outline.

All site, section, and file pages can be moved around the site hierarchy and into other site outlines using the drag-and-drop methods learned above under "Moving Outline Items." Cut-and-paste and copy-and-paste methods can also be used to move pages around site outlines. Read about these methods at the beginning of this chapter under "Working with the Outlining Features."

Although files added to sites often hold many pages, they appear in a Web site as one long scrolling page. If you want to move a certain page within a file, you must recreate the page as a file of its own. Place that file into a site outline and move it as you please within the confines of where a file can be moved.

Cut, clear, delete, and remove methods are used to remove pages from site outlines. To remove any outline page (site, section, or file) from a site map, highlight its name in the hierarchical view by clicking it, then select Edit ➪ Clear and click the Remove button. Take comfort in the fact that a removed site item, along with all of its pages, can be imported back into the site map as a copy. Select Edit ➪ Cut to delete pages that paste back immediately in the event that you change your mind about cutting them. Select Edit ➪ Clear and then click Delete to permanently remove pages and their resultant files or folders from both the site map and the staging area.

Additions, removals, and rearrangements to the pages of a site are reflected when the site is updated (converted). Read about updating sites later in this chapter under "Updating Pages."

Adding, Moving, and Removing Sections

Click a site or section item and press the Create section icon to add a section or subsection to its contents. Select Create ➪ Section to perform the same task. When the new section drops into the outline, the cursor will flash in the new section's name box. Type in a name for the new section. This name will read as the title on the section page upon conversion. To edit a section name, add a description (subtitle) for the section, or change a section's properties, right-click the name of the section in the site outline. Select Properties from the drop-down menu and the Section Properties dialog box will appear onscreen. By the way, while that section name is highlighted, you can press Alt+Enter or Edit ➪ Properties to open this same dialog box. Figure 30-5 shows the editable properties for a section. A section's title, subtitle, and Web SmartMaster Look can be edited using this dialog box.

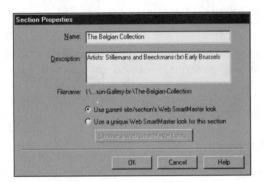

Figure 30-5: Use the Section Properties dialog box to change a section's editable properties.

Click within the Section Properties Name text box to edit a section name. Click within the Description text box to add or edit a descriptive subtitle for the section. The other options in this dialog box concerning a section's Web SmartMaster Look become clearer after reading a later section of this chapter entitled "Choosing Another Look," so leave those decisions for the moment. Click OK to accept edits in this dialog box, or Cancel to escape any changes made.

Use drag-and-drop methods detailed above under "Moving Outline Items" to move sections around, and into, site maps. Refer to the term "Section item," in the bulleted list at the end of that section to learn more about where a section can be moved and what happens when you move it. The cut-and-paste, and-copy-and paste methods detailed earlier under "Working with the Outlining Features" are also viable methods for moving section items around the site outline.

Remove sections from a site outline using cut or clear methods. Highlight a section in the site hierarchy by right-clicking its name, then select Edit ➪ Cut if you think you might want to paste the section back immediately. Select Edit ➪ Clear and then click Delete if you are sure you want the section and its contents, along with any resulting files or folders created in the staging area, removed from both the site map and disk. To perform the same operation in several other ways, right-click a section name, select Delete from the drop-down menu, and then click the Delete button; or press the Delete key and then Enter. Because the Delete button is preselected in the Remove Confirmation dialog box, pressing Enter confirms the selection.

Inserting Other Sites

When a site is removed from the site map using Edit ➪ Clear and then Remove, it can be inserted back into the site pane. Removing a site from this pane view does only that; it removes it from view, while leaving its site files and folders in their staging area directories.

When a site is created and named, FastSite creates an identically named file folder and places it in the staging area. This folder then holds all of a site's files and folders as they are created by FastSite. Select File ➪ User Preferences and click the File Locations tab to review the path of your Staging directory. The default name of this directory is FastSite; its default path is lotus\Work\FastSite.

Experiment with re-inserting a site back into the site pane. Click the "Web Site Solutions by Lotus FastSite" site item you created at the beginning of this chapter and select Edit ➪ Clear and then click the Remove button. This removes the site from view, while retaining its files and folders in the staging area.. Now, open the Import Site dialog box you see in Figure 30-6 by selecting File ➪ Import Site from the menus. Use the Look In list of this dialog box to navigate to the Staging directory whose path you just reviewed in the User Preferences dialog box. When you see its folder appear in the Import Site dialog box, double-click its folder icon to open and view its contents. You will then see the "Web Site Solutions by Lotus FastSite" site folder. Double-click this folder to open it. Next, locate and click the file named "Web Site Solutions by Lotus FastSite.FST" to both highlight the file name and insert it into the File Name text box. Click the Import button to insert a copy of this site back into the site pane.

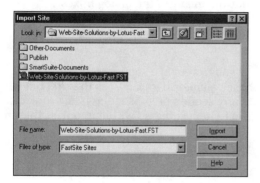

Figure 30-6: Insert a removed site back into the site pane by importing it.

After a site copy enters the site pane view, a dialog box opens onscreen. This dialog box informs you that the imported site has a Web SmartMaster Look saved with it. You are given the option to keep the Web SmartMaster Look or select another. Click No to keep the original Web SmartMaster Look or click Yes to pick a new one. An imported site inserts into the site pane named as a "Copy of" the original site name. A copy of the original site and all its contents is placed in both the site pane and the staging area. Rename the copy and work with it as you would any other site.

What is the benefit of importing a removed (stored) site? Stored sites are template sites. Other network users can use your stored site by inserting it into their FastSite site pane. They can then use the site as is, add the site as a section in another site, or edit the site copy for their needs. This is beneficial in keeping a uniform site look throughout a network. Well-designed site templates can be used as a basis for creating any number of other sites, and that saves time!

Refresh yourself on the quick steps through the site import process. Click a test site item showing in the site pane to highlight its name. Select Edit ➪ Clear and then click the Remove button to remove the site from view. Select File ➪ Import Site to bring the Import dialog box onscreen. Navigate to the Staging directory. When it shows in the Import Site dialog box, double-click its folder icon to open it. Locate the folder of the test site item you just removed, within the Import Site dialog box viewing area. Double-click its folder icon to open it. Locate and click the site's .FST file name, to both highlight the file and insert its name into the File Name text box. Next, click the Import button to bring the site back into the site pane as a copy.

Choosing Another Look

By the time a site or section item hits the site hierarchy, a Web SmartMaster Look of some sort has been established for it. Whether the look was chosen in the site creation process or arrived at by default, it can be changed. A site, section, or even a subsection's Web SmartMaster Look is easily switched to another of FastSite's packaged looks. If those looks don't suit your taste, create a customized look and apply it to your pages. FastSite is flexible. If at any point in editing a look you don't like your changes, select the Cancel button on any of the dialog boxes.

A Look for the Section

When you create a section in a site, or subsection in a section, it inherits its immediate parent's look. This establishes a uniform look across the site, but what if a uniform look isn't what you want? Any section or subsection item's look can be altered. Its new look then trickles down to items created within it, unless they, too, are customized.

To quickly change a section or subsection's current Web SmartMaster Look to one of the default FastSite looks, or to a previously saved look, click its name in the site map. Select File ⇨ Choose Another Web SmartMaster Look and then select For Current Section, to bring the Choose Web SmartMaster Look for Current Section dialog box onscreen. This dialog box is similar to the Create Site — Web SmartMaster Look dialog box you passed through when creating your first new site, and it is used in the same way. Click a look option in the Select a Web SmartMaster scrolling list and preview the look in the other frames of the dialog box. If your selection is satisfactory, click OK to accept the change and a dialog box appears onscreen. This box reminds you that a Web page has to be converted to reflect changes made to it. Click Yes if you are ready to convert the page immediately, or No to convert the page later.

The Choose Web SmartMaster Look for Current Section dialog box offers a Browse for More Looks button. On the first click of the button you might feel a bit mystified; don't be. Web SmartMaster Looks are easily customized and saved. If you've ever customized a look and saved it to a special directory, clicking this button lets you navigate to the look and select it for your section or subsection. Read more about Web SmartMaster Look customization under "Customizing a Look for a Section or Site," later in this chapter.

A Look for the Site

What do you want your site visitors' first impressions to be? The Web SmartMaster Look you choose for your site home page is the one that will either set their teeth on edge or relax and welcome them. If you are hoping to quickly create your site and want to do so with the least amount of effort, set your site's look to one that you will feel comfortable with throughout the site. Unless otherwise customized, all pages added to a site carry the look of their parent site.

The first step in changing a site item's look is to highlight the site item in the hierarchical view. Use the arrow keys to move up the site map to the site item or click to select its name. Select File ⇨ Choose Another Web SmartMaster Look and then select For Site. When you do, the Choose Web SmartMaster Look for Site dialog box opens. Scroll through the list of looks available in the Select a Web SmartMaster scrolling list and click the name of one you want to preview. Using the other scrolling frames in this dialog box, look over the background, text, and navigators the look offers. The Browse for More Looks button permits those who have saved looks to locate them and select one. If you haven't done this, you'll want to ignore this button for the time being and read more about it as you continue. When you find the look that meets your needs, click OK and a dialog box will open onscreen. Pages will not reflect edits made to their look until they are converted; select Yes if you would like to convert your page and see your changes now. Select No if you prefer to convert it later.

Customizing a Look for a Section or Site

The following paragraphs assist you in creating a custom Web SmartMaster Look to apply to your Web sites. When you have finished, you will save the look for future use. Before proceeding, review the location selected for the current Web SmartMaster Look directory. You may later decide to change this directory, but for now it is helpful to know where it is found. Select File ⇨ User Preferences and click the File Locations tab. Write down the path noted in the Web SmartMaster Look directory box and then click Cancel to exit the box. If the FastSite Web SmartMaster Looks are too generic for you, and your creative juices are flowing, you'll want to create a unique look for your site, section, or subsection items using the look editing tools. Because the dialog boxes used to edit looks for home and section pages, or section and subsection pages, are nearly clones, they will both be discussed together. If your focus is to change a site's look, highlight a site name in your site map. If your focus is to change a section's look, highlight a section item.

For a site, select Edit ⇨ Site's Web SmartMaster Look to open the Edit Site's Web SmartMaster Look dialog box shown in Figure 30-7. For a section, select Edit ⇨ Section's Web SmartMaster Look to open a nearly identical dialog box.

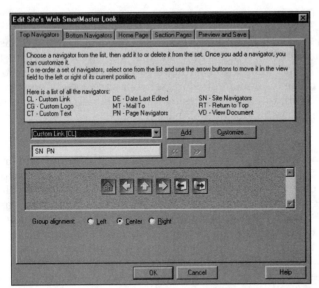

Figure 30-7: Customize the look of a site's home and section pages using the Edit Site's Web SmartMaster Look dialog box.

The major differences between the Edit Site's Web SmartMaster Look dialog box and the Edit Current Section's Web SmartMaster Look dialog box are the page looks they permit you to customize. The former offers look customization of a site's home page and the section pages that will form under it (read across the tabs in the dialog box). The latter offers look customization of a currently selected section page and the subsection pages that will form under it (again, peek at the panels). Even after altering section and subsection page looks using either of these dialog boxes, you can later focus on a particular section or subsection and customize its look.

Each panel of either the Edit Site's Web SmartMaster Look dialog box or the Edit Current Section's Web SmartMaster Look dialog box includes instructions on how to make the changes its options offer. Click either the Top Navigators or Bottom Navigators tab present in one of these dialog boxes to view its panel of options. Look at the list of items shown in Figure 30-7. This list is identical on all Top or Bottom Navigator panels. The items you see listed are the abbreviations for, and text descriptions of, FastSite's available navigator set options. Some of these navigator items are already present, appearing as navigator buttons, on your site or section pages. They came as part of your page's Web SmartMaster Look package. The Top and Bottom Navigator panels give you the option to delete, add and, once added, customize most navigator items that can be available on your pages. Among the list of items you can add and customize are custom links (in text or image form), custom logos, and a "Mail to" item that can also appear in text or image form. When these navigator items are added during the look editing process, they will appear amidst your site page's navigator sets on conversion of your site.

Maybe you've noticed that Top Navigators often appear in a type of box, separated from the rest of one of your site's pages. You can see this when you click a link on a home page, accessing its page. These boxes are actually called *HTML- created frames*. Your FastSite browser permits you to customize the size of these frames. You can drag the bottom line of the frame up or down if you want to get a better view of what is inside it. In the Preview Web Pages tab, with a converted section page showing, and its Navigator frame at the top, place your mouse pointer over the frame line dividing the navigators from the Web page. When the pointer turns into a double arrow, press and hold the left mouse button and drag up or down to shrink or expand the navigator frame. Resizing HTML frames in the FastSite browser is handy for looking over your customization of navigator items in FastSite. Once you have done this, however, recheck your customization work using the browsers that you think your site's audience will use.

Using the Top and Bottom Navigator panel options you customize the navigator sets that will be present on your site's pages. In doing so, you can highlight the name of one of your currently available navigator items in the drop-down list you see (such as site navigators [SN] or page navigators [PN]). When you do, its abbreviation will be highlighted in the view field and, using the right or left double-arrows to the right of this view field, you can then shuffle this item into another order. Additionally, you can change the alignment of the navigator set, shifting it right, left, or center. The moment you alter any navigator item for use in your site, you can see the changes in the preview window of these panels.

Practice editing a navigator item by adding a Mail To button to a site's Bottom Navigators. To do so, highlight a site item in the site map and select Edit ⇨ Site's Web SmartMaster Look. Click the Bottom Navigators tab, and then click the down-arrow available to the right of the list box available in this panel. Scroll the list and select the Mail To [MT] selection when you see it in the list. With the Mail To [MT] selection highlighted and showing in the list box, click the Add button. Type your name into the User name text box, and your e-mail address into the Email address text box of the Customize Mail To dialog box. Click OK to accept the entries and drop "MT" into the View Field box showing just below the list box. With the MT item highlighted in the view field, click the left directional arrow button, located to the right of the View Field box, one time. This action shuffles the MT item left and into a different position in the navigator button arrangement. Click the right directional arrow once if you want to replace it where it was. Notice that the Mail To button is added to your Bottom Navigator preview window. In fact, click that Mail To item to test it. It should open your default mail program, ready to create a message. Close the mail program, click OK to exit from the Edit Site's Web SmartMaster Look dialog box and select Yes to convert your site. Every page in your site, unless otherwise customized, will now have a Bottom Navigator button that site visitors can click to send you a pre-addressed e-mail.

Continue your customization process by again opening the Edit Site's or Section's Web SmartMaster Look dialog box and clicking one of the dialog box's two tabs with the word *Page* in them. Read through your options and have a little fun experimenting. Any changes you like can be kept, while any you don't can be changed again. Moreover, all changes can be canceled.

If you are proficient in HTML, you can HTML-edit Home or Section pages. To do so, select either Edit ⇨ Site's Web SmartMaster Look and the Home Page tab or Edit ⇨ Section's Web SmartMaster Look and the Current Section Page tab, then click the Advanced Edits button. Dialog boxes provide information and guidance. The editor that will be opened is the one selected using the File ⇨ User Preferences HTML Editor tab.

Click the Preview and Save tab when you're ready to review your edits. This panel's Preview radio buttons let you preview how all the changes you've made will translate to home, section, and subsection pages upon conversion. Click OK to accept the look immediately and convert your page, or consider saving the look beforehand.

Custom looks can be saved to use in future site design. If you like the new look you've created, save it. Click the Save as a Named Web SmartMaster Look button to open the Save Web SmartMaster Look dialog box. When it appears onscreen, type in a name for your new look and then tab into the Location text box to enter the directory path for the new look's folder. To ensure that the look is available as a selectable option in the Choose Another Web SmartMaster Look dialog boxes, save it to the Web SmartMaster Look directory path you wrote down earlier in this chapter when you selected File ⇨ User Preferences and clicked the File Locations tab. Now, click in the Description text box and type in a description for the look. With all dialog box entries made, click OK. Another dialog box appears. When you save a Web SmartMaster Look, a folder named after the look must be created to hold its contents. This dialog box merely wants to know if that is what you want to occur. Click Yes, and FastSite saves the look where you directed. A pop-up dialog box notifies you that the save was successful. Click OK to escape the dialog box and return to the Preview and Save tab. With your new look previewed and saved, click OK to accept your changes, and Yes to convert your page immediately. If you prefer to convert your page later, click No.

Have a Little Fun with the Web!

There are many items, available from the Web, that can be used in your FastSite Web sites. In fact, at times you may be online viewing a Web page with a background that you find attractive. While on the Internet browsing that Web page with the Preview Web Pages pane as your browser, right-click the Web page and notice the drop-down menu. You can select Save Background As and bring that background into your machine as a file, normally a .gif file. When you select Save Background As, a Save Picture dialog box will open with the file's name in its File Name box. Find a folder location on your drive to place the file, then click Save to save that file to the folder. You can rename that file or keep its name. Just be sure to keep its .gif extension attached to the file name (for example, mybackgd.gif). After you have the file on disk, you can change the look of your Web page, assuming that it isn't a copyrighted background.

Select your site in the hierarchical view, then select Edit ⇨ Site's Web SmartMaster Look. Click the Home Page tab to view its panel. Locate the Custom Image radio button in the Home Page Background area of the panel. Click the Custom Image radio button and then click Browse to locate that new background file on disk. Once you find the file, select it so that its name appears in the File Name text box of the Open dialog box. Click Open; the .gif file's name is now printed to the right of the Custom Image button text on the panel. Select OK to accept the edit to your Web page's background. The next time you view your newly converted Web page, it should have the background you appreciated.

There are many sites throughout the Web that invite you to download all manner of .gif and .jpg files. The graphics of the files are often on display in these sites, and instructions are handy to help you download them. These files can be used for custom bullets, backgrounds, and decoration. The custom logo offered in the Top and Bottom Navigator panel of the Edit Site's Web SmartMaster Look dialog box, does not have to be a logo. It can be customized as a decorative graphic and inserted in your navigators. Using downloaded files to edit a site or section's look in some way can be as easy as inserting a background file. Techniques learned while customizing the site background and the Mail To navigator item can be applied, in combination, to customize many other aspects of a site or section's look.

Updating Pages

In this chapter, you have learned how to flex your FastSite editing muscles. Wonderful, but unless you update your Web pages, they will be out of date or unreadable to your public; and they won't be much fun for you, in terms of seeing your progress. In this section, you get a firm grip on this part of the process. Updating pages is converting them to readable, Web-ready pages. Not only that, it is a process of having fun with FastSite along the way.

You can actually right-click any unconverted item in your site outline and select Convert to Web Pages any time that you want to see what your work has produced. So try it; first, add a file to a site or section item you have in your site hierarchy. Click the site or section item, click the Add File icon and navigate to a file you want to see in a site. Select its file name in the Add Files dialog box, and with its name in the File Name text box, click Add to place it in your site map. The file should be highlighted and sitting in the hierarchical view, waiting for you to type in a name for it. Type a name in and press Enter, or just press Enter to accept the file item with its own name. Now, right-click the new file item and select Convert to Web Pages from the drop-down menu. Let FastSite do its thing. After conversion the Preview Web Pages pane appears onscreen displaying your newly converted page. Does it look like you had hoped?

If a document doesn't look like you wish after conversion, you can try another type of file conversion for the file, if it is available. Right-click the file item name and press Alt+Enter or right-click the file name and select Properties. This will open the File Properties dialog box. Look at the radio buttons listed for Conversion format. Depending on the file item you placed in your site, you may have more than one conversion option or "Publishing Options." Options that you do not have will be grayed out; those that you can try will be ready for you to click. Click another format and then click OK to exit this dialog box. Now, make sure the file is highlighted and right-click it again, selecting Convert to Web Pages from the drop-down menu. Better? If not, there are still other options for you with this document file item.

Documents that you hope to place in your site may have to be worked with a bit, especially if they were not created in Lotus and other products that FastSite supports well (look in the FastSite Help Index for file types supported by FastSite). If the documents can be opened in your Lotus products using file filters (file of type), they can probably then be saved into Lotus product file format. Open a troublesome file in a Lotus application, then save it to the Lotus file format. Next, use the Lotus application to save the file into HTML or Internet format. In Word Pro, the beginning menu items to get you going in this process are File ➪ Internet, and then HTML Export Assistant. Work through an application's dialog boxes and offerings, saving the file to Internet format. Once that process is complete, again make sure your file item is placed in your site map, and convert it again.

File items created in Lotus and numerous other products should convert wonderfully. Work a bit on those that don't, before you give up on them. Use file conversion tactics wherever there are questions.

You can convert one site map item at a time. And, you can also convert a whole site at once. Or, with a click of a few buttons, you can convert those that have been marked by FastSite as needing updating.

Select a site you are ready to convert by clicking its name in the site map. Click File ⇨ Convert to Web Pages or click the Convert to Web Pages icon to open the Convert to Web Pages dialog box shown in Figure 30-8.

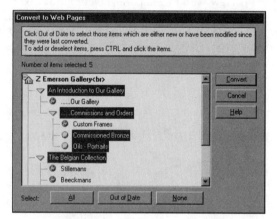

Figure 30-8: Update your site using the Convert to Web Pages dialog box.

This dialog box is the same one to which you were introduced in Figure 29-22. When you open it, you can select the All or Out of Date buttons, or you can click, Ctrl+click or Shift+click individual items to highlight those you wish to convert. Click Convert to prime your site for the Web. After the Converting to Web Pages dialog box clears the screen, your site is ready to preview and test. Flip through all the pages, test all the links, and gloat.

Printing

At any point in your Web creation process you can highlight either a site or section item in your site map and print out a detailed summary of the action it includes. Summary printouts are headed with the site or section name you select to print, and they include a number of details, including, but not limited to: the site or section items description (title), the number of files in the item, source path and names of files included in the item, the date that source files included in the item were last modified, the date the file was last converted to Web format, the staging area of the item, other section items included in the item (with details about their contents), when the site was last posted, and the location of the server the site was posted to. Some things are best seen, so highlight a site map item and select File ⇨ Print. Next, select Site Information and have a look at a printout. Ah, yes, make sure your printer is turned on and filled with paper.

Several other print options are available with FastSite. If you'd like to print a document that has been included in the site map, click the file item that represents it, and select File ➪ Print and then Document to print it out.

Have you ever been surfing the Web and wanted a printout of a Web page you were looking at? Click the Preview Web Pages tab and bring one of your locally converted Web site pages into view. Or . . . make an online connection and locate an Internet Web page using FastSite's Preview Web Pages pane as a browser. With either one of these Web pages showing in the Preview Web Pages pane, select File ➪ Print, and then Web Page to print a copy of the page. This works so much easier than scribbling down details found on a Web page. The next thing you know, someone will be scribbling down details from yours!

✦   ✦   ✦

Using Common SmartSuite Internet Features

The advent of the World Wide Web, just a few years ago, transformed the entire computer industry. Once a little-known backwater of the online community, the Internet has now achieved prominence as the world's central nervous system. Whereas we once used our computers in isolation, or as part of smaller-scale networks, now our computers are tied into other computers planet-wide. It's no wonder, then, that Lotus has included key Internet features in its newest SmartSuite package. These features offer convenient Web browsing, and the ability to link to Internet documents, create and publish HTML Web documents, and open or save documents to Internet (or intranet) servers.

In this chapter, we assume that you already have access to the Internet via a dial-up or cable-modem account with an Internet Service Provider, or can reach the Internet via your company's network. It's also taken for granted that you have basic Internet literacy, such as having used a Web browser and sent and received electronic mail. Your computer should already have a Web browser installed, preferably either Netscape Navigator/Communicator or Microsoft Internet Explorer.

Basic Internet Access

SmartSuite lets you take advantage of the Internet by publishing documents (or parts of documents, such as a range of spreadsheet cells) on the Internet. This topic is discussed in Chapter 32, "Creating Web Documents with SmartSuite Applications." In the current chapter, we focus on some Internet fundamentals.

Getting Help from the Web

The Lotus SuiteHelp drawer is on the far right of the SmartCenter bar. Use the arrow button on the bar to move to that drawer if you can't see it. When you click the drawer, you can choose either the Lotus Online or SmartSuite Tips folder. (You'll need to be online to use these features, because they pull their information from the Lotus Web site.)

Lotus Online

Use Lotus Online to go to the Lotus Home Page, Lotus Customer Support, to access the Lotus File Transfer Protocol (FTP) site, or to post a technical question. You can also get more information on the LotusScript programming language, or view the sites for SmartSuite Partners, which sell products and services for SmartSuite users.

Clicking any of these links opens that page using the Web browser. In Figure 31-1, we've chosen the Lotus Customer Support page.

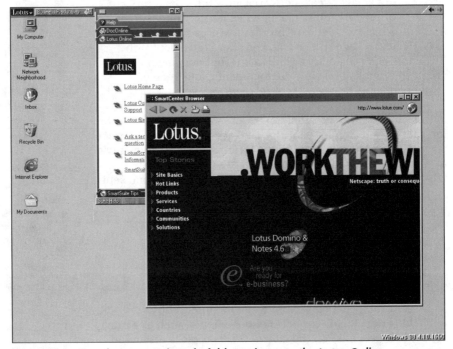

Figure 31-1: Use the Lotus SuiteHelp folder to jump to the Lotus Online resources.

Note that the Lotus site tends to be very busy; you may sometimes need to wait until after business hours before you can get to it. One way to work around this is to use one of the secondary Lotus servers. For example, use `http://www2.lotus.com` to open the same Web site that you'd get with `www.lotus.com`. Don't spread this tip around too widely, however, or this site will get just as busy as the main one!

Downloading Files

Although the Lotus Online drawer offers quick access to files on the Lotus FTP server, you can go directly to the Lotus FTP server by entering **ftp.lotus.com** in the Address or Location box in your Web browser. Alternately, you may wish to use FTP client software such as WS_FTP, CuteFTP, or FTP Explorer, all available as shareware at `http://www.shareware.com/`.

In Figure 31-2, we've clicked the Lotus FTP Site item in the Lotus Online drawer. The FTP site is displayed as a list of folders. Click a folder name to go to (and view) that folder's contents. To download a file to your computer, click a file's link (underlined).

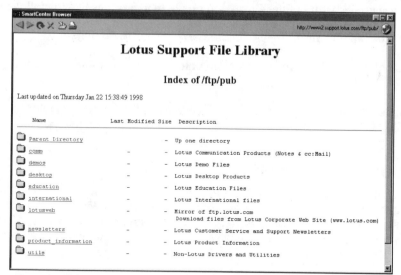

Figure 31-2: The Lotus FTP site offers files that you can download to your computer.

The Lotus FTP site lets you download a variety of files, including software updates, additional documentation, newsletters, and utilities. We encourage you to explore the FTP site so that you know what's available for download.

SmartSuite Tips

When you click the SmartSuite Tips folder, SmartCenter connects to the TipWorld site to display the SmartSuite tip of the day. *PC World* magazine's TipWorld editors regularly update the tips site with new tips and tricks for using SmartSuite applications.

SmartSuite Internet Features

Each application of SmartSuite can create and publish Web documents, although only Word Pro offers full-featured Web page generation. Word Pro includes ready-to-use HTML templates and HTML tools, and adapts Word Pro features for Web page creation. For example, graphics in a document are automatically translated to GIF or JPEG format when published to the Web. Word Pro tables are reformatted as HTML tables. Word Pro wallpaper becomes a Web page background graphic. You can also insert links between pages or to locations on the Internet.

You don't have to know anything about HTML to publish to the Web. For example, if you type a sentence with boldface, you don't have to insert tags like the following:

```
The quick <B>brown</B> fox jumped over the lazy dogs.
```

Just highlight the word brown and click the Boldface button on the Word Pro toolbar.

For a detailed discussion of how to create Web pages with SmartSuite, refer to Chapter 32, "Creating Web Documents with SmartSuite Applications."

Common Internet Features

SmartSuite applications have a few Internet features in common. You can use the File menu to publish a document (or part of a document) as a Web page. You can open files from a Web server or FTP site, and you can save documents to an FTP server. These commands are available on the File ➪ Internet submenu, as shown in Figure 31-3.

Another convenient way to get to the Internet features is to turn on the Internet toolbar. If the toolbar is not displayed, use the View ➪ Show/Hide ➪ Internet Tools menu selection. The Internet toolbar is shown here in Figure 31-4.

Note   In some applications, you simply use View ➪ Internet Tools. Also, some of these toolbar buttons are not shown in some SmartSuite applications. For example, Approach does not show a button for Create/Edit Hyperlink.

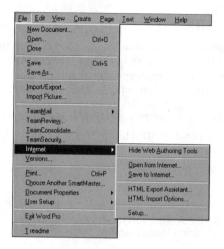

Figure 31-3: The Internet submenu on the File menu is common to most SmartSuite applications.

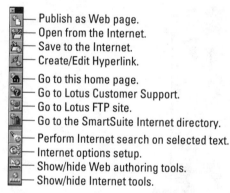

— Publish as Web page.
— Open from the Internet.
— Save to the Internet.
— Create/Edit Hyperlink.

— Go to this home page.
— Go to Lotus Customer Support.
— Go to Lotus FTP site.
— Go to the SmartSuite Internet directory.

— Perform Internet search on selected text.
— Internet options setup.
— Show/hide Web authoring tools.
— Show/hide Internet tools.

Figure 31-4: The Internet Tools toolbar offers convenient access to common Internet features.

The three Go To buttons take you to one of several Lotus Web pages. You can open the Lotus Home Page, the Customer Support site, or the file transfer site, just as you can via the SmartSuite Help drawer. The SmartSuite Internet Dictionary, located at http://www.lotus.com/smartctr/ss97ref.htm, is the same thing as the SmartSuite Web Reference.

The Perform Internet Search button allows you to select a word, phrase, sentence, or any part of a document. When you click the Search button, your Web browser opens and the selected text is piped into Yahoo! as the search criteria.

The two Show buttons are self-explanatory. They are convenient ways to display or remove the two Internet-related toolbars from the application's user interface.

SmartSuite Internet Publishing

Most SmartSuite applications let you create HTML documents or convert existing documents to HTML format. You can save these documents to an FTP server, or open files from the FTP server. An FTP server is a computer on the Internet or on a local intranet that uses Internet protocols to transfer files either from your computer to the remote computer (uploading), or from the remote computer to your computer (downloading). You can also use the FTP server to store non-HTML files, but these can't be opened by a Web browser. Instead, you use the FTP server as a storage bin that lets multiple users share documents over the Internet.

Creating Internet Content

Lotus Word Pro is the easiest way to create Web documents, so we'll use it as an example of how to prepare a document for the Web. To get started, click File ⇨ New (or click the New Document toolbar button) and choose one of the HTML style sheets, as shown in Figure 31-5.

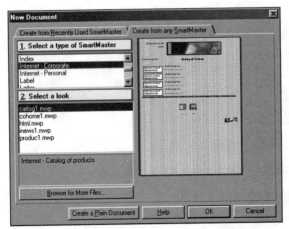

Figure 31-5: Word Pro offers several SmartMaster templates for HTML Web publishing.

Figure 31-6 shows the Internet Corporate Newsletter SmartMaster, ready for customization. You complete the template by clicking in various regions and typing text or importing graphics. It's a quick way to create a Web page.

Again, you should refer to Chapter 32, "Creating Web Documents with SmartSuite Applications," to find out how to create and publish other types of SmartSuite documents for use with the Internet. We'll use Word Pro to demonstrate the common Internet features of SmartSuite; other SmartSuite applications work similarly.

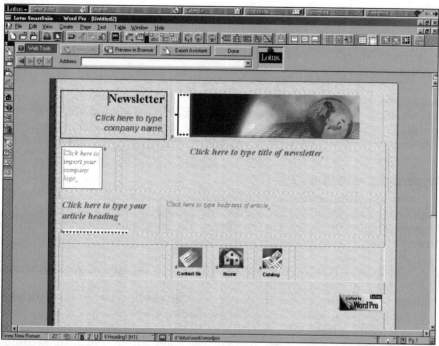

Figure 31-6: Click any region to customize the newsletter for your purposes.

Inserting Hyperlinks

While you can publish a SmartSuite document as a Web page, for real interactivity you need a way to let the user jump to another page. This is accomplished by inserting a hyperlink on the page. A *hyperlink* is a word or phrase, underlined and set off in a distinctive color, whose text is associated with a hyperlink reference, or Web page address. When the user clicks the link, the Web browser opens the page referenced by the link.

A graphic can also be used as a hyperlink, although this is not always as obvious to the visitor to your Web. Some simple browsers can't display graphics, and some users turn off graphics to speed up browsing, so you should probably use a text-based hyperlink in addition to any graphical hyperlinks you use.

In addition to jumping to another page, a hyperlink can be used to solicit feedback via electronic mail. Instead of the prefix `http://`, use the prefix `mailto:` followed by the e-mail address to which you want to send the mail. When the user clicks a mailto link, the e-mail software associated with the Web browser opens up a new (empty) mail message, with the e-mail address already filled in.

SmartSuite takes the hyperlink concept one step further. Rather than linking to another Web site, you can link to another document. This means that you can use hyperlinks to connect various SmartSuite documents. You don't need a Web server, because no Web pages are involved. You're simply jumping from one document to another.

Some SmartSuite applications offer other interesting hyperlink variations. Lotus 1-2-3 lets you use a hyperlink to jump to another region of the spreadsheet. Freelance lets you attach a hyperlink to text or to a graphic; and during a slide show, clicking a link can jump to another slide, start an animation, play a sound, and so forth.

Hyperlinks with Word Pro

Creating a hyperlink is easy in Word Pro. Just type some text and select it (or select some existing text). Or, click a graphic to select it. Click the Create/Edit Hyperlink button on the Internet toolbar, or use the menu option Create ⇨ Hyperlink.

Figure 31-7 shows how Word Pro's Create Hyperlink dialog box changes when you choose different hyperlink actions. You can create links to Web sites, Web pages, bookmarks, and Domino servers (same as a Web site). Just enter the Web address (URL) in the Link To text box. Use the drop-down arrow to select from addresses you've recently entered. (When used with the bookmark option, this list displays all the bookmarks in the document that you can choose from. You must have already created some bookmarks before you can link to them.)

You can also click Browse to fill in the Link To box. Your Web browser opens, and you can use it to find the Web page you want to link to. When you return to your application (that is, Word Pro or other SmartSuite application), the address of the Web page is filled in automatically.

A link can start a file transfer with the `ftp://` protocol, or send an e-mail message. Less useful are options that let you display the results of a gopher search (an obsolete way to index documents on the Internet), open a newsgroup (using a built-in or external newsreader program), or start a Telnet session to interact with another computer in terminal mode.

Note   If you choose None for Action, you simply remove the hyperlink status from the selected text or graphic — it will no longer be an active link.

You can also edit an existing hyperlink. Select the hyperlink and click the same button you used to create the hyperlink, the Create/Edit Hyperlink button. This brings up the dialog box you used to create the link, in which you can change the Link To destination or the type of link.

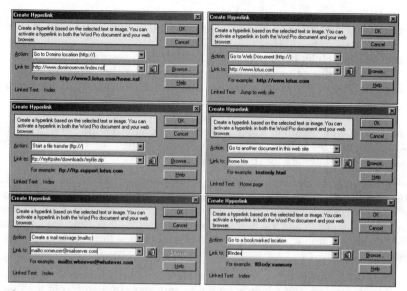

Figure 31-7: This figure demonstrates the types of hyperlinks you can create. Use the paste pot icon to paste the text in the clipboard into the text box.

Hyperlinks with 1-2-3

To create a hyperlink in 1-2-3, move to the cell to which you want to attach the link, and click the Create/Edit Hyperlink button on the Internet toolbar. You can also use Create ➪ Hyperlink.

The options for creating a hyperlink in 1-2-3 are shown in Figure 31-8. As you can see, the range of choices is somewhat simpler. You can either choose None (to remove an existing hyperlink), Go to an Internet Location, Go to Another File, or Go to a Range or Object in This Workbook.

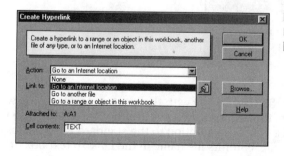

Figure 31-8: 1-2-3 lets you jump to an Internet location, to another file, or another location in the current workbook.

As with the Word Pro Create Hyperlink dialog box, you can use Browse to surf for the location you want to link to. For an Internet location, the Web browser starts up. If you choose to go to another file, the Browse button opens a standard file open dialog box, which lets you choose from the files on your computer or network. The most interesting option lets you jump to another location in the spreadsheet workbook. If you have a large, complicated workbook divided into several zones, this option lets you tie them together conveniently.

Hot Stuff

You can also insert a button in a spreadsheet cell and attach a hyperlink to the button. When you click the button, the hyperlink action is carried out. This lets you create a slick-looking user interface for your workbooks.

By default, the Create Internet Button icon is not displayed on the Internet toolbar. Use User Setup ⇨ SmartIcons Setup (or right-click any toolbar and choose SmartIcons Setup from the context menu). Choose Internet Tools from the Bar Name drop-down text box so that you can add the button to your Internet toolbar. Drag the SmartIcon labeled "Create a button with a link to a URL" (the fourth one from the bottom) to the Internet toolbar.

You can then click that button whenever you want to insert a button. Drag a rectangle to draw the outline of the button on the screen. You can then fill out the Create Hyperlink dialog box to specify to which location the button should jump.

Hyperlinks with Freelance

Lotus Freelance lets you attach a hyperlink to any text or graphic in your presentation. When running the presentation, clicking one of these objects performs one of the following actions, as shown in Figure 31-9: Go to an Internet Location, Go to Another File, Go to Another Page, Run Application, Play Sound, or Play Movie.

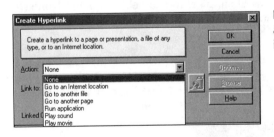

Figure 31-9: You can attach various actions when hyperlinking objects in Freelance.

After choosing an action, fill in the Link To box with the location to which you want to jump. With Internet Location, this will be a Web page (although you can also use variations such as `ftp://` and `mailto:` in addition to the standard `http://` for a Web page). To jump to another file, enter its file name in the Link To text box or click Browse to select a file on your computer's hard drive (or from the network).

If you select Go to Another Page, you can choose to jump to the next page (the default), the previous page, the first page, the last page, or the last page viewed. You can also use Link To to pause/resume the presentation, list all pages (so you can jump to one), or quit the presentation.

Configuring Internet Options

To get ready to save your work to the Internet, you should first configure the Internet options. This lets you set up the information for FTP servers.

Why would you want to open or save files to an FTP server? It's really the only way to share files over the Internet using open Internet standards. You can't save a file directly to a Web site, though, because HTTP doesn't let a client computer upload pages. However, if you have a Web site, you can probably publish HTML files to the Web site via the FTP protocol. Armed with the address of the FTP server and the folder (directory) name where the Web content is stored, you can open and save Web documents (or any kind of SmartSuite document).

If your company runs an intranet on the local area network, you can also open and save files to the FTP server on your network. There are usually easier ways to access network folders, but sometimes, for security reasons, the FTP protocol is the only way you're allowed to publish documents to the intranet.

To configure the FTP server you want to use, click the Internet Options Setup button or choose the File ➪ Internet ➪ Setup menu option. The Internet Options Setup dialog box appears, as shown in Figure 31-10.

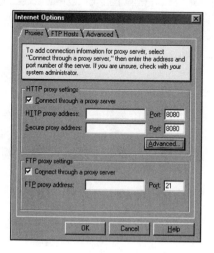

Figure 31-10: Use the Proxies tab if you access the Internet via your company's local area network.

Figure 31-10 shows the Proxies tab heading of the Internet Setup dialog box. You only need to use the Proxies tab if you have to go through your company network to access the Internet. In that case, ask your network administrator for the names or IP addresses of the Web server and the FTP server, and make sure you also get the correct port number.

You may also need a username and password (not necessarily what you use to log into the network) for security reasons. In that case, click the Advanced button to pull up the HTTP Advanced Options dialog box (not shown here). You can also use the HTTP Advanced Options dialog box to set up exceptions; that is, sites that should not be accessed via the proxy server.

Configuring for a Proxy Server

A proxy server is a computer on your network that is attached to the Internet, often via a firewall. The firewall screens network traffic to allow you to view external Internet sites and send basic information, such as e-mail, but restricts access to the corporate network by Internet users. The proxy server relays your computer's request for Internet access.

To configure the proxy, you need to know the name or IP address of the proxy server, and the port number used for HTTP (usually 8080). Note that the default is 80, which is the port normally used for Web access on your computer. If you have a modem connection in addition to a network connection, you won't be able to access the Internet via your modem connection if you use 80 for the proxy server. That's why port 8080 is normally used instead.

Some proxy servers require a username and password to authenticate or restrict access to the Internet, so you can enter that here as well. If you aren't sure what to use for this dialog box, contact your network administrator.

The Passive check box engages passive transfer mode. You should only engage passive transfer mode if both of the following conditions apply:

1. You are FTPing through a firewall or some other kind of gateway.

2. You get weird errors, particularly "failed data channel" errors.

Basically, the check box is there to give you something to try if you're having trouble getting files through a firewall.

We get to the meat of the dialog box in Figure 31-11. Here's where you can set up FTP servers. You may only have one FTP server, or you may work with several.

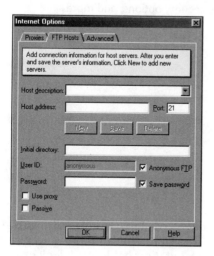

Figure 31-11: After entering a plain-English description and FTP address, click Save to store the site in your list of FTP sites.

To configure an FTP site (host), you need the address of the server (for example, `ftp.myserver.com`), the port used by the FTP server (usually 21), and what directory to use for opening and saving files (leave blank to save to the root directory). For an anonymous FTP server, leave the check box selected for Anonymous FTP. If you have to be authenticated, turn off that check box and enter your User ID and password. Uncheck Save password if you're concerned that someone with access to your computer may not be authorized to save to the FTP server. If you access this site via the proxy server configured in the Proxies tab, check Use Proxy.

Also enter a meaningful name in the Host Description text box. This is the name of the FTP server you'll choose when opening or saving a file to the Internet. After entering all relevant information, click Save. If you have additional FTP servers to configure, click New. You can use Delete to remove an obsolete or incorrectly configured FTP server. (To edit an FTP account, choose its name from the Host Description text box by clicking the arrow to the right of the box. After editing the information displayed, click Save.)

Advanced Internet Options

Figure 31-12 shows the third tab of the Internet Options dialog box, Advanced, which lets you set a few other miscellaneous options. (This tab only appears with Word Pro, not other applications like 1-2-3.)

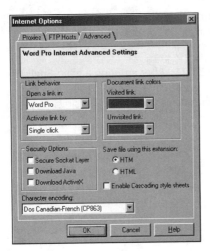

Figure 31-12: The Advanced tab (only shown in Word Pro) lets you choose how links are handled, set default colors for hyperlinks, choose security options, and more.

If you want to create hyperlinks, consider how you'd like to handle those links. By default, clicking a link will open that page within Word Pro. Word Pro does its best to convert HTML into word processing format, but it probably won't look exactly how it would in the browser. So if you'd rather have a link open in your Web browser, click the Open a Link In box and choose Default Browser. To move to a document pointed to by a link, you'd normally simply click the link. To avoid accidentally moving to another page (and having to wait for the page to load), you may wish to change the Activate Link By option to Double-Click.

The colors for Visited Link and Unvisited Link are normally set to the standard for HTML, violet and blue. If this conflicts with the color scheme you've set up for your page (for example, the dark purple may not show up on a dark blue background), you can customize these colors. Keep in mind that many people are accustomed to the default colors and may be disoriented by your custom colors. (They'll get over it.)

The Security Options affect how pages are opened by Word Pro. Enable Secure Socket Layer if you want to be able to open pages stored on a Web server supporting SSL. (Web documents on a secure site are preceded by the prefix `https://`.) By default, this is disabled, along with the ability to download Java or ActiveX controls. These aren't features that you can edit with Word Pro, so you might as well leave them turned off.

Because Web pages are often stored on Windows-based servers, the default filename extension is .HTM. Some UNIX Web servers insist on using the suffix .HTML, though, so this is something you can change in the Advanced Options dialog box.

If you want to give Word Pro more latitude in converting word processing documents to HTML, click the check box for Enable Cascading Style Sheets. This also allows Word Pro to convert CSS information and display it appropriately in the Word Pro document.

More Info

Cascading Style Sheets (CSS) are a part of the new HTML 3.0 standard. A CSS can redefine any standard tag, such as <H1> for a Level 1 Heading, or introduce new formatting tags. A redefined tag can use a custom font and font treatment. CSS also allows fine control over line spacing, something sorely lacking in the older HTML standard. Only versions of Internet Explorer or Netscape Navigator 3.0 or later support CSS, however, so if you want your pages viewable on the widest variety of browsers, leave this check box turned off.

Character Encoding is an esoteric option of little importance to most users. Most Web pages already specify which character set to use. (Some fonts offer different versions of their character set to support special language symbols.) If a page doesn't specify a character set, the option set here is used.

Saving to the Internet

When you are ready to publish your document to the Internet, you can choose either File ➪ Internet ➪ Save to Internet, or use Save As and click the Internet button.

When you save a file to the Internet, you'll see a dialog box like the one shown in Figure 31-13. If you don't see the Save to Internet dialog box, you haven't set up any servers yet. Click the Setup button on the dialog box you *do* get, and configure it as discussed in "Configuring Internet Options".

Before you can save your document, you have to establish a connection to the FTP server. Choose a server from the FTP Servers list, then click Connect. If you'd rather connect automatically, check Auto-Connect To This Server Next Time. (If you're not already online, Connect will usually start your Internet dialer, if it's configured to autodial. If not, establish an Internet connection manually before clicking Connect.)

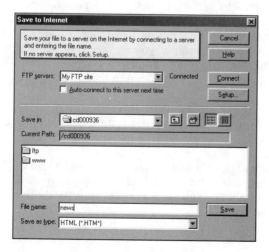

Figure 31-13: Choose an FTP server from the list and click Connect. You can then view the folders (directories) on the site, and save your document.

Once you're connected, you can browse the folders on the server by double-clicking the folder icons (if any). You can also navigate by choosing a folder from the Save In list box. To the right of this box are icons for Up, New Folder, Small Icons, and Details. Use Details if you want to view things such as the file size, date, and time.

Enter the file name of your document in the File Name text box. By default, documents saved to the Internet are saved with the .HTM extension. (As mentioned a few paragraphs earlier, you can change the default to .HTML if your server requires it. Few do.)

You don't have to save your document as an HTML document. If you're using an FTP site to share files over the Internet, you can save it as a standard Word Pro document.

Also keep in mind what operating system runs on the Web server. If it's an old DOS or Windows 3.1 server, you'll be limited to the old eight-character file name limitation, with no lowercase. A Windows 95 or Windows NT server allows file names of up to 253 characters long, including spaces. Uppercase or lowercase is preserved, but is not significant — a Web page named JumpStart could be opened as jumpstart.htm, Jumpstart.htm, JUMPSTART.HTM, and so on.

Most UNIX servers, on the other hand, do not allow spaces in file names and are picky when it comes to uppercase and lowercase. If you have a folder named Cricket, you can't open a page within it with the browser by typing `www.cutecat.com/cricket/default.htm`; you'd have to be exact, as in `www.cutecat.com/Cricket/default.htm`. For this reason, it's best to stick to lowercase file names with no spaces or other punctuation.

You may have problems connecting to the server. In this case, click Setup and make sure you have the correct settings for your FTP server.

Opening Documents from the Internet

You have two ways to open documents from the Internet. You can open files from an FTP server or directly from the World Wide Web. The latter is a great way to learn how to put together Web pages. Open a page from a site that you appreciate, and you can then edit it with Word Pro. For example, you can see that many authors use tables with invisible borders to format text in columns. Of course, you shouldn't *steal* from other Internet authors, but it *can* lead to inspiration.

Opening pages from the Internet also lets you use Word Pro as a Web browser, albeit a slow and somewhat clunky one (not all pages translate well as Word Pro documents).

More typically, you'll use the ability to open pages from an FTP site. As you work on your Web site, you'll save your pages to the Internet, so obviously you'll need a way to open them at a later time. (You could keep all your work on your hard drive and only transfer it to the Internet as needed.)

Before trying to open a page from the Internet, configure settings for the FTP server(s) you wish to use as discussed in "Configuring Internet Options." Choose File ➪ Internet ➪ Open from Internet. You can also use the Open toolbar icon and click the Internet button, or use the Open icon on the Internet toolbar. No matter how you get there, the Open from Internet dialog box should appear, as shown in Figure 31-14.

Figure 31-14: Type a URL address to open a page from the Internet.

To open from a Web site, type the address (URL), including the name of the HTML document, in the Address text box, and click Open.

To open from an FTP site, click the radio button for FTP. The appearance of the dialog box changes (see Figure 31-15). You can now choose one of the FTP servers you've set up, connect to it, navigate to a desired folder, and choose a file to open.

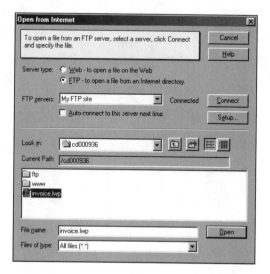

Figure 31-15: Choose an FTP server, click Connect, double-click a folder to open it (optionally), and then double-click on a file name to open it using Word Pro.

✦   ✦   ✦

Creating Web Documents with SmartSuite Applications

Using Word Pro to Work with Web Pages

This book has already discussed a multitude of ways in which you can work with documents in Word Pro. In addition to all those capabilities, you can use Word Pro to create and edit documents destined to be used on the Internet. Chapter 31, "Using Common SmartSuite Internet Features," discussed how to create hyperlinks, but you can also save a document in the Internet's native HTML format, open an Internet document for editing, and publish an Internet document back to the Internet. Using the Web authoring tools and Word Pro's ability to work with HTML (as covered below), you can create Internet documents.

Displaying and Hiding the Web Authoring Tools

Word Pro provides a set of special Web authoring tools (see Figure 32-1). To display the Web authoring tools, choose Show Web Authoring Tools from the Internet item in the File menu. Alternately, you can click the Show/Hide Web Authoring Tools SmartIcon in the Internet tools SmartIcon bar. Once you display the Web authoring tools, the menu option is renamed Hide Web Authoring Tools, and clicking the menu option (or clicking the Show/Hide Web Authoring tools SmartIcon) hides the Web authoring tools.

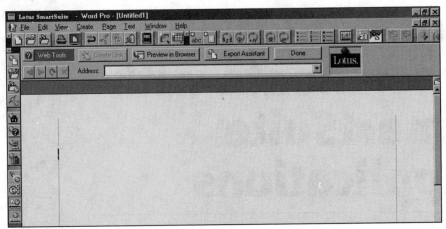

Figure 32-1: The Web authoring tools enable you to move through documents, specify an Internet address, create hyperlinks, and engage the Export Assistant.

The Web authoring tools consist of a series of buttons that enable you to perform the following actions:

✦ **Left Arrow.** Displays the previous open document. This arrow is only available if multiple documents are open in Word Pro, and you are not currently viewing the first document.

✦ **Right Arrow.** Displays the next open document. This arrow is only available if multiple documents are open in Word Pro, and you are not currently viewing the last document.

✦ **Reload.** Reloads a document from the Internet. The address is given by the Address: line in the Web authoring tools. The document is loaded using the current HTML Import options (see "Setting the HTML Import Options," later in this chapter). This command is not available if you are not viewing a document from the Internet.

✦ **Stop.** Stops loading the specified Web page from the Internet.

✦ **Address.** The Address text line enables you to enter an Internet address (such as `www.lotus.com/default.htm`) for retrieving a document. You can click the drop-down arrow to choose a recently accessed Internet address from the list.

✦ **Create Link/Edit Link.** The first button alongside the words "Web Tools" is labeled either Create Link (if the text insertion point is *not* on a hyperlink) or Edit Link (if the text insertion point *is* on a hyperlink). These commands enable you to either create a hyperlink or edit an existing hyperlink (see Chapter 31, "Using Common SmartSuite Internet Features," for more information on hyperlinks).

✦ **Preview in Browser.** Saves the current document as an HTML (Web) document and then opens it in your default browser. This enables you to see what the document will look like if it is opened from the Internet using a browser.

✦ **Export Assistant.** The HTML Export Assistant walks you through the process of setting up the HTML export options and saving your file in Internet format. For more information, see "Using the HTML Export Assistant," later in this chapter.

✦ **Done.** When you are done using the Web authoring tools, you can click the Done button to remove the Web authoring tools from the screen and regain the space.

Saving a Document in HTML Format on Your Hard Drive

When you are building Web pages using the many tools in Word Pro, you need to save the pages in the Internet format that browsers can open and display. These files are called HTML (HyperText MarkUp Language) files. You can save HTML files either to your hard drive or directly to the Internet.

To save an HTML file to your hard drive, use the following steps:

1. Open the document you want to convert to HTML (choose Open from the File menu) or create the document in Word Pro.

2. Choose Save As from the File menu. Word Pro opens the Save As dialog box (see Figure 32-2).

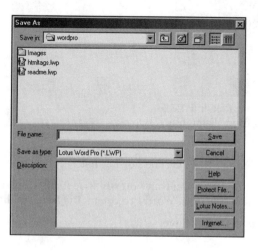

Figure 32-2: Use the Save As dialog box to convert a Word Pro file to an HTML (or any other available format) file.

3. Use the folder controls to navigate to the location on your hard drive where you want to save the file, and type the name of the file into the File Name text box.

4. Choose the HTML (*.HTM*) option from the Save As Type drop-down list. If Word Pro warns you that you will lose formatting, click the Yes button to continue with the save.

Note

HTML cannot represent all the different formatting options you can specify in Word Pro. Thus, you should preview the converted document in a browser to make sure it still looks the way you want it to after the conversion.

5. Click Save. Word Pro converts the file to HTML format and saves it to the selected location on your hard drive.

You can also use Word Pro's export function to export a file in HTML format. Use the following steps:

1. Open the document you want to export to HTML (choose Open from the File menu) or create the document in Word Pro.

2. Choose Import/Export from the File menu. Word Pro opens the Import or Export dialog box. Choose Export Your Document into Another File Format from selection 1 in the dialog box (see Figure 32-3).

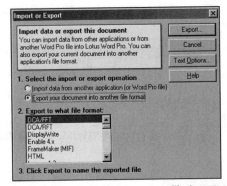

Figure 32-3: You can export a file in HTML format using the Import/Export dialog box.

3. Choose HTML from the Export to What File Format list.

4. Choose Export. If Word Pro warns you that you will lose formatting, click the Yes button to continue with the save. Word Pro opens the Save As dialog box.

5. Enter the name of the file and click Save.

Publishing an HTML File to the Internet

You can publish an HTML file directly to the Internet. This can be handy when the file is part of an existing Web site and you just need to make a small change to the page and then publish the change to the Web site. To publish an HTML file to the Internet, you must have a live Internet connection. After you have established the connection, use the following steps:

1. Open the document you want to export to HTML (choose Open from the File menu) or create the document in Word Pro.

2. Choose Save to Internet from the Internet item of the File menu. Word Pro opens the Save to Internet dialog box (see Figure 32-4).

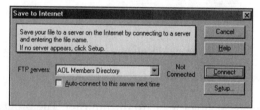

Figure 32-4: The Save to Internet dialog box enables you to directly publish your Word Pro document to an FTP site.

3. Choose the FTP server to which you want to upload the file from the FTP Servers drop-down list. Click the Setup button if you need to define another FTP server (see Chapter 31, "Using Common SmartSuite Internet Features," for details on how to set up a FTP server for the list).

4. Click the Connect button and wait for the words "Not Connected" to change to "Connected." Once the connection has been established, the path to the target FTP server is displayed in the lower portion of the dialog box (see Figure 32-5).

5. If your FTP server permits it, you can use the folder controls to navigate to another directory on the server. The current path is (not too surprisingly) displayed in the Current Path text box.

6. Type the file name for the file into the File Name text box. Make sure the Save As type drop-down list is set to HTML (*.HTM*).

Note

Most FTP servers are more restrictive than Windows when it comes to naming files. For example, the AOL FTP server does not allow spaces and other special characters in its file names. You'll have to check with your FTP server provider to find out their rules, but you can pretty much stay out of trouble by following standard DOS naming conventions. DOS naming allows for up to eight characters, a period (.), and then up to three characters. You should not use special characters such as *, &, ^, %, $, #, @, !, and ~.

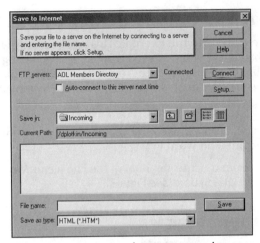

Figure 32-5: Once you have connected to an FTP site, you can specify the file name and location of the site to save the file to.

7. Click Save. Word Pro begins saving the file to the Internet. The progress of the save is displayed in the Internet File Progress dialog box (see Figure 32-6).

Figure 32-6: The Internet File Progress dialog box shows you the progress in publishing the file to the FTP site.

Setting the HTML Import Options

Word Pro enables you to open a Web page for editing, make changes to the Web page, and save it back to a Web site. You can control many aspects of both importing and exporting the Web page.

To set the options Word Pro uses when importing HTML pages, choose HTML Import Options from the Internet item in the File menu. Word Pro displays the HTML Import Options dialog box (see Figure 32-7).

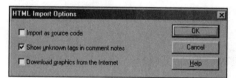

Figure 32-7: The HTML Import Options dialog box enables you to set the options Word Pro uses when it imports an HTML (Web) page.

You can set the following options:

✦ **Import as source code.** Turn this option on if you know HTML and wish to modify the HTML formatting commands in the document. With this option set, you see the actual HTML formatting commands (displayed as ordinary text in the document), rather than a formatted HTML document.

✦ **Show unknown tags in comment notes.** Because the HTML "standard" continues to evolve, there may be some HTML "tags" (snippets of HTML code) that Word Pro does not recognize. If you set this option, Word Pro places unrecognized HTML tags in the text of the document and marks them with a unique character style so they are recognized as commands. This is especially important if you did not set the Import As Source Code option. In that case, you will see an HTML document that is formatted using the HTML tags that Word Pro understands, and the unknown tags will appear as text for you to view, modify, or remove.

✦ **Download graphics from the Internet.** If you set this option, Word Pro will download graphics referenced by the Web page on the Internet. Downloading the graphics from the Internet takes more time, but provides a more complete view of the page you have downloaded. If you don't set this option, the Web page will display frames with question marks (?) in place of the graphic. You may want to select this option if you are just changing some of the text on a page and you intend to upload the changed page back to the Web site. The name and locations of the graphics are maintained in the Word Pro document, so the document will look "normal" again (the graphics will display) once you have uploaded the page back to the Web site and view it through a browser.

Using the HTML Export Assistant

Word Pro's HTML Export Assistant can provide step-by-step help for exporting any document as a Web page. Use the following steps:

1. Open or create the Web page you want to export.

2. Choose HTML Export Assistant from the Internet item in the File menu. Word Pro opens the HTML Export Assistant dialog box (see Figure 32-8).

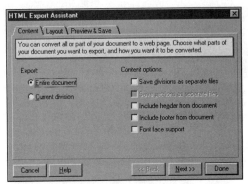

Figure 32-8: The HTML Export Assistant dialog box helps you export any file as a Web page.

3. Choose the options you want to use in the Content panel. You can export the entire document as a single HTML document by choosing the Entire Document option. Alternately, you can export just the current division by choosing Current Division. You can also save the divisions (and sections within divisions) as separate files. This is handy for breaking up a long document into individual Web pages.

   You can also decide to include the header (choose Include Header from Document) or footer (choose Include Footer from Document) in the Web pages. If you do, each page will include the specified header and/or footer.

4. Click the Next> button or click the Layout tab to open the Layout panel (see Figure 32-9).

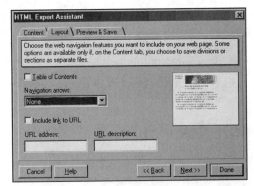

Figure 32-9: The Layout panel enables you to specify how you want to navigate between pages.

5. Choose the options you want from the Layout panel. You can add a link to another Web page (hyperlink) by checking the Include Link to URL option. Enter the URL address of the linked page and the optional URL description. If you enter a URL description, the automatically created hyperlink text uses your description instead of the URL address in the document.

If you set any of the options in the Content panel that create multiple pages from your document, you can choose to create a table of contents by clicking the Table of Contents check box. The table of contents option provides a list of the pages on the left side of each page, with an automatically created hyperlink to each page. This makes it easy to choose any of the pages and jump to them easily. You can also add navigation arrows between the pages by choosing the location of the arrows from the Navigation Arrows drop-down list.

Note The options that create multiple pages from your document are on the Content panel. They are the Save Divisions As Separate Files and Save Sections As Separate Files options.

6. Click the Next> button or click the Preview & Save tab to open it (see Figure 32-10).

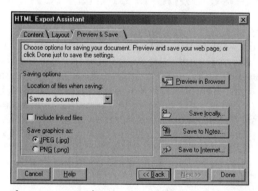

Figure 32-10: The Preview & Save panel enables you to view the page in your browser and save it on your hard drive, to Notes, or to the Internet.

7. Choose the options you want from the Preview & Save panel (see "Understanding the Save Options of the Preview & Save Panel," later in this chapter).

8. If you just want to set the export options, click Done. Otherwise, choose one of the buttons on the right side of the Preview & Save dialog box:

- **Preview in Browser.** Click this button if you want to see how your browser will display the document. Word Pro opens your default Internet browser and displays the document.

- **Save locally.** To save the Web page(s) to your local hard drive, choose this button. Word Pro opens the Browse dialog box so you can specify the hard drive location. Choose the file location and enter the name of the file in the File Name text box. Then click Save. Depending on how you set the Saving options (see "Understanding the Save Options of the Preview & Save Panel"), Word Pro will ask you for file location and file name as many times as needed.

- **Save to Notes.** To save the document to a Notes server, choose this button.

- **Save to Internet.** To save the Web page(s) to the Internet, choose this button (you must have a connection to the Internet for this work). After Word Pro displays the Save to Internet dialog box, follow Steps 2–6 in the section "Publishing an HTML File to the Internet."

Understanding the Save Options of the Preview & Save Panel

When you use the HTML Export Assistant to set how you want to export a document, you must choose how you want to save the files that are referenced by your document. These files are normally graphics that appear in the document, but can also be automatically generated graphics, such as navigation arrows. Because of the way HTML works, the graphics must be saved as separate files from the main document. It is important to set the file location properly, or the main HTML file (created from your document) won't be able to reference the graphics — and the graphics won't appear in the document when you view it with a browser. You set Saving options from the Preview & Save panel of the HTML Export Assistant.

The options are as follows:

✦ **Location of files when saving.** If you choose to have Word Pro create the graphics files referenced in the document, you can choose where the graphics files will be saved. There are three possibilities:

✦ **Same as document.** All related files will be saved to the same directory as the main document. When you save the document, you only need to specify the name and directory for the main document.

✦ **Single directory.** All related files will be saved to a single directory, which does not need to be the same as the document directory. When you save the document, you specify the name and directory for the main document, as well as the directory for the related files. If you choose Cancel when Word Pro queries you for the related files directory, the related files will be saved in the same directory as the document.

✦ **Different directory.** All related files can be saved into different directories, which do not need to be the same as the document directory. When you save the document, you specify the name and directory for the main document, as well as the directory for each of the related files.

✦ **Include linked files.** If you check this option, Word Pro will automatically create files for the graphics. These graphics files will then be saved along with the main HTML document. If you don't check this option, the graphics file won't be created. However, if they already exist on the Web (as they would if you were opening an existing Web page for editing), then the document will still reference the graphics properly once you have saved it back to the Web site.

✦ **Save graphic as.** If you choose to have Word Pro create the graphics files referenced in the document, you can choose from either JPEG or PNG format. For consistency with all Web browsers, you should always use the default choice of JPEG.

Opening and Editing a Web Page

With the ability to modify text, perform formatting changes, create and edit tables, and create and edit hyperlinks, Word Pro can serve as an excellent tool for making modifications to Web pages. To modify a Web page, you must open the Web page from the Internet, perform the modifications you want to make, and upload the changed page back to the Internet (see "Publishing an HTML File to the Internet," earlier in this chapter).

To open a Web page, you must have a live Internet connection. After you have established the connection, use the following steps:

1. Choose Open from Internet from the Internet item in the File menu (or click the Open from Internet SmartIcon). Word Pro displays the Open from Internet dialog box (see Figure 32-11).

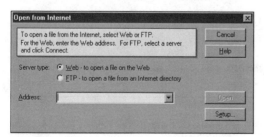

Figure 32-11: The Open from Internet dialog box enables you to specify the URL (Web address) to download the page from.

2. Make sure the server type is set to Web, and either type in the URL (Web address) of the page you want to open or choose from a list of recently opened pages from the Address drop-down list.

Note

Unlike a "standard" Web URL (such as `www.lotus.com`), the URL that you use for opening a Web page from the Internet *must* specify an actual page in the target Web site. For example, you could specify `www.lotus.com/default.htm`. A Web page URL must include the Web site designator (for example, `www.lotus.com`) as well as the path to the Web page on the Web site (for example, `/default.htm`).

3. Click the Open button.

4. Word Pro connects to the Web site, locates the Web page, downloads it to your computer, and displays the Web page using the HTML Import options settings (see "Setting HTML Import Options," earlier in this chapter).

Once you have opened the Web page, Word Pro displays the page (see Figure 32-12). You can then make changes to the page and republish it to the Web site.

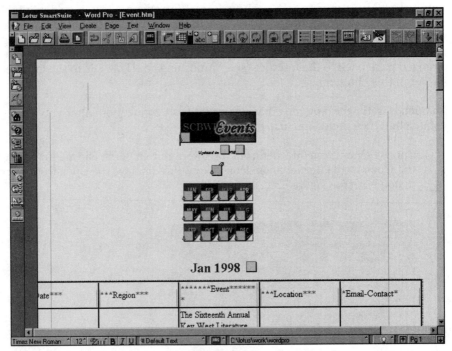

Figure 32-12: A Web page opened in Word Pro.

Using 1-2-3 to Work with Web Pages

You can publish spreadsheets (or portions of spreadsheets) that you create with Lotus 1-2-3 to the Internet, making the contents of the spreadsheets available on the Web. You can also access a Web page and edit the contents of the page in 1-2-3.

To publish a spreadsheet to the Web, you must first decide how much of the spreadsheet file you want to distribute. You can publish the entire workbook, just the current sheet, or a selected range. Because the options for publishing a range are quite different from publishing a workbook or single sheet, we'll discuss them separately.

Publishing a 1-2-3 Workbook to the Internet

To publish an entire 1-2-3 workbook or a single sheet to the Internet, use the following steps:

1. Open the workbook you want to publish.

2. Select Convert to Web Pages from the Internet item in the File menu. 1-2-3 displays the Convert to Web Pages dialog box (see Figure 32-13).

Figure 32-13: The Convert to Web Pages dialog box enables you to prepare a 1-2-3 spreadsheet for the Internet.

3. Enter a file name in the File Name for Web Page text box. Make sure the file ends in .htm if you want to be able to view the file from a browser.

4. In the What to Convert section, choose either Entire Workbook or Current Sheet (for a discussion of the Selected Range option, see "Publishing a 1-2-3 Range," later in this chapter).

Note

Only the jDoc option is available in the Format section. The workbook or single sheet is saved as a graphic along with the .htm file you specified earlier. In a browser, it will look much like it did in 1-2-3.

5. Choose Next> to advance to the next panel (see Figure 32-14).

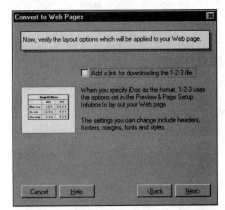

Figure 32-14: This panel of the Convert to Web Pages dialog box enables you to create a button for downloading the file from your Web site.

6. If you want the Web page to include a hyperlink that downloads the file to a viewer's computer, click the check box entitled Add a Link for Downloading the 1-2-3 File.

7. Click the Next> button to advance to the next panel (see Figure 32-15).

8. From this panel, you can choose to save the Web pages either on your local hard drive or directly to an Internet server by choosing the appropriate option for location. If you choose to save on your local hard drive, you can enter the directory in the Directory text box. You can also click the Browse button to open the Browse for Folder dialog box in its hard drive version (see Figure 32-16). Choose the directory and click OK.

If you choose to save to the Internet (you need an Internet connection for this), you can enter the URL to save to in the Directory text box. Alternately, you can click the Browse button to open the Browse for Directory dialog box in its Internet version, which looks identical to the Save to Internet dialog box (see Figure 32-4). Select the FTP server you want from the list, and press the Connect button to connect to the server. Once connected, navigate to the directory on the FTP server and click the OK button.

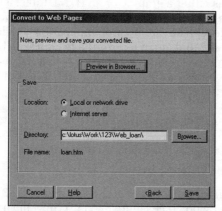

Figure 32-15: The last panel enables you to choose a destination and save your Web pages.

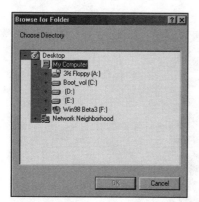

Figure 32-16: Choose a directory on your local hard drive for saving the Web pages.

9. Click the Save button. 1-2-3 saves the file either to your hard drive or directly to the Internet.

Publishing a 1-2-3 Range to the Internet

As an alternative to saving an entire workbook or a single sheet, you can save a specified 1-2-3 range to the Internet. There are some significant advantages to publishing a range. While a workbook or single sheet can *only* be published as a graphic, a range can be published as either a graphic or an HTML table. If you do publish the range as an HTML table (recommended!), you can open the Web page and modify the contents of the table with any number of applications, including 1-2-3, Word Pro, or any Web publishing tool (such as FrontPage Express). Unlike an HTML table, you can't work with the contents of a graphic—that is, you can't change a graphic back into a spreadsheet or a Word Pro document for editing, the way you can with an HTML table.

To publish a 1-2-3 range to the Internet, use the following steps:

1. Open the workbook that contains the range you want to publish.

2. Highlight the range you want to publish.

3. Select Convert to Web Pages from the Internet in the File menu. 1-2-3 opens the Convert to Web Pages dialog box (see Figure 32-17). Type a file name into the File Name for Web Page text box. Notice that the Selected Range option is now available (and selected by default), and the Format options now include HTML Table. You can type the range into the Selected Range text box, or click the button alongside the text box to select a range.

Figure 32-17: Use the Convert to Web Pages dialog box to save the worksheet as a web page.

4. If you choose to convert either an entire workbook or a single sheet, or if you choose the jDoc format, the rest of the steps are identical to Steps 5–8 in the section "Publishing a 1-2-3 Workbook to the Internet."

5. Click the Next> button to move to the next panel of the Convert to Web Pages dialog box (see Figure 32-18).

Figure 32-18: This panel enables you to set the table options for publishing the range to the Web.

6. Choose the options you want to use from this panel. As you check each option, the sample table to the left side of the dialog box displays a thumbnail view of what the table will look like. The options are as follows:

- **Header.** Check this option and enter the text of the header in the text box. The header is located above the table, separated from the table (and any description — see next bullet) by a horizontal line.

- **Description.** Check this option and enter the text of the description in the text box. The description is located between the header and the table.

- **Show table borders.** Check this option to turn on the lines around the cells in the table.

- **Add a link for downloading the 1-2-3 file.** Check this option to provide a hyperlink below the table. Clicking this hyperlink in a browser downloads a copy of the HTML page containing the table to the user's computer.

- **Author name.** Check this option and enter the text of the author's name in the text box. The author's name is located below the table, separated from the table by a horizontal line.

- **E-mail address.** Check this option and enter the text of the e-mail address in the text box. The e-mail address is located below the author's name (if any). From a browser, a user can click the e-mail address to send a note to that address.

7. Click Next> to move to the next panel of the Convert to Web Pages dialog box (see Figure 32-15). From here, follow Steps 7 and 8 in "Publishing a 1-2-3 Workbook to the Internet," above.

Importing Data from a Web Page into 1-2-3

Lotus 1-2-3 makes it easy to import the contents of a Web page into 1-2-3, where you can work with the data as a spreadsheet. You must have a connection to the Internet to import data from a Web site. To import a Web page into 1-2-3, use the following steps:

1. Open the workbook into which you want to import Web data.

2. Select the range of cells that will receive the imported data.

3. Choose Get Data from Web from the Internet item in the File menu. 1-2-3 opens the Get Data from Web dialog box (see Figure 32-19).

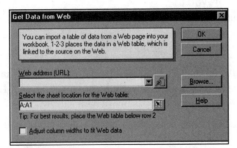

Figure 32-19: Use the Get Data From Web dialog box to import a Web page into 1-2-3.

4. Type a Web address (URL) into the Web Address drop-down list, or choose a recently accessed Web address from the drop-down list.

You can also click the Browse button to open your Web browser. Once your Web browser is open, navigate to the site from which you want to import data. Then, select and copy the URL (press Ctrl+C) in the address line of your browser. Switch back to 1-2-3 and paste the URL into the Web Address drop-down list (press Ctrl+V to paste the URL).

5. Click OK to import the data. 1-2-3 imports only the contents of HTML tables, and places the URL address in the first cell of the range (see Figure 32-20).

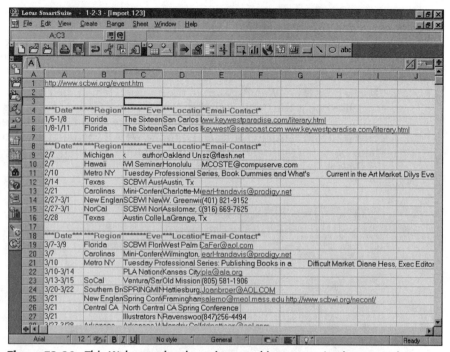

Figure 32-20: This Web page has been imported into 1-2-3 (and converted to a worksheet so the contents can be edited).

Note

As you can see from Figure 32-20, the imported table isn't very pretty. However, you can use the formatting options in 1-2-3 (such as adjusting column width and word wrap) to format the table more attractively.

Publishing a Freelance Presentation to the Internet

Freelance is a powerful tool for creating multislide presentations. And it could be very convenient to view a Freelance presentation from a Web site. If your presentation were available for someone to look at using their browser, you wouldn't have to distribute the presentation to them, or update that distribution when you update the presentation. Of course, to view a Freelance presentation from a Web site, you need an easy way to convert the Freelance presentation to a set of Web pages and upload them to a Web site. Freelance makes this simple.

To convert a Freelance presentation to a set of linked Web pages, you need an Internet connection. Then, use the following steps:

1. Open the Freelance presentation that you want to convert and send to a Web site.

2. Choose Convert to Web Pages from the Internet item in the File menu. Freelance opens the Convert to Web Pages—Overview dialog box (see Figure 32-21). This dialog box walks you through the steps you'll need to perform to convert the presentation and send it to the Web. If you don't want to see this dialog box each time you convert a presentation to a set of Web pages, click in the Do Not Show Me This Message Again check box.

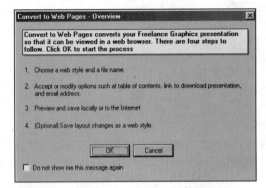

Figure 32-21: The Convert to Web Pages— Overview dialog box lays out the steps you'll need to follow to convert your presentation to a set of Web pages.

3. Click OK to display the Convert to Web Pages—Step 1 dialog box (see Figure 32-22). Choose a style from the list in the Web Style box. The options are as follows:

   • **Single Image.** This option converts each page to a single image. Web pages that use this option look the most like the Freelance presentation, but take the longest to load into a browser over the Internet.

   • **Tiled Background.** This option separates the text and background into separate files, and converts the background of a page to a tiled image. This works best for text on a plain background or a textured background that can be tiled. A tiled background is built from a single repeated image, and the image (the "tile") can be quite small, speeding up the load time considerably over a complex graphic background.

- **Screen Show with Plug-in.** With the two options listed above, a person viewing the presentation in a browser is limited to simply viewing the slides and clicking graphic buttons to move between slides. Any fancy effects you built into the original presentation, such as slide transitions and builds, are lost when you post the presentation on a Web site. Using the Lotus plug-in, however, the user can run the presentation in a browser and see the transitions, builds, and animations. The user needs to have the plug-in (available from the Lotus Web site) in order for this to work. Alternately, you can copy the plug-in to your own Web site and provide a button that enables the user to download the plug-in.

- **Screen Show with ActiveX.** As with the plug-in, this option enables the user to view the presentation in a browser and still see the transitions, builds, and animations. The ActiveX control they need is downloaded automatically to their browser and run whenever they run the presentation. The automatic nature of ActiveX is convenient, but the ActiveX control must be downloaded to the user each time they run the presentation, which causes a delay while the download takes place.

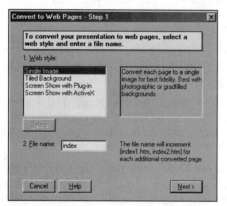

Figure 32-22: Step 1 of the Convert to Web Pages dialog box enables you to specify how the Web pages will be created and the file name to use.

4. Choose a file name and type it into the File Name text box. Each slide will use the file name, followed by a number. For example, if you use the default "index" file name, the slides in the presentation will be created as index1.htm, index2.htm, and so on.

5. Click Next> to move to the next panel of the Convert to Web Pages dialog box (see Figure 32-23).

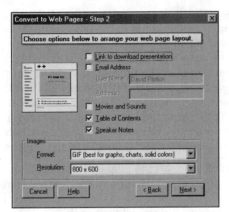

Figure 32-23: Step 2 of the Convert to Web Pages dialog box enables you to format the resulting presentation.

6. Choose the check box options you want to set. As you select each option, a thumbnail view of the presentation page displays a sample of what the page will look like. The options are as follows:

- **Link to download presentation (not available for screen shows).** This option places a small hypertext link in the header of each slide. Clicking the link downloads the presentation to the user's computer.

- **E-mail Address.** This option places the User Name and Address (if supplied) in the footer of each slide. When you check this option, the text boxes for the User Name and Address become available for you to enter appropriate information.

- **Movies and Sounds (not available for screen shows).** This option places any movies and sounds that you included in the presentation on the Web site. If the user's browser is configured to play movies and sound files, the movies and sounds will play at the appropriate place in the presentation (provided they have the necessary players).

- **Table of Contents.** This option places a table of contents on the left side of each slide. The table of contents consists of a listing of all the slide titles. Clicking a slide title jumps right to that slide.

- **Speaker Notes.** This option places the speaker notes for each slide below the slide.

7. Set the image format from the two drop-down lists in the Images section of the dialog box. The Format drop-down list enables you to pick from GIF format (best for graphs, charts, and solid colors) or JPEG (best for photographs, gradient fills, and other complex graphics).

The Resolution drop-down list enables you to pick the resolution of the slide on the Web site. Lower resolutions (such as 640×480) load faster, require less space on the Web site, and fit well on VGA-resolution screens. Higher resolutions (such as 1024×768 or 1280×1024) provide finer detail, but the files can get very large and require a lot of scrolling for people with low-resolution screens.

A resolution of 800x600 is a good compromise between file size and resolution. Most computers today have a higher resolution than 640x480, and 800x600 provides sufficient detail to display a presentation on the Web.

8. Click Next> to advance to the next panel. Freelance runs a utility to convert the slides to the specified graphics images, and then displays the Convert to Web Pages — Step 3 dialog box (see Figure 32-24).

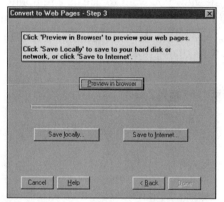

Figure 32-24: Step 3 of the Convert to Web Pages dialog box enables you to preview the presentation in a browser or save the file.

9. From the Step 3 dialog box, you can choose to preview the presentation in your browser by clicking the Preview in Browser button. You can also choose to save the presentation on your hard drive or on the Internet.

To save the presentation on your hard drive, click the Save Locally button. Freelance opens the Browse for Folder dialog box in its hard drive version (see Figure 32-16). Navigate to the folder in which you want to save the presentation files and click OK.

To save the presentation to the Internet, you need an Internet connection. Freelance opens the Browse For directory in its Internet version, which looks identical to the Save to Internet dialog box (see Figure 32-4). Select the FTP server you want from the list, and press the Connect button to connect to the server. Once connected, navigate to the directory on the FTP server and click the OK button.

10. Click Done to complete the conversion to Web pages.

Publishing an Approach View to the Internet

Approach provides the ability to enter data and customize how you see the data using *views* (forms, reports, form letters, charts, crosstabs, and mailing labels). If your Approach views were available on the Internet, others could see your data. Of course, to see an Approach view on a Web site, you need an easy way to convert the Approach views to a set of Web pages and upload them to the Web site.

To convert an Approach view to a set of linked Web pages, you need an Internet connection. Then, use the following steps:

1. Open the Approach file that contains the view you want to use to create the Web page. Then, navigate to the view you want to use as a template for the Web page. Choose the record that contains the data you want to display.

2. Choose Convert View to Web Pages from the Internet item in the File menu. Approach opens the Save View As dialog box (see Figure 32-25).

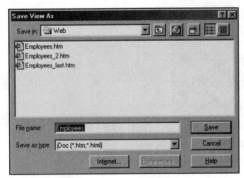

Figure 32-25: Use the Save View As dialog box to save the view to your hard drive or the Internet.

3. Enter a file name in the File Name text box. This name will be used as the "root" for creating the Web page names. For example, if you provide a file name of "Employees," the Web pages will be called Employees.htm, Employees_2.htm, and so on.

4. If you want to save to your local hard drive, use the Save View As dialog box to navigate to the directory in which you want to save the Web pages. Then, click the Save button.

5. Alternately, if you want to save the views to the Internet (you need an Internet connection for this), click the Internet button. Approach opens the Save to Internet dialog box (see Figure 32-26). Choose the FTP server from the FTP Servers drop-down list, and click the Connect button to connect to the server. Navigate to the directory on the server and click the Save button.

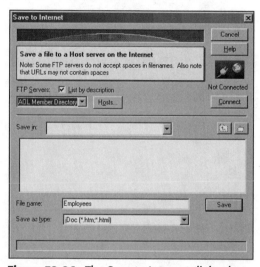

Figure 32-26: The Save to Internet dialog box enables you to pick a destination on the Internet, and save your Approach view Web pages.

✦   ✦   ✦

Working with Communications and Team Editing Features

More often than not, a finished business document results from collaborating with a group overtime—not from a one-time brain dump and subsequent editing session. Before the advent of e-mail, soliciting feedback involved photocopying your document, sending it via interoffice or regular mail, making follow-up calls or simply waiting for changes to come back, then reviewing each marked-up copy and incorporating the best suggestions by hand. With e-mail and SmartSuite's *team computing* features, that routine is toast. You can use TeamMail to e-mail all or part of a file and a message. Or, you can route the information so that your collaborators review it in a particular order. In addition, you can use TeamReview and TeamConsolidate features in Word Pro, 1-2-3, and Freelance to determine which changes you want to incorporate into the routed information. If you want to prevent certain changes to a Word Pro or Approach file, use the TeamSecurity features to limit access to that file. Finally, you can deliver your Freelance Graphics presentation live over a network using TeamShow. Use this chapter to get on the ball with SmartSuite team computing features.

"Printing" to Fax a File

If you have a fax modem and faxing software installed in your computer (many new systems do), you can use that fax modem to fax an open SmartSuite file. This saves you the trouble of printing a hard copy of the file, going to your fax machine, and running the pages through the machine (hoping that it doesn't jam). When you or your computer vendor installed your fax modem, the process included installing driver software for the fax modem as well as faxing software such as WinFax Pro. Some versions of Windows also offer faxing software called Microsoft Fax.

You can fax a Word Pro document; a Freelance Graphics presentation; a 1-2-3 worksheet; an Approach form, worksheet, or report; or an Organizer section.

Assuming your fax modem and its accompanying software have been set up correctly, use the following steps to fax an open file from a SmartSuite application:

1. Open the file you want to fax. If you're working in 1-2-3, select the worksheet to fax. In Approach, display the view to print. In Organizer, select the section to fax.

2. Choose File ⇨ Print. The Print dialog box opens.

3. Open the Print To drop-down list, and select the name of your faxing software, such as Microsoft Fax. For example, Figure 33-1 shows the Compaq Fax program selected as the printer.

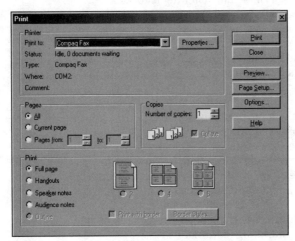

Figure 33-1: To fax a file, select the name of your fax software from the Print To drop-down list.

4. Choose any other needed printing options.

5. Choose Print. After a pause, the dialog box for sending a fax in your fax software appears (Figure 33-2 shows an example).

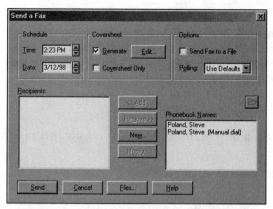

Figure 33-2: Your fax software displays a dialog box that enables you to specify fax recipients and create a cover sheet.

6. Use the options in the dialog box to specify one or more fax recipients (you may need to manually enter the name and number in some software), create a cover sheet, or set other faxing options. Consult the documentation or online Help for your fax software to learn what features it offers.

7. Choose Send or the equivalent command for sending the fax in your software. The software creates a copy of your file in a faxable, electronic format, dials the fax phone number, sends the fax, and shuts down automatically. You can then work with your SmartSuite file, or simply save and close it.

Dialing a Phone Number in Approach

Your team might organize key contact information such as a list of customers or vendors in an Approach database, rather than in Lotus Organizer, because Approach can capture more information and offers more ways for managing and using that data. As such, there's no reason for a team to duplicate certain lists of contact information if it's not warranted.

If an Approach database includes contact phone numbers, you can use your modem to dial one of those phone numbers. This saves you the trouble of looking up the phone number in another area. You can connect a handset phone to your data-only modem and use it to make the call.

Note Approach doesn't automatically recognize your modem, so you have to check its modem settings. Choose File ➪ User Setup ➪ Approach Preferences, then click the Dialer tab. Specify the settings for your modem, such as the COM (communications) port it's configured to use, then click OK.

Follow these steps to dial a call from Approach:

1. Start Approach and open the database that holds the number or numbers to call.

2. Display the view you want to work in (choosing a data entry form or worksheet works best).

3. Click in the field that holds the phone number to dial.

4. Choose Browse ➪ Dial or Worksheet ➪ Dial, depending on the view you're working in. The Dialing dialog box appears (see Figure 33-3) to tell you it's dialing the number.

Figure 33-3: Approach informs you as it dials the specified number.

5. When the call connects, pick up your phone handset.

6. After conducting your call, hang up the handset or the modem.

Using TeamMail

SmartSuite's TeamMail command enables you to send all or part of a SmartSuite file from within your SmartSuite application. You leave the file open and use the TeamMail command to send the message. TeamMail works along with your existing e-mail application, such as cc:Mail, Lotus Mail, or Outlook. TeamMail prepares and sends a message to your e-mail program's outbox, from which you can then send the message to the designated recipients.

The types of TeamMail messages you can send vary depending on which SmartSuite application you're sending from. Therefore, this section first looks at the differences between how the process starts in the various applications, then moves on to discuss common options and how to finish the send operation. To start the process in any application, open the file you'd like to send along with your TeamMail message; if you want to send only selected information from that file, also select the information to send.

Note

You can use the Team SmartIcon bar to send and manage TeamMail messages and work with other Team features in each SmartSuite application. Right-click any SmartIcon bar, then click Team to display the Team SmartIcon bar. It offers the Send an E-mail SmartIcon first. Click it to initiate a TeamMail message.

In Word Pro

Choose File ➪ TeamMail ➪ Send New Message to display the TeamMail dialog box for Word Pro (see Figure 33-4). In the Send area, choose the option button that defines exactly what to send: a Message Only, a Message with Current Selection's Text as Message Body, or the Current Document, as an Attachment. After you make your selection, click OK to continue sending the message, as described later under "Finishing the Message."

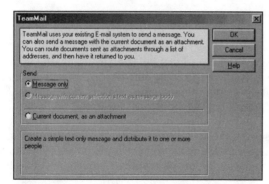

Figure 33-4: Use the TeamMail dialog box in Word Pro to control what type of message you send.

In 1-2-3

In 1-2-3, you only need choose File ➪ TeamMail. In the TeamMail dialog box that appears, choose an option under Send: Workbook with Message or Message Only. If you choose Message Only, you can check the Paste in a Picture of the Selection check box to insert a graphic of the selected range in the body of the message. (Your recipients cannot edit the information in this graphic.) Click OK to continue sending the message, as described later under "Finishing the Message."

In Freelance Graphics

In Freelance, choose File ➪ TeamMail. In the TeamMail dialog box that appears, choose an option under Send: Message Only; Specified Pages, As An Attachment; or Current Presentation, As An Attachment. If you choose Current Presentation, As An Attachment, you can check the Attach Mobile Screen Show Player, Too check box to also e-mail a copy of the Mobile Screen Show Player program, so that your recipient can play the presentation even if he or she doesn't have the Freelance Graphics program. Note that the file for the Mobile Screen Show Player is rather large, so attaching it adds to your transmission time and will take some time to be received by the recipient's system. Click OK to continue sending the message, as described later under "Finishing the Message." If you chose Specified Pages, As An Attachment in the TeamMail dialog box, the Mail Selected Pages dialog box appears. Click to place a check mark in the lower-left corner of each page to include, then click OK to continue sending the message.

 See the section called "Mobile Screen Show Player" in Chapter 19, "Creating and Running an Onscreen Show," to learn more about installing and distributing the Mobile Screen Show Player program.

In Approach

Choose File ➪ TeamMail ➪ Send New Message to display the TeamMail dialog box for Approach. To send a message only, click the Send button without selecting any options in the dialog box. Alternately, select the Snapshot of the Current View check box under Send to insert a graphic of the selected view in the body of the message. Or, select the Approach File With check box, then click an option button to indicate whether you want to send the Current View Only or All of the Views; to limit the file data you e-mail, also check Include Data From and choose the database information to e-mail from the accompanying drop-down list. Then, click Send to continue sending the message.

In Organizer

Choose File ➪ TeamMail to display the TeamMail dialog box for Organizer. In the Send area, choose the option button you want: Message Only or Message with Selected Entries as Message Body. (The latter option saves you the trouble of typing a message and ensures that you communicate dates and times accurately.) In the To area, choose People I Select from the Mail Directory if you want to address the message as described next under "Finishing the Message." Or, if you selected some Address section entries before choosing the TeamMail command, choose People from the Selected Addresses to address the message to those recipients. If you don't want to list those recipients in the message itself, also check Don't Include Address Entries in Message Body. Then, click OK and continue as described next to send the message.

Finishing the Message

After you click OK or Send from a SmartSuite application to continue sending a TeamMail message, Windows may display a Choose Profile dialog box, prompting you to select a user profile for use by Windows Messaging or Microsoft Exchange. Choose the profile to use from the Profile Name drop-down list, then click OK. Another TeamMail dialog box appears, offering two tabs you use to specify who should receive the file or message and how it should be routed.

Use the Basics tab to build the list of recipients, determine whether to route the message, and type the message text. In the Recipient column of the grid near the top of the tab, type an e-mail address on each line, or click the button with the envelope and pencil that appears at the right of the current line. Use the Names dialog box that appears to select the recipient. Choose the address book to use from the Show Names From The drop-down list.

To select each recipient, click the recipient name in the left list of the Names dialog box, then click the Name button. Click OK to finish specifying the recipients. Back on the Basics tab, you can click in the cell beside each recipient and type an individual message to that recipient. If you want to route the message, open the Select How to Distribute drop-down list, and choose Route from One Address to the Next. Check Return Document to Originator when Done to tell the SmartSuite application to include a Return to Originator command or button for the last recipient who works with the message, prompting that person to return the message to you. Choose a priority for the message from the Delivery Priority drop-down list. Then, enter the subject and message in the Subject and Message to All text boxes. Figure 33-5 shows example message information on the Basics tab.

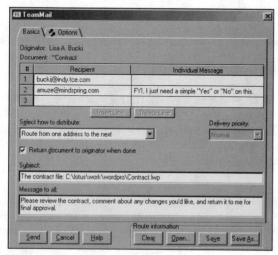

Figure 33-5: Enter your recipients and message information on the Basics tab.

TeamMail routes the message to the recipients in the order in which you list them in the Basics tab. Make sure you enter the recipients in the order you want, especially if one recipient needs to review comments made by an earlier recipient.

Before you continue sending the message, click the Options tab to make any settings you need before sending the document on. The top four check boxes only become active if you route the message. The first two check boxes (Send Message to Originator when Document Is Forwarded or Send Message to Alternate when Document Is Forwarded) automatically generate a tracking message each time a recipient forwards the message to the next recipient: either the originator (you) or an alternate person whose e-mail address you specify in the text box below the second check box.

Check Include Routed Document with Tracking Messages if you want to also receive a current copy of the routed document with each tracking message. Check the fourth check box, Allow Recipient to Modify Route, if you want to give recipients the flexibility to change the routing order. The final two options are available for regular or routed messages. Check Send Return Mail Receipt When Mail Message Is Opened if you want to receive an e-mail receipt as soon as the recipient opens the message (letting you know that you can then discuss the message, if needed). Check Save a Copy of This Message to keep a copy of the message so you can check it later, if needed.

Your Simple MAPI Client

Suppose you try to click Send to send a TeamMail message, see an error message, and click OK, which shuts down your SmartSuite application. This clearly means that TeamMail is having a problem communicating with your e-mail program. The *MAPI* (*Messaging Application Program Interface*) software installed behind the scenes on your system routes messages from individual applications like the TeamMail messages in SmartSuite applications to the e-mail program you want to use. For this to work, your e-mail program needs to be configured as the *simple MAPI client*. Some e-mail programs automatically configure themselves to be the simple MAPI client, such as Microsoft Exchange or Windows Messaging. In other instances, you must set up the application to be the simple MAPI client or choose which one to use if you have multiple e-mail programs installed on your system. The steps will vary between e-mail programs, but here's one example: In Outlook Express, choose Tools ➪ Options. On the General tab, check Make Outlook Express My Default Simple MAPI Client. An Options dialog box appears, warning you that checking this option disables MAPI features for other e-mail programs installed on your system. Click Yes to continue, then click OK. A message box warns you that you must restart your system. Click OK to close the message, then restart your system for the change to take effect. If you can't discover how to set your e-mail program as the MAPI client or otherwise get it to work, consult with your system administrator, or Lotus Technical Support and the Technical Support department for your e-mail program.

When you've specified all the information you need on the Basics and Options tab, click Send.

Sending the Message from Your E-mail Outbox

Depending on how you've configured your e-mail program, clicking Send may launch your e-mail program, dial your Internet connection or connect to your network, and then send the message. If you haven't set up your system to e-mail messages automatically, the messages go to your e-mail program's outbox (see the example in Figure 33-6). You need to manually open your e-mail program and send the message by clicking the Send (or Send and Receive) button or choosing the appropriate menu command. Your e-mail program connects to the Internet or network, if needed, and then sends the message.

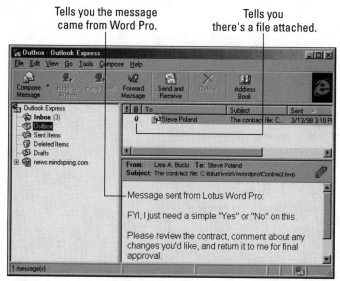

Figure 33-6: TeamMail messages go to your e-mail outbox, as shown here, if your mail program doesn't send them automatically.

Receiving and Responding to TeamMail Messages

Anyone receiving a TeamMail message likewise receives it in the inbox for his or her regular e-mail program. Of course, to receive the message, you or your recipient must start the e-mail program, connect to the Internet or Network as needed, and then issue the command for retrieving messages. (We'll assume from here that you're the recipient.) Then, open the message just like any regular e-mail message. The message will open, showing any file attachment sent as part of the TeamMail message, as shown in Figure 33-7. You can use the normal commands in your e-mail program for replying to or forwarding the message. You can save the file attachment, or double-click it to save it to disk or open it in the appropriate SmartSuite application.

When you open a routed file in Word Pro, Freelance, or Approach, the Send to Next Stop and Edit Route commands on the File ➪ TeamMail submenu become enabled. First make your changes and corrections to the file (marking the revisions or including comment notes, if needed), and save the file. If you want to change the routing order, use the File ➪ TeamMail ➪ Edit Route command to display the Basics tab of the TeamMail dialog box, in which you can only change the routing order for recipients. Make your changes to the order, then click Send to send the message. To stick with the original routing order, choose File ➪ TeamMail ➪ Send to Next Stop to forward the message to its next recipient. A message box asks whether you want to "Send to (Next Recipient)?" Click OK. TeamMail sends the file/message to your e-mail outbox. If your e-mail program doesn't send messages immediately, you'll need to send the message from your outbox manually.

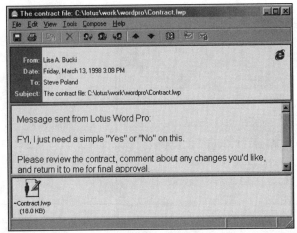

Figure 33-7: A received TeamMail message looks just like a regular e-mail message.

Note   If you're the last recipient of a routed message, use the File ➪ TeamMail ➪ Return to Originator command to route the file into which everyone has inserted comments back to its sender.

When you open a routed file in 1-2-3, the routing works a bit differently. When you open the routed file, a TeamMail (flow control) dialog box appears. The Contributor/Action list lists all the recipients, in order, with your name at the top of the list. ("Originator" appears beside the name of the person who sent the message. Type your comment about the file in the Comment text box, then click Send to Next to route the message to its next recipient, or Return to Originator if you're the last recipient.

The flow control dialog box doesn't offer any kind of close button. If you want to consider the file further and send your response at a later time, click the Close button for the file window. You can then later reopen the file attachment from your e-mail program.

Managing a Group Document Review

The TeamReview and TeamConsolidate (collectively called *team editing*) features in some of the SmartSuite applications work alone or in concert with TeamMail to help you request comments from colleagues, review those comments, and choose which comments to keep or discard. Word Pro, 1-2-3, and Freelance each offer some form of team editing capability, as detailed in this section.

Approach doesn't offer any team editing capabilities, because entering and using database information typically doesn't require collaboration, and because large database files are more likely to be stored on a network server, where other users can open them and use their information.

In Word Pro

Word Pro's team editing capabilities far outstrip those in the other SmartSuite applications, because text documents tend to be the most subject to revision (primarily because sentences are more subjective in nature than discrete values). Word Pro makes it easy to capture and track changes from different users, via such features as revision mark options, file versions, and TeamReview and TeamConsolidate.

Choosing Revision Mark Options

The revision markup options you set, along with the Personal tab information you enter in the Word Pro Preferences dialog box, identify your edits not only when you're marking up edits in your own files, but also how edits are handled when you're working with team editing features. As such, you may want to check the markup options you've selected. To do so, choose File ➪ User Setup ➪ Word Pro Preferences.

On the General tab, click the Markup Options button. The Markup Options for (Your Name) dialog box appears. Use the Markup for Insertions drop-down list to specify how to format insertions. Below that list, check Text Color and/or Background Color to apply one or both of those colors to inserted text, then choose the color to use from the accompanying drop-down lists. Use the Markup for Deletions drop-down list to specify how Word Pro marks deleted text. Then, choose the Same Colors as Insertions or Different Colors for Deletions option button. If you choose the latter, use its Text Color and Background Color check boxes/drop-down lists to apply a particular color. Finally, select a color for document highlighting from the Highlighter/Comment Color drop-down list. Click OK, then click OK again to close the Word Pro Preferences dialog box and finalize your choices.

Working with Versions

If you've ever used the File ➪ Save As command to copy a file under a new name, you've used a rudimentary form of *versioning*. Word Pro automates the process of creating versions of a file, whether each version was created by you or another editor. To create and work with versions in a file, choose File ➪ Versions. The Versions for File dialog box appears.

The most recent version appears at the top of the list (see Figure 33-8). You can edit only the most recent version. To do so, click it in the list, then click OK. You can click another version in the list and then click OK to open it, but the opened file version will be read-only, meaning that you cannot edit it. If you want to be able to edit an older version, click it in the list, then click the Save As File button, and specify a name and location under which to save the file.

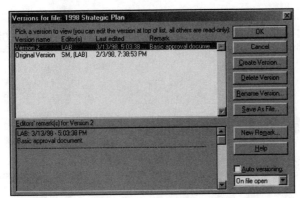

Figure 33-8: Create and work with versions in this dialog box.

To create a new version, click the Create Version button in the Versions for File dialog box. In the Create Document Version dialog box that appears, edit the name for the version in the Version Name text box, type any descriptive information about the file that you want in the Editor's Remark text box, then click OK.

To delete a version, select it in the list and then click the Delete Version button. In the warning message box that appears, click Yes to delete the version. To rename the selected version, click the Rename Version button, enter or edit the version name in the New Name For text box, then click OK. To add an additional remark for the selected version, click the New Remark button. Type the new remark in the Please Enter a New Editor's Remark text box, then click OK. Word Pro appends the new remark to the top of the list of remarks for that version.

If you want to have Word Pro automatically create versions for a file in case you forget to do so, check the Auto Versioning check box, then open the drop-down list below it, and specify whether to create each new version On File Open, Every Day, or Every Week. Finally, to close the Versions for File dialog box without opening a particular version, click Cancel.

Using TeamReview and TeamConsolidate

In Word Pro, TeamReview and TeamConsolidate work hand in hand.

TeamReview enables you to specify who you want to review a file, control what types of changes each reviewer can make, and determine how to distribute the file to those reviewers. Use the following steps to use TeamReview to prepare a file for editing by your colleagues:

1. Open the file that you want to send or route for review by others.

2. Choose File ⇨ TeamReview. The TeamReview Assistant dialog box appears.

3. Use the Step 1: Who tab to specify who you want to allow to edit the file or who to route it to. Open the Verify Editors By drop-down list, and choose whether you want to identify each editor by Word Pro User Name (as entered in the Personal tab of the Word Pro Preferences dialog box), OS Login (the name the person uses to log on to Windows or the network), or E-mail Login. Then, to add each editor, click the Add button, enter the name in the New Editor's Name dialog box, then click OK. Click Next after you've finished specifying all the editors.

4. Use the Step 2: What tab to control how Word Pro handles edits made by the various reviewers; set the options you want, then click Next:

   • Leave Set Options for All People to Review and Comment selected if you don't want to change the default reviewing options or set specific options for specific users.

   • Choose the Set Specific Options for All People Sharing the Document to set limits on how each reviewer can comment on the document, enabling the three drop-down lists below that option button. Open the Edits Are drop-down list, and choose an option from the list to specify where each user may make changes, such as only in comment notes; your choice in this drop-down list controls what the next two drop-down lists offer, or whether both remain active. Open the Limited To drop-down list, and click to check each rule you want to enforce (such as preventing printing or specifying that all edits will be marked), then click the check to close the drop-down list. Use the Greeting Will Suggest drop-down list to display one or more greetings that suggests a particular user action; click to check each greeting, then click the drop-down list check to close it.

- If you want different editors to be able to perform different types of edits, click the Set Specific Options for Specific People drop-down list, then click the Options button to display the Editing Rights tab of the TeamSecurity dialog box. Set the rights for each editor (see the later discussion of TeamSecurity), then click OK.

- To display a greeting when each editor opens the file, check Display Greeting with This Text, then type the greeting in the text box below.

- Check Request Editor's Remark on Close to display a message box prompting the reviewer to enter a remark before the file closes.

5. Open the Distribute Document By drop-down list on the Step 3: How tab to determine how you will distribute the document. Choose Saving Document to a File to simply save a copy of the file so that you can give team members a disk copy. Choose Saving Document to a File on Internet or Saving Document to Notes to save the file to an Internet location or in a Notes database. Choose Saving Documents and Sending Via E-mail or Saving Document and Routing Via E-mail to send or route the file via TeamMail.

6. Click Done. Depending on your choice in Step 5, Word Pro will either display the Save As dialog box so you can name and save the file, prompt you for an Internet location or Notes database to save it to, or start a TeamMail message, which you can then send to others.

When you or another user opens a file that's been set up with TeamReview, Word Pro displays any greeting you specified in a Document Greeting Message dialog box. The dialog box explains any editing rules set up for the file. Leave Edit in New Version selected from the Would You Like To drop-down list, unless you want to open a read-only version of the file.

To automatically open the Review & Comment Tools SmartIcon bar, check Show Review and Comment Tools. Click the Markup Style icon to choose options for marking up your edits (you only need to do this if you want to use markup formatting other than what you specified by clicking the Markup Options button on the General tab of the Word Pro Preferences dialog box). Click OK. Word Pro creates a new version, if needed, to hold the marked edits, and turns on the markup edits feature. Make your changes and comments, then save and close the file. If you're prompted to enter an editor's remark, enter it in the Editor's Remark Please dialog box and click OK.

After you've gathered the various copies of the reviewed file, use the following steps to consolidate the edits:

1. If you want to consolidate the edits into the original file, open it in Word Pro. Or, if you prefer, open a new, blank file into which you'd like to consolidate the edits.

2. Choose File ➪ TeamConsolidate. The TeamConsolidate dialog box appears.

3. For each reviewer file (or routed file) you've received, click the Add Files button beside Select the Files to Compare to Your Current File. In the Browse dialog box that appears, navigate to and select the file you want to add to the list of those to consolidate, then click Open. Similarly, if you stored the file in an Internet location or in a Notes database, use the Internet or Notes button to retrieve the file or copies of it from the location where you placed it for TeamReview.

4. Under Protect Current Version of This Document?, leave the top option button selected to create a new version of the document; or click No, Consolidate and Markup into the Current Version of This Document, to insert all the comments in a new file version.

5. Under What Do You Want to Do with the Consolidated Document, leave the top option button selected to insert the consolidated version into the currently open file. To insert the consolidated version in a completely new file, click Put the Consolidated Document into a Copy of This File.

6. Click OK. TeamConsolidate consolidates all the edits in a new file version, in the current file, or a new file, and displays the Review Bar, so you can review each edit and decide whether to keep or reject it. See "Marking and Reviewing Revisions, Highlighting, and Comment Notes" in Chapter 3, "Creating and Working with Documents," to learn how to work with the Review bar.

7. After you've worked through the revisions, save and close the file.

In 1-2-3

1-2-3 provides more limited TeamReview features, as questions about worksheets often revolve around verifying a range of numbers or formulas. To start the process, select the range about which you need feedback. Choose File ➪ TeamReview. The TeamReview dialog box appears (see Figure 33-9). If you didn't first select the range to send, click the select range button at the right end of the Range text box, drag on the worksheet to select the range, then click the green Enter check box in the Range Selected dialog box to redisplay the TeamReview dialog box. Then, beside As, click Formulas and Values or Values Only to specify whether you want your reviewers to check the formulas and results, or the resulting values only. Click OK.

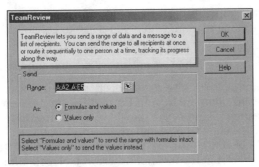

Figure 33-9: You can distribute a range of worksheet cells for comment using 1-2-3's TeamReview dialog box.

Another TeamReview dialog box appears, and the work area changes to display only the range you selected to send for TeamReview. The dialog box prompts you to make any changes you want to the data. Make them, and then click Send. 1-2-3 displays the TeamMail dialog box, so you can send or route the message to a list of recipients and set message and routing options, as described earlier under "Finishing the Message," and then click Send to save the file and send the message to your e-mail program. From there, your e-mail program will send it automatically, or you may need to send it manually from your outbox, as described earlier.

When you or a recipient receives a 1-2-3 range sent for TeamReview, the range appears as an e-mail message attachment, and any additional message appears as the body of the e-mail message. Double-click the file attachment to open it in 1-2-3 (specifying that you want to open the file if prompted). The range appears in 1-2-3, along with a different TeamReview (flow control) dialog box. Your name appears at the top of the Contributor/Action list in the TeamReview dialog box. Make any changes you want to apply to the range, enter needed notes in the Comment text box of the TeamReview dialog box, and then click Send to Next or Return to Originator. The message routes back via your e-mail program.

If you've received e-mail messages containing replies to TeamMail you've sent via the TeamReview feature in 1-2-3, when you open the attachment in 1-2-3, the TeamReview (flow control) dialog box opens. Enter the notes you have in the Comment text box, then make any changes needed in the range itself. Click Send to Next or Return to Originator to send your changes and comments on to the next routing recipient via your e-mail program.

When you've received an e-mail message that contains an attachment you earlier routed for TeamReview, the TeamReview (flow control) dialog box opens when you open the sent or routed attachment. Click the Merge button to merge all the routed changes or Range (then selecting the range(s) to merge) to merge the reviewers' changes. Choose File ➪ Save or File ➪ Save As to save the changes you've incorporated into your worksheet.

In Freelance

In Freelance, you can distribute only the whole presentation for review. To do so, open the presentation file and choose File ➪ TeamReview. Read the instructions in the TeamReview dialog box that appears, then click OK. The Distribute for TeamReview dialog box appears. Open the Distribute Presentation By drop-down list, then specify whether you want to distribute the file by Posting in a Notes Database, Posting in a Public Directory, Routing via E-mail, or Save to a Floppy Disk(s). If you're posting to a Notes database, enter the path and file name in the Notes Database text box. If you chose to post to a network directory, enter the path to that shared directory in the Path and File Name text box. In either case, leave the Notify Reviewers by E-mail check box checked to also send an e-mail message notifying the reviewers of the location of the file to review.

Choose one of the option buttons beside Reviewer Privileges. You can choose Commenting Only to restrict the reviewers to including comment notes, or Commenting or Editing to enable reviewers to enter presentation content. Click OK. The Set Password for Editing dialog box appears if you specified that recipients can edit the presentation in addition to including comment notes. If you want to create a password, enter it in the Password text box, then enter it again in the Verify text box. Click OK. A dialog box appears to prompt you to specify where to send the presentation, depending on your choice from the Distribute Presentation By drop-down list. For example, if you're creating copies of the file to send, the Distribute Presentation on Floppy Disk dialog box appears. Specify a Drive and a File Name, and click OK. When prompted by the Insert Floppy Disk dialog box, insert a floppy disk into the drive, then click OK. After Freelance makes one floppy disk copy, the Make Another Copy? Dialog box appears. Click Yes to repeat the process, or No to finish making copies. When the Distribution Complete dialog box appears, choose Save and Close the Presentation to finish working with the presentation, or Save and Resume Editing the Presentation if you want to continue working. Click OK to close the dialog box and proceed.

If you open a Freelance file or message attachment that's been distributed for TeamReview, the TeamReview Access Rights dialog box appears. Choose your name from the Name drop-down list, then click Add comments using TeamReview Commenting Tools or Edit the Presentation Content to specify how you want to edit the presentation. Then, enter the password in the Password text box and click OK. If the Merge Now dialog box appears, click Merge Now to merge the comments directly into the original file; otherwise, click Cancel. If the Instructions for Reviewers dialog box appears, review the instructions for adding comments to the file, then click OK.

When the Freelance file opens for your edits and comments, make your changes, or click the buttons that appear to the left of the displayed page to create comments. When you finish making your comments, choose File ➪ Save to save the file. Then, choose File ➪ Done Reviewing – Notify Author. The Browse for Folder dialog box appears. Select the folder in which to store your copy of the file, then click OK. The TeamMail dialog box appears. Verify where to send or route the message, edit the Subject or Message to All text boxes, then click Send to e-mail the file directly or to send it to your e-mail program's outbox.

If you open the original file you previously distributed for TeamReview in Freelance Graphics, a Warning dialog box appears. It reminds you that when you receive and open copies of the review file, you should choose Yes if Freelance asks whether you want to merge the changes. Click Open to continue opening the file. Then, choose File ➪ TeamReview ➪ Consolidate Comments for each reviewed file that holds comments to incorporate. In the Consolidate Comments dialog box that appears, use the Browse button to select the file that holds comments to incorporate, then click OK. Choose the command and use the Browse button again to incorporate comments from other reviewer copies of the file.

Alternately, if you open an individual file returned to you by a reviewer, it appears onscreen, showing comments, as shown in Figure 33-10. Choose File ➪ TeamReview ➪ Merge Comments into Parent if you want to add that reviewer's comments into the original presentation file. In the Merge Comments into Parent dialog box that appears, edit the path and file name for the original file in the Parent File Name text box, or use the Browse button to find the file. Click OK to merge the comments into the original presentation file. When you've incorporated comments from all the needed files, choose File ➪ TeamReview ➪ End Review to finish reviewing the file.

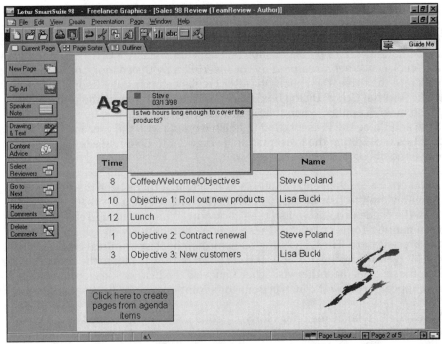

Figure 33-10: Freelance TeamReview comments look like Word Pro comment notes.

Using TeamSecurity to Protect Your Work

The lone downside to team editing occurs when an unintended collaborator makes changes to or even ruins a file. Fortunately, Word Pro and Approach offer protection against such occurrences by offering TeamSecurity features that enable you to limit who can access and edit your files.

As you learned in the preceding TeamReview section, you don't route entire files in 1-2-3 and in Freelance; you can open each individual review file before you consolidate its comments. So, 1-2-3 and Freelance don't have an urgent need for security features. However, because you may frequently route Word Pro files to a number of users and because users often access Approach databases from a shared network drive, both these applications offer TeamSecurity. You apply TeamSecurity settings to individual files, as described in this section. Start by opening the file that needs security protection. After selecting the TeamSecurity features you want, save the file to enable those security features.

In Word Pro

Choose File ⇨ TeamSecurity to display the TeamSecurity dialog box, shown in Figure 33-11. The first tab, Access, enables you to create passwords and control who can open the file or change security settings. The first area, Who Can Open (Access) This File, offers the choices for controlling who can open and edit the file. Anyone (Unprotected) removes any previously selected protection. Current Editors Only tells Word Pro that only users you list on the Editing Rights tab of the TeamSecurity dialog box can open the file. Original Author Only sets up the file so that only you can open it. Selecting Anyone with This Password enables the Change button; click that button, type a new password of up to 50 characters in the Enter New File Password dialog box, then click OK.

Under Who Can Open This Dialog, and Change Access, Editing Rights, and Other Protection Options, choose Anyone (Unprotected) if you want to enable any user to be able to change the TeamSecurity settings for the file. If you don't, click the Only option button, then select the editor who you want to control the file's security. To allow access by several people, choose Anyone with This Password and click the Change button; type a new password of up to 50 characters in the Enter New File Password dialog box, then click OK. Open the Verify Editors Using drop-down list, and choose whether Word Pro will check the Word Pro User Name, OS Login, or E-mail Login to verify that the person is indeed an editor allowed access to the file. If you choose OS Login or E-mail Login, make sure the Allow Alternate Verification check box remains checked, to ensure that Word Pro checks the specified type of login name.

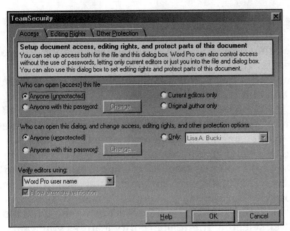

Figure 33-11: In Word Pro, you can use TeamSecurity to assign passwords, control what users can edit, and more.

Click the Editing Rights tab to designate (by Word Pro User Name or login name) who can edit the file (if you selected Current Editors Only on the Access tab). For each new editor, click the New Editor button to display the New Editor dialog box. Type the editor's exact Word Pro User Name, OS Login name, or E-mail Login in the New Editor's Name text box, and click OK. Then, to specify what type of edits the editor can make, click the editor's name in the list, and make your selections from the Edits Are, Limited To, and Greeting Will Suggest drop-down lists.

Your selection from the Edits Are drop-down list specifies where each editor may make changes, such as only in comment notes; whatever you select in this drop-down list determines what the next two drop-down lists offer, or whether both remain active. Open the Limited To drop-down list, and click to check each rule you want to enforce (such as preventing printing or specifying that all edits will be marked), then click the check to close the drop-down list.

Use the Greeting Will Suggest drop-down list to select one or more greetings (which appear when the editor opens the file) that suggest particular editor action or guide the editor as to where he or she can make changes; click to check each greeting, then click the drop-down list check to close it. You also can click the Markup button to display the dialog box for controlling the appearance of the editor's insertions and deletions. Add as many editors as needed, and set the editing rights for each. Finally, to display a custom greeting when any editor opens the file, check Display Greeting with This Text, and then type the greeting in the text box below. Check Request Editor's Remark on Close to display a message box prompting each editor to enter a remark before the file closes.

The final tab, Other Protection, enables you to control whether editors can see certain parts of the document. For example, you may want editors to fine-tune language in one document division without seeing sensitive financial information in another section. Under Division Protection, check Display All Division Tabs in Document to ensure that editors may display the division tabs, even if you hide one or more divisions. Then, open the Protection Settings for Division drop-down list, and select the division for which you want to add special protection; your selections in the remaining four check boxes in that area of the dialog box then apply to the selected division only. Check Hide Entire Division to hide the selected division. Check Honor Protection on Frames and Table Cells to prevent editors from making changes to them. Select Allow Editing of Protected Text if you want to temporarily turn off text protection. Check Show Hidden Text to display that text in the protected division; clear the check box to prevent editors from viewing that hidden text.

Note

Remember: You have to use an InfoBox to assign protection to document elements or hide or protect selected text. On the Font, Attribute, and Color tab of the Text InfoBox, choose Hidden or Protected from the Attributes list to hide or protect the selection. To protect a selected frame, display the Frame InfoBox, click the Misc. tab, and select Protect Frame from the Other Options drop-down list. For a table, first protect individual cells by checking the Protect Cell check box on the Misc. tab of the Table Cell InfoBox. Then, on the Misc. tab of the Table InfoBox, check Prevent Editing of Protected Cells to prevent anyone from editing the contents of cells you've protected, or Protect Entire Table to protect the contents of all the table cells.

The Team Protection Options area of the dialog box enables you to control some facets of team editing for the whole protected file. Check Disable Version Review to prevent TeamReview and the creation of versions within the protected document. Checking Disable Notes/FX of TeamSecurity Fields prevents the protected document from exchanging information with a Notes database. Use Require Running of Startup Scripts to ensure that all startup scripts for the document run when the document opens. To enable any editor to change the prompts for Click Here blocks, select the Edit Click Here Block Prompts On-Screen check box.

After you specify all the TeamSecurity settings for the document, click OK to apply them and close the dialog box.

In Approach

Choosing File ➪ TeamSecurity in Approach displays a TeamSecurity dialog box that lists different users who have access to the file. You also can display this dialog box by choosing File ➪ User Setup ➪ Approach Preferences, and then the TeamSecurity button on the Password tab. Typically, you'll need to set up new access for a single user or a group of users.

Using Protection to Create and Use Preprinted Forms

You can use Word Pro's TeamSecurity features and printing features in combination to create preprinted fill-in forms, and later print the fill-in information in only selected areas (blanks) of the form. For example, you can create a table that includes each fill-in "prompt" in the left column, as well as borders for the table cells. Leave the right-hand cells blank, and then print your "form." Next, apply protection to the prompt text in the left-hand cells. (You don't need to protect the whole table.) Open the TeamSecurity dialog box and select its Other Protection tab. Select the name of the division that holds the table from the Protection Settings for Division drop-down list, check Honor Protection on Frames and Cells, and clear the check beside Allow Editing of Protected text. Click OK and save the document. Then, you open the document for the form, and type your specific responses to fill in the right column of table cells. Insert one of the blank forms you printed earlier into the printer, remembering to place it face up or face down as required by your particular printer. Choose File ⇨ Print, click the Options button, then check On Preprinted Form under Print Options. Click OK, then Print to print your responses on the preprinted form.

Click the New button to display the Edit TeamSecurity dialog box. Enter the name of the group or user for whom you want to restrict access in the Group or User Name text box. The name you enter doesn't have to be the user's OS login or network group name; it can be any descriptive label you want to make up for the user or group. To require the user or group member to enter a password in order to open the file, type the password you want in the Approach File Password text box.

The bottom of the dialog box offers three tabs: Database, View, and Advanced. On the Database and View tabs, click to check each database or view that you want to enable the user or group members to be able to open. Clear the check beside any element you want to prevent the user or group members from opening. On the Advanced tab, select the Designer Privileges check box to enable the designated user or group members to make changes to the database and report structures. When it's available, check the Change Passwords check box to enable the user or group to change the passwords you've assigned.

Finally, you can assign passwords to specific databases on the database tab, requiring the user or group members to enter a password before they can work with a database. To do so, click the Database tab, then check the Require Passwords for Each Database check box. Then, click the Database Password button. On the Password tab of the Approach Preferences dialog box, select the database to protect from the Database drop-down list, check Read/Write Password, then type the password to use in the accompanying text box. Repeat the process for other databases, then click OK to close the Approach Preferences dialog box.

Click OK again to close the Edit TeamSecurity dialog box and finish specifying the access settings for the new user or group. The user or group name appears in the list in the TeamSecurity dialog box. You can use the New button to create new user or group entries. Or, you can click an entry in the list, and use the Delete button to delete it, or the Edit button to change the access settings you previously specified. When you finish specifying TeamSecurity settings, click Done to close the TeamSecurity dialog box and apply those settings to the Approach file.

Using TeamShow to "Broadcast" a Freelance Presentation

If you've tried to schedule a meeting lately, you know how tough it can be to gather all your audience members in the same room at the same time. To overcome this problem, Freelance Graphics enables you to broadcast a presentation over your company's network so that no one has to leave his or her office. Ideally, you'll want to simultaneously conference call with those users so that you can deliver your oral presentation along with the onscreen one. This section covers how to work with TeamShow, whether you're the sender or the receiver.

Sending a TeamShow

Team Show uses TCP/IP, the same network "language" that computers use to communicate over the Internet. A network with TCP/IP uses a machine or TCP/IP name (as in `bucki.lotus.com`) or an IP address (four groups of numbers separated by periods, as in 000.00.000.00) to identify each computer connected to the network. To send information to a specific computer, you need to tell the network which TCP/IP name or IP address to send to. So, the first step in preparing to broadcast a TeamShow is to gather a list of the TCP/IP names or IP addresses for all computers (and therefore, all users) to which you want to broadcast the show. Each receiver connected to a company network can find this information by choosing File ⇨ TeamShow ⇨ Receive, then clicking Next to display the TeamShow: Your Computer's Identity dialog box, which lists the machine name and IP address for the system. Alternately, your network system administrator can generally provide this information for a list of users.

Once you've compiled a list of users and machine names or IP addresses, keep it handy for future use and reference. Your computer must be connected to the network and logged on, obviously; but you won't need the machine name or IP address for your system.

The fact that the Internet uses TCP/IP doesn't necessarily mean it's easy to broadcast a TeamShow to a colleague over the Internet. That's because most Internet Service Providers (ISPs) assign IP addresses dynamically. That is, the ISP's server computer assigns a different available IP address for an individual user's system each time that user logs on. In some cases, users can make arrangements with the ISP to receive a static IP address. In other instances, the ISP can tell a user how to check the IP address being used for the current connection, so that the user can call you with that address; however, he or she will have to remain connected until you complete the broadcast. If your receivers have their own site connected to the Internet, you may instead be able to use the machine name for the site. The last problem, though, is if either network is protected by a *firewall*. Firewalls prevent the transmission of TeamShow presentations.

IP addresses generally are easier for TCP/IP to understand than machine names. Anything numeric, such as an IP address, is easier for a computer to understand than alphanumeric information, such as a machine name. So, if you're having trouble connecting via machine names, try IP addresses instead.

Once you have your list of IP addresses, you can start Freelance and open the presentation you want to broadcast. Choose File ➪ TeamShow ➪ Send. A Welcome dialog box appears. Review the information it presents, then click Next. The TeamShow: Connecting by Network dialog box appears. You use this dialog box to specify the IP addresses to which Freelance broadcasts the show. To specify each machine (TCP/IP) name or IP address, enter it in the Type in the TCP/IP Name or IP Address of the New Site text box, then click the Add button to add it to the Select the Remote Sites for This Session list (see Figure 33-12). If your list already contains some sites, click to check each site to which you want to broadcast the show, or clear the check beside each name or address to which you don't want to broadcast the show.

After you've selected your broadcast list, a dialog box informs you that Freelance is ready to connect to your audience and send the show. Click the Finish button to do so.

Receiving a TeamShow

Receiving a TeamShow requires much less effort than broadcasting the show. If you're scheduled to receive a TeamShow, choose File ➪ TeamShow ➪ Receive. The TeamShow: Preparing to Receive Remove Screenshow dialog box appears. Review the information it offers, then click Next. The TeamShow: Your Computer's Identity dialog box appears. Provide the identity information about your computer to the TeamShow sender, if needed, then click Next. The TeamShow: Ready to Receive Remove Presentation dialog box appears. Review its instructions, then click Finish. The TeamShow: Waiting for Sender dialog box appears. As soon as the sender begins broadcasting the show, that dialog box disappears, and the show begins playing on your system.

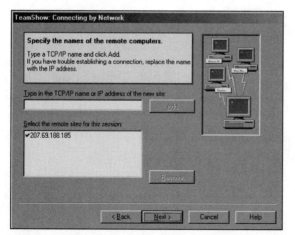

Figure 33-12: When you send a TeamShow, you specify the TCP/IP name or IP address of each computer to which you want to broadcast the show.

✦　　✦　　✦

Exploiting Other Features

This part covers special-purpose SmartSuite features. The ScreenCam chapter tells you how to capture onscreen keystrokes and commands and voice over as a movie that other users can replay. (This is a great way to show team members exactly what to do with a document.) See here how to record and save a movie, rerecord the screentrack or soundtrack, or add captions. You'll also explore how to create a movie in segments that you can later rearrange. When you finish, e-mail your movie to colleagues who need it.

In this part, you'll also learn what linking and embedding is, and how you can use it to integrate the SmartSuite applications. You'll also find out about how you can use your voice to select commands and enter content in specific SmartSuite applications.

Using ScreenCam

Lotus ScreenCam is a utility that enables you to capture a sequence of actions into a "movie," complete with video and audio. Movies made with ScreenCam can be used to illustrate how to perform a complex action in an application. You can use a series of movies to provide computer-based training, or simply to walk someone through the procedure for carrying out a task.

Once you have recorded a ScreenCam movie, you can give it to someone else. Anyone can play a ScreenCam movie — they don't have to have a copy of ScreenCam, nor do they have to have the application you were demonstrating in ScreenCam. You can either provide the recipient with a free "player" program (which can play any ScreenCam movie), or create a self-running movie. You can even send someone the movie over the Internet.

The video portion of a ScreenCam movie is a recording of whatever is happening on your screen, including opening applications, choosing menu options, moving the mouse, editing text, pressing onscreen buttons, and almost any other action you can perform on your screen. This video portion is referred to as a *screentrack*. Typically, you use a ScreenCam movie to show how to perform a sequence of actions in an application such as Approach or 1-2-3.

To create the audio portion of a ScreenCam movie, you need a microphone and sound card. While you are performing the screentrack actions on the screen, you can record an audio explanation of what is happening on the screen. This audio portion is known as a *soundtrack,* or sometimes as a *voice-over.*

In addition to the soundtrack, you can also add text captions that pop up on the screen at strategic times to add additional explanation, or provide explanations to people who don't have sound cards (and thus can't hear the soundtrack).

Note   Keep in mind that ScreenCam movies can get huge. If you have a high-resolution monitor and choose high quality sound for your recordings, the files can reach multi-megabyte sizes in a hurry. Use the minimum screen resolution that will get your point across, and choose radio or telephone quality (more on this later) sound—this quality is sufficient for a voice-over.

Preparing to Create a ScreenCam Movie

Like a screenplay, a ScreenCam movie should be based on a written script. In the script, you should figure out what actions you want to accomplish, and the dialogue you want to use in the movie. It is best to create multiple short "scenes" for your movie, just as they do for films. This is because it is easy to make a mistake during the recording, and if you do, you must "reshoot" the scene. Short scenes (under a page of script) are easier to reshoot, and also easier to memorize for recording the scene (because you must watch the screen and not the script page during the recording). You don't have to worry about creating the final movie from the scenes because ScreenCam makes it easy to create a complete movie from a series of scenes.

Reviewing the ScreenCam Controls

When you first open ScreenCam, you get a control panel (see Figure 34-1) that provides all the buttons you need to record, control, and playback your recording. The control panel looks much like the front panel of a VCR, and contains many of the same controls.

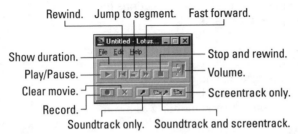

Figure 34-1: The main ScreenCam control panel gives you all the controls for recording and playing back your movie.

The following list describes what the controls on the control panel do:

✦ **Play/Pause.** This control plays or pauses the current movie. If there is movie in memory (either one you recorded or one that you opened from the File menu), this button enables you to play the movie. While the movie is playing, you can click this same button to pause the playback.

✦ **Rewind.** This control rewinds the current movie. While a movie is playing (or paused), clicking this button sends the movie back to the beginning. It then begins playing at the beginning again.

✦ **Jump to Segment.** This control jumps to a segment during playback. If you have built a movie using segments (See "Working with Segments," later in this chapter), you can click this button to see a list of the segments in the movie. You can then choose a segment, and ScreenCam will jump directly to that segment and start playing it.

✦ **Fast Forward.** This control fast forwards the current movie. While a movie is playing (or paused) clicking this button advances the movie quickly (like fast forward on a tape deck or VCR).

✦ **Stop and Rewind.** This control stops the current movie right where it is and rewinds it back to the beginning.

✦ **Show Duration.** This control shows the duration of the movie. The line that advances through the duration bar graphically shows how much of the movie has finished playing.

✦ **Volume.** This control adjusts the sound volume during playback. To adjust the sound volume during playback, click the slider and drag it up (to increase volume) or down (to decrease volume).

✦ **Record.** This control starts a ScreenCam recording. There is a pause before the recording starts, so make sure to wait until after the pause. To tell when ScreenCam is ready to record, wait for the Stop Panel to appear. If you have turned off the Stop Panel using Preferences (see "Using Preferences to Control Movie Parameters" later in this chapter), then just wait until the title bar of the current application becomes active (not "grayed-out").

✦ **Clear Movie.** This control clears the current movie from memory. If you haven't saved the movie, ScreenCam asks if you want to save the movie before deleting it.

✦ **Soundtrack Only.** When this control (with a small picture of a microphone on it) is selected, ScreenCam records only the voice-over soundtrack. None of the movements of the mouse or the screen are recorded.

✦ **Soundtrack and Screentrack.** When this control is selected, both the soundtrack (voice-over) and the screentrack (screen movements) are recorded as part of the ScreenCam movie.

✦ **Screentrack Only.** When this control is selected, the screentrack is recorded, but the soundtrack is ignored and not included as part of the ScreenCam movie.

Preparing to Record

ScreenCam provides a number of preferences and controls for configuring how it will work. First of all, you can configure the keyboard keys (known as *hotkeys*) that you use for controlling ScreenCam. Next, you can configure a set of preferences that control how the movie is recorded, which controls are available on the screen during the recording, items that are included in the ScreenCam recording, and parameters that control sound quality. You can also set the location for storing temporary ScreenCam files created during a recording (this can be an important issue if your hard drive is nearly full). Finally, you can configure the display and playback options (called *object settings*) that will be used when you include a ScreenCam movie in another document.

Setting the Hotkeys

While you are recording a movie, you need to control certain aspects of recording. For example, you might need to pause a recording. You can't use your mouse to perform these actions because the mouse movement would be recorded as part of the movie. Instead, ScreenCam enables you to use the keyboard to perform these actions. These keyboard keys are known as *hotkeys*. To set the hotkeys you use for controlling ScreenCam from the keyboard, choose Hot Keys from the Edit menu. ScreenCam opens the Hot Keys dialog box (see Figure 34-2). The dialog box is split into three sections: For Recording, For Playback, and For Captions.

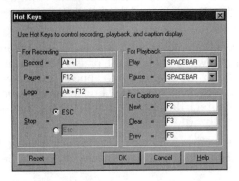

Figure 34-2: The Hot Keys dialog box enables you to configure the keys you use to control ScreenCam.

Setting the "For Recording" Hotkeys

You can set the following keys:

   ✦ **Record.** This key (default is F12) starts the recording. The Record/Pause key is handy for starting and pausing a recording if you have chosen not to display the Stop Panel (which provides buttons for recording and pausing a recording). Without the Stop panel on the screen, you must use the Record/Pause hotkey to perform these actions.

✦ **Pause.** While you are recording, you can press the Pause key (default is F12) to pause the recording sequence. As you will see later, you can build a whole series of short movie "scenes" by pausing.

✦ **Logo.** This key (default is Alt+F12) toggles the onscreen logo off and on. The *logo* is a graphic that you can choose to display (see "Using Preferences to Control Movie Parameters," later in this chapter) so people viewing the recording know it is a ScreenCam recording. Under preferences you can choose to use the default logo or choose another graphic.

✦ **Stop.** To stop the recording altogether, press the Stop key (default is Esc).

Setting the "For Playback" Hotkeys

You can set the following keys:

✦ **Play.** The play key (default is the spacebar) starts a playback of the current movie in memory.

✦ **Pause.** While the movie is playing back, you can press the Pause key (default is the spacebar) to pause the playback.

Setting the "For Captions" Hotkeys

You can set the following keys:

✦ **Next.** When you are recording a movie, and you have created text captions (see "Using Captions for Clarity," below), pressing the Next button (default is F2) displays the next caption in the sequence at the position you designated when building the caption.

✦ **Clear.** When you are recording a movie and you have placed a caption on the screen, you can remove the current caption (leaving no captions on the screen) by pressing the Clear key (default is F3).

✦ **Previous.** When you are recording a movie and you have created text captions, pressing the Prev button (default is F5) displays the previous caption in the sequence at the position you designated when building the caption.

Using Preferences to Control Movie Parameters

To edit ScreenCam's various preferences, choose Preferences from the Edit menu. ScreenCam displays the Preferences dialog box (see Figure 34-3). The dialog box has three tabs: Panel, Settings, and Temp Files. Each of these tabs is discussed in the following sections.

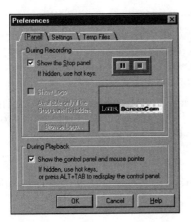

Figure 34-3: Configure ScreenCam the way you want using the Preferences dialog box. Displayed here is the Panel tab.

The Panel Tab

Using the Panel tab, you can choose the following options:

✦ Whether to show the Stop panel while recording. The Stop panel provides two small buttons for starting, pausing, and stopping a recording. If you choose to show the Stop panel, it is visible in your ScreenCam recording, as are the mouse movements to and from the Stop panel to use its controls. If you don't want to use the Stop panel, you can control the progress of the recording using the hotkeys defined in the last section.

✦ If you choose not to show the Stop panel, you might want some other way to let observers of the movie know it is a movie and not "the real thing." If you don't display the Stop panel, this next option becomes available—to show a logo on the screen. You can click on the Browse logo button to pick any bmp graphic file as the logo.

✦ During playback, you can choose whether to show or hide the ScreenCam control panel and mouse pointer. If you hide these items, the playback looks like a "live" demo of the application recorded in the movie. Otherwise, the ScreenCam control panel appears, and the mouse pointer looks like a bit of film. If you choose to hide these items, you'll have to control the playback using the hot keys defined in the last section.

The Settings Tab

The settings in this tab (see Figure 34-4) control the fine detail of the recording—and have quite an impact on the size of the resulting movie file. The options are as follows:

✦ **Allow Resizing of the movie view during playback.** By checking this option, you can focus on a specific part of the movie by resizing the movie window, and then change the portion of the movie that displays in that window.

✦ **Emphasize font fidelity during recording.** If you want the fonts (which are small and finely detailed) to look just like they did in the original application, you can check this option. However, the movie file must record more detail, and is subsequently larger than it would be otherwise.

✦ **Show ToolTips and Show All hidden help messages.** While you are recording the movie, various tool tips (the yellow flags that remind you what an icon does), and other help messages may appear in the application you are recording. If you don't check these options, they won't be recorded into the ScreenCam movie.

✦ **Set the Sound Recording Quality.** In general, ScreenCam does not take advantage of high-quality sound, but using high-quality sound *will* significantly increase the size of the movie file because the sound requires more data. This option enables you to pick three quantities that set the sound quality. The defaults work well, but you can change the sample rate, sample size, and number of channels.

The sample rate corresponds to how often the voice recording is sampled. The more often the recording is sampled, the more fidelity there is in the recording. For example, a "telephone quality" sampling occurs at about 11kHz, while a CD-audio quality sampling occurs at 44kHz.

The sample size corresponds to how many discrete "steps" the measured sample can be broken up into. An 8-bit sample has 256 steps, while a 16-bit sample has 65,536 discrete steps. The more steps, the truer the sound — but a 16-bit sample takes up twice as much room as an 8-bit sample.

Finally, the number of channels has only two values: mono and stereo. If you record in mono, both the speakers connected to your sound card will have the same signal. Because you will undoubtedly use a single microphone, the recorded signal is inherently mono anyway — so why create a voice track that is stereo (and twice the size of a mono soundtrack)?

Figure 34-4: The Settings Tab enables you to set quantities that impact the quality of the recording — and the size.

The Temp Files Tab

ScreenCam generates some *really* big temporary files while it is working. This tab enables you to specify where you want the temporary files stored. If you have only a single hard drive, you don't have much choice; if you have access to a Jazz drive or other removable storage, you might want to consider placing your temporary files there.

You have two options in setting the file location. If you choose the first radio button, ScreenCam will place the temporary files in the default Temp directory on your main hard drive. If you choose the second radio button, you can specify the location to store the temporary files. This location can be in another folder on your main hard drive (C), or on another hard drive.

Adjusting Object Settings

As you will learn in Chapter 35, "Sharing Information Between Documents," you can embed the output of one application (such as ScreenCam) in another application (such as Approach or Word Pro). The object settings enable you to specify exactly how the ScreenCam movie will behave when it is embedded and opened in another application. To set the object settings, choose Object Settings from the Edit menu. ScreenCam opens the Object Settings dialog box (see Figure 34-5).

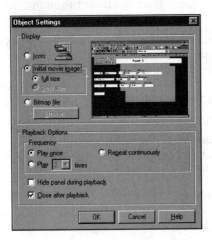

Figure 34-5: The Object Settings dialog box enables you to control ScreenCam's behavior when it is embedded in another application.

You can choose the following options:

✦ Whether to display an icon in the OLE container (such as an Approach PicturePlus field) or the initial image of the movie. You can also display a bitmap file. This can be handy if the first frame isn't very indicative of what the movie contains. In this case, you can build a bitmap file using a paint program and use that as the display image instead.

✦ The playback options. You can choose to play the movie just once, a user-specified number of times (choose the number from the Play drop-down list) or repeat continuously.

✦ Hide the panel during playback. If you don't choose this option, the ScreenCam control panel is visible during playback of the movie.

✦ Close after playback. If you don't choose this option, ScreenCam remains open and available after the movie ends (assuming you didn't choose repeat continuously).

Performing a Basic Recording

Creating a basic recording in ScreenCam is really very simple. Use the following steps:

1. Start ScreenCam. The control panel appears with the controls.

2. Open the application that you want to use during the recording.

3. Choose whether you want to record the sound (soundtrack), the screentrack, or both — and click the button in the control panel to make your choice.

4. Click the Record button on the control panel or press the default hotkey (F12) to start the recording. ScreenCam displays the Lotus ScreenCam 98 — Stop Panel Visible dialog box (see Figure 34-6) with some basic instructions. If you don't want to see this dialog box each time you record, check the Click Here to Hide This Message check box. Click OK to start the recording.

Figure 34-6: The Stop Panel Visible dialog box provides basic instructions before beginning a recording.

5. Perform the operations you want to record, including recording the voice track into the microphone.

Note   While you are recording, the control panel isn't visible. In fact, the only portion of ScreenCam you see (if it is enabled) is the Stop panel, which displays two buttons — one to stop the recording, and another to pause the recording. If the Stop panel is displayed, then the mouse action you use at the end of the recording to stop the movie is recorded as part of the movie.

One of the options discussed above is hiding the Stop panel, in which case (if you didn't enable the logo display) there is no indication that ScreenCam is running on the screen. You'll have to use the hotkey to stop the recording (default is Esc).

6. Click the Stop button in the Stop panel or press the Esc key to finish the recording when you are done.

Saving the ScreenCam Movie

Once you finish recording the movie, it exists only in memory — it will disappear once you turn the computer off or exit ScreenCam. You can save a ScreenCam movie in one of three different formats:

✦ **As a standard ScreenCam movie.** To play back this type of file, you must have the full retail version of ScreenCam or the ScreenCam movie player (see "Playing a Recording," later in this chapter). To save a standard ScreenCam movie file, choose Save from the File menu. ScreenCam opens the Save As dialog box. Type a file name into the File Name field, and click the Save button.

✦ **As a self-playing movie.** This option creates an actual program (exe file) that someone can simply double-click to run. They don't need ScreenCam or the ScreenCam movie player. However, a self-playing movie file is much bigger than a standard movie — almost 800KB bigger. So, if you are distributing multiple movies, you are better off distributing the movie player and regular ScreenCam movies.

✦ **To save a self-playing movie, choose Save from the File menu. ScreenCam opens the Save As dialog box.** Choose the Stand-alone Movies option from the Save As Type drop-down list. Type a file name into the File Name text box, and click Save.

✦ **As a Video for Windows (avi) file.** This is a "standard" windows animation file. If you want people to run the animation from an Internet browser (such as Netscape Navigator) or to access the movie from standard graphics tools, this is a good choice. However, depending on the options you choose, the file can be very large. For example, using the default options, a 185KB ScreenCam file becomes a 2.4MB Video for Windows file!

✦ **To save a Video for Windows file, choose Save from the File menu.** ScreenCam opens the Save As dialog box. Choose Video for Windows from the Save As Type drop-down list. Type a file name into the File Name text box, and click Save.

The Save dialog box provides a number of options to customize the saved file. From the Save As dialog box, click the Options button to open the Save Options dialog box (see Figure 34-7)

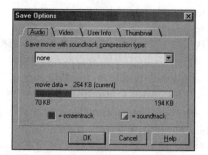

Figure 34-7: The Save Options dialog box enables you to set the options for saving a ScreenCam movie file.

The tabs in the Save Options dialog box guide you through setting the following options:

✦ **Audio.** The audio panel enables you to further compress the soundtrack, saving space in the movie. For example, in a short, 109KB movie, about half the space is used by the soundtrack and half by the screentrack. If you choose the VocalTec IMA ADPCM compression from the drop-down list, the movie size drops to 82KB, because the soundtrack size is cut in half.

✦ **Video.** This panel enables you to set options for saving a file as a Video for Windows (avi) file. You can choose the frames per second from the drop-down list, and choose whether to create the video using the full movie size or the current screen size. Of course, if you want the video saved in a lower resolution (which creates a smaller file), you'll have to change your screen to a lower resolution.

✦ **User Info.** This option enables you to replace the author information for the movie with the name of the person to whom ScreenCam is registered (you specified this information when you installed SmartSuite).

✦ **Thumbnail.** This panel simply enables you to add a thumbnail (preview) to a movie or update an existing thumbnail. The thumbnail can be used when the ScreenCam file is embedded via OLE into another application.

Making Corrections

You aren't always going to get both the screentrack and the soundtrack perfect! Sometimes, for example, you might maneuver the mouse correctly, but stumble over a word in the soundtrack. ScreenCam makes it possible to rerecord just the screentrack or just the soundtrack. Whichever item (screentrack or soundtrack) you choose to rerecord, the *other* item plays back while you rerecord. Thus, if you rerecord the soundtrack, the mouse and screen actions (the screentrack) play back by themselves so you can focus on just recording the right words.

To rerecord either the screentrack or the soundtrack, use the following steps:

1. Ensure that the movie you want to correct is currently open. If it is not, open the movie.

2. To rerecord the *soundtrack,* choose Clear Soundtrack from the Edit menu. The soundtrack is discarded, and the Microphone button (soundtrack) is selected in the control panel.

   To rerecord the *screentrack,* choose Clear Screentrack from the Edit menu. The screentrack is discarded, and the video camera button (screentrack) is selected in the control panel.

3. Click the Record button in the control panel, and rerecord the screentrack or soundtrack as you normally would.

4. Click the Stop button or press Esc to end the recording. Save your movie.

Working with Segments

The shorter you make your movies, the less chance you have of making an error during the recording—and having to rerecord the movie. ScreenCam enables you to break a movie up into small sections called *segments* (sort of like scenes) that not only let you shorten each recording (while still creating a long movie), but also remove "dead space," such as when you have to switch applications or adjust preferences between segments.

Building Segmented Movies

You can create segments in one of two ways. The first way is while you are recording a movie. Just push the Pause button (or use F12) to pause the recording. Then push the Play button (or use F12) to start recording again. Each time you perform this Pause-Play action, you create another segment.

You can also create segments in a movie by appending movies together. To do so, choose Open from the File menu to display the Open dialog box and open the movie that will comprise the first segment. Choose Open again to redisplay the Open dialog box. This time, after choosing the file to open, ScreenCam will display the Open Preferences dialog box. Choose the radio button to Append onto Existing Movie. Continue opening and appending movies to create the segments. You can also choose to replace or add just the screentrack or just the soundtrack from the new movie.

Don't forget to save your movie when you are done appending segments.

Note   When creating segments using the Open dialog box, the movies must have the same quality sound and must have been recorded at the same screen size and resolution.

Working with Segments

Once you've built a movie from segments, you can customize the segments to name them and rearrange them. To work with the segments, choose Segments from the Edit menu. The ScreenCam dialog box appears (see Figure 34-8).

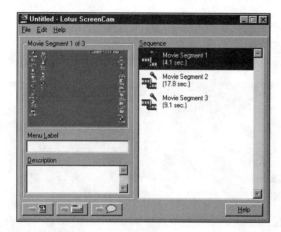

Figure 34-8: This ScreenCam dialog box enables you to name, describe, and rearrange segments.

On the right side of the dialog box is a Sequence list of segments. To work with a segment, click it. A thumbnail of the first frame appears in the box on the left side of the dialog box. You can type a name into the Menu Label text box, as well as a description into the Description box. The name you type into the Menu Label text box appears when you click the Jump to Segment button while playing the movie.

To rearrange the order of the segments, select the segment you want to move, and choose Cut from the Edit menu. Then click the segment after which you want the cut segment to appear. Choose Paste from the Edit menu and the segment is inserted into the movie. When playing a movie, you can jump to a particular segment by clicking the Jump to Segment button in the control panel. A list of segments appears, and you can click the one you want to play. ScreenCam immediately begins playing the selected segment.

Using Captions for Clarity

In addition to the sound track, you can add the equivalent of subtitles (or *close captioning*) to your ScreenCam movie. Captions are blocks of text that appear on the screen in the positions you designate. You create the captions prior to beginning the recording, saving them in a special caption file. You can specify the position, text, background, and font for each caption. During the recording, you call up each caption as you need it.

Creating Captions

To create captions for a ScreenCam movie, use the following steps:

1. Choose Captions from the Edit menu in the ScreenCam control panel. ScreenCam displays the Caption Script dialog box, along with a caption window (see Figure 34-9).

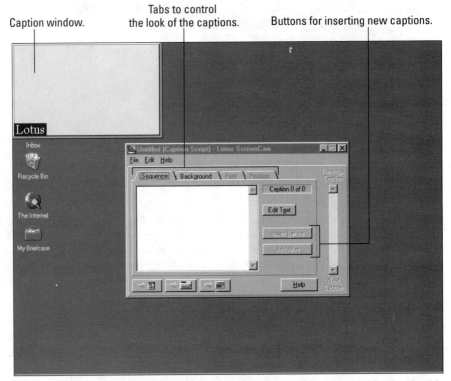

Caption window.   Tabs to control the look of the captions.   Buttons for inserting new captions.

Figure 34-9: The Caption Script dialog box provides all the tools you need to build captions for your ScreenCam movie.

2. If you want to use a caption file you've already created, choose Open from the File menu and load the file.

3. Click the Background tab to choose a bitmap (bmp) file to use as a background for the first caption. In the Location window (see Figure 34-10) navigate to a location that contains bitmaps (lotus\scrcam\captions, which is the default setting, is a good place), and the list of bitmaps will appear in the File list. Choose the bitmap you want to use.

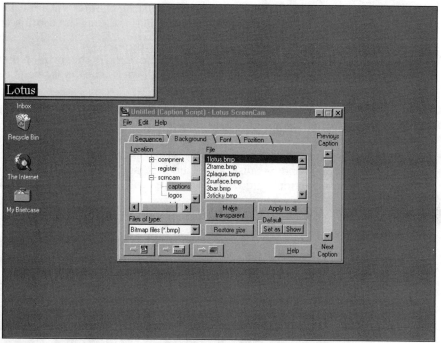

Figure 34-10: Pick a bitmap to provide a background for the caption.

4. Click the Font tab to specify the font, size, style, color, and alignment for the text of the caption.

Note

If you click the Apply to All button in the Font or Background tabs, the choice you make will apply to all the captions you have defined, rather than just the current caption you are defining. And Set As Default will apply your settings to all new captions you create from this point on.

5. Click the Position tab to specify the location at which the caption will appear on the screen. If you choose the Leave at Freehand Position option, the caption will appear where the caption window appears on the screen when you are done defining the caption. You can click and drag the onscreen caption window to a new location on the screen, or resize it, and the new location and size will define where the caption appears.

The Align All with Top Left Caption Corner button overrides the location option you have set for all captions. All caption windows will be displayed at the position of the current caption window.

If you choose the Center on Screen option, the caption will appear centered on the screen, regardless of where you click and drag the caption window to while defining the caption.

The Center all Captions Onscreen button overrides the location option you have set for all captions. All caption windows will be displayed at the center of the screen.

6. Click the Sequence tab, and then click the Edit Text button. This moves the text insertion point to the caption window, where you can type in the text of the caption. You can drag and resize the caption window as well as the text area within the window (see Figure 34-11) as needed to get all the text to fit. The caption window must be resized first, and then the text area can be sized within the caption window. The text area will not accept any more text than will fit.

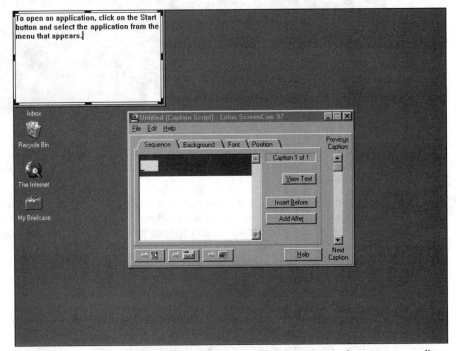

Figure 34-11: Type the text for the caption into the caption window. You can adjust the size and location of the caption window and the text area within the caption window.

7. Click the Add After button when you are finished writing the text of the caption. ScreenCam moves to the next caption, and the text from the previous caption appears in the Sequence window. The next caption uses all the same properties (size in megabytes), background, font, and position) as the previous caption.

Note

To insert a caption before an existing caption, click on the existing caption and then click Insert Before. This action inserts a new, blank caption prior to the selected caption. This new caption has all the same properties as the selected caption.

8. Repeat Steps 6 and 7 to add more captions, or use some of the previous steps to adjust the properties of the individual captions. Remember to save the caption file when you are done!

Editing a Caption

You can edit the text of a caption as well as rearrange the order of captions. To edit the text of a caption, choose the caption in the Sequence tab. The selected caption appears in the caption window. Then, click the Edit Text button. You can now edit the text of the caption just like any other text in a SmartSuite application. You can also change the properties of a caption using the various tabs in the Caption Script dialog box.

To rearrange the order of the captions, select the caption you want to move, and choose Cut from the Edit menu. Then click the caption after which you want the cut caption to appear. Choose Paste from the Edit menu and the caption is inserted into the sequence.

Recording Using Captions

To use the captions in a recording, you must instruct ScreenCam where to place the captions (at the prespecified locations) during the recording. To do so, use the following steps:

1. Choose Captions from the Edit menu, and then choose Open from the File menu to open the caption file you want to use.

2. Choose Movie from the Edit menu and then File ➪ New, or use F12 to begin recording the movie as usual.

3. When you get to the place in the movie where you want to display the first caption, use the hotkey F2 for Next Caption to display the first caption.

4. As the recording progresses, use the Next F2, Clear F3, and Prev F5 hotkeys to display the captions in the correct order.

5. When the movie is finished, click the Stop button or use the Stop Esc hotkey to end the movie, and File ➪ Save As to save it.

6. When you play back the movie, the captions will appear just as you specified.

✦   ✦   ✦

Sharing Information Between Documents

The applications included with SmartSuite enable you to create many different kinds of documents — schedules; spreadsheets and charts; database forms, reports, charts, mailing labels and worksheets; word processing documents; and presentations. It would be handy, however, to be able to share the information from a document in one application (such as Word Pro) with a document created in another application (such as Freelance).

You can accomplish this sharing between documents in different applications in two ways: by copying and pasting information between documents created in different applications, and by using a special Windows feature called *Object Linking and Embedding (OLE)*. You'll learn both techniques in this chapter.

Simple Copying and Pasting Between Applications

You've undoubtedly used the cutting, copying, and pasting features of Windows to make changes to your SmartSuite documents. You can also copy information from a document in one application, and paste that information into a document in another application. However, there are a number of disadvantages to this approach. First of all, while you can paste text and graphics (such as Word Pro text or the contents of a field in an Approach form), you can't use this technique to paste entire documents. For example, you can't simply paste an Approach view into a Freelance slide. In addition, some formatting is usually lost when you perform a paste. For instance, you can select the contents of an entire Freelance slide and paste it into Word Pro — but the resulting Word Pro document won't look much like the Freelance slide because background, font formatting, color, and bullets are all lost in the transfer from one application to another. OLE resolves all these issues, but is somewhat more complex to use. OLE works with *all* OLE-compliant programs.

Using Copy with Paste

To copy a portion of a document in one SmartSuite application and paste it into a document in another SmartSuite application, use the following steps:

1. Open the document that contains the material you want to copy from one SmartSuite application to another. For example, you could open a Word Pro document containing a bulleted list (see figure 35-1) that you want to copy to a Freelance presentation.

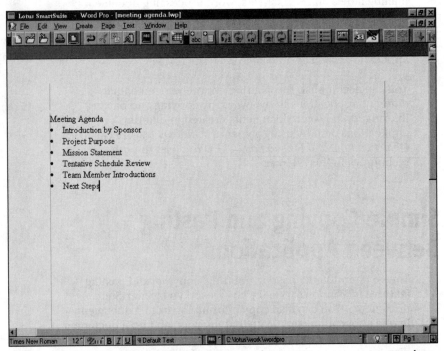

Figure 35-1: Word Pro is a good place to create documents you want to paste into documents in other applications.

2. Select the portion of the document that you want to copy, and choose Copy from the Edit menu. Windows places the copied object in the Clipboard.

3. Open the document in the application into which you want to paste the contents of the Clipboard.

4. Click the location in the receiving document where you want to paste the Clipboard contents, and choose Paste from the Edit menu. Windows pastes the contents of the Clipboard into the receiving document. Figure 35-2 shows the bulleted list pasted into a Freelance presentation.

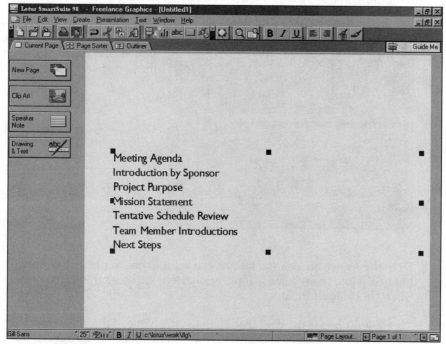

Figure 35-2: The bulleted list from Word Pro appears in Freelance.

5. Make any changes you need to the receiving document, and save your changes.

Note

The Windows Clipboard does not preserve all formatting when transferring items between applications. As a result, the pasted item may not look exactly as it did in the source document. For example, the bullets that appear in the list in Word Pro (see Figure 35-1) have been lost in Freelance (see Figure 35-2). To fix this, you'll need to edit the pasted text in Freelance (using Freelance's text-editing tools). To preserve all formatting, it is best to use OLE (see "OLE: What It Is and What It Does," later in this chapter).

Using Copy with Paste Special

The Windows Clipboard actually stores cut or copied items in several different formats. When you use Paste (see previous section), the paste is carried out using the default Clipboard format. In the case of text from Word Pro, this format is "unformatted text" — which is why the fancy bullets disappeared in our last example. However, you can choose which of the Clipboard formats you want to use for pasting. To do so, follow Steps 1–3 in the previous section. Then, click the location in the receiving document where you want to paste the Clipboard contents, and choose Paste Special from the Edit menu. The receiving application (Freelance, in our example) opens the Paste Special dialog box (see Figure 35-3).

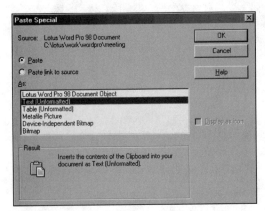

Figure 35-3: The Paste Special dialog box enables you to pick the format of the pasted item, or use OLE for pasting.

From the As list, choose the format you want to use to paste the contents of the Clipboard into the receiving application. Here are some things to keep in mind when choosing a format:

✦ If you choose the item that includes the name of the source application (Lotus Word Pro Document Object, in our example), the Paste Special operation actually links or embeds an OLE object in the document. Using Paste Special is the only way to create an OLE object from just a portion of a document (rather than the whole document), and is explained further in the section "Linking and Embedding Using Paste Special," later in this chapter.

✦ The exact options that appear in the As list depend on what you cut or copied. For example, the list will be different for a piece of clip art than for text.

✦ If you choose a graphic format (for example, Metafile picture, Device-independent Bitmap, or Bitmap), the resulting paste will look exactly like it did in the originating document. For example, the bulleted list will include the bullets and any font formatting. However, the pasted object is a graphic — you can't edit it like a text object.

OLE: What It Is and What It Does

Object Linking and Embedding (OLE) is a special feature of Windows that enables you to create a *compound document.* With OLE, a document (such as a Word Pro document) can include multiple OLE objects, which are actually documents you created using another application. For example, a Word Pro document can include a 1-2-3 worksheet, or a Freelance slide can include an Approach form. And a training manual you build in Freelance or Word Pro can include ScreenCam movies. The OLE object in the document looks *exactly* like it did when you created it, and when you need to edit the OLE object, you actually run the originating application, giving you access to all of the tools you used to build the OLE object in the first place. However, the resulting document can get quite large.

Note

Because OLE is built into Windows, you aren't limited to using only SmartSuite applications to create compound documents. Many other applications can create OLE objects for use in a document as well.

OLE Objects

OLE objects are files created using special Windows applications that can act as *OLE server applications.* An OLE server application is any application that can create an OLE object for use by another application; all the SmartSuite applications can act this way. When you install an OLE server application, that application notifies Windows and is added to a list of OLE servers. When you instruct an application to insert an OLE object, you can pick the type of object from the list of OLE server applications.

OLE objects (created using an OLE server application) are added to a document that you create using an application referred to as an *OLE client application.* An OLE client application is any application that can use an OLE object created by an OLE server application. For example, if you are embedding a ScreenCam movie into a Freelance presentation, ScreenCam is the OLE server application, and Freelance is the OLE client application. A particular application (such as Freelance) can play the role of OLE server application in one instance (adding a Freelance slide to a Word Pro document) and play the role of OLE client application in another instance (adding a ScreenCam movie to a Freelance presentation).

Understanding the Two Flavors of OLE Connections

When you place an OLE object into an OLE client application (such as adding a ScreenCam movie to a Freelance presentation), you can specify whether the OLE object is *embedded* or *linked.* Each type of OLE connection has advantages and disadvantages. Both types of connections are discussed in the following sections.

Embedding Objects

Embedding an OLE object in an OLE client application stores the OLE object directly in the OLE client application file. For example, the ScreenCam movie is actually stored within the Freelance presentation file. This makes the overall size of the OLE client application file larger (it must actually hold the contents of the OLE object), but it also makes the OLE client application file more portable. That is, you can give the OLE client application file (such as the Freelance file) to someone else who has the OLE client application, and they will be able to open the file and modify the OLE object (provided they have the OLE server application that created the object). You only need to transfer a single file (the OLE client application file) to someone else. You can only view the embedded object (and modify it) from within the OLE client application file where it is embedded.

Linking Objects

Linking an object works differently than embedding one. Instead of storing the OLE object in the OLE client application file, it is stored externally as a regular file, and a link is established from the OLE client application file to the linked OLE server file. The OLE client application file is smaller, because it stores only a link to the OLE server file, not the whole file. However, this configuration is also less portable — when you give someone an OLE client application file that contains links to OLE objects, you must give them the linked OLE server files as well. You can also run into problems if you move the linked file (using Explorer, for example), because the link then won't be able to locate the file, and you'll have to reestablish the link.

Another key advantage to linking is that multiple OLE client files can reference the same OLE object, and you can modify the OLE object directly using the OLE server application that created it. If you do modify the OLE object, all the OLE client files that are linked to it will use the new version.. For example, you can link the same ScreenCam recording (OLE object) of how to create an Approach database to multiple Freelance presentations (OLE client application) that train people how to use Approach. If you modify the recording (for example, creating a new soundtrack), all the Freelance presentations will use updated version.

Creating an Embedded or Linked Object

To embed or link an OLE object to a document, use the following steps:

1. Open the OLE client application into which you want to embed an OLE object, and open the file that will include the embedded object.

2. Choose Object from the Create menu. The application displays the Create Object dialog box (see Figure 35-4).

Note If you are in Approach in Browse mode, you must select a PicturePlus field or the Object item in the Create menu is unavailable. In Organizer, you must be in a Note page, or the Object item in the Create menu is unavailable.

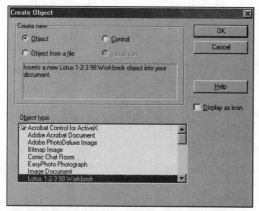

Figure 35-4: Use the Create Object dialog box to create a new OLE object or to insert an existing one into the OLE client file.

3. Choose either the Create a New Object radio button or the Create an Object from File radio button. Create a New Object means that you will use an OLE server application to create an OLE object that does not already exist. The next few steps assume that you chose the Create a New Object radio button.

4. Choose the object type from the Object Type list. This is a list of all the OLE server applications you have installed on your computer.

5. Click the OK button. The selected OLE server application opens on your screen. Use the capabilities of the application to create the OLE object.

6. When you have completed creating the object, return to the client application by using the Exit and Return to selection in the File menu. The OLE object you created is embedded and displayed in the OLE client application document. For example, in Figure 35-5, a 1-2-3 worksheet has been embedded in a Word Pro document.

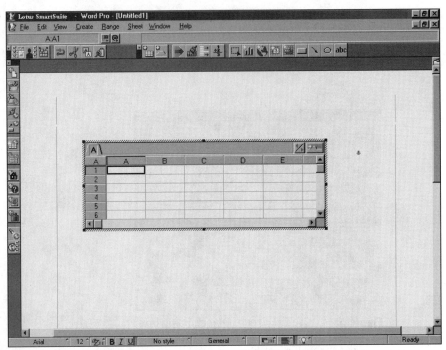

Figure 35-5: You can do very useful things with OLE, such as embed a 1-2-3 worksheet in a Word Pro document.

If you choose to create an object from a file (see Step 3), then you need to proceed a little differently. The Create Object dialog box changes to reflect your choices (see Figure 35-6).

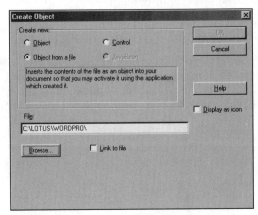

Figure 35-6: The Create Object dialog box changes if you choose Create from a File.

Objects You Can Create with SmartSuite Applications

While the types of objects you can create varies depending on the OLE server applications you have installed on your machine, you can create many different types of OLE objects from the applications in SmartSuite:

✦ **Approach** allows you to create all of the following: entire applications, charts, crosstabs, envelopes, form letters, forms, mailing labels, reports, and worksheets.

✦ **ScreenCam** allows you to create a movie.

✦ **1-2-3** allows you to create a workbook.

✦ **Freelance** allows you to create a drawing or a presentation.

✦ **Word Pro** allows you to create a document.

Use the following steps after choosing the Create New Object from a File radio button in the Create Object dialog box:

1. Specify the file from which to create the OLE object by either typing it into the File text box or clicking the Browse button and choosing the file from the Browse dialog box.

2. Choose from the two following check boxes available in the Create Object dialog box:

   • **Link**. Click this box if you want to link the file, rather than embed it.

   • **Display as Icon**. Click this box if you would rather display the OLE object as an icon (which speeds up displaying the document in which it is linked or embedded).

3. Click OK to link or embed the OLE object in the document. The document displays the linked or embedded OLE object.

Note

In Approach, the Create Object dialog box is called "Insert Object," and the two options are labeled "Create New" and "Create from File." However, except for these minor differences, embedding or linking an OLE object in Approach works the same.

Linking and Embedding Using Paste Special

As discussed earlier, you can copy items from a source document by selecting the items and choosing Copy from the Edit menu. Once these items are in the Windows Clipboard, you can use Paste Special in the Edit menu (see Figure 35-3) to control how the items are pasted into your target document. If the document in which you created and copied the items is an OLE server application, you can use Paste Special to create an OLE object from the copied items and embed or link them into another document.

Note If the creating application is an OLE server application, the list of available pasting formats in the Paste Special dialog box has an option that refers to the creating application.

Hot Stuff Using Paste Special is the only way to create an OLE object from just a portion of an existing document. "Normal" object embedding and linking creates an OLE object from only an entire document or file.

It's easier to see how to use Paste Special to perform OLE by walking through an example:

1. Run Word Pro and open a Word Pro document.

2. Copy some text by selecting the text and choosing Copy from the Edit menu. This places the copied text in the Windows Clipboard.

3. Run Freelance and open a Freelance presentation. Navigate to the location into which you want to embed or link the Word Pro text.

4. Choose Paste Special from the Edit menu. Freelance opens the Paste Special dialog box.

5. Choose "Lotus Word Pro Document Object" from the list of formats for pasting.

6. Choose one of the following radio button options:

   • **Paste.** The pasted items are embedded in the document using OLE.

   • **Paste Link to Source.** The pasted items are linked to the document using OLE.

7. Click OK to complete the Paste Special.

Editing, Deleting, and Playing OLE Objects

Once you have embedded or linked an OLE object into an OLE client application document, you can edit the object, delete it, or play it (discussed at the end of this section).

Editing OLE Objects

To edit an OLE object, use the following steps:

1. Select the area in the OLE client application document that contains the OLE object you want to edit.

2. Right-click the OLE object to display the pop-up menu, or click the new menu that appears when you selected the OLE object. This OLE Object menu refers to the type of OLE object, but the exact name varies between applications. For example, if you embed a 1-2-3 workbook in Word Pro, the menu is called "Workbook." However, if you embed a 1-2-3 workbook in Freelance or Approach, the menu is called "Workbook Object."

3. From either the pop-up menu or the new OLE Object menu described in Step 2, navigate to the menu options that permit editing. This varies from one application to another, and even varies between the OLE Object menu and the pop-up menu within a given application. If, for example, you embed or link a 1-2-3 workbook in Word Pro, the OLE Object menu contains both the Edit and Open menu options. However, the pop-up OLE object menu in Word Pro contains a Workbook Object, and the additional menu that appears when you click the Workbook Object menu item contains the Edit and Open items. However, in Freelance, both the OLE Object menu and the pop-up menu contain the items Edit Workbook and Open Workbook. Figure 35-7 shows the OLE Object Edit menu for Word Pro.

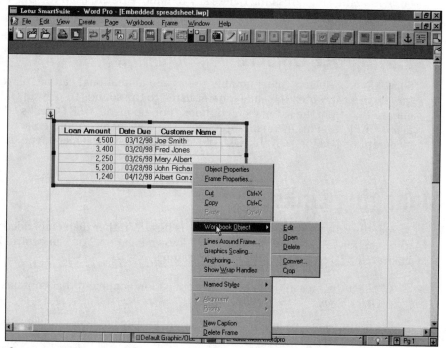

Figure 35-7: The OLE object menu enables you to open or edit the OLE object.

Note Choosing the Open menu option always opens the OLE object in the creating application in a separate window (which usually makes it easier to make your editing changes). However, what happens when you choose the Edit option varies depending on whether the OLE object is linked or embedded. For embedded objects, the OLE container area turns into an Edit window in which you can make the changes you want. For linked objects, the OLE object opens in a separate window in the creating application, just as if you had chosen the Open menu option.

4. Make the changes to the document in the creating application.

5. If the OLE object was embedded, simply exit the creating application, as described earlier. If the OLE object was linked, save the changes as you would normally, then exit the creating application.

Deleting OLE Objects

To delete an OLE object, click the area that contains the OLE object to highlight the borders of the area. Press the Delete key or choose Delete from the OLE object's editing menu (described in Step 3, above).

Playing OLE Objects

Some kinds of objects (most notably sound and animations) can be "played" — that is, you can watch the animation or listen to the sound. To play an OLE object, choose Play from the list of menu options (pop-up menu, OLE Object's editing menu, or PicturePlus menu in Approach). The Play menu option replaces the Open menu option (that is, playable OLE objects do not have an Open menu option).

Managing Links

As mentioned earlier, an OLE object that is linked (rather than embedded) has a connection to an actual file stored at a known location. You can control how the links are updated by using the following steps:

1. Select the area in the OLE client application document that contains a linked OLE object.

2. Choose Manage Links from the Edit menu. The application opens the Manage Links dialog box (see Figure 35-8).

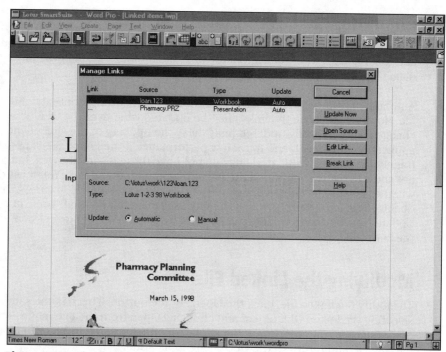

Figure 35-8: The Manage Links dialog box enables you to modify the configuration of your linked OLE objects.

3. If multiple links are displayed (because you have multiple files linked to the OLE client application document), choose the link you want to work with.

4. (Optional) Perform the actions you want to apply to the selected link, as described in "Understanding Link Actions," below.

5. When you are done working with the links, exit the Manage Links dialog box by clicking the Done button (the Cancel button changes to read "Done" after you have modified at least one link) or the Cancel button.

Understanding Link Actions

The Manage Links dialog box provides all the tools you need to manage the links to OLE objects you've created in a document. You can control how the links update, break links, and remap a "lost" link. These options are discussed in the following sections.

Changing the Link Update Method

A link can be updated either automatically or manually. To choose the update method, choose either the Automatic or Manual radio button in the Manage Links dialog box.

Automatically updated links always show the most current contents of the linked file. However, because the links must be updated whenever the OLE object file changes, automatically updated links delay the opening of the OLE client application document, and may slow performance if the linked file is updated frequently. Manually updated links do not have these disadvantages, but also do not show the latest version of the file until you update the link. You must decide whether having the latest version of the OLE object displayed in the OLE client document is important to you. If the link uses manual updating, you can click the Update Now button to update the link and display the most current contents of the linked file.

Modifying the Linked File

To modify the linked file, click the Open Source button. This has the same effect as selecting the linked OLE object and choosing Open from the File menu — the file opens in a separate window in the application that created it. You can modify the file, save it, and return to the OLE client application.

Changing the Referenced File

If you want to change which file is linked to the OLE client document, choose the Change Source button and select the new file to link to from the Change Source dialog box.

You can also use the Change Source button to fix a broken link. Occasionally, a file may be moved to another location on your hard drive or the network (or you may remap a network drive). If this happens the link will be broken because the client application is unable to locate the linked file. To remedy this situation, you can choose the Change Source button and select the file's new location on your hard drive or the network.

Breaking a Link

Choose the Break Link button to break the link between the contents of the container in the OLE client application document and the linked file. The OLE client document may still display a representation of what was in the file when the link was broken (for example, text or a graphic or an icon); however, changes to the contents of the formerly linked file are not reflected in the OLE client document.

✦   ✦   ✦

Using ViaVoice

"**I** talk, it types." IBM's advertising for the standalone ViaVoice product provides a great snapshot of how ViaVoice enhances a computer's usefulness and reduces manual labor. Lotus' parent company now offers you the opportunity to use ViaVoice along with Word Pro. SmartSuite Millennium Edition includes a version of ViaVoice that you can install and use to dictate information into Word Pro. This chapter explains how to set up and work with ViaVoice, so you can say about your computer, "I talk, it types."

Deciding Whether to Use Voice Technology

Despite all the recent hullabaloo, voice dictation programs have been around for some time. Several years ago, sound cards became a hot upgrade and then a standard part for every computer system. Users focused on how sound cards could help a computer output sound, for multimedia presentations and gaming purposes. A few companies, however, considered how users could use the sound card and a microphone to get information into a computer, and developed *voice,* or *speech, recognition programs.* Speech recognition programs enable users to dictate entries and select commands by speaking into a microphone.

As recently as 1994, however, speech recognition wasn't catching on very well. The new generation of speech recognition programs are getting a better reception today, due to timing—let's face it, any computer purchased within the last two years has plenty of firepower—and significant headway and luck in overcoming technological hurdles. Headset microphones have become inexpensive and widely available, and most computers sold today feature a Pentium or better processor with 32MB of RAM. Speech recognition programs from the previous generation required the user to speak very carefully and pause distinctly between words (called *discrete speech recognition*). This required as much concentration and effort as using the keyboard or mouse to give commands. Furthermore, older programs could only accept dictated text (or other input) at a relatively slow rate; anyone with halfway decent typing skills could outpace the speech recognition program.

Now, speech recognition programs use *continuous speech recognition* technology. Basically, this means that you don't have to pause carefully between words when dictating to a speech recognition program; you can speak at a normal, conversational pace. In fact, ViaVoice can enter 70 words per minute or more, well beyond the typing prowess of most users. The full-blown version of ViaVoice boasts a 22,000-word dictionary, and you can train it to recognize more than 42,000 words.

Now that speech recognition technology has caught up with user needs, what benefits can it offer you? For one thing, the same freedom as a hands-free phone headset. You can be leafing through files to find the facts you need to dictate into a document. And, if your hands or wrists ever become irritated through too much keyboard time, you won't have to type. You also can enjoy improved spelling. ViaVoice types entries correctly every time. Finally, your document content might improve a bit because it's likely to be more conversational and less stilted.

Installing ViaVoice

If you opted not to install ViaVoice using the SmartSuite Install program (covered in the Appendix), you can instead install it separately from the SmartSuite CD-ROM. After the basic installation process finishes, ViaVoice displays a User Wizard that enables you to *enroll* yourself as a user. The Wizard also helps you connect your microphone and set it up to work with ViaVoice.

You may have received a free noise-reducing headset microphone with SmartSuite. If you didn't receive a free mic, you can purchase a headset mic designed specifically for speech recognition for as little as $60 from your local computer store or a computer mail-order catalog like PC Connection (800-800-5555).

The ViaVoice setup process takes at least 30 minutes, so perform the setup during a quiet time when you're not likely to be interrupted. Use the following steps to install ViaVoice and complete the enrollment process:

1. Insert the SmartSuite CD-ROM in your CD-ROM drive. When the Lotus SmartSuite Millennium Edition window appears, click the Extras button to open a My Computer window showing the Extras folders on the CD. (Alternately, choose Start ➪ Programs ➪ Windows Explorer to launch the Windows Explorer, click the icon for the CD-ROM drive in the folder tree at the left, then double-click the Extra folder in the pane at the right.)

2. In the My Computer or Explorer window, double-click the Viavoice folder icon. Then, double-click the icon for the Setup.exe file, which includes a computer and a software box.

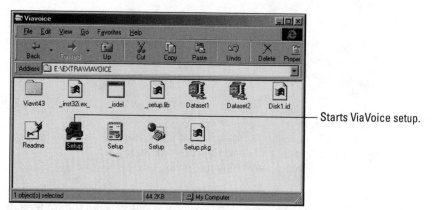

Starts ViaVoice setup.

Figure 36-1: Install ViaVoice by running the Setup.exe file in the \Extra\Viavoice folder on the SmartSuite CD-ROM.

3. The Setup program launches and the Welcome screen appears. Review its information, then choose Next.

4. A message box informs you that you need to install the IBM ViaVoice Runtimes. Click Yes to continue and do so.

5. Next, the Select Language to View License Agreement dialog box appears. Select a language option button, then click Next.

6. Review the terms of the license agreement that appear in the Software License Agreement dialog box, then click Yes to accept the terms and continue.

7. Another Welcome screen appears, welcoming you to the setup for ViaVoice itself. Review the information, then click Next to continue.

8. Enter or correct your name in the Name text box of the User Information dialog box, then click Next.

9. In the Choose Destination Location dialog box, use the Browse button to specify the disk and folder to which you want to install ViaVoice, if you don't want to install it to the default location, C:\ViaVoice\. Click Next.

10. The Select Program Folder dialog box appears (see Figure 36-2). By default, it suggests that the Setup program place the ViaVoice startup command in the IBM ViaVoice folder on the Programs submenu of the Windows Start menu. You can edit that folder name in the Program Folders text box. Or, you can choose one of the Existing Folders, such as the Lotus SmartSuite folder, to include the ViaVoice startup command in that folder, instead. Click Next.

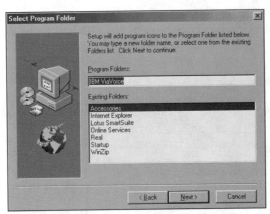

Figure 36-2: Specify a folder on the Start menu to
hold the ViaVoice program using this dialog box.

11. The Start Copying Files dialog box appears. It verifies the folder settings
    you've specified. Use the Back button to back up to prior dialog boxes to
    change those settings, if needed. Otherwise, click Next.

12. The Setup program copies the ViaVoice Runtime files to your computer. When
    it finishes, the Setup Complete dialog box informs you that Setup has finished
    copying the Runtime files to your computer. Click Finish to install ViaVoice
    itself.

13. Another Software License Agreement window appears. This one covers the
    installation of Word Pro with ViaVoice. Review the terms, then click Yes.

14. In the Choose Destination Location dialog box, use the Browse button to
    specify the disk and folder to which you want to install Word Pro with
    ViaVoice, if you don't want to install it to the default location, C:\Program
    Files\ViaVoice Seamlessly Integrated\. Click Next.

15. Setup copies the files to your system. When it finishes, the Setup Complete
    dialog box appears. Leave the Yes, I Want to Restart My Computer Now option
    button selected, then click Finish. The Setup Program exits and restarts your
    computer.

16. The Lotus Word Pro New User Wizard dialog box appears immediately after
    your system reboots.

17. If you want, edit the user name in the Name text box. Click Next.

18. The next Wizard dialog box, labeled Setting Up the Microphone, lets you know
    that your microphone needs to be set up to work with ViaVoice. Click Next.

19. The Microphone Setup Wizard dialog box appears. It displays welcome
    information, and lets you know that the Wizard will guide you through the mic
    setup process. Click Next.

20. The next Wizard dialog box, titled Selecting a Sound Card, displays Input and Output drop-down lists that you can use to select the sound card to use for mic input and output. (Note that this dialog box may not appear if the Wizard finds only one set of sound card software drivers on your system.) In general, the Wizard displays the best input and output options, so you can click Next to continue.

21. The next Wizard dialog box is titled Gathering Information. In the Sound Output area, select the option button for the type of device to use to output ViaVoice sound. If your system has External Speakers, leaving that option selected is the best all-around choice. However, if you work in an open office environment, consider clicking the Microphone Headset option so that dictation will play back to the headset only. In the Click on Microphone Parts area of the dialog box, click the picture for each microphone part you received. This helps the Wizard tell you how to connect the mic correctly. Click Next.

22. The next Wizard dialog box, Testing Audio Playback, enables you to specify a volume level for played-back dictation. Click the Test button, then use the mouse to drag the volume slider to the volume you want. Repeat the process by clicking the Re-Test button. When you're satisfied with the volume, click Next.

23. The next Wizard dialog box lists steps for Adjusting the Headset. Follow the steps, then click Next.

24. The Wizard displays Connecting the Microphone information and a picture that shows how to plug the microphone into the system unit (the box that holds the brains and the disk drives) for your computer. Plug the mic in as shown, then click Next.

25. The Wizard next directs you through the process of Testing the Microphone. Click the Test button, then wait as the Wizard records room noise. Then click Continue and read the sentence specified by the Wizard. Click Next.

26. The Wizard verifies that you've correctly connected the microphone by displaying Microphone Connection Complete information. Click Next.

27. Follow the Adjusting the Audio Level steps in the next Wizard dialog box. Click Start, then say each word that the Wizard highlights. If your microphone levels aren't set correctly, a dialog box may appear with instructions for adjusting your setup. For example, the Signal Adapter Required dialog box may inform you that you need to add a signal adapter for the microphone (which should have come with the mic), providing a picture of how to do so. Make the needed adjustment, then click OK. Click the Re-Start button to re-perform the test. When the top of the dialog box displays "Audio Level Adjustment Complete," click Next.

28. The next step is Testing Speech Recognition. Click Start, then say each word when the Wizard highlights it. If the Wizard doesn't recognize all the words as you speak them, it tells you so at the top of the dialog box. Click Re-Start to re-perform the test as many times as needed. When the top of the dialog box displays "Microphone Setup Wizard Completed Successfully," click Finish.

29. The Lotus Word Pro New User Wizard dialog box reappears, and displays its Quick Training (1 of 3) information screens. Click Start, then say the highlighted sentence. When the dialog box tells you the Wizard has recorded and processed your speech sample, click Next.

30. Repeat the process as directed by the Quick Training (2 of 3) and Quick Training (3 of 3) screens for the Wizard.

Note   The Quick Training screens of the Wizard are intended to train both you and ViaVoice. The screens explain how to include punctuation as you dictate (by saying "COMMA," for example) and how to stop the dictation by saying "STOP DICTATION." Anything that appears in capital letters identifies a command or punctuation mark that ViaVoice understands.

31. The What's Next? screen of the New User Wizard appears. Click an option button to start Word Pro, beginning the enrollment process (described in the next section), or None of the Above (which takes you to Windows), then click Finish.

Enrolling Users and Training ViaVoice

The *enrollment process* teaches ViaVoice how your voice sounds, so it will be able to recognize and execute the commands and dictation you give. It gives ViaVoice the chance to adapt to unique aspects of your voice, such as an accent. If you don't take the time to complete the enrollment or if you get excited or drowsy and don't sound the same as when you enrolled, you likely won't be satisfied with how ViaVoice interprets what you say. Furthermore, ViaVoice stores any vocabulary entries or macros you create with the user name and enrollment you specify, so that different users can customize ViaVoice without interfering with another user's setup. For example, if you have a job-sharing arrangement with someone else who will be using the same computer system, each of you should set up a separate user name and enrollment under ViaVoice. You can set up multiple enrollments for each user name, so that each user can choose a different enrollment for different situations. For instance, you could set up one enrollment to use for creating casual correspondence (including slang terms) in Word Pro, and another for business-oriented correspondence (including jargon).

To start the enrollment process if you didn't elect to do so from the last screen of the New User Wizard, choose Start ➪ Programs ➪ IBM ViaVoice ➪ Tools ➪ Enrollment. The IBM ViaVoice Enrollment dialog box appears.

Click your name in the User Names list. Or, to add a user name, click Create, enter a Name in the User Information dialog box, and click OK to run the User Wizard and set up the user. With the correct name selected in the User Names list, click Enroll. The Enrollments dialog box appears. To create a new enrollment for the selected user name, click the New button and enter a description (name) for the enrollment in the Enrollment Description dialog box. Click OK. Select the enrollment to work with by clicking it, as shown in Figure 36-3. (You can use the Description button to edit the enrollment name.)

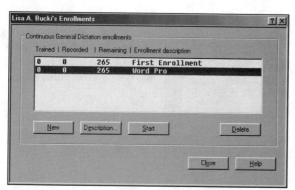

Figure 36-3: Create and select enrollments in this dialog box.

To begin "training" ViaVoice to recognize the words in the selected enrollment, click Start. The Continuous General Dictation Enrollment Sample dialog box appears. It lets you know that you need to speak continuously and naturally during the training process. Click the Continuous button to hear a sample of the correct speaking technique. Click Next. A message appears to inform you that you need to record 50 phrases before training. Click OK to continue and display the Continuous General Dictation dialog box (see Figure 36-4). Click Start, then begin reading the displayed sentences aloud. Also read any punctuation mark that's spelled out in CAPITAL LETTERS. If you don't say the punctuation marks out loud, ViaVoice won't know where to include punctuation in the phrases and sentences you dictate. After you read each sentence, ViaVoice immediately displays the next one (unless you specify otherwise by clicking the Options button). Continue reading the sentences, which provide information about how to dictate effectively to ViaVoice. If you need to take a break, click the Stop button. Click Start to resume recording from where you left off. The counter in the upper-left corner of the dialog box tracks the number of sentences you've recorded. Remember, you have to finish at least 50 of the sentences before you can continue the enrollment process.

> The enrollment sentences provide useful descriptions and hints about how to dictate most effectively to ViaVoice. If you have time, you should read all the sentences, not only to enhance ViaVoice's ability to recognize your speech, but also to learn more about using the product.

As you'll discover after you read the first dozen sentences or so, if a sentence you just read turns red onscreen, ViaVoice didn't understand you. An Unrecognized Information dialog box may appear, giving you possible suggestions for correcting the sentence. Click OK to close the dialog box. You can click the Playback button to hear a recording of how you said the sentence, to get an idea of what you may have done wrong. Then, click Start and reread the sentence. Repeat the process until ViaVoice understands your pronunciation and continues to the next sentence. Or, click Next to skip the red sentence and move on to the next sentence.

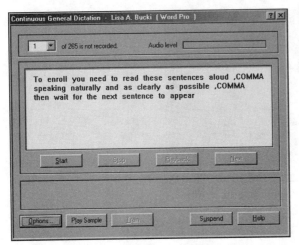

Figure 36-4: Click Start, then read the sentences (including the punctuation marks spelled out in CAPITAL LETTERS) that the dialog box displays.

After you dictate 50 sentences, the Enrollment Increment Complete dialog box appears. It describes your options for proceeding when you return to the Continuous General Dictation dialog box: Click Train to begin training, Suspend to suspend the enrollment process so you can come back to it later, or Start to continue recording sentences. Click OK to close the Enrollment Increment Complete dialog box, then choose how to proceed.

If you click Train, a slightly different Enrollment Increment Complete dialog box appears. (If you continue recording instead, click Stop when you think you've recorded enough, then click Train.) Click OK to proceed with the training. The Enrollments dialog box appears, showing you how many sentences you've recorded and displaying the progress of the training. The training process takes several minutes, and lasts longer if you've recorded more sentences. A message box informs you when the training finishes. Click OK to close the message box. The Default User message box appears to ask whether you want to choose the new enrollment as the default user for ViaVoice. Click Yes to do so, or No to close the message box without doing so.

Click Close to close the Enrollments dialog box, then click Exit at the IBM ViaVoice Enrollment dialog box to complete the user setup and enrollment process.

Note

If you need to suspend the enrollment, you can restart the process by choosing Start ➪ Programs ➪ IBM ViaVoice ➪ Tools ➪ Enrollment. Choose your User Name, then click Enroll. Select the enrollment to work with, then click Start. Click Start again to record more sentences. Click Stop to end recording (or record all sentences if you see a message box informing you that you must do so), then click Train. In the Enrollment Increment Complete dialog box, click the Backup button to backup the previous training.

Number of
recorded sentences
being used
for the training.

Indicates the
training progress.

Figure 36-5: ViaVoice uses the sentences you recorded
to train the enrollment to recognize your speech patterns.

Choosing the User and Setting Other Options

Before you begin any dictation session within a SmartSuite application that
supports ViaVoice, you must first select the user and enrollment that ViaVoice
should use for the session. You change this setting in the same dialog box that
offers other general options for ViaVoice. Use the following steps to specify other
options along with selecting the user and enrollment:

1. Choose Start ➪ Programs ➪ IBM ViaVoice ➪ Tools ➪ ViaVoice Options. The IBM
   ViaVoice Options dialog box appears.

2. The first tab, Audio, offers a limited number of settings for working with
   sound input and output. You generally don't need to change anything in the
   Input area. Leave the Microphone option button selected beside Input Jack.
   However, if you will be using a dictation recorder (there are now ones
   specially designed to work with speech recognition software) to input the
   dictation, click Line In and adjust the Line In Volume slider. To adjust the
   audio volume ViaVoice uses when it reads material back, drag the Output
   (for Audio Playback) slider.

3. Click the User tab to display its options (see Figure 36-6). Choose your user
   name from the top drop-down list, and the enrollment you want to use from
   the second drop-down list. If you've created a vocabulary file (words you've
   trained ViaVoice to recognize) that you want to use, choose it from the
   Vocabulary drop-down list.

4. Click the Voice tab, which offers settings that help you fine-tune ViaVoice's
   speed and accuracy (see Figure 36-7). Drag the Recognition Sensitivity slider
   to control how close your pronunciation has to be in order for ViaVoice to
   recognize words, or how much background noise ViaVoice can tolerate. The

Best Guess end of the continuum gives you more pronunciation latitude, but means that you need to work in a quiet environment. Dragging the slider toward Exact Match means your pronunciation must be more accurate, but that ViaVoice can filter out a lot of background noise. In the Recognition Performance area, click Fast if you want to dictate at a rapid speed, but be aware that this might result in ViaVoice making some mistakes; however, this setting might be preferable if you're just putting together a first draft of a document. Click Accurate to tell ViaVoice to slow down and concentrate on getting the words right. Use Balanced if you want to proceed at a normal pace, and have the time to check for the typical number of mistakes that ViaVoice might make. To return all the tab settings to the defaults, click the Default Settings button. (Don't change the Diagnostic Level setting unless you're told to do so by a Lotus technical support representative.)

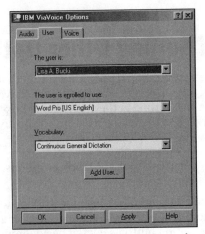

Figure 36-6: Choose the user and enrollment to use for your next dictation session on this tab.

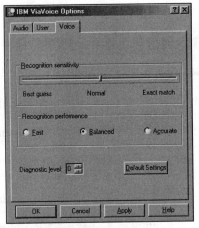

Figure 36-7: Use these settings to help ViaVoice work either faster or with greater accuracy.

5. Click OK to close the dialog box and apply your new settings.

Dictating Entries

You don't actually start ViaVoice to use it for dictation. You open the ViaVoice-enabled version of Word Pro, and create or open the document in which you want to use dictation. After installing the ViaVoice Runtimes and ViaVoice-enabled version of Word Pro, the Word Pro application includes a Dictation menu with commands for performing dictation. The SpeechBar above the title bar displays visual cues that help guide you through the dictation process, and includes a Microphone button for turning the microphone on and off. In addition, the application talks to you in a pleasant voice, prompting you to begin dictation and confirming the commands you give it.

To learn some of the basic ViaVoice commands, say "WHAT CAN I SAY?" into your microphone. Figure 36-8 shows the command listing and the tools in the ViaVoice-enabled version of Word Pro. If you want to temporarily disable your ViaVoice, so that you can concentrate on typing, say "GO TO SLEEP." To reactivate ViaVoice, say "WAKE UP." You can turn ViaVoice off and on within the application using the Dictation ⇨ Stop ViaVoice and Dictation ⇨ Start ViaVoice commands.

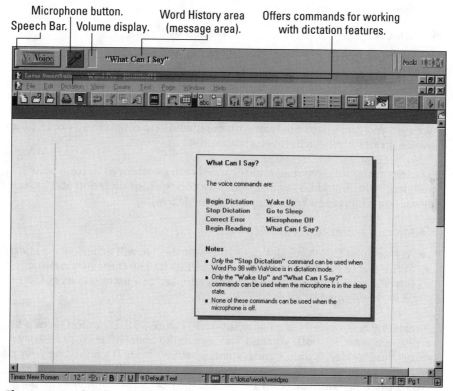

Figure 36-8: ViaVoice-enabled application versions include special dictation tools.

Choose Help ⇨ ViaVoice Help Topics to get online Help about ViaVoice. You also can click the menu button at the left end of the SpeechBar to display useful commands.

Dictating

To begin the dictation process, position the insertion point where you want to insert the dictated material, then choose Dictation ➪ Begin Dictation (Alt+B) or say "BEGIN DICTATION." After the application says "Begin Dictating" to verify your command, you can begin dictating your text in a natural, relaxed tone.

In Word Pro, say the following commands to punctuate your material (ViaVoice uses capital letters for these commands to remind you to *say* them):

COMMA	CLOSE-QUOTE
PERIOD	NEW-PARAGRAPH
QUESTION-MARK	NEW-LINE
COLON	SPACE-BAR
SEMI-COLON	LOWERCASE
EXCLAMATION-POINT	UPPERCASE
OPEN-QUOTE	NO-SPACE

Make sure you don't pause in two-word commands (to remind you not to pause, ViaVoice inserts hyphens in these commands).

Because you should have read and recorded many sentences to train your enrollment, you should be familiar with how to speak for dictation and include the punctuation commands. For example, say the following:

✦ Monthly report NEW-PARAGRAPH

✦ At this point COMMA sales data still indicates we will experience a shortfall at the end of the second fiscal quarter PERIOD The three new products introduced last month have not been adopted by customers as quickly as we had hoped PERIOD NEW-PARAGRAPH

The resulting text resembles what is shown in Figure 36-9. Dictation takes a bit of practice, however, for both you and ViaVoice. If the SpeechBar Word History Area displays Pardon Me?, it didn't understand what you said. Try adjusting your pace or speaking more distinctly. In some cases, too, you'll need to pause and let ViaVoice catch up with you. Your best bet is to speak at an even, natural pace.

When you've finished dictating, choose Dictation ➪ Stop Dictation (Alt+P) or say, "STOP DICTATION." Also note that you can't use the mouse or keyboard to enter or edit text while dictating, so stop dictation if you need to make changes.

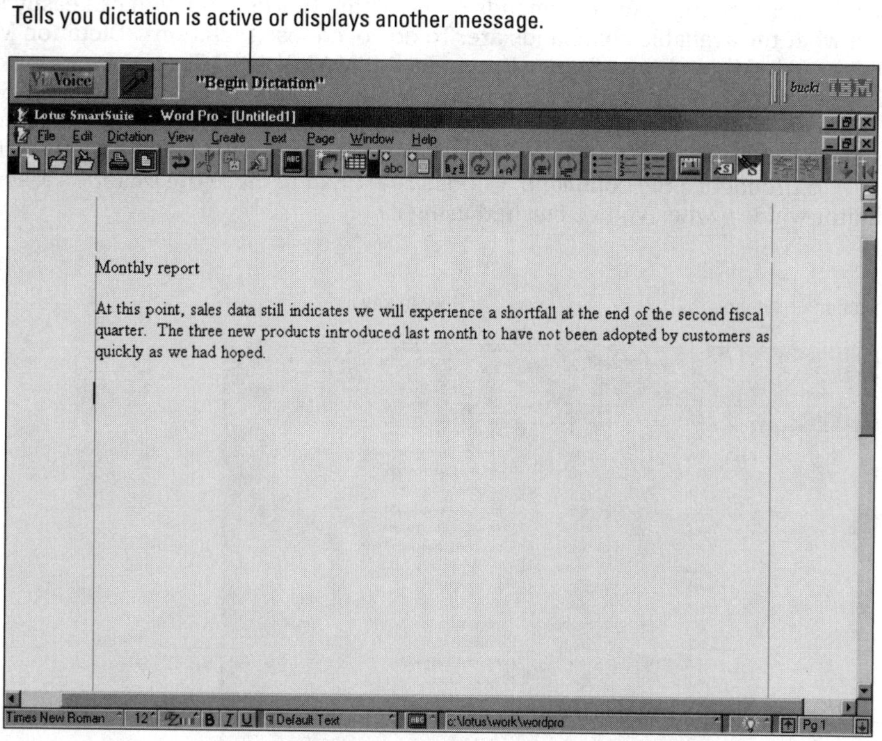
Tells you dictation is active or displays another message.
"Begin Dictation"
Lotus SmartSuite - Word Pro - [Untitled1]
File Edit Dictation View Create Text Page Window Help
Monthly report
At this point, sales data still indicates we will experience a shortfall at the end of the second fiscal quarter. The three new products introduced last month to have not been adopted by customers as quickly as we had hoped.
Times New Roman
Default Text
c:\lotus\work\wordpro
Pg 1

Figure 36-9: Text and punctuation you dictate appear at the insertion point.

Danger Zone

From time to time, you may need to recalibrate the microphone's input levels, especially if ViaVoice begins having trouble understanding your dictation. Choose Start ➪ Programs ➪ IBM ViaVoice ➪ Tools ➪ Microphone Setup. Under Select Setup, click the Adjust the Audio Level option button, then click Next and follow the Microphone Setup Wizard's subsequent instructions. Also check how close the microphone is to your mouth. If it's too close or far away, dictation won't work correctly.

Learning Symbols and Other Commands

There are even more commands that you can use to format text as you dictate, and symbols you can include. For example, you can say the "UPPERCASE" command before a word to have ViaVoice enter the word (and only that word) in all capital letters. Or, you can use the "SPACEBAR" command to enter a space, or the "DOLLAR-SIGN" or "PERCENT-SIGN" commands to enter those characters.

While there are too many commands to list within this chapter, you can easily find out what the available commands are. To do so, choose Dictation ⇨ Dictation Macro Editor (Alt+M) or choose Start ⇨ Programs ⇨ IBM ViaVoice ⇨ Tools ⇨ Dictation Macro Editor. The Dictation Macro Editor window opens, as shown in Figure 36-10. The Name column lists each symbol or command action. Scroll down the column to view the command or symbol you need, then check the far right column to verify how to pronounce the command. Choose File ⇨ Exit to close the Dictation Macro Editor window when you've finished using it.

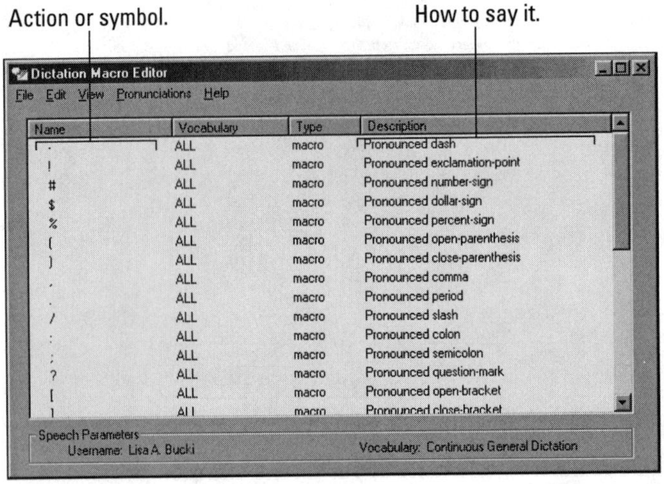

Action or symbol.   How to say it.

Figure 36-10: This window lists the commands you can use to enter special symbols or perform a command.

See "Training Commands and Creating Macros" near the end of this chapter to learn how to use the Dictation Macro Editor to help ViaVoice better recognize the commands you give it.

Having ViaVoice Read Material Back

ViaVoice can read text and numbers back to you, which serves as a great way to proof documents, especially if you've typed information, rather than dictated it. While your own eyes might skip over a wrong word or awkward phrase, when ViaVoice reads your text back to you, you get exactly what you've entered.

To start, position the insertion point at the beginning of the text to read, or select a specific portion of text if you want to hear only that selection. Then, choose Dictation ⇨ Begin Reading or say, "BEGIN READING." The reader appears onscreen (see Figure 36-11) and begins reading the text back to you. You can click the Pause button on the Reader to stop the reading. To resume reading, click the microphone button on the SpeechBar, and then say, "BEGIN READING."

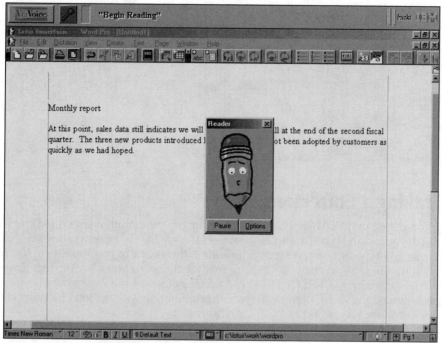

Figure 36-11: Use the Reader to proofread your text.

You can change how the Reader looks and sounds. To do so, choose Dictation ⇨ Reading Options (Alt+R) or click the Options button on the Reader. The Virtual Voice Control Properties dialog box appears. On the first tab, Voice Models, use the Selected Voice drop-down list to choose a different speaking voice for the reader, and then click the Sample Voice button to hear a preview. (The voices are rather comical, because they all are variations of the *same* voice.)

If you want to spend time experimenting, you can create and save your own voice by clicking the Advanced Voice Settings button; we'll leave that process for you to explore on your own. On the text tab, you can click the Use Wave button, then click the Browse button to find a WAV file for the Reader to play; for everyday use, though, just leave the Use Text option button selected so the reader will read back the document text. On the Actor Gallery tab, use the scroll bar beside the actor at the left (see Figure 36-12) to choose another character as your Reader. Choose a Default Expression from that drop-down list, then check or clear Use Animated Face, depending on whether you want the Reader's mouth to move as it reads. Click OK to apply your changes and close the dialog box.

To finish working with the Reader, click the Close button on the Reader window. Then, click the microphone button on the SpeechBar to turn the microphone back on.

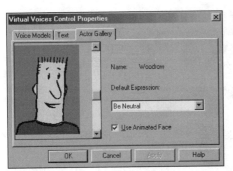

Figure 36-12: Use the scroll bar near the example at the left to choose another actor.

Making a Correction

If you notice that ViaVoice has mistaken your pronunciation and entered the wrong word, you can use ViaVoice to help correct the mistake. (It cannot, however, correct words you type in.) Stop dictating, if needed, then click to position the insertion point on the word to correct. Then, right-click the word and click Correct Error (Ctrl+F2), or say, "CORRECT ERROR." ViaVoice plays its recording of how you pronounced the word, then displays a shortcut menu with options for correcting the word (see Figure 36-13).

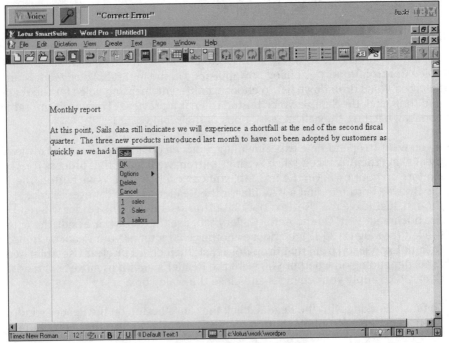

Figure 36-13: Say "CORRECT ERROR" to display a shortcut menu with options for correcting the word containing the insertion point.

You can simply click one of the numbered words at the bottom of the menu to insert it in place of the selected word. Or, you can enter another correction in the text box at the top of the menu, then click OK to use that correction to replace the word. To change the formatting for the word, click Options, then click one of the submenu choices: Capitalize, Lowercase, Uppercase, Numeric, Spell Out, or Add Phrase (when available). Click Delete to remove the selected word, or Cancel to close the correction menu without making a change.

If you decide you don't want the correction you made, choose Edit ➪ Undo or click the Undo Last Command or Action SmartIcon.

Working with Vocabulary

The vocabulary file for each enrollment holds the recordings of words you have spoken, so that ViaVoice will recognize the words when you say them and type them correctly into a document. You should spend some time adding to the vocabulary for your enrollments, to increase your dictation efficiency. For example, you might want to add your name, your company name, jargon terms and acronyms you work with, and so on. Use the following steps to add and train ViaVoice to recognize new words:

1. Click the menu button at the left end of the SpeechBar, choose User Options, and use the User tab in the IBM ViaVoice Options dialog box to ensure you've selected the right user name, enrollment, and vocabulary file. Click OK.

2. Make sure the microphone is on. If the "Mic Off" message appears in the SpeechBar, click the Microphone button to turn it back on.

3. Choose Dictation ➪ Vocabulary Expander or choose Start ➪ Programs ➪ IBM ViaVoice ➪ Tools ➪ Vocabulary Expander. The Vocabulary Expander window appears.

4. Use the File ➪ Open command to open any rich text format (.RTF) or plain text file (.TXT) that holds the vocabulary words you'd like to add. Or, type the words into the window, as shown in Figure 36-14.

5. Choose Analyze ➪ Text or click the Analyze Text button to have the Vocabulary Expander go through the window contents and identify any words that don't already appear in the selected vocabulary file. The Missing Vocabulary Words dialog box appears.

6. In the list at the left, click the first word to add to the vocabulary, then press and hold the Ctrl key and click each additional word to add to the vocabulary (see Figure 36-15). Click Add.

Analyze Text button.

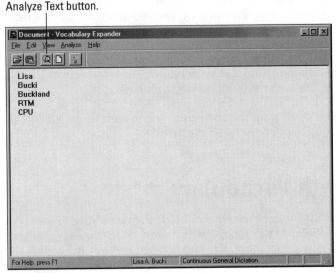

Figure 36-14: Enter or open a file that holds the vocabulary words to add.

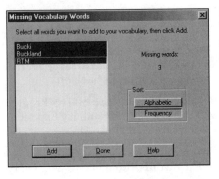

Figure 36-15: In the list that the Vocabulary Expander generates, select the words to add to the vocabulary, then click Add.

7. The Training Required dialog box appears, informing you that you need to train some of the new words. Click the Train button.

8. Use the Vocabulary Expander Train Word dialog box that appears (see Figure 36-16) to record how you say each word, which trains ViaVoice to recognize it. Select each word in the Written Like list, click the record button, say the word, click the Stop button, then click Add to add the recorded pronunciation. (Or, click the Play button to review your recording, and record over it if you're not satisfied.) Click Done to close the dialog box when you finish recording each word.

Danger Zone

When making recordings for training, make sure you don't have too much "dead air" time before and after your pronunciation, which can make the word more difficult to recognize.

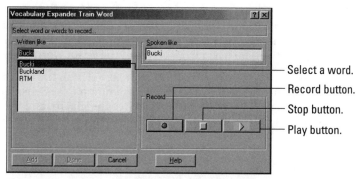

Figure 36-16: After you add a new word to the vocabulary, you have to train ViaVoice to recognize the word by recording how you say it.

9. The Words in Context dialog box appears, asking if the analyzed text is typical of your writing style and the context in which you typically use the newly trained words. If you opened a document containing the new words and the prior statement is true, click Yes. If you simply typed a list of words or if the document you opened didn't reflect your typical writing or typical usage for those words, click No.

10. The Vocabulary Expander Statistics dialog box appears, telling you how many words it analyzed and added to the vocabulary. Click OK.

11. Choose File ➪ Exit to close the Vocabulary Expander. You do not have to save the file.

Training Commands and Creating Macros

ViaVoice may need a bit of additional work to help it keep up with you. For one thing, you may want to provide it with some extra training to help it recognize how you pronounce commands. Or, you may want to create your own commands or shortcuts for dictating lengthy entries, so you can give a two-word command to enter your company name and address in a document, for example. You accomplish both feats in the Dictation Macro Editor, using the following steps:

1. Make sure the microphone is on. If the "Mic Off" message appears in the SpeechBar, click the Microphone button to turn it back on.

2. Choose Dictation ➪ Dictation Macro Editor (Alt+M) or choose Start ➪ Programs ➪ IBM ViaVoice ➪ Tools ➪ Dictation Macro Editor. The Dictation Macro Editor window opens.

3. To train a command such as the SPACE-BAR command, select the command in the list. Choose Pronunciations ➪ Train. Click the Advanced button in the Train Word dialog box, then click the Keep Other Pronunciations option

button. (This ensures you can have multiple recordings of how you say the command, to help ViaVoice recognize it more readily.) Click the Record button, say the command, and then click the Stop button. Click Add to add the new pronunciation, and then Done to close the Train Word dialog box.

4. To create a new macro, choose Edit ➪ Create Macro (F5) in the Dictation Macro Editor window. In the Modify Macro dialog box, enter a Case-Sensitive Name, a Description that tells ViaVoice how to pronounce the macro, and the Macro Text. Figure 36-17 shows an example. Click Save to finish the macro entry.

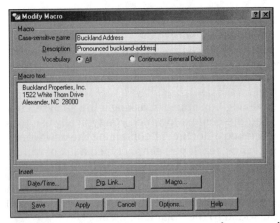

Figure 36-17: You can create a two-word command that enters a larger chunk of text when you're dictating.

Note

You have numerous other macro options available to you. Click the Help button in the Modify Macro dialog box or experiment with the other dialog box options on your own to learn more.

Danger Zone

Always use two words for your macro commands. Otherwise, ViaVoice will become confused and won't know whether you want it to enter a single word or treat the word as your command. Also, make sure you choose two words that form an unusual combination. If you use a common phrase like "Thank-you" as your command, ViaVoice might be confused as to whether it should enter the phrase "Thank-You" or the macro text if you say "Thank-you" while dictating.

5. Back in the Dictation Macro Editor Window, select the macro you just created, and train ViaVoice to recognize how you say it, as described in Step 3.

6. Repeat Steps 3–5 to train ViaVoice for more commands and create any additional macros.

7. Choose File ➪ Exit to close the Dictation Macro Editor when you've finished.

Installing SmartSuite

Installing programs has become a much more matter-of-fact process than it was even a few years ago. With the Millennium Edition of SmartSuite, you can complete installation by making just a few simple choices. SmartSuite does offer additional installation options, however, and the installation process you follow may depend on whether you're using a standalone system or working on a network. Furthermore, if you find you no longer use a particular SmartSuite application, you can remove it from your system. This appendix helps you understand installation issues and options, and explains how to install and remove SmartSuite applications.

Preparing to Install

Most of us can't wait to install and use a new software package, but rushing forward without laying the proper groundwork can have unexpected consequences, no matter how "intelligent" the installation program seems to be. Before you install SmartSuite or any other software, you should perform the following maintenance steps to prepare your system for the installation and safeguard against disasters:

◆ **Check for available hard disk space.** Depending on how you set it up, SmartSuite can take more than 240MB of hard disk space. If you're low on space, empty the Recycle Bin and delete old backup (.BAK) files and temporary (.TMP) files in the \Windows\Temp folder. Move older data files that you rarely or never use to floppy or Zip disks, or some alternative media such as a tape backup drive or another type of removable disk.

✦ **Run disk maintenance and backup tools.** Checking the drive for errors and defragmenting the drive can free up disk space (delete the resulting .CHK files) and ensure that SmartSuite installs to a contiguous area on the hard disk, which allows the SmartSuite applications to run more efficiently. If you haven't backed up your system files recently, you should do so before installing software. To access the maintenance and backup tools in Windows, right-click the drive icon in Windows Explorer or My Computer. Choose Properties, then click the Tools tab. This tab offers the options you use to error-check, defragment, or back up the disk.

✦ **If you're installing over a previous SmartSuite version, back up your documents, worksheets, and so on.** Even though the folder structure for SmartSuite separates data files from program files (so that installing a new version installs over old program files only), you should still back up your data files or copy them to another folder from the applicable \lotus\Work subfolder, for good measure. In addition, if you've created any custom SmartMaster files or have saved any changes to the default SmartMasters, you should copy those files to another location, too, so that you don't install over the SmartMasters and obliterate your changes.

Note The advice in the preceding bulleted point also applies if you're removing a SmartSuite application, as described later in this appendix. Even though uninstalling should leave all your data files and changed files (such as SmartMasters) intact, copying those crucial files could save you work later if something unexpected happens.

The SmartSuite installation CD-ROM also contains resources you should review before installing SmartSuite. If you're installing to a standalone or end-user system, open and review the Readme.wri file in the \Lotus folder on the CD-ROM. This file covers general installation issues, known problems that might occur when you try to run the applications in different scenarios, and what features install by default for each application. In addition, it can help you install SmartSuite applications in multiple languages, should you need that capability.

In addition, the CD-ROM offers another *Readme.wri* file that's specific to each application. For example, the \Lotus\Wordpro folder holds the Readme.wri file for Word Pro. Each of these Readme.wri files provides valuable, application-specific information. If you have installation concerns, want to install a single SmartSuite application only, or have problems with an application after installation, consult the Readme.wri file for that application.

Hot Stuff The individual Readme.wri files also install to your hard disk when you install SmartSuite. To review one of those files after installation, choose Start ➪ Programs ➪ Lotus SmartSuite ➪ Lotus User Assistance, then click the Product Updates command for the application you'd like to learn more about.

If you're a network administrator, you should open and review the general Readme.wri file, the application-specific Readme.wri files, and Readnet.txt, also found in the \Lotus folder on the CD-ROM. This file contains information about installing to a variety of networked environments, including NetWare, Windows NT, OS/2 Warp, and Notes (using various types of clients).

Choosing and Performing Your Installation

After you've laid the groundwork, it's time to begin the installation process. While the Install program provides a good deal of automation, you still have to make some choices and give it some direction along the way. For example, you can choose different types of installations to control how many files and features install on your system, thereby controlling how much hard disk space SmartSuite consumes and what features it offers.

No matter what type of installation you ultimately choose, use the following steps to begin the installation process:

1. Shut down any open applications, including open SmartSuite applications, if you're installing over an existing version of SmartSuite.

2. Insert the SmartSuite CD-ROM in your CD-ROM drive. The installation program automatically launches and displays the Lotus SmartSuite window shown in Figure A-1. If the window shown in Figure A-1 doesn't appear by itself, double-click the icon for your CD-ROM drive in either My Computer or Windows Explorer.

Figure A-1: SmartSuite's installation program launches automatically when you insert the CD-ROM. Click the option you want to continue installing.

The icons at the bottom of the window enable you to choose the installation you'd like. The rest of this section covers key installation options.

Choosing a QuickInstall

If you don't want to take the time to heavily customize your installation and want to keep your choices to the minimum, click the QuickInstall icon (it's second from the left) at the bottom of the Lotus SmartSuite window. The QuickInstall dialog box appears (see Figure A-2).

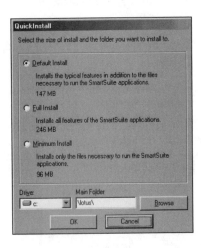

Figure A-2: When you choose QuickInstall, the installation program limits you to these options for controlling how much of SmartSuite to install, and where to install it.

The QuickInstall enables you to choose from three general types of installations, to control how much hard disk space SmartSuite occupies. The Default install, selected by default, presents the option most users should find adequate: It installs the most common features for all the SmartSuite applications. If you want every single feature to be available and have no hard disk space limitations, choose Full Install. If you want to conserve disk space, such as when you're installing to a notebook or to an older system, click Minimum Install. The Drive and Main Folder settings specify the hard disk and folder where you'd like to install SmartSuite. You can use either the Drive drop-down list or Main Folder text box to specify another folder to hold SmartSuite, or click the Browse button and use the Select a Folder dialog box that appears to navigate to and select the location you'd like.

After you choose an install size and location, click OK to proceed with the QuickInstall. Review the information in the Lotus Software Agreement, and then click I Agree to continue. In the Welcome to Lotus SmartSuite Install Program dialog box, enter your name in the applicable text box, then click Next to continue the installation. QuickInstall copies the SmartSuite files to your system, creating folders and subfolders as needed. After it finishes, a message informs you that installation is complete. Click OK. If you're prompted to restart your system, do so to ensure that SmartSuite will work correctly. When the system reboots, the opening screen of the Online Registration program appears. You can either follow its onscreen prompts to register your copy of SmartSuite, or click Exit and then Yes and OK to skip the registration and begin working.

If you're extremely low on hard disk space, you can click the Run from CD-ROM icon near the bottom of the Lotus SmartSuite window and follow the onscreen prompts to install a minimal number of files to your hard disk. Under this type of installation, before you can start a SmartSuite application, you have to insert the SmartSuite CD-ROM in your CD-ROM drive. If you have an older system with a slower (4x, 2x, and so on) CD-ROM drive, however, SmartSuite will likely run substantially slower than it would if it were installed to your hard disk. So, choose this type of installation only if you have very little hard disk space and don't mind digging up your CD every time you need it.

Using an Automatic Install

QuickInstall basically enables you to specify how much hard disk space to use to install SmartSuite. If you instead want to choose which applications to install based on your needs, you need to use a different installation process that takes a bit more time but provides you with more options.

For increased flexibility in where you install SmartSuite and which specific applications you install, follow these steps from the SmartSuite windows:

1. Click the Install icon in the bottom, right corner of the SmartSuite window. The Lotus Software Agreement dialog box presents the Lotus user agreement. Review the terms of the agreement, then click the I Agree button to continue.

2. The Welcome to the Lotus SmartSuite Install Program dialog box appears, as shown in Figure A-3. Enter the correct information in the Your Name and Company Name text boxes, then click Next. Click Yes when the Confirm Names dialog box appears to verify your entries, and continue installing SmartSuite.

3. When the Specify Lotus SmartSuite Folder dialog box appears, use the Drive drop-down list and Folder text box to change the disk and folder to install to, if you want to install to a location other than the default. You also can click the Browse button to display the Browse for Folder dialog box, which you can use to select another drive or folder. Click Next.

If you have another, earlier version of SmartSuite installed, the Install program displays a dialog box asking you to verify that you want to replace the older version. Click Next to do so and continue installation, or Exit Install to stop installing the new version. You may also see a message asking if you want to back up any SmartMasters installed on your system after Step 5. Click Yes to do so, No to skip the backup and continue the installation, or Exit Install to quit.

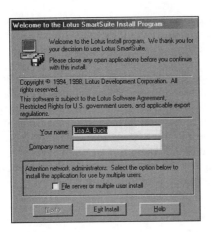

Figure A-3: You have to enter your name and your company name, no matter which installation method you choose, in order to be able to continue installing SmartSuite. The name you enter becomes your user name within the applications.

4. The Select Lotus SmartSuite Applications dialog box (see Figure A-4) lists each of the SmartSuite applications and the specific folder that will hold it after installation. Click to clear the check mark beside each application you don't wish to install. Or, if you want to change the folder to which a specific application installs, click the application in the list, then use the Drive drop-down list and Folder text box (or Browse button), to choose another location to hold the application. Click Next.

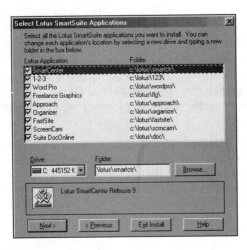

Figure A-4: Click to clear the check mark beside any application you don't wish to install.

5. In the Install Options dialog box that appears, select one of the top two options: Default Features – Automatic Install or Minimum Features – Automatic Install. As shown in Figure A-5, the dialog box tells you how much hard disk space each option requires, based on the applications you chose to install in the Select Lotus SmartSuite Applications dialog box (Figure A-4). After you choose which type of Automatic Install to perform, click Next.

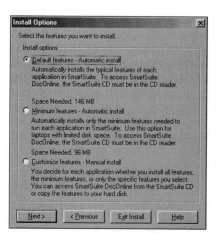

Figure A-5: This dialog box shows you how much disk space either of the Automatic Install options requires, based on the choices you made in the dialog box shown in Figure A-4.

Danger Zone

If you chose to install Lotus Organizer, the Choose Your Organizer Configuration dialog box may appear. Click PIM Only to use Organizer by itself. If you also use Lotus Notes 4.5, you can click PIM with Group Scheduling instead, which enables you to use Organizer (along with Notes) to coordinate team schedules and meetings. After you make your choice, click Next.

6. In the Select Program Folder dialog box that appears, specify which folder on the Programs submenu of the Start menu will hold the startup commands (shortcuts) for the SmartSuite applications. Edit the Folder Name entry if you wish to use a name other than Lotus SmartSuite. Click Next.

7. The Begin Copying Files dialog box asks if you want to start copying the SmartSuite files to your hard disk. Click Yes to continue.

8. As the Lotus Install program copies files to your hard disk, it informs you of its progress. Different messages appear at the top of the screen to introduce you to key features in SmartSuite.

9. When the Lotus Install program finishes copying files to your system and configuring your SmartSuite installation, the Install Complete dialog box appears, prompting you to reboot your system so that you can use SmartSuite. Click Yes.

10. Before it reboots, the Install program displays the SmartSuite Extras dialog box, which gives you the option of installing certain program extras (from the \Extras folder on the CD-ROM), such as ViaVoice and data synchronization software for using Lotus Organizer with a PalmPilot or other hand-held computer. Click to check an extra to install, then click the Install button. Follow the install process for the selected application. Back at the SmartSuite Extras dialog box, repeat the process to install additional extras.

11. When you finish installing extras, click Done in the SmartSuite Extras dialog box to complete the installation and reboot your system.

12. When your system reboots, the Online Registration program starts. (Or, if you installed ViaVoice, its New User Wizard will appear. Follow the wizard prompts to continue working with your computer. See Chapter 36 for more details on setting up ViaVoice.) You can follow its prompts to complete the online registration, or click Exit, Yes, and OK to close the program and begin working with SmartSuite.

Performing a Custom Install

You've seen how to control installation by choosing how much disk space it can use and by choosing which applications to install. For even greater control, you can use a custom installation, selecting which features install for each SmartSuite application you install. For example, if you need only the basic features for Freelance Graphics but need the advanced features for 1-2-3, you should execute a custom install, as follows:

1. Perform Steps 1–4 of the preceding automatic install procedure.

Again, if you have another, earlier, version of SmartSuite installed, the Install program displays a dialog box asking you to verify that you want to replace the older version. Click Next to do so and continue installation, or Exit Install to stop installing the new version. You may also later (after Step 8) see a message asking if you want to back up any SmartMasters installed on your system. Click Yes to do so, No to skip the backup and continue the installation, or Exit Install to quit.

2. In the Install Options dialog box, click the Customize Features-Manual Install option, then click Next. The Select SmartSuite Applications to Customize dialog box appears (see Figure A-6).

3. In the list of applications that you've chosen to install, click the application to customize.

4. Open the Install Option dialog box, then specify whether you want to use the Default (installs typical features), Custom (you select which features to install), or Minimum (installs the minimum possible number of files) installation for the application.

5. If you left the Custom option selected for the application in Step 4, click the Customize button to display the Customize dialog box for the application (see the example for 1-2-3 in Figure A-7), which you can use to specify each feature that you'd like to install. Click the check box for a feature to select it, or clear the check beside it; only checked features install. When a feature is checked, click the feature name (not the check box), then click the Change Feature

button to select a different folder to hold the files for the selected feature. Depending on the application you're customizing, the dialog box may contain several different tabs of features. Click each tab to review its features, or use the arrow buttons near the upper-right corner of the dialog box to display additional tabs. Click OK to close the Customize dialog box.

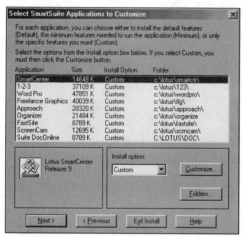

Figure A-6: Use this dialog box to select each application you want to customize, and to indicate how to customize it.

6. Each application uses several subfolders within the main SmartSuite folder to hold particular types of files, such as backup files. If you want to examine and perhaps change any of those folders for the application you selected in Step 3, click the Folders button in the Select SmartSuite Applications to Customize dialog box. Change any drive and folder settings (see the example in Figure A-8), then click OK.

7. Repeat Steps 3–6 to customize the settings for as many additional applications as needed.

8. Click Next in the Select SmartSuite Applications to Customize dialog box, then complete the installation as described in Steps 7–12 of the preceding automatic install procedure.

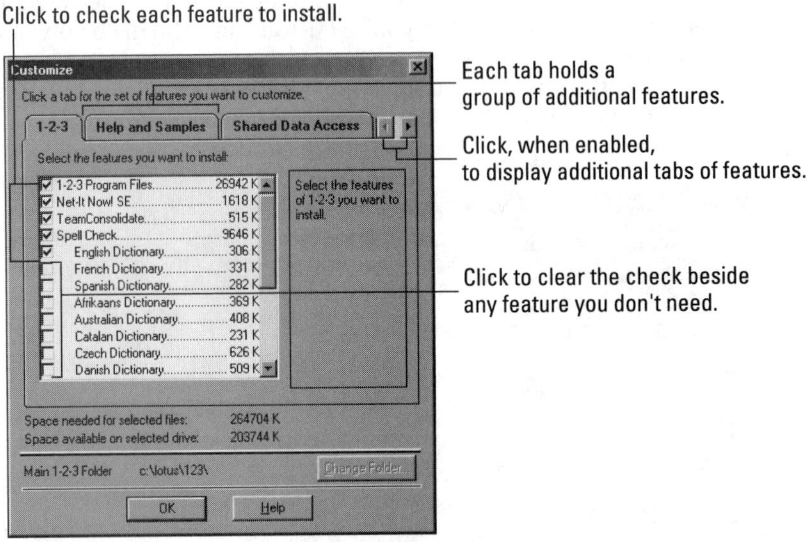

Click to check each feature to install.

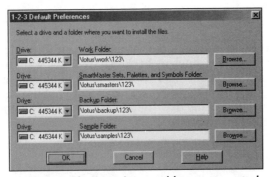

Each tab holds a group of additional features.

Click, when enabled, to display additional tabs of features.

Select the features of 1-2-3 you want to install.

Click to clear the check beside any feature you don't need.

Figure A-7: Customize the application installation using a dialog box like this example for 1-2-3, which specifies which features install.

Figure A-8: These settings enable you to control where an application stores work (the files you create), SmartMasters and palettes, backup files, and sample files.

Hot Stuff

If you want to add or remove individual application features in an existing SmartSuite installation, run a custom install (without uninstalling anything first).

Uninstalling SmartSuite Features

After you gain experience and comfort working with an application, you develop a pretty clear picture of which features you use and which you never touch. Similarly, when you install a suite of applications, you may find that you don't take advantage of all of them. This section explains how to remove parts of SmartSuite to free up disk space.

Deleting the Registration Files

After you install SmartSuite, you'll be prompted to complete an online registration process. You enter the requested registration information, and then send the information via modem to Lotus. Some users, though, may not need to complete the online registration. You may opt to complete and mail the registration card enclosed with the software instead. Or, your copy of SmartSuite might be covered under your company's multi-user license, so you don't need to register individually.

After you've used the online registration, or if you don't want to use it at all, you can remove the registration files from your hard disk to free about 1MB of space — enough for several very large documents. If you're running SmartSuite on a notebook computer, in particular, you might need the room.

Use the following steps to delete the SmartSuite registration files from your system:

1. Using the Windows Explorer or My Computer, delete the \register subfolder of the \lotus folder on your hard disk. (If you installed SmartSuite to a folder other than C:\lotus, look for the subfolder within that folder instead.) Figure A-9 shows this subfolder in a My Computer window. Click the folder to select it, then press Delete or click the Delete button. In the Confirm Folder Delete dialog box, click Yes.

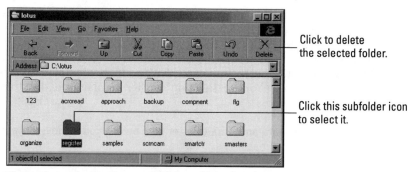

Figure A-9: The \register subfolder within the \lotus folder holds files you can safely delete.

2. Choose Start ⇨ Settings ⇨ Taskbar & Start Menu.

3. Choose the Start Menu Programs tab in the Taskbar Properties dialog box, then click the Remove button on the tab.

4. In the Remove Shortcuts/Folders dialog box, click the plus (+) sign beside the Startup folder, then click the Lotus SmartSuite Release 9 Registration option, as shown in Figure A-10.

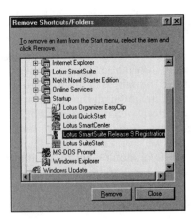

Figure A-10: You can use this dialog box to remove commands that appear on the Windows Start menu, such as the selected Lotus SmartSuite Registration command shown here.

5. Click Remove, then click Close to close the Remove Shortcuts/Folder dialog box.

6. Click OK to close the Taskbar Properties dialog box.

7. Reboot your system.

Removing Applications

You may need to reclaim even more hard disk space, especially if you discover that you don't at all need a particular SmartSuite application. For example, if you have an older system with less than 1.2 gigabytes of hard disk space and you find that you don't ever use Lotus Approach, you can delete Approach from your system without much hassle. Of course, you can always rerun the installation program (see "Choosing and Performing Your Installation" earlier in this Appendix) to reinstall an application you've deleted.

Danger Zone Copy or back up key data and SmartMaster files before you remove an application, just as an added safety measure.

Use the following steps to run the Lotus Uninstall program to remove one or more SmartSuite applications from your system:

1. If you're planning to remove SmartCenter or all of SmartSuite, close the SmartCenter and SuiteStart, as well as any other SmartSuite features that are running behind the scenes. To close the SmartCenter, click the Lotus button at the left end of the SmartCenter, then click Exit SmartCenter. To shut down SuiteStart, press Ctrl+Alt+Delete. In the Close Program dialog box, select SmartCenter, then click End Task. If you press Ctrl+Alt+Delete and see Suitest, Easyclip, and Remind32 listed, you also need to end each of those tasks. Select one or the other, then click End Task; redisplay the Close Program dialog box, and end the other task.

2. Close any other SmartSuite applications that you're running, such as Word Pro.

3. Choose Start ⇨ Settings ⇨ Control Panel. The Control Panel window opens.

4. Double-click the Add/Remove Programs icon. The Add/Remove Programs Properties dialog box appears, with the Install/Uninstall tab selected by default.

5. In the scrolling list at the bottom of the dialog box, select Lotus SmartSuite Release 9, then click the Add/Remove button below the list. The Select Lotus SmartSuite Applications dialog box appears.

6. To remove all of SmartSuite, select the top option button, Uninstall All of SmartSuite. Or, to remove some applications while leaving others installed, leave the bottom option button, Uninstall Selected SmartSuite Applications, selected; then, click to check each individual application to remove. Figure A-11 shows Approach selected for removal, for example.

7. Click OK. The Lotus Uninstall dialog box appears, asking you to verify the selection you've made for deletion.

8. Click Yes to continue the uninstall process.

9. At points, Lotus Uninstall may display a message telling you that a particular file version doesn't match the one that was originally installed. In such a case, you can click Skip to leave the file intact on your hard disk (for instances when the file might be a SmartMaster you've edited and want to keep), or Remove to remove the file. After you make a selection, the installation continues.

10. If Uninstall tries to remove a folder that's not empty, it'll give you the option to Skip or Retry the deletion. Make your selection to continue the uninstall process. However, if you click Retry a few times and Uninstall continues to be unable to remove the folder, make a note of the folder path so that you can delete it manually, if needed, after Uninstall finishes.

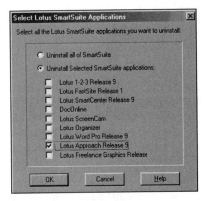

Figure A-11: In this dialog box, select which SmartSuite applications to uninstall. For example, leave the bottom option button selected, then click Approach to remove the Approach application only.

11. Lotus Uninstall informs you when the uninstall process completes, displaying a dialog box that informs you all features and files have been removed. Click OK to close the dialog box.

12. Finally, Lotus Uninstall tells you that it can reclaim disk space if you restart the computer. Click Restart Now to do so (the recommended option), or Skip to simply close the Lotus Uninstall program. If you choose Skip, you can then click OK to close the Add/Remove Programs Properties dialog box, and close the Control Panel window.

✦　　✦　　✦

Index

(continued)

(continued)

(continued)